# MILLENNIUM STAR ATLAS
## VOLUME III

# MILLENNIUM STAR ATLAS

*An All-Sky Atlas Comprising*
*One Million Stars to Visual Magnitude Eleven*
*from the Hipparcos and Tycho Catalogues*
*and Ten Thousand Nonstellar Objects*

## VOLUME III: 16 TO 24 HOURS

### Roger W. Sinnott

*Sky & Telescope*

### Michael A. C. Perryman

EUROPEAN SPACE AGENCY
FOR THE HIPPARCOS PROJECT

1997

SKY PUBLISHING CORPORATION

*Cambridge, Massachusetts*

EUROPEAN SPACE AGENCY

*ESTEC, Noordwijk, The Netherlands*

## Principal Collaborators

### TYCHO CATALOGUE

Erik Høg

Ulrich Bastian          Valeri V. Makarov
Claus Fabricius         Jean-Louis Halbwachs
Volkmar Großmann        Andreas Wicenec

### HIPPARCOS CATALOGUE

Hans Schrijver

Michel Grenon           Lennart Lindegren
Jean Kovalevsky         François Mignard
Floor van Leeuwen       Catherine Turon

### SKY PUBLISHING CORPORATION

Sally M. MacGillivray

E. Talmadge Mentall     Imelda B. Joson
Richard Tresch Fienberg Samantha Parker
Gregg Dinderman         Leif J. Robinson

LIBRARY OF CONGRESS CATALOGUING-IN-PUBLICATION DATA

Sinnott, Roger W.
    Millennium Star Atlas: an all-sky atlas comprising one million stars to visual magnitude eleven from the Hipparcos and Tycho Catalogues and ten thousand nonstellar objects / Roger W. Sinnott, Michael A. C. Perryman.
        p.       cm.
    Includes bibliographical references and index.
    Contents: v.1. 0 to 8 hours — v.2. 8 to 16 hours — v.3. 16 to 24 hours.
    ISBN 0-933346-84-0 (3-vol. set: alk. paper).—ISBN 0-933346-81-6 (Vol. I: alk. paper).—ISBN 0-933346-82-4 (Vol. II: alk. paper).—ISBN 0-933346-83-2 (Vol. III: alk. paper).
    1. Stars—Atlases. 2. Astronomy—Charts, diagrams, etc. I. Perryman, Michael A. C. II. Title.
    QB65.S62    1997                                  97-2552
                                                    CIP

# CONTENTS

# HOW TO USE THIS ATLAS

THE *MILLENNIUM STAR ATLAS* contains about 1,058,000 stars, all those observed by the European Space Agency's Hipparcos spacecraft. More than 10,000 nonstellar objects have been included from other sources. The chart arrangement and scale have been chosen to make the atlas practical and efficient to use, considering the wealth of information it contains.

The atlas divides the celestial sphere into three lunes, or gores, each spanning a particular range of right ascension from pole to pole. Volume I covers from $0^h$ to $8^h$, Volume II from $8^h$ to $16^h$, and Volume III from $16^h$ to $24^h$. Often just one of the three, encompassing the sky overhead and along the meridian from north to south, is all that will be needed for an observing session at the telescope. The following table tells which volume is most useful during specific seasons and observing times:

| MONTH OF YEAR | TIME OF NIGHT | | | | |
|---|---|---|---|---|---|
| | *8 pm* | *10 pm* | *Midnight* | *2 am* | *4 am* |
| January | I | I | | II | II |
| February | I | | II | II | II |
| March | | II | II | II | |
| April | II | II | II | | III |
| May | II | II | | III | III |
| June | II | | III | III | III |
| July | | III | III | III | |
| August | III | III | III | | I |
| September | III | III | | I | I |
| October | III | | I | I | I |
| November | | I | I | I | |
| December | I | I | I | | II |

## CHART SCALE AND GRID LINES

Each chart embraces a very small sky area, roughly that seen with a pair of 7 × 50 binoculars. North is up. Right ascensions are labeled along the top and bottom of each page, and declinations are printed at 1° intervals along the side of the chart. The grid lines, based on the International Celestial Reference System (ICRS), are consistent with coordinates measured from the 2000.0 equator and equinox.

The chart scale is 100 arcseconds per millimeter throughout. The 1° spacing of the declination grid lines may also be used to estimate angular separations on the sky.

Constellation boundaries are shown as gray lines. The ecliptic, the Sun's apparent path in the course of the year, is a dashed line marked at 1° intervals with ecliptic longitude. Another dashed line traces the galactic equator, the adopted plane of the Milky Way; it is labeled at 1° intervals with galactic longitude.

## FINDING A CELESTIAL OBJECT

At the end of each volume, four chart keys show at a glance the region of sky covered. Chart numbers are the large numerals at the lower outside corner of each atlas page. Charts 1 through 516 are found in Volume I, 517 through 1032 in Volume II, and 1033 through 1548 in Volume III. An index lists the charts containing bright or unusual stars and deep-sky objects bearing popular names.

Within each volume, the charts start at the north celestial pole and work southward through consecutive declination bands in 6° steps. The central declination of the band is printed in large numerals at the upper outside corner of each chart.

If you know only the ICRS or 2000.0 coordinates of an object you are seeking, three steps will quickly locate the chart on which it lies: (1) Select the volume covering the general range of right ascension. (2) Flip through the pages to the desired declination band. (3) Turn consecutive pages left or right to locate the right ascension being sought.

Each pair of facing charts forms a continuous stretch of sky with a narrow overlap down the middle. Turning pages from front to back through the volume moves west, toward decreasing right ascension. Turning the pages from back to front moves east, toward increasing right ascension. (These rules apply until a volume boundary is reached at right ascension $0^h$, $8^h$, or $16^h$. While the chart immediately west of chart 763 is 764 in Volume II, that to its east is 1302 in Volume III, as the chart keys in both volumes make clear.)

Centered near the top of each chart is a small up arrow labeled with the chart number(s) immediately to the north. At the bottom of each chart, a down arrow identifies adjacent chart(s) to the south.

## THE STARS

In the legend at the bottom of each left-hand page, a tapered scale of black disks shows the range of symbols used for individual stars. The smaller the disk the fainter the star, particular sizes being shown for visual ($V$) magnitude 2.0 (brightest), 3.0, 4.0, and so on up to 11.0 (faintest). The stars on the charts themselves can have these or any intermediate sizes, so that relative brightnesses are faithfully portrayed. An exception has been made for the four dozen brightest stars of all, listed in Table IV on page XI of Volume I. To avoid excessively large disks, these well-known stars are plotted as if they, too, were of magnitude 2.0.

Only stars brighter than about magnitude 6 are visible to the naked eye. Some of these have popular names, such as Sirius or Polaris, while many more carry a Flamsteed number, a Bayer (Greek-letter) designation, or both.

Finally, every star that was found by Hipparcos to lie within 200 light-years of the Sun is labeled with its measured distance in light-years (ly). The light-year value, divided by 3.26, gives the distance in parsecs.

**Variable stars.** A black disk surrounded by some type of open circle identifies a variable star listed in the Hipparcos Catalogue. A variable is also identified by its standard designation, either an uppercase Roman letter from R to Z, a two-letter pair such as AX or CQ, or the letter V followed by 334 or a higher number. The constellation is omitted, even though it would always be included when mentioning the star in speech or writing, because a constellation label appears elsewhere on the same chart.

The size of a variable star's central disk corresponds to its median magnitude, as measured by Hipparcos, rather than to its maximum or minimum value. A surrounding dotted circle means that the amplitude of the light fluctuations is less than 0.1 magnitude. A dashed circle means the variation falls in the range of 0.1 to 1.0 magnitude. A solid circle implies the range is 1.0 or greater, and in this case the changes are obvious in a telescope even to the casual observer.

Next to the star or its designation, in parentheses, a lowercase italic letter identifies the broad class to which the variable belongs and a single digit its approximate period (expressed logarithmically), according to the following schemes:

| Variability Class | | Period in Days |
|---|---|---|
| (*e*) Eclipsing | (*s*) Semiregular | (*o*) Less than 1 |
| (*c*) Cepheid | (*i*) Irregular | (*1*) 1 to 9 |
| (*m*) Mira | (*f*) UV Ceti | (*2*) 10 to 99 |
| (*d*) δ Scuti | (*x*) Novalike | (*3*) 100 to 999 |
| (*r*) RR Lyrae | (*v*) Other | (*4*) 1,000 or more |

Mnemonically, it may help to note that the period code equals the number of digits used to express the whole number of days in the period.

For example, a star marked "RV (*e1*)" appears on chart 1274 of a region in Ophiuchus. The label tells us the star is RV Ophiuchi, an eclipsing binary with a period between 1 and 9 days. For more about the plotting of variable stars, including the complete correspondence between these variability classes and the standard variable-star types, see page XII of Volume I.

Some well-known variable stars were not observed by Hipparcos, generally because of their faint magnitude at the time of the mission, and they have been added from other sources. For example, locations of historical novae and supernovae are marked with a simple × and the letters N or SN followed by the year of appearance. Mira variables that spend much of the time near or fainter than the cutoff magnitude appear as small open circles. They can be distinguished from face-on galaxies by their designations.

**Stars of high proper motion.** All stars found in the Hipparcos Catalogue to have a proper motion greater than 0.2 arcsecond per year are plotted with an attached arrow showing the direction of this motion. The arrow's length represents the angular distance the star will move on the sky during one millennium. For example, at the chart scale of 100 arcseconds per millimeter, a 5-mm arrow means the star will move 500 arcseconds in 1,000 years. The length of an arrow should always be measured from just outside the rim of the star's disk (where the shaft begins) to the tip of the arrowhead.

**Double and multiple stars.** When the components of a double or multiple star are separated by more than 30 arcseconds, they are plotted individually with overlapping disks. But if the separation is less than 30 arcseconds, a single, enlarged disk representing the combined light is plotted at the brightest member's location with a protruding "tick" for each companion. The orientation and length of this tick, derived from Hipparcos measurements, show the state of the system at the catalogue epoch (1991.25). Most double and multiple stars with separations larger than a few tenths of an arcsecond retain nearly the same configuration for many decades.

To express angular separations meaningfully, the lengths of double-star ticks are greatly exaggerated. They are plotted on a logarithmic scale so that the closer, more interesting pairs are better distinguished. Three examples are shown in the legend, but ticks with lengths corresponding to any separation from 0.1 to 30 arcseconds are found throughout the atlas. Each tick begins just outside the rim of the primary star's enlarged disk and extends radially outward in the companion star's direction on the sky. When using the atlas at the telescope, it is important to remember that many optical systems present an inverted or mirror-reversed view.

## NONSTELLAR OBJECTS

The legend on the right-hand chart pages explains the symbols used for nebulae, star clusters, galaxies, galaxy clusters, and quasars. Many of the brightest and most striking nonstellar objects are still best known from Charles Messier's observations with small comet-seeking telescopes in the late 18th century; they carry the letter M followed by a number from 1 to 110. Thousands of other objects were enumerated by J. L. E. Dreyer in his famous *New General Catalogue* (1888), or in its two supplements together known as the *Index Catalogue* (1895 and 1908). In this atlas NGC numbers (from 1 to 7840) are printed without any prefix; IC numbers (1 to 5386) are preceded by the letters IC.

**Nebulae.** Large, bright nebulae are plotted with a continuous, irregular outline that indicates their approximate extent on long-exposure photographs. Those measuring about 10 arcminutes across or smaller are marked with an open square. Similarly, dark nebulae are shown by a dashed outline when large, or by a small dashed square when they span 10 arcminutes or less. Planetary nebulae are usually too small to plot to scale; the symbols in the legend give an idea of their diameter, including any extremely faint outer halo that may be present. When not identified by an NGC or IC number, nebulae carry the designations assigned by the astronomers who discovered or studied them, as explained in the Introduction (Volume I).

**Open and globular star clusters.** For many clusters the brighter stars are plotted individually. Open clusters are marked by a dashed open circle and globular clusters by a solid open circle and cross. The circle's diameter represents the approximate visual extent of the cluster. A minimal symbol, given in the legend, marks clusters smaller than 5 arcminutes across. When lacking an NGC or IC number, a cluster is designated by the name of an astronomer or observatory and a serial number.

**Galaxies.** The completeness limit for galaxies is a total visual magnitude brighter than about 13.5, though a number of fainter ones are included as well. All large galaxies are shown by an ellipse whose aspect ratio and orientation correspond to those on time-exposure photographs with large telescopes or CCD images. If a galaxy's major axis is smaller than 2 arcminutes it is plotted as 2 arcminutes, and if the minor axis is smaller than 1 arcminute it is plotted as 1 arcminute. This procedure preserves some idea of the orientation, even for very tiny objects.

**Quasars.** An open-centered cross is used for objects that are nearly stellar in appearance but well below the atlas's magnitude cutoff for stars. They are included for their astrophysical aura. Extragalactic quasars and their cousins, the BL Lacertae objects, make up the great majority of these, selected to be 16th magnitude or brighter visually. They are identified by such prefixes as PKS for a number in the Parkes radio survey and 3C for a number in the revised third Cambridge radio survey. The same open-cross symbol has been used for a handful of high-energy sources within our own galaxy, even though they are not quasars. These include several pulsars, the Geminga gamma-ray source, and the galactic center itself.

**Galaxy clusters.** A pentagon symbol marks a rich cluster of galaxies that has at least 10 members of 16th magnitude or brighter. In many cases, along with the pentagon, several of the brightest member galaxies are plotted individually. The prefix A refers to a number from the original northern and southern Abell catalogues; AS denotes a cluster in the southern supplement. The pentagon simply marks the cluster's location without indicating its angular extent. Most galaxy clusters in the atlas are smaller than $\frac{1}{4}°$ across.

# CHARTS 1O33–1548

Right Ascension 16 to 24 Hours

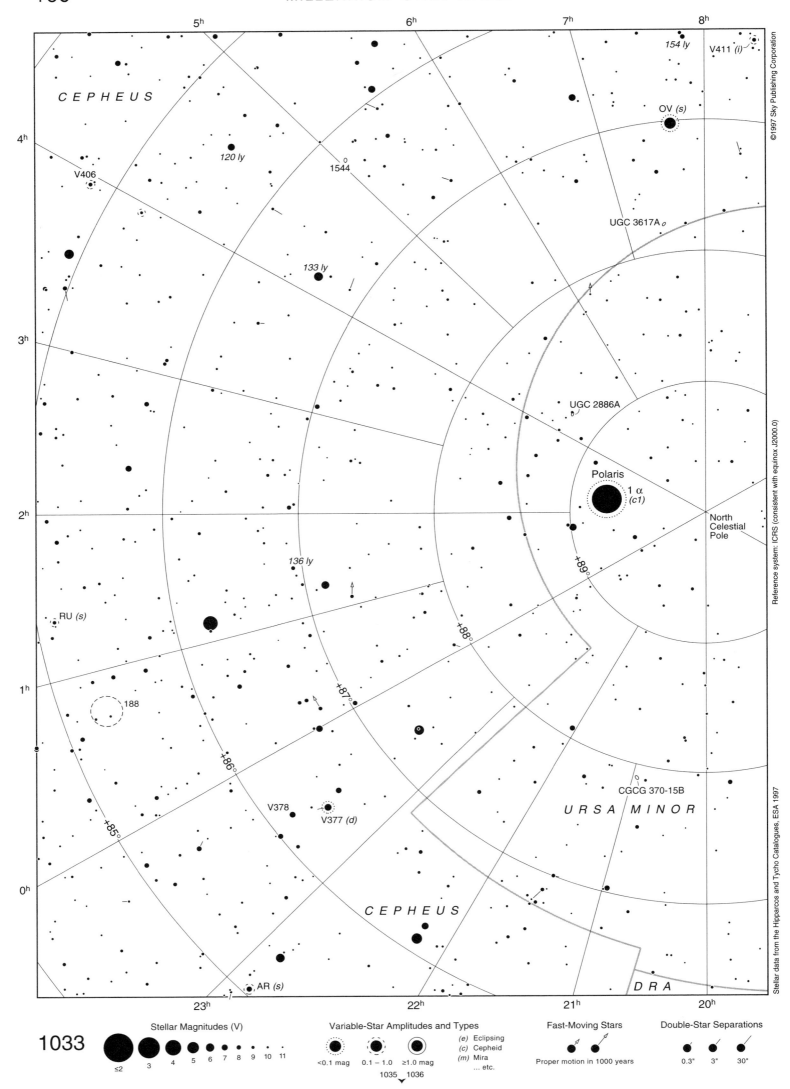

Reference system: ICRS (consistent with equinox J2000.0)

Stellar data from the Hipparcos and Tycho Catalogues, ESA 1997

CEPHEUS

V406

120 ly

1544

154 ly

V411 (i)

OV (s)

UGC 3617A

133 ly

UGC 2886A

Polaris
1 α
(c1)

North
Celestial
Pole

+89°

136 ly

+88°

RU (s)

+87°

188

+86°

CGCG 370-15B

URSA MINOR

V378

+85°

V377 (d)

CEPHEUS

AR (s)

DRA

**1033**

Stellar Magnitudes (V)

≤2   3   4   5   6   7   8   9   10  11

Variable-Star Amplitudes and Types

<0.1 mag   0.1 – 1.0   ≥1.0 mag

1035   1036

(e) Eclipsing
(c) Cepheid
(m) Mira
... etc.

Fast-Moving Stars

Proper motion in 1000 years

Double-Star Separations

0.3"   3"   30"

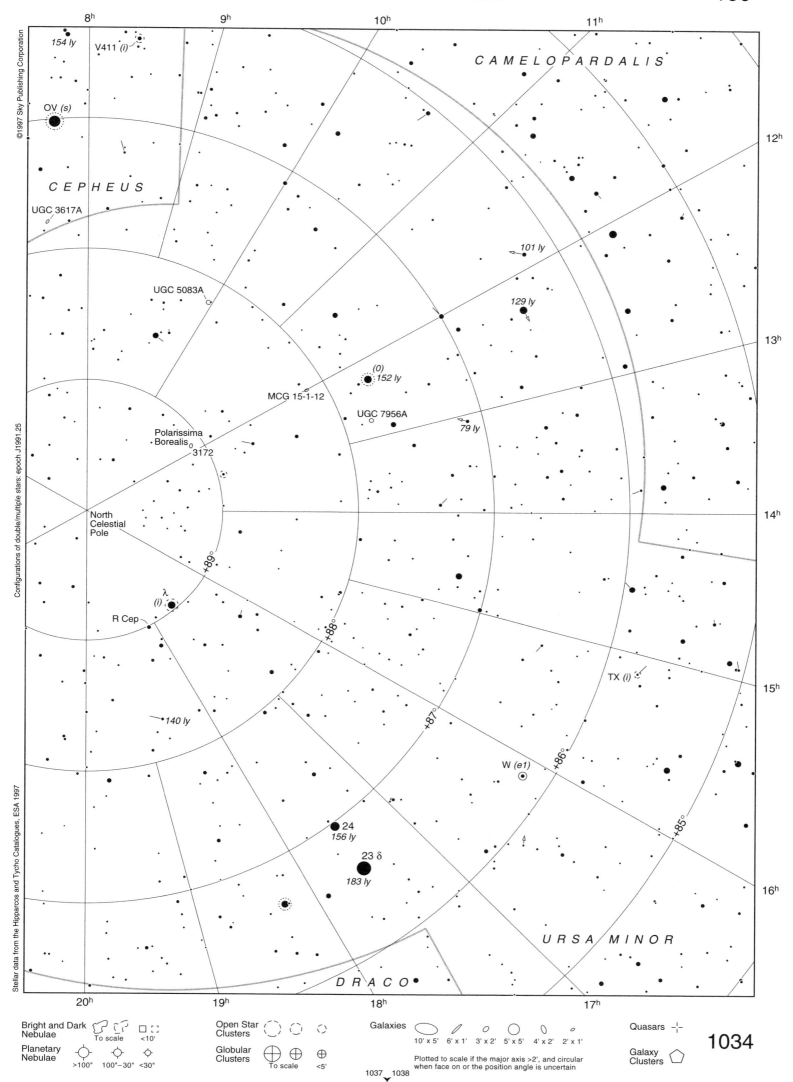

8ʰ
9ʰ
10ʰ
11ʰ
12ʰ
13ʰ
14ʰ
15ʰ
16ʰ

20ʰ
19ʰ
18ʰ
17ʰ

154 ly
V411 (i)
OV (s)

CAMELOPARDALIS

CEPHEUS

UGC 3617A

101 ly

129 ly

UGC 5083A

(0) 152 ly

MCG 15-1-12

UGC 7956A

79 ly

Polarissima
Borealis
3172

North
Celestial
Pole

+89°

λ
(i)
R Cep

+88°

TX (i)

+87°

140 ly

+86°

W (e1)

+85°

24
156 ly

23 δ
183 ly

URSA MINOR

DRACO

Bright and Dark
Nebulae
To scale    <10'
Planetary
Nebulae
>100"  100"–30"  <30"

Open Star
Clusters
Globular
Clusters
To scale    <5'

Galaxies
10' x 5'  6' x 1'  3' x 2'  5' x 5'  4' x 2'  2' x 1'

Plotted to scale if the major axis >2', and circular
when face on or the position angle is uncertain

Quasars

Galaxy
Clusters

1034

1037 1038

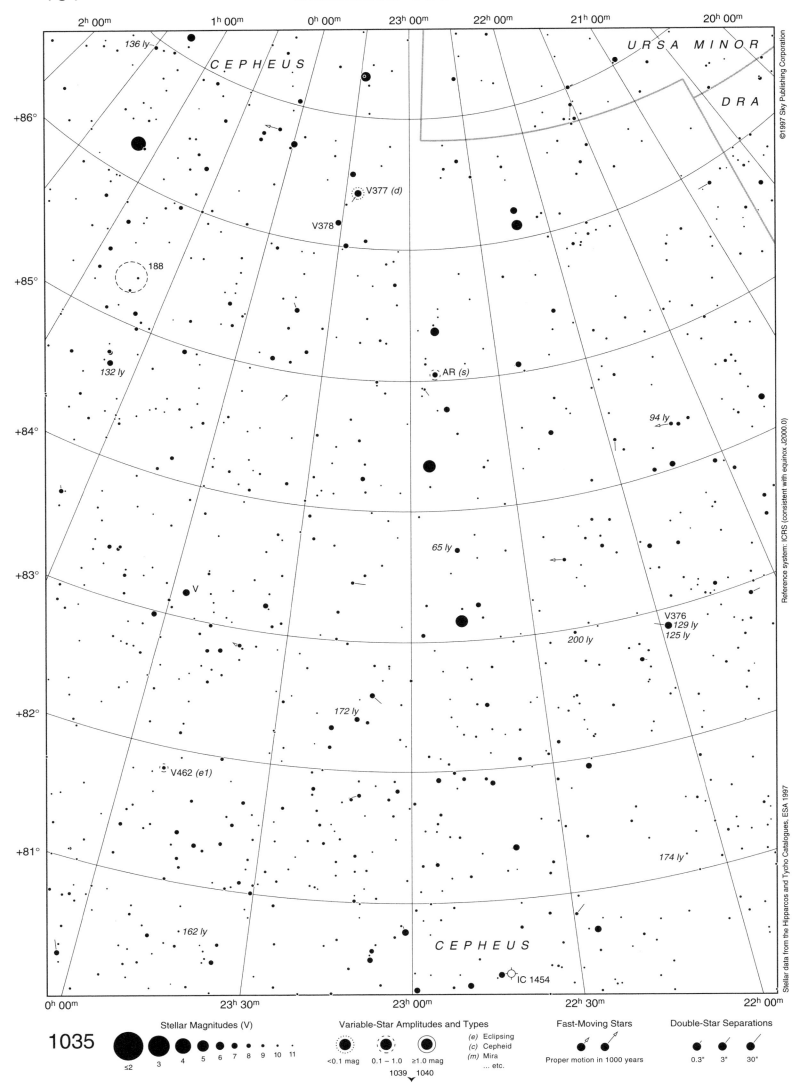

1035

Stellar Magnitudes (V)

≤2  3  4  5  6  7  8  9  10  11

Variable-Star Amplitudes and Types

<0.1 mag   0.1 – 1.0   ≥1.0 mag

(e) Eclipsing
(c) Cepheid
(m) Mira
... etc.

1039  1040

Fast-Moving Stars

Proper motion in 1000 years

Double-Star Separations

0.3"   3"   30"

# MILLENNIUM STAR ATLAS

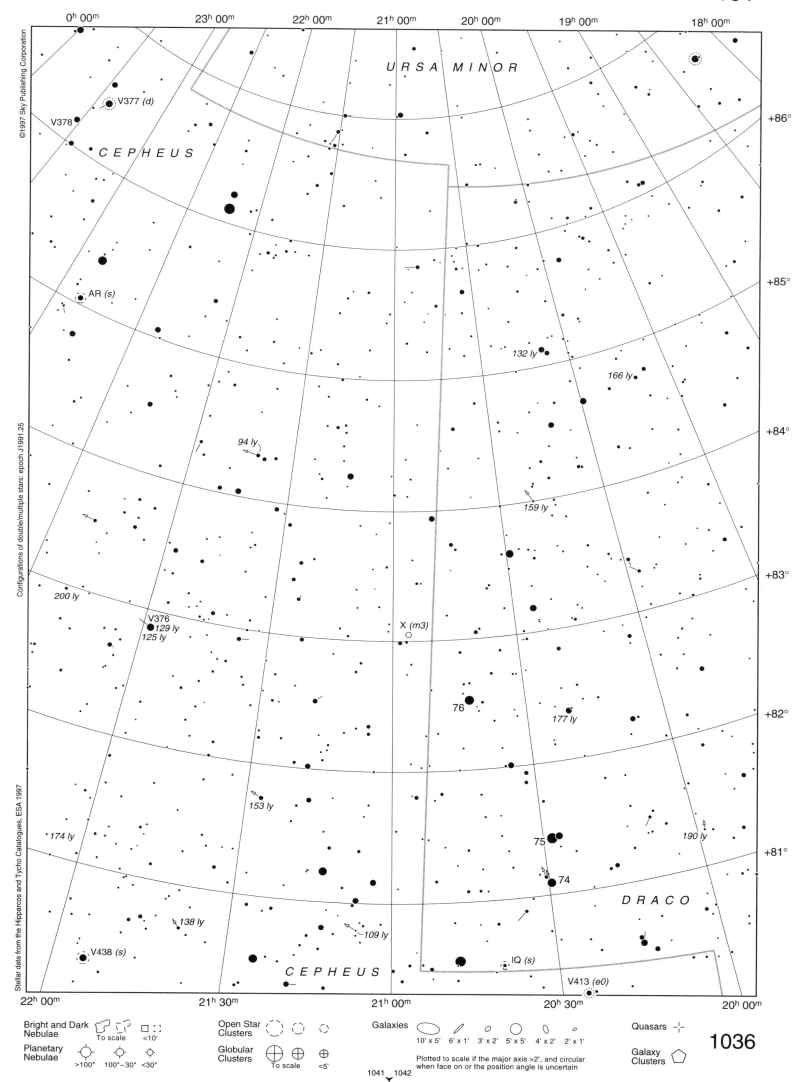

©1997 Sky Publishing Corporation

Configurations of double/multiple stars: epoch J1991.25

Stellar data from the Hipparcos and Tycho Catalogues, ESA 1997

URSA MINOR

CEPHEUS

V377 (d)

V378

AR (s)

132 ly

166 ly

94 ly

159 ly

200 ly

V376
129 ly
125 ly

X (m3)

76

177 ly

153 ly

174 ly

190 ly

75

74

138 ly

DRACO

109 ly

V438 (s)

CEPHEUS

IQ (s)

V413 (e0)

+86°

+85°

+84°

+83°

+82°

+81°

0h 00m    23h 00m    22h 00m    21h 00m    20h 00m    19h 00m    18h 00m

22h 00m    21h 30m    21h 00m    20h 30m    20h 00m

| Bright and Dark Nebulae | Open Star Clusters | Galaxies | Quasars |
|---|---|---|---|

Bright and Dark Nebulae
To scale   <10'

Planetary Nebulae
>100"   100"–30"   <30"

Open Star Clusters

Globular Clusters
To scale   <5'

Galaxies
10' x 5'   6' x 1'   3' x 2'   5' x 5'   4' x 2'   2' x 1'

Plotted to scale if the major axis >2', and circular when face on or the position angle is uncertain

Quasars

Galaxy Clusters

1036

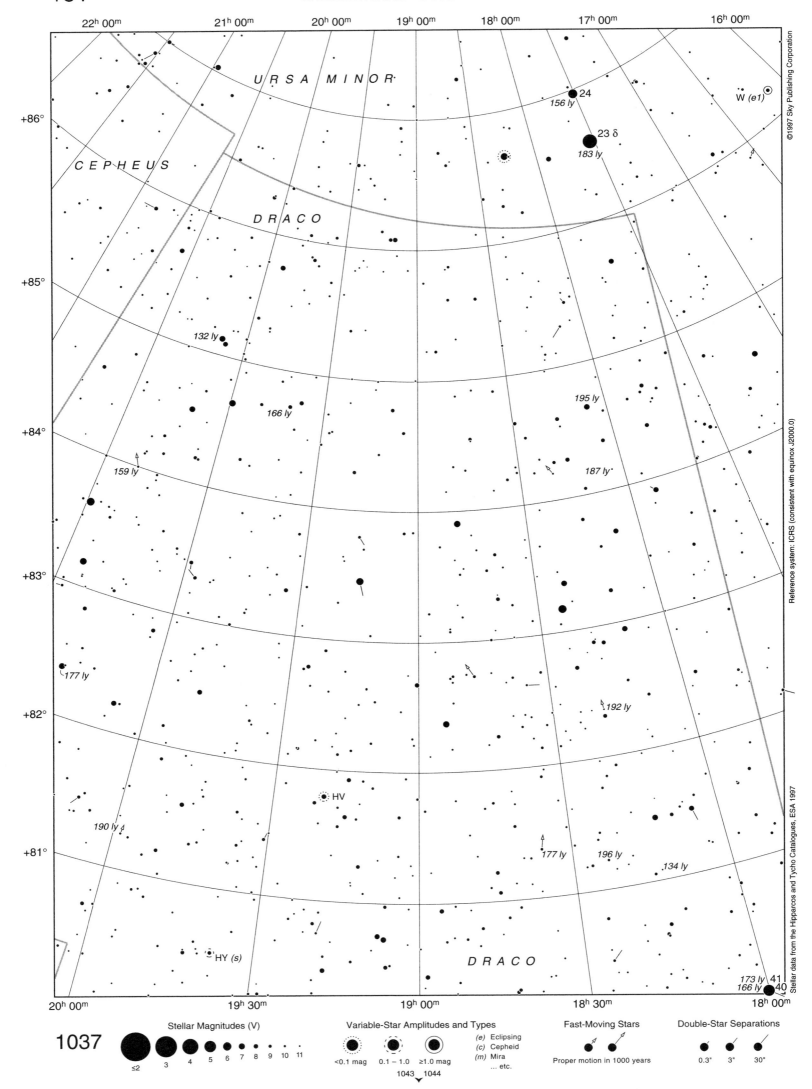

©1997 Sky Publishing Corporation

Reference system: ICRS (consistent with equinox J2000.0)

Stellar data from the Hipparcos and Tycho Catalogues, ESA 1997

U R S A   M I N O R

C E P H E U S

D R A C O

D R A C O

24
156 ly

23 δ
183 ly

W (e1)

132 ly

166 ly

159 ly

195 ly

187 ly

177 ly

192 ly

HV

190 ly

177 ly    196 ly    134 ly

HY (s)

173 ly  41
166 ly  40

1037

**Stellar Magnitudes (V)**

≤2   3   4   5   6   7   8   9   10   11

**Variable-Star Amplitudes and Types**

<0.1 mag    0.1 – 1.0    ≥1.0 mag

(e) Eclipsing
(c) Cepheid
(m) Mira
... etc.

1043   1044

**Fast-Moving Stars**

Proper motion in 1000 years

**Double-Star Separations**

0.3"    3"    30"

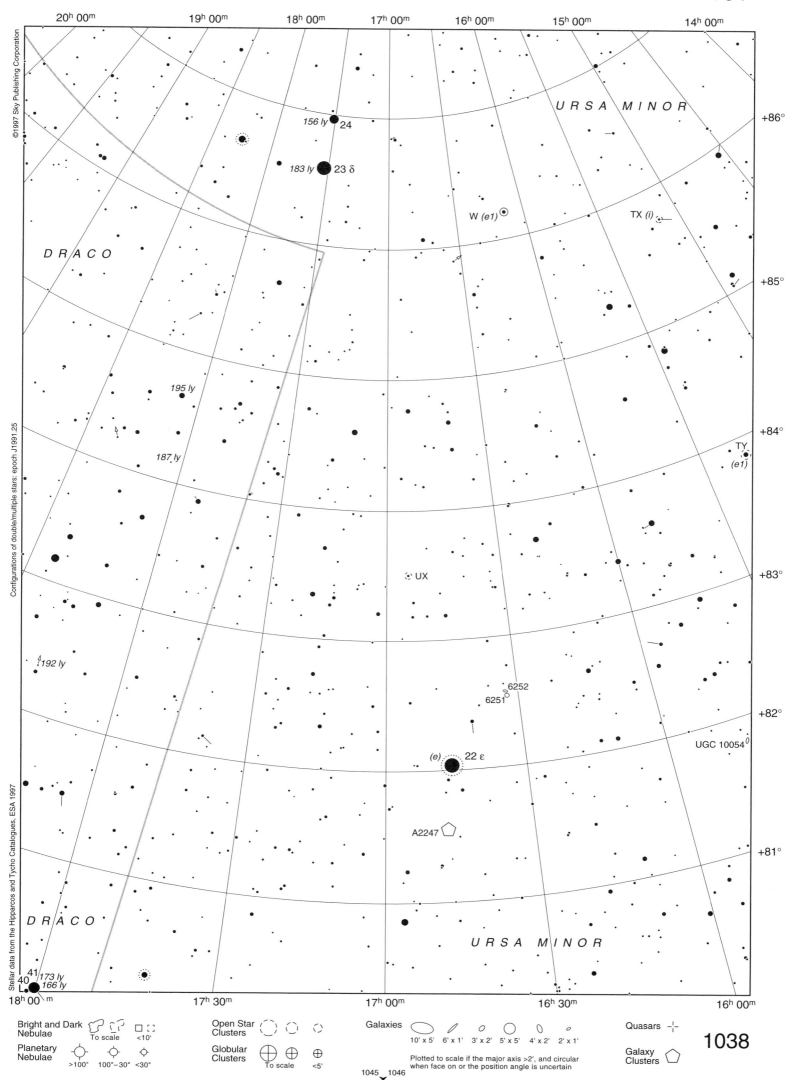

U R S A   M I N O R

156 ly 24

183 ly 23 δ

W (e1)

TX (i)

D R A C O

+86°

+85°

195 ly

187 ly

TY
(e1)

+84°

UX

+83°

192 ly

6252
6251

+82°

UGC 10054

(e) 22 ε

A2247

+81°

D R A C O

U R S A   M I N O R

41 173 ly
40
L 166 ly

18h 00m          17h 30m          17h 00m          16h 30m          16h 00m

20h 00m      19h 00m      18h 00m      17h 00m      16h 00m      15h 00m      14h 00m

| Bright and Dark Nebulae | Open Star Clusters | Galaxies | Quasars |
| --- | --- | --- | --- |

Bright and Dark Nebulae
To scale   <10'

Planetary Nebulae
>100"   100"–30"   <30"

Open Star Clusters

Globular Clusters
To scale   <5'

Galaxies
10' x 5'   6' x 1'   3' x 2'   5' x 5'   4' x 2'   2' x 1'

Plotted to scale if the major axis >2', and circular
when face on or the position angle is uncertain

Quasars

Galaxy Clusters

1038

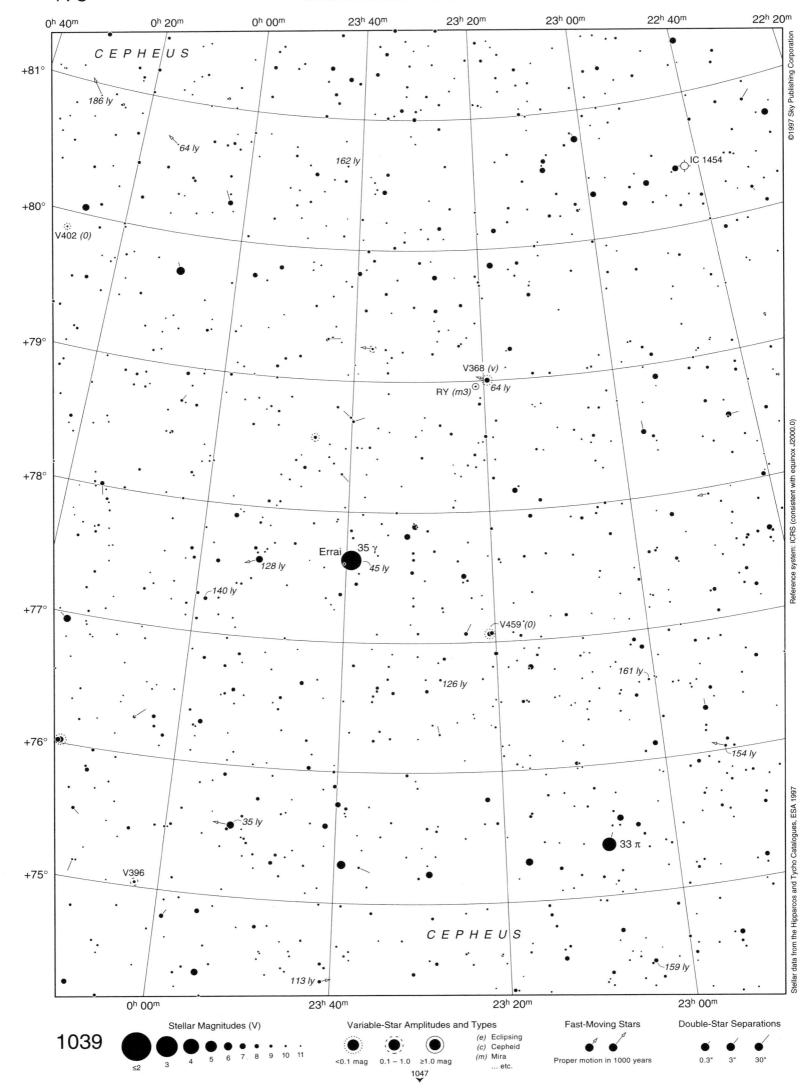

©1997 Sky Publishing Corporation

Reference system: ICRS (consistent with equinox J2000.0)

Stellar data from the Hipparcos and Tycho Catalogues, ESA 1997

1039

Stellar Magnitudes (V)

≤2  3  4  5  6  7  8  9  10  11

Variable-Star Amplitudes and Types

<0.1 mag   0.1 – 1.0   ≥1.0 mag

(e) Eclipsing
(c) Cepheid
(m) Mira
... etc.

Fast-Moving Stars

Proper motion in 1000 years

Double-Star Separations

0.3"   3"   30"

# MILLENNIUM STAR ATLAS

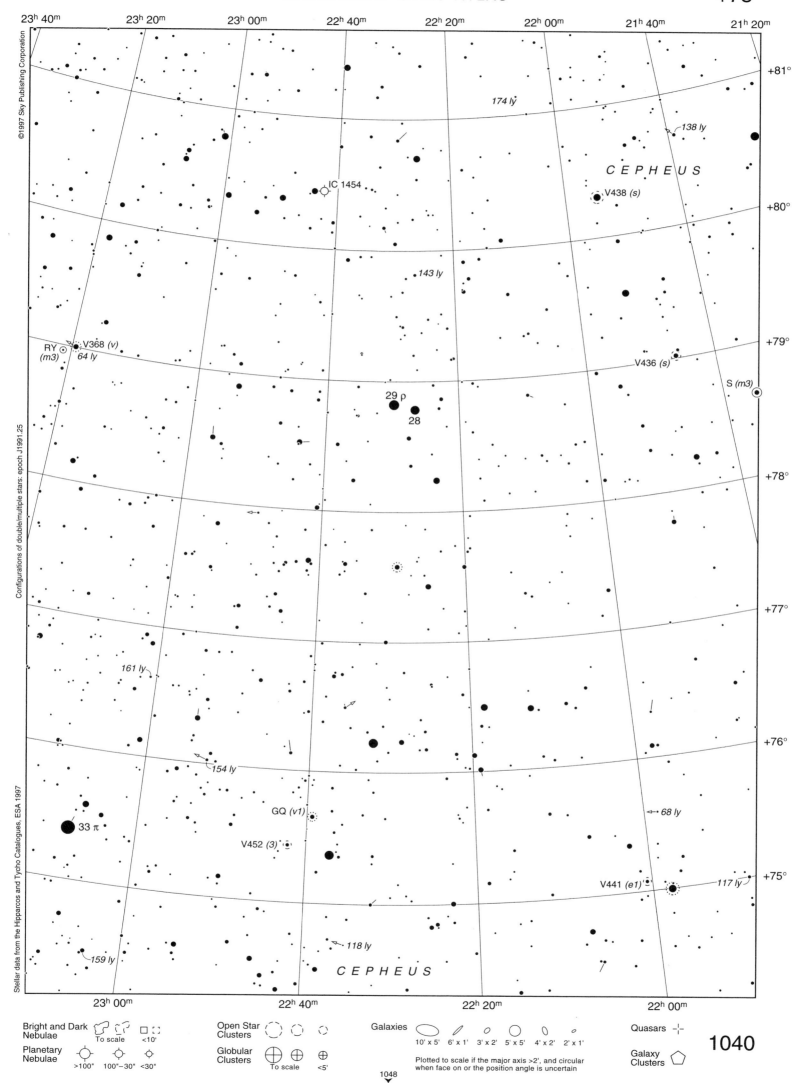

©1997 Sky Publishing Corporation

Configurations of double/multiple stars: epoch J1991.25

Stellar data from the Hipparcos and Tycho Catalogues, ESA 1997

23ʰ 40ᵐ   23ʰ 20ᵐ   23ʰ 00ᵐ   22ʰ 40ᵐ   22ʰ 20ᵐ   22ʰ 00ᵐ   21ʰ 40ᵐ   21ʰ 20ᵐ

+81°
+80°
+79°
+78°
+77°
+76°
+75°

174 ly
138 ly

C E P H E U S

IC 1454
V438 (s)

143 ly

RY
(m3)
V368 (v)
64 ly
V436 (s)
S (m3)

29 ρ
28

161 ly

154 ly

33 π
GQ (v1)
68 ly
V452 (3)
V441 (e1)
117 ly

118 ly
159 ly

C E P H E U S

23ʰ 00ᵐ   22ʰ 40ᵐ   22ʰ 20ᵐ   22ʰ 00ᵐ

Bright and Dark Nebulae
To scale   <10'
Planetary Nebulae
>100"   100"–30"   <30'

Open Star Clusters
Globular Clusters
To scale   <5'

Galaxies
10' x 5'   6' x 1'   3' x 2'   5' x 5'   4' x 2'   2' x 1'
Plotted to scale if the major axis >2', and circular when face on or the position angle is uncertain

Quasars

Galaxy Clusters

1040

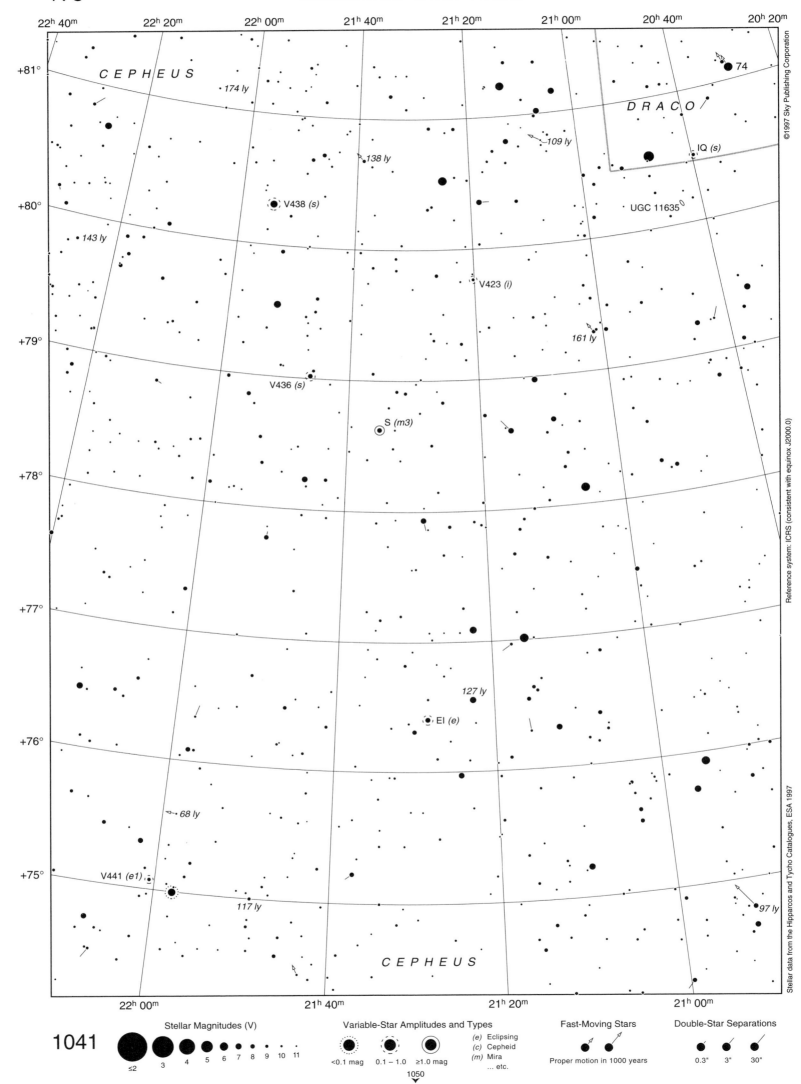

©1997 Sky Publishing Corporation

Reference system: ICRS (consistent with equinox J2000.0)

Stellar data from the Hipparcos and Tycho Catalogues, ESA 1997

C E P H E U S
174 ly
143 ly
V438 (s)
138 ly
109 ly
D R A C O
74
IQ (s)
UGC 11635
V423 (i)
161 ly
V436 (s)
S (m3)
127 ly
El (e)
68 ly
V441 (e1)
117 ly
97 ly
C E P H E U S

1041

Stellar Magnitudes (V)

●  ●  ●  ● ● ● · · · ·
≤2  3  4  5 6 7 8 9 10 11

Variable-Star Amplitudes and Types

⊙  ⊙  ⊙
<0.1 mag   0.1 – 1.0   ≥1.0 mag

(e) Eclipsing
(c) Cepheid
(m) Mira
... etc.

Fast-Moving Stars

Proper motion in 1000 years

Double-Star Separations

●  ●  ●
0.3"   3"   30"

# MILLENNIUM STAR ATLAS

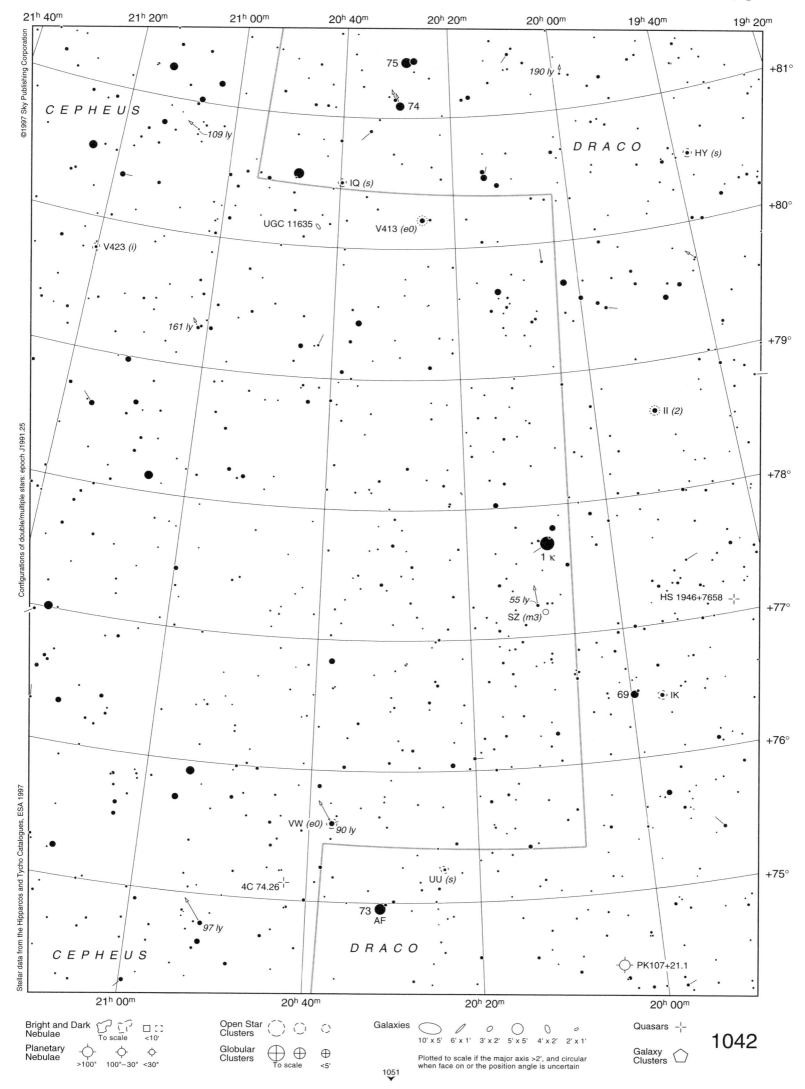

Configurations of double/multiple stars: epoch J1991.25

Stellar data from the Hipparcos and Tycho Catalogues. ESA 1997

21h 40m     21h 20m     21h 00m     20h 40m     20h 20m     20h 00m     19h 40m     19h 20m

C E P H E U S

D R A C O

75

74

190 ly

HY (s)

109 ly

IQ (s)

UGC 11635

V413 (e0)

V423 (i)

161 ly

II (2)

1 κ

55 ly

SZ (m3)

HS 1946+7658

69     IK

VW (e0)     90 ly

4C 74.26

UU (s)

73
AF

PK107+21.1

C E P H E U S

D R A C O

+81°

+80°

+79°

+78°

+77°

+76°

+75°

21h 00m     20h 40m     20h 20m     20h 00m

| Bright and Dark Nebulae | Open Star Clusters | Galaxies | Quasars |

Bright and Dark Nebulae     To scale     <10'
Planetary Nebulae     >100"     100"–30"     <30"

Open Star Clusters
Globular Clusters     To scale     <5'

Galaxies     10' x 5'   6' x 1'   3' x 2'   5' x 5'   4' x 2'   2' x 1'
Plotted to scale if the major axis >2', and circular when face on or the position angle is uncertain

Quasars

Galaxy Clusters

1042

1051

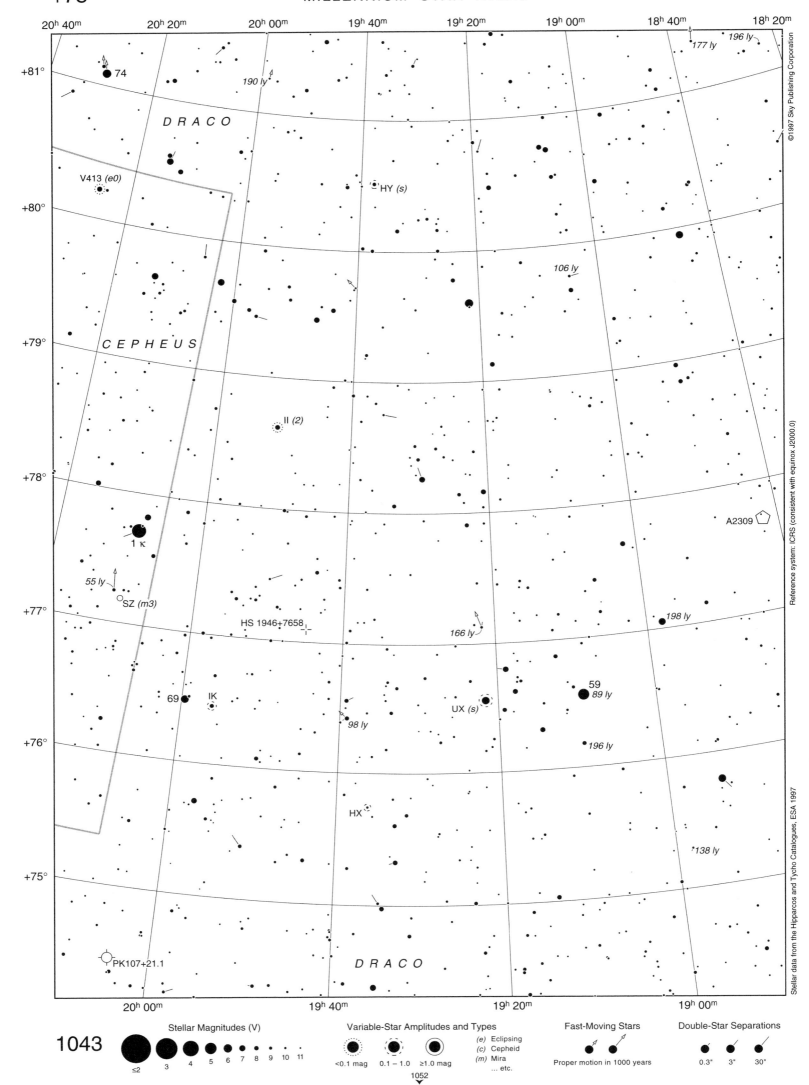

©1997 Sky Publishing Corporation

Reference system: ICRS (consistent with equinox J2000.0)

Stellar data from the Hipparcos and Tycho Catalogues, ESA 1997

1043

Stellar Magnitudes (V)

≤2   3   4   5   6   7  8  9  10 11

Variable-Star Amplitudes and Types

<0.1 mag    0.1 − 1.0    ≥1.0 mag

(e) Eclipsing
(c) Cepheid
(m) Mira
... etc.

Fast-Moving Stars

Proper motion in 1000 years

Double-Star Separations

0.3"   3"   30"

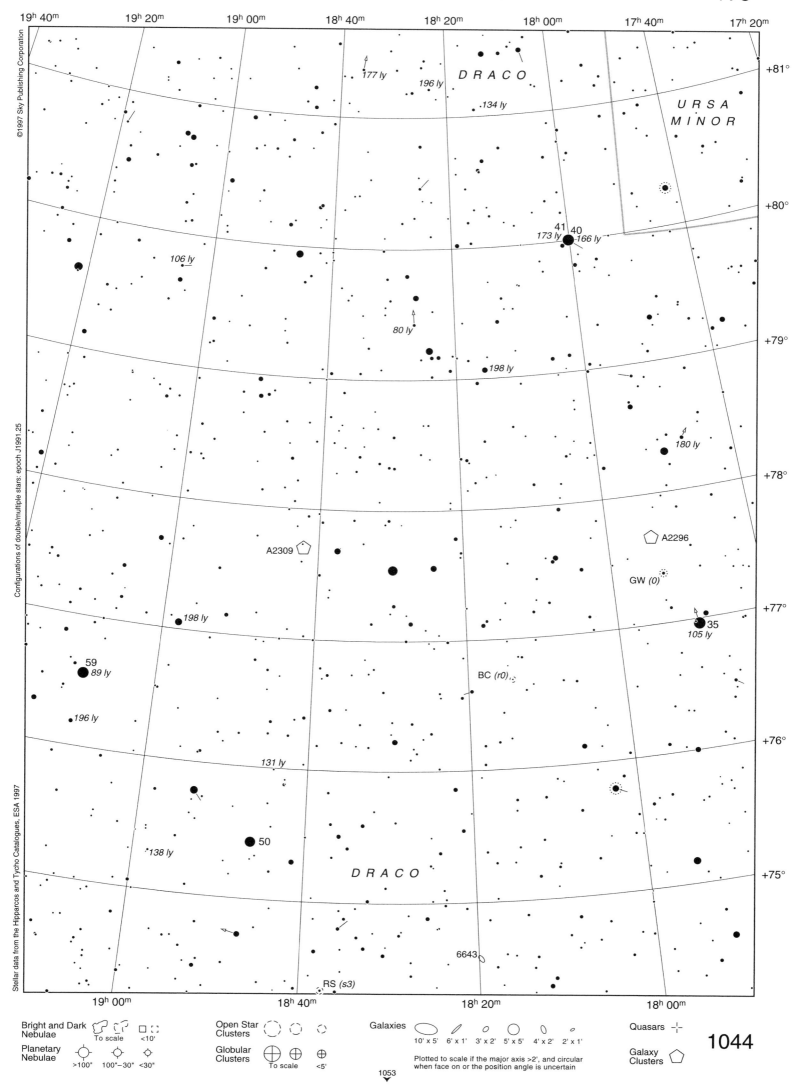

Configurations of double/multiple stars: epoch J1991.25

Stellar data from the Hipparcos and Tycho Catalogues, ESA 1997

D R A C O

U R S A
M I N O R

177 ly

196 ly

134 ly

41 40
173 ly 166 ly

106 ly

80 ly

198 ly

180 ly

A2296

A2309

GW (0)

198 ly

35
105 ly

59
89 ly

BC (r0)

196 ly

131 ly

50

138 ly

D R A C O

6643

RS (s3)

Bright and Dark
Nebulae
To scale    <10'

Planetary
Nebulae
>100"  100"–30"  <30"

Open Star
Clusters

Globular
Clusters
To scale    <5'

Galaxies

10' x 5'  6' x 1'  3' x 2'  5' x 5'  4' x 2'  2' x 1'

Plotted to scale if the major axis >2', and circular
when face on or the position angle is uncertain

Quasars

Galaxy
Clusters

1044

1053

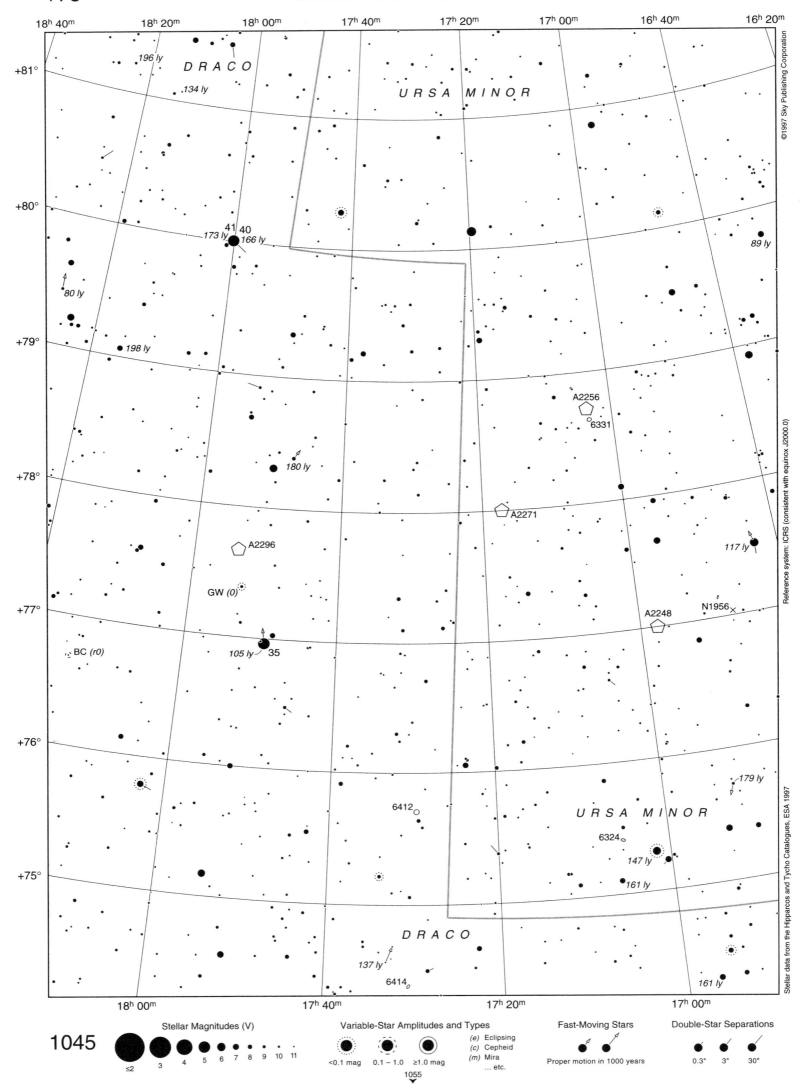

**1045**

Stellar Magnitudes (V)

≤2    3    4    5   6  7  8  9 10 11

Variable-Star Amplitudes and Types

<0.1 mag    0.1 − 1.0    ≥1.0 mag

(e) Eclipsing
(c) Cepheid
(m) Mira
... etc.

Fast-Moving Stars

Proper motion in 1000 years

Double-Star Separations

0.3"    3"    30"

1055

# MILLENNIUM STAR ATLAS

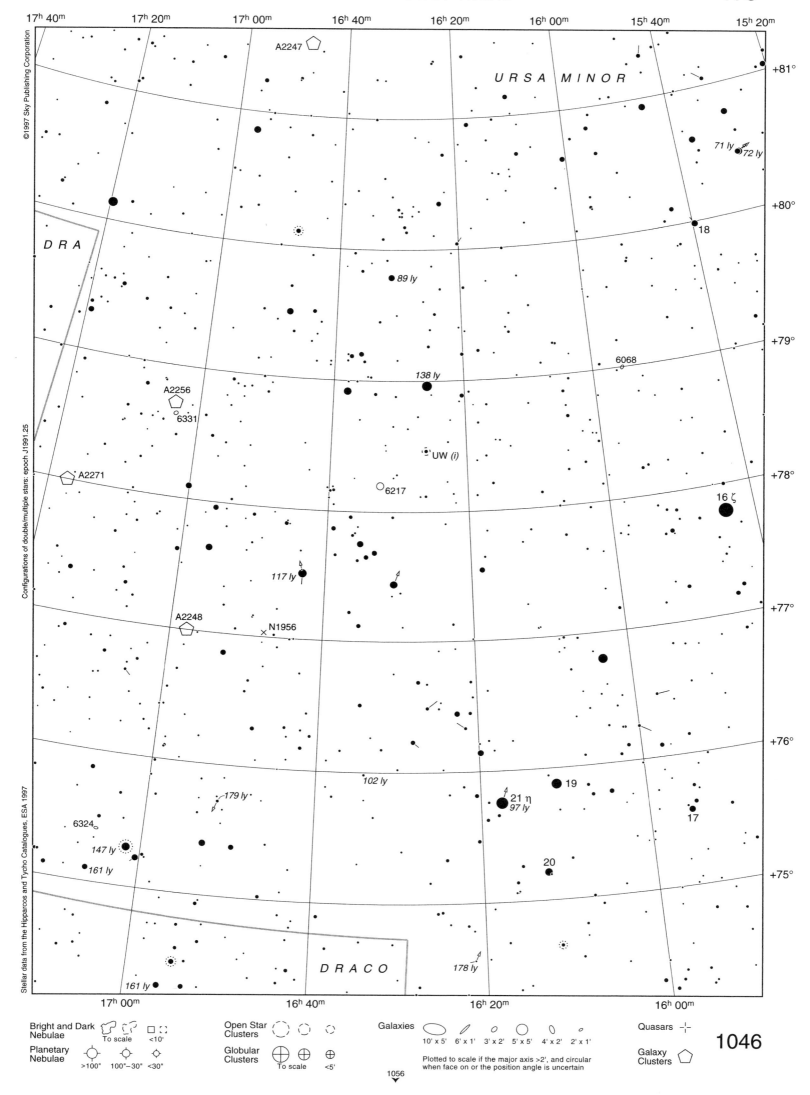

Configurations of double/multiple stars: epoch J1991.25

Stellar data from the Hipparcos and Tycho Catalogues, ESA 1997

URSA MINOR

DRA

DRACO

+81°
+80°
+79°
+78°
+77°
+76°
+75°

17h 40m  17h 20m  17h 00m  16h 40m  16h 20m  16h 00m  15h 40m  15h 20m

17h 00m  16h 40m  16h 20m  16h 00m

A2247

71 ly  72 ly

18

89 ly

138 ly

6068

A2256
6331

UW (i)

A2271

6217

16 ζ

117 ly

A2248

N1956

102 ly

179 ly

19

21 η
97 ly

17

6324

147 ly

20

161 ly

161 ly

178 ly

| | | | |
|---|---|---|---|
| Bright and Dark Nebulae | Open Star Clusters | Galaxies | Quasars −|− |
| Planetary Nebulae | Globular Clusters | | Galaxy Clusters |

Bright and Dark Nebulae — To scale — <10'

Planetary Nebulae — >100" — 100"–30" — <30"

Open Star Clusters

Globular Clusters — To scale — <5'

Galaxies — 10' x 5'  6' x 1'  3' x 2'  5' x 5'  4' x 2'  2' x 1'

Plotted to scale if the major axis >2', and circular when face on or the position angle is uncertain

Quasars

Galaxy Clusters

1046

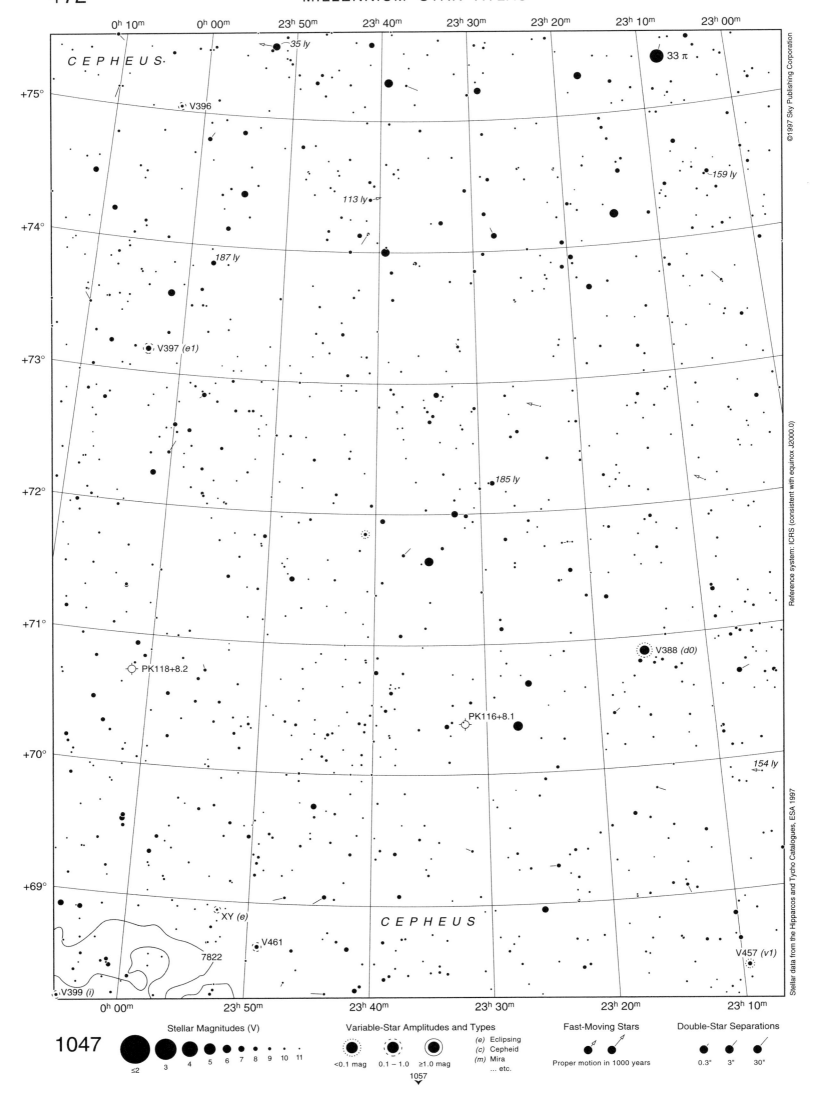

©1997 Sky Publishing Corporation

Reference system: ICRS (consistent with equinox J2000.0)

Stellar data from the Hipparcos and Tycho Catalogues, ESA 1997

C E P H E U S

V396

35 ly

33 π

159 ly

113 ly

187 ly

V397 (e1)

185 ly

V388 (d0)

PK118+8.2

PK116+8.1

154 ly

C E P H E U S

XY (e)

V461

7822

V457 (v1)

V399 (i)

1047

| Stellar Magnitudes (V) | Variable-Star Amplitudes and Types | Fast-Moving Stars | Double-Star Separations |
|---|---|---|---|

Stellar Magnitudes (V)
≤2   3   4   5   6 7 8 9 10 11

Variable-Star Amplitudes and Types
<0.1 mag    0.1 – 1.0    ≥1.0 mag

(e) Eclipsing
(c) Cepheid
(m) Mira
... etc.

Fast-Moving Stars
Proper motion in 1000 years

Double-Star Separations
0.3"   3"   30"

1057

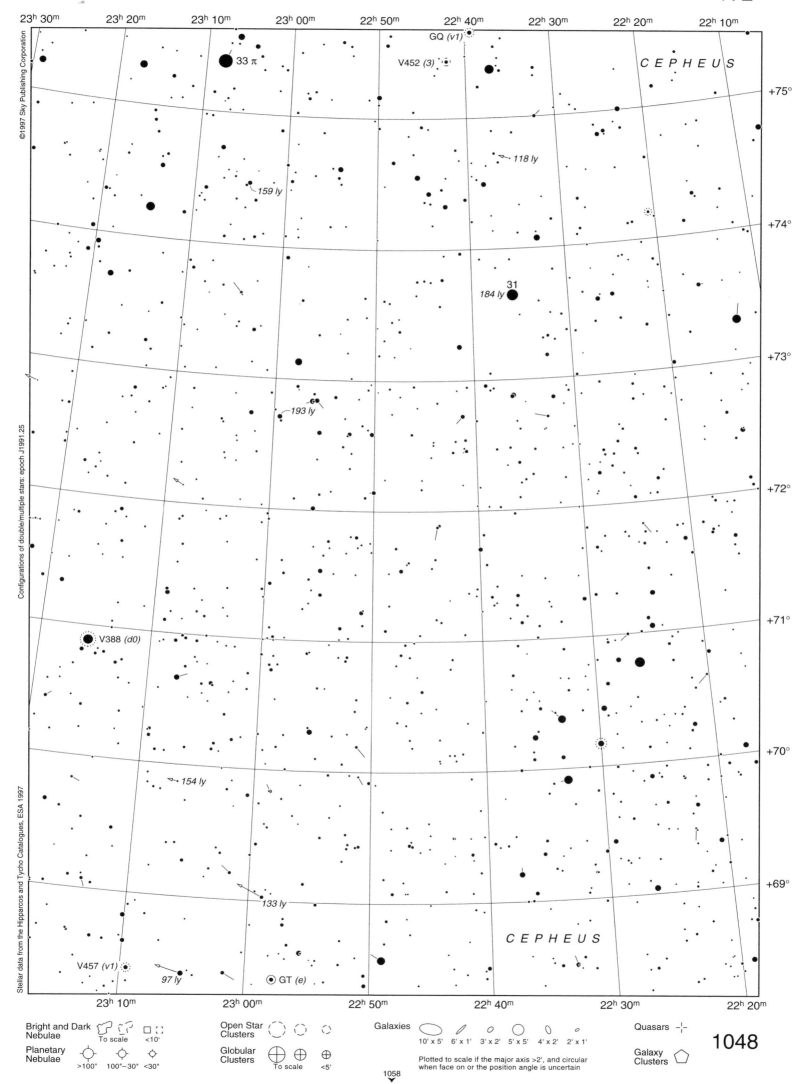

# MILLENNIUM STAR ATLAS

+72°

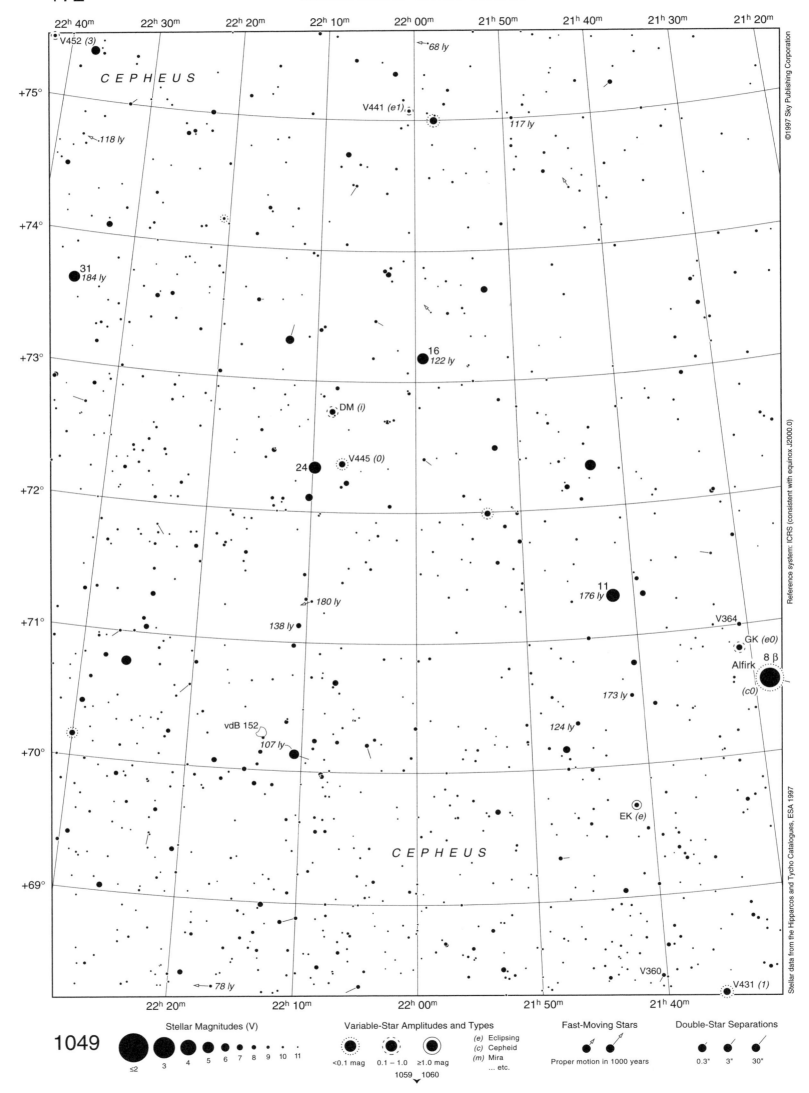

©1997 Sky Publishing Corporation

Reference system: ICRS (consistent with equinox J2000.0)

Stellar data from the Hipparcos and Tycho Catalogues, ESA 1997

V452 (3)

C E P H E U S

118 ly

68 ly

V441 (e1)

117 ly

31
184 ly

16
122 ly

DM (i)

V445 (0)

24

11
176 ly

V364

GK (e0)

8 β
Alfirk
(c0)

180 ly

138 ly

173 ly

124 ly

vdB 152

107 ly

EK (e)

C E P H E U S

V360

78 ly

V431 (1)

**1049**

### Stellar Magnitudes (V)
≤2   3   4   5   6   7   8   9   10   11

### Variable-Star Amplitudes and Types
<0.1 mag   0.1 – 1.0   ≥1.0 mag

(e) Eclipsing
(c) Cepheid
(m) Mira
... etc.

1059   1060

### Fast-Moving Stars
Proper motion in 1000 years

### Double-Star Separations
0.3"   3"   30"

# MILLENNIUM STAR ATLAS

**+72°**

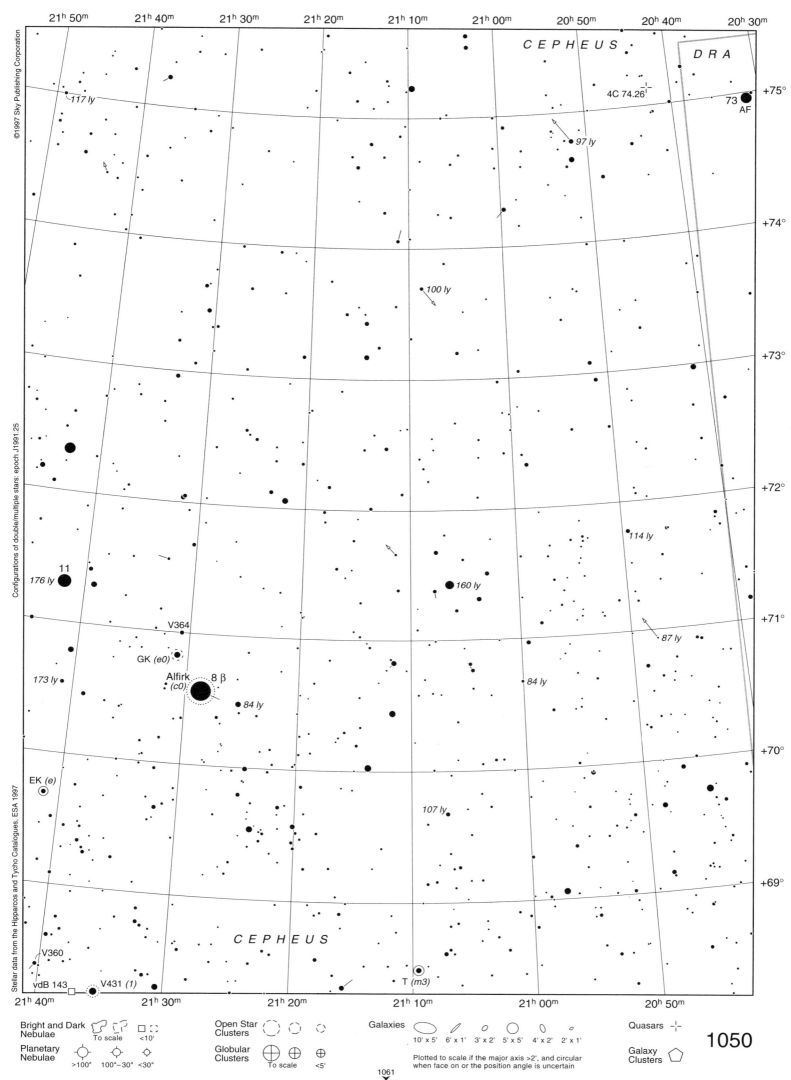

©1997 Sky Publishing Corporation

Configurations of double/multiple stars: epoch J1991.25

Stellar data from the Hipparcos and Tycho Catalogues, ESA 1997

21h 50m   21h 40m   21h 30m   21h 20m   21h 10m   21h 00m   20h 50m   20h 40m   20h 30m

C E P H E U S          D R A

4C 74.26

73
AF

+75°

117 ly

97 ly

+74°

100 ly

+73°

+72°

11
176 ly

114 ly

160 ly

+71°
87 ly

V364

GK (e0)

173 ly

Alfirk   8 β
(c0)
84 ly

84 ly

84 ly

+70°

EK (e)

107 ly

+69°

C E P H E U S

V360

vdB 143   V431 (1)

T (m3)

21h 40m   21h 30m   21h 20m   21h 10m   21h 00m   20h 50m

| | |
|---|---|
| **Bright and Dark Nebulae** | To scale   <10' |
| **Planetary Nebulae** | >100"   100"–30"   <30" |
| **Open Star Clusters** | |
| **Globular Clusters** | To scale   <5' |
| **Galaxies** | 10' x 5'   6' x 1'   3' x 2'   5' x 5'   4' x 2'   2' x 1' |
| | Plotted to scale if the major axis >2', and circular when face on or the position angle is uncertain |
| **Quasars** | |
| **Galaxy Clusters** | |

**1050**

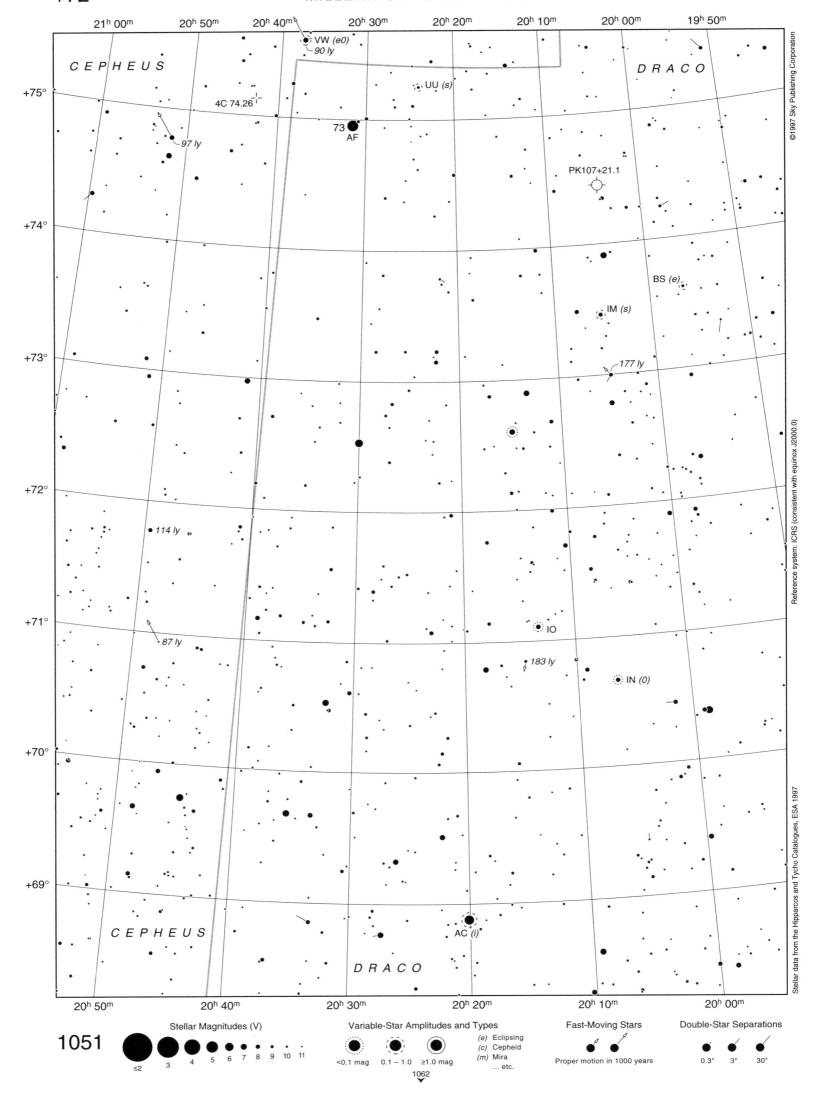

©1997 Sky Publishing Corporation

Reference system: ICRS (consistent with equinox J2000.0)

Stellar data from the Hipparcos and Tycho Catalogues, ESA 1997

C E P H E U S

D R A C O

VW *(e0)*
90 ly

4C 74.26

UU *(s)*

97 ly

73
AF

PK107+21.1

BS *(e)*

IM *(s)*

177 ly

114 ly

IO

183 ly

87 ly

IN *(0)*

C E P H E U S

AC *(i)*

D R A C O

1051

### Stellar Magnitudes (V)

≤2   3   4   5   6   7   8   9   10   11

### Variable-Star Amplitudes and Types

<0.1 mag    0.1 – 1.0    ≥1.0 mag

*(e)* Eclipsing
*(c)* Cepheid
*(m)* Mira
... etc.

### Fast-Moving Stars

Proper motion in 1000 years

### Double-Star Separations

0.3"   3"   30"

1062

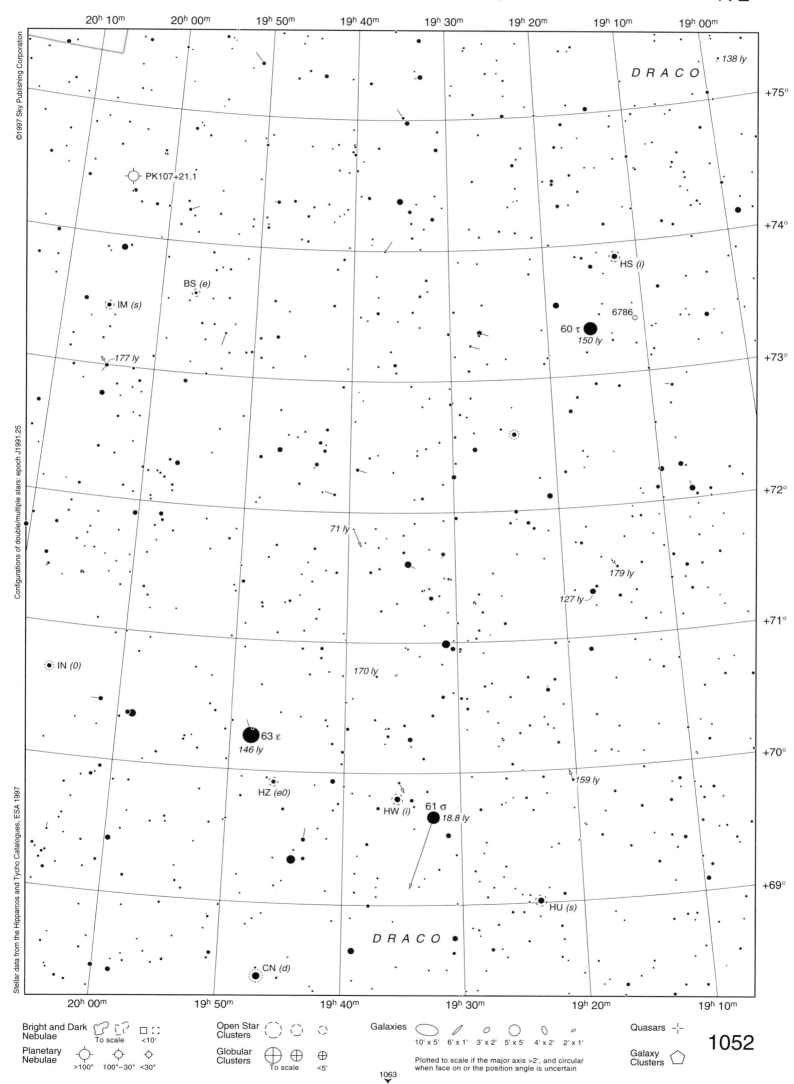

DRACO

*138 ly*

PK107+21.1

HS *(i)*

BS *(e)*

IM *(s)*

6786

60 τ
*150 ly*

*177 ly*

*71 ly*

*179 ly*

*127 ly*

IN *(0)*

*170 ly*

63 ε
*146 ly*

*159 ly*

HZ *(e0)*

HW *(i)*

61 σ
*18.8 ly*

HU *(s)*

DRACO

CN *(d)*

| Bright and Dark Nebulae | | | Open Star Clusters | | | Galaxies | | | | | | | Quasars |
|---|---|---|---|---|---|---|---|---|---|---|---|---|---|
| | To scale | <10' | | To scale | <5' | | | | | | | | |

Planetary Nebulae
>100"  100"–30"  <30"

Globular Clusters

Galaxies
10' x 5'  6' x 1'  3' x 2'  5' x 5'  4' x 2'  2' x 1'

Galaxy Clusters

Plotted to scale if the major axis >2', and circular when face on or the position angle is uncertain

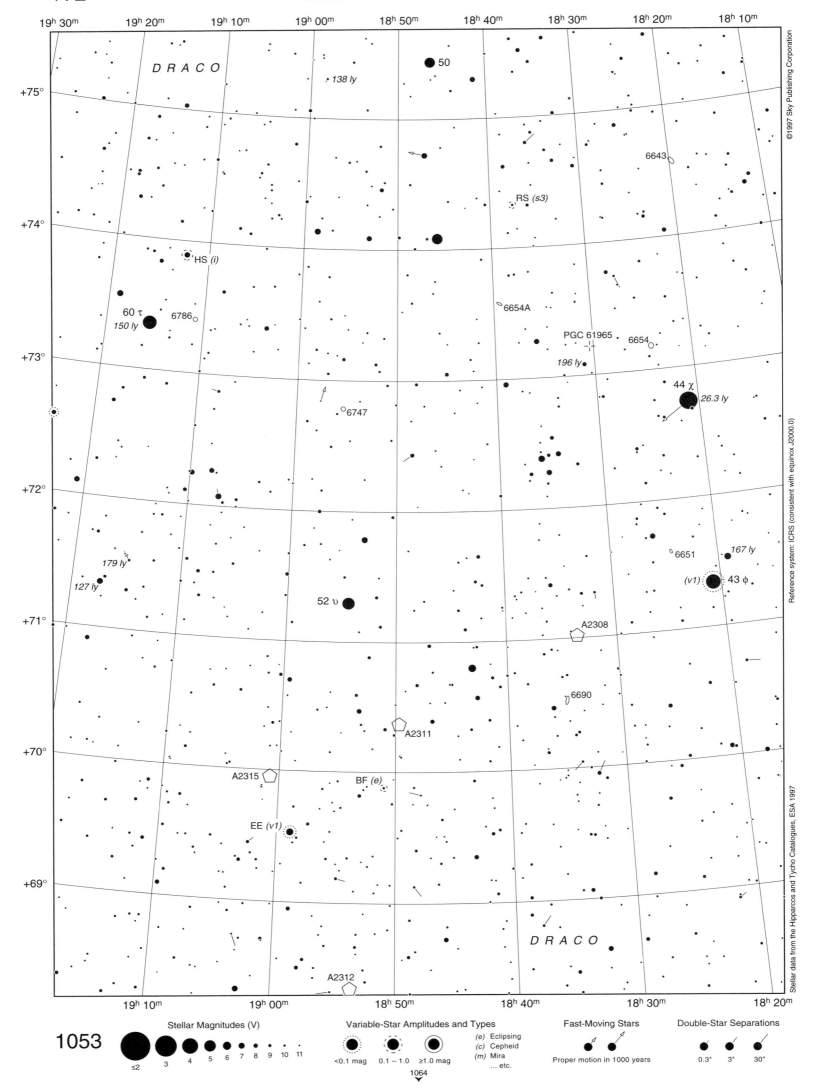

©1997 Sky Publishing Corporation

Reference system: ICRS (consistent with equinox J2000.0)

Stellar data from the Hipparcos and Tycho Catalogues, ESA 1997

DRACO

50

138 ly

6643

RS (s3)

HS (i)

60 τ
150 ly          6786

6654A

PGC 61965          6654

196 ly

44 χ     26.3 ly

6747

6651          167 ly

179 ly

(v1)     43 φ

127 ly

52 υ

A2308

θ 6690

A2311

A2315

BF (e)

EE (v1)

DRACO

A2312

1053

Stellar Magnitudes (V)

≤2   3   4   5   6   7   8   9   10   11

Variable-Star Amplitudes and Types

<0.1 mag   0.1 – 1.0   ≥1.0 mag

(e) Eclipsing
(c) Cepheid
(m) Mira
... etc.

Fast-Moving Stars

Proper motion in 1000 years

Double-Star Separations

0.3"   3"   30"

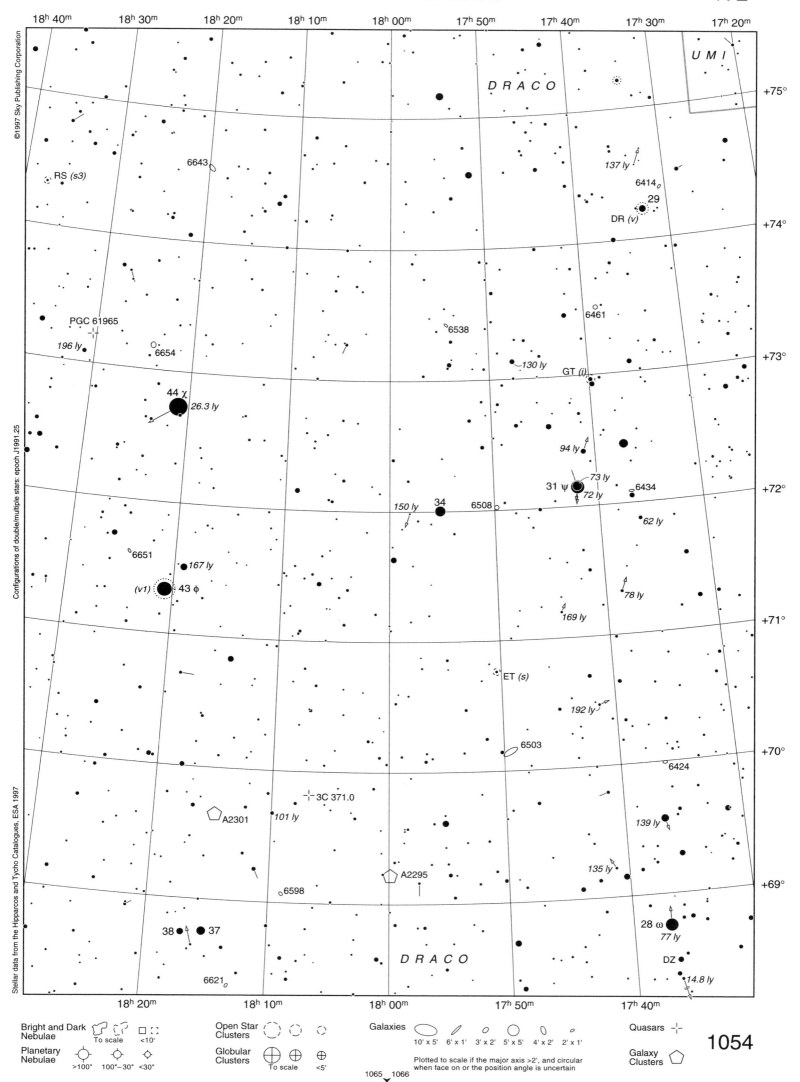

18ʰ 40ᵐ  18ʰ 30ᵐ  18ʰ 20ᵐ  18ʰ 10ᵐ  18ʰ 00ᵐ  17ʰ 50ᵐ  17ʰ 40ᵐ  17ʰ 30ᵐ  17ʰ 20ᵐ

U M I

D R A C O

+75°

©1997 Sky Publishing Corporation

6643

RS (s3)

137 ly

6414

29

DR (v)

+74°

6461

PGC 61965

6538

196 ly

6654

130 ly

GT (i)

+73°

44 χ   26.3 ly

94 ly

31 ψ   73 ly

6434

72 ly

Configurations of double/multiple stars: epoch J1991.25

150 ly

34

6508

+72°

62 ly

6651

167 ly

78 ly

(v1)   43 φ

169 ly

+71°

ET (s)

192 ly

6503

+70°

6424

3C 371.0

A2301

101 ly

139 ly

Stellar data from the Hipparcos and Tycho Catalogues, ESA 1997

A2295

135 ly

6598

+69°

38   37

28 ω

77 ly

D R A C O

DZ

6621

14.8 ly

18ʰ 20ᵐ  18ʰ 10ᵐ  18ʰ 00ᵐ  17ʰ 50ᵐ  17ʰ 40ᵐ

Bright and Dark Nebulae — To scale — <10'

Open Star Clusters — To scale

Galaxies — 10' x 5'  6' x 1'  3' x 2'  5' x 5'  4' x 2'  2' x 1'

Quasars

Planetary Nebulae — >100"  100"–30"  <30"

Globular Clusters — To scale — <5'

Plotted to scale if the major axis >2', and circular when face on or the position angle is uncertain

Galaxy Clusters

1054

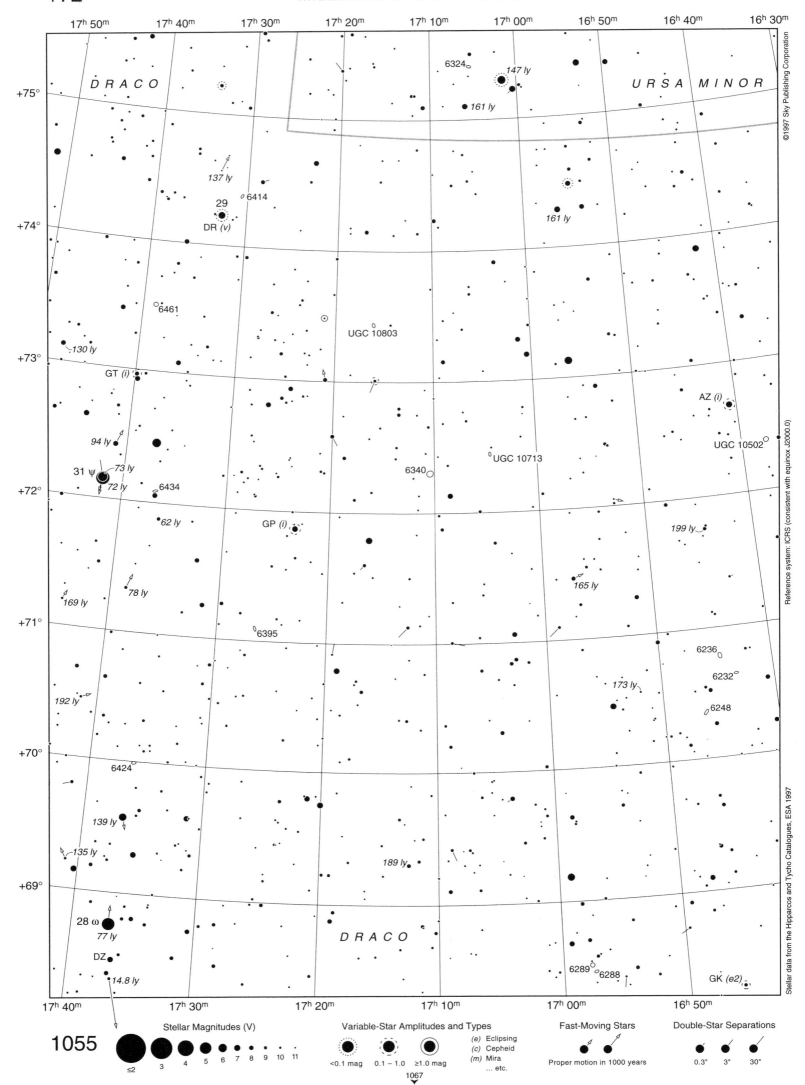

D R A C O

U R S A   M I N O R

6324

147 ly

161 ly

137 ly

29
DR (v)

6414

161 ly

6461

UGC 10803

130 ly

GT (i)

AZ (i)

UGC 10502

94 ly

31 ψ    73 ly
72 ly    6434

6340

UGC 10713

62 ly

GP (i)

199 ly

78 ly

165 ly

169 ly

6395

6236

192 ly

6232

173 ly

6248

6424

D R A C O

139 ly

135 ly

189 ly

28 ω
77 ly

DZ

6289    6288

GK (e2)

14.8 ly

1055

Stellar Magnitudes (V)

≤2    3    4    5    6    7    8    9    10    11

Variable-Star Amplitudes and Types

<0.1 mag    0.1 – 1.0    ≥1.0 mag

(e) Eclipsing
(c) Cepheid
(m) Mira
... etc.

Fast-Moving Stars

Proper motion in 1000 years

Double-Star Separations

0.3"    3"    30"

1067

# MILLENNIUM STAR ATLAS

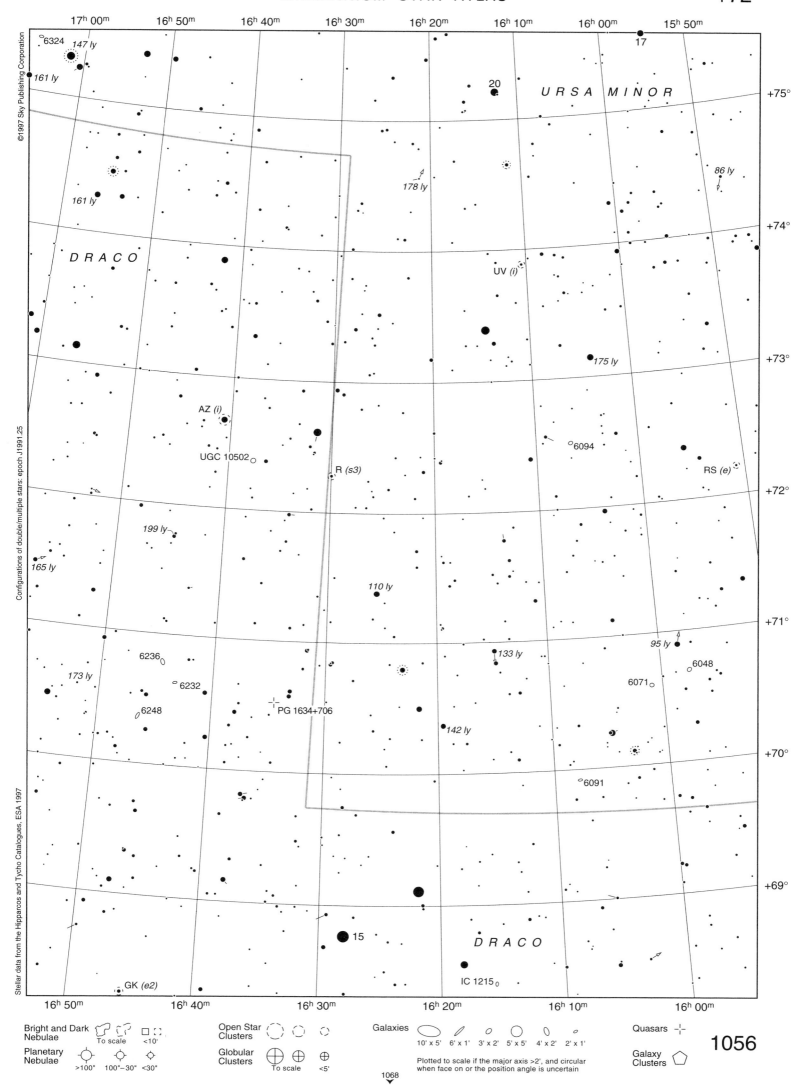

©1997 Sky Publishing Corporation

Configurations of double/multiple stars: epoch J1991.25

Stellar data from the Hipparcos and Tycho Catalogues, ESA 1997

17ʰ 00ᵐ   16ʰ 50ᵐ   16ʰ 40ᵐ   16ʰ 30ᵐ   16ʰ 20ᵐ   16ʰ 10ᵐ   16ʰ 00ᵐ   15ʰ 50ᵐ

6324  147 ly

161 ly

161 ly

D R A C O

U R S A   M I N O R

17

20

178 ly

86 ly

UV (i)

175 ly

AZ (i)

6094

RS (e)

UGC 10502

R (s3)

199 ly

165 ly

110 ly

95 ly

133 ly

6236

6048

173 ly

6232

6071

6248

PG 1634+706

142 ly

6091

D R A C O

15

IC 1215

GK (e2)

+75°

+74°

+73°

+72°

+71°

+70°

+69°

16ʰ 50ᵐ   16ʰ 40ᵐ   16ʰ 30ᵐ   16ʰ 20ᵐ   16ʰ 10ᵐ   16ʰ 00ᵐ

| Bright and Dark Nebulae | To scale | <10' |
|---|---|---|

Planetary Nebulae  >100"  100"–30"  <30"

Open Star Clusters

Globular Clusters  To scale  <5'

Galaxies  10' x 5'  6' x 1'  3' x 2'  5' x 5'  4' x 2'  2' x 1'

Plotted to scale if the major axis >2', and circular when face on or the position angle is uncertain

Quasars

Galaxy Clusters

**1056**

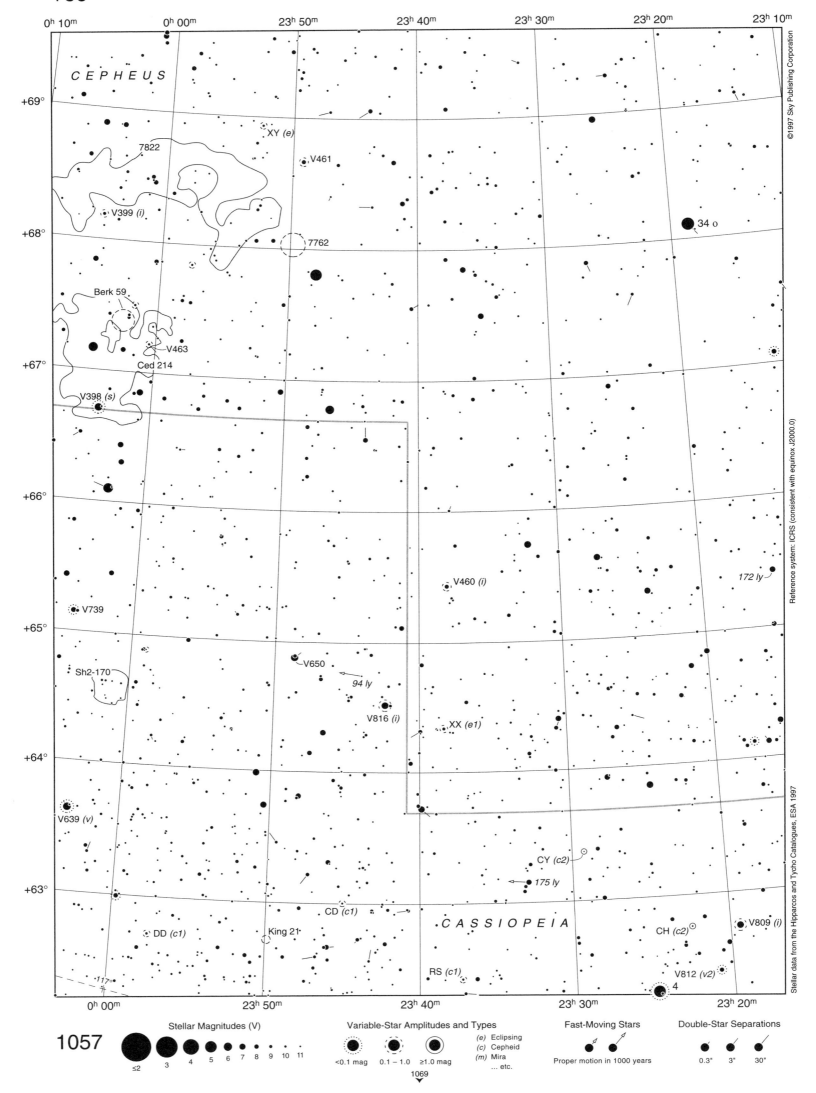

©1997 Sky Publishing Corporation

Reference system: ICRS (consistent with equinox J2000.0)

Stellar data from the Hipparcos and Tycho Catalogues, ESA 1997

CEPHEUS

CASSIOPEIA

XY (e)
V461
7822
V399 (i)
7762
34 o
Berk 59
V463
Ced 214
V398 (s)
172 ly
V460 (i)
V739
V650
94 ly
Sh2-170
V816 (i)
XX (e1)
V639 (v)
CY (c2)
175 ly
CD (c1)
King 21
DD (c1)
CH (c2)
V809 (i)
RS (c1)
V812 (v2)
117°
4

**1057**

Stellar Magnitudes (V)

≤2  3  4  5  6  7  8  9  10  11

Variable-Star Amplitudes and Types

<0.1 mag   0.1 – 1.0   ≥1.0 mag

(e) Eclipsing
(c) Cepheid
(m) Mira
... etc.

Fast-Moving Stars

Proper motion in 1000 years

Double-Star Separations

0.3"   3"   30"

# MILLENNIUM STAR ATLAS

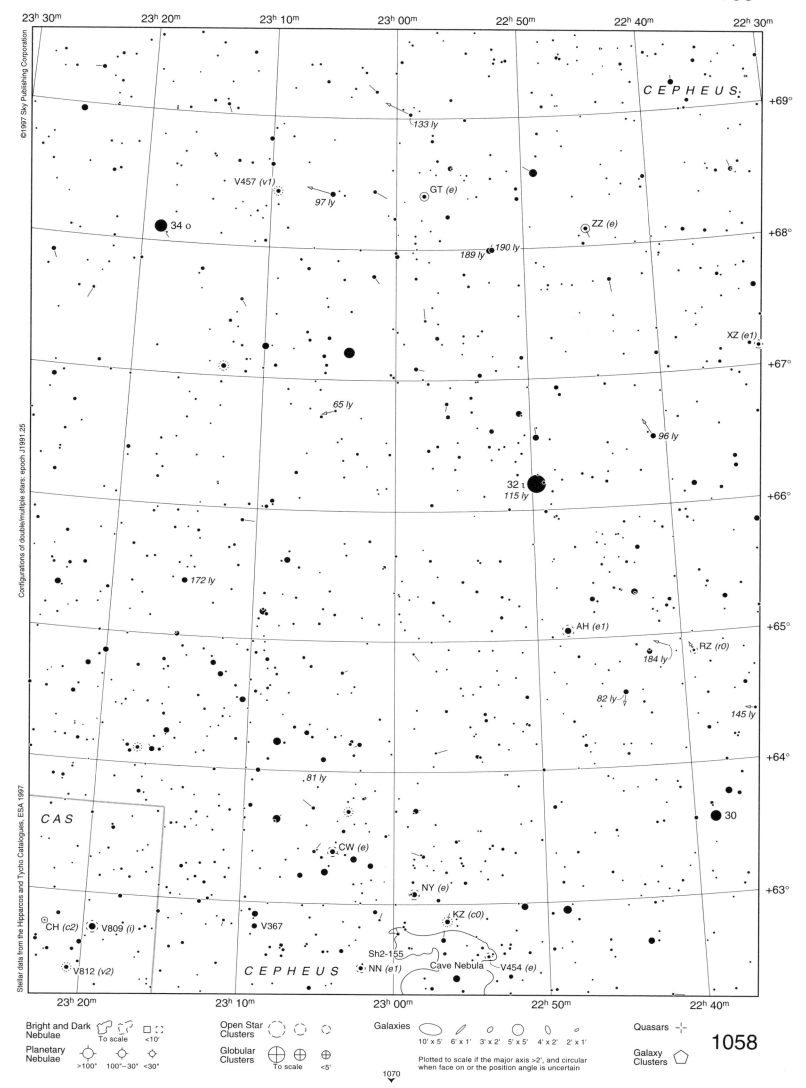

C E P H E U S

+69°

+68°

+67°

+66°

+65°

+64°

+63°

133 ly

V457 (v1)

GT (e)

ZZ (e)

97 ly

34 o

189 ly    190 ly

XZ (e1)

65 ly

96 ly

32 ι
115 ly

172 ly

AH (e1)

RZ (r0)

184 ly

82 ly

145 ly

30

81 ly

C A S

CW (e)

NY (e)

KZ (c0)

CH (c2)    V809 (i)

V367

Sh2-155

V812 (v2)

C E P H E U S

NN (e1)

Cave Nebula    V454 (e)

| Bright and Dark Nebulae | Open Star Clusters | Galaxies | Quasars |
| To scale    <10' | | 10' x 5'   6' x 1'   3' x 2'   5' x 5'   4' x 2'   2' x 1' | |
| Planetary Nebulae | Globular Clusters | | Galaxy Clusters |
| >100"   100"–30"   <30" | To scale    <5' | Plotted to scale if the major axis >2', and circular when face on or the position angle is uncertain | |

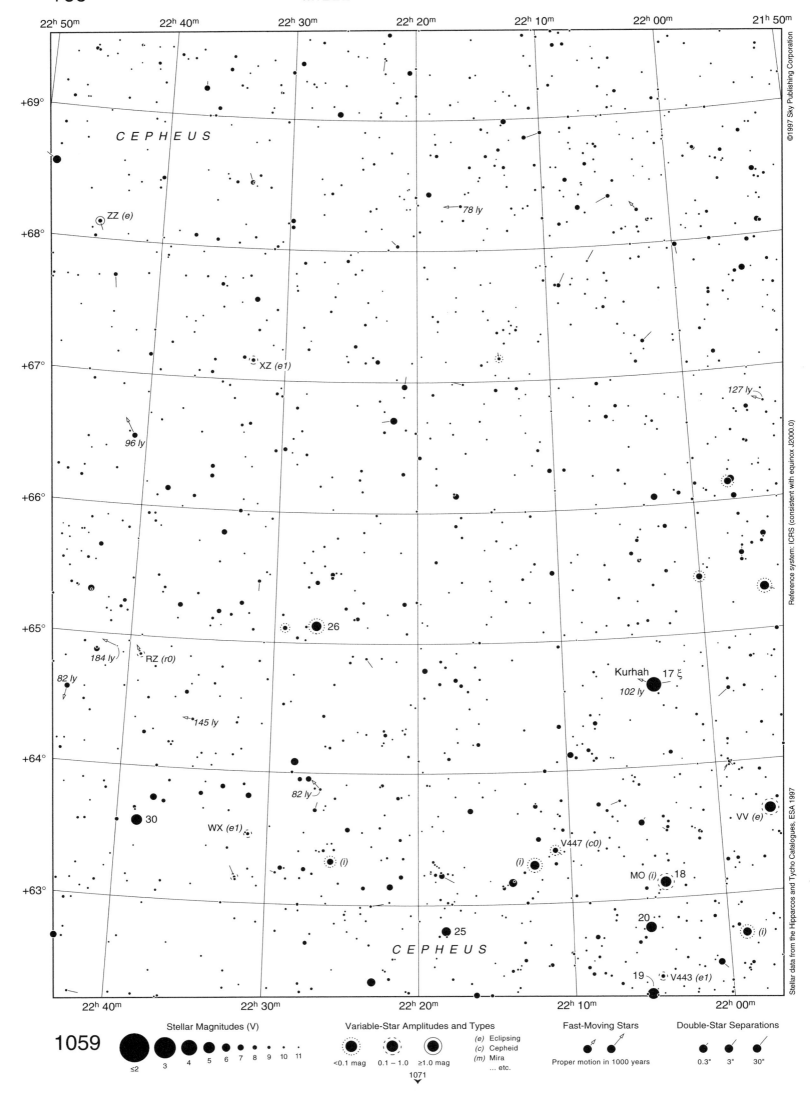

C E P H E U S

ZZ (e)

78 ly

XZ (e1)

127 ly

96 ly

26

184 ly

RZ (r0)

Kurhah   17 ξ

82 ly

102 ly

145 ly

82 ly

30

WX (e1)

VV (e)

(i)

V447 (c0)

(i)

MO (i)  18

20

25

(i)

C E P H E U S

19   V443 (e1)

©1997 Sky Publishing Corporation

Reference system: ICRS (consistent with equinox J2000.0)

Stellar data from the Hipparcos and Tycho Catalogues, ESA 1997

**1059**

| Stellar Magnitudes (V) | Variable-Star Amplitudes and Types | Fast-Moving Stars | Double-Star Separations |
|---|---|---|---|
| ≤2  3  4  5  6  7  8  9  10  11 | <0.1 mag   0.1 – 1.0   ≥1.0 mag | Proper motion in 1000 years | 0.3"   3"   30" |

(e) Eclipsing
(c) Cepheid
(m) Mira
... etc.

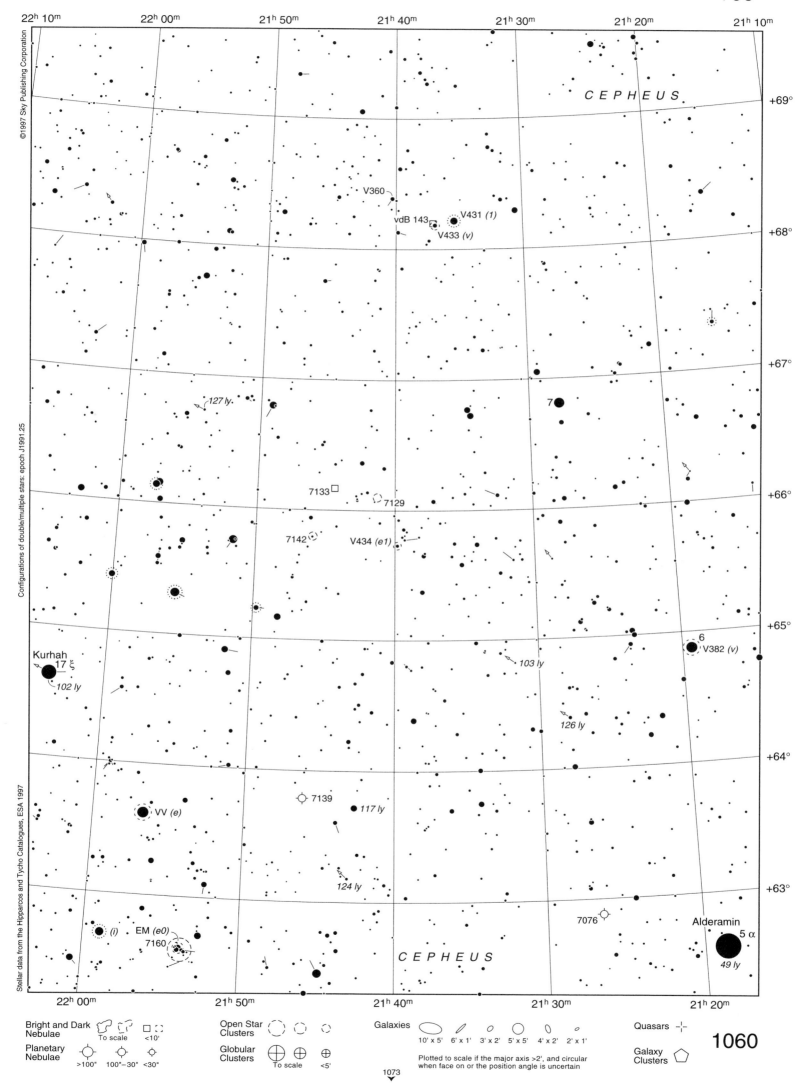

CEPHEUS

+69°

V360

V431 *(1)*
vdB 143
V433 *(v)*

+68°

127 ly

7

+67°

7133
7129

+66°

7142
V434 *(e1)*

Kurhah
17 ξ
102 ly

6
V382 *(v)*

+65°

103 ly

126 ly

+64°

7139
117 ly

VV *(e)*

124 ly

+63°

7076
Alderamin
5 α
49 ly

*(i)*
EM *(e0)*
7160

CEPHEUS

Bright and Dark Nebulae    To scale    <10'
Planetary Nebulae    >100"    100"–30"    <30"
Open Star Clusters
Globular Clusters    To scale    <5'
Galaxies    10' x 5'    6' x 1'    3' x 2'    5' x 5'    4' x 2'    2' x 1'
Plotted to scale if the major axis >2', and circular when face on or the position angle is uncertain
Quasars
Galaxy Clusters

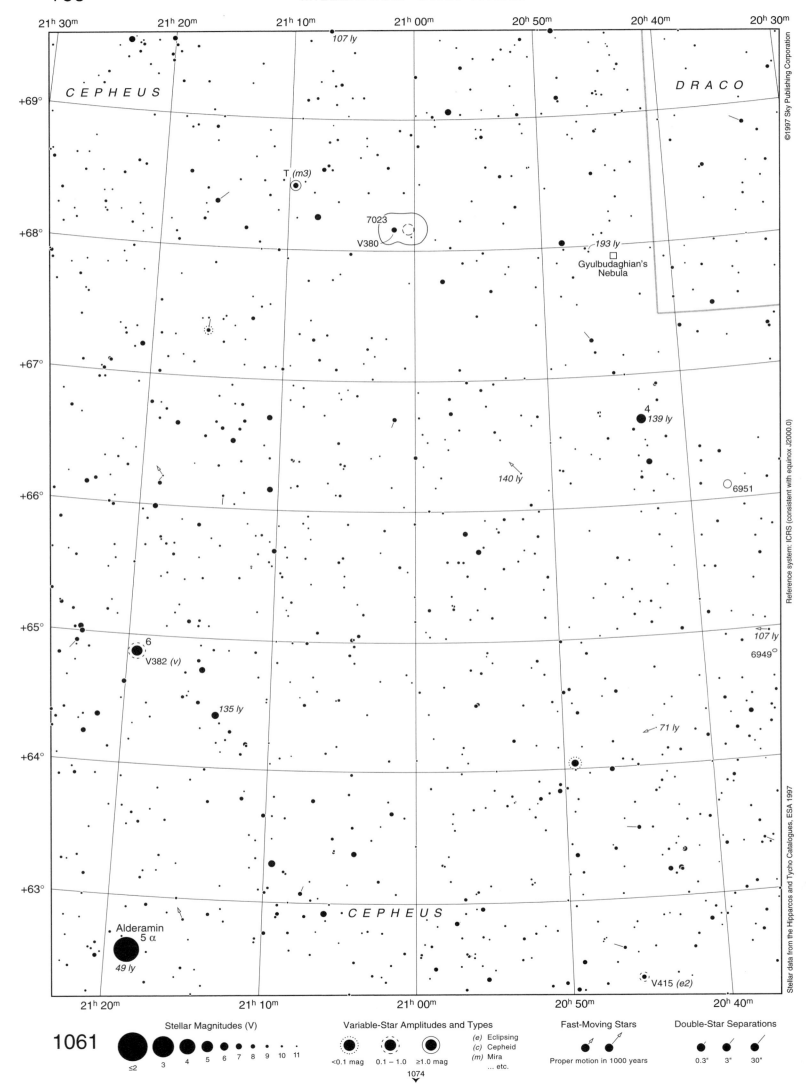

©1997 Sky Publishing Corporation

21ʰ 30ᵐ  21ʰ 20ᵐ  21ʰ 10ᵐ  21ʰ 00ᵐ  20ʰ 50ᵐ  20ʰ 40ᵐ  20ʰ 30ᵐ

C E P H E U S

D R A C O

+69°

107 ly

T (m3)

7023

+68°

V380

193 ly

Gyulbudaghian's
Nebula

+67°

4
139 ly

○ 6951

+66°

140 ly

+65°

6
V382 (v)

107 ly

6949 ○

135 ly

71 ly

+64°

C E P H E U S

+63°

Alderamin
5 α

49 ly

V415 (e2)

21ʰ 20ᵐ  21ʰ 10ᵐ  21ʰ 00ᵐ  20ʰ 50ᵐ  20ʰ 40ᵐ

Reference system: ICRS (consistent with equinox J2000.0)

Stellar data from the Hipparcos and Tycho Catalogues, ESA 1997

1061

Stellar Magnitudes (V)

≤2  3  4  5  6  7  8  9  10  11

Variable-Star Amplitudes and Types

<0.1 mag   0.1 – 1.0   ≥1.0 mag

(e) Eclipsing
(c) Cepheid
(m) Mira
... etc.

Fast-Moving Stars

Proper motion in 1000 years

Double-Star Separations

0.3"   3"   30"

1074

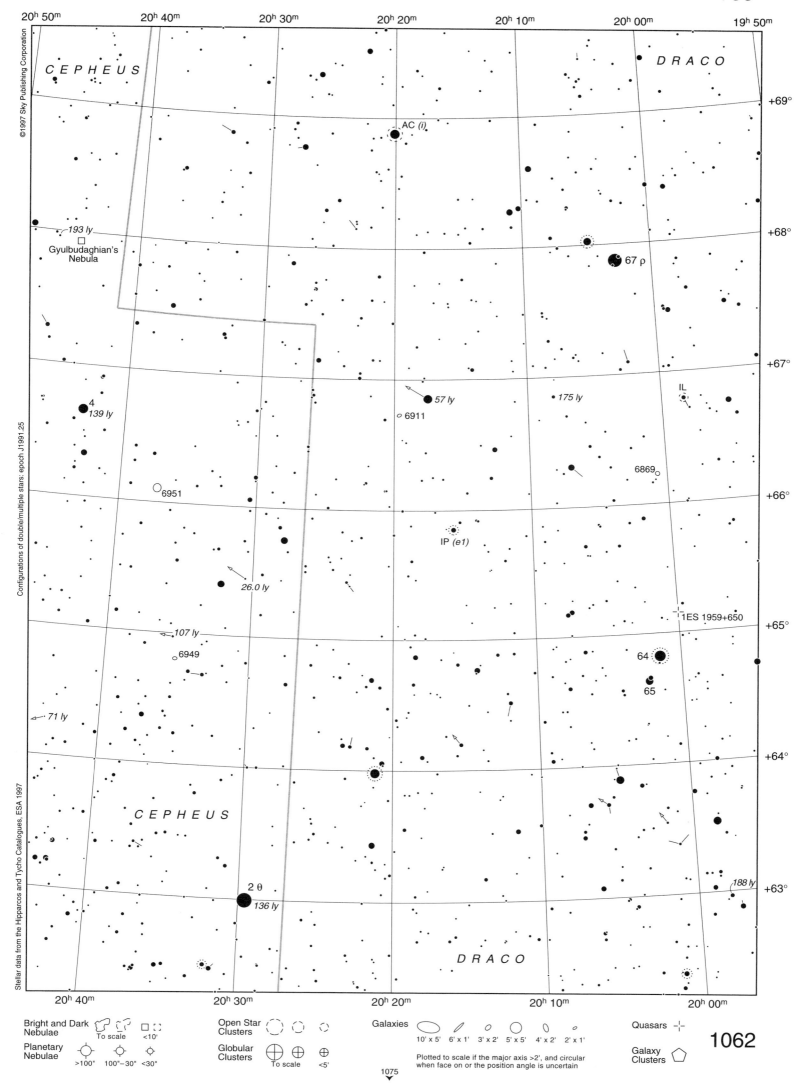

©1997 Sky Publishing Corporation

Configurations of double/multiple stars: epoch J1991.25

Stellar data from the Hipparcos and Tycho Catalogues, ESA 1997

CEPHEUS

DRACO

+69°

+68°

+67°

+66°

+65°

+64°

+63°

20h 50m
20h 40m
20h 30m
20h 20m
20h 10m
20h 00m
19h 50m

AC (i)

193 ly
Gyulbudaghian's Nebula

67 ρ

4
139 ly

57 ly
6911

175 ly

IL

6951

6869

IP (e1)

26.0 ly

1ES 1959+650

107 ly

6949

64

65

71 ly

CEPHEUS

2 θ
136 ly

DRACO

188 ly

20h 40m
20h 30m
20h 20m
20h 10m
20h 00m

Bright and Dark Nebulae
To scale
<10'

Open Star Clusters

Galaxies
10' × 5'  6' × 1'  3' × 2'  5' × 5'  4' × 2'  2' × 1'

Quasars

Planetary Nebulae
>100"  100"–30"  <30"

Globular Clusters
To scale  <5'

Plotted to scale if the major axis >2', and circular when face on or the position angle is uncertain

Galaxy Clusters

1062

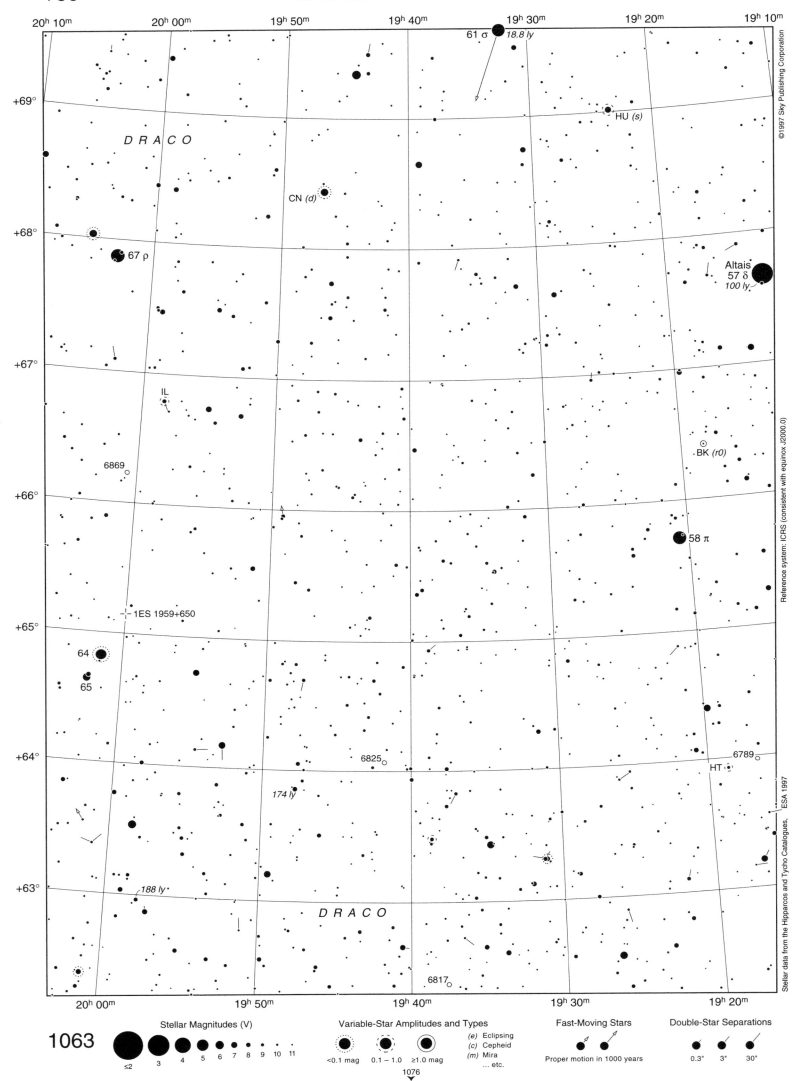

©1997 Sky Publishing Corporation

+69°

D R A C O

61 σ    18.8 ly

HU (s)

CN (d)

67 ρ

Altais
57 δ
100 ly

+68°

IL

BK (r0)

6869

+66°

58 π

Reference system: ICRS (consistent with equinox J2000.0)

1ES 1959+650

+65°

64

65

6825

6789

HT

174 ly

ESA 1997

+63°

188 ly

D R A C O

6817

20h 00m    19h 50m    19h 40m    19h 30m    19h 20m

Stellar data from the Hipparcos and Tycho Catalogues,

Stellar Magnitudes (V)

≤2    3    4    5    6    7    8    9    10    11

Variable-Star Amplitudes and Types

<0.1 mag    0.1 – 1.0    ≥1.0 mag

(e) Eclipsing
(c) Cepheid
(m) Mira
... etc.

Fast-Moving Stars

Proper motion in 1000 years

Double-Star Separations

0.3"    3"    30"

# MILLENNIUM STAR ATLAS

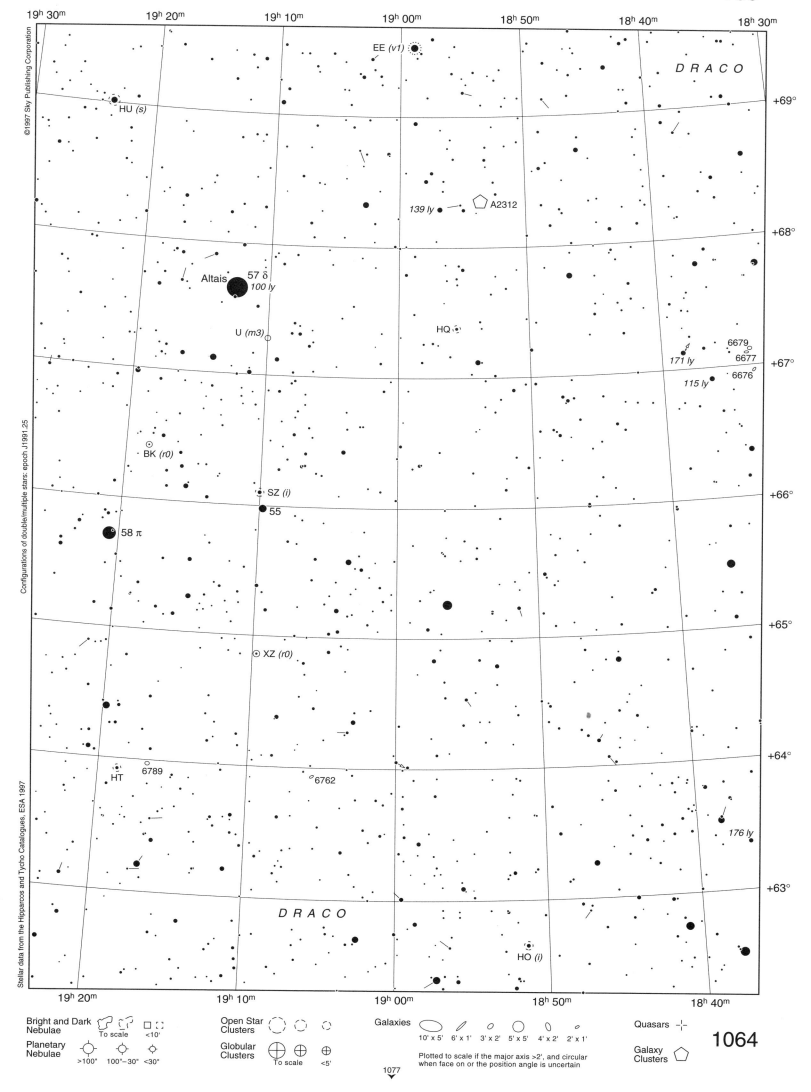

©1997 Sky Publishing Corporation

Configurations of double/multiple stars: epoch J1991.25

Stellar data from the Hipparcos and Tycho Catalogues, ESA 1997

DRACO

EE (v1)

HU (s)

+69°

139 ly  A2312

+68°

Altais  57 δ
100 ly

U (m3)

HQ

6679
6677
171 ly
6676
115 ly

+67°

BK (r0)

SZ (i)
55

58 π

+66°

XZ (r0)

+65°

+64°

HT  6789

6762

176 ly

+63°

DRACO

HO (i)

19h 20m   19h 10m   19h 00m   18h 50m   18h 40m

| | | | | |
|---|---|---|---|---|
| Bright and Dark Nebulae | Open Star Clusters | Galaxies | | Quasars |
| To scale  <10' | | 10' x 5'  6' x 1'  3' x 2'  5' x 5'  4' x 2'  2' x 1' | | |
| Planetary Nebulae | Globular Clusters | | | Galaxy Clusters |
| >100"  100"−30"  <30" | To scale  <5' | Plotted to scale if the major axis >2', and circular when face on or the position angle is uncertain | | |

**1064**

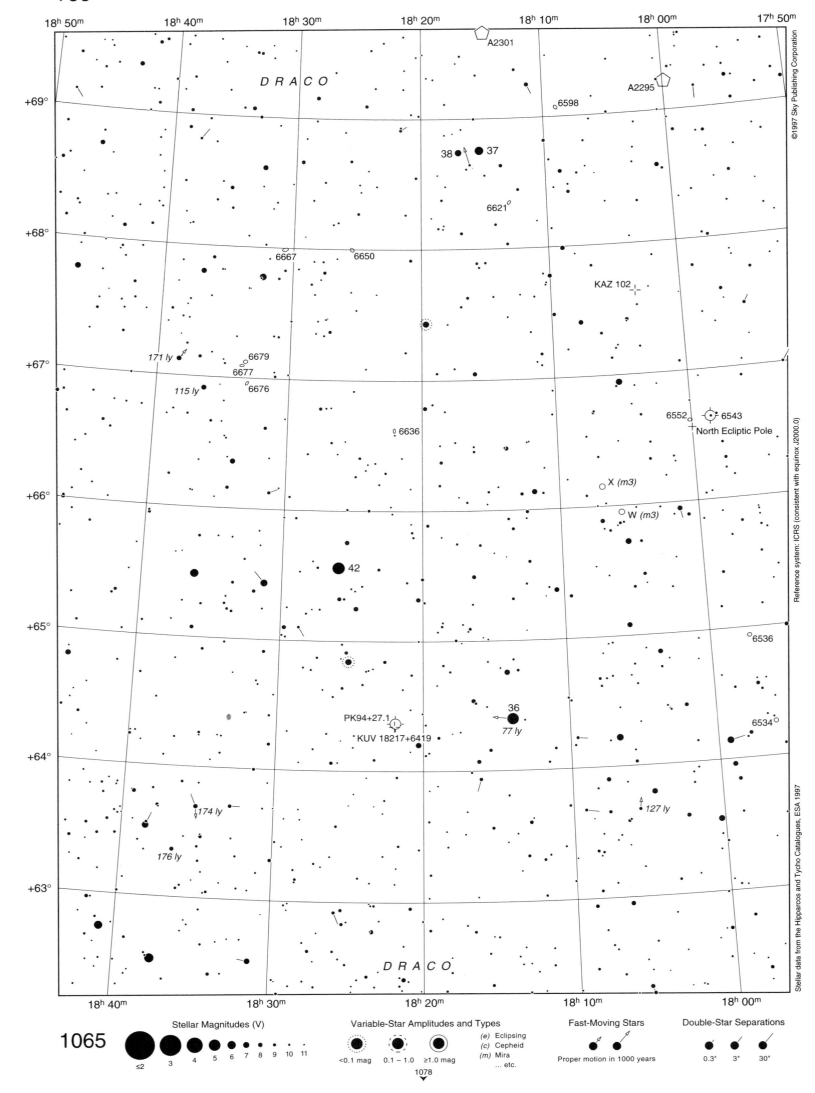

©1997 Sky Publishing Corporation

Reference system: ICRS (consistent with equinox J2000.0)

Stellar data from the Hipparcos and Tycho Catalogues, ESA 1997

1065

Stellar Magnitudes (V)

≤2   3   4   5   6   7   8   9   10   11

Variable-Star Amplitudes and Types

<0.1 mag   0.1 – 1.0   ≥1.0 mag

(e) Eclipsing
(c) Cepheid
(m) Mira
... etc.

1078

Fast-Moving Stars

Proper motion in 1000 years

Double-Star Separations

0.3"   3"   30"

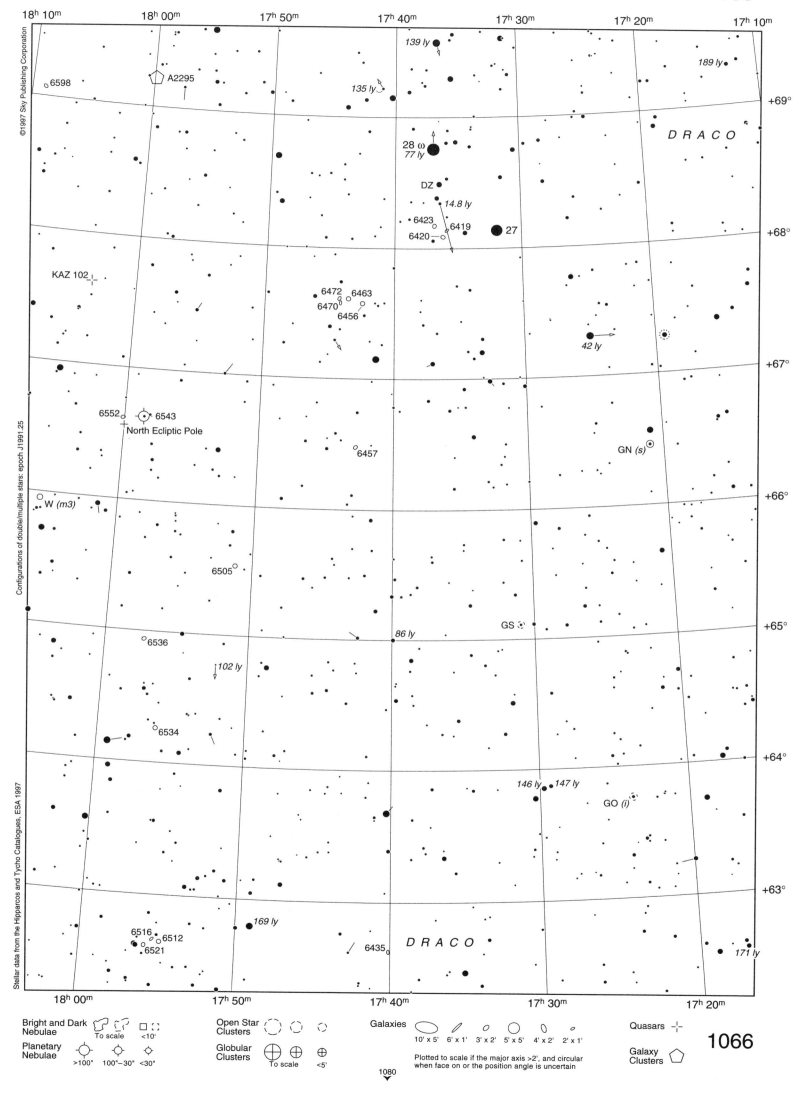

©1997 Sky Publishing Corporation

Configurations of double/multiple stars: epoch J1991.25

Stellar data from the Hipparcos and Tycho Catalogues, ESA 1997

6598

A2295

139 ly

135 ly

D R A C O

189 ly

28 ω
77 ly

DZ

14.8 ly

6423   6419
6420      27

KAZ 102

6472   6463
6470
6456

42 ly

6552   6543
North Ecliptic Pole

6457

GN (s)

W (m3)

6505

GS

86 ly

6536

102 ly

6534

146 ly   147 ly

GO (i)

D R A C O

169 ly

6516   6512
6521

6435

171 ly

18h 10m    18h 00m    17h 50m    17h 40m    17h 30m    17h 20m    17h 10m

+69°

+68°

+67°

+66°

+65°

+64°

+63°

18h 00m    17h 50m    17h 40m    17h 30m    17h 20m

| Bright and Dark Nebulae | | | | | | |
|---|---|---|---|---|---|---|
| To scale | <10' | | | | | |

Planetary Nebulae
>100"   100"–30"   <30"

Open Star Clusters

Globular Clusters
To scale   <5'

Galaxies
10' x 5'   6' x 1'   3' x 2'   5' x 5'   4' x 2'   2' x 1'

Plotted to scale if the major axis >2', and circular when face on or the position angle is uncertain

Quasars

Galaxy Clusters

1066

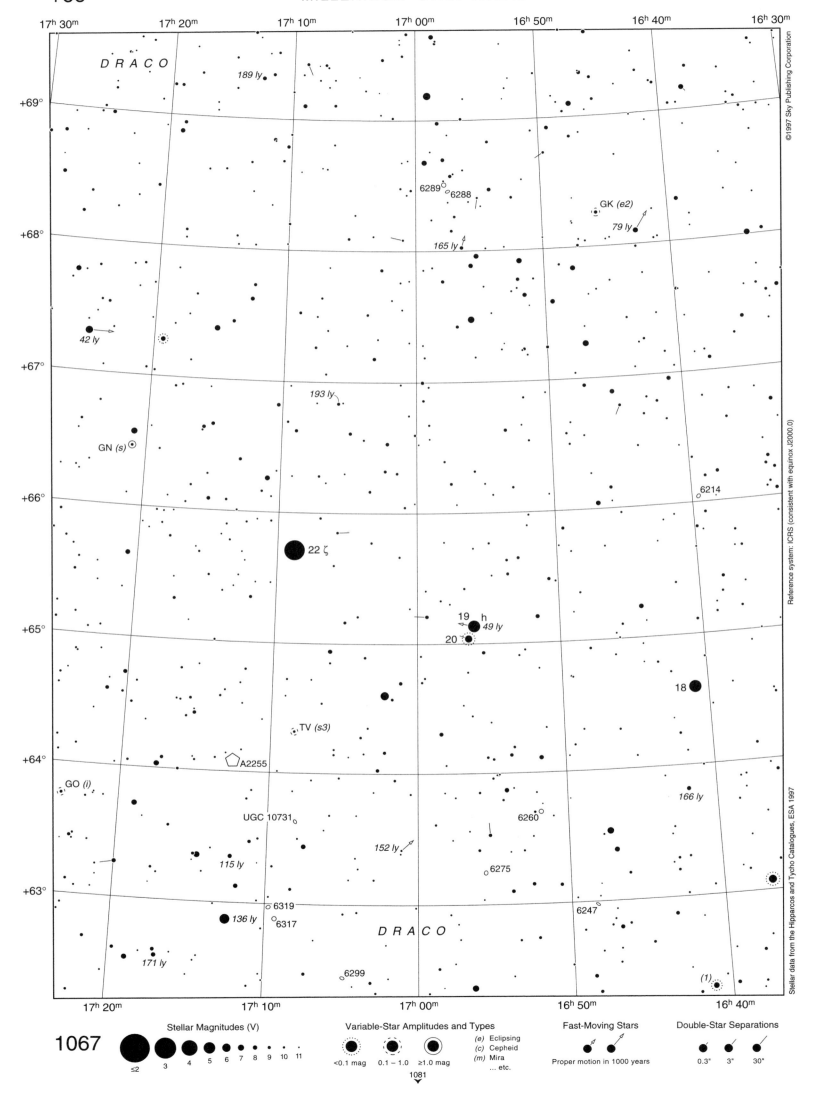

1067

**Stellar Magnitudes (V)**

≤2   3   4   5   6   7   8   9   10   11

**Variable-Star Amplitudes and Types**

<0.1 mag    0.1 – 1.0    ≥1.0 mag

(e) Eclipsing
(c) Cepheid
(m) Mira
... etc.

**Fast-Moving Stars**

Proper motion in 1000 years

**Double-Star Separations**

0.3"   3"   30"

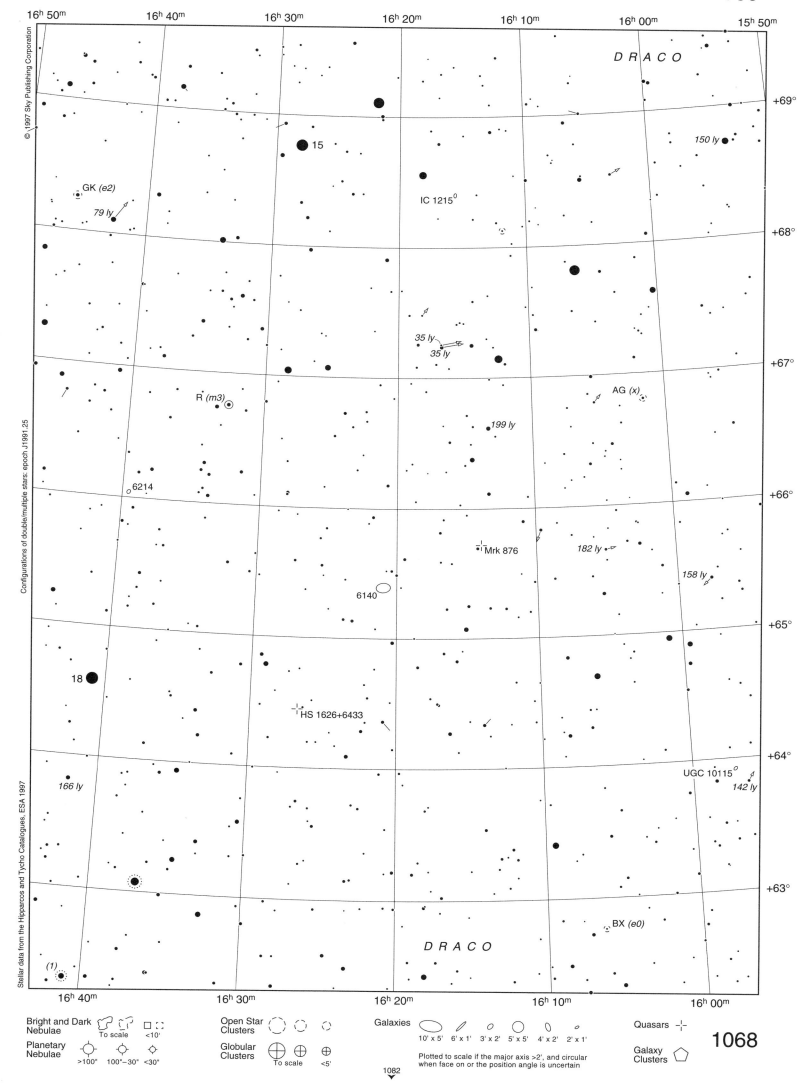

D R A C O

16h 50m    16h 40m    16h 30m    16h 20m    16h 10m    16h 00m    15h 50m

+69°

150 ly

15

GK (e2)

IC 1215

79 ly

+68°

35 ly
35 ly

+67°

R (m3)

AG (x)

199 ly

6214

+66°

Mrk 876

182 ly

158 ly

6140

+65°

18

166 ly

HS 1626+6433

+64°

UGC 10115

142 ly

+63°

BX (e0)

(1)

D R A C O

16h 40m    16h 30m    16h 20m    16h 10m    16h 00m

© 1997 Sky Publishing Corporation

Configurations of double/multiple stars: epoch J1991.25

Stellar data from the Hipparcos and Tycho Catalogues, ESA 1997

**Bright and Dark Nebulae**
To scale    <10'

**Planetary Nebulae**
>100"    100"–30"    <30"

**Open Star Clusters**

**Globular Clusters**
To scale    <5'

**Galaxies**
10' x 5'    6' x 1'    3' x 2'    5' x 5'    4' x 2'    2' x 1'

Plotted to scale if the major axis >2', and circular when face on or the position angle is uncertain

**Quasars**

**Galaxy Clusters**

1068

1082

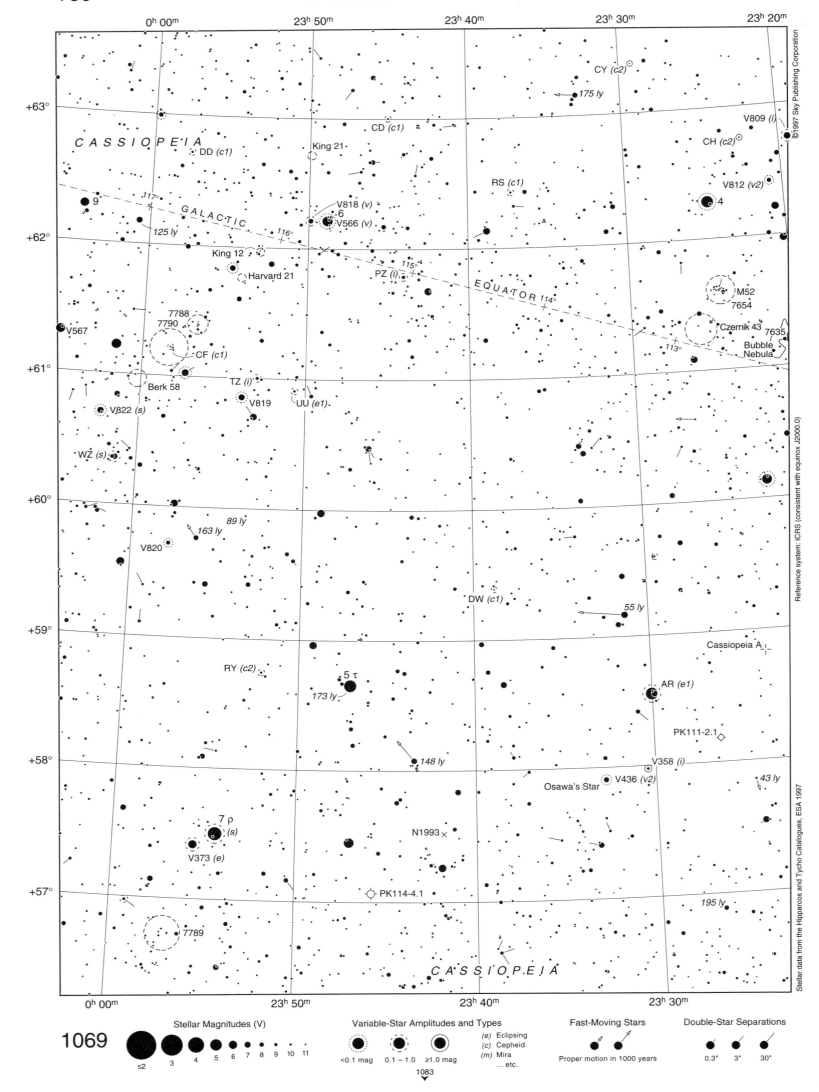

©1997 Sky Publishing Corporation

Reference system: ICRS (consistent with equinox J2000.0)

Stellar data from the Hipparcos and Tycho Catalogues, ESA 1997

Stellar Magnitudes (V)

≤2  3  4  5  6  7  8  9  10  11

Variable-Star Amplitudes and Types

<0.1 mag    0.1 – 1.0    ≥1.0 mag

(e) Eclipsing
(c) Cepheid
(m) Mira
... etc.

Fast-Moving Stars

Proper motion in 1000 years

Double-Star Separations

0.3"    3"    30"

# MILLENNIUM STAR ATLAS

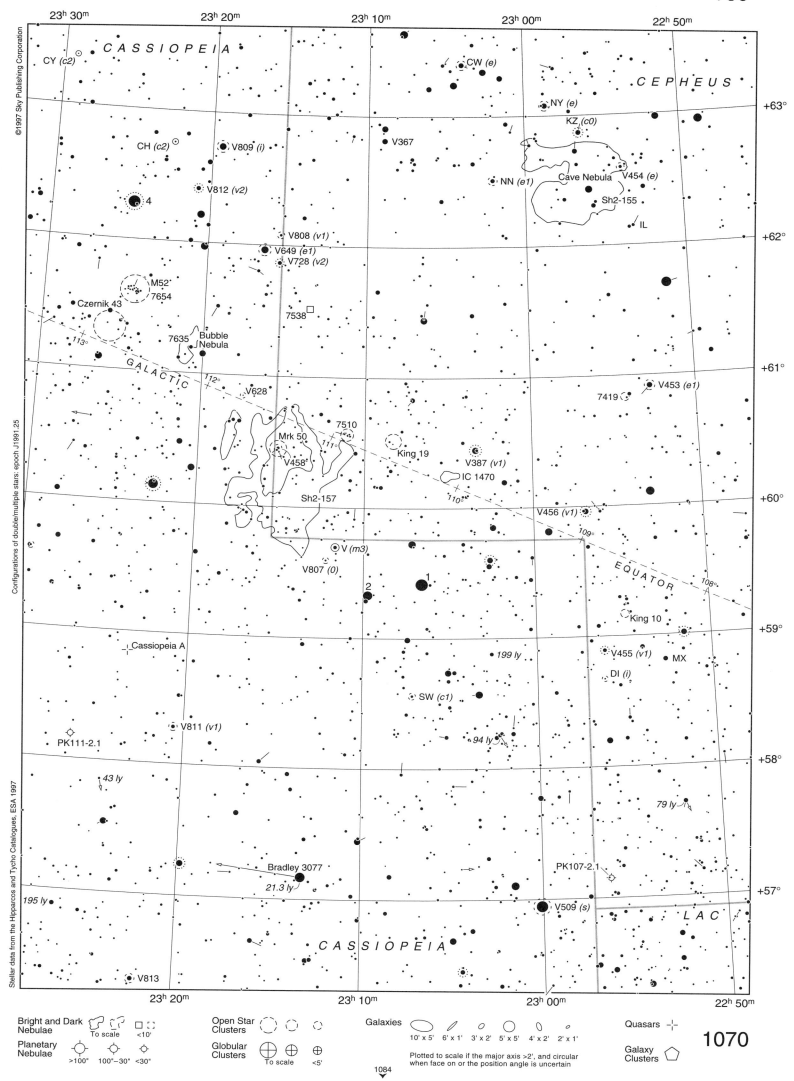

*CASSIOPEIA*

CY *(c2)*

CH *(c2)*

V809 *(i)*

V812 *(v2)*

4

V808 *(v1)*

V649 *(e1)*
V728 *(v2)*

M52
7654

Czernik 43

113°

GALACTIC

7635  Bubble
Nebula

112°

V628

Mrk 50

7510

111°

V458

Sh2-157

110°

V *(m3)*

V807 *(0)*

2

1

Cassiopeia A

V811 *(v1)*

PK111-2.1

43 ly

Bradley 3077

21.3 ly

195 ly

*CASSIOPEIA*

V813

V367

CW *(e)*

NY *(e)*

KZ *(c0)*

*CEPHEUS*

NN *(e1)*

Cave Nebula  V454 *(e)*

Sh2-155

IL

7538

7419

V453 *(e1)*

King 19

V387 *(v1)*

IC 1470

109°

V456 *(v1)*

*EQUATOR*

108°

King 10

199 ly

V455 *(v1)*  MX

DI *(i)*

SW *(c1)*

94 ly

79 ly

PK107-2.1

V509 *(s)*

*LAC*

## Legend

| Bright and Dark Nebulae | | | Open Star Clusters | | | Galaxies | | | | | | Quasars |
|---|---|---|---|---|---|---|---|---|---|---|---|---|
| | To scale | <10' | | | | 10' x 5' | 6' x 1' | 3' x 2' | 5' x 5' | 4' x 2' | 2' x 1' | |

Planetary Nebulae
>100"  100"–30"  <30"

Globular Clusters
To scale  <5'

Galaxy Clusters

Plotted to scale if the major axis >2', and circular when face on or the position angle is uncertain

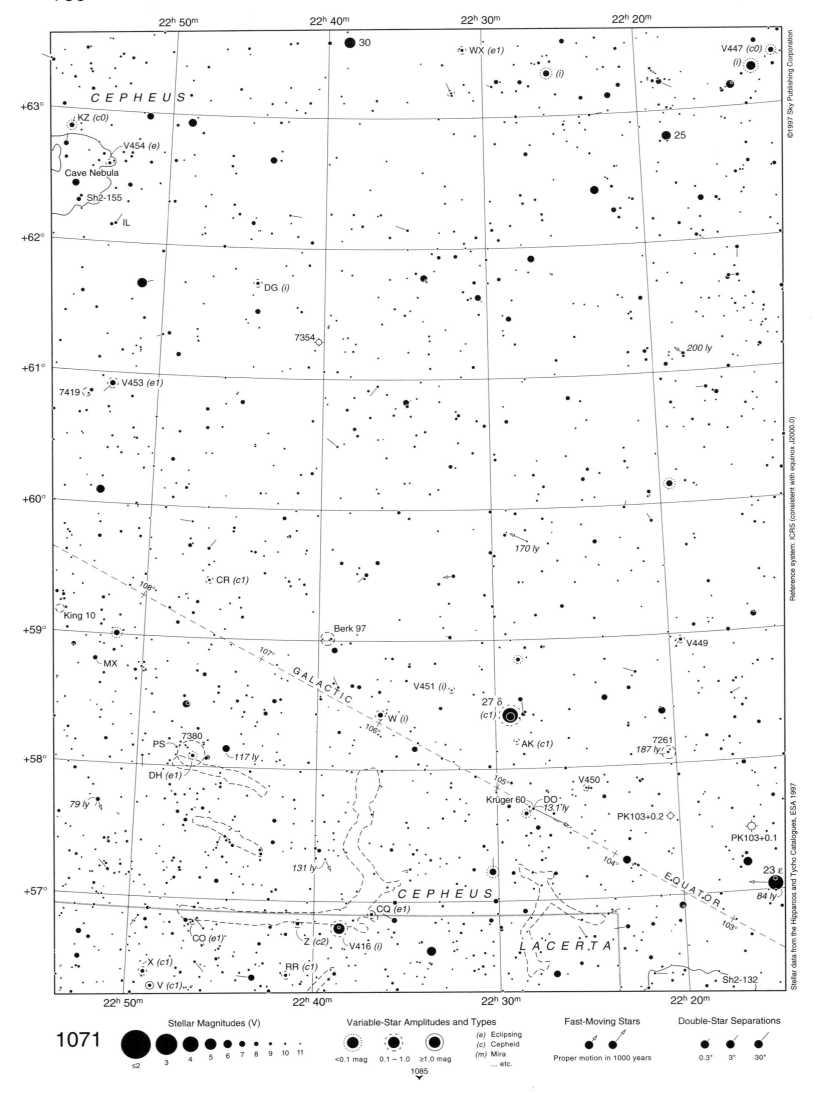

©1997 Sky Publishing Corporation

Reference system: ICRS (consistent with equinox J2000.0)

Stellar data from the Hipparcos and Tycho Catalogues, ESA 1997

1071

Stellar Magnitudes (V)

≤2    3    4    5    6    7    8    9   10   11

Variable-Star Amplitudes and Types

<0.1 mag    0.1 – 1.0    ≥1.0 mag

(e) Eclipsing
(c) Cepheid
(m) Mira
... etc.

Fast-Moving Stars

Proper motion in 1000 years

Double-Star Separations

0.3"    3"    30"

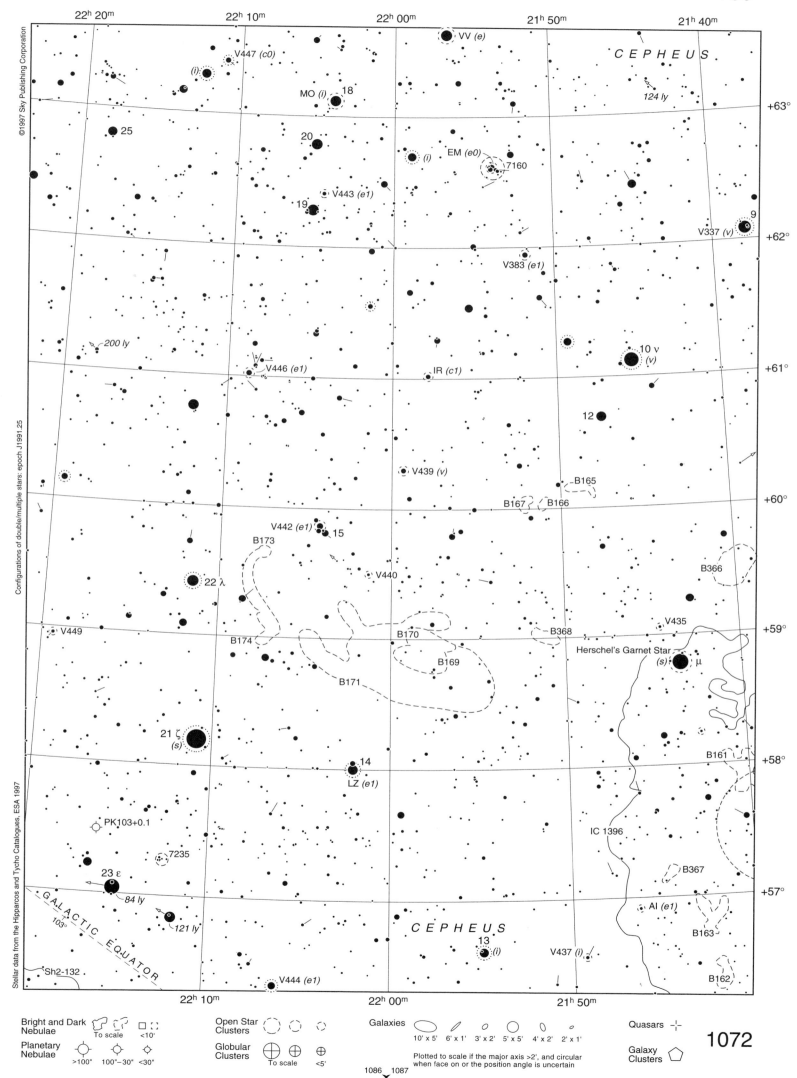

22h 20m    22h 10m    22h 00m    21h 50m    21h 40m

CEPHEUS

VV (e)

V447 (c0)

(i)

MO (i)    18

124 ly

+63°

25

20

(i)    EM (e0)
7160

V443 (e1)

19

9
V337 (v)

+62°

V383 (e1)

200 ly

V446 (e1)

IR (c1)

10 ν
(v)

+61°

12

V439 (v)

B165

B167    B166

+60°

V442 (e1)    15

B173

V440

B366

22 λ

B174    B170    B368    V435

V449    B169    Herschel's Garnet Star
(s)    μ    +59°

B171

B161

21 ζ
(s)

14

+58°

LZ (e1)

PK103+0.1

IC 1396

7235    B367

23 ε    +57°

84 ly    AI (e1)

121 ly    B163

13
(i)    V437 (i)

C E P H E U S    B162

GALACTIC EQUATOR
103°

Sh2-132    V444 (e1)

22h 10m    22h 00m    21h 50m

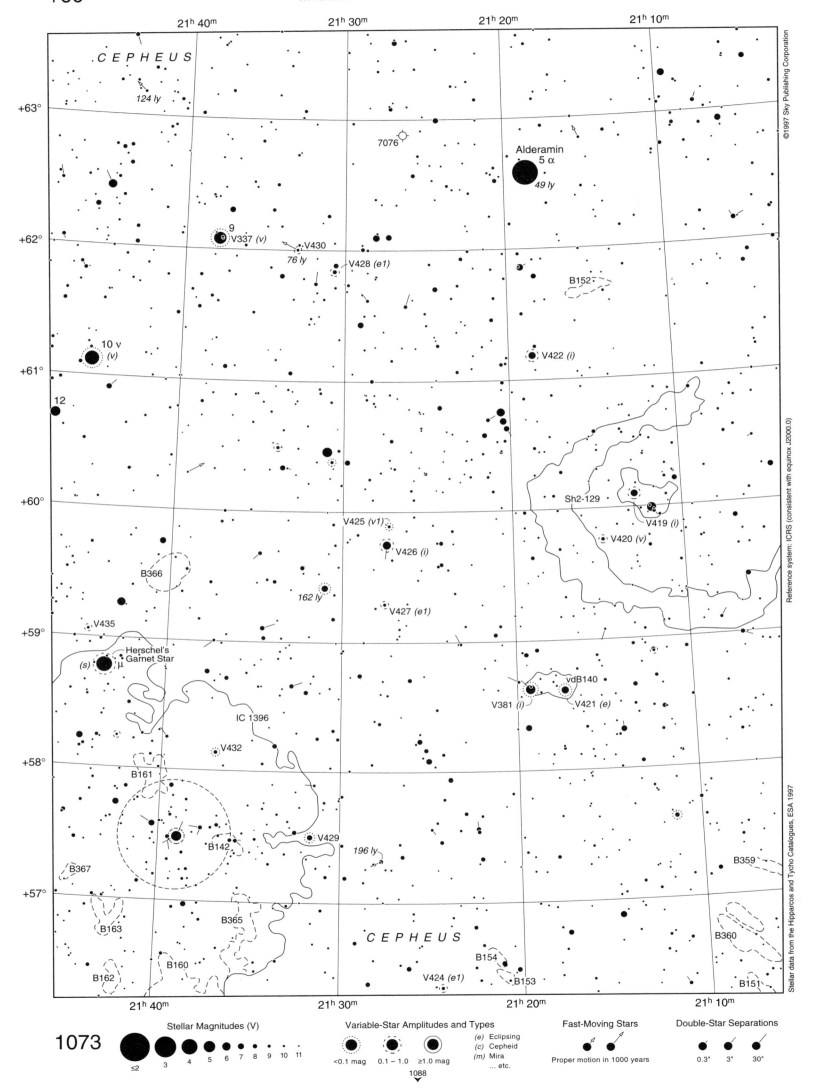

C E P H E U S

*124 ly*

7076

Alderamin
5 α
*49 ly*

9
θ
V337 *(v)*
V430
*76 ly*
V428 *(e1)*

B152

10 ν
*(v)*

V422 *(i)*

12

Sh2-129

V425 *(v1)*

V426 *(i)*

V419 *(i)*

B366

V420 *(v)*

*162 ly*

V427 *(e1)*

V435

Herschel's
Garnet Star
*(s)*  μ

vdB140

V381 *(i)*
V421 *(e)*

IC 1396

V432

B161

V429

*196 ly*

B359

B367

B142

B163

B365

C E P H E U S

B154

B160

B153

B360

V424 *(e1)*

B162

B151

©1997 Sky Publishing Corporation

Reference system: ICRS (consistent with equinox J2000.0)

Stellar data from the Hipparcos and Tycho Catalogues, ESA 1997

**1073**

Stellar Magnitudes (V)

≤2   3   4   5   6   7   8   9   10   11

Variable-Star Amplitudes and Types

<0.1 mag   0.1 – 1.0   ≥1.0 mag

(e) Eclipsing
(c) Cepheid
(m) Mira
... etc.

1088
ᴠ

Fast-Moving Stars

Proper motion in 1000 years

Double-Star Separations

0.3"   3"   30"

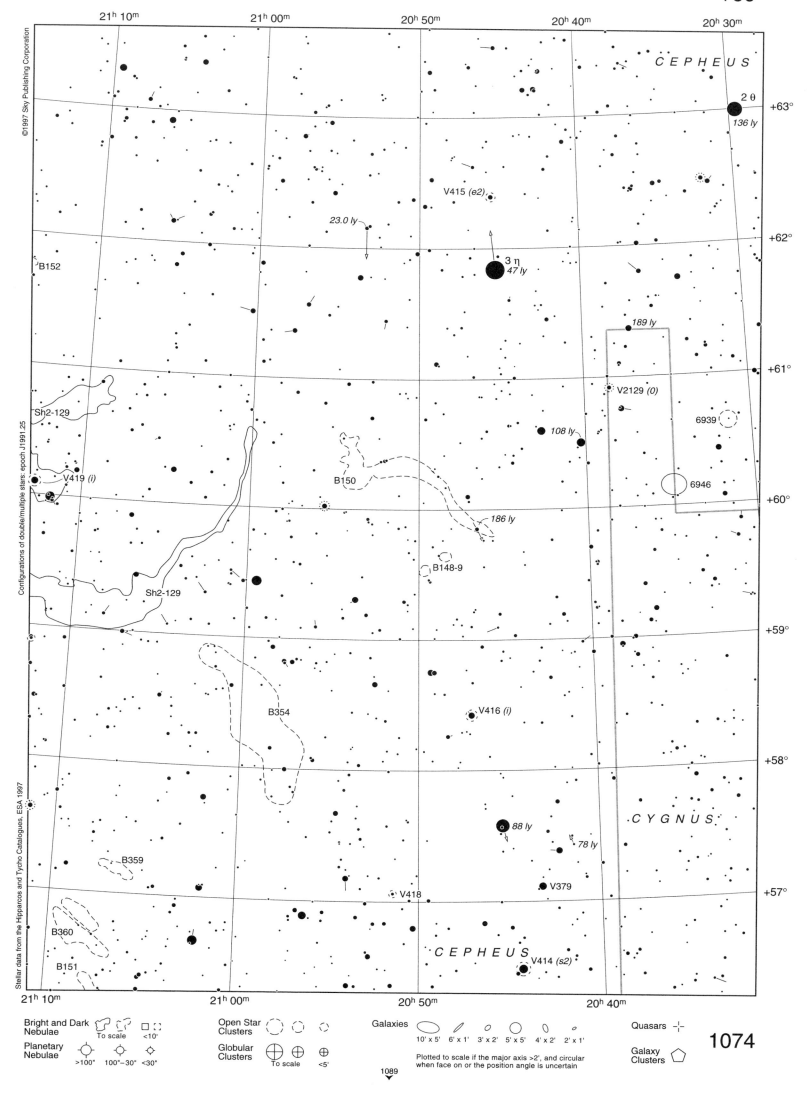

Configurations of double/multiple stars: epoch J1991.25

Stellar data from the Hipparcos and Tycho Catalogues, ESA 1997

21ʰ 10ᵐ  21ʰ 00ᵐ  20ʰ 50ᵐ  20ʰ 40ᵐ  20ʰ 30ᵐ

C E P H E U S

2 θ
136 ly

V415 (e2)

23.0 ly

3 η
47 ly

189 ly

+63°

+62°

+61°

B152

Sh2-129

V419 (i)

V2129 (0)

6939

108 ly

B150

6946

186 ly

B148-9

Sh2-129

+60°

+59°

B354

V416 (i)

C Y G N U S

88 ly

78 ly

B359

V379

+58°

+57°

B360

V418

B151

C E P H E U S

V414 (s2)

21ʰ 10ᵐ  21ʰ 00ᵐ  20ʰ 50ᵐ  20ʰ 40ᵐ

| | | | |
|---|---|---|---|
| **Bright and Dark Nebulae** | **Open Star Clusters** | **Galaxies** | **Quasars** |
| To scale   <10' | To scale   <10' | 10' x 5'  6' x 1'  3' x 2'  5' x 5'  4' x 2'  2' x 1' | |
| **Planetary Nebulae** | **Globular Clusters** | | **Galaxy Clusters** |
| >100"  100"-30"  <30" | To scale   <5' | Plotted to scale if the major axis >2', and circular when face on or the position angle is uncertain | |

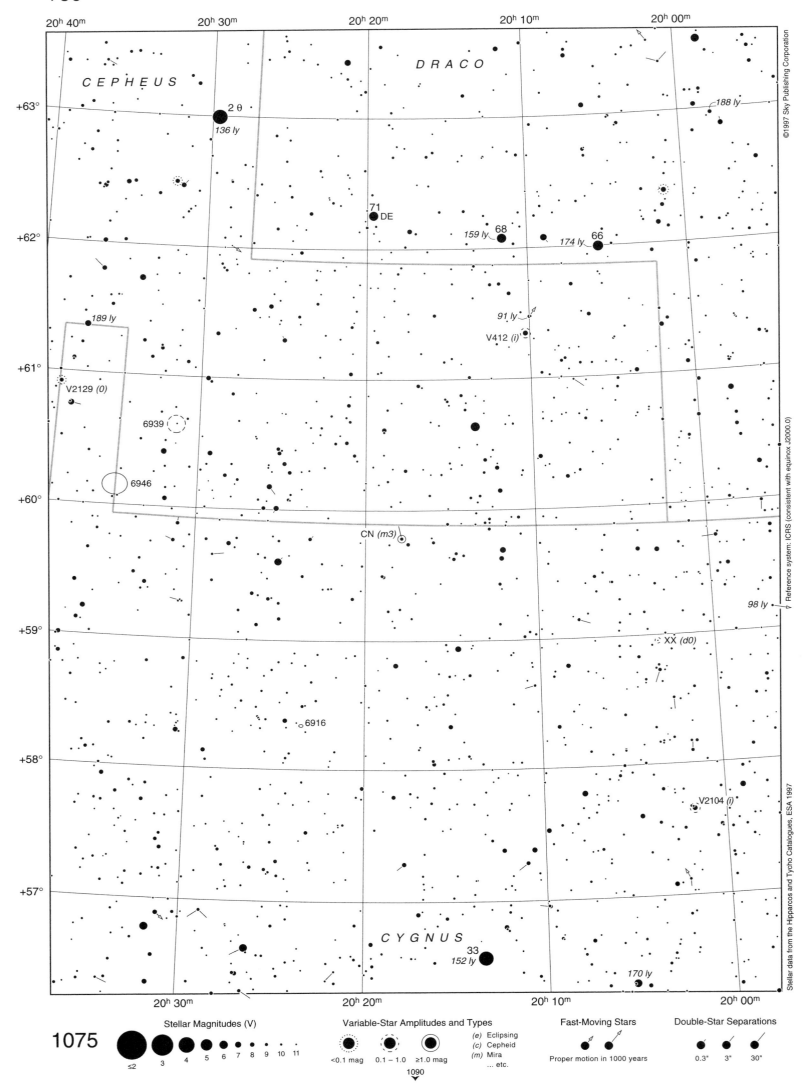

©1997 Sky Publishing Corporation

↓ Reference system: ICRS (consistent with equinox J2000.0)

Stellar data from the Hipparcos and Tycho Catalogues, ESA 1997

C E P H E U S

D R A C O

+63°    2 θ
        *136 ly*

71
DE

159 ly  68        174 ly  66

188 ly

91 ly

V412 *(i)*

189 ly

V2129 *(0)*

6939

6946

CN *(m3)*

98 ly

XX *(d0)*

6916

V2104 *(i)*

C Y G N U S

33
*152 ly*        170 ly

1075

**Stellar Magnitudes (V)**

≤2   3   4   5   6   7   8   9  10  11

**Variable-Star Amplitudes and Types**

<0.1 mag    0.1 – 1.0    ≥1.0 mag

*(e)* Eclipsing
*(c)* Cepheid
*(m)* Mira
... etc.

**Fast-Moving Stars**

Proper motion in 1000 years

**Double-Star Separations**

0.3"    3"    30"

1090

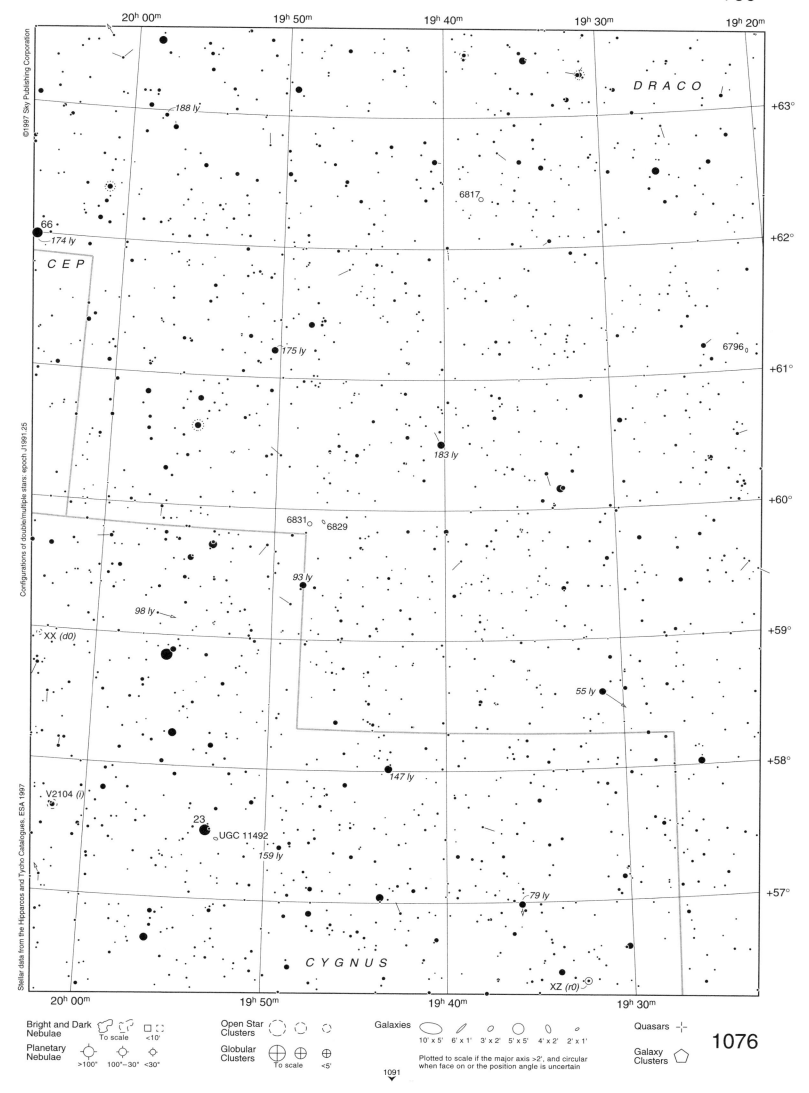

20h 00m 19h 50m 19h 40m 19h 30m 19h 20m

+63°
+62°
+61°
+60°
+59°
+58°
+57°

DRACO

CEP

CYGNUS

6817

6796

188 ly

66
174 ly

175 ly

183 ly

6831 6829

93 ly

98 ly

XX (d0)

55 ly

147 ly

V2104 (i)

23
UGC 11492

159 ly

79 ly

XZ (r0)

20h 00m 19h 50m 19h 40m 19h 30m

© 1997 Sky Publishing Corporation

Configurations of double/multiple stars: epoch J1991.25

Stellar data from the Hipparcos and Tycho Catalogues, ESA 1997

| Bright and Dark Nebulae | | | Open Star Clusters | | | Galaxies | | | | | | | Quasars |
|---|---|---|---|---|---|---|---|---|---|---|---|---|---|
| | To scale | <10' | | | | | | | | | | | |
| Planetary Nebulae | | | Globular Clusters | | | 10' x 5' | 6' x 1' | 3' x 2' | 5' x 5' | 4' x 2' | 2' x 1' | Galaxy Clusters |
| >100" | 100"–30" | <30" | | To scale | <5' | Plotted to scale if the major axis >2', and circular when face on or the position angle is uncertain | | | | | | |

1076

1091

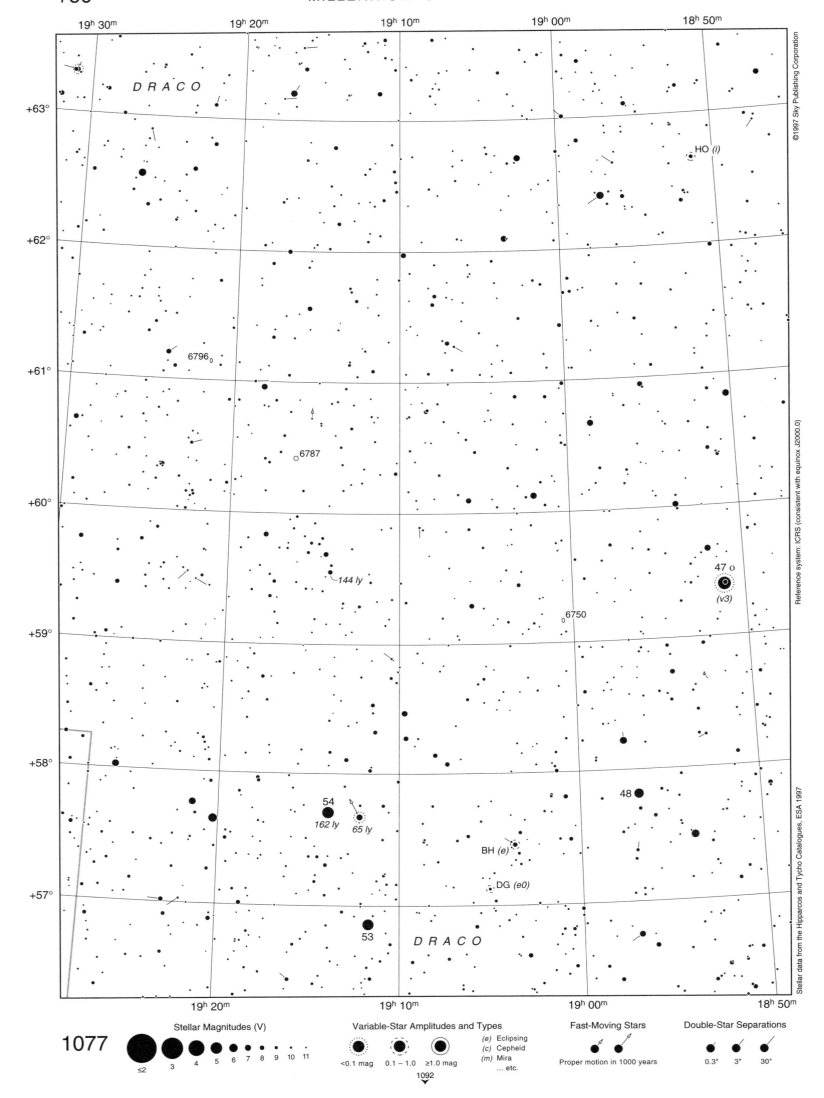

DRACO

6796₀

6787

144 ly

6750

47 o
(v3)

HO (i)

54
162 ly
65 ly

48

BH (e)

DG (e0)

53

DRACO

©1997 Sky Publishing Corporation

Reference system: ICRS (consistent with equinox J2000.0)

Stellar data from the Hipparcos and Tycho Catalogues, ESA 1997

1077

Stellar Magnitudes (V)

≤2   3   4   5   6   7  8  9 10 11

Variable-Star Amplitudes and Types

<0.1 mag   0.1 – 1.0   ≥1.0 mag

(e) Eclipsing
(c) Cepheid
(m) Mira
... etc.

Fast-Moving Stars

Proper motion in 1000 years

Double-Star Separations

0.3"   3"   30"

# MILLENNIUM STAR ATLAS

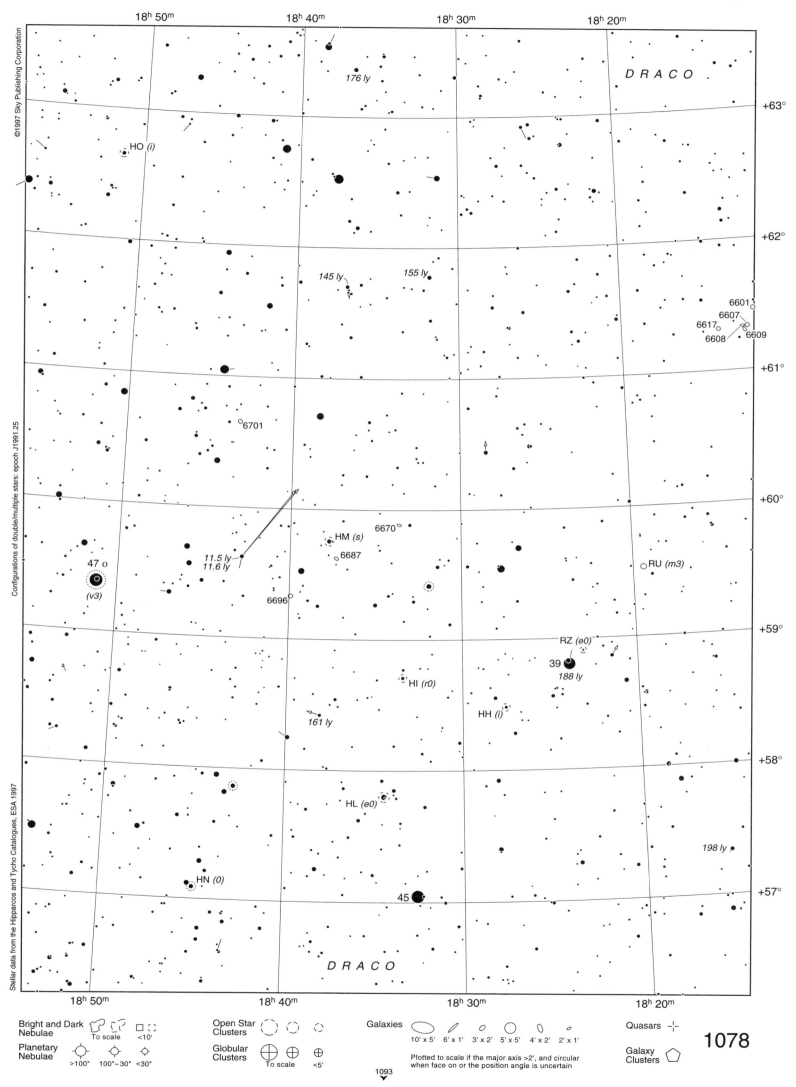

18h 50m   18h 40m   18h 30m   18h 20m

*D R A C O*

176 ly

HO *(i)*

+63°

+62°

145 ly   155 ly

6601
6607
6617
6608   6609

+61°

6701

+60°

HM *(s)*   6670

11.5 ly   6687
11.6 ly

47 o   6696   RU *(m3)*

*(v3)*

+59°

RZ *(e0)*

39
188 ly

HI *(r0)*

HH *(i)*

161 ly

+58°

198 ly

HL *(e0)*

HN *(0)*

+57°

45

*D R A C O*

18h 50m   18h 40m   18h 30m   18h 20m

Bright and Dark
Nebulae
To scale   <10'

Open Star
Clusters
To scale

Galaxies
10' x 5'   6' x 1'   3' x 2'   5' x 5'   4' x 2'   2' x 1'

Quasars

Planetary
Nebulae
>100"   100"–30"   <30"

Globular
Clusters
To scale   <5'

Plotted to scale if the major axis >2', and circular
when face on or the position angle is uncertain

Galaxy
Clusters

+60°

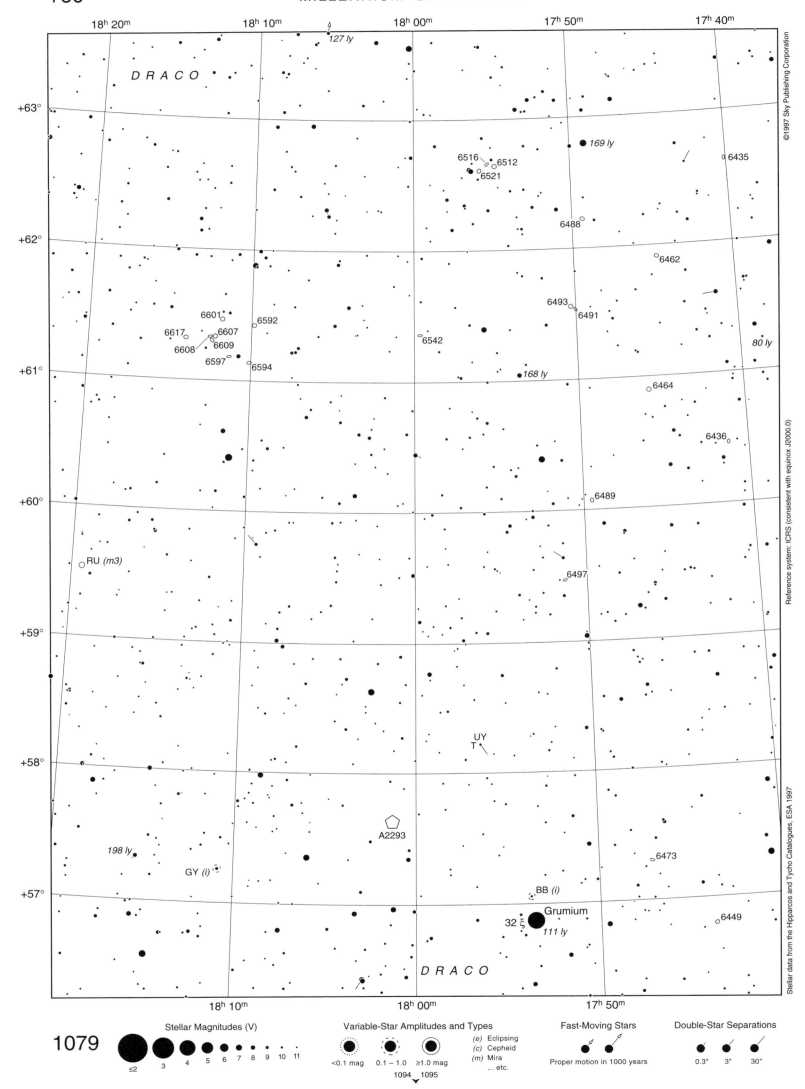

D R A C O

127 ly

169 ly

6516 6512
6521

6488

6462

6601 6592
6617 6607
6608 6609
6597 6594

6493
6491

6542

168 ly

80 ly

6464

6436

RU (m3)

6489

6497

UY
T

A2293

198 ly

GY (i)

6473

BB (i)

Grumium
32 ξ    111 ly

6449

D R A C O

©1997 Sky Publishing Corporation

Reference system: ICRS (consistent with equinox J2000.0)

Stellar data from the Hipparcos and Tycho Catalogues, ESA 1997

1079

**Stellar Magnitudes (V)**

≤2   3   4   5   6   7   8   9   10   11

**Variable-Star Amplitudes and Types**

<0.1 mag   0.1 – 1.0   ≥1.0 mag

(e) Eclipsing
(c) Cepheid
(m) Mira
... etc.

1094   1095

**Fast-Moving Stars**

Proper motion in 1000 years

**Double-Star Separations**

0.3"   3"   30"

# MILLENNIUM STAR ATLAS

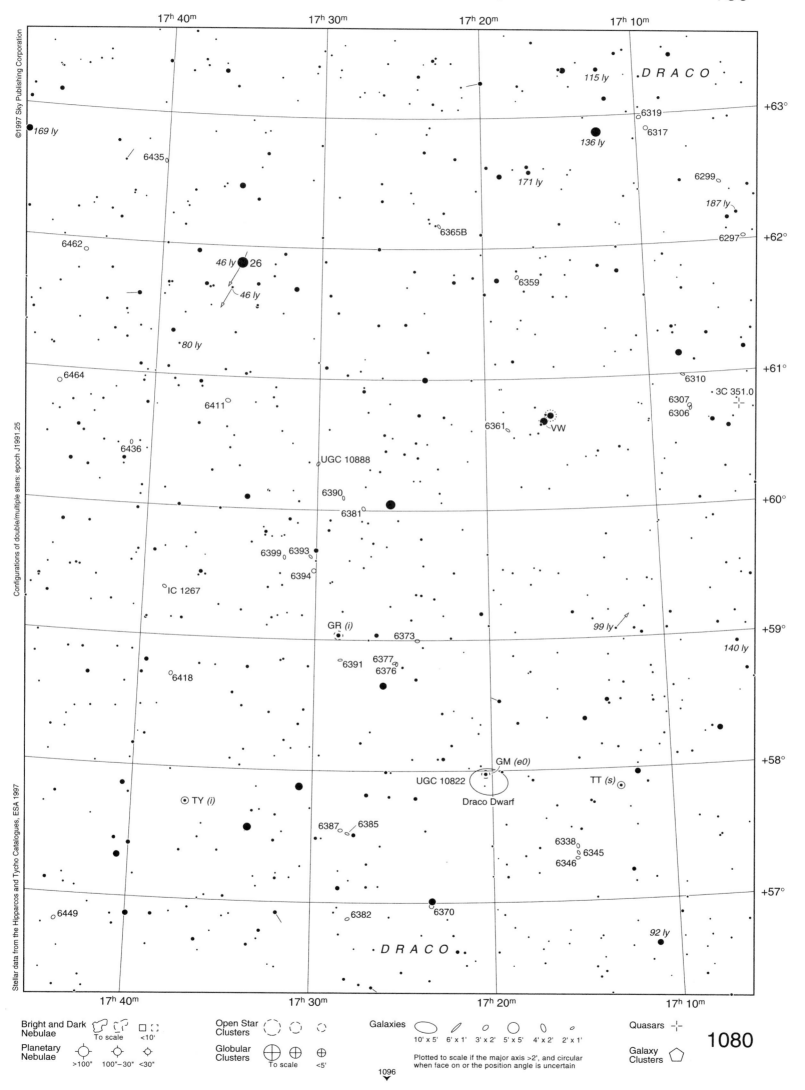

Configurations of double/multiple stars: epoch J1991.25

Stellar data from the Hipparcos and Tycho Catalogues, ESA 1997

17h 40m    17h 30m    17h 20m    17h 10m

DRACO

169 ly

6435

6462

46 ly  26
46 ly
80 ly

6464

6411

6436

UGC 10888

6390
6381

6399  6393
6394

IC 1267

GR (i)
6373
6391  6377
6376

6418

TY (i)

6387  6385

6449

6382  6370

DRACO

115 ly
6319
6317
136 ly
6299
171 ly
187 ly
6365B  6297

6359

6310  3C 351.0
6307
6306

6361
VW

99 ly
140 ly

GM (e0)
UGC 10822        TT (s)
Draco Dwarf

6338
6345
6346

92 ly

17h 40m    17h 30m    17h 20m    17h 10m

+63°

+62°

+61°

+60°

+59°

+58°

+57°

| Bright and Dark Nebulae | Open Star Clusters | Galaxies | Quasars |
|---|---|---|---|

Bright and Dark Nebulae
To scale    <10'

Planetary Nebulae
>100"  100"–30"  <30'

Open Star Clusters

Globular Clusters
To scale    <5'

Galaxies
10' x 5'  6' x 1'  3' x 2'  5' x 5'  4' x 2'  2' x 1'

Plotted to scale if the major axis >2', and circular when face on or the position angle is uncertain

Quasars

Galaxy Clusters

1080

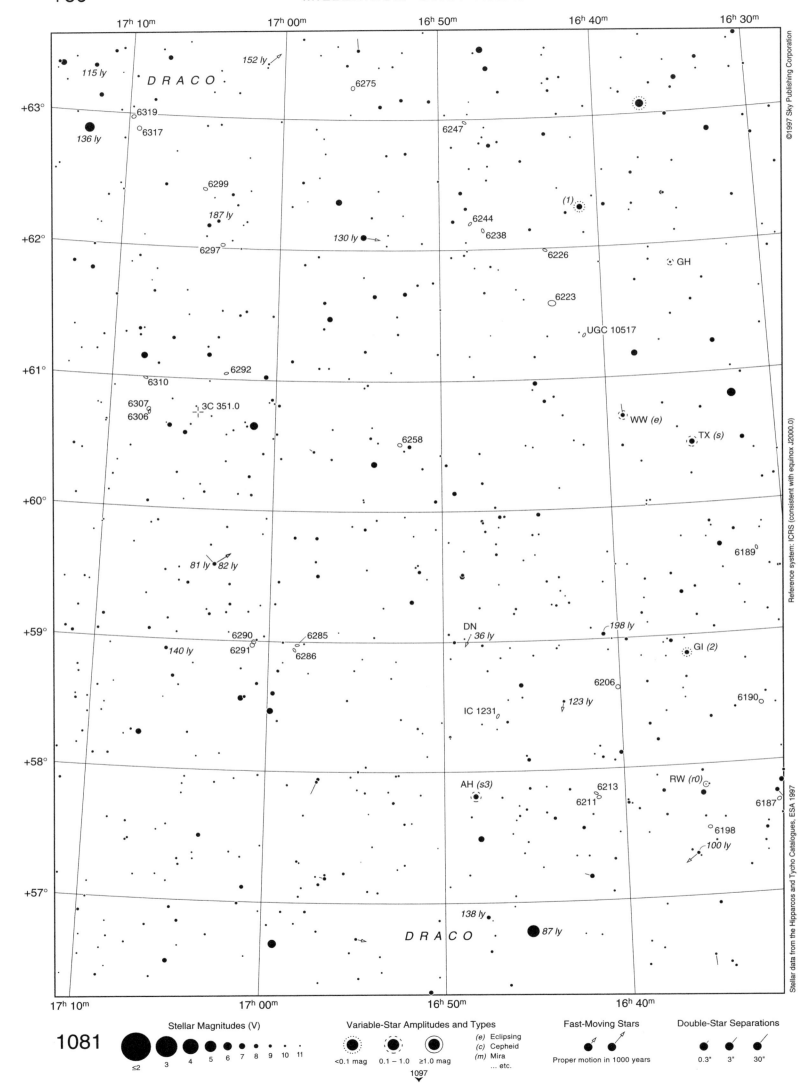

D R A C O

115 ly

152 ly

6275

6319
6317
136 ly

6247

(1)

6244
6238

6226

GH

6223

UGC 10517

6299

187 ly

6297

130 ly

6292

6310

6307
6306

3C 351.0

6258

6189

WW (e)

TX (s)

81 ly 82 ly

198 ly

GI (2)

DN
36 ly

6290
6291
140 ly

6285
6286

6206

123 ly

IC 1231

6190

AH (s3)

RW (r0)

6213
6211

6187

6198

100 ly

138 ly

87 ly

D R A C O

17h 10m
+63°
+62°
+61°
+60°
+59°
+58°
+57°

17h 00m   16h 50m   16h 40m   16h 30m

17h 10m   17h 00m   16h 50m   16h 40m

1081

Stellar Magnitudes (V)

≤2   3   4   5   6   7   8   9   10   11

Variable-Star Amplitudes and Types

<0.1 mag   0.1 – 1.0   ≥1.0 mag

(e) Eclipsing
(c) Cepheid
(m) Mira
... etc.

1097

Fast-Moving Stars

Proper motion in 1000 years

Double-Star Separations

0.3"   3"   30"

# MILLENNIUM STAR ATLAS

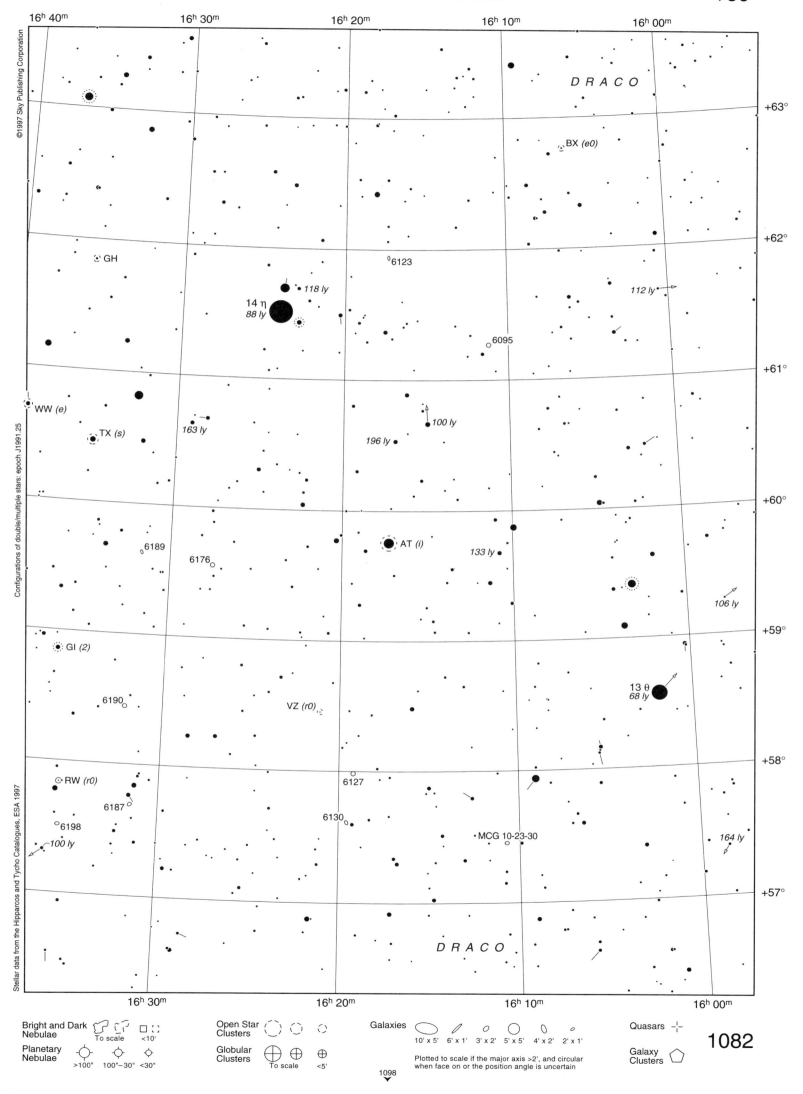

16ʰ 40ᵐ   16ʰ 30ᵐ   16ʰ 20ᵐ   16ʰ 10ᵐ   16ʰ 00ᵐ

*D R A C O*

BX *(e0)*

GH

6123

14 η
88 ly

118 ly

112 ly →

6095

WW *(e)*

TX *(s)*

163 ly

100 ly

196 ly

106 ly

6189

6176

AT *(i)*

133 ly

GI *(2)*

6190

VZ *(r0)*

13 θ
68 ly

RW *(r0)*

6187

6127

6198

6130

100 ly

MCG 10-23-30

164 ly

*D R A C O*

16ʰ 30ᵐ   16ʰ 20ᵐ   16ʰ 10ᵐ   16ʰ 00ᵐ

+63°
+62°
+61°
+60°
+59°
+58°
+57°

| Bright and Dark Nebulae | | | Open Star Clusters | | | Galaxies | | | | | | Quasars |
|---|---|---|---|---|---|---|---|---|---|---|---|---|
| To scale | <10' | | | | | 10' x 5' | 6' x 1' | 3' x 2' | 5' x 5' | 4' x 2' | 2' x 1' | |
| Planetary Nebulae | | | Globular Clusters | | | | | | | | | Galaxy Clusters |
| >100" | 100"–30" | <30" | To scale | <5' | | Plotted to scale if the major axis >2', and circular when face on or the position angle is uncertain | | | | | | |

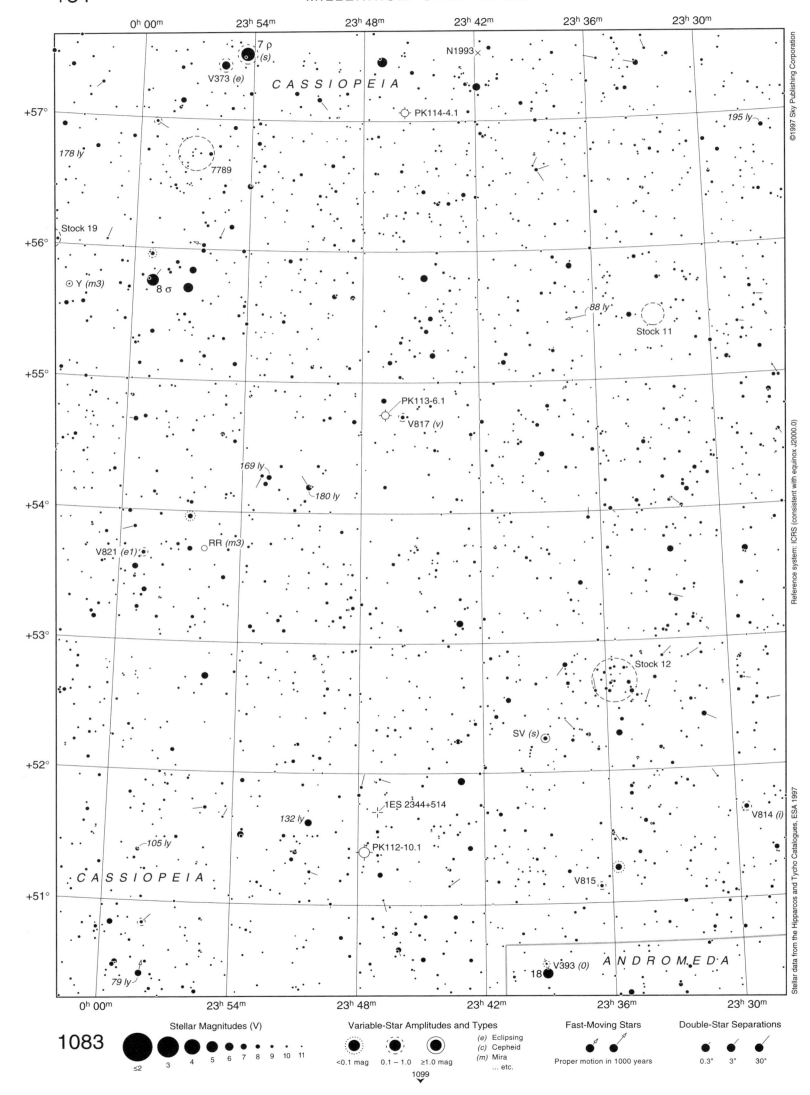

CASSIOPEIA

7 ρ (s)
V373 (e)
N1993
PK114-4.1
7789
195 ly
178 ly
Stock 19
Y (m3)
8 σ
88 ly
Stock 11
PK113-6.1
V817 (v)
169 ly
180 ly
V821 (e1)
RR (m3)
Stock 12
SV (s)
1ES 2344+514
132 ly
105 ly
PK112-10.1
V814 (i)
V815
CASSIOPEIA
V393 (0)
18
ANDROMEDA
79 ly

1083

**Stellar Magnitudes (V)**
≤2   3   4   5   6   7   8   9   10   11

**Variable-Star Amplitudes and Types**
<0.1 mag   0.1 – 1.0   ≥1.0 mag

(e) Eclipsing
(c) Cepheid
(m) Mira
... etc.

1099

**Fast-Moving Stars**
Proper motion in 1000 years

**Double-Star Separations**
0.3"   3"   30"

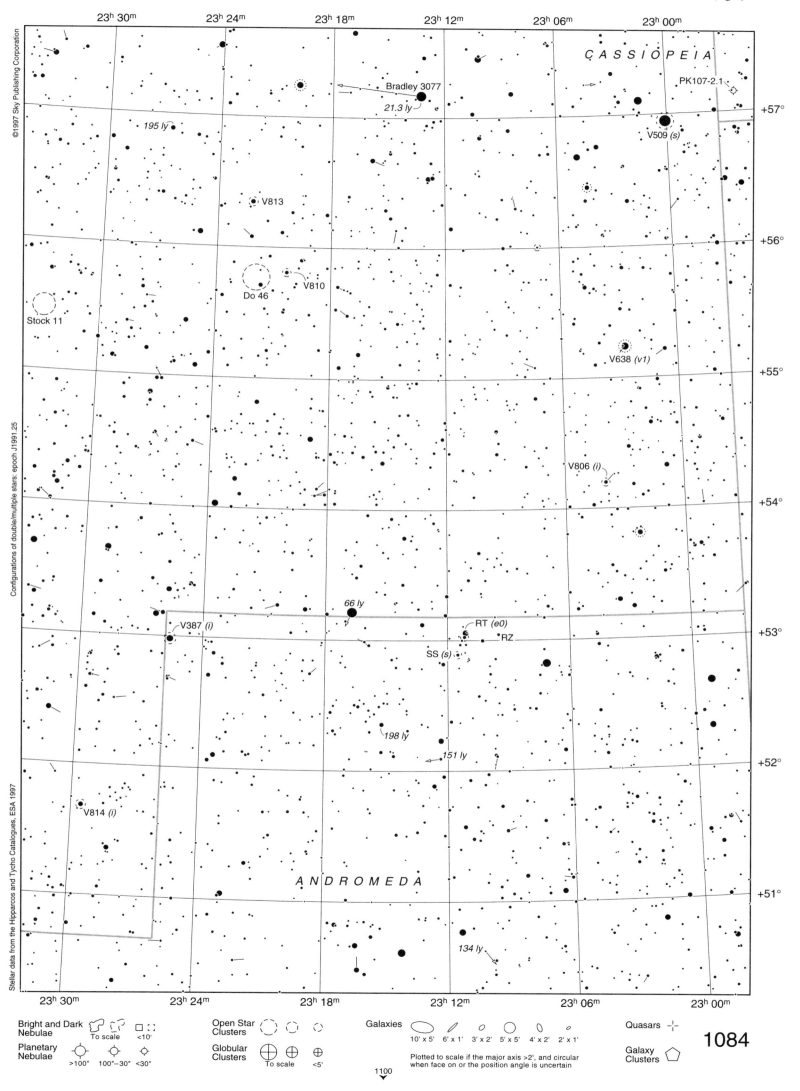

23h 30m    23h 24m    23h 18m    23h 12m    23h 06m    23h 00m

*CASSIOPEIA*

PK107-2.1

Bradley 3077
*21.3 ly*

+57°

195 ly

V509 *(s)*

V813

+56°

V810

Do 46

Stock 11

V638 *(v1)*

+55°

V806 *(i)*

+54°

66 ly

V387 *(i)*

RT *(e0)*

RZ

SS *(s)*

+53°

198 ly

151 ly

+52°

V814 *(i)*

*ANDROMEDA*

+51°

134 ly

23h 30m    23h 24m    23h 18m    23h 12m    23h 06m    23h 00m

Bright and Dark Nebulae — To scale — <10'

Planetary Nebulae — >100" — 100"–30" — <30"

Open Star Clusters

Globular Clusters — To scale — <5'

Galaxies — 10' x 5' — 6' x 1' — 3' x 2' — 5' x 5' — 4' x 2' — 2' x 1'

Plotted to scale if the major axis >2', and circular when face on or the position angle is uncertain

Quasars

Galaxy Clusters

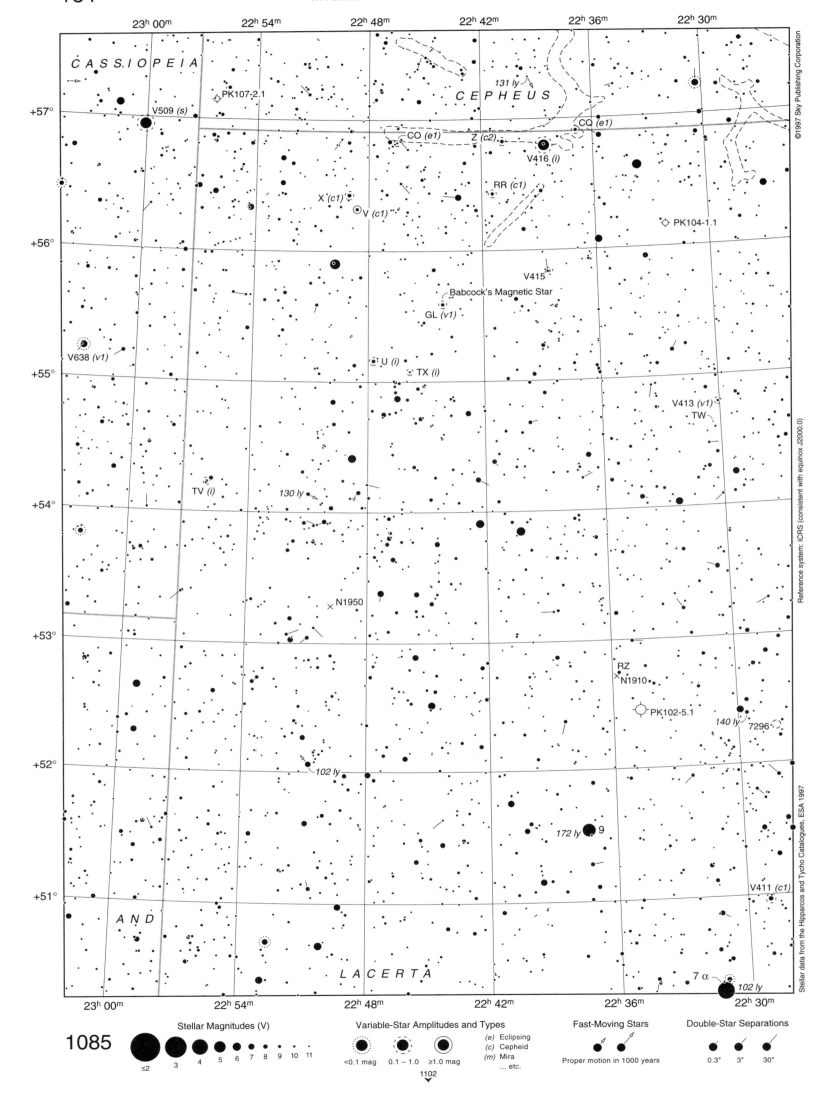

©1997 Sky Publishing Corporation

Reference system: ICRS (consistent with equinox J2000.0)

Stellar data from the Hipparcos and Tycho Catalogues, ESA 1997

1085

Stellar Magnitudes (V)

≤2   3   4   5   6   7   8   9   10   11

Variable-Star Amplitudes and Types

<0.1 mag   0.1 – 1.0   ≥1.0 mag

(e) Eclipsing
(c) Cepheid
(m) Mira
... etc.

1102
▼

Fast-Moving Stars

Proper motion in 1000 years

Double-Star Separations

0.3"   3"   30"

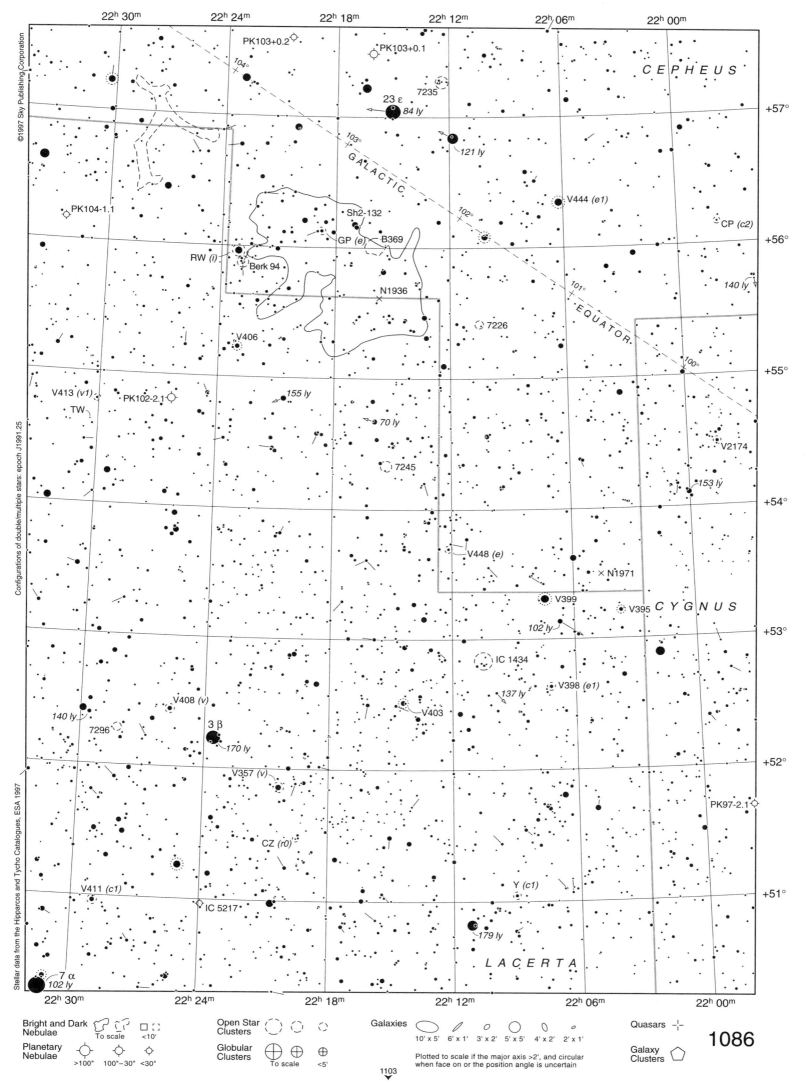

CEPHEUS

22ʰ 30ᵐ  22ʰ 24ᵐ  22ʰ 18ᵐ  22ʰ 12ᵐ  22ʰ 06ᵐ  22ʰ 00ᵐ

PK103+0.2
PK103+0.1
104°
7235
23 ε
84 ly
GALACTIC
103°
121 ly
102°
V444 (e1)
CP (c2)
PK104-1.1
Sh2-132
GP (e)    B369
RW (i)
Berk 94
+57°
+56°
EQUATOR
101°
140 ly
N1936
7226
V406
100°
+55°
V413 (v1)
PK102-2.1
155 ly
TW
70 ly
V2174
7245
153 ly
+54°
V448 (e)
N1971
V399
CYGNUS
V395
102 ly
IC 1434
V398 (e1)
+53°
137 ly
V408 (v)
140 ly
7296
V403
3 β
170 ly
V357 (v)
+52°
CZ (r0)
PK97-2.1
V411 (c1)
Y (c1)
+51°
IC 5217
179 ly
LACERTA
7 α
102 ly

22ʰ 30ᵐ  22ʰ 24ᵐ  22ʰ 18ᵐ  22ʰ 12ᵐ  22ʰ 06ᵐ  22ʰ 00ᵐ

Bright and Dark Nebulae     To scale    <10'
Planetary Nebulae    >100"  100"–30"  <30"
Open Star Clusters
Globular Clusters    To scale    <5'
Galaxies    10' x 5'   6' x 1'   3' x 2'   5' x 5'   4' x 2'   2' x 1'
Plotted to scale if the major axis >2', and circular when face on or the position angle is uncertain
Quasars
Galaxy Clusters

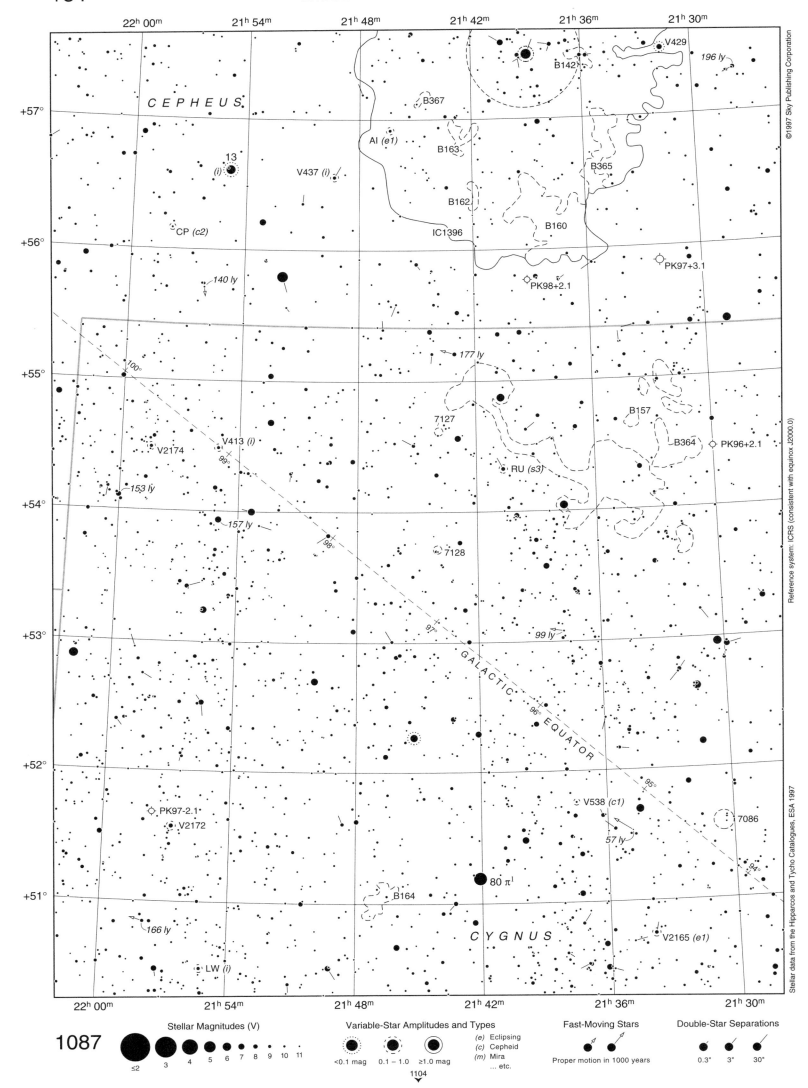

**1087**

Stellar Magnitudes (V)
≤2  3  4  5  6  7  8  9  10  11

Variable-Star Amplitudes and Types
<0.1 mag    0.1 – 1.0 mag    ≥1.0 mag

(e) Eclipsing
(c) Cepheid
(m) Mira
... etc.

1104

Fast-Moving Stars
Proper motion in 1000 years

Double-Star Separations
0.3"  3"  30"

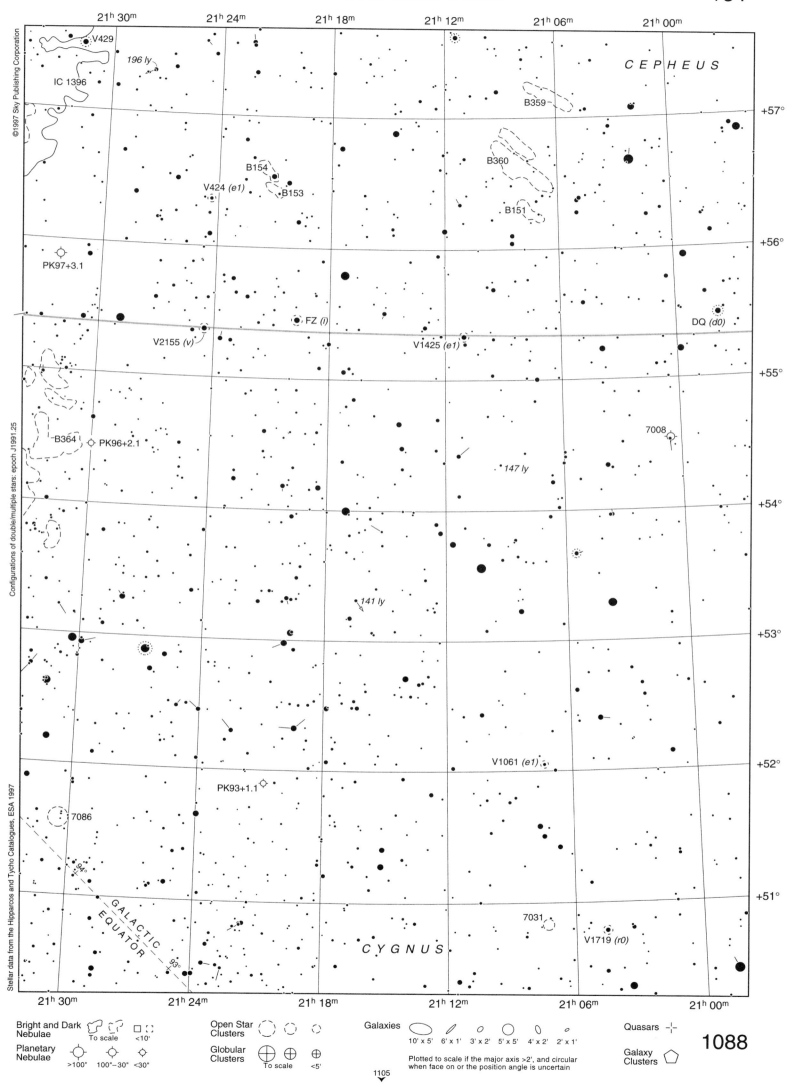

Configurations of double/multiple stars: epoch J1991.25

Stellar data from the Hipparcos and Tycho Catalogues, ESA 1997

CEPHEUS

CYGNUS

GALACTIC EQUATOR

IC 1396
196 ly
V429
B154
V424 (e1)
B153
B359
B360
B151
PK97+3.1
FZ (i)
V2155 (v)
V1425 (e1)
DQ (d0)
B364
PK96+2.1
7008
147 ly
141 ly
7086
PK93+1.1
V1061 (e1)
7031
V1719 (r0)
94°
93°

| Bright and Dark Nebulae | To scale | <10' | | Open Star Clusters | | | Galaxies | | | | | | | Quasars | |
| Planetary Nebulae | >100" | 100"–30" | <30" | Globular Clusters | To scale | <5' | 10' x 5' | 6' x 1' | 3' x 2' | 5' x 5' | 4' x 2' | 2' x 1' | | Galaxy Clusters | |

Plotted to scale if the major axis >2', and circular when face on or the position angle is uncertain

1088

1105

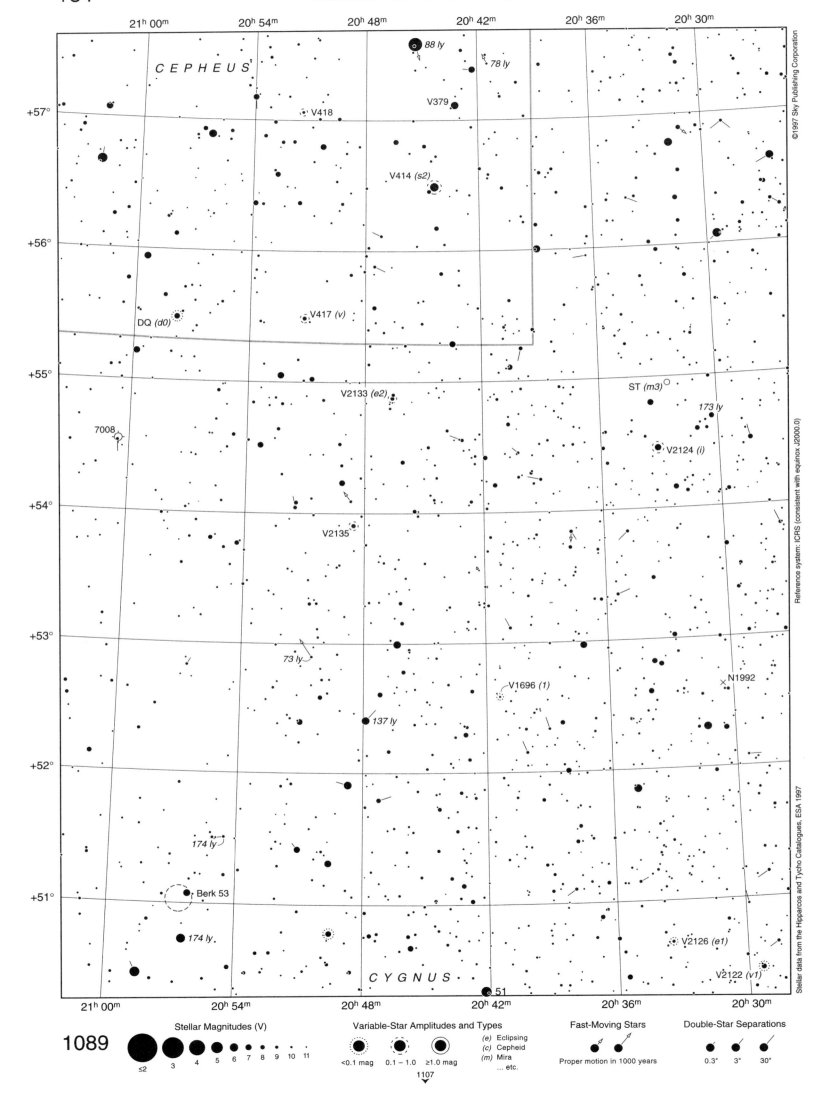

©1997 Sky Publishing Corporation

Reference system: ICRS (consistent with equinox J2000.0)

Stellar data from the Hipparcos and Tycho Catalogues, ESA 1997

C E P H E U S

88 ly

78 ly

V379

V418

V414 (s2)

V417 (v)

DQ (d0)

V2133 (e2)

ST (m3)

173 ly

7008

V2124 (i)

V2135

73 ly

V1696 (1)

N1992

137 ly

174 ly

Berk 53

174 ly

V2126 (e1)

V2122 (v1)

C Y G N U S

51

Stellar Magnitudes (V)

≤2    3    4    5    6    7    8    9    10   11

Variable-Star Amplitudes and Types

<0.1 mag    0.1 – 1.0    ≥1.0 mag

(e) Eclipsing
(c) Cepheid
(m) Mira
... etc.

Fast-Moving Stars

Proper motion in 1000 years

Double-Star Separations

0.3"    3"    30"

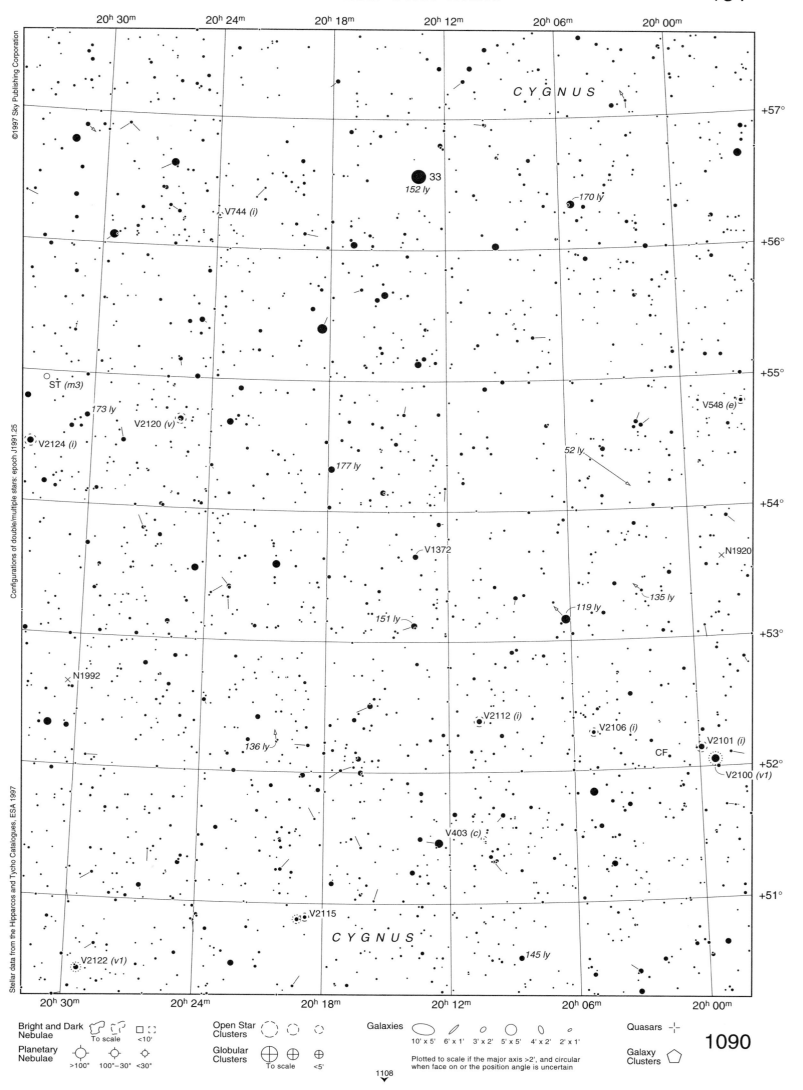

20h 30m    20h 24m    20h 18m    20h 12m    20h 06m    20h 00m

*C Y G N U S*

33
*152 ly*
*170 ly*

V744 *(i)*

ST *(m3)*

*173 ly*
V548 *(e)*

V2120 *(v)*
*52 ly*

V2124 *(i)*

*177 ly*

V1372
N1920

*135 ly*

*119 ly*
*151 ly*

N1992

V2112 *(i)*

V2106 *(i)*

V2101 *(i)*
*136 ly*
CF
V2100 *(v1)*

V403 *(c)*

V2115

*C Y G N U S*

V2122 *(v1)*
*145 ly*

20h 30m    20h 24m    20h 18m    20h 12m    20h 06m    20h 00m

+57°
+56°
+55°
+54°
+53°
+52°
+51°

| Bright and Dark Nebulae | Open Star Clusters | Galaxies | Quasars |
|---|---|---|---|

Bright and Dark
Nebulae      To scale   <10'

Open Star
Clusters

Galaxies

Quasars

Planetary
Nebulae
>100"  100"-30"  <30"

Globular
Clusters
To scale    <5'

10' x 5'  6' x 1'  3' x 2'  5' x 5'  4' x 2'  2' x 1'

Galaxy
Clusters

Plotted to scale if the major axis >2', and circular
when face on or the position angle is uncertain

1090

1108

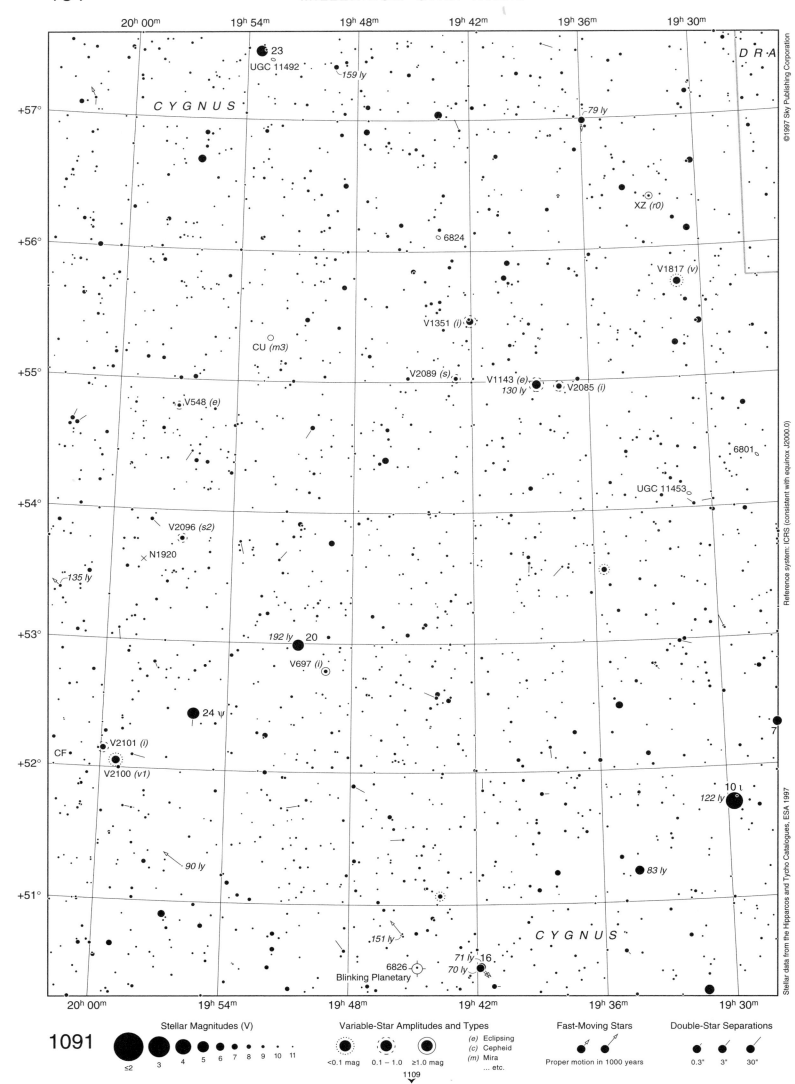

D R A

C Y G N U S

+57°
+56°
+55°
+54°
+53°
+52°
+51°

20ʰ 00ᵐ    19ʰ 54ᵐ    19ʰ 48ᵐ    19ʰ 42ᵐ    19ʰ 36ᵐ    19ʰ 30ᵐ

23
UGC 11492
159 ly
79 ly
XZ (r0)
6824
V1817 (v)
V1351 (i)
CU (m3)
V2089 (s)
V1143 (e)
130 ly
V2085 (i)
V548 (e)
6801
UGC 11453
V2096 (s2)
N1920
135 ly
192 ly    20
V697 (i)
24 ψ
7
V2101 (i)
CF
V2100 (v1)
10 ι
122 ly
90 ly
83 ly
C Y G N U S
151 ly
71 ly  16
6826    70 ly
Blinking Planetary

1091

**Stellar Magnitudes (V)**

≤2   3   4   5   6   7   8   9  10  11

**Variable-Star Amplitudes and Types**

<0.1 mag    0.1 – 1.0    ≥1.0 mag

(e) Eclipsing
(c) Cepheid
(m) Mira
... etc.

**Fast-Moving Stars**

Proper motion in 1000 years

**Double-Star Separations**

0.3"    3"    30"

1109

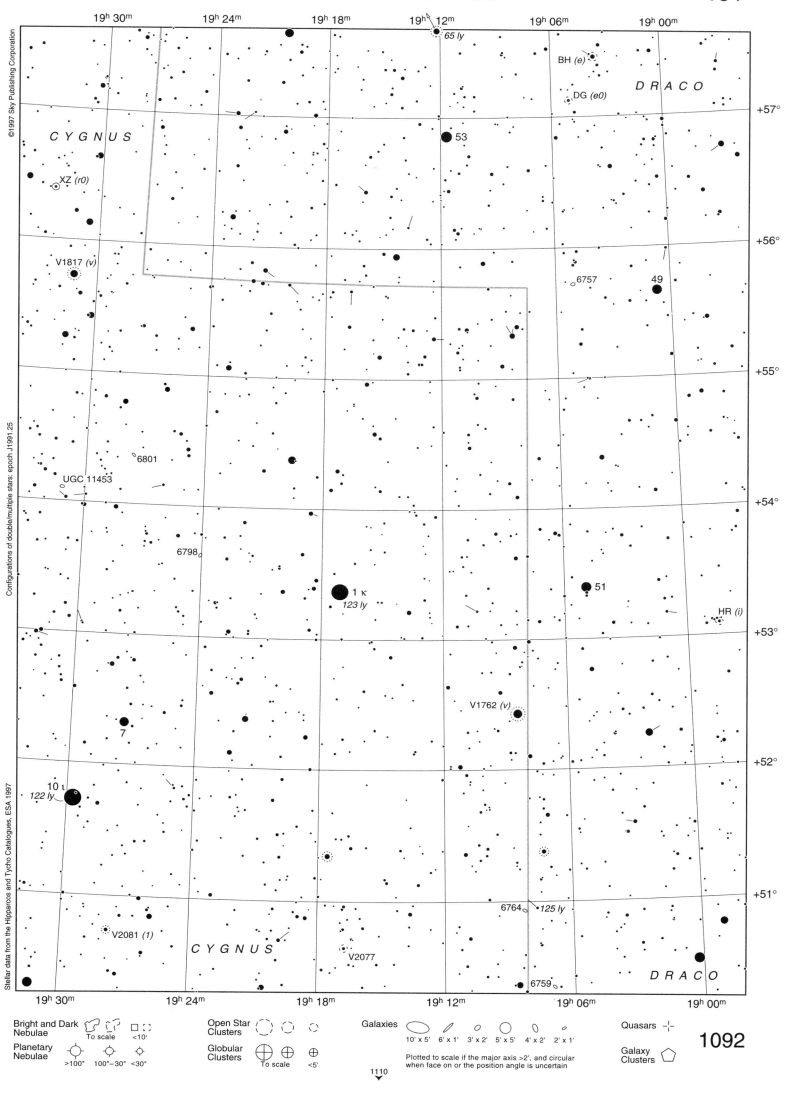

Configurations of double/multiple stars: epoch J1991.25

Stellar data from the Hipparcos and Tycho Catalogues, ESA 1997

19h 30m    19h 24m    19h 18m    19h 12m    19h 06m    19h 00m

DRACO

CYGNUS

65 ly

BH (e)

DG (e0)

53

XZ (r0)

V1817 (v)

6757

49

6801

UGC 11453

6798

1 κ
123 ly

51

HR (i)

V1762 (v)

7

10 ι
122 ly

6764   125 ly

V2081 (1)

CYGNUS

V2077

6759

DRACO

19h 30m    19h 24m    19h 18m    19h 12m    19h 06m    19h 00m

+57°

+56°

+55°

+54°

+53°

+52°

+51°

Bright and Dark
Nebulae
To scale   <10'

Planetary
Nebulae
>100"   100"–30"   <30"

Open Star
Clusters

Globular
Clusters
To scale   <5'

Galaxies

10' x 5'   6' x 1'   3' x 2'   5' x 5'   4' x 2'   2' x 1'

Plotted to scale if the major axis >2', and circular
when face on or the position angle is uncertain

Quasars

Galaxy
Clusters

1092

1110

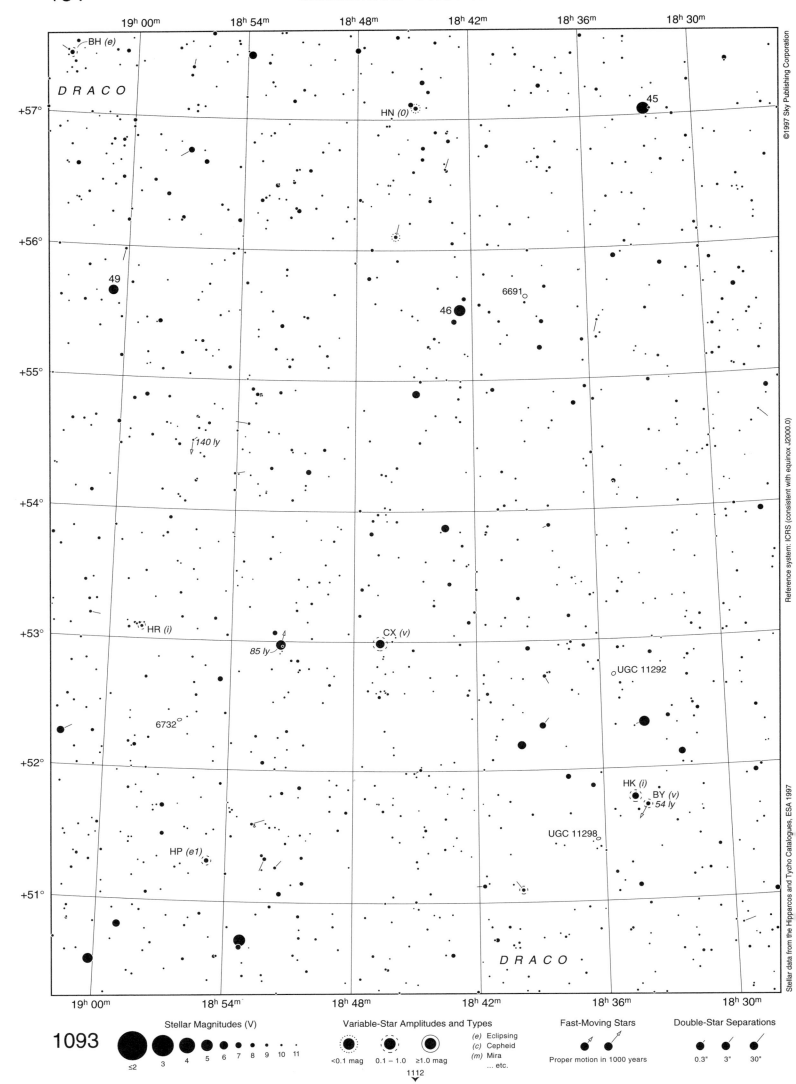

©1997 Sky Publishing Corporation

Reference system: ICRS (consistent with equinox J2000.0)

Stellar data from the Hipparcos and Tycho Catalogues, ESA 1997

1093

Stellar Magnitudes (V)

≤2   3   4   5   6   7   8   9   10   11

Variable-Star Amplitudes and Types

<0.1 mag    0.1 – 1.0    ≥1.0 mag

(e) Eclipsing
(c) Cepheid
(m) Mira
... etc.

Fast-Moving Stars

Proper motion in 1000 years

Double-Star Separations

0.3"   3"   30"

1112

# MILLENNIUM STAR ATLAS

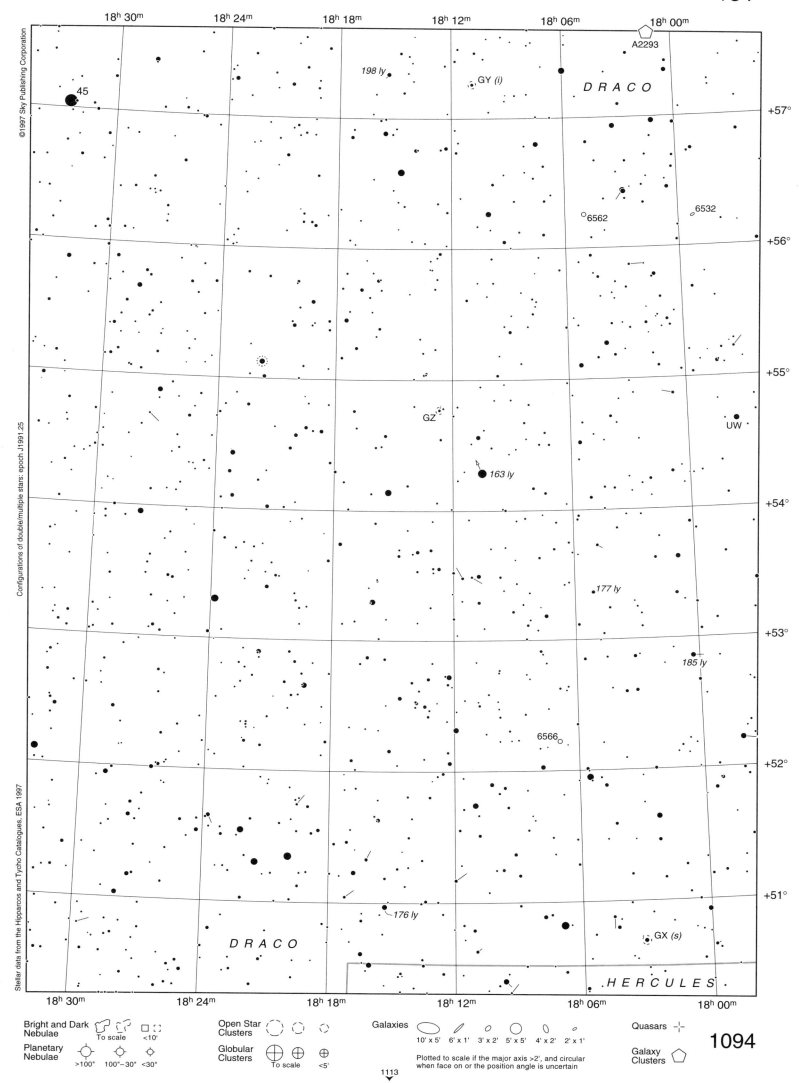

©1997 Sky Publishing Corporation

Configurations of double/multiple stars: epoch J1991.25

Stellar data from the Hipparcos and Tycho Catalogues, ESA 1997

18h 30m    18h 24m    18h 18m    18h 12m    18h 06m    18h 00m

A2293

198 ly          GY (i)          D R A C O

45

6562          6532

+57°

+56°

+55°

GZ

UW

163 ly

+54°

177 ly

+53°

185 ly

6566

+52°

+51°

176 ly          GX (s)

D R A C O          H E R C U L E S

18h 30m    18h 24m    18h 18m    18h 12m    18h 06m    18h 00m

| Bright and Dark Nebulae | Open Star Clusters | Galaxies | Quasars |
| Planetary Nebulae | Globular Clusters | | Galaxy Clusters |

To scale    <10'
>100"    100"–30"    <30"

To scale    <5'

10' x 5'   6' x 1'   3' x 2'   5' x 5'   4' x 2'   2' x 1'

Plotted to scale if the major axis >2', and circular when face on or the position angle is uncertain

1094

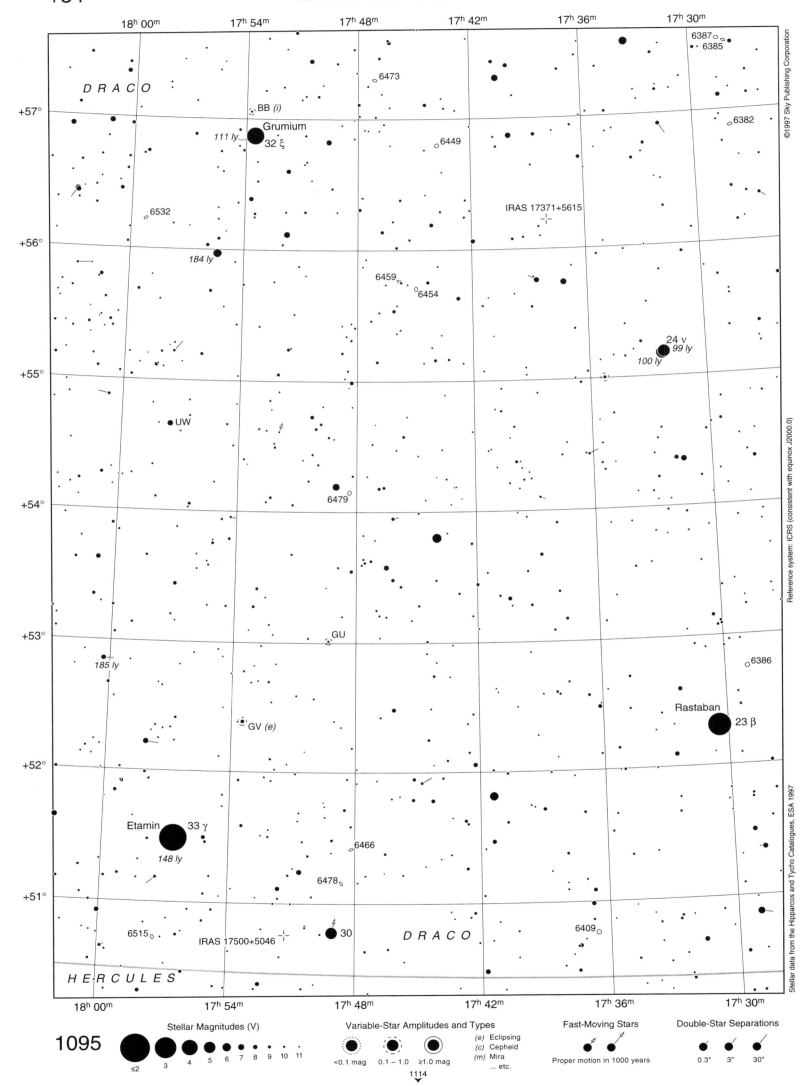

©1997 Sky Publishing Corporation

Reference system: ICRS (consistent with equinox J2000.0)

Stellar data from the Hipparcos and Tycho Catalogues, ESA 1997

1095

Stellar Magnitudes (V)

≤2   3   4   5   6   7   8   9   10   11

Variable-Star Amplitudes and Types

<0.1 mag   0.1 – 1.0   ≥1.0 mag

(e) Eclipsing
(c) Cepheid
(m) Mira
... etc.

Fast-Moving Stars

Proper motion in 1000 years

Double-Star Separations

0.3"   3"   30"

1114

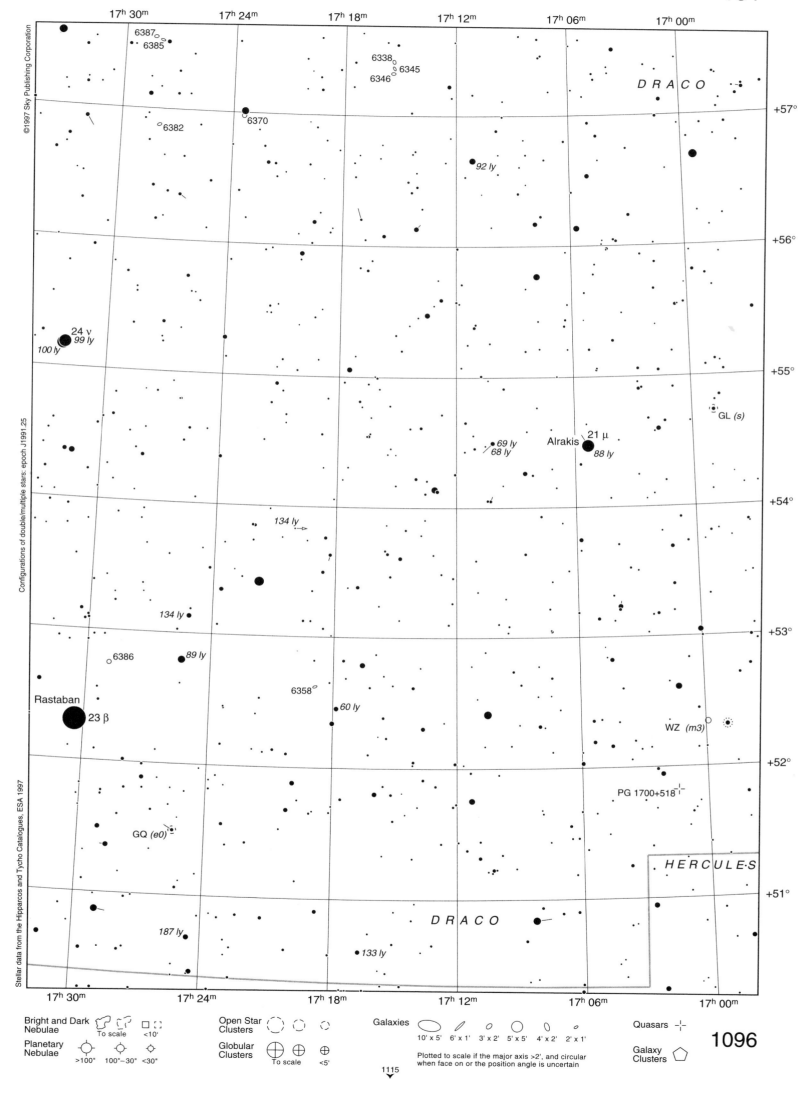

17h 30m   17h 24m   17h 18m   17h 12m   17h 06m   17h 00m

+57°
+56°
+55°
+54°
+53°
+52°
+51°

DRACO

6387
6385
6338
6346  6345
6382
6370
92 ly
24 ν
99 ly
100 ly
Alrakis  21 μ
69 ly
68 ly
88 ly
GL (s)
134 ly
134 ly
6386  89 ly
6358
60 ly
Rastaban
23 β
WZ (m3)
PG 1700+518
GQ (e0)
HERCULES
DRACO
187 ly
133 ly

17h 30m   17h 24m   17h 18m   17h 12m   17h 06m   17h 00m

Bright and Dark
Nebulae
To scale    <10'

Planetary
Nebulae
>100"  100"–30"  <30"

Open Star
Clusters

Globular
Clusters
To scale    <5'

Galaxies
10' x 5'  6' x 1'  3' x 2'  5' x 5'  4' x 2'  2' x 1'
Plotted to scale if the major axis >2', and circular
when face on or the position angle is uncertain

Quasars

Galaxy
Clusters

1096

1115

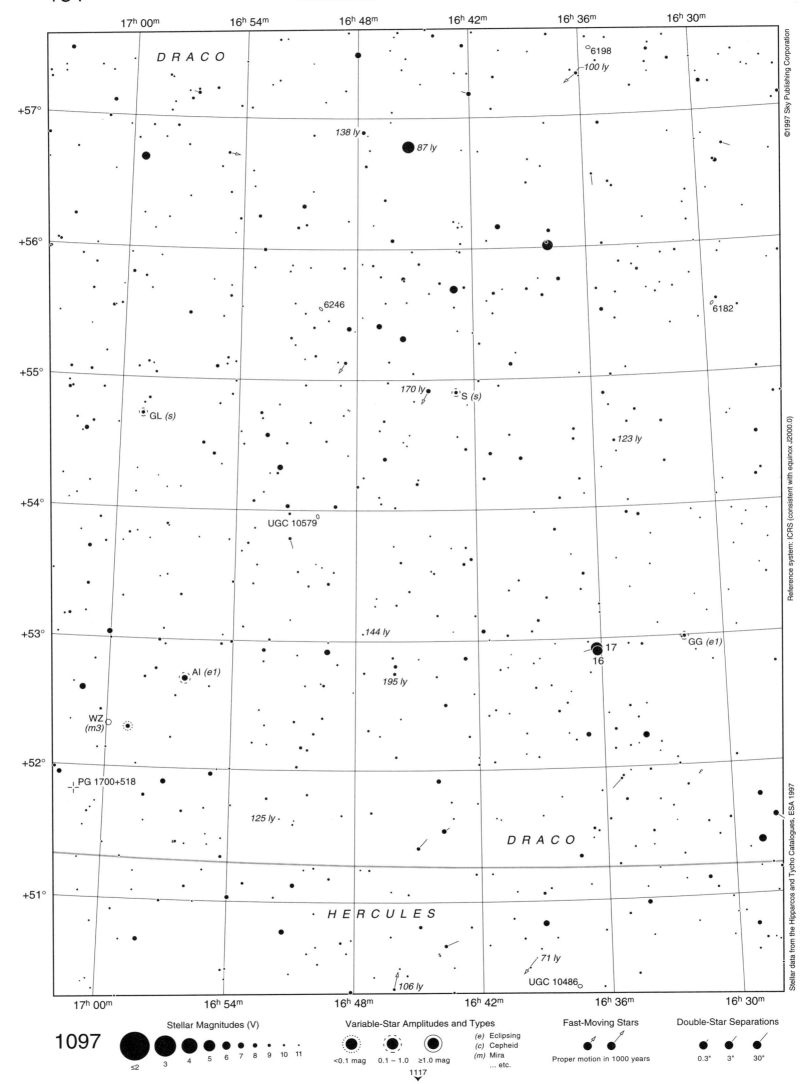

©1997 Sky Publishing Corporation

Reference system: ICRS (consistent with equinox J2000.0)

Stellar data from the Hipparcos and Tycho Catalogues, ESA 1997

DRACO

○6198
↙ 100 ly

138 ly
87 ly

6246

○ 6182

170 ly
◎ S (s)

GL (s)

123 ly

UGC 10579

144 ly

GG (e1)

17
16

Al (e1)

195 ly

WZ ○
(m3)

PG 1700+518

125 ly

DRACO

HERCULES

71 ly

106 ly

UGC 10486 ○

1097

Stellar Magnitudes (V)

≤2   3   4   5   6   7  8  9 10 11

Variable-Star Amplitudes and Types

<0.1 mag   0.1 – 1.0   ≥1.0 mag

(e) Eclipsing
(c) Cepheid
(m) Mira
... etc.

1117

Fast-Moving Stars

Proper motion in 1000 years

Double-Star Separations

0.3"   3"   30"

# MILLENNIUM STAR ATLAS

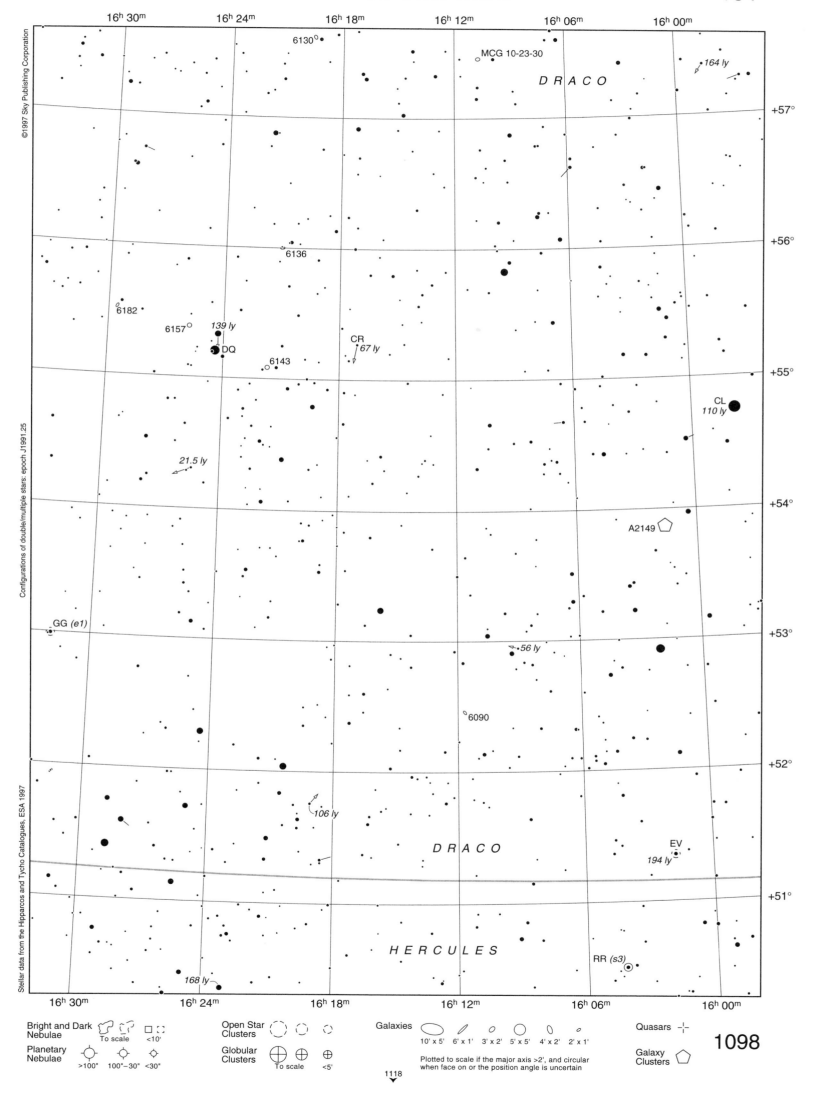

16h 30m    16h 24m    16h 18m    16h 12m    16h 06m    16h 00m

6130

MCG 10-23-30

D R A C O

164 ly

+57°

+56°

6136

6182

6157    139 ly

DQ

6143

CR
67 ly

+55°

CL
110 ly

21.5 ly

+54°

A2149

GG (e1)

+53°

56 ly

6090

+52°

106 ly

D R A C O

EV
194 ly

+51°

H E R C U L E S

RR (s3)

168 ly

16h 30m    16h 24m    16h 18m    16h 12m    16h 06m    16h 00m

| Bright and Dark Nebulae | | | Open Star Clusters | | | Galaxies | | | | | | Quasars |
|---|---|---|---|---|---|---|---|---|---|---|---|---|
| To scale | | <10' | | | | 10' x 5' | 6' x 1' | 3' x 2' | 5' x 5' | 4' x 2' | 2' x 1' | |
| Planetary Nebulae | | | Globular Clusters | | | | | | | | | Galaxy Clusters |
| >100" | 100"–30" | <30" | To scale | | <5' | | | | | | | |

Plotted to scale if the major axis >2', and circular when face on or the position angle is uncertain

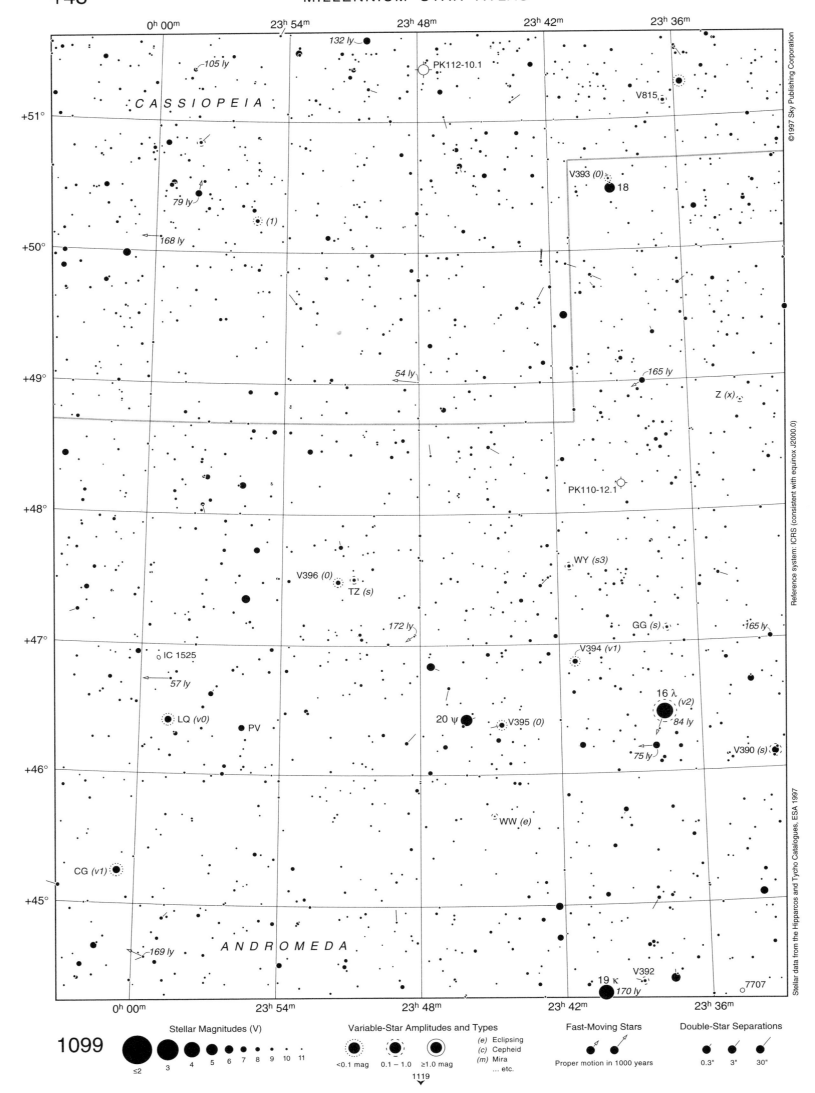

Stellar Magnitudes (V)

Variable-Star Amplitudes and Types

Fast-Moving Stars

Double-Star Separations

**1099**

≤2   3   4   5   6 7 8 9 10 11

<0.1 mag    0.1 – 1.0    ≥1.0 mag

(e) Eclipsing
(c) Cepheid
(m) Mira
... etc.

Proper motion in 1000 years

0.3"   3"   30"

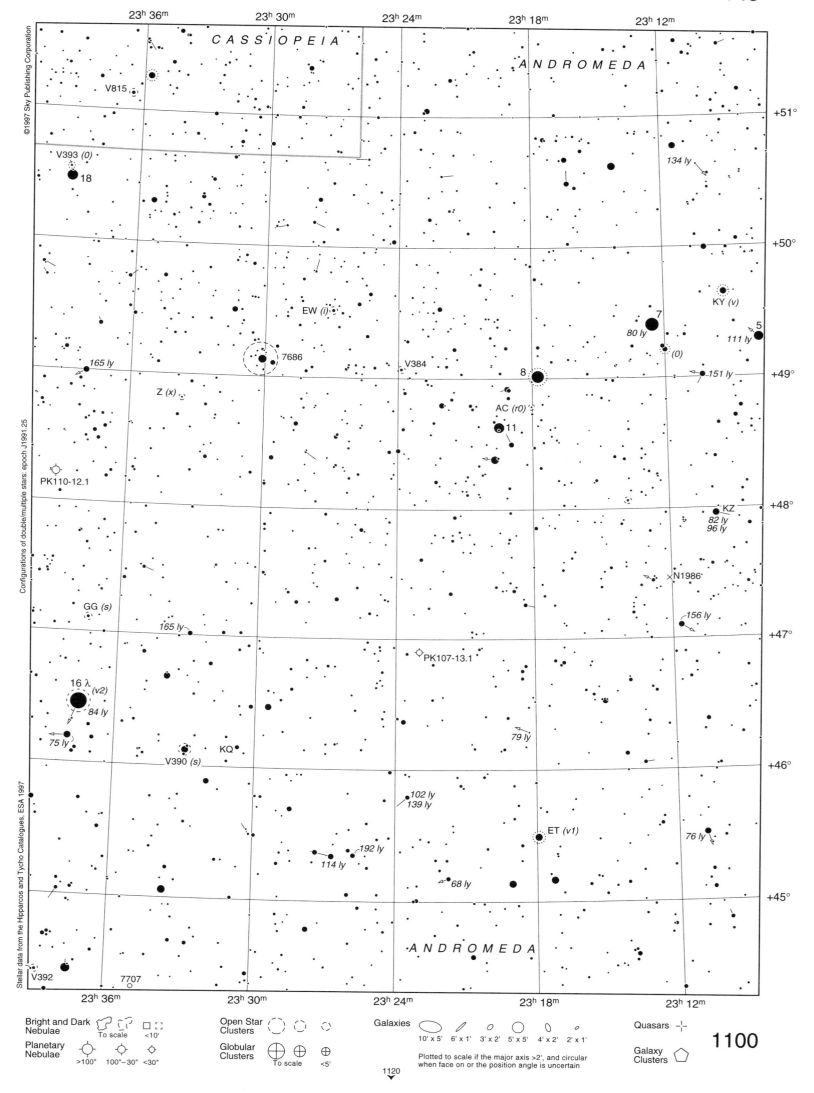

CASSIOPEIA

ANDROMEDA

V815

V393 (0)
18

134 ly

+51°

+50°

KY (v)

EW (i)

7
80 ly

5
111 ly

7686

V384

(0)

165 ly

8

151 ly

+49°

Z (x)

AC (r0)

11

PK110-12.1

KZ
82 ly
96 ly

+48°

N1986

GG (s)

156 ly

165 ly

+47°

PK107-13.1

16 λ (v2)
84 ly

75 ly

79 ly

76 ly

KQ
V390 (s)

102 ly
139 ly

ET (v1)

192 ly
114 ly

68 ly

+46°

+45°

ANDROMEDA

V392

7707

23h 36m          23h 30m          23h 24m          23h 18m          23h 12m

Bright and Dark Nebulae — To scale — <10'

Planetary Nebulae — >100" — 100"–30" — <30"

Open Star Clusters

Globular Clusters — To scale — <5'

Galaxies — 10' x 5' — 6' x 1' — 3' x 2' — 5' x 5' — 4' x 2' — 2' x 1'

Plotted to scale if the major axis >2', and circular when face on or the position angle is uncertain

Quasars

Galaxy Clusters

1100

# MILLENNIUM STAR ATLAS

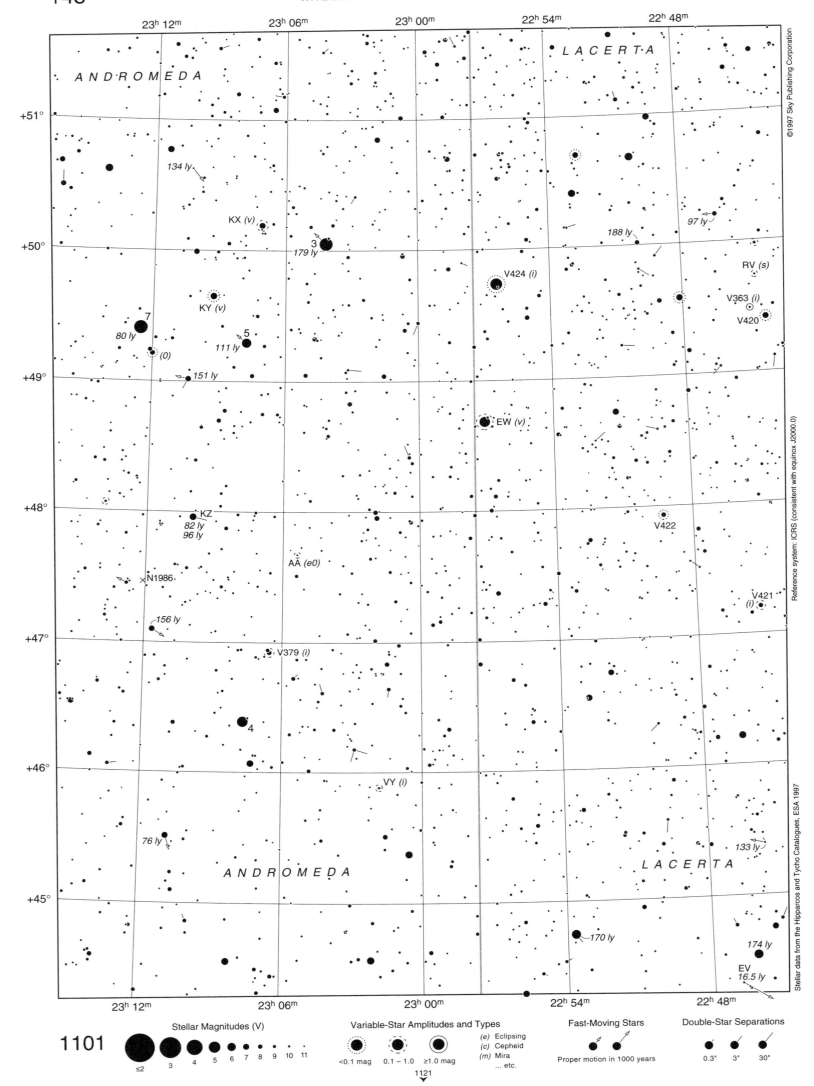

©1997 Sky Publishing Corporation

Reference system: ICRS (consistent with equinox J2000.0)

Stellar data from the Hipparcos and Tycho Catalogues, ESA 1997

**1101**

**Stellar Magnitudes (V)**
≤2  3  4  5  6  7  8  9  10  11

**Variable-Star Amplitudes and Types**
<0.1 mag   0.1 – 1.0   ≥1.0 mag

(e) Eclipsing
(c) Cepheid
(m) Mira
... etc.

**Fast-Moving Stars**
Proper motion in 1000 years

**Double-Star Separations**
0.3"   3"   30"

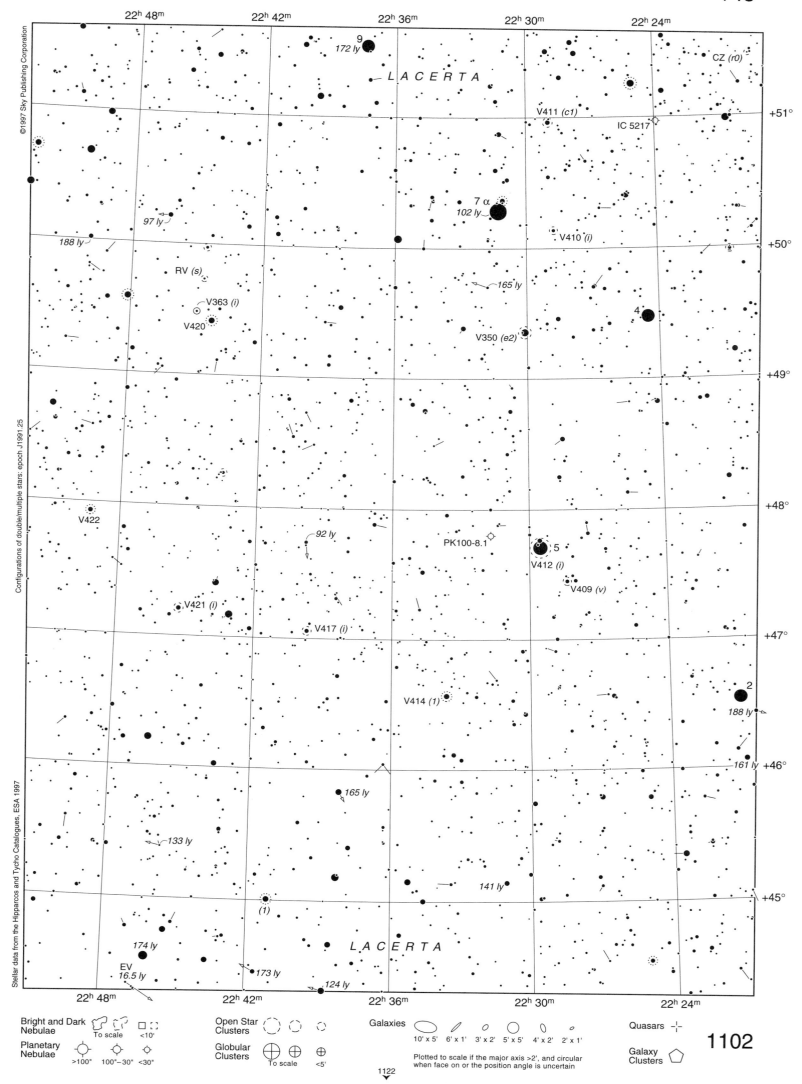

22h 48m   22h 42m   22h 36m   22h 30m   22h 24m

9
172 ly

LACERTA

CZ (r0)

V411 (c1)
IC 5217

+51°

7 α
102 ly

V410 (i)

+50°

97 ly

188 ly

RV (s)

165 ly

V363 (i)
V420

V350 (e2)

4

+49°

V422

92 ly

PK100-8.1

V412 (i)

5

+48°

V409 (v)

V421 (i)

V417 (i)

2
188 ly

V414 (1)

+47°

161 ly   +46°

165 ly

133 ly

141 ly

+45°

(1)

LACERTA

174 ly

EV
16.5 ly   173 ly

124 ly

22h 48m   22h 42m   22h 36m   22h 30m   22h 24m

Bright and Dark Nebulae
To scale   <10'

Planetary Nebulae
>100"   100"–30"   <30"

Open Star Clusters

Globular Clusters
To scale   <5'

Galaxies
10' x 5'   6' x 1'   3' x 2'   5' x 5'   4' x 2'   2' x 1'

Plotted to scale if the major axis >2', and circular when face on or the position angle is uncertain

Quasars

Galaxy Clusters

1102

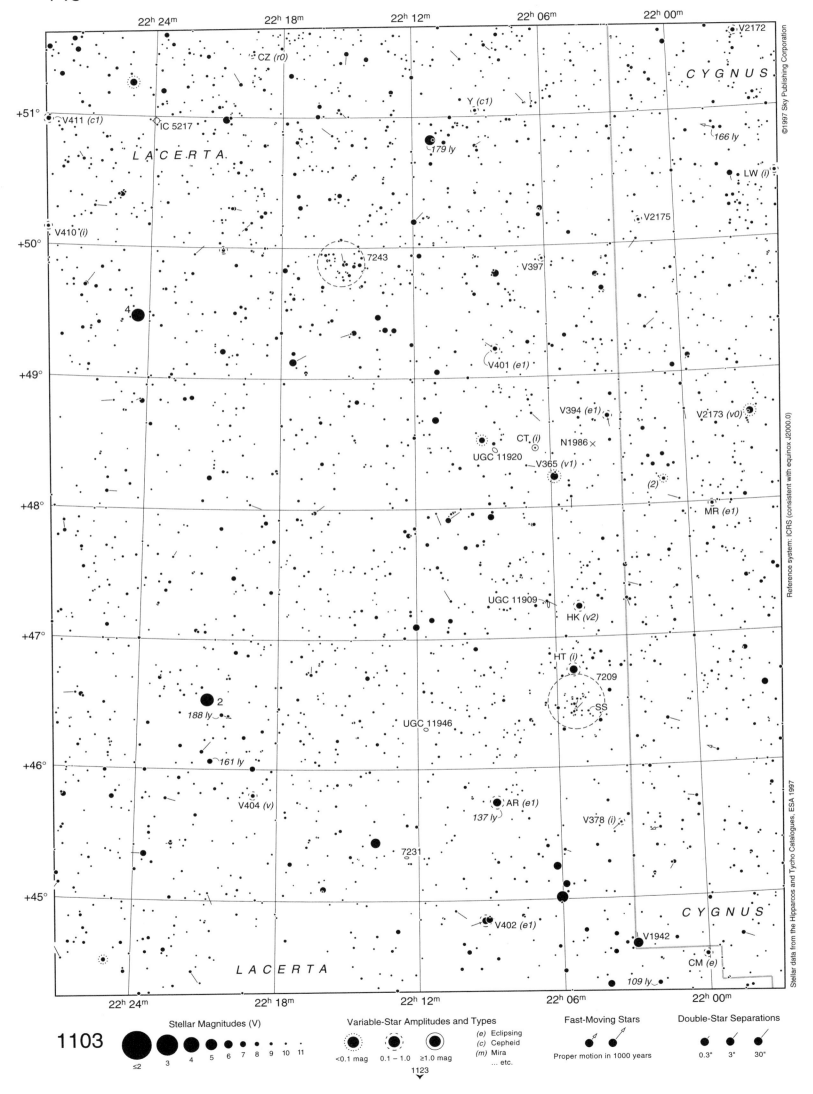

©1997 Sky Publishing Corporation

Reference system: ICRS (consistent with equinox J2000.0)

Stellar data from the Hipparcos and Tycho Catalogues, ESA 1997

Stellar Magnitudes (V)

Variable-Star Amplitudes and Types

Fast-Moving Stars

Double-Star Separations

1103

≤2   3   4   5   6   7  8  9  10  11

<0.1 mag   0.1 – 1.0   ≥1.0 mag

(e) Eclipsing
(c) Cepheid
(m) Mira
... etc.

Proper motion in 1000 years

0.3"   3"   30"

1123

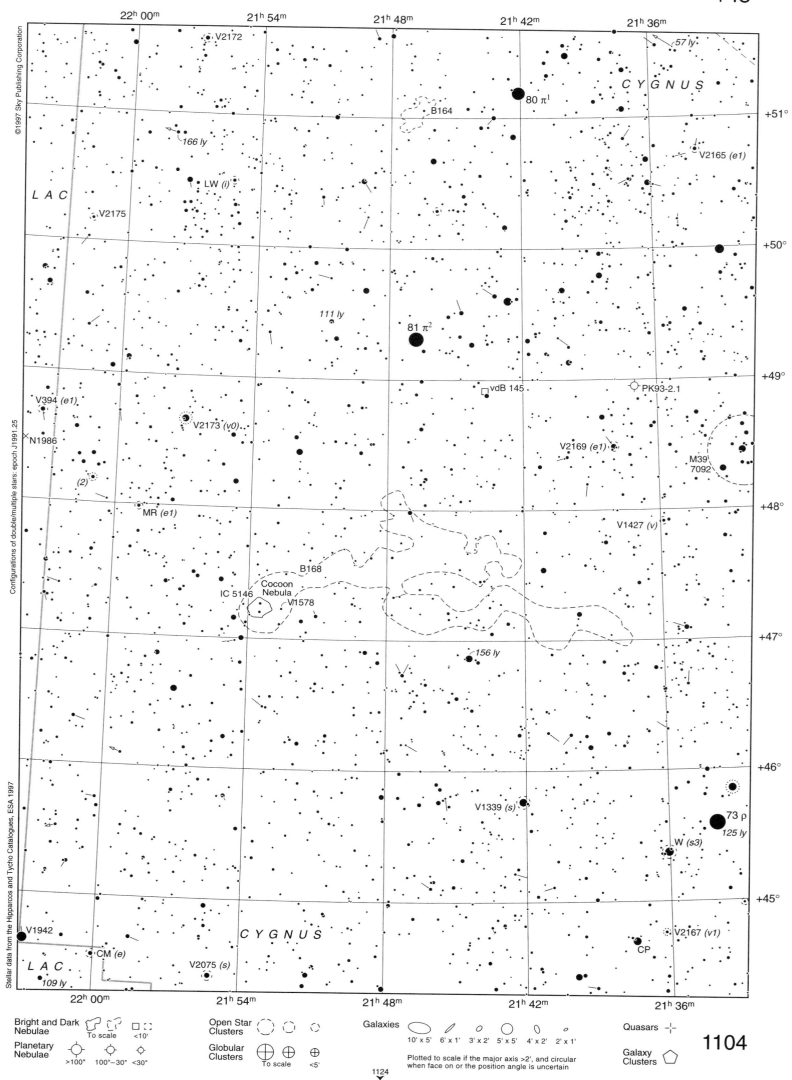

©1997 Sky Publishing Corporation

Configurations of double/multiple stars: epoch J1991.25

Stellar data from the Hipparcos and Tycho Catalogues, ESA 1997

22ʰ 00ᵐ          21ʰ 54ᵐ          21ʰ 48ᵐ          21ʰ 42ᵐ          21ʰ 36ᵐ

V2172

57 ly

C Y G N U S

80 π¹
B164

+51°

V2165 (e1)

166 ly

L A C

LW (i)

+50°

V2175

111 ly

81 π²

+49°

vdB 145          PK93-2.1

V394 (e1)

V2173 (v0)

V2169 (e1)

M39
7092

N1986

(2)

+48°

MR (e1)

V1427 (v)

B168

Cocoon
Nebula

IC 5146          V1578

+47°

156 ly

+46°

V1339 (s)

73 ρ
125 ly

W (s3)

+45°

V1942

V2167 (v1)

C Y G N U S

CP

CM (e)

L A C

V2075 (s)

109 ly

22ʰ 00ᵐ          21ʰ 54ᵐ          21ʰ 48ᵐ          21ʰ 42ᵐ          21ʰ 36ᵐ

Bright and Dark
Nebulae         To scale   <10'

Open Star
Clusters

Galaxies

10' x 5'  6' x 1'  3' x 2'  5' x 5'  4' x 2'  2' x 1'

Quasars

Planetary
Nebulae    >100"  100"–30"  <30"

Globular
Clusters   To scale   <5'

Galaxy
Clusters

Plotted to scale if the major axis >2', and circular
when face on or the position angle is uncertain

1104

1124

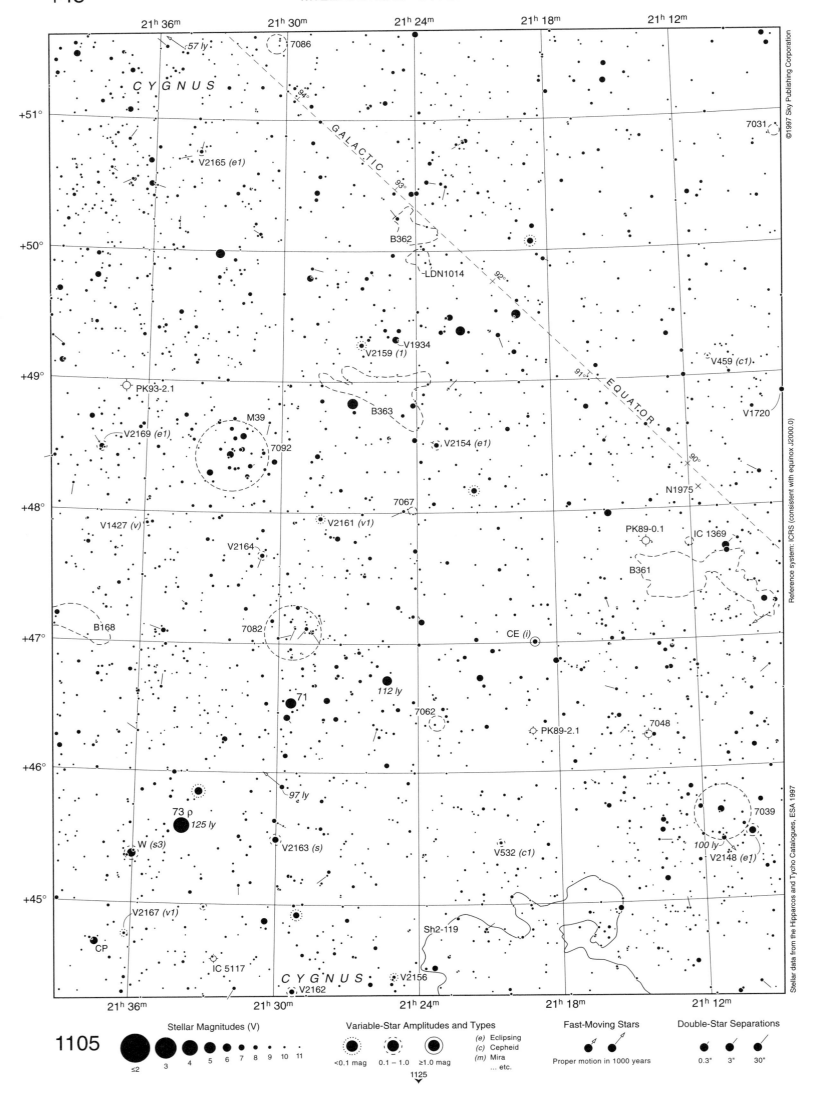

©1997 Sky Publishing Corporation

Reference system: ICRS (consistent with equinox J2000.0)

Stellar data from the Hipparcos and Tycho Catalogues, ESA 1997

CYGNUS

57 ly

7086

94°

GALACTIC

V2165 (e1)

B362

LDN1014

92°

93°

V1934

V2159 (1)

V459 (c1)

91°

EQUATOR

PK93-2.1

M39

B363

V1720

V2169 (e1)

7092

V2154 (e1)

90°

N1975

7067

PK89-0.1    IC 1369

V1427 (v)

V2161 (v1)

B361

V2164

B168

7082

CE (i)

71

112 ly

7062

PK89-2.1    7048

97 ly

73 ρ    125 ly

7039

W (s3)

V2163 (s)

V532 (c1)    100 ly

V2148 (e1)

V2167 (v1)

CP

Sh2-119

IC 5117

CYGNUS

V2156

V2162

Stellar Magnitudes (V)

≤2    3    4    5    6    7    8    9    10    11

Variable-Star Amplitudes and Types

<0.1 mag    0.1 – 1.0    ≥1.0 mag

(e) Eclipsing
(c) Cepheid
(m) Mira
... etc.

Fast-Moving Stars

Proper motion in 1000 years

Double-Star Separations

0.3"    3"    30"

# MILLENNIUM STAR ATLAS

**+48°**

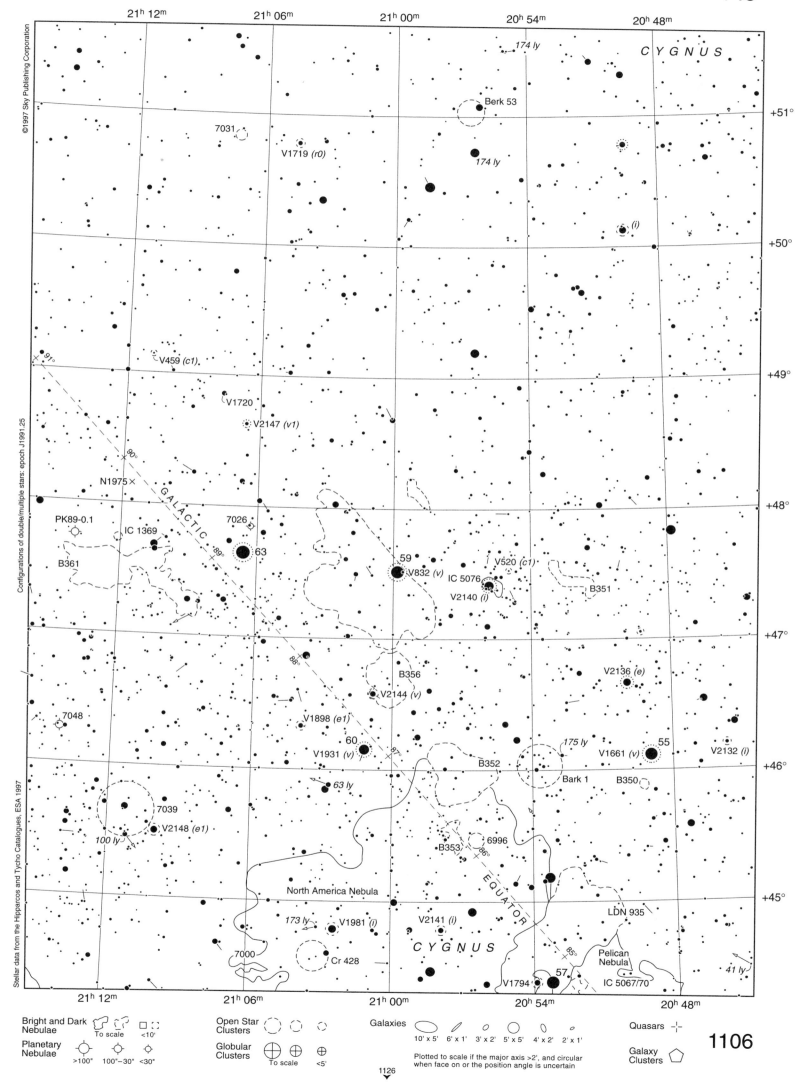

Configurations of double/multiple stars: epoch J1991.25

Stellar data from the Hipparcos and Tycho Catalogues, ESA 1997

21ʰ 12ᵐ  21ʰ 06ᵐ  21ʰ 00ᵐ  20ʰ 54ᵐ  20ʰ 48ᵐ

C Y G N U S

174 ly
Berk 53

7031
V1719 (r0)
174 ly

(i)

V459 (c1)

V1720
V2147 (v1)

91°
90°
N1975

GALACTIC
89°

PK89-0.1
IC 1369
7026
63
59
V832 (v)
V520 (c1)
IC 5076
V2140 (i)
B351

B361

88°

B356
V2144 (v)
V2136 (e)

7048
V1898 (e1)
60
V1931 (v)
87°
175 ly
B352
Bark 1
V1661 (v)
55
V2132 (i)
B350

63 ly

7039
V2148 (e1)
100 ly
86°
6996
B353
EQUATOR

North America Nebula
LDN 935
85°

173 ly
V1981 (i)
V2141 (i)
Pelican Nebula

7000
Cr 428
C Y G N U S
57
V1794
IC 5067/70
41 ly

21ʰ 12ᵐ  21ʰ 06ᵐ  21ʰ 00ᵐ  20ʰ 54ᵐ  20ʰ 48ᵐ

+51°
+50°
+49°
+48°
+47°
+46°
+45°

**Bright and Dark Nebulae**  To scale  <10'

**Planetary Nebulae**  >100"  100"–30"  <30"

**Open Star Clusters**  To scale  <5'

**Globular Clusters**  To scale  <5'

**Galaxies**  10' x 5'  6' x 1'  3' x 2'  5' x 5'  4' x 2'  2' x 1'

Plotted to scale if the major axis >2', and circular when face on or the position angle is uncertain

**Quasars**

**Galaxy Clusters**

**1106**

+48°

# MILLENNIUM STAR ATLAS

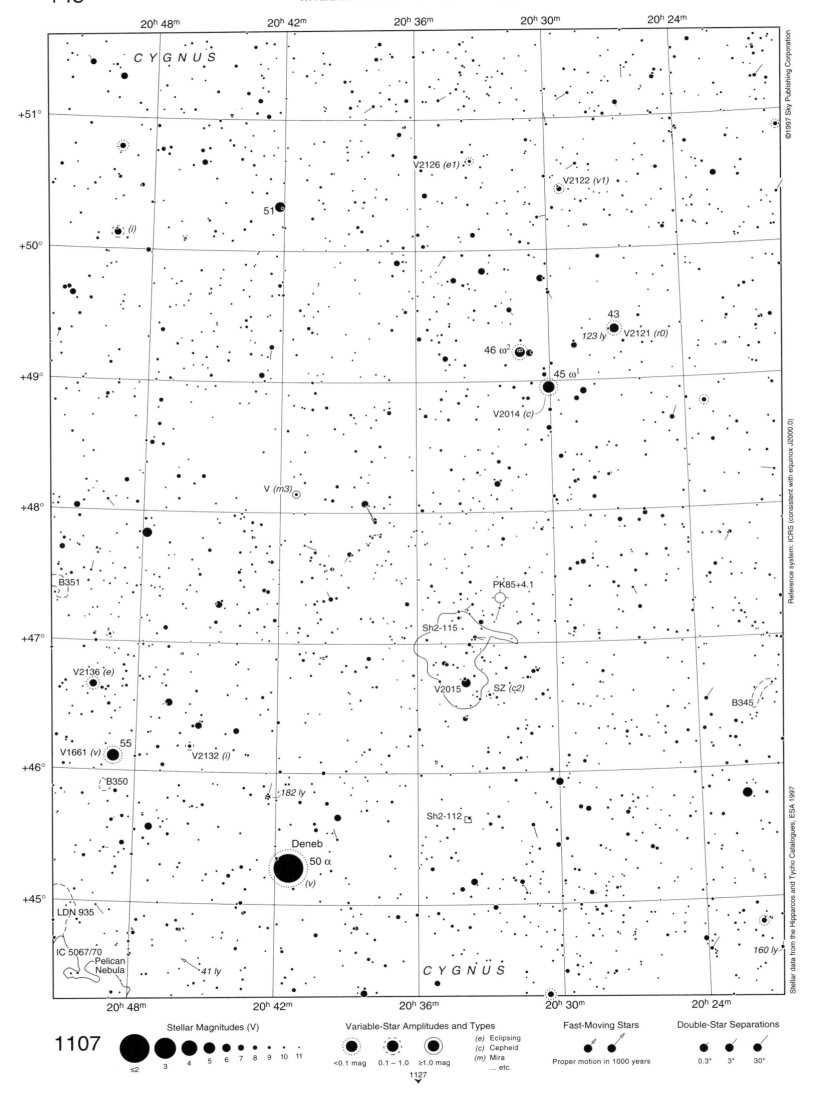

C Y G N U S

V2126 (e1)

V2122 (v1)

51

(i)

43
123 ly   V2121 (r0)

46 ω²

45 ω¹

V2014 (c)

V (m3)

B351

PK85+4.1

Sh2-115

V2136 (e)

V2015   SZ (ç2)

B345

V1661 (v)   55

V2132 (i)

B350

182 ly

Sh2-112

Deneb
50 α
(v)

LDN 935

IC 5067/70
Pelican
Nebula

41 ly

160 ly

C Y G N U S

## 1107

**Stellar Magnitudes (V)**

≤2   3   4   5   6   7   8   9   10   11

**Variable-Star Amplitudes and Types**

<0.1 mag   0.1 – 1.0   ≥1.0 mag

(e) Eclipsing
(c) Cepheid
(m) Mira
... etc.

**Fast-Moving Stars**

Proper motion in 1000 years

**Double-Star Separations**

0.3"   3"   30"

# MILLENNIUM STAR ATLAS

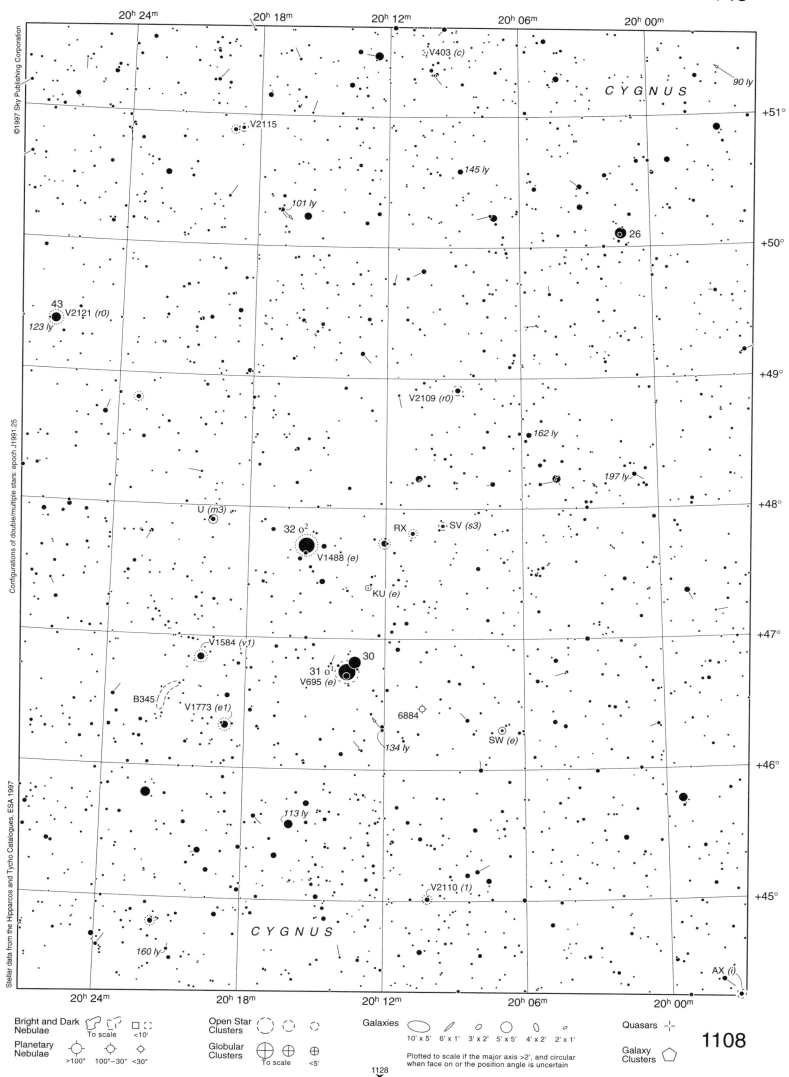

©1997 Sky Publishing Corporation

Configurations of double/multiple stars: epoch J1991.25

Stellar data from the Hipparcos and Tycho Catalogues, ESA 1997

20h 24m    20h 18m    20h 12m    20h 06m    20h 00m

+51°
+50°
+49°
+48°
+47°
+46°
+45°

CYGNUS

V403 (c)
90 ly
V2115
145 ly
101 ly
26
43
V2121 (r0)
123 ly
V2109 (r0)
162 ly
197 ly
U (m3)
32 o²
RX    SV (s3)
V1488 (e)
KU (e)
V1584 (v1)
31 o¹    30
V695 (e)
B345
V1773 (e1)
6884
134 ly
SW (e)
113 ly
V2110 (1)
CYGNUS
160 ly
AX (i)

Bright and Dark Nebulae          Open Star Clusters          Galaxies                                                              Quasars
To scale    <10'                                                    10' x 5'  6' x 1'  3' x 2'  5' x 5'  4' x 2'  2' x 1'

Planetary Nebulae                  Globular Clusters                                                                               Galaxy Clusters
>100"  100"–30"  <30"          To scale    <5'          Plotted to scale if the major axis >2', and circular
                                                                      when face on or the position angle is uncertain

1108

1128

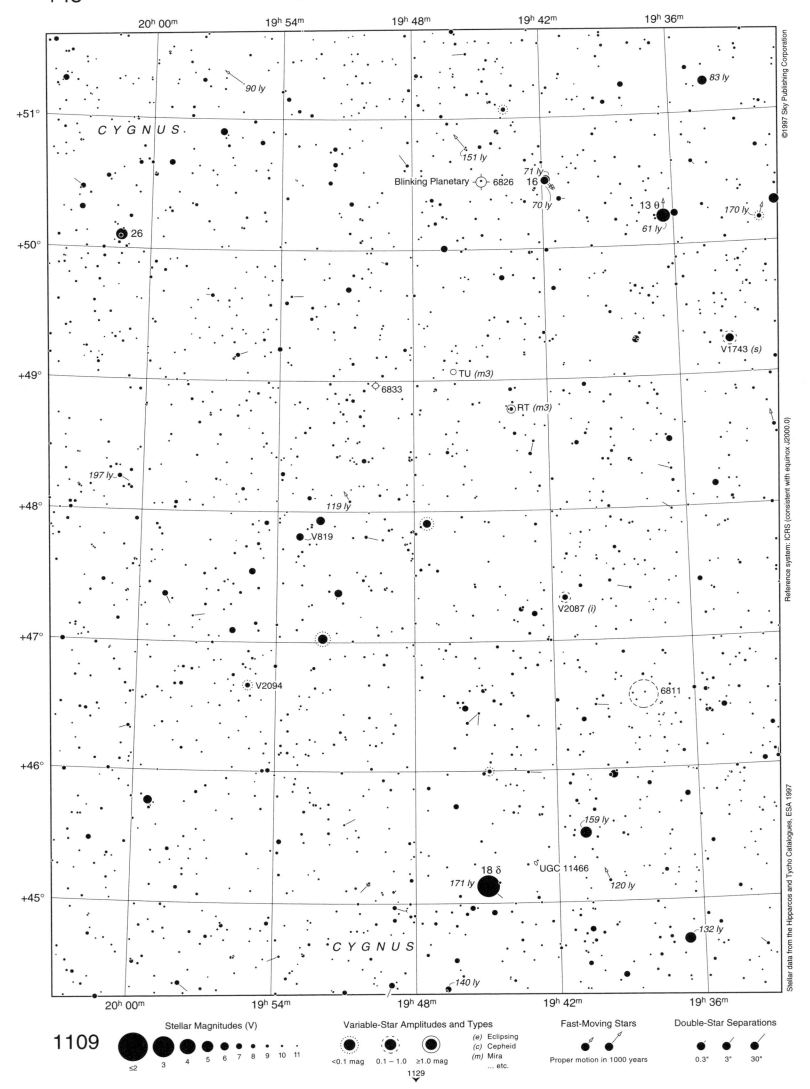

©1997 Sky Publishing Corporation

Reference system: ICRS (consistent with equinox J2000.0)

Stellar data from the Hipparcos and Tycho Catalogues, ESA 1997

90 ly

CYGNUS

151 ly

Blinking Planetary ⊙ 6826    16    71 ly

70 ly

13 θ

61 ly

83 ly

170 ly

26

V1743 (s)

TU (m3)

6833

RT (m3)

197 ly

119 ly

V819

V2087 (i)

V2094

6811

159 ly

18 δ    UGC 11466

171 ly    120 ly

CYGNUS

132 ly

140 ly

1109

Stellar Magnitudes (V)

≤2    3    4    5    6    7    8    9    10    11

Variable-Star Amplitudes and Types

<0.1 mag    0.1 – 1.0    ≥1.0 mag

(e) Eclipsing
(c) Cepheid
(m) Mira
... etc.

1129

Fast-Moving Stars

Proper motion in 1000 years

Double-Star Separations

0.3"    3"    30"

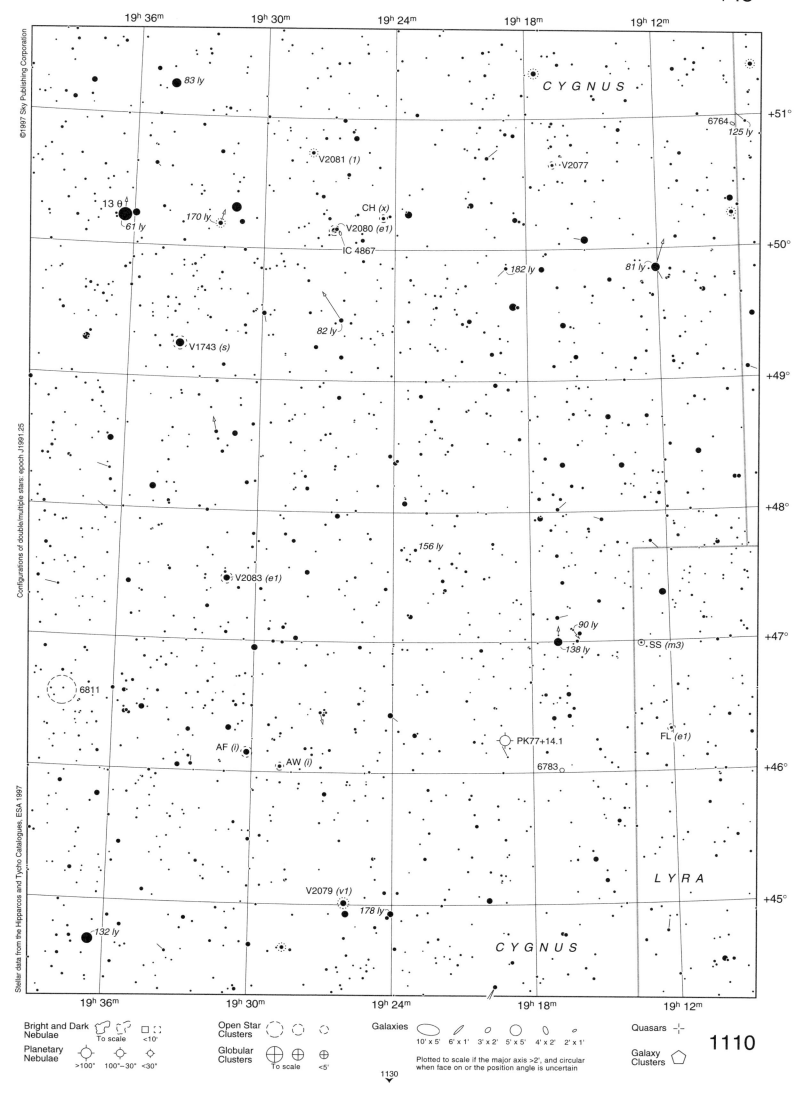

19h 36m          19h 30m          19h 24m          19h 18m          19h 12m

+51°

*C Y G N U S*

83 ly

6764
125 ly

V2081 (1)

V2077

13 θ

CH (x)

61 ly          170 ly          V2080 (e1)
                               IC 4867

81 ly

+50°

182 ly

82 ly

V1743 (s)

+49°

+48°

156 ly

V2083 (e1)

90 ly
138 ly

⊙ SS (m3)

+47°

6811

FL (e1)

AF (i)          PK77+14.1

AW (i)          6783

+46°

*L Y R A*

V2079 (v1)

+45°

132 ly          178 ly

*C Y G N U S*

+48°

19h 36m          19h 30m          19h 24m          19h 18m          19h 12m

+48°

# MILLENNIUM STAR ATLAS

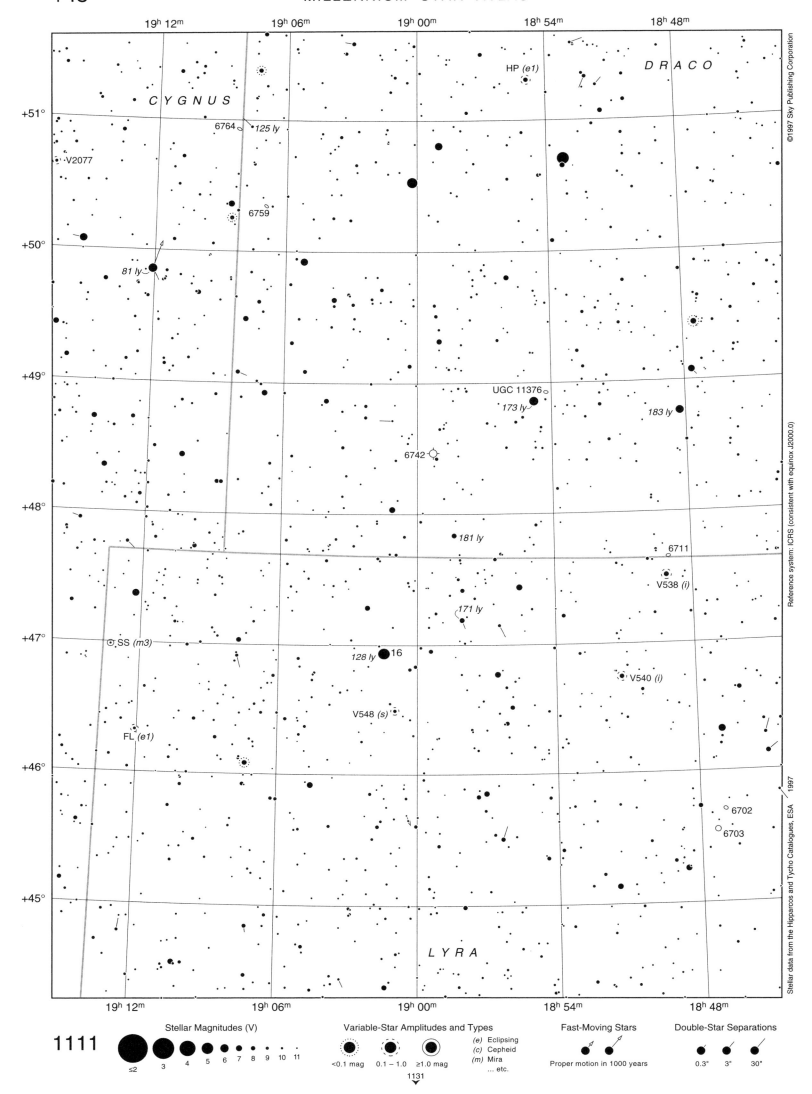

CYGNUS

DRACO

HP *(e1)*

6764 — *125 ly*

V2077

6759

*81 ly*

UGC 11376

*173 ly*

*183 ly*

6742

*181 ly*

6711

V538 *(i)*

*171 ly*

SS *(m3)*

*128 ly* 16

V540 *(i)*

V548 *(s)*

FL *(e1)*

6702

6703

LYRA

1111

### Stellar Magnitudes (V)

≤2   3   4   5   6   7   8   9   10   11

### Variable-Star Amplitudes and Types

<0.1 mag   0.1 – 1.0   ≥1.0 mag

*(e)* Eclipsing
*(c)* Cepheid
*(m)* Mira
... etc.

### Fast-Moving Stars

Proper motion in 1000 years

### Double-Star Separations

0.3"   3"   30"

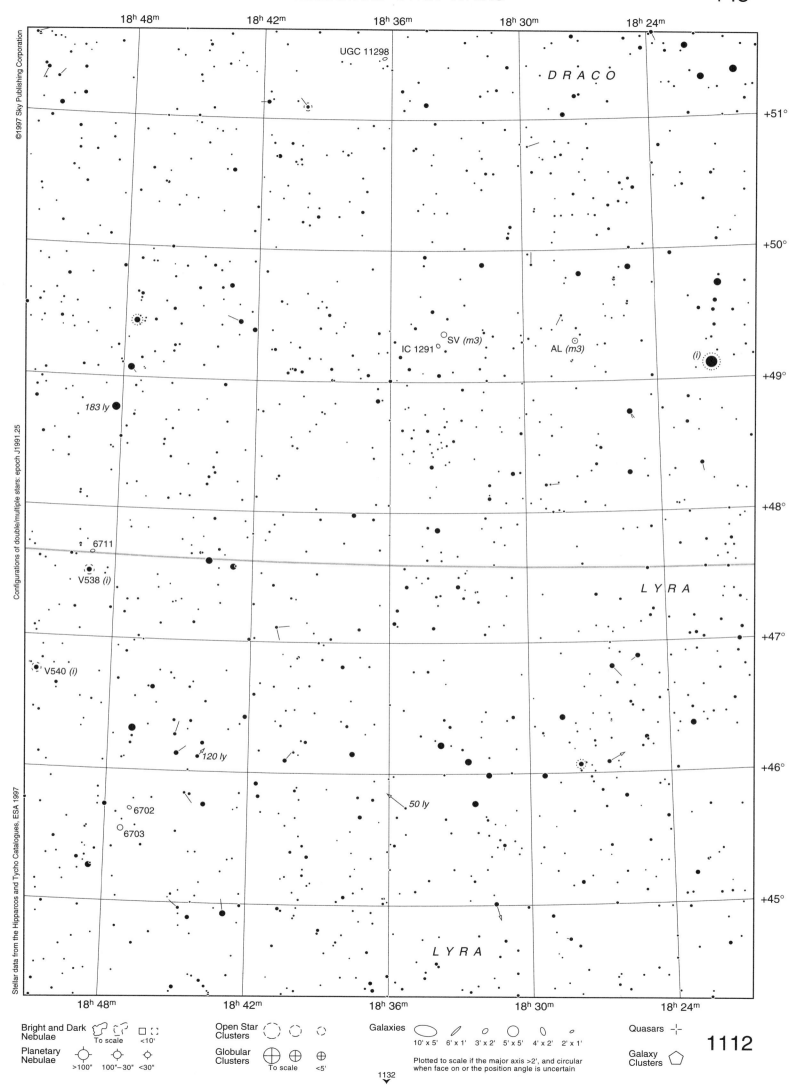

18h 48m    18h 42m    18h 36m    18h 30m    18h 24m

UGC 11298

*D R A C O*

+51°

+50°

IC 1291 ○    SV *(m3)*    AL *(m3)*

*(i)*

+49°

*183 ly*

+48°

6711

V538 *(i)*    *L Y R A*

+47°

V540 *(i)*

120 ly

6702    50 ly

6703

*L Y R A*

+46°

+45°

18h 48m    18h 42m    18h 36m    18h 30m    18h 24m

Bright and Dark Nebulae — To scale — <10'

Planetary Nebulae — >100" — 100"–30" — <30'

Open Star Clusters

Globular Clusters — To scale — <5'

Galaxies — 10' x 5' — 6' x 1' — 3' x 2' — 5' x 5' — 4' x 2' — 2' x 1'

Plotted to scale if the major axis >2', and circular when face on or the position angle is uncertain

Quasars

Galaxy Clusters

1112

1132

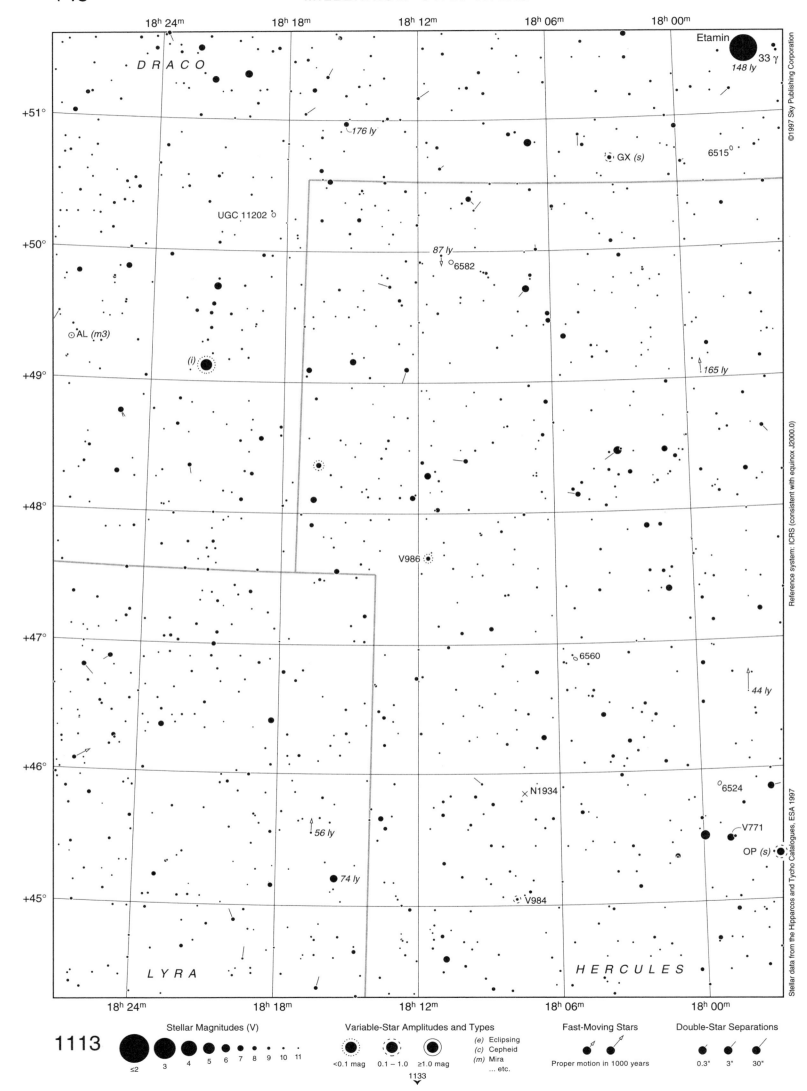

DRACO

Etamin
33 γ
148 ly

176 ly

GX (s)
6515

UGC 11202

AL (m3)

(i)

87 ly
6582

165 ly

V986

6560

44 ly

N1934
6524

56 ly
V771

OP (s)

74 ly

V984

LYRA

HERCULES

1113

**Stellar Magnitudes (V)**
≤2   3   4   5   6   7   8   9   10   11

**Variable-Star Amplitudes and Types**
<0.1 mag   0.1 – 1.0   ≥1.0 mag

(e) Eclipsing
(c) Cepheid
(m) Mira
... etc.

1133

**Fast-Moving Stars**
Proper motion in 1000 years

**Double-Star Separations**
0.3"   3"   30"

# MILLENNIUM STAR ATLAS

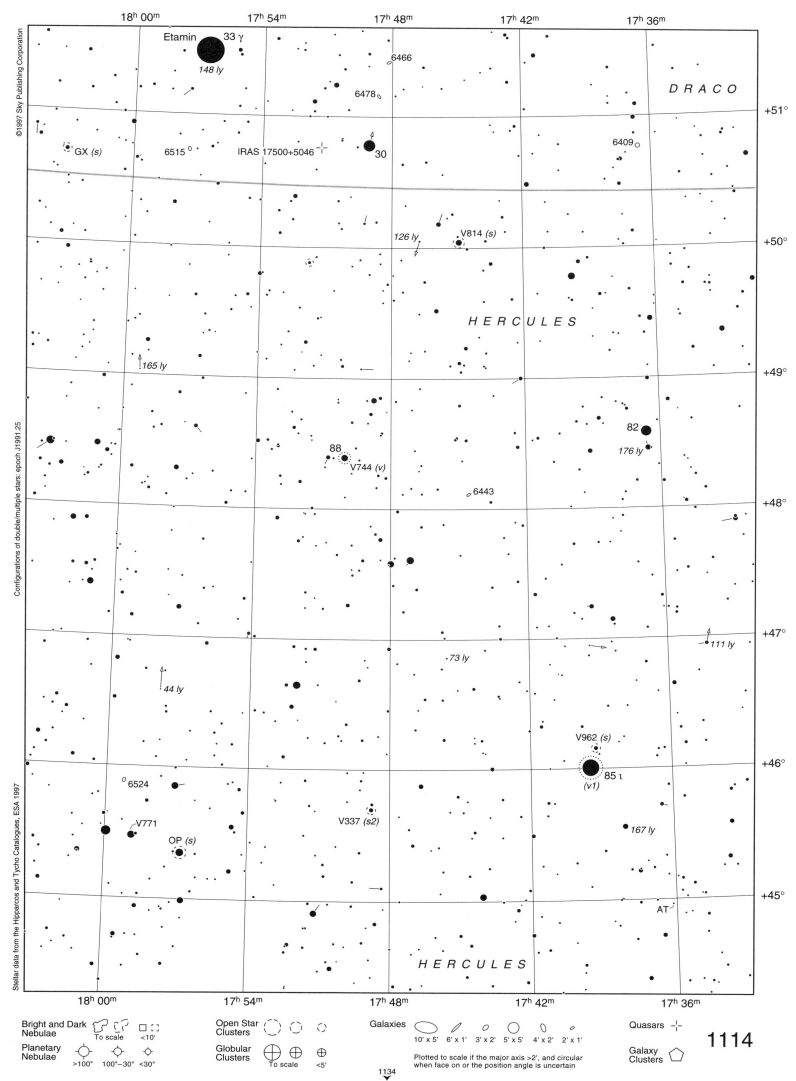

©1997 Sky Publishing Corporation

Configurations of double/multiple stars: epoch J1991.25

Stellar data from the Hipparcos and Tycho Catalogues, ESA 1997

18h 00m    17h 54m    17h 48m    17h 42m    17h 36m

+51°
+50°
+49°
+48°
+47°
+46°
+45°

DRACO

HERCULES

HERCULES

Etamin    33 γ
148 ly
6466
6478
GX (s)    6515    IRAS 17500+5046    30
6409
V814 (s)
126 ly
165 ly
82
176 ly
88
V744 (v)
6443
73 ly
111 ly
44 ly
V962 (s)
85 ι
(v1)
6524
V337 (s2)
167 ly
V771
OP (s)
AT

18h 00m    17h 54m    17h 48m    17h 42m    17h 36m

| Bright and Dark Nebulae | Open Star Clusters | Galaxies | Quasars |

Bright and Dark Nebulae    To scale    <10'

Planetary Nebulae    >100"    100"–30"    <30'

Open Star Clusters

Globular Clusters    To scale    <5'

Galaxies    10' x 5'    6' x 1'    3' x 2'    5' x 5'    4' x 2'    2' x 1'

Plotted to scale if the major axis >2', and circular when face on or the position angle is uncertain

Quasars

Galaxy Clusters

1114

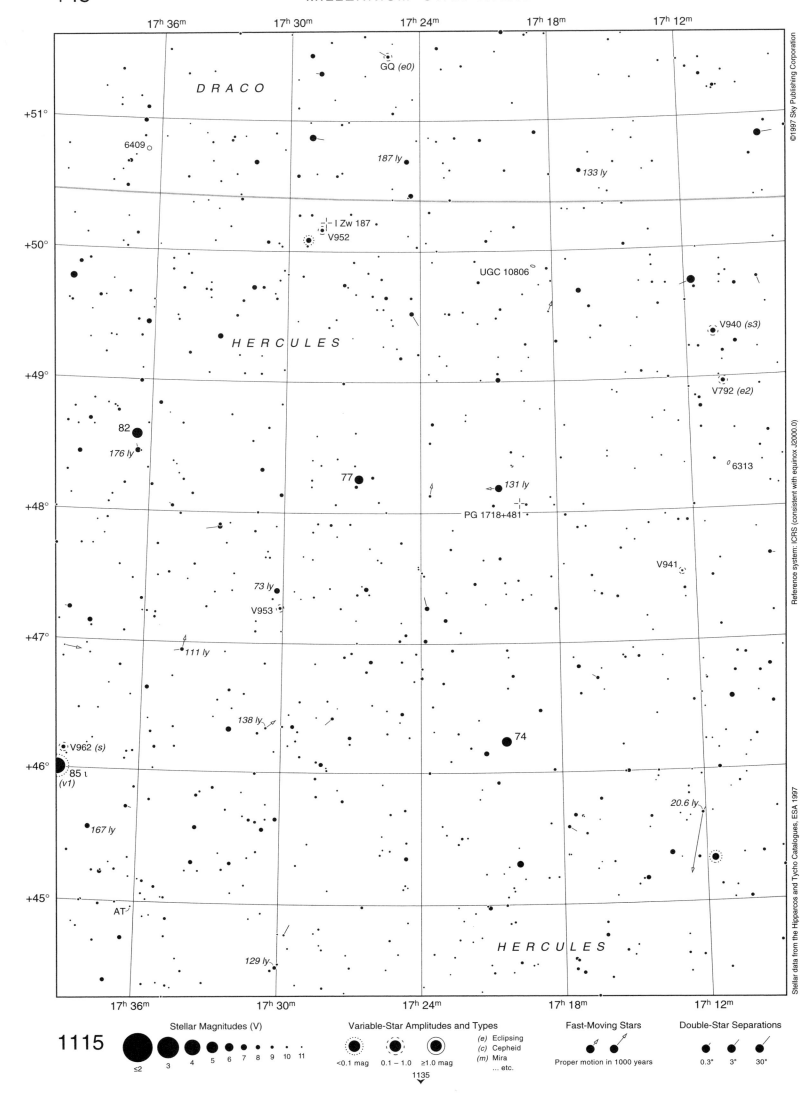

©1997 Sky Publishing Corporation

Reference system: ICRS (consistent with equinox J2000.0)

Stellar data from the Hipparcos and Tycho Catalogues, ESA 1997

Stellar Magnitudes (V)

≤2  3  4  5  6  7  8  9  10  11

Variable-Star Amplitudes and Types

<0.1 mag   0.1 – 1.0   ≥1.0 mag

(e) Eclipsing
(c) Cepheid
(m) Mira
... etc.

Fast-Moving Stars

Proper motion in 1000 years

Double-Star Separations

0.3"   3"   30"

1135

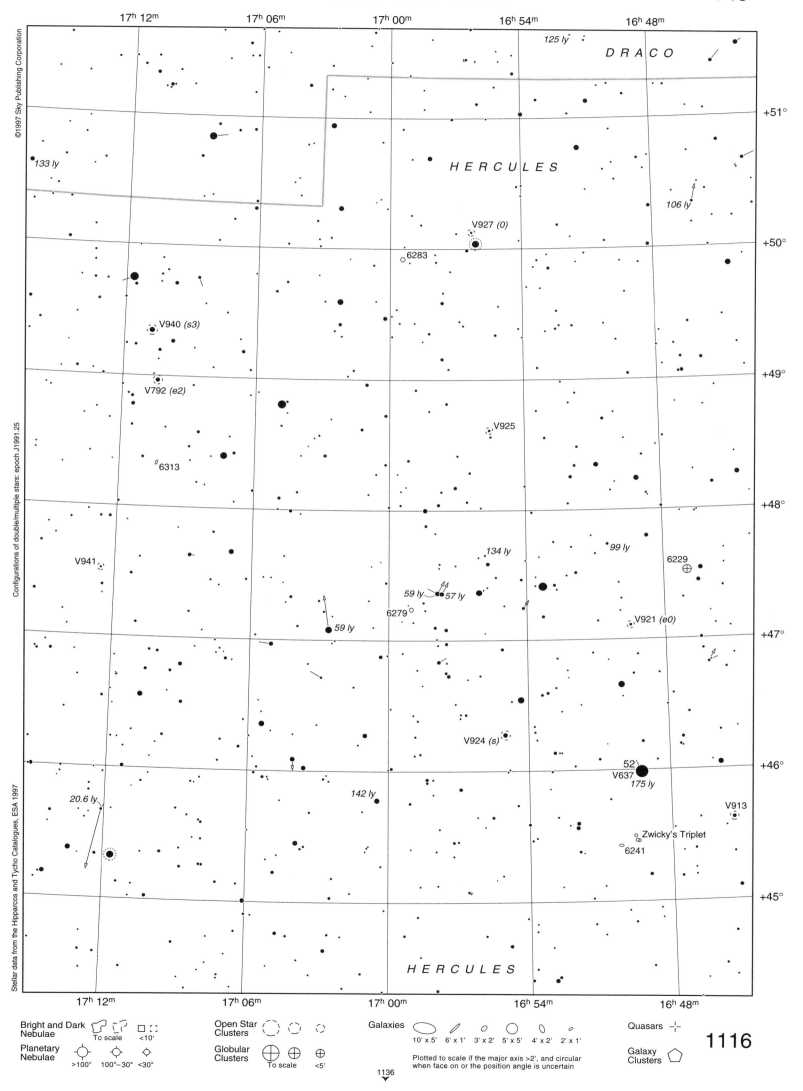

Configurations of double/multiple stars: epoch J1991.25

Stellar data from the Hipparcos and Tycho Catalogues, ESA 1997

17ʰ 12ᵐ    17ʰ 06ᵐ    17ʰ 00ᵐ    16ʰ 54ᵐ    16ʰ 48ᵐ

125 ly

D R A C O

+51°

133 ly

H E R C U L E S

106 ly

V927 (0)

+50°

6283

V940 (s3)

V792 (e2)

+49°

V925

6313

+48°

134 ly          99 ly

6229

V941              59 ly ⟋ 57 ly

6279          V921 (e0)

59 ly    +47°

V924 (s)

52
V637
175 ly    +46°

20.6 ly          142 ly          V913

Zwicky's Triplet
6241

+45°

17ʰ 12ᵐ    17ʰ 06ᵐ    17ʰ 00ᵐ    16ʰ 54ᵐ    16ʰ 48ᵐ

H E R C U L E S

| Bright and Dark Nebulae | Open Star Clusters | Galaxies | Quasars |
|---|---|---|---|

Bright and Dark Nebulae    To scale    <10'

Open Star Clusters

Galaxies    10' x 5'   6' x 1'   3' x 2'   5' x 5'   4' x 2'   2' x 1'

Quasars

Planetary Nebulae    >100"   100"–30"   <30"

Globular Clusters    To scale    <5'

Plotted to scale if the major axis >2', and circular when face on or the position angle is uncertain

Galaxy Clusters

1116

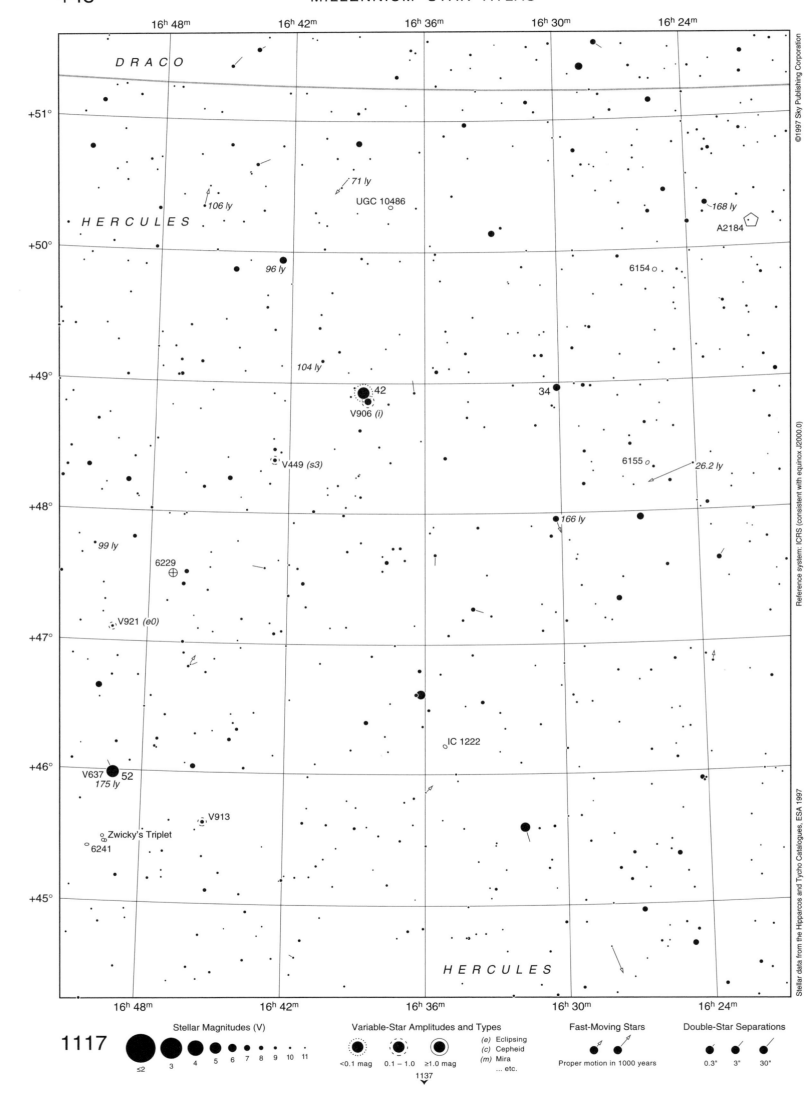

16h 48m   16h 42m   16h 36m   16h 30m   16h 24m

DRACO

HERCULES

71 ly
UGC 10486

106 ly

168 ly
A2184

96 ly

6154 ○

104 ly

42
V906 (i)

34

V449 (s3)

6155 ○   26.2 ly

166 ly

99 ly

6229 ⊕

V921 (e0)

IC 1222

V637   52
175 ly

V913

Zwicky's Triplet
6241

HERCULES

1117

### Stellar Magnitudes (V)
≤2   3   4   5   6   7   8   9   10   11

### Variable-Star Amplitudes and Types
<0.1 mag   0.1 – 1.0   ≥1.0 mag
(e) Eclipsing
(c) Cepheid
(m) Mira
... etc.

1137

### Fast-Moving Stars
Proper motion in 1000 years

### Double-Star Separations
0.3"   3"   30"

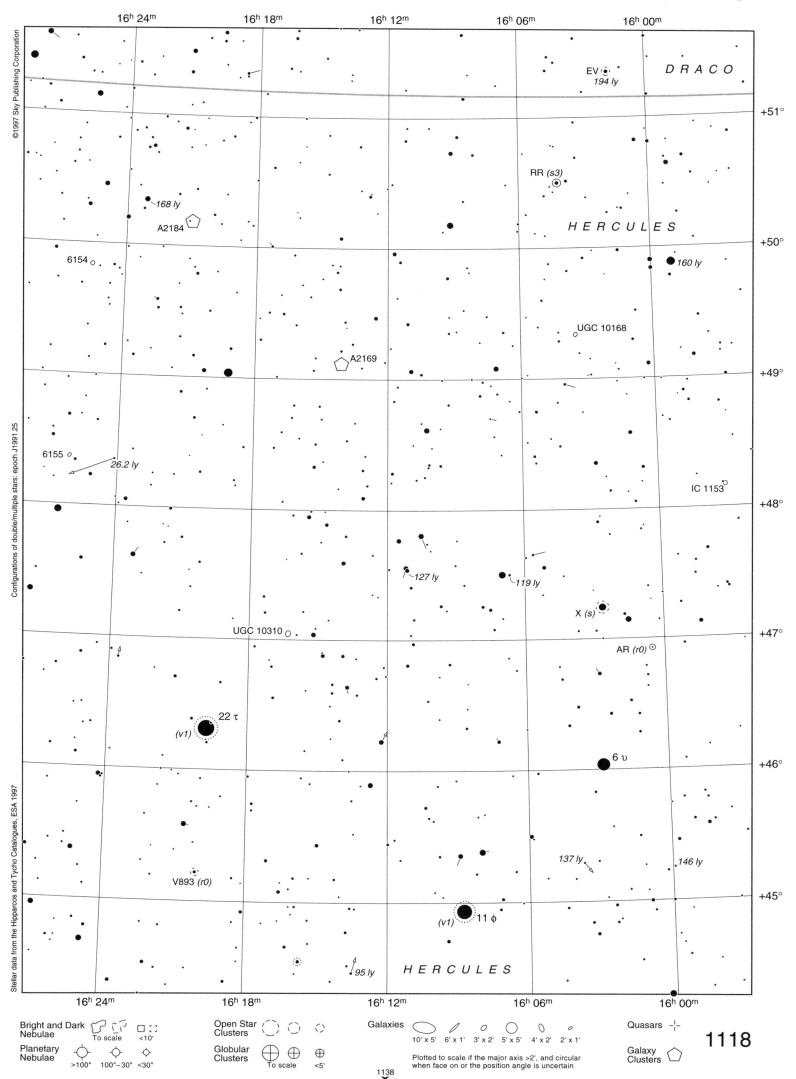

DRACO

EV
194 ly

RR (s3)

HERCULES

+51°

168 ly

A2184

+50°

6154

160 ly

UGC 10168

A2169

+49°

6155

26.2 ly

IC 1153

+48°

127 ly

119 ly

X (s)

UGC 10310

+47°

AR (r0)

22 τ

(v1)

6 υ

+46°

137 ly

146 ly

V893 (r0)

+45°

(v1)

11 φ

95 ly

HERCULES

16h 24m    16h 18m    16h 12m    16h 06m    16h 00m

Bright and Dark
Nebulae
To scale    <10'

Planetary
Nebulae
>100"  100"–30"  <30"

Open Star
Clusters

Globular
Clusters
To scale    <5'

Galaxies
10' x 5'  6' x 1'  3' x 2'  5' x 5'  4' x 2'  2' x 1'

Plotted to scale if the major axis >2', and circular
when face on or the position angle is uncertain

Quasars

Galaxy
Clusters

1118

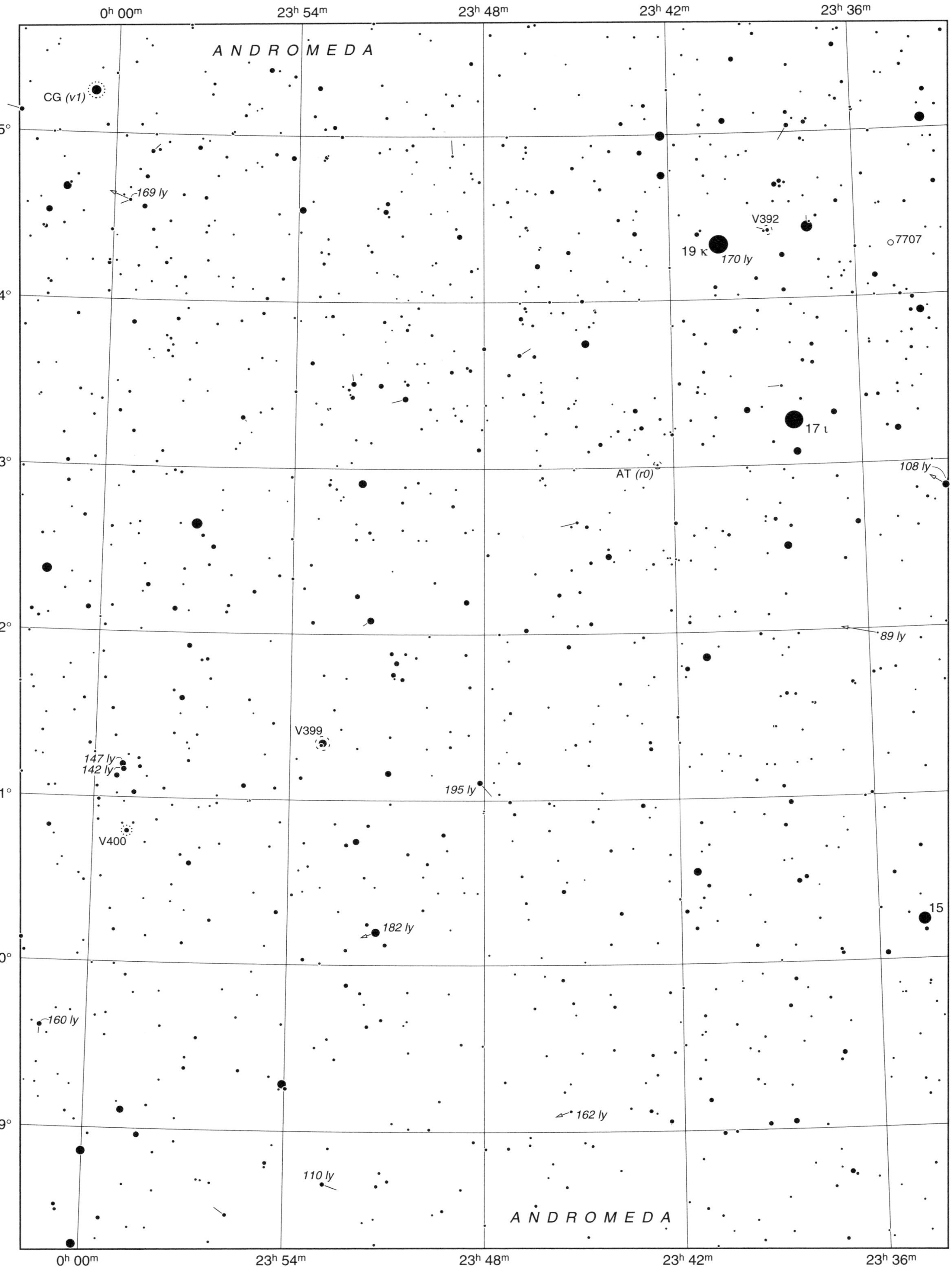
0h 00m
23h 54m
23h 48m
23h 42m
23h 36m
ANDROMEDA
CG (v1)
+45°
169 ly
V392
19 κ
170 ly
7707
+44°
17 ι
+43°
AT (r0)
108 ly
+42°
89 ly
V399
147 ly
142 ly
195 ly
+41°
V400
182 ly
15
+40°
160 ly
+39°
162 ly
110 ly
ANDROMEDA
0h 00m
23h 54m
23h 48m
23h 42m
23h 36m



Reference system: ICRS (consistent with equinox J2000.0)

Stellar data from the Hipparcos and Tycho Catalogues, ESA 1997



Stellar Magnitudes (V)
≤2 3 4 5 6 7 8 9 10 11

Variable-Star Amplitudes and Types
<0.1 mag 0.1 – 1.0 ≥1.0 mag
(e) Eclipsing
(c) Cepheid
(m) Mira
... etc.

Fast-Moving Stars
Proper motion in 1000 years

Double-Star Separations
0.3" 3" 30"

1139

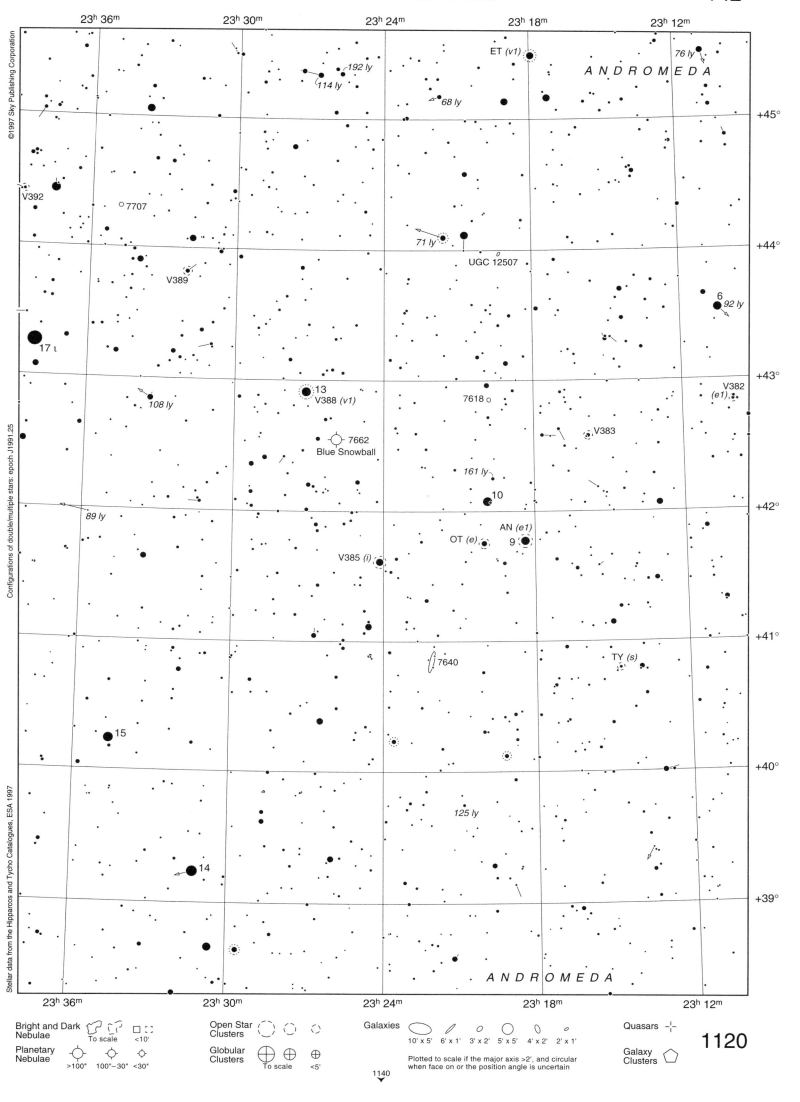

23h 36m    23h 30m    23h 24m    23h 18m    23h 12m

+45°
+44°
+43°
+42°
+41°
+40°
+39°

A N D R O M E D A

ET (v1)
76 ly

192 ly
114 ly
68 ly

V392
7707

71 ly
UGC 12507

V389
6  92 ly

17 ι

13
V388 (v1)
108 ly
7618
V382 (e1)
V383

7662
Blue Snowball
161 ly
10

89 ly
AN (e1)
OT (e)   9
V385 (i)

7640
TY (s)

15

125 ly

14

A N D R O M E D A

23h 36m    23h 30m    23h 24m    23h 18m    23h 12m

Bright and Dark Nebulae
To scale   <10'

Planetary Nebulae
>100"  100"–30"  <30"

Open Star Clusters

Globular Clusters
To scale   <5'

Galaxies
10' x 5'  6' x 1'  3' x 2'  5' x 5'  4' x 2'  2' x 1'

Plotted to scale if the major axis >2', and circular when face on or the position angle is uncertain

Quasars

Galaxy Clusters

1120

1140

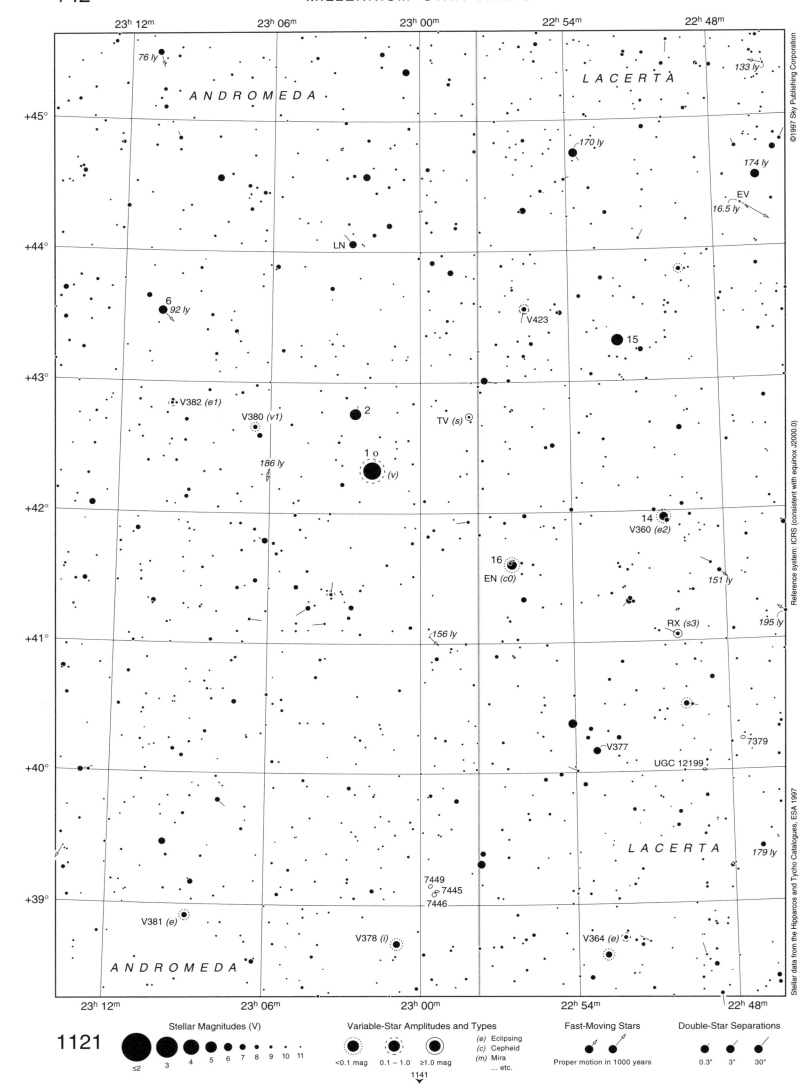

1121

Stellar Magnitudes (V)

≤2  3  4  5  6  7  8  9  10  11

Variable-Star Amplitudes and Types

<0.1 mag    0.1 – 1.0    ≥1.0 mag

(e) Eclipsing
(c) Cepheid
(m) Mira
... etc.

Fast-Moving Stars

Proper motion in 1000 years

Double-Star Separations

0.3"   3"   30"

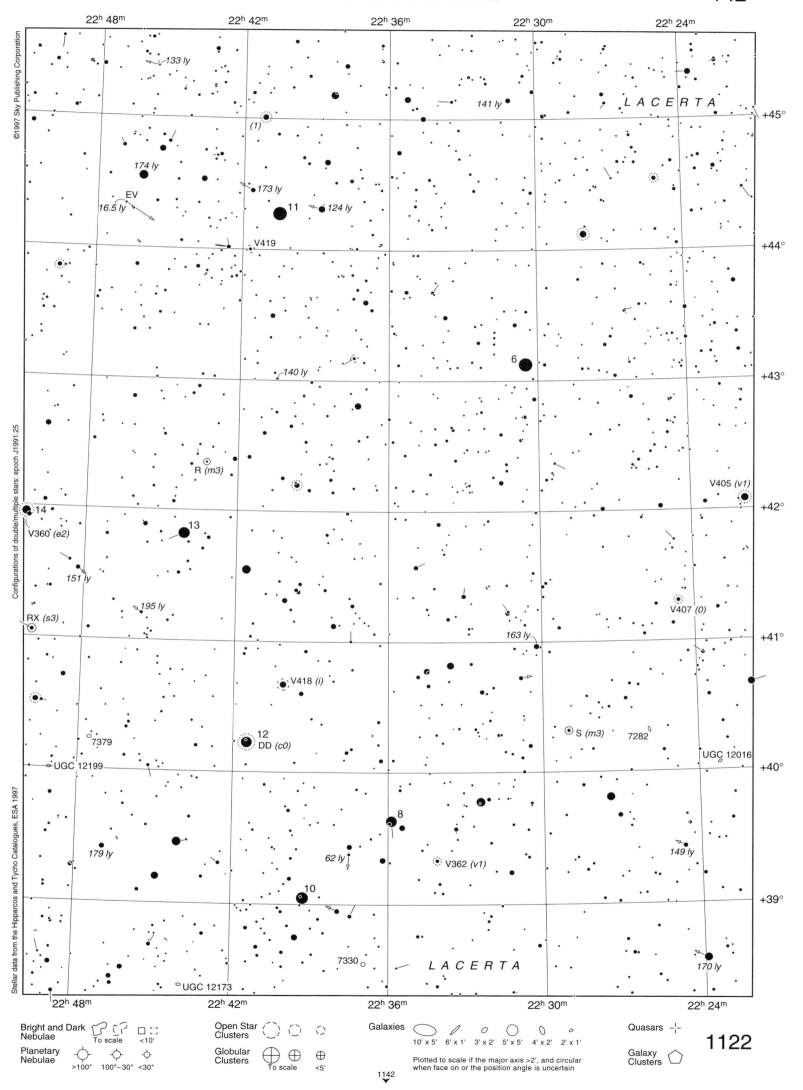

Configurations of double/multiple stars: epoch J1991.25

Stellar data from the Hipparcos and Tycho Catalogues, ESA 1997

1102

*L A C E R T A*

22ʰ 48ᵐ          22ʰ 42ᵐ          22ʰ 36ᵐ          22ʰ 30ᵐ          22ʰ 24ᵐ

+45°
+44°
+43°
+42°
+41°
+40°
+39°

*133 ly*
*141 ly*
*(1)*
*174 ly*
EV
*173 ly*
*16.5 ly*
11   *124 ly*
V419
*140 ly*
6
R *(m3)*
V405 *(v1)*
14
V360 *(e2)*
13
*151 ly*
V407 *(0)*
*195 ly*
RX *(s3)*
*163 ly*
V418 *(i)*
S *(m3)*   7282
7379
12
DD *(c0)*
UGC 12016
UGC 12199
8
*179 ly*
*62 ly*
V362 *(v1)*
*149 ly*
10
7330
*L A C E R T A*
*170 ly*
UGC 12173

22ʰ 48ᵐ          22ʰ 42ᵐ          22ʰ 36ᵐ          22ʰ 30ᵐ          22ʰ 24ᵐ

| Bright and Dark Nebulae | | | Open Star Clusters | | | Galaxies | | | | | | Quasars |
|---|---|---|---|---|---|---|---|---|---|---|---|---|
| To scale | | <10' | | | | 10' x 5' | 6' x 1' | 3' x 2' | 5' x 5' | 4' x 2' | 2' x 1' | |
| Planetary Nebulae | | | Globular Clusters | | | | | | | | | Galaxy Clusters |
| >100" | 100"–30" | <30" | To scale | | <5' | Plotted to scale if the major axis >2', and circular when face on or the position angle is uncertain | | | | | | |

1122

1142

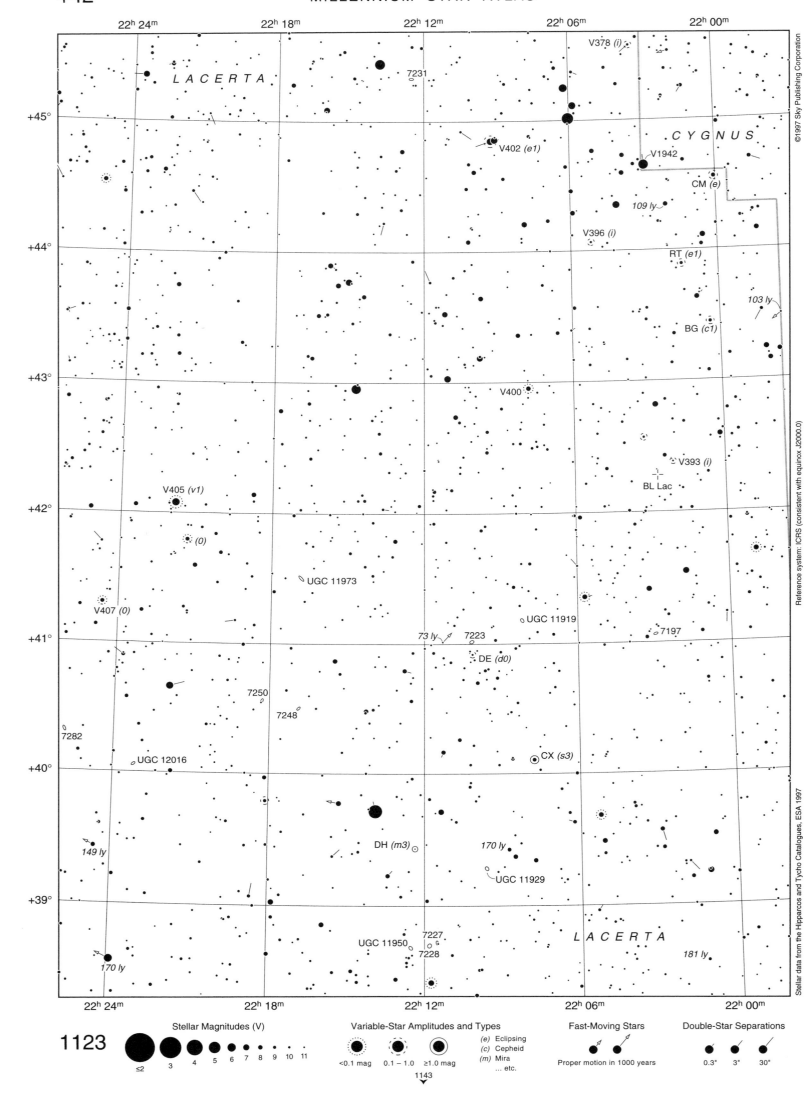

**Stellar Magnitudes (V)**

≤2  3  4  5  6  7  8  9  10  11

**Variable-Star Amplitudes and Types**

<0.1 mag    0.1 – 1.0    ≥1.0 mag

*(e)* Eclipsing
*(c)* Cepheid
*(m)* Mira
... etc.

**Fast-Moving Stars**

Proper motion in 1000 years

**Double-Star Separations**

0.3"  3"  30"

**1123**

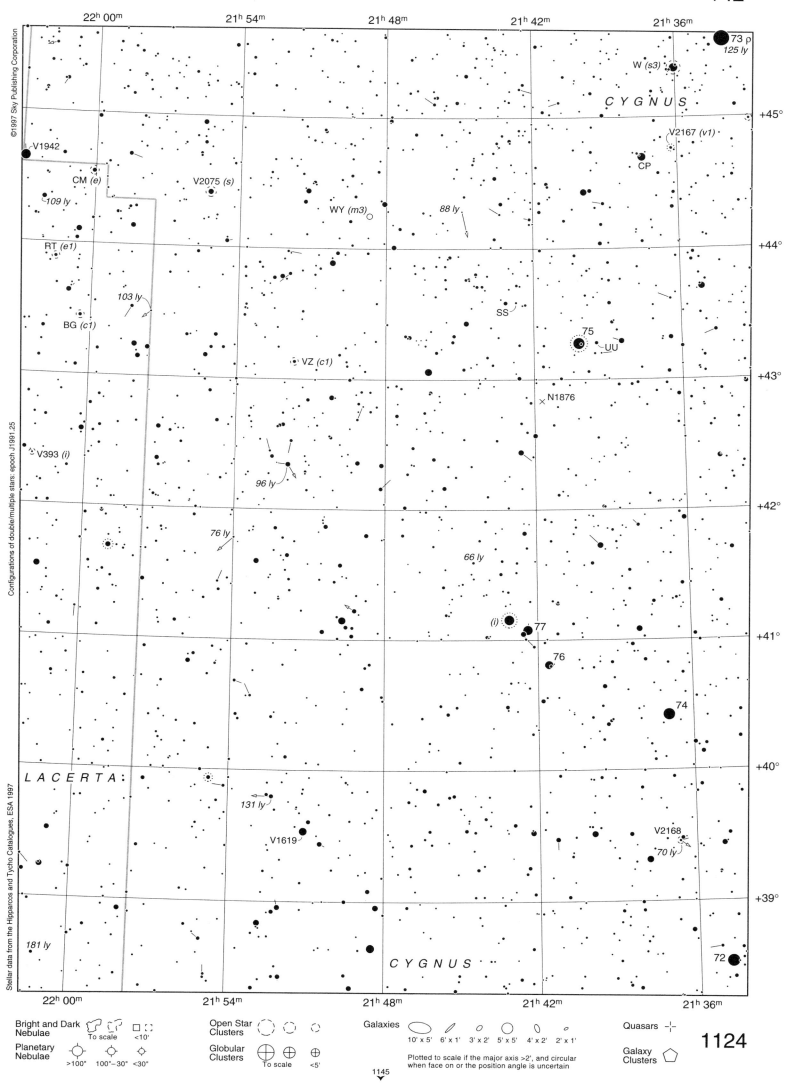

Configurations of double/multiple stars: epoch J1991.25

Stellar data from the Hipparcos and Tycho Catalogues, ESA 1997

22h 00m  21h 54m  21h 48m  21h 42m  21h 36m

73 ρ
*125 ly*

W *(s3)*

*C Y G N U S*

V2167 *(v1)*

+45°

V1942

CP

CM *(e)*

V2075 *(s)*

WY *(m3)*

*88 ly*

*109 ly*

RT *(e1)*

+44°

SS

*103 ly*

75

BG *(c1)*

UU

VZ *(c1)*

+43°

N1876

V393 *(i)*

*96 ly*

+42°

*76 ly*

*66 ly*

*(i)*  77

76

*131 ly*

74

*L A C E R T A*

+40°

V1619

V2168

*70 ly*

+39°

*181 ly*

*C Y G N U S*

72

22h 00m  21h 54m  21h 48m  21h 42m  21h 36m

Bright and Dark Nebulae  ☁ ☁  □ ⬚  To scale  <10'
Planetary Nebulae  ⬡ ⬦ ◇  >100"  100"–30"  <30"

Open Star Clusters  ◠ ◡ ◌
Globular Clusters  ⊕ ⊕ ⊕  To scale  <5'

Galaxies  ⬭ ╱ ○ ◯ ◯ ◦
10' x 5'  6' x 1'  3' x 2'  5' x 5'  4' x 2'  2' x 1'

Plotted to scale if the major axis >2', and circular when face on or the position angle is uncertain

Quasars  -¦-

Galaxy Clusters  ⬠

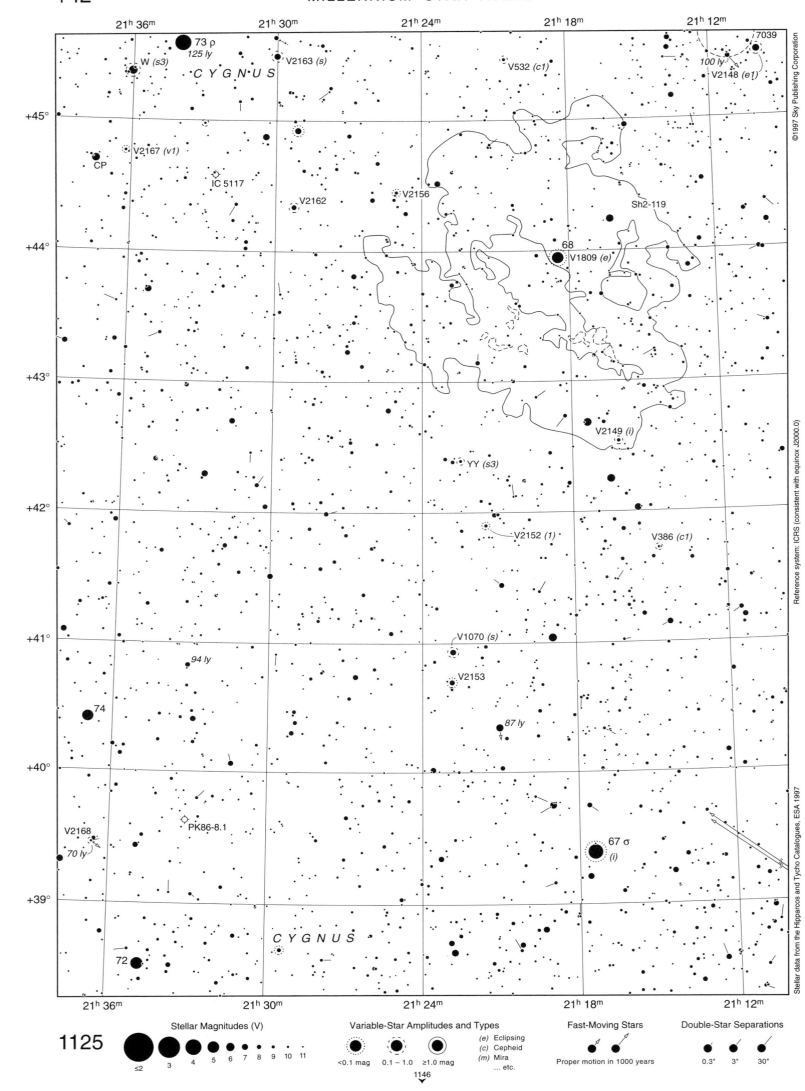

1125

Stellar Magnitudes (V)

≤2    3    4    5    6    7    8    9    10    11

Variable-Star Amplitudes and Types

<0.1 mag    0.1 – 1.0    ≥1.0 mag

(e) Eclipsing
(c) Cepheid
(m) Mira
... etc.

Fast-Moving Stars

Proper motion in 1000 years

Double-Star Separations

0.3"    3"    30"

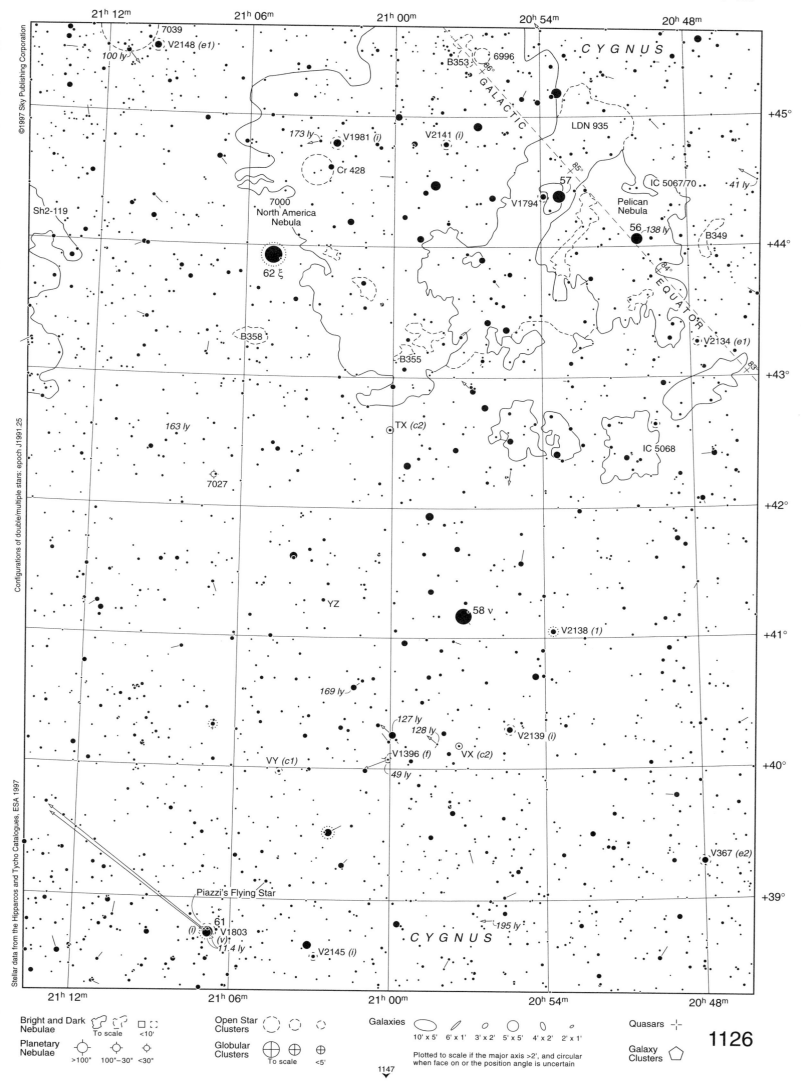

Configurations of double/multiple stars: epoch J1991.25

Stellar data from the Hipparcos and Tycho Catalogues, ESA 1997

7039
V2148 (e1)
100 ly

*C Y G N U S*

6996
B353
LDN 935

GALACTIC

173 ly
V1981 (i)
V2141 (i)

Cr 428

57
V1794
IC 5067/70
Pelican Nebula
41 ly

Sh2-119

7000
North America
Nebula

56  138 ly
B349

EQUATOR

62 ξ

85°

84°

B358

V2134 (e1)

B355

83°

TX (c2)

IC 5068

7027

58 ν

YZ

V2138 (1)

169 ly

127 ly
128 ly

V2139 (i)

V1396 (f)
VX (c2)

VY (c1)

49 ly

V367 (e2)

Piazzi's Flying Star

195 ly

61
(i)  V1803
(v)
11.4 ly

*C Y G N U S*

V2145 (i)

| Bright and Dark Nebulae | | Open Star Clusters | | Galaxies | | Quasars |
|---|---|---|---|---|---|---|
| To scale | <10' | To scale | <5' | 10' x 5'  6' x 1'  3' x 2'  5' x 5'  4' x 2'  2' x 1' | | Galaxy Clusters |

Planetary Nebulae
>100"  100"-30"  <30"

Globular Clusters
To scale  <5'

Plotted to scale if the major axis >2', and circular when face on or the position angle is uncertain

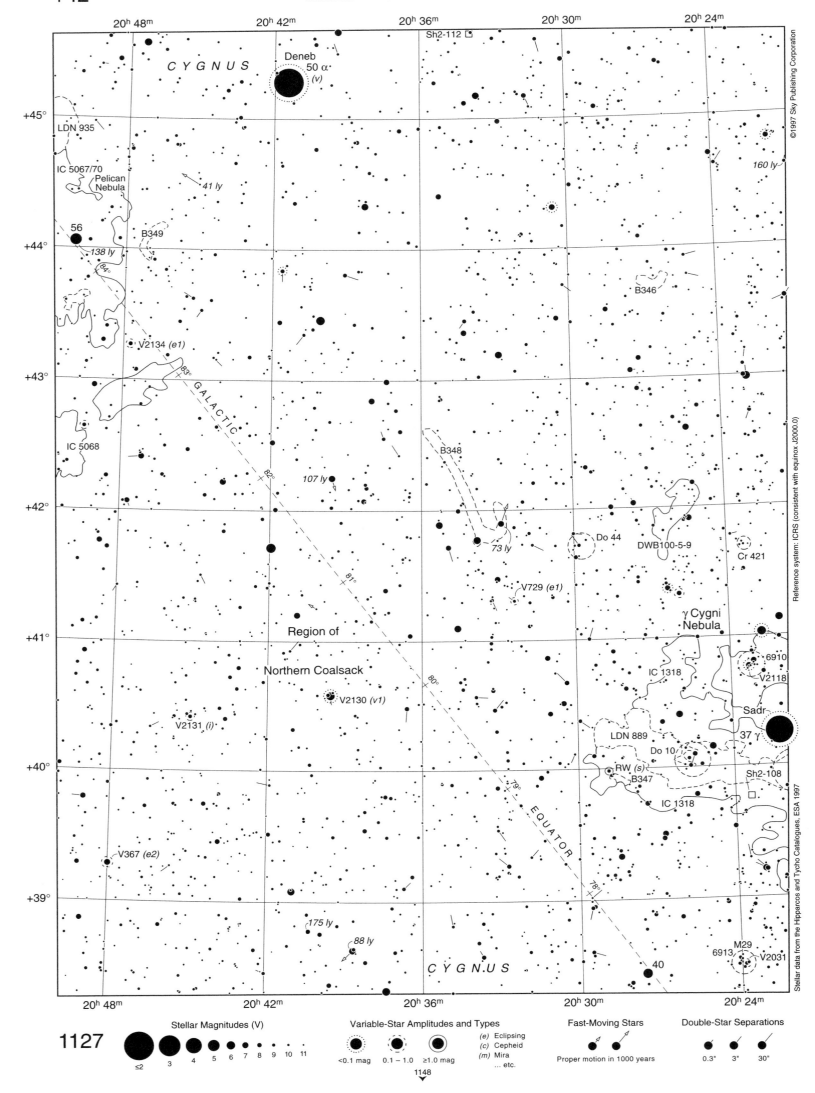

©1997 Sky Publishing Corporation

Reference system: ICRS (consistent with equinox J2000.0)

Stellar data from the Hipparcos and Tycho Catalogues, ESA 1997

Stellar Magnitudes (V)

≤2  3  4  5  6  7  8  9  10  11

Variable-Star Amplitudes and Types

<0.1 mag   0.1 – 1.0   ≥1.0 mag

(e) Eclipsing
(c) Cepheid
(m) Mira
... etc.

Fast-Moving Stars

Proper motion in 1000 years

Double-Star Separations

0.3"   3"   30"

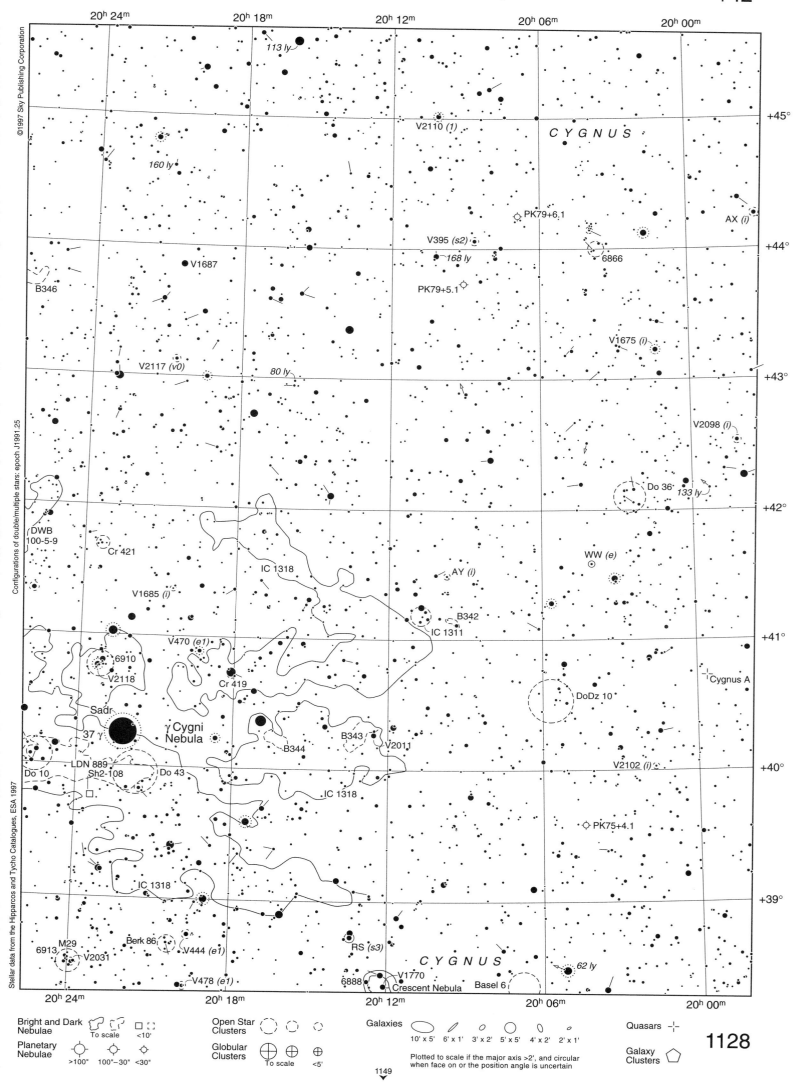

20h 24m    20h 18m    20h 12m    20h 06m    20h 00m

113 ly

V2110 (1)        C Y G N U S        +45°

160 ly

PK79+6.1

AX (i)

V395 (s2)

V1687        168 ly        6866        +44°

B346        PK79+5.1

V1675 (i)

V2117 (v0)        80 ly        +43°

V2098 (i)

Do 36    133 ly

+42°

DWB
100-5-9        WW (e)

Cr 421

IC 1318        AY (i)

V1685 (i)        B342
IC 1311        +41°

V470 (e1)

6910        Cr 419        B343    V2011        Cygnus A

V2118        DoDz 10

Sadr
37 γ    γ Cygni
Nebula        B344        V2102 (i)    +40°

Do 10    LDN 889    Do 43
Sh2-108        IC 1318

PK75+4.1

IC 1318

M29
6913        Berk 86
V2031        V444 (e1)        RS (s3)        62 ly

V478 (e1)        6888    V1770    Basel 6
Crescent Nebula        C Y G N U S

20h 24m    20h 18m    20h 12m    20h 06m    20h 00m        +39°

+44°
+43°
+42°
+41°
+40°

Bright and Dark
Nebulae        To scale    <10'        Open Star
Clusters        Galaxies        10' x 5'  6' x 1'  3' x 2'  5' x 5'  4' x 2'  2' x 1'        Quasars

Planetary
Nebulae        >100"  100"−30"  <30"        Globular
Clusters        To scale    <5'        Plotted to scale if the major axis >2', and circular
when face on or the position angle is uncertain        Galaxy
Clusters

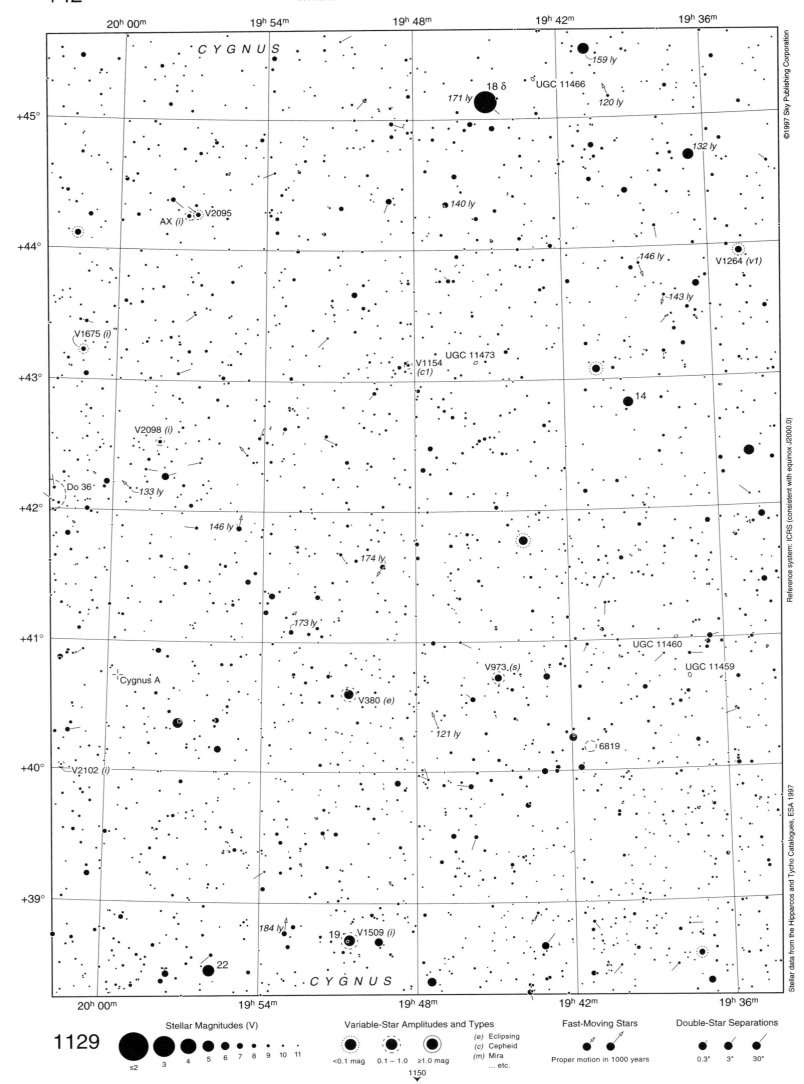

©1997 Sky Publishing Corporation

Reference system: ICRS (consistent with equinox J2000.0)

Stellar data from the Hipparcos and Tycho Catalogues, ESA 1997

Stellar Magnitudes (V)

≤2  3  4  5  6  7  8  9 10 11

Variable-Star Amplitudes and Types

<0.1 mag   0.1 – 1.0   ≥1.0 mag

(e) Eclipsing
(c) Cepheid
(m) Mira
... etc.

Fast-Moving Stars

Proper motion in 1000 years

Double-Star Separations

0.3"   3"   30"

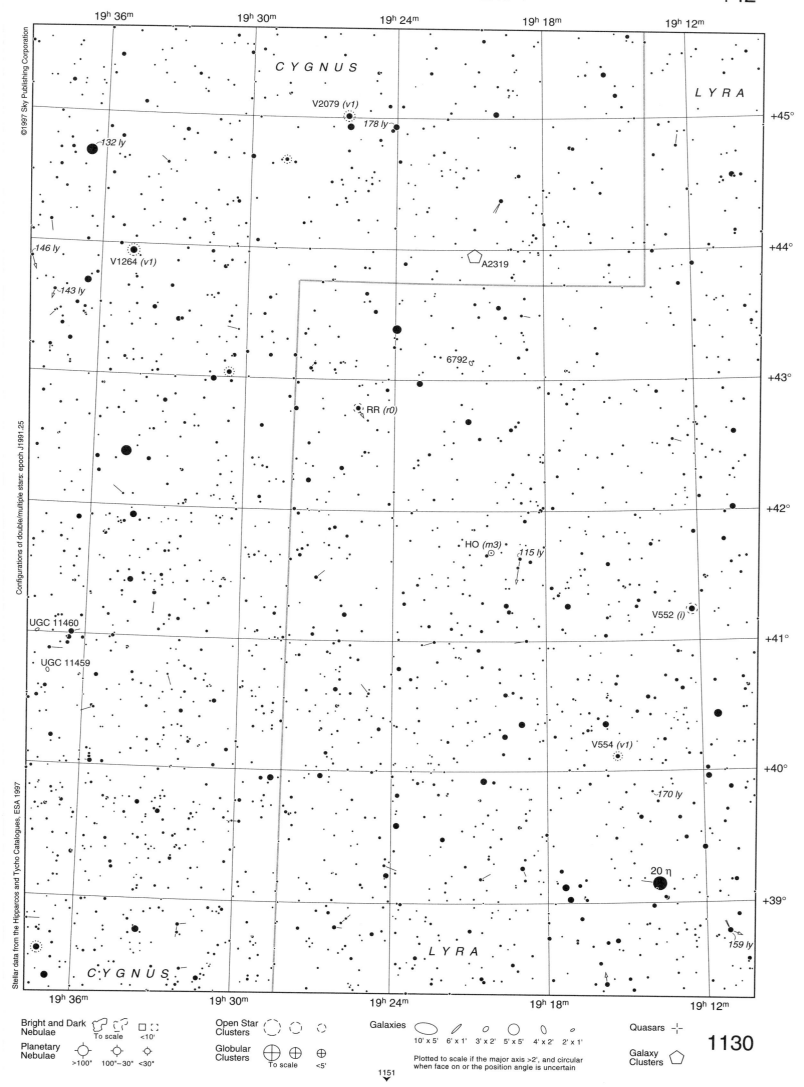

C Y G N U S

L Y R A

V2079 *(v1)*

178 ly

132 ly

146 ly

V1264 *(v1)*

143 ly

A2319

6792

RR *(r0)*

HO *(m3)*

115 ly

V552 *(i)*

UGC 11460

UGC 11459

V554 *(v1)*

170 ly

20 η

+45°

+44°

+43°

+42°

+41°

+40°

+39°

19h 36m

19h 30m

19h 24m

19h 18m

19h 12m

L Y R A

159 ly

C Y G N U S

| Bright and Dark Nebulae | Open Star Clusters | Galaxies | Quasars |
|---|---|---|---|
| To scale    <10' | | 10' x 5'   6' x 1'   3' x 2'   5' x 5'   4' x 2'   2' x 1' | |
| Planetary Nebulae | Globular Clusters | | Galaxy Clusters |
| >100"   100"-30"   <30" | To scale   <5' | Plotted to scale if the major axis >2', and circular when face on or the position angle is uncertain | |

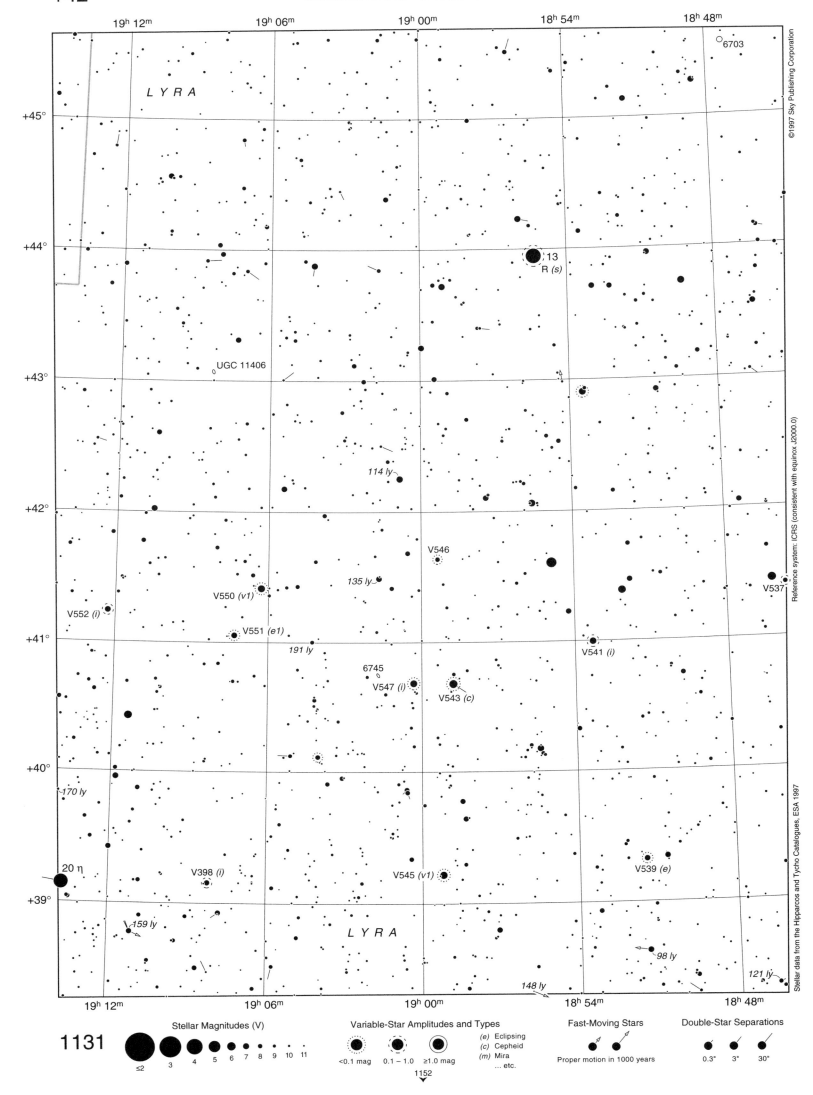

©1997 Sky Publishing Corporation

Reference system: ICRS (consistent with equinox J2000.0)

Stellar data from the Hipparcos and Tycho Catalogues, ESA 1997

LYRA

UGC 11406

13
R (s)

114 ly

V546

135 ly

V550 (v1)

V552 (i)

V551 (e1)

191 ly

V541 (i)

6745

V547 (i)

V543 (c)

V537

20 η

170 ly

V398 (i)

V545 (v1)

V539 (e)

159 ly

LYRA

98 ly

148 ly

121 ly

6703

**1131**

Stellar Magnitudes (V)

≤2   3   4   5   6   7   8   9  10  11

Variable-Star Amplitudes and Types

<0.1 mag    0.1 – 1.0    ≥1.0 mag

(e) Eclipsing
(c) Cepheid
(m) Mira
... etc.

Fast-Moving Stars

Proper motion in 1000 years

Double-Star Separations

0.3"    3"    30"

1152

# MILLENNIUM STAR ATLAS

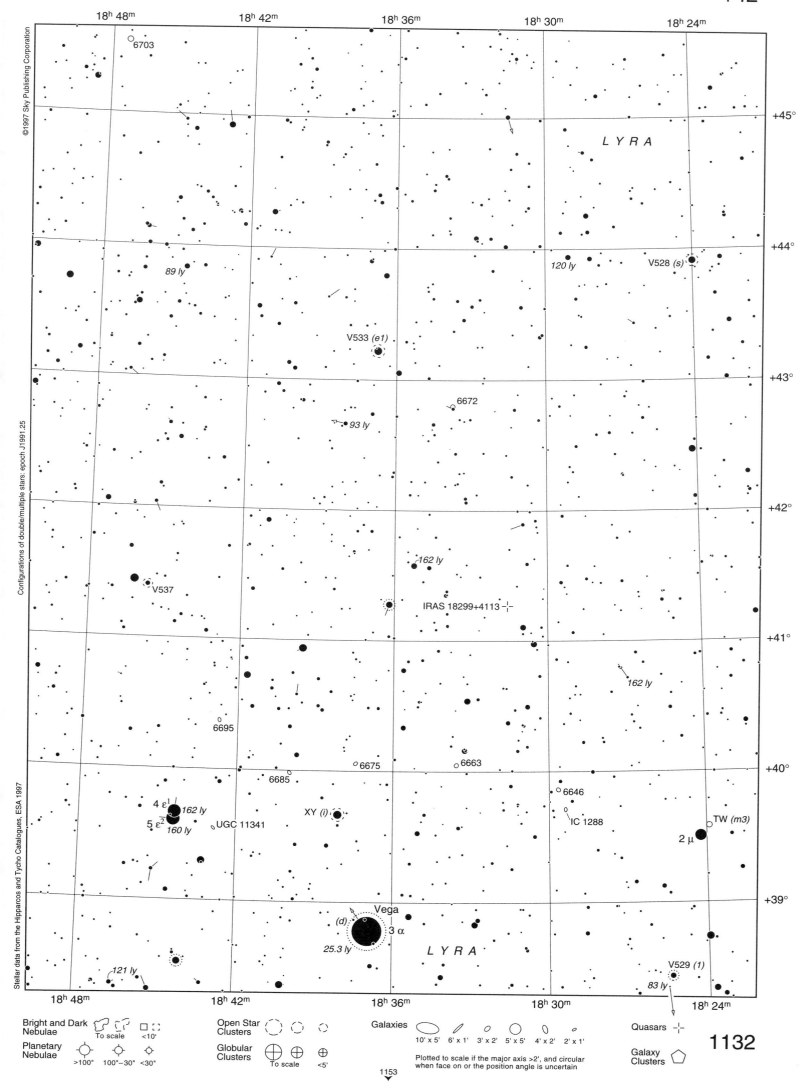

Configurations of double/multiple stars: epoch J1991.25

Stellar data from the Hipparcos and Tycho Catalogues, ESA 1997

18h 48m    18h 42m    18h 36m    18h 30m    18h 24m

+45°
+44°
+43°
+42°
+41°
+40°
+39°

*L Y R A*

6703

89 ly

V533 (e1)

120 ly        V528 (s)

6672

93 ly

162 ly

V537          IRAS 18299+4113

162 ly

6695

6675      6663

6685

6646

4 ε¹  162 ly
5 ε²  160 ly   UGC 11341      XY (i)      IC 1288      TW (m3)
                                                        2 μ

Vega
(d)        3 α
25.3 ly    *L Y R A*

121 ly                                    V529 (1)
                                           83 ly

18h 48m    18h 42m    18h 36m    18h 30m    18h 24m

| Bright and Dark Nebulae | Open Star Clusters | Galaxies | Quasars |
|---|---|---|---|

To scale   <10'

To scale

Planetary Nebulae
>100"  100"-30"  <30"

Globular Clusters
To scale   <5'

10' x 5'  6' x 1'  3' x 2'  5' x 5'  4' x 2'  2' x 1'

Plotted to scale if the major axis >2', and circular when face on or the position angle is uncertain

Galaxy Clusters

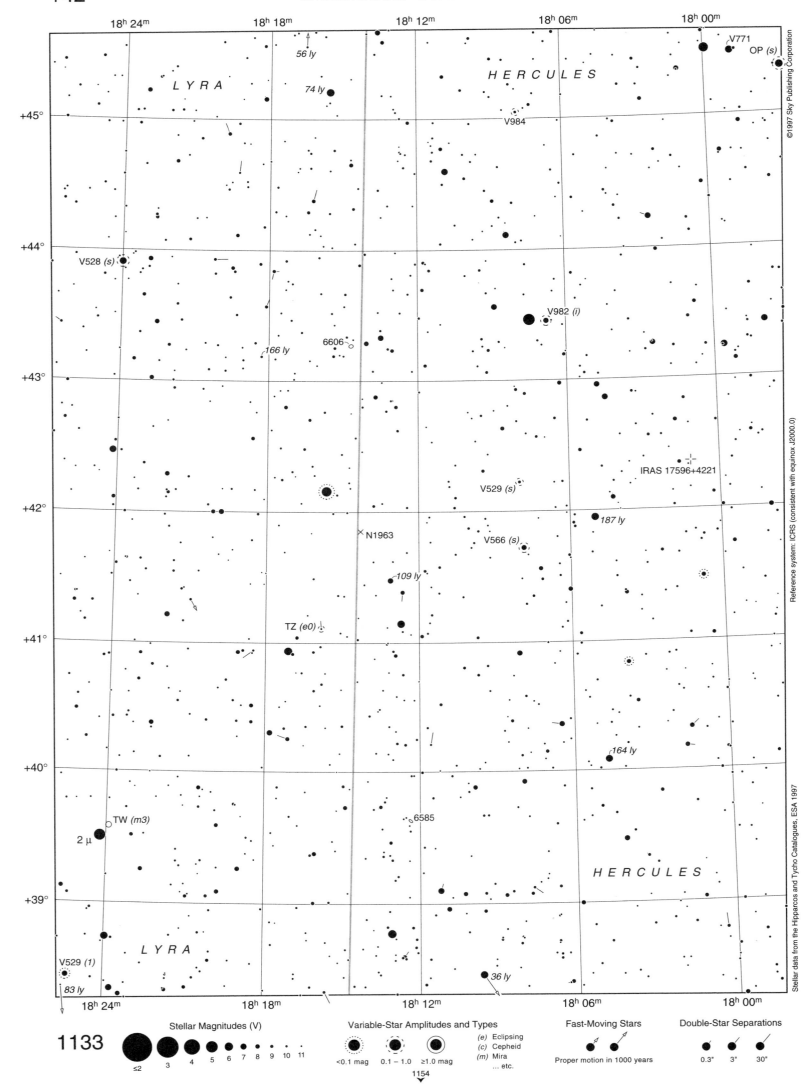

1133

Stellar Magnitudes (V)

≤2   3   4   5   6   7   8   9   10   11

Variable-Star Amplitudes and Types

<0.1 mag   0.1 – 1.0   ≥1.0 mag

(e) Eclipsing
(c) Cepheid
(m) Mira
... etc.

Fast-Moving Stars

Proper motion in 1000 years

Double-Star Separations

0.3"   3"   30"

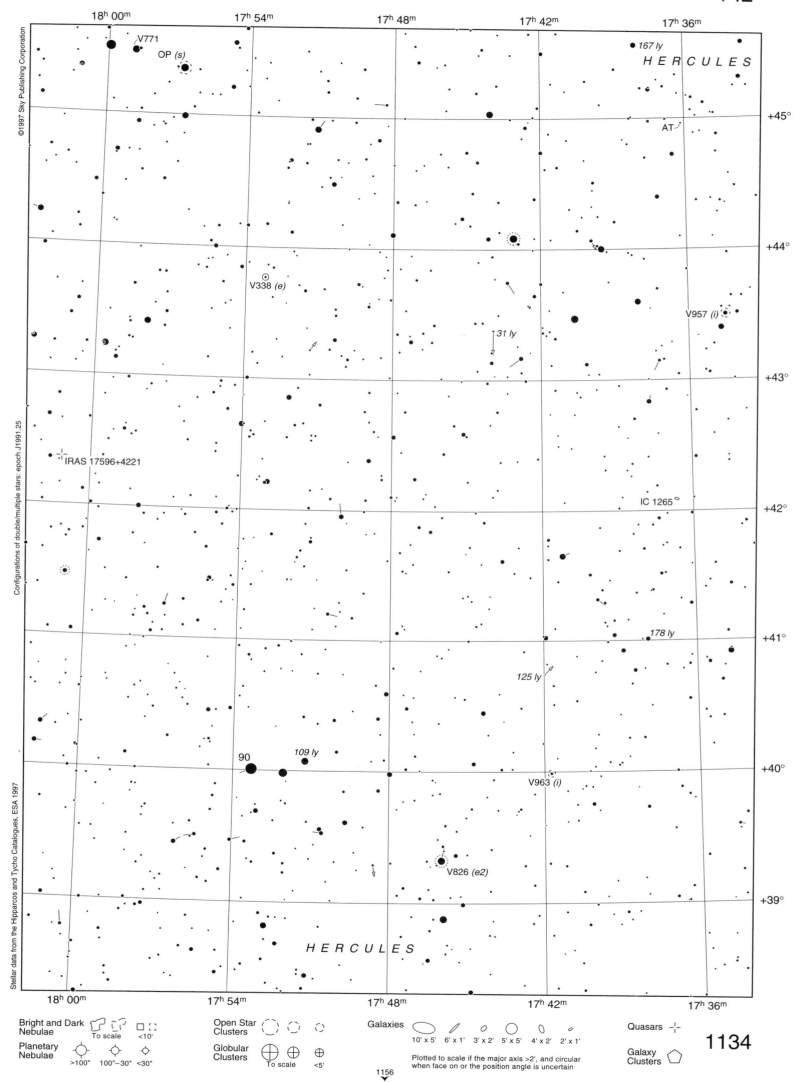

© 1997 Sky Publishing Corporation

Configurations of double/multiple stars: epoch J1991.25

Stellar data from the Hipparcos and Tycho Catalogues, ESA 1997

HERCULES

V771
OP *(s)*
167 ly
AT
V957 *(i)*
V338 *(e)*
31 ly
IRAS 17596+4221
IC 1265
178 ly
125 ly
90
109 ly
V963 *(i)*
V826 *(e2)*

HERCULES

18h 00m        17h 54m        17h 48m        17h 42m        17h 36m

+45°
+44°
+43°
+42°
+41°
+40°
+39°

**Bright and Dark Nebulae**    To scale    <10'

**Planetary Nebulae**    >100"    100"–30"    <30"

**Open Star Clusters**

**Globular Clusters**    To scale    <5'

**Galaxies**    10' x 5'    6' x 1'    3' x 2'    5' x 5'    4' x 2'    2' x 1'

Plotted to scale if the major axis >2', and circular when face on or the position angle is uncertain

**Quasars**

**Galaxy Clusters**

1134

1156

+42°

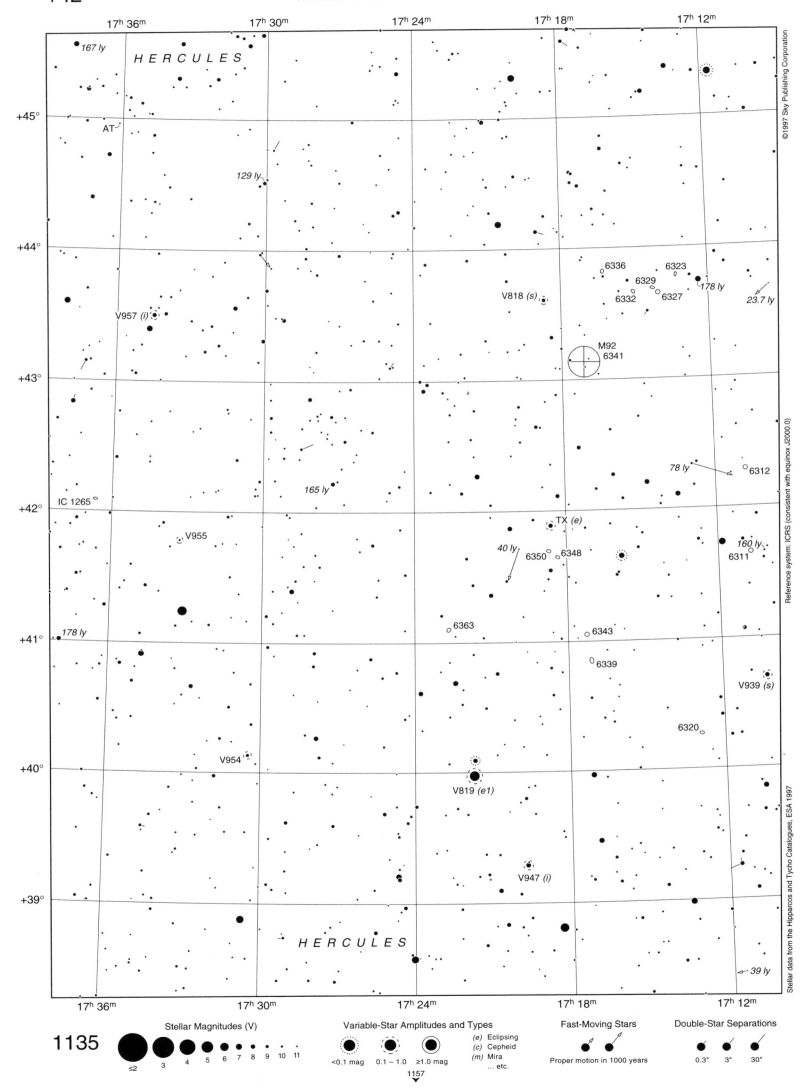

Reference system: ICRS (consistent with equinox J2000.0)

Stellar data from the Hipparcos and Tycho Catalogues, ESA 1997

1135

Stellar Magnitudes (V)

≤2   3   4   5   6   7   8   9   10   11

Variable-Star Amplitudes and Types

<0.1 mag    0.1 – 1.0    ≥1.0 mag

(e)  Eclipsing
(c)  Cepheid
(m)  Mira
...  etc.

Fast-Moving Stars

Proper motion in 1000 years

Double-Star Separations

0.3"    3"    30"

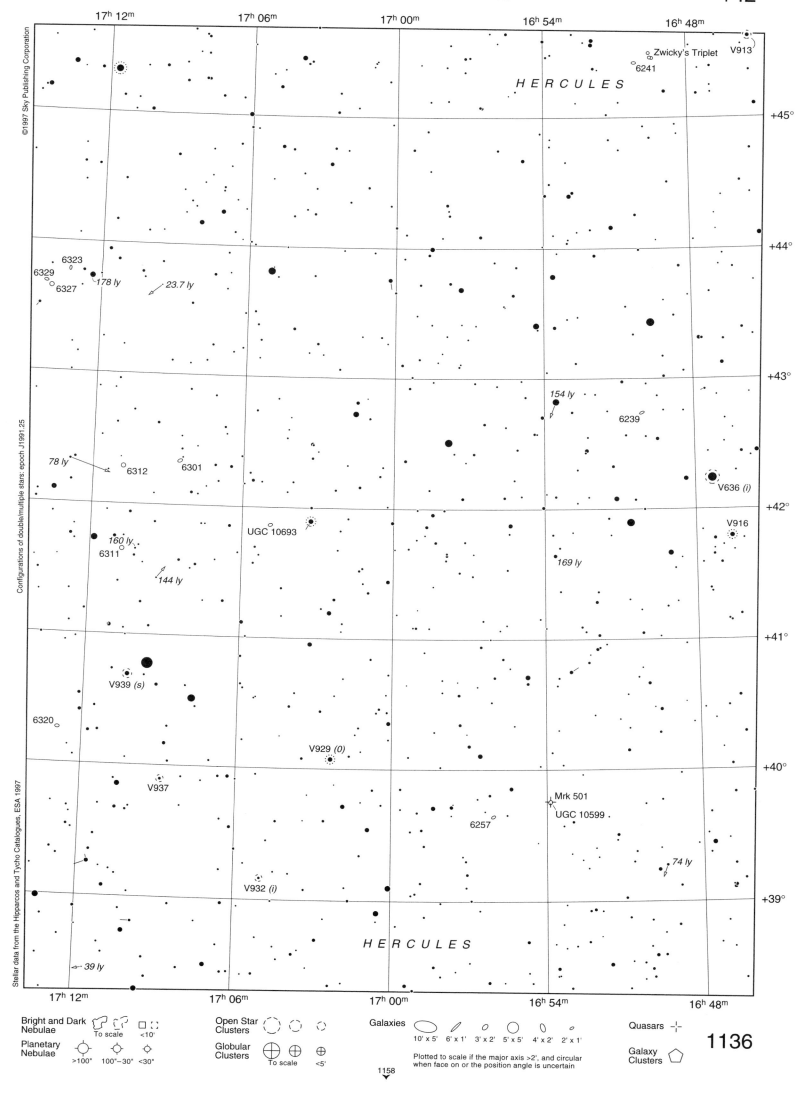

Configurations of double/multiple stars: epoch J1991.25

Stellar data from the Hipparcos and Tycho Catalogues, ESA 1997

HERCULES

Zwicky's Triplet
V913
6241

+45°

+44°

6323
6329
6327
178 ly
23.7 ly

+43°

154 ly
6239

78 ly
6312
6301
V636 (i)

+42°

UGC 10693
V916

160 ly
6311
169 ly

144 ly

+41°

V939 (s)

6320

V929 (0)

+40°

V937

Mrk 501
UGC 10599
6257

74 ly

V932 (i)

+39°

HERCULES

39 ly

17ʰ 12ᵐ    17ʰ 06ᵐ    17ʰ 00ᵐ    16ʰ 54ᵐ    16ʰ 48ᵐ

| Bright and Dark Nebulae | Open Star Clusters | Galaxies | Quasars |
| To scale    <10' | | 10' x 5'   6' x 1'   3' x 2'   5' x 5'   4' x 2'   2' x 1' | |
| Planetary Nebulae | Globular Clusters | | Galaxy Clusters |
| >100"   100"–30"   <30" | To scale   <5' | Plotted to scale if the major axis >2', and circular when face on or the position angle is uncertain | |

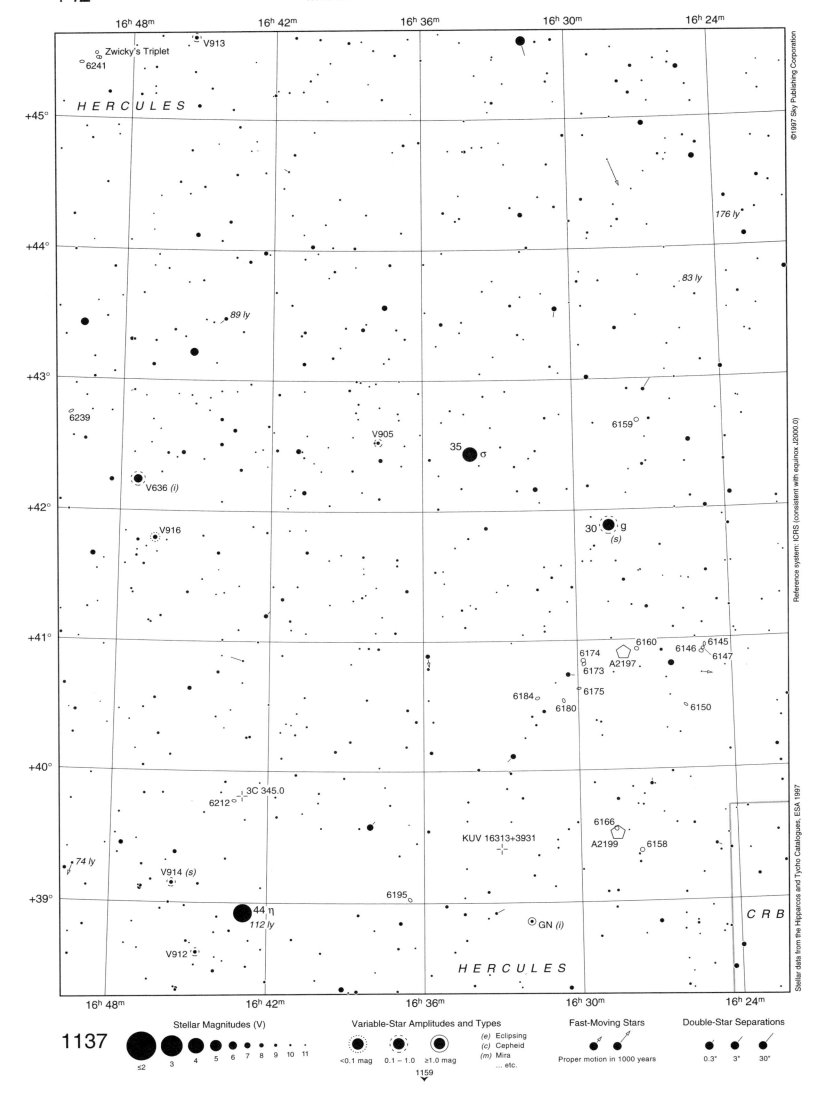

1137

Stellar Magnitudes (V)

≤2  3  4  5  6  7  8  9  10  11

Variable-Star Amplitudes and Types

<0.1 mag   0.1 – 1.0   ≥1.0 mag

(e) Eclipsing
(c) Cepheid
(m) Mira
... etc.

Fast-Moving Stars

Proper motion in 1000 years

Double-Star Separations

0.3"   3"   30"

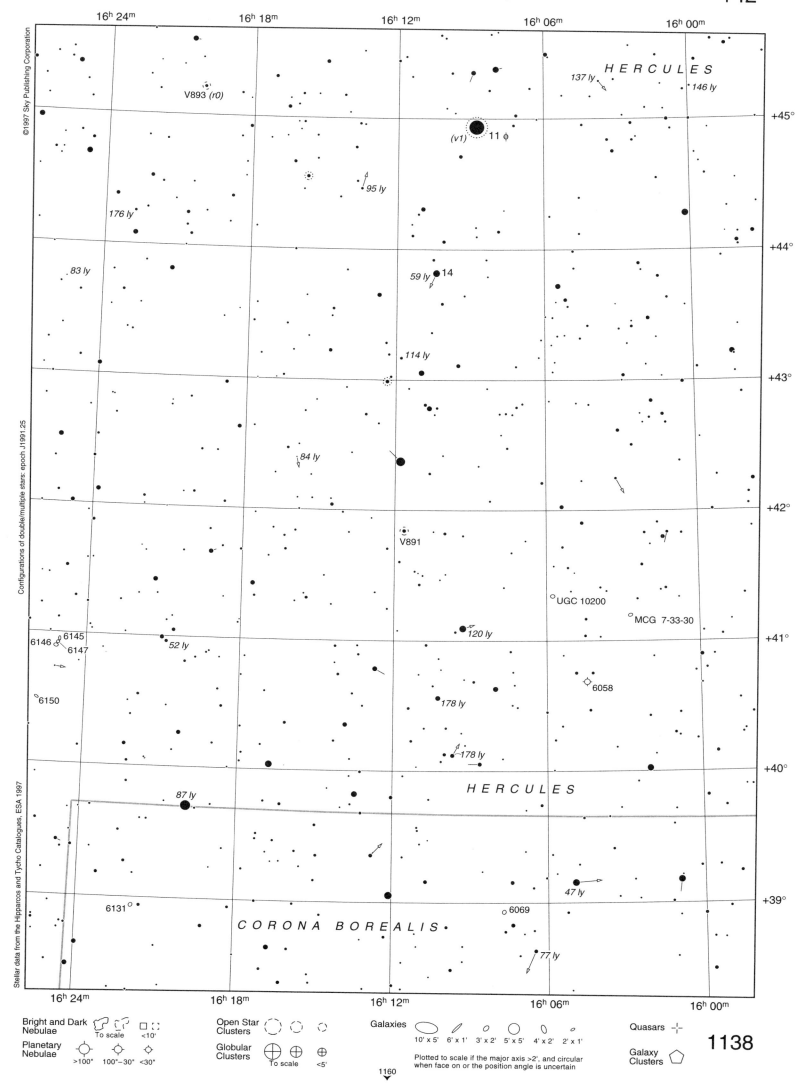

16h 24m        16h 18m        16h 12m        16h 06m        16h 00m

H E R C U L E S

V893 (r0)

137 ly        146 ly

(v1)   11 φ

95 ly                                                          +45°

176 ly

83 ly                                                          +44°

59 ly  14

114 ly                                                        +43°

84 ly                                                          +42°

V891

UGC 10200

MCG 7-33-30

6146   6145                                                   +41°
6147              52 ly
                                    120 ly
6150                                                6058

                                    178 ly

                                    178 ly

                                                              +40°

H E R C U L E S

87 ly

                                                              +39°
6131                       6069
                                              47 ly
C O R O N A   B O R E A L I S

                                    77 ly

16h 24m        16h 18m        16h 12m        16h 06m        16h 00m

Bright and Dark    Open Star       Galaxies                         Quasars
Nebulae            Clusters                                                    1138
      To scale          <10'                10' x 5'  6' x 1'  3' x 2'  5' x 5'  4' x 2'  2' x 1'
Planetary
Nebulae            Globular                                         Galaxy
                   Clusters                                         Clusters
    >100"  100"–30"  <30"      To scale    <5'   Plotted to scale if the major axis >2', and circular
                                                  when face on or the position angle is uncertain

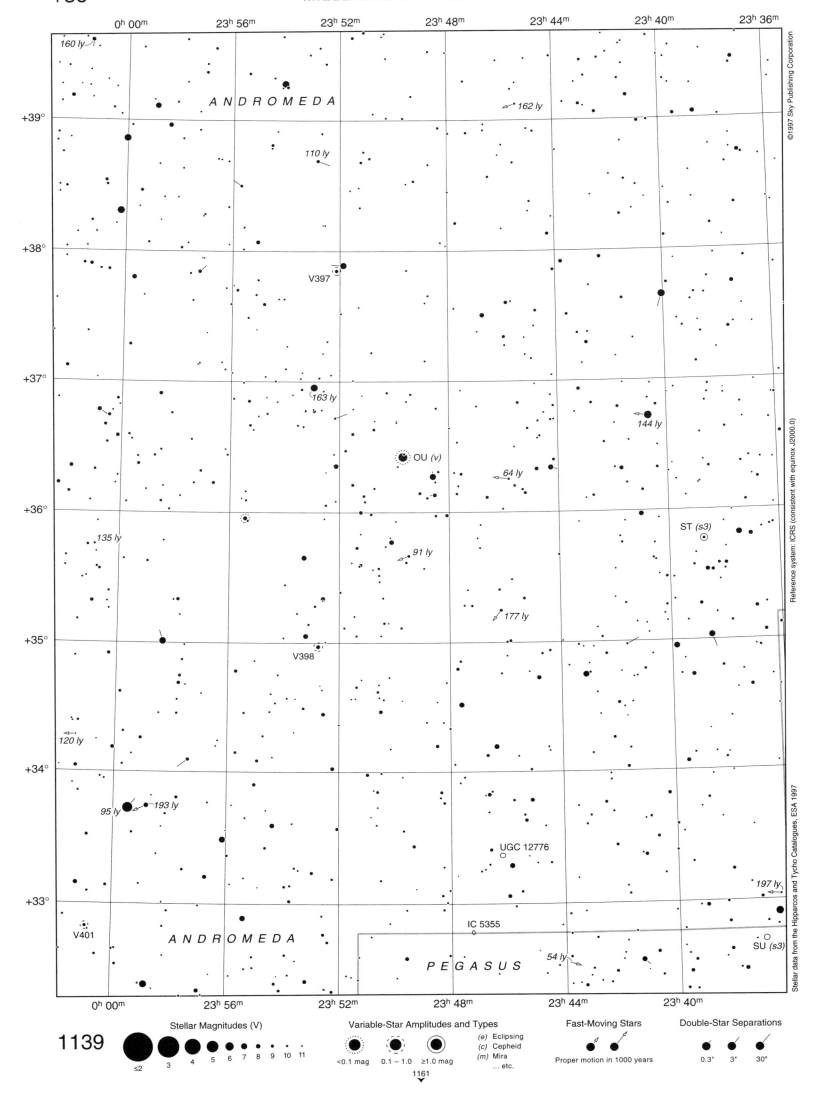

1139

Stellar Magnitudes (V)

≤2  3  4  5  6  7  8  9  10  11

Variable-Star Amplitudes and Types

<0.1 mag   0.1 – 1.0   ≥1.0 mag

(e) Eclipsing
(c) Cepheid
(m) Mira
... etc.

Fast-Moving Stars

Proper motion in 1000 years

Double-Star Separations

0.3"  3"  30"

# MILLENNIUM STAR ATLAS

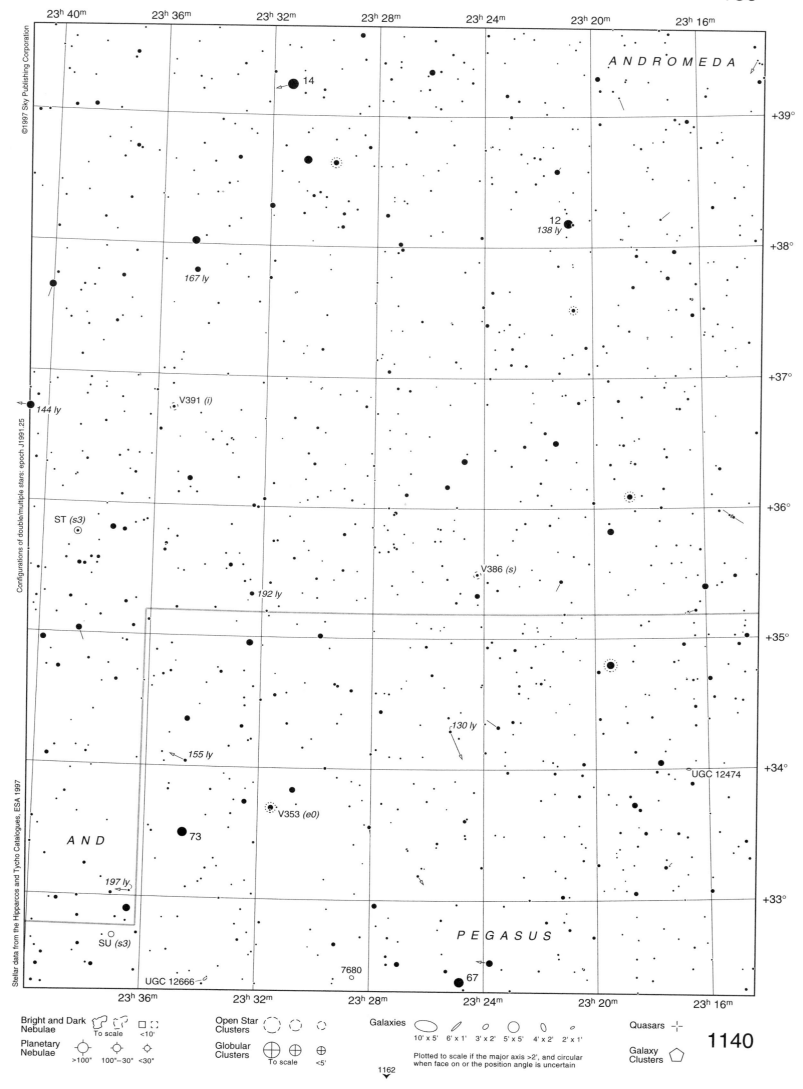

©1997 Sky Publishing Corporation

Configurations of double/multiple stars: epoch J1991.25

Stellar data from the Hipparcos and Tycho Catalogues, ESA 1997

A N D R O M E D A

14

12
*138 ly*

167 ly

144 ly

V391 *(i)*

ST *(s3)*

192 ly

V386 *(s)*

130 ly

155 ly

UGC 12474

V353 *(e0)*

A N D

73

197 ly

SU *(s3)*

UGC 12666

P E G A S U S

7680

67

| Bright and Dark Nebulae | Open Star Clusters | Galaxies | Quasars |
|---|---|---|---|
| To scale   <10' | | 10' x 5'   6' x 1'   3' x 2'   5' x 5'   4' x 2'   2' x 1' | |
| Planetary Nebulae | Globular Clusters | | Galaxy Clusters |
| >100"   100"–30"   <30" | To scale   <5' | Plotted to scale if the major axis >2', and circular when face on or the position angle is uncertain | |

**1140**

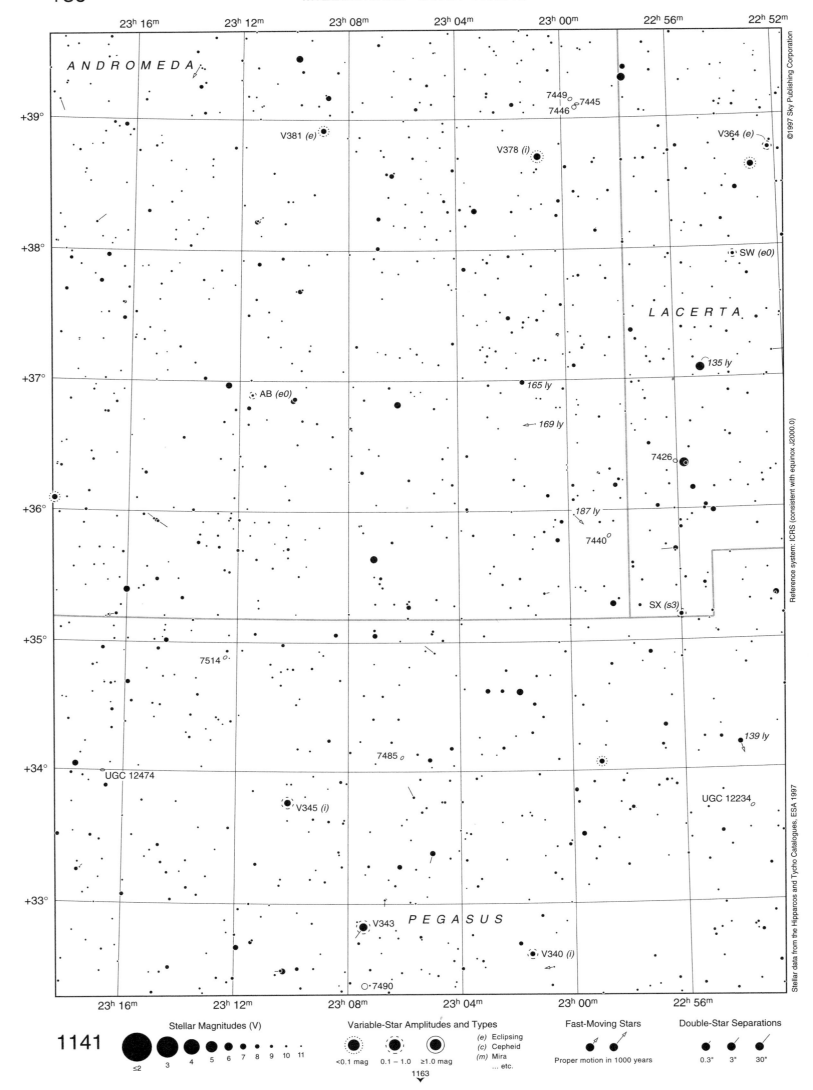

©1997 Sky Publishing Corporation

Reference system: ICRS (consistent with equinox J2000.0)

Stellar data from the Hipparcos and Tycho Catalogues, ESA 1997

ANDROMEDA

7449 7445
7446

V381 (e)

V378 (i)

V364 (e)

SW (e0)

LACERTA

135 ly

AB (e0)

165 ly

169 ly

7426

187 ly

7440

SX (s3)

7514

7485

139 ly

UGC 12474

UGC 12234

V345 (i)

PEGASUS

V343

V340 (i)

7490

1141

Stellar Magnitudes (V)

≤2   3   4   5   6   7  8  9 10 11

Variable-Star Amplitudes and Types

<0.1 mag   0.1 – 1.0   ≥1.0 mag

(e) Eclipsing
(c) Cepheid
(m) Mira
... etc.

Fast-Moving Stars

Proper motion in 1000 years

Double-Star Separations

0.3"   3"   30"

# MILLENNIUM STAR ATLAS

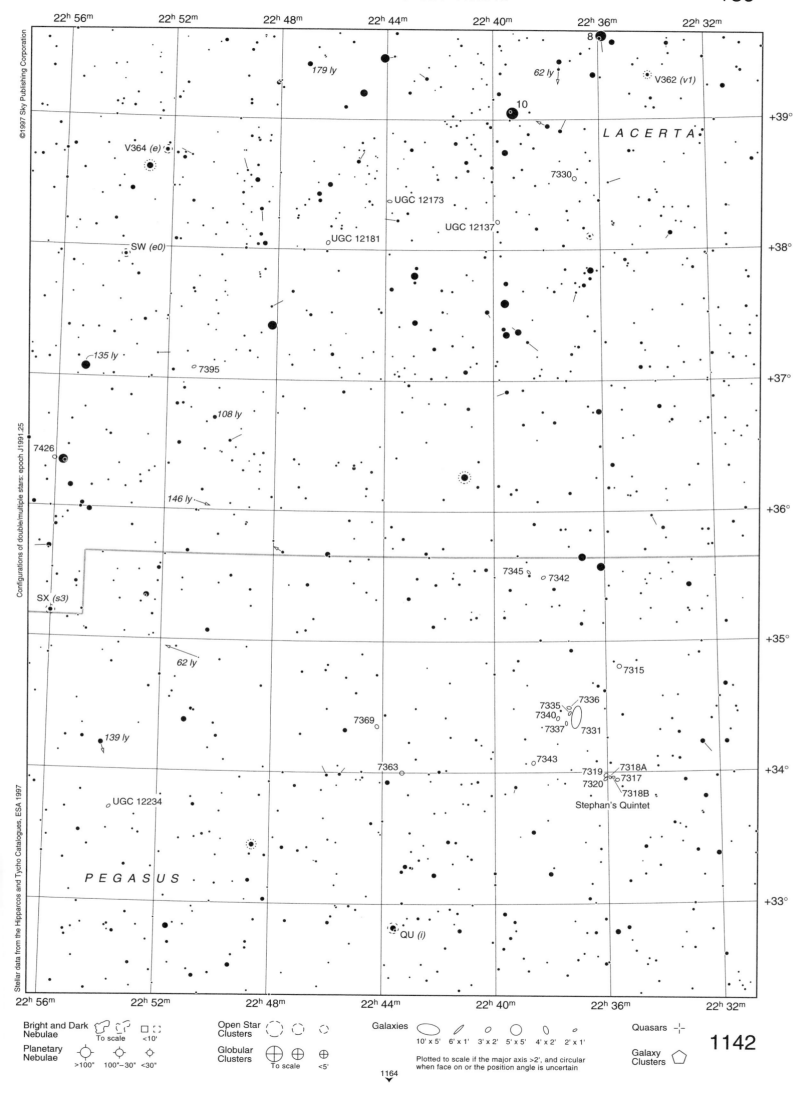

22h 56m    22h 52m    22h 48m    22h 44m    22h 40m    22h 36m    22h 32m

179 ly

62 ly

V362 (v1)

10

LACERTA

7330

UGC 12173

UGC 12137

V364 (e)

SW (e0)

135 ly

7395

108 ly

7426

146 ly

SX (s3)

62 ly

7345    7342

7315

139 ly

7335    7336
7340
7337    7331

7369

7343

7363

7319    7318A
7320    7317
7318B

UGC 12234

Stephan's Quintet

PEGASUS

QU (i)

+39°

+38°

+37°

+36°

+35°

+34°

+33°

22h 56m    22h 52m    22h 48m    22h 44m    22h 40m    22h 36m    22h 32m

Configurations of double/multiple stars: epoch J1991.25

Stellar data from the Hipparcos and Tycho Catalogues, ESA 1997

| Bright and Dark Nebulae | Open Star Clusters | Galaxies | Quasars |
| To scale    <10' | To scale    <10' | 10' x 5'   6' x 1'   3' x 2'   5' x 5'   4' x 2'   2' x 1' | |

Planetary Nebulae
>100"   100"-30"   <30"

Globular Clusters
To scale   <5'

Plotted to scale if the major axis >2', and circular when face on or the position angle is uncertain

Galaxy Clusters

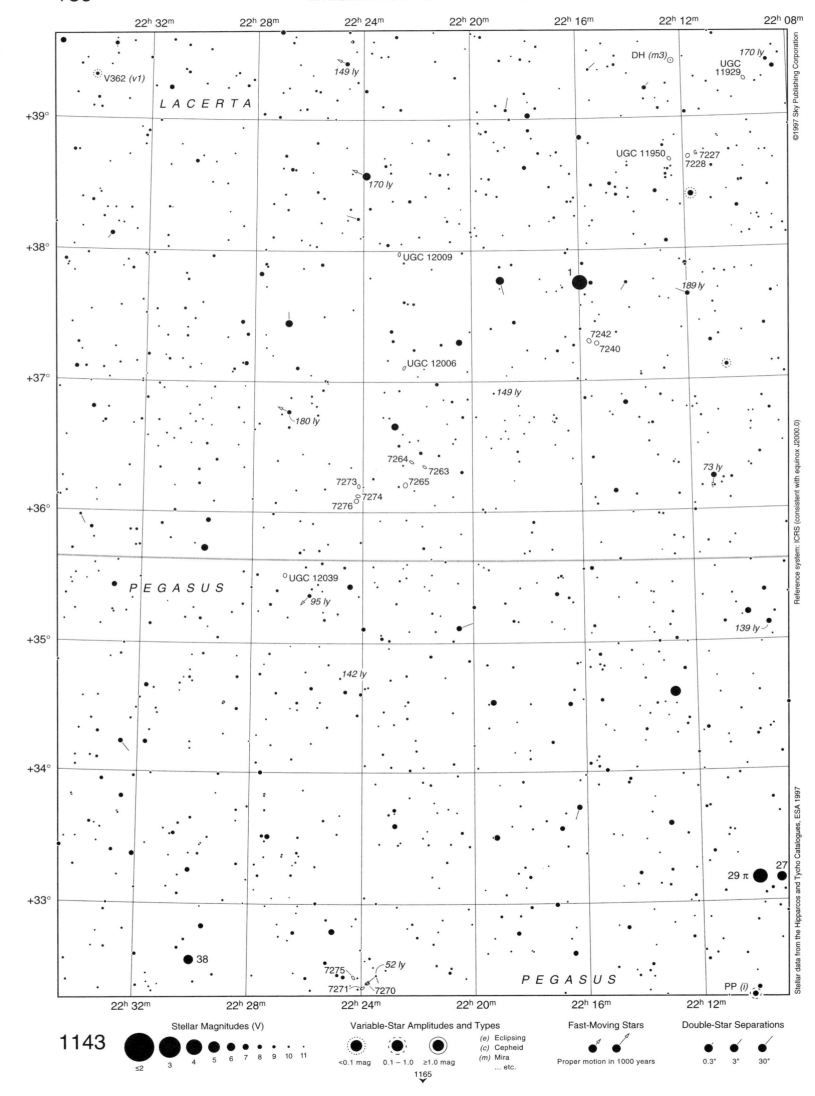

©1997 Sky Publishing Corporation

Reference system: ICRS (consistent with equinox J2000.0)

Stellar data from the Hipparcos and Tycho Catalogues, ESA 1997

1143

Stellar Magnitudes (V)

≤2   3   4   5   6   7   8   9   10   11

Variable-Star Amplitudes and Types

<0.1 mag   0.1 – 1.0   ≥1.0 mag

(e) Eclipsing
(c) Cepheid
(m) Mira
... etc.

Fast-Moving Stars

Proper motion in 1000 years

Double-Star Separations

0.3"   3"   30"

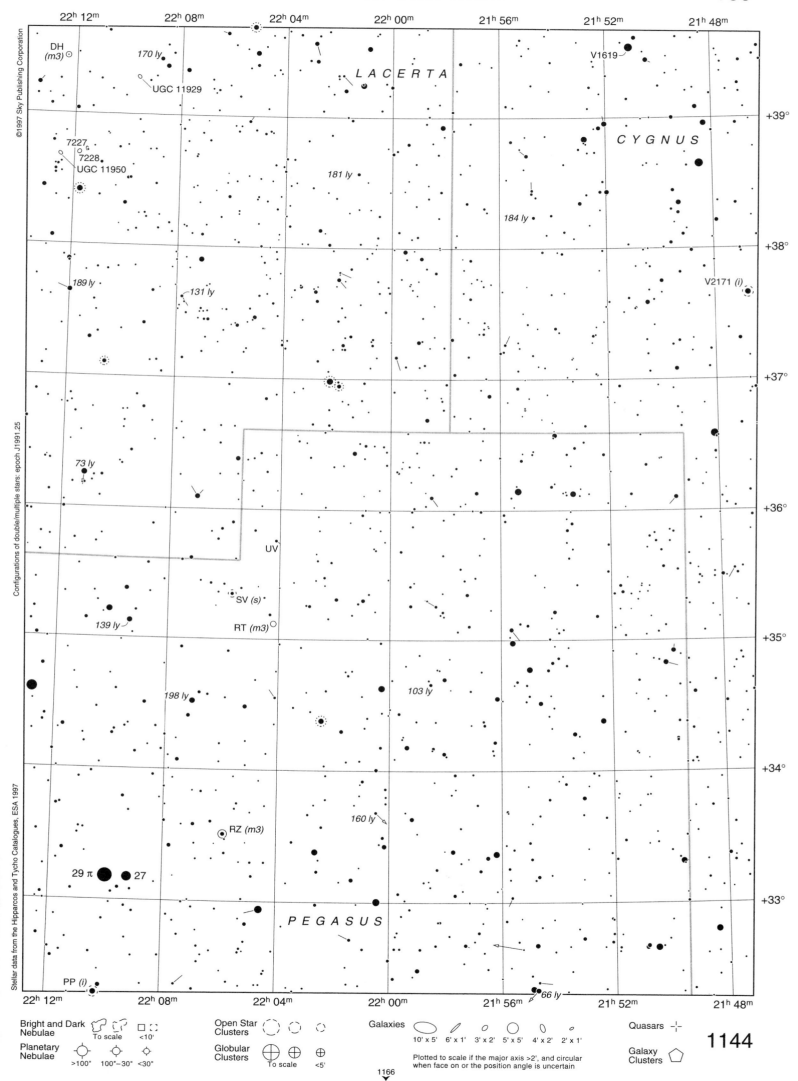

22h 12m    22h 08m    22h 04m    22h 00m    21h 56m    21h 52m    21h 48m

DH
(m3)

170 ly

UGC 11929

*LACERTA*

V1619

*CYGNUS*

+39°

7227
7228
UGC 11950

181 ly

184 ly

+38°

189 ly

131 ly

V2171 (i)

+37°

73 ly

+36°

UV

SV (s)

RT (m3)

139 ly

198 ly

103 ly

+35°

+34°

160 ly

RZ (m3)

29 π    27

+33°

*PEGASUS*

PP (i)

66 ly

22h 12m    22h 08m    22h 04m    22h 00m    21h 56m    21h 52m    21h 48m

©1997 Sky Publishing Corporation

Configurations of double/multiple stars: epoch J1991.25

Stellar data from the Hipparcos and Tycho Catalogues, ESA 1997

Bright and Dark Nebulae
To scale    <10'
Planetary Nebulae
>100"    100"−30"    <30"

Open Star Clusters
Globular Clusters
To scale    <5'

Galaxies
10' x 5'    6' x 1'    3' x 2'    5' x 5'    4' x 2'    2' x 1'

Plotted to scale if the major axis >2', and circular when face on or the position angle is uncertain

Quasars

Galaxy Clusters

**1144**

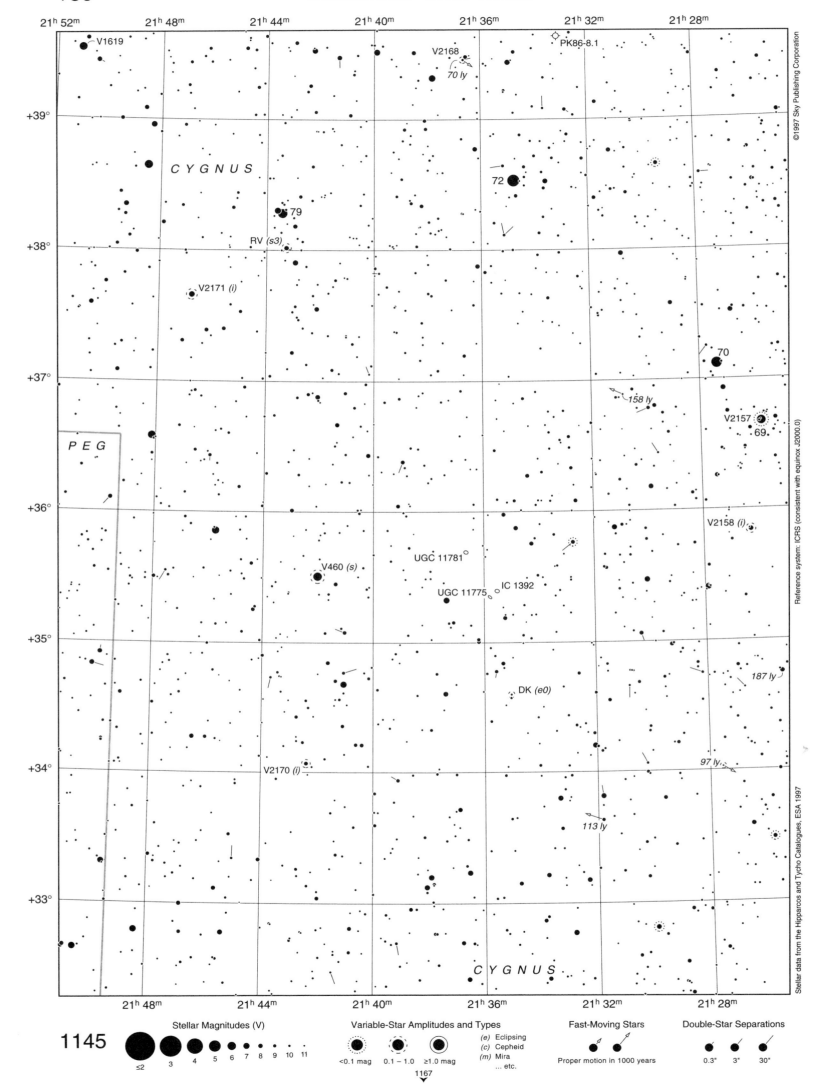

1145

Stellar Magnitudes (V)

≤2   3   4   5   6   7   8   9   10   11

Variable-Star Amplitudes and Types

<0.1 mag    0.1 – 1.0    ≥1.0 mag

(e) Eclipsing
(c) Cepheid
(m) Mira
... etc.

Fast-Moving Stars

Proper motion in 1000 years

Double-Star Separations

0.3"   3"   30"

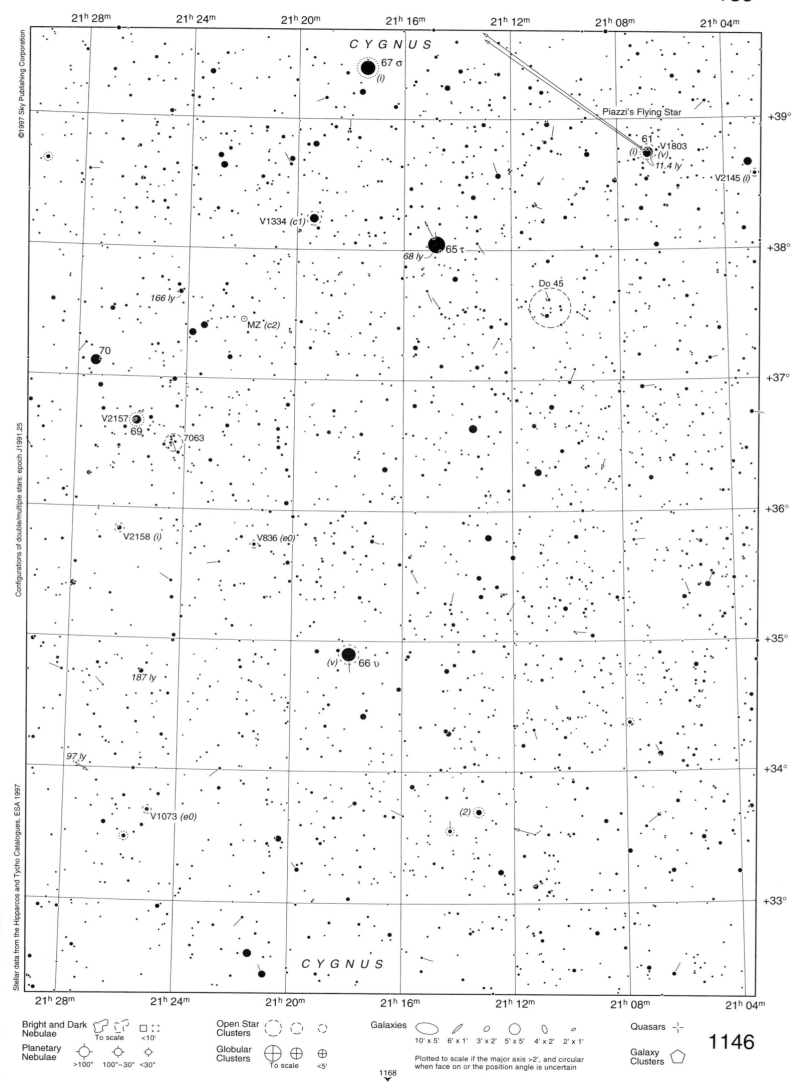

Configurations of double/multiple stars: epoch J1991.25

Stellar data from the Hipparcos and Tycho Catalogues, ESA 1997

CYGNUS

67 σ
(i)

Piazzi's Flying Star

61
V1803
(i)   (v)
11.4 ly
V2145 (i)

V1334 (c1)

65 τ
68 ly

Do 45

166 ly

MZ (c2)

70

V2157
69

7063

V2158 (i)

V836 (e0)

66 υ
(v)

187 ly

97 ly

V1073 (e0)

(2)

CYGNUS

+39°
+38°
+37°
+36°
+35°
+34°
+33°

21h 28m   21h 24m   21h 20m   21h 16m   21h 12m   21h 08m   21h 04m

Bright and Dark
Nebulae
To scale   <10'

Open Star
Clusters

Galaxies
10' x 5'   6' x 1'   3' x 2'   5' x 5'   4' x 2'   2' x 1'

Quasars

1146

Planetary
Nebulae
>100"   100"–30"   <30"

Globular
Clusters
To scale   <5'

Plotted to scale if the major axis >2', and circular
when face on or the position angle is uncertain

Galaxy
Clusters

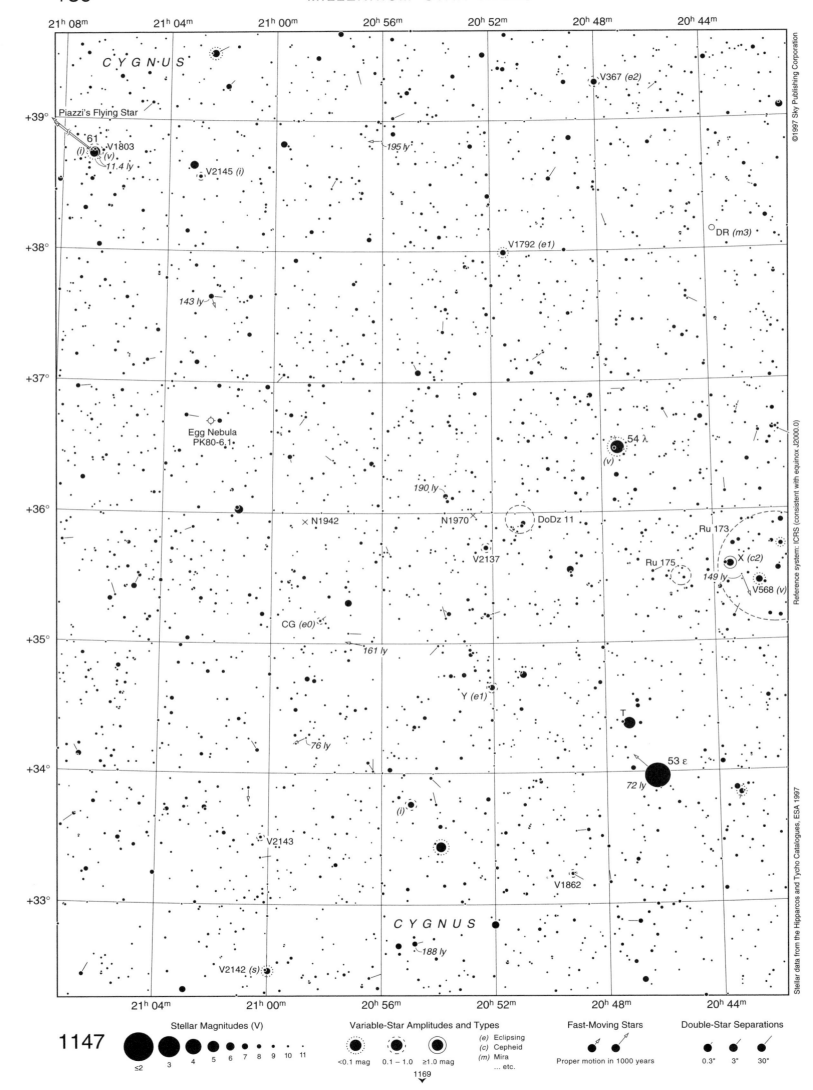

CYGNUS

Piazzi's Flying Star

61
(i)   V1803
(v)
11.4 ly

V2145 (i)

195 ly

V367 (e2)

DR (m3)

V1792 (e1)

143 ly

Egg Nebula
PK80-6.1

54 λ
(v)

190 ly

Ru 173

× N1942          N1970 ×          DoDz 11

Ru 175

X (c2)

149 ly

V568 (v)

V2137

CG (e0)

161 ly

Y (e1)

T

76 ly

53 ε

72 ly

(i)

V2143

V1862

CYGNUS

188 ly

V2142 (s)

Stellar Magnitudes (V)

≤2   3   4   5   6   7   8   9   10   11

Variable-Star Amplitudes and Types

<0.1 mag   0.1 – 1.0   ≥1.0 mag

(e) Eclipsing
(c) Cepheid
(m) Mira
... etc.

Fast-Moving Stars

Proper motion in 1000 years

Double-Star Separations

0.3"   3"   30"

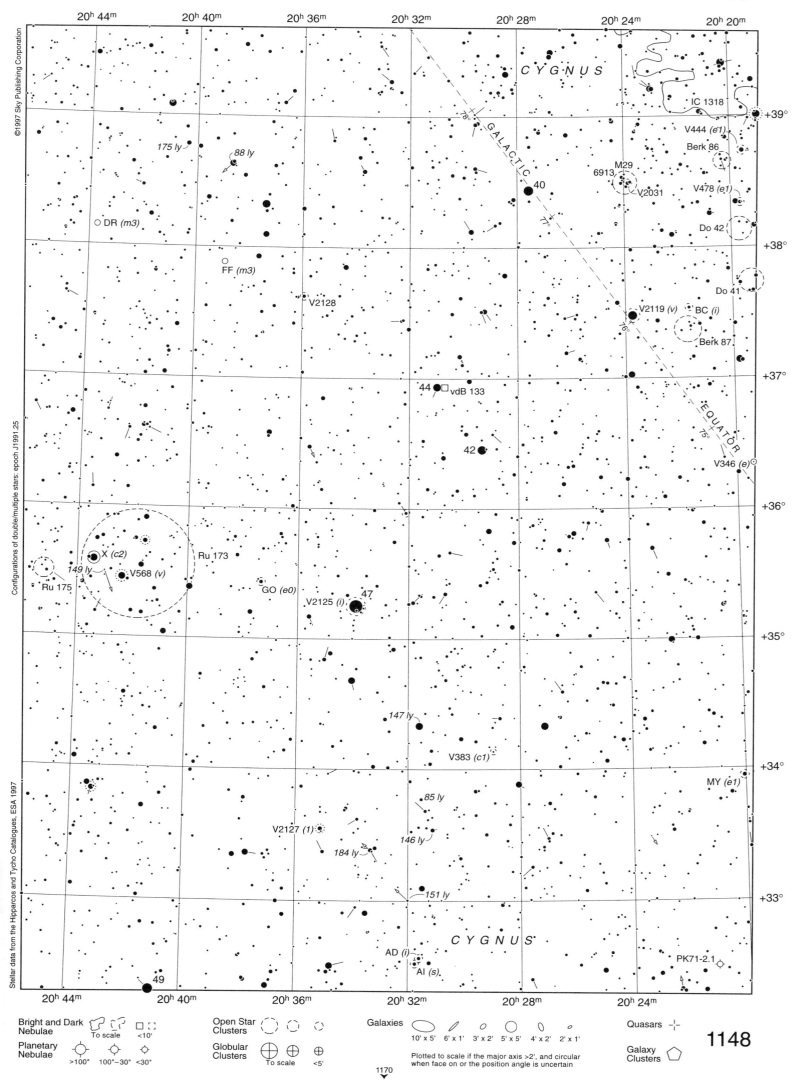

20h 44m    20h 40m    20h 36m    20h 32m    20h 28m    20h 24m    20h 20m

C Y G N U S

IC 1318

+39°

V444 (e1)

Berk 86

175 ly

88 ly

M29

6913

V2031

V478 (e1)

40

Do 42

+38°

DR (m3)

FF (m3)

Do 41

V2128

V2119 (v)    BC (i)

Berk 87

+37°

44    vdB 133

EQUATOR

42

V346 (e)

+36°

X (c2)    Ru 173

149 ly

Ru 175    V568 (v)

GO (e0)

47

V2125 (i)

+35°

147 ly

V383 (c1)

+34°

MY (e1)

85 ly

V2127 (1)

146 ly

184 ly

151 ly

+33°

C Y G N U S

AD (i)

PK71-2.1

Al (s)

49

20h 44m    20h 40m    20h 36m    20h 32m    20h 28m    20h 24m

GALACTIC

78°    77°    76°    75°

Bright and Dark
Nebulae    To scale    <10'

Planetary
Nebulae    >100"  100"-30"  <30"

Open Star
Clusters

Globular
Clusters    To scale    <5'

Galaxies

10' x 5'  6' x 1'  3' x 2'  5' x 5'  4' x 2'  2' x 1'

Plotted to scale if the major axis >2', and circular
when face on or the position angle is uncertain

Quasars

Galaxy
Clusters

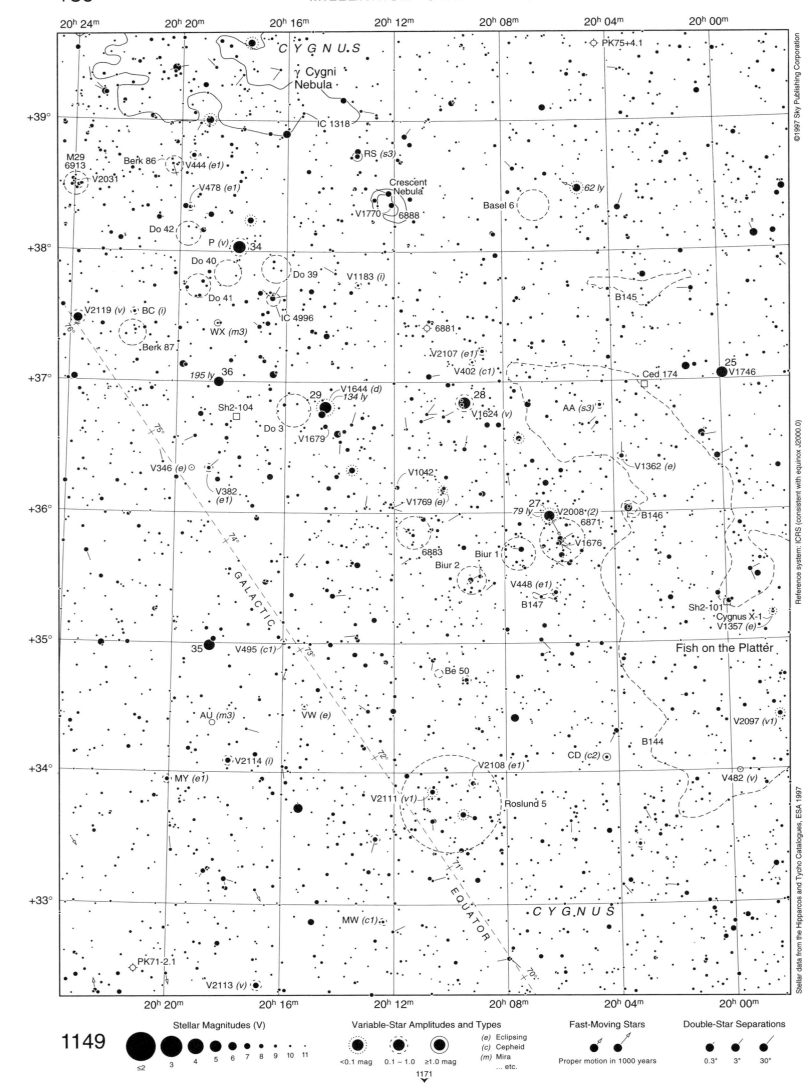

©1997 Sky Publishing Corporation

Reference system: ICRS (consistent with equinox J2000.0)

Stellar data from the Hipparcos and Tycho Catalogues, ESA 1997

CYGNUS

γ Cygni Nebula

IC 1318

M29 6913
Berk 86
V2031
V444 (e1)
V478 (e1)
Do 42
P (v)  34
Do 40
Do 39
Do 41
IC 4996
V1183 (i)
V2119 (v)  BC (i)
WX (m3)
Berk 87
36  195 ly
Sh2-104
29  V1644 (d)  134 ly
Do 3
V1679
V346 (e) ⊙
V382 (e1)
V1042
V1769 (e)
6883
Biur 2  Biur 1
35  V495 (c1)
Be 50
AU (m3)
VW (e)
V2114 (i)
MY (e1)
V2111 (v1)
Roslund 5
V2108 (e1)
MW (c1)
PK71-2.1
V2113 (v)

RS (s3)
Crescent Nebula
V1770  6888
Basel 6
62 ly
B145
6881
V2107 (e1) ⊙
V402 (c1)
28
V1624 (v)
AA (s3)
V1362 (e)
27  V2008 (2)
79 ly  6871
V1676
V448 (e1)
B147
B146
Sh2-101
Cygnus X-1
V1357 (e)
Fish on the Platter
V2097 (v1)
B144
CD (c2) ⊙
V482 (v)
Ced 174
25  V1746
PK75+4.1

GALACTIC

EQUATOR

CYGNUS

+39°
+38°
+37°
+36°
+35°
+34°
+33°

20h 24m  20h 20m  20h 16m  20h 12m  20h 08m  20h 04m  20h 00m

76°  75°  74°  73°  72°  71°  70°

Stellar Magnitudes (V)

≤2  3  4  5  6  7  8  9  10  11

Variable-Star Amplitudes and Types

<0.1 mag  0.1 – 1.0  ≥1.0 mag

(e) Eclipsing
(c) Cepheid
(m) Mira
... etc.

Fast-Moving Stars

Proper motion in 1000 years

Double-Star Separations

0.3"  3"  30"

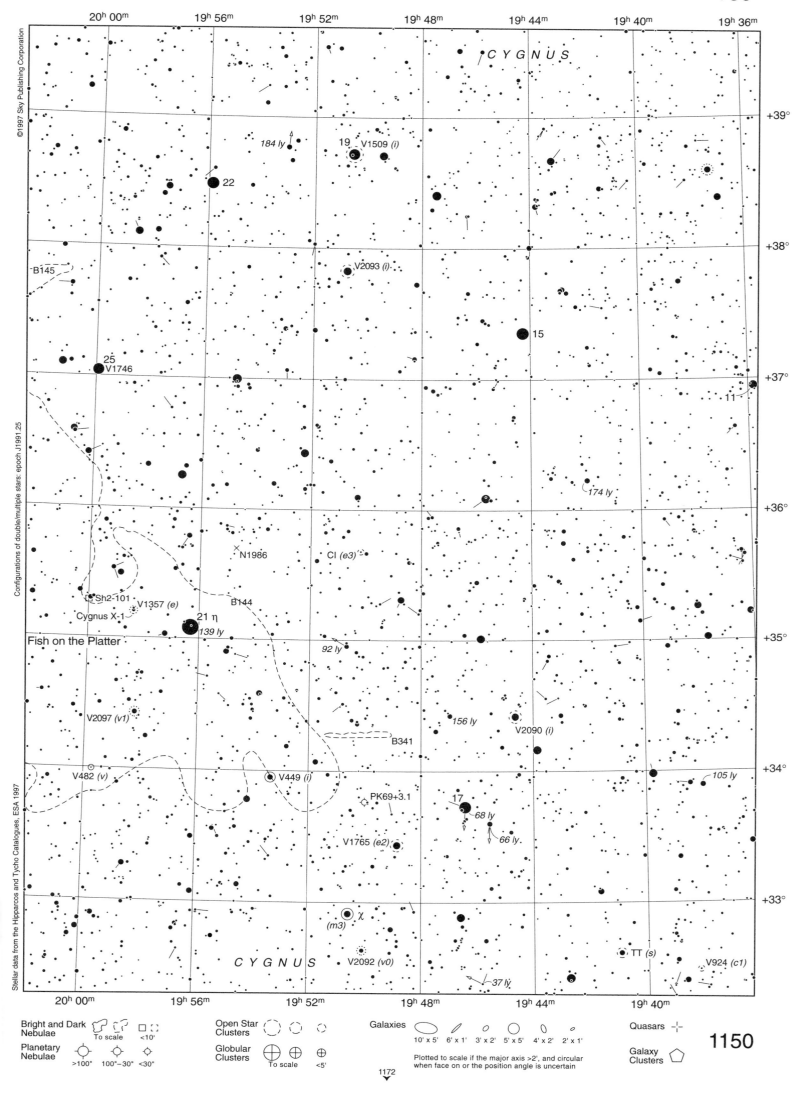

Configurations of double/multiple stars: epoch J1991.25

Stellar data from the Hipparcos and Tycho Catalogues, ESA 1997

CYGNUS

184 ly

19  V1509 (i)

22

V2093 (i)

15

25
V1746

11

N1986

Cl (e3)

174 ly

Sh2-101
V1357 (e)          B144
Cygnus X-1

21 η
139 ly

Fish on the Platter

92 ly

V2097 (v1)

156 ly

V2090 (i)

B341

V482 (v)              V449 (i)

105 ly

PK69+3.1

17
68 ly

66 ly.

V1765 (e2)

χ
(m3)

CYGNUS

TT (s)

V2092 (v0)

V924 (c1)

37 ly

| Bright and Dark Nebulae | Open Star Clusters | Galaxies | Quasars |
| --- | --- | --- | --- |

Bright and Dark Nebulae    To scale    <10'

Open Star Clusters

Galaxies    10' x 5'   6' x 1'   3' x 2'   5' x 5'   4' x 2'   2' x 1'

Quasars

Planetary Nebulae   >100"   100"-30"   <30"

Globular Clusters   To scale   <5'

Galaxy Clusters

Plotted to scale if the major axis >2', and circular when face on or the position angle is uncertain

1150

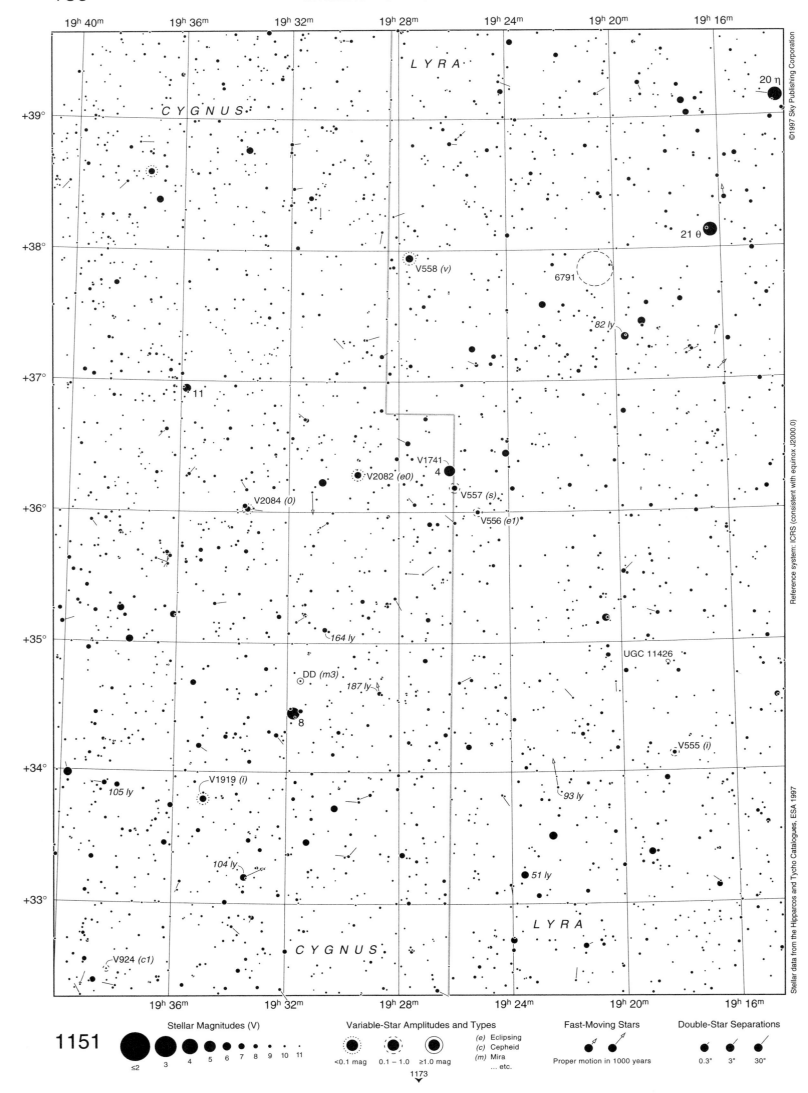

LYRA

CYGNUS

20 η

21 θ

V558 (v)

6791

82 ly

11

V1741

V2082 (e0)

4

V557 (s)

V2084 (0)

V556 (e1)

164 ly

UGC 11426

DD (m3)

187 ly

8

V555 (i)

V1919 (i)

93 ly

105 ly

104 ly

51 ly

LYRA

CYGNUS

V924 (c1)

Stellar Magnitudes (V)

≤2  3  4  5  6  7  8  9  10  11

Variable-Star Amplitudes and Types

<0.1 mag    0.1 – 1.0    ≥1.0 mag

(e) Eclipsing
(c) Cepheid
(m) Mira
... etc.

Fast-Moving Stars

Proper motion in 1000 years

Double-Star Separations

0.3"    3"    30"

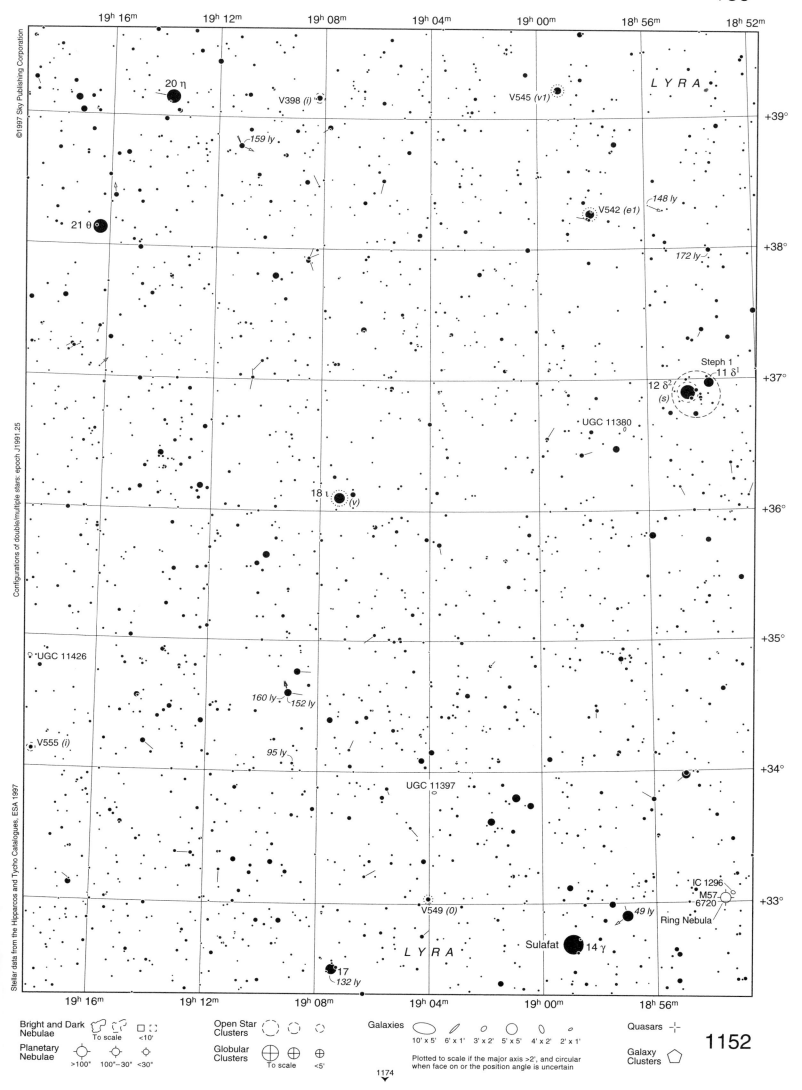

Configurations of double/multiple stars: epoch J1991.25

Stellar data from the Hipparcos and Tycho Catalogues, ESA 1997

L Y R A

20 η

V398 (i)

V545 (v1)

159 ly

21 θ

V542 (e1)

148 ly

172 ly

Steph 1
11 δ¹

12 δ²
(s)

UGC 11380

18 ι
(v)

+39°

+38°

+37°

+36°

+35°

+34°

+33°

UGC 11426

160 ly    152 ly

V555 (i)

95 ly

UGC 11397

IC 1296
M57
6720
Ring Nebula

49 ly

V549 (0)

Sulafat    14 γ

L Y R A

17
132 ly

19h 16m    19h 12m    19h 08m    19h 04m    19h 00m    18h 56m

Bright and Dark Nebulae    To scale    <10'
Planetary Nebulae    >100"    100"–30"    <30"

Open Star Clusters
Globular Clusters    To scale    <5'

Galaxies    10' x 5'    6' x 1'    3' x 2'    5' x 5'    4' x 2'    2' x 1'
Plotted to scale if the major axis >2', and circular when face on or the position angle is uncertain

Quasars

Galaxy Clusters

1152

1174
▼

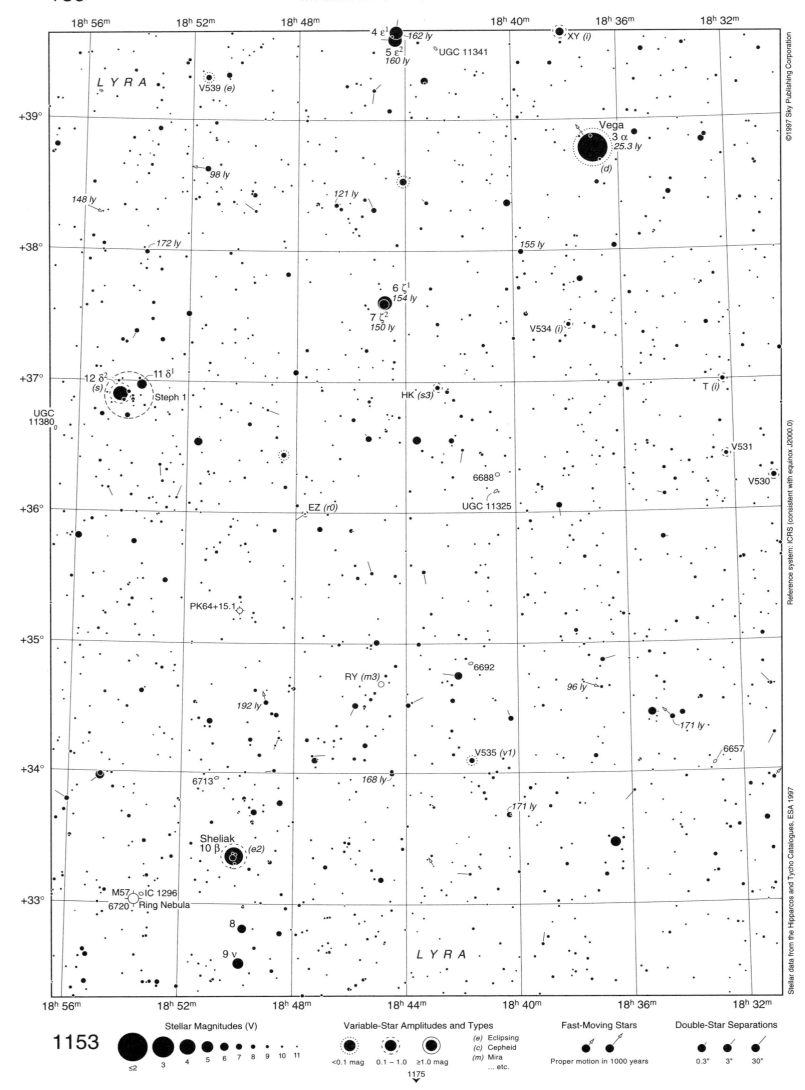

LYRA

4 ε¹ — 162 ly
5 ε² — 160 ly

XY (i)

UGC 11341

V539 (e)

Vega
3 α
25.3 ly
(d)

98 ly

148 ly

121 ly

172 ly

155 ly

6 ζ¹
154 ly
7 ζ²
150 ly

V534 (i)

12 δ²
(s)    11 δ¹
Steph 1

HK (s3)

T (i)

UGC
11380

V531

V530

6688

UGC 11325

EZ (r0)

PK64+15.1

RY (m3)

6692

96 ly

171 ly

6657

V535 (v1)

6713    168 ly

171 ly

Sheliak
10 β    (e2)

M57    IC 1296
6720    Ring Nebula

8

9 ν

L Y R A

Stellar Magnitudes (V)

≤2    3    4    5    6    7    8    9    10    11

Variable-Star Amplitudes and Types

<0.1 mag    0.1 – 1.0    ≥1.0 mag

(e) Eclipsing
(c) Cepheid
(m) Mira
... etc.

Fast-Moving Stars

Proper motion in 1000 years

Double-Star Separations

0.3"    3"    30"

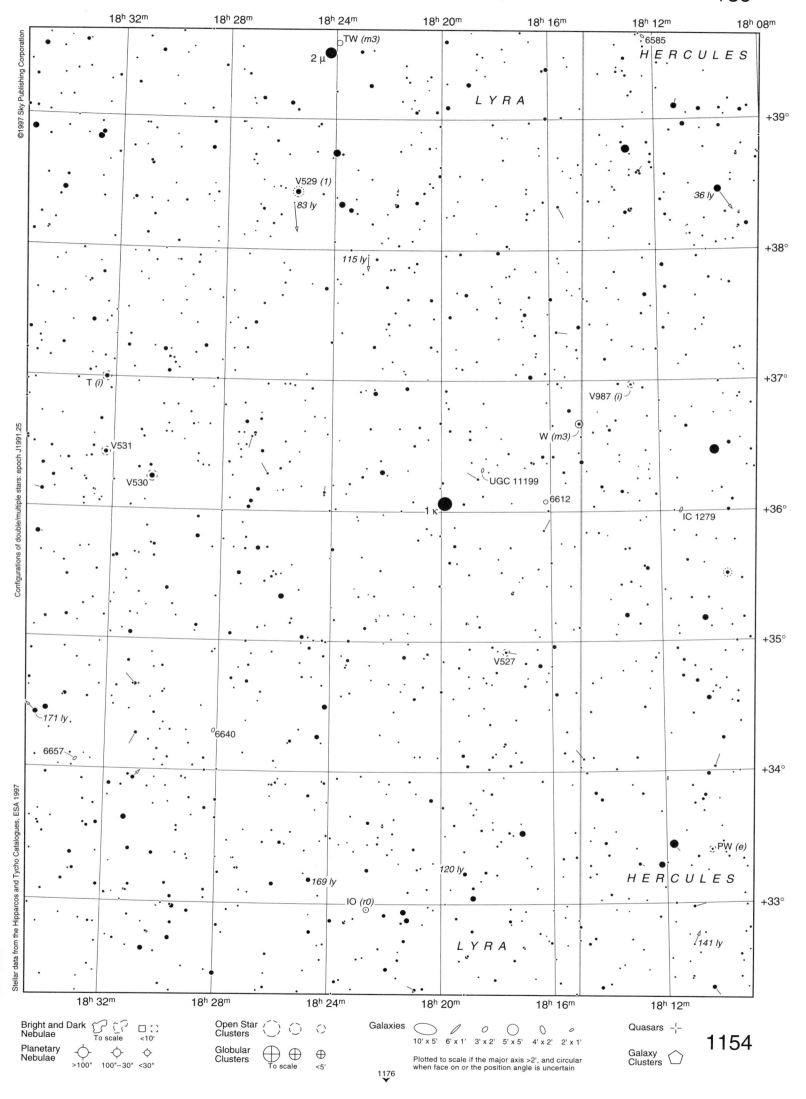

18h 32m  18h 28m  18h 24m  18h 20m  18h 16m  18h 12m  18h 08m

TW (m3)
6585
HERCULES
2 μ
LYRA
+39°

V529 (1)
36 ly
83 ly
+38°
115 ly

T (i)
V987 (i)
+37°
W (m3)
V531
UGC 11199
V530
6612
1 κ
IC 1279
+36°

+35°
V527

171 ly
6640
6657
+34°

PW (e)
HERCULES
120 ly
169 ly
IO (r0)
+33°
LYRA
141 ly

18h 32m  18h 28m  18h 24m  18h 20m  18h 16m  18h 12m

Bright and Dark Nebulae
To scale   <10'
Open Star Clusters
Galaxies
10' x 5'  6' x 1'  3' x 2'  5' x 5'  4' x 2'  2' x 1'
Quasars

Planetary Nebulae
>100"  100"–30"  <30"
Globular Clusters
To scale   <5'
Galaxy Clusters

Plotted to scale if the major axis >2', and circular when face on or the position angle is uncertain

1154

# MILLENNIUM STAR ATLAS

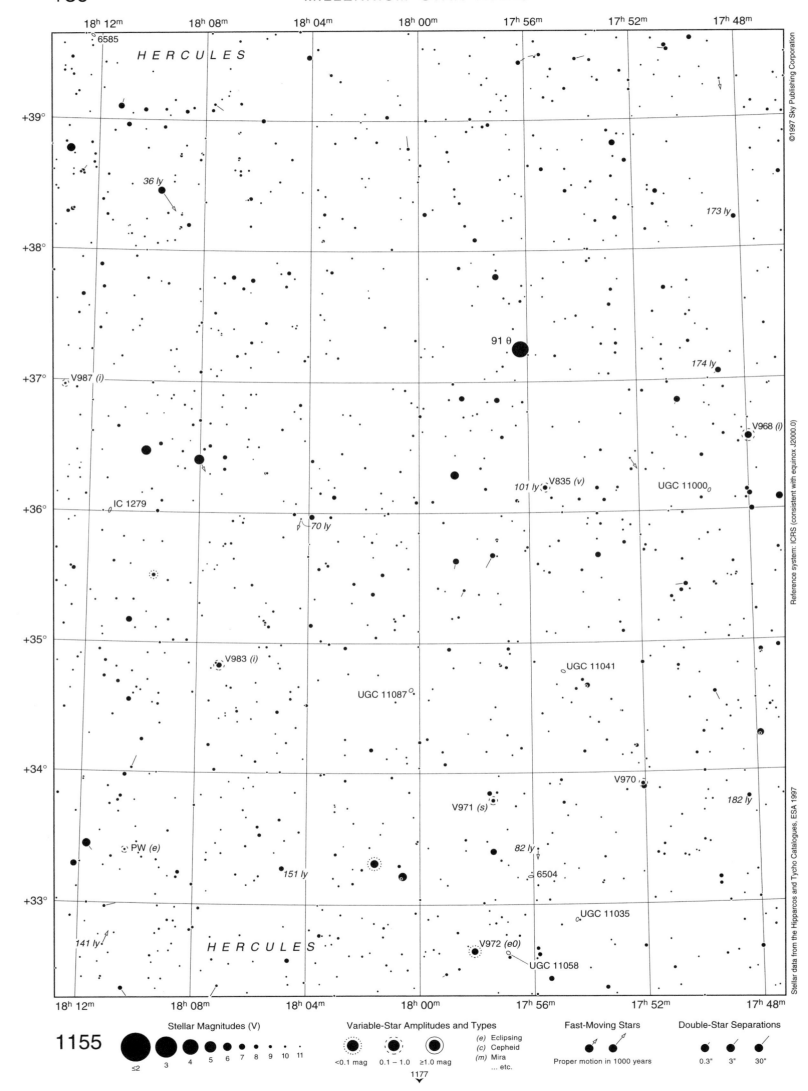

H E R C U L E S

6585

36 ly

173 ly

91 θ

174 ly

V987 (i)

V968 (i)

IC 1279

V835 (v)

101 ly

UGC 11000

70 ly

V983 (i)

UGC 11041

UGC 11087

V970

182 ly

V971 (s)

PW (e)

82 ly

151 ly

6504

UGC 11035

141 ly

H E R C U L E S

V972 (e0)

UGC 11058

©1997 Sky Publishing Corporation

Reference system: ICRS (consistent with equinox J2000.0)

Stellar data from the Hipparcos and Tycho Catalogues, ESA 1997

**1155**

**Stellar Magnitudes (V)**

≤2    3    4    5   6  7  8  9 10 11

**Variable-Star Amplitudes and Types**

<0.1 mag   0.1 – 1.0   ≥1.0 mag

(e) Eclipsing
(c) Cepheid
(m) Mira
... etc.

**Fast-Moving Stars**

Proper motion in 1000 years

**Double-Star Separations**

0.3"    3"    30"

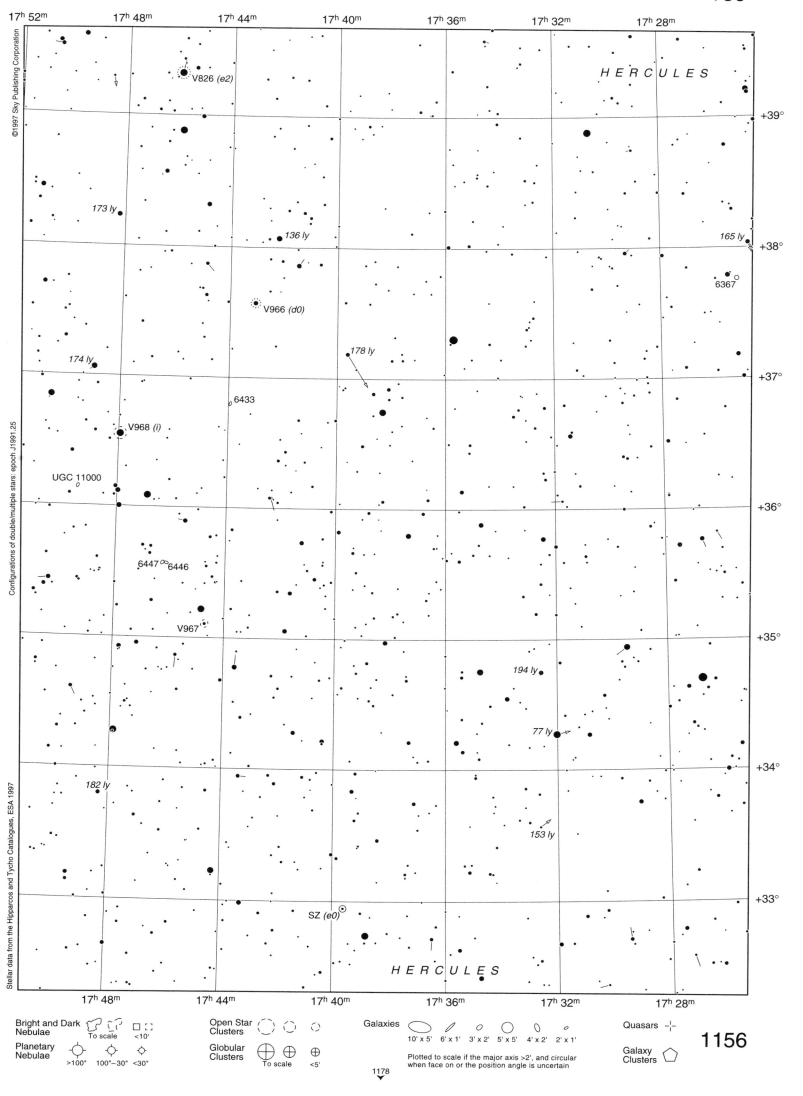

HERCULES

V826 (e2)

173 ly

136 ly

165 ly

6367

V966 (d0)

178 ly

174 ly

6433

V968 (i)

UGC 11000

6447 ∞ 6446

V967

194 ly

77 ly

182 ly

153 ly

SZ (e0)

HERCULES

| Bright and Dark Nebulae | Open Star Clusters | Galaxies | Quasars |
|---|---|---|---|

Bright and Dark Nebulae
To scale    <10'

Planetary Nebulae
>100"    100"–30"    <30"

Open Star Clusters

Globular Clusters
To scale    <5'

Galaxies
10' x 5'    6' x 1'    3' x 2'    5' x 5'    4' x 2'    2' x 1'

Plotted to scale if the major axis >2', and circular
when face on or the position angle is uncertain

Quasars

Galaxy Clusters

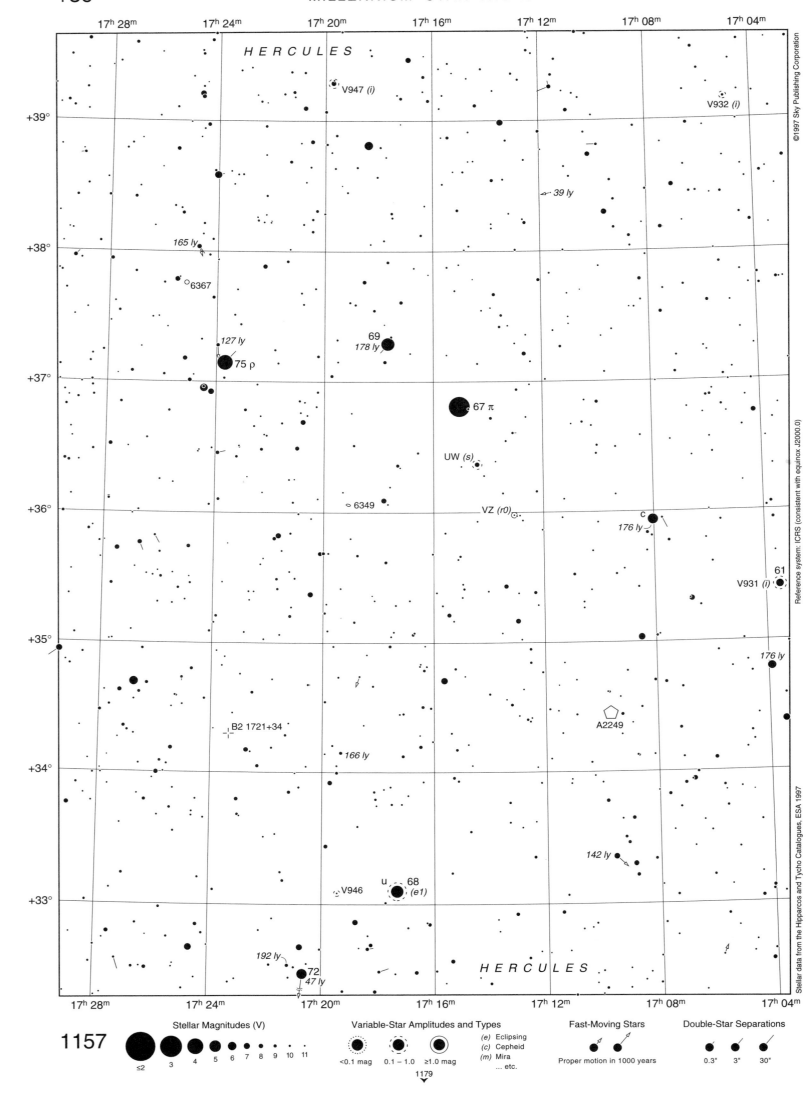

HERCULES

V947 (i)

V932 (i)

39 ly

165 ly

○6367

127 ly

69
178 ly

75 ρ

67 π

UW (s)

○ 6349

VZ (r0)

c
176 ly

61
V931 (i)

176 ly

A2249

B2 1721+34

166 ly

142 ly

u    68
V946    (e1)

HERCULES

192 ly

72
47 ly

1157

**Stellar Magnitudes (V)**

≤2   3   4   5   6   7  8  9  10  11

**Variable-Star Amplitudes and Types**

<0.1 mag    0.1 – 1.0    ≥1.0 mag

(e) Eclipsing
(c) Cepheid
(m) Mira
... etc.

1179

**Fast-Moving Stars**

Proper motion in 1000 years

**Double-Star Separations**

0.3"    3"    30"

# MILLENNIUM STAR ATLAS

+36°

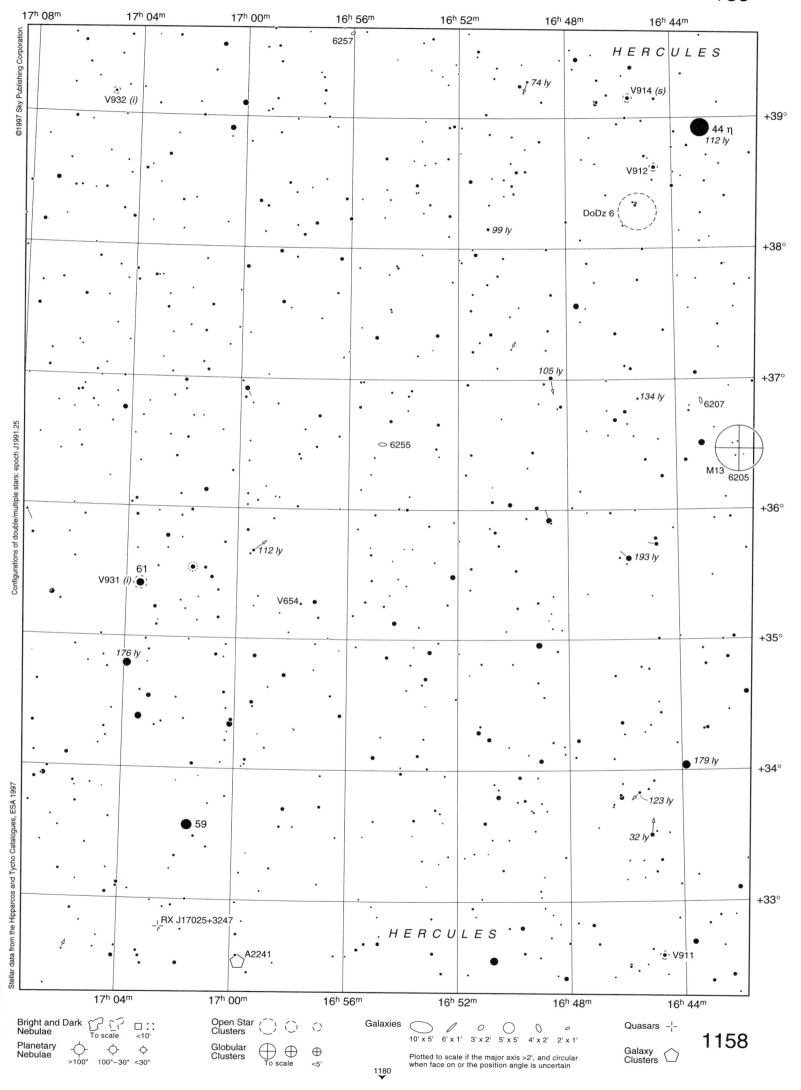

HERCULES

6257

74 ly

V914 (s)

V932 (i)

+39°

44 η
112 ly

V912

DoDz 6

99 ly

+38°

+37°

105 ly

134 ly

⁰6207

6255

M13
6205

+36°

112 ly

193 ly

61
V931 (i)

V654

+35°

176 ly

179 ly

123 ly

59

32 ly

+34°

+33°

RX J17025+3247

HERCULES

A2241

V911

17h 08m   17h 04m   17h 00m   16h 56m   16h 52m   16h 48m   16h 44m

17h 04m   17h 00m   16h 56m   16h 52m   16h 48m   16h 44m

| Bright and Dark Nebulae | Open Star Clusters | Galaxies | Quasars |
|---|---|---|---|

To scale   <10'

To scale   <10'

Planetary Nebulae
>100"  100"–30"  <30"

Globular Clusters
To scale   <5'

10' x 5'  6' x 1'  3' x 2'  5' x 5'  4' x 2'  2' x 1'

Galaxy Clusters

Plotted to scale if the major axis >2', and circular when face on or the position angle is uncertain

1158

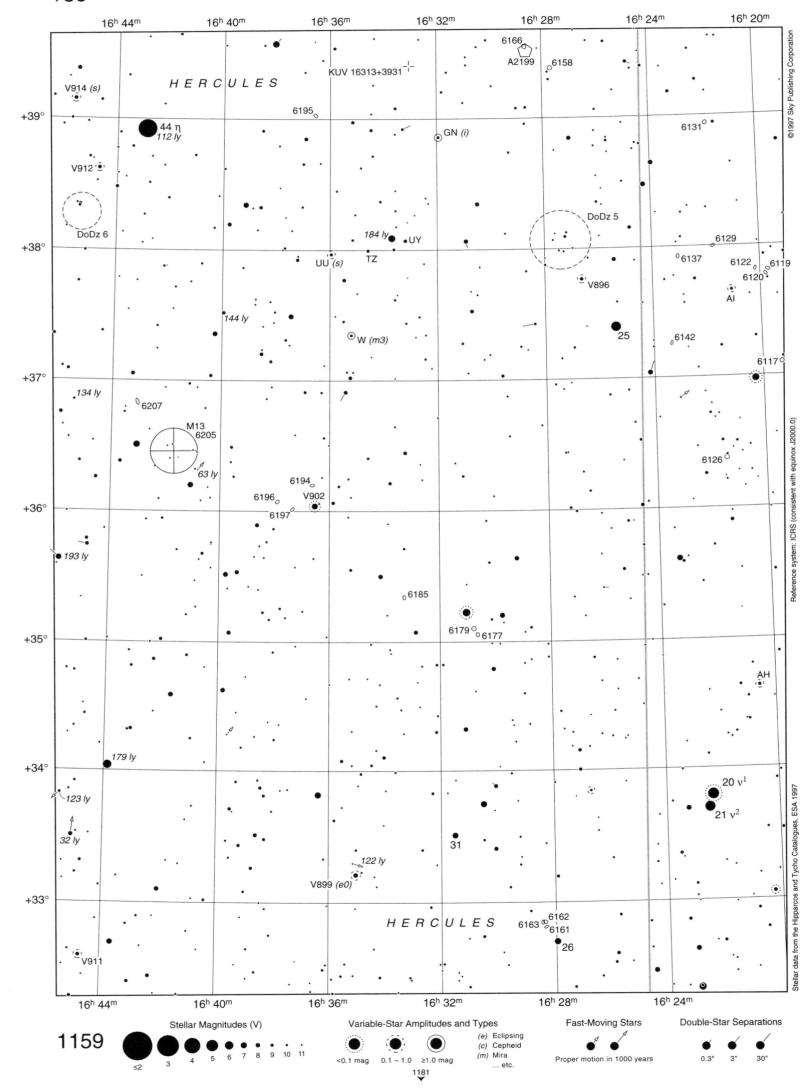

©1997 Sky Publishing Corporation

Reference system: ICRS (consistent with equinox J2000.0)

Stellar data from the Hipparcos and Tycho Catalogues, ESA 1997

HERCULES

HERCULES

V914 (s)
44 η
112 ly
V912
DoDz 6
V911

6166
A2199
6158
KUV 16313+3931
6195
GN (i)
6131
DoDz 5
184 ly    UY
UU (s)    TZ
6129
V896
6137
6122  6119
6120
AI
144 ly
W (m3)
25
6142
6117
134 ly
6207
6126
M13
6205
63 ly
6194
6196    V902
6197
193 ly
6185
6179  6177
AH
179 ly
123 ly
20 ν¹
32 ly
21 ν²
31
122 ly
V899 (e0)
6162
6163  6161
26

1159

Stellar Magnitudes (V)

≤2    3    4    5    6    7    8    9    10    11

Variable-Star Amplitudes and Types

<0.1 mag    0.1 – 1.0    ≥1.0 mag

(e) Eclipsing
(c) Cepheid
(m) Mira
... etc.

Fast-Moving Stars

Proper motion in 1000 years

Double-Star Separations

0.3"    3"    30"

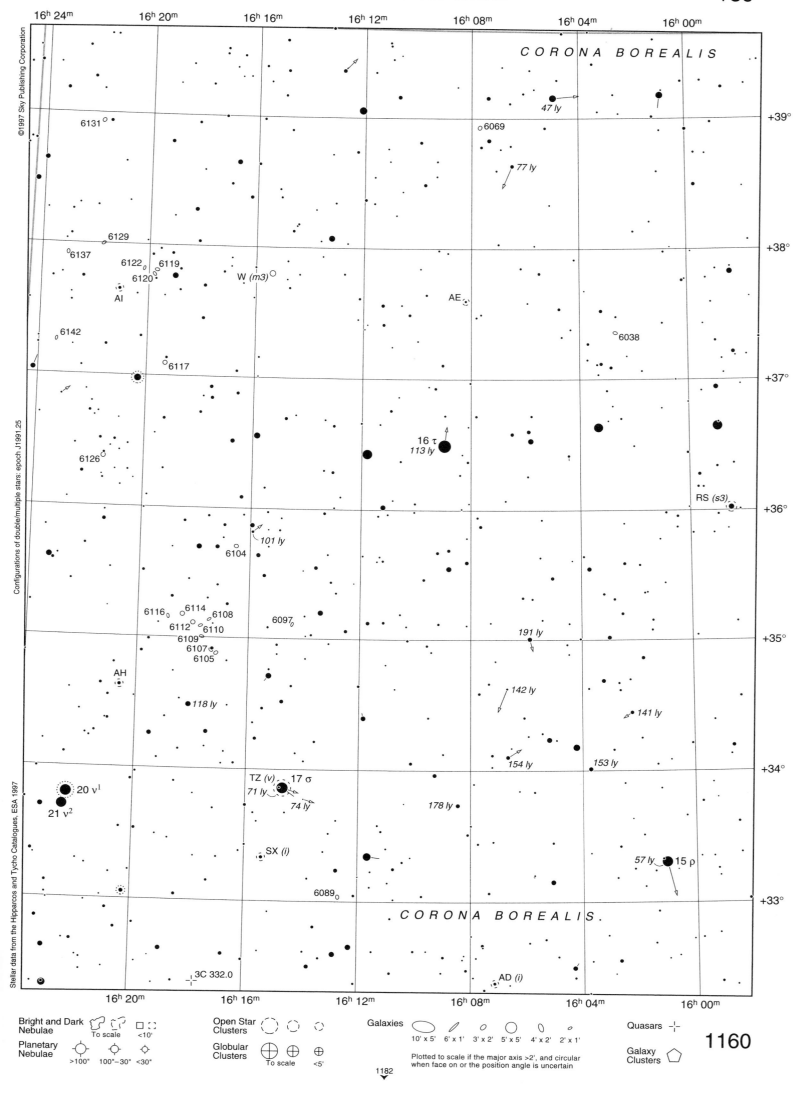

CORONA BOREALIS

16h 24m   16h 20m   16h 16m   16h 12m   16h 08m   16h 04m   16h 00m

+39°
+38°
+37°
+36°
+35°
+34°
+33°

6131
6069
47 ly
77 ly
6129
6137
6122
6119
6120
AI
W (m3)
AE
6038
6142
6117
16 τ
113 ly
6126
RS (s3)
101 ly
6104
6116  6114  6108
6112  6110
6109
6107  6105
6097
191 ly
AH
118 ly
142 ly
141 ly
154 ly
153 ly
TZ (v)   17 σ
20 ν¹
71 ly   74 ly
178 ly
21 ν²
SX (i)
57 ly   15 ρ
6089
CORONA BOREALIS.
3C 332.0
AD (i)

16h 20m   16h 16m   16h 12m   16h 08m   16h 04m   16h 00m

Bright and Dark
Nebulae            To scale   <10'

Planetary
Nebulae      >100"  100"–30"  <30"

Open Star
Clusters

Globular
Clusters     To scale   <5'

Galaxies

10' x 5'  6' x 1'  3' x 2'  5' x 5'  4' x 2'  2' x 1'

Plotted to scale if the major axis >2', and circular
when face on or the position angle is uncertain

Quasars

Galaxy
Clusters

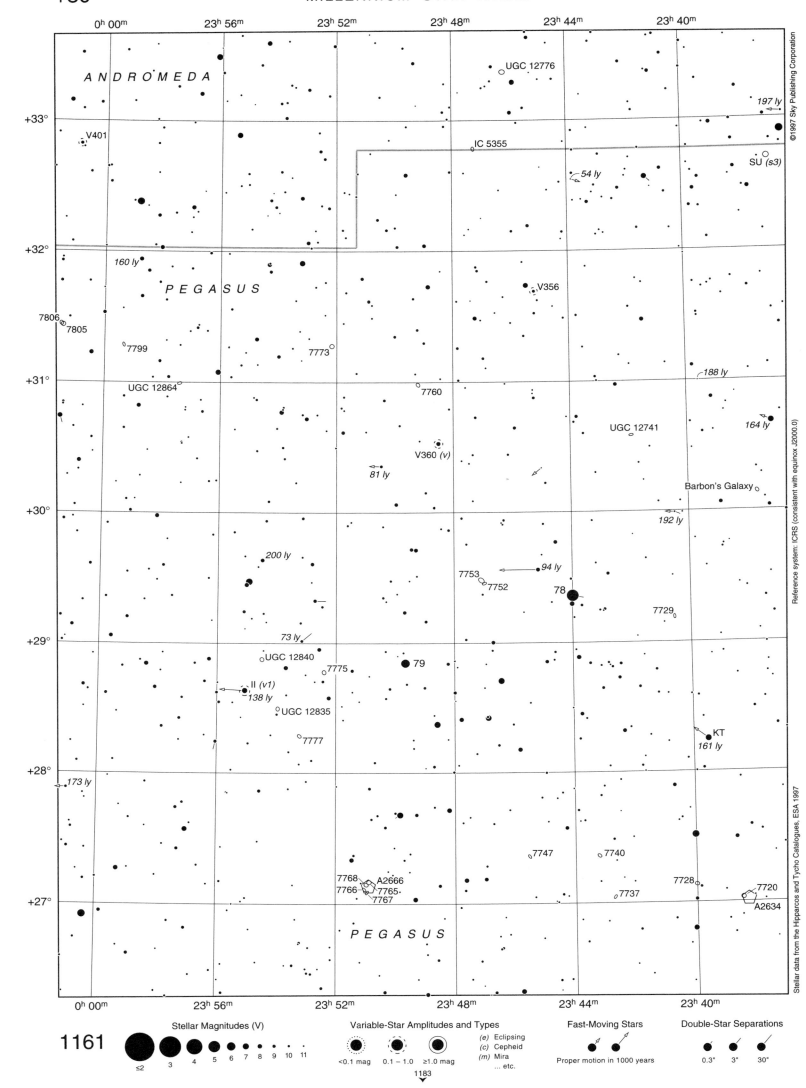

Reference system: ICRS (consistent with equinox J2000.0)

Stellar data from the Hipparcos and Tycho Catalogues, ESA 1997

ANDROMEDA

UGC 12776

197 ly

+33°

V401

IC 5355

SU (s3)

54 ly

+32°

160 ly

PEGASUS

V356

7806
7805

7799

7773

188 ly

+31°

UGC 12864

7760

164 ly

UGC 12741

V360 (v)

Barbon's Galaxy

81 ly

+30°

192 ly

200 ly

94 ly

7753

7752

78

7729

+29°

73 ly

UGC 12840

79

7775

II (v1)

138 ly

UGC 12835

KT

7777

161 ly

+28°

173 ly

7747

7740

7768

A2666

7728

7720

7766

7765

7737

A2634

7767

+27°

PEGASUS

Stellar Magnitudes (V)

≤2    3    4    5    6    7    8    9  10  11

Variable-Star Amplitudes and Types

<0.1 mag   0.1 – 1.0   ≥1.0 mag

(e) Eclipsing
(c) Cepheid
(m) Mira
... etc.

1183

Fast-Moving Stars

Proper motion in 1000 years

Double-Star Separations

0.3"    3"    30"

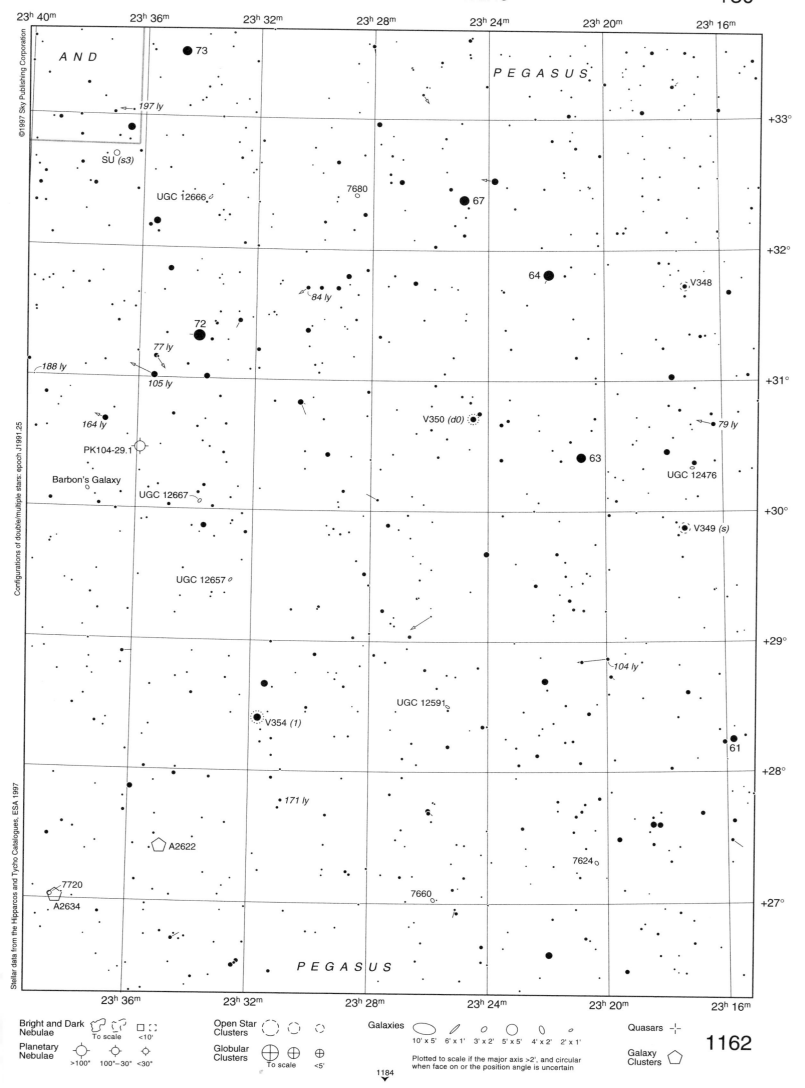

23h 40m · 23h 36m · 23h 32m · 23h 28m · 23h 24m · 23h 20m · 23h 16m

A N D

©1997 Sky Publishing Corporation

P E G A S U S

+33°

73

197 ly

SU (s3)

UGC 12666

7680

67

+32°

84 ly

64

V348

72

77 ly

188 ly

105 ly

+31°

164 ly

V350 (d0)

79 ly

PK104-29.1

63

Barbon's Galaxy

UGC 12476

UGC 12667

+30°

V349 (s)

UGC 12657

Configurations of double/multiple stars: epoch J1991.25

+29°

104 ly

UGC 12591

61

V354 (1)

+28°

171 ly

Stellar data from the Hipparcos and Tycho Catalogues, ESA 1997

A2622

7624

7720

7660

A2634

+27°

P E G A S U S

23h 36m · 23h 32m · 23h 28m · 23h 24m · 23h 20m · 23h 16m

Bright and Dark Nebulae · To scale · <10'
Open Star Clusters
Galaxies · 10' x 5' · 6' x 1' · 3' x 2' · 5' x 5' · 4' x 2' · 2' x 1'
Quasars

Planetary Nebulae · >100" · 100"–30" · <30"
Globular Clusters · To scale · <5'
Galaxy Clusters

Plotted to scale if the major axis >2', and circular when face on or the position angle is uncertain

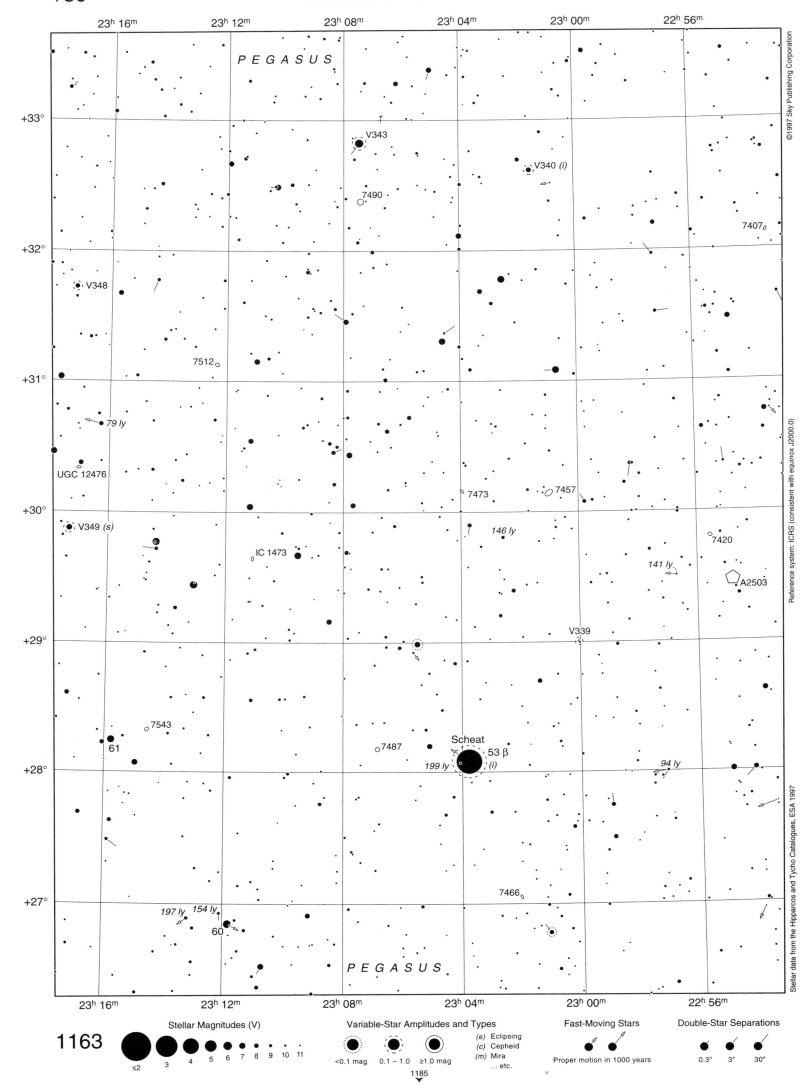

PEGASUS

V343
V340 (i)
7490
7407
V348
7512
79 ly
UGC 12476
7473
7457
7420
V349 (s)
146 ly
IC 1473
141 ly
A2503
V339
7543
7487
Scheat
61
53 β
199 ly
(i)
94 ly
7466
197 ly   154 ly
60
PEGASUS

1163

Stellar Magnitudes (V)

≤2  3  4  5  6  7  8  9  10  11

Variable-Star Amplitudes and Types

<0.1 mag    0.1 – 1.0    ≥1.0 mag

(e) Eclipsing
(c) Cepheid
(m) Mira
... etc.

Fast-Moving Stars

Proper motion in 1000 years

Double-Star Separations

0.3"   3"   30"

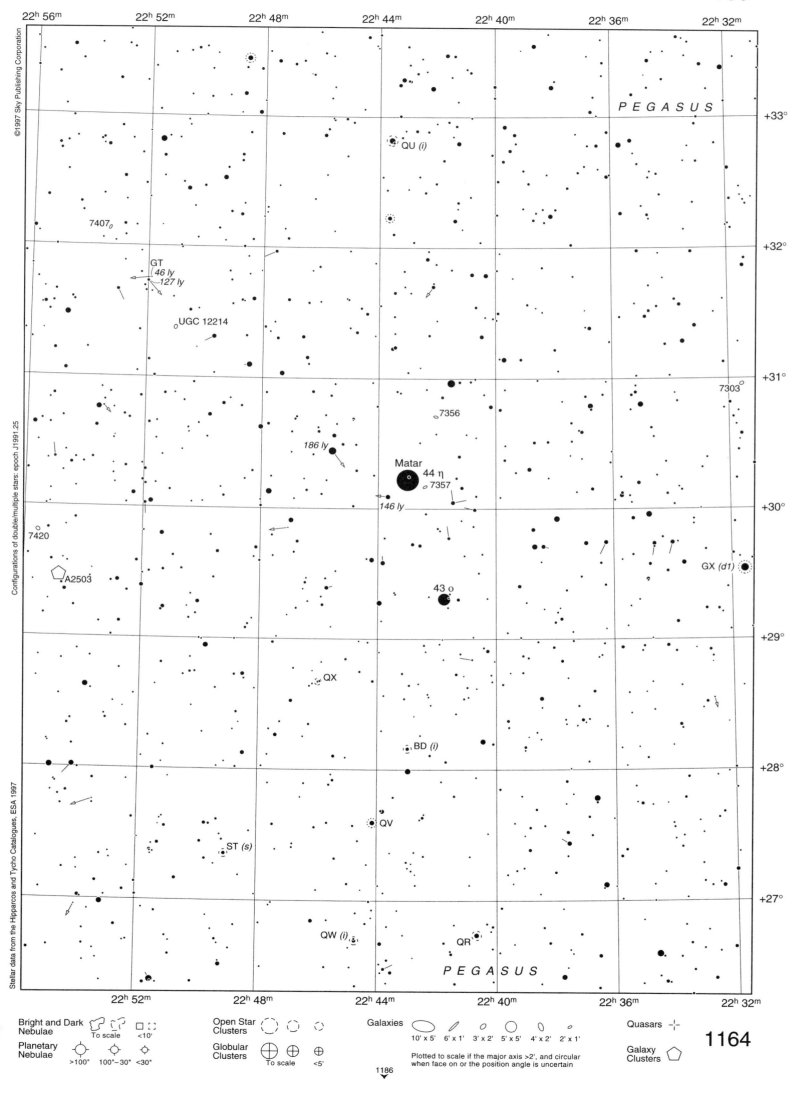

PEGASUS

22h 56m    22h 52m    22h 48m    22h 44m    22h 40m    22h 36m    22h 32m

QU (i)

7407₀

GT
(46 ly
127 ly

UGC 12214

7303₀

7356

186 ly

Matar
44 η
7357

146 ly

7420₀

A2503

GX (d1)

43 o

QX

BD (i)

QV

ST (s)

QW (i)

QR

PEGASUS

22h 52m    22h 48m    22h 44m    22h 40m    22h 36m    22h 32m

+33°
+32°
+31°
+30°
+29°
+28°
+27°

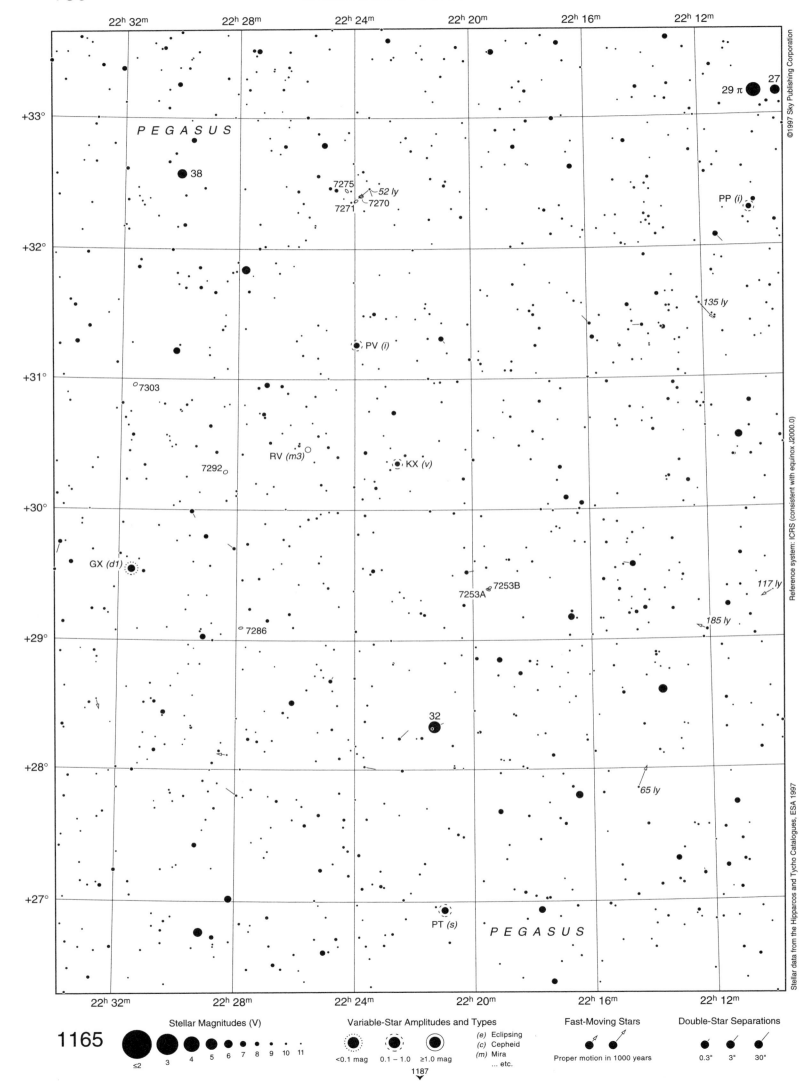

MILLENNIUM STAR ATLAS

1143

©1997 Sky Publishing Corporation

Reference system: ICRS (consistent with equinox J2000.0)

Stellar data from the Hipparcos and Tycho Catalogues, ESA 1997

PEGASUS

38

7275
52 ly
7271
7270

29 π
27

PP (i)

135 ly

PV (i)

7303

RV (m3)

7292

KX (v)

GX (d1)

7253A    7253B

117 ly

7286

185 ly

32

65 ly

PT (s)

PEGASUS

**Stellar Magnitudes (V)**

≤2   3   4   5   6   7  8  9  10  11

**Variable-Star Amplitudes and Types**

<0.1 mag    0.1 – 1.0    ≥1.0 mag

(e) Eclipsing
(c) Cepheid
(m) Mira
... etc.

1187

**Fast-Moving Stars**

Proper motion in 1000 years

**Double-Star Separations**

0.3"    3"    30"

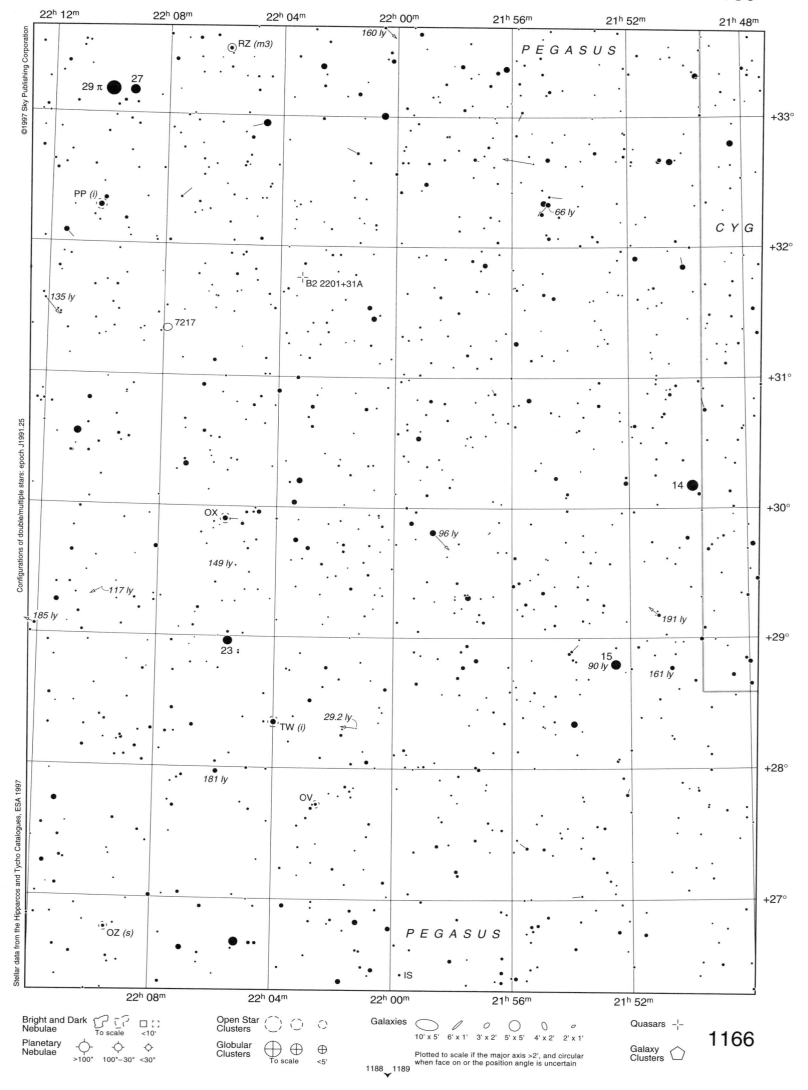

22h 12m    22h 08m    22h 04m    22h 00m    21h 56m    21h 52m    21h 48m

RZ (m3)
160 ly

P E G A S U S

29 π    27

+33°

PP (i)
66 ly

C Y G

+32°

135 ly

B2 2201+31A

7217

+31°

14

+30°

OX
96 ly

149 ly

117 ly

191 ly

185 ly

+29°

23
15
90 ly    161 ly

TW (i)    29.2 ly

181 ly

+28°

OV

+27°

OZ (s)

P E G A S U S

IS

22h 08m    22h 04m    22h 00m    21h 56m    21h 52m

| Bright and Dark Nebulae | | To scale | <10' | Open Star Clusters | | Galaxies | 10' x 5' | 6' x 1' | 3' x 2' | 5' x 5' | 4' x 2' | 2' x 1' | Quasars |
| Planetary Nebulae | >100" | 100"-30" | <30" | Globular Clusters | To scale | <5' | | | Galaxy Clusters | |

Plotted to scale if the major axis >2', and circular when face on or the position angle is uncertain

1166

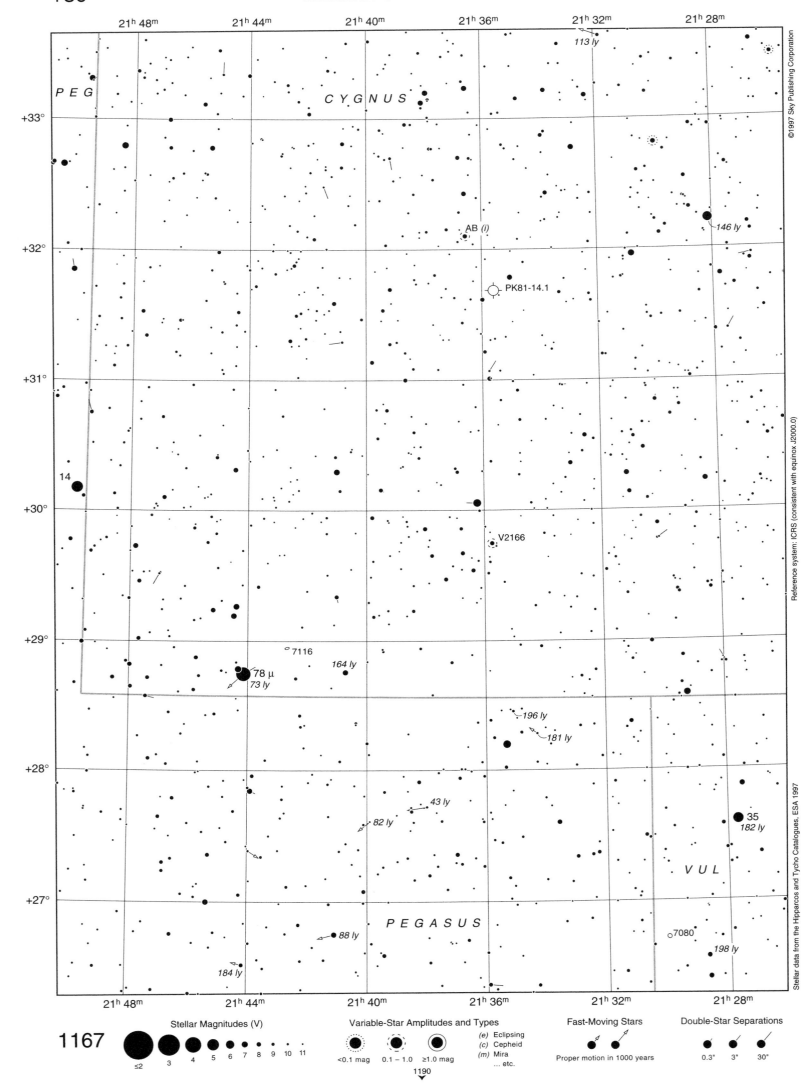

Reference system: ICRS (consistent with equinox J2000.0)

Stellar data from the Hipparcos and Tycho Catalogues, ESA 1997

PEG

CYGNUS

113 ly

146 ly

AB (i)

PK81-14.1

14

V2166

7116

164 ly

78 μ
73 ly

196 ly

181 ly

43 ly

82 ly

35
182 ly

VUL

88 ly

PEGASUS

7080

198 ly

184 ly

Stellar Magnitudes (V)

≤2  3  4  5  6  7  8  9  10  11

Variable-Star Amplitudes and Types

<0.1 mag   0.1 – 1.0   ≥1.0 mag

(e) Eclipsing
(c) Cepheid
(m) Mira
... etc.

1190

Fast-Moving Stars

Proper motion in 1000 years

Double-Star Separations

0.3"  3"  30"

# MILLENNIUM STAR ATLAS

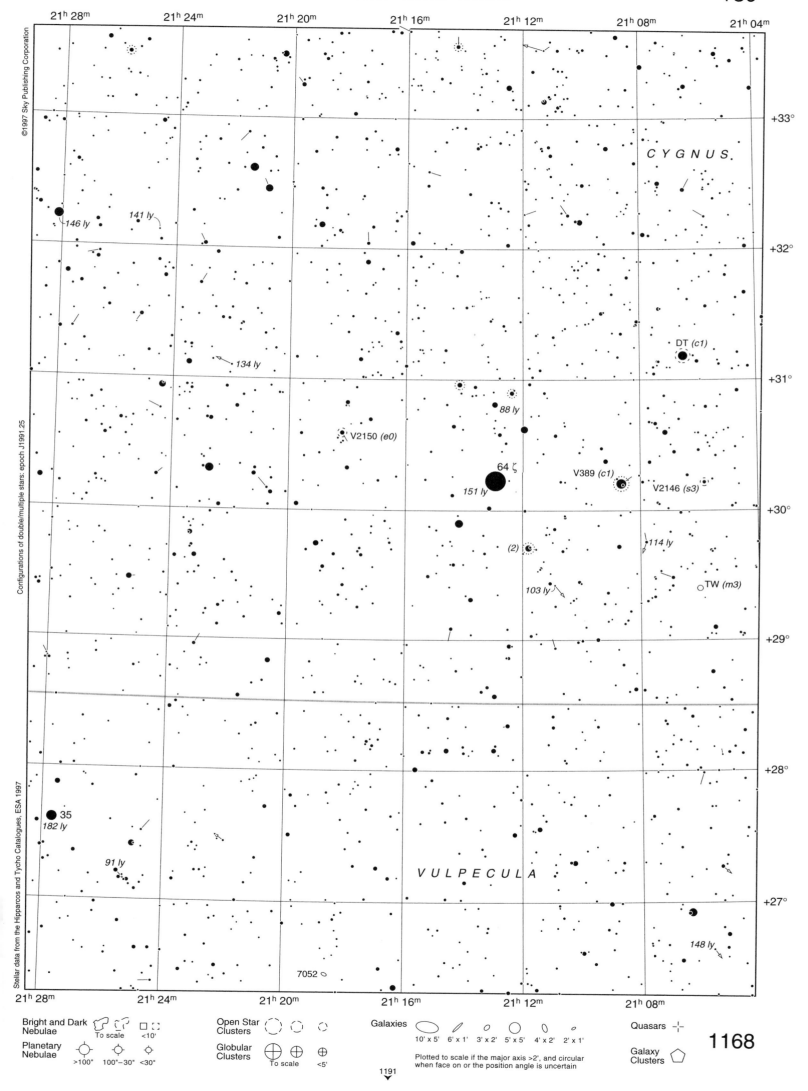

21h 28m  21h 24m  21h 20m  21h 16m  21h 12m  21h 08m  21h 04m

+33°
+32°
+31°
+30°
+29°
+28°
+27°

*C Y G N U S*

DT (c1)

88 ly

V2150 (e0)

64 ζ

V389 (c1)

V2146 (s3)

151 ly

114 ly

(2)

103 ly

TW (m3)

146 ly

141 ly

134 ly

35

182 ly

91 ly

*V U L P E C U L A*

7052

148 ly

21h 28m  21h 24m  21h 20m  21h 16m  21h 12m  21h 08m

| Bright and Dark Nebulae | Open Star Clusters | Galaxies | Quasars |
|---|---|---|---|

To scale   <10'

Planetary Nebulae
>100"   100"–30"   <30"

Globular Clusters
To scale   <5'

10' x 5'   6' x 1'   3' x 2'   5' x 5'   4' x 2'   2' x 1'

Plotted to scale if the major axis >2', and circular when face on or the position angle is uncertain

Galaxy Clusters

1168

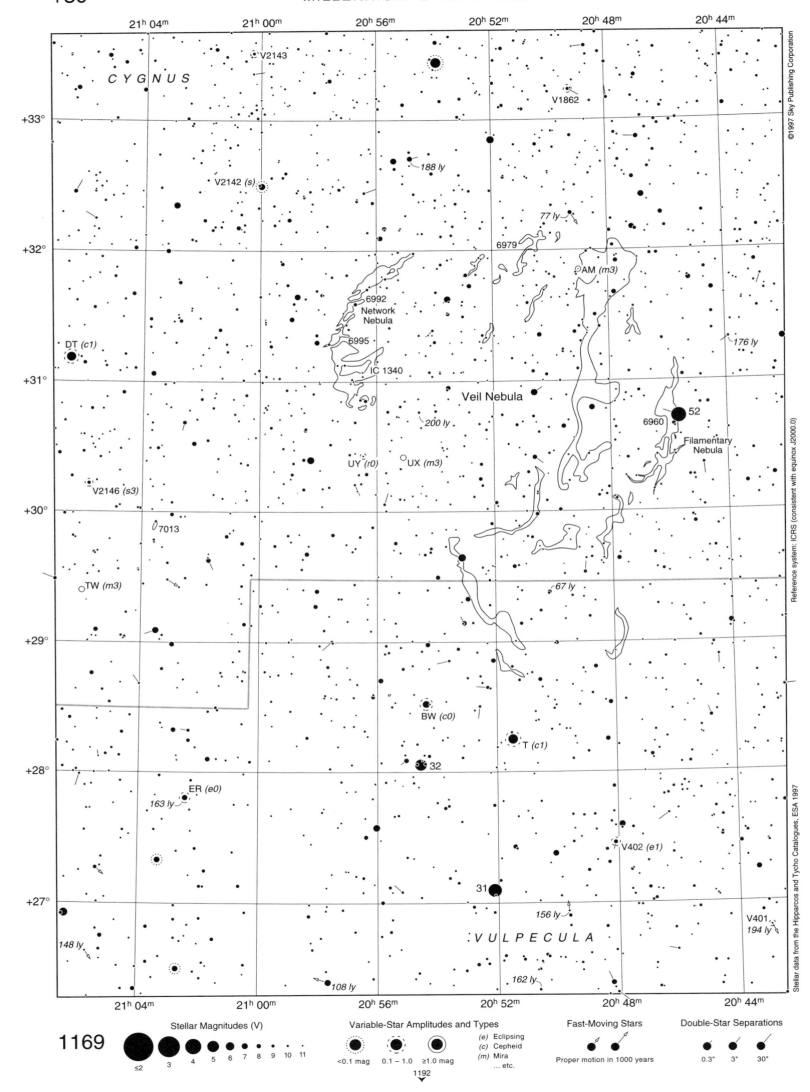

C Y G N U S

V2143

V1862

188 ly

V2142 (s)

77 ly

6979

AM (m3)

6992
Network
Nebula

6995

IC 1340

DT (c1)

Veil Nebula

176 ly

52
6960
Filamentary
Nebula

200 ly

UY (r0)      UX (m3)

V2146 (s3)

7013

67 ly

TW (m3)

BW (c0)

T (c1)

32

ER (e0)

163 ly

V402 (e1)

31

156 ly

V401
194 ly

148 ly

V U L P E C U L A

162 ly

108 ly

©1997 Sky Publishing Corporation

Reference system: ICRS (consistent with equinox J2000.0)

Stellar data from the Hipparcos and Tycho Catalogues, ESA 1997

**1169**

Stellar Magnitudes (V)

≤2   3   4   5   6   7   8   9   10   11

Variable-Star Amplitudes and Types

<0.1 mag    0.1 – 1.0    ≥1.0 mag

(e) Eclipsing
(c) Cepheid
(m) Mira
... etc.

Fast-Moving Stars

Proper motion in 1000 years

Double-Star Separations

0.3"   3"   30"

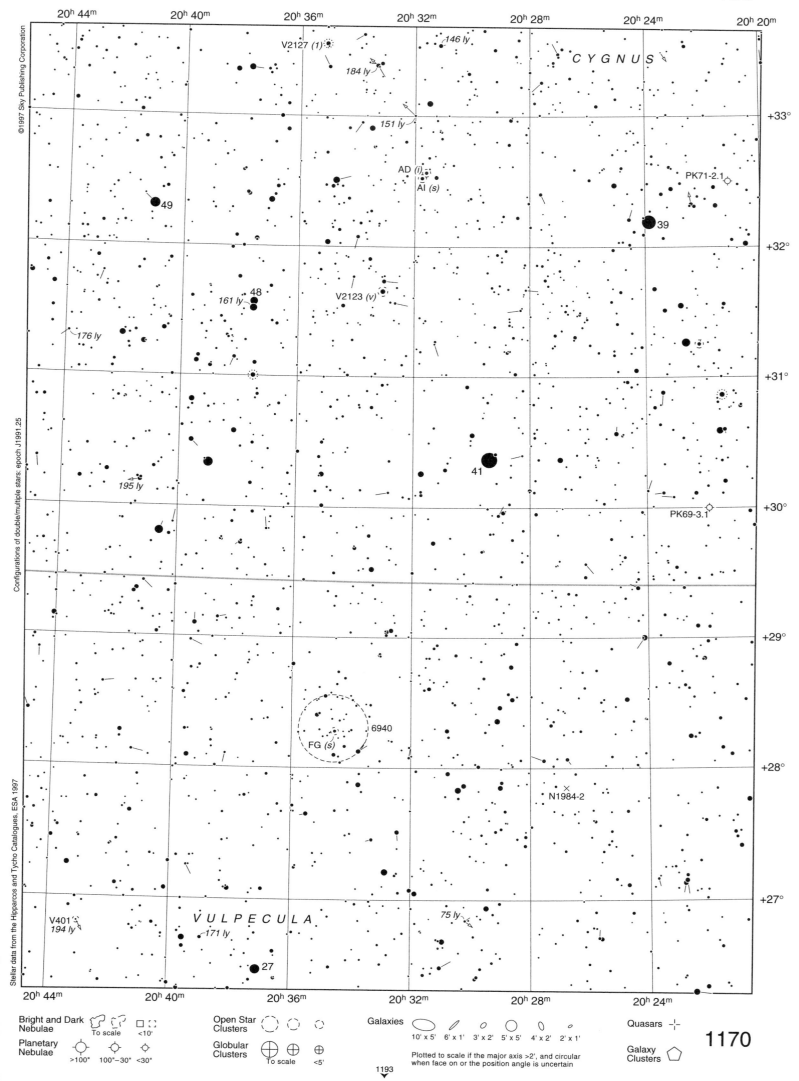

Configurations of double/multiple stars: epoch J1991.25

Stellar data from the Hipparcos and Tycho Catalogues, ESA 1997

20h 44m    20h 40m    20h 36m    20h 32m    20h 28m    20h 24m    20h 20m

V2127 (1)

146 ly

CYGNUS

+33°

184 ly

151 ly

PK71-2.1

AD (i)
AI (s)

49

39    +32°

48
161 ly    V2123 (v)

176 ly    +31°

41    PK69-3.1    +30°

195 ly

6940

FG (s)    +28°

N1984-2

+27°

V401
194 ly    VULPECULA    75 ly

171 ly

27

20h 44m    20h 40m    20h 36m    20h 32m    20h 28m    20h 24m

Bright and Dark
Nebulae          To scale    <10'          Open Star
Clusters          Galaxies          Quasars

Planetary
Nebulae          Globular
Clusters                Plotted to scale if the major axis >2', and circular
when face on or the position angle is uncertain          Galaxy
Clusters

>100"  100"-30"  <30"          To scale  <5'          10' x 5'  6' x 1'  3' x 2'  5' x 5'  4' x 2'  2' x 1'

1170

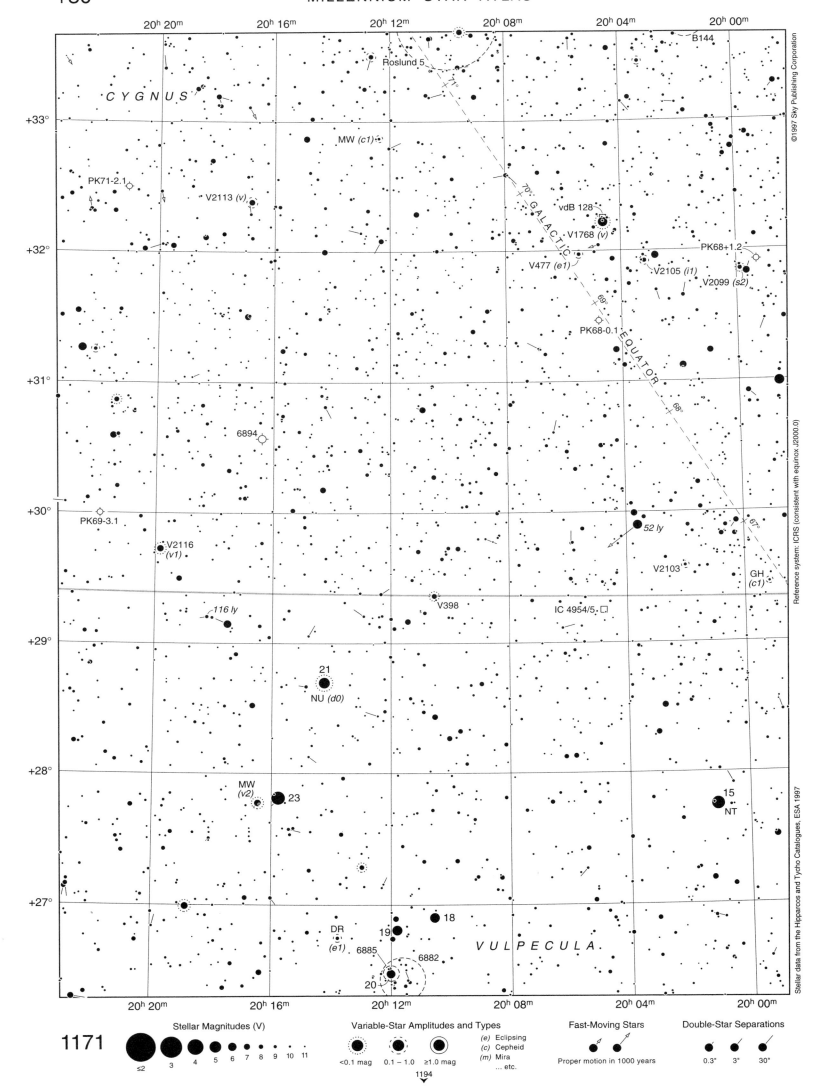

Stellar Magnitudes (V)

≤2   3   4   5   6   7   8   9   10   11

Variable-Star Amplitudes and Types

<0.1 mag   0.1 – 1.0   ≥1.0 mag

(e) Eclipsing
(c) Cepheid
(m) Mira
... etc.

Fast-Moving Stars

Proper motion in 1000 years

Double-Star Separations

0.3"   3"   30"

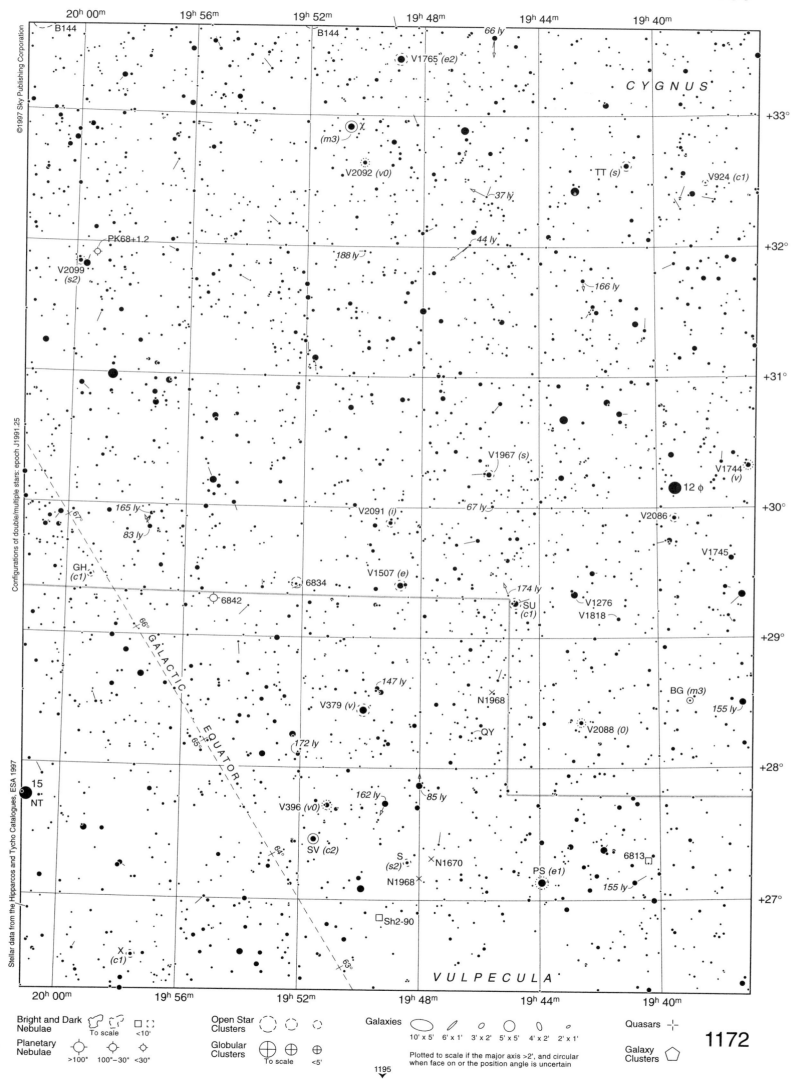

*C Y G N U S*

B144

V1765 *(e2)*

66 ly

χ
*(m3)*

V2092 *(v0)*

37 ly

TT *(s)*

V924 *(c1)*

PK68+1.2

44 ly

166 ly

V2099
*(s2)*

188 ly

V1967 *(s)*

V1744
*(v)*

12 φ

165 ly

V2091 *(i)*

67 ly

V2086

83 ly

V1745

GH
*(c1)*

6834

V1507 *(e)*

174 ly

6842

SU
*(c1)*

V1276

V1818

*G A L A C T I C*

147 ly

N1968

BG *(m3)*

V379 *(v)*

155 ly

QY

V2088 *(0)*

*E Q U A T O R*

172 ly

15
NT

162 ly

85 ly

V396 *(v0)*

SV *(c2)*

S
*(s2)*

N1670

6813

PS *(e1)*

N1968

155 ly

Sh2-90

X
*(c1)*

*V U L P E C U L A*

+33°

+32°

+31°

+30°

+29°

+28°

+27°

| Bright and Dark Nebulae | | Open Star Clusters | | Galaxies | | | | | | Quasars |
| --- | --- | --- | --- | --- | --- | --- | --- | --- | --- | --- |
| To scale | <10' | | | 10' x 5' | 6' x 1' | 3' x 2' | 5' x 5' | 4' x 2' | 2' x 1' | |
| Planetary Nebulae | | Globular Clusters | | | | | | | | Galaxy Clusters |
| >100" | 100"–30" | <30" | To scale | <5' | | | | | | |

Plotted to scale if the major axis >2', and circular when face on or the position angle is uncertain

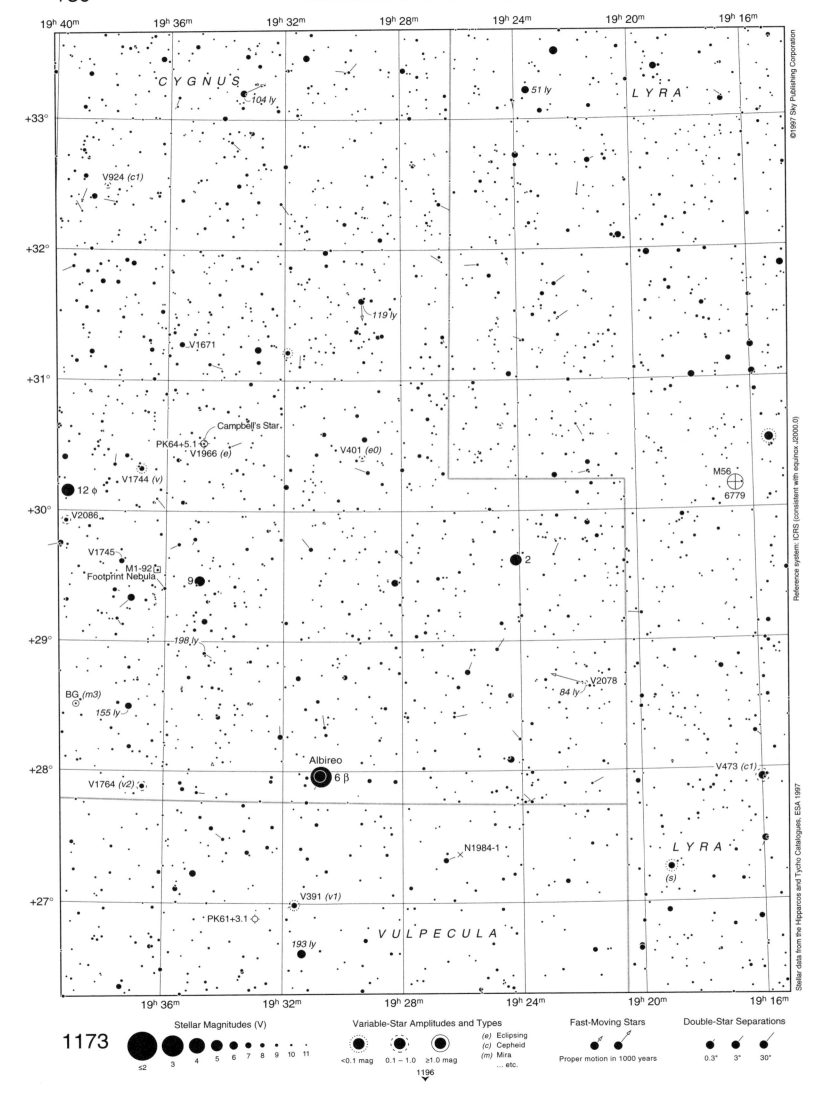

CYGNUS

LYRA

104 ly

V924 (c1)

51 ly

119 ly

V1671

Campbell's Star

PK64+5.1

V1966 (e)

V401 (e0)

M56
6779

V1744 (v)

12 φ

V2086

V1745

2

M1-92
Footprint Nebula

9

198 ly

V2078

84 ly

BG (m3)

155 ly

Albireo

6 β

V473 (c1)

V1764 (v2)

LYRA

N1984-1

(s)

V391 (v1)

PK61+3.1

VULPECULA

193 ly

1173

Stellar Magnitudes (V)

≤2    3    4    5    6   7  8  9  10 11

Variable-Star Amplitudes and Types

<0.1 mag    0.1 – 1.0    ≥1.0 mag

(e) Eclipsing
(c) Cepheid
(m) Mira
... etc.

1196

Fast-Moving Stars

Proper motion in 1000 years

Double-Star Separations

0.3"    3"    30"

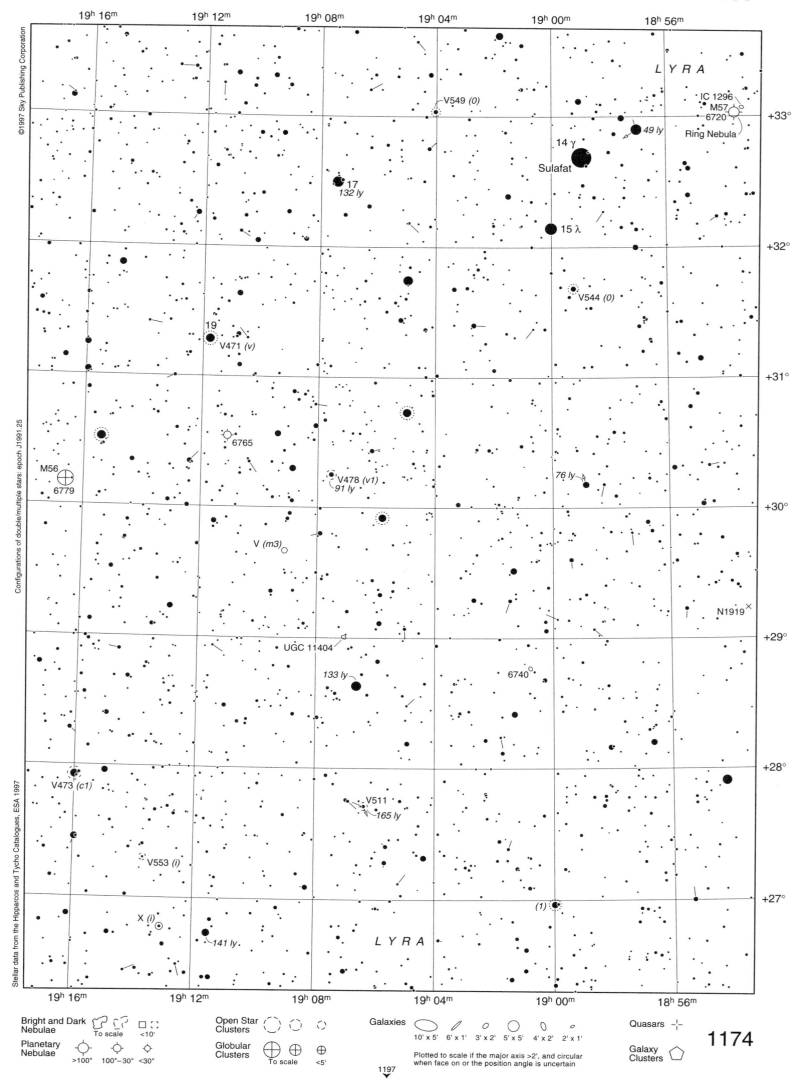

*L Y R A*

IC 1296
M57
6720
Ring Nebula

49 ly

14 γ
Sulafat

15 λ

V549 (0)

17
132 ly

V544 (0)

19
V471 (v)

6765

M56
6779

V478 (v1)
91 ly

76 ly

V (m3)

N1919

UGC 11404

6740

133 ly

V473 (c1)

V511
165 ly

V553 (i)

(1)

X (i)

141 ly

*L Y R A*

| Bright and Dark Nebulae | Open Star Clusters | Galaxies | Quasars |
| --- | --- | --- | --- |

Bright and Dark Nebulae
To scale      <10'

Planetary Nebulae
>100"   100"–30"   <30"

Open Star Clusters

Globular Clusters
To scale   <5'

Galaxies
10' x 5'   6' x 1'   3' x 2'   5' x 5'   4' x 2'   2' x 1'

Plotted to scale if the major axis >2', and circular when face on or the position angle is uncertain

Quasars

Galaxy Clusters

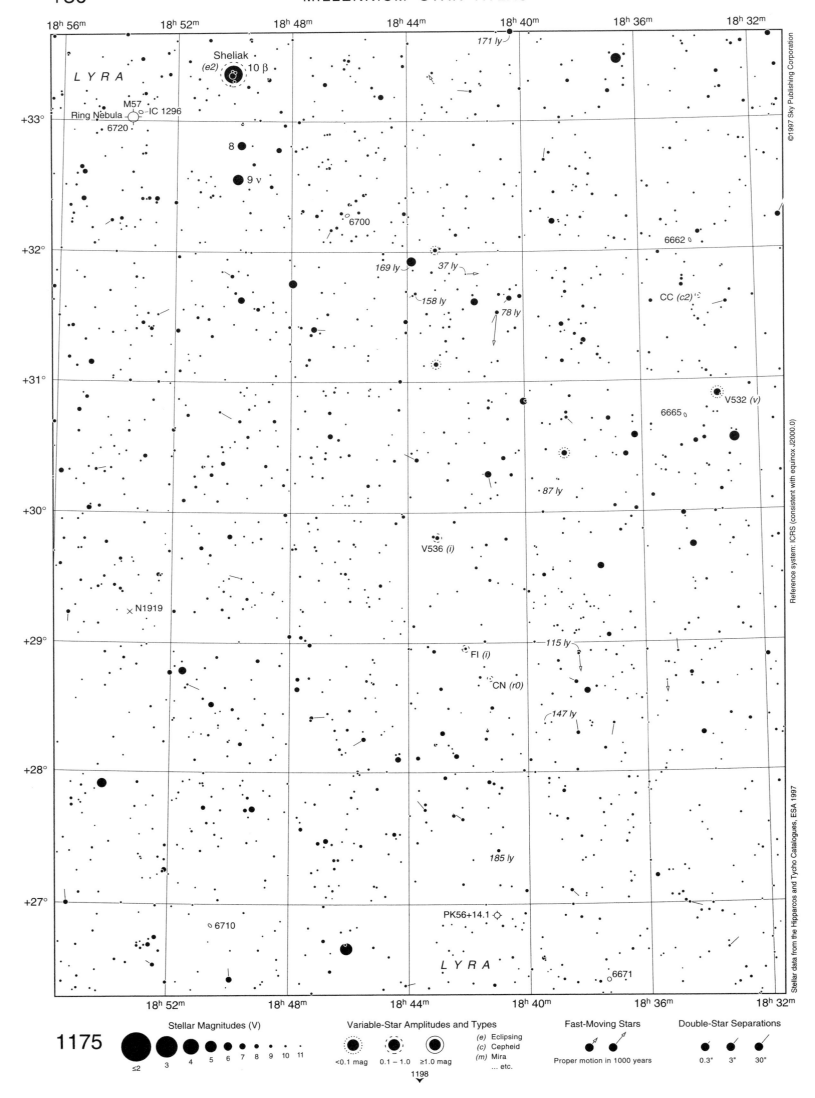

©1997 Sky Publishing Corporation

Reference system: ICRS (consistent with equinox J2000.0)

Stellar data from the Hipparcos and Tycho Catalogues, ESA 1997

1175

Stellar Magnitudes (V)

≤2   3   4   5   6   7   8   9   10   11

Variable-Star Amplitudes and Types

<0.1 mag   0.1 – 1.0   ≥1.0 mag

(e) Eclipsing
(c) Cepheid
(m) Mira
... etc.

Fast-Moving Stars

Proper motion in 1000 years

Double-Star Separations

0.3"   3"   30"

1198

# MILLENNIUM STAR ATLAS

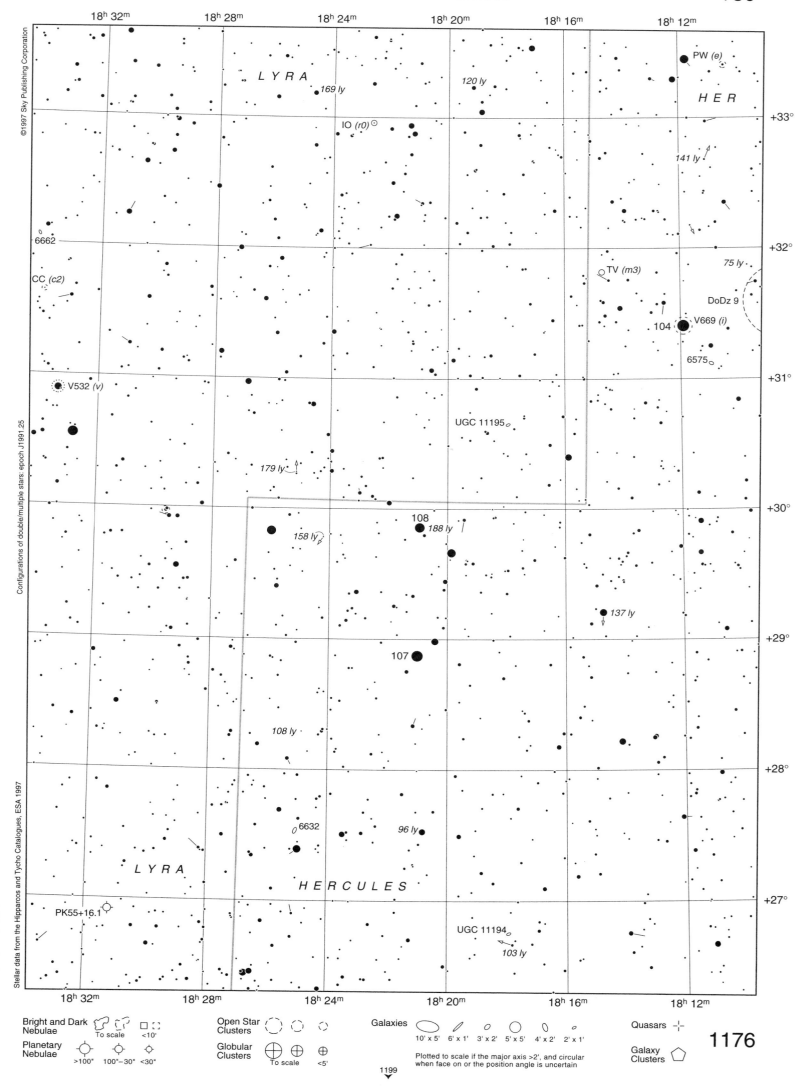

18h 32m   18h 28m   18h 24m   18h 20m   18h 16m   18h 12m

+33°
+32°
+31°
+30°
+29°
+28°
+27°

L Y R A

H E R

PW (e)

169 ly
120 ly

IO (r0)

141 ly

6662

CC (c2)

TV (m3)

75 ly

DoDz 9

104  V669 (i)

6575

V532 (v)

UGC 11195

179 ly

108  188 ly

158 ly

137 ly

107

108 ly

6632

96 ly

L Y R A

H E R C U L E S

PK55+16.1

UGC 11194

103 ly

Bright and Dark Nebulae     To scale     <10'

Planetary Nebulae     >100"   100"-30"   <30"

Open Star Clusters

Globular Clusters     To scale     <5'

Galaxies     10' x 5'   6' x 1'   3' x 2'   5' x 5'   4' x 2'   2' x 1'

Plotted to scale if the major axis >2', and circular when face on or the position angle is uncertain

Quasars

Galaxy Clusters

**1176**

+30°

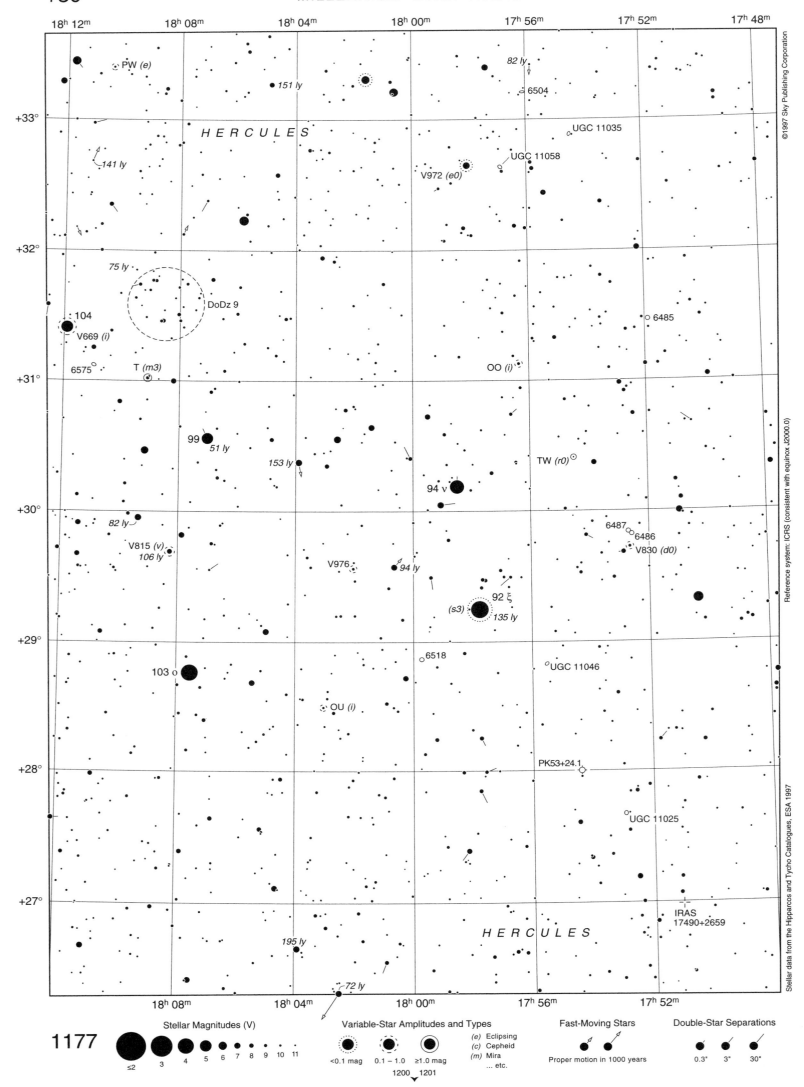

H E R C U L E S

PW (e)
151 ly
82 ly
6504
UGC 11035
UGC 11058
V972 (e0)
141 ly
75 ly
DoDz 9
104
V669 (i)
6485
6575
T (m3)
OO (i)
99
51 ly
153 ly
TW (r0)
94 ν
82 ly
6487
6486
V815 (v)
V830 (d0)
106 ly
V976
94 ly
92 ξ
(s3)
135 ly
6518
UGC 11046
103 o
OU (i)
PK53+24.1
UGC 11025
IRAS
17490+2659
H E R C U L E S
195 ly
72 ly

1177

Stellar Magnitudes (V)
≤2  3  4  5  6 7 8 9 10 11

Variable-Star Amplitudes and Types
<0.1 mag   0.1 – 1.0   ≥1.0 mag
1200   1201

(e) Eclipsing
(c) Cepheid
(m) Mira
... etc.

Fast-Moving Stars
Proper motion in 1000 years

Double-Star Separations
0.3"  3"  30"

©1997 Sky Publishing Corporation

Reference system: ICRS (consistent with equinox J2000.0)

Stellar data from the Hipparcos and Tycho Catalogues, ESA 1997

# MILLENNIUM STAR ATLAS

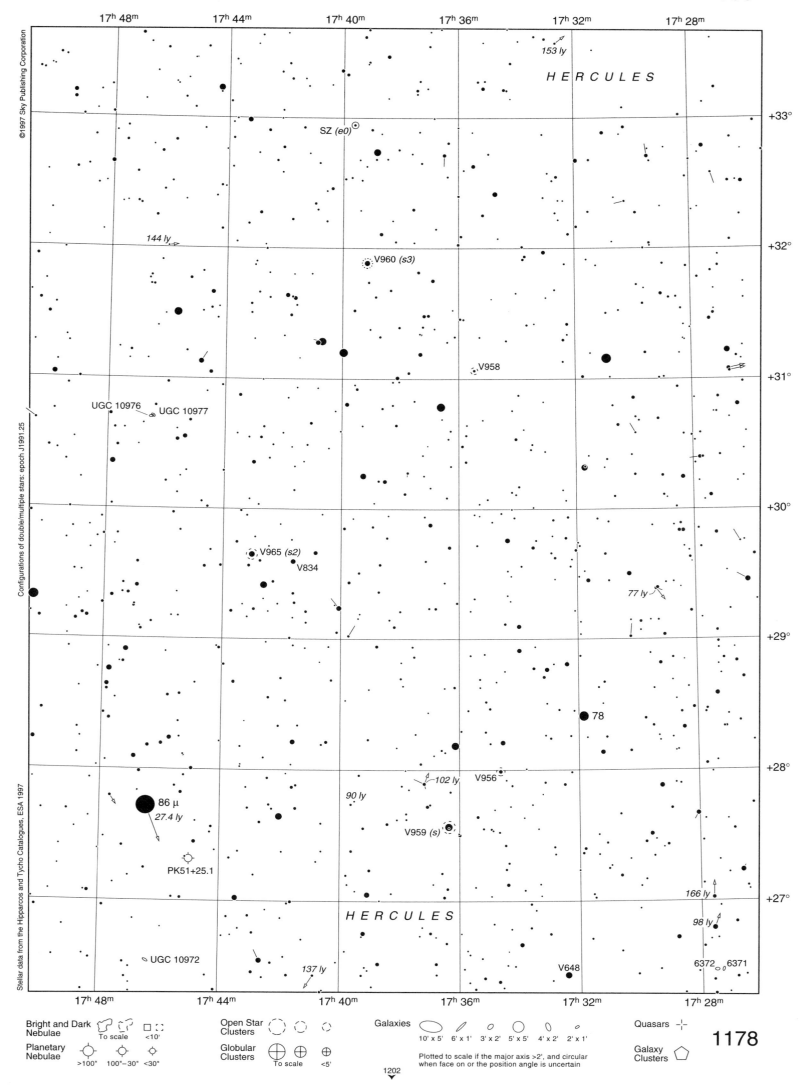

Configurations of double/multiple stars: epoch J1991.25

Stellar data from the Hipparcos and Tycho Catalogues, ESA 1997

H E R C U L E S

153 ly

SZ (e0)

+33°

144 ly

V960 (s3)

+32°

V958

+31°

UGC 10976    UGC 10977

V965 (s2)
V834

77 ly

+30°

+29°

78

86 μ
27.4 ly

102 ly
90 ly

V956

+28°

V959 (s)

PK51+25.1

166 ly

+27°

H E R C U L E S

98 ly

UGC 10972

137 ly

V648

6372  6371

17ʰ 48ᵐ    17ʰ 44ᵐ    17ʰ 40ᵐ    17ʰ 36ᵐ    17ʰ 32ᵐ    17ʰ 28ᵐ

| Bright and Dark Nebulae | Open Star Clusters | Galaxies | Quasars |
|---|---|---|---|

Bright and Dark Nebulae    To scale    <10'

Open Star Clusters

Galaxies
10' x 5'   6' x 1'   3' x 2'   5' x 5'   4' x 2'   2' x 1'

Quasars

Planetary Nebulae
>100"   100"-30"   <30"

Globular Clusters
To scale   <5'

Plotted to scale if the major axis >2', and circular
when face on or the position angle is uncertain

Galaxy Clusters

1178

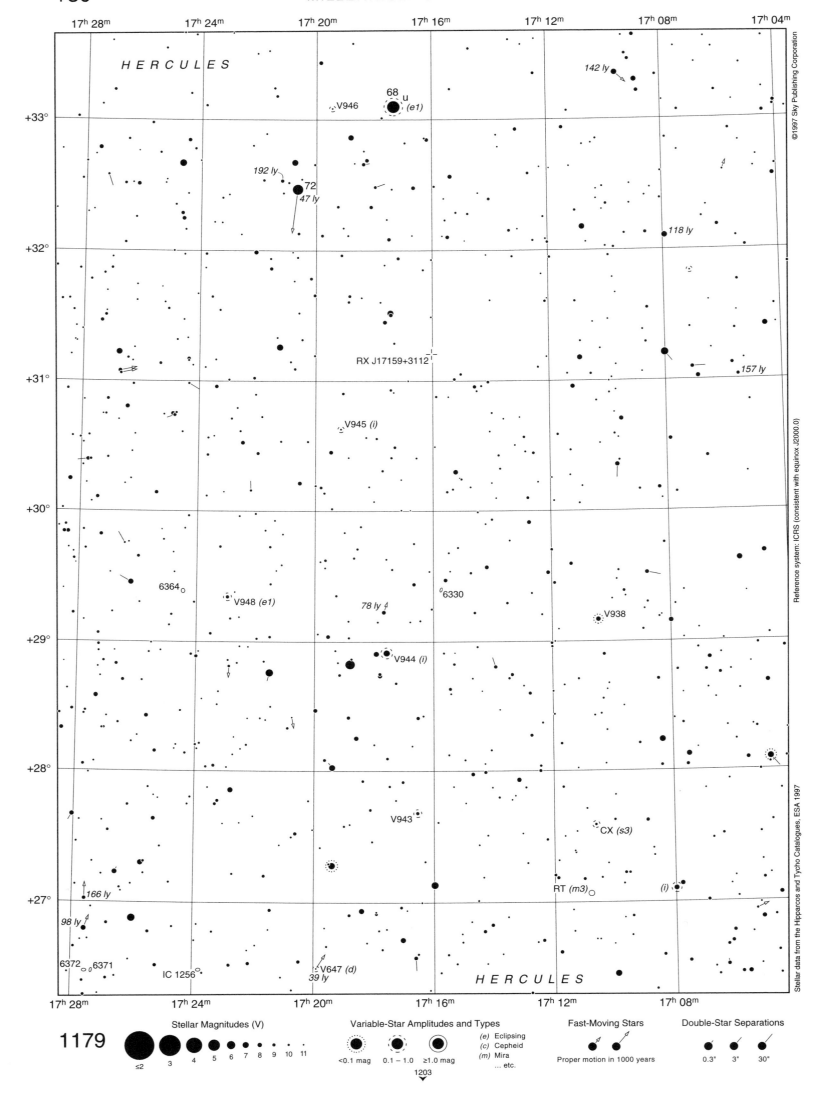

©1997 Sky Publishing Corporation

Reference system: ICRS (consistent with equinox J2000.0)

Stellar data from the Hipparcos and Tycho Catalogues, ESA 1997

HERCULES

68 u
(e1)
V946

192 ly
72
47 ly

142 ly

118 ly

157 ly

RX J17159+3112

V945 (i)

6364
V948 (e1)
78 ly
6330
V938

V944 (i)

V943
CX (s3)

RT (m3)
(i)

166 ly

98 ly

6372  6371
IC 1256
V647 (d)
39 ly

HERCULES

1179

Stellar Magnitudes (V)
≤2  3  4  5  6  7  8  9  10  11

Variable-Star Amplitudes and Types
<0.1 mag    0.1 – 1.0    ≥1.0 mag

(e) Eclipsing
(c) Cepheid
(m) Mira
... etc.

Fast-Moving Stars
Proper motion in 1000 years

Double-Star Separations
0.3"    3"    30"

1203

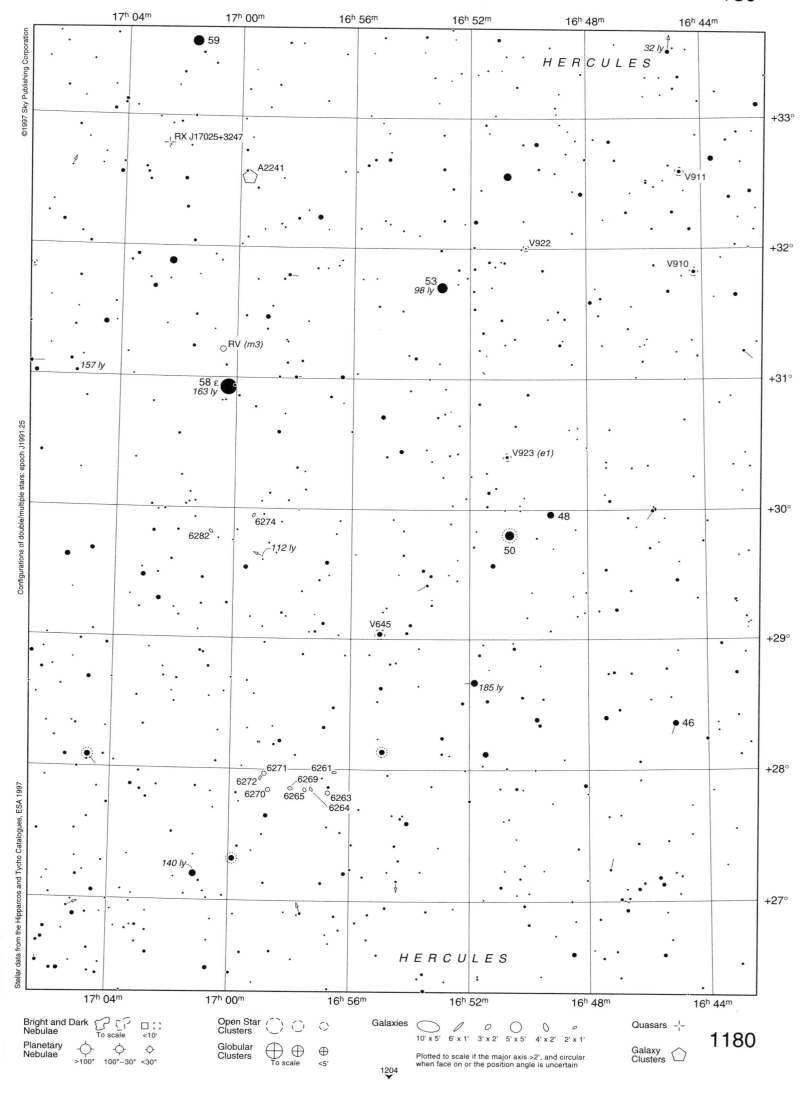

HERCULES

RX J17025+3247

A2241

V911

V922

53
98 ly

RV (m3)

V910

58 ε
163 ly

157 ly

V923 (e1)

6274

48

6282

50

112 ly

V645

185 ly

46

6271   6261
6272   6269
6270   6265   6263
              6264

140 ly

HERCULES

17ʰ 04ᵐ      17ʰ 00ᵐ      16ʰ 56ᵐ      16ʰ 52ᵐ      16ʰ 48ᵐ      16ʰ 44ᵐ

+33°
+32°
+31°
+30°
+29°
+28°
+27°

Bright and Dark
Nebulae
To scale        <10'

Planetary
Nebulae
>100"   100"–30"   <30"

Open Star
Clusters

Globular
Clusters
To scale        <5'

Galaxies
10' x 5'   6' x 1'   3' x 2'   5' x 5'   4' x 2'   2' x 1'

Plotted to scale if the major axis >2', and circular
when face on or the position angle is uncertain

Quasars

Galaxy
Clusters

1180

▼
1204

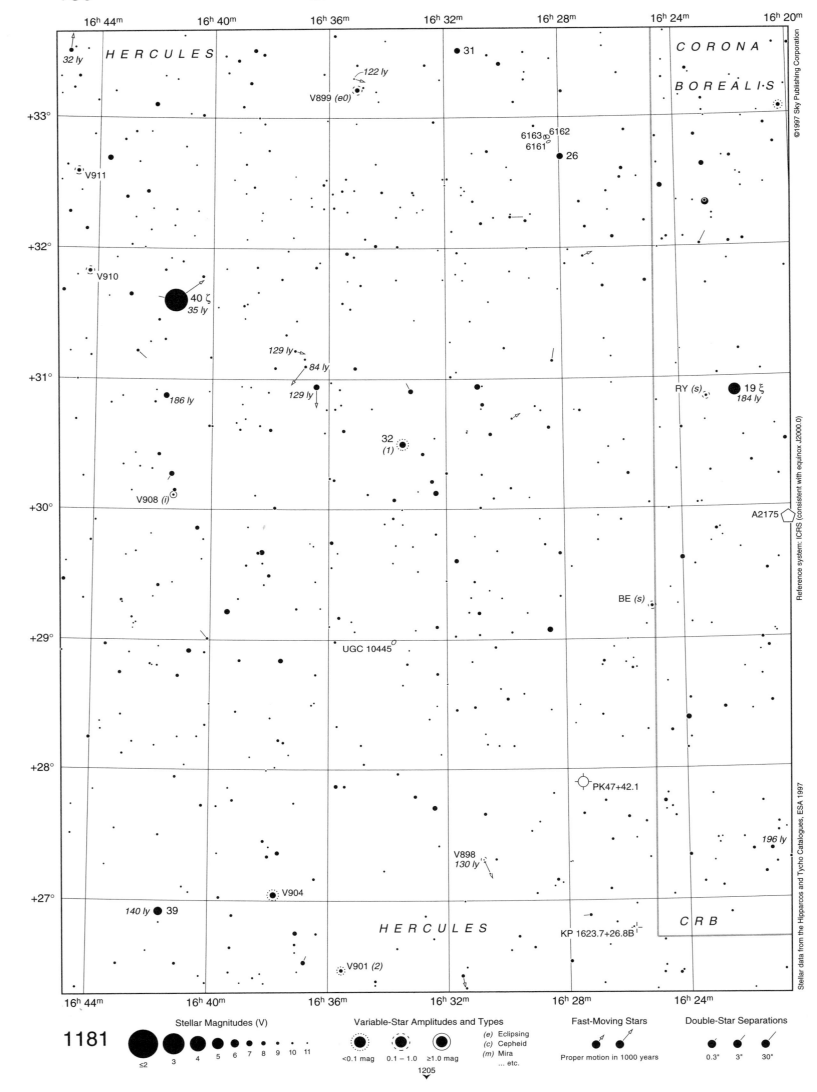

Reference system: ICRS (consistent with equinox J2000.0)

Stellar data from the Hipparcos and Tycho Catalogues, ESA 1997

Stellar Magnitudes (V)

≤2    3    4    5   6   7   8   9  10  11

Variable-Star Amplitudes and Types

<0.1 mag    0.1 – 1.0    ≥1.0 mag

(e) Eclipsing
(c) Cepheid
(m) Mira
... etc.

1205

Fast-Moving Stars

Proper motion in 1000 years

Double-Star Separations

0.3"    3"    30"

MILLENNIUM STAR ATLAS

+30°

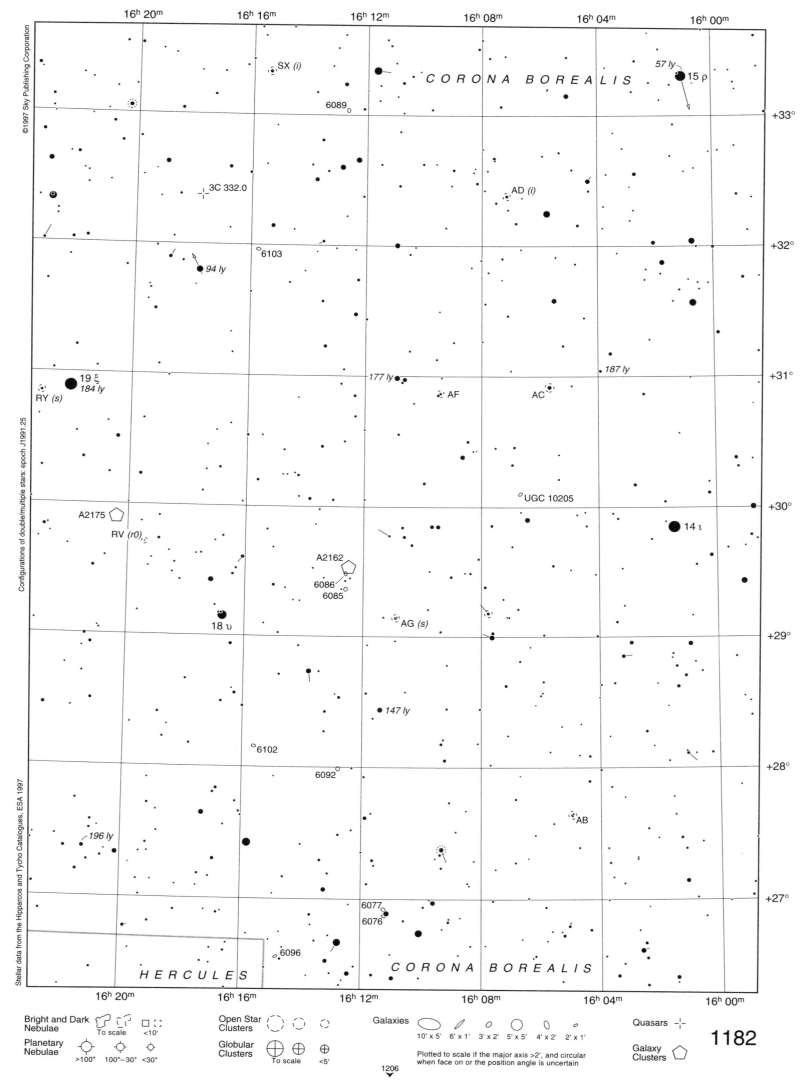

16h 20m   16h 16m   16h 12m   16h 08m   16h 04m   16h 00m

+33°

+32°

+31°

+30°

+29°

+28°

+27°

SX (i)
6089

*C O R O N A   B O R E A L I S*

*57 ly*
15 ρ

3C 332.0

AD (i)

6103

*94 ly*

19 ξ
*184 ly*
RY (s)

*177 ly*
AF

AC

*187 ly*

UGC 10205

A2175

RV (r0)

A2162
6086
6085

AG (s)

14 ι

18 υ

*147 ly*

6102

6092

AB

*196 ly*

6077
6076

6096

*H E R C U L E S*

*C O R O N A   B O R E A L I S*

16h 20m   16h 16m   16h 12m   16h 08m   16h 04m   16h 00m

| Bright and Dark Nebulae | Open Star Clusters | Galaxies | Quasars |
|---|---|---|---|

To scale    <10'

Planetary Nebulae    >100"  100"–30"  <30'

Globular Clusters    To scale  <5'

10' x 5'  6' x 1'  3' x 2'  5' x 5'  4' x 2'  2' x 1'

Galaxy Clusters

Plotted to scale if the major axis >2', and circular when face on or the position angle is uncertain

1182

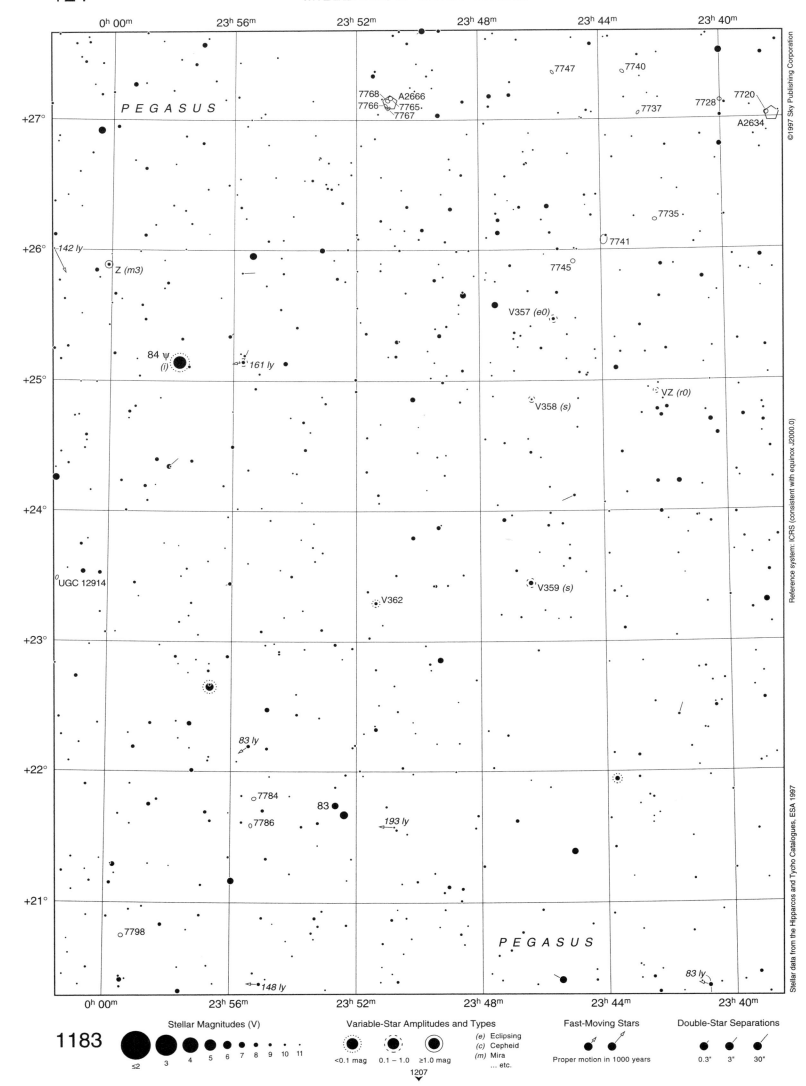

PEGASUS

7747
7740
7768 A2666
7766 7765
7767
7728 7720
7737
A2634

142 ly
Z (m3)
7735

7741
7745

V357 (e0)

84 ψ
(i)
161 ly
VZ (r0)

V358 (s)

UGC 12914
V359 (s)

V362

83 ly

7784
7786
83
193 ly

7798

148 ly
PEGASUS
83 ly

1183

Stellar Magnitudes (V)

≤2  3  4  5  6  7  8  9  10  11

Variable-Star Amplitudes and Types

<0.1 mag   0.1 – 1.0   ≥1.0 mag

(e) Eclipsing
(c) Cepheid
(m) Mira
... etc.

1207

Fast-Moving Stars

Proper motion in 1000 years

Double-Star Separations

0.3"   3"   30"

# MILLENNIUM STAR ATLAS

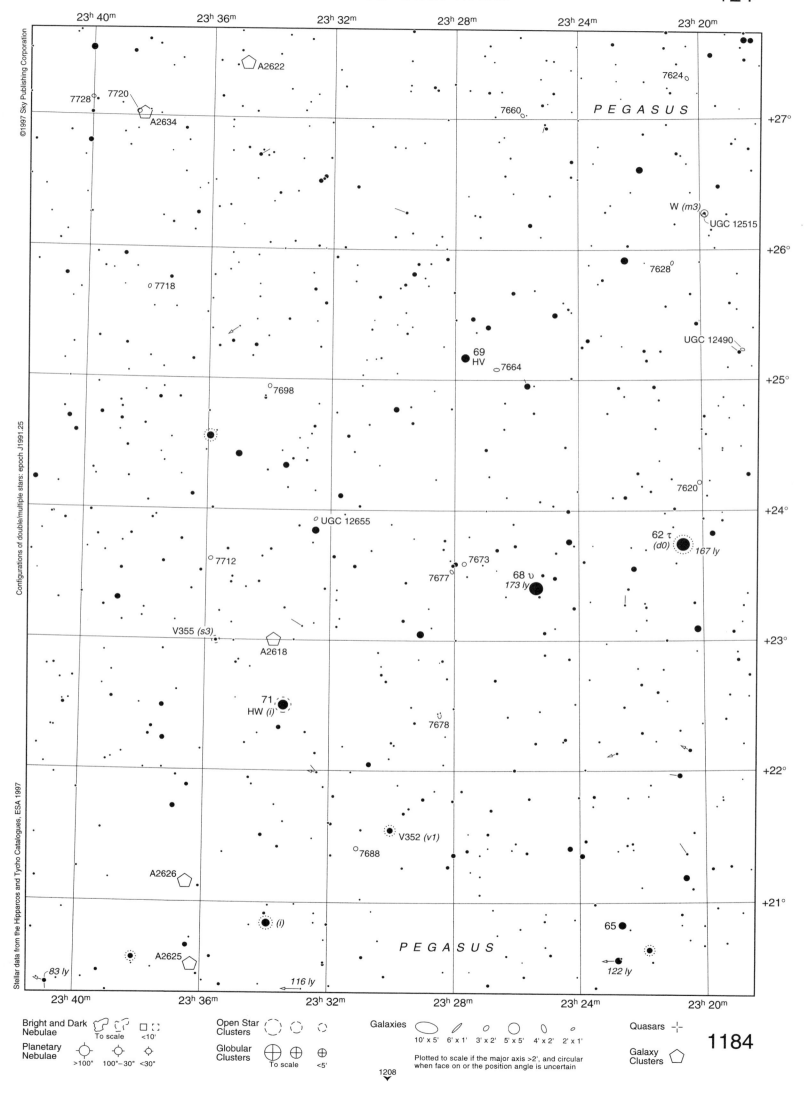

Configurations of double/multiple stars: epoch J1991.25

Stellar data from the Hipparcos and Tycho Catalogues, ESA 1997

23h 40m   23h 36m   23h 32m   23h 28m   23h 24m   23h 20m

A2622

7728   7720
A2634

7660

P E G A S U S

7624

+27°

W *(m3)*
UGC 12515

7718

7628

+26°

UGC 12490

69
HV

7664

+25°

7698

7620

+24°

UGC 12655

62 τ
*(d0)*   *167 ly*

7712

7673

68 υ
*173 ly*

7677

V355 *(s3)*

A2618

+23°

71

7678

HW *(i)*

+22°

V352 *(v1)*

7688

A2626

+21°

*(i)*

65

A2625

*83 ly*

P E G A S U S

*122 ly*

*116 ly*

23h 40m   23h 36m   23h 32m   23h 28m   23h 24m   23h 20m

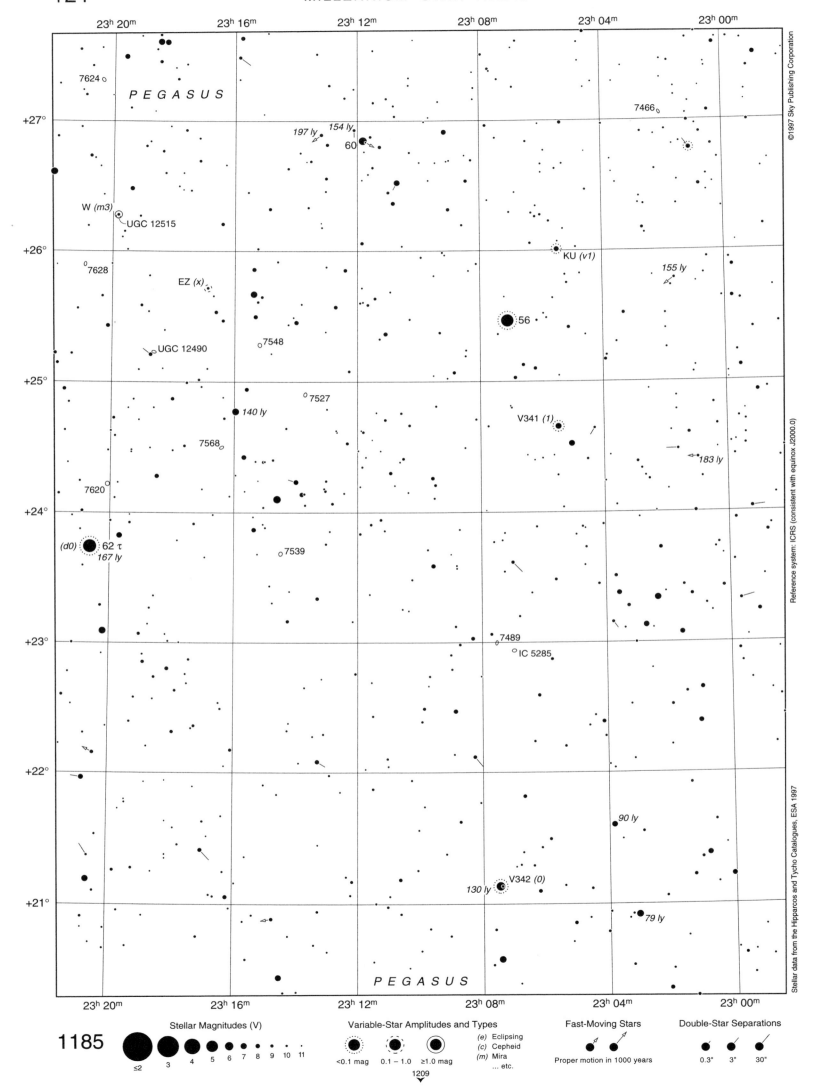

PEGASUS

7624

197 ly    154 ly
60

W (m3)
UGC 12515

7466

KU (v1)

7628

EZ (x)

155 ly

56

UGC 12490    7548

7527

140 ly

V341 (1)

7568

183 ly

7620

(d0)  62 τ
167 ly

7539

7489
IC 5285

90 ly

V342 (0)
130 ly

79 ly

PEGASUS

1185

Stellar Magnitudes (V)

≤2    3    4    5    6    7    8    9    10    11

Variable-Star Amplitudes and Types

<0.1 mag    0.1 – 1.0    ≥1.0 mag

(e) Eclipsing
(c) Cepheid
(m) Mira
... etc.

Fast-Moving Stars

Proper motion in 1000 years

Double-Star Separations

0.3"    3"    30"

1209

# MILLENNIUM STAR ATLAS

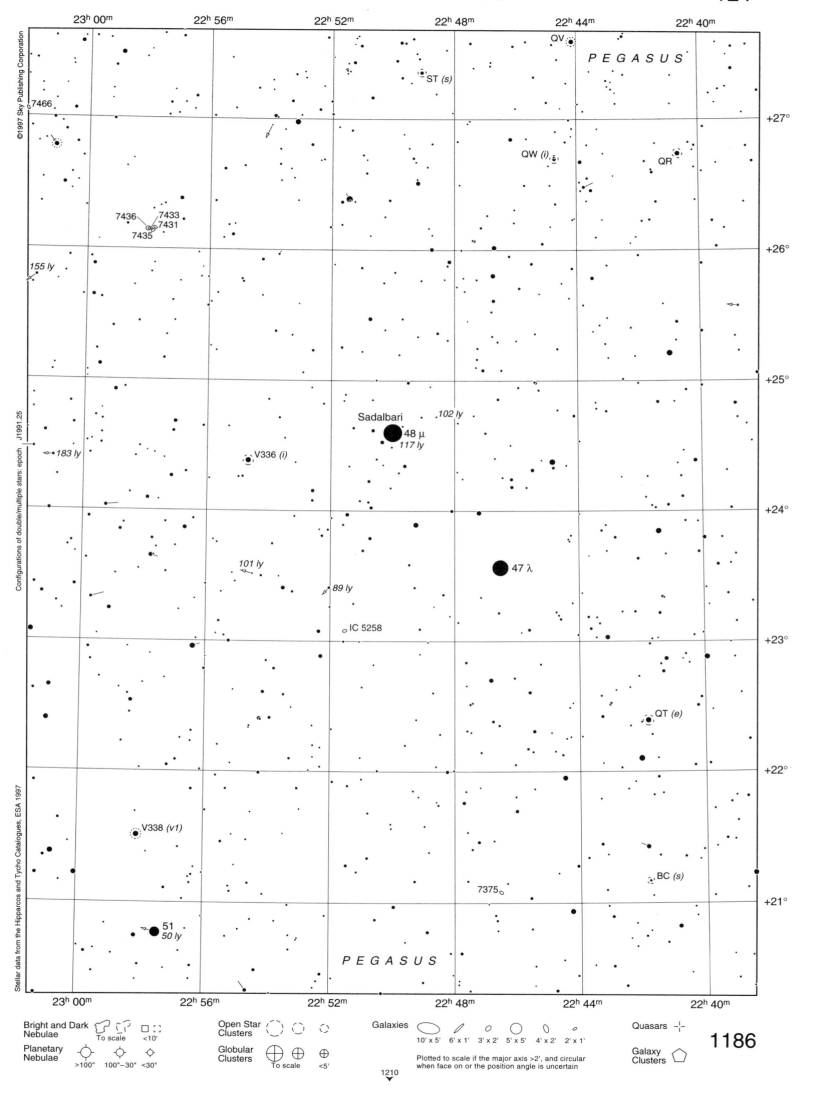

Configurations of double/multiple stars: epoch J1991.25

Stellar data from the Hipparcos and Tycho Catalogues, ESA 1997

23h 00m   22h 56m   22h 52m   22h 48m   22h 44m   22h 40m

PEGASUS

QV

ST (s)

QW (i)

QR

7466

7436  7433
7431
7435

+27°

+26°

155 ly

183 ly

Sadalbari    102 ly
48 μ
117 ly

V336 (i)

+25°

47 λ

101 ly

89 ly

IC 5258

+24°

+23°

QT (e)

BC (s)

7375

+22°

V338 (v1)

51
50 ly

PEGASUS

+21°

23h 00m   22h 56m   22h 52m   22h 48m   22h 44m   22h 40m

Bright and Dark
Nebulae
To scale   <10'

Planetary
Nebulae
>100"  100"–30"  <30"

Open Star
Clusters

Globular
Clusters
To scale   <5'

Galaxies
10' x 5'  6' x 1'  3' x 2'  5' x 5'  4' x 2'  2' x 1'

Plotted to scale if the major axis >2', and circular
when face on or the position angle is uncertain

Quasars

Galaxy
Clusters

1186

1210

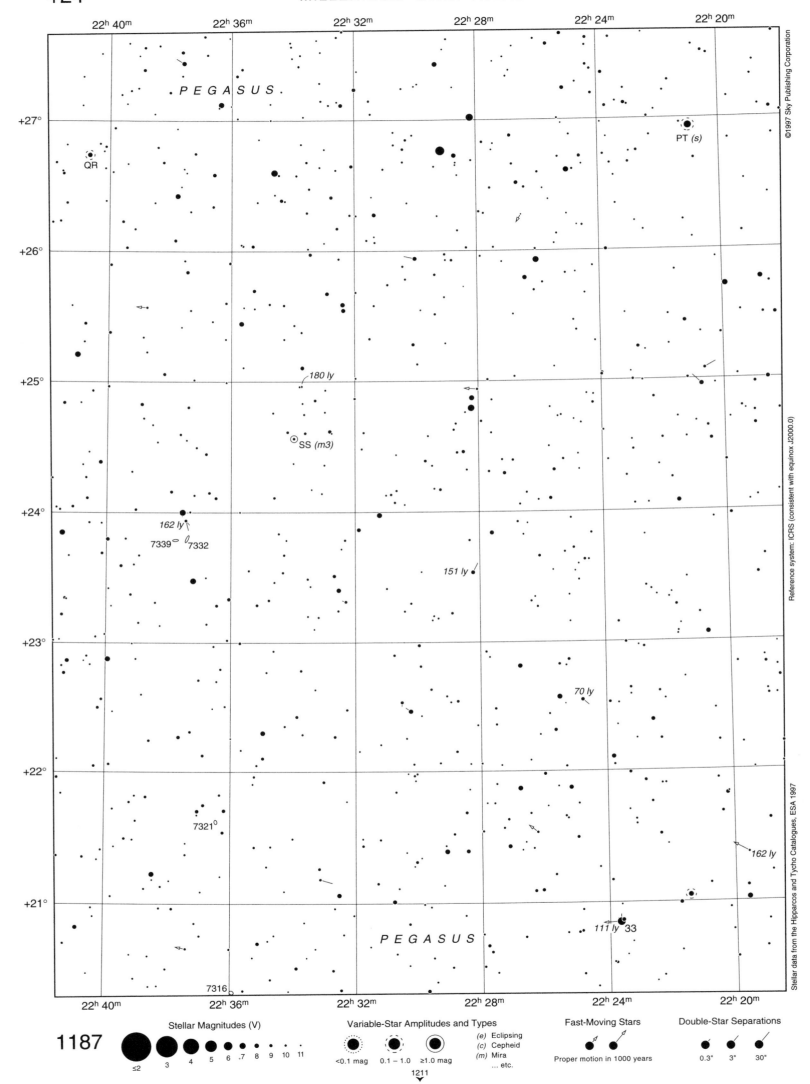

©1997 Sky Publishing Corporation

Reference system: ICRS (consistent with equinox J2000.0)

Stellar data from the Hipparcos and Tycho Catalogues, ESA 1997

P E G A S U S

+27°

PT (s)

QR

180 ly

SS (m3)

+24°

162 ly

7339 ○ ○ 7332

151 ly •

+23°

70 ly

+22°

7321 ○

162 ly

+21°

111 ly 33

P E G A S U S

7316 ○

1187

Stellar Magnitudes (V)

≤2    3    4    5    6   .7  8  9  10  11

Variable-Star Amplitudes and Types

<0.1 mag   0.1 – 1.0   ≥1.0 mag

(e) Eclipsing
(c) Cepheid
(m) Mira
... etc.

Fast-Moving Stars

Proper motion in 1000 years

Double-Star Separations

0.3"   3"   30"

# MILLENNIUM STAR ATLAS

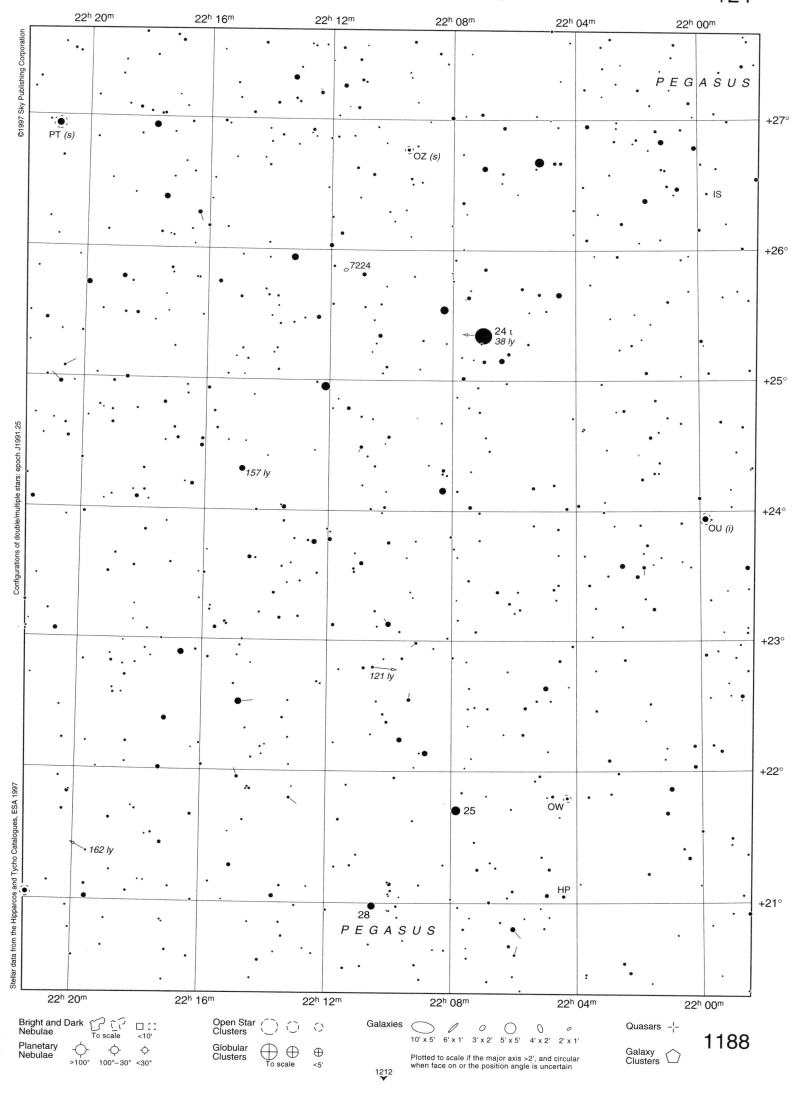

PEGASUS

PT (s)

OZ (s)

IS

7224

24 ι
38 ly

157 ly

OU (i)

121 ly

162 ly

25

OW

HP

28

PEGASUS

| Bright and Dark Nebulae | Open Star Clusters | Galaxies | Quasars |
|---|---|---|---|

To scale    <10'

Planetary Nebulae
>100"  100"–30"  <30"

Open Star Clusters

Globular Clusters
To scale    <5'

Galaxies
10' x 5'   6' x 1'   3' x 2'   5' x 5'   4' x 2'   2' x 1'

Plotted to scale if the major axis >2', and circular when face on or the position angle is uncertain

Quasars

Galaxy Clusters

1188

1212

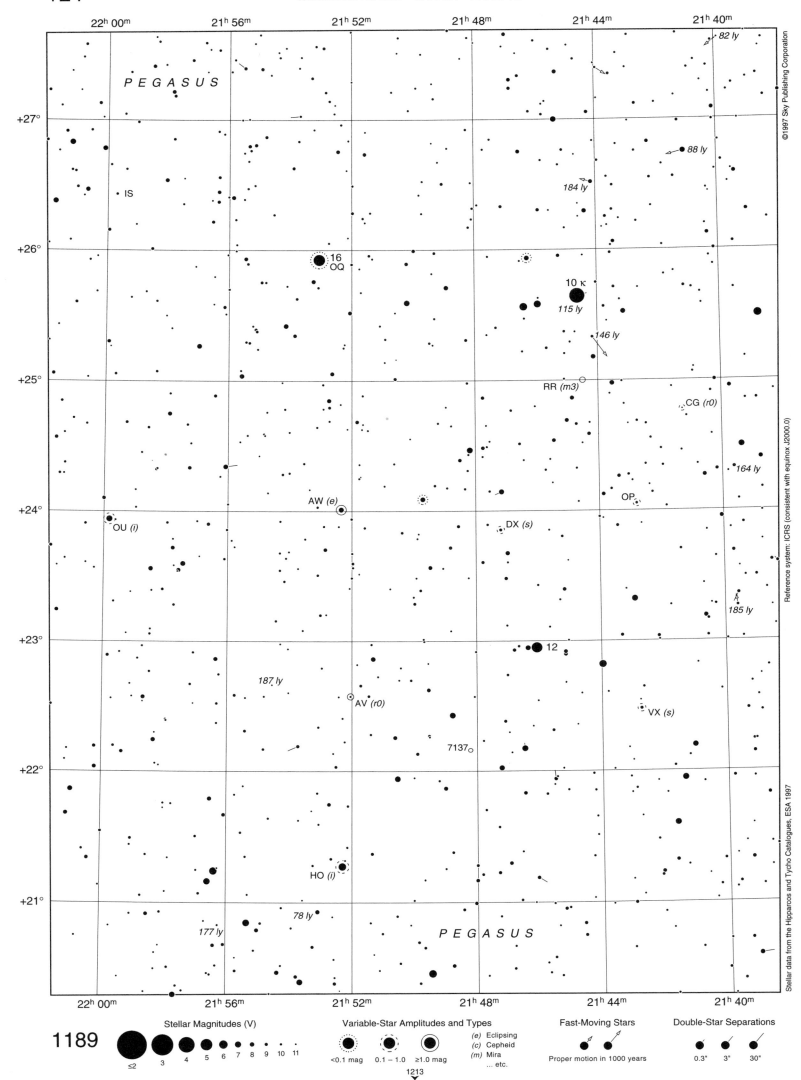

©1997 Sky Publishing Corporation

Reference system: ICRS (consistent with equinox J2000.0)

Stellar data from the Hipparcos and Tycho Catalogues, ESA 1997

PEGASUS

IS

16 OQ

10 κ
115 ly

146 ly

RR (m3)

CG (r0)

164 ly

OP

AW (e)

DX (s)

OU (i)

185 ly

12

187 ly

AV (r0)

VX (s)

7137

HO (i)

78 ly

177 ly

PEGASUS

1189

Stellar Magnitudes (V)
≤2 3 4 5 6 7 8 9 10 11

Variable-Star Amplitudes and Types
<0.1 mag    0.1 – 1.0    ≥1.0 mag

(e) Eclipsing
(c) Cepheid
(m) Mira
... etc.

Fast-Moving Stars
Proper motion in 1000 years

Double-Star Separations
0.3"  3"  30"

# MILLENNIUM STAR ATLAS

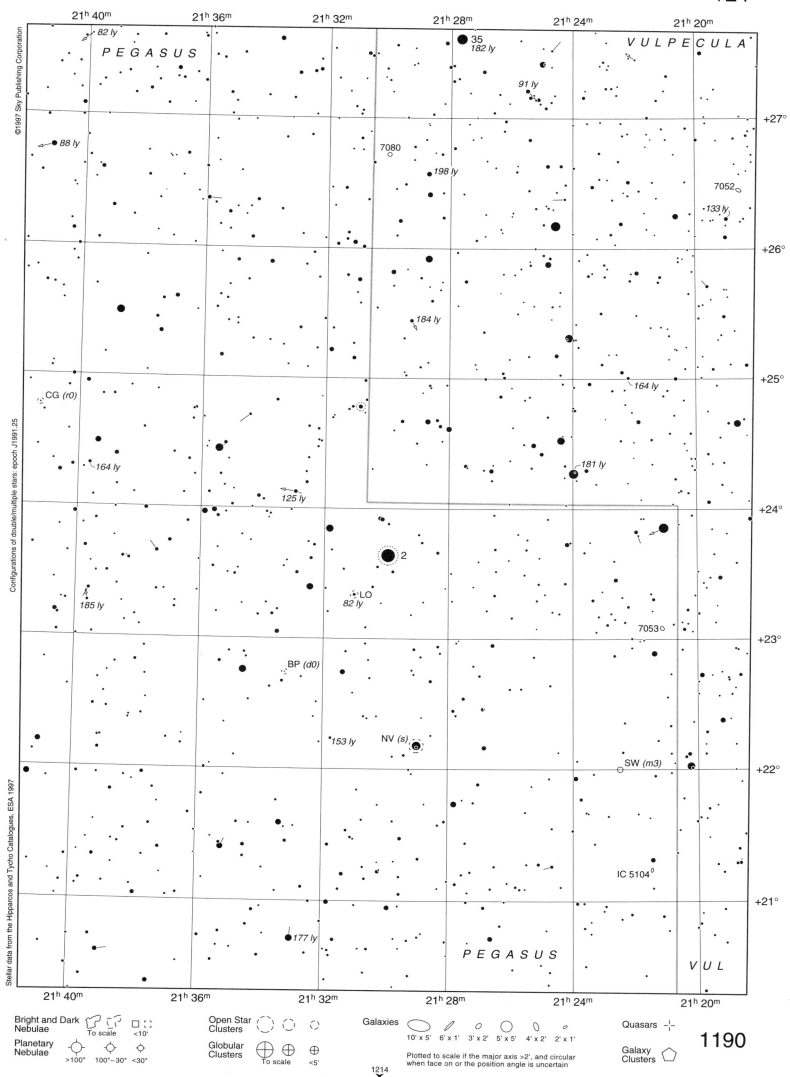

©1997 Sky Publishing Corporation

Configurations of double/multiple stars: epoch J1991.25

Stellar data from the Hipparcos and Tycho Catalogues, ESA 1997

21h 40m  21h 36m  21h 32m  21h 28m  21h 24m  21h 20m

P E G A S U S

V U L P E C U L A

82 ly
35
182 ly
91 ly
7080
198 ly
7052
133 ly
+27°
+26°
184 ly
164 ly
+25°
CG (r0)
181 ly
164 ly
125 ly
+24°
2
185 ly
LO
82 ly
7053
+23°
BP (d0)
153 ly
NV (s)
SW (m3)
+22°
IC 5104
+21°
177 ly

P E G A S U S

V U L

88 ly

Bright and Dark Nebulae    To scale    <10'
Planetary Nebulae    >100"  100"–30"  <30"

Open Star Clusters
Globular Clusters    To scale    <5'

Galaxies
10' x 5'  6' x 1'  3' x 2'  5' x 5'  4' x 2'  2' x 1'
Plotted to scale if the major axis >2', and circular when face on or the position angle is uncertain

Quasars

Galaxy Clusters

**1190**

1168

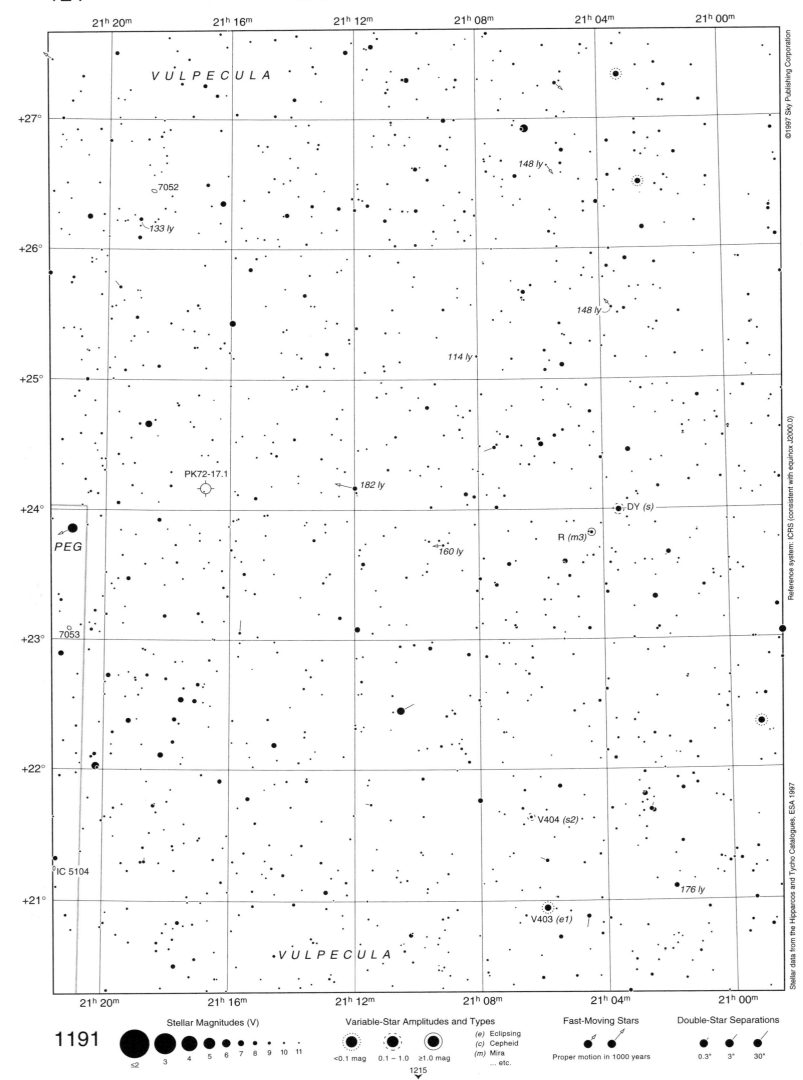

©1997 Sky Publishing Corporation

Reference system: ICRS (consistent with equinox J2000.0)

Stellar data from the Hipparcos and Tycho Catalogues, ESA 1997

1191

**Stellar Magnitudes (V)**

≤2   3   4   5   6   7   8   9   10   11

**Variable-Star Amplitudes and Types**

<0.1 mag    0.1 – 1.0 mag    ≥1.0 mag

(e) Eclipsing
(c) Cepheid
(m) Mira
... etc.

1215

**Fast-Moving Stars**

Proper motion in 1000 years

**Double-Star Separations**

0.3"    3"    30"

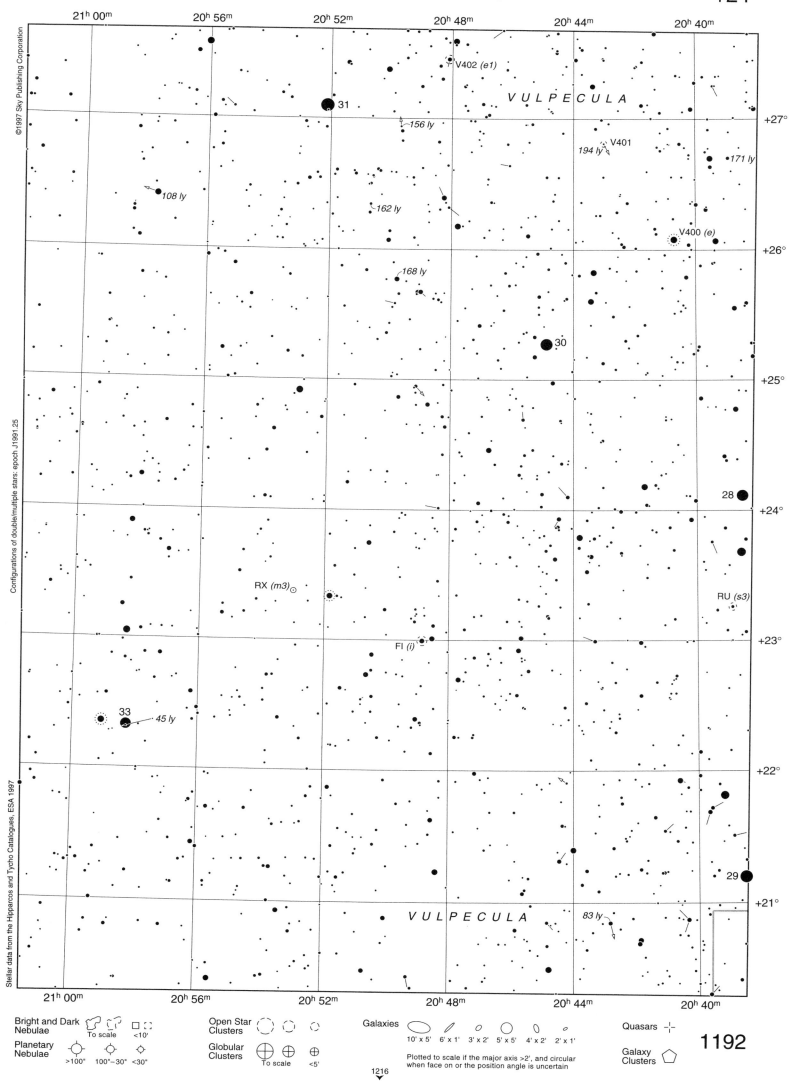

21h 00m    20h 56m    20h 52m    20h 48m    20h 44m    20h 40m

V402 (e1)

V U L P E C U L A

156 ly

194 ly  V401

171 ly

108 ly

162 ly

V400 (e)

168 ly

30

RX (m3)

RU (s3)

28

FI (i)

33    45 ly

29

V U L P E C U L A    83 ly

+27°
+26°
+25°
+24°
+23°
+22°
+21°

31

21h 00m    20h 56m    20h 52m    20h 48m    20h 44m    20h 40m

Bright and Dark
Nebulae          To scale   <10'

Planetary
Nebulae     >100"   100"–30"   <30"

Open Star
Clusters

Globular
Clusters    To scale   <5'

Galaxies

10' x 5'  6' x 1'  3' x 2'  5' x 5'  4' x 2'  2' x 1'

Plotted to scale if the major axis >2', and circular
when face on or the position angle is uncertain

Quasars

Galaxy
Clusters

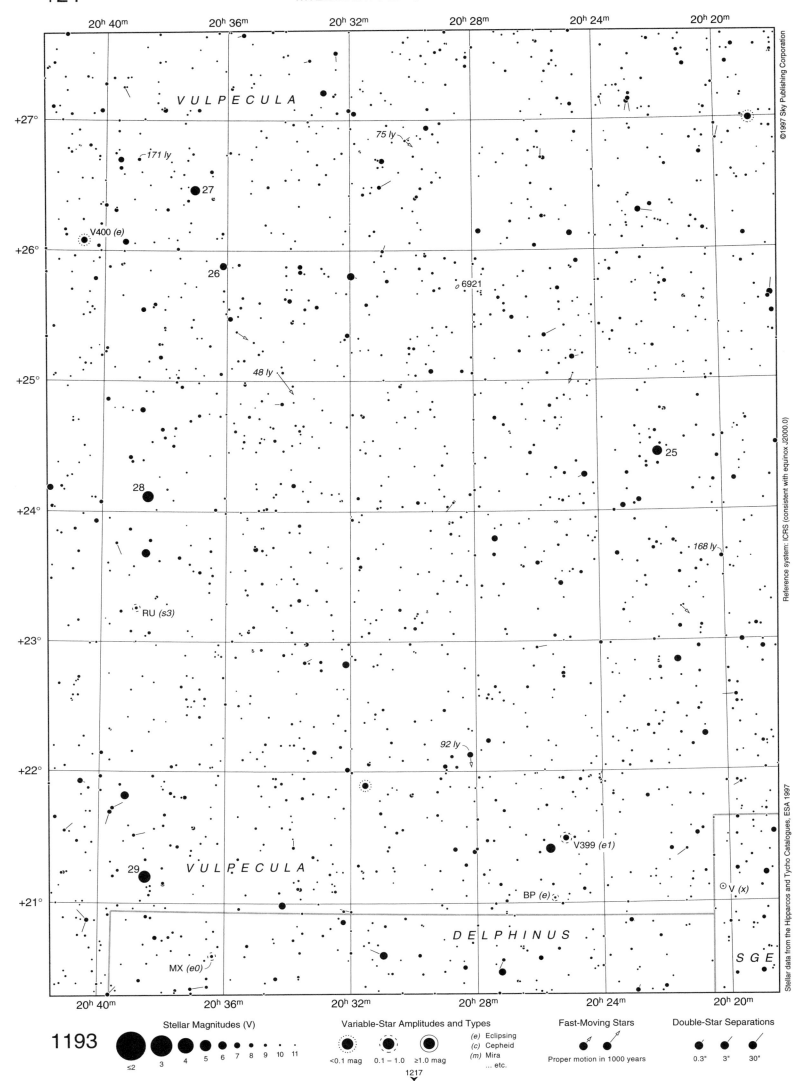

1193

Stellar Magnitudes (V)

≤2  3  4  5  6  7  8  9  10  11

Variable-Star Amplitudes and Types

<0.1 mag    0.1 − 1.0    ≥1.0 mag

(e) Eclipsing
(c) Cepheid
(m) Mira
... etc.

Fast-Moving Stars

Proper motion in 1000 years

Double-Star Separations

0.3"    3"    30"

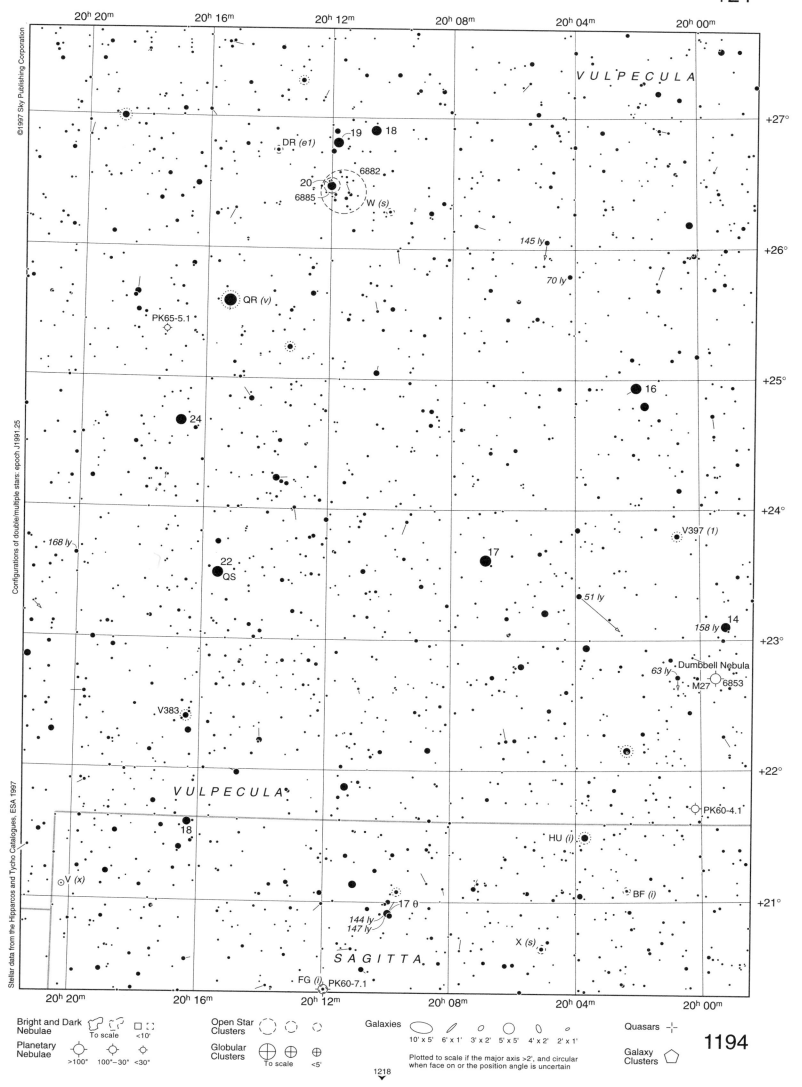

Configurations of double/multiple stars: epoch J1991.25

Stellar data from the Hipparcos and Tycho Catalogues, ESA 1997

20h 20m    20h 16m    20h 12m    20h 08m    20h 04m    20h 00m

*VULPECULA*

+27°

19  18
DR *(e1)*

6882
20  6885    W *(s)*

+26°
145 ly

70 ly

QR *(v)*
PK65-5.1

+25°
16

24

22
QS

17

+24°

168 ly

51 ly

14
158 ly

+23°

63 ly    Dumbbell Nebula
M27  6853

V383

V397 *(1)*

+22°

*VULPECULA*

18

PK60-4.1

HU *(i)*

V *(x)*

17 θ    BF *(i)*

+21°
144 ly
147 ly

X *(s)*

*SAGITTA*

FG *(i)*  PK60-7.1

20h 20m    20h 16m    20h 12m    20h 08m    20h 04m    20h 00m

Bright and Dark Nebulae — To scale — <10'
Planetary Nebulae — >100" — 100"–30" — <30"
Open Star Clusters
Globular Clusters — To scale — <5'
Galaxies — 10' x 5' — 6' x 1' — 3' x 2' — 5' x 5' — 4' x 2' — 2' x 1'
Plotted to scale if the major axis >2', and circular when face on or the position angle is uncertain
Quasars
Galaxy Clusters

1194

1218

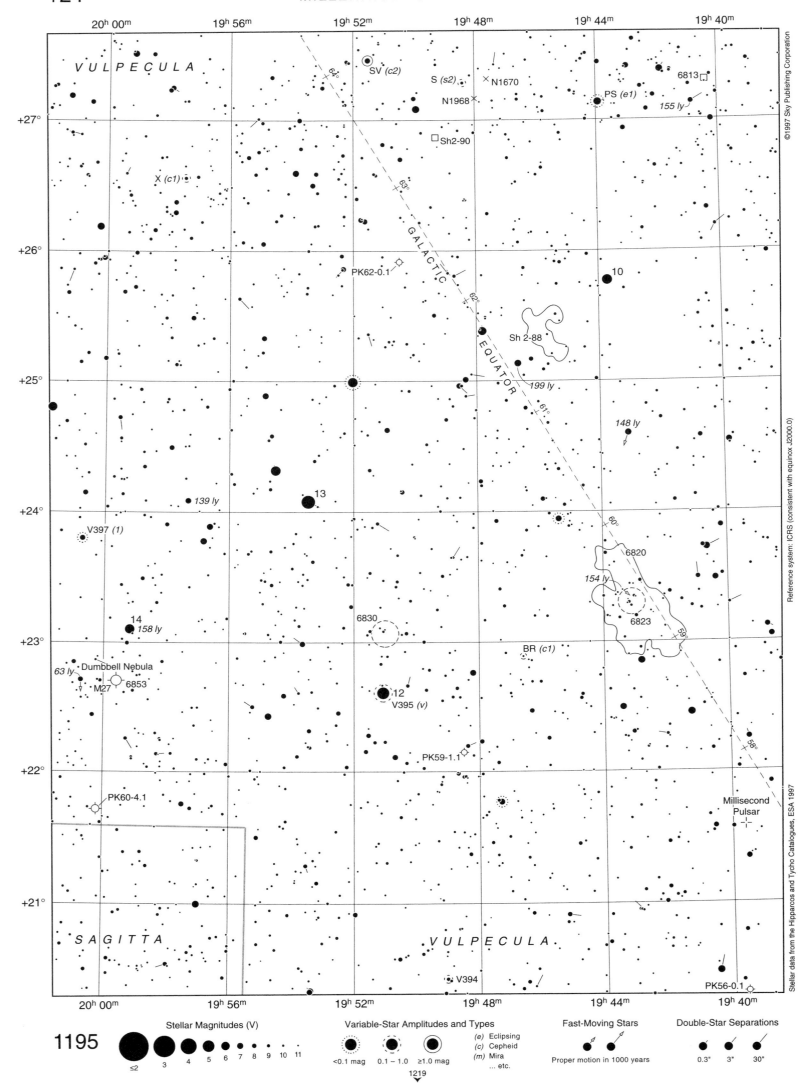

VULPECULA

SV (c2)

S (s2)    × N1670

N1968 ×

□ Sh2-90

PS (e1)

6813 □

155 ly

X (c1)

PK62-0.1

10

Sh 2-88

199 ly

148 ly

13

139 ly

V397 (1)

6820

154 ly

6823

14

158 ly

6830

BR (c1)

63 ly    Dumbbell Nebula

M27  6853

12

V395 (v)

PK59-1.1

PK60-4.1

Millisecond
Pulsar

+21°

SAGITTA

VULPECULA

V394

PK56-0.1

**Stellar Magnitudes (V)**

3   4   5   6   7   8   9   10  11

≤2

**Variable-Star Amplitudes and Types**

<0.1 mag    0.1 – 1.0    ≥1.0 mag

(e) Eclipsing
(c) Cepheid
(m) Mira
... etc.

**Fast-Moving Stars**

Proper motion in 1000 years

**Double-Star Separations**

0.3"    3"    30"

1219

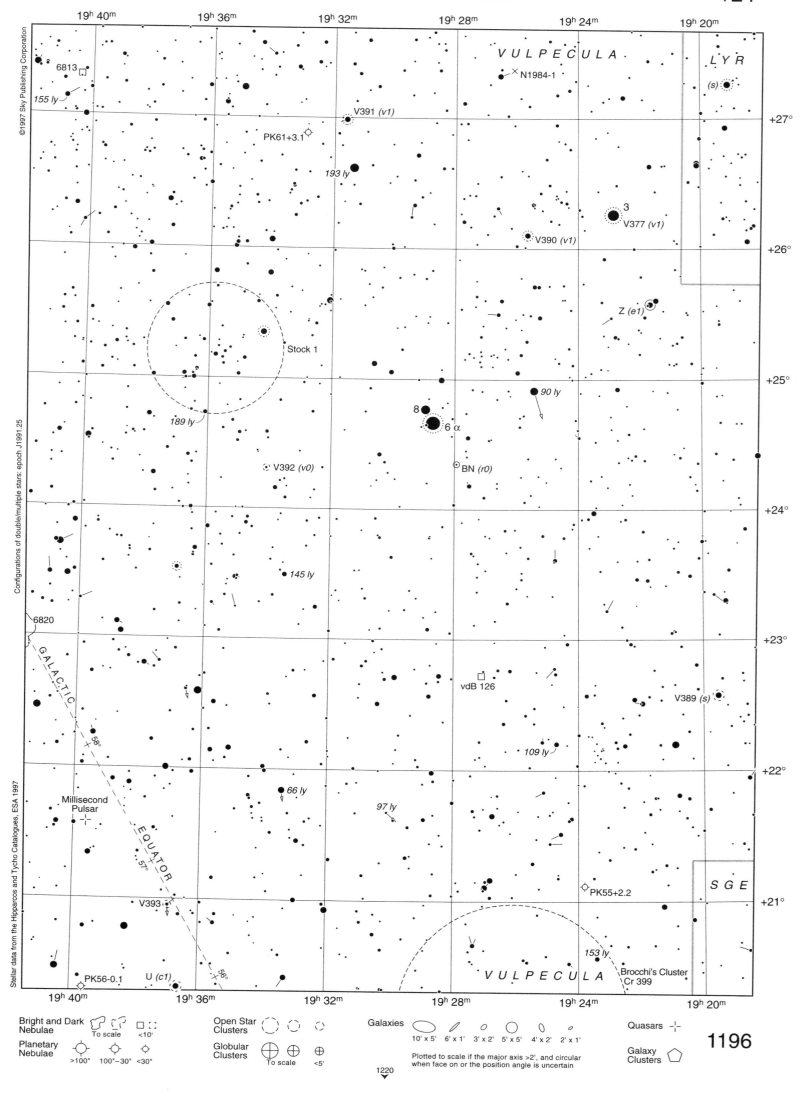

Configurations of double/multiple stars: epoch J1991.25

Stellar data from the Hipparcos and Tycho Catalogues, ESA 1997

6813
155 ly

V391 (v1)
PK61+3.1
193 ly

VULPECULA

N1984-1

LYR
(s)

3
V377 (v1)
V390 (v1)

Z (e1)

Stock 1
189 ly

90 ly

8
6 α

V392 (v0)
BN (r0)

145 ly

6820

GALACTIC

58°

V389 (s)

vdB 126

109 ly

66 ly

97 ly

Millisecond
Pulsar

EQUATOR
57°

V393

56°

PK55+2.2

SGE

153 ly

PK56-0.1    U (c1)

VULPECULA

Brocchi's Cluster
Cr 399

+27°

+26°

+25°

+24°

+23°

+22°

+21°

19h 40m    19h 36m    19h 32m    19h 28m    19h 24m    19h 20m

Bright and Dark
Nebulae
To scale    <10'

Planetary
Nebulae
>100"    100"–30"    <30"

Open Star
Clusters

Globular
Clusters
To scale    <5'

Galaxies
10' x 5'    6' x 1'    3' x 2'    5' x 5'    4' x 2'    2' x 1'

Plotted to scale if the major axis >2', and circular
when face on or the position angle is uncertain

Quasars

Galaxy
Clusters

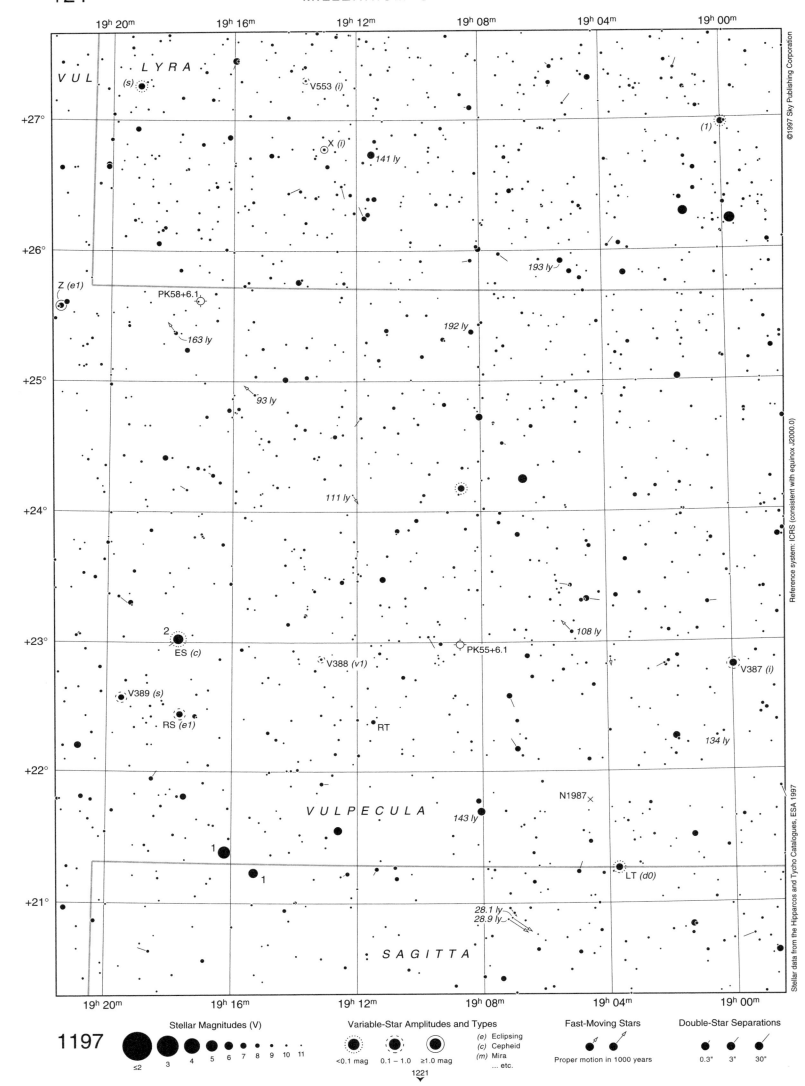

©1997 Sky Publishing Corporation

Reference system: ICRS (consistent with equinox J2000.0)

Stellar data from the Hipparcos and Tycho Catalogues, ESA 1997

**Stellar Magnitudes (V)**

≤2   3   4   5   6   7   8   9   10   11

**Variable-Star Amplitudes and Types**

<0.1 mag    0.1 – 1.0    ≥1.0 mag

(e) Eclipsing
(c) Cepheid
(m) Mira
... etc.

**Fast-Moving Stars**

Proper motion in 1000 years

**Double-Star Separations**

0.3"    3"    30"

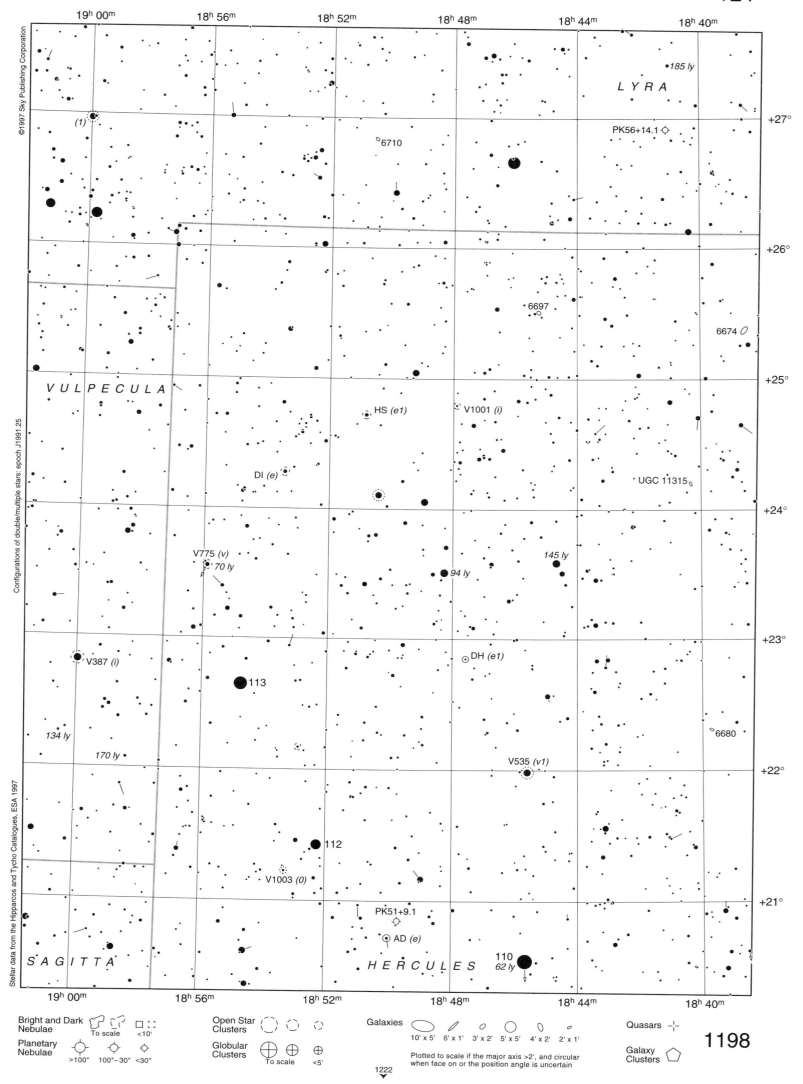

*LYRA*

*185 ly*

PK56+14.1

6710

6697

6674

*VULPECULA*

HS (e1)

V1001 (i)

DI (e)

UGC 11315

V775 (v)
70 ly

94 ly

145 ly

DH (e1)

V387 (i)

113

6680

134 ly

170 ly

V535 (v1)

112

V1003 (0)

PK51+9.1

AD (e)

110
62 ly

*SAGITTA*

*HERCULES*

| Bright and Dark Nebulae | | Open Star Clusters | | | Galaxies | | | | | | Quasars |
|---|---|---|---|---|---|---|---|---|---|---|---|
| To scale | <10' | | | | 10' x 5' | 6' x 1' | 3' x 2' | 5' x 5' | 4' x 2' | 2' x 1' | |

Planetary Nebulae
>100"  100"–30"  <30"

Globular Clusters
To scale  <5'

Plotted to scale if the major axis >2', and circular when face on or the position angle is uncertain

Galaxy Clusters

**1198**

1222

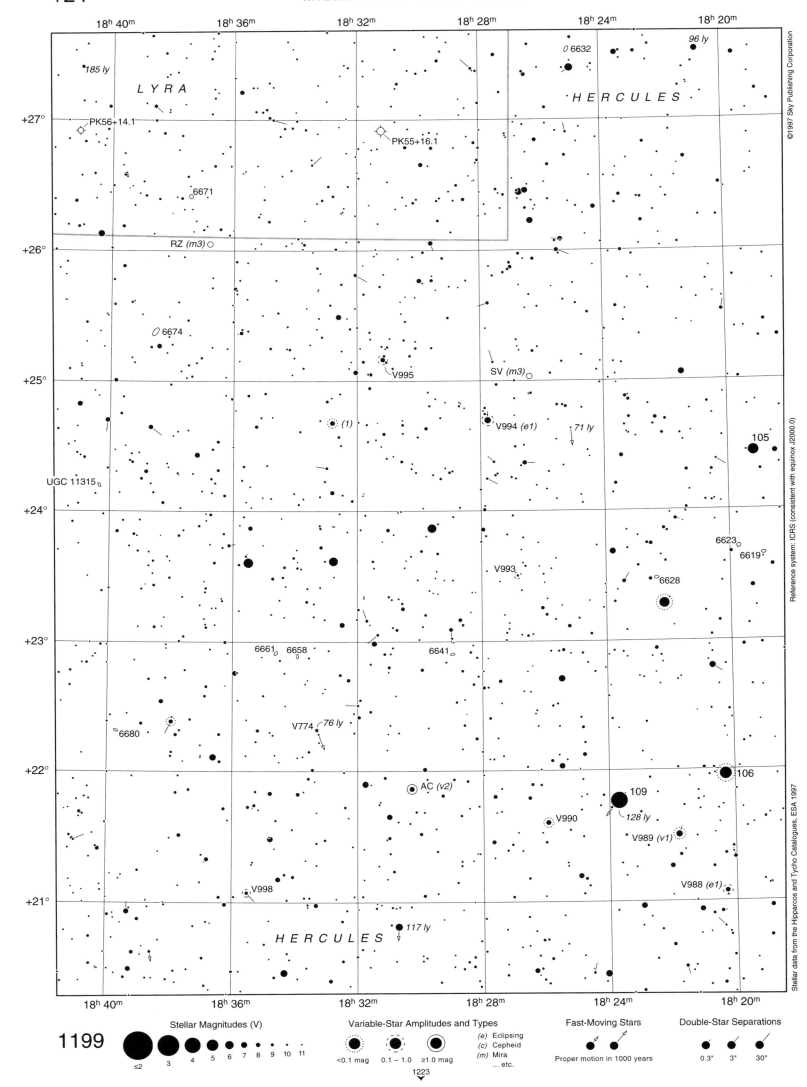

LYRA

HERCULES

185 ly

PK56+14.1

PK55+16.1

6671

96 ly

0 6632

+27°

RZ (m3) ○

+26°

0 6674

V995

SV (m3) ○

+25°

UGC 11315 ○

(1)

V994 (e1)

71 ly

105

+24°

6623 ○
6619 ○

V993

6628 ○

6661 ○　6658 ○

6641 ○

+23°

6680 ○

V774 　76 ly

+22°

AC (v2)

V990

109

128 ly

V989 (v1)

106

V998

V988 (e1)

+21°

HERCULES

117 ly

1199

**Stellar Magnitudes (V)**

≤2　3　4　5　6　7　8　9　10　11

**Variable-Star Amplitudes and Types**

<0.1 mag　0.1 – 1.0　≥1.0 mag

(e) Eclipsing
(c) Cepheid
(m) Mira
... etc.

1223

**Fast-Moving Stars**

Proper motion in 1000 years

**Double-Star Separations**

0.3"　3"　30"

# MILLENNIUM STAR ATLAS

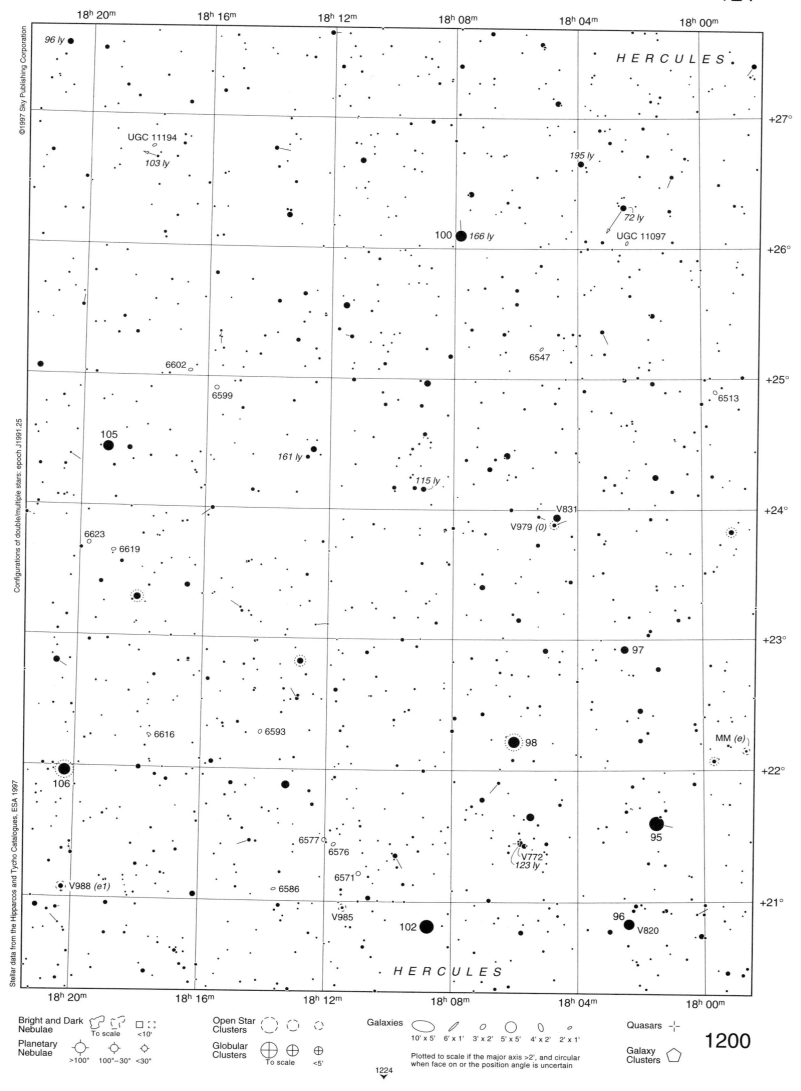

Configurations of double/multiple stars: epoch J1991.25

Stellar data from the Hipparcos and Tycho Catalogues, ESA 1997

HERCULES

96 ly

18h 20m    18h 16m    18h 12m    18h 08m    18h 04m    18h 00m

UGC 11194
103 ly

195 ly

72 ly
UGC 11097

100  166 ly

6547

6602

6599

6513

105

161 ly

115 ly

V831
V979 (0)

+27°
+26°
+25°
+24°
+23°
+22°
+21°

6623
6619

97

6616    6593

98

MM (e)

106

95

6577
6576

V772
123 ly

6571

6586

V988 (e1)

V985

96
V820

102

HERCULES

18h 20m    18h 16m    18h 12m    18h 08m    18h 04m    18h 00m

Bright and Dark
Nebulae
    To scale    <10'

Planetary
Nebulae
    >100"  100"–30"  <30"

Open Star
Clusters

Globular
Clusters
    To scale    <5'

Galaxies
    10' x 5'  6' x 1'  3' x 2'  5' x 5'  4' x 2'  2' x 1'

Plotted to scale if the major axis >2', and circular
when face on or the position angle is uncertain

Quasars

Galaxy
Clusters

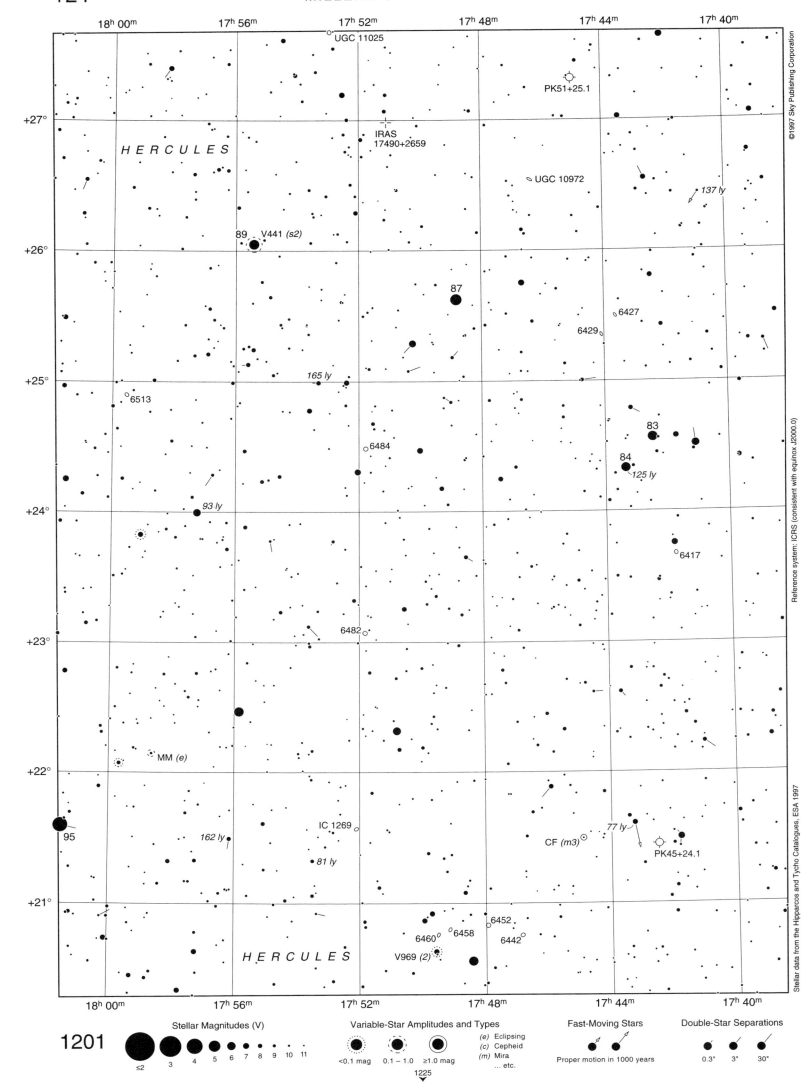

©1997 Sky Publishing Corporation

Reference system: ICRS (consistent with equinox J2000.0)

Stellar data from the Hipparcos and Tycho Catalogues, ESA 1997

HERCULES

UGC 11025

PK51+25.1

IRAS
17490+2659

UGC 10972

137 ly

89   V441 (s2)

87

6427

6429

6513

165 ly

83

6484

84

125 ly

93 ly

6417

6482

MM (e)

IC 1269

77 ly

95

162 ly

CF (m3)

81 ly

PK45+24.1

6452

6460   6458   6442

V969 (2)

HERCULES

1201

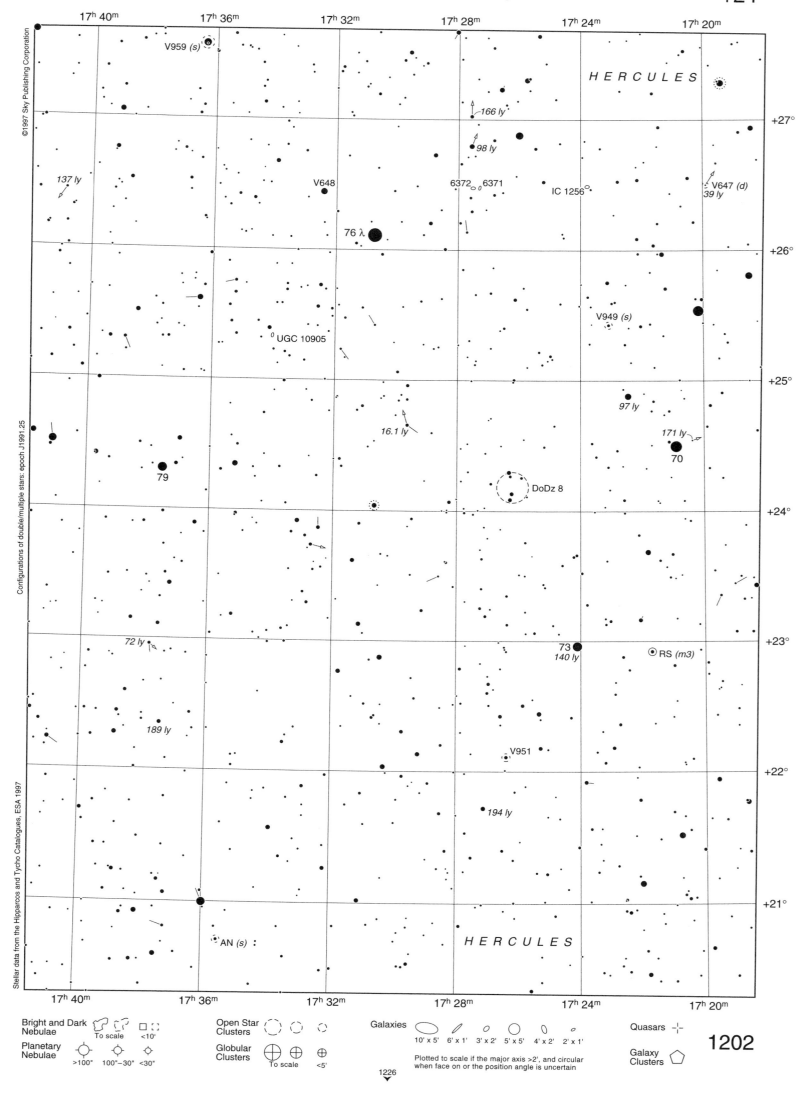

V959 (s)

H E R C U L E S

17ʰ 40ᵐ    17ʰ 36ᵐ    17ʰ 32ᵐ    17ʰ 28ᵐ    17ʰ 24ᵐ    17ʰ 20ᵐ

+27°

166 ly

98 ly

137 ly

V648    6372  6371    IC 1256    V647 (d)
                                 39 ly

76 λ

+26°

V949 (s)

UGC 10905

+25°

97 ly

16.1 ly    171 ly

70

79

DoDz 8    +24°

72 ly    73    RS (m3)
         140 ly

189 ly

+23°

V951

194 ly    +22°

+21°

AN (s)

H E R C U L E S

17ʰ 40ᵐ    17ʰ 36ᵐ    17ʰ 32ᵐ    17ʰ 28ᵐ    17ʰ 24ᵐ    17ʰ 20ᵐ

Bright and Dark Nebulae    Open Star Clusters    Galaxies    Quasars
To scale    <10'    To scale    10' x 5'  6' x 1'  3' x 2'  5' x 5'  4' x 2'  2' x 1'

Planetary Nebulae    Globular Clusters    Galaxy Clusters    1202
>100"  100"–30"  <30"    To scale    <5'    Plotted to scale if the major axis >2', and circular when face on or the position angle is uncertain

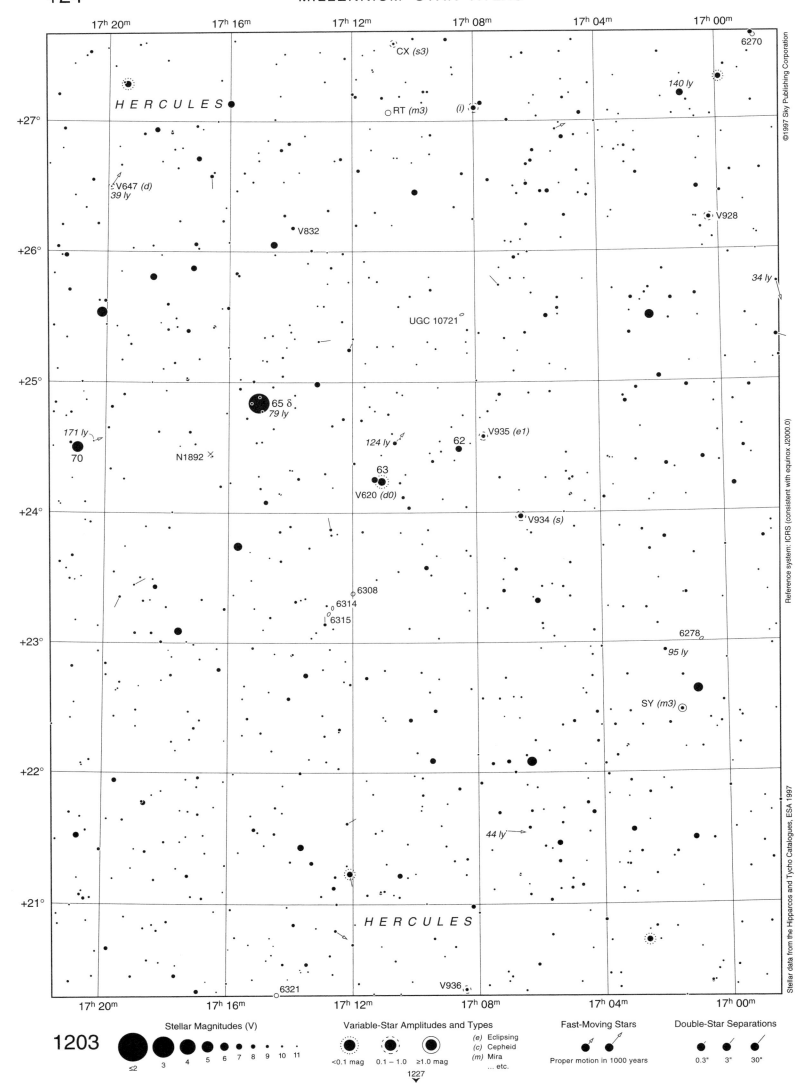

HERCULES

CX (s3)

RT (m3)    (i)

6270

140 ly

V928

V647 (d)
39 ly

V832

34 ly

UGC 10721

65 δ
79 ly

171 ly

70

N1892

124 ly

62

V935 (e1)

63

V620 (d0)

V934 (s)

6308

6314
6315

6278
95 ly

SY (m3)

44 ly

HERCULES

6321

V936

**1203**

Stellar Magnitudes (V)

≤2  3  4  5  6  7  8  9  10  11

Variable-Star Amplitudes and Types

<0.1 mag    0.1 – 1.0    ≥1.0 mag

(e) Eclipsing
(c) Cepheid
(m) Mira
... etc.

1227
▼

Fast-Moving Stars

Proper motion in 1000 years

Double-Star Separations

0.3"   3"   30"

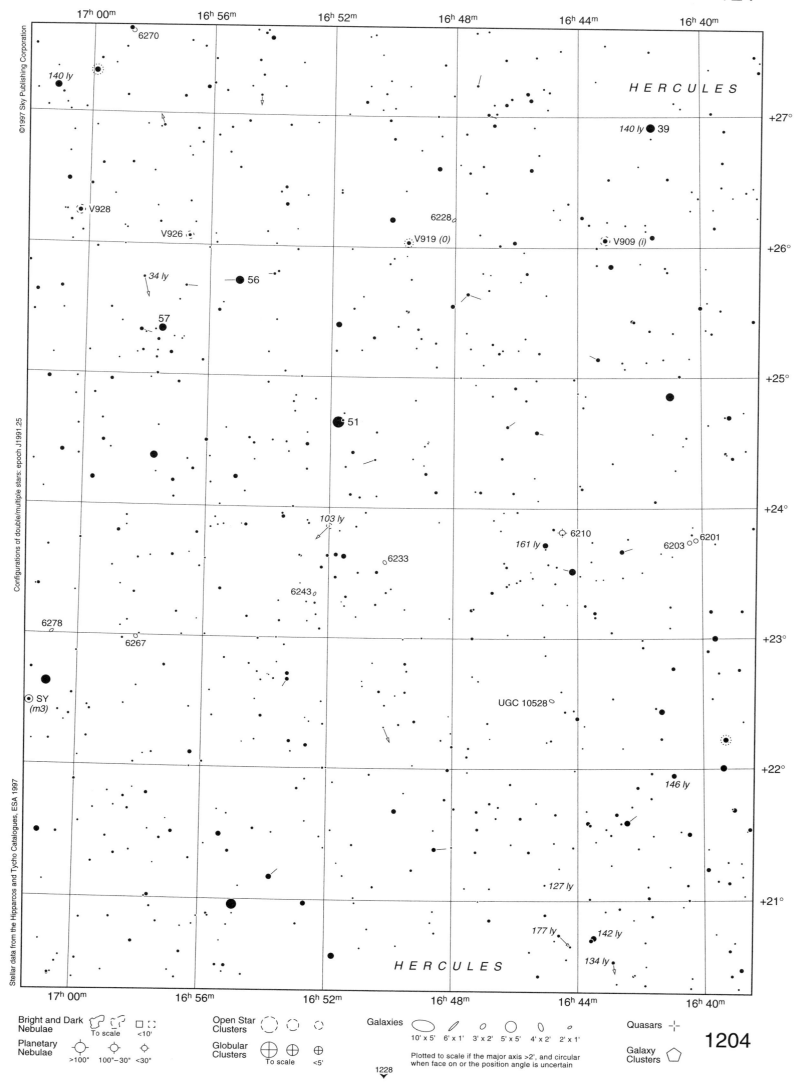

©1997 Sky Publishing Corporation

Configurations of double/multiple stars: epoch J1991.25

Stellar data from the Hipparcos and Tycho Catalogues, ESA 1997

HERCULES

17h 00m   16h 56m   16h 52m   16h 48m   16h 44m   16h 40m

+27°
+26°
+25°
+24°
+23°
+22°
+21°

6270
140 ly
V928
V926
6228
V919 (0)
V909 (i)
140 ly  39
34 ly
56
57
51
103 ly
6233
6243
6278
6267
SY (m3)
6210
161 ly
6203  6201
UGC 10528
146 ly
127 ly
177 ly  142 ly
134 ly

HERCULES

17h 00m   16h 56m   16h 52m   16h 48m   16h 44m   16h 40m

| Bright and Dark Nebulae | To scale | <10' |
| Open Star Clusters | | |
| Galaxies | 10'x5' 6'x1' 3'x2' 5'x5' 4'x2' 2'x1' | |
| Quasars | | |
| Planetary Nebulae | >100" 100"–30" <30" | Globular Clusters | To scale <5' | Plotted to scale if the major axis >2', and circular when face on or the position angle is uncertain | Galaxy Clusters | |

1204

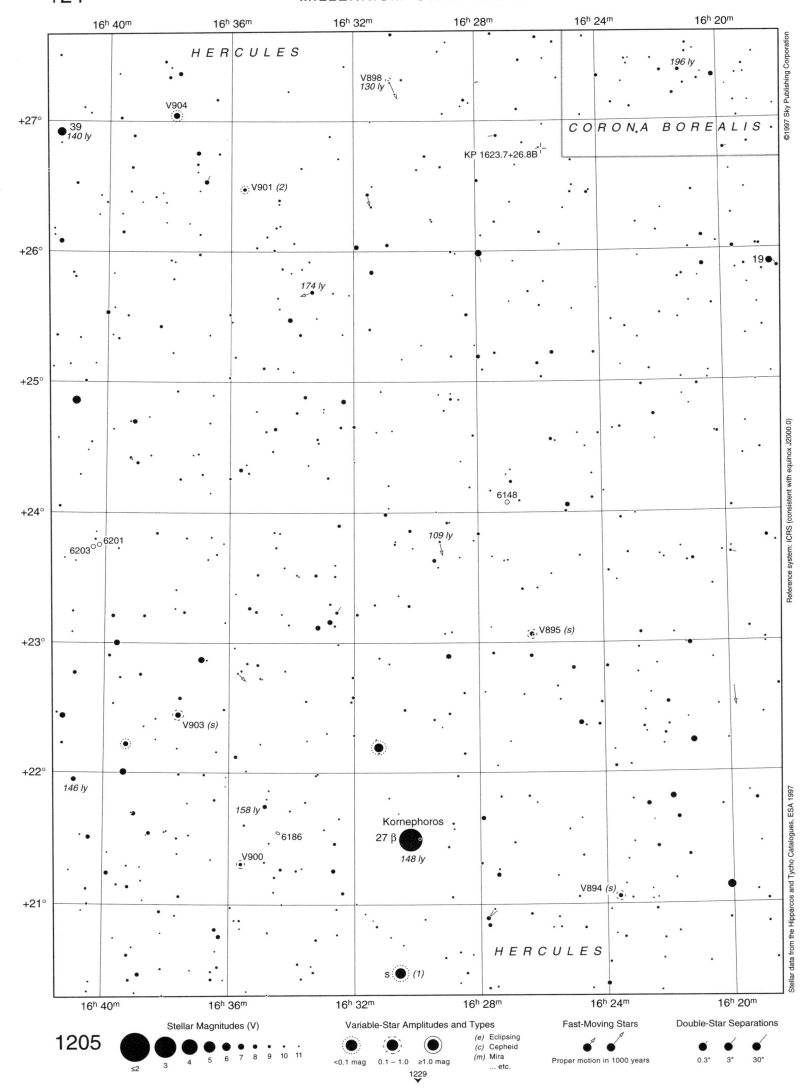

HERCULES

CORONA BOREALIS

V898
130 ly

V904

39
140 ly

V901 (2)

KP 1623.7+26.8B

196 ly

19

174 ly

6148

6203 ○○ 6201

109 ly

V895 (s)

V903 (s)

146 ly

158 ly

6186

Kornephoros
27 β
148 ly

V900

V894 (s)

HERCULES

s (1)

©1997 Sky Publishing Corporation

Reference system: ICRS (consistent with equinox J2000.0)

Stellar data from the Hipparcos and Tycho Catalogues, ESA 1997

1205

Stellar Magnitudes (V)

≤2  3  4  5  6  7  8  9  10  11

Variable-Star Amplitudes and Types

<0.1 mag   0.1 – 1.0   ≥1.0 mag

(e) Eclipsing
(c) Cepheid
(m) Mira
... etc.

Fast-Moving Stars

Proper motion in 1000 years

Double-Star Separations

0.3"  3"  30"

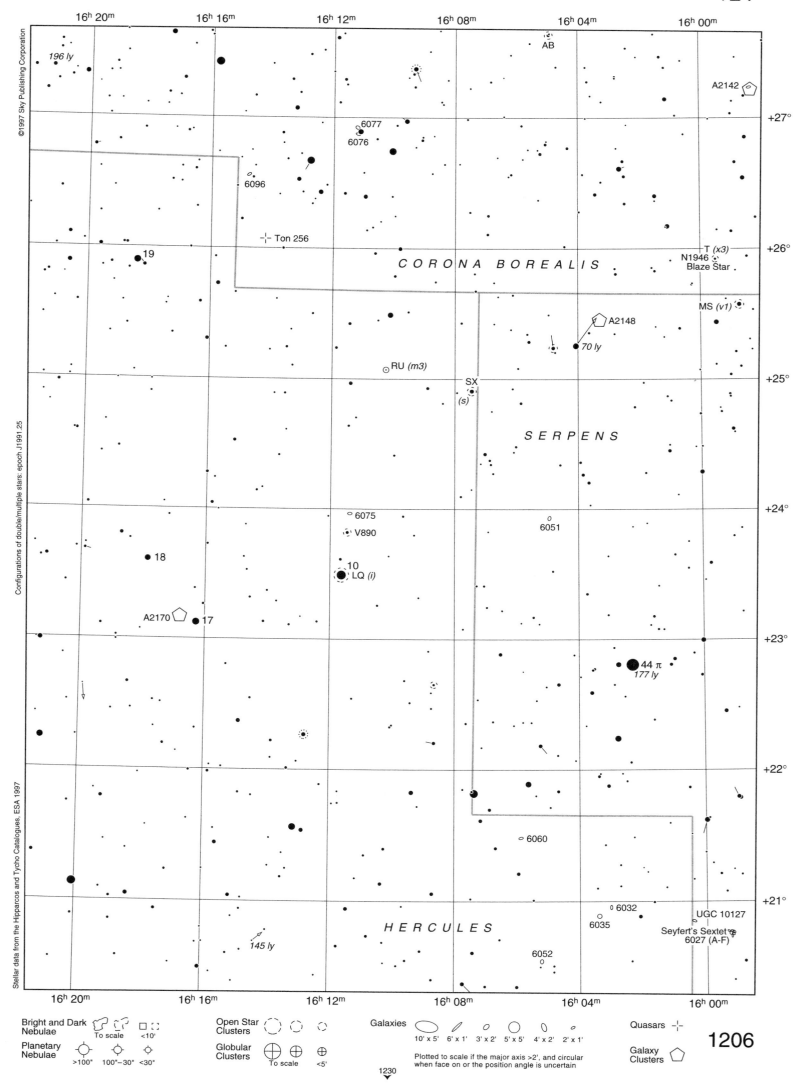

16h 20m  16h 16m  16h 12m  16h 08m  16h 04m  16h 00m

+27°
+26°
+25°
+24°
+23°
+22°
+21°

*196 ly*

A2142

AB

6077
6076

6096

Ton 256

*C O R O N A   B O R E A L I S*

T *(x3)*
N1946
Blaze Star

19

A2148

MS *(v1)*

*70 ly*

RU *(m3)*

SX
*(s)*

*S E R P E N S*

6075

6051

V890

18

10
LQ *(i)*

A2170

17

44 π
*177 ly*

6060

6032

UGC 10127

6035

Seyfert's Sextet
6027 (A-F)

*H E R C U L E S*

*145 ly*

6052

16h 20m  16h 16m  16h 12m  16h 08m  16h 04m  16h 00m

| Bright and Dark Nebulae | | | Open Star Clusters | | | Galaxies | | | | | | | Quasars |
| To scale | | <10' | | | | 10' x 5' | 6' x 1' | 3' x 2' | 5' x 5' | 4' x 2' | 2' x 1' | |
| Planetary Nebulae | | | Globular Clusters | | | | | | | | | Galaxy Clusters |
| >100" | 100"–30" | <30" | To scale | | <5' | | | | | | | |

Plotted to scale if the major axis >2', and circular
when face on or the position angle is uncertain

**1206**

1230

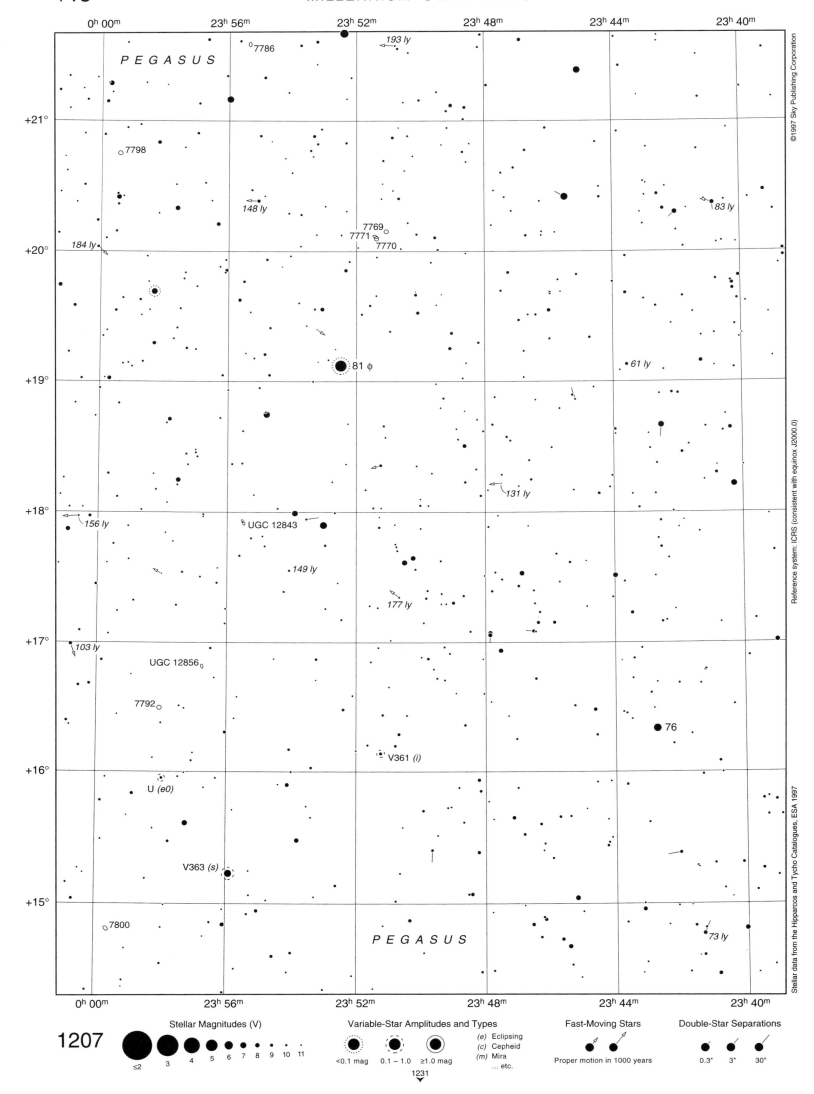

1183

MILLENNIUM STAR ATLAS

0ʰ 00ᵐ   23ʰ 56ᵐ   23ʰ 52ᵐ   23ʰ 48ᵐ   23ʰ 44ᵐ   23ʰ 40ᵐ

P E G A S U S

7786

193 ly

7798

148 ly

83 ly

7769
7771
7770

184 ly

+21°

+20°

61 ly

81 φ

+19°

131 ly

156 ly

UGC 12843

149 ly

177 ly

+18°

103 ly

UGC 12856

7792

76

V361 (i)

+17°

U (e0)

+16°

V363 (s)

7800

P E G A S U S

73 ly

+15°

0ʰ 00ᵐ   23ʰ 56ᵐ   23ʰ 52ᵐ   23ʰ 48ᵐ   23ʰ 44ᵐ   23ʰ 40ᵐ

©1997 Sky Publishing Corporation

Reference system: ICRS (consistent with equinox J2000.0)

Stellar data from the Hipparcos and Tycho Catalogues, ESA 1997

**1207**

Stellar Magnitudes (V)

≤2   3   4   5   6   7   8   9   10   11

Variable-Star Amplitudes and Types

<0.1 mag    0.1 – 1.0    ≥1.0 mag

(e) Eclipsing
(c) Cepheid
(m) Mira
... etc.

Fast-Moving Stars

Proper motion in 1000 years

Double-Star Separations

0.3"    3"    30"

1231

# MILLENNIUM STAR ATLAS

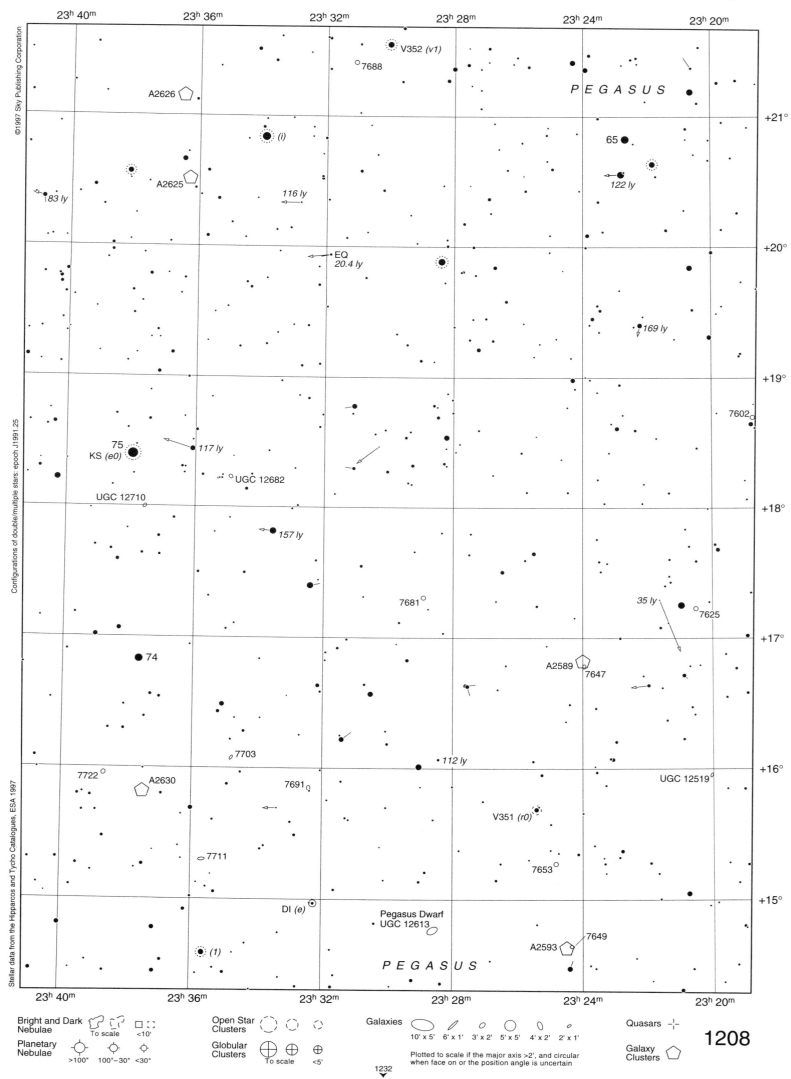

©1997 Sky Publishing Corporation

Configurations of double/multiple stars: epoch J1991.25

Stellar data from the Hipparcos and Tycho Catalogues, ESA 1997

*P E G A S U S*

*P E G A S U S*

V352 *(v1)*

7688

A2626

A2625

*(i)*

*83 ly*

*116 ly*

65

*122 ly*

EQ
*20.4 ly*

*169 ly*

7602

75
KS *(e0)*

*117 ly*

UGC 12682

UGC 12710

*157 ly*

*35 ly*

7625

7681

74

A2589
7647

7703

*112 ly*

7722

A2630

7691

UGC 12519

V351 *(r0)*

7711

7653

DI *(e)*

Pegasus Dwarf
UGC 12613

*(1)*

A2593
7649

## Legend

Bright and Dark Nebulae — To scale — <10'

Planetary Nebulae — >100" — 100"–30" — <30"

Open Star Clusters

Globular Clusters — To scale — <5'

Galaxies — 10' x 5'  6' x 1'  3' x 2'  5' x 5'  4' x 2'  2' x 1'

Plotted to scale if the major axis >2', and circular when face on or the position angle is uncertain

Quasars

Galaxy Clusters

1208

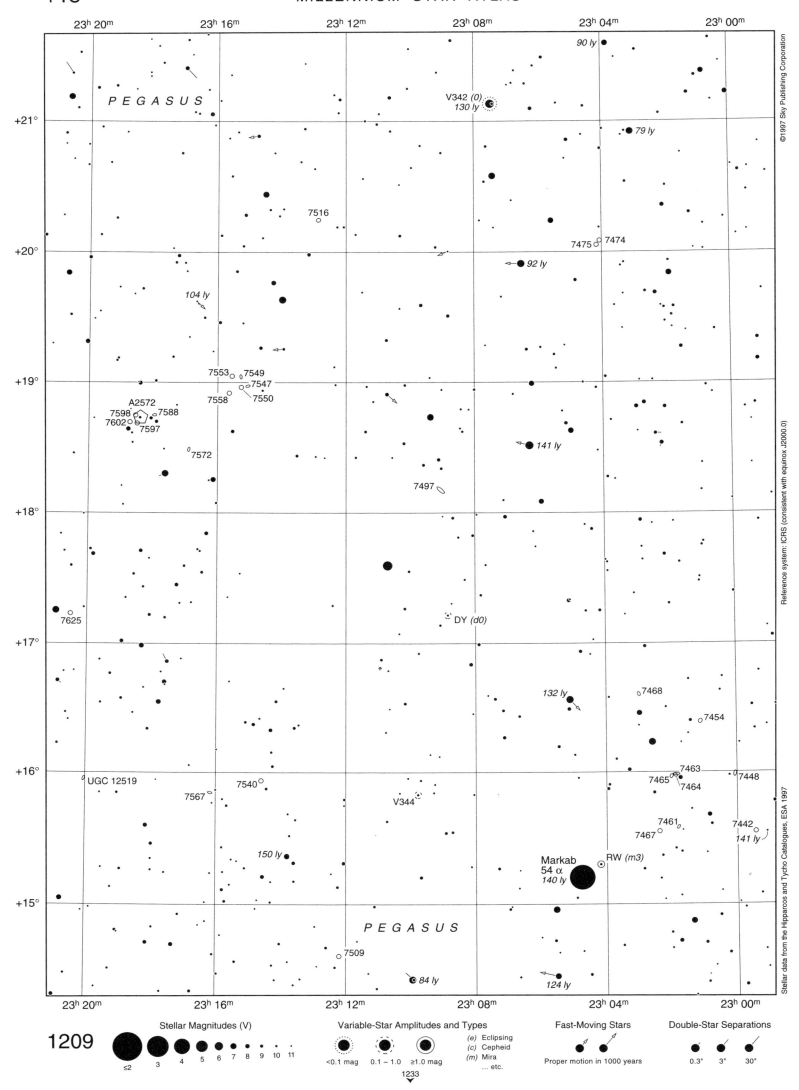

Stellar Magnitudes (V)

≤2   3   4   5   6  7  8  9 10 11

Variable-Star Amplitudes and Types

<0.1 mag   0.1 – 1.0   ≥1.0 mag

(e) Eclipsing
(c) Cepheid
(m) Mira
... etc.

Fast-Moving Stars

Proper motion in 1000 years

Double-Star Separations

0.3"    3"    30"

1209

1233

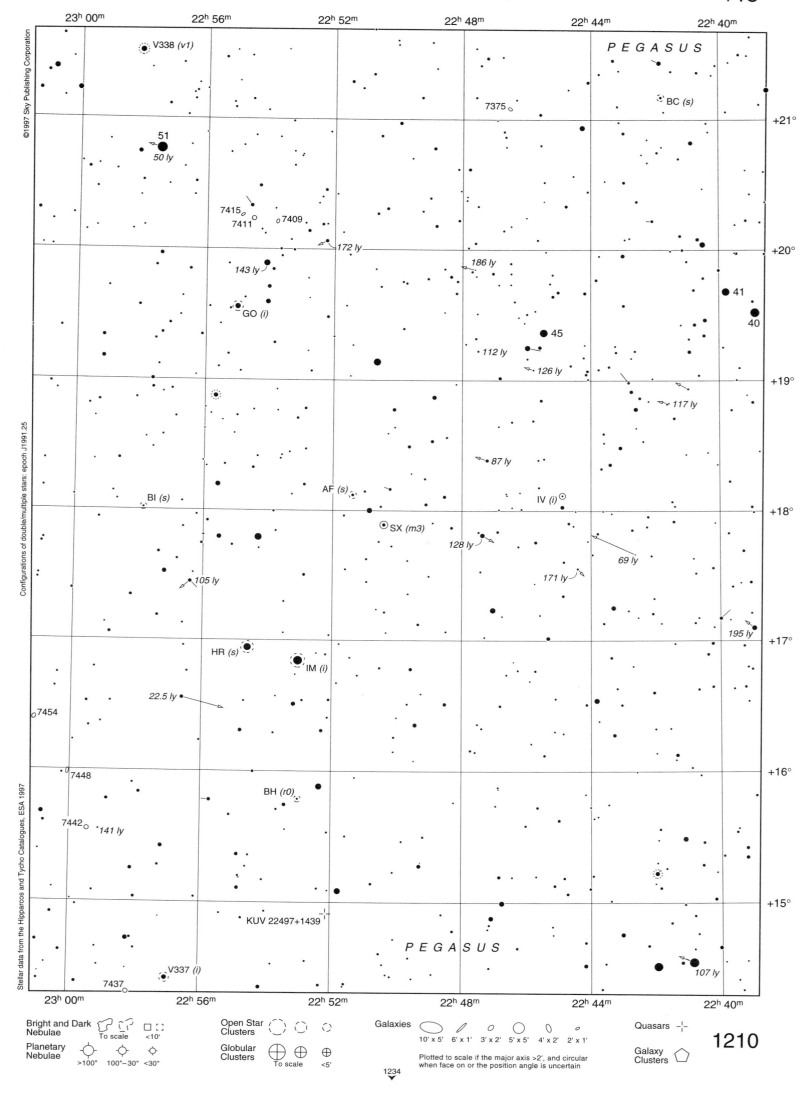

PEGASUS

V338 (v1)

7375

BC (s)

51
50 ly

7415
7411    7409

172 ly

143 ly

186 ly

GO (i)

41

40

45

112 ly

126 ly

117 ly

87 ly

BI (s)

AF (s)

IV (i)

SX (m3)

128 ly

69 ly

105 ly

171 ly

195 ly

HR (s)

IM (i)

22.5 ly

7454

7448

BH (r0)

7442    141 ly

KUV 22497+1439

PEGASUS

V337 (i)

107 ly

7437

©1997 Sky Publishing Corporation

Configurations of double/multiple stars: epoch J1991.25

Stellar data from the Hipparcos and Tycho Catalogues, ESA 1997

+21°

+20°

+19°

+18°

+17°

+16°

+15°

23h 00m   22h 56m   22h 52m   22h 48m   22h 44m   22h 40m

Bright and Dark Nebulae    To scale    <10'

Planetary Nebulae    >100"   100"–30"   <30"

Open Star Clusters

Globular Clusters    To scale    <5'

Galaxies    10' x 5'   6' x 1'   3' x 2'   5' x 5'   4' x 2'   2' x 1'

Plotted to scale if the major axis >2', and circular when face on or the position angle is uncertain

Quasars

Galaxy Clusters

1210

+18°

# MILLENNIUM STAR ATLAS

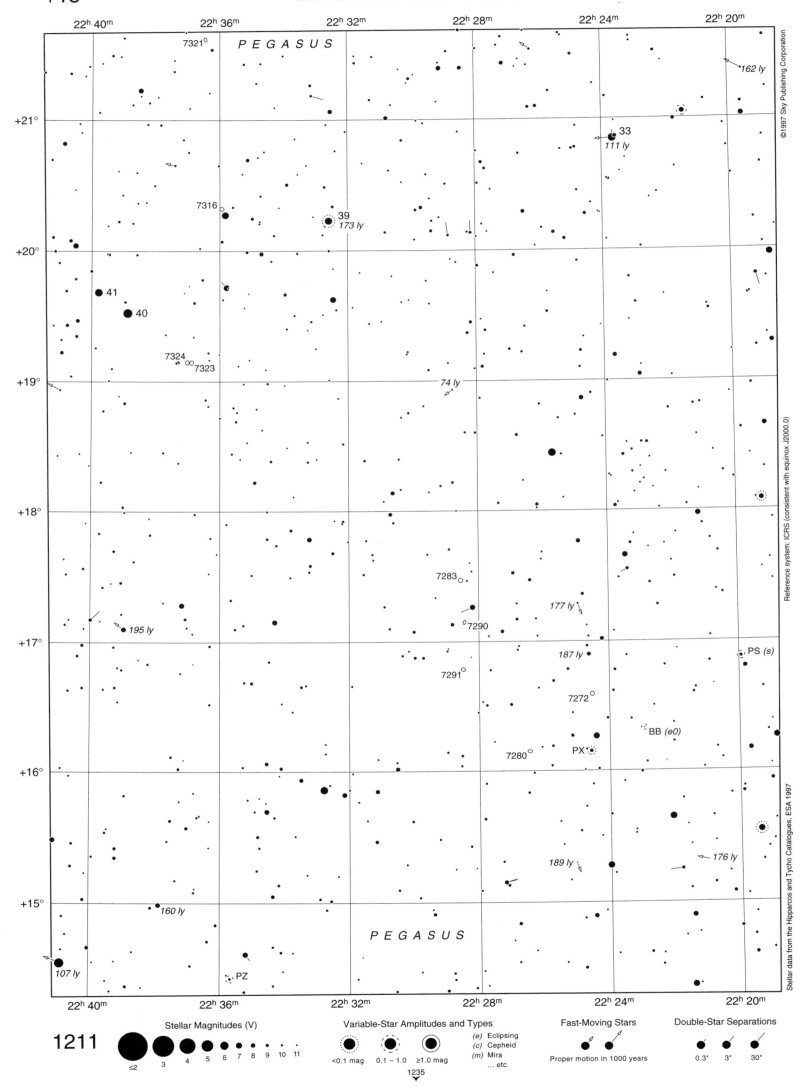

©1997 Sky Publishing Corporation

Reference system: ICRS (consistent with equinox J2000.0)

Stellar data from the Hipparcos and Tycho Catalogues, ESA 1997

P E G A S U S

7321°

7316

39
173 ly

33
111 ly

162 ly

41

40

7324 ∞ 7323

74 ly

7283 ○

7290 °

177 ly

7291 ○

187 ly

PS (s)

7272 ○

BB (e0)

7280 ○    PX

195 ly

189 ly

176 ly

160 ly

P E G A S U S

107 ly

PZ

1211

### Stellar Magnitudes (V)

≤2    3    4    5    6    7    8    9   10   11

### Variable-Star Amplitudes and Types

<0.1 mag    0.1 – 1.0    ≥1.0 mag

(e) Eclipsing
(c) Cepheid
(m) Mira
... etc.

1235

### Fast-Moving Stars

Proper motion in 1000 years

### Double-Star Separations

0.3"    3"    30"

# MILLENNIUM STAR ATLAS

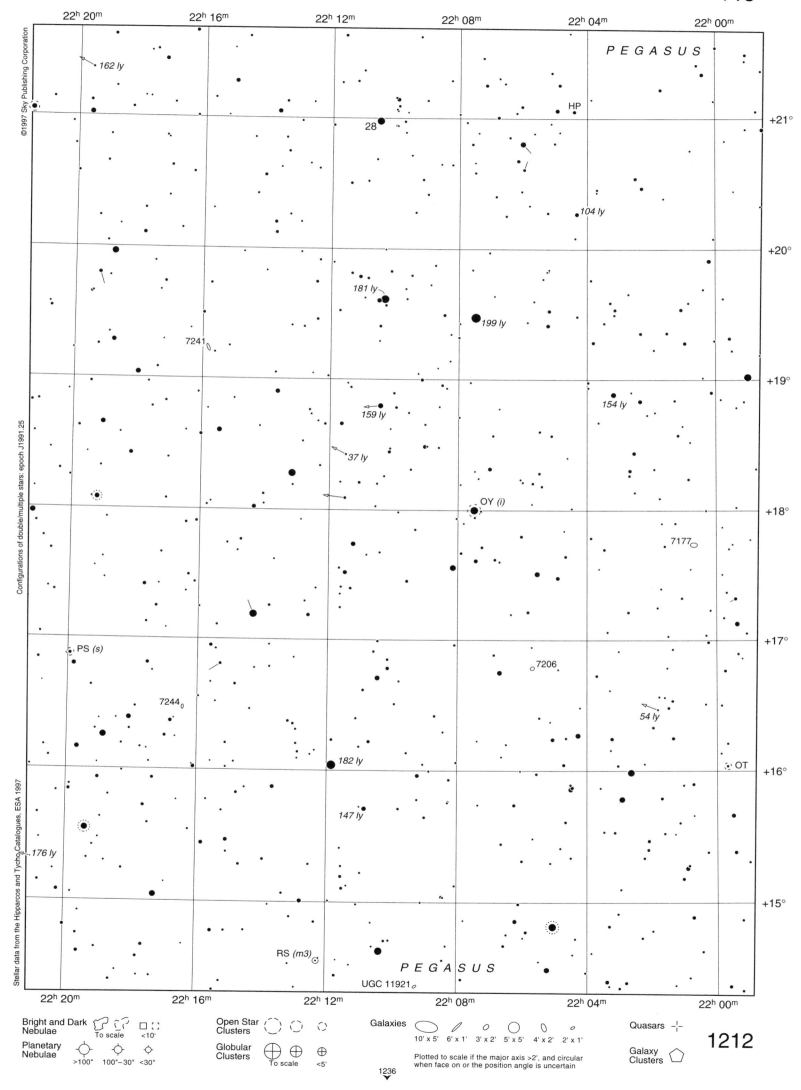

Configurations of double/multiple stars: epoch J1991.25

Stellar data from the Hipparcos and Tycho Catalogues, ESA 1997

PEGASUS

162 ly

28

HP

104 ly

181 ly

199 ly

7241

159 ly

154 ly

37 ly

OY (i)

7177

PS (s)

7206

7244

54 ly

182 ly

OT

147 ly

176 ly

RS (m3)

PEGASUS

UGC 11921

22h 20m    22h 16m    22h 12m    22h 08m    22h 04m    22h 00m

+21°   +20°   +19°   +18°   +17°   +16°   +15°

Bright and Dark Nebulae   To scale   <10'

Planetary Nebulae   >100"   100"–30"   <30"

Open Star Clusters

Globular Clusters   To scale   <5'

Galaxies   10' x 5'   6' x 1'   3' x 2'   5' x 5'   4' x 2'   2' x 1'

Plotted to scale if the major axis >2', and circular when face on or the position angle is uncertain

Quasars

Galaxy Clusters

**1212**

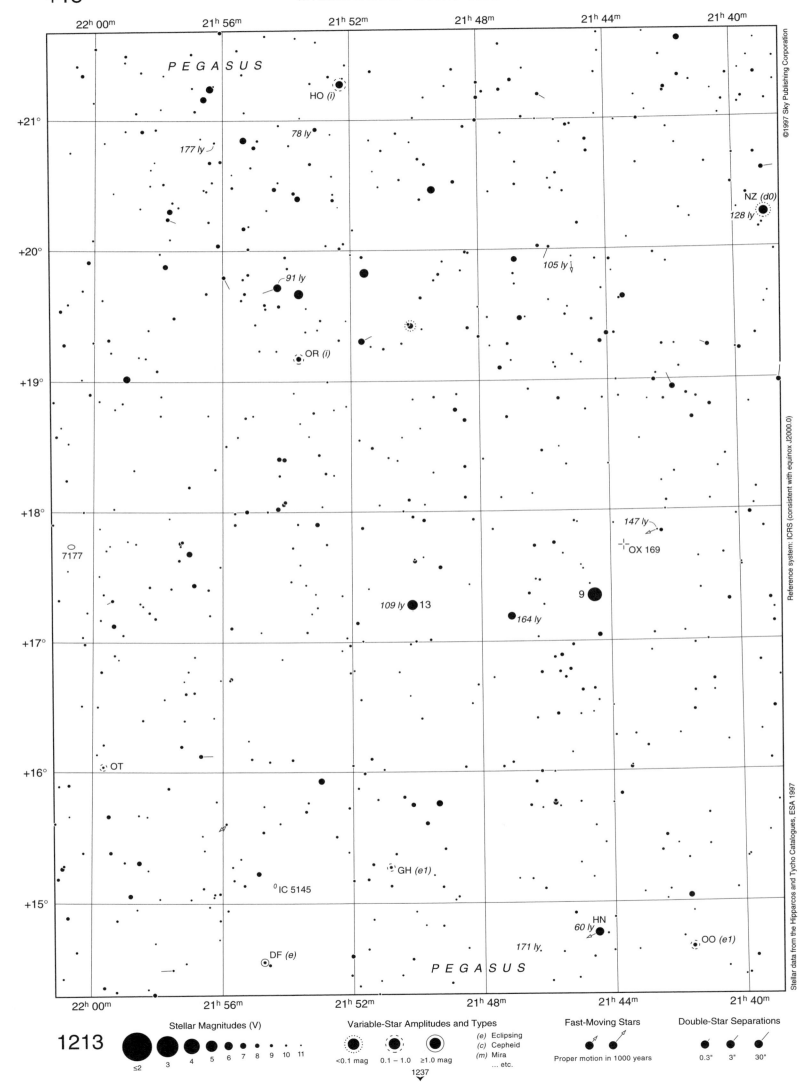

PEGASUS

HO (i)

177 ly

78 ly

NZ (d0)

128 ly

91 ly

105 ly

OR (i)

7177

147 ly

OX 169

9

109 ly 13

164 ly

OT

GH (e1)

0 IC 5145

HN

60 ly

171 ly.

OO (e1)

DF (e)

PEGASUS

1213

**Stellar Magnitudes (V)**

≤2  3  4  5  6  7  8  9  10  11

**Variable-Star Amplitudes and Types**

<0.1 mag    0.1 – 1.0    ≥1.0 mag

(e) Eclipsing
(c) Cepheid
(m) Mira
... etc.

**Fast-Moving Stars**

Proper motion in 1000 years

**Double-Star Separations**

0.3"    3"    30"

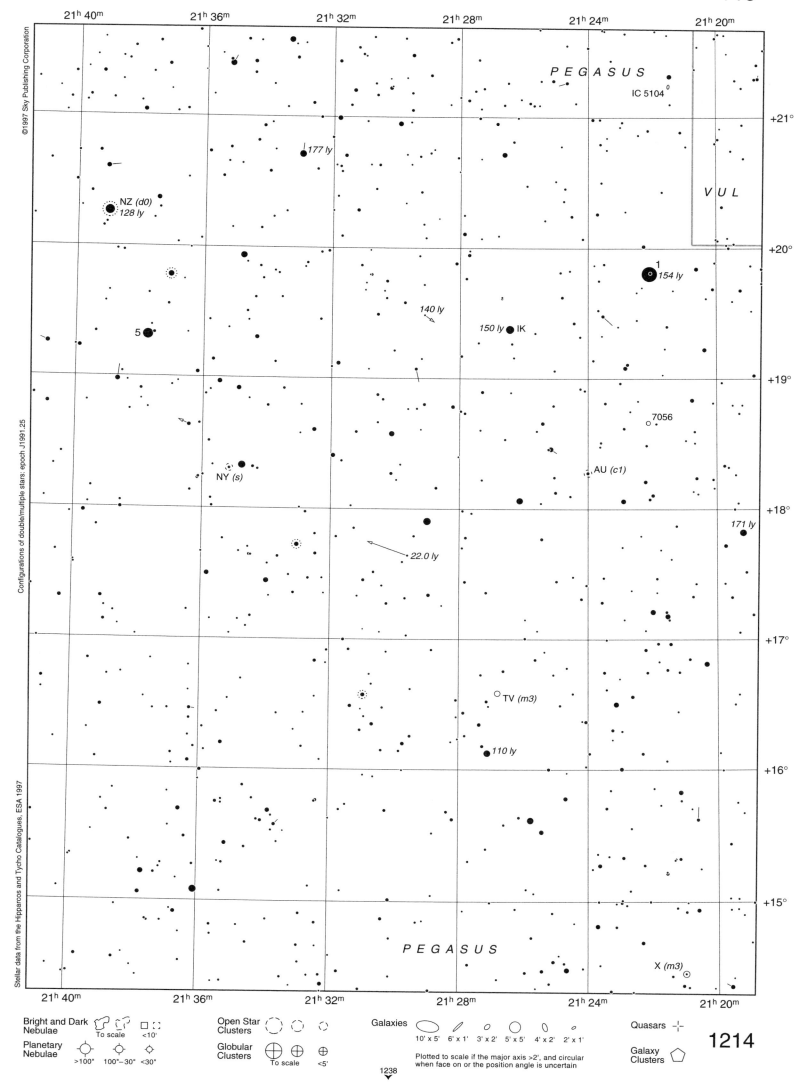

Configurations of double/multiple stars: epoch J1991.25
Stellar data from the Hipparcos and Tycho Catalogues, ESA 1997

21h 40m    21h 36m    21h 32m    21h 28m    21h 24m    21h 20m

P E G A S U S

IC 5104 °

V U L

+21°

177 ly

NZ (d0)
128 ly

1
154 ly

+20°

5

140 ly

150 ly ● IK

7056

+19°

NY (s)

AU (c1)

+18°

171 ly

22.0 ly

+17°

TV (m3)

110 ly

+16°

+15°

P E G A S U S

X (m3)

21h 40m    21h 36m    21h 32m    21h 28m    21h 24m    21h 20m

Bright and Dark Nebulae
To scale        <10'
Planetary Nebulae
>100"  100"–30"  <30"

Open Star Clusters
Globular Clusters
To scale    <5'

Galaxies
10' x 5'  6' x 1'  3' x 2'  5' x 5'  4' x 2'  2' x 1'
Plotted to scale if the major axis >2', and circular
when face on or the position angle is uncertain

Quasars

Galaxy Clusters

1214

1238

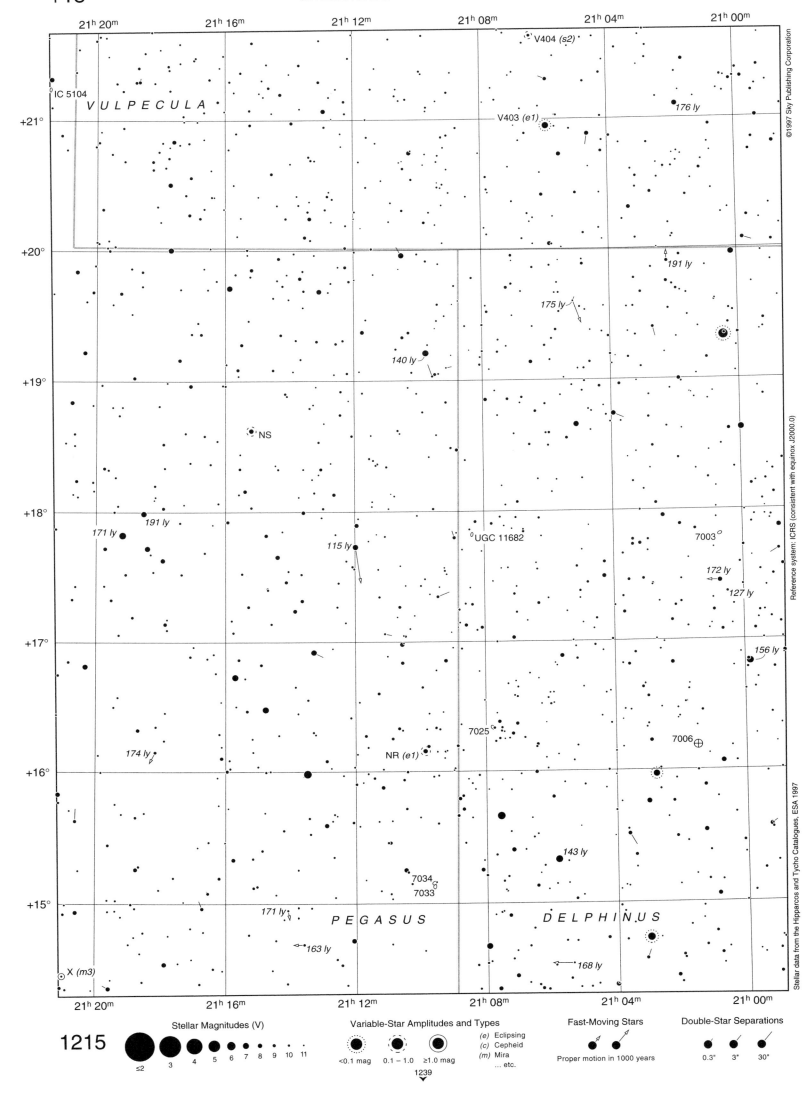

VULPECULA

PEGASUS

DELPHINUS

©1997 Sky Publishing Corporation

Reference system: ICRS (consistent with equinox J2000.0)

Stellar data from the Hipparcos and Tycho Catalogues, ESA 1997

Stellar Magnitudes (V)

≤2   3   4   5   6   7   8   9   10   11

Variable-Star Amplitudes and Types

<0.1 mag    0.1 – 1.0    ≥1.0 mag

(e) Eclipsing
(c) Cepheid
(m) Mira
... etc.

Fast-Moving Stars

Proper motion in 1000 years

Double-Star Separations

0.3"    3"    30"

1239

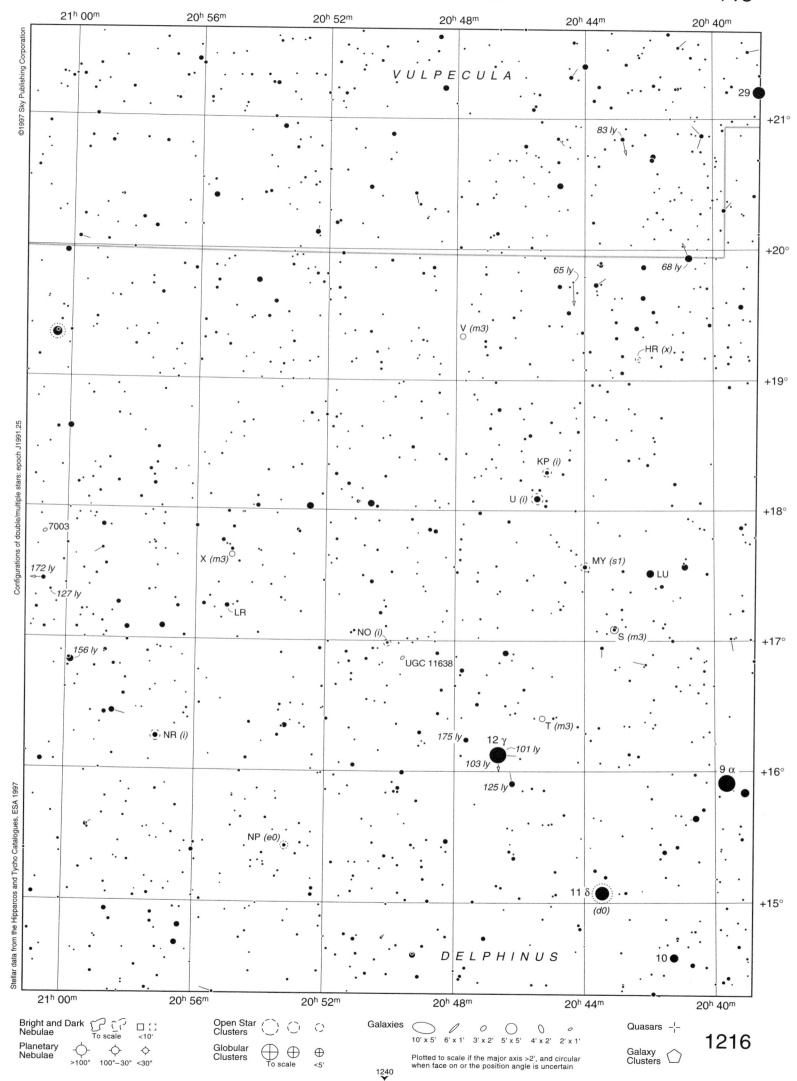

VULPECULA

29

83 ly

+21°

65 ly          68 ly          +20°

V (m3)

HR (x)

+19°

KP (i)

U (i)          +18°

7003

X (m3)          MY (s1)          LU

172 ly          LR

127 ly          NO (i)          S (m3)          +17°

156 ly          UGC 11638

T (m3)

NR (i)          175 ly          12 γ          101 ly

103 ly          9 α          +16°

125 ly

NP (e0)          11 δ          +15°

(d0)

DELPHINUS          10

©1997 Sky Publishing Corporation

Configurations of double/multiple stars: epoch J1991.25

Stellar data from the Hipparcos and Tycho Catalogues, ESA 1997

21h 00m          20h 56m          20h 52m          20h 48m          20h 44m          20h 40m

| Bright and Dark Nebulae | Open Star Clusters | Galaxies | Quasars |
| --- | --- | --- | --- |

To scale     <10'          To scale          10' x 5'   6' x 1'   3' x 2'   5' x 5'   4' x 2'   2' x 1'

Planetary Nebulae          Globular Clusters          Galaxy Clusters

>100"   100"–30"   <30"          To scale   <5'          Plotted to scale if the major axis >2', and circular when face on or the position angle is uncertain

1216

1240

# MILLENNIUM STAR ATLAS

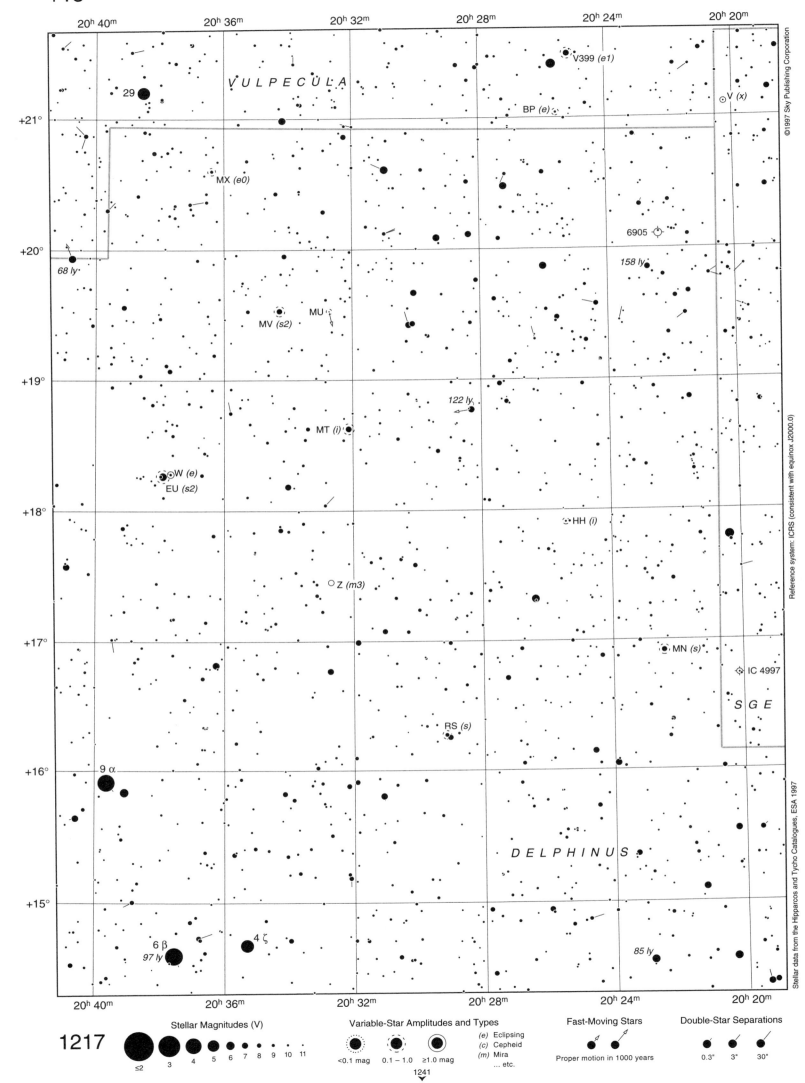

V399 (e1)

BP (e)

V (x)

6905

158 ly

MX (e0)

MV (s2)   MU

MT (i)

122 ly

W (e)
EU (s2)

HH (i)

Z (m3)

MN (s)

IC 4997

RS (s)

68 ly

97 ly

9 α

6 β

4 ζ

85 ly

V U L P E C U L A

D E L P H I N U S

S G E

## 1217

**Stellar Magnitudes (V)**

≤2    3    4    5    6    7    8    9    10    11

**Variable-Star Amplitudes and Types**

<0.1 mag    0.1 – 1.0    ≥1.0 mag

(e) Eclipsing
(c) Cepheid
(m) Mira
... etc.

**Fast-Moving Stars**

Proper motion in 1000 years

**Double-Star Separations**

0.3"    3"    30"

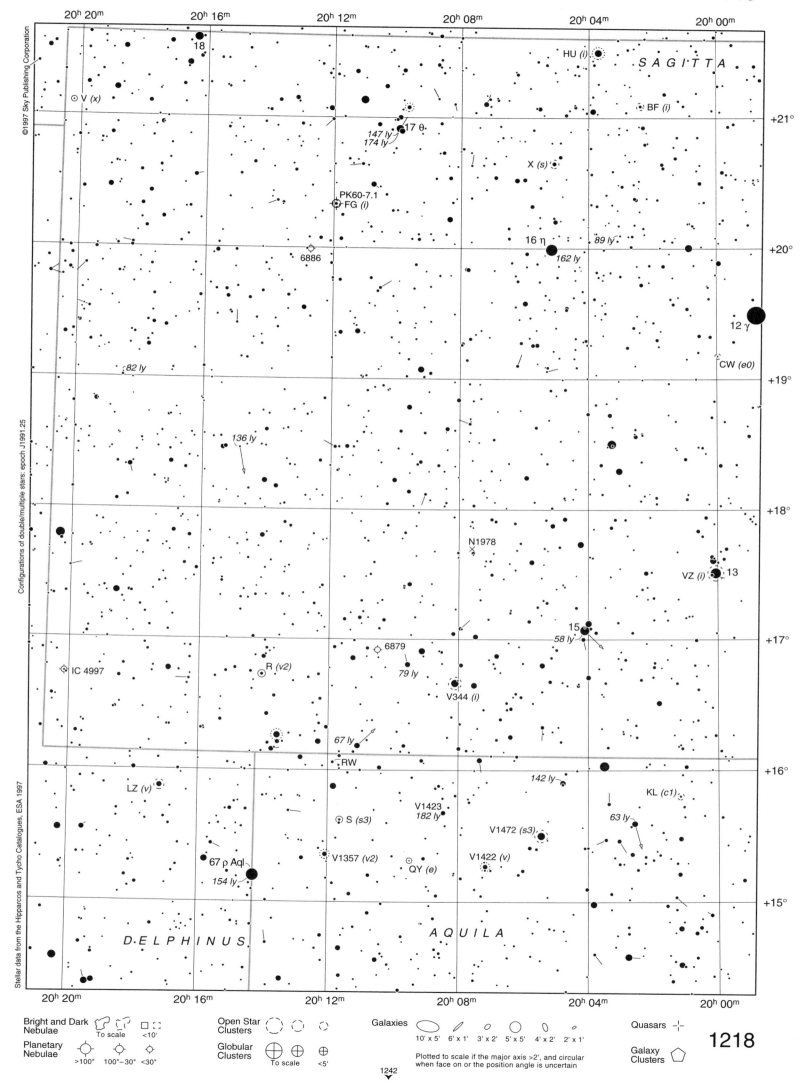

© 1997 Sky Publishing Corporation

Configurations of double/multiple stars: epoch J1991.25

Stellar data from the Hipparcos and Tycho Catalogues, ESA 1997

20h 20m   20h 16m   20h 12m   20h 08m   20h 04m   20h 00m

18

V (x)

HU (i)

SAGITTA

BF (i)

+21°

17 θ
147 ly
174 ly

X (s)

PK60-7.1
FG (i)

16 η
162 ly

89 ly

+20°

6886

12 γ

82 ly

CW (e0)

+19°

136 ly

+18°

N1978

VZ (i)   13

15
58 ly

+17°

IC 4997

R (v2)

6879

79 ly

V344 (i)

67 ly

RW

142 ly

+16°

LZ (v)

KL (c1)

V1423
182 ly

63 ly

S (s3)

V1472 (s3)

V1357 (v2)

QY (e)

V1422 (v)

67 ρ Aql
154 ly

DELPHINUS

AQUILA

+15°

20h 20m   20h 16m   20h 12m   20h 08m   20h 04m   20h 00m

Bright and Dark Nebulae
To scale   <10'

Open Star Clusters

Galaxies
10' x 5'   6' x 1'   3' x 2'   5' x 5'   4' x 2'   2' x 1'

Quasars

Planetary Nebulae
>100"   100"–30"   <30"

Globular Clusters
To scale   <5'

Plotted to scale if the major axis >2', and circular when face on or the position angle is uncertain

Galaxy Clusters

1218

1242

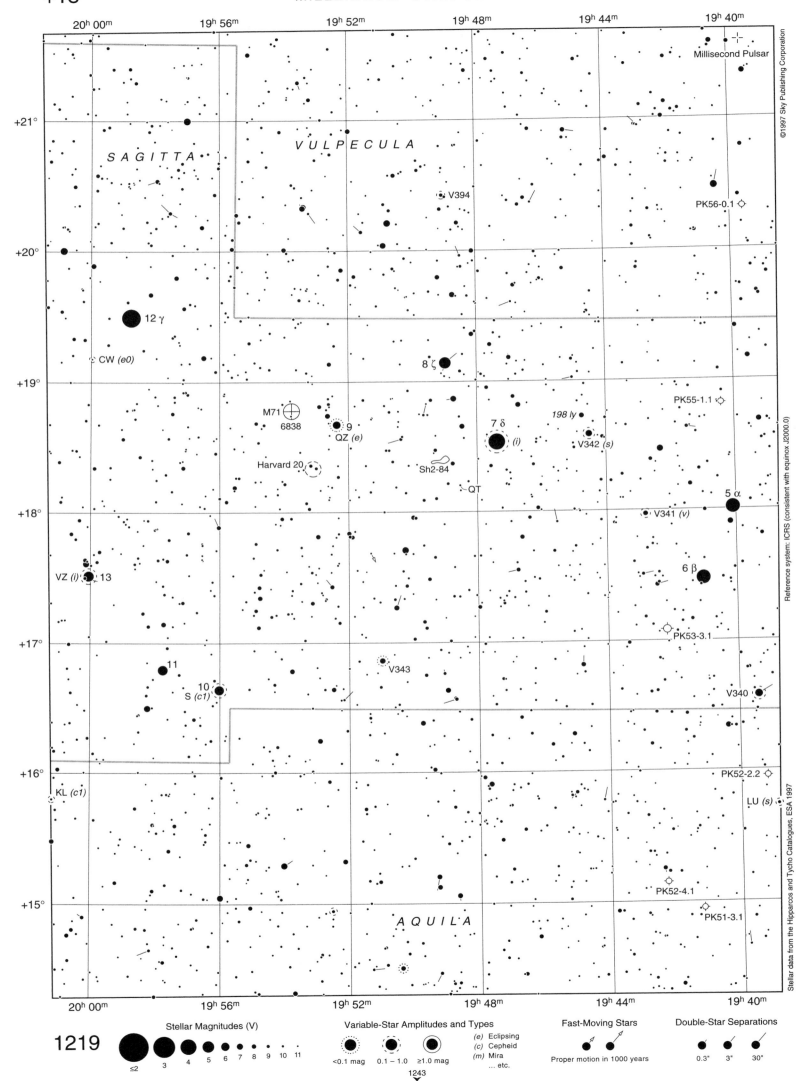

Reference system: ICRS (consistent with equinox J2000.0)

Stellar data from the Hipparcos and Tycho Catalogues, ESA 1997

20ʰ 00ᵐ    19ʰ 56ᵐ    19ʰ 52ᵐ    19ʰ 48ᵐ    19ʰ 44ᵐ    19ʰ 40ᵐ

+21°

+20°

+19°

+18°

+17°

+16°

+15°

SAGITTA

VULPECULA

AQUILA

Millisecond Pulsar

PK56-0.1

V394

8 ζ

12 γ

CW (e0)

M71
6838

9
QZ (e)

Harvard 20

Sh2-84

QT

7 δ
(i)

198 ly

V342 (s)

PK55-1.1

5 α

V341 (v)

6 β

PK53-3.1

V340

VZ (i)  13

11

10
S (c1)

V343

PK52-2.2

LU (s)

KL (c1)

PK52-4.1

PK51-3.1

20ʰ 00ᵐ    19ʰ 56ᵐ    19ʰ 52ᵐ    19ʰ 48ᵐ    19ʰ 44ᵐ    19ʰ 40ᵐ

1219

Stellar Magnitudes (V)

≤2    3    4    5    6    7    8    9   10  11

Variable-Star Amplitudes and Types

<0.1 mag    0.1 – 1.0    ≥1.0 mag

(e) Eclipsing
(c) Cepheid
(m) Mira
... etc.

Fast-Moving Stars

Proper motion in 1000 years

Double-Star Separations

0.3"    3"    30"

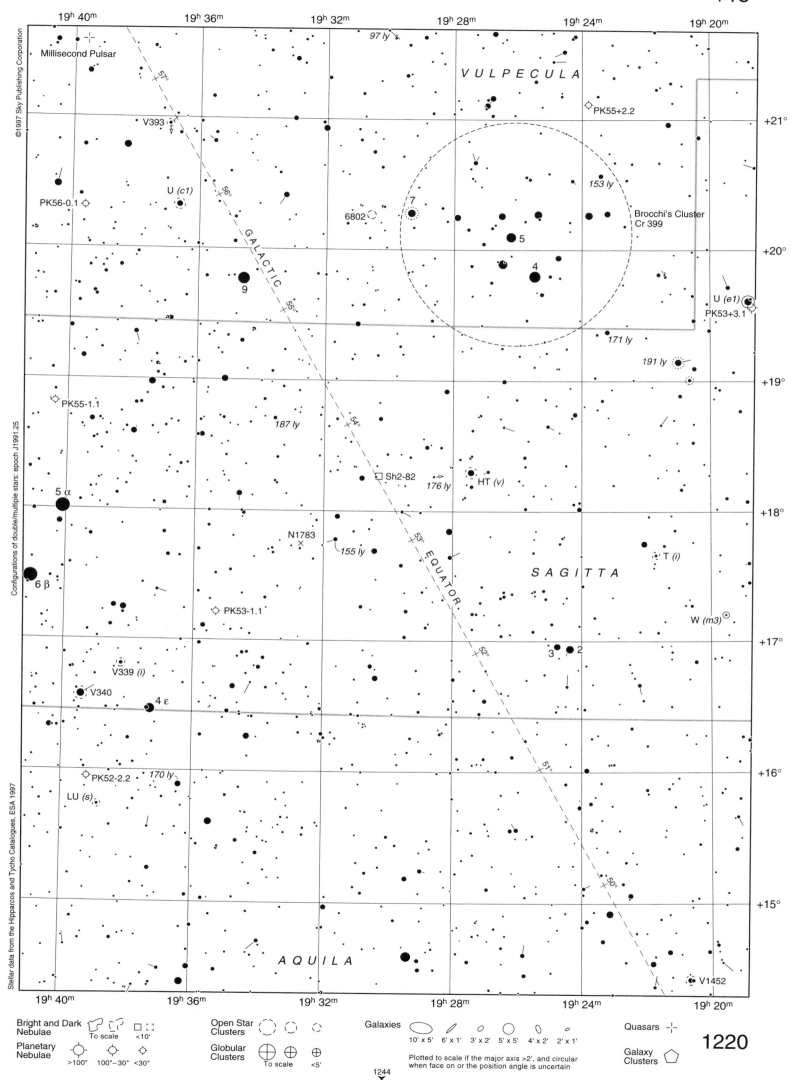

19h 40m   19h 36m   19h 32m   19h 28m   19h 24m   19h 20m

©1997 Sky Publishing Corporation

Millisecond Pulsar

V393

U (c1)

PK56-0.1

PK55-1.1

5 α

6 β

Configurations of double/multiple stars: epoch J1991.25

Stellar data from the Hipparcos and Tycho Catalogues, ESA 1997

97 ly

*VULPECULA*

PK55+2.2

153 ly

6802   7

5

9   4

Brocchi's Cluster
Cr 399

U (e1)
PK53+3.1

171 ly

191 ly

187 ly

Sh2-82

176 ly   HT (v)

54°

N1783

155 ly

*EQUATOR*

PK53-1.1

53°

*SAGITTA*

T (i)

W (m3)

52°

3   2

V339 (i)

V340

4 ε

51°

PK52-2.2   170 ly

LU (s)

50°

*AQUILA*

V1452

19h 40m   19h 36m   19h 32m   19h 28m   19h 24m   19h 20m

+21°

+20°

+19°

+18°

+17°

+16°

+15°

Bright and Dark
Nebulae
To scale   <10'

Planetary
Nebulae
>100"  100"–30"  <30"

Open Star
Clusters

Globular
Clusters
To scale   <5'

Galaxies
10' x 5'  6' x 1'  3' x 2'  5' x 5'  4' x 2'  2' x 1'

Plotted to scale if the major axis >2', and circular
when face on or the position angle is uncertain

Quasars

Galaxy
Clusters

1220

1244

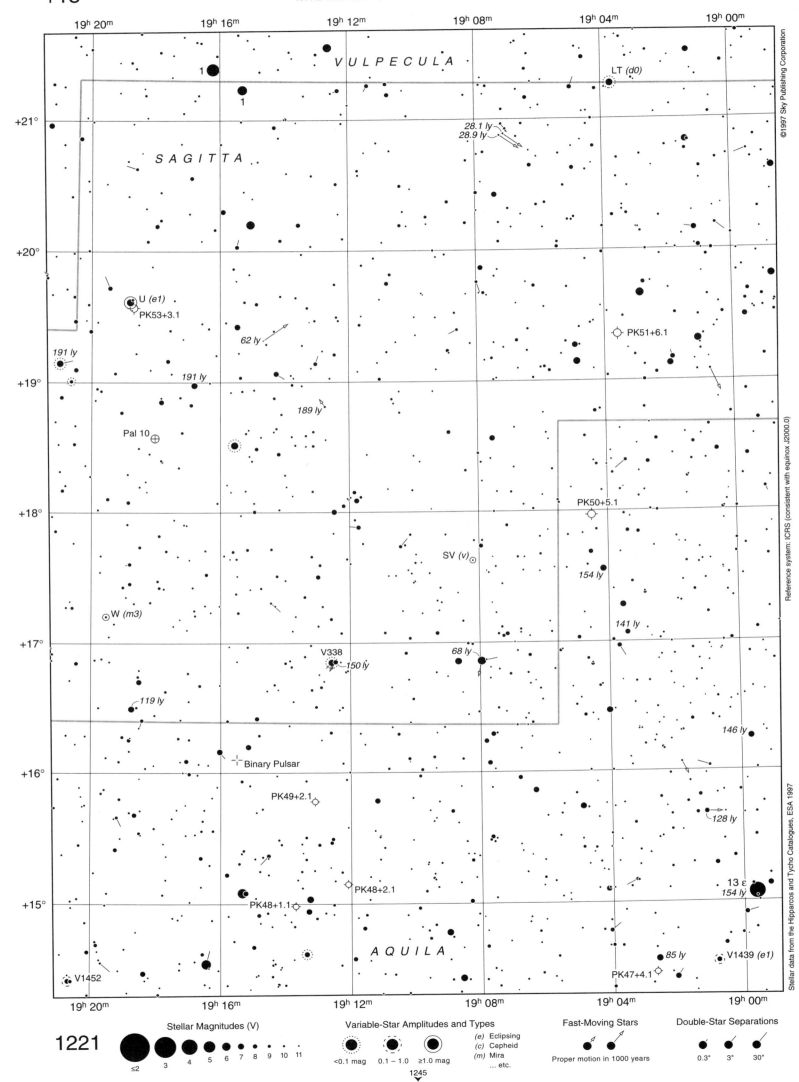

1221

Stellar Magnitudes (V)
≤2  3  4  5  6  7  8  9 10 11

Variable-Star Amplitudes and Types
<0.1 mag    0.1 – 1.0    ≥1.0 mag

(e) Eclipsing
(c) Cepheid
(m) Mira
... etc.

Fast-Moving Stars
Proper motion in 1000 years

Double-Star Separations
0.3"   3"   30"

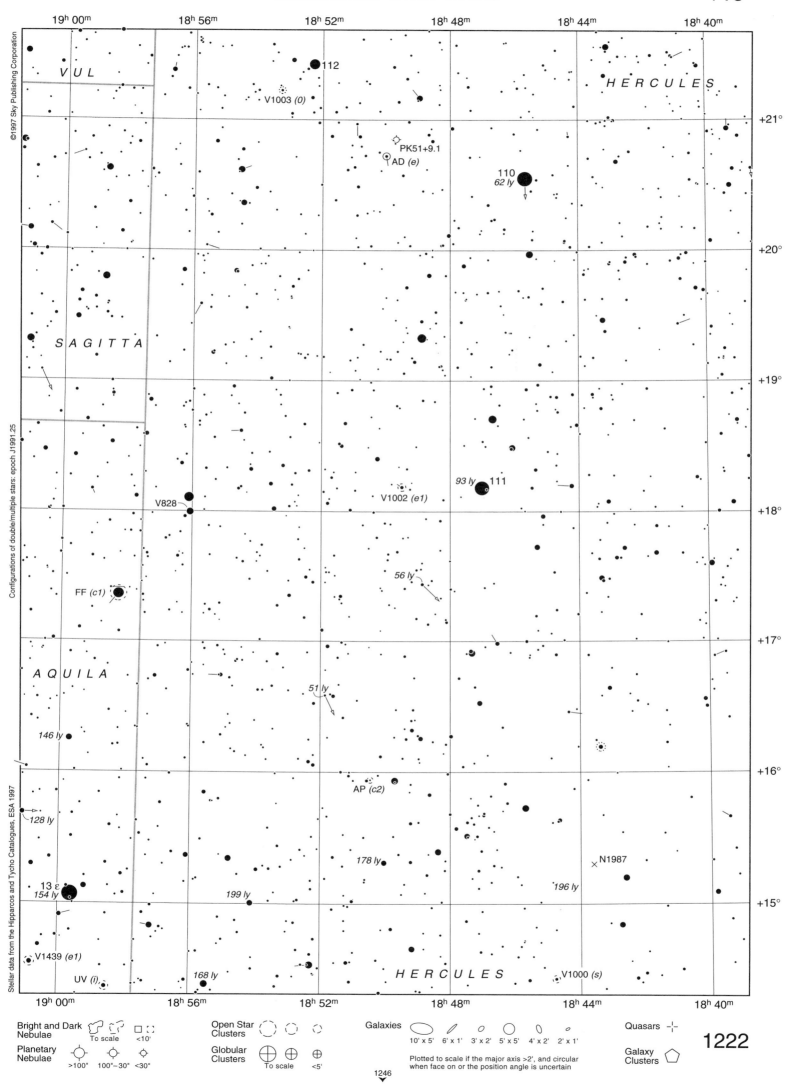

VUL

HERCULES

112

V1003 (0)

PK51+9.1
AD (e)

110
62 ly

+21°

+20°

SAGITTA

+19°

V828

93 ly 111

V1002 (e1)

+18°

56 ly

FF (c1)

51 ly

+17°

AQUILA

146 ly

AP (c2)

+16°

128 ly

178 ly

N1987

13 ε
154 ly        199 ly        196 ly

+15°

V1439 (e1)

UV (i)        168 ly        HERCULES        V1000 (s)

19h 00m        18h 56m        18h 52m        18h 48m        18h 44m        18h 40m

| Bright and Dark Nebulae | Open Star Clusters | Galaxies | Quasars |
| Planetary Nebulae | Globular Clusters | | Galaxy Clusters |

To scale   <10'

To scale   <5'

>100"  100"–30"  <30"

10' x 5'   6' x 1'   3' x 2'   5' x 5'   4' x 2'   2' x 1'

Plotted to scale if the major axis >2', and circular
when face on or the position angle is uncertain

+18°

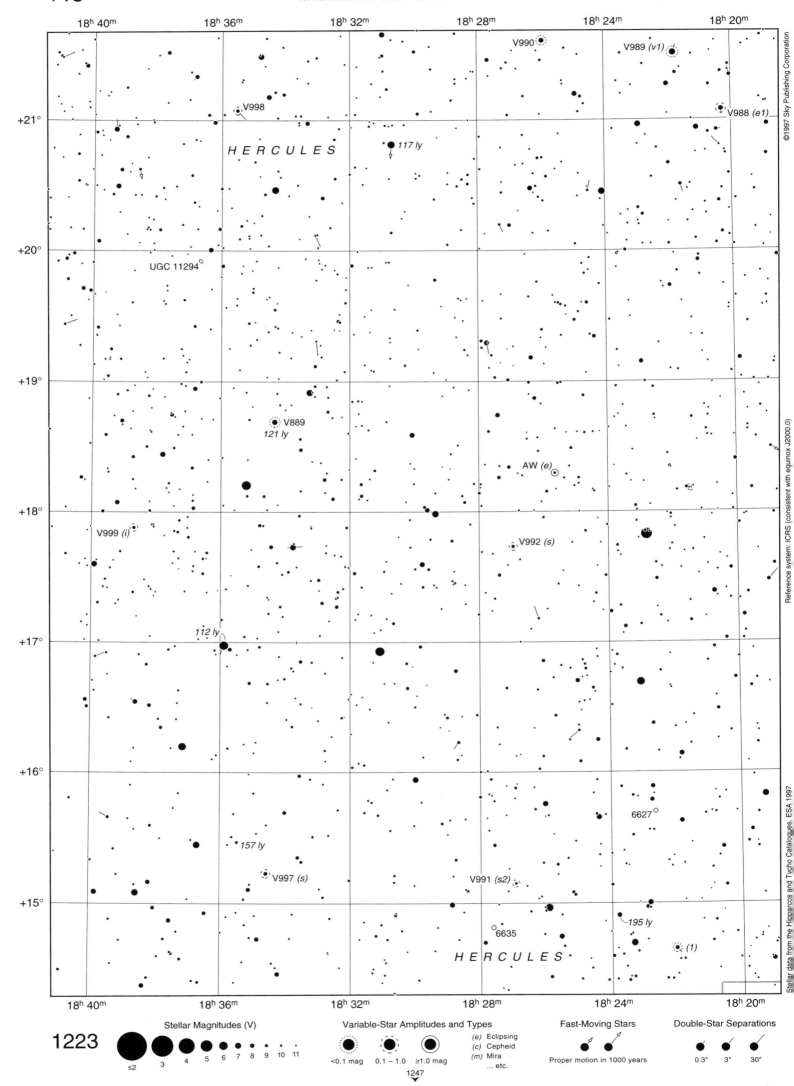

HERCULES

V998

V990

V989 (v1)

V988 (e1)

117 ly

+21°

UGC 11294

+20°

+19°

V889

121 ly

AW (e)

+18°

V999 (i)

V992 (s)

112 ly

+17°

6627

+16°

157 ly

V997 (s)

V991 (s2)

195 ly

6635

(1)

+15°

HERCULES

©1997 Sky Publishing Corporation

Reference system: ICRS (consistent with equinox J2000.0)

Stellar data from the Hipparcos and Tycho Catalogues, ESA 1997

18ʰ 40ᵐ   18ʰ 36ᵐ   18ʰ 32ᵐ   18ʰ 28ᵐ   18ʰ 24ᵐ   18ʰ 20ᵐ

**1223**

Stellar Magnitudes (V)

≤2   3   4   5   6   7   8   9   10   11

Variable-Star Amplitudes and Types

<0.1 mag   0.1 – 1.0   ≥1.0 mag

(e) Eclipsing
(c) Cepheid
(m) Mira
... etc.

Fast-Moving Stars

Proper motion in 1000 years

Double-Star Separations

0.3"   3"   30"

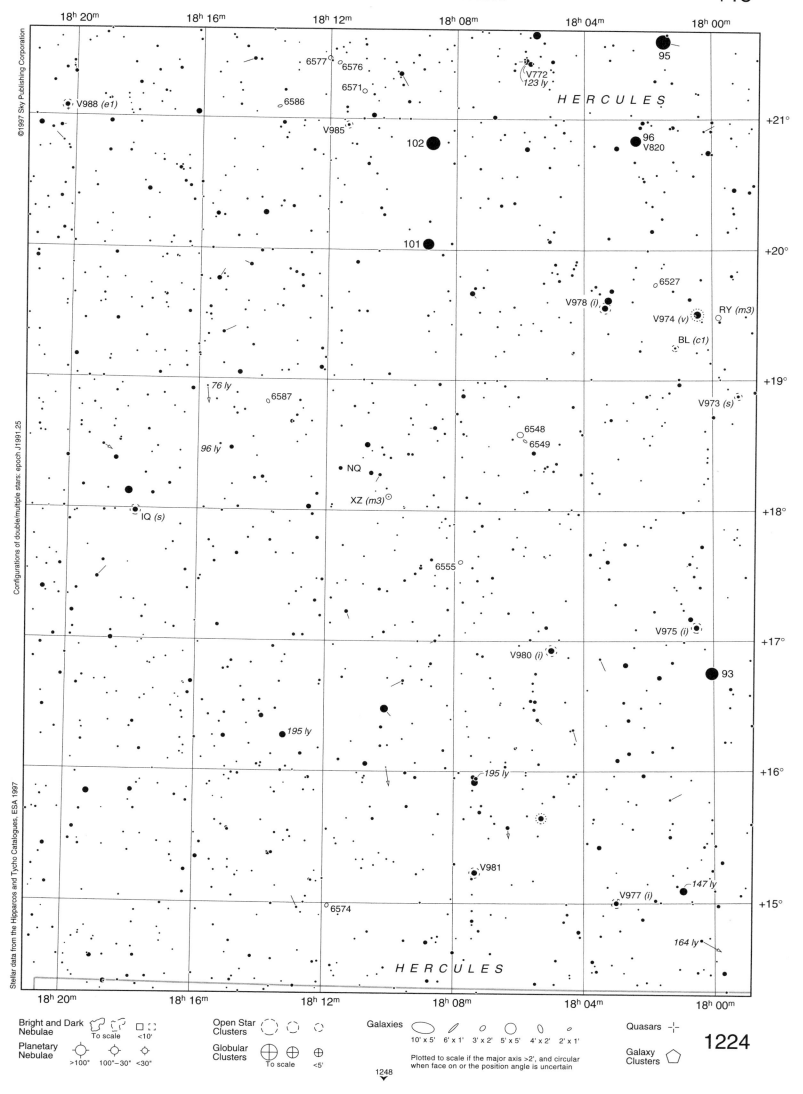

©1997 Sky Publishing Corporation

Configurations of double/multiple stars: epoch J1991.25

Stellar data from the Hipparcos and Tycho Catalogues, ESA 1997

18h 20m   18h 16m   18h 12m   18h 08m   18h 04m   18h 00m

+21°
+20°
+19°
+18°
+17°
+16°
+15°

HERCULES

V988 (e1)
6577  6576
6571
6586
V985
102
101
V772
123 ly
95
96
V820
6527
V978 (i)
V974 (v)
RY (m3)
BL (c1)
V973 (s)
76 ly
6587
6548
6549
96 ly
NQ
XZ (m3)
IQ (s)
6555
V975 (i)
V980 (i)
93
195 ly
195 ly
V981
V977 (i)
147 ly
6574
164 ly

HERCULES

1224

1248

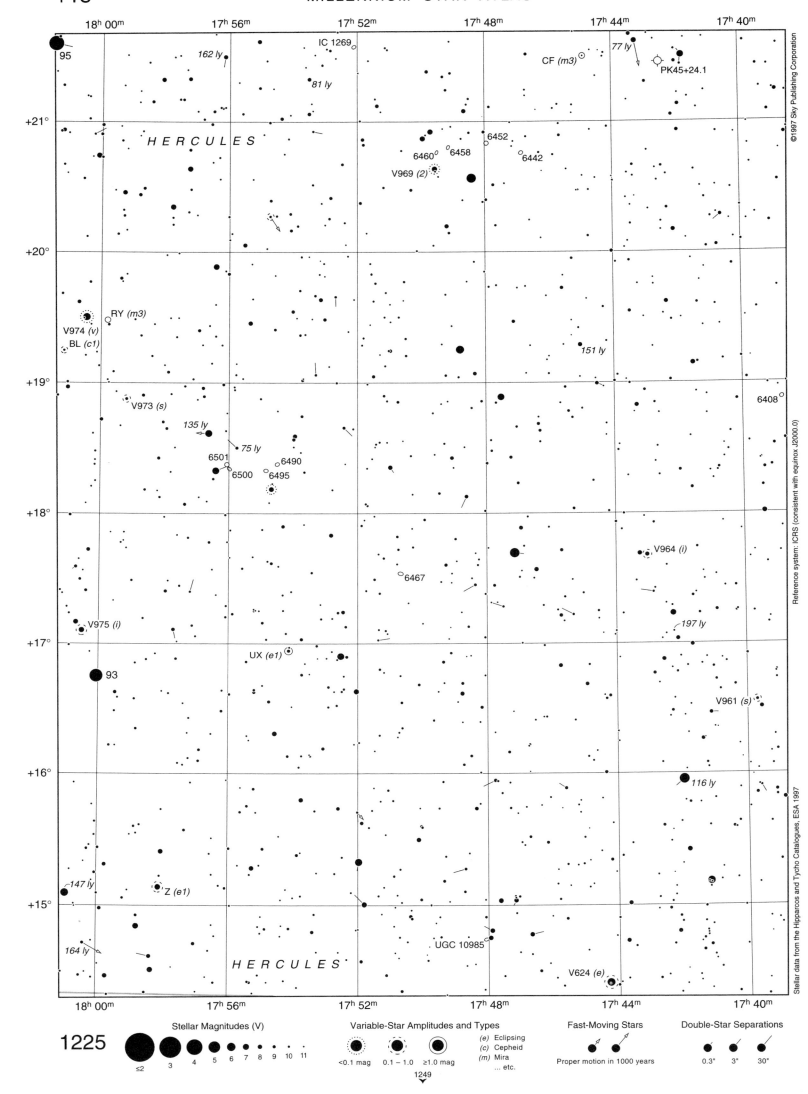

©1997 Sky Publishing Corporation

Reference system: ICRS (consistent with equinox J2000.0)

Stellar data from the Hipparcos and Tycho Catalogues, ESA 1997

1225

Stellar Magnitudes (V)

≤2   3   4   5   6   7   8   9   10   11

Variable-Star Amplitudes and Types

<0.1 mag    0.1 – 1.0    ≥1.0 mag

(e) Eclipsing
(c) Cepheid
(m) Mira
... etc.

Fast-Moving Stars

Proper motion in 1000 years

Double-Star Separations

0.3"   3"   30"

1249

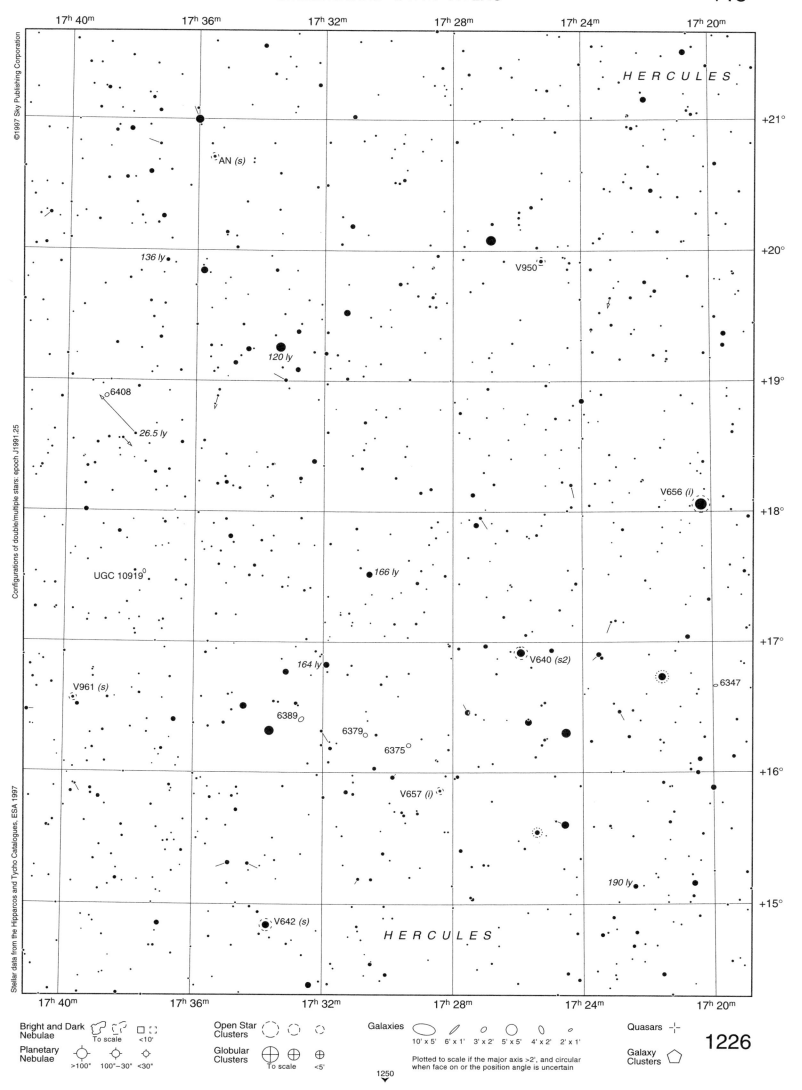

HERCULES

AN *(s)*

136 ly

120 ly

6408

26.5 ly

V950

V656 *(i)*

UGC 10919

166 ly

V640 *(s2)*

6347

V961 *(s)*

164 ly

6389

6379

6375

V657 *(i)*

190 ly

V642 *(s)*

HERCULES

| | | | | |
|---|---|---|---|---|
| 17h 40m | 17h 36m | 17h 32m | 17h 28m | 17h 24m | 17h 20m |

+21°
+20°
+19°
+18°
+17°
+16°
+15°

Bright and Dark Nebulae
To scale  <10'

Planetary Nebulae
>100"  100"–30"  <30"

Open Star Clusters

Globular Clusters
To scale  <5'

Galaxies
10' x 5'  6' x 1'  3' x 2'  5' x 5'  4' x 2'  2' x 1'
Plotted to scale if the major axis >2', and circular when face on or the position angle is uncertain

Quasars

Galaxy Clusters

**1226**

1250

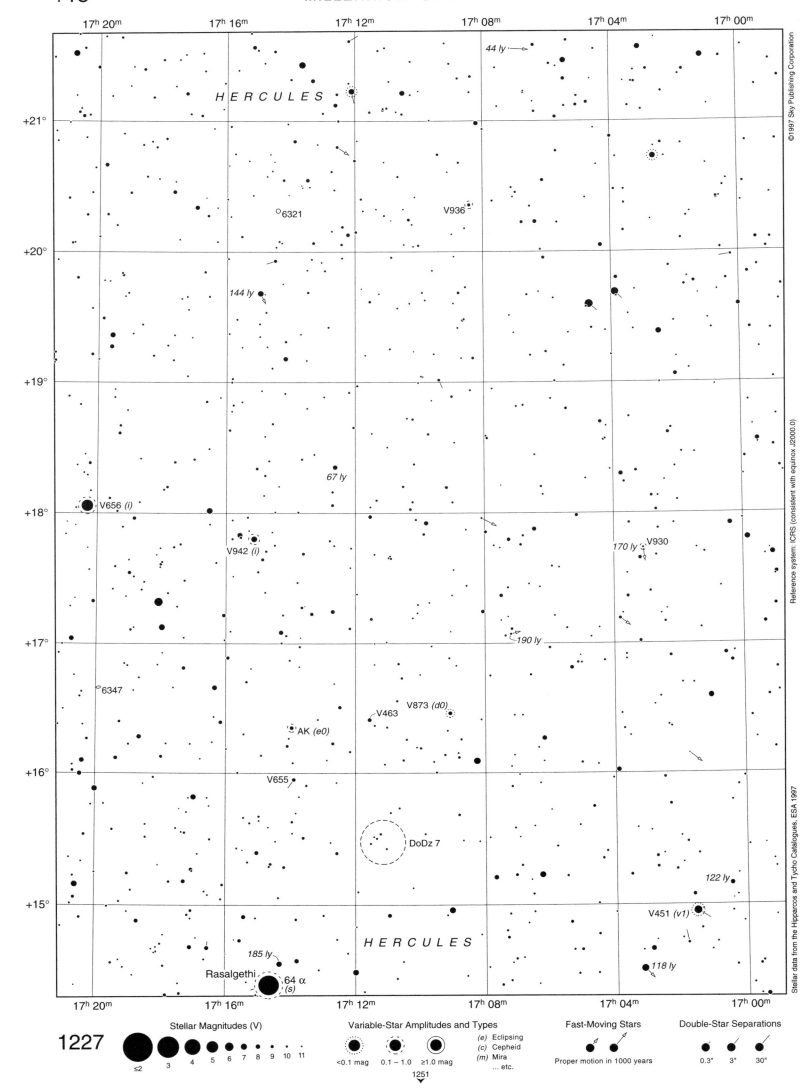

©1997 Sky Publishing Corporation

Reference system: ICRS (consistent with equinox J2000.0)

Stellar data from the Hipparcos and Tycho Catalogues, ESA 1997

H E R C U L E S

44 ly

6321

V936

144 ly

67 ly

V656 (i)

V942 (i)

170 ly   V930

190 ly

6347

V873 (d0)
V463

AK (e0)

V655

DoDz 7

122 ly

V451 (v1)

H E R C U L E S

185 ly

118 ly

Rasalgethi    64 α
              (s)

Stellar Magnitudes (V)

≤2   3   4   5   6   7   8   9  10  11

Variable-Star Amplitudes and Types

<0.1 mag    0.1 – 1.0    ≥1.0 mag

(e) Eclipsing
(c) Cepheid
(m) Mira
... etc.

Fast-Moving Stars

Proper motion in 1000 years

Double-Star Separations

0.3"   3"   30"

1251

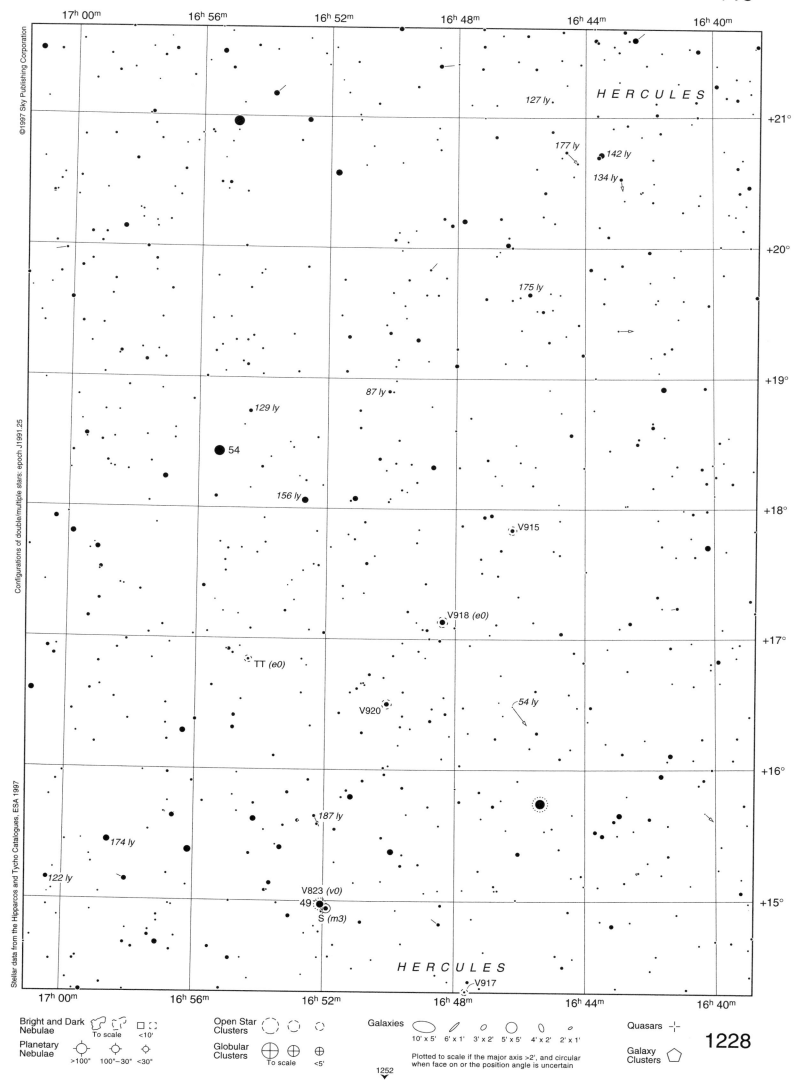

HERCULES

127 ly

177 ly
142 ly
134 ly

175 ly

87 ly
129 ly

54

156 ly

V915

V918 (e0)

TT (e0)

V920

54 ly

187 ly

174 ly

122 ly

V823 (v0)
49
S (m3)

HERCULES

V917

Bright and Dark
Nebulae
To scale  <10'

Planetary
Nebulae
>100"  100"-30"  <30"

Open Star
Clusters

Globular
Clusters
To scale  <5'

Galaxies
10' x 5'  6' x 1'  3' x 2'  5' x 5'  4' x 2'  2' x 1'

Plotted to scale if the major axis >2', and circular
when face on or the position angle is uncertain

Quasars

Galaxy
Clusters

1228

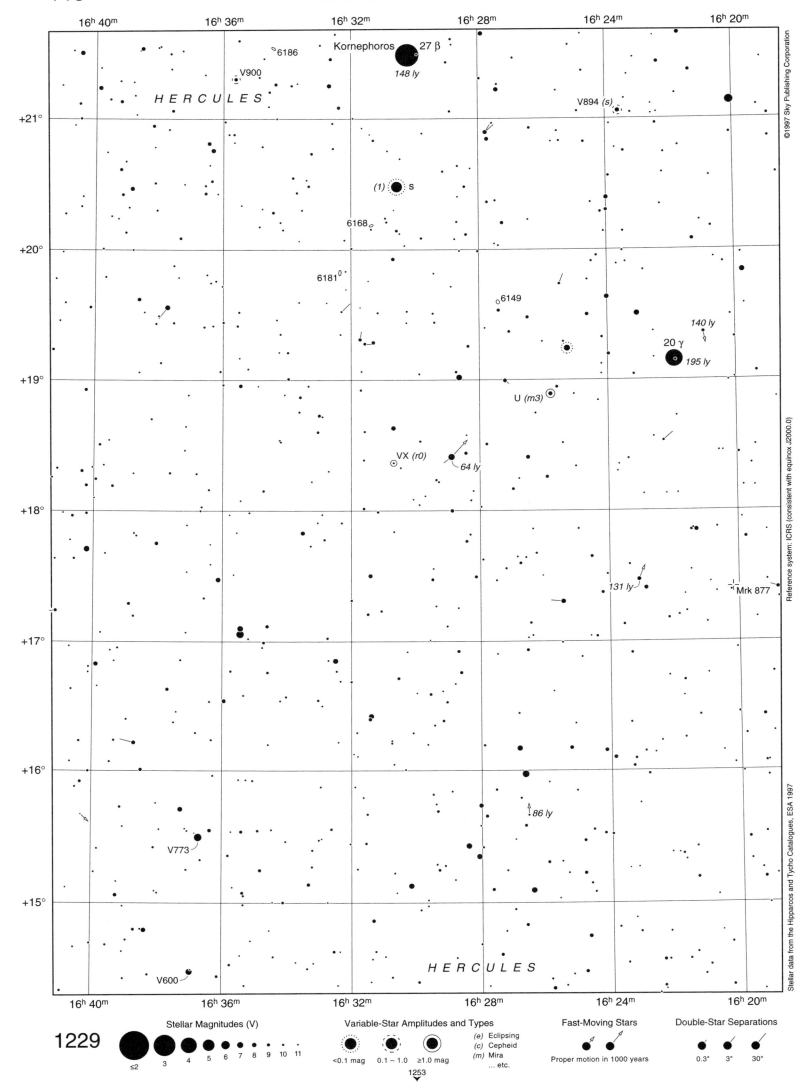

**1229**

Stellar Magnitudes (V)

≤2  3  4  5  6  7  8  9  10  11

Variable-Star Amplitudes and Types

<0.1 mag    0.1 – 1.0    ≥1.0 mag

(e) Eclipsing
(c) Cepheid
(m) Mira
... etc.

Fast-Moving Stars

Proper motion in 1000 years

Double-Star Separations

0.3"   3"   30"

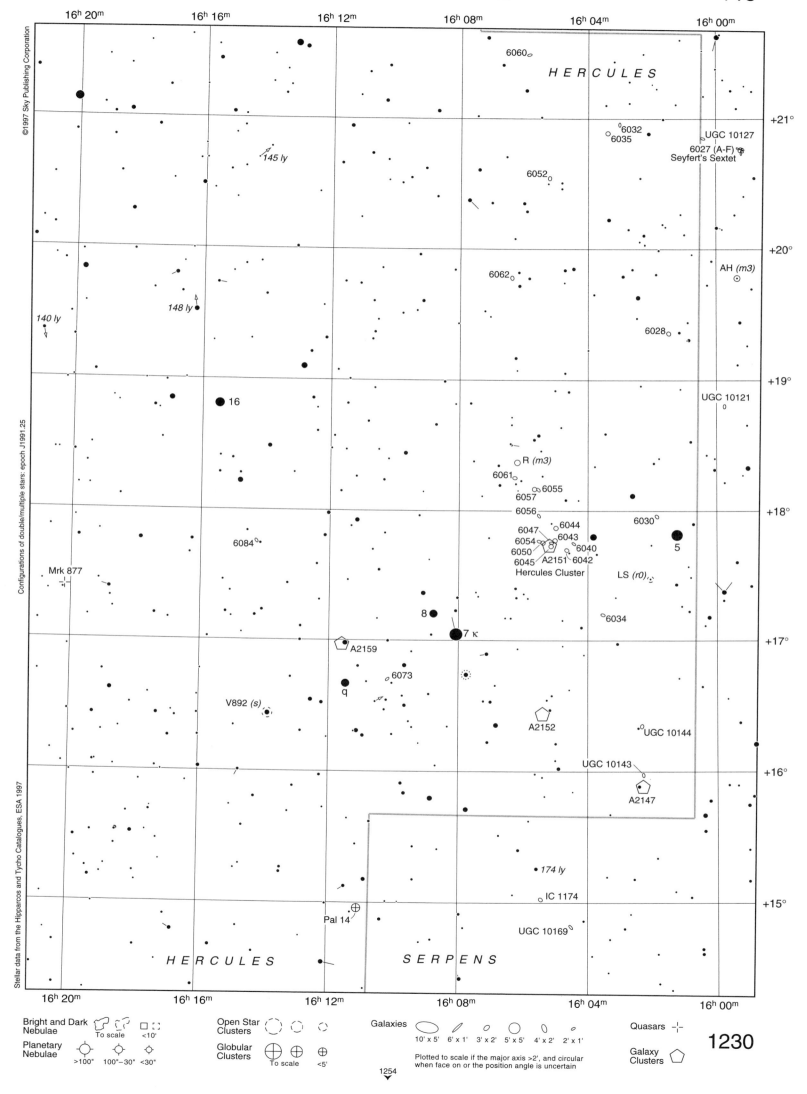

H E R C U L E S

6060

6032
6035
UGC 10127
6027 (A-F)
Seyfert's Sextet

6052

6062

AH *(m3)*

6028

145 ly

148 ly

140 ly

16

UGC 10121

R *(m3)*
6061
6055
6057
6056
6047 6044
6054 6043
6050 6040
6045 A2151 6042
Hercules Cluster
6030
6084
LS *(r0)*
5
Mrk 877
6034
8
7 κ
A2159
6073
q
A2152
V892 *(s)*
UGC 10144
UGC 10143
A2147

174 ly

IC 1174
Pal 14
UGC 10169

H E R C U L E S        S E R P E N S

©1997 Sky Publishing Corporation

Configurations of double/multiple stars: epoch J1991.25

Stellar data from the Hipparcos and Tycho Catalogues, ESA 1997

| | | |
|---|---|---|
| Bright and Dark Nebulae | Open Star Clusters | Galaxies |
| Planetary Nebulae | Globular Clusters | |

Bright and Dark Nebulae
To scale    <10'

Planetary Nebulae
>100"   100"–30"   <30"

Open Star Clusters

Globular Clusters
To scale    <5'

Galaxies
10' x 5'   6' x 1'   3' x 2'   5' x 5'   4' x 2'   2' x 1'

Plotted to scale if the major axis >2', and circular when face on or the position angle is uncertain

Quasars

Galaxy Clusters

# MILLENNIUM STAR ATLAS

+12°

©1997 Sky Publishing Corporation

Reference system: ICRS (consistent with equinox J2000.0)

Stellar data from the Hipparcos and Tycho Catalogues, ESA 1997

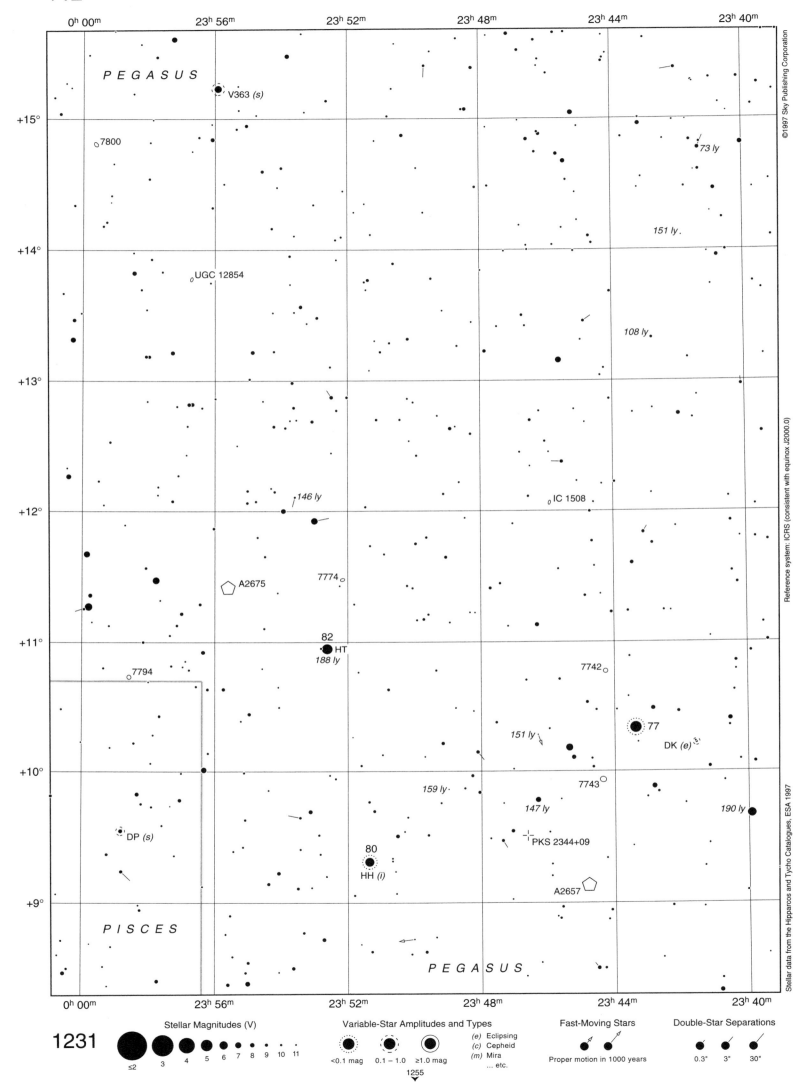

P E G A S U S

V363 (s)

7800

UGC 12854

73 ly

151 ly

108 ly

146 ly

IC 1508

A2675

7774

82
HT
188 ly

7742

7794

77
DK (e)

7743

151 ly

159 ly

147 ly

190 ly

DP (s)

PKS 2344+09

80
HH (i)

A2657

P I S C E S

P E G A S U S

## Stellar Magnitudes (V)

≤2  3  4  5  6  7  8  9  10  11

## Variable-Star Amplitudes and Types

<0.1 mag   0.1 – 1.0   ≥1.0 mag

(e) Eclipsing
(c) Cepheid
(m) Mira
... etc.

## Fast-Moving Stars

Proper motion in 1000 years

## Double-Star Separations

0.3"  3"  30"

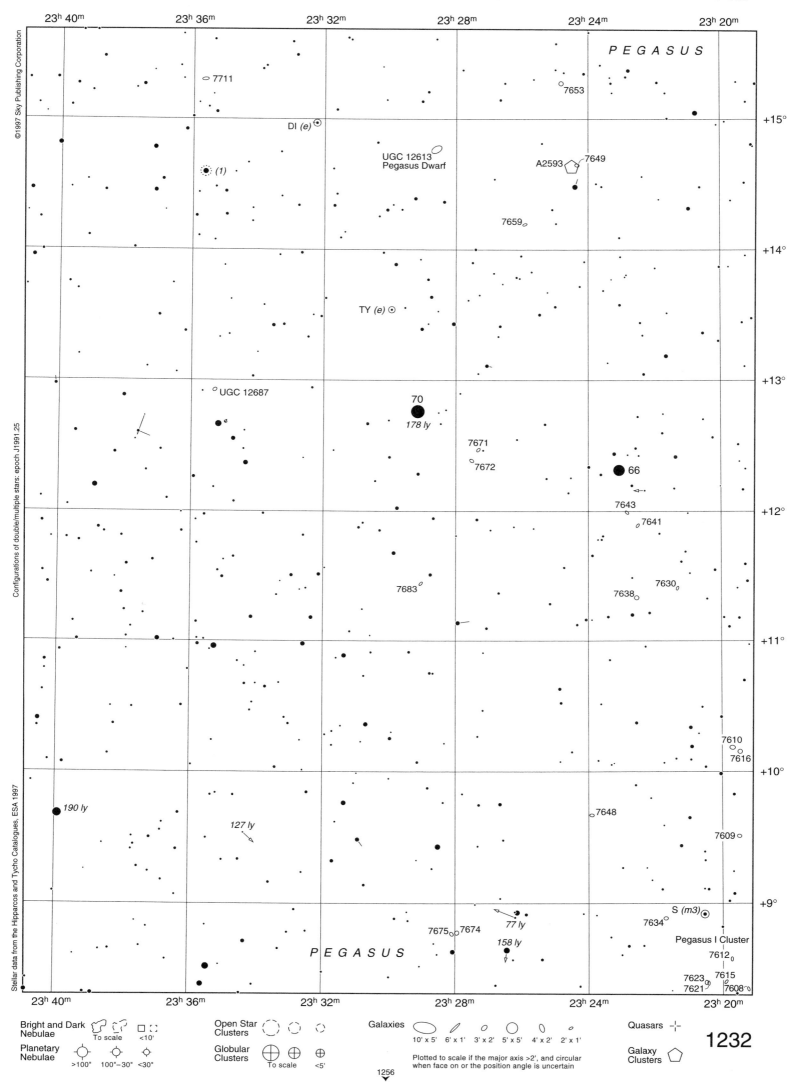

Configurations of double/multiple stars: epoch J1991.25

Stellar data from the Hipparcos and Tycho Catalogues, ESA 1997

PEGASUS

7711

7653

DI (e)

UGC 12613
Pegasus Dwarf

A2593        7649

(1)

7659

+15°

+14°

TY (e)

UGC 12687

70
178 ly

7671
7672

66

7643
7641

+13°

+12°

7683

7630
7638

7610
7616

190 ly

7648

7609

127 ly

S (m3)
7634

77 ly

7675 7674

Pegasus I Cluster

7612

7623    7615
7621    7608

158 ly

PEGASUS

+11°

+10°

+9°

Bright and Dark
Nebulae
To scale    <10'

Planetary
Nebulae
>100"  100"–30"  <30'

Open Star
Clusters

Globular
Clusters
To scale    <5'

Galaxies
10' x 5'   6' x 1'   3' x 2'   5' x 5'   4' x 2'   2' x 1'

Plotted to scale if the major axis >2', and circular
when face on or the position angle is uncertain

Quasars

Galaxy
Clusters

# MILLENNIUM STAR ATLAS

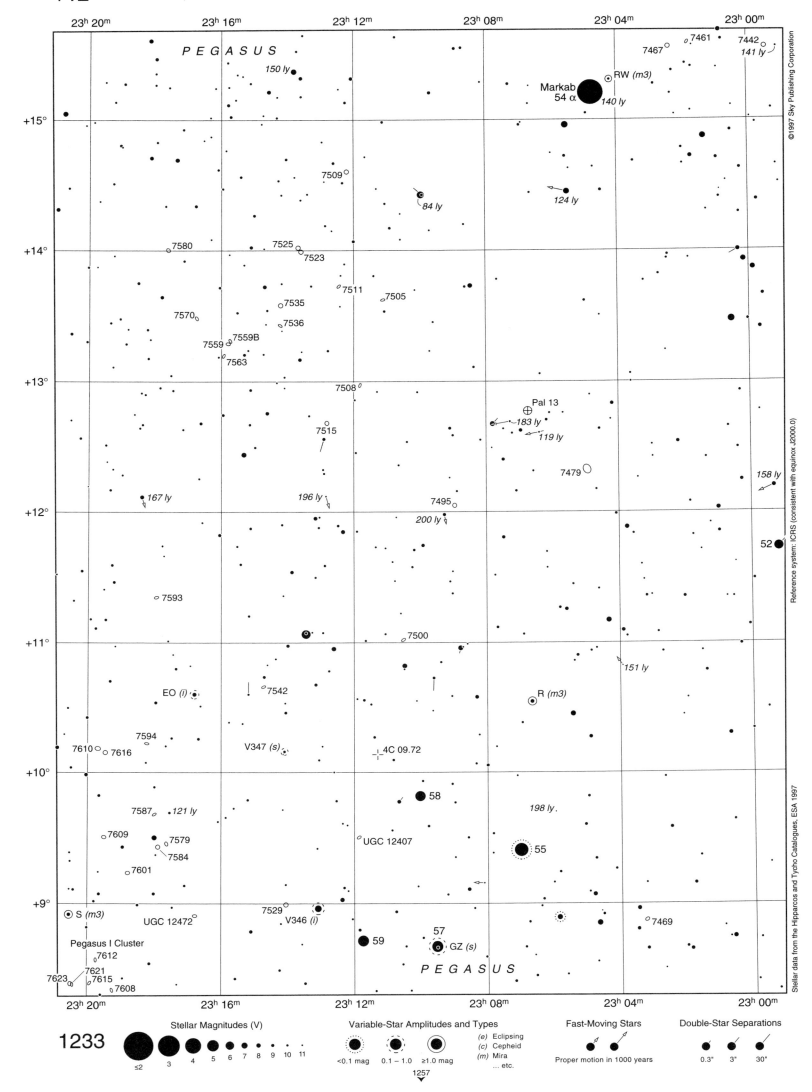

©1997 Sky Publishing Corporation

Reference system: ICRS (consistent with equinox J2000.0)

Stellar data from the Hipparcos and Tycho Catalogues, ESA 1997

1233

**Stellar Magnitudes (V)**

≤2  3  4  5  6  7  8  9  10  11

**Variable-Star Amplitudes and Types**

<0.1 mag   0.1 – 1.0   ≥1.0 mag

(e) Eclipsing
(c) Cepheid
(m) Mira
... etc.

**Fast-Moving Stars**

Proper motion in 1000 years

**Double-Star Separations**

0.3"  3"  30"

1257

# MILLENNIUM STAR ATLAS

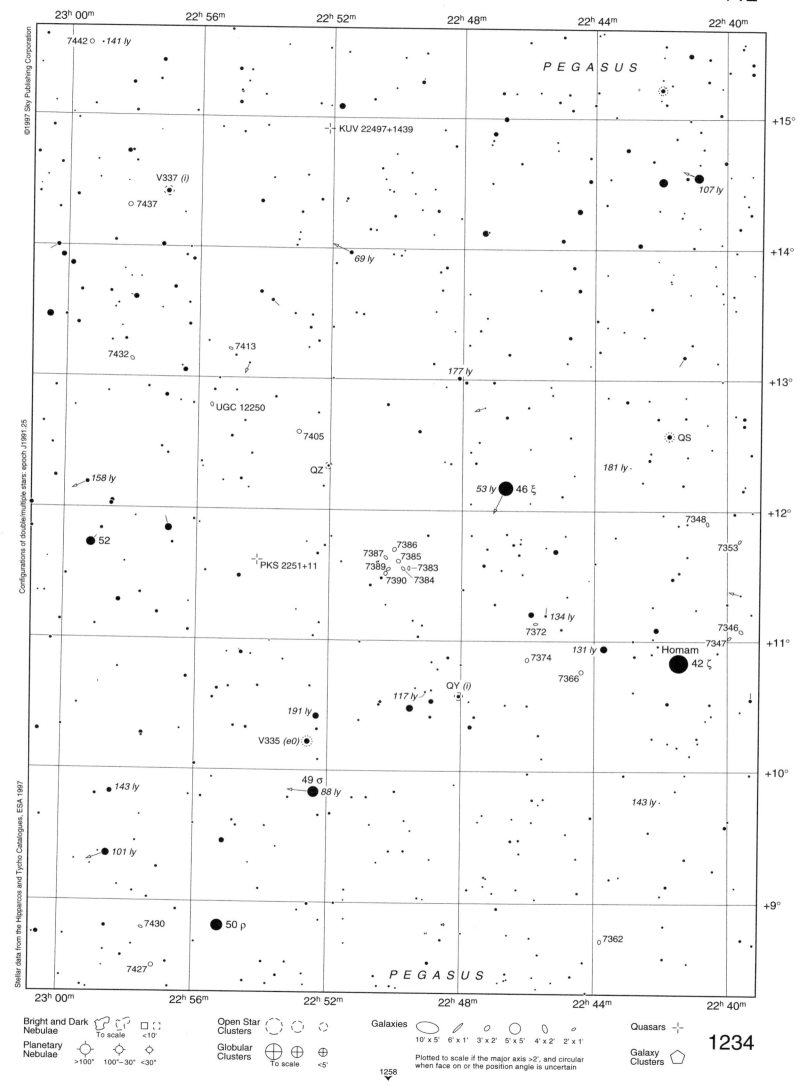

Configurations of double/multiple stars: epoch J1991.25

Stellar data from the Hipparcos and Tycho Catalogues, ESA 1997

23h 00m          22h 56m          22h 52m          22h 48m          22h 44m          22h 40m

P E G A S U S

7442 ○ ·141 ly

+15°

KUV 22497+1439

V337 (i)

○ 7437

107 ly

69 ly

+14°

7432 ○          ○ 7413

177 ly

QS

○ UGC 12250

+13°

○ 7405

181 ly

QZ

158 ly

53 ly ● 46 ξ

+12°

7348 ○

● 52

7353 ○

7386
7387 ○  ○ 7385
PKS 2251+11    7389 ○  ○ ○—7383
            7390  7384

134 ly

7346 ○

7372 ○

7347 ○

131 ly ●          Homam

+11°

○ 7374                    42 ζ

7366 ○

QY (i)

117 ly

191 ly ●

V335 (e0) ⊙

+10°

49 σ
143 ly ●    ● 88 ly

143 ly ·

101 ly ●

+9°

○ 7430    ● 50 ρ

7362 ○

7427 ○

P E G A S U S

23h 00m          22h 56m          22h 52m          22h 48m          22h 44m          22h 40m

---

Bright and Dark
Nebulae                    □    Open Star    ⊙  ○  ○    Galaxies    ⬭  ╱  ○  ○  ◖  ◠    Quasars    ┤├
            To scale   <10'   Clusters                              10'x5' 6'x1' 3'x2' 5'x5' 4'x2' 2'x1'
Planetary                                                                                    Galaxy      ⬠
Nebulae    ◇  ◇  ◇    Globular    ⊕  ⊕  ⊕                                                     Clusters
        >100" 100"–30" <30"   Clusters   To scale  <5'   Plotted to scale if the major axis >2', and circular
                                                          when face on or the position angle is uncertain

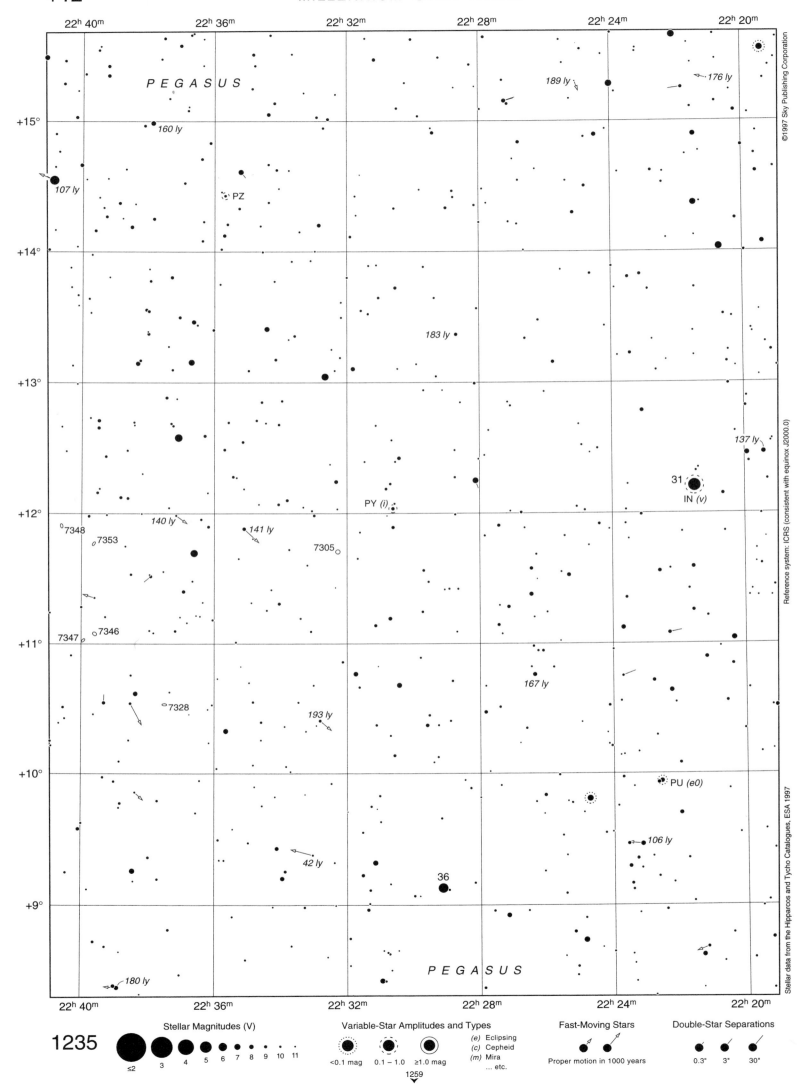

©1997 Sky Publishing Corporation

Reference system: ICRS (consistent with equinox J2000.0)

Stellar data from the Hipparcos and Tycho Catalogues, ESA 1997

PEGASUS

160 ly

PZ

189 ly

176 ly

107 ly

183 ly

137 ly

31

IN (v)

PY (i)

140 ly

7348    7353

141 ly

7305

7347    7346

7328

167 ly

193 ly

PU (e0)

106 ly

42 ly

36

PEGASUS

180 ly

Stellar Magnitudes (V)

≤2    3    4    5    6    7    8    9   10   11

Variable-Star Amplitudes and Types

<0.1 mag    0.1 – 1.0    ≥1.0 mag

(e) Eclipsing
(c) Cepheid
(m) Mira
... etc.

Fast-Moving Stars

Proper motion in 1000 years

Double-Star Separations

0.3"    3"    30"

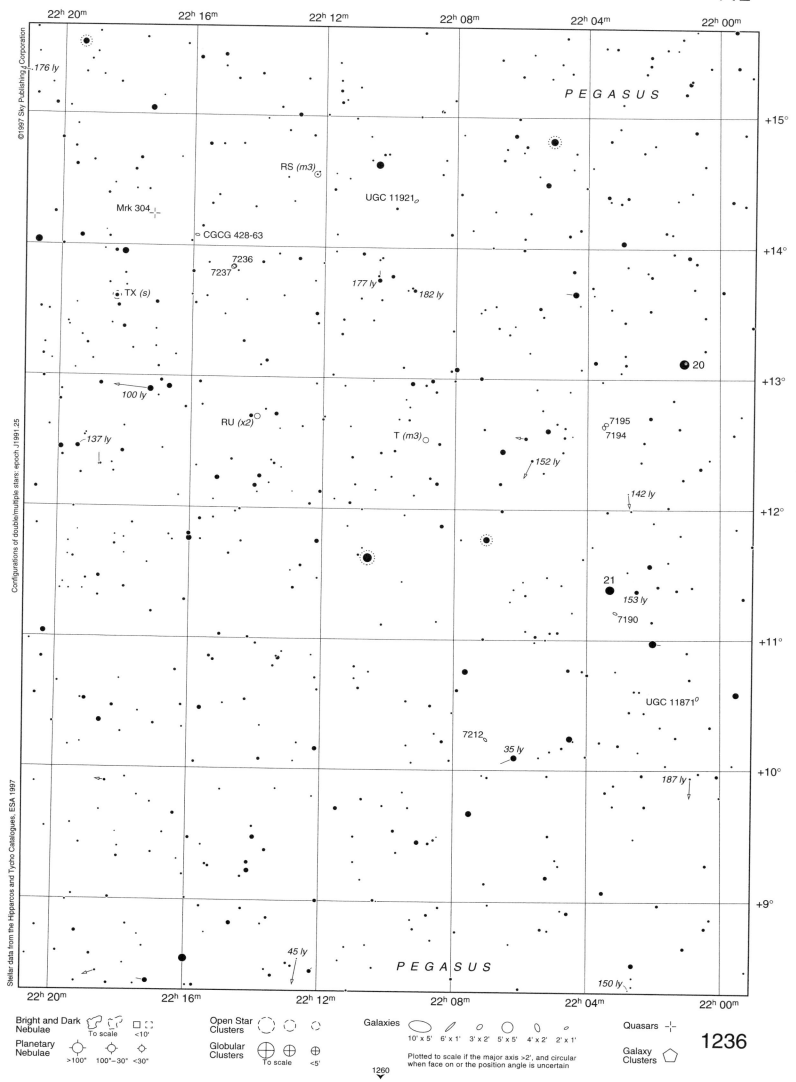

Configurations of double/multiple stars: epoch J1991.25

Stellar data from the Hipparcos and Tycho Catalogues, ESA 1997

P E G A S U S

22h 20m     22h 16m     22h 12m     22h 08m     22h 04m     22h 00m

+15°

RS (m3)

UGC 11921

Mrk 304

CGCG 428-63

+14°

7236
7237

TX (s)

177 ly

182 ly

20

+13°

100 ly

RU (x2)

T (m3)

7195
7194

137 ly

152 ly

142 ly

+12°

21

153 ly

7190

+11°

UGC 11871

7212

35 ly

187 ly

+10°

+9°

45 ly

P E G A S U S

150 ly

22h 20m     22h 16m     22h 12m     22h 08m     22h 04m     22h 00m

Bright and Dark Nebulae — To scale — <10'
Planetary Nebulae — >100" 100"–30" <30"
Open Star Clusters
Globular Clusters — To scale — <5'
Galaxies — 10' x 5' 6' x 1' 3' x 2' 5' x 5' 4' x 2' 2' x 1'
Plotted to scale if the major axis >2', and circular when face on or the position angle is uncertain
Quasars
Galaxy Clusters

1236

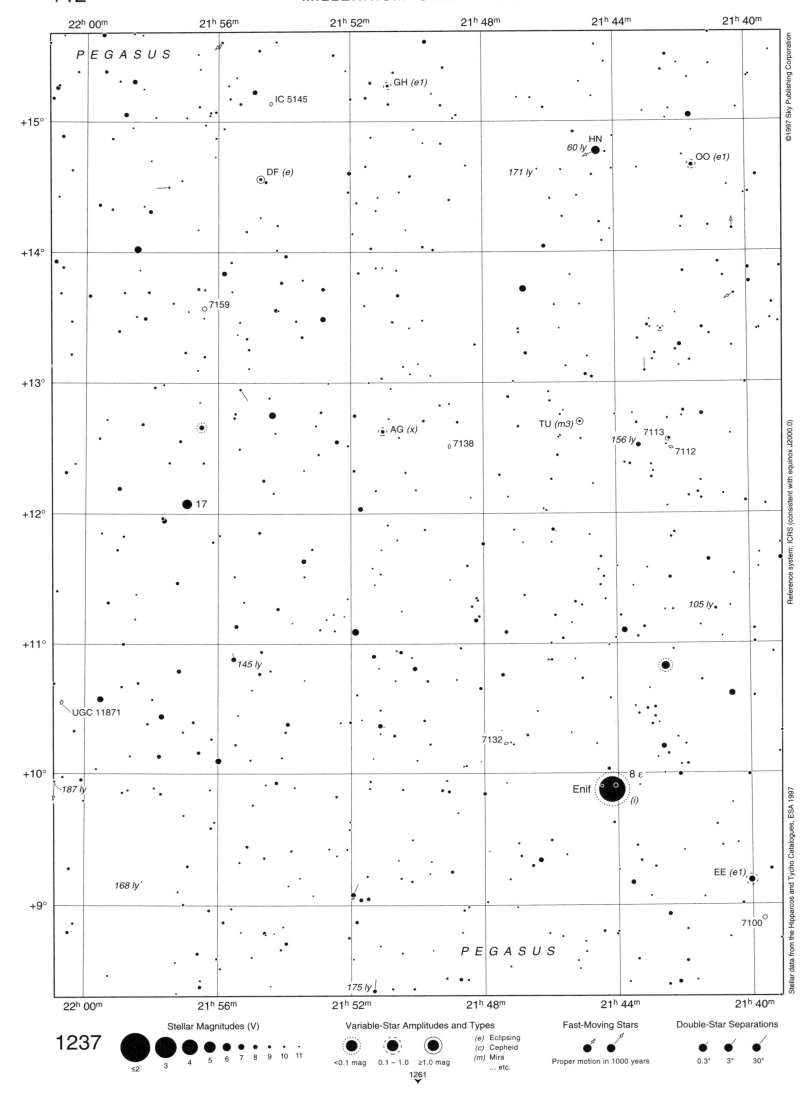

©1997 Sky Publishing Corporation

Reference system: ICRS (consistent with equinox J2000.0)

Stellar data from the Hipparcos and Tycho Catalogues, ESA 1997

PEGASUS

IC 5145

GH (e1)

HN
60 ly

OO (e1)

171 ly

DF (e)

7159

AG (x)

7138

TU (m3)

156 ly    7113
          7112

17

105 ly

145 ly

UGC 11871

7132

187 ly

8 ε
Enif    (i)

168 ly

EE (e1)

9°

7100

PEGASUS

175 ly

1237    Stellar Magnitudes (V)

≤2   3   4   5   6  7  8 9 10 11

Variable-Star Amplitudes and Types

<0.1 mag    0.1 – 1.0    ≥1.0 mag

(e) Eclipsing
(c) Cepheid
(m) Mira
... etc.

Fast-Moving Stars

Proper motion in 1000 years

Double-Star Separations

0.3"   3"   30"

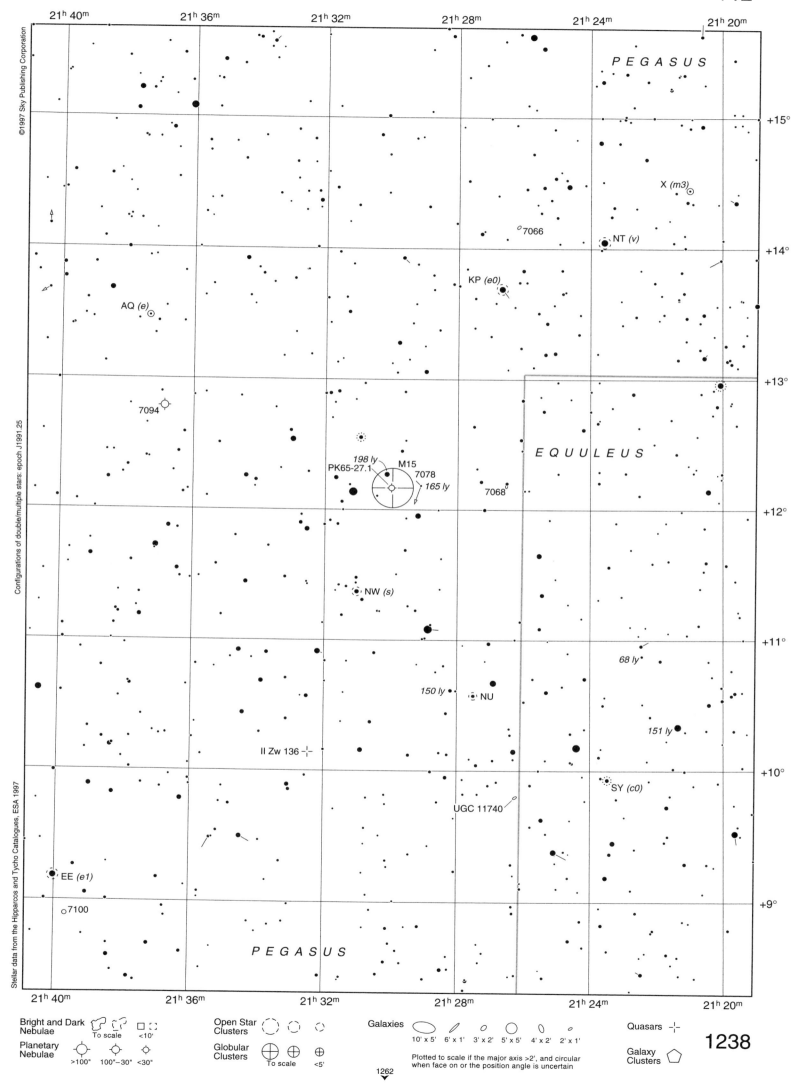

*P E G A S U S*

X (m3)

°7066

NT (v)

KP (e0)

AQ (e)

7094

*E Q U U L E U S*

198 ly    M15
PK65-27.1    7078
165 ly

7068

NW (s)

68 ly

150 ly    NU

151 ly

II Zw 136

SY (c0)

UGC 11740

EE (e1)

°7100

*P E G A S U S*

| Bright and Dark Nebulae | | | Open Star Clusters | | | Galaxies | | | | | | Quasars |
|---|---|---|---|---|---|---|---|---|---|---|---|---|
| To scale | | <10' | | | | 10' x 5' | 6' x 1' | 3' x 2' | 5' x 5' | 4' x 2' | 2' x 1' | |

| Planetary Nebulae | | | Globular Clusters | | | | Galaxy Clusters |
|---|---|---|---|---|---|---|---|
| >100" | 100"-30" | <30" | To scale | | <5' | | |

Plotted to scale if the major axis >2', and circular
when face on or the position angle is uncertain

1238

1262

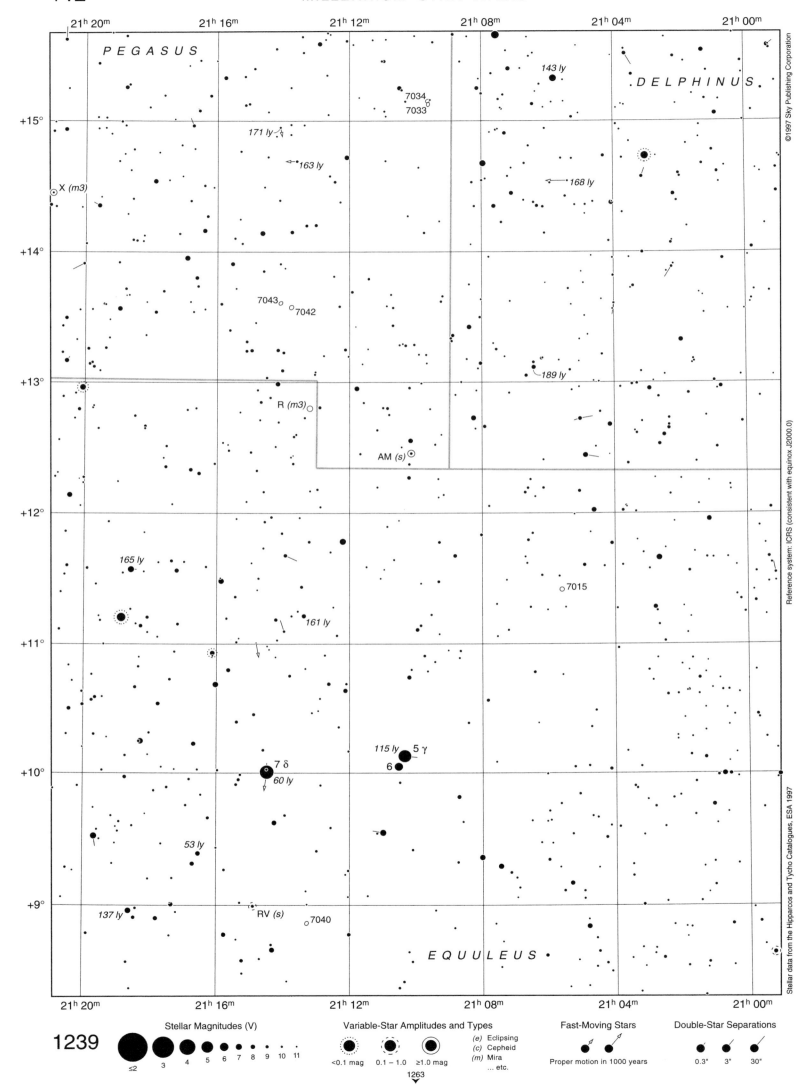

©1997 Sky Publishing Corporation

Reference system: ICRS (consistent with equinox J2000.0)

Stellar data from the Hipparcos and Tycho Catalogues, ESA 1997

PEGASUS

DELPHINUS

171 ly

163 ly

168 ly

7034
7033

143 ly

X (m3)

7043 o  o 7042

189 ly

R (m3) o

AM (s) o

7015

165 ly

161 ly

115 ly   5 γ
6

7 δ
60 ly

53 ly

137 ly

RV (s)
o 7040

EQUULEUS

Stellar Magnitudes (V)

≤2   3   4   5   6   7   8   9  10  11

Variable-Star Amplitudes and Types

<0.1 mag    0.1 – 1.0    ≥1.0 mag

(e) Eclipsing
(c) Cepheid
(m) Mira
... etc.

1263

Fast-Moving Stars

Proper motion in 1000 years

Double-Star Separations

0.3"    3"    30"

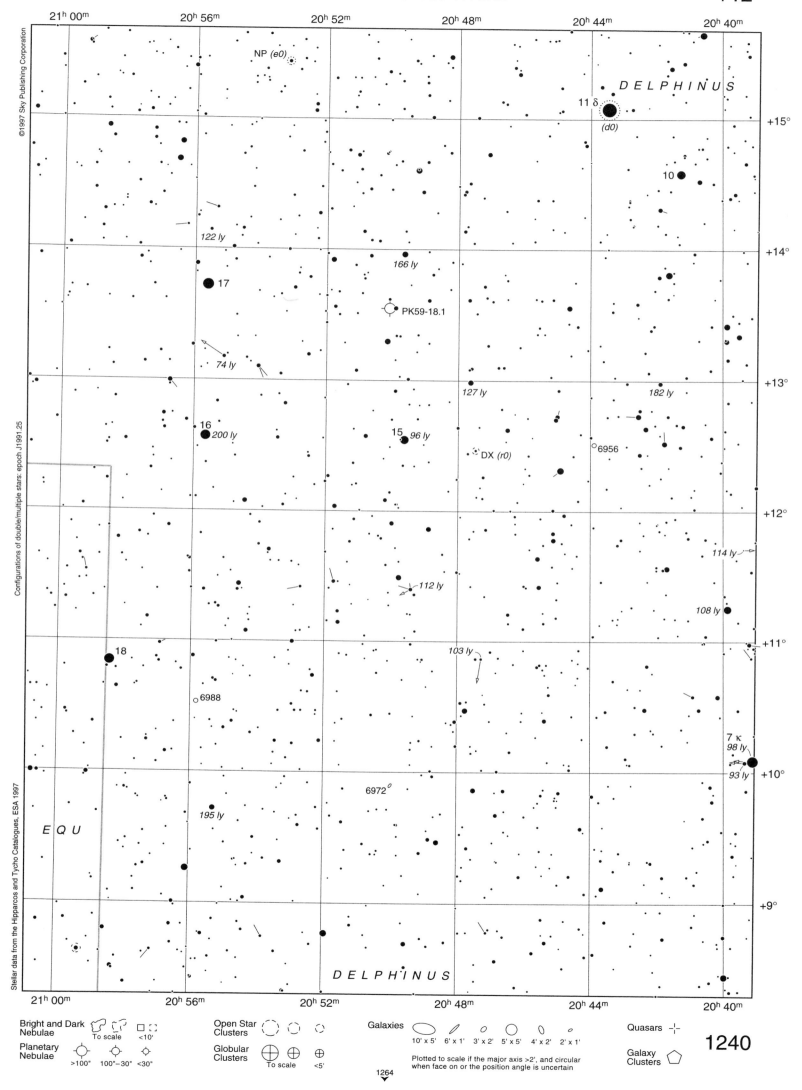

21h 00m   20h 56m   20h 52m   20h 48m   20h 44m   20h 40m

NP *(e0)*

*DELPHINUS*

11 δ

*(d0)*

+15°

10

122 ly

+14°

166 ly

17

PK59-18.1

74 ly

127 ly   182 ly   +13°

16
200 ly   15   96 ly

DX *(r0)*

6956

+12°

114 ly

112 ly

108 ly   +11°

18

103 ly

6988

7 κ
98 ly

93 ly   +10°

195 ly   6972

*EQU*

+9°

21h 00m   20h 56m   20h 52m   20h 48m   20h 44m   20h 40m

*DELPHINUS*

Bright and Dark Nebulae
To scale   <10'

Planetary Nebulae
>100"   100"–30"   <30"

Open Star Clusters
To scale   <5'

Globular Clusters
To scale   <5'

Galaxies
10' x 5'   6' x 1'   3' x 2'   5' x 5'   4' x 2'   2' x 1'

Plotted to scale if the major axis >2', and circular when face on or the position angle is uncertain

Quasars

Galaxy Clusters

1240

1264

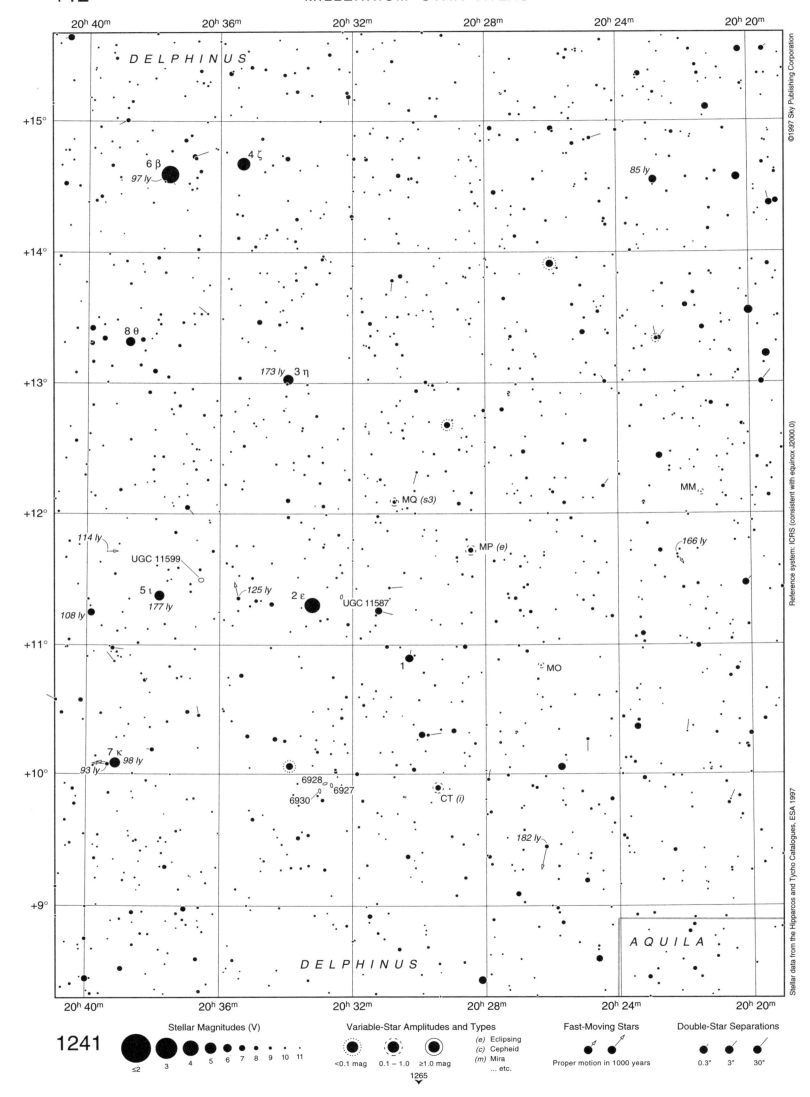

©1997 Sky Publishing Corporation

20ʰ 40ᵐ    20ʰ 36ᵐ    20ʰ 32ᵐ    20ʰ 28ᵐ    20ʰ 24ᵐ    20ʰ 20ᵐ

*D E L P H I N U S*

+15°

6 β
97 ly
4 ζ
85 ly

+14°

8 θ

173 ly  3 η

+13°

+12°

MQ (s3)

MM

+11°

114 ly
UGC 11599
5 ι
177 ly
125 ly
2 ε
UGC 11587
166 ly
MP (e)

108 ly

1
MO

7 κ  98 ly
93 ly

+10°

6928    6927
6930
CT (i)

182 ly

+9°

*A Q U I L A*

*D E L P H I N U S*

20ʰ 40ᵐ    20ʰ 36ᵐ    20ʰ 32ᵐ    20ʰ 28ᵐ    20ʰ 24ᵐ    20ʰ 20ᵐ

Reference system: ICRS (consistent with equinox J2000.0)

Stellar data from the Hipparcos and Tycho Catalogues, ESA 1997

Stellar Magnitudes (V)

≤2  3  4  5  6  7  8  9  10  11

Variable-Star Amplitudes and Types

<0.1 mag   0.1 – 1.0   ≥1.0 mag

(e) Eclipsing
(c) Cepheid
(m) Mira
... etc.

▽
1265

Fast-Moving Stars

Proper motion in 1000 years

Double-Star Separations

0.3″   3″   30″

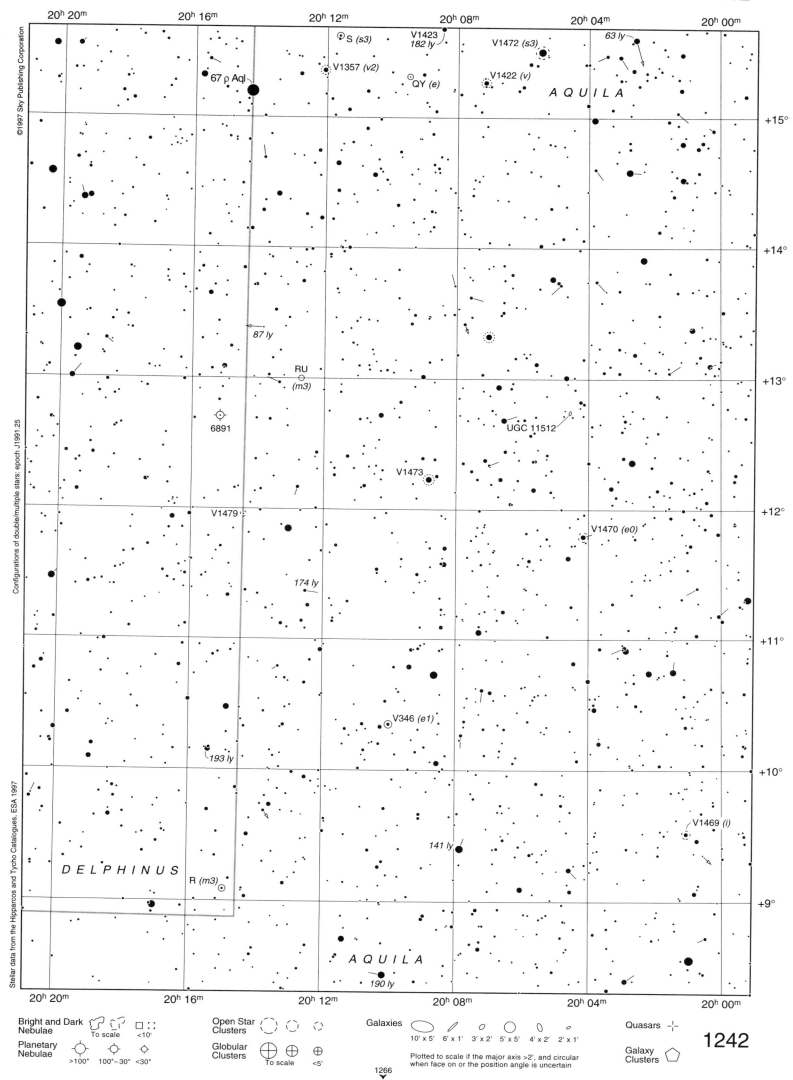

20h 20m
20h 16m
20h 12m
20h 08m
20h 04m
20h 00m

V1423
182 ly
S (s3)
V1472 (s3)
63 ly
V1357 (v2)
67 ρ Aql
QY (e)
V1422 (v)
AQUILA

+15°

+14°

87 ly

RU
(m3)

+13°

6891

UGC 11512

V1473

+12°

V1479

V1470 (e0)

174 ly

+11°

V346 (e1)

193 ly

+10°

V1469 (i)

141 ly

DELPHINUS

R (m3)

+9°

AQUILA

190 ly

20h 20m
20h 16m
20h 12m
20h 08m
20h 04m
20h 00m

Bright and Dark
Nebulae
To scale    <10'

Open Star
Clusters

Galaxies
10' x 5'   6' x 1'   3' x 2'   5' x 5'   4' x 2'   2' x 1'

Quasars

Planetary
Nebulae
>100"   100"–30"   <30'

Globular
Clusters
To scale   <5'

Plotted to scale if the major axis >2', and circular
when face on or the position angle is uncertain

Galaxy
Clusters

1242

1266

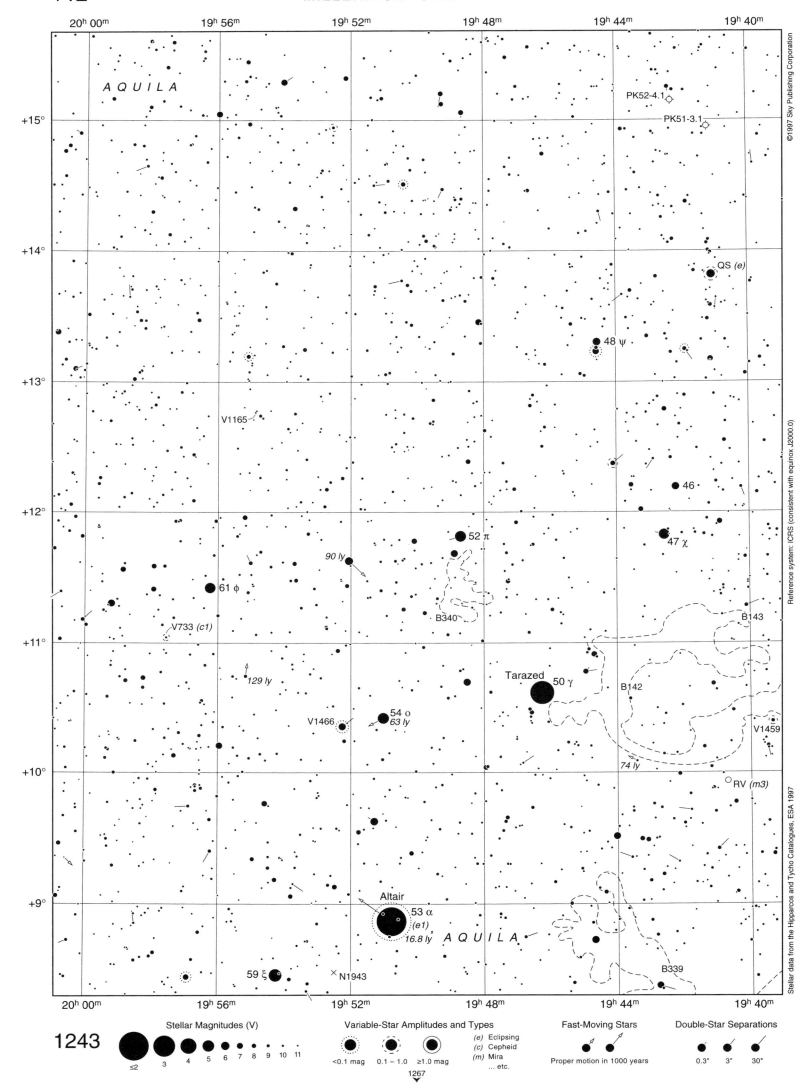

©1997 Sky Publishing Corporation

Reference system: ICRS (consistent with equinox J2000.0)

Stellar data from the Hipparcos and Tycho Catalogues, ESA 1997

1219

AQUILA

PK52-4.1
PK51-3.1

QS (e)

48 ψ

46

V1165

47 χ

52 π

90 ly

61 φ

B340

B143

V733 (c1)

Tarazed  50 γ

B142

129 ly

V1459

V1466

54 o
63 ly

74 ly

RV (m3)

Altair

53 α
(e1)
16.8 ly

AQUILA

59 ξ

× N1943

B339

**1243**

| Stellar Magnitudes (V) | Variable-Star Amplitudes and Types | Fast-Moving Stars | Double-Star Separations |
|---|---|---|---|

Stellar Magnitudes (V)
≤2　3　4　5　6　7　8　9　10　11

Variable-Star Amplitudes and Types
<0.1 mag　0.1 – 1.0　≥1.0 mag

(e) Eclipsing
(c) Cepheid
(m) Mira
... etc.

Fast-Moving Stars
Proper motion in 1000 years

Double-Star Separations
0.3"　3"　30"

1267

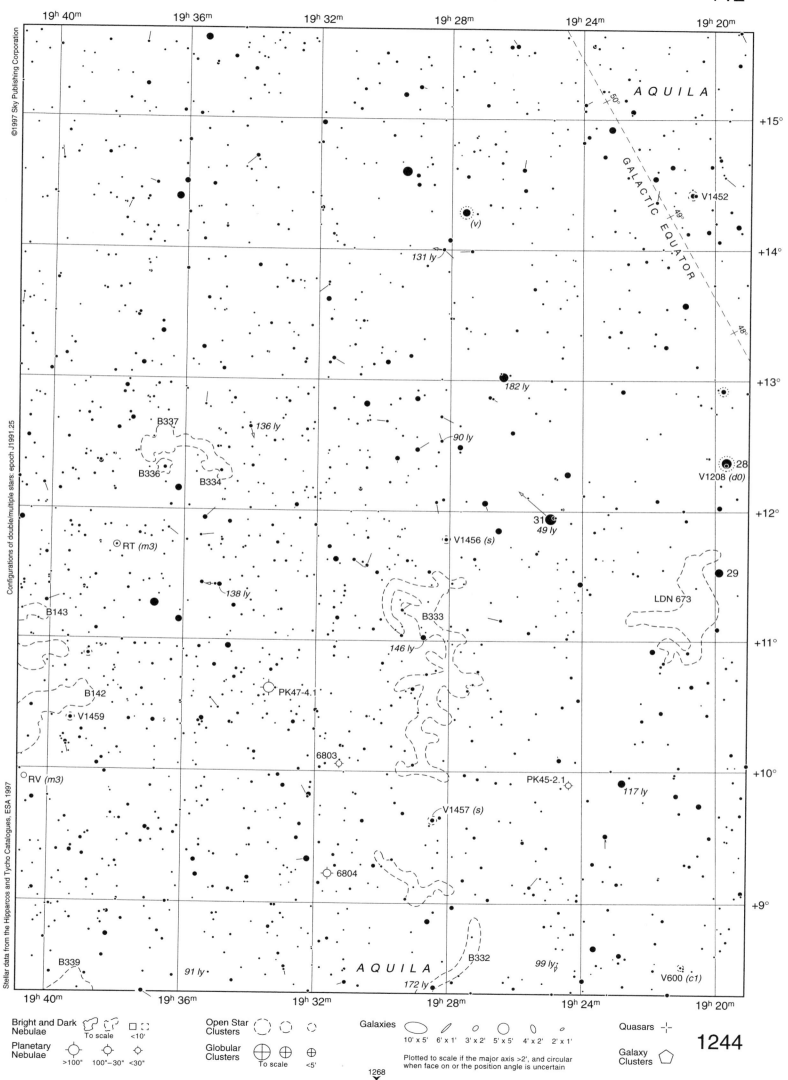

Bright and Dark
Nebulae                To scale       <10'

Planetary
Nebulae
          >100"  100"–30"  <30'

Open Star
Clusters

Globular
Clusters
          To scale        <5'

Galaxies

10' x 5'   6' x 1'   3' x 2'   5' x 5'   4' x 2'   2' x 1'

Plotted to scale if the major axis >2', and circular
when face on or the position angle is uncertain

Quasars   –|–

Galaxy
Clusters

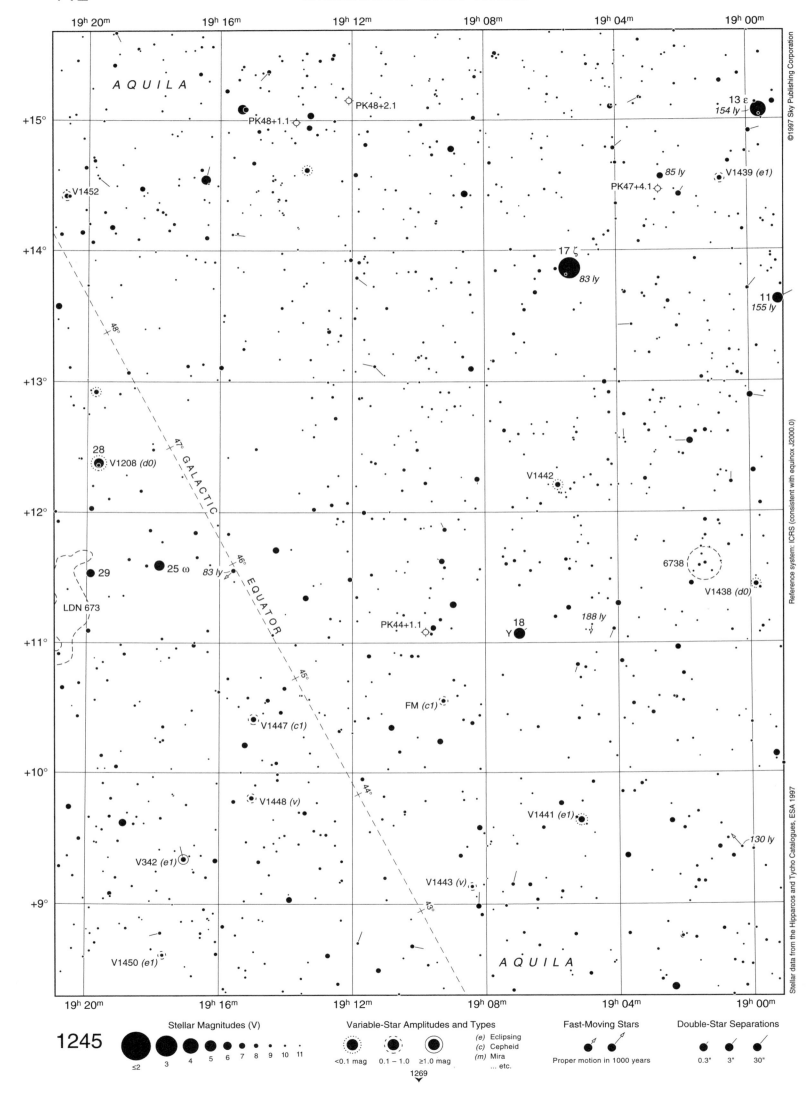

### Stellar Magnitudes (V)

≤2  3  4  5  6  7  8  9  10  11

### Variable-Star Amplitudes and Types

<0.1 mag   0.1 – 1.0   ≥1.0 mag

(e) Eclipsing
(c) Cepheid
(m) Mira
... etc.

### Fast-Moving Stars

Proper motion in 1000 years

### Double-Star Separations

0.3"   3"   30"

1269

# MILLENNIUM STAR ATLAS

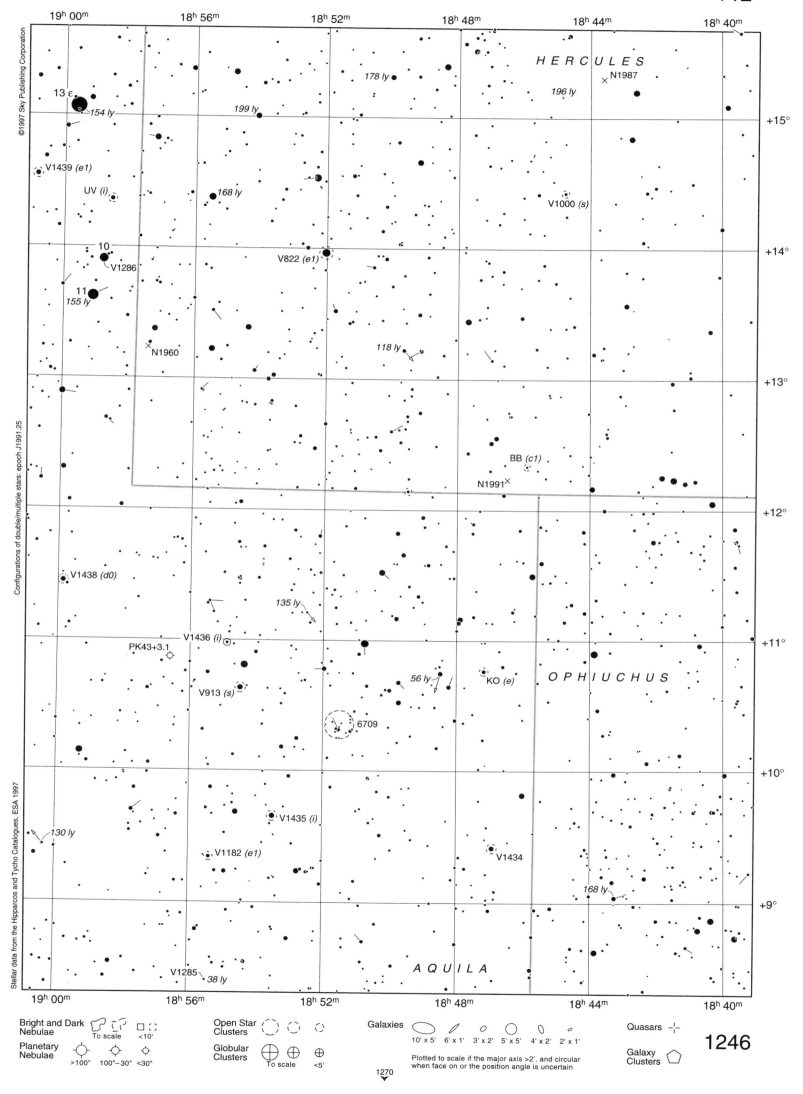

Configurations of double/multiple stars: epoch J1991.25

Stellar data from the Hipparcos and Tycho Catalogues, ESA 1997

HERCULES

OPHIUCHUS

AQUILA

| | | |
|---|---|---|
| Bright and Dark Nebulae | | |
| Planetary Nebulae | >100" 100"–30" <30" | |
| Open Star Clusters | | |
| Globular Clusters | To scale <5' | |
| Galaxies | 10' x 5'  6' x 1'  3' x 2'  5' x 5'  4' x 2'  2' x 1' | |
| Quasars | | |
| Galaxy Clusters | | |

To scale <10'

Plotted to scale if the major axis >2', and circular when face on or the position angle is uncertain

1246

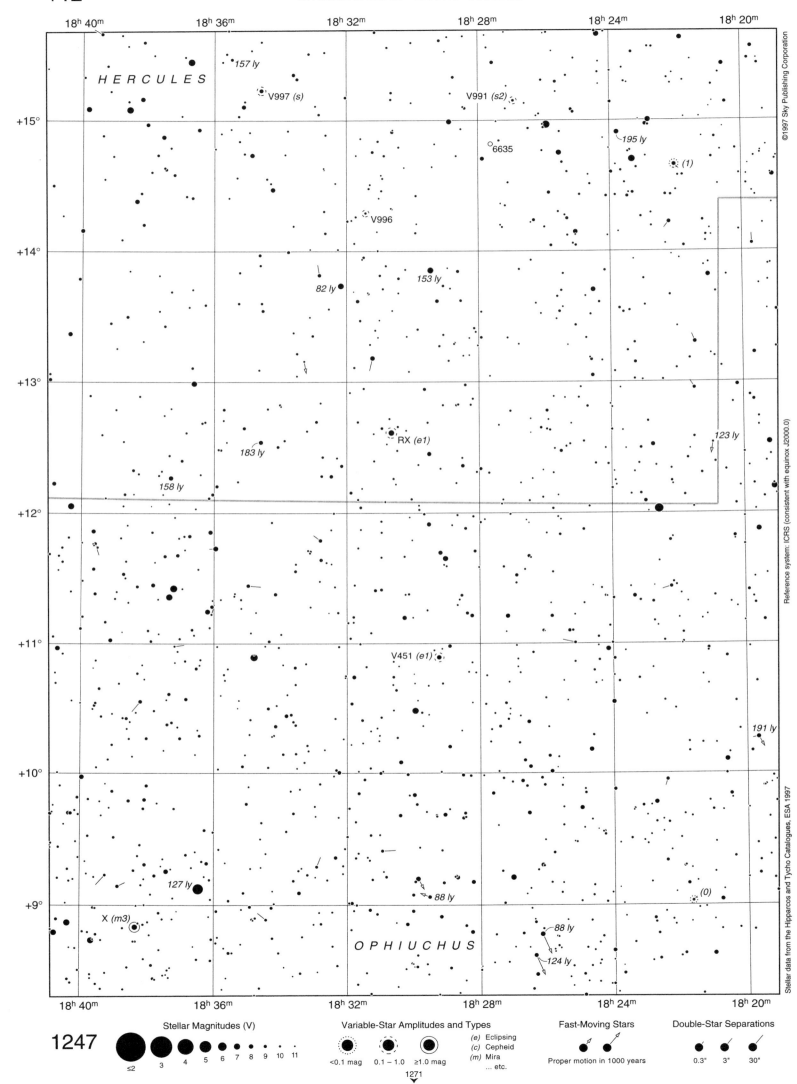

| Stellar Magnitudes (V) | Variable-Star Amplitudes and Types | Fast-Moving Stars | Double-Star Separations |
|---|---|---|---|
| ≤2  3  4  5  6 7 8 9 10 11 | <0.1 mag   0.1 − 1.0   ≥1.0 mag   (e) Eclipsing (c) Cepheid (m) Mira ... etc. | Proper motion in 1000 years | 0.3″  3″  30″ |

# MILLENNIUM STAR ATLAS

**+12°**

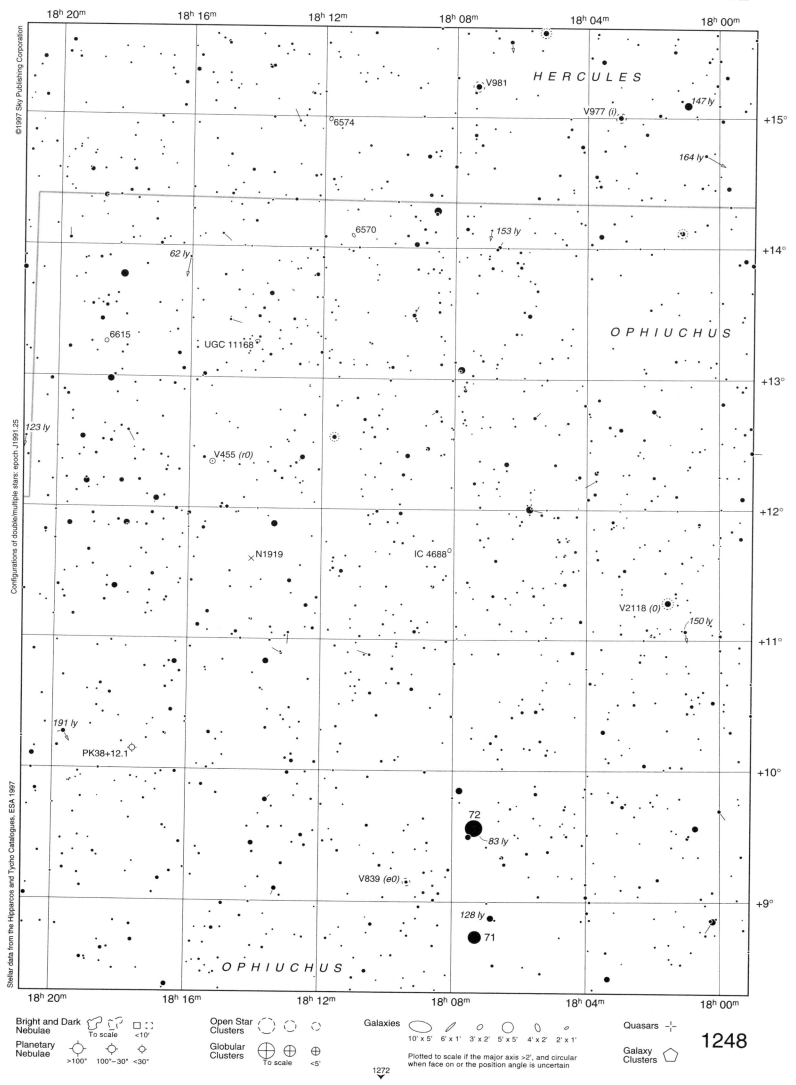

18h 20m   18h 16m   18h 12m   18h 08m   18h 04m   18h 00m

H E R C U L E S

V981

147 ly

V977 (i)

+15°

164 ly

6574

6570

153 ly

+14°

62 ly

O P H I U C H U S

6615

UGC 11168

+13°

123 ly

V455 (r0)

+12°

N1919

IC 4688

V2118 (0)

150 ly

+11°

191 ly

PK38+12.1

+10°

72

83 ly

V839 (e0)

+9°

128 ly

71

O P H I U C H U S

18h 20m   18h 16m   18h 12m   18h 08m   18h 04m   18h 00m

| Bright and Dark Nebulae | Open Star Clusters | Galaxies | Quasars |
| --- | --- | --- | --- |

To scale   <10'

To scale   <10'

Open Star Clusters

Globular Clusters

To scale   <5'

Galaxies

10' x 5'   6' x 1'   3' x 2'   5' x 5'   4' x 2'   2' x 1'

Plotted to scale if the major axis >2', and circular when face on or the position angle is uncertain

Planetary Nebulae

>100"   100"–30"   <30"

Quasars

Galaxy Clusters

**1248**

1272

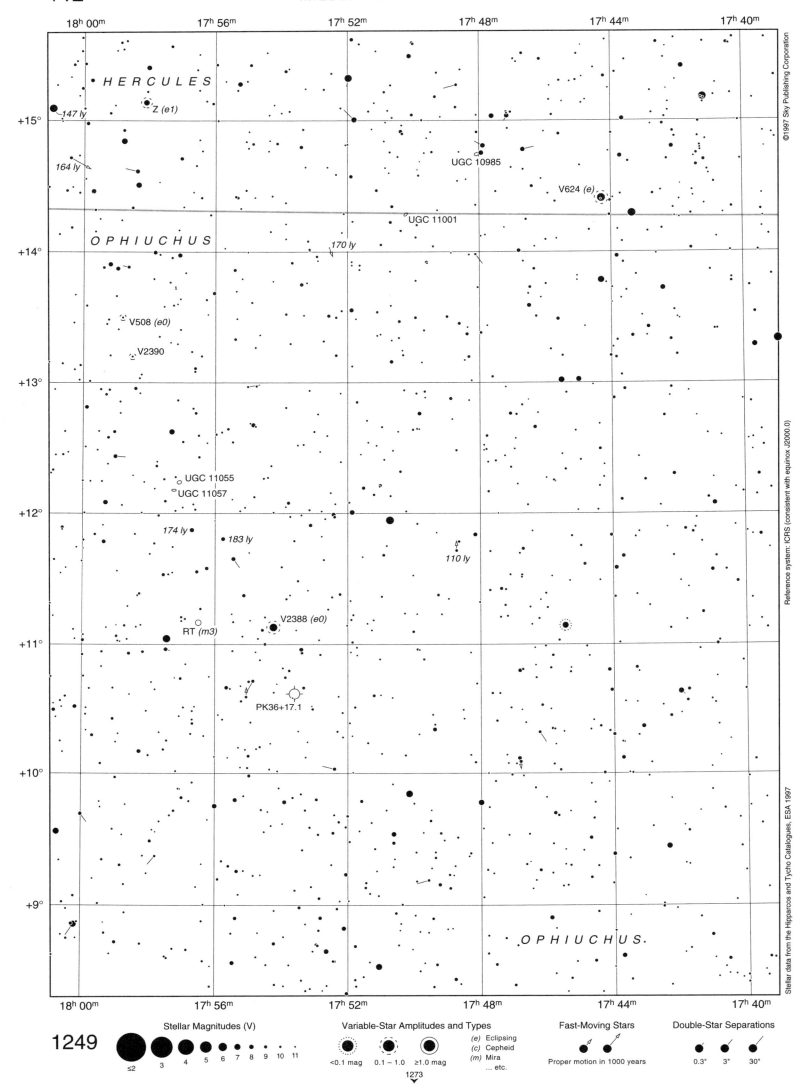

18ʰ 00ᵐ     17ʰ 56ᵐ     17ʰ 52ᵐ     17ʰ 48ᵐ     17ʰ 44ᵐ     17ʰ 40ᵐ

HERCULES

Z (e1)

147 ly

+15°

164 ly

UGC 10985

V624 (e)

UGC 11001

OPHIUCHUS

+14°

170 ly

V508 (e0)

V2390

+13°

UGC 11055
UGC 11057

+12°

174 ly    183 ly

110 ly

V2388 (e0)

RT (m3)

+11°

PK36+17.1

+10°

+9°

OPHIUCHUS

18ʰ 00ᵐ     17ʰ 56ᵐ     17ʰ 52ᵐ     17ʰ 48ᵐ     17ʰ 44ᵐ     17ʰ 40ᵐ

©1997 Sky Publishing Corporation

Reference system: ICRS (consistent with equinox J2000.0)

Stellar data from the Hipparcos and Tycho Catalogues, ESA 1997

**1249**

| Stellar Magnitudes (V) | Variable-Star Amplitudes and Types | Fast-Moving Stars | Double-Star Separations |
|---|---|---|---|

Stellar Magnitudes (V)
≤2   3   4   5   6   7   8   9   10   11

Variable-Star Amplitudes and Types
<0.1 mag   0.1 – 1.0   ≥1.0 mag

(e) Eclipsing
(c) Cepheid
(m) Mira
... etc.

Fast-Moving Stars
Proper motion in 1000 years

Double-Star Separations
0.3"   3"   30"

1273

# MILLENNIUM STAR ATLAS

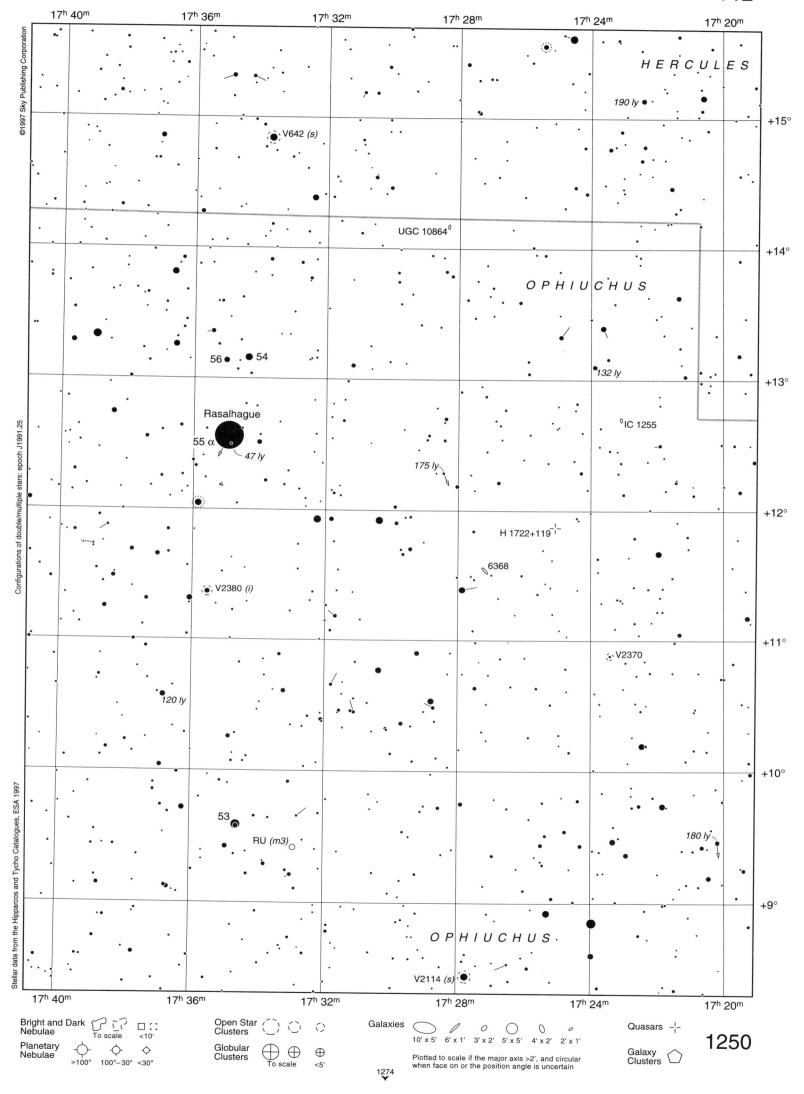

HERCULES

*190 ly*

OPHIUCHUS

UGC 10864 $^0$

V642 *(s)*

56 ● 54

*132 ly*

Rasalhague

$^0$IC 1255

55 α

*47 ly*

*175 ly*

H 1722+119

6368

V2380 *(i)*

V2370

*120 ly*

53

*180 ly*

RU *(m3)*

OPHIUCHUS

V2114 *(s)*

©1997 Sky Publishing Corporation

Configurations of double/multiple stars: epoch J1991.25

Stellar data from the Hipparcos and Tycho Catalogues, ESA 1997

| Bright and Dark Nebulae | | | | Open Star Clusters | | | Galaxies | | | | | | Quasars |
|---|---|---|---|---|---|---|---|---|---|---|---|---|---|
| To scale | | <10' | | | | | 10' x 5' | 6' x 1' | 3' x 2' | 5' x 5' | 4' x 2' | 2' x 1' | |
| Planetary Nebulae | | | | Globular Clusters | | | | | | | | | Galaxy Clusters |
| >100" | 100"–30" | <30" | | To scale | | <5' | Plotted to scale if the major axis >2', and circular when face on or the position angle is uncertain | | | | | | |

**1250**

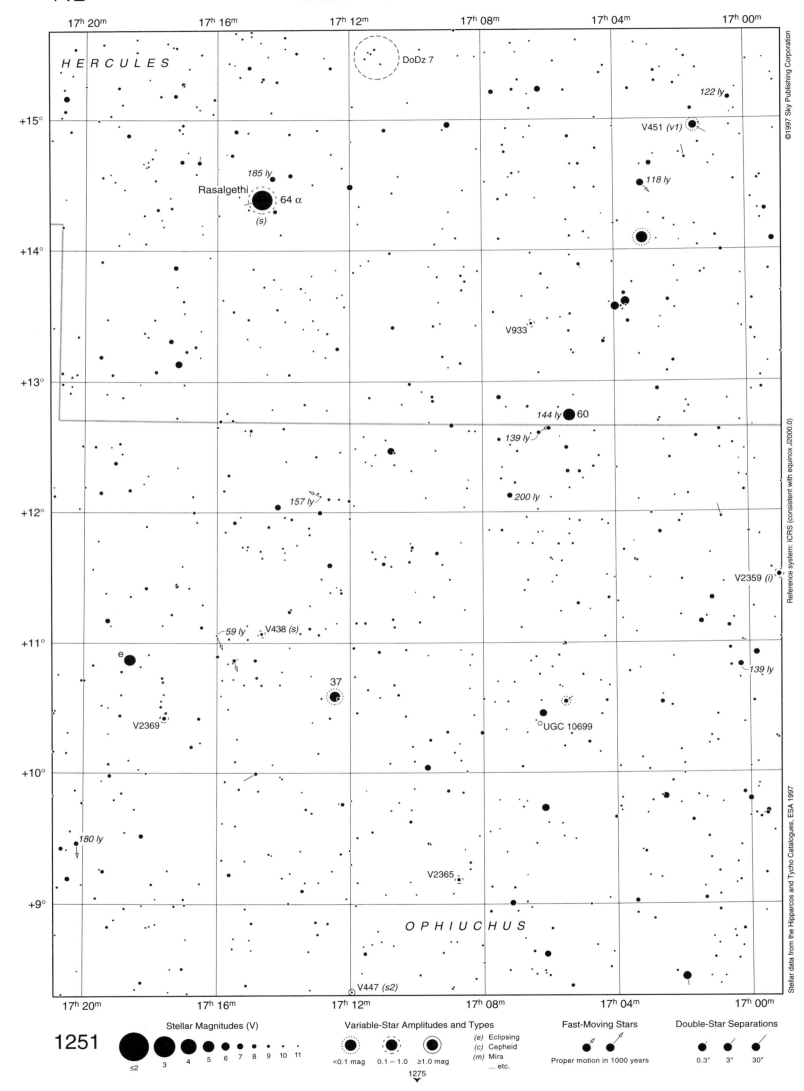

©1997 Sky Publishing Corporation

Reference system: ICRS (consistent with equinox J2000.0)

Stellar data from the Hipparcos and Tycho Catalogues, ESA 1997

HERCULES

DoDz 7

122 ly

V451 (v1)

118 ly

Rasalgethi

185 ly

64 α

(s)

V933

144 ly 60

139 ly

157 ly

200 ly

V2359 (i)

e

59 ly

V438 (s)

139 ly

37

V2369

UGC 10699

180 ly

V2365

V447 (s2)

OPHIUCHUS

Stellar Magnitudes (V)

≤2  3  4  5  6  7  8  9  10  11

Variable-Star Amplitudes and Types

<0.1 mag    0.1 – 1.0    ≥1.0 mag

(e) Eclipsing
(c) Cepheid
(m) Mira
... etc.

Fast-Moving Stars

Proper motion in 1000 years

Double-Star Separations

0.3"  3"  30"

1275

# MILLENNIUM STAR ATLAS

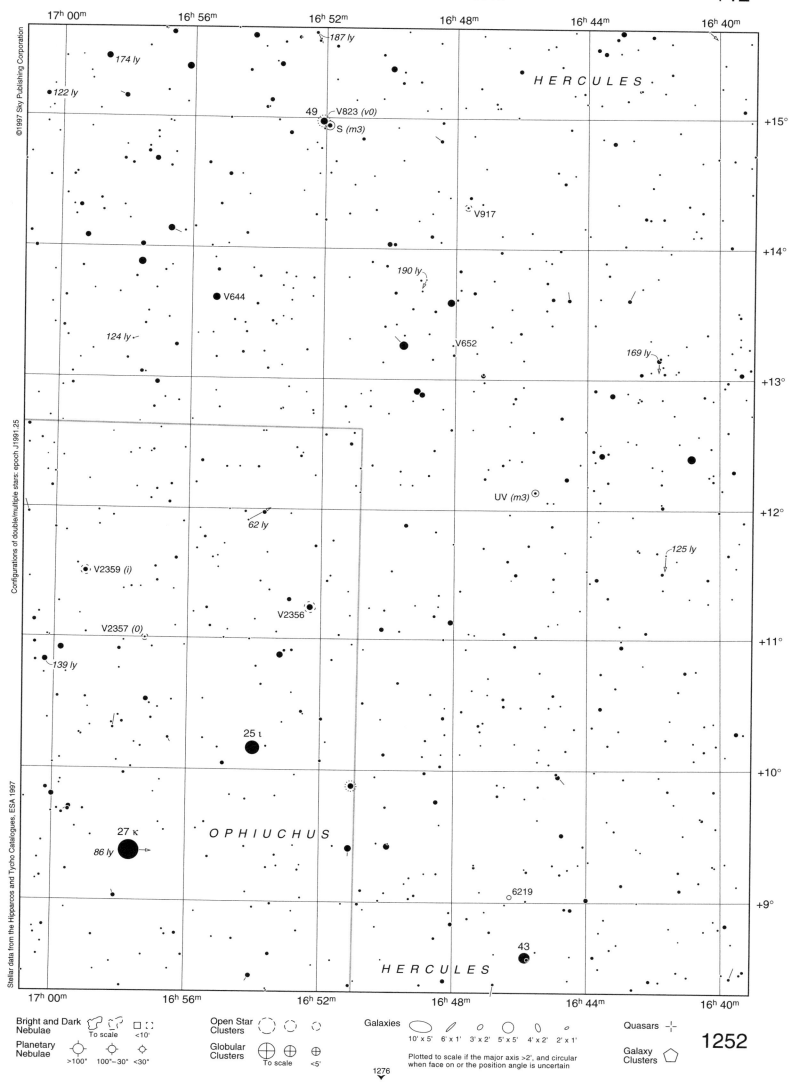

17h 00m   16h 56m   16h 52m   16h 48m   16h 44m   16h 40m

174 ly

122 ly

H E R C U L E S

49   V823 (v0)
S (m3)

V917   +15°

190 ly

V644

124 ly

V652   +14°

169 ly   +13°

UV (m3)

62 ly   +12°

125 ly

V2359 (i)

V2356

V2357 (0)   +11°

139 ly

25 ι

+10°

27 κ   O P H I U C H U S

86 ly

6219   +9°

43

H E R C U L E S

17h 00m   16h 56m   16h 52m   16h 48m   16h 44m   16h 40m

| Bright and Dark Nebulae | | | Open Star Clusters | | | Galaxies | | | | | | Quasars |
|---|---|---|---|---|---|---|---|---|---|---|---|---|
| To scale | <10' | | | | | 10' x 5' | 6' x 1' | 3' x 2' | 5' x 5' | 4' x 2' | 2' x 1' | |
| Planetary Nebulae | | | Globular Clusters | | | | | | | | | Galaxy Clusters |
| >100" | 100"–30" | <30" | To scale | <5' | | Plotted to scale if the major axis >2', and circular when face on or the position angle is uncertain | | | | | | |

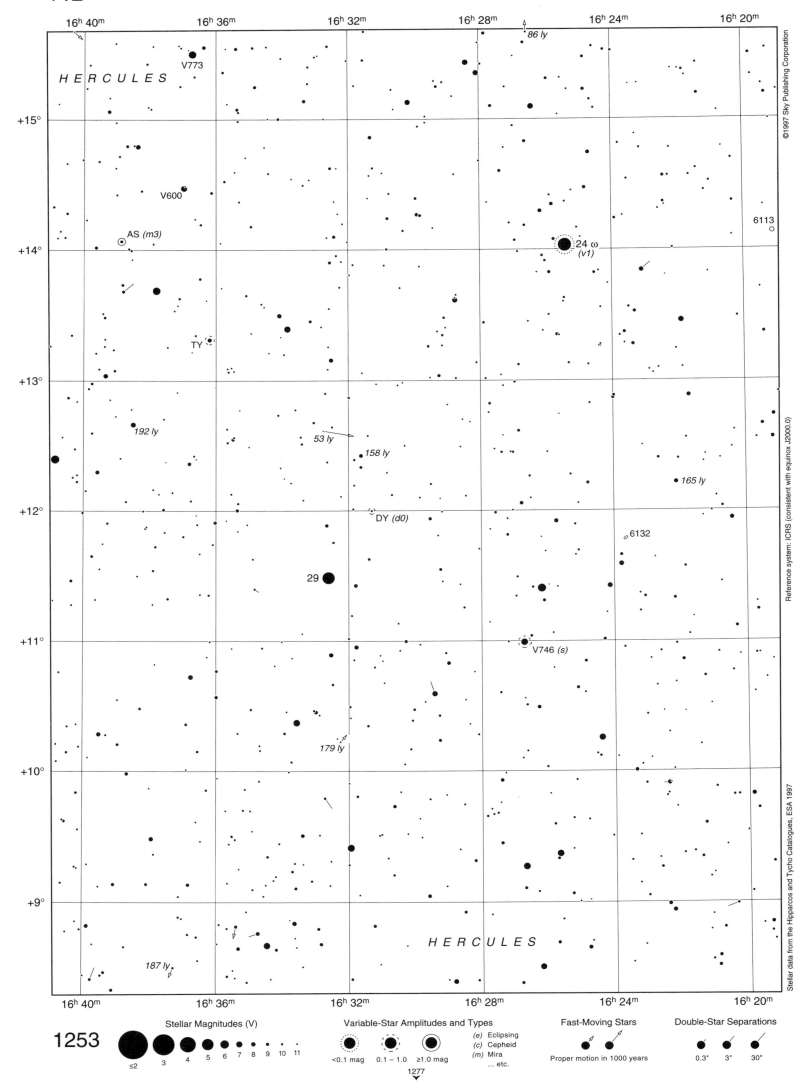

©1997 Sky Publishing Corporation

Reference system: ICRS (consistent with equinox J2000.0)

Stellar data from the Hipparcos and Tycho Catalogues, ESA 1997

1253

Stellar Magnitudes (V)

≤2   3   4   5   6   7   8   9   10   11

Variable-Star Amplitudes and Types

<0.1 mag    0.1 – 1.0    ≥1.0 mag

(e) Eclipsing
(c) Cepheid
(m) Mira
... etc.

Fast-Moving Stars

Proper motion in 1000 years

Double-Star Separations

0.3"   3"   30"

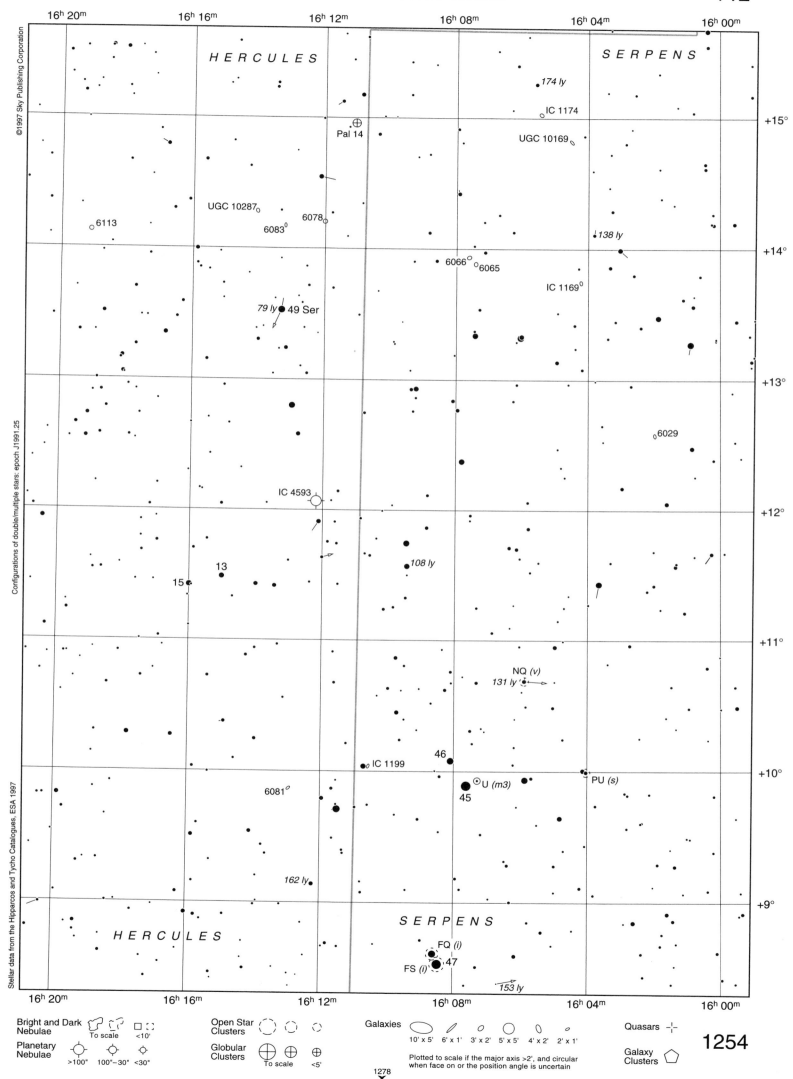

HERCULES

SERPENS

*174 ly*

IC 1174

Pal 14

UGC 10169

UGC 10287    6078

6113    6083

*138 ly*

6066   6065

IC 1169

*79 ly* 49 Ser

6029

IC 4593

13

*108 ly*

15

NQ *(v)*

*131 ly*

46

IC 1199

U *(m3)*

PU *(s)*

6081

45

*162 ly*

SERPENS

HERCULES

FQ *(i)*

FS *(i)* 47

*153 ly*

Configurations of double/multiple stars: epoch J1991.25

Stellar data from the Hipparcos and Tycho Catalogues, ESA 1997

Bright and Dark
Nebulae
To scale    <10'

Planetary
Nebulae
>100"    100"–30"    <30"

Open Star
Clusters

Globular
Clusters
To scale    <5'

Galaxies
10' x 5'   6' x 1'   3' x 2'   5' x 5'   4' x 2'   2' x 1'

Plotted to scale if the major axis >2', and circular
when face on or the position angle is uncertain

Quasars

Galaxy
Clusters

**1254**

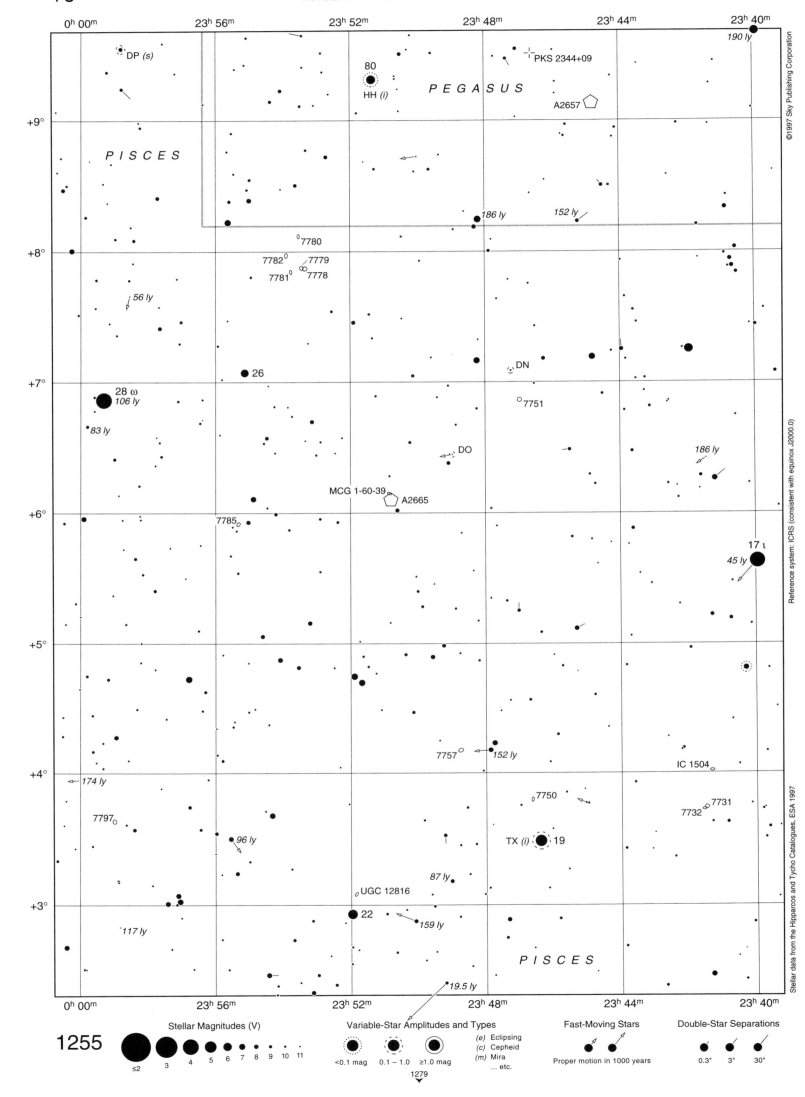

+9°

+8°

+7°

+6°

+5°

+4°

+3°

PISCES

PEGASUS

DP (s)

80
HH (i)

PKS 2344+09

A2657

186 ly

152 ly

°7780

7782° °7779
7781° °7778

56 ly

26

28 ω
106 ly

83 ly

DN

°7751

DO

186 ly

MCG 1-60-39
A2665

7785°

17 ι
45 ly

7757°
152 ly

IC 1504°

174 ly

7750°

7731
7732°

7797°

96 ly

TX (i)  19

87 ly

UGC 12816

22
159 ly

117 ly

19.5 ly

PISCES

©1997 Sky Publishing Corporation

Reference system: ICRS (consistent with equinox J2000.0)

Stellar data from the Hipparcos and Tycho Catalogues, ESA 1997

1255

Stellar Magnitudes (V)

≤2    3    4    5    6   7  8  9 10 11

Variable-Star Amplitudes and Types

<0.1 mag    0.1 – 1.0    ≥1.0 mag

(e) Eclipsing
(c) Cepheid
(m) Mira
... etc.

Fast-Moving Stars

Proper motion in 1000 years

Double-Star Separations

0.3"    3"    30"

1279

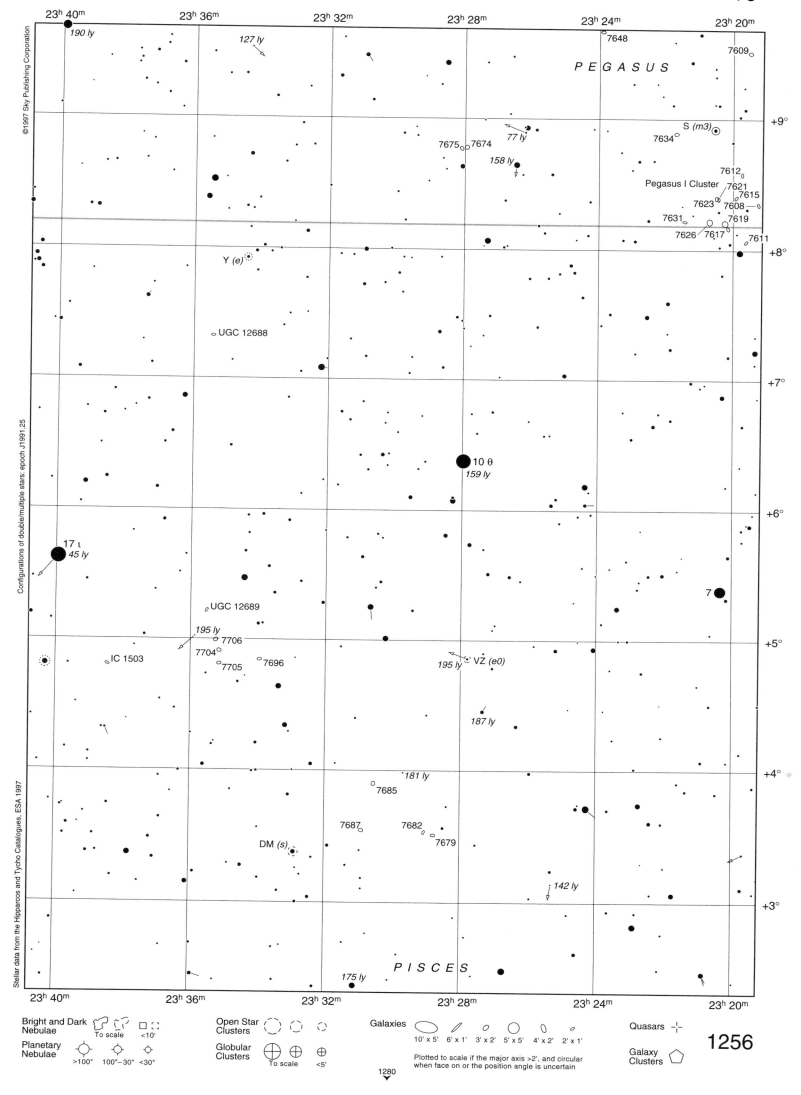

23h 40m · 190 ly
127 ly
7648
7609
PEGASUS
+9°
S (m3)
7675 7674
77 ly
7634
158 ly
7612
Pegasus I Cluster 7621
7615
7623 7608
7631 7619
7626 7617 7611
Y (e)
+8°
UGC 12688
+7°
10 θ
159 ly
+6°
17 ι
45 ly
7
UGC 12689
195 ly 7706
7704
7705 7696
+5°
IC 1503
195 ly VZ (e0)
187 ly
+4°
181 ly
7685
7687 7682
7679
DM (s)
142 ly
+3°
PISCES
175 ly
23h 40m 23h 36m 23h 32m 23h 28m 23h 24m 23h 20m

| Bright and Dark Nebulae | Open Star Clusters | Galaxies | Quasars |
|---|---|---|---|
| To scale <10' | | 10' x 5' 6' x 1' 3' x 2' 5' x 5' 4' x 2' 2' x 1' | |
| Planetary Nebulae | Globular Clusters | | Galaxy Clusters |
| >100" 100"-30" <30" | To scale <5' | Plotted to scale if the major axis >2', and circular when face on or the position angle is uncertain | |

1256

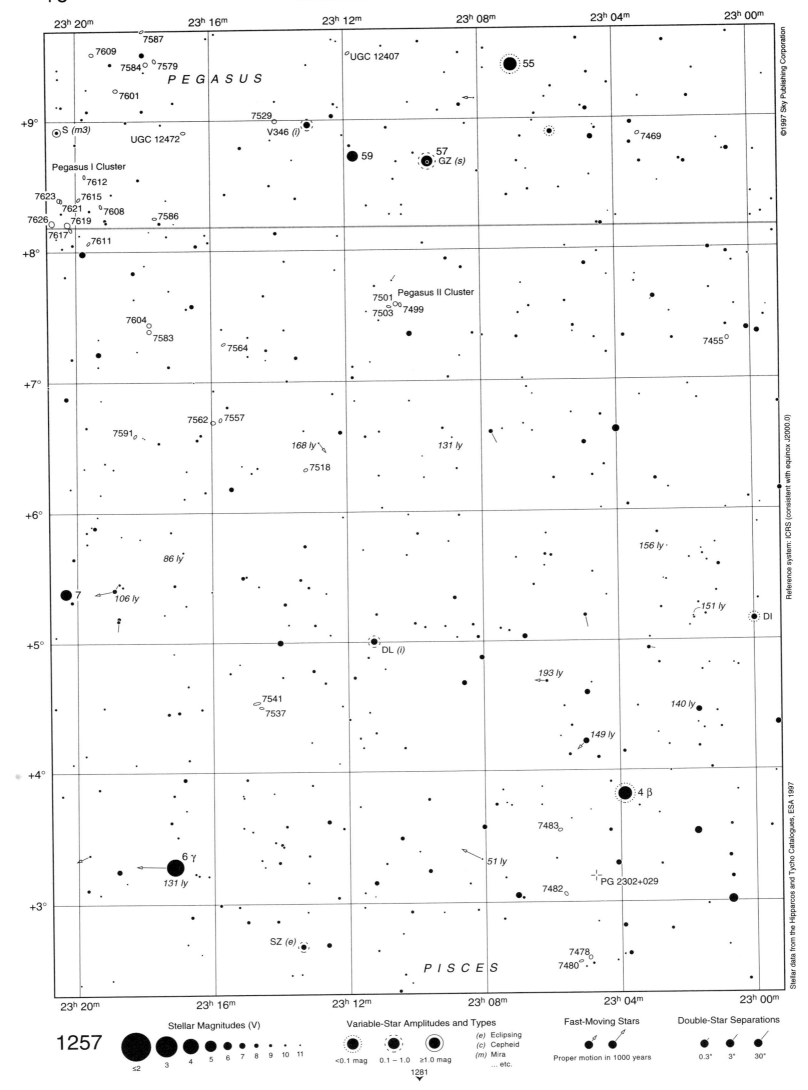

23h 20m   23h 16m   23h 12m   23h 08m   23h 04m   23h 00m

7587
7609
7584  7579
7601
PEGASUS
UGC 12407
55

+9°
S (m3)
UGC 12472
7529
V346 (i)
59
57
GZ (s)
7469

Pegasus I Cluster
7612
7623   7615
7621   7608
7626   7619   7586
7617
7611

Pegasus II Cluster
7501
7503  7499
7455

7604
7583
7564

+8°

+7°
7562  7557
7591
168 ly
131 ly
7518

+6°
86 ly
156 ly

7
106 ly
151 ly
DI

+5°
DL (i)
193 ly
7541
7537
140 ly
149 ly

+4°
4 β
7483
51 ly
6 γ
131 ly
7482
PG 2302+029

+3°
SZ (e)
7478
7480
PISCES

23h 20m   23h 16m   23h 12m   23h 08m   23h 04m   23h 00m

©1997 Sky Publishing Corporation

Reference system: ICRS (consistent with equinox J2000.0)

Stellar data from the Hipparcos and Tycho Catalogues, ESA 1997

Stellar Magnitudes (V)

1257

≤2   3   4   5   6   7   8   9  10  11

Variable-Star Amplitudes and Types

<0.1 mag   0.1 – 1.0   ≥1.0 mag

(e) Eclipsing
(c) Cepheid
(m) Mira
... etc.

1281

Fast-Moving Stars

Proper motion in 1000 years

Double-Star Separations

0.3"   3"   30"

# MILLENNIUM STAR ATLAS

+6°

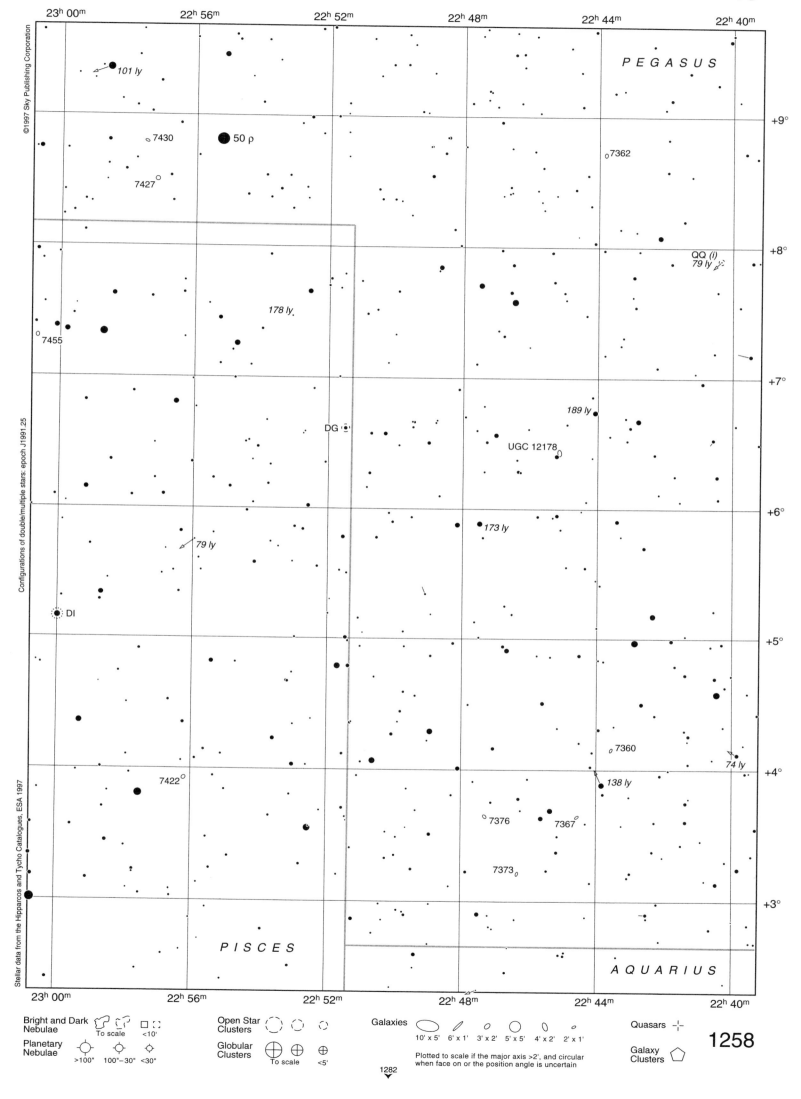

PEGASUS

23h 00m  22h 56m  22h 52m  22h 48m  22h 44m  22h 40m

101 ly

50 ρ
7430
7427
7362

+9°

+8°
QQ (i)
79 ly

178 ly
7455

189 ly

+7°

DG
UGC 12178

+6°
79 ly
173 ly

DI

+5°

7360
74 ly

+4°
7422
138 ly

7376   7367
7373

+3°

PISCES

AQUARIUS

23h 00m  22h 56m  22h 52m  22h 48m  22h 44m  22h 40m

| Bright and Dark Nebulae | Open Star Clusters | Galaxies | Quasars |
| To scale  <10' | | 10' x 5'  6' x 1'  3' x 2'  5' x 5'  4' x 2'  2' x 1' | |
| Planetary Nebulae | Globular Clusters | | Galaxy Clusters |
| >100"  100"−30"  <30" | To scale  <5' | Plotted to scale if the major axis >2', and circular when face on or the position angle is uncertain | |

1258

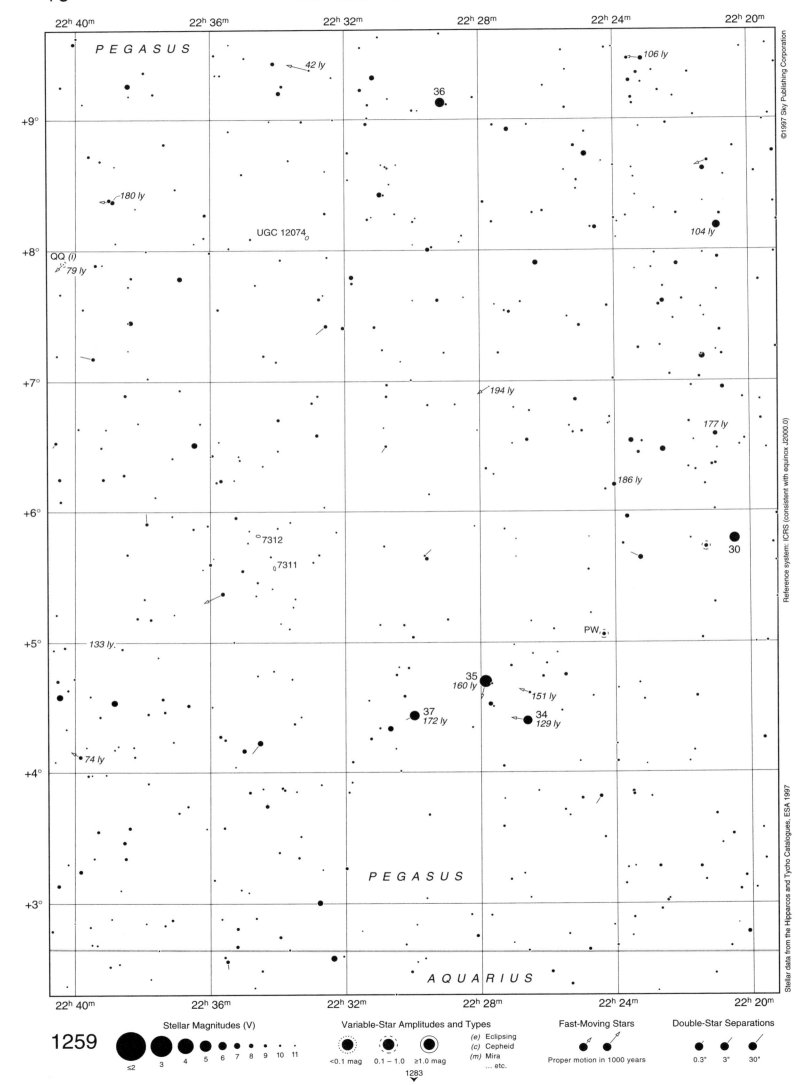

©1997 Sky Publishing Corporation

Reference system: ICRS (consistent with equinox J2000.0)

Stellar data from the Hipparcos and Tycho Catalogues, ESA 1997

PEGASUS

42 ly

36

106 ly

180 ly

UGC 12074

104 ly

QQ (i)

79 ly

194 ly

177 ly

186 ly

7312

30

7311

PW

133 ly.

35
160 ly

151 ly

37
172 ly

34
129 ly

74 ly

PEGASUS

AQUARIUS

1259

Stellar Magnitudes (V)

≤2   3   4   5   6 7 8 9 10 11

Variable-Star Amplitudes and Types

<0.1 mag   0.1 – 1.0   ≥1.0 mag

(e) Eclipsing
(c) Cepheid
(m) Mira
... etc.

1283

Fast-Moving Stars

Proper motion in 1000 years

Double-Star Separations

0.3"   3"   30"

# MILLENNIUM STAR ATLAS

+6°

Configurations of double/multiple stars: epoch J1991.25

Stellar data from the Hipparcos and Tycho Catalogues, ESA 1997

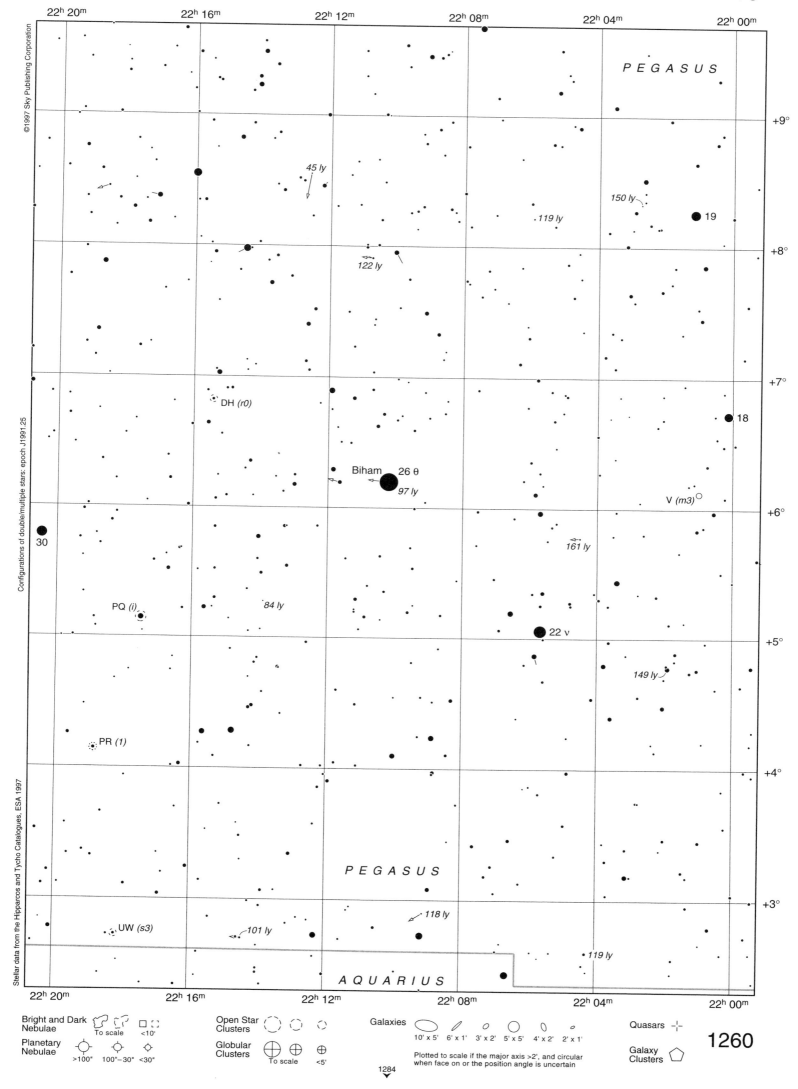

*P E G A S U S*

*45 ly*

*150 ly*

*119 ly*

19

*122 ly*

DH *(r0)*

18

Biham    26 θ

*97 ly*

V *(m3)*

30

*161 ly*

PQ *(i)*

*84 ly*

22 ν

*149 ly*

PR *(1)*

*P E G A S U S*

*118 ly*

UW *(s3)*

*101 ly*

*119 ly*

*A Q U A R I U S*

| Bright and Dark Nebulae | Open Star Clusters | Galaxies | Quasars |

To scale    <10'

Planetary Nebulae

>100"    100"−30"    <30"

Globular Clusters

To scale    <5'

10' x 5'   6' x 1'   3' x 2'   5' x 5'   4' x 2'   2' x 1'

Plotted to scale if the major axis >2', and circular when face on or the position angle is uncertain

Galaxy Clusters

1260

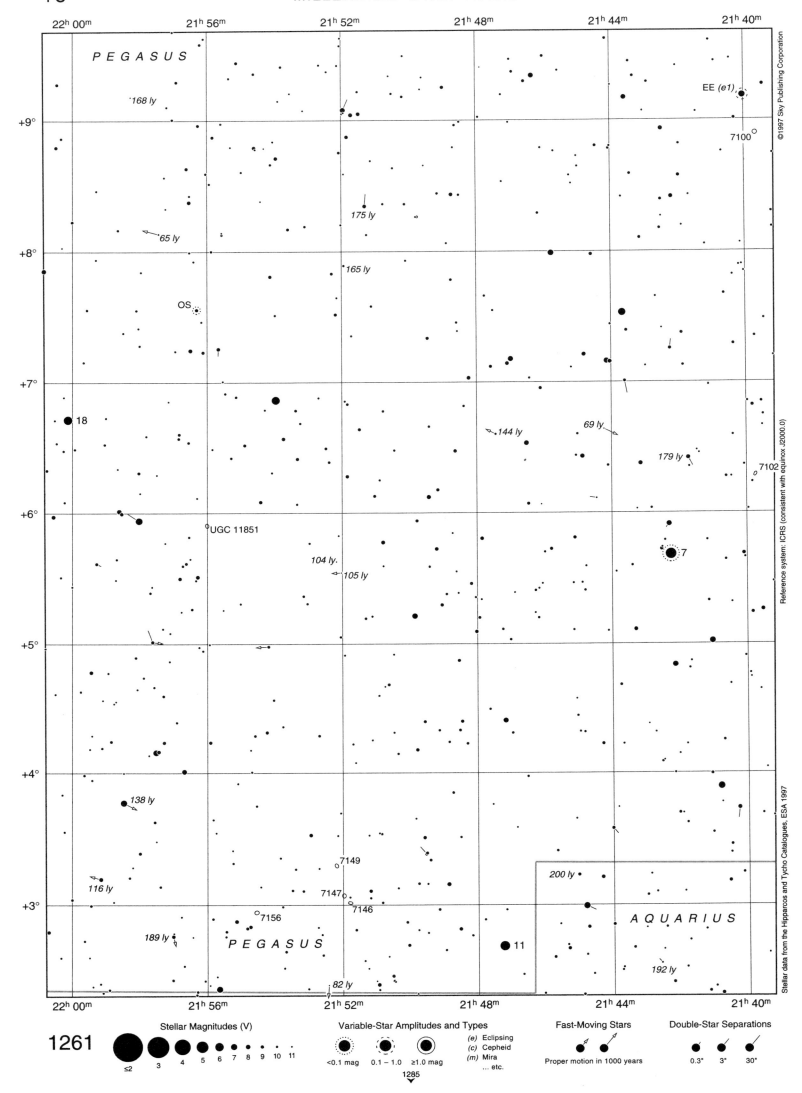

PEGASUS

22h 00m   21h 56m   21h 52m   21h 48m   21h 44m   21h 40m

EE *(e1)*

7100

*168 ly*

+9°

*175 ly*

*65 ly*

+8°

*165 ly*

OS

+7°

18

*144 ly*

*69 ly.*

*179 ly*

7102

+6°

UGC 11851

7

*104 ly.*
*105 ly*

+5°

*138 ly*

+4°

*200 ly*

*116 ly*

7149

AQUARIUS

7147

7146

*189 ly*

7156

PEGASUS

11

*192 ly*

*82 ly*

©1997 Sky Publishing Corporation

Reference system: ICRS (consistent with equinox J2000.0)

Stellar data from the Hipparcos and Tycho Catalogues, ESA 1997

1261

Stellar Magnitudes (V)

≤2   3   4   5   6   7   8   9   10   11

Variable-Star Amplitudes and Types

<0.1 mag   0.1 – 1.0   ≥1.0 mag

*(e)* Eclipsing
*(c)* Cepheid
*(m)* Mira
... etc.

Fast-Moving Stars

Proper motion in 1000 years

Double-Star Separations

0.3"   3"   30"

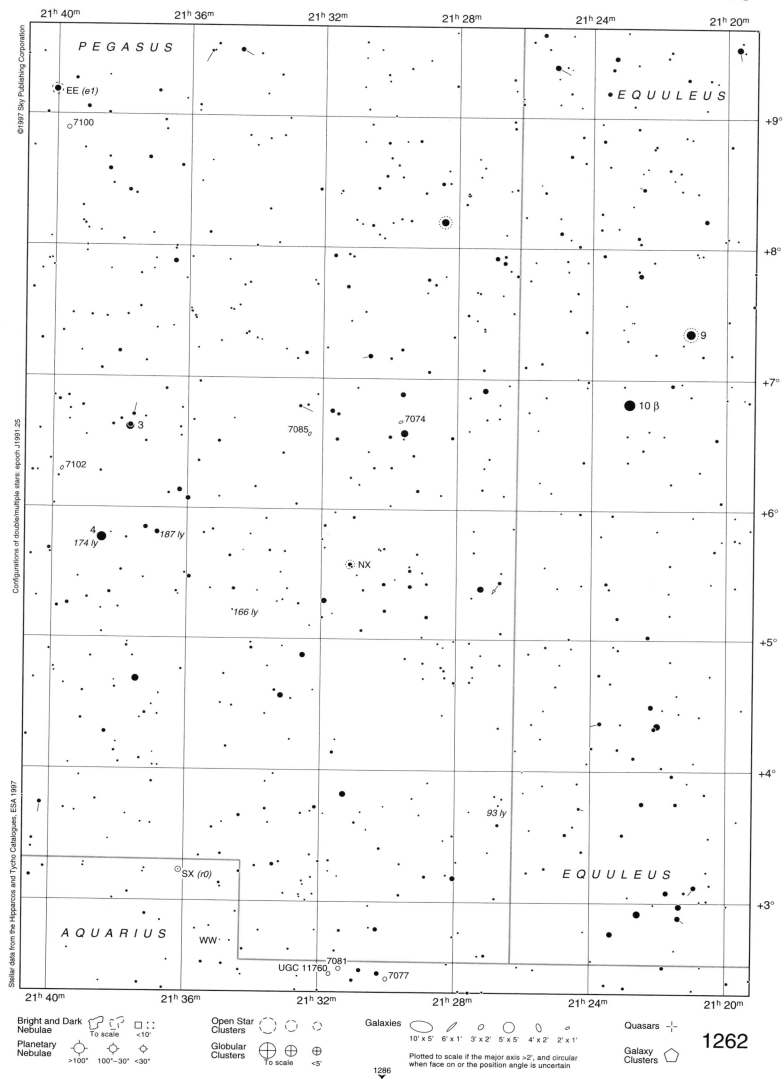

P E G A S U S

EE *(e1)*

7100

E Q U U L E U S

9

3

7102

7085

7074

10 β

4

174 ly

187 ly

NX

166 ly

93 ly

E Q U U L E U S

SX *(r0)*

A Q U A R I U S

WW

7081
UGC 11760

7077

Bright and Dark
Nebulae
To scale    <10'

Planetary
Nebulae
>100"  100"–30"  <30"

Open Star
Clusters

Globular
Clusters
To scale    <5'

Galaxies

10' x 5'  6' x 1'  3' x 2'  5' x 5'  4' x 2'  2' x 1'

Plotted to scale if the major axis >2', and circular
when face on or the position angle is uncertain

Quasars

Galaxy
Clusters

# +6°

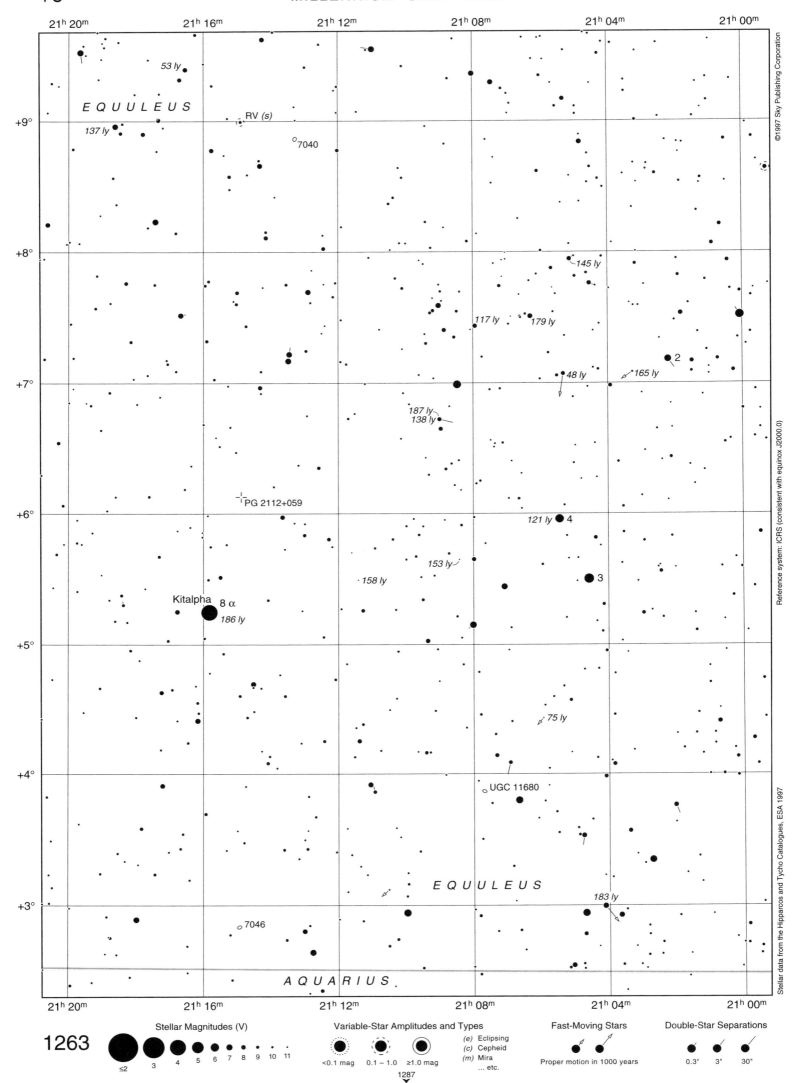

Reference system: ICRS (consistent with equinox J2000.0)

Stellar data from the Hipparcos and Tycho Catalogues, ESA 1997

E Q U U L E U S

RV (s)

7040

53 ly

137 ly

145 ly

117 ly    179 ly

2

48 ly    165 ly

187 ly
138 ly

PG 2112+059

121 ly    4

153 ly

158 ly    3

Kitalpha    8 α
186 ly

75 ly

UGC 11680

E Q U U L E U S

183 ly

7046

A Q U A R I U S

**1263**

**Stellar Magnitudes (V)**

≤2    3    4    5    6    7    8    9    10    11

**Variable-Star Amplitudes and Types**

<0.1 mag    0.1 – 1.0    ≥1.0 mag

(e) Eclipsing
(c) Cepheid
(m) Mira
... etc.

**Fast-Moving Stars**

Proper motion in 1000 years

**Double-Star Separations**

0.3"    3"    30"

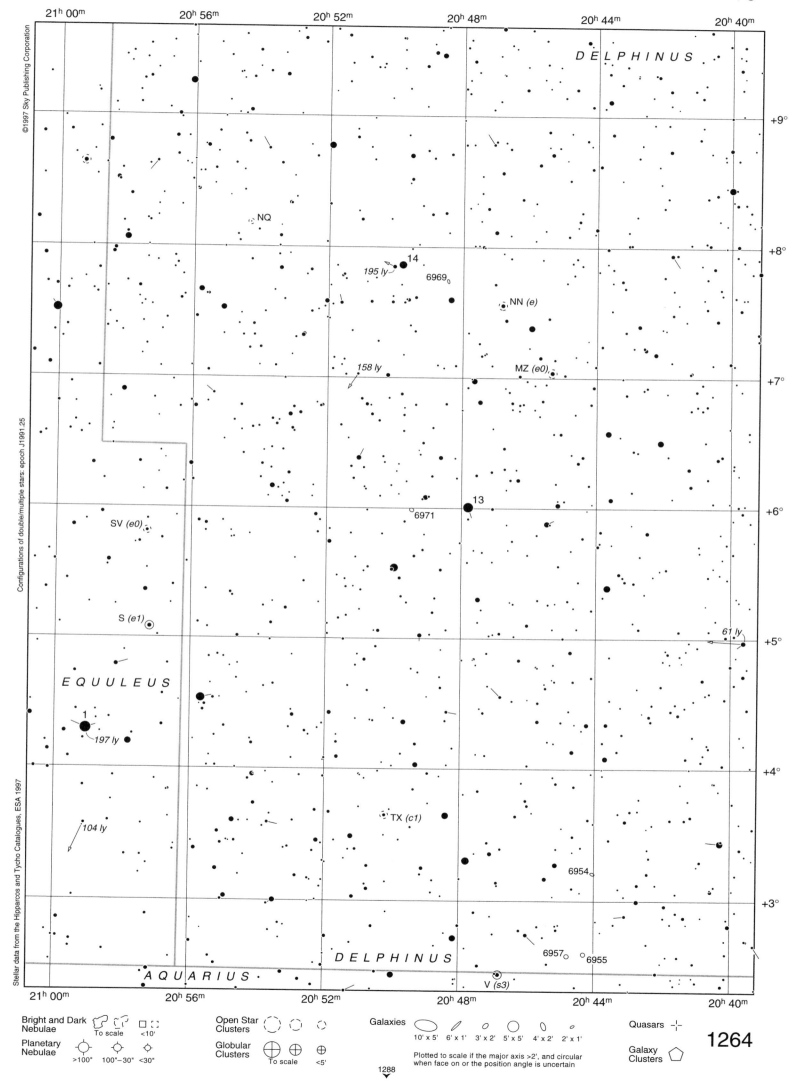

Configurations of double/multiple stars: epoch J1991.25

Stellar data from the Hipparcos and Tycho Catalogues, ESA 1997

21h 00m        20h 56m        20h 52m        20h 48m        20h 44m        20h 40m

DELPHINUS

+9°

NQ

+8°

14
195 ly
6969

NN (e)

158 ly

MZ (e0)

+7°

13

6971                                                +6°

SV (e0)

S (e1)

61 ly
+5°

EQUULEUS

1
197 ly

+4°

104 ly

TX (c1)

6954

+3°

DELPHINUS

6957   6955

AQUARIUS

V (s3)

21h 00m        20h 56m        20h 52m        20h 48m        20h 44m        20h 40m

Bright and Dark Nebulae        To scale        <10'
Planetary Nebulae        >100"        100"–30"        <30"

Open Star Clusters
Globular Clusters        To scale        <5'

Galaxies        10' x 5'   6' x 1'   3' x 2'   5' x 5'   4' x 2'   2' x 1'
Plotted to scale if the major axis >2', and circular when face on or the position angle is uncertain

Quasars

Galaxy Clusters

1264

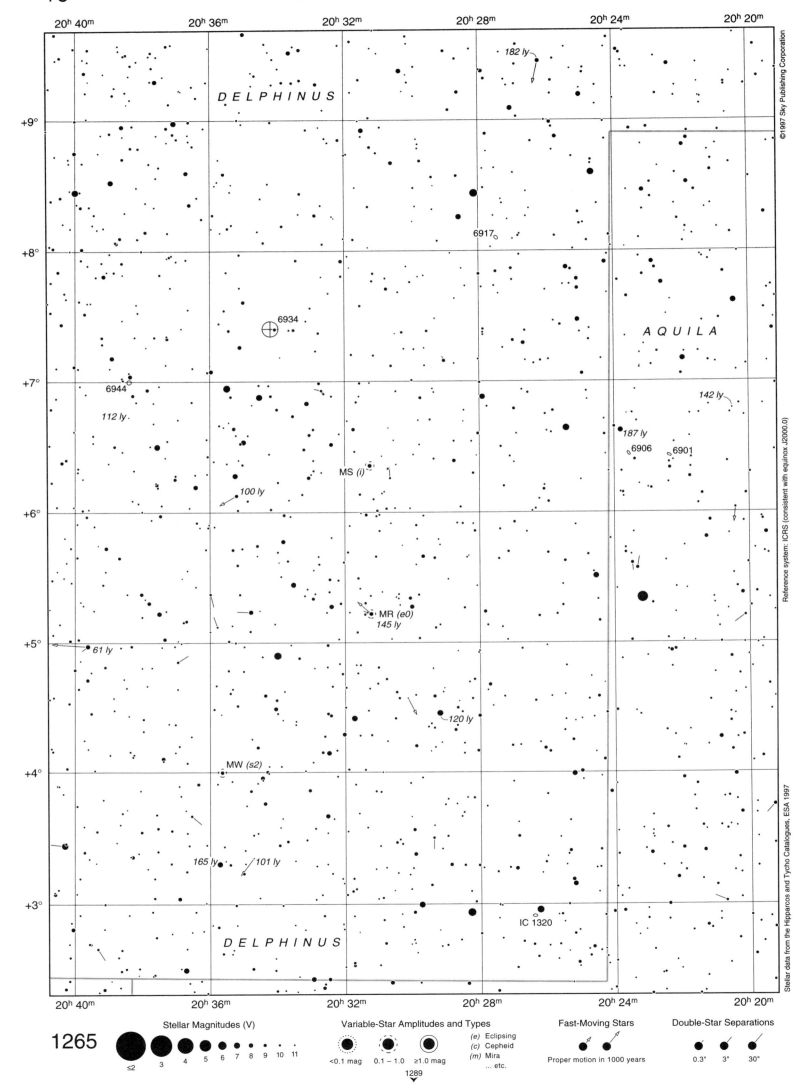

©1997 Sky Publishing Corporation

Reference system: ICRS (consistent with equinox J2000.0)

Stellar data from the Hipparcos and Tycho Catalogues, ESA 1997

DELPHINUS

AQUILA

DELPHINUS

182 ly

6917

6934

6944

112 ly

142 ly

187 ly
6906     6901

MS (i)

100 ly

MR (e0)
145 ly

61 ly

120 ly

MW (s2)

165 ly    101 ly

IC 1320

1265

Stellar Magnitudes (V)

≤2   3   4   5   6   7  8  9 10 11

Variable-Star Amplitudes and Types

<0.1 mag   0.1 – 1.0   ≥1.0 mag

(e) Eclipsing
(c) Cepheid
(m) Mira
... etc.

Fast-Moving Stars

Proper motion in 1000 years

Double-Star Separations

0.3"   3"   30"

1289

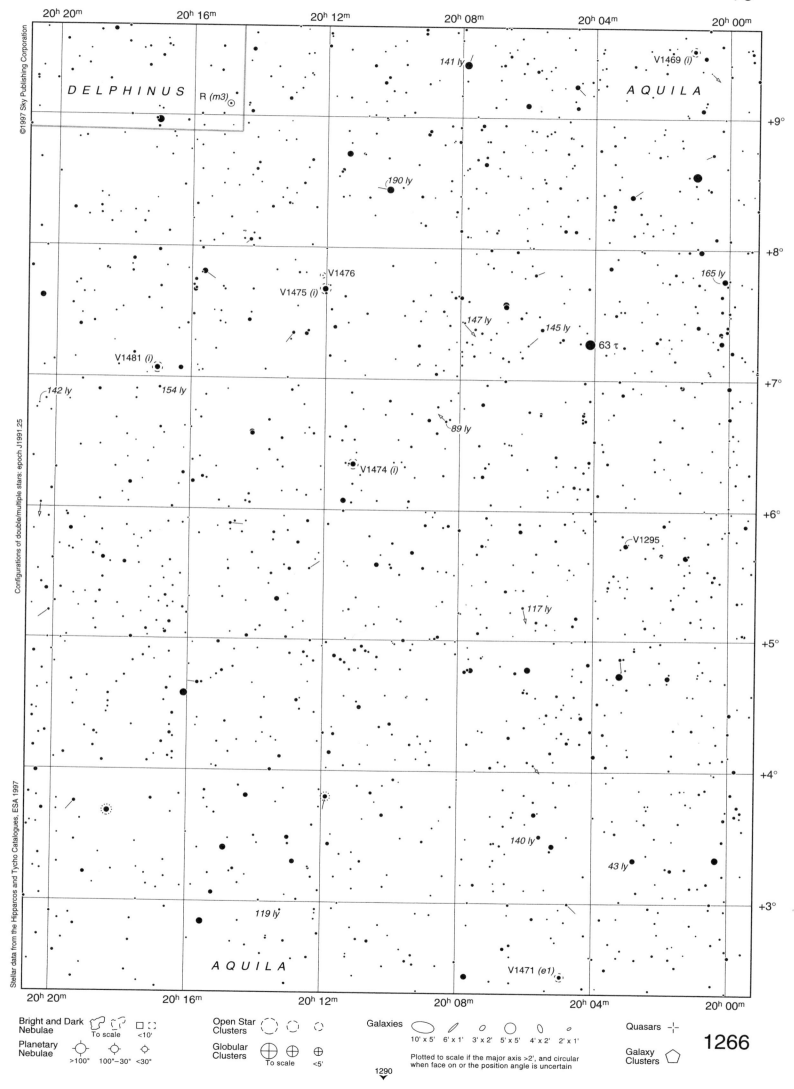

DELPHINUS

R (m3)

AQUILA

V1469 (i)

141 ly

190 ly

+9°

+8°

165 ly

V1476
V1475 (i)
147 ly
145 ly
63 τ

V1481 (i)

142 ly        154 ly

+7°

89 ly

V1474 (i)

+6°

V1295

117 ly

+5°

+4°

140 ly

43 ly

+3°

119 ly

AQUILA

V1471 (e1)

Configurations of double/multiple stars: epoch J1991.25

Stellar data from the Hipparcos and Tycho Catalogues, ESA 1997

Bright and Dark
Nebulae          To scale      <10'
Planetary
Nebulae      >100"   100"–30"   <30"

Open Star
Clusters
Globular
Clusters    To scale    <5'

Galaxies
10' x 5'  6' x 1'  3' x 2'  5' x 5'  4' x 2'  2' x 1'
Plotted to scale if the major axis >2', and circular
when face on or the position angle is uncertain

Quasars

Galaxy
Clusters

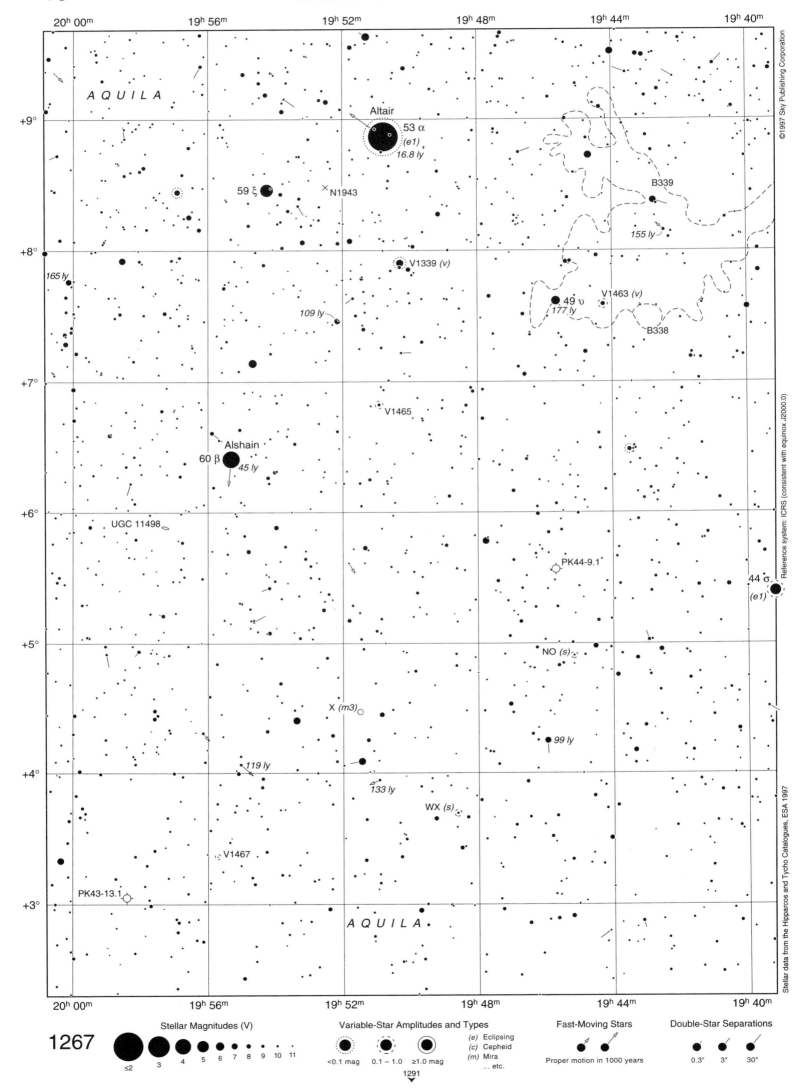

©1997 Sky Publishing Corporation

Reference system: ICRS (consistent with equinox J2000.0)

Stellar data from the Hipparcos and Tycho Catalogues, ESA 1997

AQUILA

Altair
53 α
(e1)
16.8 ly

59 ξ
×N1943

B339
155 ly

V1339 (v)

165 ly

109 ly

49 υ
177 ly
V1463 (v)
B338

V1465

Alshain
60 β
45 ly

UGC 11498
PK44-9.1
44 σ
(e1)

NO (s)

X (m3)
99 ly

119 ly
133 ly

WX (s)

V1467

PK43-13.1

AQUILA

1267

Stellar Magnitudes (V)
≤2    3    4   5  6  7 8 9 10 11

Variable-Star Amplitudes and Types
<0.1 mag    0.1 – 1.0    ≥1.0 mag

(e) Eclipsing
(c) Cepheid
(m) Mira
... etc.

Fast-Moving Stars
Proper motion in 1000 years

Double-Star Separations
0.3"    3"    30"

# MILLENNIUM STAR ATLAS

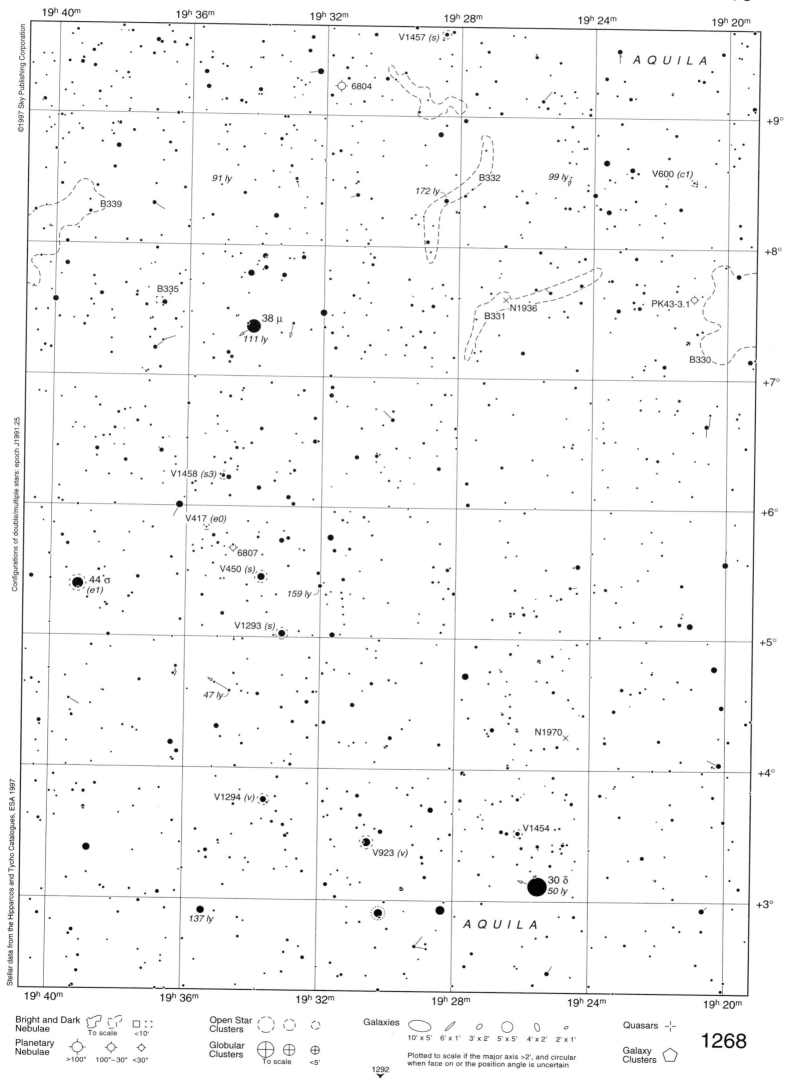

| | | |
|---|---|---|
| 19h 40m | 19h 36m | 19h 32m | 19h 28m | 19h 24m | 19h 20m |

V1457 (s)

AQUILA

6804

91 ly

B332

99 ly

V600 (c1)

172 ly

B339

+9°

B335

+8°

N1936

38 μ

B331

PK43-3.1

111 ly

B330

+7°

V1458 (s3)

V417 (e0)

+6°

6807

44 σ
(e1)

V450 (s)

159 ly

V1293 (s)

+5°

47 ly

N1970

+4°

V1294 (v)

V1454

V923 (v)

30 δ
50 ly

137 ly

AQUILA

+3°

| | | |
|---|---|---|
| 19h 40m | 19h 36m | 19h 32m | 19h 28m | 19h 24m | 19h 20m |

Bright and Dark
Nebulae
To scale        <10'

Planetary
Nebulae
>100"   100"–30"   <30"

Open Star
Clusters

Globular
Clusters
To scale        <5'

Galaxies

10' x 5'   6' x 1'   3' x 2'   5' x 5'   4' x 2'   2' x 1'

Plotted to scale if the major axis >2', and circular
when face on or the position angle is uncertain

Quasars

Galaxy
Clusters

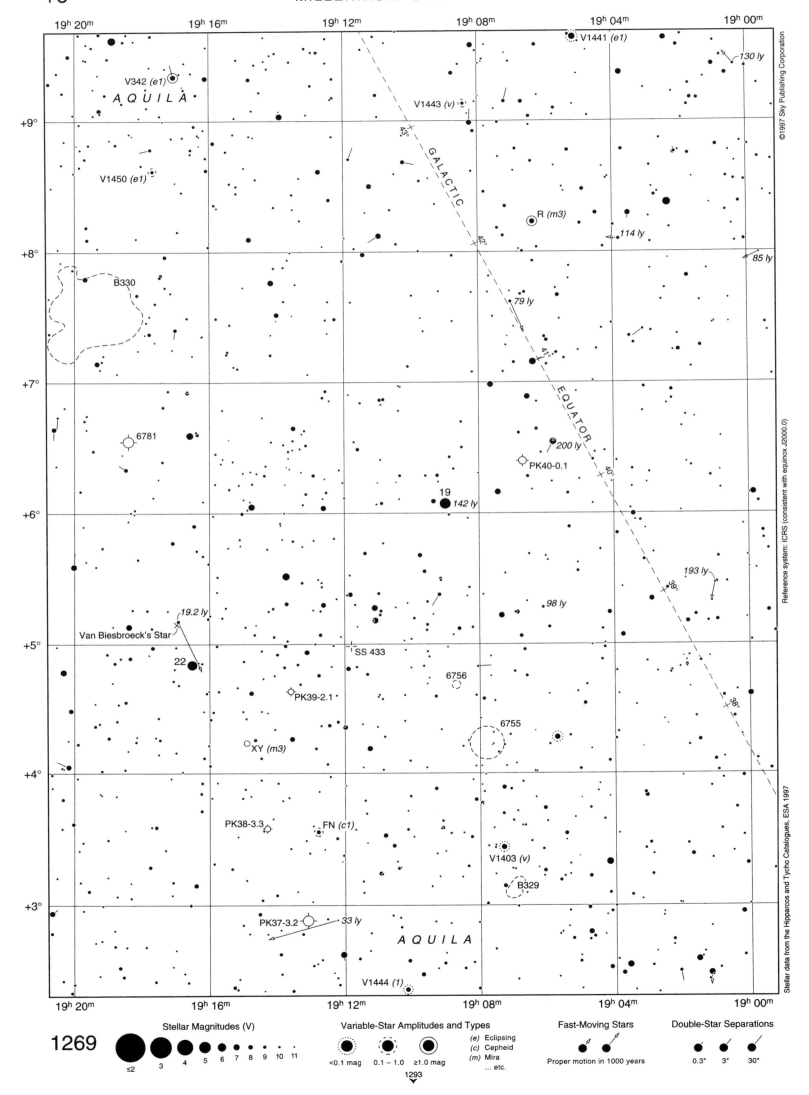

©1997 Sky Publishing Corporation

Reference system: ICRS (consistent with equinox J2000.0)

Stellar data from the Hipparcos and Tycho Catalogues, ESA 1997

19ʰ 20ᵐ    19ʰ 16ᵐ    19ʰ 12ᵐ    19ʰ 08ᵐ    19ʰ 04ᵐ    19ʰ 00ᵐ

V1441 (e1)
130 ly
V342 (e1)
A Q U I L A
V1443 (v)
GALACTIC
43°
+9°
V1450 (e1)
42°
R (m3)
114 ly
85 ly
+8°
B330
79 ly
41°
+7°
EQUATOR
6781
200 ly
PK40-0.1
40°
19    142 ly
+6°
193 ly
39°
98 ly
19.2 ly
Van Biesbroeck's Star
SS 433
+5°
22
6756
38°
PK39-2.1
6755
XY (m3)
+4°
PK38-3.3    FN (c1)
V1403 (v)
B329
+3°
PK37-3.2    33 ly
A Q U I L A
V1444 (1)

19ʰ 20ᵐ    19ʰ 16ᵐ    19ʰ 12ᵐ    19ʰ 08ᵐ    19ʰ 04ᵐ    19ʰ 00ᵐ

**1269**

Stellar Magnitudes (V)

≤2   3   4   5   6   7   8   9   10   11

Variable-Star Amplitudes and Types

<0.1 mag    0.1 – 1.0    ≥1.0 mag

(e) Eclipsing
(c) Cepheid
(m) Mira
... etc.

Fast-Moving Stars

Proper motion in 1000 years

Double-Star Separations

0.3"    3"    30"

1293

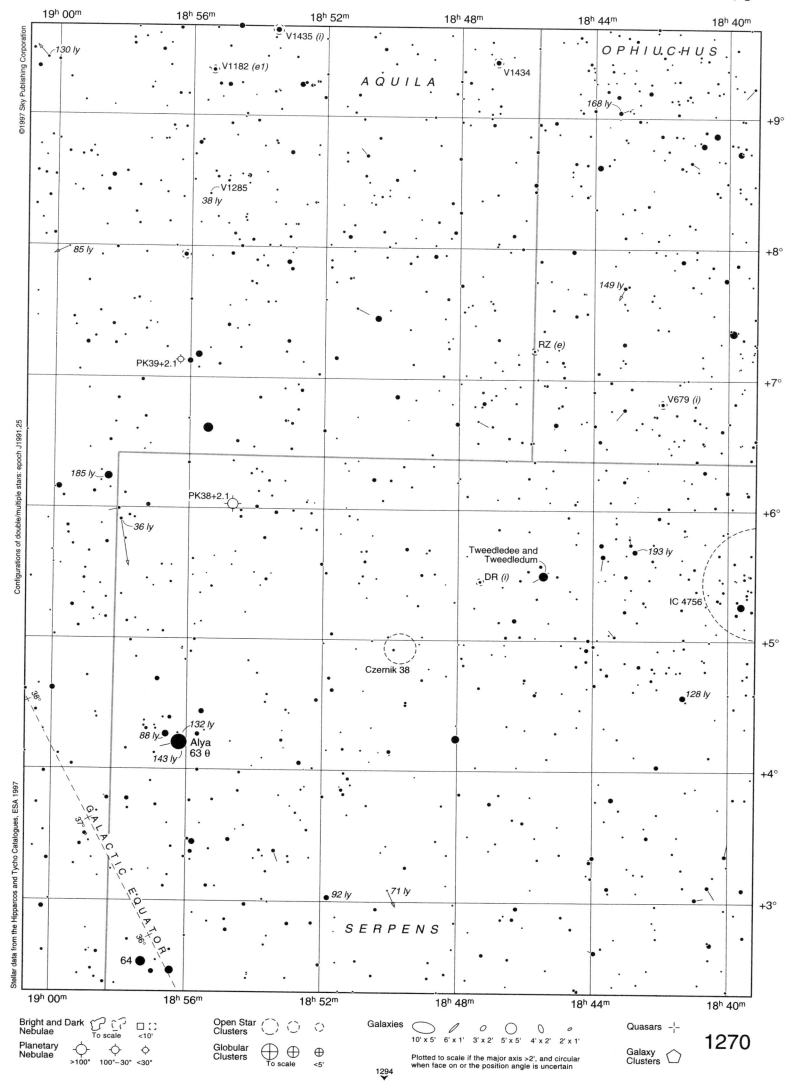

Configurations of double/multiple stars: epoch J1991.25

Stellar data from the Hipparcos and Tycho Catalogues, ESA 1997

19h 00m · 18h 56m · 18h 52m · 18h 48m · 18h 44m · 18h 40m

OPHIUCHUS

AQUILA

SERPENS

V1435 (i)
V1182 (e1)
V1285
38 ly
130 ly
85 ly
PK39+2.1
185 ly
PK38+2.1
36 ly
Alya
63 θ
132 ly
88 ly
143 ly
64
92 ly
71 ly
V1434
168 ly
149 ly
RZ (e)
V679 (i)
Tweedledee and
Tweedledum
DR (i)
193 ly
IC 4756
Czernik 38
128 ly
36°
GALACTIC EQUATOR
37°
36°

+9°
+8°
+7°
+6°
+5°
+4°
+3°

Bright and Dark
Nebulae
To scale    <10'
Planetary
Nebulae
>100"  100"–30"  <30"

Open Star
Clusters
Globular
Clusters
To scale    <5'

Galaxies
10' x 5'  6' x 1'  3' x 2'  5' x 5'  4' x 2'  2' x 1'
Plotted to scale if the major axis >2', and circular
when face on or the position angle is uncertain

Quasars
Galaxy
Clusters

1270

1294

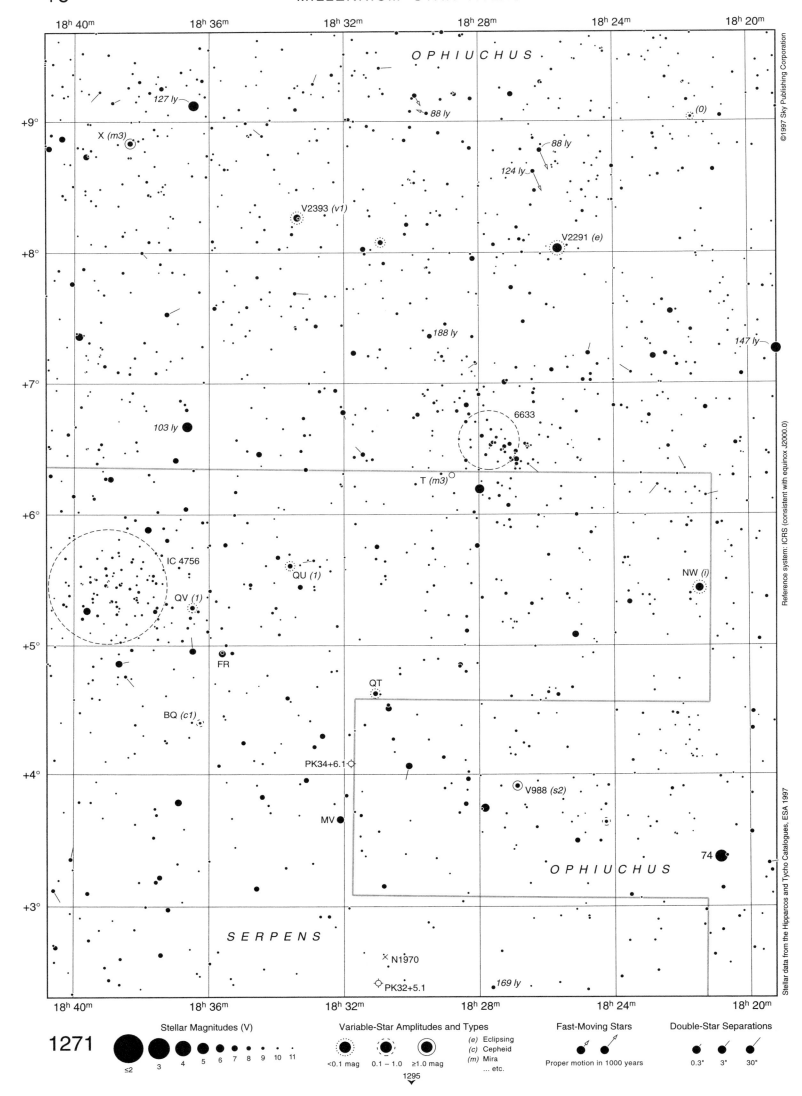

©1997 Sky Publishing Corporation

Reference system: ICRS (consistent with equinox J2000.0)

Stellar data from the Hipparcos and Tycho Catalogues, ESA 1997

OPHIUCHUS

88 ly

88 ly

124 ly

V2393 (v1)

V2291 (e)

X (m3)

127 ly

188 ly

147 ly

103 ly

6633

T (m3)

NW (i)

IC 4756

QU (1)

QV (1)

FR

QT

BQ (c1)

PK34+6.1

V988 (s2)

MV

74

OPHIUCHUS

SERPENS

N1970

PK32+5.1

169 ly

**1271**

Stellar Magnitudes (V)

≤2  3  4  5  6  7  8  9  10  11

Variable-Star Amplitudes and Types

<0.1 mag   0.1 – 1.0   ≥1.0 mag

(e) Eclipsing
(c) Cepheid
(m) Mira
... etc.

Fast-Moving Stars

Proper motion in 1000 years

Double-Star Separations

0.3"  3"  30"

1295

# MILLENNIUM STAR ATLAS

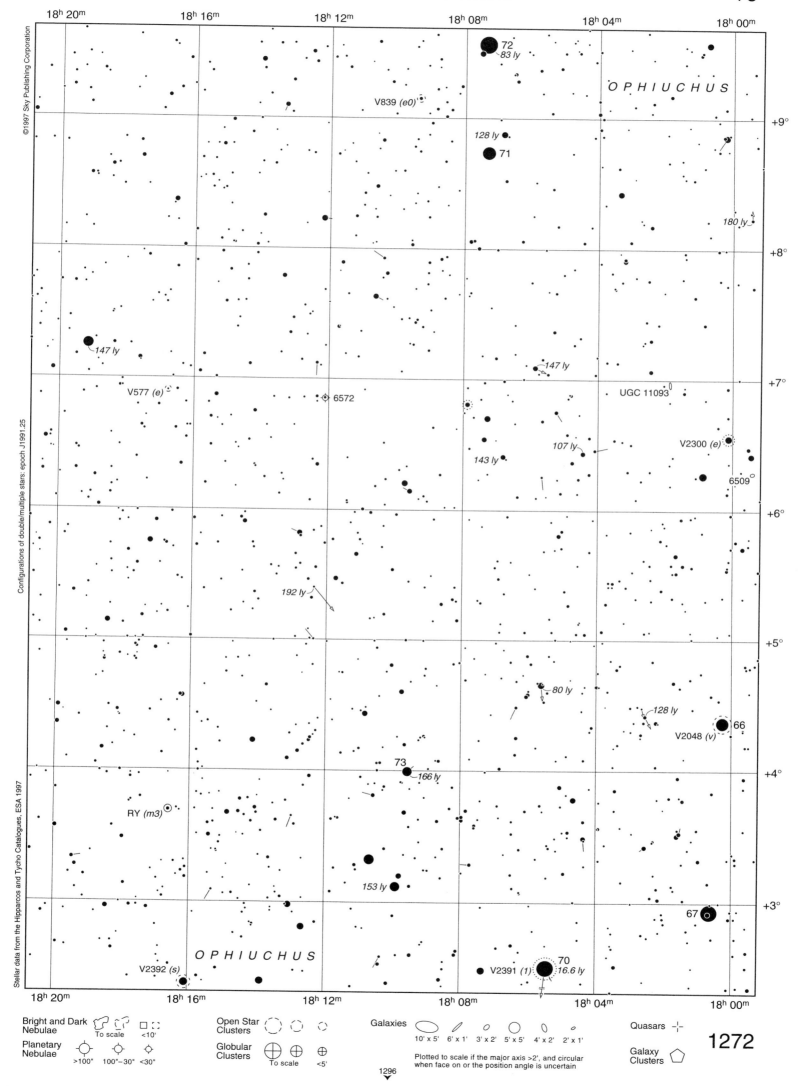

18h 20m  18h 16m  18h 12m  18h 08m  18h 04m  18h 00m

O P H I U C H U S

72
83 ly

V839 (e0)

128 ly
71

180 ly

+9°

+8°

147 ly

147 ly

V577 (e)

6572

UGC 11093

107 ly

+7°

143 ly

V2300 (e)

6509

+6°

192 ly

80 ly

+5°

128 ly

V2048 (v)
66

73
166 ly

+4°

RY (m3)

153 ly

67

+3°

O P H I U C H U S

V2392 (s)

V2391 (1)
70
16.6 ly

18h 20m  18h 16m  18h 12m  18h 08m  18h 04m  18h 00m

| Bright and Dark Nebulae | | To scale | | <10' |
|---|---|---|---|---|

Open Star Clusters

Globular Clusters    To scale    <5'

Galaxies
10' x 5'   6' x 1'   3' x 2'   5' x 5'   4' x 2'   2' x 1'
Plotted to scale if the major axis >2', and circular when face on or the position angle is uncertain

Planetary Nebulae   >100"   100"–30"   <30"

Quasars

Galaxy Clusters

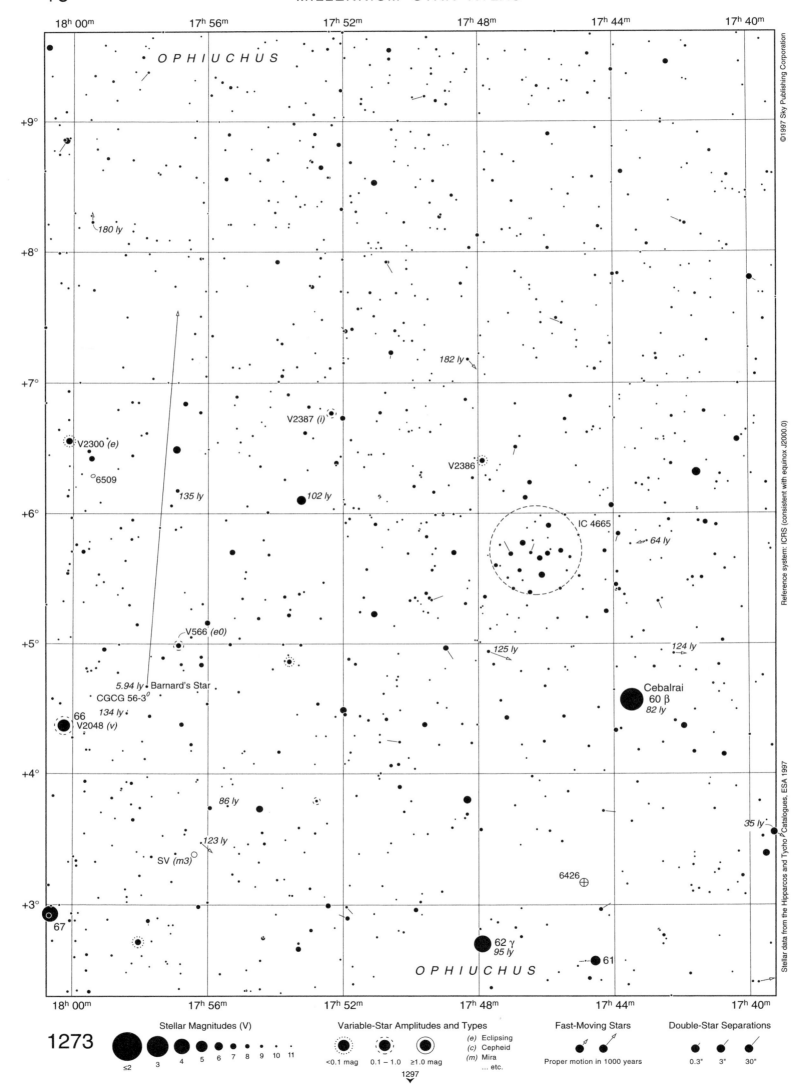

O P H I U C H U S

18h 00m · 17h 56m · 17h 52m · 17h 48m · 17h 44m · 17h 40m

+9°
+8°
+7°
+6°
+5°
+4°
+3°

180 ly

182 ly

V2387 (i)

V2300 (e)

6509

135 ly

102 ly

V2386

IC 4665

64 ly

V566 (e0)

125 ly

124 ly

5.94 ly · Barnard's Star
CGCG 56-3⁰
134 ly

Cebalrai
60 β
82 ly

66
V2048 (v)

86 ly

35 ly

123 ly

SV (m3)

6426

67

62 γ
95 ly

61

O P H I U C H U S

©1997 Sky Publishing Corporation

Reference system: ICRS (consistent with equinox J2000.0)

Stellar data from the Hipparcos and Tycho Catalogues, ESA 1997

Stellar Magnitudes (V)
≤2  3  4  5  6  7  8  9  10  11

Variable-Star Amplitudes and Types
<0.1 mag    0.1 – 1.0    ≥1.0 mag

(e) Eclipsing
(c) Cepheid
(m) Mira
... etc.

Fast-Moving Stars
Proper motion in 1000 years

Double-Star Separations
0.3"  3"  30"

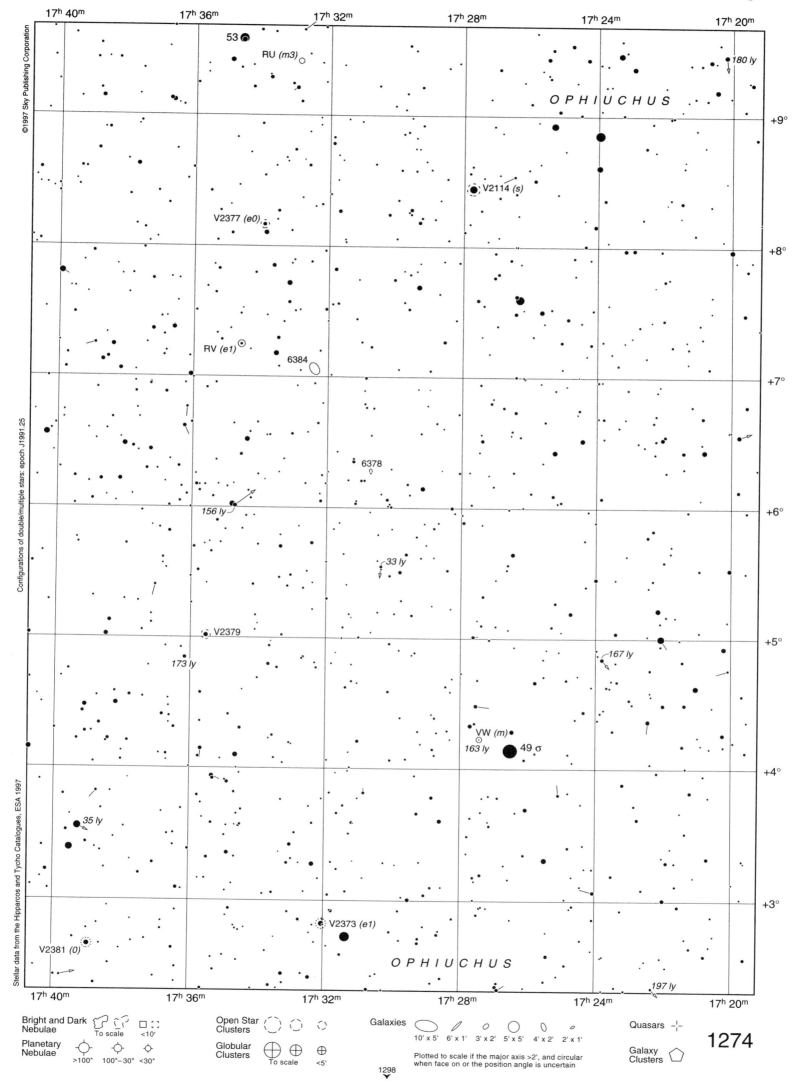

Configurations of double/multiple stars: epoch J1991.25

Stellar data from the Hipparcos and Tycho Catalogues, ESA 1997

53

RU (m3)

180 ly

OPHIUCHUS

V2114 (s)

V2377 (e0)

RV (e1)

6384

6378

156 ly

33 ly

V2379

173 ly

167 ly

VW (m)

163 ly    49 σ

35 ly

V2373 (e1)

V2381 (0)

OPHIUCHUS

197 ly

| Bright and Dark Nebulae | | | | Open Star Clusters | | | Galaxies | | | | | | Quasars |
|---|---|---|---|---|---|---|---|---|---|---|---|---|---|
| | To scale | | <10' | To scale | | | 10' x 5' | 6' x 1' | 3' x 2' | 5' x 5' | 4' x 2' | 2' x 1' | |
| Planetary Nebulae | | | | Globular Clusters | | | | | | | | | Galaxy Clusters |
| | >100" | 100"–30" | <30" | To scale | | <5' | Plotted to scale if the major axis >2', and circular when face on or the position angle is uncertain | | | | | | |

1274

+6°

# MILLENNIUM STAR ATLAS

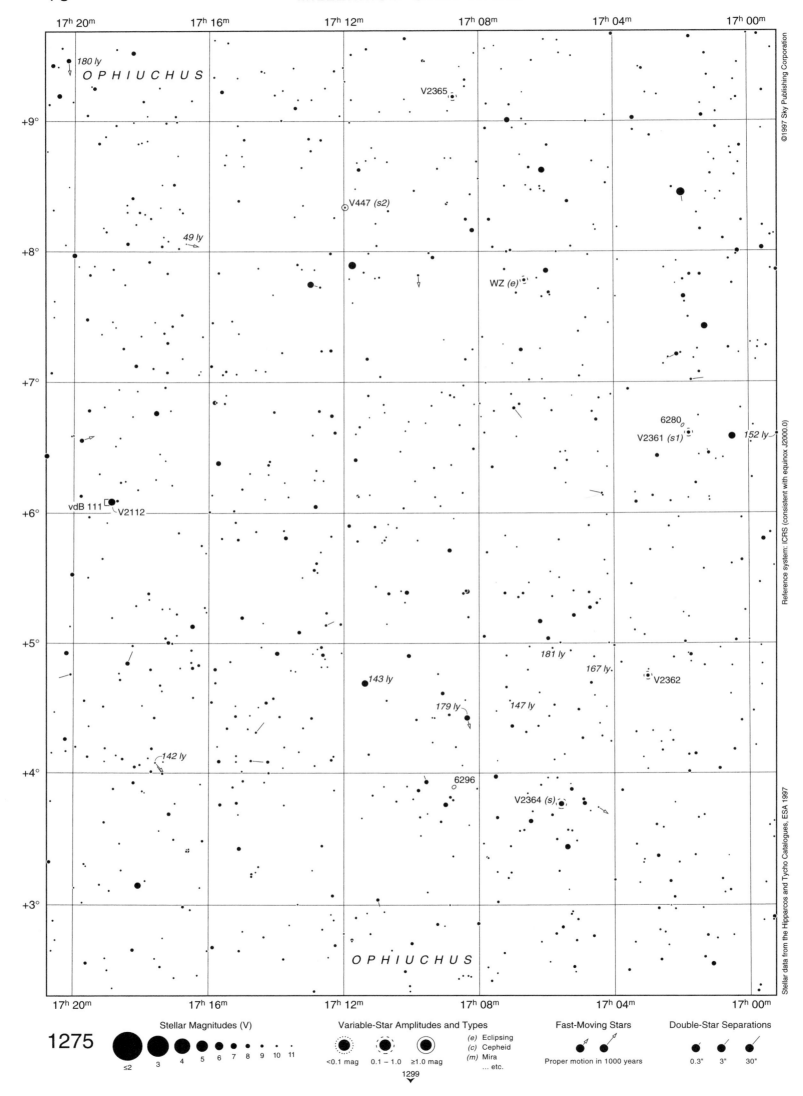

O P H I U C H U S

180 ly

V2365

V447 (s2)

49 ly

WZ (e)

6280

V2361 (s1)

152 ly

vdB 111
V2112

181 ly

167 ly

V2362

143 ly

179 ly

147 ly

142 ly

6296

V2364 (s)

O P H I U C H U S

**1275**

Stellar Magnitudes (V)

≤2  3  4  5  6  7  8  9  10  11

Variable-Star Amplitudes and Types

<0.1 mag    0.1 – 1.0    ≥1.0 mag

(e) Eclipsing
(c) Cepheid
(m) Mira
... etc.

Fast-Moving Stars

Proper motion in 1000 years

Double-Star Separations

0.3"    3"    30"

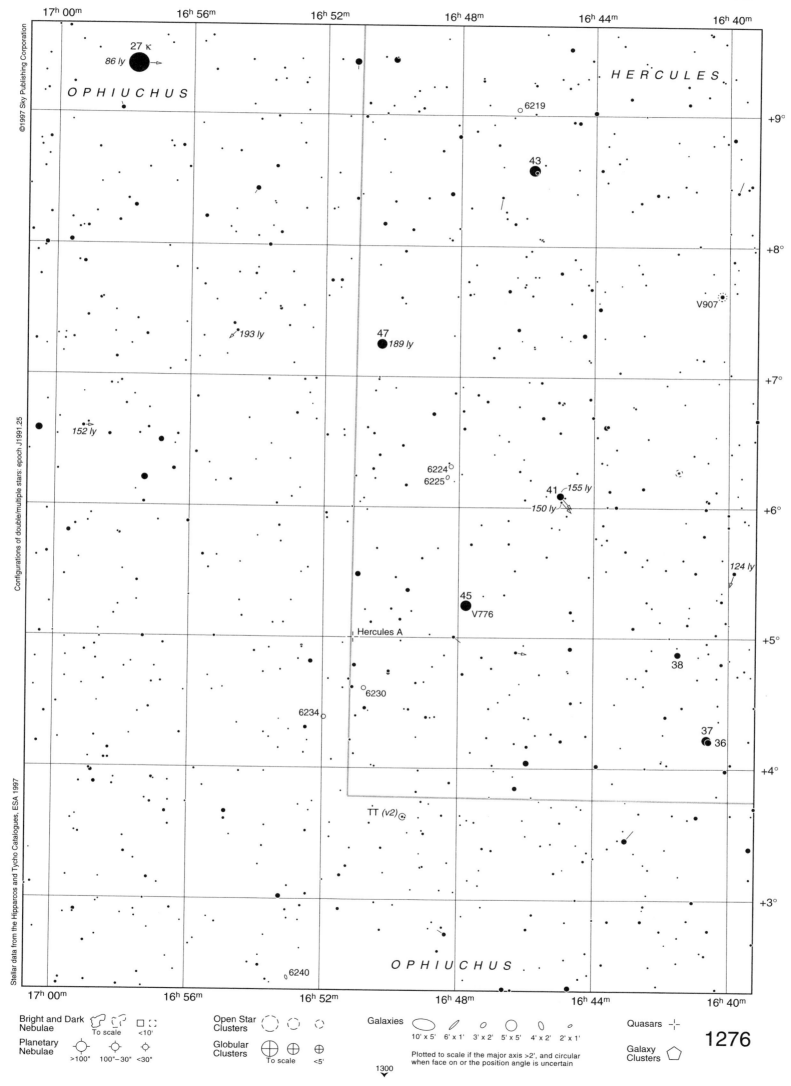

Configurations of double/multiple stars: epoch J1991.25

Stellar data from the Hipparcos and Tycho Catalogues, ESA 1997

17h 00m    16h 56m    16h 52m    16h 48m    16h 44m    16h 40m

27 κ
86 ly

O P H I U C H U S

H E R C U L E S

6219

43

V907

193 ly

47
189 ly

152 ly

6224
6225

41 — 155 ly
150 ly

124 ly

45
V776

Hercules A

38

6230

6234

37
36

124 ly

TT (v2)

O P H I U C H U S

6240

+9°
+8°
+7°
+6°
+5°
+4°
+3°

| Bright and Dark Nebulae | Open Star Clusters | Galaxies | Quasars |
|---|---|---|---|
| To scale   <10' | | 10' x 5'   6' x 1'   3' x 2'   5' x 5'   4' x 2'   2' x 1' | |
| Planetary Nebulae | Globular Clusters | | Galaxy Clusters |
| >100"   100"-30"   <30" | To scale   <5' | Plotted to scale if the major axis >2', and circular when face on or the position angle is uncertain | |

1276

1300

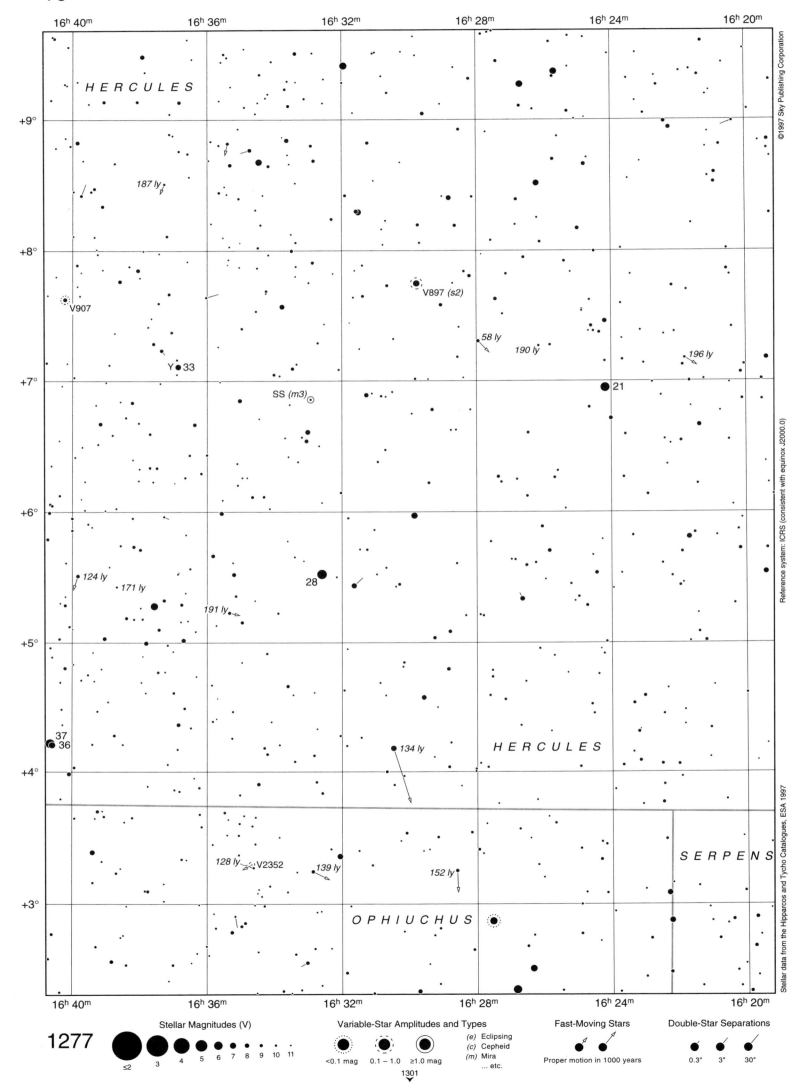

HERCULES

V907

Y● 33

V897 (s2)

58 ly

190 ly

196 ly

SS (m3)⊙

21

187 ly

124 ly

171 ly

28

191 ly

37
36

134 ly

HERCULES

128 ly    V2352

139 ly

152 ly

SERPENS

OPHIUCHUS

| Stellar Magnitudes (V) | | | | | | | | | | | Variable-Star Amplitudes and Types | | | | Fast-Moving Stars | | Double-Star Separations | | |
|---|---|---|---|---|---|---|---|---|---|---|---|---|---|---|---|---|---|---|---|
| ≤2 | 3 | 4 | 5 | 6 | 7 | 8 | 9 | 10 | 11 | | <0.1 mag | 0.1 – 1.0 | ≥1.0 mag | | | | 0.3" | 3" | 30" |

(e) Eclipsing
(c) Cepheid
(m) Mira
... etc.

Proper motion in 1000 years

1301

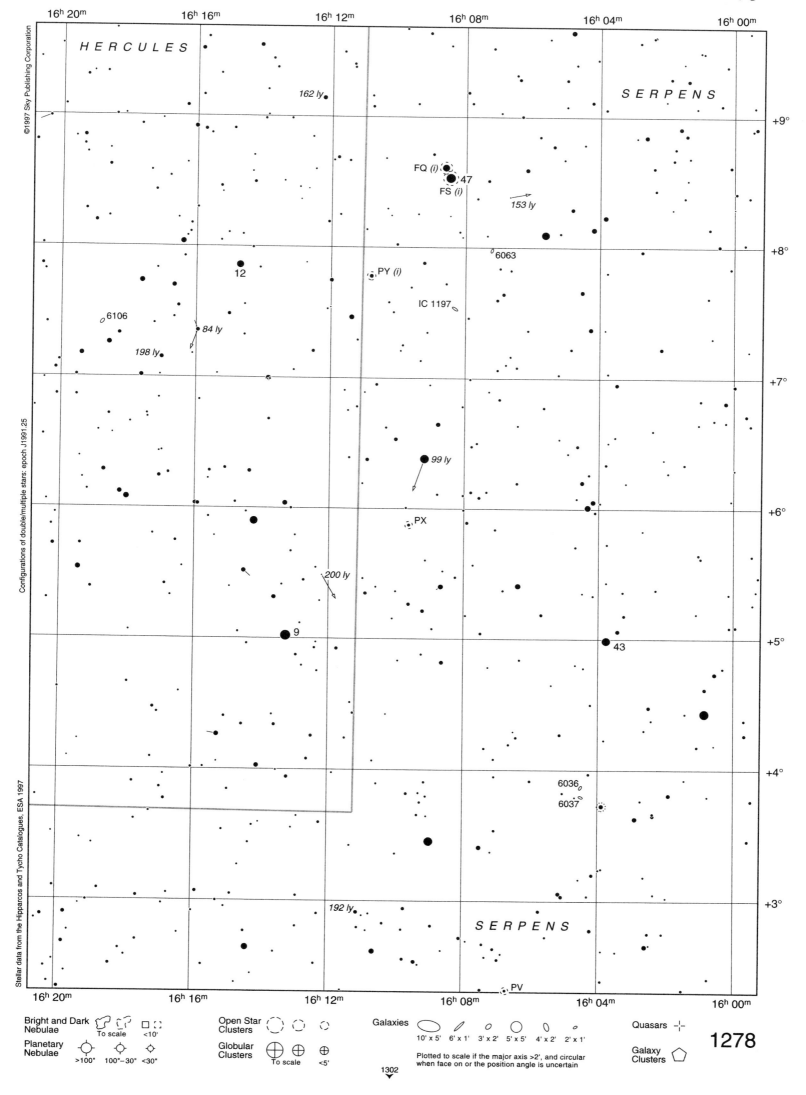

HERCULES

SERPENS

162 ly

FQ (i)
47
FS (i)
153 ly

6063

12

PY (i)

IC 1197

6106

84 ly

198 ly

99 ly

PX

200 ly

9

43

6036
6037

192 ly

SERPENS

PV

Bright and Dark
Nebulae
To scale      <10'

Planetary
Nebulae
>100"   100"–30"   <30"

Open Star
Clusters

Globular
Clusters
To scale    <5'

Galaxies
10' x 5'   6' x 1'   3' x 2'   5' x 5'   4' x 2'   2' x 1'

Plotted to scale if the major axis >2', and circular
when face on or the position angle is uncertain

Quasars

Galaxy
Clusters

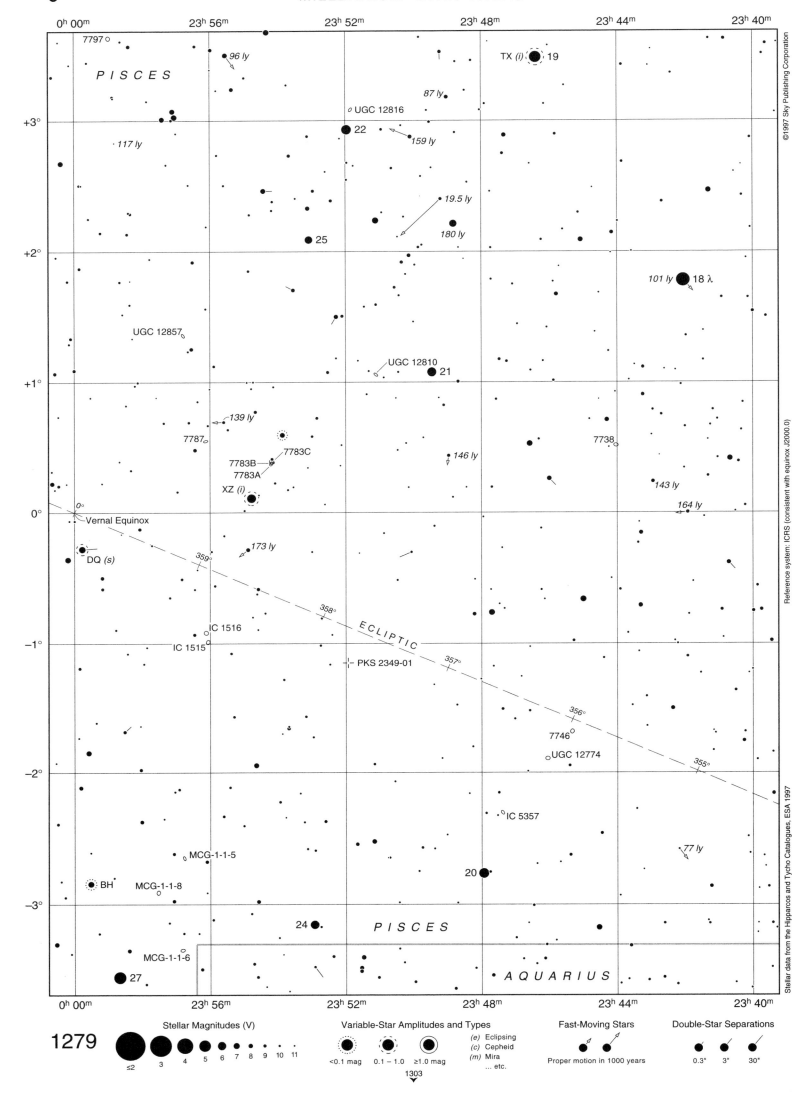

7797 ○

*P I S C E S*

96 ly

TX *(i)* 19

87 ly

*o* UGC 12816

22

159 ly

· 117 ly

19.5 ly

25

180 ly

101 ly 18 λ

UGC 12857 ○

UGC 12810

21

+3°

+2°

+1°

139 ly

7787 ○

7738 ○

7783B — 7783C

7783A

146 ly

143 ly

XZ *(i)*

164 ly

0°

Vernal Equinox

0°

173 ly

DQ *(s)*

359°

358°

*E C L I P T I C*

IC 1516

IC 1515

PKS 2349-01

357°

356°

7746 ○

UGC 12774 ○

355°

IC 5357 ○

77 ly

MCG-1-1-5 ○

20

BH ○

MCG-1-1-8 ○

24

*P I S C E S*

MCG-1-1-6 ○

*A Q U A R I U S*

27

-1°

-2°

-3°

0h 00m      23h 56m      23h 52m      23h 48m      23h 44m      23h 40m

©1997 Sky Publishing Corporation

Reference system: ICRS (consistent with equinox J2000.0)

Stellar data from the Hipparcos and Tycho Catalogues, ESA 1997

1279

Stellar Magnitudes (V)

≤2   3   4   5   6   7   8   9   10   11

Variable-Star Amplitudes and Types

<0.1 mag    0.1 – 1.0    ≥1.0 mag

*(e)* Eclipsing
*(c)* Cepheid
*(m)* Mira
... etc.

Fast-Moving Stars

Proper motion in 1000 years

Double-Star Separations

0.3"    3"    30"

# MILLENNIUM STAR ATLAS

0°

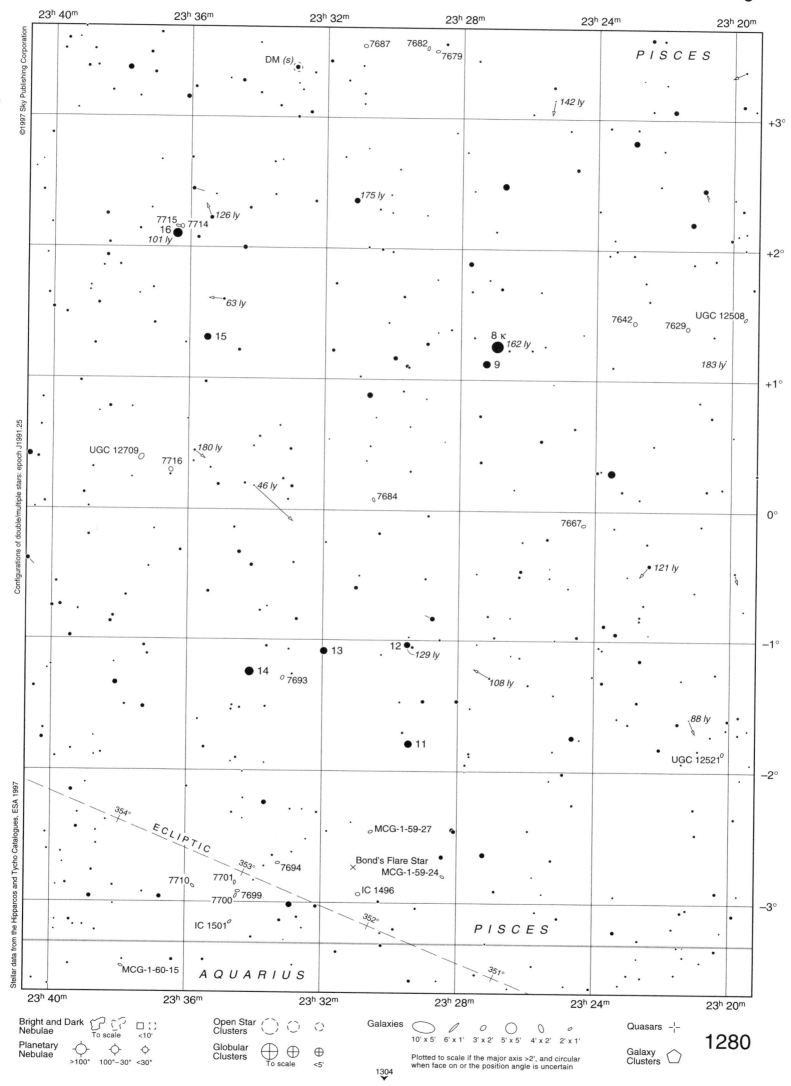

Stellar data from the Hipparcos and Tycho Catalogues, ESA 1997

Configurations of double/multiple stars: epoch J1991.25

P I S C E S

23h 40m    23h 36m    23h 32m    23h 28m    23h 24m    23h 20m

DM (s)

7687    7682    7679

142 ly

+3°

175 ly

7715 7714    126 ly
16
101 ly

+2°

63 ly

15

8 κ    162 ly
9

7642    7629    UGC 12508

183 ly

+1°

UGC 12709    180 ly
7716

46 ly

7684

7667

0°

121 ly

13
12    129 ly

14    7693

108 ly

88 ly

11

UGC 12521

-1°

-2°

ECLIPTIC

354°

MCG-1-59-27

353°    7694

Bond's Flare Star
MCG-1-59-24

7710    7701

7700    7699

IC 1496

IC 1501

352°

P I S C E S

-3°

MCG-1-60-15

A Q U A R I U S

351°

23h 40m    23h 36m    23h 32m    23h 28m    23h 24m    23h 20m

Bright and Dark Nebulae
To scale    <10'

Open Star Clusters

Galaxies
10' x 5'    6' x 1'    3' x 2'    5' x 5'    4' x 2'    2' x 1'

Quasars

Planetary Nebulae
>100"    100"-30"    <30"

Globular Clusters
To scale    <5'

Plotted to scale if the major axis >2', and circular when face on or the position angle is uncertain

Galaxy Clusters

1280

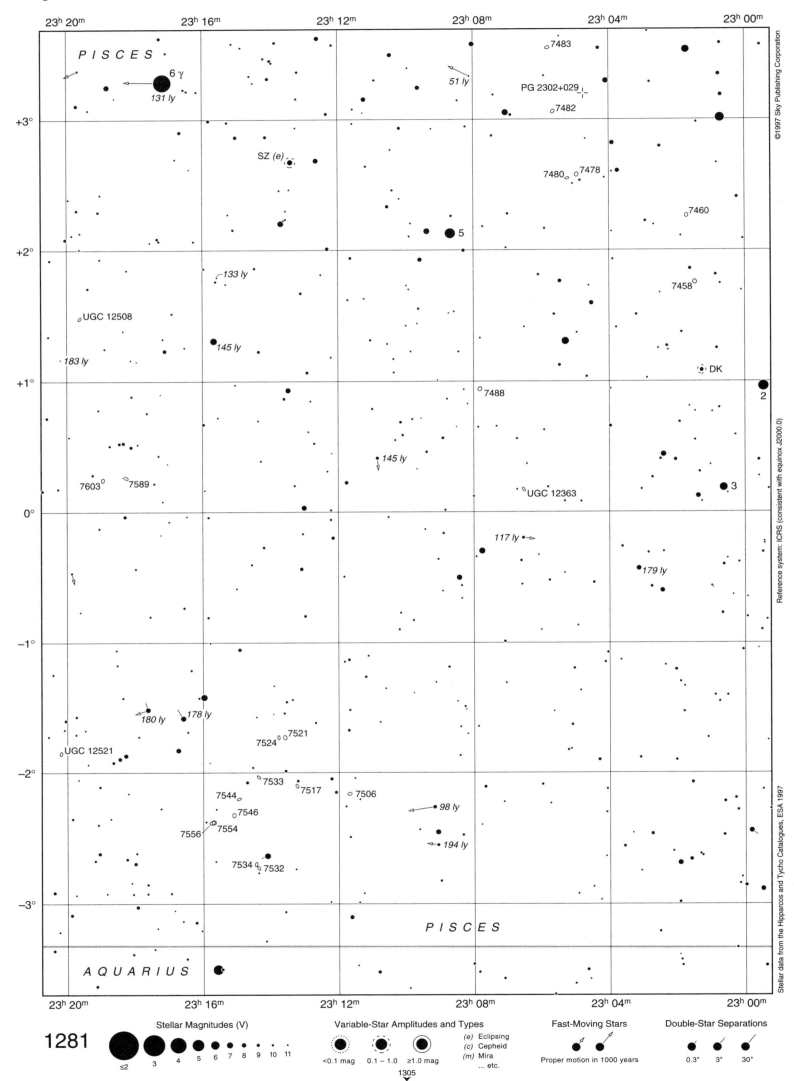

©1997 Sky Publishing Corporation

Reference system: ICRS (consistent with equinox J2000.0)

Stellar data from the Hipparcos and Tycho Catalogues, ESA 1997

**1281**

| Stellar Magnitudes (V) | Variable-Star Amplitudes and Types | Fast-Moving Stars | Double-Star Separations |
|---|---|---|---|

Stellar Magnitudes (V): ≤2  3  4  5  6  7  8  9  10  11

Variable-Star Amplitudes and Types:
<0.1 mag   0.1 – 1.0   ≥1.0 mag

(e) Eclipsing
(c) Cepheid
(m) Mira
... etc.

Fast-Moving Stars: Proper motion in 1000 years

Double-Star Separations: 0.3"  3"  30"

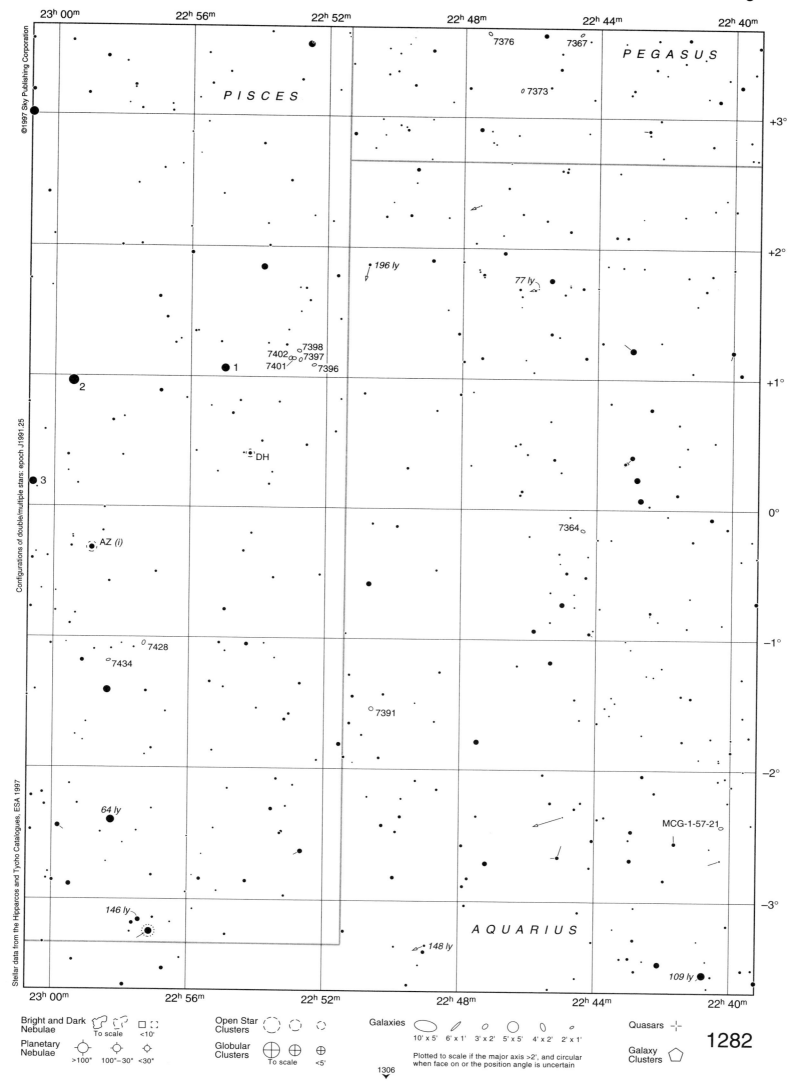

P E G A S U S

P I S C E S

7376
7367

7373

196 ly

77 ly

7398
7402 7397
7401 7396

1
2

3

DH

AZ (i)

7364

7428
7434

7391

64 ly

MCG-1-57-21

146 ly

A Q U A R I U S
148 ly

109 ly

| Bright and Dark Nebulae | | | | Open Star Clusters | | | Galaxies | | | | | | | Quasars |
| To scale | | <10' | | | | | 10' x 5' | 6' x 1' | 3' x 2' | 5' x 5' | 4' x 2' | 2' x 1' | |
| Planetary Nebulae | | | | Globular Clusters | | | | | | | | | | Galaxy Clusters |
| >100" | 100"–30" | <30" | | To scale | | <5' | | Plotted to scale if the major axis >2', and circular when face on or the position angle is uncertain | | | | | | |

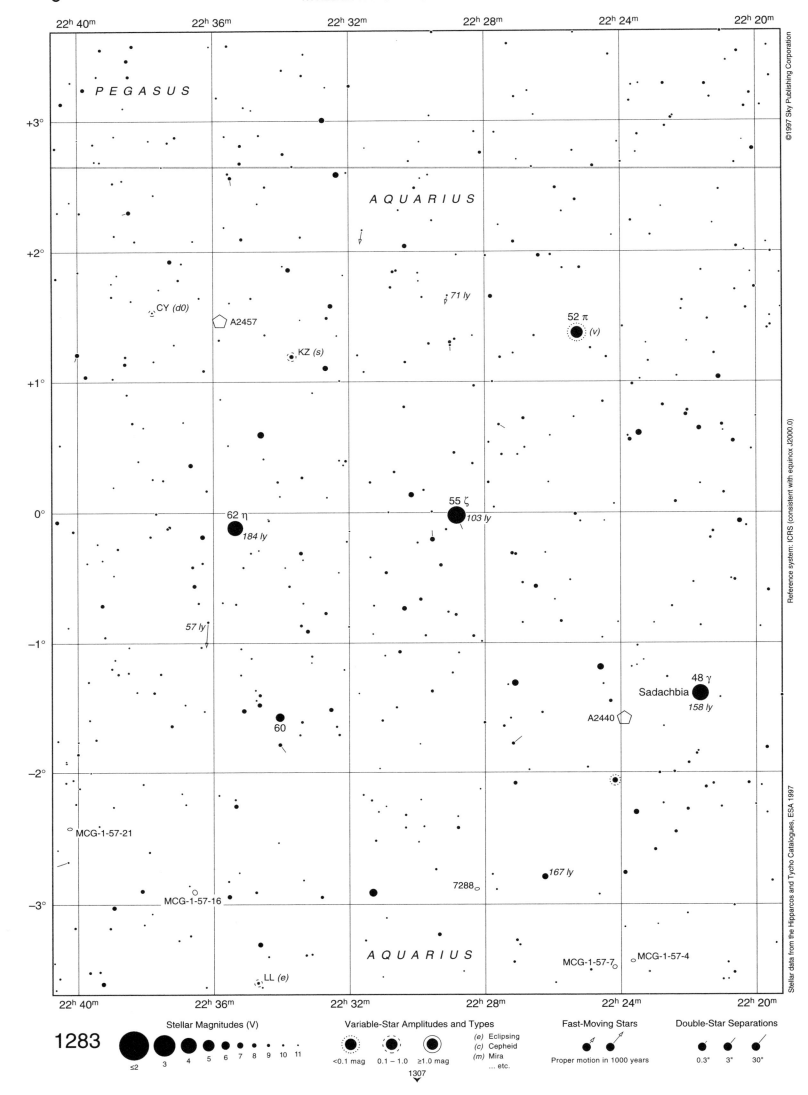

Reference system: ICRS (consistent with equinox J2000.0)

Stellar data from the Hipparcos and Tycho Catalogues, ESA 1997

PEGASUS

AQUARIUS

CY (d0)

A2457

KZ (s)

71 ly

52 π (v)

62 η
184 ly

55 ζ 103 ly

57 ly

48 γ
Sadachbia
158 ly

A2440

60

MCG-1-57-21

167 ly

7288

MCG-1-57-16

MCG-1-57-7

MCG-1-57-4

AQUARIUS

LL (e)

1283

Stellar Magnitudes (V)

≤2  3  4  5  6  7  8  9  10  11

Variable-Star Amplitudes and Types

<0.1 mag    0.1 – 1.0    ≥1.0 mag

(e) Eclipsing
(c) Cepheid
(m) Mira
... etc.

1307

Fast-Moving Stars

Proper motion in 1000 years

Double-Star Separations

0.3"    3"    30"

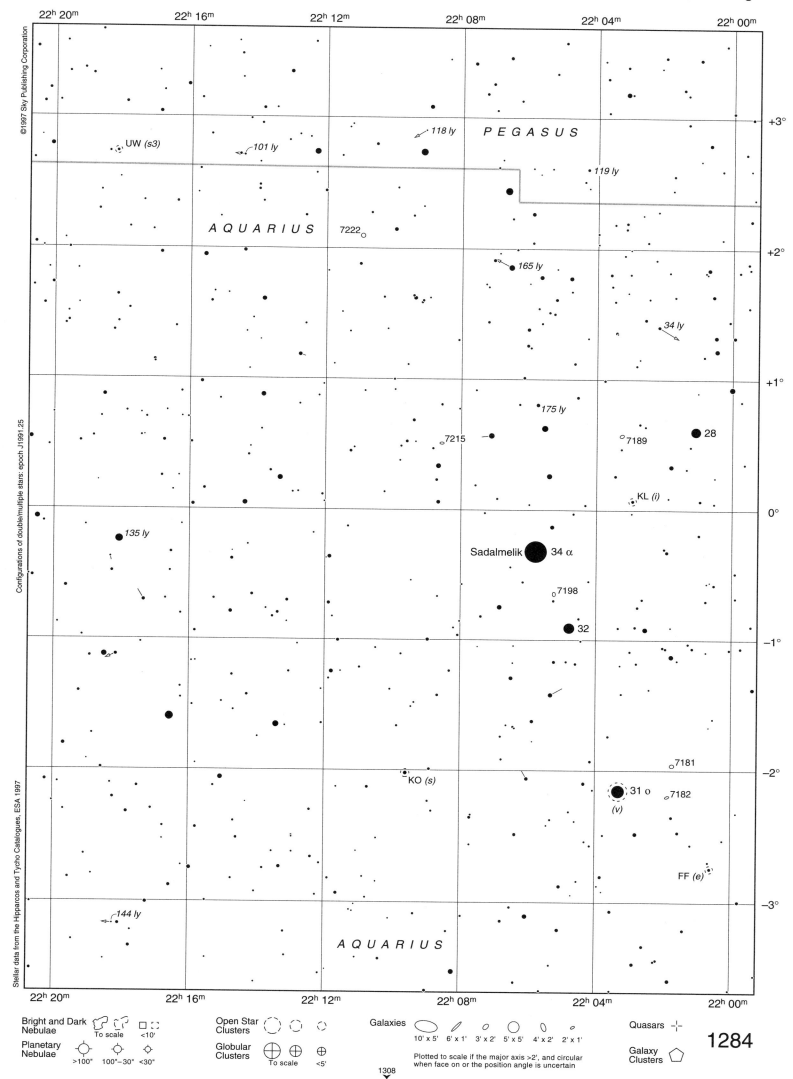

PEGASUS

AQUARIUS

AQUARIUS

UW (s3)
101 ly
118 ly
119 ly
7222
165 ly
34 ly
175 ly
7215
7189
28
KL (i)
135 ly
Sadalmelik
34 α
7198
32
KO (s)
7181
31 o
7182
(v)
FF (e)
144 ly

22h 20m
22h 16m
22h 12m
22h 08m
22h 04m
22h 00m
+3°
+2°
+1°
0°
-1°
-2°
-3°

22h 20m
22h 16m
22h 12m
22h 08m
22h 04m
22h 00m

Bright and Dark
Nebulae
To scale
<10'

Planetary
Nebulae
>100"
100"–30"
<30"

Open Star
Clusters

Globular
Clusters
To scale
<5'

Galaxies
10' x 5'
6' x 1'
3' x 2'
5' x 5'
4' x 2'
2' x 1'

Plotted to scale if the major axis >2', and circular
when face on or the position angle is uncertain

Quasars

Galaxy
Clusters

1284

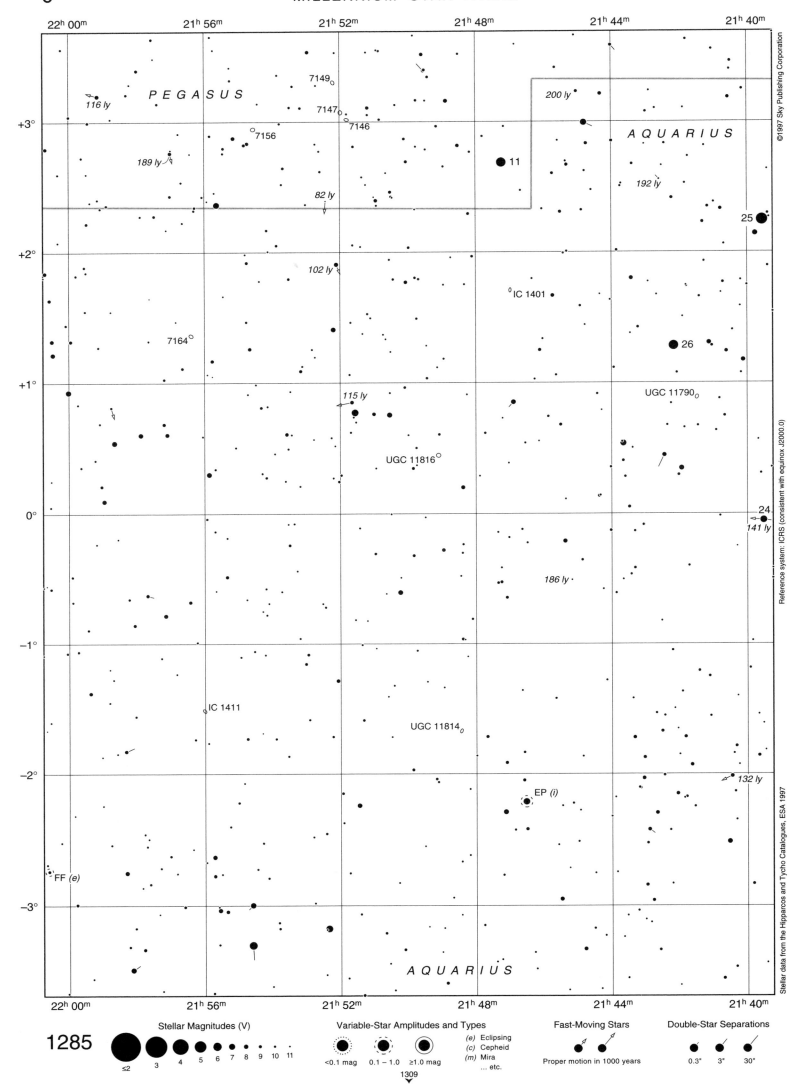

©1997 Sky Publishing Corporation

Reference system: ICRS (consistent with equinox J2000.0)

Stellar data from the Hipparcos and Tycho Catalogues, ESA 1997

P E G A S U S

A Q U A R I U S

A Q U A R I U S

1285

**Stellar Magnitudes (V)**

≤2   3   4   5   6   7   8   9   10   11

**Variable-Star Amplitudes and Types**

<0.1 mag   0.1 – 1.0   ≥1.0 mag

(e) Eclipsing
(c) Cepheid
(m) Mira
... etc.

**Fast-Moving Stars**

Proper motion in 1000 years

**Double-Star Separations**

0.3"   3"   30"

1309

# MILLENNIUM STAR ATLAS

0°

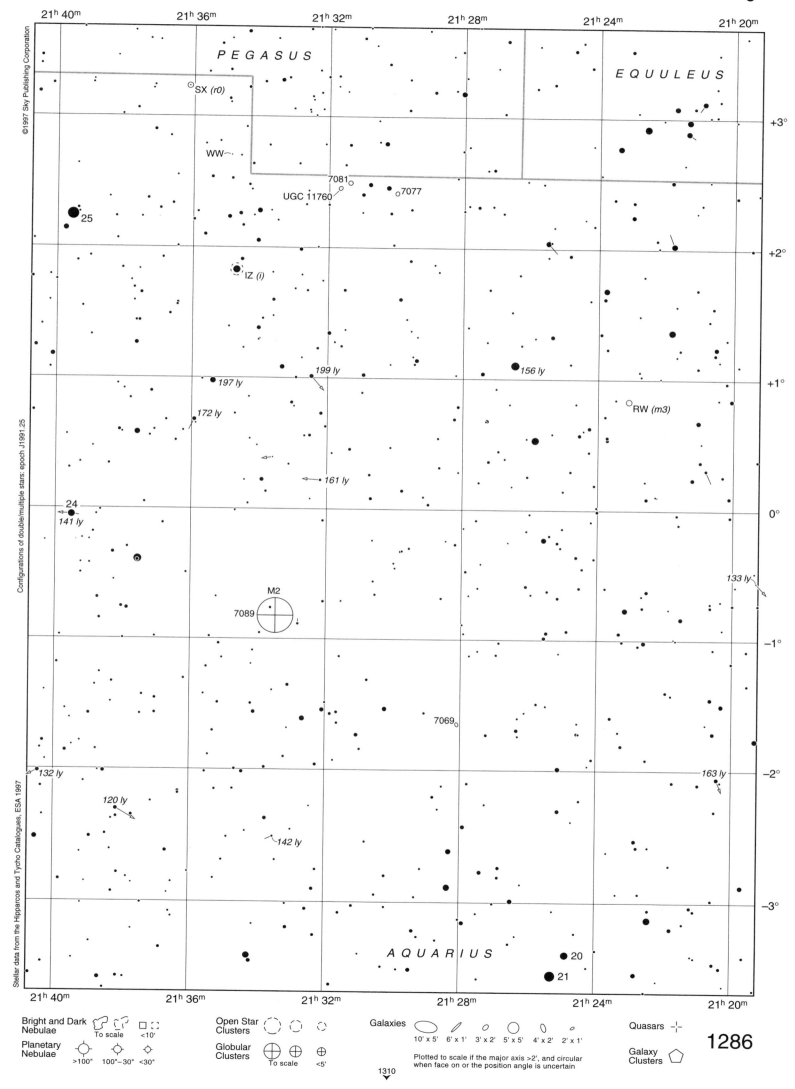

21ʰ 40ᵐ    21ʰ 36ᵐ    21ʰ 32ᵐ    21ʰ 28ᵐ    21ʰ 24ᵐ    21ʰ 20ᵐ

P E G A S U S

E Q U U L E U S

SX (r0)

WW

7081
UGC 11760    7077

25

IZ (i)

199 ly

197 ly    156 ly

172 ly    RW (m3)

24
141 ly

133 ly

M2
7089

7069

132 ly    163 ly

120 ly

142 ly

A Q U A R I U S    20

21

21ʰ 40ᵐ    21ʰ 36ᵐ    21ʰ 32ᵐ    21ʰ 28ᵐ    21ʰ 24ᵐ    21ʰ 20ᵐ

+3°
+2°
+1°
0°
−1°
−2°
−3°

Configurations of double/multiple stars: epoch J1991.25

Stellar data from the Hipparcos and Tycho Catalogues, ESA 1997

Bright and Dark Nebulae
To scale    <10'

Planetary Nebulae
>100"    100"–30"    <30"

Open Star Clusters

Globular Clusters
To scale    <5'

Galaxies
10' x 5'    6' x 1'    3' x 2'    5' x 5'    4' x 2'    2' x 1'

Plotted to scale if the major axis >2', and circular when face on or the position angle is uncertain

Quasars

Galaxy Clusters

1286

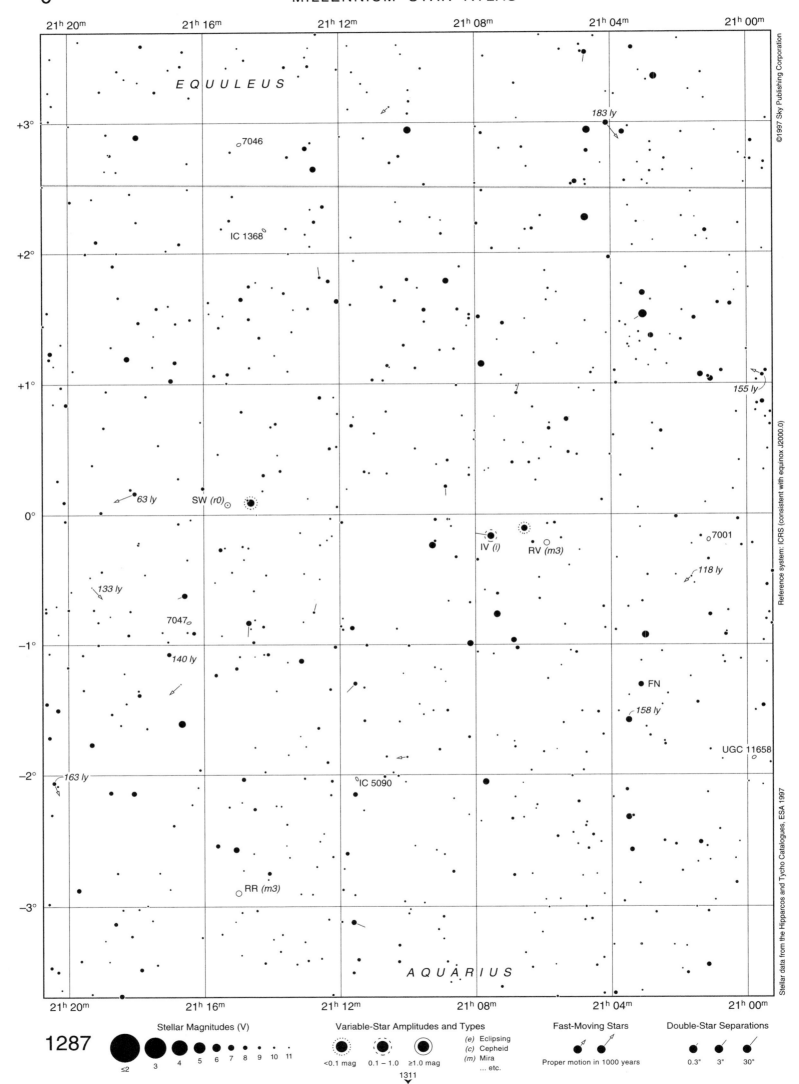

©1997 Sky Publishing Corporation

Reference system: ICRS (consistent with equinox J2000.0)

Stellar data from the Hipparcos and Tycho Catalogues, ESA 1997

E Q U U L E U S

7046

IC 1368

183 ly

155 ly

63 ly

SW (r0)

7001

IV (i)

RV (m3)

118 ly

133 ly

7047

140 ly

FN

158 ly

UGC 11658

163 ly

IC 5090

RR (m3)

A Q U A R I U S

1287

| Stellar Magnitudes (V) | Variable-Star Amplitudes and Types | Fast-Moving Stars | Double-Star Separations |

≤2    3    4    5    6    7    8    9    10    11

<0.1 mag    0.1 – 1.0    ≥1.0 mag

(e) Eclipsing
(c) Cepheid
(m) Mira
... etc.

Proper motion in 1000 years

0.3"    3"    30"

1311

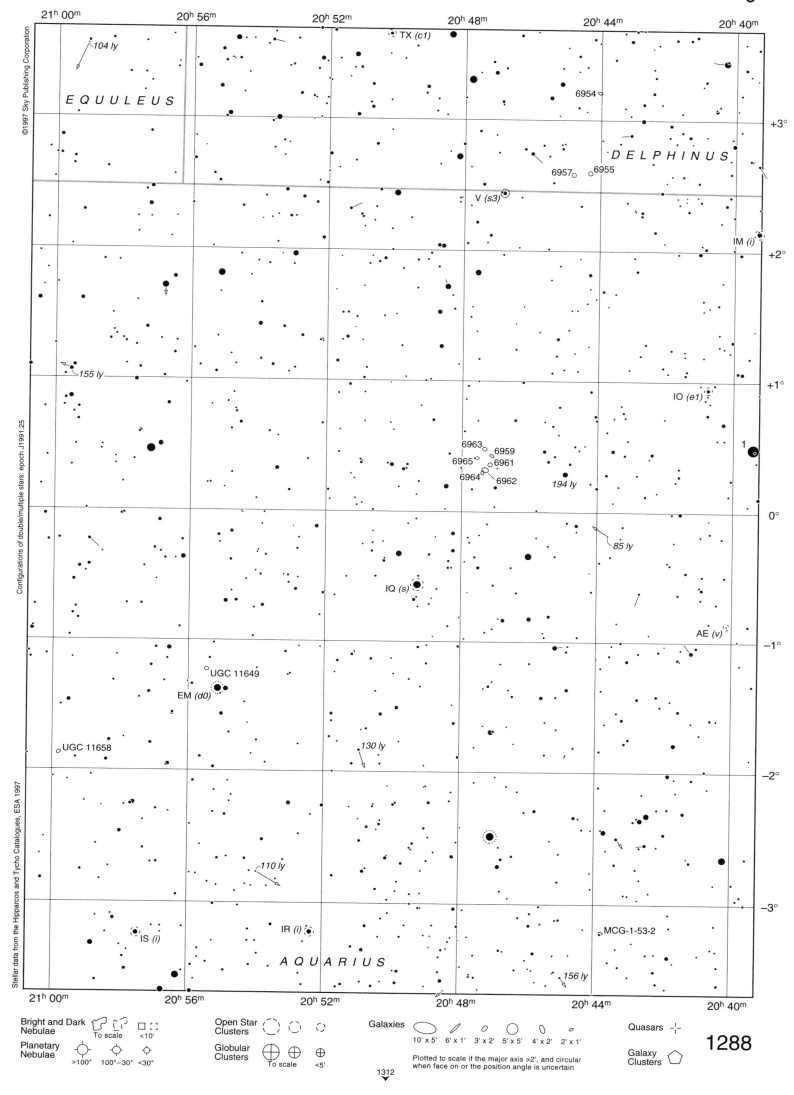

Configurations of double/multiple stars: epoch J1991.25

Stellar data from the Hipparcos and Tycho Catalogues, ESA 1997

*E Q U U L E U S*

104 ly

TX (c1)

6954

*D E L P H I N U S*

6957○  ○6955

V (s3)

IM (i)

+3°

+2°

155 ly

IO (e1)

+1°

6963 ○    ○6959
6965 ○ ○ 6961
6964 ○ ○ 6962

194 ly

1

0°

85 ly

IQ (s)

AE (v)

−1°

UGC 11649

EM (d0)

UGC 11658

130 ly

−2°

110 ly

−3°

IS (i)

IR (i)

MCG-1-53-2

*A Q U A R I U S*

156 ly

## Legend

| Bright and Dark Nebulae | To scale | <10' |
|---|---|---|

| Planetary Nebulae | >100" | 100"–30" | <30" |
|---|---|---|---|

| Open Star Clusters | | |
|---|---|---|

| Globular Clusters | To scale | <5' |
|---|---|---|

Galaxies

10' x 5'  6' x 1'  3' x 2'  5' x 5'  4' x 2'  2' x 1'

Plotted to scale if the major axis >2', and circular when face on or the position angle is uncertain

Quasars

Galaxy Clusters

1288

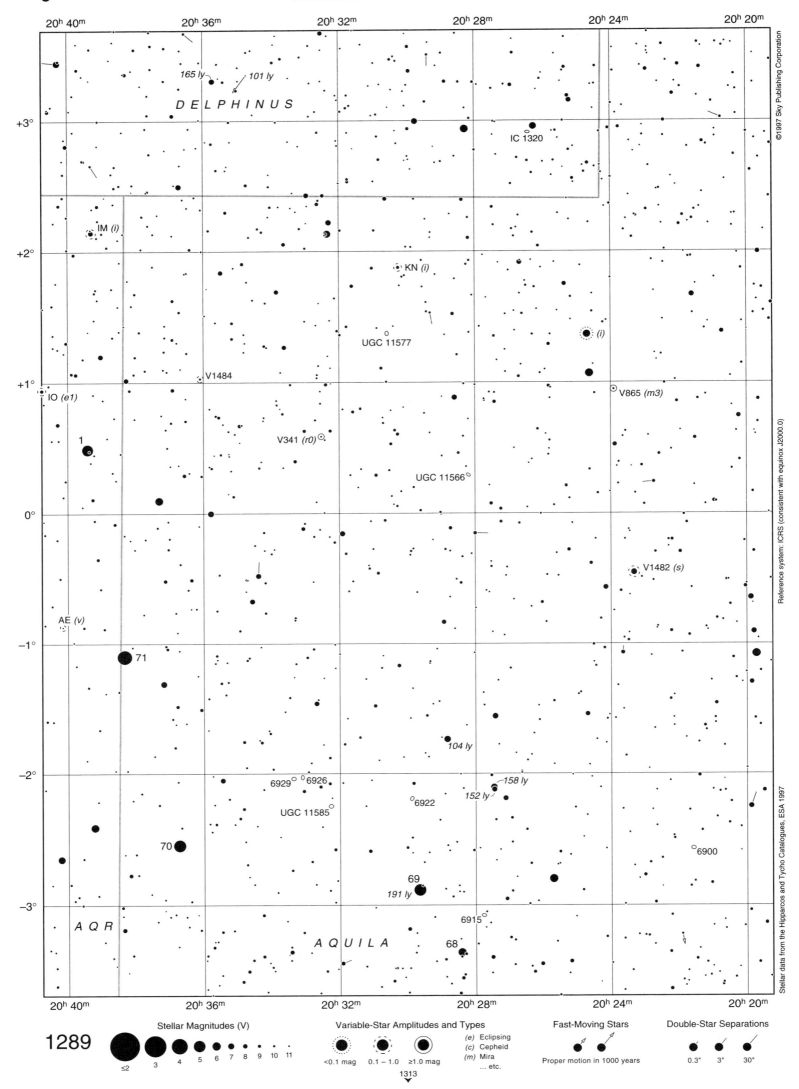

©1997 Sky Publishing Corporation

Reference system: ICRS (consistent with equinox J2000.0)

Stellar data from the Hipparcos and Tycho Catalogues, ESA 1997

165 ly    101 ly

*D E L P H I N U S*

IC 1320

IM *(i)*

KN *(i)*

UGC 11577

*(i)*

V1484

V865 *(m3)*

IO *(e1)*

1

V341 *(r0)*

UGC 11566

V1482 *(s)*

AE *(v)*

71

104 ly

-2°

6929  6926

158 ly

6922

152 ly

UGC 11585

70

6900

69

191 ly

6915

*A Q R*

*A Q U I L A*

68

1289

Stellar Magnitudes (V)

≤2   3   4   5   6   7   8   9   10   11

Variable-Star Amplitudes and Types

<0.1 mag   0.1 – 1.0   ≥1.0 mag

*(e)* Eclipsing
*(c)* Cepheid
*(m)* Mira
… etc.

Fast-Moving Stars

Proper motion in 1000 years

Double-Star Separations

0.3"   3"   30"

# MILLENNIUM STAR ATLAS

0°

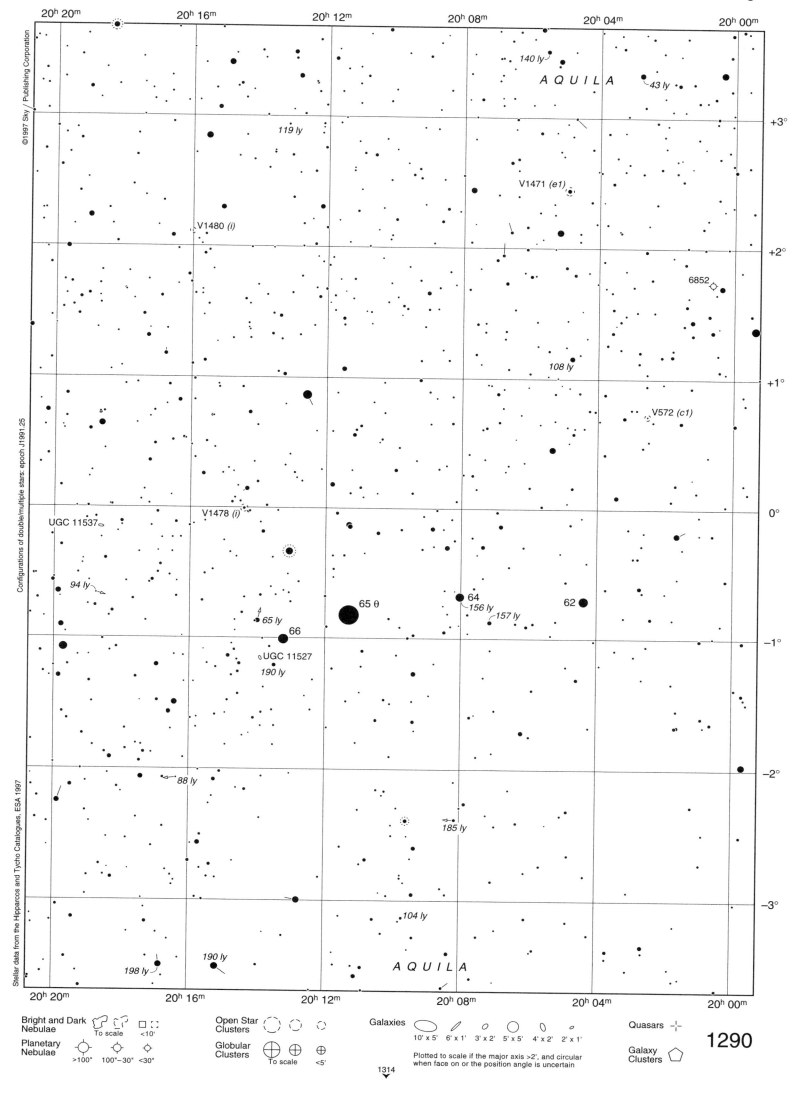

20h 20m    20h 16m    20h 12m    20h 08m    20h 04m    20h 00m

140 ly

A Q U I L A

43 ly

+3°

119 ly

V1471 (e1)

+2°

V1480 (i)

6852

108 ly

+1°

V572 (c1)

V1478 (i)

0°

UGC 11537

94 ly

64

156 ly

62

65 θ

157 ly

66

65 ly

-1°

UGC 11527

190 ly

88 ly

-2°

185 ly

104 ly

-3°

A Q U I L A

190 ly

198 ly

Configurations of double/multiple stars: epoch J1991.25

Stellar data from the Hipparcos and Tycho Catalogues, ESA 1997

Bright and Dark Nebulae    To scale    <10'

Open Star Clusters

Galaxies    10' x 5'   6' x 1'   3' x 2'   5' x 5'   4' x 2'   2' x 1'

Quasars

Planetary Nebulae    >100"   100"-30"   <30"

Globular Clusters    To scale    <5'

Plotted to scale if the major axis >2', and circular when face on or the position angle is uncertain

Galaxy Clusters

1290

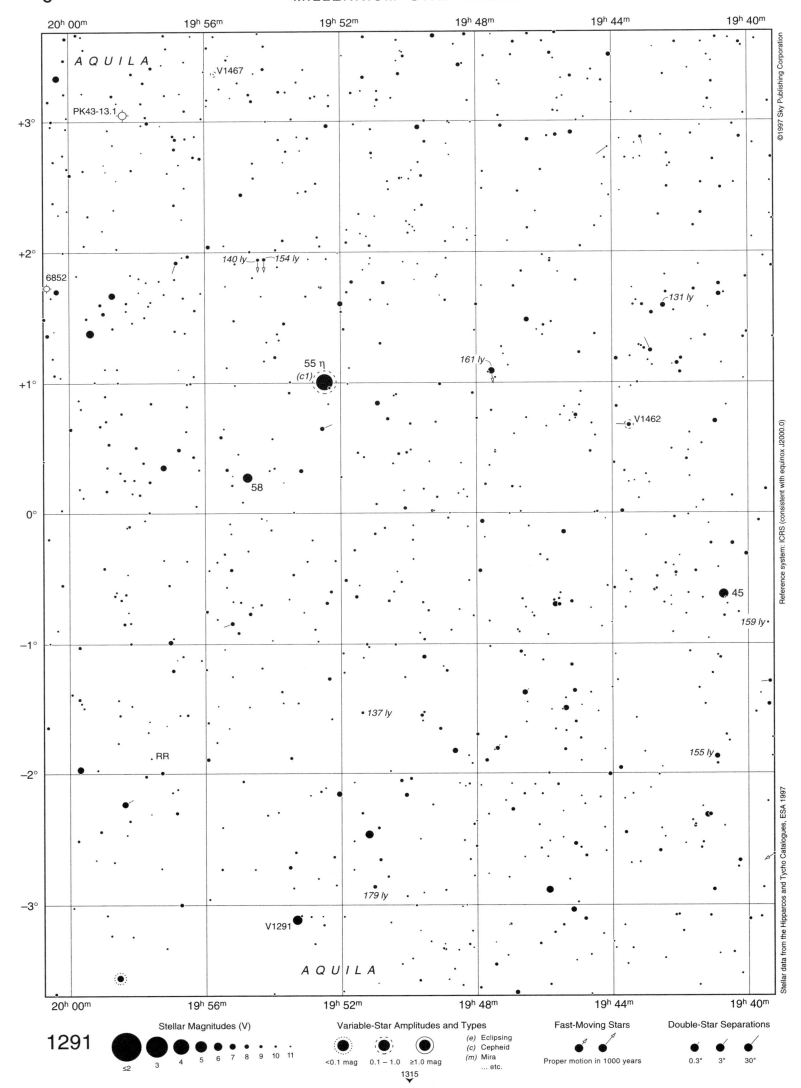

©1997 Sky Publishing Corporation

Reference system: ICRS (consistent with equinox J2000.0)

Stellar data from the Hipparcos and Tycho Catalogues, ESA 1997

1291

Stellar Magnitudes (V)

≤2   3   4   5   6   7   8   9   10   11

Variable-Star Amplitudes and Types

<0.1 mag    0.1 – 1.0    ≥1.0 mag

(e) Eclipsing
(c) Cepheid
(m) Mira
... etc.

Fast-Moving Stars

Proper motion in 1000 years

Double-Star Separations

0.3"    3"    30"

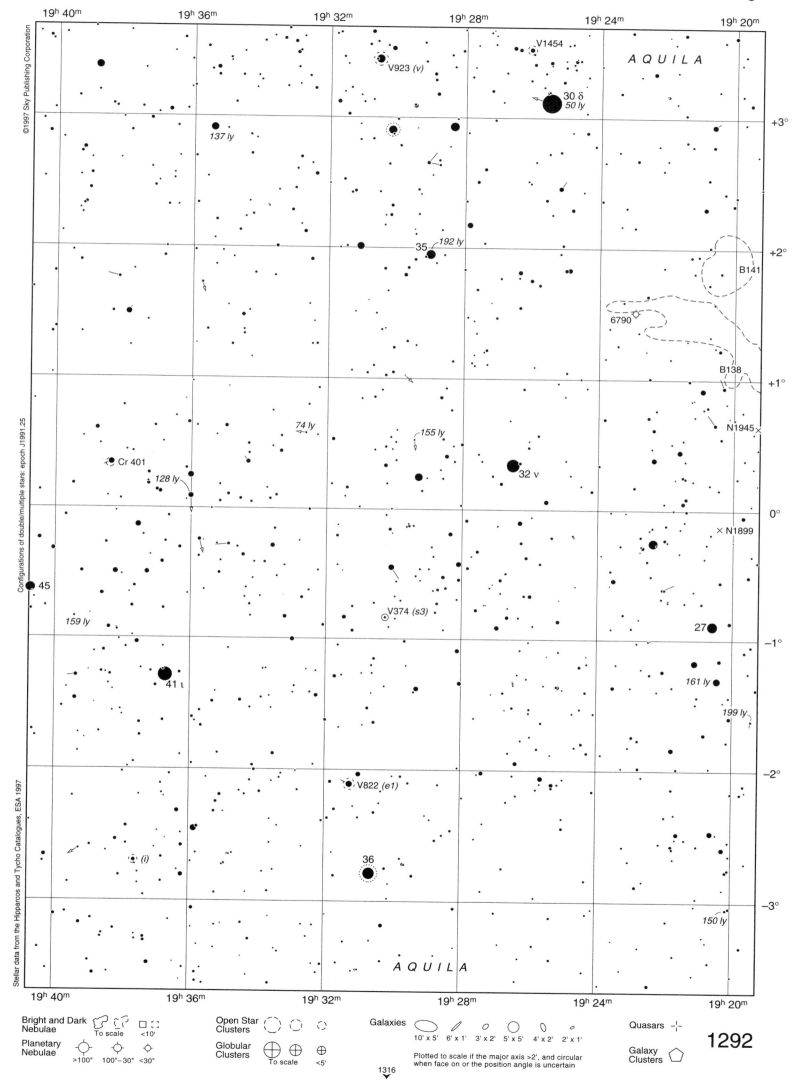

©1997 Sky Publishing Corporation

Configurations of double/multiple stars: epoch J1991.25

Stellar data from the Hipparcos and Tycho Catalogues, ESA 1997

19h 40m    19h 36m    19h 32m    19h 28m    19h 24m    19h 20m

V1454

V923 (v)

AQUILA

30 δ
50 ly

+3°

137 ly

35   192 ly
+2°

B141

6790

B138
+1°

74 ly

155 ly

N1945

Cr 401

32 ν

128 ly

0°

N1899

45

V374 (s3)

27

159 ly

41 ι

161 ly

199 ly

-1°

V822 (e1)
-2°

(i)

36

150 ly

-3°

AQUILA

19h 40m    19h 36m    19h 32m    19h 28m    19h 24m    19h 20m

Bright and Dark Nebulae    Open Star Clusters    Galaxies    Quasars
To scale    <10'    To scale    10' x 5'  6' x 1'  3' x 2'  5' x 5'  4' x 2'  2' x 1'

Planetary Nebulae    Globular Clusters    Galaxy Clusters
>100"  100"–30"  <30"    To scale    <5'    Plotted to scale if the major axis >2', and circular when face on or the position angle is uncertain

1292

1316 ▼

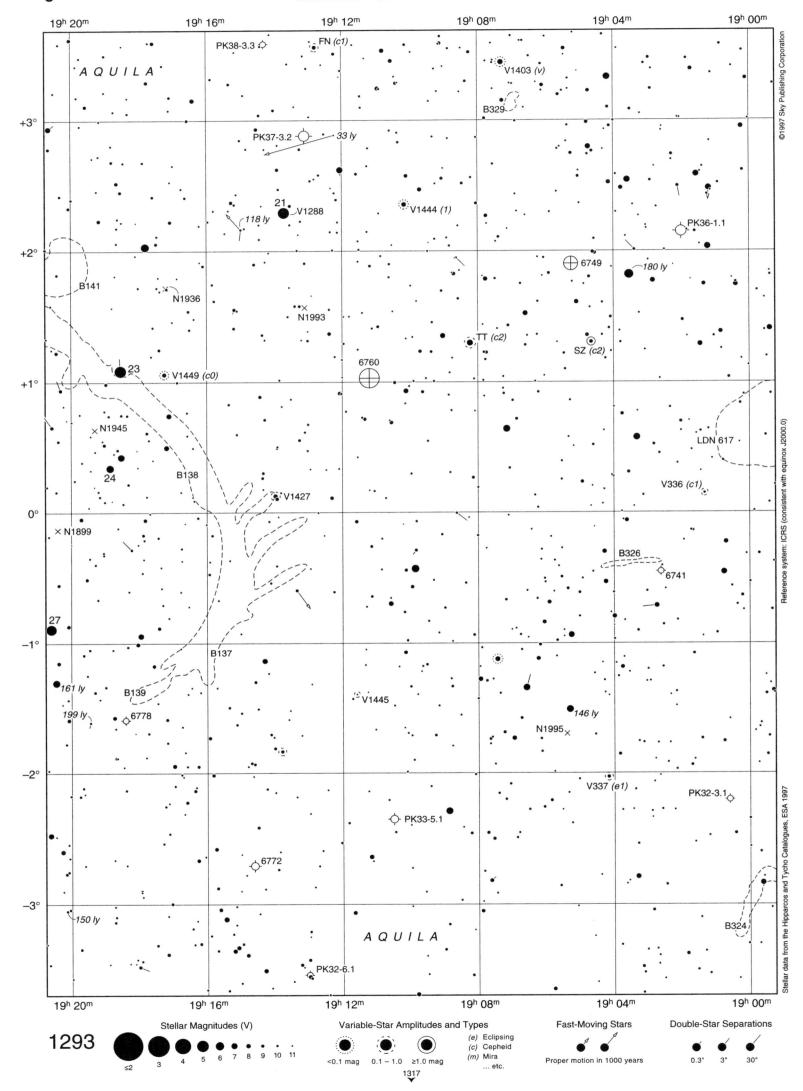

©1997 Sky Publishing Corporation

Reference system: ICRS (consistent with equinox J2000.0)

Stellar data from the Hipparcos and Tycho Catalogues, ESA 1997

1293

Stellar Magnitudes (V)

≤2   3   4   5   6   7   8   9  10  11

Variable-Star Amplitudes and Types

<0.1 mag   0.1 – 1.0   ≥1.0 mag

(e) Eclipsing
(c) Cepheid
(m) Mira
... etc.

Fast-Moving Stars

Proper motion in 1000 years

Double-Star Separations

0.3"   3"   30"

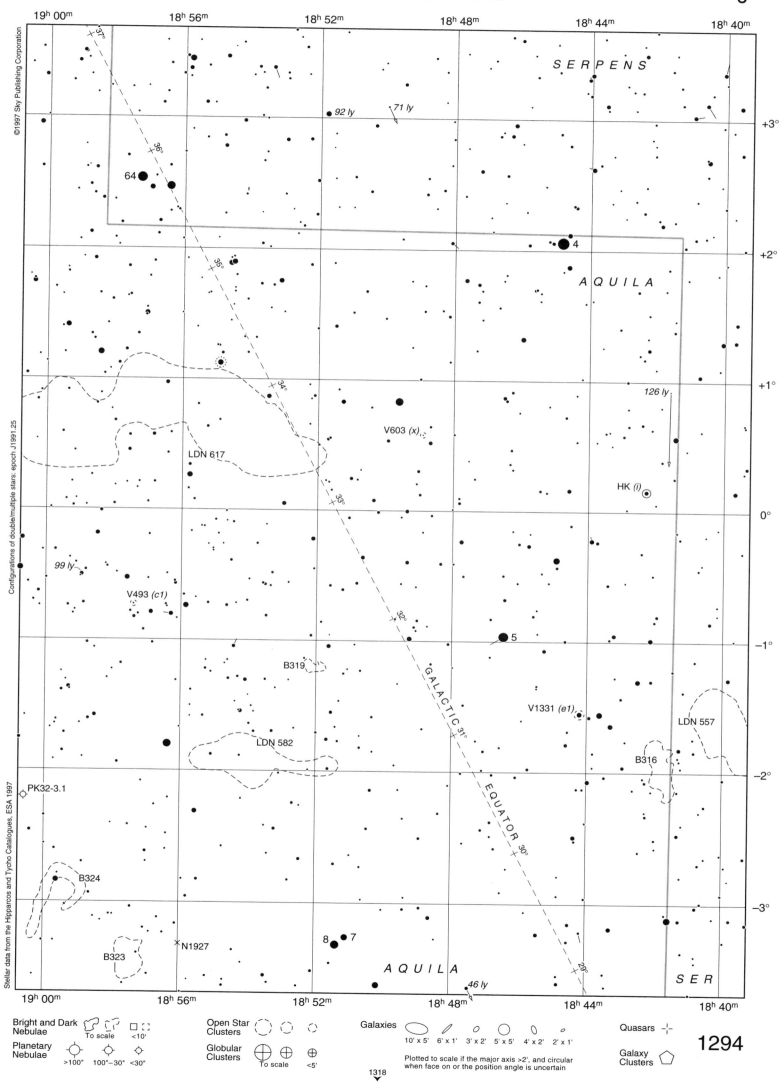

19h 00m    18h 56m    18h 52m    18h 48m    18h 44m    18h 40m

S E R P E N S

92 ly    71 ly

+3°

64

+2°

4

A Q U I L A

126 ly

+1°

V603 (x)

LDN 617

HK (i)

0°

99 ly

V493 (c1)

-1°

5

B319

V1331 (e1)

LDN 557

LDN 582

B316

-2°

PK32-3.1

B324

-3°

B323

N1927

8  7

A Q U I L A

S E R

46 ly

19h 00m    18h 56m    18h 52m    18h 48m    18h 44m    18h 40m

Bright and Dark Nebulae — To scale — <10'
Planetary Nebulae — >100" — 100"–30" — <30"

Open Star Clusters
Globular Clusters — To scale — <5'

Galaxies
10' x 5'   6' x 1'   3' x 2'   5' x 5'   4' x 2'   2' x 1'
Plotted to scale if the major axis >2', and circular when face on or the position angle is uncertain

Quasars
Galaxy Clusters

1294

1318

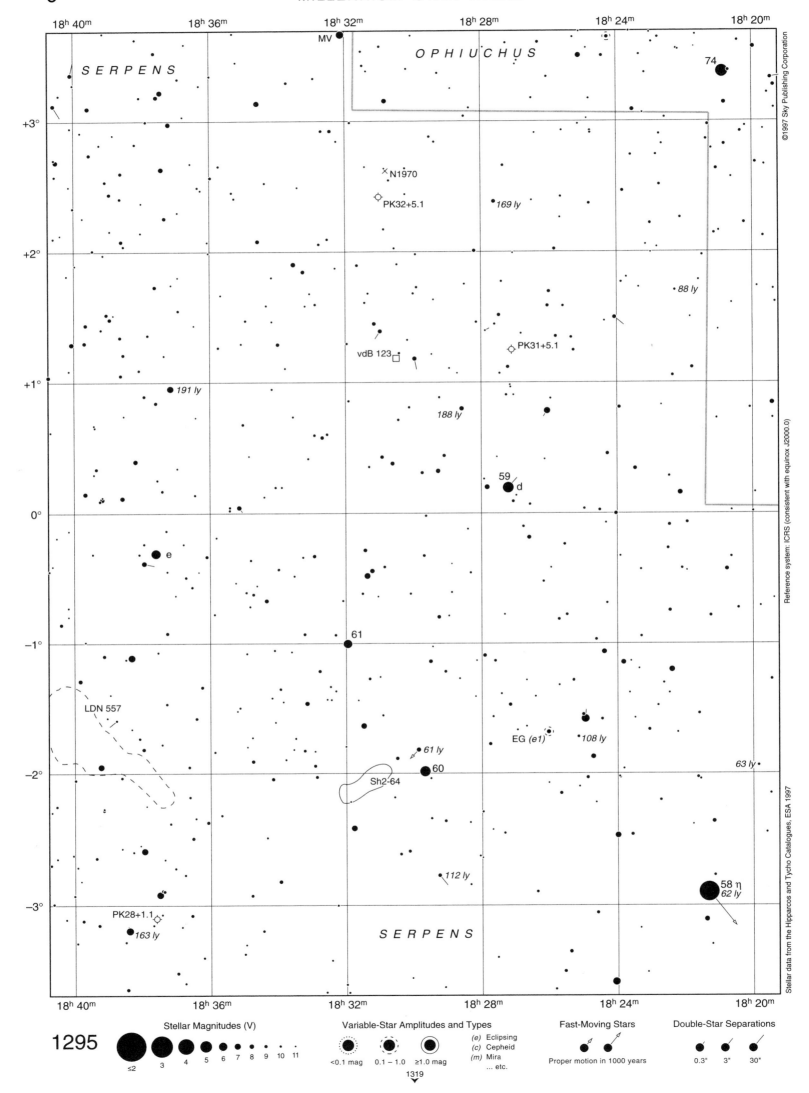

©1997 Sky Publishing Corporation

Reference system: ICRS (consistent with equinox J2000.0)

Stellar data from the Hipparcos and Tycho Catalogues, ESA 1997

18ʰ 40ᵐ      18ʰ 36ᵐ      18ʰ 32ᵐ      18ʰ 28ᵐ      18ʰ 24ᵐ      18ʰ 20ᵐ

S E R P E N S

O P H I U C H U S

74

+3°

N1970

PK32+5.1

169 ly

+2°

88 ly

vdB 123

PK31+5.1

+1°

191 ly

188 ly

59 d

0°

e

61

-1°

LDN 557

EG (e1)    108 ly

61 ly

63 ly

60

Sh2-64

112 ly

58 η
62 ly

-2°

PK28+1.1

163 ly

-3°

S E R P E N S

18ʰ 40ᵐ      18ʰ 36ᵐ      18ʰ 32ᵐ      18ʰ 28ᵐ      18ʰ 24ᵐ      18ʰ 20ᵐ

MV

**1295**

| Stellar Magnitudes (V) | Variable-Star Amplitudes and Types | Fast-Moving Stars | Double-Star Separations |
|---|---|---|---|
| ≤2  3  4  5  6 7 8 9 10 11 | <0.1 mag   0.1 – 1.0   ≥1.0 mag   (e) Eclipsing (c) Cepheid (m) Mira ... etc. | Proper motion in 1000 years | 0.3"  3"  30" |

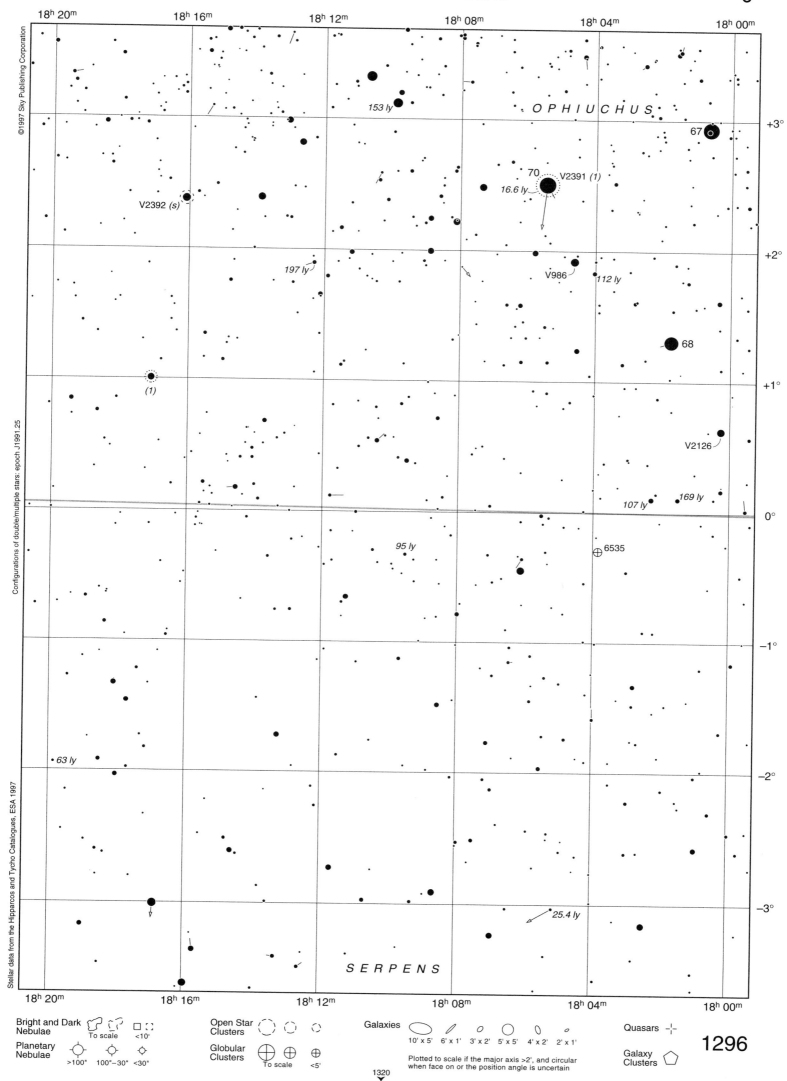

O P H I U C H U S

S E R P E N S

18h 20m    18h 16m    18h 12m    18h 08m    18h 04m    18h 00m

+3°
+2°
+1°
0°
-1°
-2°
-3°

153 ly
67
70    V2391 (1)
16.6 ly
V2392 (s)
197 ly
V986    112 ly
68
(1)
V2126
107 ly    169 ly
95 ly
6535
63 ly
25.4 ly

| Bright and Dark Nebulae | | | | Open Star Clusters | | | Galaxies | | | | | | | Quasars | |
| --- | --- | --- | --- | --- | --- | --- | --- | --- | --- | --- | --- | --- | --- | --- | --- |
| To scale | | <10' | | | | | 10' x 5' | 6' x 1' | 3' x 2' | 5' x 5' | 4' x 2' | 2' x 1' | | | |

Planetary Nebulae
>100"   100"-30"   <30"

Globular Clusters
To scale   <5'

Plotted to scale if the major axis >2', and circular when face on or the position angle is uncertain

Galaxy Clusters

1296

0°

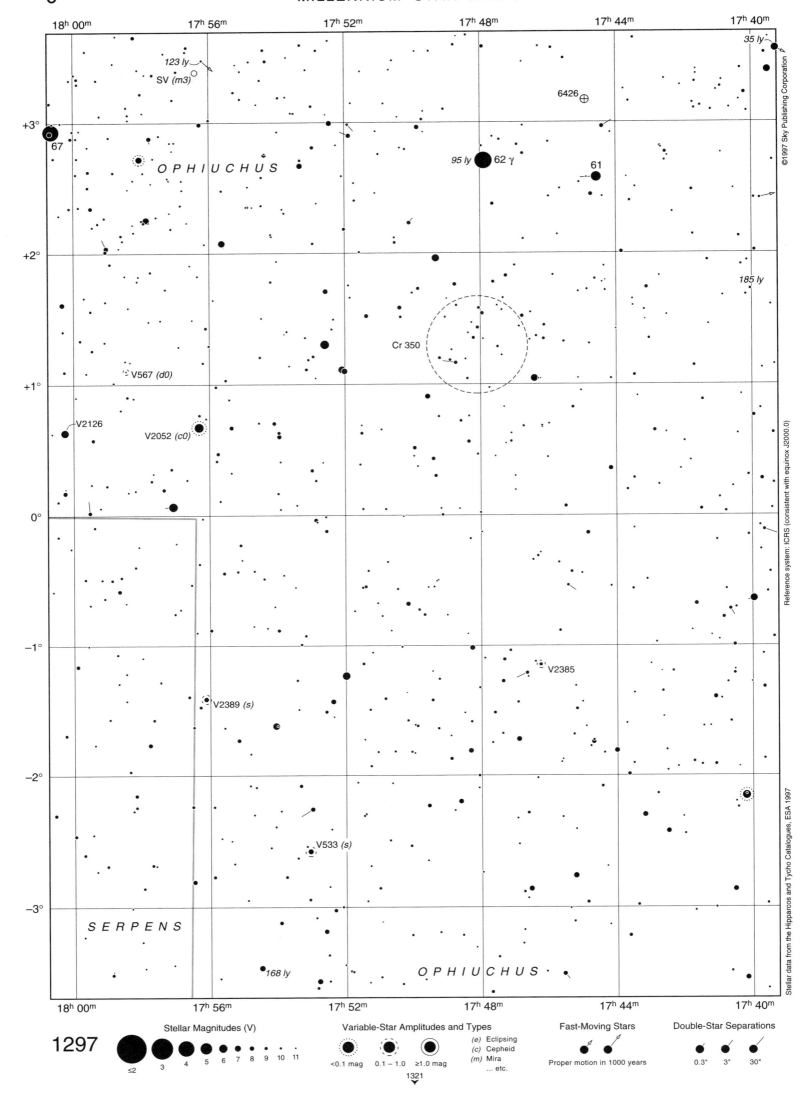

©1997 Sky Publishing Corporation

Reference system: ICRS (consistent with equinox J2000.0)

Stellar data from the Hipparcos and Tycho Catalogues, ESA 1997

**1297**

| Stellar Magnitudes (V) | Variable-Star Amplitudes and Types | Fast-Moving Stars | Double-Star Separations |

Stellar Magnitudes (V)
≤2  3  4  5  6  7  8  9  10  11

Variable-Star Amplitudes and Types
<0.1 mag   0.1 – 1.0   ≥1.0 mag

(e) Eclipsing
(c) Cepheid
(m) Mira
... etc.

Fast-Moving Stars
Proper motion in 1000 years

Double-Star Separations
0.3"  3"  30"

0°

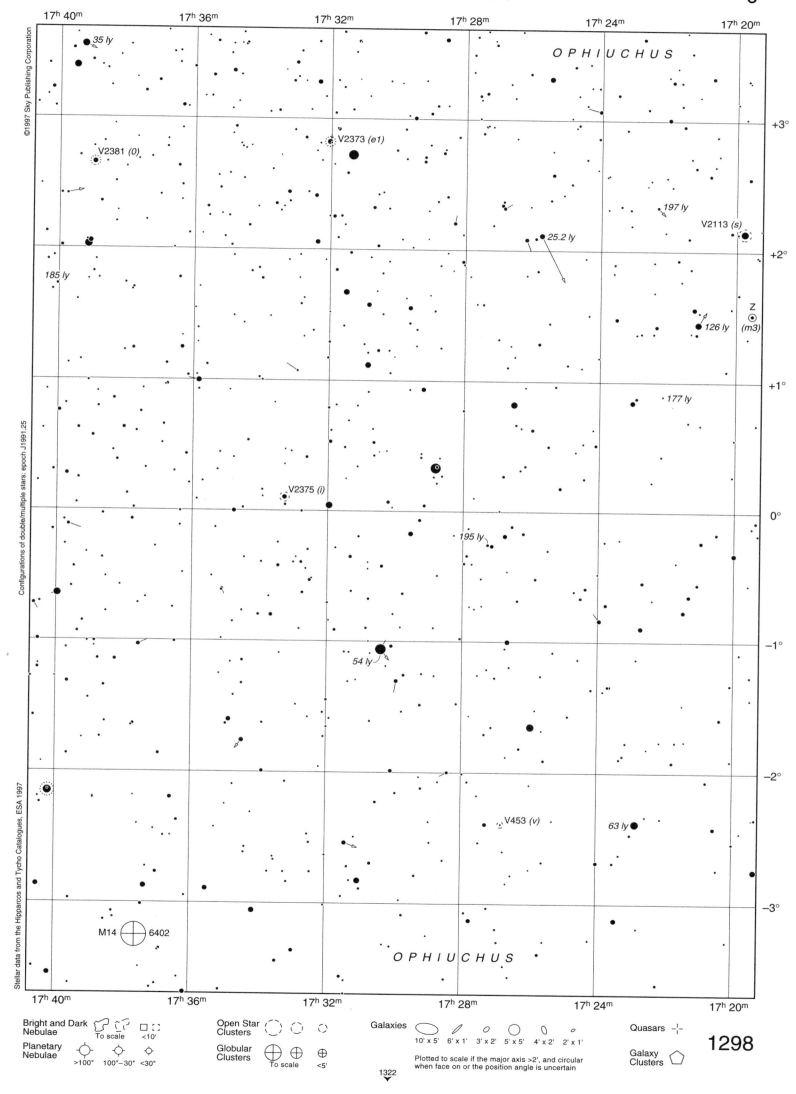

Configurations of double/multiple stars: epoch J1991.25

Stellar data from the Hipparcos and Tycho Catalogues, ESA 1997

OPHIUCHUS

35 ly

V2381 (0)

V2373 (e1)

197 ly

V2113 (s)

25.2 ly

185 ly

Z
⊙
(m3)

126 ly

177 ly

V2375 (i)

195 ly

54 ly

V453 (v)

63 ly

M14 ⊕ 6402

OPHIUCHUS

17ʰ 40ᵐ   17ʰ 36ᵐ   17ʰ 32ᵐ   17ʰ 28ᵐ   17ʰ 24ᵐ   17ʰ 20ᵐ

+3°
+2°
+1°
0°
−1°
−2°
−3°

Bright and Dark
Nebulae

To scale   <10'

Planetary
Nebulae

>100"  100"−30"  <30"

Open Star
Clusters

Globular
Clusters

To scale   <5'

Galaxies

10' x 5'  6' x 1'  3' x 2'  5' x 5'  4' x 2'  2' x 1'

Plotted to scale if the major axis >2', and circular
when face on or the position angle is uncertain

Quasars

Galaxy
Clusters

1298

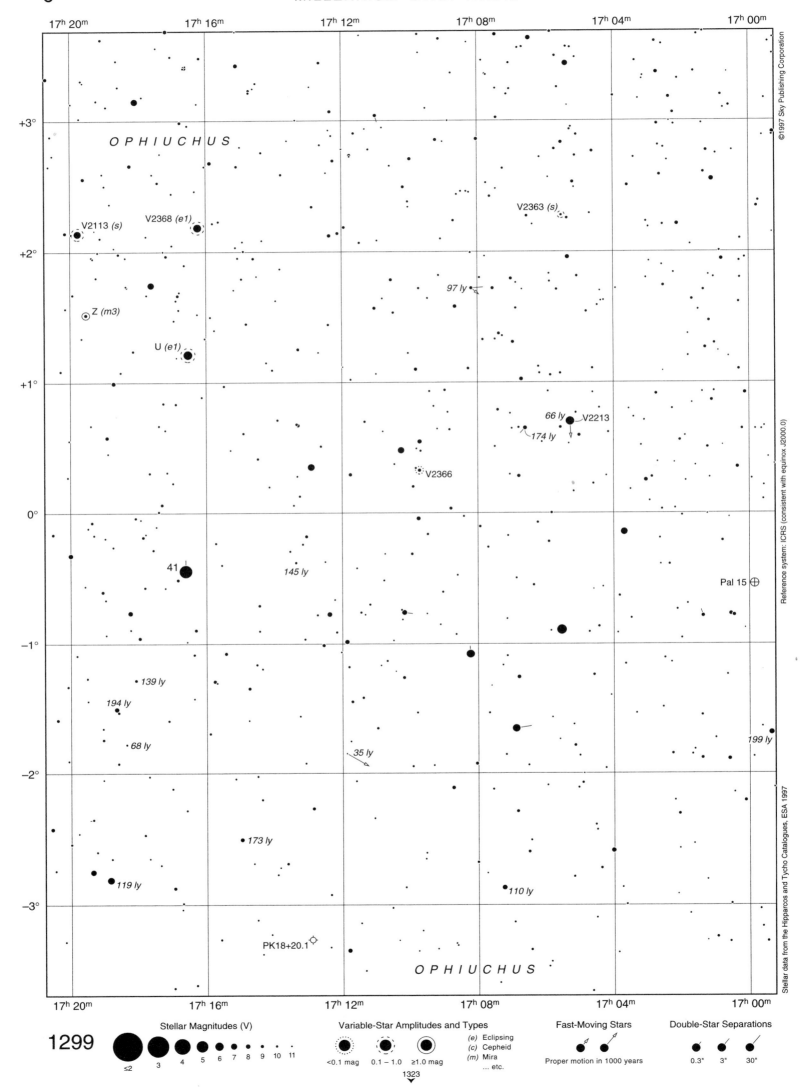

O P H I U C H U S

V2113 (s)
V2368 (e1)
V2363 (s)

97 ly

Z (m3)

U (e1)

66 ly    V2213
174 ly

V2366

41

145 ly

Pal 15

139 ly

194 ly

68 ly

199 ly

35 ly

173 ly

119 ly

110 ly

PK18+20.1

O P H I U C H U S

©1997 Sky Publishing Corporation

Reference system: ICRS (consistent with equinox J2000.0)

Stellar data from the Hipparcos and Tycho Catalogues, ESA 1997

1299

Stellar Magnitudes (V)

≤2    3    4    5    6    7    8    9    10   11

Variable-Star Amplitudes and Types

<0.1 mag    0.1 – 1.0    ≥1.0 mag

(e) Eclipsing
(c) Cepheid
(m) Mira
... etc.

Fast-Moving Stars

Proper motion in 1000 years

Double-Star Separations

0.3"    3"    30"

1323

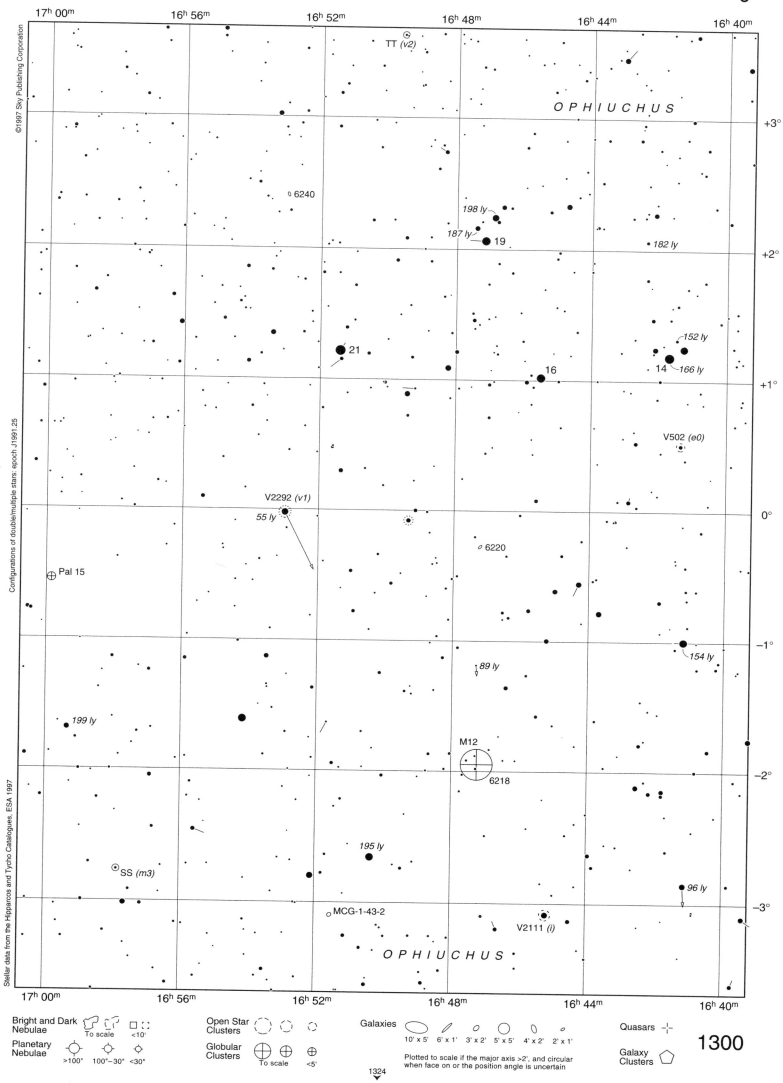

# MILLENNIUM STAR ATLAS

0°

Configurations of double/multiple stars: epoch J1991.25

Stellar data from the Hipparcos and Tycho Catalogues, ESA 1997

17ʰ 00ᵐ    16ʰ 56ᵐ    16ʰ 52ᵐ    16ʰ 48ᵐ    16ʰ 44ᵐ    16ʰ 40ᵐ

TT *(v2)*

*O P H I U C H U S*

+3°

6240

*198 ly*

*187 ly*  19

*182 ly*    +2°

*152 ly*

21    14  *166 ly*

16    +1°

V502 *(e0)*

V2292 *(v1)*

*55 ly*    0°

6220

Pal 15

*154 ly*    −1°

↕ *89 ly*

*199 ly*

M12

6218    −2°

*195 ly*

SS *(m3)*

*96 ly*

MCG-1-43-2    −3°

V2111 *(i)*

*O P H I U C H U S*

17ʰ 00ᵐ    16ʰ 56ᵐ    16ʰ 52ᵐ    16ʰ 48ᵐ    16ʰ 44ᵐ    16ʰ 40ᵐ

| Bright and Dark Nebulae | | | | Open Star Clusters | | | Galaxies | | | | | | | Quasars |
|---|---|---|---|---|---|---|---|---|---|---|---|---|---|---|
| To scale | | <10' | | | | | 10' x 5' | 6' x 1' | 3' x 2' | 5' x 5' | 4' x 2' | 2' x 1' | | |
| Planetary Nebulae | | | | Globular Clusters | | | | | | | | | | |
| >100" | 100"−30" | <30" | | To scale | | <5' | | | | | | | | Galaxy Clusters |

Plotted to scale if the major axis >2', and circular when face on or the position angle is uncertain

1300

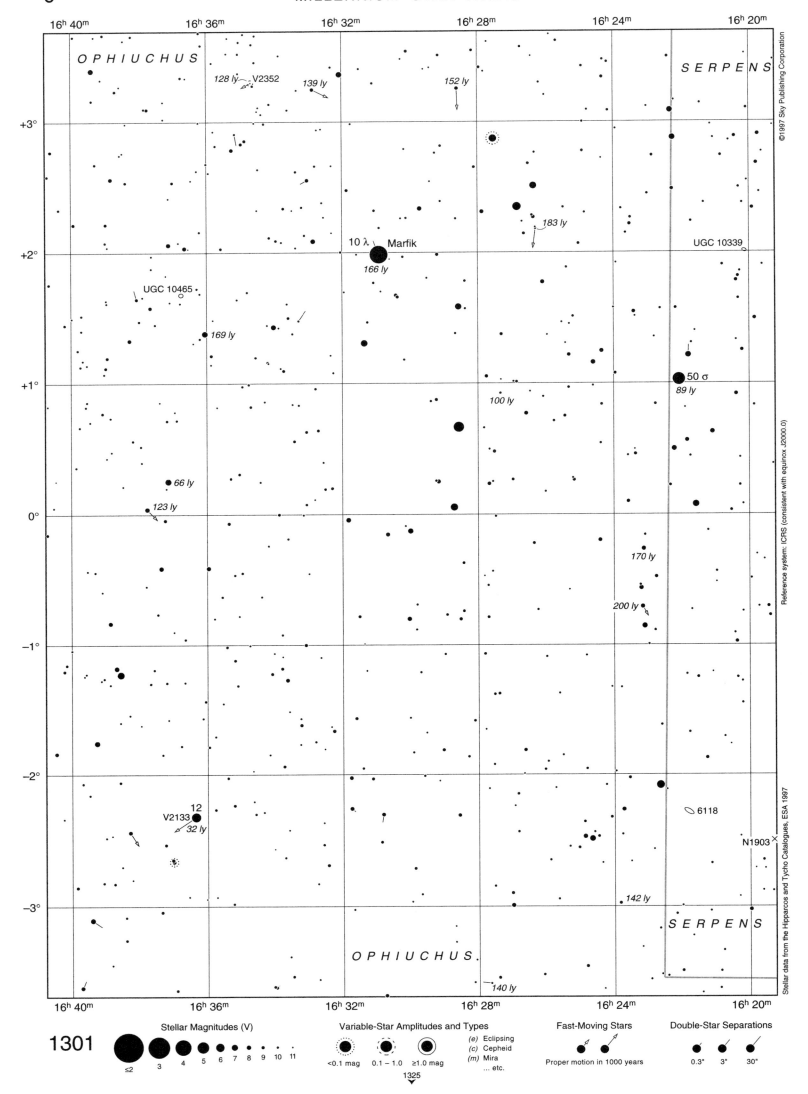

O P H I U C H U S

S E R P E N S

128 ly    V2352    139 ly    152 ly

+3°

10 λ    Marfik    183 ly    UGC 10339

+2°    166 ly

UGC 10465    169 ly

50 σ    +1°    89 ly

100 ly

66 ly

123 ly    170 ly    0°

200 ly

−1°

12    −2°
V2133    6118
32 ly    N1903

142 ly    −3°

S E R P E N S

O P H I U C H U S

140 ly

**Stellar Magnitudes (V)**

1301    ≤2    3    4    5    6    7    8    9    10    11

**Variable-Star Amplitudes and Types**

<0.1 mag    0.1 – 1.0    ≥1.0 mag

(e) Eclipsing
(c) Cepheid
(m) Mira
... etc.

**Fast-Moving Stars**

Proper motion in 1000 years

**Double-Star Separations**

0.3"    3"    30"

# MILLENNIUM STAR ATLAS

0°

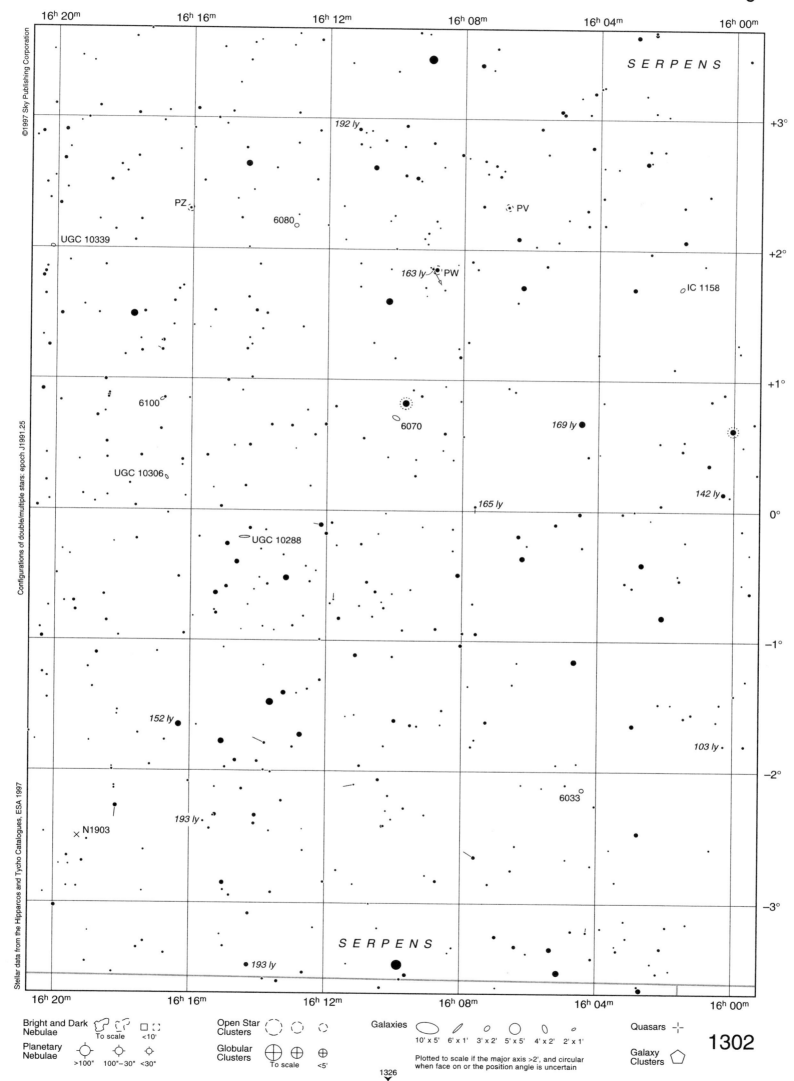

*S E R P E N S*

16h 20m  16h 16m  16h 12m  16h 08m  16h 04m  16h 00m

+3°
+2°
+1°
0°
−1°
−2°
−3°

192 ly
PZ
6080
UGC 10339
PV
163 ly  PW
IC 1158
6100
6070
169 ly
UGC 10306
142 ly
165 ly
UGC 10288
152 ly
103 ly
193 ly
6033
N1903
193 ly
*S E R P E N S*
193 ly

| Bright and Dark Nebulae | Open Star Clusters | Galaxies | Quasars |

Bright and Dark Nebulae — To scale — <10'

Planetary Nebulae — >100" 100"−30" <30"

Open Star Clusters

Globular Clusters — To scale — <5'

Galaxies — 10' x 5'  6' x 1'  3' x 2'  5' x 5'  4' x 2'  2' x 1'

Plotted to scale if the major axis >2', and circular when face on or the position angle is uncertain

Quasars

Galaxy Clusters

1302

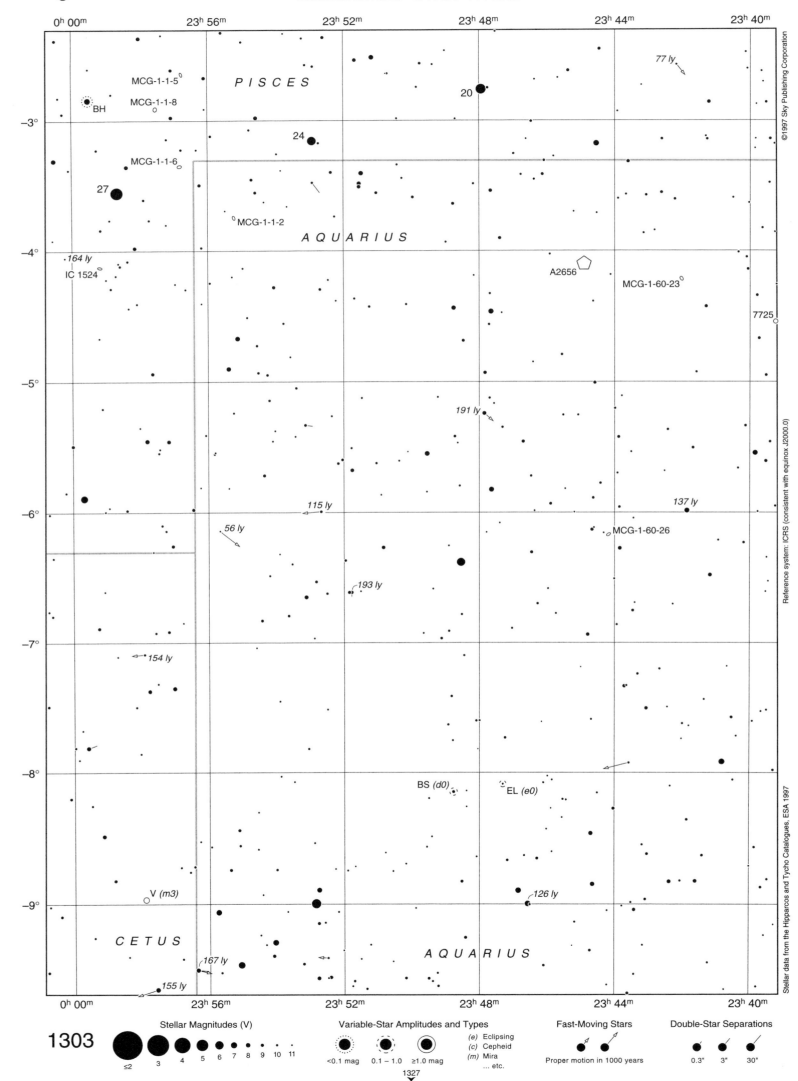

©1997 Sky Publishing Corporation

Reference system: ICRS (consistent with equinox J2000.0)

Stellar data from the Hipparcos and Tycho Catalogues, ESA 1997

0h 00m   23h 56m   23h 52m   23h 48m   23h 44m   23h 40m

PISCES

MCG-1-1-5

BH

MCG-1-1-8

20

77 ly

24

MCG-1-1-6

27

AQUARIUS

MCG-1-1-2

164 ly

IC 1524

A2656

MCG-1-60-23

7725

191 ly

137 ly

115 ly

MCG-1-60-26

56 ly

193 ly

154 ly

BS (d0)

EL (e0)

V (m3)

126 ly

CETUS

AQUARIUS

167 ly

155 ly

0h 00m   23h 56m   23h 52m   23h 48m   23h 44m   23h 40m

1303

Stellar Magnitudes (V)

≤2   3   4   5   6   7   8   9   10   11

Variable-Star Amplitudes and Types

<0.1 mag   0.1 – 1.0   ≥1.0 mag

(e) Eclipsing
(c) Cepheid
(m) Mira
... etc.

Fast-Moving Stars

Proper motion in 1000 years

Double-Star Separations

0.3"   3"   30"

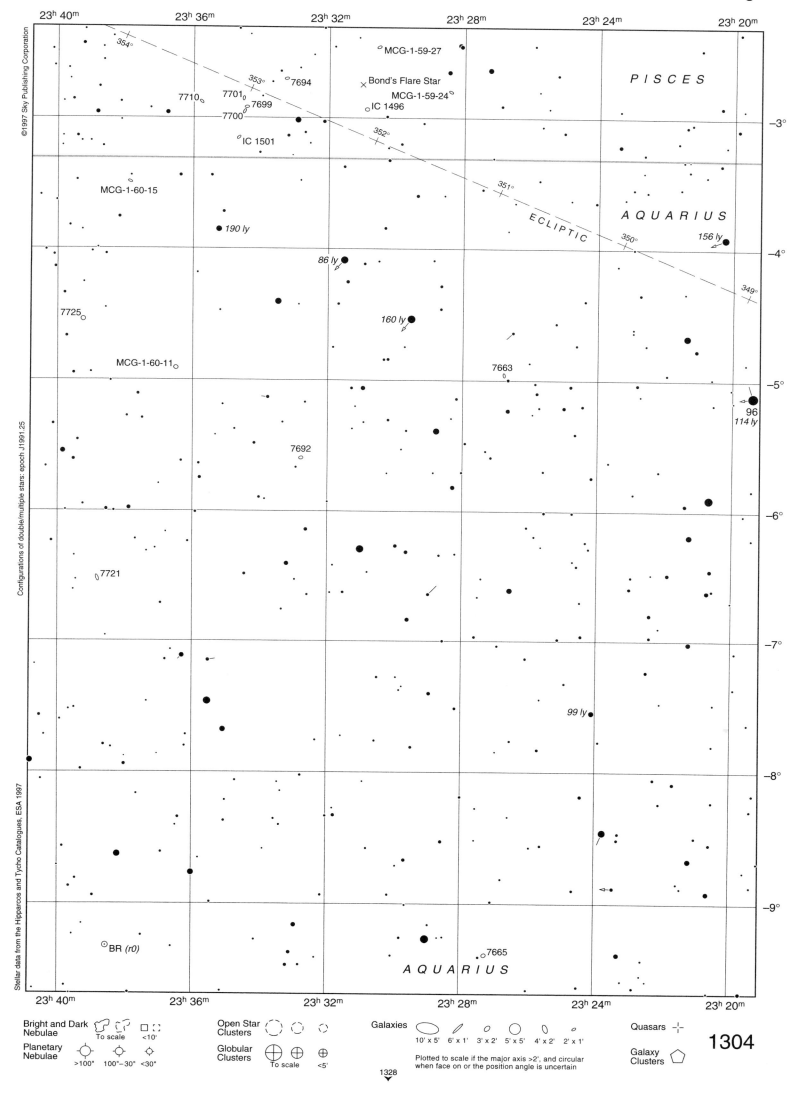

PISCES

AQUARIUS

ECLIPTIC

MCG-1-59-27

Bond's Flare Star

MCG-1-59-24

IC 1496

7694

7710   7701

7699

7700

IC 1501

MCG-1-60-15

190 ly

156 ly

86 ly

160 ly

7725

MCG-1-60-11

7663

96
114 ly

7692

7721

99 ly

BR (r0)

7665

AQUARIUS

−3°

−4°

−5°

−6°

−7°

−8°

−9°

354°

353°

352°

351°

350°

349°

23ʰ 40ᵐ   23ʰ 36ᵐ   23ʰ 32ᵐ   23ʰ 28ᵐ   23ʰ 24ᵐ   23ʰ 20ᵐ

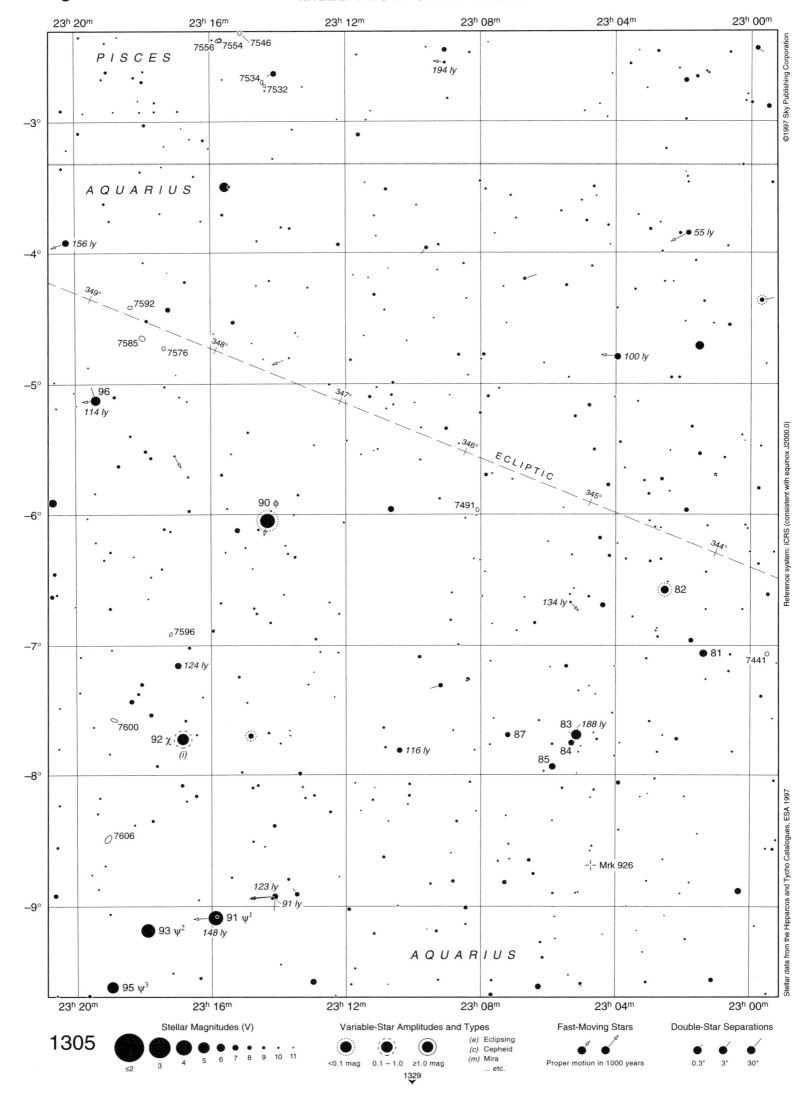

©1997 Sky Publishing Corporation

Reference system: ICRS (consistent with equinox J2000.0)

Stellar data from the Hipparcos and Tycho Catalogues, ESA 1997

PISCES

AQUARIUS

194 ly

55 ly

156 ly

349°

348°

100 ly

347°

346°

ECLIPTIC

345°

344°

90 φ

7491

82

134 ly

7596

81

7441

124 ly

83  188 ly

87

84

116 ly

85

92 χ

(i)

7600

Mrk 926

7606

123 ly

91 ly

91 ψ¹

93 ψ²

148 ly

AQUARIUS

95 ψ³

Stellar Magnitudes (V)

≤2  3  4  5  6  7  8  9  10  11

Variable-Star Amplitudes and Types

<0.1 mag    0.1 – 1.0    ≥1.0 mag

(e) Eclipsing
(c) Cepheid
(m) Mira
... etc.

Fast-Moving Stars

Proper motion in 1000 years

Double-Star Separations

0.3"    3"    30"

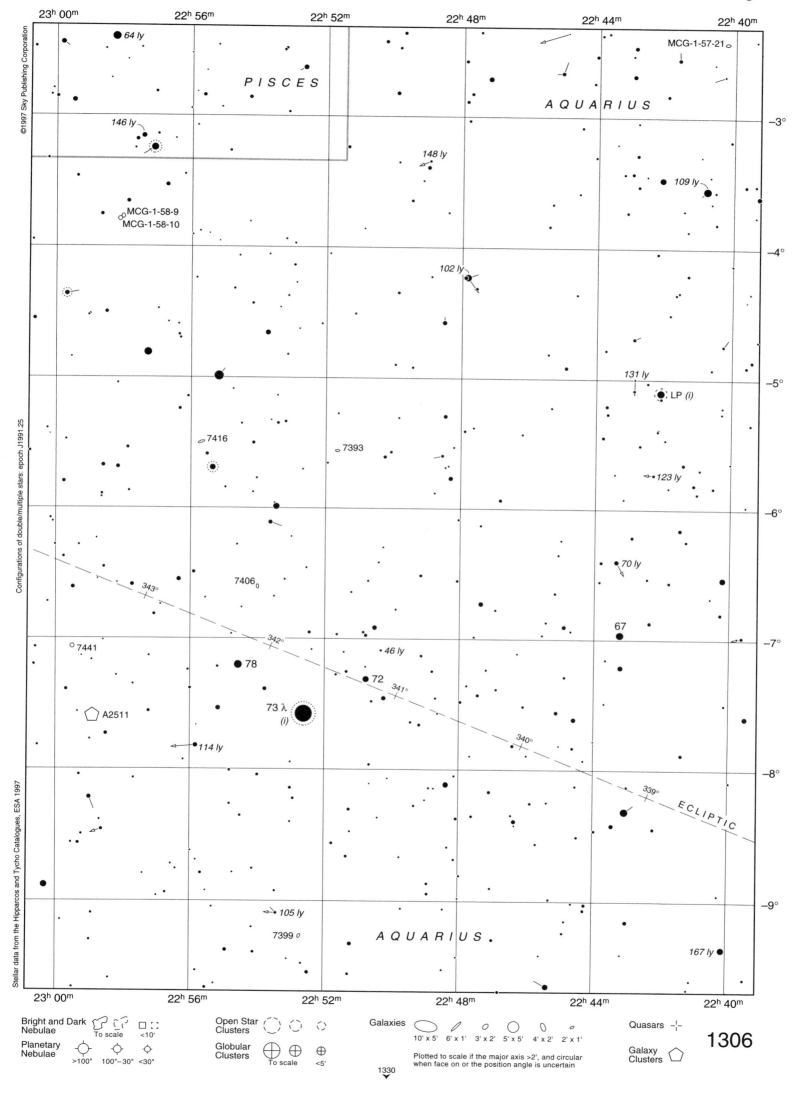

PISCES

AQUARIUS

MCG-1-57-21

64 ly

146 ly

148 ly

109 ly

MCG-1-58-9
MCG-1-58-10

102 ly

131 ly

LP (i)

7416

7393

123 ly

70 ly

7406

343°

67

342°

7441

78

46 ly

72

341°

73 λ
(i)

A2511

340°

114 ly

339°

ECLIPTIC

AQUARIUS

105 ly

7399

167 ly

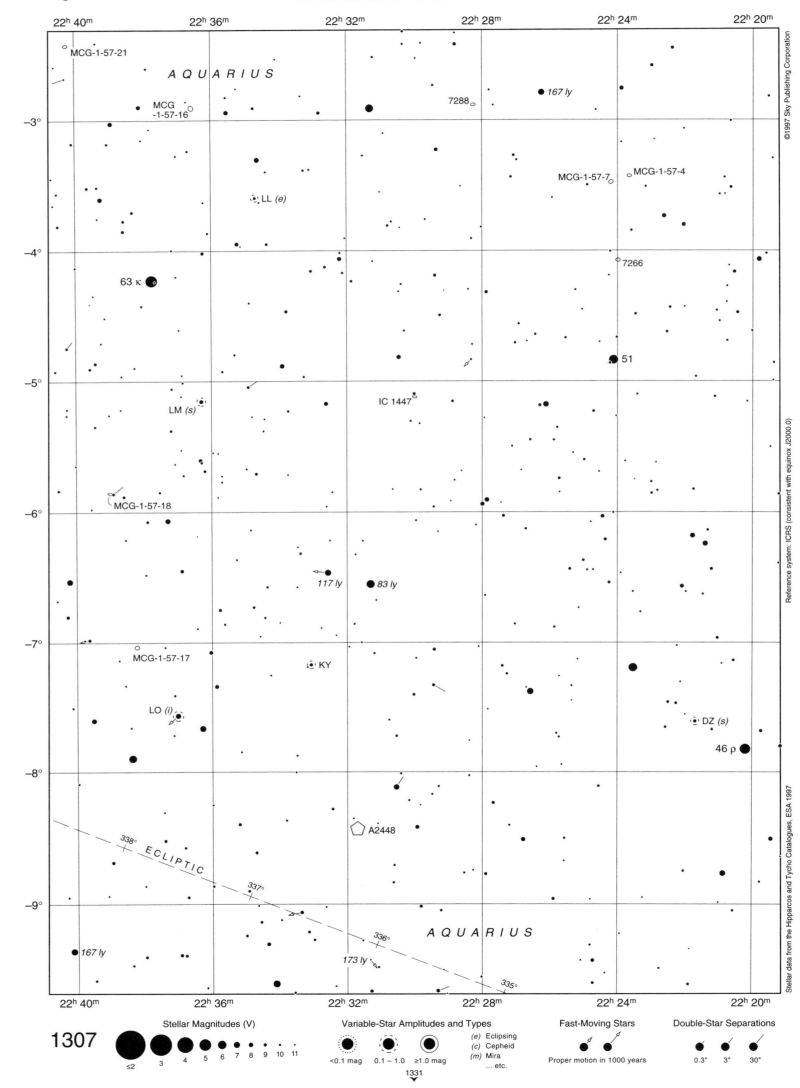

©1997 Sky Publishing Corporation

Reference system: ICRS (consistent with equinox J2000.0)

Stellar data from the Hipparcos and Tycho Catalogues, ESA 1997

MCG-1-57-21
AQUARIUS
MCG-1-57-16
7288
167 ly
MCG-1-57-7
MCG-1-57-4
LL (e)
7266
63 κ
51
LM (s)
IC 1447
MCG-1-57-18
117 ly
83 ly
MCG-1-57-17
KY
DZ (s)
LO (i)
46 ρ
A2448
338° ECLIPTIC
337°
336°
335°
AQUARIUS
167 ly
173 ly

1307

Stellar Magnitudes (V)
≤2    3    4    5    6    7    8    9   10   11

Variable-Star Amplitudes and Types
<0.1 mag    0.1 – 1.0    ≥1.0 mag

(e) Eclipsing
(c) Cepheid
(m) Mira
... etc.

Fast-Moving Stars
Proper motion in 1000 years

Double-Star Separations
0.3"    3"    30"

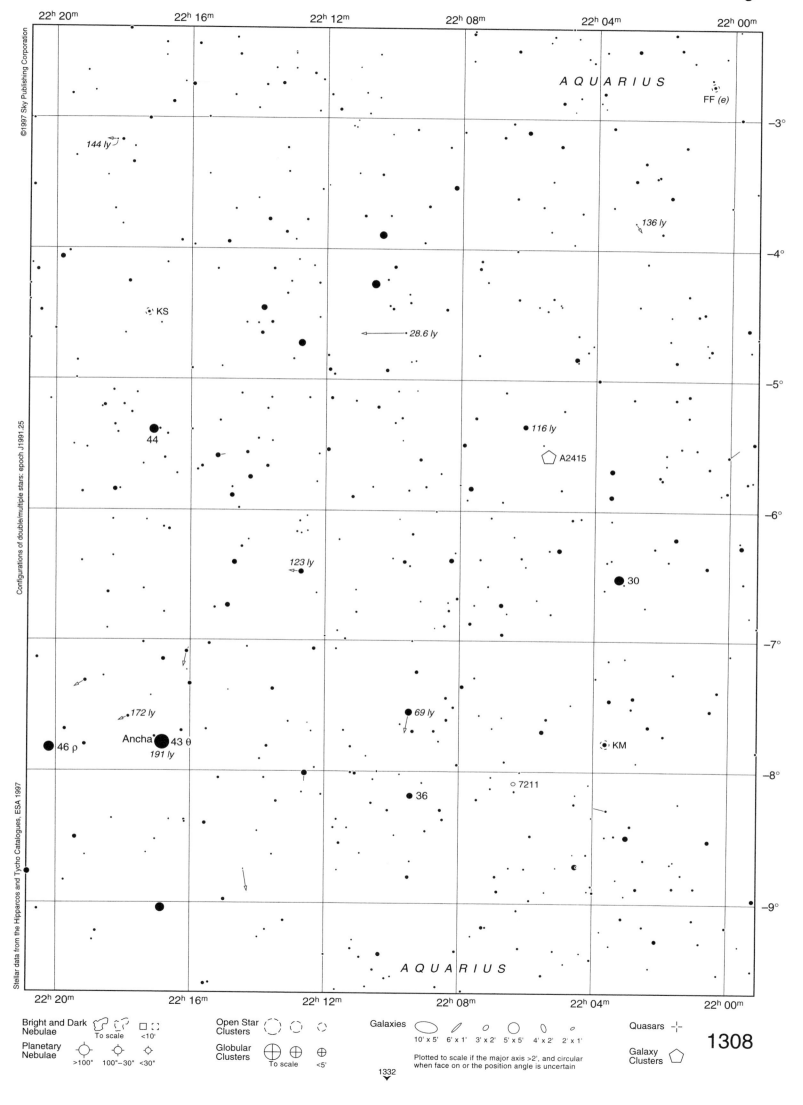

22h 20m  22h 16m  22h 12m  22h 08m  22h 04m  22h 00m

AQUARIUS

FF (e)

−3°

144 ly

136 ly

KS

−4°

28.6 ly

−5°

44

116 ly

A2415

−6°

123 ly

30

−7°

172 ly

69 ly

46 ρ  Ancha  43 θ

191 ly

KM

−8°

36

7211

−9°

AQUARIUS

22h 20m  22h 16m  22h 12m  22h 08m  22h 04m  22h 00m

Bright and Dark
Nebulae
To scale      <10'

Planetary
Nebulae
>100"  100"−30"  <30"

Open Star
Clusters

Globular
Clusters
To scale      <5'

Galaxies

10' x 5'   6' x 1'   3' x 2'   5' x 5'   4' x 2'   2' x 1'

Plotted to scale if the major axis >2', and circular
when face on or the position angle is uncertain

Quasars

Galaxy
Clusters

1308

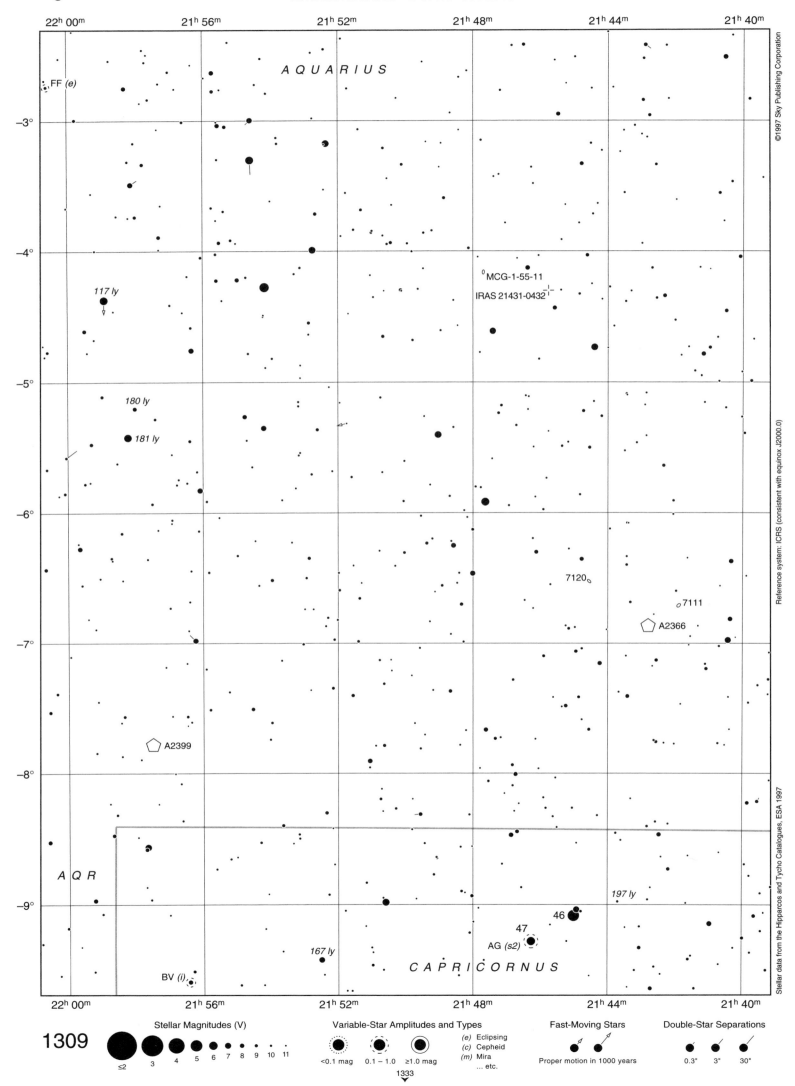

| Stellar Magnitudes (V) | Variable-Star Amplitudes and Types | Fast-Moving Stars | Double-Star Separations |
|---|---|---|---|

**1309**

≤2  3  4  5  6  7  8  9  10  11

<0.1 mag   0.1 – 1.0   ≥1.0 mag

(e) Eclipsing
(c) Cepheid
(m) Mira
... etc.

Proper motion in 1000 years

0.3"  3"  30"

▼
1333

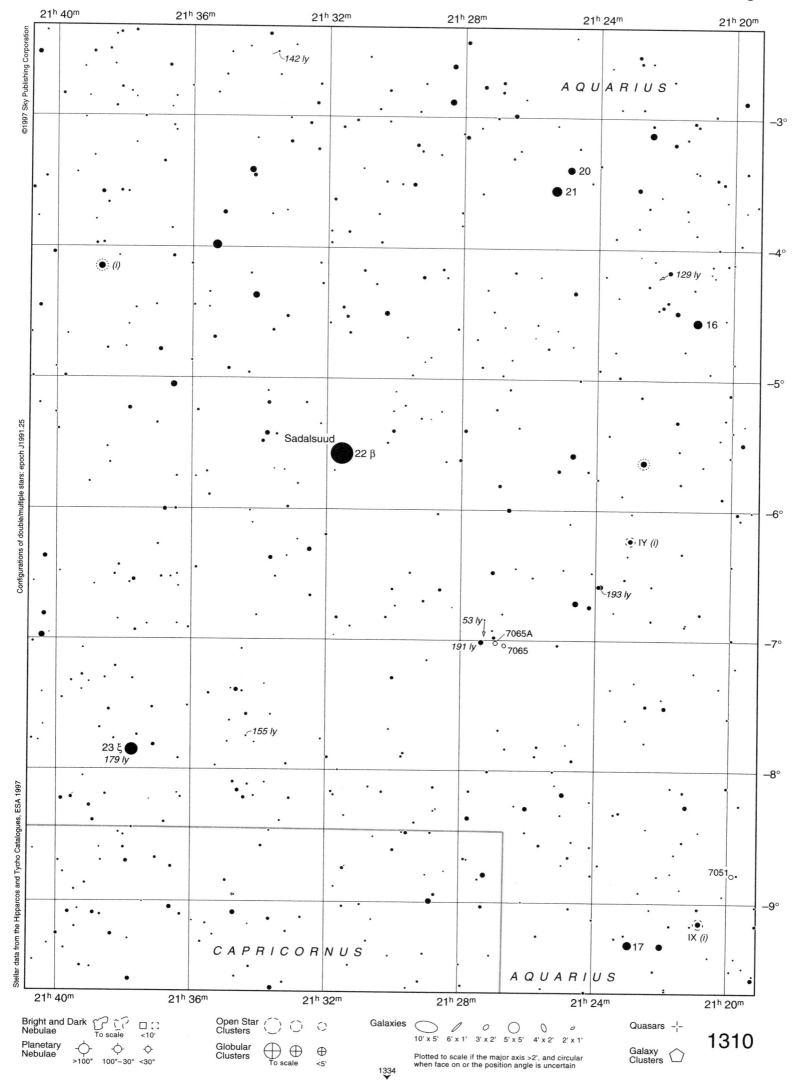

A Q U A R I U S

142 ly

20
21

(i)

129 ly

16

Sadalsuud
22 β

IY (i)

193 ly

53 ly
7065A
191 ly
7065

155 ly

23 ξ
179 ly

7051

IX (i)

C A P R I C O R N U S

17

A Q U A R I U S

Bright and Dark Nebulae
To scale   <10'
Planetary Nebulae
>100"   100"-30"   <30"

Open Star Clusters
Globular Clusters
To scale   <5'

Galaxies
10' x 5'   6' x 1'   3' x 2'   5' x 5'   4' x 2'   2' x 1'

Plotted to scale if the major axis >2', and circular
when face on or the position angle is uncertain

Quasars

Galaxy Clusters

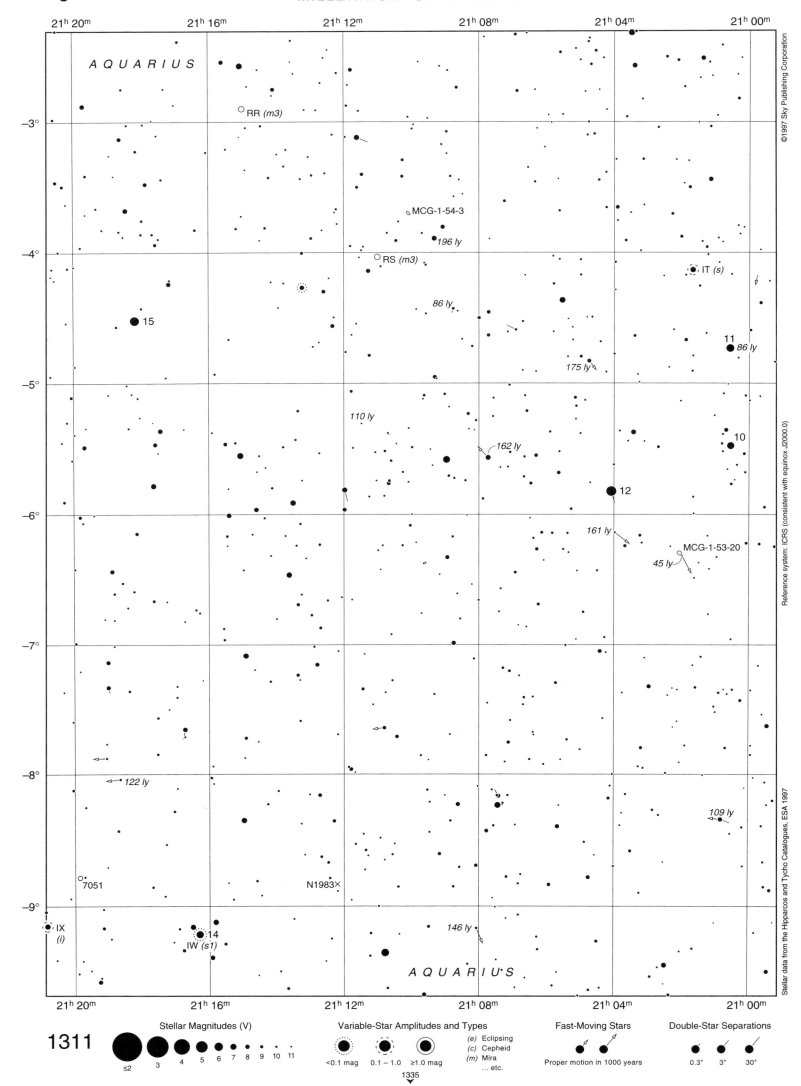

A Q U A R I U S

RR *(m3)*

MCG-1-54-3

*196 ly*

RS *(m3)*

IT *(s)*

*86 ly*

15

11  *86 ly*

*175 ly*

*110 ly*

10

*162 ly*

12

*161 ly*

MCG-1-53-20

*45 ly*

*122 ly*

*109 ly*

7051

N1983✕

*146 ly*

IX
*(i)*

14

IW *(s1)*

A Q U A R I U S

©1997 Sky Publishing Corporation

Reference system: ICRS (consistent with equinox J2000.0)

Stellar data from the Hipparcos and Tycho Catalogues, ESA 1997

**1311**

Stellar Magnitudes (V)

≤2  3  4  5  6  7  8  9  10  11

Variable-Star Amplitudes and Types

<0.1 mag    0.1 − 1.0    ≥1.0 mag

*(e)* Eclipsing
*(c)* Cepheid
*(m)* Mira
... etc.

1335 ▽

Fast-Moving Stars

Proper motion in 1000 years

Double-Star Separations

0.3"    3"    30"

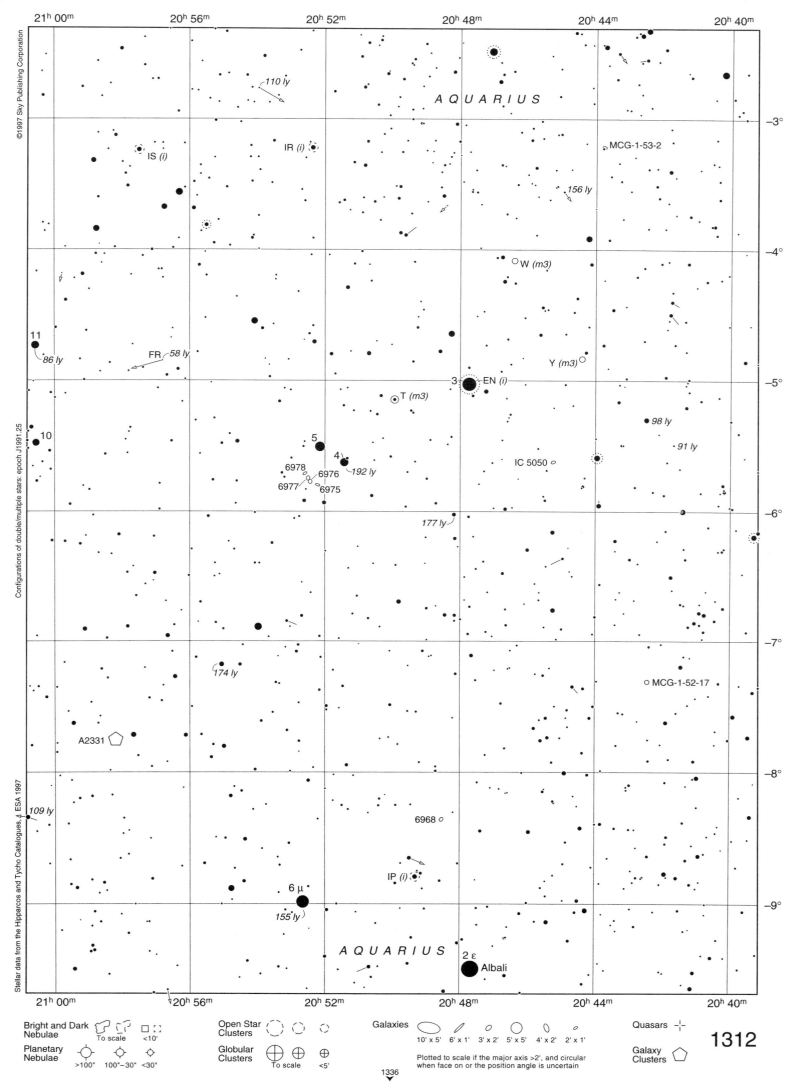

A Q U A R I U S

110 ly

IS *(i)*

IR *(i)*

MCG-1-53-2

−3°

156 ly

−4°

W *(m3)*

11

86 ly

FR 58 ly

Y *(m3)*

3 EN *(i)*

−5°

T *(m3)*

98 ly

10

5

91 ly

4 192 ly

IC 5050

6978 6976
6977 6975

−6°

177 ly

−7°

174 ly

MCG-1-52-17

A2331

−8°

109 ly

6968

IP *(i)*

6 μ

−9°

155 ly

A Q U A R I U S

2 ε
Albali

Bright and Dark
Nebulae
To scale   <10'

Planetary
Nebulae
>100"  100"–30"  <30"

Open Star
Clusters

Globular
Clusters
To scale   <5'

Galaxies
10' x 5'  6' x 1'  3' x 2'  5' x 5'  4' x 2'  2' x 1'

Plotted to scale if the major axis >2', and circular
when face on or the position angle is uncertain

Quasars

Galaxy
Clusters

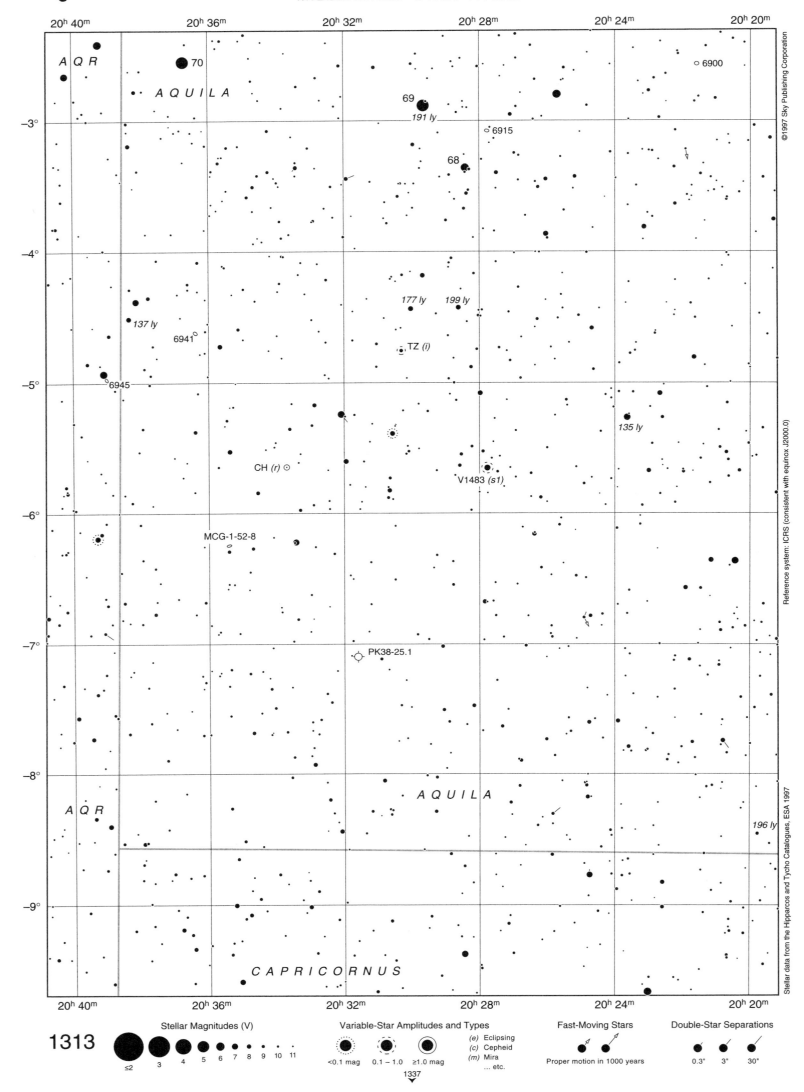

A Q R

70

A Q U I L A

69
191 ly

6900

6915

68

6941

137 ly

6945

177 ly    199 ly

TZ (i)

135 ly

CH (r) ⊙

V1483 (s1)

MCG-1-52-8

PK38-25.1

A Q R

A Q U I L A

196 ly

C A P R I C O R N U S

1313

Stellar Magnitudes (V)

≤2    3    4    5    6    7    8    9   10   11

Variable-Star Amplitudes and Types

<0.1 mag    0.1 − 1.0    ≥1.0 mag

1337

(e) Eclipsing
(c) Cepheid
(m) Mira
... etc.

Fast-Moving Stars

Proper motion in 1000 years

Double-Star Separations

0.3"    3"    30"

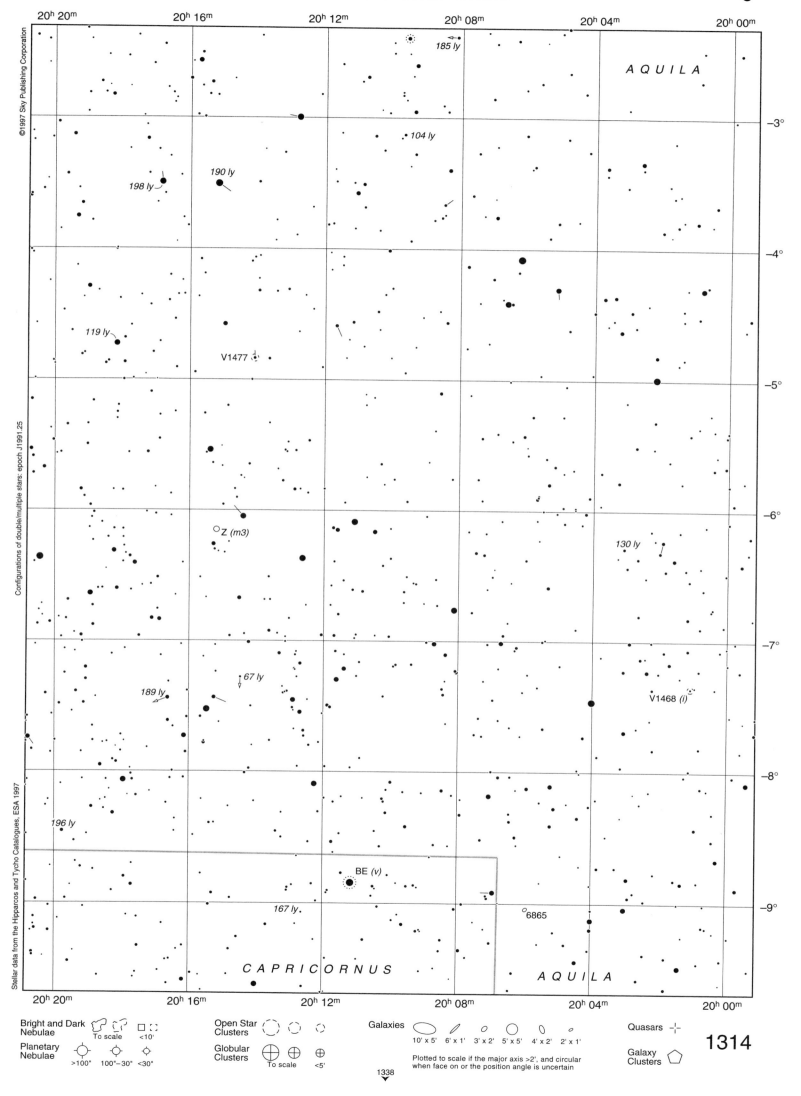

20h 20m · 20h 16m · 20h 12m · 20h 08m · 20h 04m · 20h 00m

-3°
-4°
-5°
-6°
-7°
-8°
-9°

AQUILA

185 ly
104 ly
190 ly
198 ly
119 ly
V1477
Z (m3)
130 ly
189 ly
67 ly
V1468 (i)
196 ly
BE (v)
167 ly
6865
CAPRICORNUS
AQUILA

Bright and Dark Nebulae
To scale   <10'
Planetary Nebulae
>100"   100"–30"   <30"

Open Star Clusters
Globular Clusters
To scale   <5'

Galaxies
10' x 5'   6' x 1'   3' x 2'   5' x 5'   4' x 2'   2' x 1'
Plotted to scale if the major axis >2', and circular when face on or the position angle is uncertain

Quasars
Galaxy Clusters

1314

1338 ▽

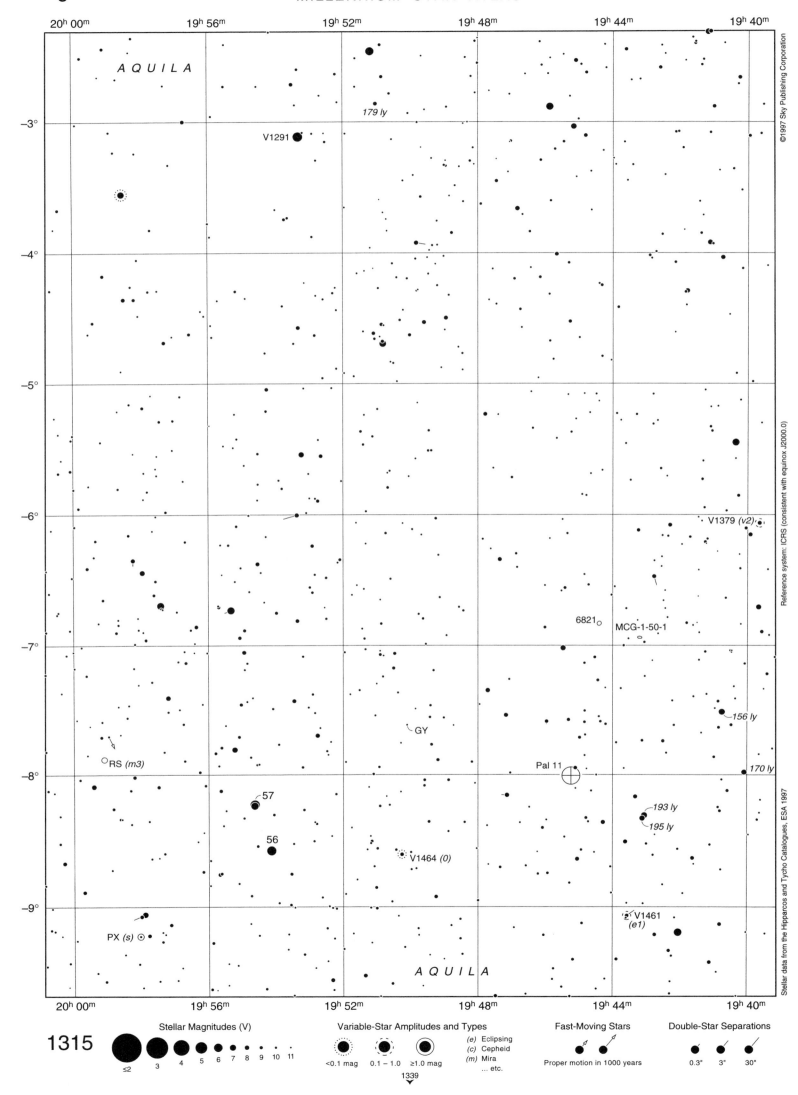

AQUILA

179 ly

V1291

V1379 (v2)

6821○   MCG-1-50-1

156 ly

GY

170 ly

○RS (m3)

Pal 11

57

193 ly

56

195 ly

V1464 (0)

V1461
(e1)

PX (s) ⊙

AQUILA

1315

Stellar Magnitudes (V)

≤2  3  4  5  6  7  8  9  10  11

Variable-Star Amplitudes and Types

<0.1 mag    0.1 – 1.0    ≥1.0 mag

(e) Eclipsing
(c) Cepheid
(m) Mira
... etc.

Fast-Moving Stars

Proper motion in 1000 years

Double-Star Separations

0.3"   3"   30"

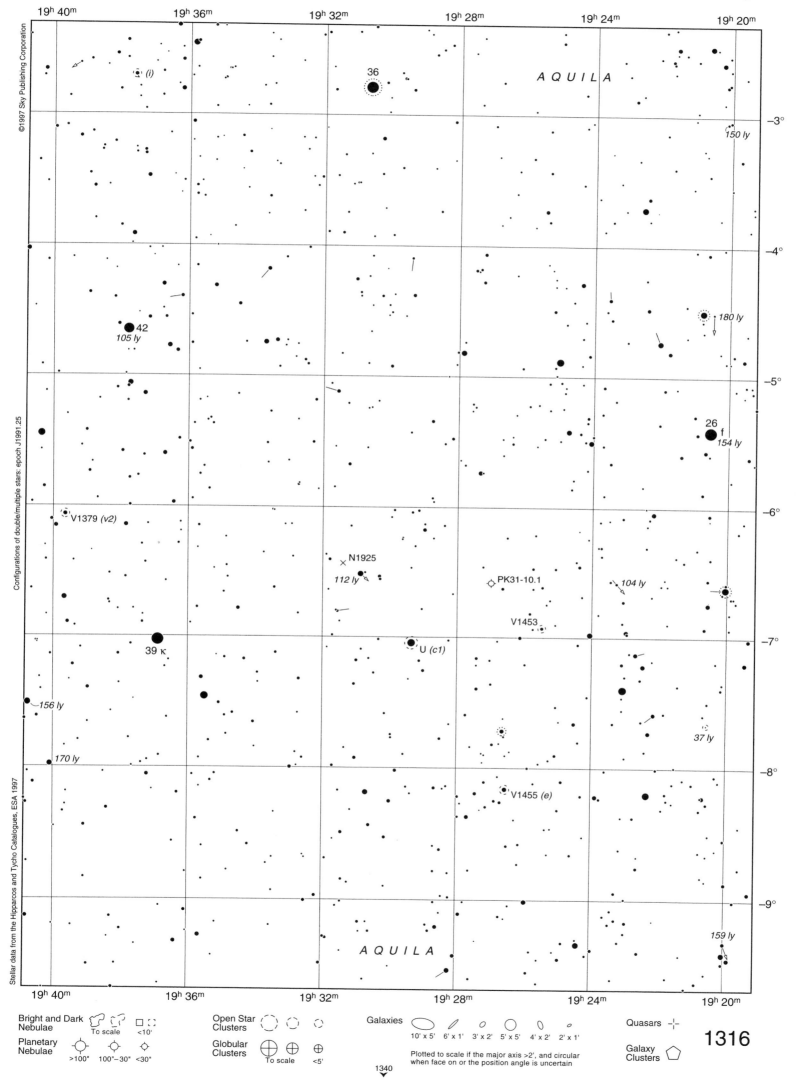

19h 40m    19h 36m    19h 32m    19h 28m    19h 24m    19h 20m

AQUILA

36

−3°

150 ly

42
105 ly

180 ly

−4°

26
f
154 ly

−5°

V1379 (v2)

−6°

N1925
112 ly

PK31-10.1

104 ly

V1453

U (c1)

−7°

39 κ

156 ly

37 ly

170 ly

−8°

V1455 (e)

159 ly

AQUILA

−9°

19h 40m    19h 36m    19h 32m    19h 28m    19h 24m    19h 20m

Bright and Dark
Nebulae
To scale    <10'

Planetary
Nebulae
>100"  100"−30"  <30"

Open Star
Clusters

Globular
Clusters
To scale    <5'

Galaxies
10' x 5'  6' x 1'  3' x 2'  5' x 5'  4' x 2'  2' x 1'

Plotted to scale if the major axis >2', and circular
when face on or the position angle is uncertain

Quasars

Galaxy
Clusters

1316

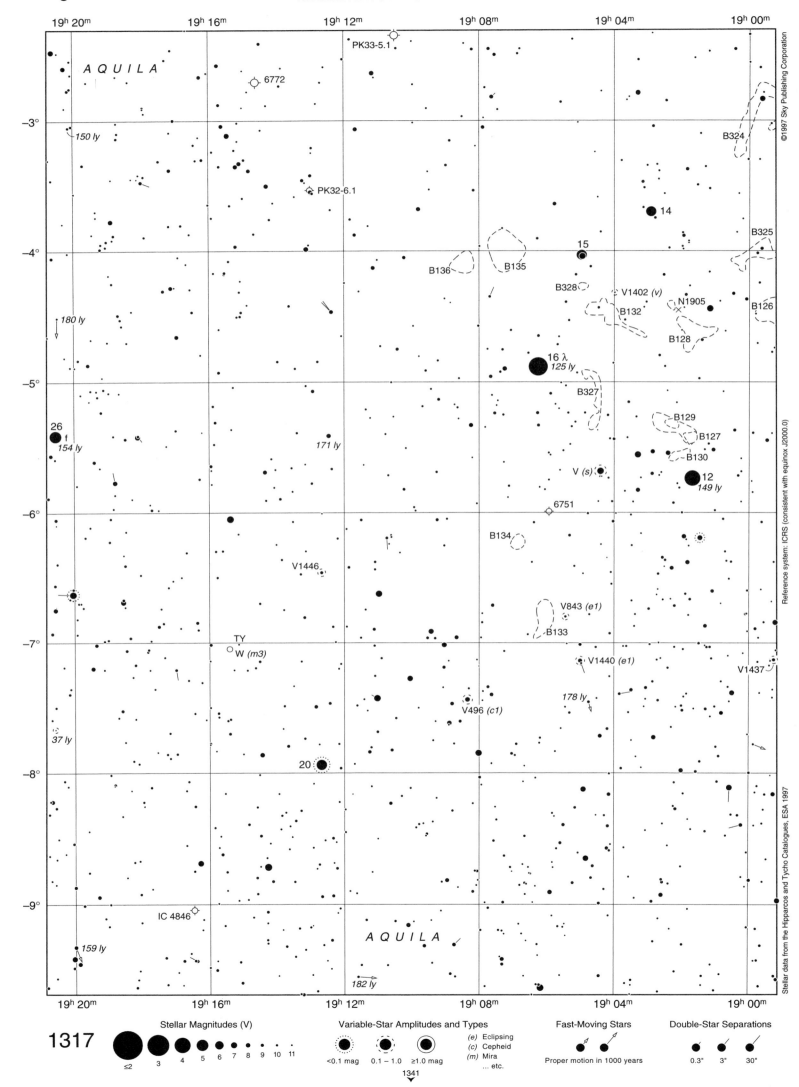

AQUILA

150 ly

6772

PK33-5.1

PK32-6.1

B324

14

15

B325

B136    B135

B328

V1402 (v)

N1905

B126

180 ly

B132

B128

16 λ
125 ly

B327

26
f
154 ly

B129

B127

B130

171 ly

V (s)

12
149 ly

6751

B134

V1446

V843 (e1)

B133

TY
W (m3)

V1440 (e1)

V1437

178 ly

37 ly

V496 (c1)

20

IC 4846

159 ly

AQUILA

182 ly

1317

Stellar Magnitudes (V)

≤2   3   4   5   6   7   8   9   10   11

Variable-Star Amplitudes and Types

<0.1 mag    0.1 – 1.0    ≥1.0 mag

(e) Eclipsing
(c) Cepheid
(m) Mira
... etc.

Fast-Moving Stars

Proper motion in 1000 years

Double-Star Separations

0.3"    3"    30"

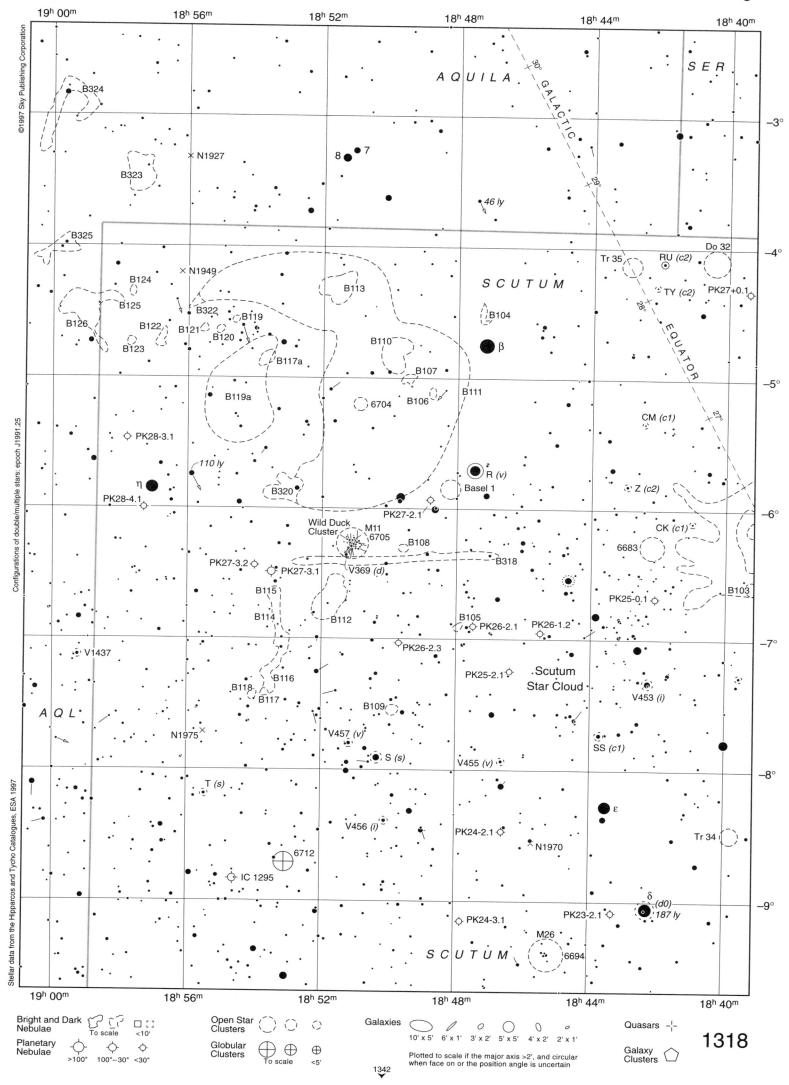

19h 00m   18h 56m   18h 52m   18h 48m   18h 44m   18h 40m

SER

AQUILA   GALACTIC

−3°

B324

N1927

B323

8  7

46 ly

29°

B325

Do 32

−4°

Tr 35   RU (c2)   PK27+0.1

B124   N1949   SCUTUM

B125   B113   TY (c2)

B126   B322   B119   B104

B122   B121   B120   B110

B123   B117a   B107

B119a   6704   B106   B111

−5°

CM (c1)

PK28-3.1

110 ly

R (v)   Z (c2)

η   Basel 1

PK28-4.1   B320   CK (c1)

PK27-2.1   −6°

6683

Wild Duck   M11   B108

Cluster   6705   B318

PK27-3.2   PK27-3.1   V369 (d)   PK25-0.1   B103

B115

B114   B112   B105   PK26-2.1   PK26-1.2

PK26-2.3   −7°

V1437   PK25-2.1   Scutum   V453 (i)

Star Cloud

B116

B118   SS (c1)

B117   B109

AQL   N1975   V457 (v)

S (s)   V455 (v)   −8°

T (s)   ε

V456 (i)

PK24-2.1   Tr 34

6712   N1970

IC 1295

δ (d0)

PK24-3.1   PK23-2.1   187 ly   −9°

M26

SCUTUM   6694

19h 00m   18h 56m   18h 52m   18h 48m   18h 44m   18h 40m

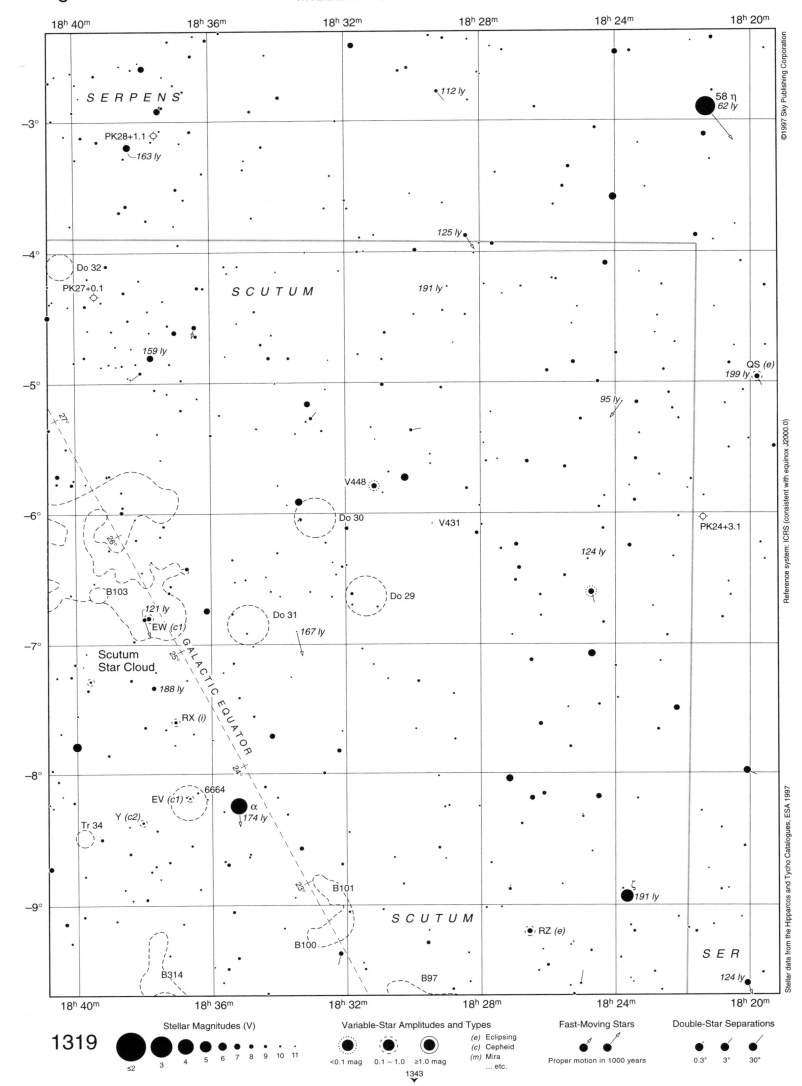

©1997 Sky Publishing Corporation

Reference system: ICRS (consistent with equinox J2000.0)

Stellar data from the Hipparcos and Tycho Catalogues, ESA 1997

1319

Stellar Magnitudes (V)

≤2   3   4   5   6   7   8   9  10  11

Variable-Star Amplitudes and Types

<0.1 mag   0.1 – 1.0   ≥1.0 mag

(e) Eclipsing
(c) Cepheid
(m) Mira
... etc.

1343

Fast-Moving Stars

Proper motion in 1000 years

Double-Star Separations

0.3"   3"   30"

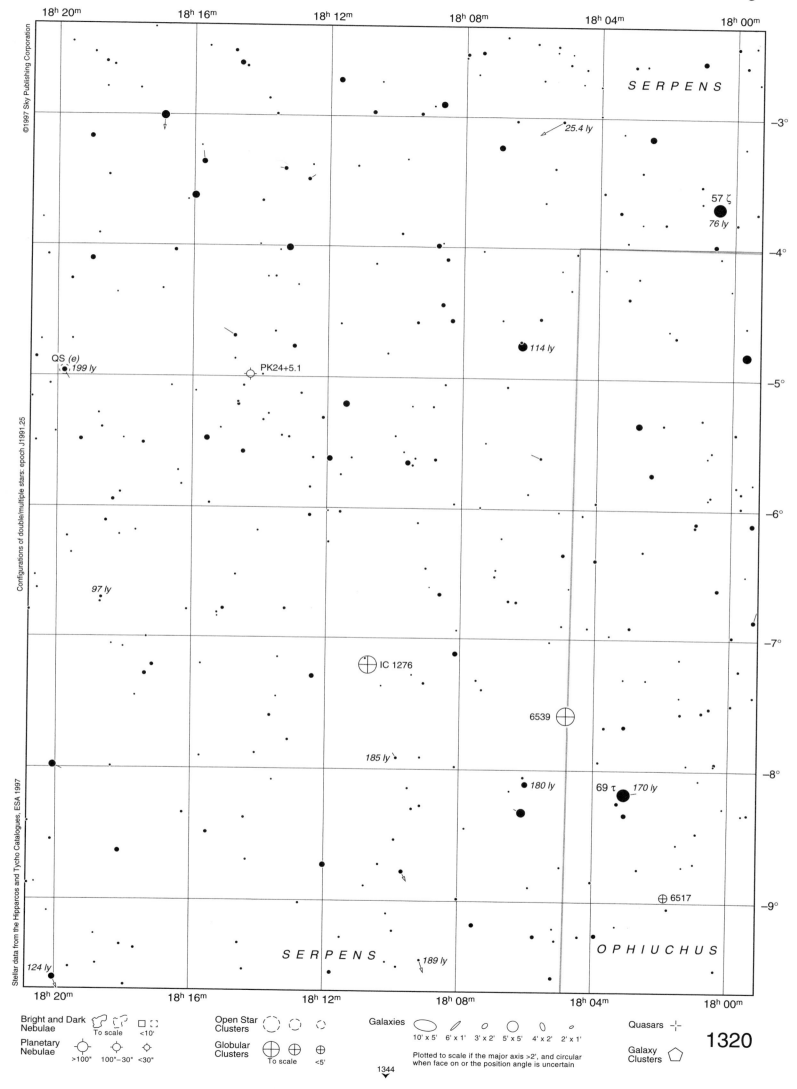

SERPENS

57 ζ
76 ly

25.4 ly

114 ly

QS (e)
199 ly

PK24+5.1

97 ly

IC 1276

6539

185 ly

180 ly

69 τ   170 ly

6517

124 ly

SERPENS

189 ly

OPHIUCHUS

| Bright and Dark Nebulae | | | Open Star Clusters | | | Galaxies | | | | | | Quasars |
|---|---|---|---|---|---|---|---|---|---|---|---|---|
| To scale | | <10' | | | | 10' x 5' | 6' x 1' | 3' x 2' | 5' x 5' | 4' x 2' | 2' x 1' | |

Planetary Nebulae
>100"   100"−30"   <30"

Globular Clusters
To scale   <5'

Galaxy Clusters

Plotted to scale if the major axis >2', and circular when face on or the position angle is uncertain

**1320**

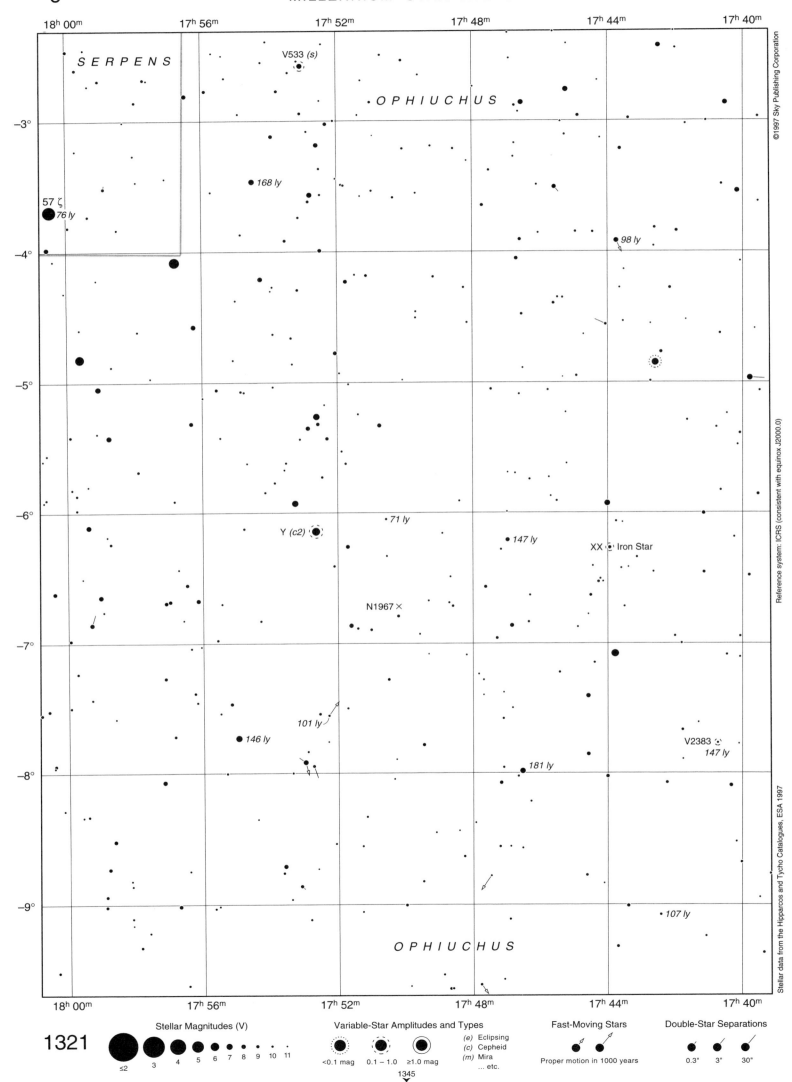

©1997 Sky Publishing Corporation

Reference system: ICRS (consistent with equinox J2000.0)

Stellar data from the Hipparcos and Tycho Catalogues, ESA 1997

SERPENS

OPHIUCHUS

V533 (s)

168 ly

57 ζ
76 ly

98 ly

Y (c2)

71 ly

147 ly

XX Iron Star

N1967 ×

101 ly

146 ly

V2383
147 ly

181 ly

107 ly

OPHIUCHUS

1321

Stellar Magnitudes (V)

≤2    3    4    5    6    7    8    9    10    11

Variable-Star Amplitudes and Types

<0.1 mag     0.1 − 1.0     ≥1.0 mag

(e) Eclipsing
(c) Cepheid
(m) Mira
... etc.

Fast-Moving Stars

Proper motion in 1000 years

Double-Star Separations

0.3"    3"    30"

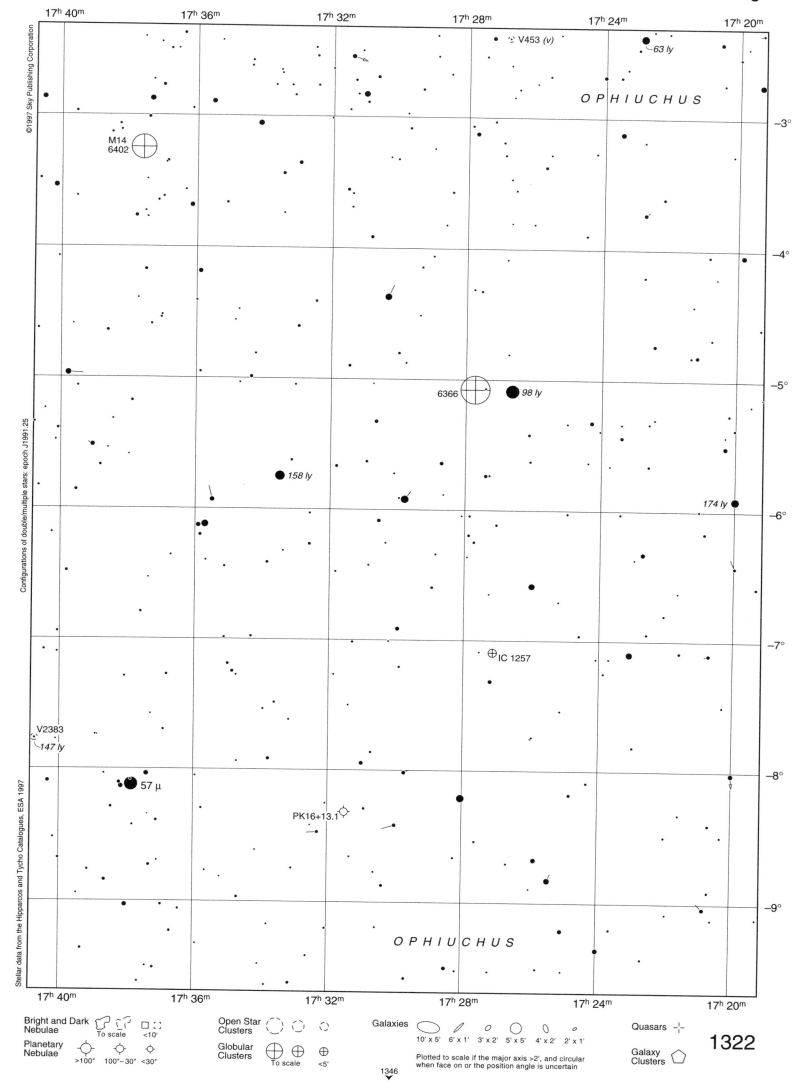

17ʰ 40ᵐ  17ʰ 36ᵐ  17ʰ 32ᵐ  17ʰ 28ᵐ  17ʰ 24ᵐ  17ʰ 20ᵐ

V453 (v)

63 ly

O P H I U C H U S

−3°

M14
6402

−4°

6366  98 ly

−5°

158 ly

174 ly

−6°

IC 1257

−7°

V2383
147 ly

−8°

57 μ

PK16+13.1

O P H I U C H U S

−9°

17ʰ 40ᵐ  17ʰ 36ᵐ  17ʰ 32ᵐ  17ʰ 28ᵐ  17ʰ 24ᵐ  17ʰ 20ᵐ

Bright and Dark Nebulae
To scale   <10'

Open Star Clusters

Galaxies
10' x 5'   6' x 1'   3' x 2'   5' x 5'   4' x 2'   2' x 1'

Quasars

Planetary Nebulae
>100"   100"−30"   <30"

Globular Clusters
To scale   <5'

Plotted to scale if the major axis >2', and circular when face on or the position angle is uncertain

Galaxy Clusters

1322

1346

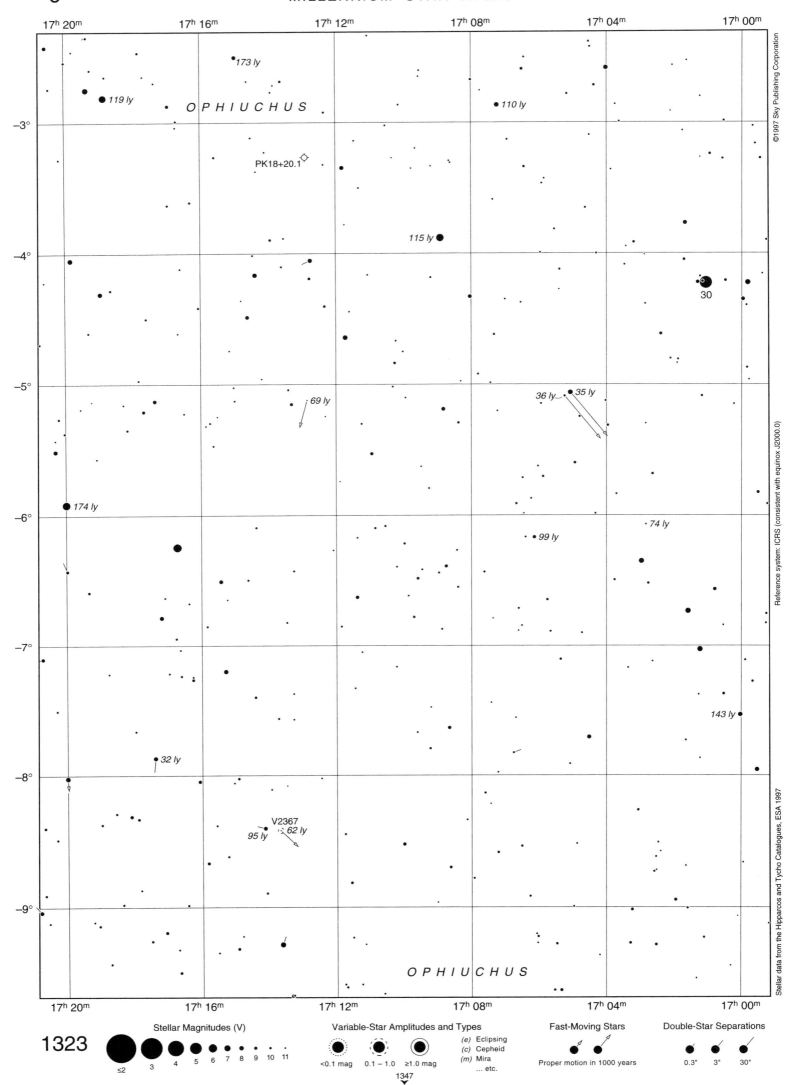

©1997 Sky Publishing Corporation

Reference system: ICRS (consistent with equinox J2000.0)

Stellar data from the Hipparcos and Tycho Catalogues, ESA 1997

OPHIUCHUS

173 ly

119 ly

PK18+20.1

110 ly

115 ly

30

69 ly

36 ly  35 ly

174 ly

99 ly

74 ly

143 ly

32 ly

V2367
95 ly  62 ly

OPHIUCHUS

Stellar Magnitudes (V)

≤2  3  4  5  6  7  8  9  10  11

Variable-Star Amplitudes and Types

<0.1 mag   0.1 − 1.0   ≥1.0 mag

(e) Eclipsing
(c) Cepheid
(m) Mira
... etc.

1347

Fast-Moving Stars

Proper motion in 1000 years

Double-Star Separations

0.3"  3"  30"

# MILLENNIUM STAR ATLAS

−6°

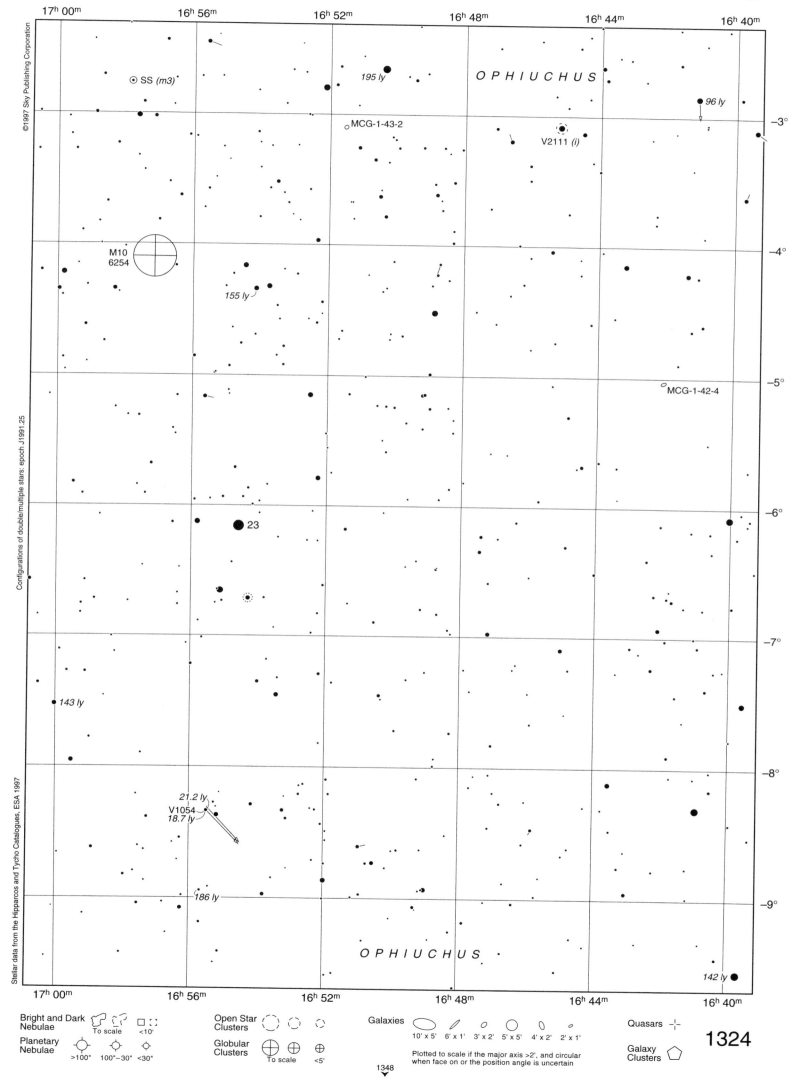

©1997 Sky Publishing Corporation

17h 00m  16h 56m  16h 52m  16h 48m  16h 44m  16h 40m

⊙ SS (m3)

195 ly

O P H I U C H U S

96 ly

−3°

○ MCG-1-43-2

V2111 (i)

M10
6254

−4°

155 ly

○ MCG-1-42-4

−5°

23

−6°

143 ly

−7°

−8°

21.2 ly
V1054
18.7 ly

186 ly

−9°

O P H I U C H U S

142 ly ●

17h 00m  16h 56m  16h 52m  16h 48m  16h 44m  16h 40m

Configurations of double/multiple stars: epoch J1991.25

Stellar data from the Hipparcos and Tycho Catalogues, ESA 1997

Bright and Dark
Nebulae
To scale  <10'

Planetary
Nebulae
>100"  100"–30"  <30"

Open Star
Clusters

Globular
Clusters
To scale  <5'

Galaxies
10' x 5'  6' x 1'  3' x 2'  5' x 5'  4' x 2'  2' x 1'

Plotted to scale if the major axis >2', and circular
when face on or the position angle is uncertain

Quasars

Galaxy
Clusters

**1324**

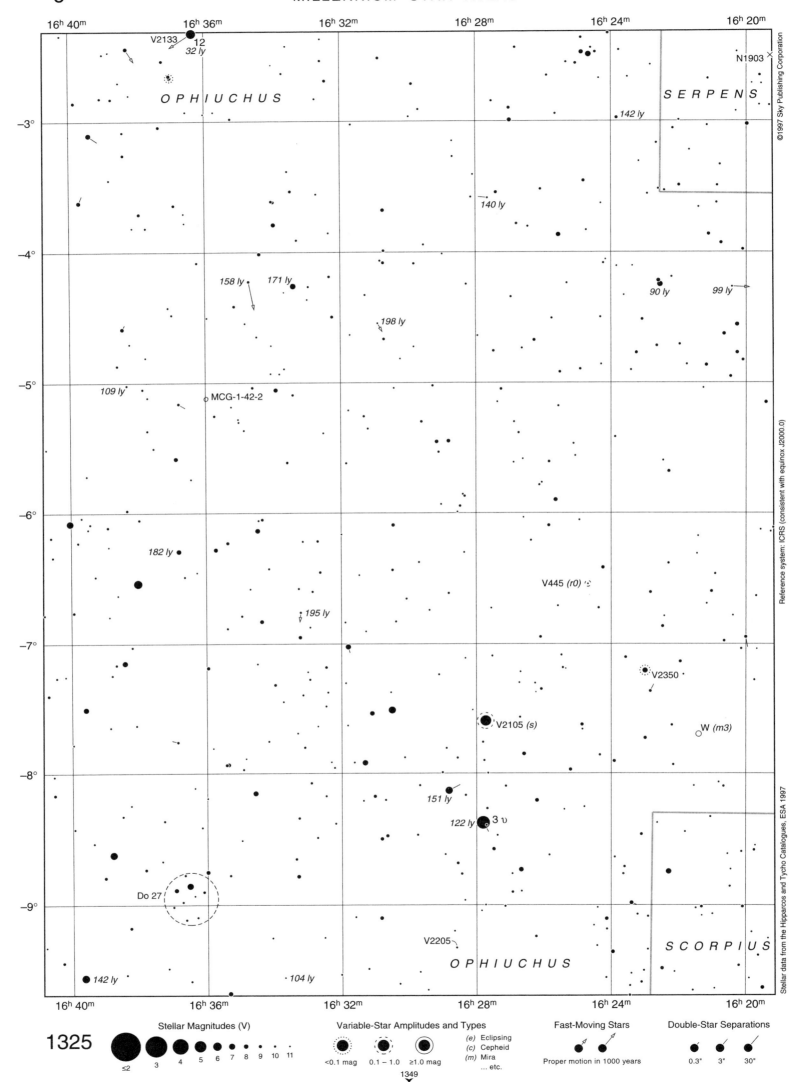

OPHIUCHUS

SERPENS

SCORPIUS

V2133
12
*32 ly*

N1903

*142 ly*

*140 ly*

*158 ly*    *171 ly*

*90 ly*    *99 ly*

*198 ly*

*109 ly*    MCG-1-42-2

*182 ly*

V445 (r0)

*195 ly*

V2350

V2105 (s)

W (m3)

*151 ly*

*122 ly*  3 υ

Do 27

V2205

*142 ly*    *104 ly*

OPHIUCHUS

**1325**

Stellar Magnitudes (V)

≤2   3   4   5   6   7   8   9   10   11

Variable-Star Amplitudes and Types

<0.1 mag   0.1 – 1.0   ≥1.0 mag

(e) Eclipsing
(c) Cepheid
(m) Mira
... etc.

Fast-Moving Stars

Proper motion in 1000 years

Double-Star Separations

0.3"   3"   30"

^1349

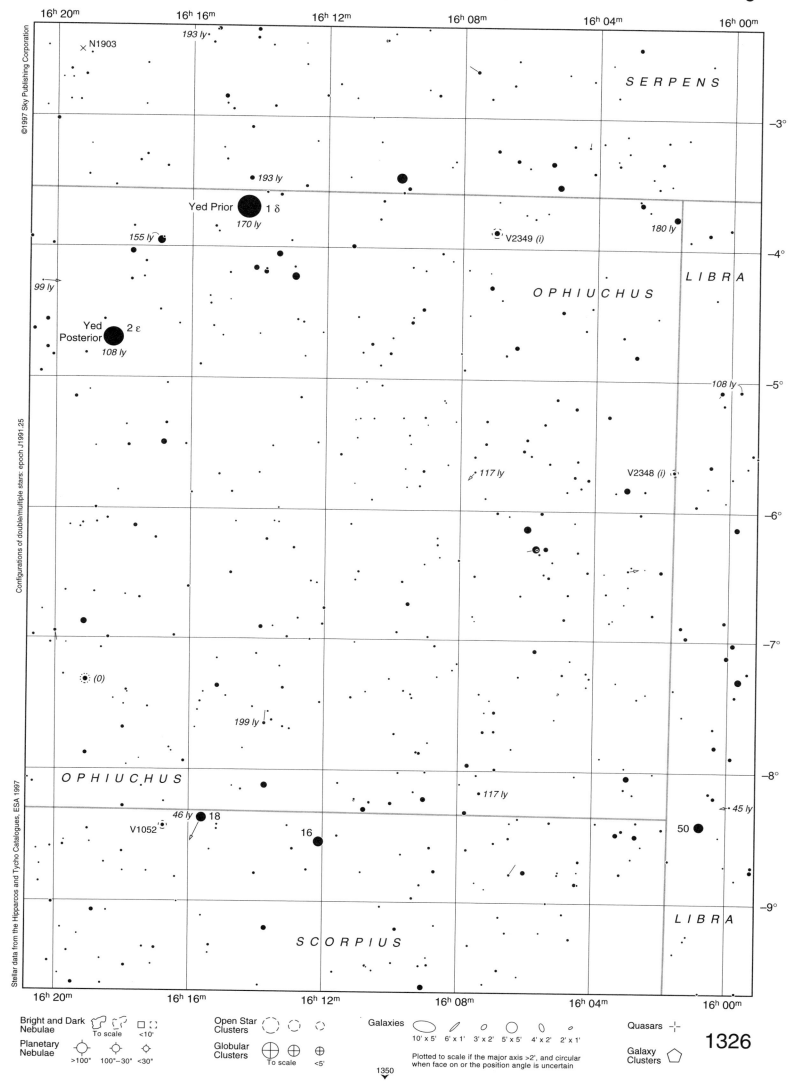

16h 20m  16h 16m  16h 12m  16h 08m  16h 04m  16h 00m

N1903

SERPENS

−3°

193 ly

193 ly

Yed Prior  1 δ
170 ly

V2349 (i)

180 ly

−4°

155 ly

LIBRA

OPHIUCHUS

99 ly

Yed
Posterior  2 ε
108 ly

108 ly  −5°

117 ly  V2348 (i)

−6°

−7°

(0)

199 ly  −8°

OPHIUCHUS

117 ly

45 ly

46 ly  18

V1052

50

16

−9°

LIBRA

SCORPIUS

16h 20m  16h 16m  16h 12m  16h 08m  16h 04m  16h 00m

| Bright and Dark Nebulae | Open Star Clusters | Galaxies | Quasars |
|---|---|---|---|

To scale  <10'

Planetary Nebulae
>100"  100"−30"  <30"

Globular Clusters
To scale  <5'

10' x 5'  6' x 1'  3' x 2'  5' x 5'  4' x 2'  2' x 1'

Galaxy Clusters

Plotted to scale if the major axis >2', and circular when face on or the position angle is uncertain

−12°

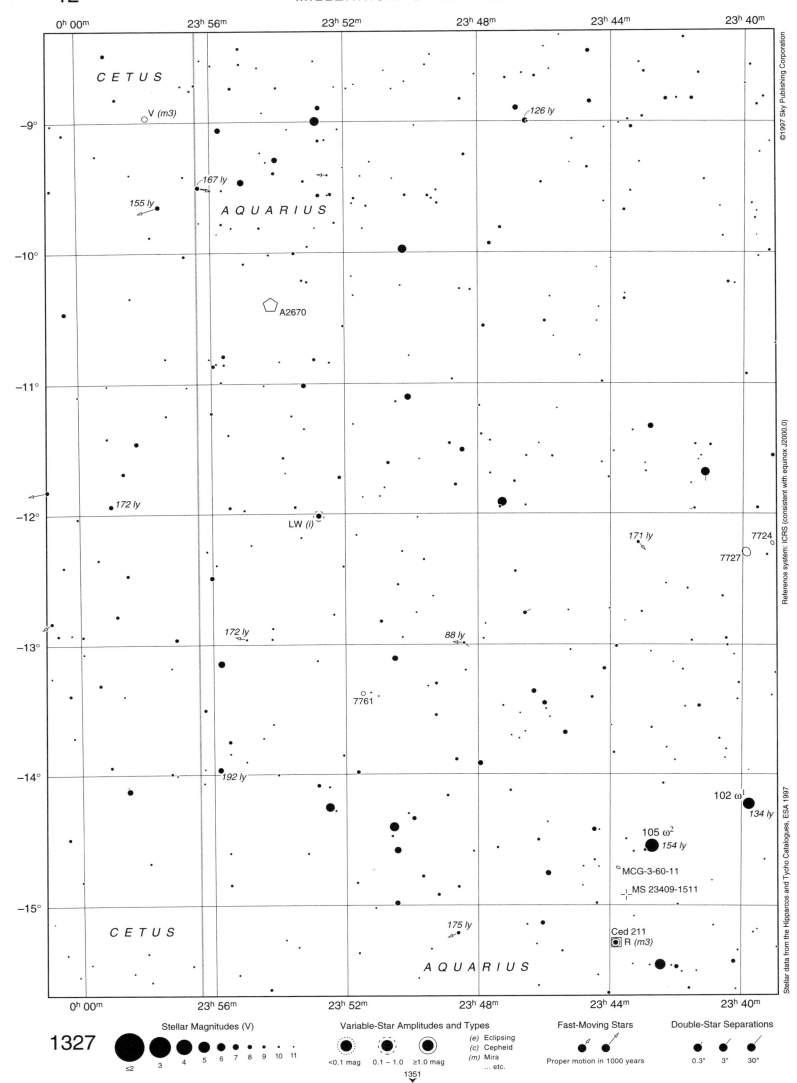

0ʰ 00ᵐ    23ʰ 56ᵐ    23ʰ 52ᵐ    23ʰ 48ᵐ    23ʰ 44ᵐ    23ʰ 40ᵐ

C E T U S

V (m3)

126 ly

167 ly

155 ly

A Q U A R I U S

−9°

−10°

A2670

−11°

172 ly

LW (i)

171 ly

7724
7727

−12°

172 ly

88 ly

−13°

7761

192 ly

−14°

102 ω¹
134 ly

105 ω²
154 ly

MCG-3-60-11

MS 23409-1511

−15°

C E T U S

175 ly

Ced 211
R (m3)

A Q U A R I U S

0ʰ 00ᵐ    23ʰ 56ᵐ    23ʰ 52ᵐ    23ʰ 48ᵐ    23ʰ 44ᵐ    23ʰ 40ᵐ

©1997 Sky Publishing Corporation

Reference system: ICRS (consistent with equinox J2000.0)

Stellar data from the Hipparcos and Tycho Catalogues, ESA 1997

1327

Stellar Magnitudes (V)

≤2   3   4   5   6   7   8   9   10   11

Variable-Star Amplitudes and Types

<0.1 mag   0.1 − 1.0   ≥1.0 mag

(e) Eclipsing
(c) Cepheid
(m) Mira
... etc.

Fast-Moving Stars

Proper motion in 1000 years

Double-Star Separations

0.3"   3"   30"

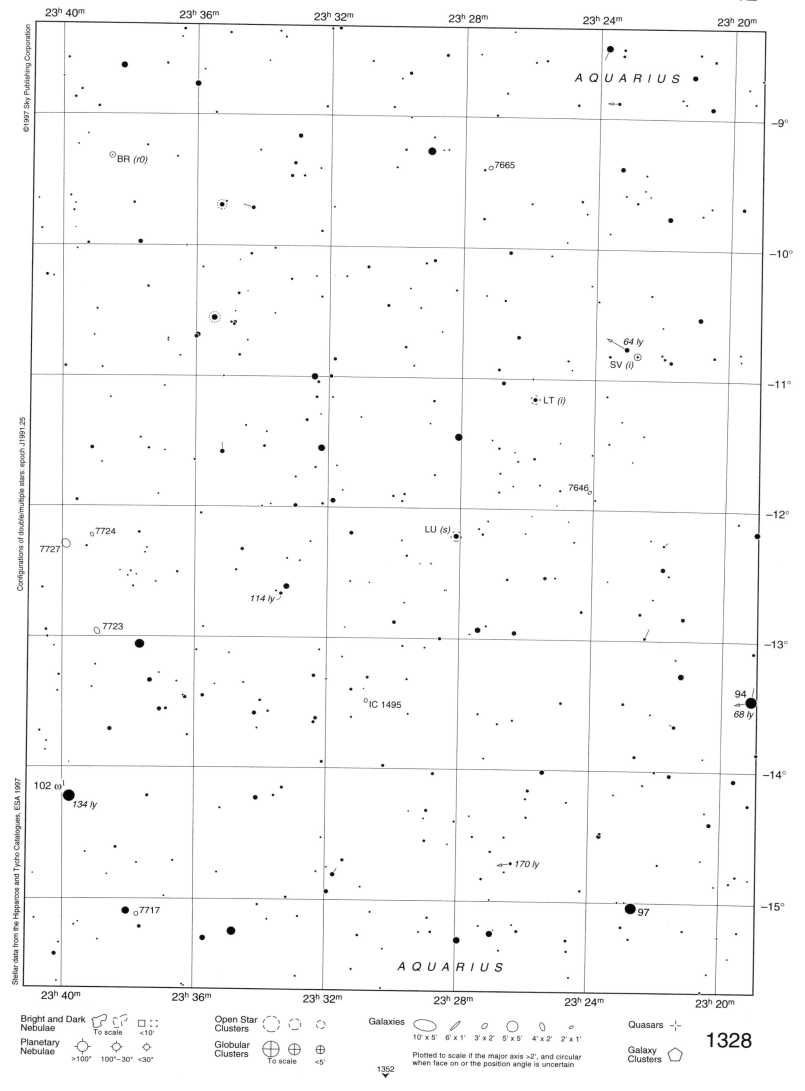

23h 40m    23h 36m    23h 32m    23h 28m    23h 24m    23h 20m

−9°
−10°
−11°
−12°
−13°
−14°
−15°

A Q U A R I U S

⊙ BR (r0)

○ 7665

64 ly
⊙
SV (i)

⊙ LT (i)

7646 ○

LU (s) ⊙

○ 7724

7727 ○

114 ly

○ 7723

○ IC 1495

94
68 ly

102 ω¹
134 ly

170 ly

○ 7717

97

A Q U A R I U S

23h 40m    23h 36m    23h 32m    23h 28m    23h 24m    23h 20m

Bright and Dark Nebulae
To scale   <10'

Planetary Nebulae
>100"  100"−30"  <30"

Open Star Clusters
To scale

Globular Clusters
To scale   <5'

Galaxies
10' x 5'  6' x 1'  3' x 2'  5' x 5'  4' x 2'  2' x 1'
Plotted to scale if the major axis >2', and circular when face on or the position angle is uncertain

1352 ▼

Quasars

Galaxy Clusters

1328

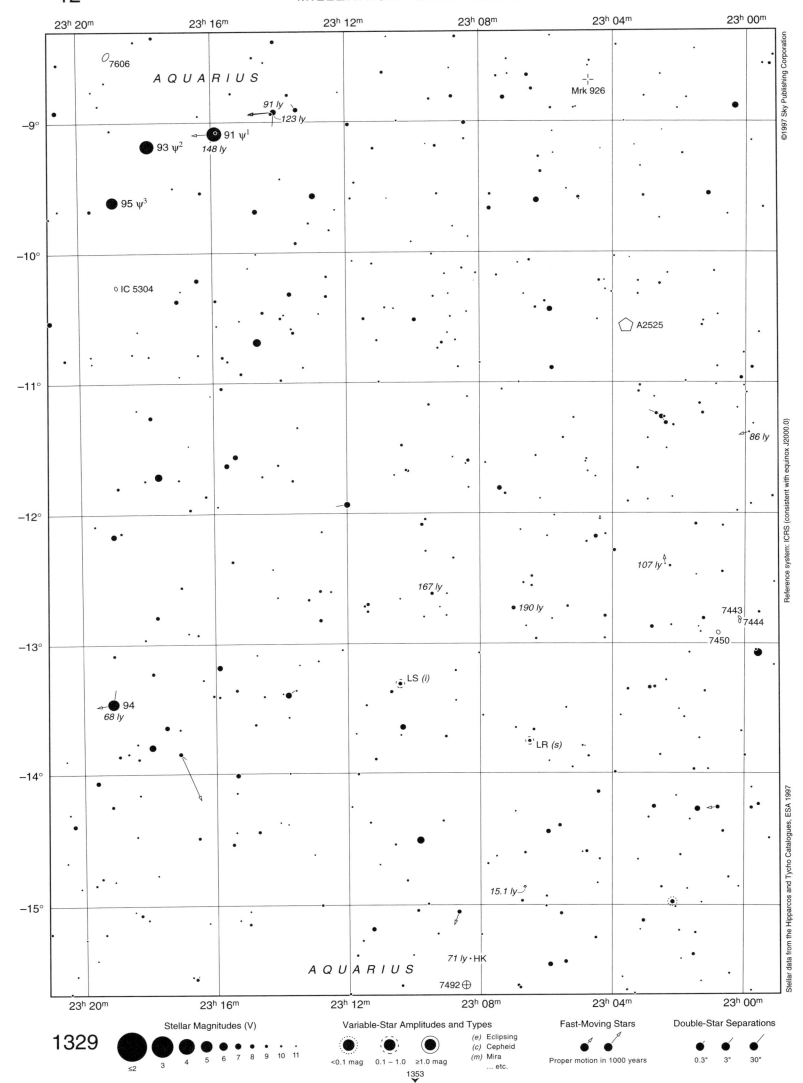

©1997 Sky Publishing Corporation

Reference system: ICRS (consistent with equinox J2000.0)

Stellar data from the Hipparcos and Tycho Catalogues, ESA 1997

1329

| Stellar Magnitudes (V) | Variable-Star Amplitudes and Types | Fast-Moving Stars | Double-Star Separations |
|---|---|---|---|

Stellar Magnitudes (V)
≤2  3  4  5  6  7  8  9  10  11

Variable-Star Amplitudes and Types
<0.1 mag   0.1 – 1.0   ≥1.0 mag

(e) Eclipsing
(c) Cepheid
(m) Mira
... etc.

Fast-Moving Stars
Proper motion in 1000 years

Double-Star Separations
0.3"   3"   30"

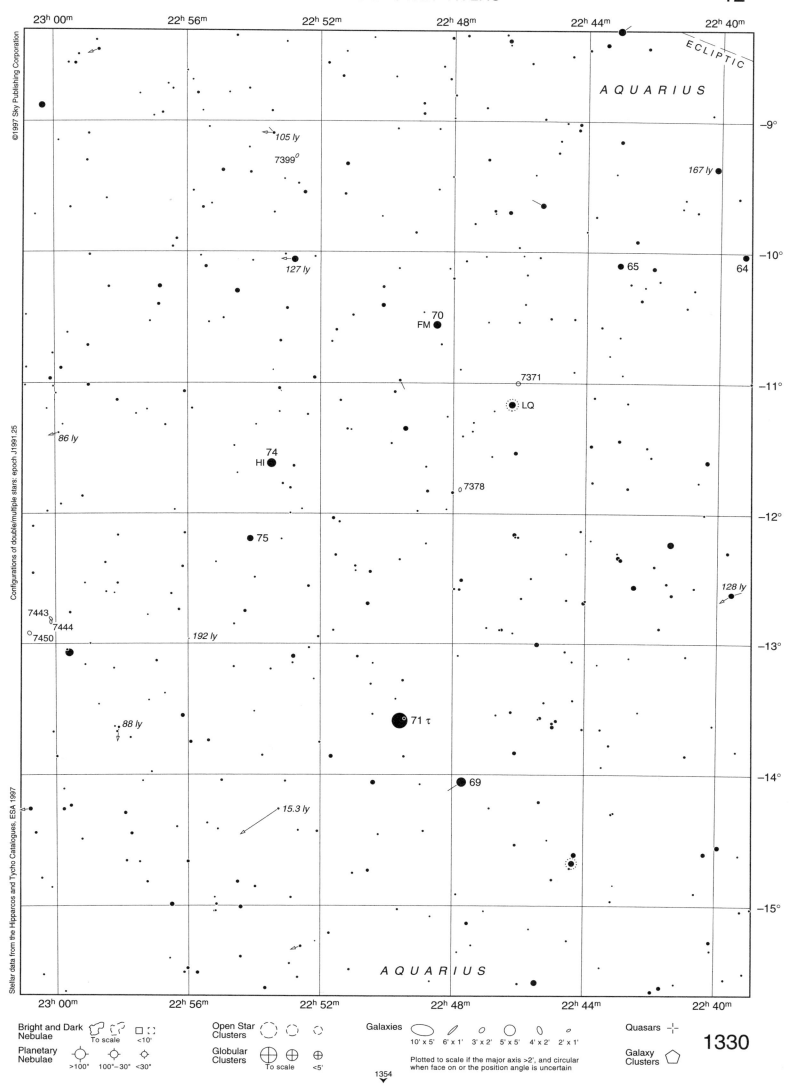

ECLIPTIC

A Q U A R I U S

105 ly

7399

167 ly

127 ly

65      64

70
FM

7371

LQ

86 ly

74
HI

7378

75

128 ly

7443
7444
7450
192 ly

88 ly

71 τ

69

15.3 ly

A Q U A R I U S

Bright and Dark Nebulae   To scale   <10'

Planetary Nebulae   >100"   100"−30"   <30"

Open Star Clusters

Globular Clusters   To scale   <5'

Galaxies   10' x 5'   6' x 1'   3' x 2'   5' x 5'   4' x 2'   2' x 1'

Plotted to scale if the major axis >2', and circular when face on or the position angle is uncertain

Quasars

Galaxy Clusters

1330

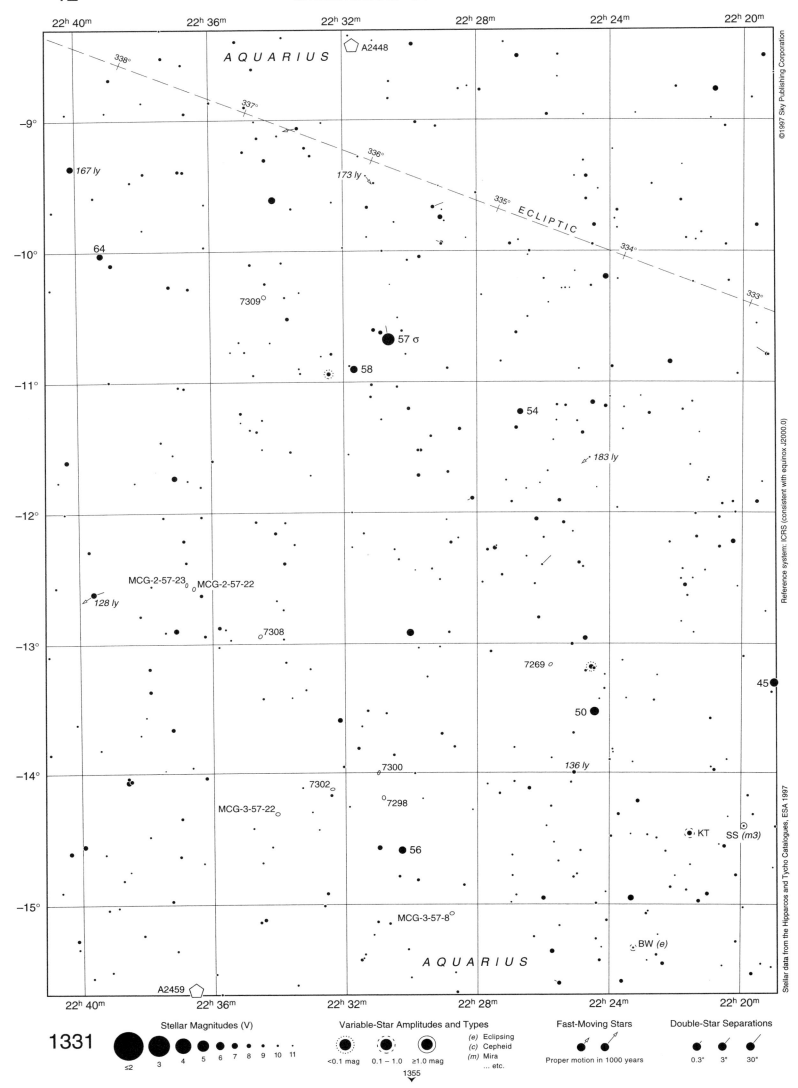

AQUARIUS

A2448

338°

337°

336°

335° ECLIPTIC

334°

333°

167 ly

173 ly

64

7309

57 σ

58

54

183 ly

128 ly

MCG-2-57-23    MCG-2-57-22

7308

7269

45

50

7300

136 ly

7302

7298

MCG-3-57-22

KT

SS (m3)

56

MCG-3-57-8

BW (e)

AQUARIUS

A2459

1331

Stellar Magnitudes (V)

≤2  3  4  5  6 7 8 9 10 11

Variable-Star Amplitudes and Types

<0.1 mag    0.1 − 1.0    ≥1.0 mag

(e) Eclipsing
(c) Cepheid
(m) Mira
... etc.

Fast-Moving Stars

Proper motion in 1000 years

Double-Star Separations

0.3"    3"    30"

1355

# MILLENNIUM STAR ATLAS

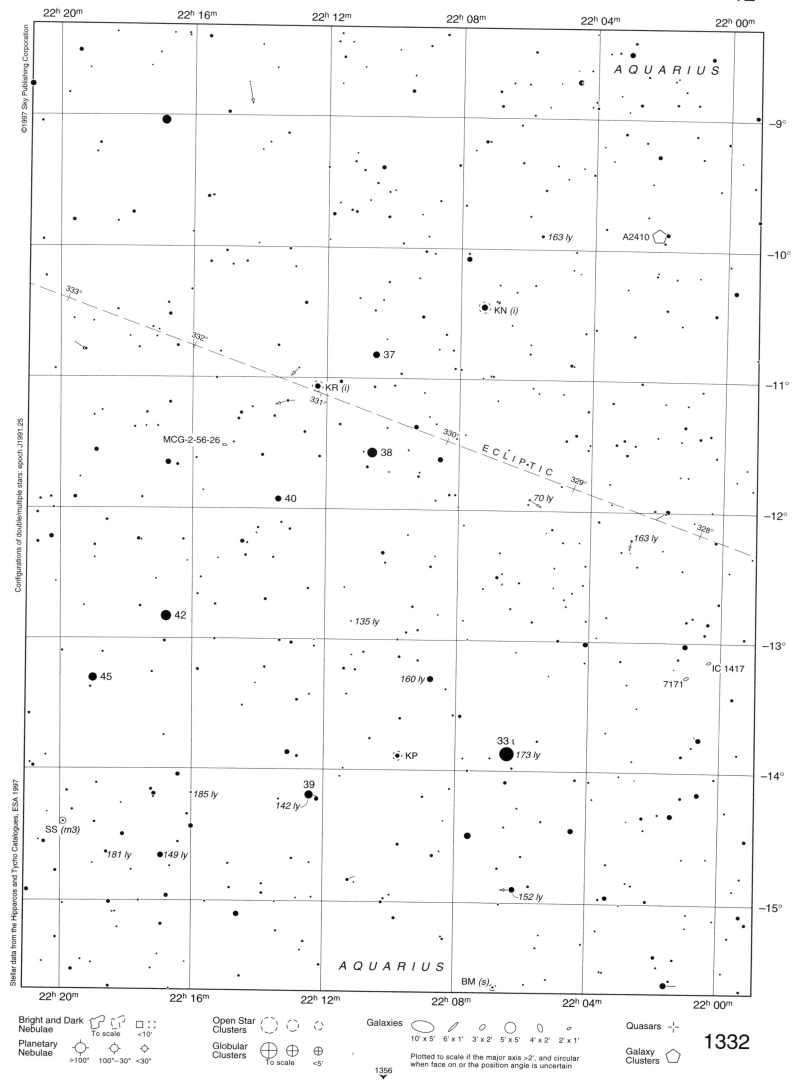

AQUARIUS

22ʰ 20ᵐ  22ʰ 16ᵐ  22ʰ 12ᵐ  22ʰ 08ᵐ  22ʰ 04ᵐ  22ʰ 00ᵐ

−9°

−10°

333°

332°

KN (i)

37

KR (i)

331°

MCG-2-56-26

330°

38

329°

ECLIPTIC

70 ly

40

328°

163 ly

135 ly

42

IC 1417

45

160 ly

7171

33 ι

173 ly

KP

39

185 ly

142 ly

SS (m3)

181 ly    149 ly

152 ly

AQUARIUS

BM (s)

22ʰ 20ᵐ  22ʰ 16ᵐ  22ʰ 12ᵐ  22ʰ 08ᵐ  22ʰ 04ᵐ  22ʰ 00ᵐ

−13°

−14°

−15°

163 ly

A2410

©1997 Sky Publishing Corporation

Configurations of double/multiple stars: epoch J1991.25

Stellar data from the Hipparcos and Tycho Catalogues, ESA 1997

| Bright and Dark Nebulae | | | Open Star Clusters | | | Galaxies | | | | | | Quasars |
| To scale | | <10' | | | | 10' x 5' | 6' x 1' | 3' x 2' | 5' x 5' | 4' x 2' | 2' x 1' | |
| Planetary Nebulae | | | Globular Clusters | | | | | | | | | Galaxy Clusters |
| >100" | 100"-30" | <30" | To scale | | <5' | Plotted to scale if the major axis >2', and circular when face on or the position angle is uncertain | | | | | | |

1332

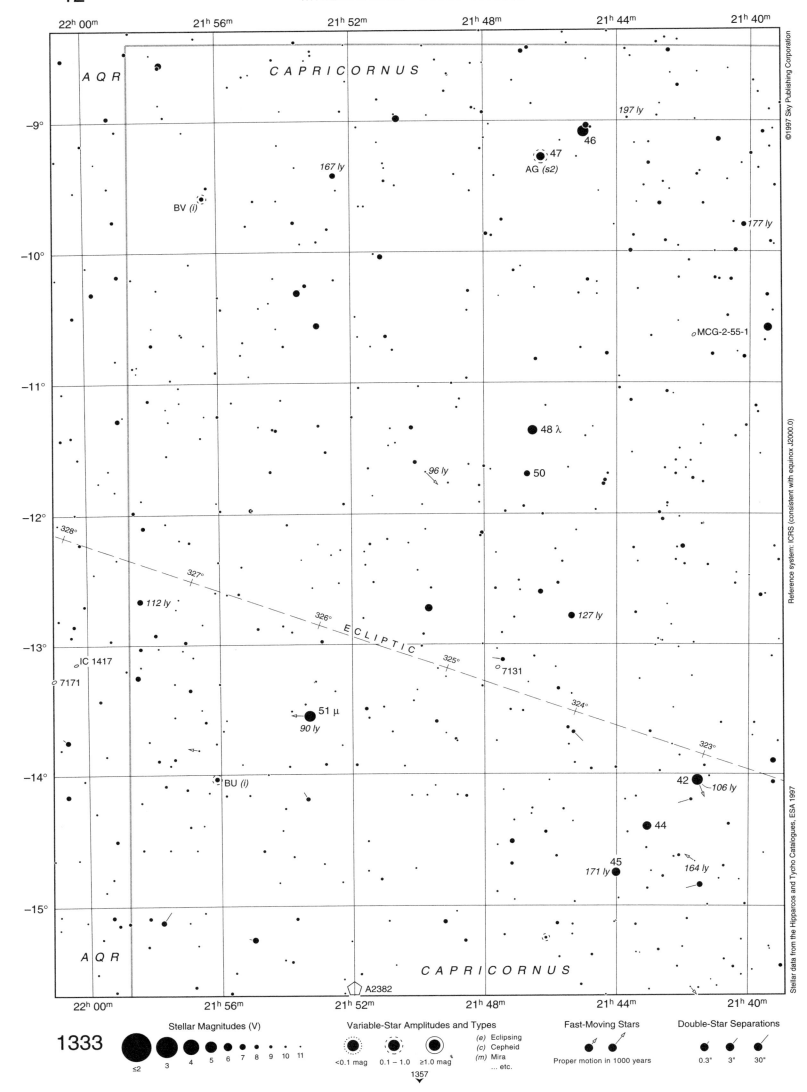
22ʰ 00ᵐ   21ʰ 56ᵐ   21ʰ 52ᵐ   21ʰ 48ᵐ   21ʰ 44ᵐ   21ʰ 40ᵐ

A Q R

C A P R I C O R N U S

197 ly

−9°

46

47
AG (s2)

167 ly

BV (i)

177 ly

−10°

MCG-2-55-1

−11°

48 λ

50

96 ly

−12°

328°

327°

112 ly

326°   E C L I P T I C   127 ly

−13°

IC 1417

7171   7131

325°

324°

51 μ

90 ly

323°

BU (i)

42   106 ly

−14°

44

45
171 ly   164 ly

−15°

A Q R

C A P R I C O R N U S

A2382

22ʰ 00ᵐ   21ʰ 56ᵐ   21ʰ 52ᵐ   21ʰ 48ᵐ   21ʰ 44ᵐ   21ʰ 40ᵐ

©1997 Sky Publishing Corporation

Reference system: ICRS (consistent with equinox J2000.0)

Stellar data from the Hipparcos and Tycho Catalogues, ESA 1997

**1333**

Stellar Magnitudes (V)
≤2   3   4   5   6   7   8   9   10   11

Variable-Star Amplitudes and Types
<0.1 mag   0.1 – 1.0   ≥1.0 mag

(e) Eclipsing
(c) Cepheid
(m) Mira
... etc.

Fast-Moving Stars
Proper motion in 1000 years

Double-Star Separations
0.3"   3"   30"

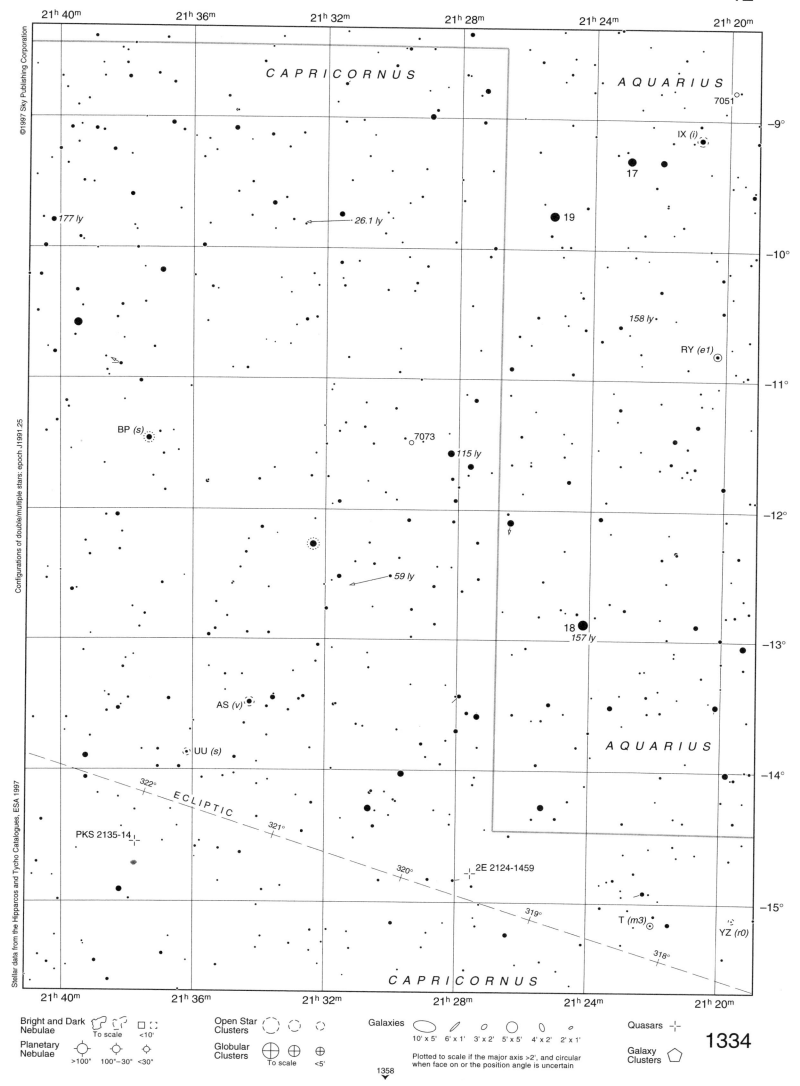

21h 40m    21h 36m    21h 32m    21h 28m    21h 24m    21h 20m

C A P R I C O R N U S

A Q U A R I U S

7051

IX (i)

17

19

−9°

177 ly

26.1 ly

−10°

158 ly

RY (e1)

BP (s)

−11°

7073

115 ly

−12°

59 ly

18

157 ly

AS (v)

A Q U A R I U S

UU (s)

−13°

−14°

322°    E C L I P T I C

321°

PKS 2135-14

320°    2E 2124-1459

319°

T (m3)

YZ (r0)

318°

−15°

C A P R I C O R N U S

21h 40m    21h 36m    21h 32m    21h 28m    21h 24m    21h 20m

Bright and Dark Nebulae     To scale     <10'
Planetary Nebulae     >100"     100"–30"     <30"
Open Star Clusters
Globular Clusters     To scale     <5'
Galaxies     10' x 5'   6' x 1'   3' x 2'   5' x 5'   4' x 2'   2' x 1'
Plotted to scale if the major axis >2', and circular when face on or the position angle is uncertain
Quasars
Galaxy Clusters

1334

1358

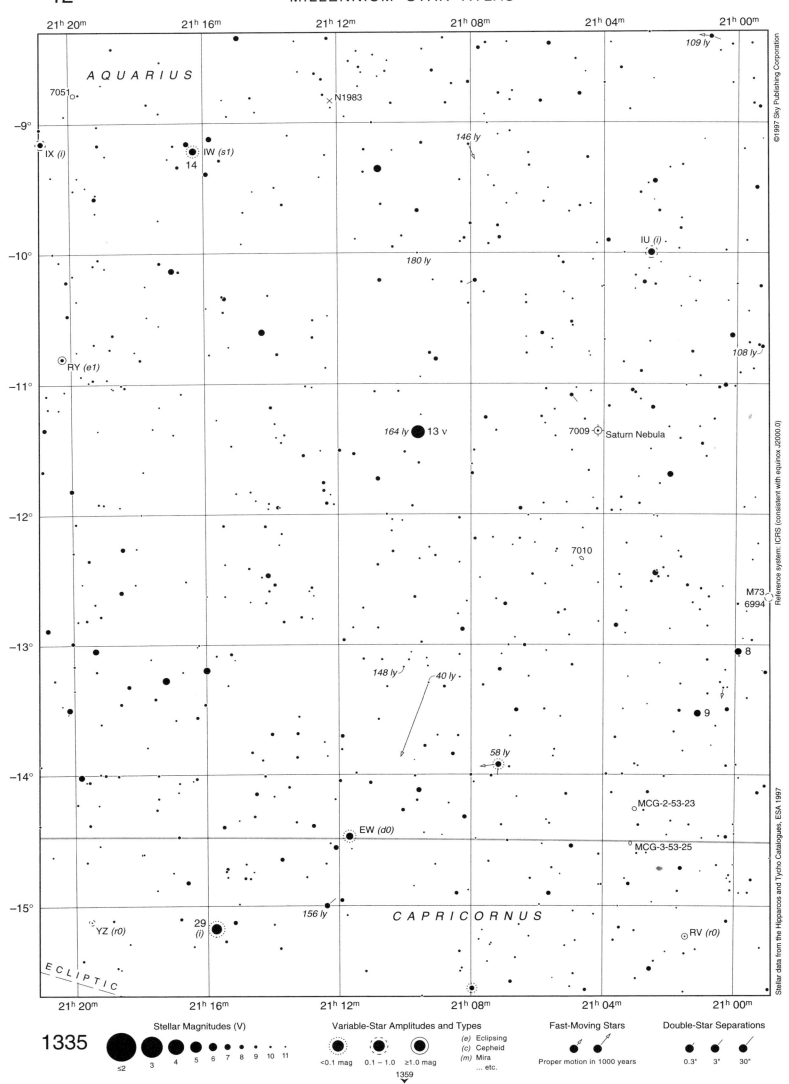

©1997 Sky Publishing Corporation

Reference system: ICRS (consistent with equinox J2000.0)

Stellar data from the Hipparcos and Tycho Catalogues, ESA 1997

1335

Stellar Magnitudes (V)

≤2  3  4  5  6  7  8  9  10  11

Variable-Star Amplitudes and Types

<0.1 mag   0.1 – 1.0   ≥1.0 mag

(e) Eclipsing
(c) Cepheid
(m) Mira
... etc.

Fast-Moving Stars

Proper motion in 1000 years

Double-Star Separations

0.3"   3"   30"

1359

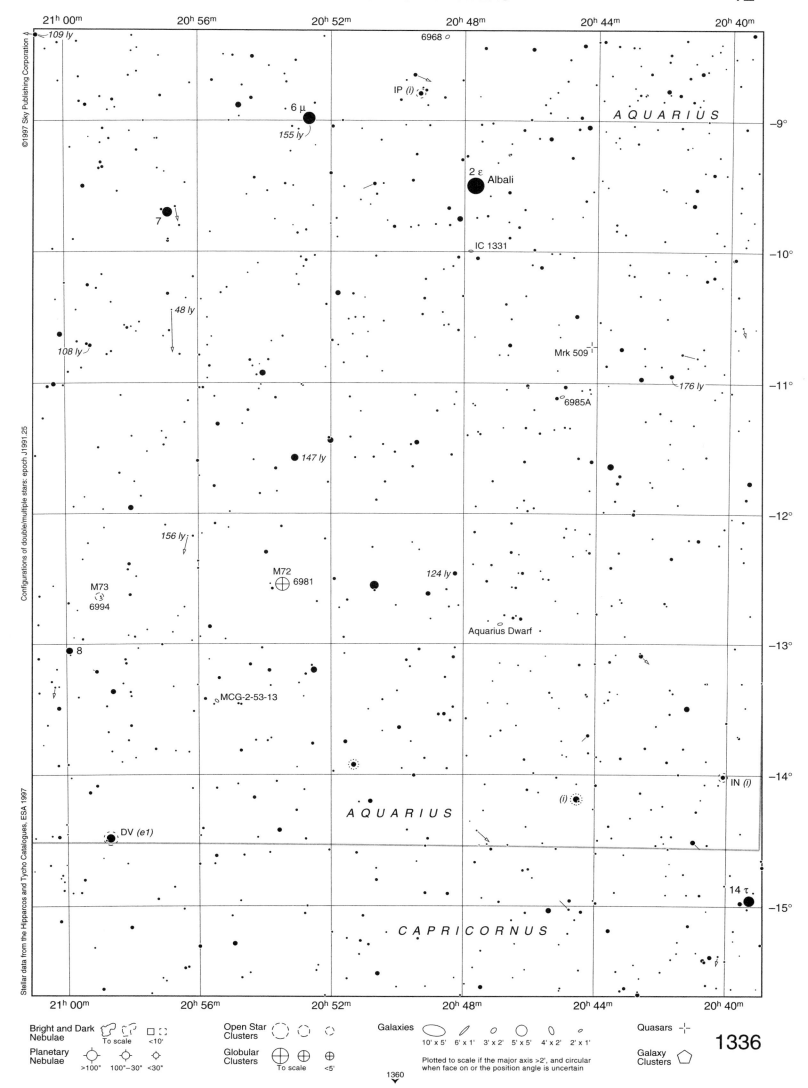
21h 00m          20h 56m          20h 52m          20h 48m          20h 44m          20h 40m

6968

IP (i)

AQUARIUS

−9°

6 μ

155 ly

2 ε   Albali

7

IC 1331

−10°

48 ly

Mrk 509

108 ly

176 ly

−11°

6985A

147 ly

−12°

156 ly

M72
6981

124 ly

M73
6994

Aquarius Dwarf

−13°

8

MCG-2-53-13

IN (i)

−14°

AQUARIUS

(i)

DV (e1)

14 τ

−15°

CAPRICORNUS

21h 00m          20h 56m          20h 52m          20h 48m          20h 44m          20h 40m

Bright and Dark
Nebulae
To scale    <10'

Open Star
Clusters

Galaxies

10' x 5'  6' x 1'  3' x 2'  5' x 5'  4' x 2'  2' x 1'

Quasars

Planetary
Nebulae
>100"  100"–30"  <30"

Globular
Clusters
To scale   <5'

Plotted to scale if the major axis >2', and circular
when face on or the position angle is uncertain

Galaxy
Clusters

1336

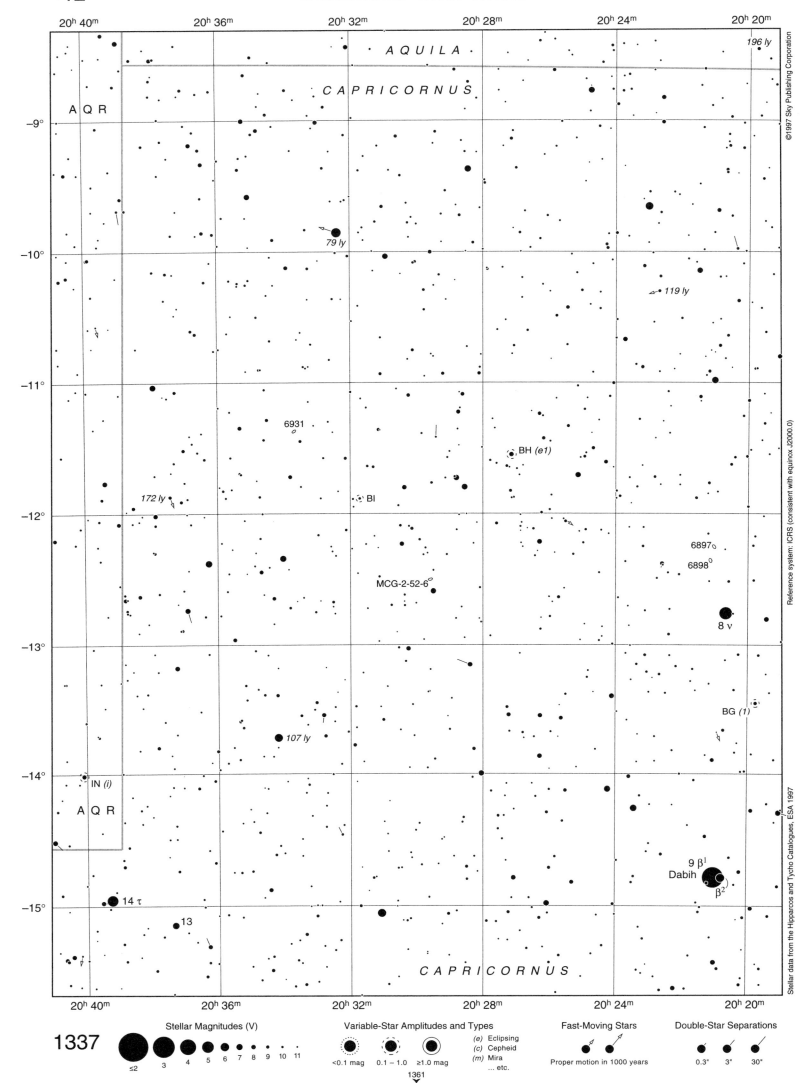

MILLENNIUM STAR ATLAS

AQUILA

CAPRICORNUS

196 ly

AQR

−9°

79 ly

−10°

119 ly

−11°

6931

BH (e1)

172 ly

BI

−12°

6897

6898

MCG-2-52-6

8 ν

−13°

BG (1)

107 ly

−14°

IN (i)

AQR

9 β¹

Dabih

β²

14 τ

−15°

13

CAPRICORNUS

20ʰ 40ᵐ   20ʰ 36ᵐ   20ʰ 32ᵐ   20ʰ 28ᵐ   20ʰ 24ᵐ   20ʰ 20ᵐ

©1997 Sky Publishing Corporation

Reference system: ICRS (consistent with equinox J2000.0)

Stellar data from the Hipparcos and Tycho Catalogues, ESA 1997

**1337**

Stellar Magnitudes (V)

≤2  3  4  5  6  7  8  9  10  11

Variable-Star Amplitudes and Types

<0.1 mag   0.1 − 1.0   ≥1.0 mag

(e) Eclipsing
(c) Cepheid
(m) Mira
... etc.

Fast-Moving Stars

Proper motion in 1000 years

Double-Star Separations

0.3"   3"   30"

1361

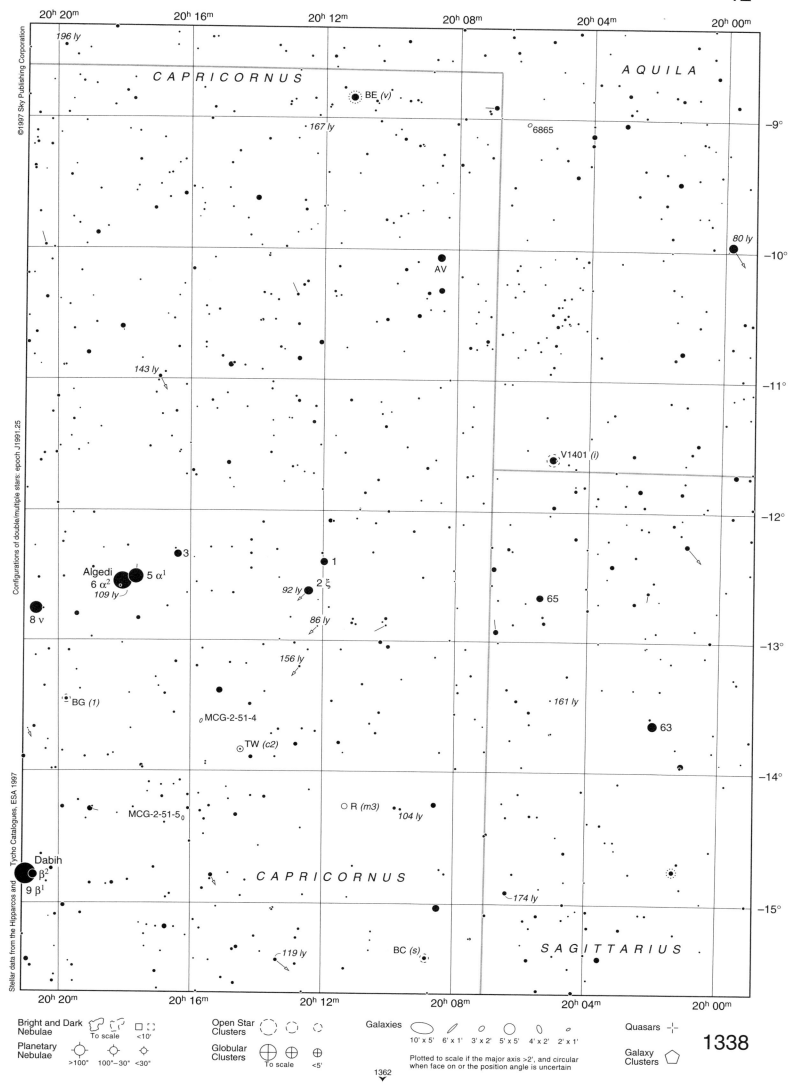

Configurations of double/multiple stars: epoch J1991.25

Stellar data from the Hipparcos and Tycho Catalogues, ESA 1997

C A P R I C O R N U S

A Q U I L A

BE (v)

196 ly

167 ly

6865

−9°

AV

80 ly

−10°

143 ly

−11°

V1401 (i)

−12°

3

1

Algedi
6 α²    5 α¹

2 ξ

65

109 ly

92 ly

8 ν

86 ly

−13°

156 ly

161 ly

BG (1)

MCG-2-51-4

63

TW (c2)

−14°

MCG-2-51-5

R (m3)

104 ly

Dabih
β²
9 β¹

C A P R I C O R N U S

174 ly

−15°

S A G I T T A R I U S

119 ly

BC (s)

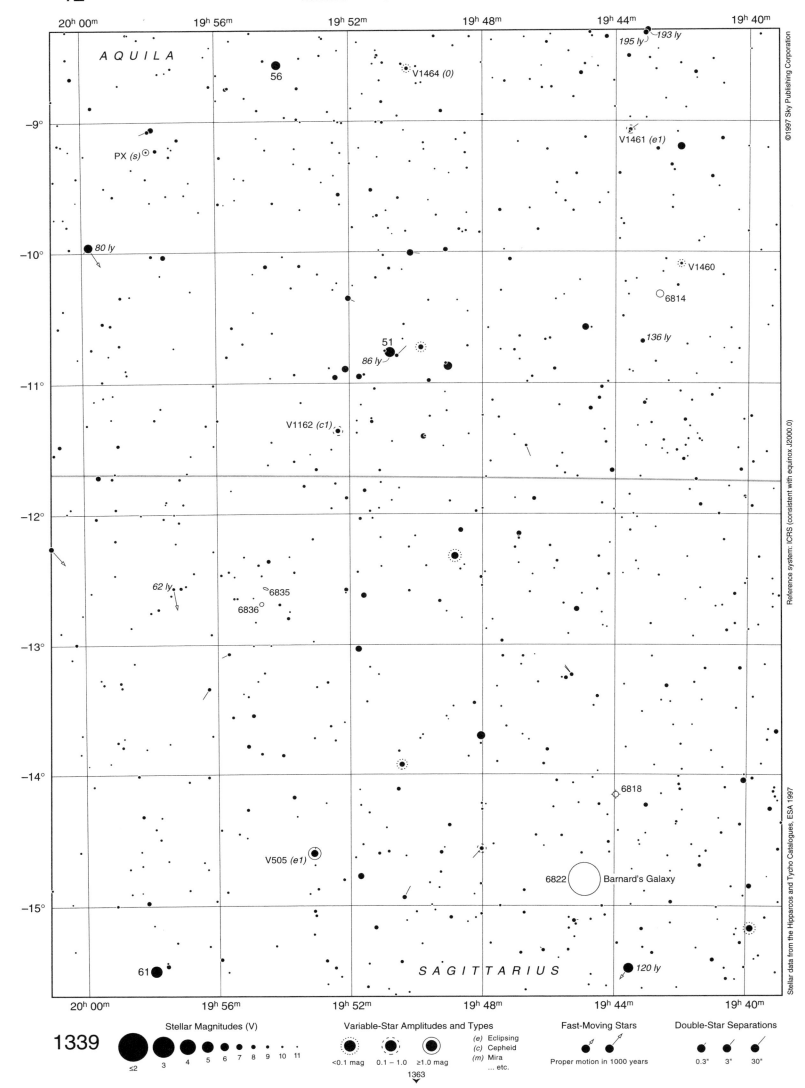

©1997 Sky Publishing Corporation

Reference system: ICRS (consistent with equinox J2000.0)

Stellar data from the Hipparcos and Tycho Catalogues, ESA 1997

Stellar Magnitudes (V)

≤2  3  4  5  6  7  8  9  10  11

Variable-Star Amplitudes and Types

<0.1 mag   0.1 – 1.0   ≥1.0 mag

(e) Eclipsing
(c) Cepheid
(m) Mira
... etc.

Fast-Moving Stars

Proper motion in 1000 years

Double-Star Separations

0.3"   3"   30"

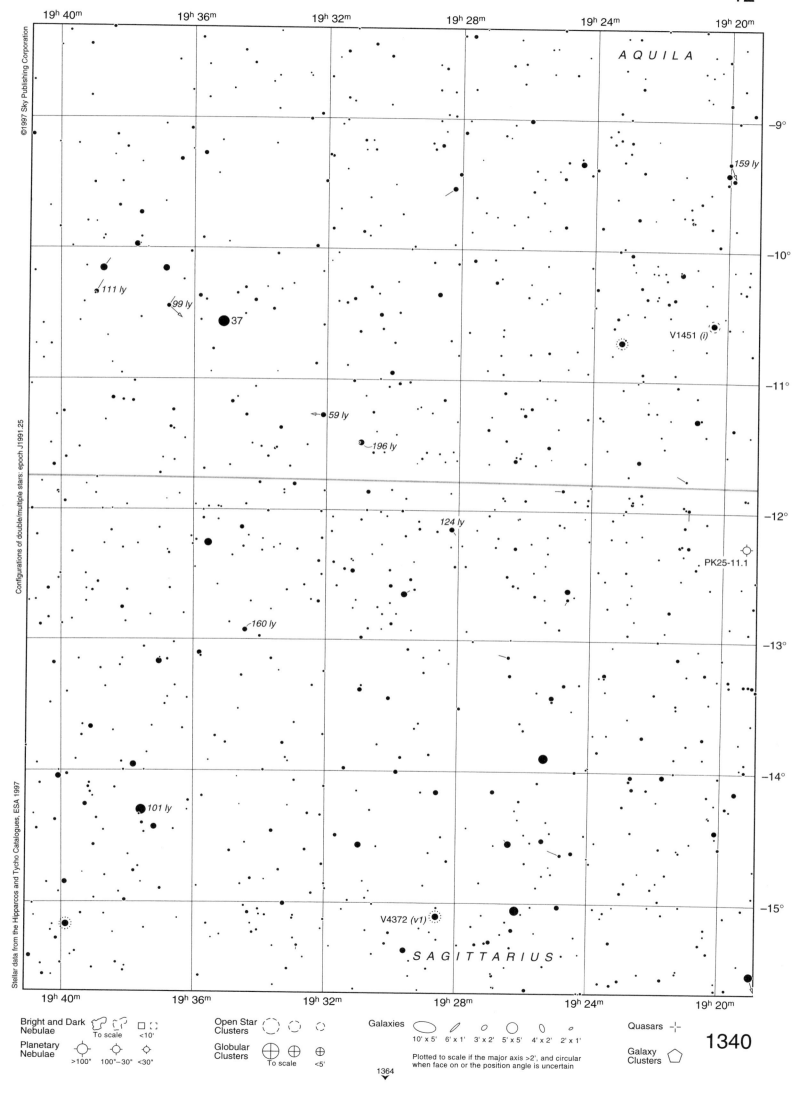

AQUILA

159 ly

111 ly

99 ly

37

V1451 (i)

59 ly

196 ly

124 ly

PK25-11.1

160 ly

101 ly

V4372 (v1)

SAGITTARIUS

Bright and Dark Nebulae
To scale    <10'

Planetary Nebulae
>100"    100"–30"    <30"

Open Star Clusters

Globular Clusters
To scale    <5'

Galaxies
10' x 5'    6' x 1'    3' x 2'    5' x 5'    4' x 2'    2' x 1'

Plotted to scale if the major axis >2', and circular when face on or the position angle is uncertain

Quasars

Galaxy Clusters

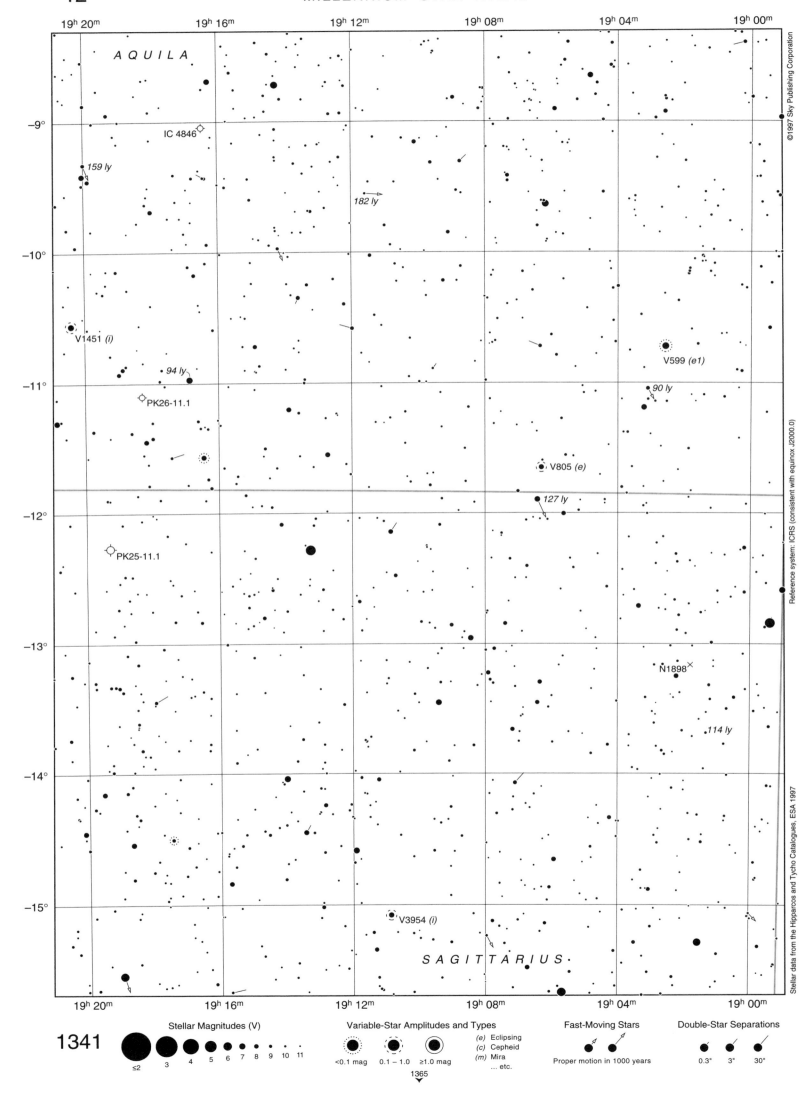

©1997 Sky Publishing Corporation

Reference system: ICRS (consistent with equinox J2000.0)

Stellar data from the Hipparcos and Tycho Catalogues, ESA 1997

1341

| Stellar Magnitudes (V) | Variable-Star Amplitudes and Types | Fast-Moving Stars | Double-Star Separations |
|---|---|---|---|

1365

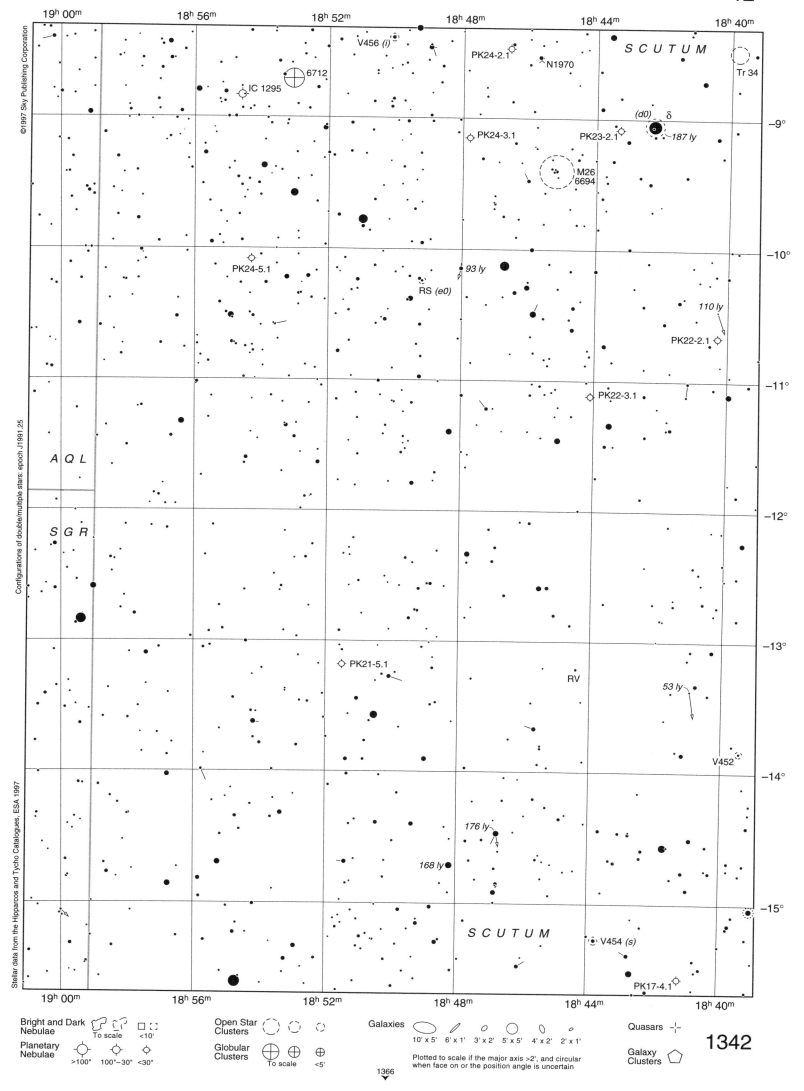

©1997 Sky Publishing Corporation

Configurations of double/multiple stars: epoch J1991.25

Stellar data from the Hipparcos and Tycho Catalogues, ESA 1997

19h 00m
18h 56m
18h 52m
18h 48m
18h 44m
18h 40m

−9°
−10°
−11°
−12°
−13°
−14°
−15°

SCUTUM
Tr 34
V456 (i)
PK24-2.1
N1970
6712
IC 1295
(d0)    δ
187 ly
PK24-3.1
PK23-2.1
M26
6694
PK24-5.1
93 ly
RS (e0)
110 ly
PK22-2.1
PK22-3.1
AQL
SGR
PK21-5.1
RV
53 ly
V452
176 ly
168 ly
SCUTUM
V454 (s)
PK17-4.1

Bright and Dark
Nebulae
To scale    <10'

Planetary
Nebulae
>100"    100"–30"    <30"

Open Star
Clusters

Globular
Clusters
To scale    <5'

Galaxies
10' x 5'    6' x 1'    3' x 2'    5' x 5'    4' x 2'    2' x 1'
Plotted to scale if the major axis >2', and circular
when face on or the position angle is uncertain

Quasars

Galaxy
Clusters

1342

1366

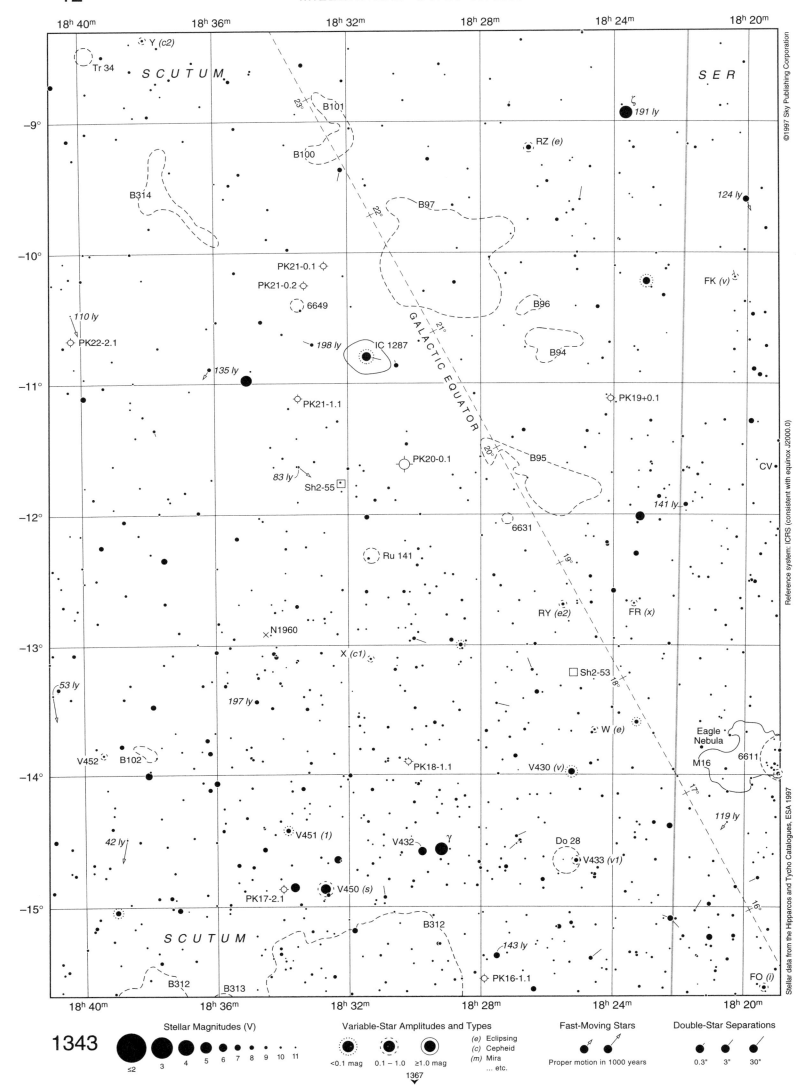

©1997 Sky Publishing Corporation

Reference system: ICRS (consistent with equinox J2000.0)

Stellar data from the Hipparcos and Tycho Catalogues, ESA 1997

1343

Stellar Magnitudes (V)

≤2   3   4   5   6   7   8   9   10   11

Variable-Star Amplitudes and Types

<0.1 mag   0.1 – 1.0   ≥1.0 mag

(e) Eclipsing
(c) Cepheid
(m) Mira
... etc.

Fast-Moving Stars

Proper motion in 1000 years

Double-Star Separations

0.3"   3"   30"

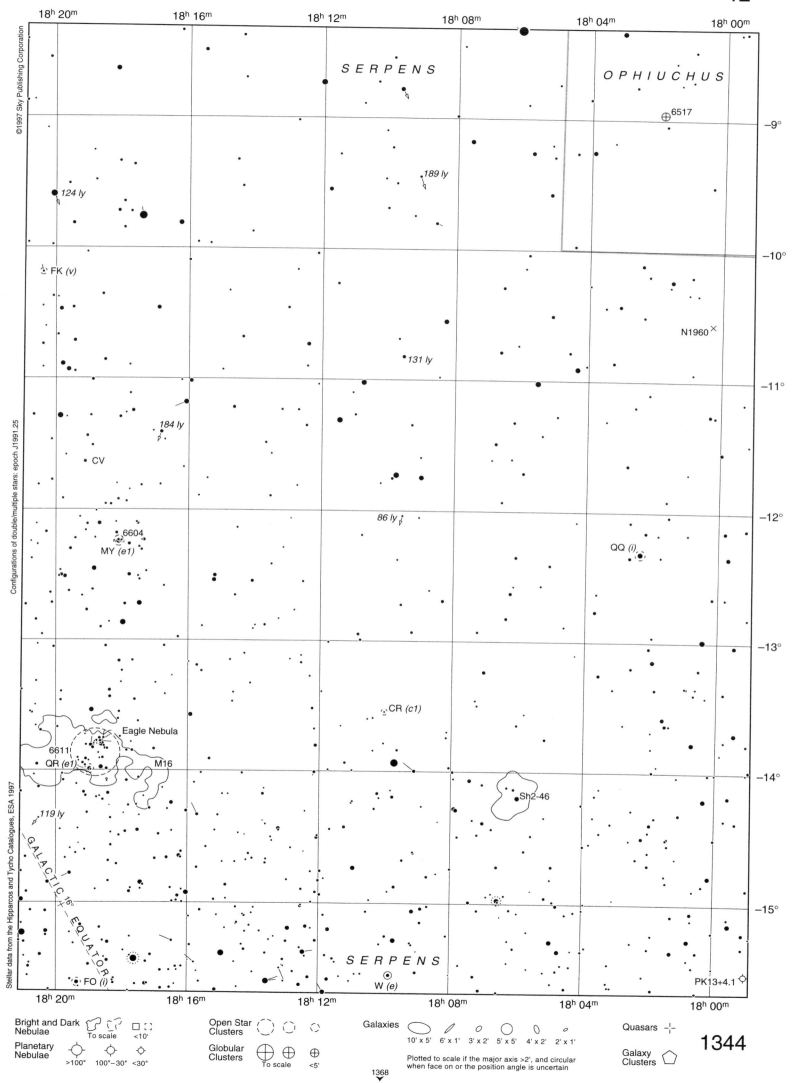

©1997 Sky Publishing Corporation

Configurations of double/multiple stars: epoch J1991.25

Stellar data from the Hipparcos and Tycho Catalogues, ESA 1997

18h 20m  18h 16m  18h 12m  18h 08m  18h 04m  18h 00m

SERPENS

OPHIUCHUS

⊕ 6517  −9°

189 ly

124 ly

FK (v)  −10°

N1960 ×

131 ly

−11°

184 ly

CV

86 ly  −12°

6604
MY (e1)

QQ (i)

−13°

CR (c1)

Eagle Nebula

6611
QR (e1)  M16  −14°

Sh2-46

119 ly

GALACTIC 16° EQUATOR

−15°

SERPENS

FO (i)  W (e)  PK13+4.1

18h 20m  18h 16m  18h 12m  18h 08m  18h 04m  18h 00m

Bright and Dark
Nebulae
To scale  <10'

Open Star
Clusters

Galaxies

10' x 5'  6' x 1'  3' x 2'  5' x 5'  4' x 2'  2' x 1'

Quasars

Planetary
Nebulae
>100"  100"−30"  <30"

Globular
Clusters
To scale  <5'

Galaxy
Clusters

Plotted to scale if the major axis >2', and circular
when face on or the position angle is uncertain

1344

1368

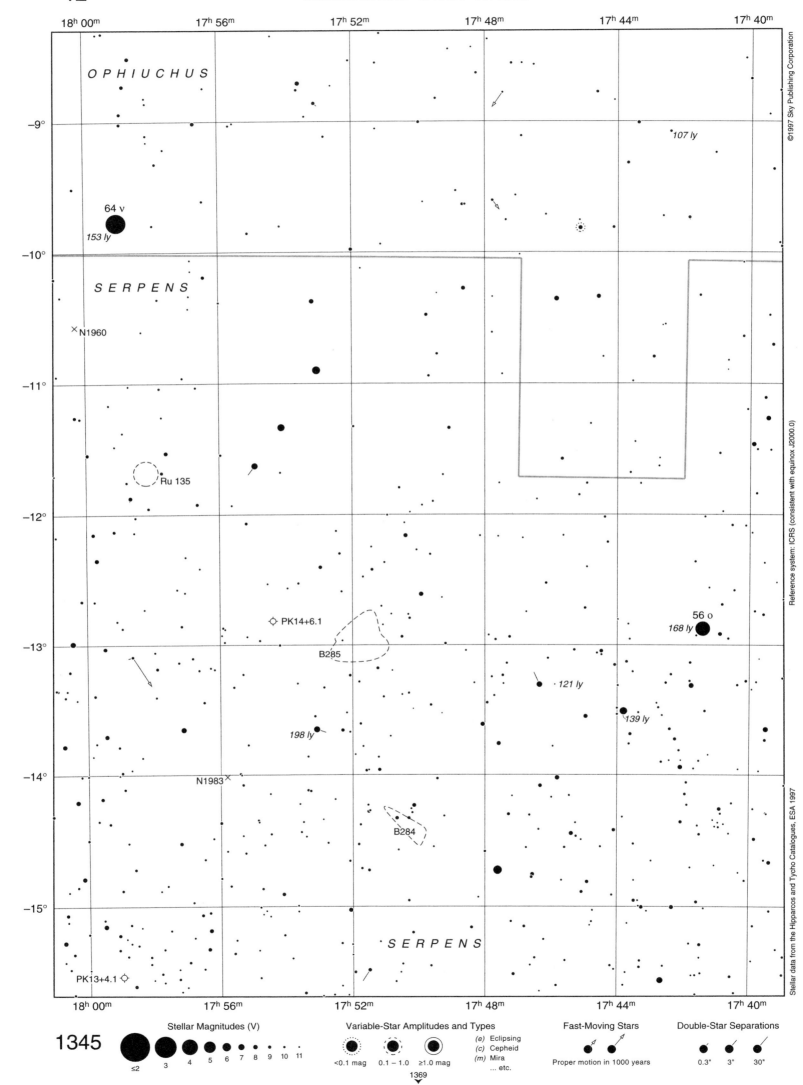

©1997 Sky Publishing Corporation

Reference system: ICRS (consistent with equinox J2000.0)

Stellar data from the Hipparcos and Tycho Catalogues, ESA 1997

1345

Stellar Magnitudes (V)

≤2   3   4   5   6   7   8   9   10   11

Variable-Star Amplitudes and Types

<0.1 mag    0.1 – 1.0    ≥1.0 mag

(e) Eclipsing
(c) Cepheid
(m) Mira
... etc.

Fast-Moving Stars

Proper motion in 1000 years

Double-Star Separations

0.3"   3"   30"

# MILLENNIUM STAR ATLAS

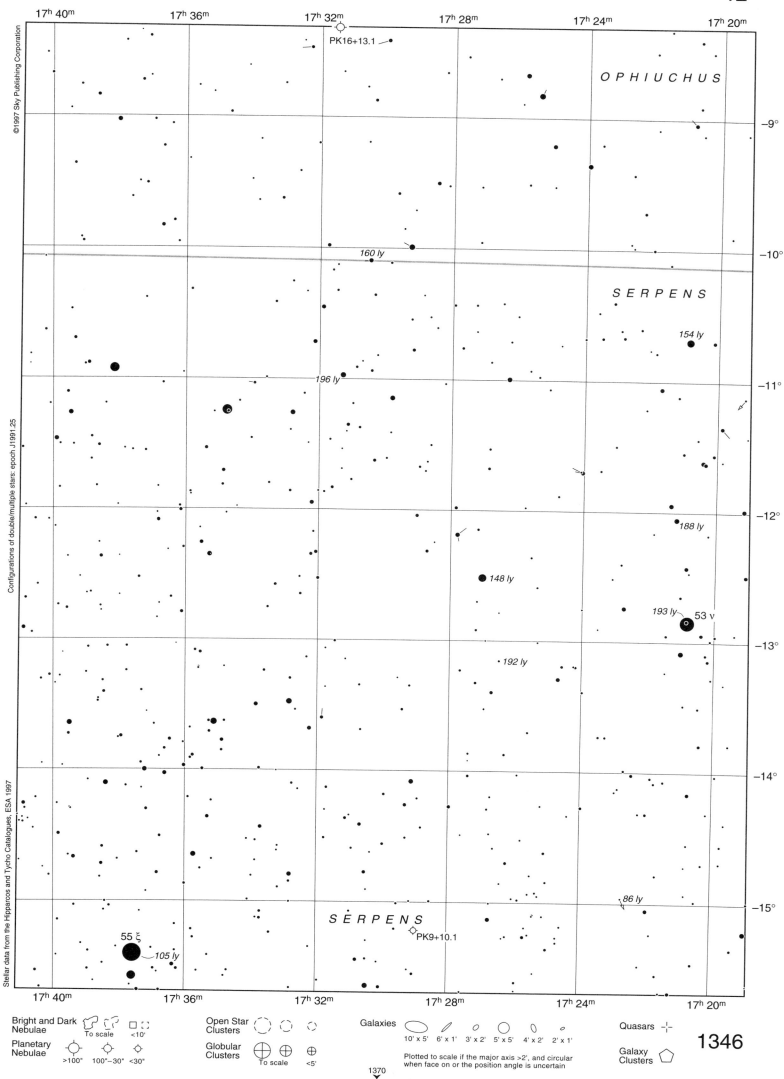

17h 40m   17h 36m   17h 32m   17h 28m   17h 24m   17h 20m

PK16+13.1

O P H I U C H U S

−9°

160 ly

−10°

S E R P E N S

154 ly

196 ly

−11°

−12°

188 ly

148 ly

193 ly   53 ν

−13°

192 ly

−14°

86 ly

−15°

S E R P E N S

PK9+10.1

55 ξ

105 ly

17h 40m   17h 36m   17h 32m   17h 28m   17h 24m   17h 20m

Bright and Dark Nebulae    To scale   <10'

Planetary Nebulae    >100"   100"–30"   <30"

Open Star Clusters

Globular Clusters    To scale   <5'

Galaxies    10' x 5'   6' x 1'   3' x 2'   5' x 5'   4' x 2'   2' x 1'

Plotted to scale if the major axis >2', and circular when face on or the position angle is uncertain

Quasars

Galaxy Clusters

**1346**

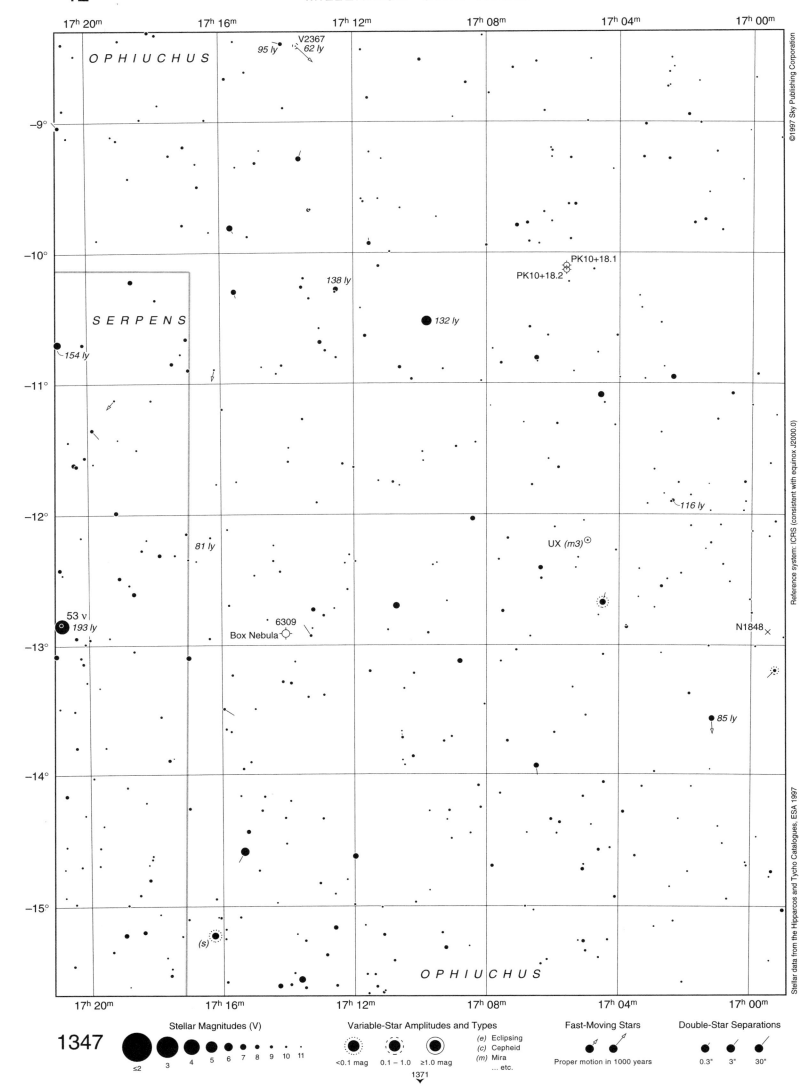

OPHIUCHUS

SERPENS

OPHIUCHUS

V2367
95 ly    62 ly

138 ly

132 ly

PK10+18.1
PK10+18.2

154 ly

116 ly

UX (m3)

81 ly

N1848

53 v
193 ly

6309
Box Nebula

85 ly

(s)

©1997 Sky Publishing Corporation

Reference system: ICRS (consistent with equinox J2000.0)

Stellar data from the Hipparcos and Tycho Catalogues, ESA 1997

**1347**

| Stellar Magnitudes (V) | Variable-Star Amplitudes and Types | Fast-Moving Stars | Double-Star Separations |
|---|---|---|---|
| ≤2  3  4  5  6 7 8 9 10 11 | <0.1 mag   0.1 – 1.0   ≥1.0 mag | Proper motion in 1000 years | 0.3"  3"  30" |

(e) Eclipsing
(c) Cepheid
(m) Mira
... etc.

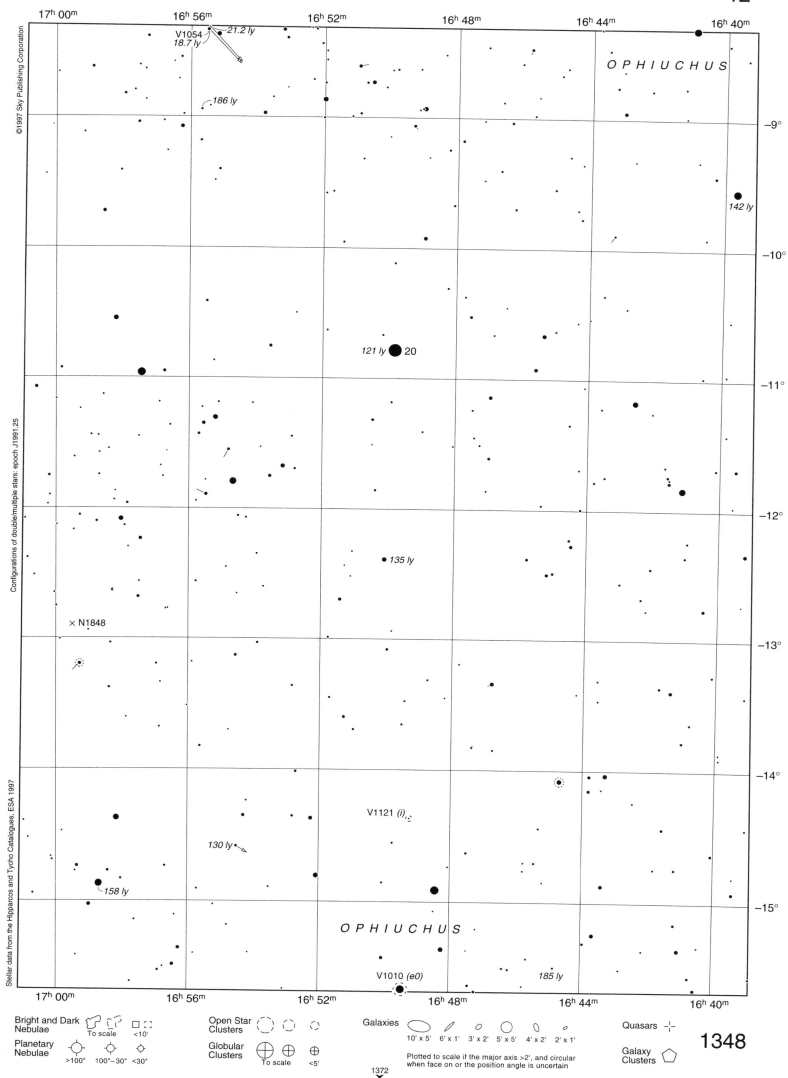

OPHIUCHUS

V1054
18.7 ly
21.2 ly
186 ly
142 ly

−9°

−10°

121 ly ● 20

−11°

135 ly

× N1848

−12°

−13°

V1121 (i)

130 ly

−14°

158 ly

OPHIUCHUS

V1010 (e0)
185 ly

−15°

Configurations of double/multiple stars: epoch J1991.25

Stellar data from the Hipparcos and Tycho Catalogues, ESA 1997

| Bright and Dark Nebulae | | | Open Star Clusters | | | Galaxies | | | | | | Quasars |
|---|---|---|---|---|---|---|---|---|---|---|---|---|
| To scale | <10' | | | | | 10' x 5' | 6' x 1' | 3' x 2' | 5' x 5' | 4' x 2' | 2' x 1' | |

| Planetary Nebulae | | | Globular Clusters | | | | | | Galaxy Clusters |
|---|---|---|---|---|---|---|---|---|---|
| >100" | 100"–30" | <30" | | To scale | <5' | | | | |

Plotted to scale if the major axis >2', and circular when face on or the position angle is uncertain

1348

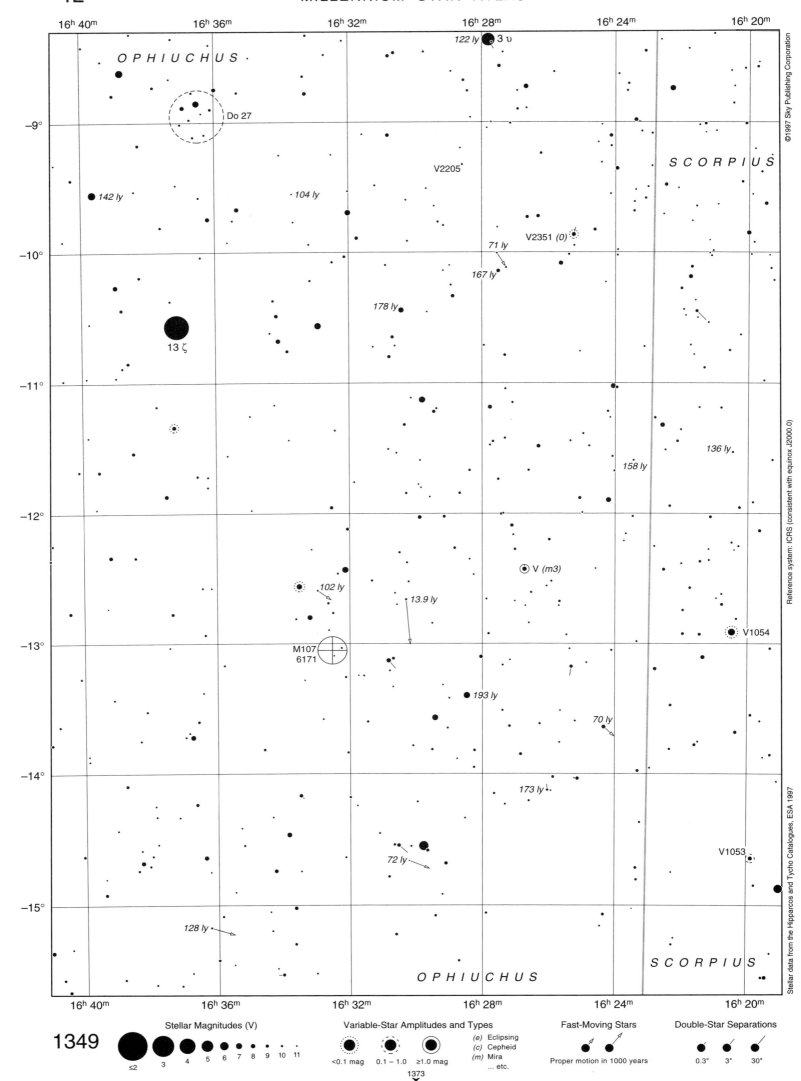

©1997 Sky Publishing Corporation

Reference system: ICRS (consistent with equinox J2000.0)

Stellar data from the Hipparcos and Tycho Catalogues, ESA 1997

1349

Stellar Magnitudes (V)

≤2   3   4   5   6   7   8   9   10   11

Variable-Star Amplitudes and Types

<0.1 mag    0.1 – 1.0    ≥1.0 mag

(e) Eclipsing
(c) Cepheid
(m) Mira
... etc.

Fast-Moving Stars

Proper motion in 1000 years

Double-Star Separations

0.3"    3"    30"

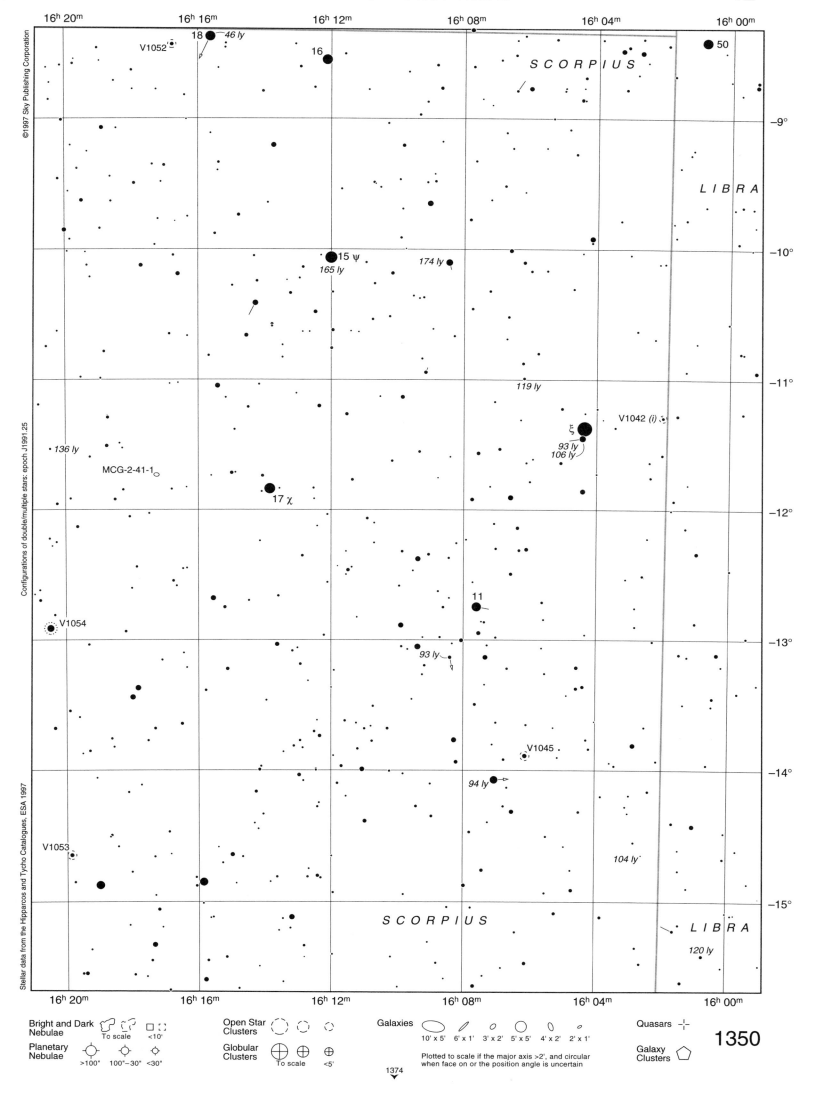

16h 20m   16h 16m   16h 12m   16h 08m   16h 04m   16h 00m

−9°

−10°

−11°

−12°

−13°

−14°

−15°

S C O R P I U S

L I B R A

V1052    18    46 ly
16    50

15 ψ    174 ly
165 ly

119 ly

136 ly    ξ    V1042 (i)
93 ly
106 ly

MCG-2-41-1

17 χ

11

V1054

93 ly

V1045

94 ly

V1053

104 ly

S C O R P I U S    L I B R A

120 ly

Bright and Dark Nebulae    To scale    <10'

Planetary Nebulae    >100"   100"−30"   <30"

Open Star Clusters

Globular Clusters    To scale    <5'

Galaxies    10' x 5'   6' x 1'   3' x 2'   5' x 5'   4' x 2'   2' x 1'

Plotted to scale if the major axis >2', and circular when face on or the position angle is uncertain

Quasars

Galaxy Clusters

1350

1374

−18°

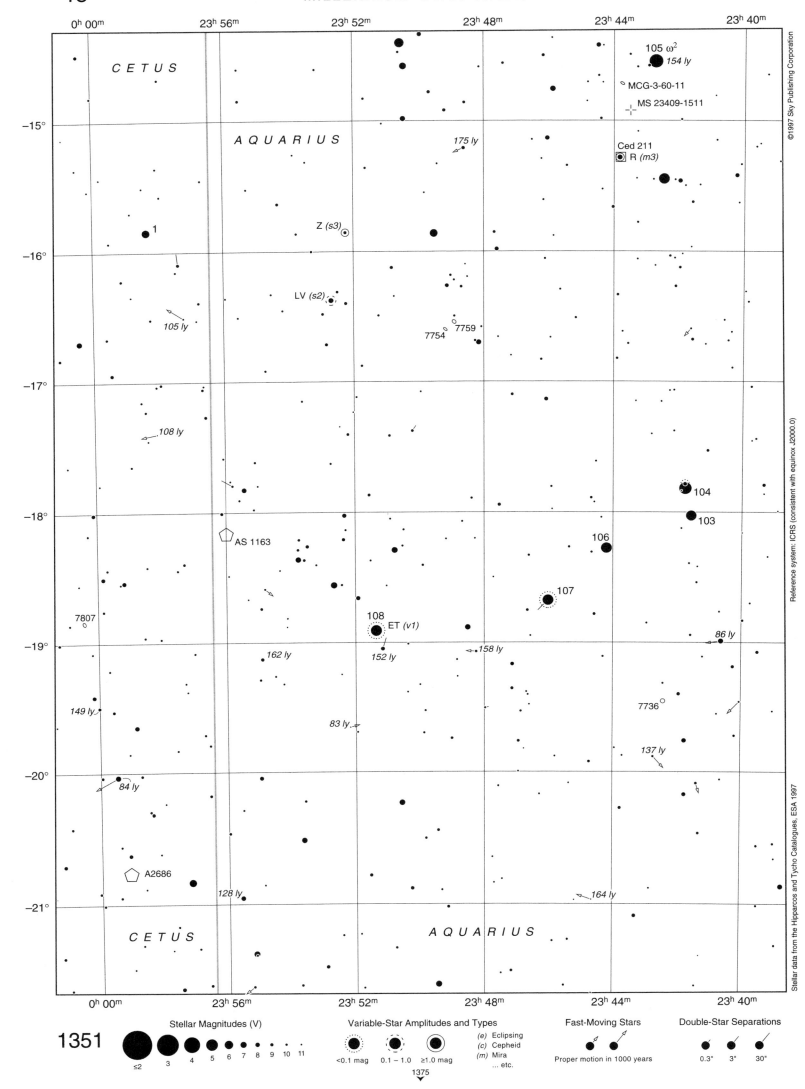

CETUS

AQUARIUS

105 ω²
*154 ly*

MCG-3-60-11

MS 23409-1511

*175 ly*

Ced 211
R *(m3)*

1

Z *(s3)*

LV *(s2)*

*105 ly*

7759
7754

*108 ly*

104

103

AS 1163

106

107

7807

108
ET *(v1)*

*86 ly*

*162 ly*
*152 ly*
*158 ly*

7736

*149 ly*

*83 ly*

*137 ly*

*84 ly*

A2686

*128 ly*

*164 ly*

CETUS

AQUARIUS

©1997 Sky Publishing Corporation

Reference system: ICRS (consistent with equinox J2000.0)

Stellar data from the Hipparcos and Tycho Catalogues, ESA 1997

1351

Stellar Magnitudes (V)

≤2  3  4  5  6  7  8  9  10  11

Variable-Star Amplitudes and Types

<0.1 mag   0.1 – 1.0   ≥1.0 mag

*(e)* Eclipsing
*(c)* Cepheid
*(m)* Mira
... etc.

1375

Fast-Moving Stars

Proper motion in 1000 years

Double-Star Separations

0.3"   3"   30"

# MILLENNIUM STAR ATLAS

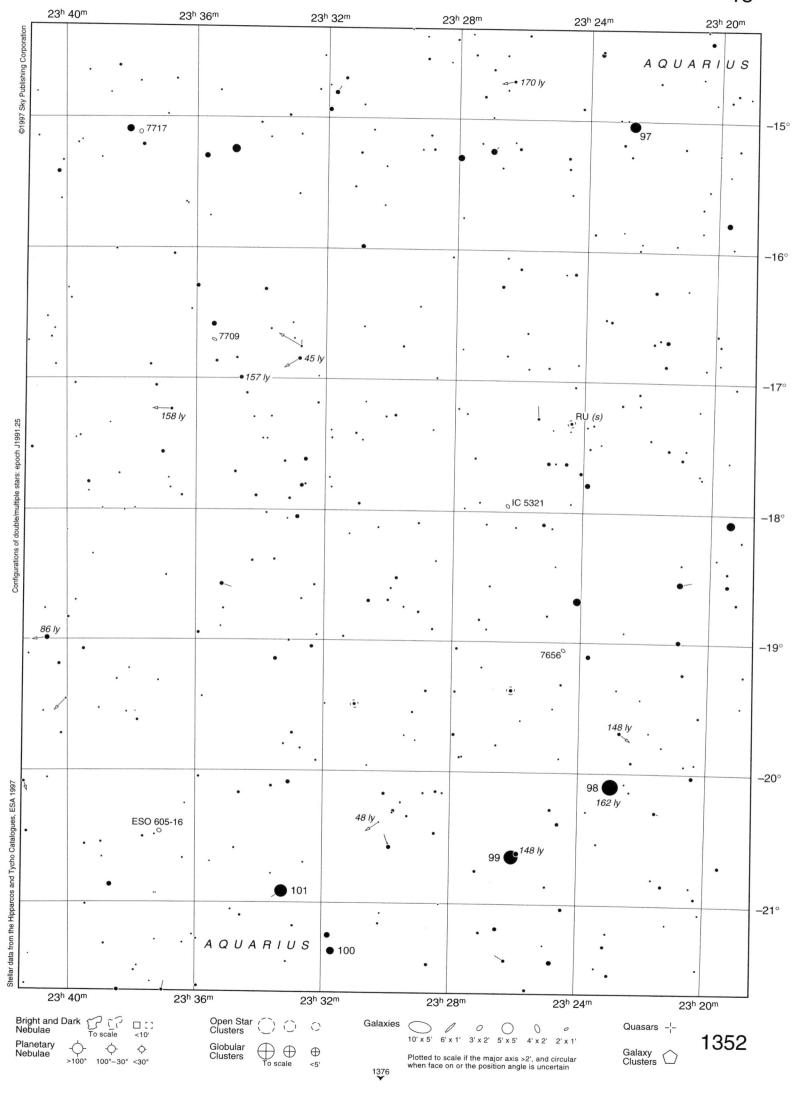

©1997 Sky Publishing Corporation

Configurations of double/multiple stars: epoch J1991.25

Stellar data from the Hipparcos and Tycho Catalogues, ESA 1997

AQUARIUS

170 ly

7717

97

7709

45 ly

157 ly

158 ly

RU (s)

IC 5321

86 ly

7656

148 ly

98
162 ly

ESO 605-16

48 ly

99   148 ly

101

AQUARIUS   100

| | 23h 40m | 23h 36m | 23h 32m | 23h 28m | 23h 24m | 23h 20m |

−15°
−16°
−17°
−18°
−19°
−20°
−21°

| Bright and Dark Nebulae | | To scale | <10' | Open Star Clusters | | | Galaxies | | | | | | Quasars |
| Planetary Nebulae | >100" | 100"−30" | <30" | Globular Clusters | To scale | <5' | 10' x 5' | 6' x 1' | 3' x 2' | 5' x 5' | 4' x 2' | 2' x 1' | Galaxy Clusters |

Plotted to scale if the major axis >2', and circular when face on or the position angle is uncertain

1352

−18°  MILLENNIUM STAR ATLAS

©1997 Sky Publishing Corporation

Reference system: ICRS (consistent with equinox J2000.0)

Stellar data from the Hipparcos and Tycho Catalogues, ESA 1997

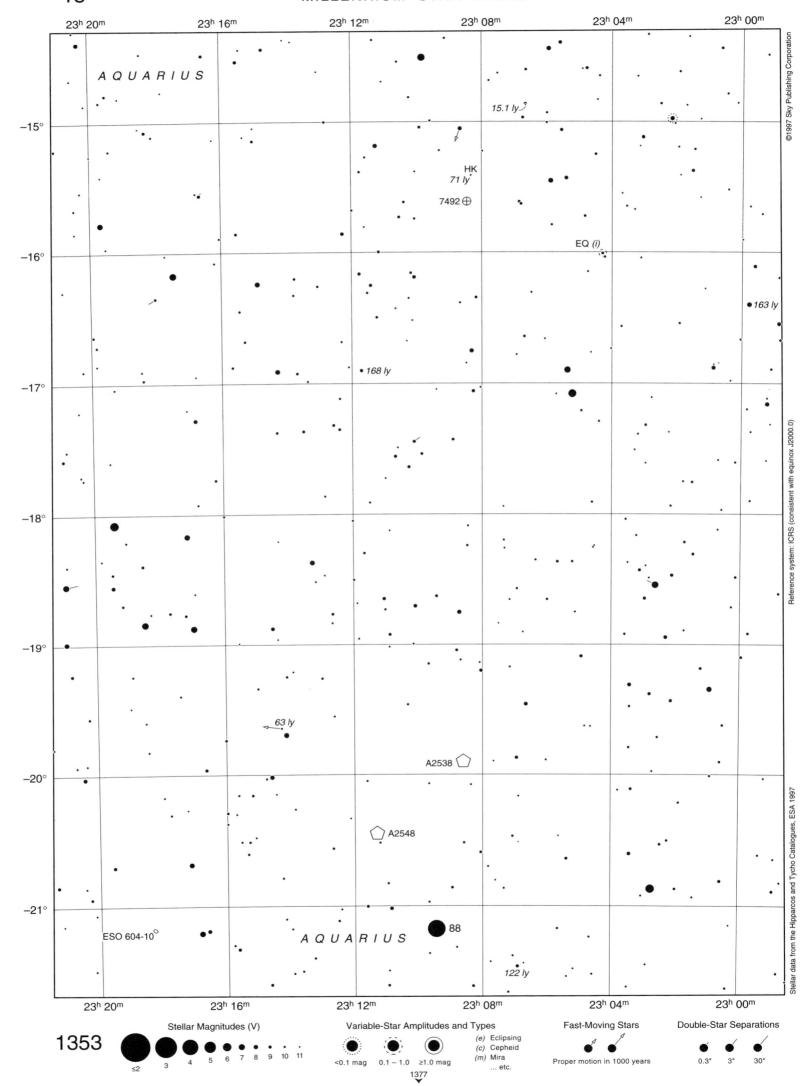

AQUARIUS

15.1 ly

HK
71 ly

7492 ⊕

EQ (i)

163 ly

168 ly

63 ly

A2538

A2548

ESO 604-10

AQUARIUS    88

122 ly

1353

**Stellar Magnitudes (V)**
≤2  3  4  5  6  7  8  9  10  11

**Variable-Star Amplitudes and Types**
<0.1 mag   0.1 − 1.0   ≥1.0 mag

(e) Eclipsing
(c) Cepheid
(m) Mira
... etc.

**Fast-Moving Stars**
Proper motion in 1000 years

**Double-Star Separations**
0.3"  3"  30"

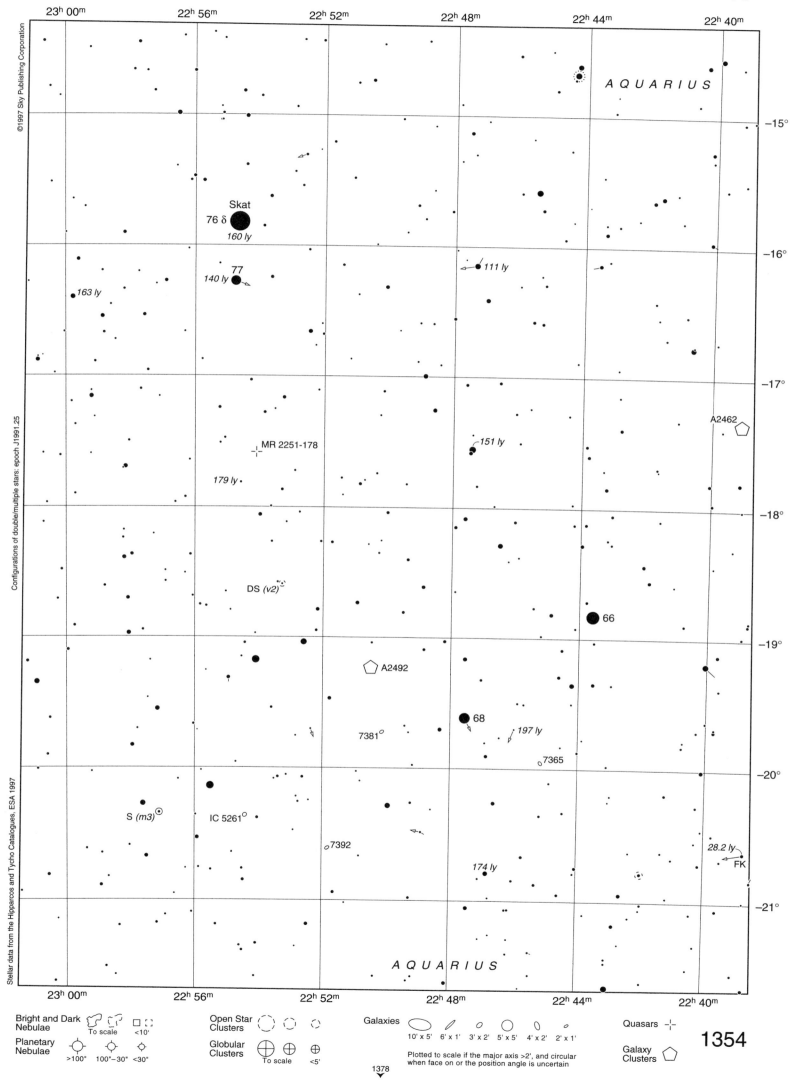

23h 00m 22h 56m 22h 52m 22h 48m 22h 44m 22h 40m

−15°
−16°
−17°
−18°
−19°
−20°
−21°

*AQUARIUS*

Skat
76 δ
*160 ly*

*163 ly*

140 ly 77

111 ly

A2462

MR 2251-178

*151 ly*

*179 ly*

DS *(v2)*

66

A2492

68
7381

*197 ly*

7365

S *(m3)*
IC 5261

7392

174 ly

*28.2 ly*
FK

*AQUARIUS*

23h 00m 22h 56m 22h 52m 22h 48m 22h 44m 22h 40m

| Bright and Dark Nebulae | | | | Open Star Clusters | | | Galaxies | | | | | | Quasars | |
|---|---|---|---|---|---|---|---|---|---|---|---|---|---|---|
| To scale | | <10' | | | | | 10' x 5' | 6' x 1' | 3' x 2' | 5' x 5' | 4' x 2' | 2' x 1' | | |

Planetary Nebulae
>100" 100"–30" <30"

Globular Clusters
To scale <5'

Galaxies
Plotted to scale if the major axis >2', and circular when face on or the position angle is uncertain

Galaxy Clusters

1354

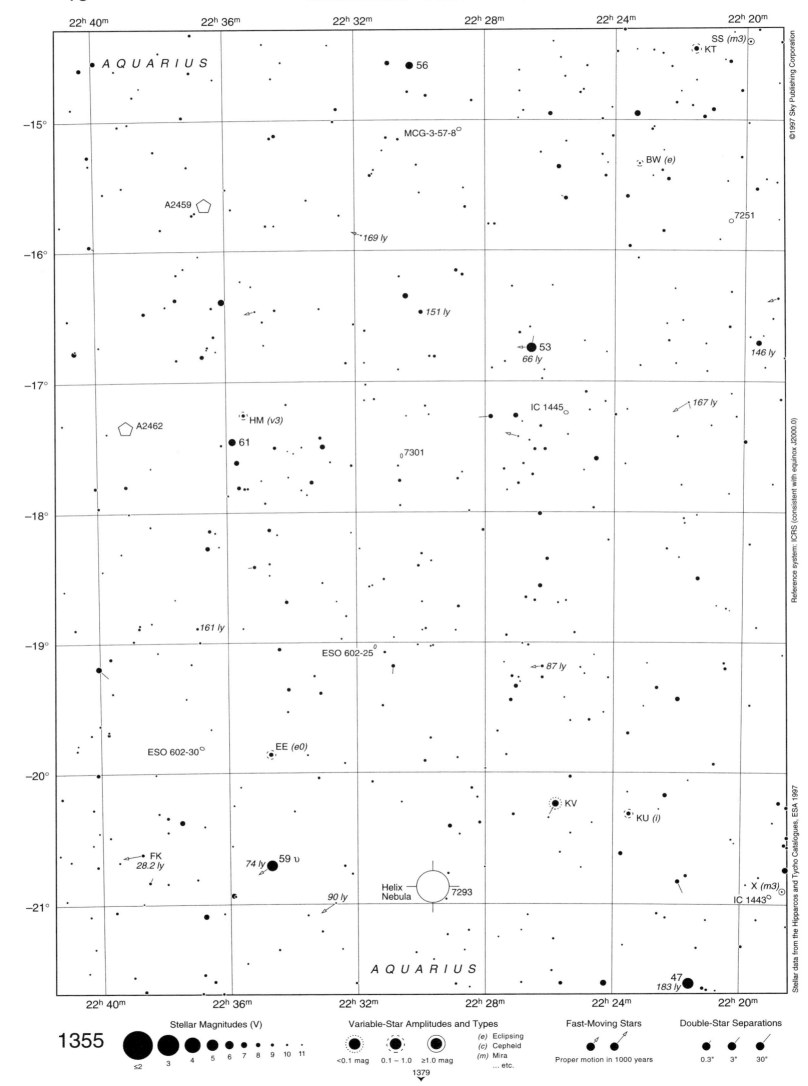

A Q U A R I U S

56

MCG-3-57-8

A2459

169 ly

151 ly

53
66 ly

146 ly

IC 1445

167 ly

HM (v3)

A2462

61

7301

SS (m3)
KT

BW (e)

7251

161 ly

ESO 602-25

87 ly

ESO 602-30

EE (e0)

KV

KU (i)

FK
28.2 ly

74 ly  59 υ

Helix
Nebula  7293

X (m3)
IC 1443

90 ly

A Q U A R I U S

47
183 ly

©1997 Sky Publishing Corporation

Reference system: ICRS (consistent with equinox J2000.0)

Stellar data from the Hipparcos and Tycho Catalogues, ESA 1997

Stellar Magnitudes (V)
≤2  3  4  5  6  7  8  9  10  11

Variable-Star Amplitudes and Types
<0.1 mag   0.1 – 1.0   ≥1.0 mag

(e) Eclipsing
(c) Cepheid
(m) Mira
... etc.

1379

Fast-Moving Stars
Proper motion in 1000 years

Double-Star Separations
0.3"  3"  30"

# MILLENNIUM STAR ATLAS

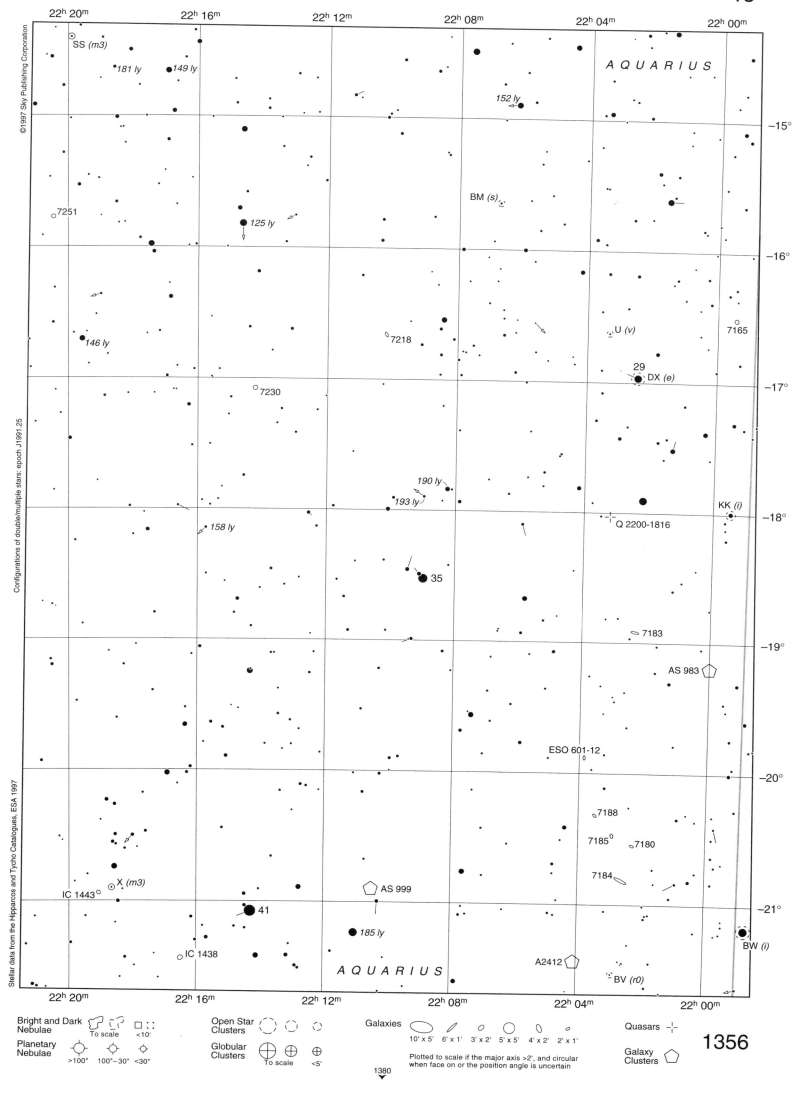

22h 20m    22h 16m    22h 12m    22h 08m    22h 04m    22h 00m

SS (m3)

A Q U A R I U S

181 ly    149 ly

152 ly

−15°

7251

BM (s)

125 ly

−16°

146 ly    7218    U (v)    7165

7230    29 DX (e)    −17°

190 ly
193 ly    KK (i)

158 ly    Q 2200-1816    −18°

35

7183    −19°

AS 983

ESO 601-12

−20°

7188
7185    7180

7184

X (m3)
IC 1443    AS 999    −21°

41    185 ly    BW (i)

IC 1438    A2412
A Q U A R I U S    BV (r0)

22h 20m    22h 16m    22h 12m    22h 08m    22h 04m    22h 00m

Bright and Dark Nebulae    To scale    <10'    Open Star Clusters    Galaxies    10' x 5'  6' x 1'  3' x 2'  5' x 5'  4' x 2'  2' x 1'    Quasars

Planetary Nebulae    >100"  100"−30"  <30"    Globular Clusters    To scale    <5'    Plotted to scale if the major axis >2', and circular when face on or the position angle is uncertain    Galaxy Clusters

1380

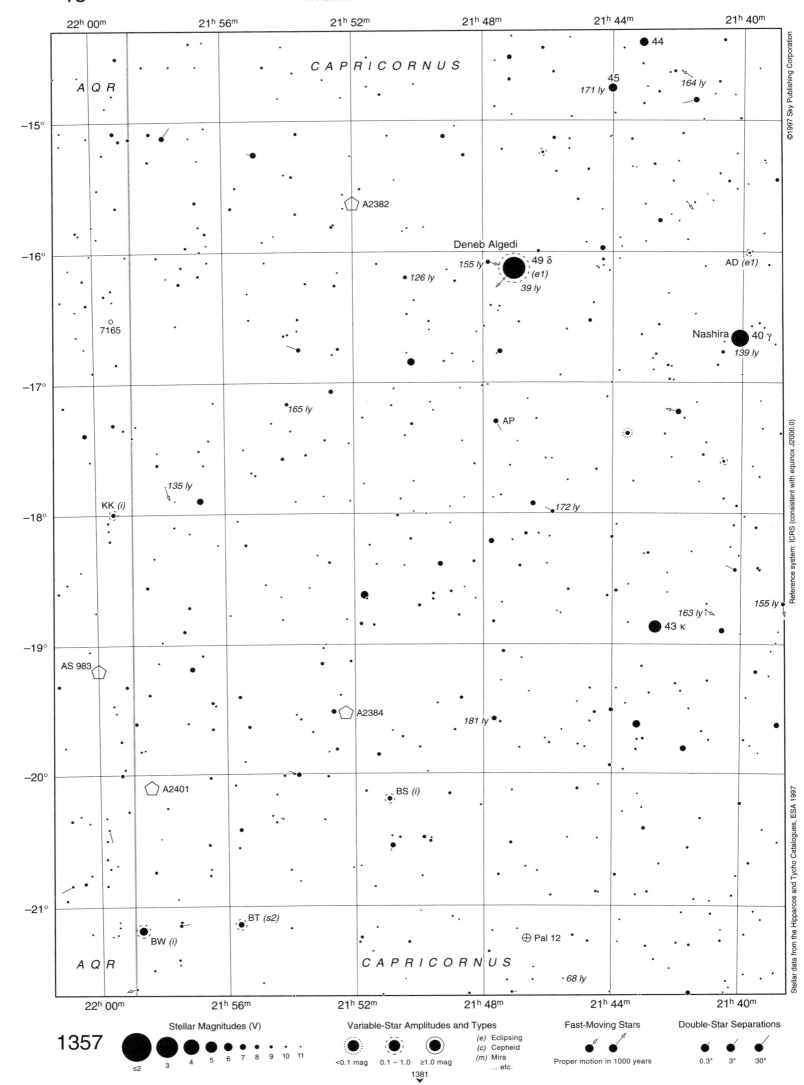

*C A P R I C O R N U S*

*A Q R*

44

45

*171 ly*

*164 ly*

A2382

Deneb Algedi

*155 ly*

49 δ
*(e1)*

*126 ly*

*39 ly*

AD *(e1)*

Nashira

40 γ

*139 ly*

○ 7165

*165 ly*

AP

*135 ly*

*172 ly*

KK *(i)*

43 κ

*163 ly*

*155 ly*

AS 983

A2384

*181 ly*

A2401

BS *(i)*

BT *(s2)*

⊕ Pal 12

BW *(i)*

*A Q R*

*C A P R I C O R N U S*

*68 ly*

**Stellar Magnitudes (V)**

≤2  3  4  5  6  7  8  9  10  11

**Variable-Star Amplitudes and Types**

<0.1 mag   0.1 – 1.0   ≥1.0 mag

*(e)* Eclipsing
*(c)* Cepheid
*(m)* Mira
... etc.

**Fast-Moving Stars**

Proper motion in 1000 years

**Double-Star Separations**

0.3"  3"  30"

1381

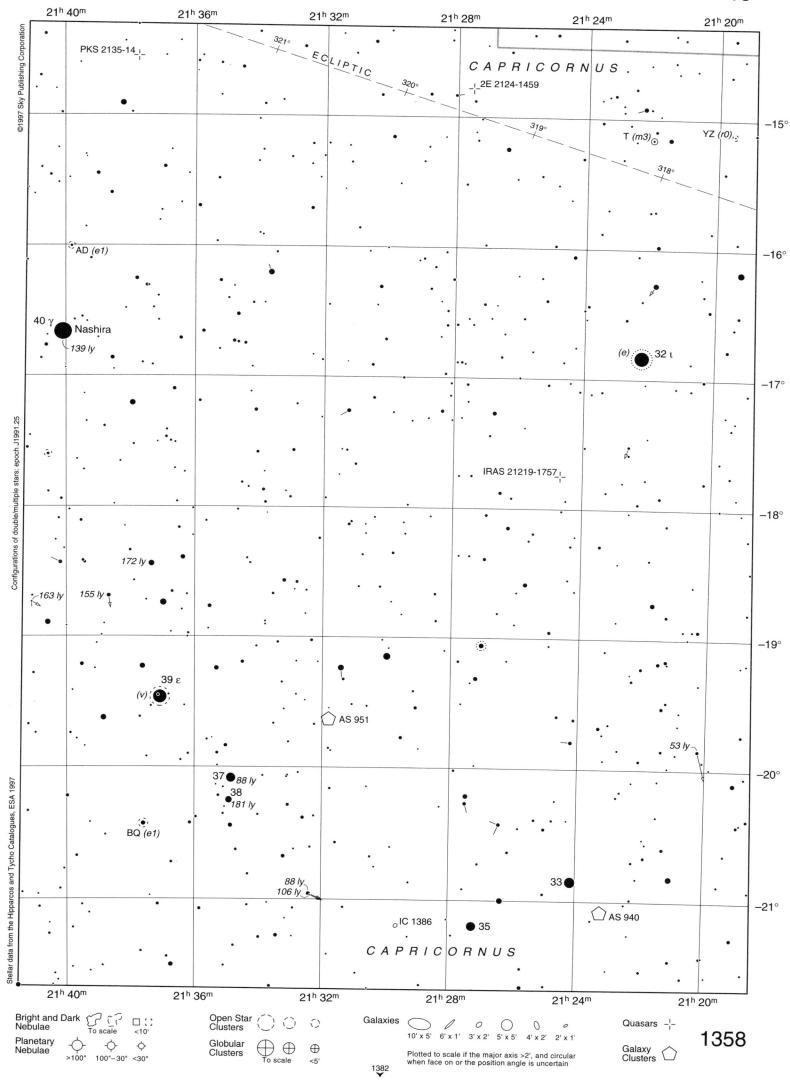

PKS 2135-14

ECLIPTIC
321°
320°
319°
318°

CAPRICORNUS

2E 2124-1459

T (m3)
YZ (r0)

AD (e1)

40 γ  Nashira
139 ly

(e) 32 ι

IRAS 21219-1757

172 ly

163 ly  155 ly

39 ε
(v)

AS 951

37  88 ly
38
181 ly

BQ (e1)

53 ly

88 ly
106 ly

33

IC 1386  35

AS 940

CAPRICORNUS

21h 40m  21h 36m  21h 32m  21h 28m  21h 24m  21h 20m

−15°
−16°
−17°
−18°
−19°
−20°
−21°

Bright and Dark
Nebulae
To scale
<10'

Planetary
Nebulae
>100"  100"−30"  <30"

Open Star
Clusters

Globular
Clusters
To scale
<5'

Galaxies
10' x 5'  6' x 1'  3' x 2'  5' x 5'  4' x 2'  2' x 1'

Plotted to scale if the major axis >2', and circular
when face on or the position angle is uncertain

Quasars

Galaxy
Clusters

1358

1382

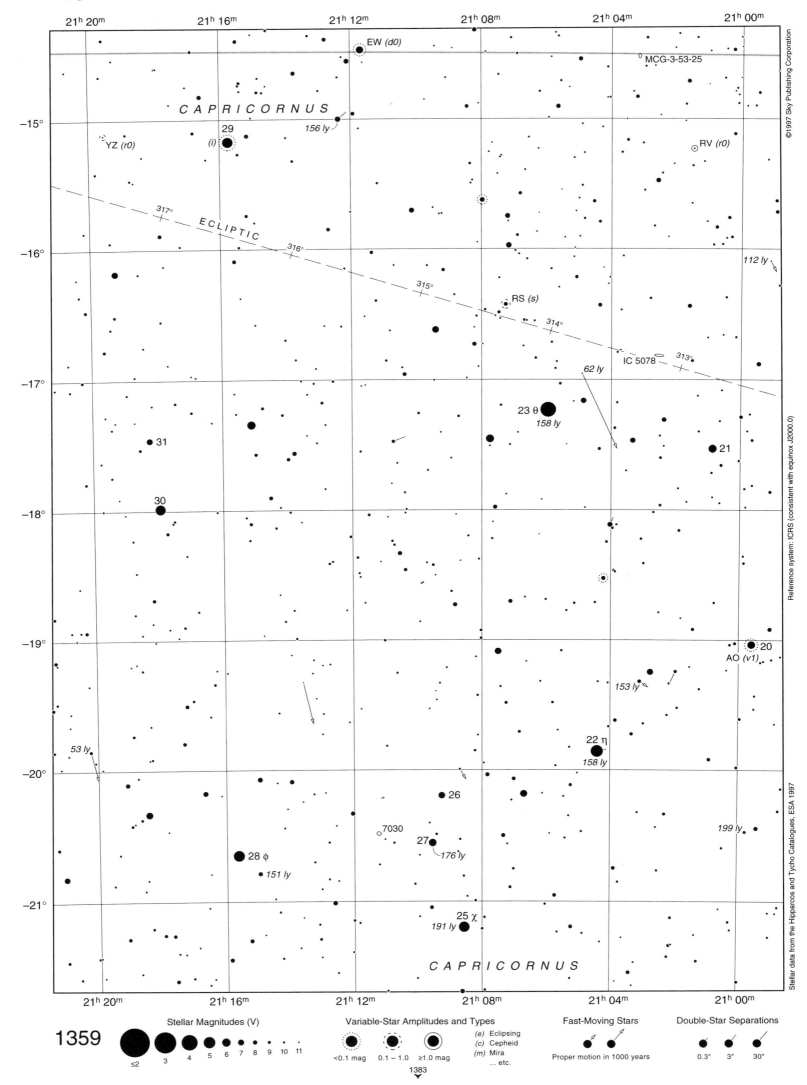

Reference system: ICRS (consistent with equinox J2000.0)

Stellar data from the Hipparcos and Tycho Catalogues, ESA 1997

1359

Stellar Magnitudes (V)

≤2  3  4  5  6  7  8  9  10  11

Variable-Star Amplitudes and Types

<0.1 mag   0.1 – 1.0   ≥1.0 mag

(e) Eclipsing
(c) Cepheid
(m) Mira
... etc.

Fast-Moving Stars

Proper motion in 1000 years

Double-Star Separations

0.3"  3"  30"

1383

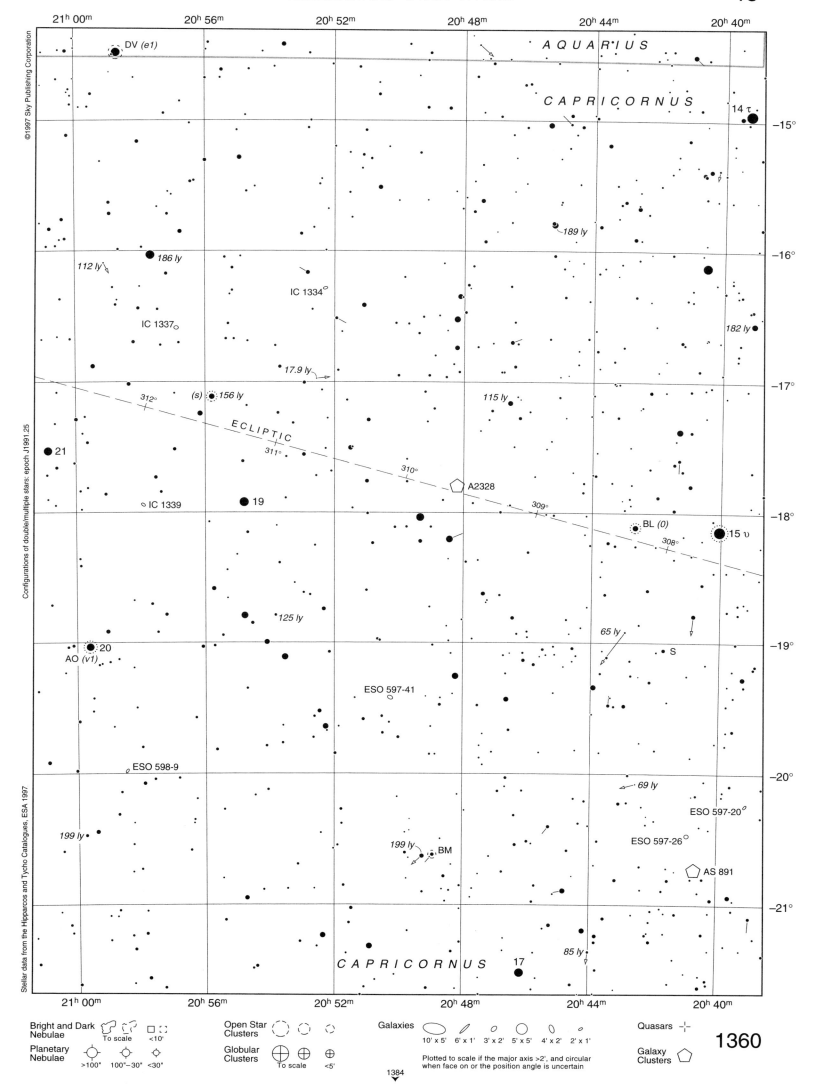

Bright and Dark Nebulae
To scale    <10'

Planetary Nebulae
>100"   100"−30"   <30"

Open Star Clusters

Globular Clusters
To scale   <5'

Galaxies
10' x 5'   6' x 1'   3' x 2'   5' x 5'   4' x 2'   2' x 1'

Plotted to scale if the major axis >2', and circular when face on or the position angle is uncertain

Quasars

Galaxy Clusters

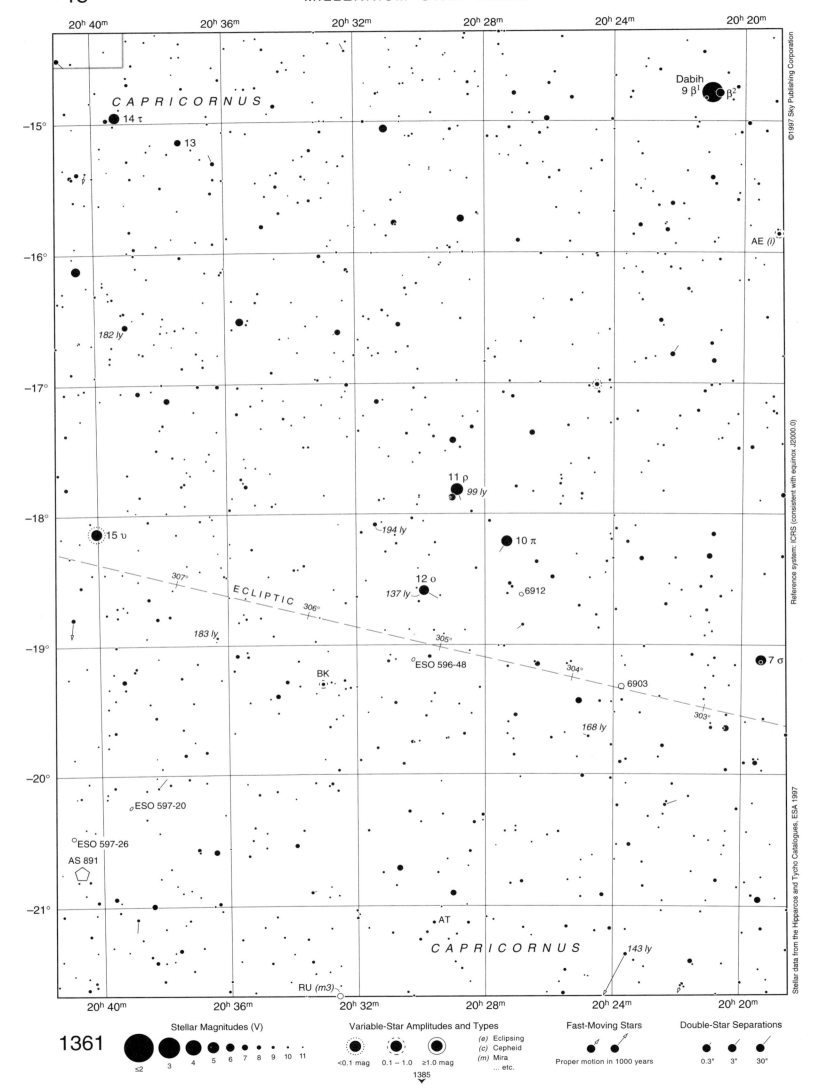

©1997 Sky Publishing Corporation

Reference system: ICRS (consistent with equinox J2000.0)

Stellar data from the Hipparcos and Tycho Catalogues, ESA 1997

20ʰ 40ᵐ    20ʰ 36ᵐ    20ʰ 32ᵐ    20ʰ 28ᵐ    20ʰ 24ᵐ    20ʰ 20ᵐ

CAPRICORNUS

Dabih
9 β¹    β²

14 τ

13

−15°

AE (i)

−16°

182 ly

−17°

11 ρ
99 ly

−18°
194 ly
15 υ
10 π
307°
ECLIPTIC  306°
12 o
137 ly
6912
183 ly
305°
−19°
7 σ
ESO 596-48
BK
304°
6903
168 ly
303°
−20°
ESO 597-20
ESO 597-26
AS 891
−21°
AT
CAPRICORNUS
143 ly
RU (m3)

20ʰ 40ᵐ    20ʰ 36ᵐ    20ʰ 32ᵐ    20ʰ 28ᵐ    20ʰ 24ᵐ    20ʰ 20ᵐ

Stellar Magnitudes (V)                    Variable-Star Amplitudes and Types        Fast-Moving Stars           Double-Star Separations

**1361**

≤2    3    4    5    6   7  8  9  10  11

<0.1 mag   0.1 – 1.0   ≥1.0 mag

1385

(e) Eclipsing
(c) Cepheid
(m) Mira
... etc.

Proper motion in 1000 years

0.3"    3"    30"

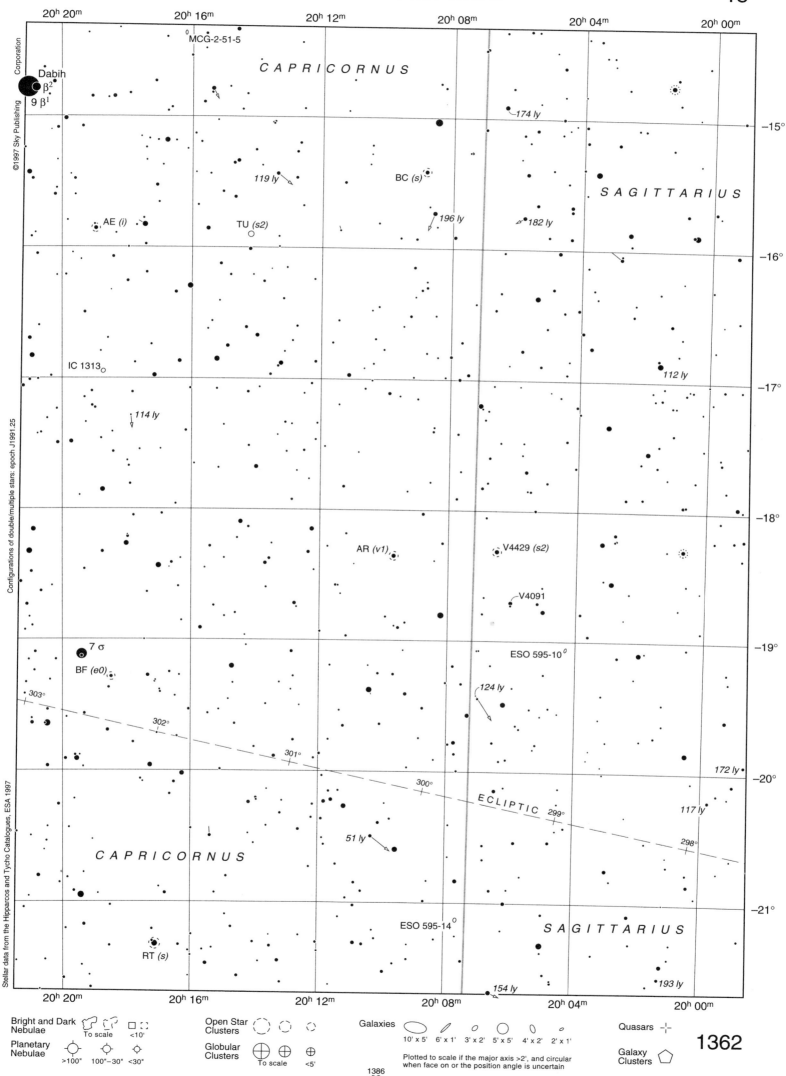

Configurations of double/multiple stars: epoch J1991.25

Stellar data from the Hipparcos and Tycho Catalogues, ESA 1997

MCG-2-51-5

Dabih
β²
9 β¹

C A P R I C O R N U S

S A G I T T A R I U S

174 ly

119 ly

BC (s)

AE (i)

TU (s2)

196 ly

182 ly

112 ly

IC 1313

114 ly

AR (v1)

V4429 (s2)

V4091

ESO 595-10

7 σ

124 ly

BF (e0)

303°

302°

301°

300°

172 ly

E C L I P T I C    299°

117 ly

51 ly

298°

C A P R I C O R N U S

ESO 595-14

S A G I T T A R I U S

RT (s)

154 ly

193 ly

| | | | | | | |
|---|---|---|---|---|---|---|
| Bright and Dark Nebulae | | To scale | <10' | Open Star Clusters | | |
| Planetary Nebulae | >100" | 100"–30" | <30" | Globular Clusters | To scale | <5' |

Galaxies
10' x 5'   6' x 1'   3' x 2'   5' x 5'   4' x 2'   2' x 1'

Plotted to scale if the major axis >2', and circular when face on or the position angle is uncertain

Quasars

Galaxy Clusters

1362

1386

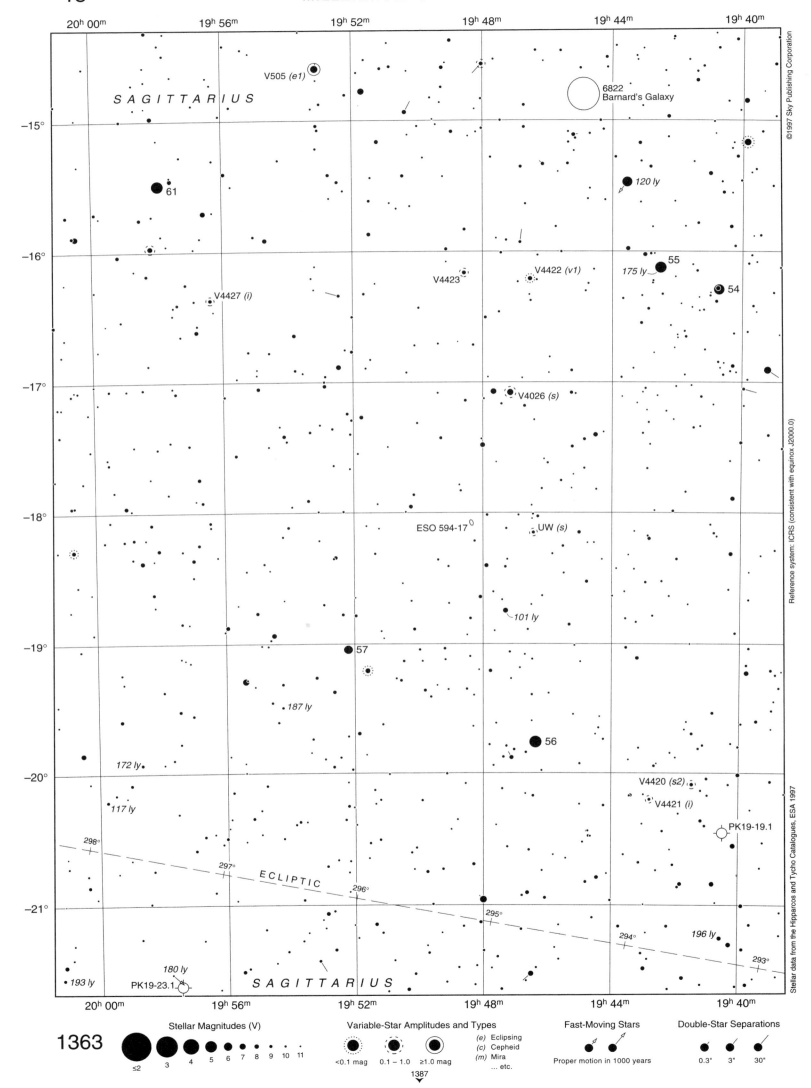

©1997 Sky Publishing Corporation

Reference system: ICRS (consistent with equinox J2000.0)

Stellar data from the Hipparcos and Tycho Catalogues, ESA 1997

SAGITTARIUS

V505 (e1)

6822
Barnard's Galaxy

61

120 ly

V4422 (v1)

V4423

175 ly     55

V4427 (i)                                          54

V4026 (s)

ESO 594-17

UW (s)

101 ly

57

187 ly

56

172 ly

V4420 (s2)

117 ly

V4421 (i)

PK19-19.1

298°

297°

ECLIPTIC

296°

295°

294°

196 ly

293°

193 ly     PK19-23.1

180 ly

SAGITTARIUS

1363

**Stellar Magnitudes (V)**

≤2   3   4   5   6   7   8   9   10   11

**Variable-Star Amplitudes and Types**

<0.1 mag     0.1 – 1.0     ≥1.0 mag

(e) Eclipsing
(c) Cepheid
(m) Mira
... etc.

**Fast-Moving Stars**

Proper motion in 1000 years

**Double-Star Separations**

0.3"   3"   30"

1387

# MILLENNIUM STAR ATLAS

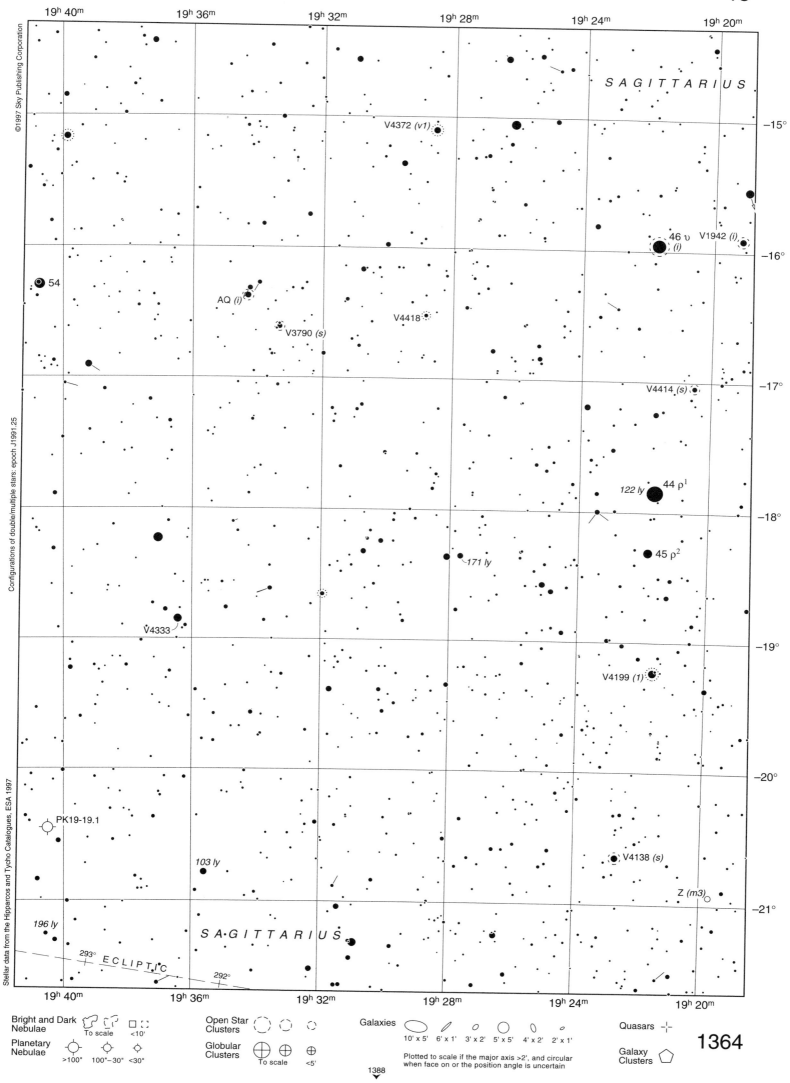

SAGITTARIUS

©1997 Sky Publishing Corporation

Configurations of double/multiple stars: epoch J1991.25

Stellar data from the Hipparcos and Tycho Catalogues, ESA 1997

V4372 *(v1)*

46 υ
*(i)*  V1942 *(i)*

54

AQ *(i)*

V4418

V3790 *(s)*

V4414 *(s)*

122 ly  44 ρ¹

45 ρ²

171 ly

V4333

V4199 *(1)*

PK19-19.1

103 ly

V4138 *(s)*

Z *(m3)*

196 ly

SAGITTARIUS

293°  E C L I P T I C

292°

19h 40m    19h 36m    19h 32m    19h 28m    19h 24m    19h 20m

−15°
−16°
−17°
−18°
−19°
−20°
−21°

| Bright and Dark Nebulae | Open Star Clusters | Galaxies | Quasars |
|---|---|---|---|

To scale    <10'

10' x 5'  6' x 1'  3' x 2'  5' x 5'  4' x 2'  2' x 1'

Planetary Nebulae

>100"  100"−30"  <30"

Globular Clusters

To scale    <5'

Galaxy Clusters

Plotted to scale if the major axis >2', and circular when face on or the position angle is uncertain

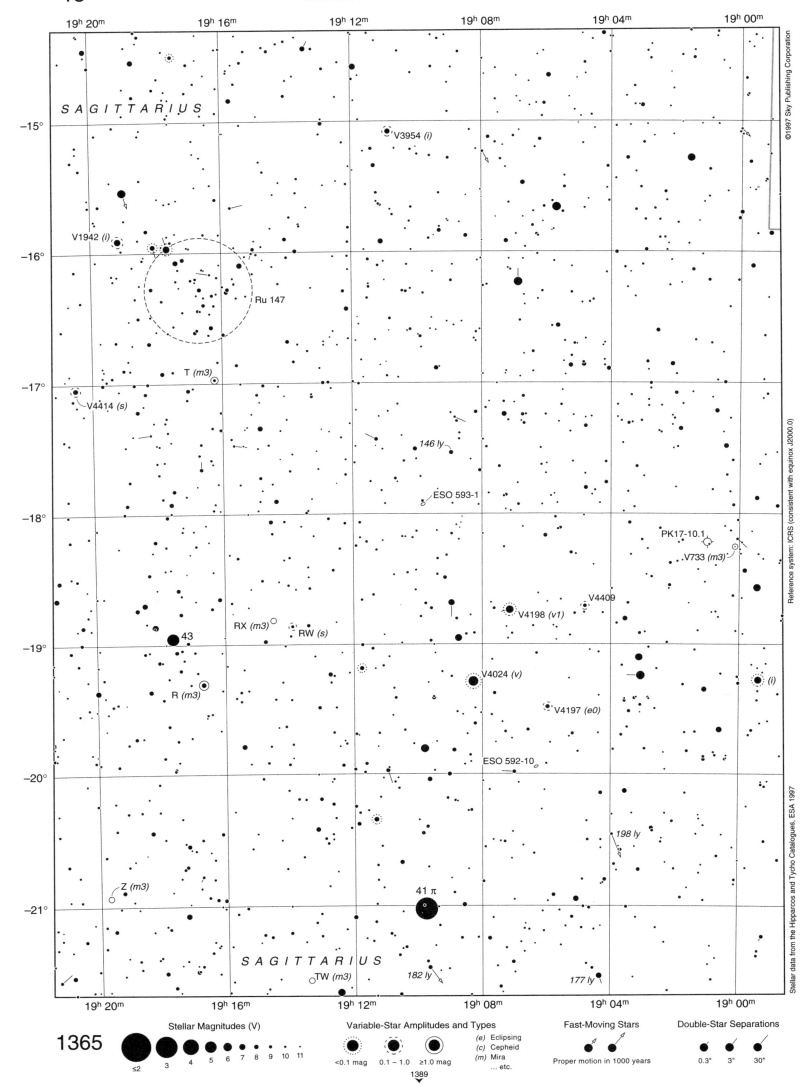

©1997 Sky Publishing Corporation

Reference system: ICRS (consistent with equinox J2000.0)

Stellar data from the Hipparcos and Tycho Catalogues, ESA 1997

SAGITTARIUS

V3954 (i)

V1942 (i)

Ru 147

T (m3)

V4414 (s)

146 ly

ESO 593-1

PK17-10.1

V733 (m3)

V4409

V4198 (v1)

RX (m3)   RW (s)

43

V4024 (v)

(i)

R (m3)

V4197 (e0)

ESO 592-10

198 ly

Z (m3)

41 π

SAGITTARIUS

TW (m3)   182 ly   177 ly

**1365**

Stellar Magnitudes (V)

≤2  3  4  5  6  7  8  9  10  11

Variable-Star Amplitudes and Types

<0.1 mag   0.1 – 1.0   ≥1.0 mag

(e) Eclipsing
(c) Cepheid
(m) Mira
... etc.

Fast-Moving Stars

Proper motion in 1000 years

Double-Star Separations

0.3"  3"  30"

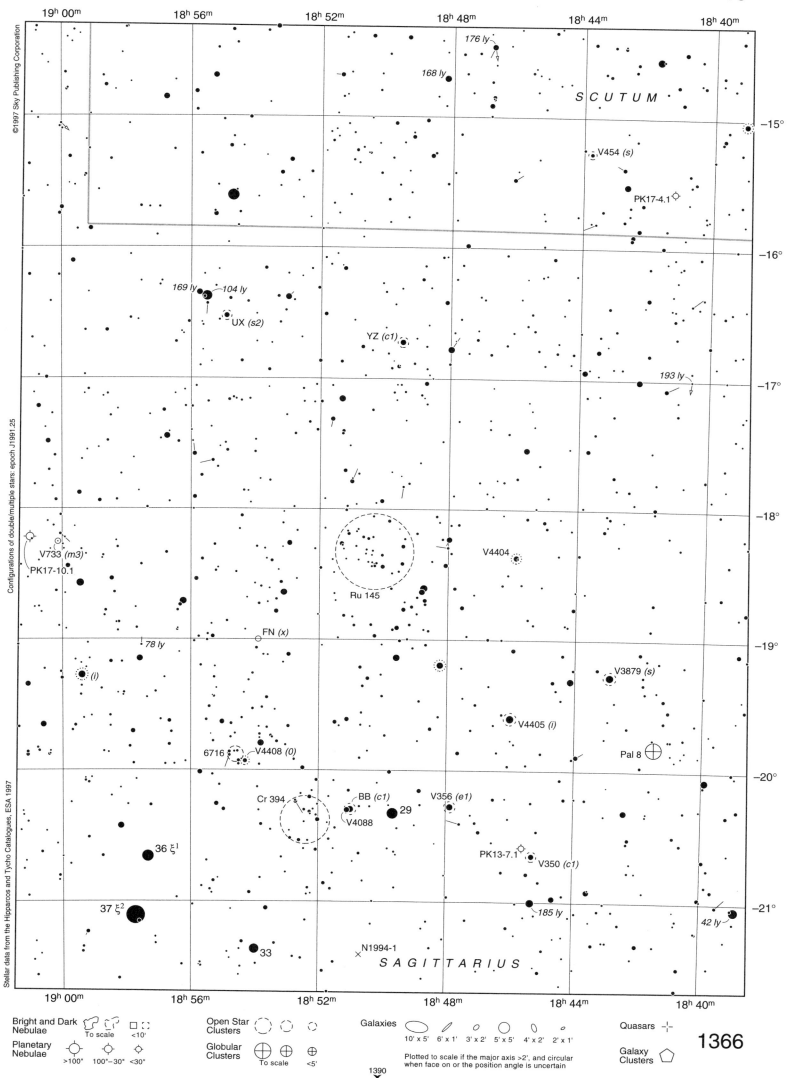

SCUTUM

SAGITTARIUS

176 ly
168 ly
V454 (s)
PK17-4.1
−15°

−16°
169 ly — 104 ly
UX (s2)
YZ (c1)
193 ly
−17°

−18°
V733 (m3)
PK17-10.1
V4404
Ru 145
−18°

FN (x)
78 ly
(i)
V3879 (s)
−19°
V4405 (i)
6716  V4408 (0)
Pal 8

−20°
Cr 394
BB (c1)
V4088
29
V356 (e1)
PK13-7.1
V350 (c1)
36 ξ¹

37 ξ²
185 ly
42 ly
−21°
33
N1994-1

Bright and Dark Nebulae
To scale   <10'
Planetary Nebulae
>100"   100"−30"   <30"

Open Star Clusters
Globular Clusters
To scale   <5'

Galaxies
10' x 5'   6' x 1'   3' x 2'   5' x 5'   4' x 2'   2' x 1'
Plotted to scale if the major axis >2', and circular when face on or the position angle is uncertain

Quasars

Galaxy Clusters

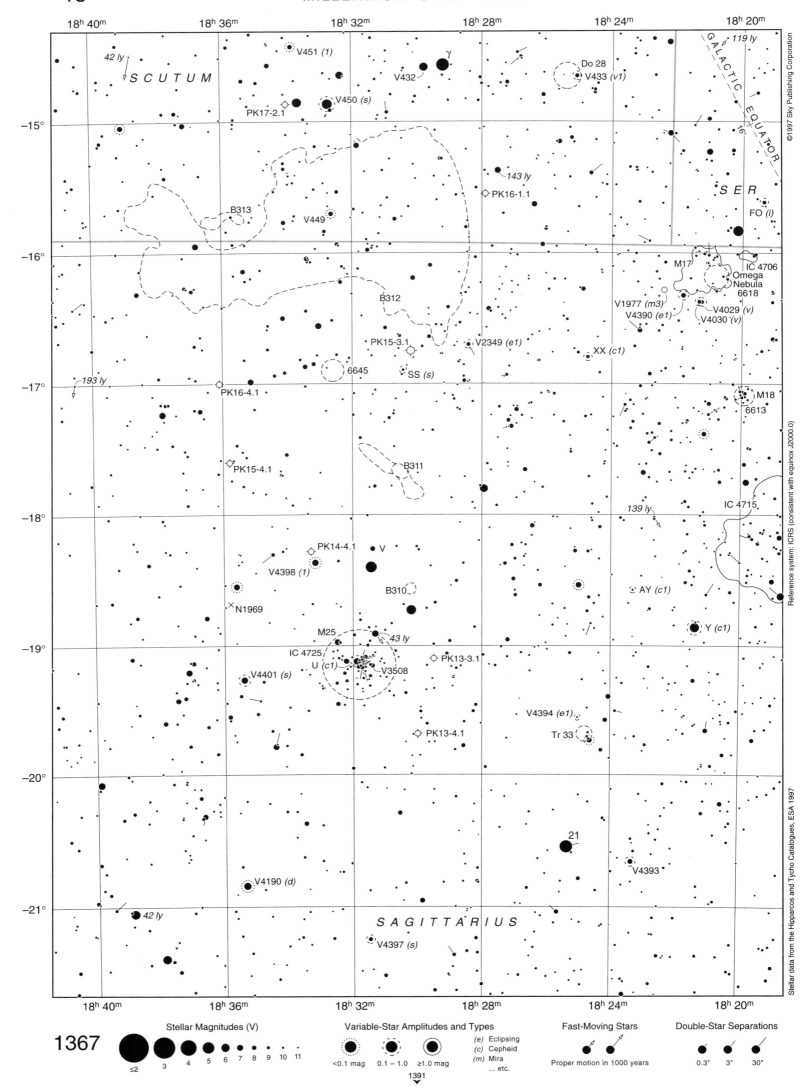

1367

Stellar Magnitudes (V)

≤2  3  4  5  6  7  8  9  10  11

Variable-Star Amplitudes and Types

<0.1 mag    0.1 − 1.0    ≥1.0 mag

(e) Eclipsing
(c) Cepheid
(m) Mira
... etc.

Fast-Moving Stars

Proper motion in 1000 years

Double-Star Separations

0.3"   3"   30"

^1391

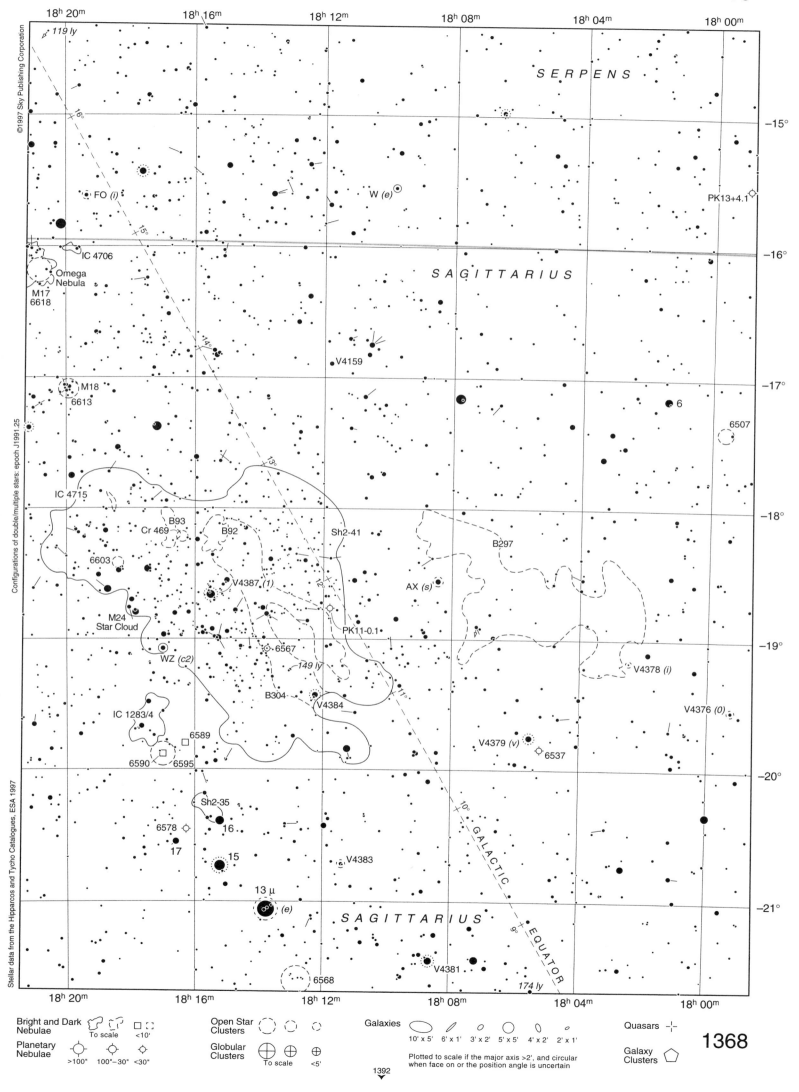

©1997 Sky Publishing Corporation

Configurations of double/multiple stars: epoch J1991.25

Stellar data from the Hipparcos and Tycho Catalogues, ESA 1997

18h 20m  18h 16m  18h 12m  18h 08m  18h 04m  18h 00m

−15°
−16°
−17°
−18°
−19°
−20°
−21°

S E R P E N S

S A G I T T A R I U S

S A G I T T A R I U S

119 ly

FO (i)

IC 4706

Omega
Nebula

M17
6618

M18
6613

IC 4715

B93
Cr 469      B92      Sh2-41

6603

V4387 (1)

M24
Star Cloud

WZ (c2)

IC 1283/4

6589
6590   6595

Sh2-35

6578

17

16

15

13 μ
(e)

6568

W (e)

PK13+4.1

V4159

6

6507

B297

AX (s)

PK11-0.1

6567

149 ly

B304

V4384

V4378 (i)

V4376 (0)

V4379 (v)
6537

V4383

V4381

174 ly

GALACTIC   EQUATOR

18h 20m  18h 16m  18h 12m  18h 08m  18h 04m  18h 00m

Bright and Dark
Nebulae
To scale   <10'

Planetary
Nebulae
>100"  100"−30"  <30"

Open Star
Clusters

Globular
Clusters
To scale   <5'

Galaxies
10' x 5'  6' x 1'  3' x 2'  5' x 5'  4' x 2'  2' x 1'

Plotted to scale if the major axis >2', and circular
when face on or the position angle is uncertain

Quasars

Galaxy
Clusters

1368

1392

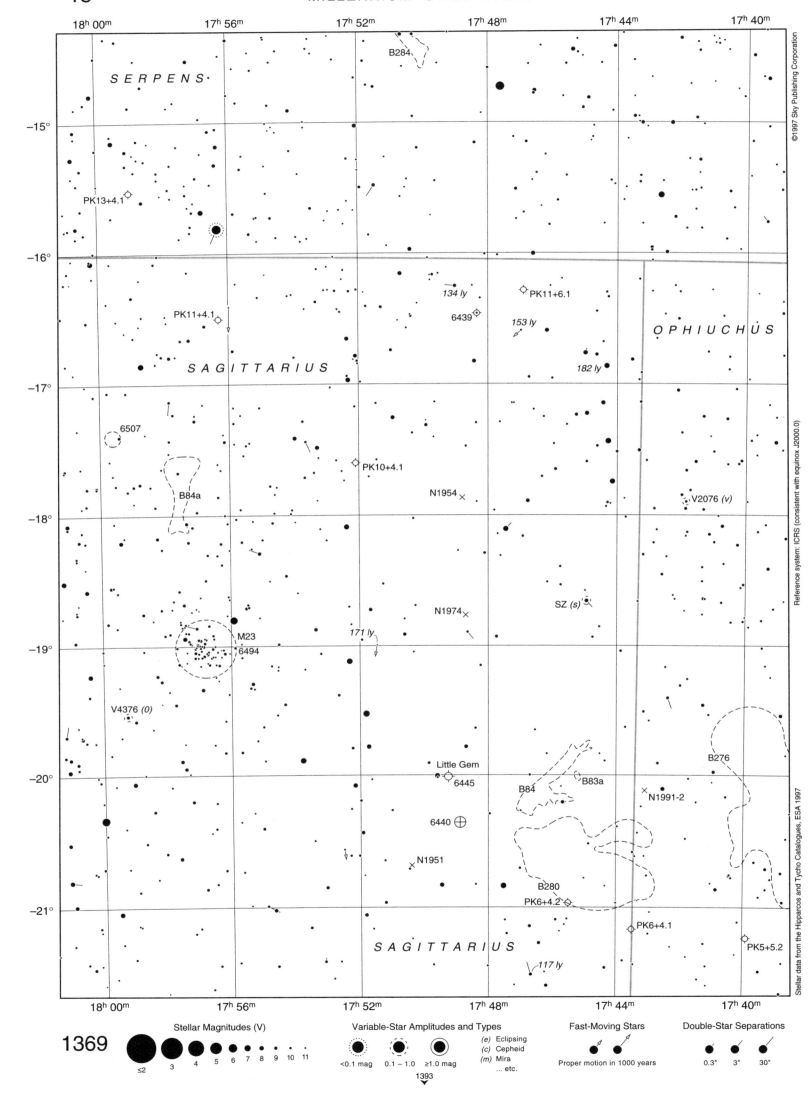

©1997 Sky Publishing Corporation

Reference system: ICRS (consistent with equinox J2000.0)

Stellar data from the Hipparcos and Tycho Catalogues, ESA 1997

1369

| Stellar Magnitudes (V) | Variable-Star Amplitudes and Types | Fast-Moving Stars | Double-Star Separations |
|---|---|---|---|

Stellar Magnitudes (V)
≤2  3  4  5  6  7  8  9  10  11

Variable-Star Amplitudes and Types
<0.1 mag    0.1 − 1.0    ≥1.0 mag

(e) Eclipsing
(c) Cepheid
(m) Mira
... etc.

Fast-Moving Stars
Proper motion in 1000 years

Double-Star Separations
0.3"   3"   30"

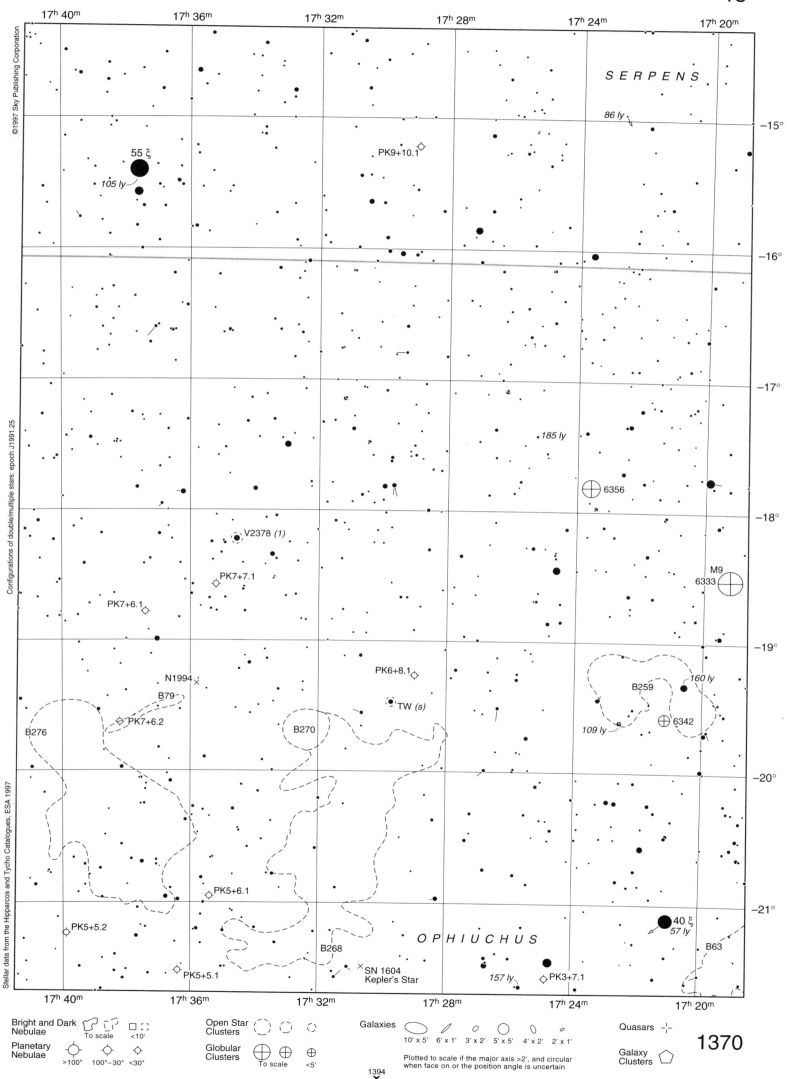

S E R P E N S

86 ly

55 ξ
105 ly

PK9+10.1

−15°

−16°

−17°

185 ly

6356

−18°

V2378 (1)

M9
6333

PK7+7.1

PK7+6.1

PK6+8.1

B259

160 ly

−19°

N1994
B79

TW (s)

6342

PK7+6.2
B276

B270

109 ly

−20°

PK5+6.1

40 ξ
57 ly

−21°

PK5+5.2

O P H I U C H U S

B63

PK5+5.1

B268

SN 1604
Kepler's Star

157 ly

PK3+7.1

| Bright and Dark Nebulae | | | | Open Star Clusters | | | Galaxies | | | | | | | Quasars |
|---|---|---|---|---|---|---|---|---|---|---|---|---|---|---|

To scale        <10'

To scale

10' x 5'   6' x 1'   3' x 2'   5' x 5'   4' x 2'   2' x 1'

Planetary Nebulae
>100"   100"−30"   <30"

Globular Clusters
To scale   <5'

Galaxy Clusters

Plotted to scale if the major axis >2', and circular
when face on or the position angle is uncertain

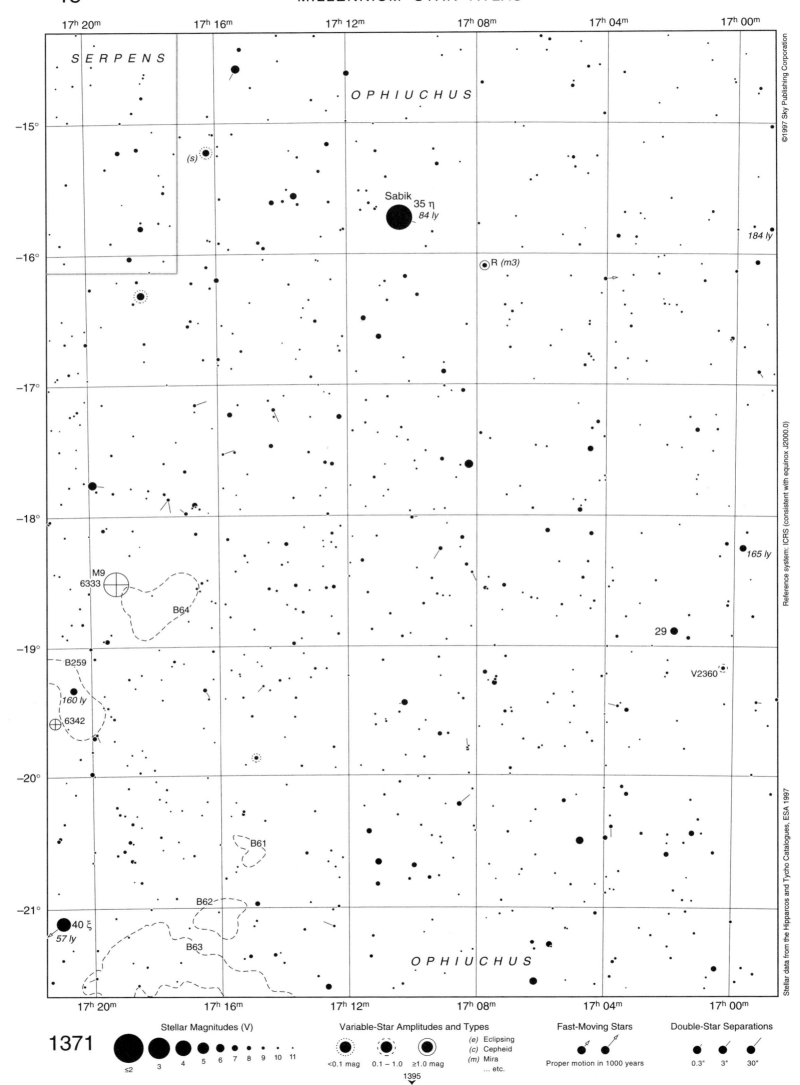

**Stellar Magnitudes (V)**

1371

≤2   3   4   5   6   7   8   9   10   11

**Variable-Star Amplitudes and Types**

<0.1 mag   0.1 – 1.0   ≥1.0 mag

(e) Eclipsing
(c) Cepheid
(m) Mira
... etc.

**Fast-Moving Stars**

Proper motion in 1000 years

**Double-Star Separations**

0.3"   3"   30"

# MILLENNIUM STAR ATLAS

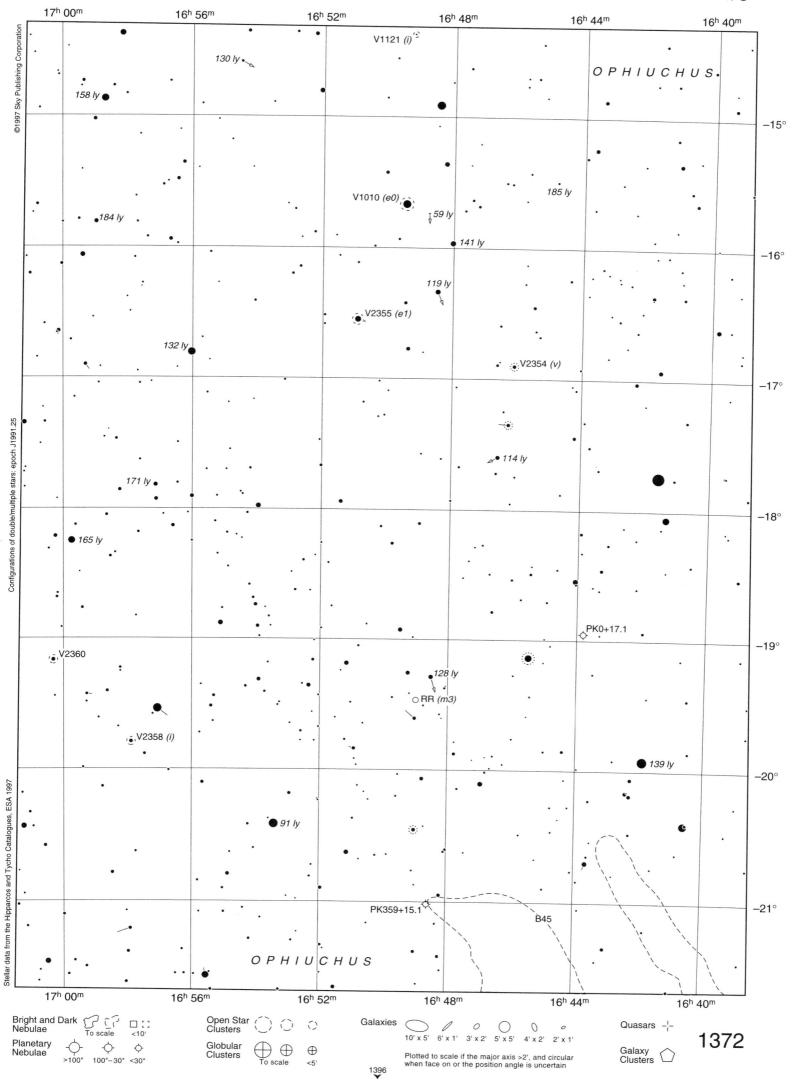

O P H I U C H U S

V1121 *(i)*

130 ly

158 ly

184 ly

V1010 *(e0)*

59 ly

185 ly

141 ly

119 ly

V2355 *(e1)*

132 ly

V2354 *(v)*

171 ly

114 ly

165 ly

PK0+17.1

V2360

128 ly

RR *(m3)*

V2358 *(i)*

139 ly

91 ly

PK359+15.1

B45

O P H I U C H U S

−15°

−16°

−17°

−18°

−19°

−20°

−21°

| Bright and Dark Nebulae | | | | Open Star Clusters | | | Galaxies | | | | | | Quasars |
|---|---|---|---|---|---|---|---|---|---|---|---|---|---|

To scale    <10'

Planetary Nebulae
>100"   100"–30"   <30'

Globular Clusters
To scale   <5'

Galaxies
10' x 5'   6' x 1'   3' x 2'   5' x 5'   4' x 2'   2' x 1'

Plotted to scale if the major axis >2', and circular
when face on or the position angle is uncertain

Quasars

Galaxy Clusters

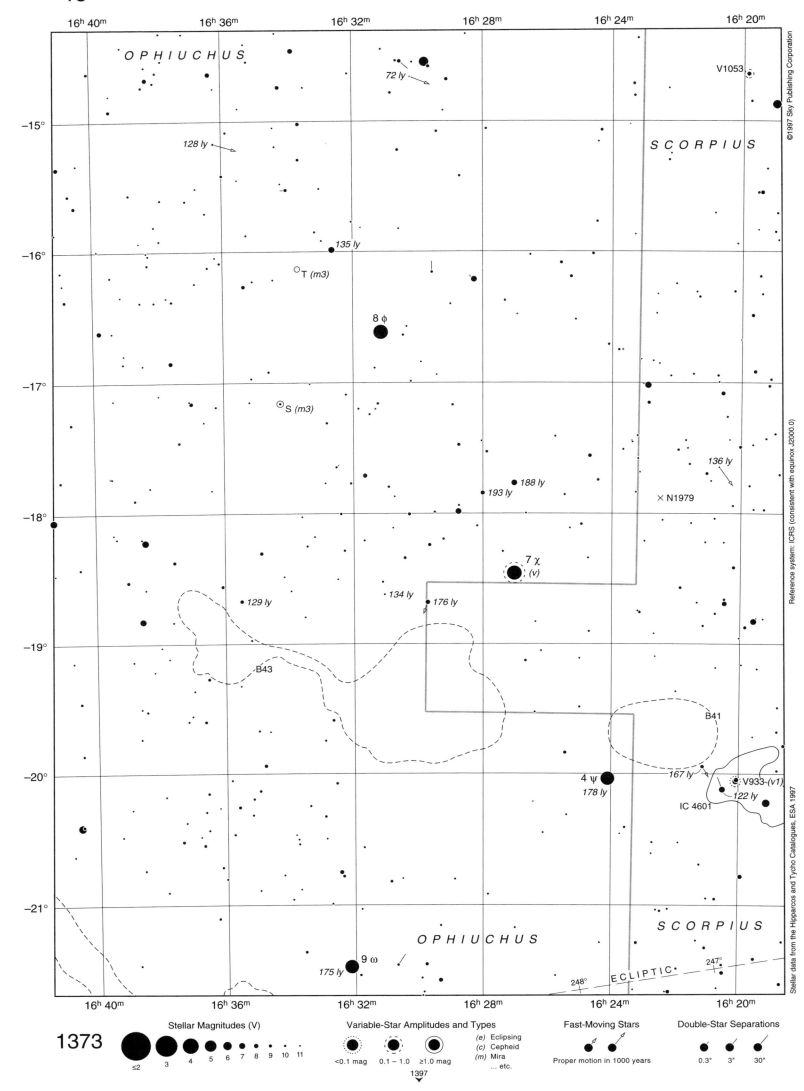

OPHIUCHUS

SCORPIUS

V1053

72 ly

128 ly

135 ly

○ T (m3)

8 φ

⊙ S (m3)

136 ly

× N1979

188 ly

193 ly

129 ly

· 134 ly

176 ly

7 χ
(v)

B43

B41

167 ly

4 ψ

178 ly

V933 (v1)

122 ly

IC 4601

OPHIUCHUS

SCORPIUS

9 ω

175 ly

248°

247°

ECLIPTIC

Stellar Magnitudes (V)

≤2  3  4  5  6  7  8  9  10  11

Variable-Star Amplitudes and Types

<0.1 mag   0.1 – 1.0   ≥1.0 mag

(e) Eclipsing
(c) Cepheid
(m) Mira
... etc.

Fast-Moving Stars

Proper motion in 1000 years

Double-Star Separations

0.3"   3"   30"

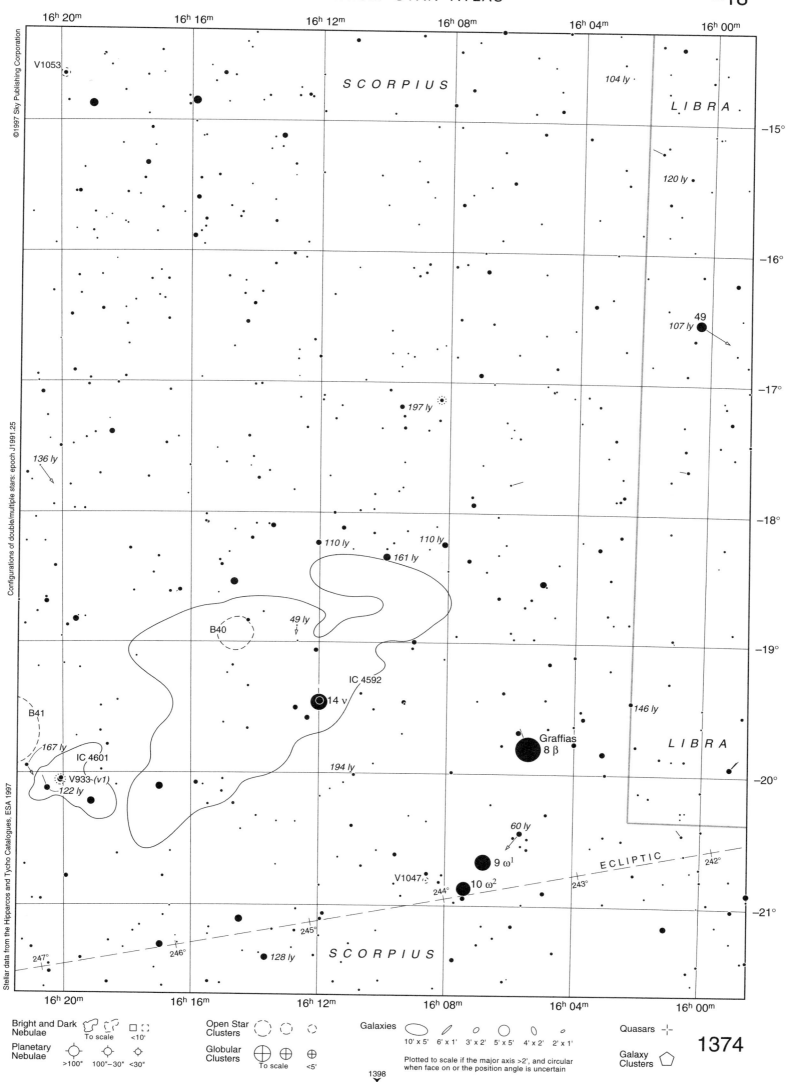

16h 20m    16h 16m    16h 12m    16h 08m    16h 04m    16h 00m

SCORPIUS

LIBRA

V1053

104 ly

−15°

120 ly

−16°

49
107 ly

−17°

197 ly

136 ly

−18°

110 ly    110 ly
161 ly

B40    49 ly

−19°

IC 4592

B41    14 ν

167 ly

IC 4601    146 ly    LIBRA

V933 (v1)    Graffias
122 ly    8 β

194 ly    −20°

60 ly

9 ω¹    242°

V1047    10 ω²    243°
244°    ECLIPTIC

−21°
245°

247°    246°    128 ly    SCORPIUS

16h 20m    16h 16m    16h 12m    16h 08m    16h 04m    16h 00m

Bright and Dark    Open Star    Galaxies    Quasars
Nebulae    Clusters
To scale    <10'    10' x 5'  6' x 1'  3' x 2'  5' x 5'  4' x 2'  2' x 1'

Planetary    Globular    Galaxy
Nebulae    Clusters    Clusters
>100"  100"–30"  <30"    To scale    <5'    Plotted to scale if the major axis >2', and circular
when face on or the position angle is uncertain

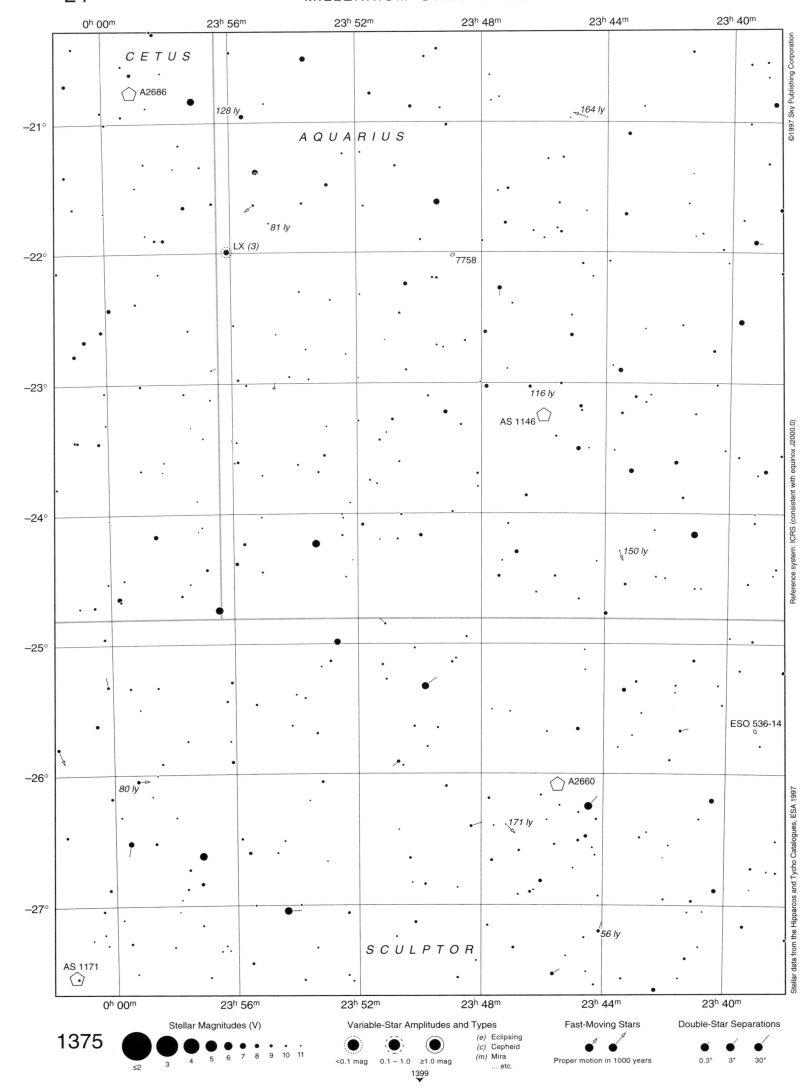

C E T U S

A2686

128 ly

164 ly

A Q U A R I U S

81 ly

LX (3)

7758

116 ly

AS 1146

150 ly

ESO 536-14

A2660

80 ly

171 ly

56 ly

S C U L P T O R

AS 1171

1375

**Stellar Magnitudes (V)**

≤2   3   4   5   6   7   8   9   10   11

**Variable-Star Amplitudes and Types**

<0.1 mag    0.1 – 1.0    ≥1.0 mag

(e) Eclipsing
(c) Cepheid
(m) Mira
... etc.

**Fast-Moving Stars**

Proper motion in 1000 years

**Double-Star Separations**

0.3"   3"   30"

1399

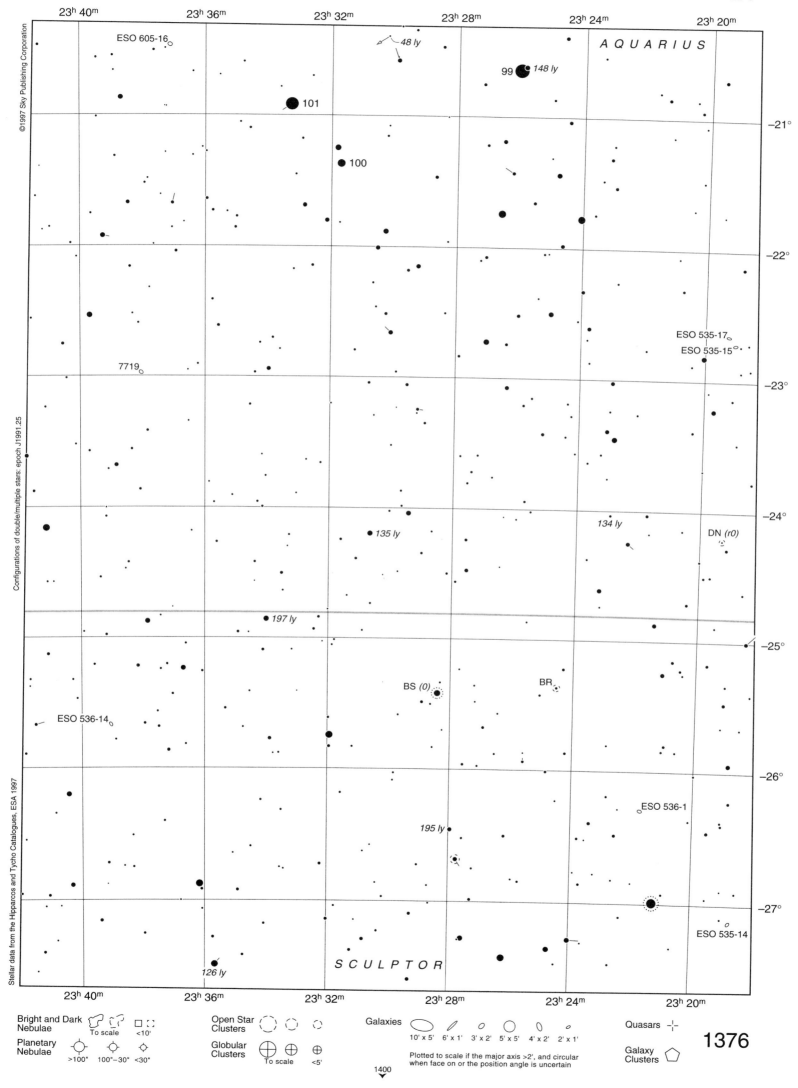

AQUARIUS

SCULPTOR

ESO 605-16

99  148 ly

101

100

48 ly

ESO 535-17
ESO 535-15

7719

135 ly

134 ly

DN (r0)

197 ly

BS (0)

BR

ESO 536-14

ESO 536-1

195 ly

ESO 535-14

126 ly

| Bright and Dark Nebulae | Open Star Clusters | Galaxies | Quasars |
|---|---|---|---|

Bright and Dark Nebulae    To scale   <10'

Planetary Nebulae   >100"   100"−30"   <30"

Open Star Clusters

Globular Clusters   To scale   <5'

Galaxies   10' x 5'   6' x 1'   3' x 2'   5' x 5'   4' x 2'   2' x 1'

Plotted to scale if the major axis >2', and circular when face on or the position angle is uncertain

Quasars

Galaxy Clusters

1376

# MILLENNIUM STAR ATLAS

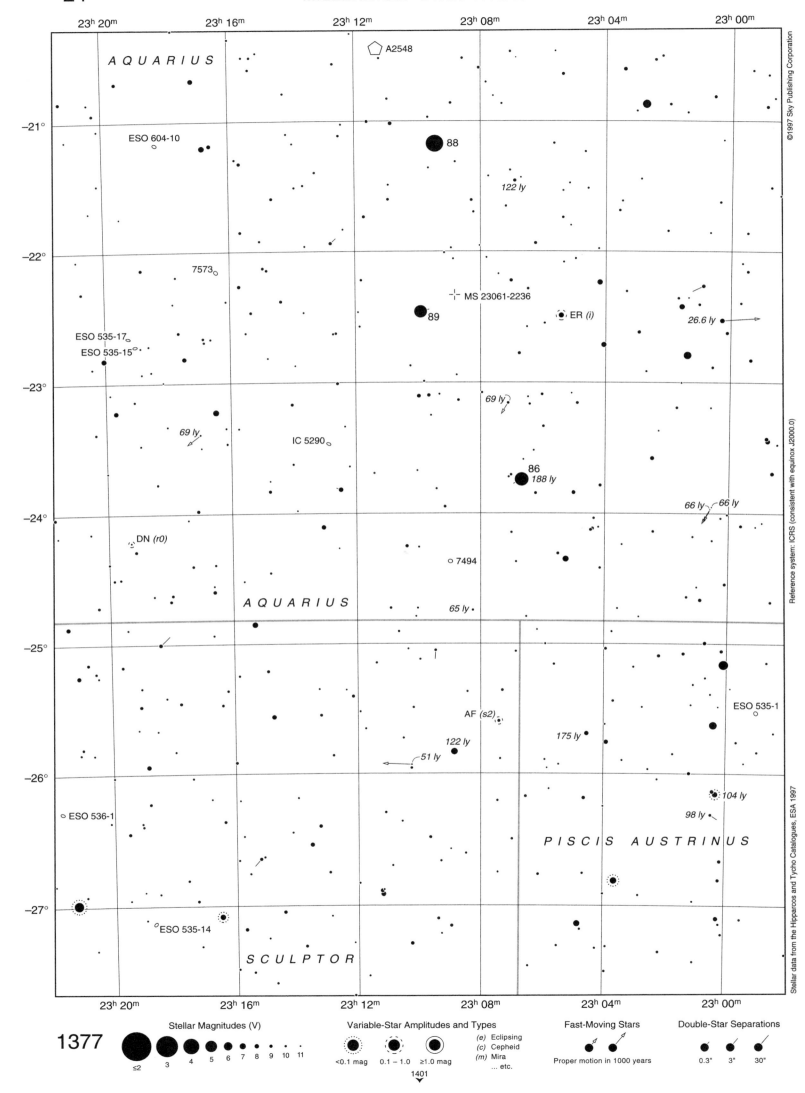

**1377**

Stellar Magnitudes (V)

≤2   3   4   5   6   7   8   9   10   11

Variable-Star Amplitudes and Types

<0.1 mag     0.1 – 1.0     ≥1.0 mag

(e) Eclipsing
(c) Cepheid
(m) Mira
... etc.

Fast-Moving Stars

Proper motion in 1000 years

Double-Star Separations

0.3"   3"   30"

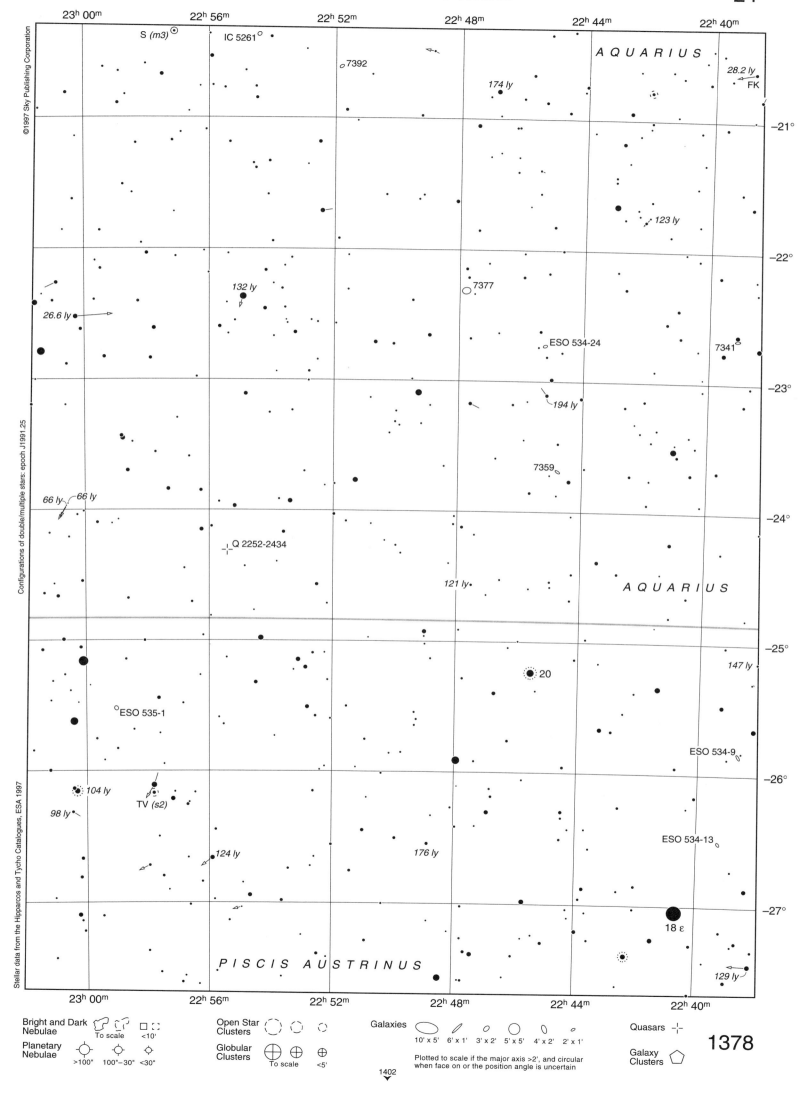

23h 00m   22h 56m   22h 52m   22h 48m   22h 44m   22h 40m

S (m3)   IC 5261

7392

A Q U A R I U S

28.2 ly
FK

174 ly

123 ly

−21°

132 ly

7377

−22°

26.6 ly

ESO 534-24

7341

194 ly

−23°

7359

66 ly   66 ly

Q 2252-2434

121 ly

A Q U A R I U S

−24°

147 ly

20

ESO 535-1

ESO 534-9

−25°

104 ly

TV (s2)

ESO 534-13

−26°

98 ly

124 ly

176 ly

18 ε

−27°

P I S C I S   A U S T R I N U S

129 ly

23h 00m   22h 56m   22h 52m   22h 48m   22h 44m   22h 40m

©1997 Sky Publishing Corporation

Configurations of double/multiple stars: epoch J1991.25

Stellar data from the Hipparcos and Tycho Catalogues, ESA 1997

| Bright and Dark Nebulae | | | | | Open Star Clusters | | | Galaxies | | | | | | | Quasars |
|---|---|---|---|---|---|---|---|---|---|---|---|---|---|---|---|
| To scale | | <10' | | | | | | 10' x 5' | 6' x 1' | 3' x 2' | 5' x 5' | 4' x 2' | 2' x 1' | | |
| Planetary Nebulae | | | | | Globular Clusters | | | | | | | | | | Galaxy Clusters |
| >100" | 100"−30" | <30" | | | To scale | | <5' | | | | | | | | |

Plotted to scale if the major axis >2', and circular when face on or the position angle is uncertain

1378

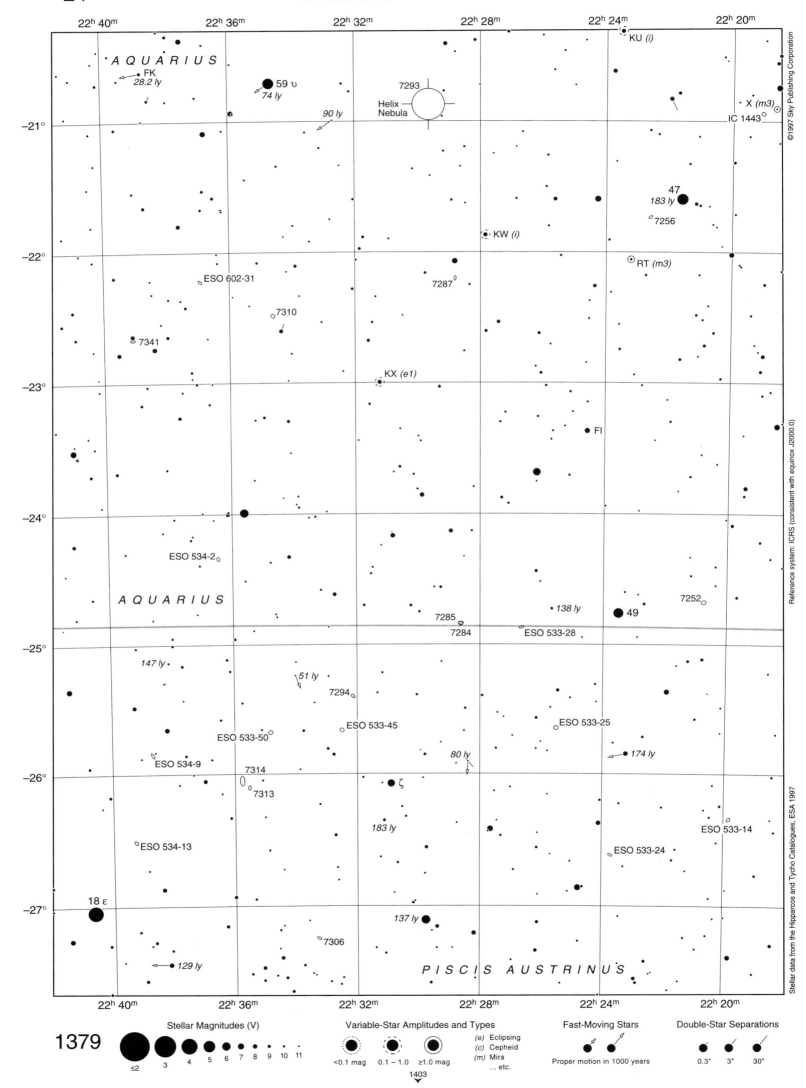

©1997 Sky Publishing Corporation

Reference system: ICRS (consistent with equinox J2000.0)

Stellar data from the Hipparcos and Tycho Catalogues, ESA 1997

22h 40m   22h 36m   22h 32m   22h 28m   22h 24m   22h 20m

AQUARIUS

FK
28.2 ly

59 υ
74 ly

90 ly

7293

Helix
Nebula

KU (i)

X (m3)

IC 1443

47
183 ly

7256

KW (i)

RT (m3)

−21°

−22°

ESO 602-31

7287

7310

7341

KX (e1)

FI

−23°

−24°

ESO 534-2

AQUARIUS

7285

7284

138 ly

49

7252

ESO 533-28

−25°

147 ly

51 ly

7294

ESO 533-45

ESO 533-50

ESO 533-25

ESO 534-9

174 ly

7314

80 ly

7313

ζ

ESO 533-14

−26°

ESO 534-13

183 ly

ESO 533-24

18 ε

137 ly

7306

−27°

129 ly

PISCIS AUSTRINUS

22h 40m   22h 36m   22h 32m   22h 28m   22h 24m   22h 20m

1379

Stellar Magnitudes (V)

≤2   3   4   5   6   7   8   9   10   11

Variable-Star Amplitudes and Types

<0.1 mag   0.1 – 1.0   ≥1.0 mag

1403

(e) Eclipsing
(c) Cepheid
(m) Mira
... etc.

Fast-Moving Stars

Proper motion in 1000 years

Double-Star Separations

0.3"   3"   30"

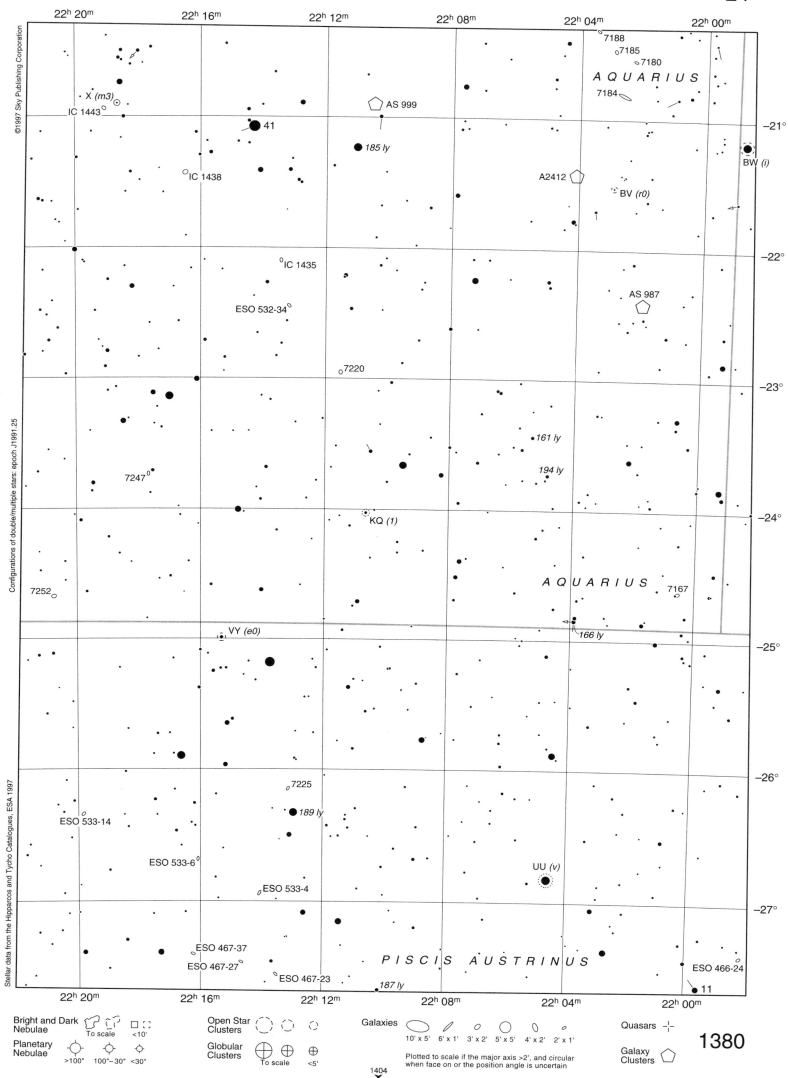

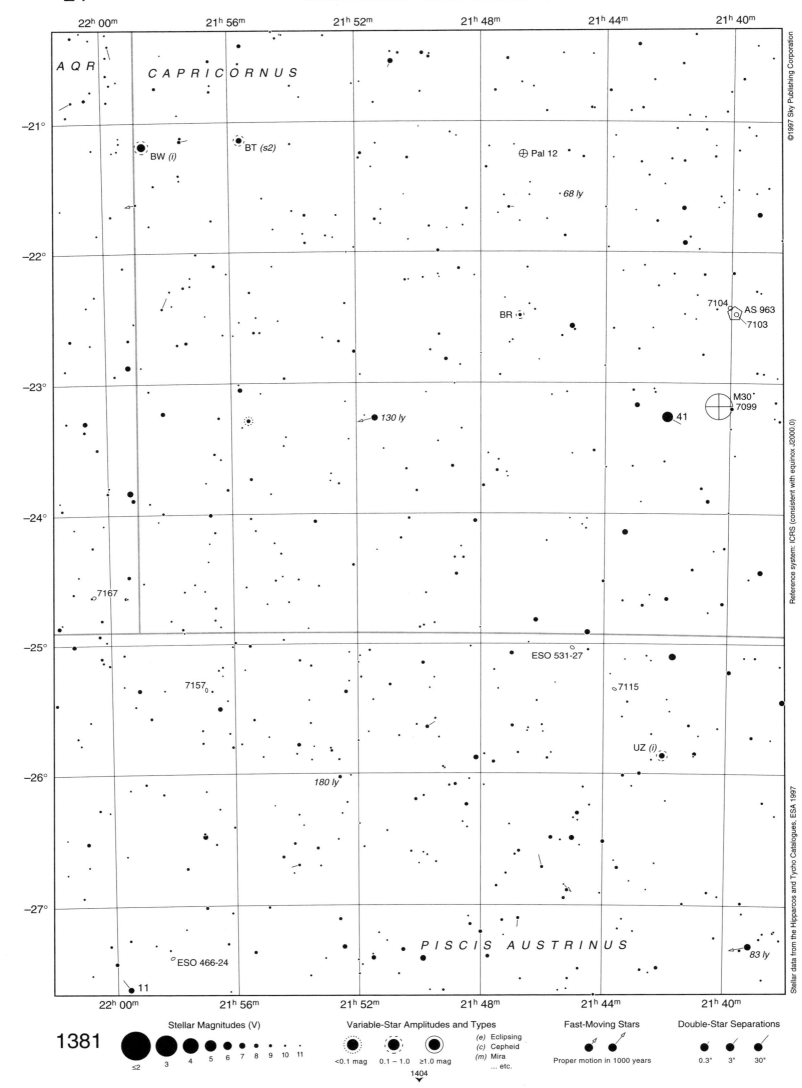

©1997 Sky Publishing Corporation

Reference system: ICRS (consistent with equinox J2000.0)

Stellar data from the Hipparcos and Tycho Catalogues, ESA 1997

1381

**Stellar Magnitudes (V)**

≤2   3   4   5   6   7   8   9   10   11

**Variable-Star Amplitudes and Types**

<0.1 mag   0.1 – 1.0   ≥1.0 mag

*(e)* Eclipsing
*(c)* Cepheid
*(m)* Mira
... etc.

**Fast-Moving Stars**

Proper motion in 1000 years

**Double-Star Separations**

0.3"   3"   30"

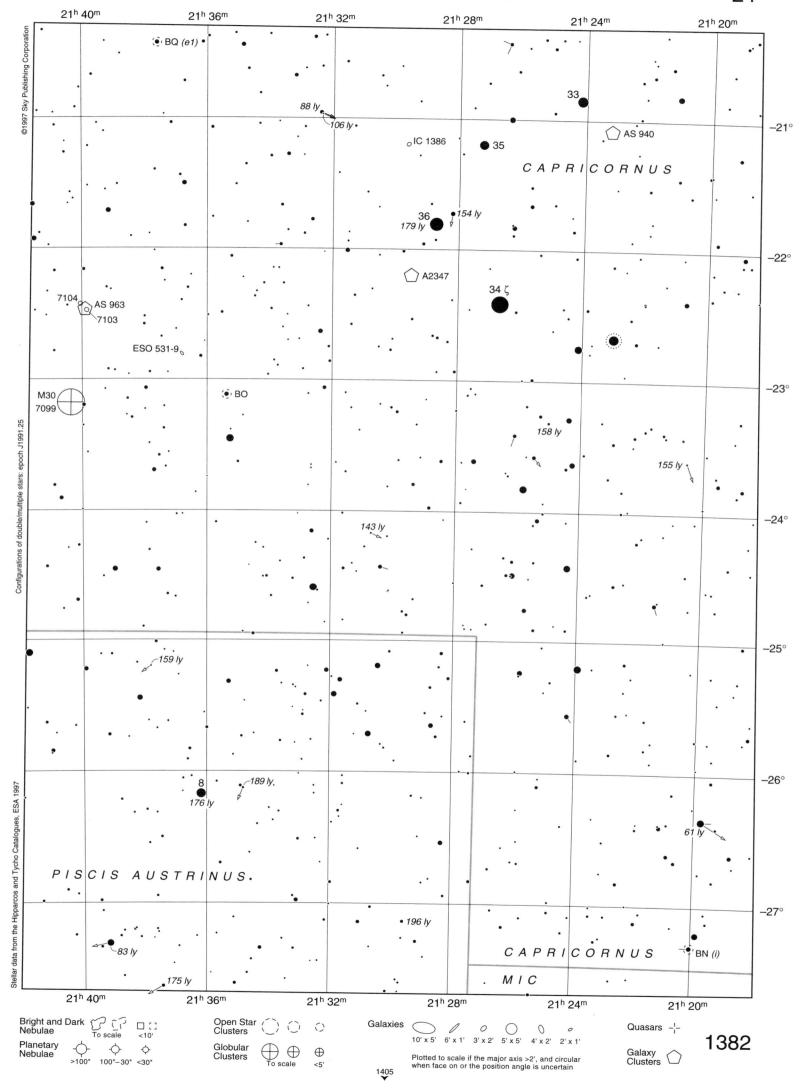

BQ (e1)

88 ly
106 ly

IC 1386

35

33

AS 940

CAPRICORNUS

36
179 ly
154 ly

A2347

34 ζ

7104
AS 963
7103

ESO 531-9

M30
7099

BO

158 ly

155 ly

143 ly

159 ly

8
176 ly
189 ly.

61 ly

PISCIS AUSTRINUS.

196 ly

83 ly

CAPRICORNUS

BN (i)

175 ly

MIC

Bright and Dark Nebulae
To scale    <10'

Planetary Nebulae
>100"   100"−30"   <30"

Open Star Clusters

Globular Clusters
To scale   <5'

Galaxies
10' x 5'   6' x 1'   3' x 2'   5' x 5'   4' x 2'   2' x 1'

Plotted to scale if the major axis >2', and circular when face on or the position angle is uncertain

Quasars

Galaxy Clusters

**1382**

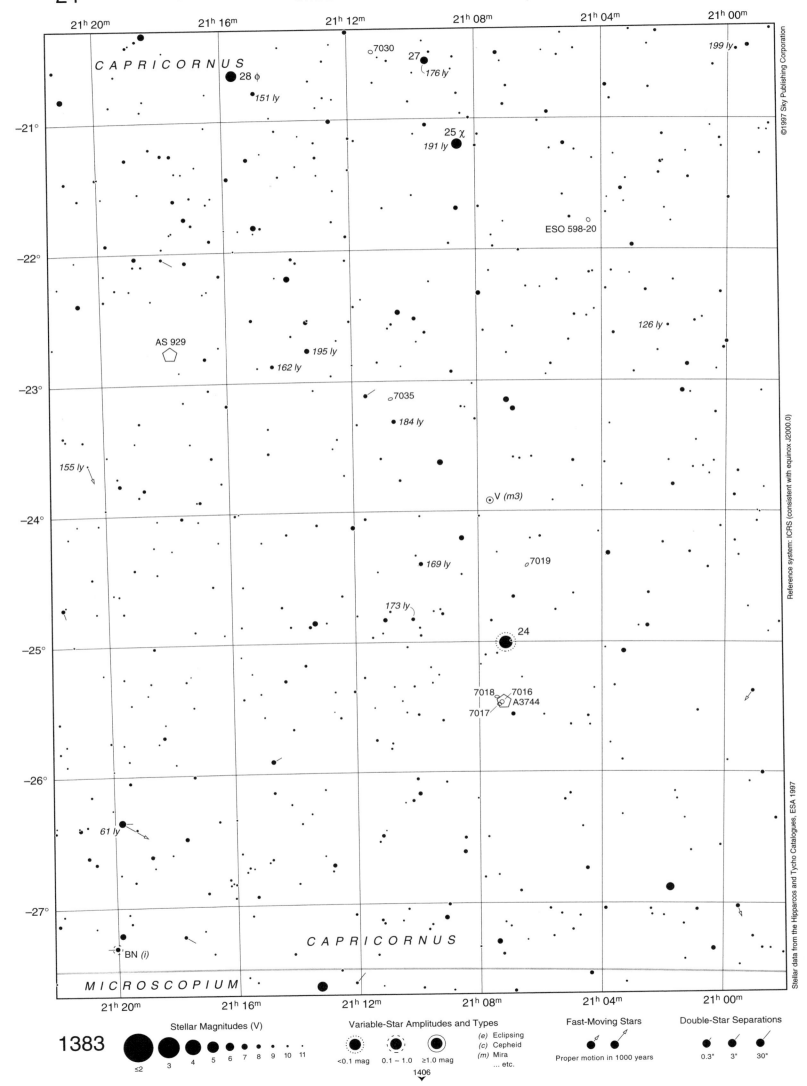

©1997 Sky Publishing Corporation

Reference system: ICRS (consistent with equinox J2000.0)

Stellar data from the Hipparcos and Tycho Catalogues, ESA 1997

21h 20m  21h 16m  21h 12m  21h 08m  21h 04m  21h 00m

CAPRICORNUS

7030

27
*176 ly*

28 φ
*151 ly*

−21°

25 χ
*191 ly*

ESO 598-20

−22°

AS 929

*195 ly*

*126 ly*

*162 ly*

−23°

7035

*184 ly*

*155 ly*

⊙ V *(m3)*

−24°

*169 ly*        7019

*173 ly*

24

−25°

7018      7016
A3744
7017

−26°

61 ly

−27°

CAPRICORNUS

BN *(i)*

MICROSCOPIUM

21h 20m  21h 16m  21h 12m  21h 08m  21h 04m  21h 00m

1383

Stellar Magnitudes (V)

≤2   3   4   5   6   7   8   9  10  11

Variable-Star Amplitudes and Types

<0.1 mag   0.1 – 1.0   ≥1.0 mag

*(e)* Eclipsing
*(c)* Cepheid
*(m)* Mira
... etc.

1406

Fast-Moving Stars

Proper motion in 1000 years

Double-Star Separations

0.3"   3"   30"

# MILLENNIUM STAR ATLAS

−24°

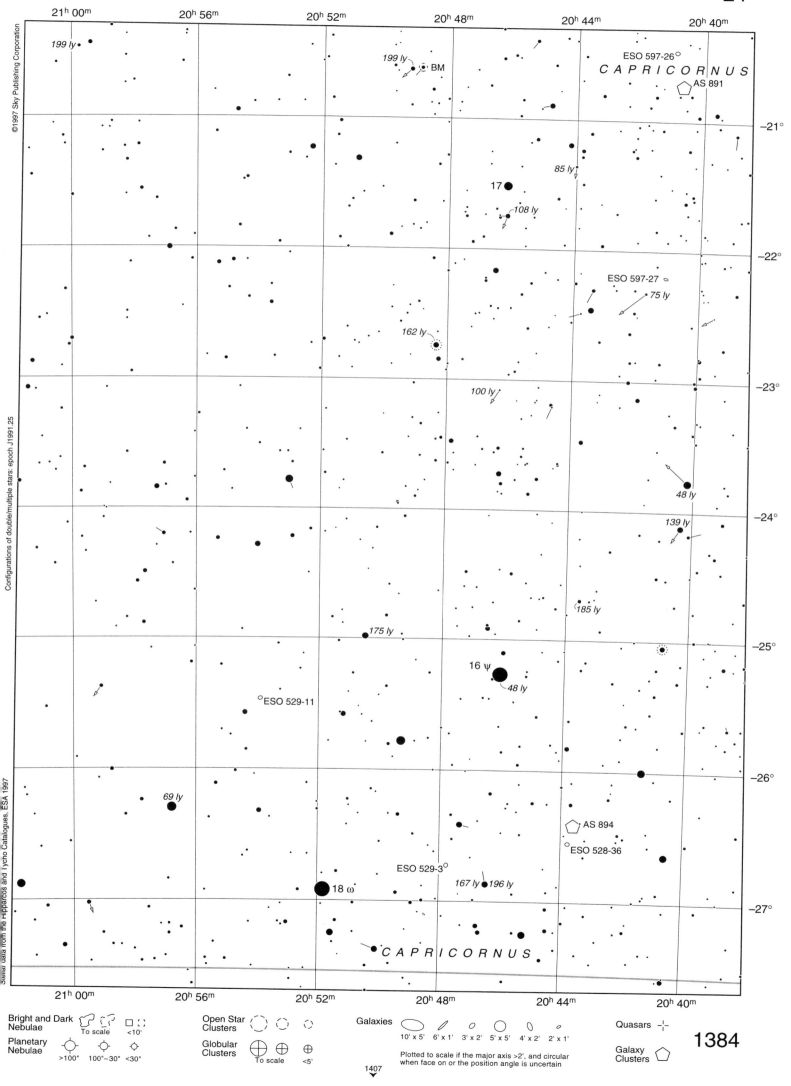

21ʰ 00ᵐ   20ʰ 56ᵐ   20ʰ 52ᵐ   20ʰ 48ᵐ   20ʰ 44ᵐ   20ʰ 40ᵐ

199 ly

199 ly ● BM

*CAPRICORNUS*

ESO 597-26 ○

AS 891

−21°

85 ly

17 ●

108 ly

−22°

ESO 597-27 ∘

75 ly

162 ly

100 ly

−23°

48 ly

139 ly

185 ly

175 ly

−24°

16 ψ ●

48 ly

ESO 529-11

−25°

69 ly

AS 894

○ ESO 528-36

−26°

ESO 529-3 ○

167 ly ● 196 ly

18 ω ●

*CAPRICORNUS*

−27°

21ʰ 00ᵐ   20ʰ 56ᵐ   20ʰ 52ᵐ   20ʰ 48ᵐ   20ʰ 44ᵐ   20ʰ 40ᵐ

**Bright and Dark Nebulae**
To scale    <10'

**Planetary Nebulae**
>100"   100"−30"   <30"

**Open Star Clusters**

**Globular Clusters**
To scale    <5'

**Galaxies**
10' x 5'   6' x 1'   3' x 2'   5' x 5'   4' x 2'   2' x 1'

Plotted to scale if the major axis >2', and circular when face on or the position angle is uncertain

**Quasars**

**Galaxy Clusters**

1384

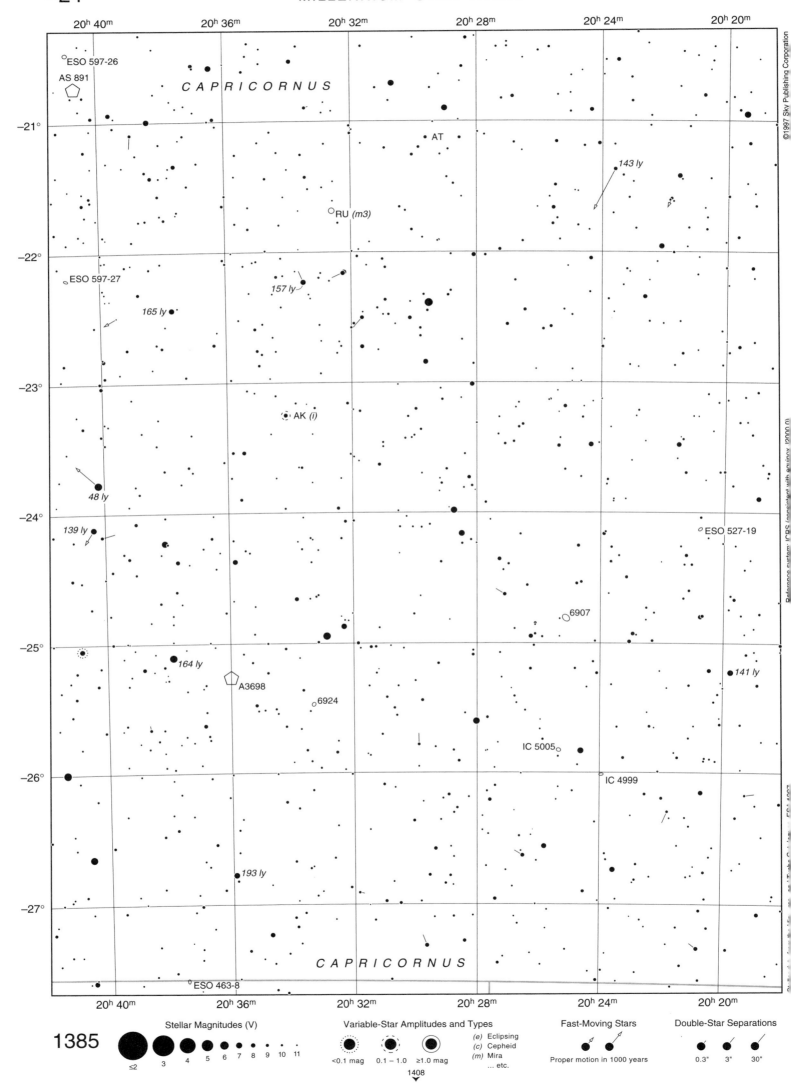

CAPRICORNUS

CAPRICORNUS

Stellar Magnitudes (V)

≤2  3  4  5  6 7 8 9 10 11

Variable-Star Amplitudes and Types

<0.1 mag   0.1 − 1.0   ≥1.0 mag

(e) Eclipsing
(c) Cepheid
(m) Mira
... etc.

Fast-Moving Stars

Proper motion in 1000 years

Double-Star Separations

0.3"   3"   30"

▼
1408

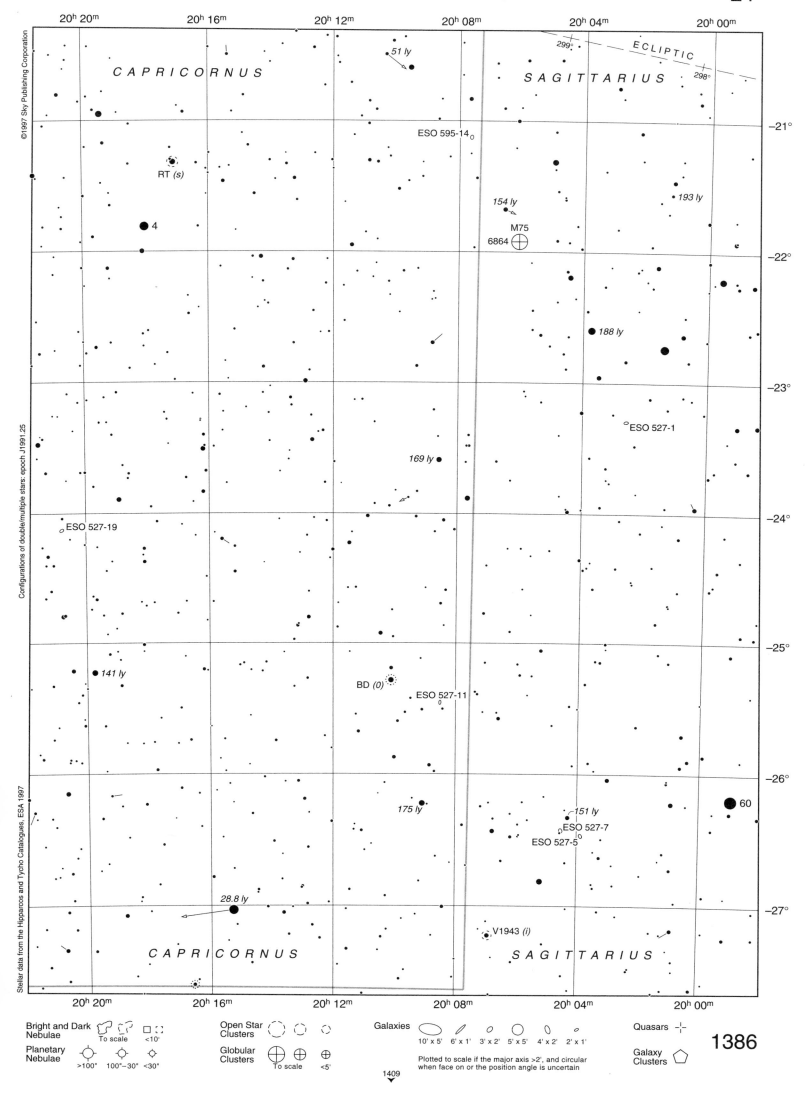

CAPRICORNUS

SAGITTARIUS

ECLIPTIC

51 ly

299°

298°

ESO 595-14

−21°

193 ly

154 ly

RT (s)

M75
6864

4

−22°

188 ly

−23°

ESO 527-1

169 ly

ESO 527-19

−24°

141 ly

BD (0)

ESO 527-11

−25°

60

175 ly

151 ly

ESO 527-7
ESO 527-5

−26°

28.8 ly

−27°

V1943 (i)

CAPRICORNUS

SAGITTARIUS

20h 20m    20h 16m    20h 12m    20h 08m    20h 04m    20h 00m

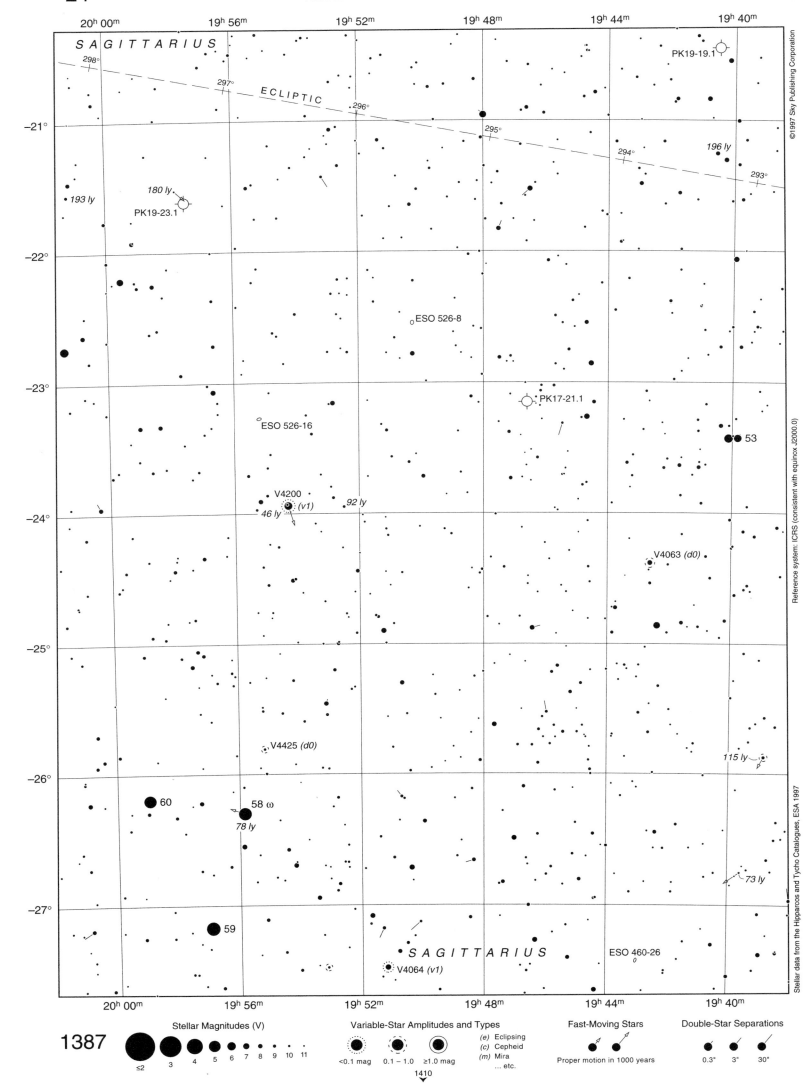

SAGITTARIUS

ECLIPTIC

298°    297°    296°    295°    294°    293°

PK19-19.1

196 ly

193 ly

180 ly

PK19-23.1

ESO 526-8

ESO 526-16

PK17-21.1

53

V4200    (v1)

92 ly

46 ly

V4063 (d0)

V4425 (d0)

115 ly

60    58 ω

78 ly

73 ly

59

SAGITTARIUS

ESO 460-26

V4064 (v1)

©1997 Sky Publishing Corporation

Reference system: ICRS (consistent with equinox J2000.0)

Stellar data from the Hipparcos and Tycho Catalogues, ESA 1997

1387

Stellar Magnitudes (V)

●  ●  ●  ●  ●  •  •  ·  ·  ·
≤2  3  4  5  6  7  8  9  10  11

Variable-Star Amplitudes and Types

<0.1 mag    0.1 – 1.0    ≥1.0 mag

(e) Eclipsing
(c) Cepheid
(m) Mira
... etc.

1410

Fast-Moving Stars

Proper motion in 1000 years

Double-Star Separations

0.3"    3"    30"

# MILLENNIUM STAR ATLAS

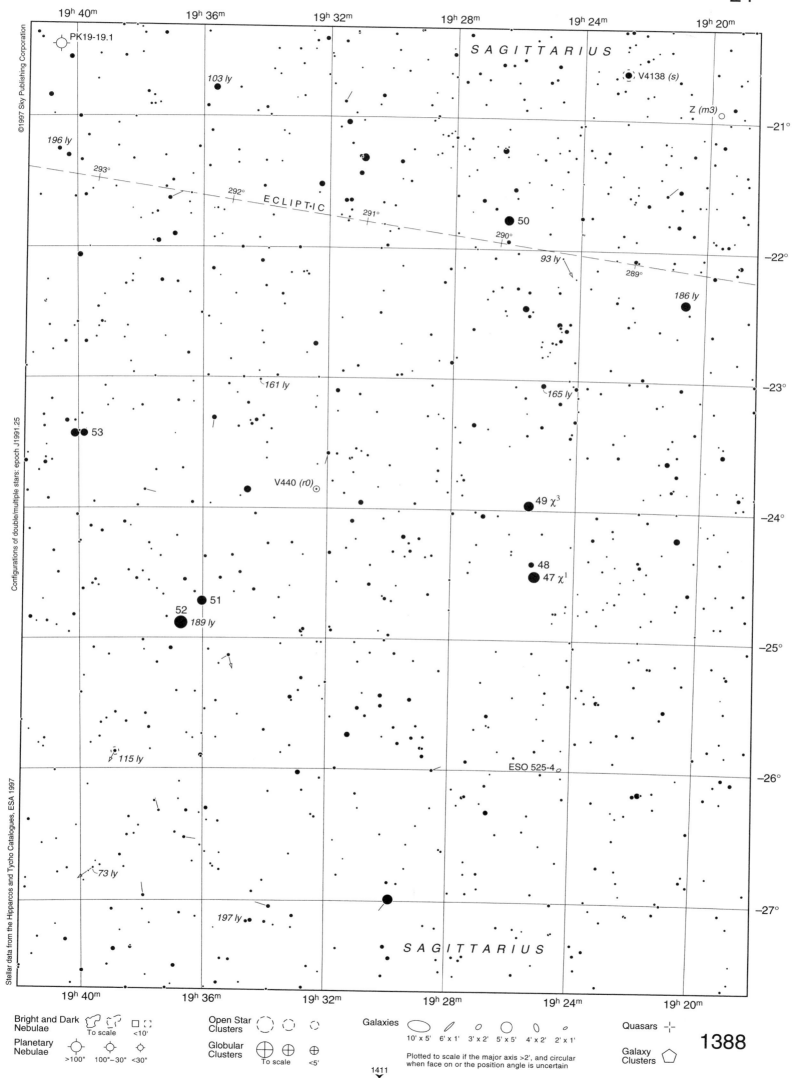

SAGITTARIUS

PK19-19.1

V4138 (s)

Z (m3)

103 ly

196 ly

293°

292°

ECLIPTIC

291°

50

290°

93 ly

289°

186 ly

161 ly

165 ly

53

V440 (r0)

49 χ³

48

47 χ¹

51

52

189 ly

115 ly

ESO 525-4

73 ly

197 ly

SAGITTARIUS

| | | | |
|---|---|---|---|
| **Bright and Dark Nebulae** | To scale | <10' | |
| **Planetary Nebulae** | >100" 100"−30" <30" | | |
| **Open Star Clusters** | | | |
| **Globular Clusters** | To scale | <5' | |
| **Galaxies** | 10' x 5' 6' x 1' 3' x 2' 5' x 5' 4' x 2' 2' x 1' | | |
| | Plotted to scale if the major axis >2', and circular when face on or the position angle is uncertain | | |
| **Quasars** | | | |
| **Galaxy Clusters** | | | |

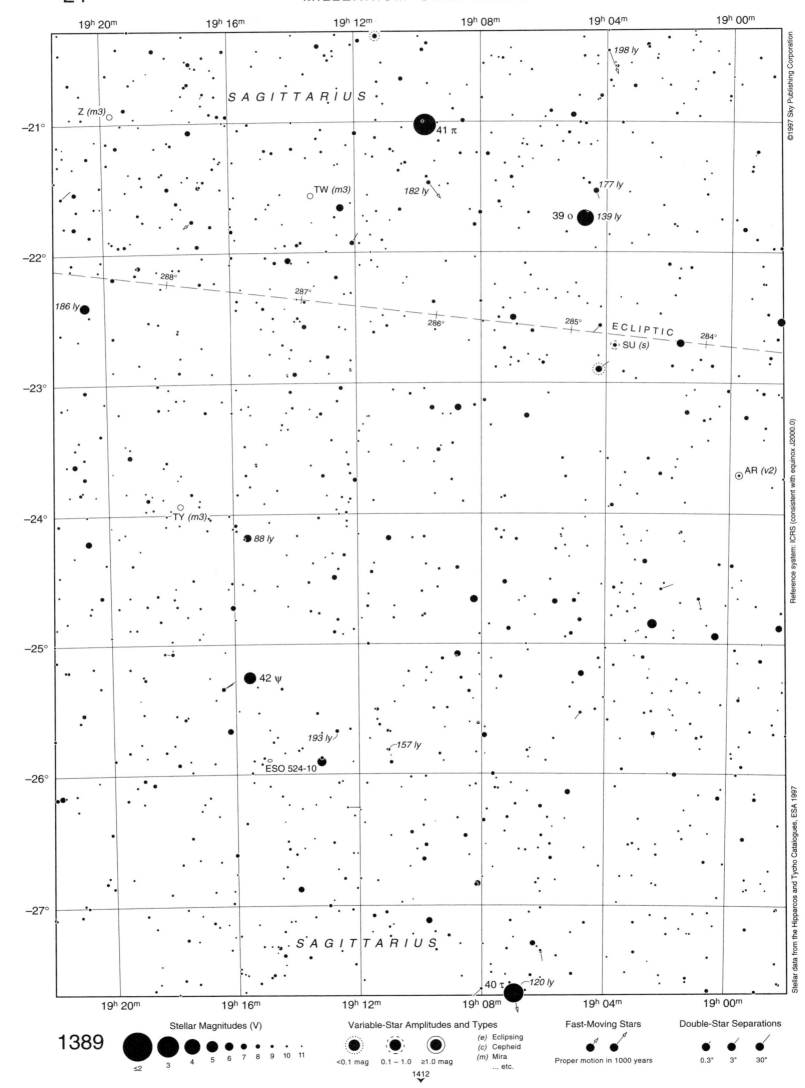

1389

Stellar Magnitudes (V)

≤2   3   4   5   6 7 8 9 10 11

Variable-Star Amplitudes and Types

<0.1 mag   0.1 – 1.0   ≥1.0 mag

(e) Eclipsing
(c) Cepheid
(m) Mira
... etc.

Fast-Moving Stars

Proper motion in 1000 years

Double-Star Separations

0.3"   3"   30"

# MILLENNIUM STAR ATLAS

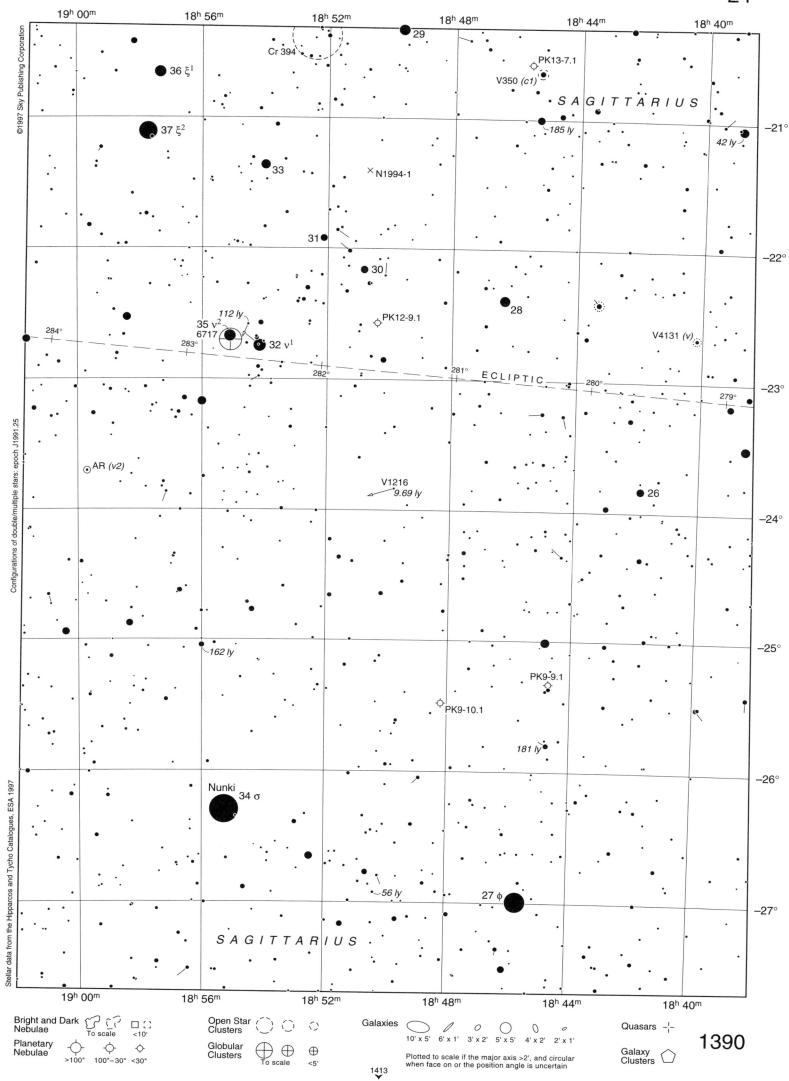

Configurations of double/multiple stars: epoch J1991.25

Stellar data from the Hipparcos and Tycho Catalogues, ESA 1997

19h 00m · 18h 56m · 18h 52m · 18h 48m · 18h 44m · 18h 40m

Cr 394

29

PK13-7.1

V350 (c1)

36 ξ¹

SAGITTARIUS

37 ξ²

−21°

185 ly

42 ly

33

N1994-1

31

30

−22°

28

112 ly

35 ν²

6717

PK12-9.1

V4131 (v)

284°

283°

32 ν¹

282°

281°

ECLIPTIC

280°

279°

−23°

AR (v2)

V1216

9.69 ly

26

−24°

162 ly

−25°

PK9-9.1

PK9-10.1

181 ly

Nunki

34 σ

−26°

56 ly

27 φ

−27°

SAGITTARIUS

19h 00m · 18h 56m · 18h 52m · 18h 48m · 18h 44m · 18h 40m

| Bright and Dark Nebulae | | Open Star Clusters | Galaxies | | | | | | Quasars |
|---|---|---|---|---|---|---|---|---|---|
| To scale | <10' | | 10' x 5' | 6' x 1' | 3' x 2' | 5' x 5' | 4' x 2' | 2' x 1' | |

| Planetary Nebulae | | | Globular Clusters | | | | | | Galaxy Clusters |
|---|---|---|---|---|---|---|---|---|---|
| >100" | 100"-30" | <30" | To scale | <5' | | Plotted to scale if the major axis >2', and circular when face on or the position angle is uncertain | | | |

−24°

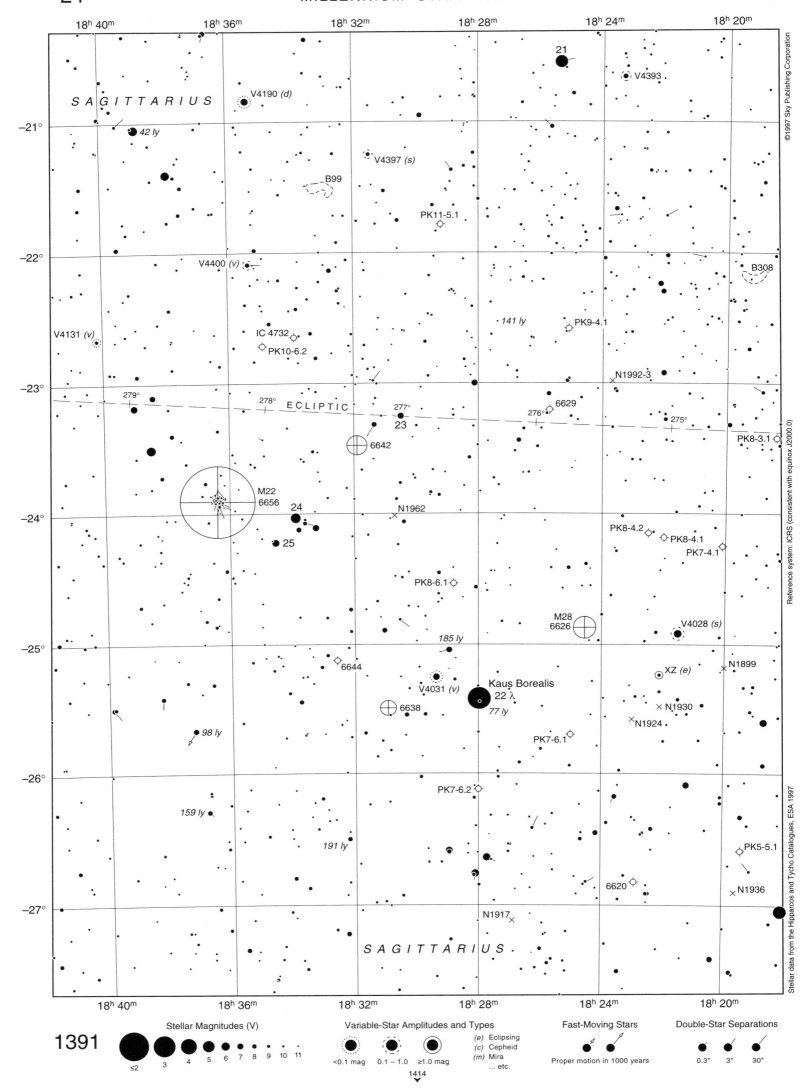

Reference system: ICRS (consistent with equinox J2000.0)

Stellar data from the Hipparcos and Tycho Catalogues, ESA 1997

SAGITTARIUS

V4190 (d)

42 ly

V4397 (s)

B99

PK11-5.1

21

V4393

V4400 (v)

B308

V4131 (v)

IC 4732
PK10-6.2

141 ly

PK9-4.1

N1992-3

279°

278° ECLIPTIC

277°
23

276° 6629

275°

PK8-3.1

6642

M22
6656

24

25

N1962

PK8-4.2 PK8-4.1
PK7-4.1

PK8-6.1

M28
6626

V4028 (s)

185 ly

6644

V4031 (v)

6638

Kaus Borealis
22 λ
77 ly

XZ (e)

N1899

N1930

N1924

98 ly

PK7-6.1

159 ly

191 ly

PK7-6.2

PK5-5.1

6620

N1936

N1917

SAGITTARIUS

1391

Stellar Magnitudes (V)

≤2   3   4   5   6   7   8   9   10   11

Variable-Star Amplitudes and Types

<0.1 mag   0.1 – 1.0   ≥1.0 mag

(e) Eclipsing
(c) Cepheid
(m) Mira
... etc.

Fast-Moving Stars

Proper motion in 1000 years

Double-Star Separations

0.3"   3"   30"

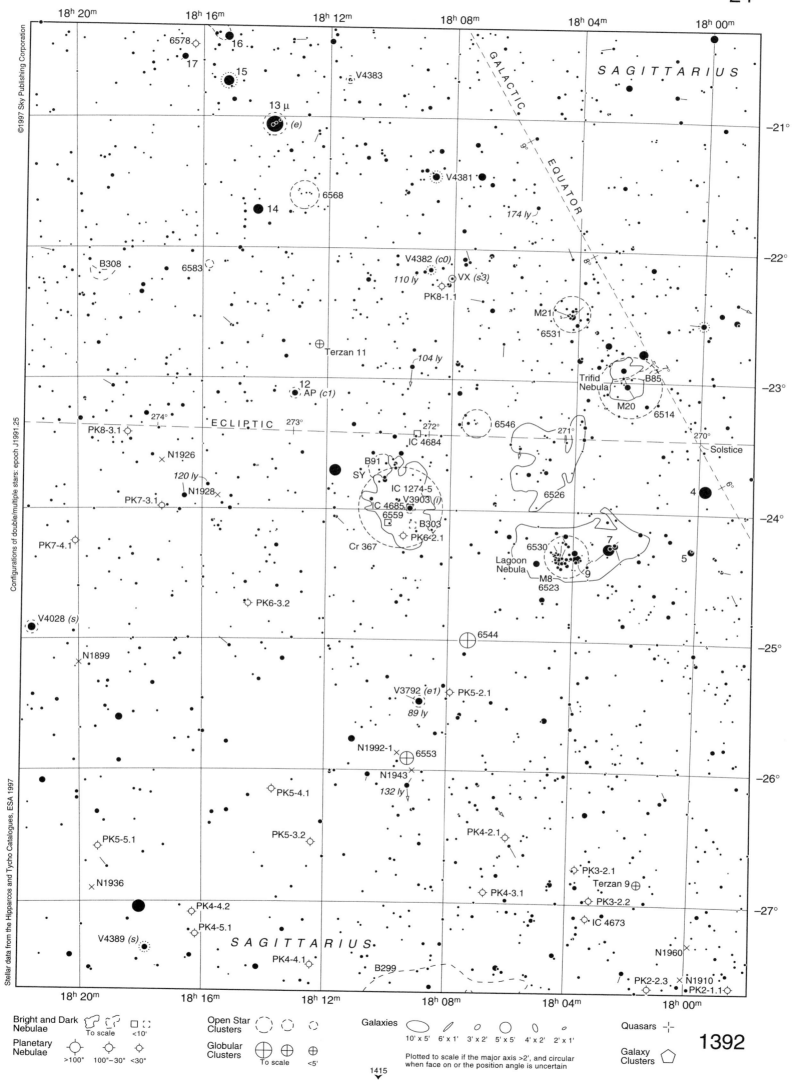

©1997 Sky Publishing Corporation

Configurations of double/multiple stars: epoch J1991.25

Stellar data from the Hipparcos and Tycho Catalogues, ESA 1997

18h 20m    18h 16m    18h 12m    18h 08m    18h 04m    18h 00m

SAGITTARIUS

−21°

−22°

−23°

−24°

−25°

−26°

−27°

6578
16
17
15
13 μ (e)
14
6568
V4383
V4381
174 ly
B308    6583
V4382 (c0)
110 ly    VX (s3)
PK8-1.1
M21
6531
Trifid Nebula    B85
M20    6514
Terzan 11
104 ly
12 AP (c1)
274°    ECLIPTIC    273°    272°    271°    270°    Solstice
PK8-3.1    6546
IC 4684
N1926
120 ly    B91    IC 1274-5
SY    V3903 (i)
N1928    IC 4685    6526
PK7-3.1    6559    B303
PK6-2.1    6530    7
Cr 367    Lagoon    9
PK7-4.1    Nebula    5
M8    4
6523
PK6-3.2
V4028 (s)
6544
N1899
V3792 (e1)    PK5-2.1
89 ly
N1992-1    6553
N1943
132 ly
PK5-4.1
PK5-3.2    PK4-2.1
PK5-5.1    PK3-2.1
Terzan 9
N1936    PK4-3.1    PK3-2.2
PK4-4.2    IC 4673
PK4-5.1    N1960
V4389 (s)    N1910
SAGITTARIUS    PK2-2.3
PK4-4.1    PK2-1.1
B299

18h 20m    18h 16m    18h 12m    18h 08m    18h 04m    18h 00m

Bright and Dark Nebulae
To scale    <10'

Planetary Nebulae
>100"    100"−30"    <30"

Open Star Clusters

Globular Clusters
To scale    <5'

Galaxies
10' x 5'    6' x 1'    3' x 2'    5' x 5'    4' x 2'    2' x 1'

Plotted to scale if the major axis >2', and circular when face on or the position angle is uncertain

Quasars

Galaxy Clusters

1392

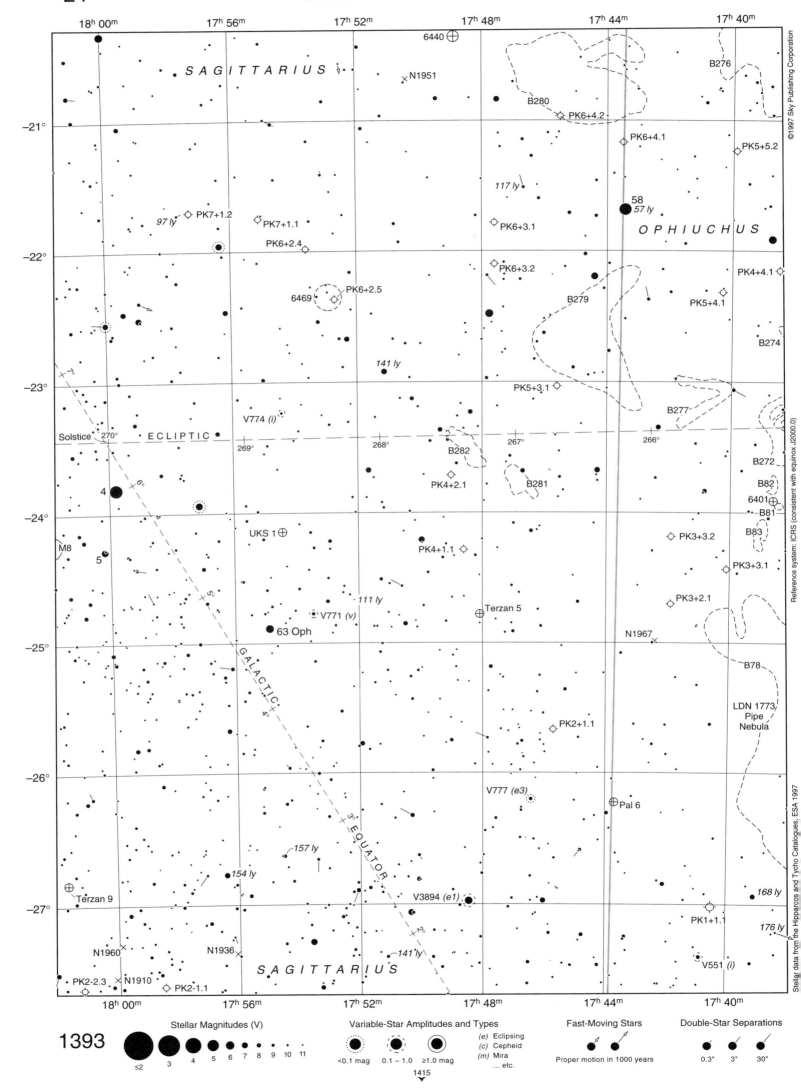

©1997 Sky Publishing Corporation

Reference system: ICRS (consistent with equinox J2000.0)

Stellar data from the Hipparcos and Tycho Catalogues, ESA 1997

SAGITTARIUS

6440

N1951

B280

PK6+4.2

PK6+4.1

PK5+5.2

B276

117 ly

58
57 ly

OPHIUCHUS

PK7+1.2

PK7+1.1

PK6+3.1

97 ly

PK6+2.4

PK6+3.2

PK4+4.1

PK5+4.1

6469

PK6+2.5

B279

B274

141 ly

PK5+3.1

B277

V774 (i)

ECLIPTIC

Solstice  270°     269°           268°        B282       267°                    266°

B272

4

PK4+2.1

B281

B82

6401

B81

UKS 1

PK4+1.1

PK3+3.2

B83

PK3+3.1

M8

5

111 ly

V771 (v)

Terzan 5

PK3+2.1

63 Oph

N1967

GALACTIC

B78

LDN 1773
Pipe
Nebula

PK2+1.1

V777 (e3)

Pal 6

157 ly

154 ly

EQUATOR

168 ly

Terzan 9

V3894 (e1)

PK1+1.1

176 ly

N1960

N1936

141 ly

V551 (i)

SAGITTARIUS

PK2-2.3    N1910    PK2-1.1

Stellar Magnitudes (V)

≤2    3    4    5    6    7    8    9    10    11

Variable-Star Amplitudes and Types

<0.1 mag    0.1 – 1.0    ≥1.0 mag

(e) Eclipsing
(c) Cepheid
(m) Mira
... etc.

Fast-Moving Stars

Proper motion in 1000 years

Double-Star Separations

0.3"    3"    30"

1415

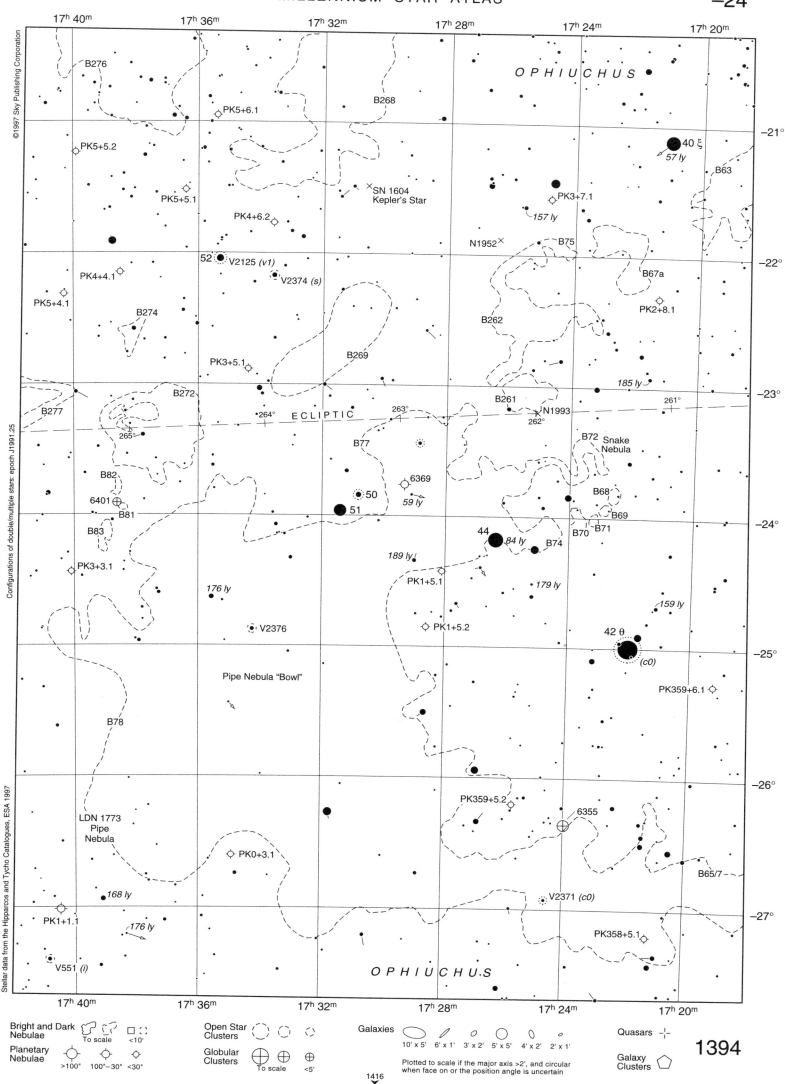

OPHIUCHUS

B276

PK5+6.1

B268

PK5+5.2

40 ξ
57 ly

B63

PK5+5.1

SN 1604
Kepler's Star

PK3+7.1
157 ly

PK4+6.2

N1952

B75

B67a

52 V2125 (v1)

PK4+4.1

V2374 (s)

B262

PK2+8.1

PK5+4.1

B274

PK3+5.1

B269

185 ly

B272

B261

N1993
262°

261°

B277

265°

ECLIPTIC   264°   263°

B77

B72   Snake
Nebula

B82

6369

6401

50

B68

B81

59 ly

B69

B83

51

44
84 ly

B74

B70   B71

PK3+3.1

189 ly

PK1+5.1

179 ly

176 ly

159 ly

V2376

PK1+5.2

42 θ

Pipe Nebula "Bowl"

(c0)

PK359+6.1

B78

PK359+5.2

6355

LDN 1773
Pipe
Nebula

PK0+3.1

B65/7

168 ly

V2371 (c0)

PK1+1.1

176 ly

PK358+5.1

V551 (i)

OPHIUCHUS

Bright and Dark
Nebulae
To scale   <10'

Planetary
Nebulae
>100"  100"–30"  <30"

Open Star
Clusters

Globular
Clusters
To scale   <5'

Galaxies
10' x 5'  6' x 1'  3' x 2'  5' x 4'  4' x 2'  2' x 1'
Plotted to scale if the major axis >2', and circular
when face on or the position angle is uncertain

Quasars

Galaxy
Clusters

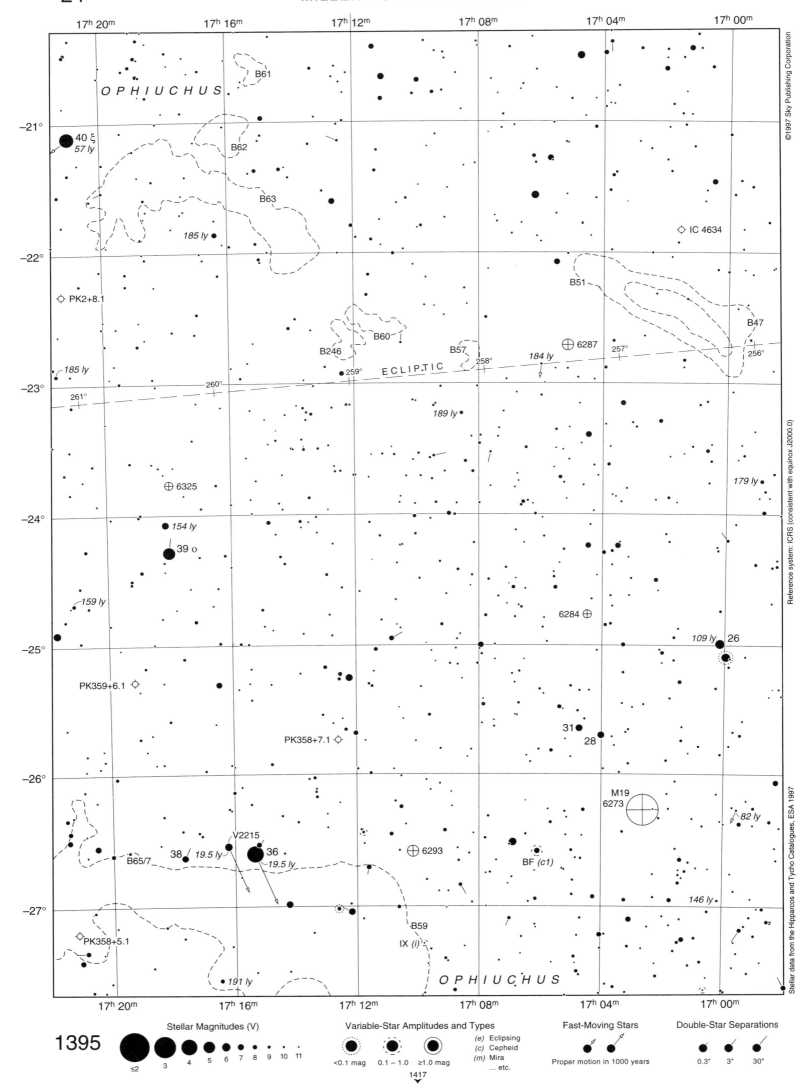

©1997 Sky Publishing Corporation

Reference system: ICRS (consistent with equinox J2000.0)

Stellar data from the Hipparcos and Tycho Catalogues, ESA 1997

1395

Stellar Magnitudes (V)

≤2  3  4  5  6  7  8  9  10  11

Variable-Star Amplitudes and Types

<0.1 mag    0.1 – 1.0    ≥1.0 mag

(e) Eclipsing
(c) Cepheid
(m) Mira
... etc.

Fast-Moving Stars

Proper motion in 1000 years

Double-Star Separations

0.3"    3"    30"

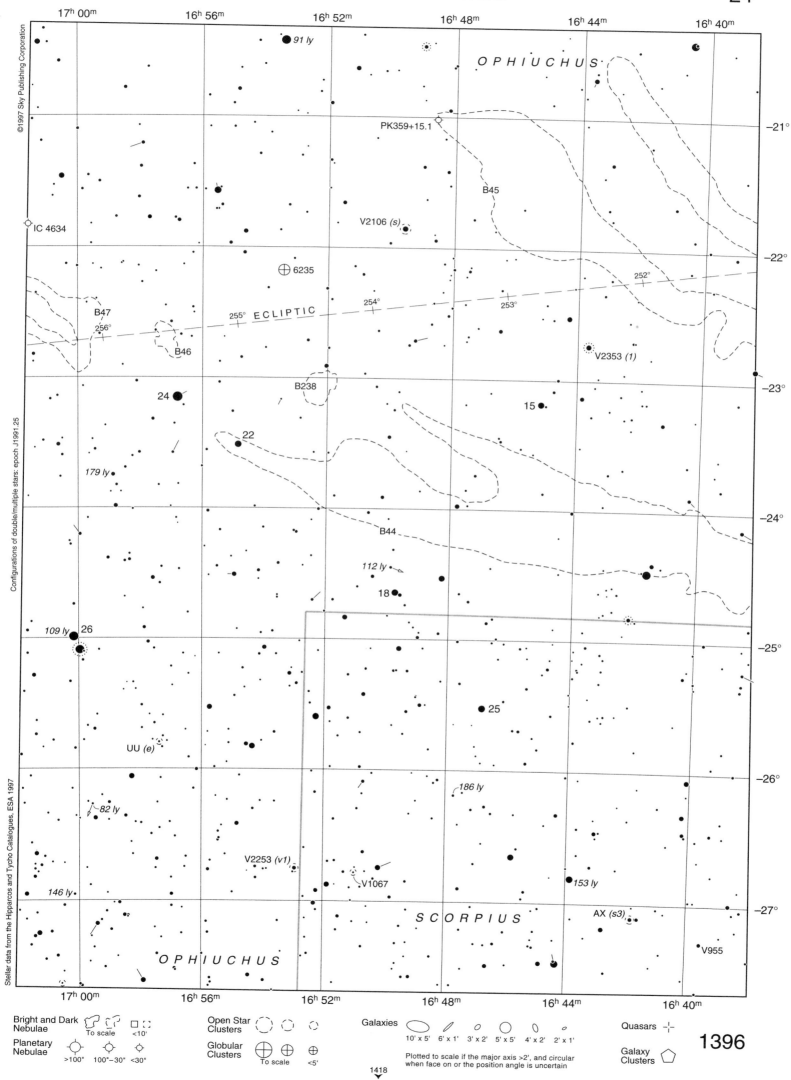

Configurations of double/multiple stars: epoch J1991.25

Stellar data from the Hipparcos and Tycho Catalogues, ESA 1997

OPHIUCHUS

PK359+15.1

B45

V2106 (s)

6235

B47

256°

255° ECLIPTIC

B46

254°

253°

252°

V2353 (1)

B238

24

22

179 ly

15

B44

112 ly

18

26

109 ly

25

UU (e)

82 ly

186 ly

V2253 (v1)

V1067

153 ly

146 ly

AX (s3)

SCORPIUS

OPHIUCHUS

V955

| Bright and Dark Nebulae | To scale | <10' |
| --- | --- | --- |
| Planetary Nebulae | >100" 100"−30" <30" | |

| Open Star Clusters | | |
| --- | --- | --- |
| Globular Clusters | To scale <5' | |

Galaxies

10' x 5'   6' x 1'   3' x 2'   5' x 5'   4' x 2'   2' x 1'

Plotted to scale if the major axis >2', and circular when face on or the position angle is uncertain

Quasars

Galaxy Clusters

1396

1418

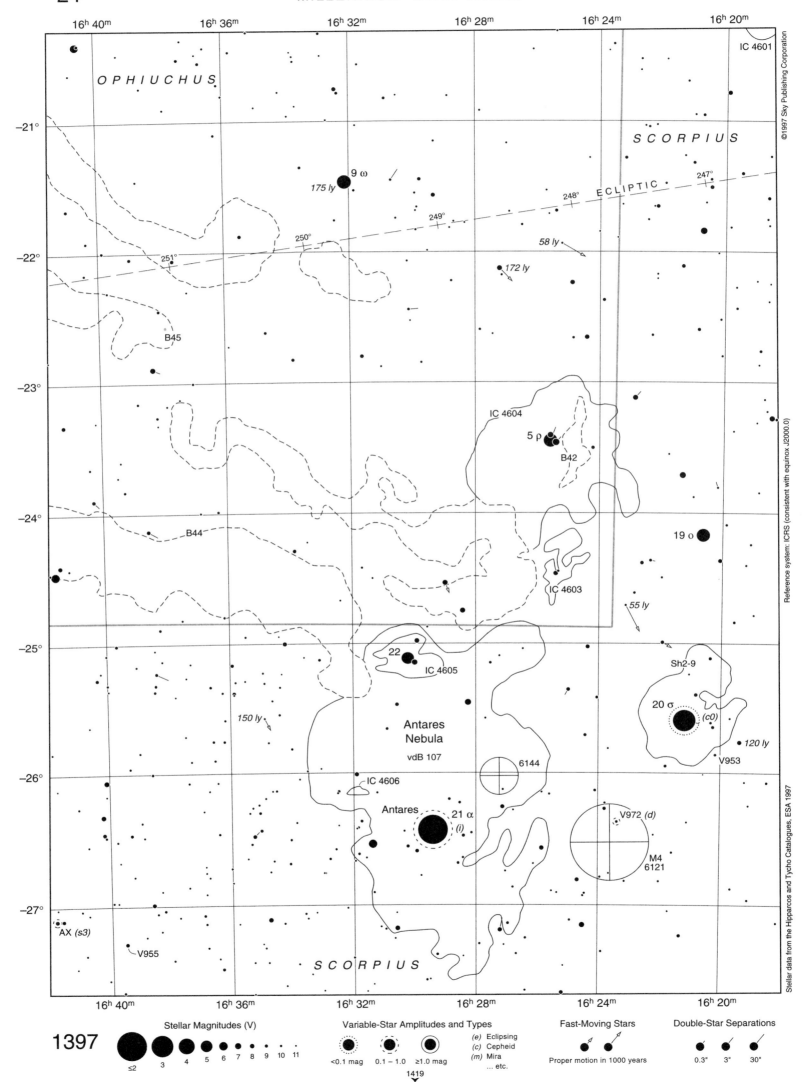

©1997 Sky Publishing Corporation

Reference system: ICRS (consistent with equinox J2000.0)

Stellar data from the Hipparcos and Tycho Catalogues, ESA 1997

1397

Stellar Magnitudes (V)

≤2   3   4   5   6   7   8   9   10   11

Variable-Star Amplitudes and Types

<0.1 mag    0.1 – 1.0    ≥1.0 mag

(e) Eclipsing
(c) Cepheid
(m) Mira
... etc.

Fast-Moving Stars

Proper motion in 1000 years

Double-Star Separations

0.3"   3"   30"

↓
1419

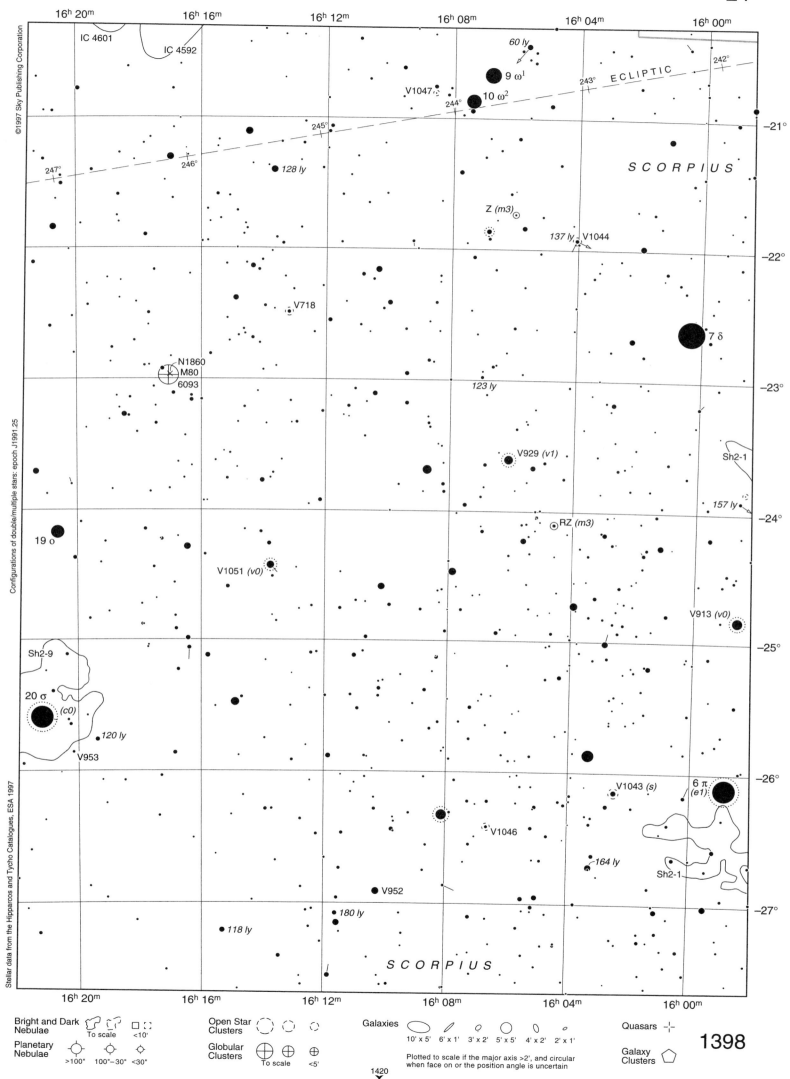

IC 4601
IC 4592
16h 20m
16h 16m
16h 12m
16h 08m
16h 04m
16h 00m

60 ly
9 ω¹
V1047
10 ω²
244°
243°
242°
ECLIPTIC
−21°
245°
SCORPIUS
247°
246°
128 ly
Z (m3)
137 ly V1044
−22°
V718
7 δ
N1860
M80
6093
123 ly
−23°
V929 (v1)
Sh2-1
157 ly
−24°
RZ (m3)
19 o
V1051 (v0)
V913 (v0)
−25°
Sh2-9
20 σ
(c0)
120 ly
V953
6 π
(e1)
V1043 (s)
−26°
V1046
164 ly
Sh2-1
V952
−27°
180 ly
118 ly
SCORPIUS

16h 20m
16h 16m
16h 12m
16h 08m
16h 04m
16h 00m

Bright and Dark Nebulae
To scale
<10'

Open Star Clusters

Galaxies
10' x 5'   6' x 1'   3' x 2'   5' x 5'   4' x 2'   2' x 1'

Quasars

Planetary Nebulae
>100"   100"−30"   <30"

Globular Clusters
To scale
<5'

Plotted to scale if the major axis >2', and circular when face on or the position angle is uncertain

Galaxy Clusters

1398

1420

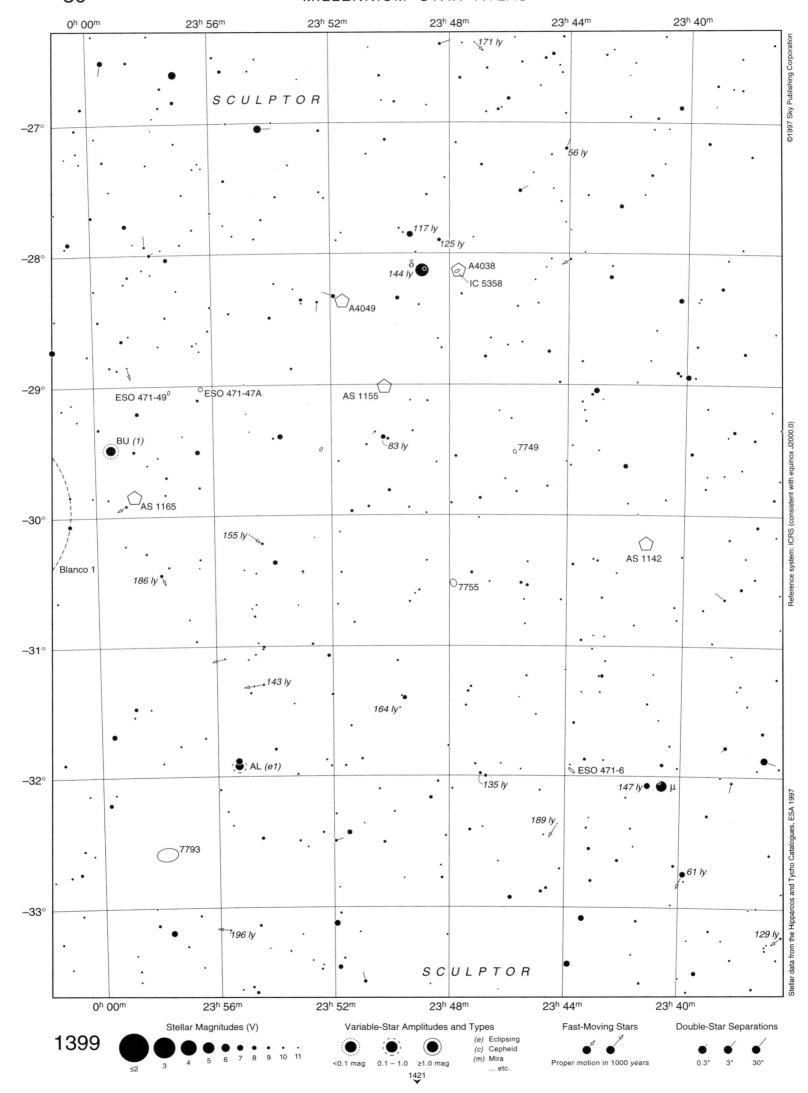

S C U L P T O R

171 ly

56 ly

117 ly
125 ly

δ
144 ly

A4038
IC 5358

A4049

AS 1155

ESO 471-49⁰    ESO 471-47A

BU (1)

7749

83 ly

AS 1165

155 ly

Blanco 1

AS 1142

186 ly

7755

143 ly

164 ly

AL (e1)

ESO 471-6

135 ly

147 ly  μ

189 ly

7793

61 ly

196 ly

129 ly

S C U L P T O R

1399

### Stellar Magnitudes (V)

≤2   3   4   5   6   7   8   9   10   11

### Variable-Star Amplitudes and Types

<0.1 mag    0.1 − 1.0    ≥1.0 mag

(e) Eclipsing
(c) Cepheid
(m) Mira
... etc.

### Fast-Moving Stars

Proper motion in 1000 years

### Double-Star Separations

0.3"   3"   30"

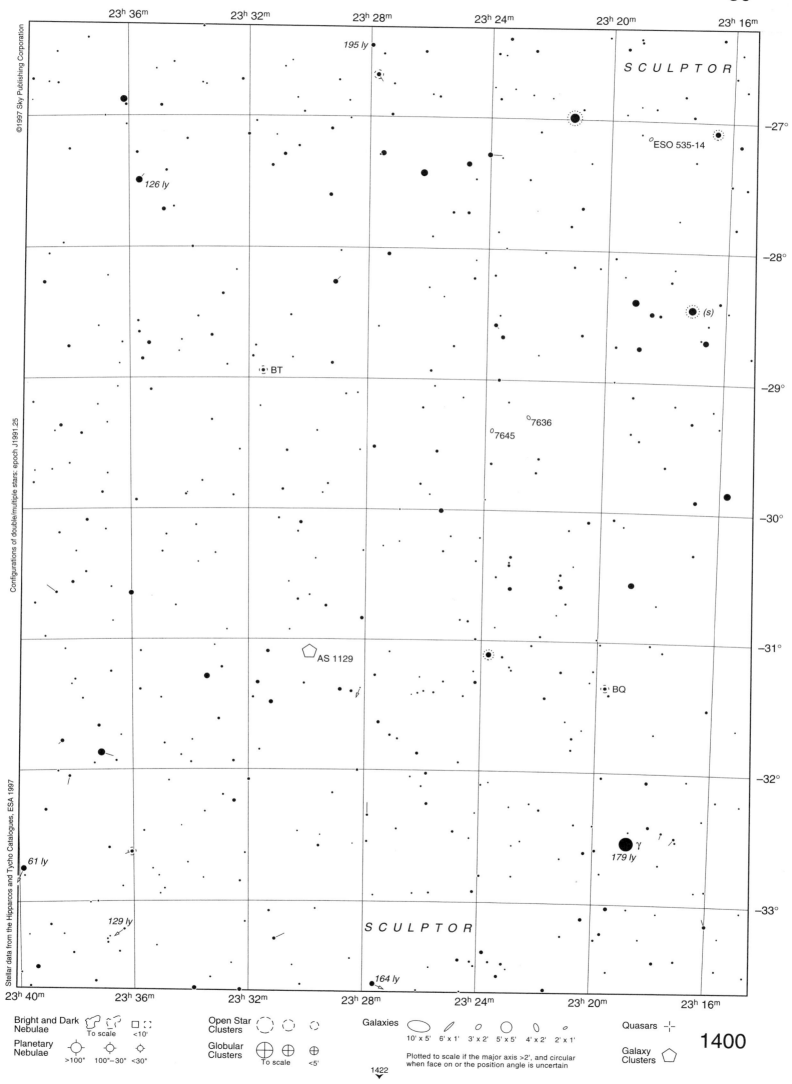

©1997 Sky Publishing Corporation

Configurations of double/multiple stars: epoch J1991.25

Stellar data from the Hipparcos and Tycho Catalogues, ESA 1997

SCULPTOR

ESO 535-14

126 ly

195 ly

(s)

BT

7636
7645

AS 1129

BQ

γ
179 ly

61 ly

129 ly

SCULPTOR

164 ly

| Bright and Dark Nebulae | Open Star Clusters | Galaxies | Quasars |
| To scale  <10' | | 10' x 5'  6' x 1'  3' x 2'  5' x 5'  4' x 2'  2' x 1' | |
| Planetary Nebulae | Globular Clusters | | Galaxy Clusters |
| >100"  100"–30"  <30" | To scale  <5' | Plotted to scale if the major axis >2', and circular when face on or the position angle is uncertain | |

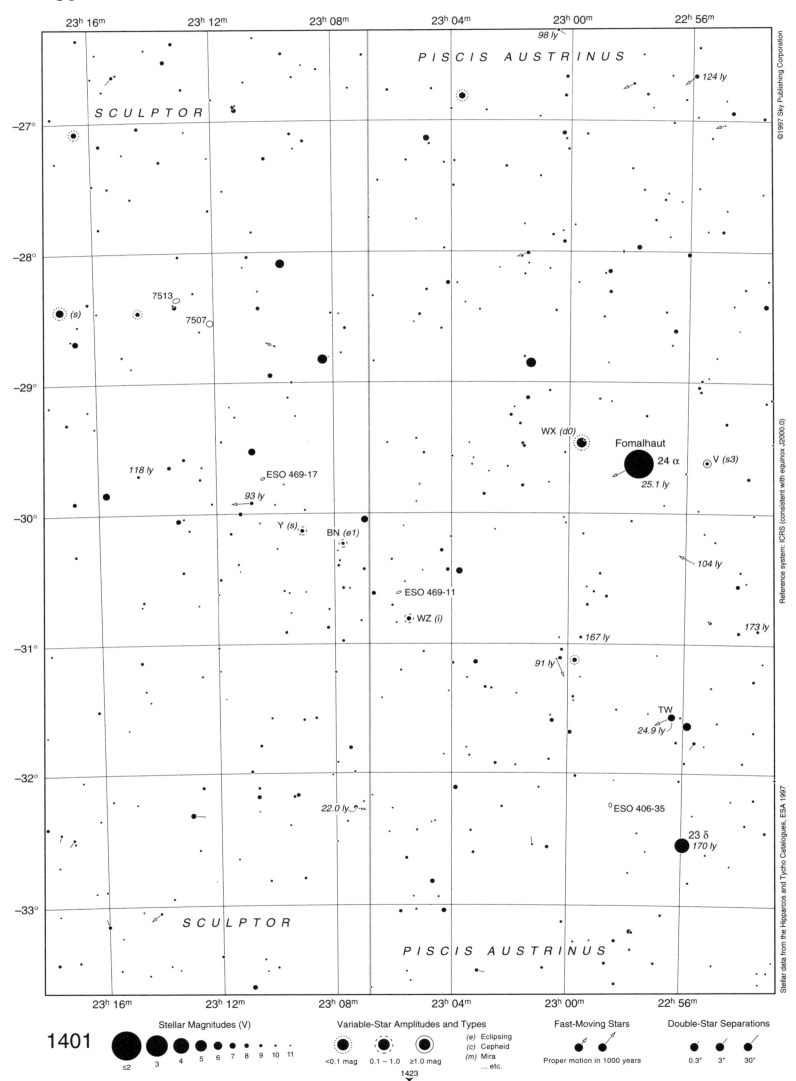

PISCIS AUSTRINUS

SCULPTOR

98 ly

124 ly

7513

7507

(s)

118 ly

ESO 469-17

93 ly

WX (d0)

Fomalhaut
24 α
25.1 ly

V (s3)

Y (s)

BN (e1)

ESO 469-11

WZ (i)

104 ly

167 ly

173 ly

91 ly

TW
24.9 ly

22.0 ly

ESO 406-35

23 δ
170 ly

SCULPTOR

PISCIS AUSTRINUS

1401

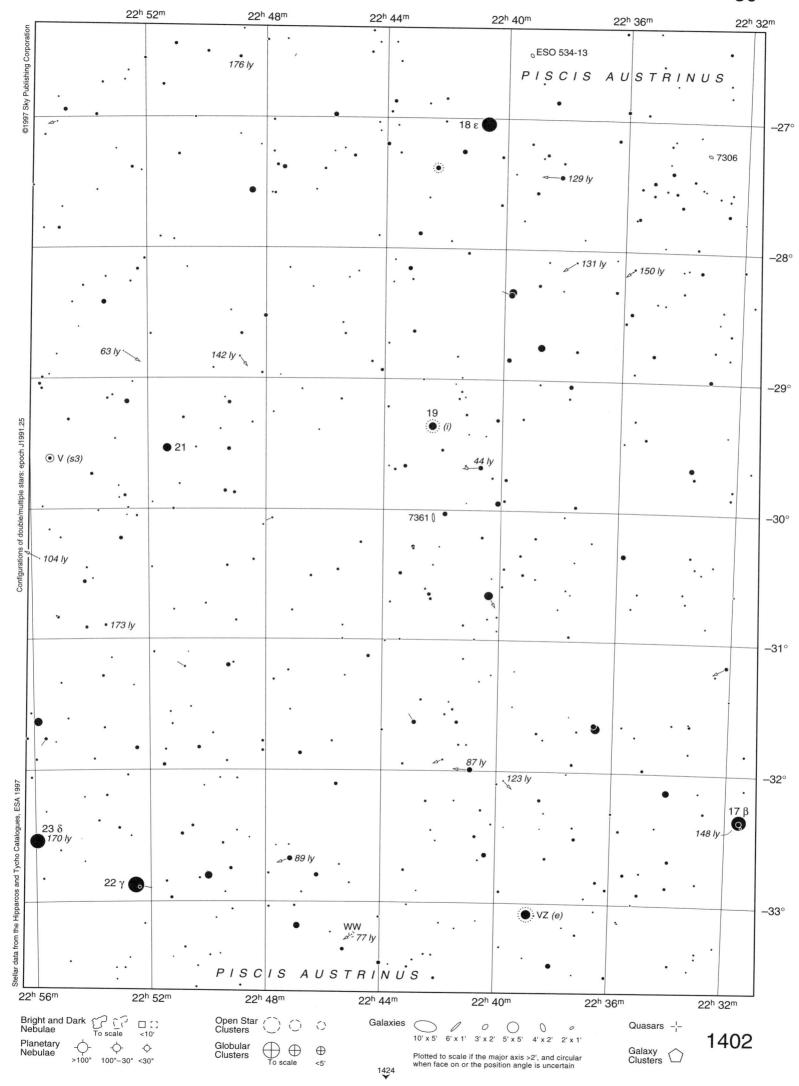

ESO 534-13

*PISCIS  AUSTRINUS*

18 ε

7306

129 ly

131 ly

150 ly

63 ly

142 ly

19

(i)

21

44 ly

V (s3)

7361

104 ly

173 ly

87 ly

123 ly

17 β

23 δ
170 ly

148 ly

22 γ

89 ly

VZ (e)

WW
77 ly

*PISCIS  AUSTRINUS*

22ʰ 52ᵐ   22ʰ 48ᵐ   22ʰ 44ᵐ   22ʰ 40ᵐ   22ʰ 36ᵐ   22ʰ 32ᵐ

−27°

−28°

−29°

−30°

−31°

−32°

−33°

22ʰ 56ᵐ   22ʰ 52ᵐ   22ʰ 48ᵐ   22ʰ 44ᵐ   22ʰ 40ᵐ   22ʰ 36ᵐ   22ʰ 32ᵐ

| Bright and Dark Nebulae | | | |
| --- | --- | --- | --- |
| To scale | <10' | | |

Planetary Nebulae
>100"  100"–30"  <30"

Open Star Clusters

Globular Clusters
To scale  <5'

Galaxies
10' x 5'  6' x 1'  3' x 2'  5' x 5'  4' x 2'  2' x 1'

Plotted to scale if the major axis >2', and circular when face on or the position angle is uncertain

Quasars

Galaxy Clusters

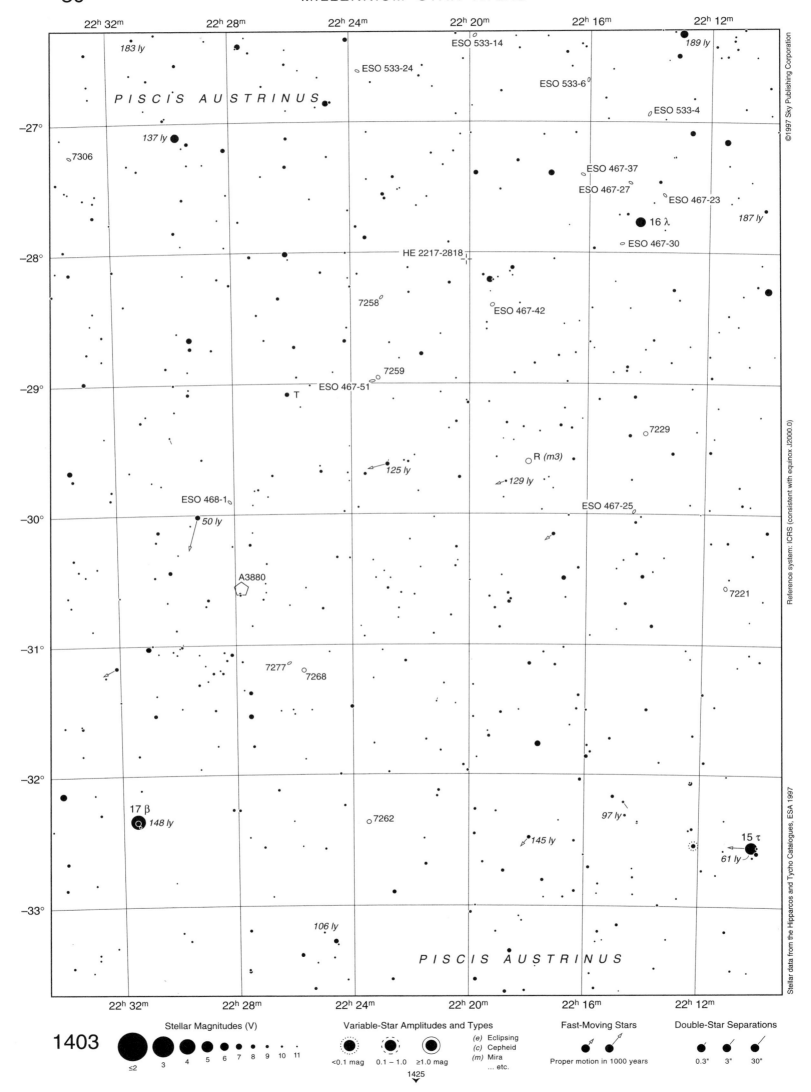

©1997 Sky Publishing Corporation

Reference system: ICRS (consistent with equinox J2000.0)

Stellar data from the Hipparcos and Tycho Catalogues, ESA 1997

22h 32m    22h 28m    22h 24m    22h 20m    22h 16m    22h 12m

183 ly

ESO 533-14

189 ly

ESO 533-24

ESO 533-6

PISCIS AUSTRINUS

ESO 533-4

−27°    137 ly

7306

ESO 467-37

ESO 467-27

ESO 467-23

187 ly

16 λ

ESO 467-30

HE 2217-2818

−28°

ESO 467-42

7258

7259

7229

ESO 467-51

−29°    T

R (m3)

125 ly    129 ly

ESO 468-1    ESO 467-25

−30°    50 ly

7221

A3880

−31°

7277    7268

−32°

17 β

97 ly

7262

15 τ

Q    148 ly    145 ly    61 ly

−33°    106 ly

PISCIS AUSTRINUS

22h 32m    22h 28m    22h 24m    22h 20m    22h 16m    22h 12m

1403    Stellar Magnitudes (V)    Variable-Star Amplitudes and Types    Fast-Moving Stars    Double-Star Separations

≤2    3    4    5    6  7  8  9 10 11    <0.1 mag    0.1 – 1.0    ≥1.0 mag    (e) Eclipsing    Proper motion in 1000 years    0.3"    3"    30"
                                                                              (c) Cepheid
                                                                              (m) Mira
                                                                              ... etc.

1425

# MILLENNIUM STAR ATLAS

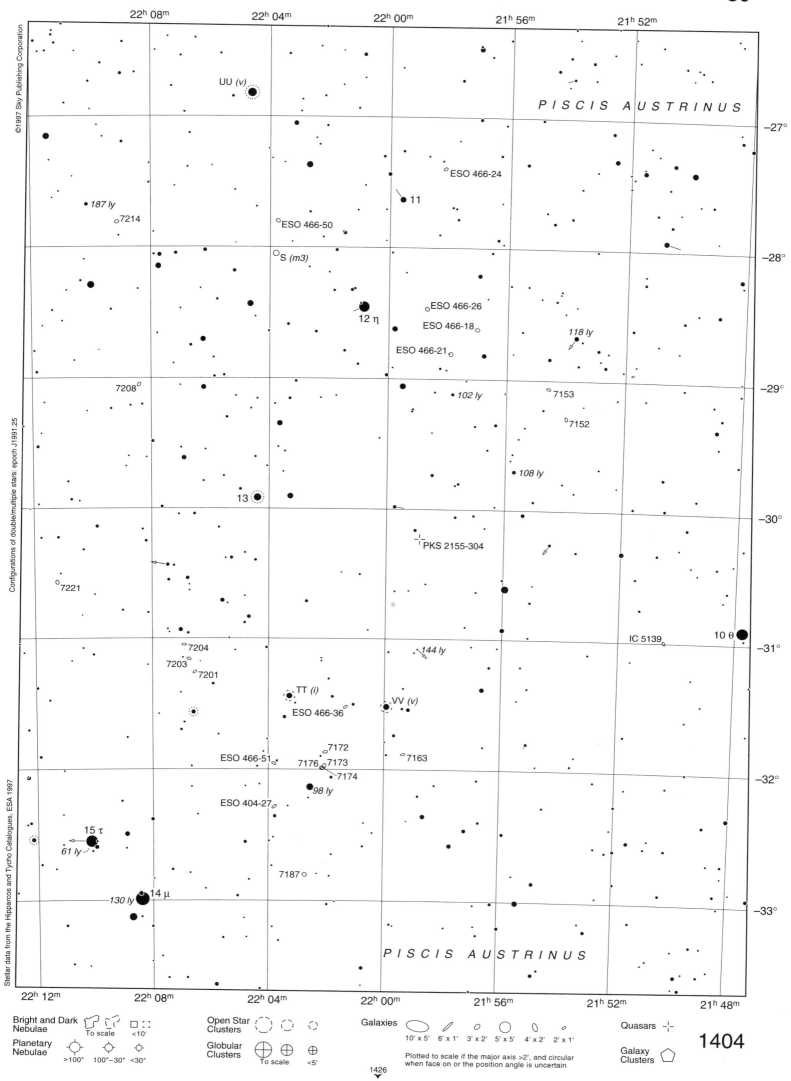

*P I S C I S   A U S T R I N U S*

UU *(v)*

−27°

ESO 466-24

11

*187 ly*

ESO 466-50
7214

ESO 466-26

S *(m3)*

−28°

12 η

ESO 466-18

*118 ly*

ESO 466-21

7208

*102 ly*

7153

−29°

7152

*108 ly*

13

−30°

PKS 2155-304

7221

IC 5139

10 θ

−31°

7204

*144 ly*

7203

7201

TT *(i)*

ESO 466-36

VV *(v)*

7172

ESO 466-51

7176  7173

7163

7174

98 ly

−32°

ESO 404-27

7187

15 τ

*61 ly*

*130 ly*  14 μ

−33°

*P I S C I S   A U S T R I N U S*

| 22h 12m | 22h 08m | 22h 04m | 22h 00m | 21h 56m | 21h 52m | 21h 48m |

Bright and Dark Nebulae
To scale
<10'

Open Star Clusters

Galaxies

Quasars

Planetary Nebulae
>100"  100"–30"  <30"

Globular Clusters
To scale
<5'

10' x 5'  6' x 1'  3' x 2'  5' x 5'  4' x 2'  2' x 1'

Galaxy Clusters

Plotted to scale if the major axis >2', and circular when face on or the position angle is uncertain

## 1404

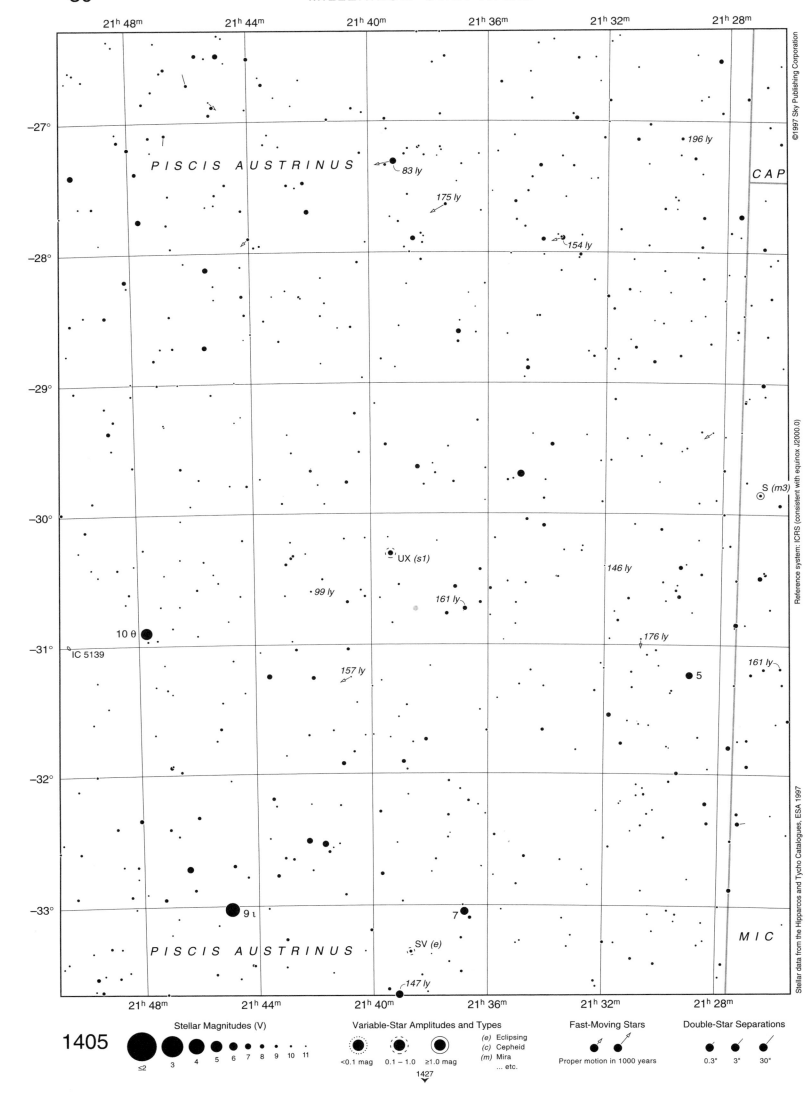

©1997 Sky Publishing Corporation

Reference system: ICRS (consistent with equinox J2000.0)

Stellar data from the Hipparcos and Tycho Catalogues, ESA 1997

PISCIS AUSTRINUS

83 ly

175 ly

154 ly

196 ly

CAP

UX (s1)

99 ly

161 ly

146 ly

176 ly

S (m3)

10 θ

IC 5139

157 ly

5

161 ly

9 ι

7

PISCIS AUSTRINUS

SV (e)

147 ly

MIC

Stellar Magnitudes (V)
≤2  3  4  5  6 7 8 9 10 11

Variable-Star Amplitudes and Types
<0.1 mag    0.1 – 1.0    ≥1.0 mag
1427

(e) Eclipsing
(c) Cepheid
(m) Mira
... etc.

Fast-Moving Stars
Proper motion in 1000 years

Double-Star Separations
0.3"   3"   30"

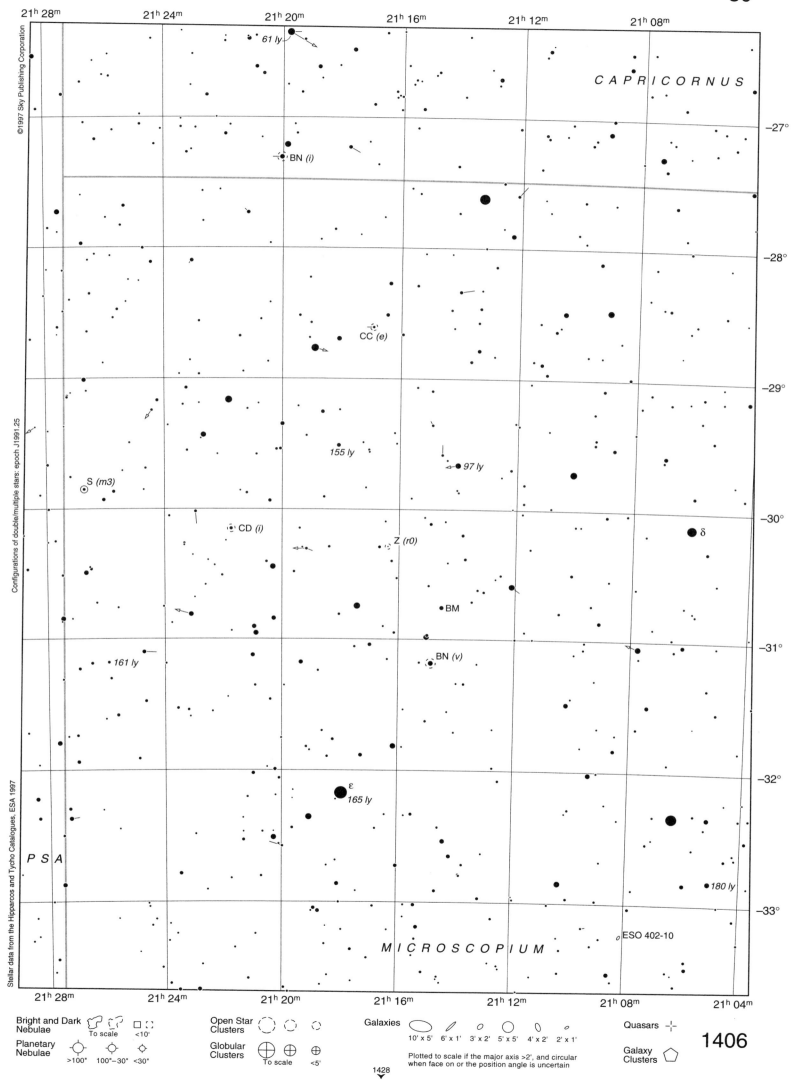

Configurations of double/multiple stars: epoch J1991.25

Stellar data from the Hipparcos and Tycho Catalogues, ESA 1997

CAPRICORNUS

BN (i)

CC (e)

61 ly

155 ly

97 ly

S (m3)

CD (i)

Z (r0)

δ

BM

BN (v)

161 ly

ε
165 ly

PSA

180 ly

ESO 402-10

MICROSCOPIUM

21h 28m   21h 24m   21h 20m   21h 16m   21h 12m   21h 08m   21h 04m

−27°
−28°
−29°
−30°
−31°
−32°
−33°

| Bright and Dark Nebulae | Open Star Clusters | Galaxies | Quasars |
|---|---|---|---|
| To scale   <10' | To scale | 10' x 5'   6' x 1'   3' x 2'   5' x 5'   4' x 2'   2' x 1' | |
| Planetary Nebulae | Globular Clusters | | Galaxy Clusters |
| >100"   100"–30"   <30" | To scale   <5' | Plotted to scale if the major axis >2', and circular when face on or the position angle is uncertain | |

1406

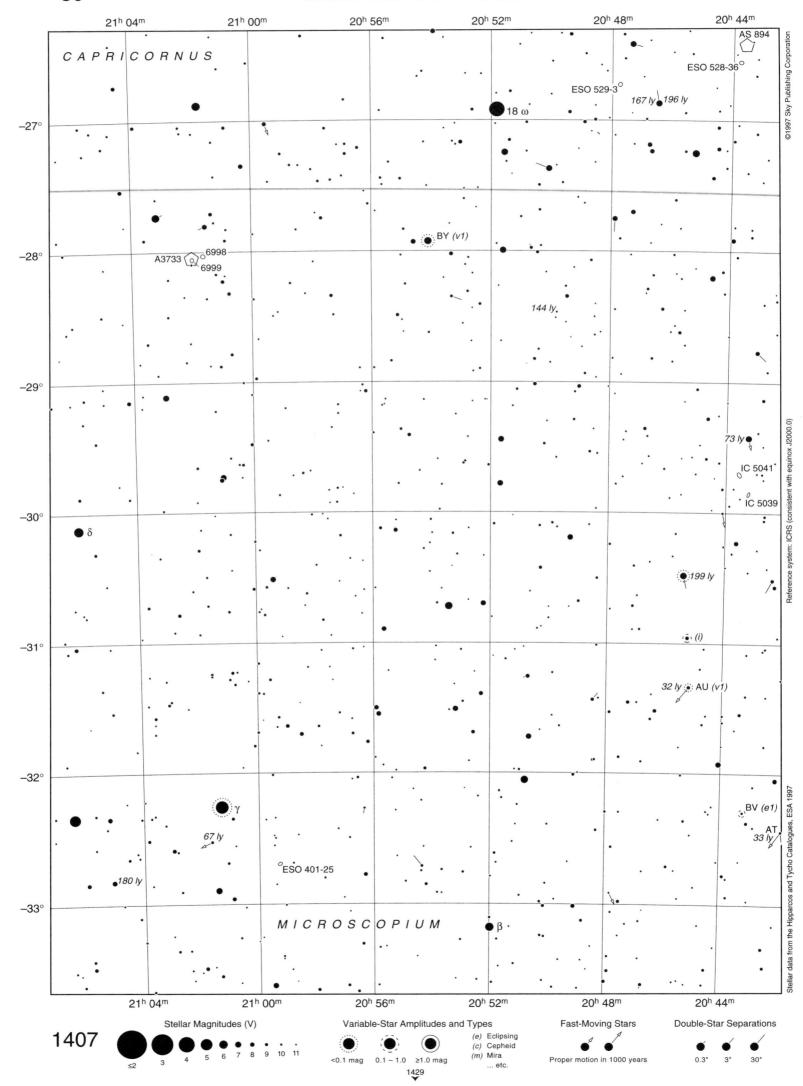

1407

Stellar Magnitudes (V)
≤2  3  4  5  6  7  8  9  10  11

Variable-Star Amplitudes and Types
<0.1 mag    0.1 – 1.0    ≥1.0 mag
(e) Eclipsing
(c) Cepheid
(m) Mira
... etc.

Fast-Moving Stars
Proper motion in 1000 years

Double-Star Separations
0.3"   3"   30"

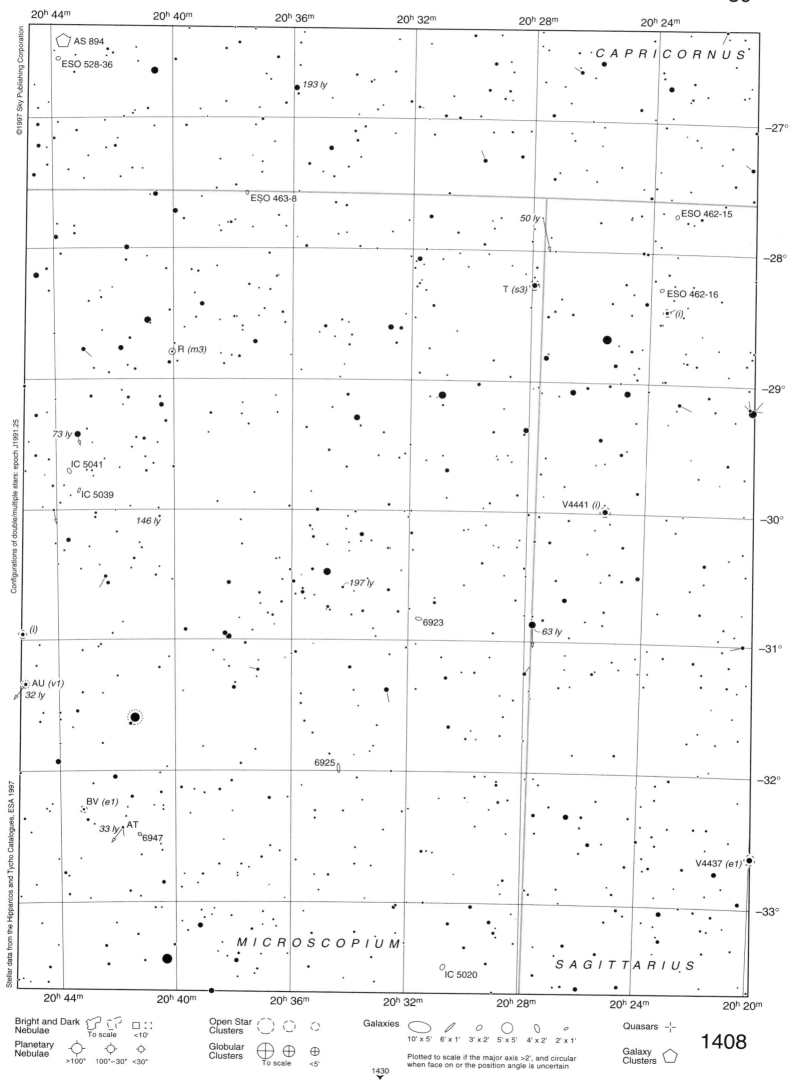

20h 44m   20h 40m   20h 36m   20h 32m   20h 28m   20h 24m

AS 894
ESO 528-36

C A P R I C O R N U S

193 ly

−27°

ESO 463-8
ESO 462-15

50 ly

−28°

T (s3)
ESO 462-16
(i)

R (m3)

−29°

73 ly
IC 5041
IC 5039

V4441 (i)

146 ly

−30°

197 ly

6923
63 ly

−31°

(i)

AU (v1)
32 ly

6925

−32°

BV (e1)

33 ly   AT
6947

V4437 (e1)

−33°

M I C R O S C O P I U M

S A G I T T A R I U S

IC 5020

20h 44m   20h 40m   20h 36m   20h 32m   20h 28m   20h 24m   20h 20m

Bright and Dark Nebulae
To scale   <10'

Open Star Clusters

Galaxies
10' x 5'   6' x 1'   3' x 2'   5' x 5'   4' x 2'   2' x 1'

Quasars

Planetary Nebulae
>100"   100"–30"   <30"

Globular Clusters
To scale   <5'

Plotted to scale if the major axis >2', and circular when face on or the position angle is uncertain

Galaxy Clusters

1408

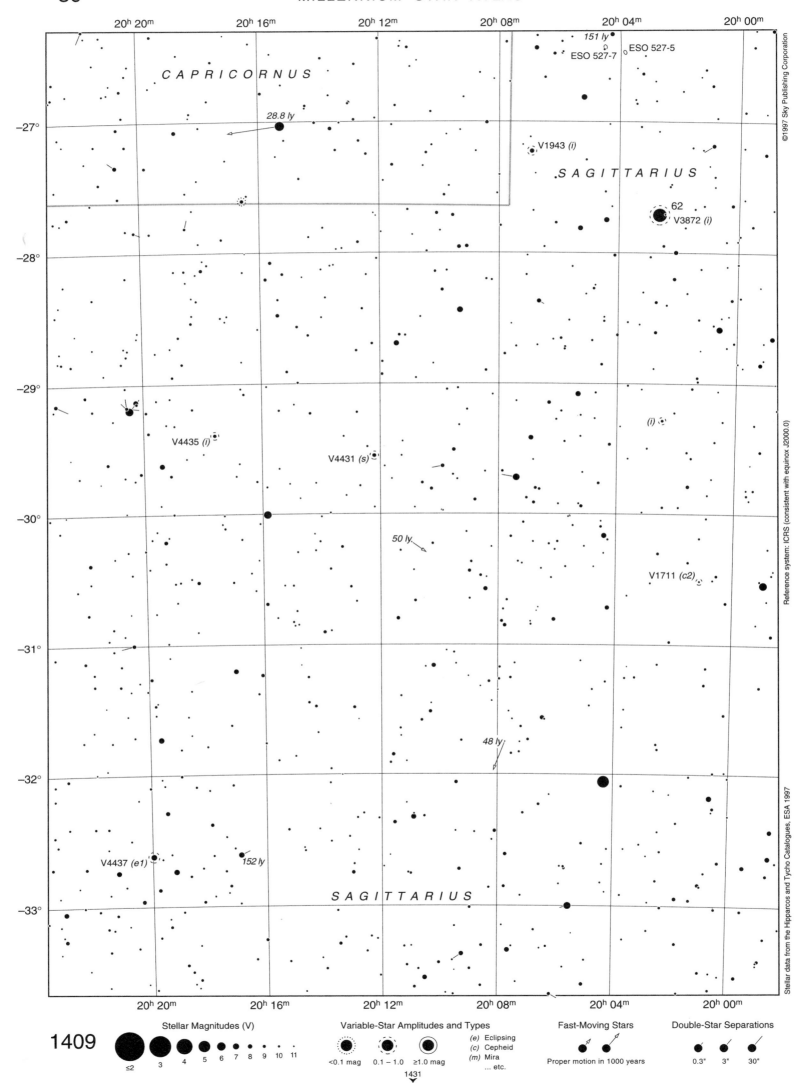

©1997 Sky Publishing Corporation

Reference system: ICRS (consistent with equinox J2000.0)

Stellar data from the Hipparcos and Tycho Catalogues, ESA 1997

CAPRICORNUS

151 ly
ESO 527-7      ESO 527-5

28.8 ly

V1943 (i)

SAGITTARIUS

62
V3872 (i)

V4435 (i)

V4431 (s)

(i)

50 ly

V1711 (c2)

48 ly

V4437 (e1)      152 ly

SAGITTARIUS

Stellar Magnitudes (V)

≤2   3   4   5   6   7   8   9   10   11

Variable-Star Amplitudes and Types

<0.1 mag   0.1 – 1.0   ≥1.0 mag

(e) Eclipsing
(c) Cepheid
(m) Mira
... etc.

Fast-Moving Stars

Proper motion in 1000 years

Double-Star Separations

0.3"   3"   30"

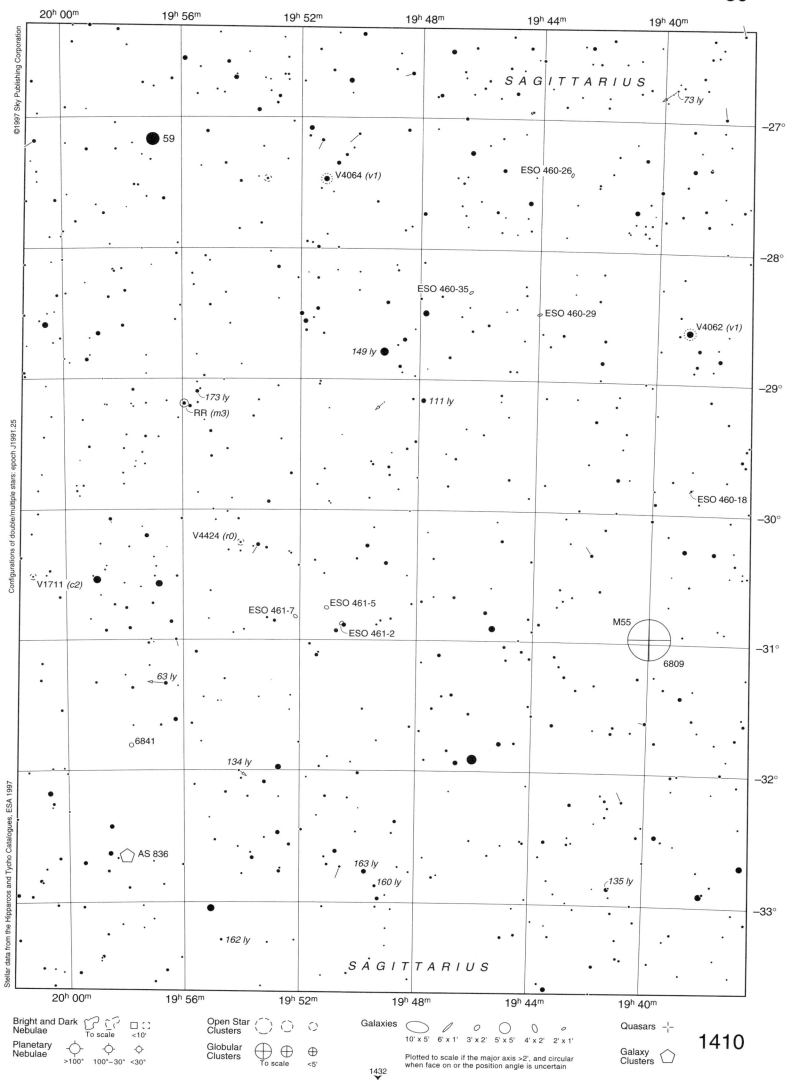

Configurations of double/multiple stars: epoch J1991.25

Stellar data from the Hipparcos and Tycho Catalogues, ESA 1997

S A G I T T A R I U S

73 ly

59

V4064 (v1)

ESO 460-26

−27°

ESO 460-35

ESO 460-29

V4062 (v1)

−28°

149 ly

173 ly

111 ly

RR (m3)

−29°

ESO 460-18

−30°

V4424 (r0)

V1711 (c2)

ESO 461-5

ESO 461-7

M55

ESO 461-2

6809

−31°

63 ly

6841

134 ly

−32°

AS 836

163 ly

135 ly

160 ly

−33°

162 ly

S A G I T T A R I U S

20h 00m   19h 56m   19h 52m   19h 48m   19h 44m   19h 40m

| Bright and Dark Nebulae | | Open Star Clusters | | | Galaxies | | | | | | Quasars |
|---|---|---|---|---|---|---|---|---|---|---|---|

Bright and Dark Nebulae
To scale   <10'

Planetary Nebulae
>100"   100"−30"   <30"

Open Star Clusters

Globular Clusters
To scale   <5'

Galaxies
10' x 5'   6' x 1'   3' x 2'   5' x 5'   4' x 2'   2' x 1'

Plotted to scale if the major axis >2', and circular
when face on or the position angle is uncertain

Quasars

Galaxy Clusters

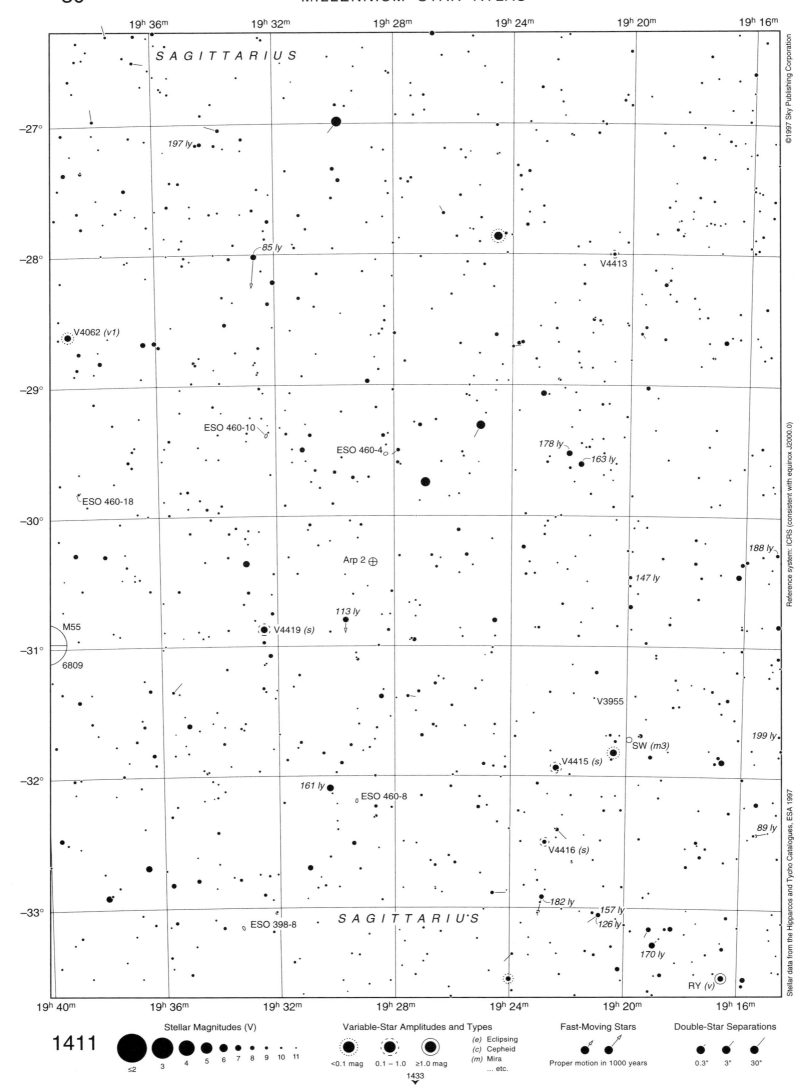

©1997 Sky Publishing Corporation

Reference system: ICRS (consistent with equinox J2000.0)

Stellar data from the Hipparcos and Tycho Catalogues, ESA 1997

SAGITTARIUS

197 ly

85 ly

V4413

V4062 (v1)

ESO 460-10

ESO 460-4

178 ly
163 ly

ESO 460-18

Arp 2

188 ly

147 ly

113 ly

M55

V4419 (s)

6809

V3955

199 ly

SW (m3)

V4415 (s)

161 ly

ESO 460-8

89 ly

V4416 (s)

182 ly
157 ly
126 ly

SAGITTARIUS

ESO 398-8

170 ly

RY (v)

1411

Stellar Magnitudes (V)
≤2  3  4  5 6 7 8 9 10 11

Variable-Star Amplitudes and Types
<0.1 mag   0.1 – 1.0   ≥1.0 mag
(e) Eclipsing
(c) Cepheid
(m) Mira
... etc.
1433

Fast-Moving Stars
Proper motion in 1000 years

Double-Star Separations
0.3"  3"  30"

# MILLENNIUM STAR ATLAS

−30°

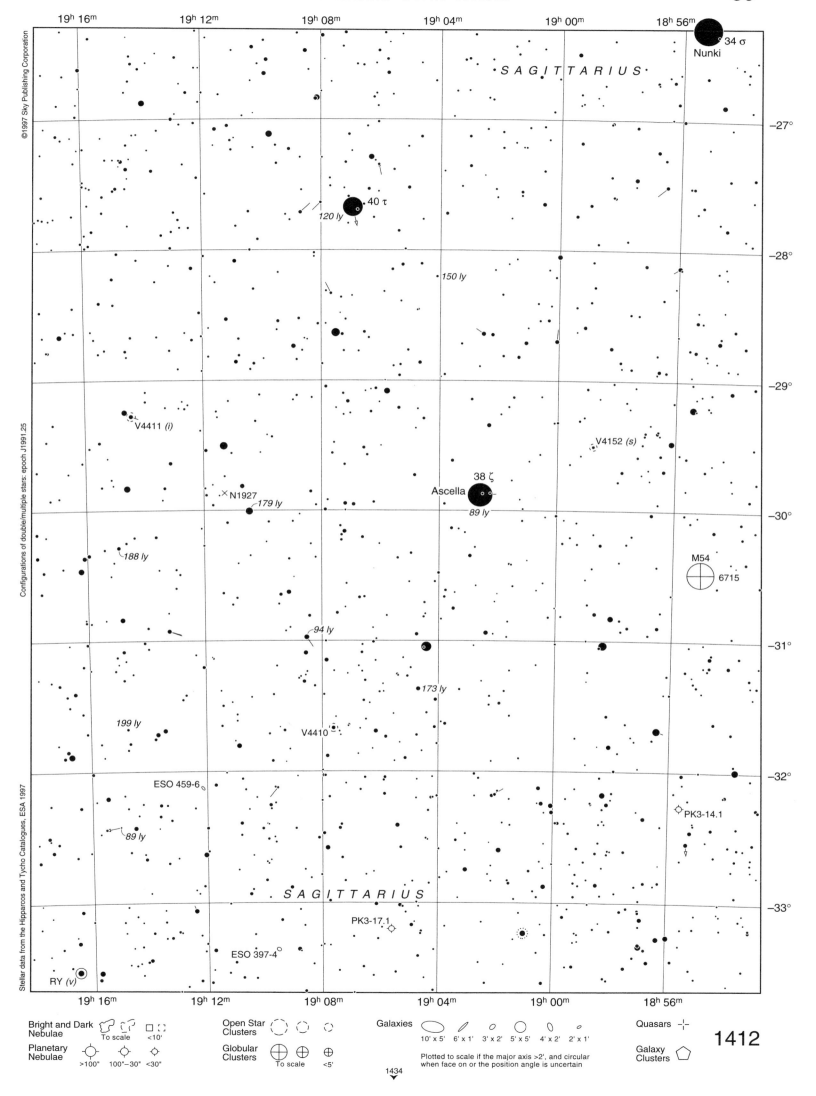

19h 16m    19h 12m    19h 08m    19h 04m    19h 00m    18h 56m

−27°

SAGITTARIUS

Nunki    34 σ

40 τ
120 ly

150 ly

−28°

V4411 (i)

V4152 (s)

−29°

38 ζ
Ascella
89 ly

× N1927
179 ly

M54
6715

188 ly

94 ly

−30°

199 ly

173 ly

V4410

−31°

ESO 459-6

PK3-14.1

89 ly

−32°

SAGITTARIUS

PK3-17.1

−33°

ESO 397-4

RY (v)

19h 16m    19h 12m    19h 08m    19h 04m    19h 00m    18h 56m

Bright and Dark
Nebulae          To scale    <10'

Open Star
Clusters

Galaxies

Quasars

1412

Planetary
Nebulae     >100"  100"−30"  <30"

Globular
Clusters    To scale    <5'

Galaxies
10' x 5'  6' x 1'  3' x 2'  5' x 5'  4' x 2'  2' x 1'

Galaxy
Clusters

Plotted to scale if the major axis >2', and circular
when face on or the position angle is uncertain

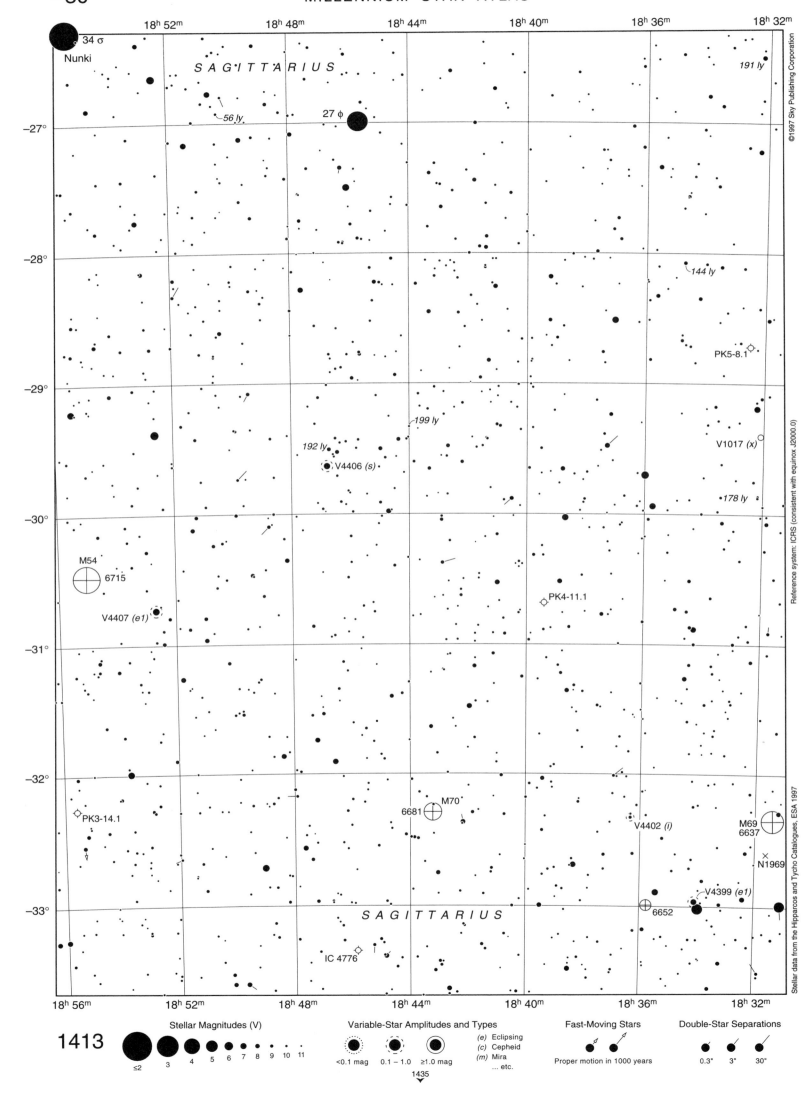

Reference system: ICRS (consistent with equinox J2000.0)

Stellar data from the Hipparcos and Tycho Catalogues, ESA 1997

1413

Stellar Magnitudes (V)

≤2　3　4　5　6　7　8　9　10　11

Variable-Star Amplitudes and Types

<0.1 mag　　0.1 – 1.0　　≥1.0 mag

(e) Eclipsing
(c) Cepheid
(m) Mira
... etc.

Fast-Moving Stars

Proper motion in 1000 years

Double-Star Separations

0.3"　3"　30"

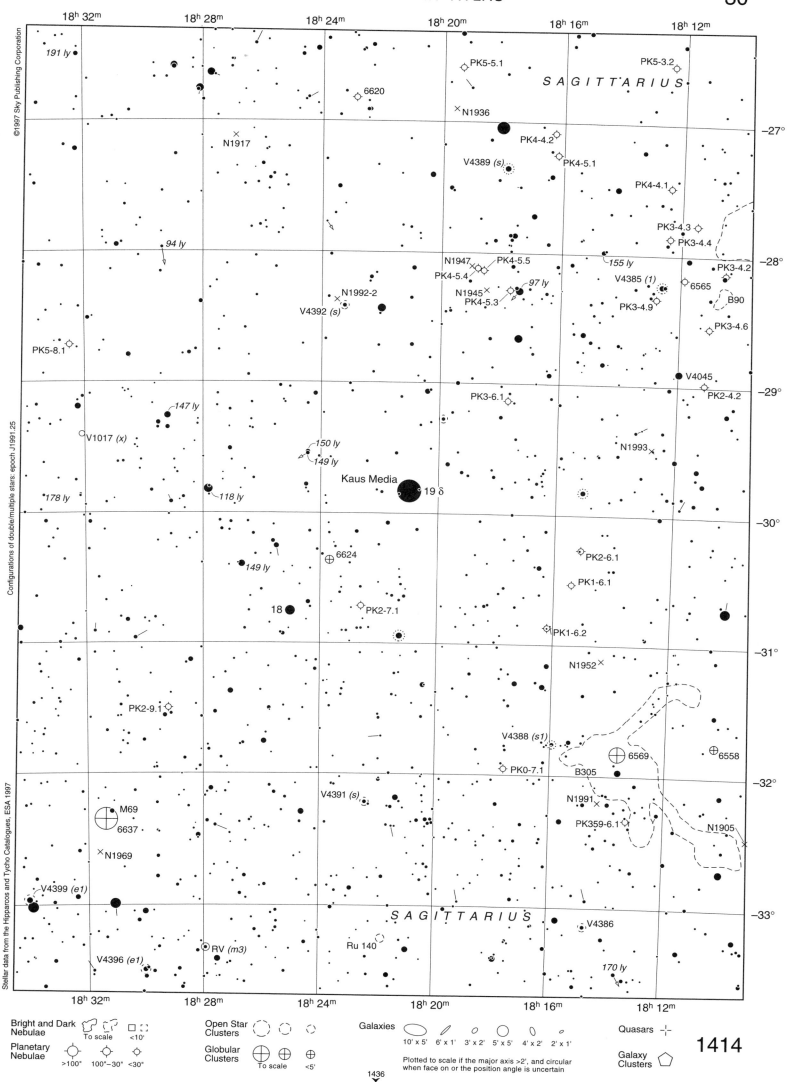

18ʰ 32ᵐ   18ʰ 28ᵐ   18ʰ 24ᵐ   18ʰ 20ᵐ   18ʰ 16ᵐ   18ʰ 12ᵐ

*191 ly*

PK5-5.1

PK5-3.2

*S A G I T T A R I U S*

6620

N1936

−27°

N1917

V4389 (s)

PK4-4.2

PK4-5.1

PK4-4.1

PK4-4.1

*94 ly*

PK3-4.3

PK3-4.4

N1947   PK4-5.5

*155 ly*

PK3-4.2

−28°

PK4-5.4

V4385 (1)

6565

N1992-2

N1945

*97 ly*

B90

V4392 (s)

PK4-5.3

PK3-4.9

PK5-8.1

PK3-4.6

V4045

PK3-6.1

PK2-4.2

−29°

*147 ly*

V1017 (x)

N1993

*150 ly*

*149 ly*

*178 ly*

Kaus Media

19 δ

*118 ly*

−30°

6624

PK2-6.1

*149 ly*

PK1-6.1

18

PK2-7.1

PK1-6.2

−31°

N1952

PK2-9.1

V4388 (s1)

6569

6558

PK0-7.1

B305

−32°

M69

V4391 (s)

N1991

6637

PK359-6.1

N1905

N1969

V4399 (e1)

*S A G I T T A R I U S*

−33°

V4386

V4396 (e1)

RV (m3)

Ru 140

*170 ly*

18ʰ 32ᵐ   18ʰ 28ᵐ   18ʰ 24ᵐ   18ʰ 20ᵐ   18ʰ 16ᵐ   18ʰ 12ᵐ

1436

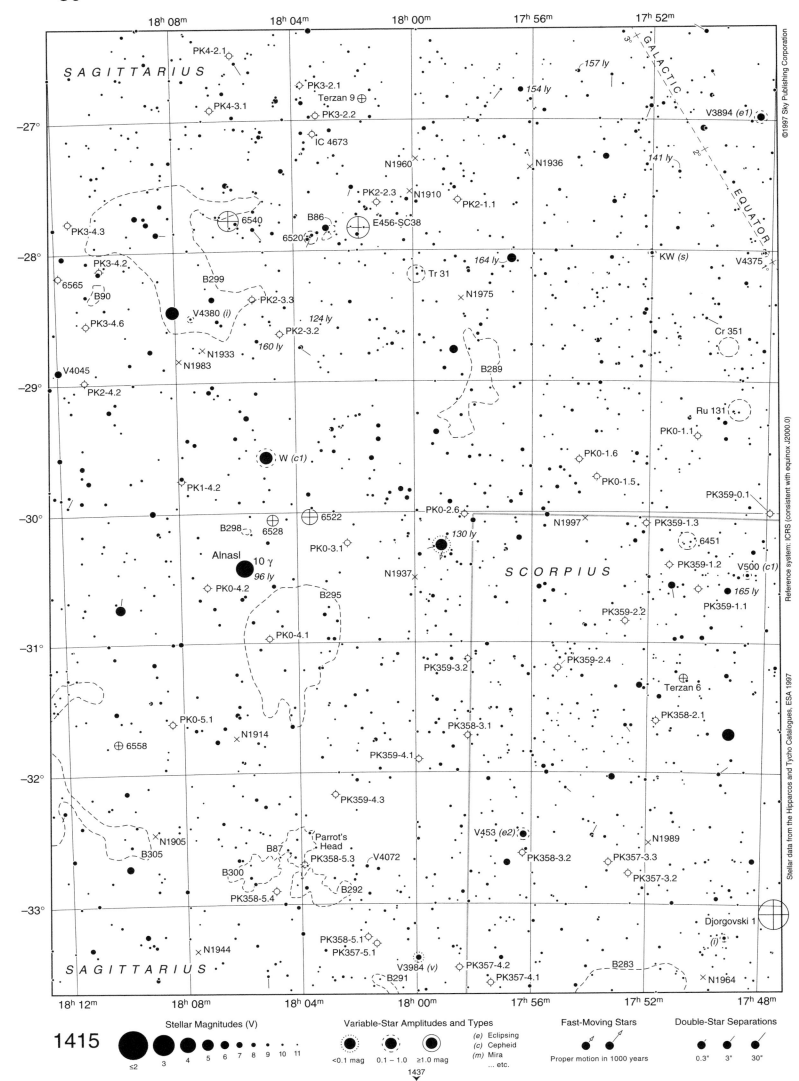

SAGITTARIUS

PK4-2.1
PK4-3.1
PK3-2.1
Terzan 9
PK3-2.2
IC 4673
N1960
PK2-2.3
N1910
PK2-1.1
157 ly
154 ly
N1936
141 ly
V3894 (e1)

6540
B86
6520
E456-SC38
KW (s)
V4375

PK3-4.3
164 ly
Tr 31
Cr 351

PK3-4.2
6565
B90
B299
PK2-3.3
N1975

V4380 (i)
124 ly
PK3-4.6
PK2-3.2
160 ly
Ru 131

N1933
B289
PK0-1.1

V4045
N1983
PK0-1.6

PK2-4.2
PK0-1.5

W (c1)
PK359-0.1

PK1-4.2
PK0-2.6
N1997
PK359-1.3

B298
6528
6522
6451

Alnasl   10 γ
96 ly
PK0-3.1
130 ly
N1937
SCORPIUS
PK359-1.2
V500 (c1)

PK0-4.2
PK359-2.2
165 ly
PK359-1.1

B295

PK0-4.1
PK359-2.4

PK359-3.2
Terzan 6

PK0-5.1
PK358-2.1

N1914
PK358-3.1

6558
PK359-4.1

PK359-4.3

Parrot's
Head
N1905
B87
PK358-5.3
V4072
V453 (e2)
N1989
B305
PK358-3.2
PK357-3.3
B300
PK358-3.2
PK357-3.2
B292

PK358-5.4
Djorgovski 1
(i)

N1944
PK358-5.1
PK357-5.1
B283

SAGITTARIUS
V3984 (v)
PK357-4.2
N1964
B291
PK357-4.1

1415

Stellar Magnitudes (V)
≤2   3   4   5   6   7   8   9   10   11

Variable-Star Amplitudes and Types
<0.1 mag   0.1 – 1.0   ≥1.0 mag
(e) Eclipsing
(c) Cepheid
(m) Mira
... etc.

Fast-Moving Stars
Proper motion in 1000 years

Double-Star Separations
0.3"   3"   30"

1437

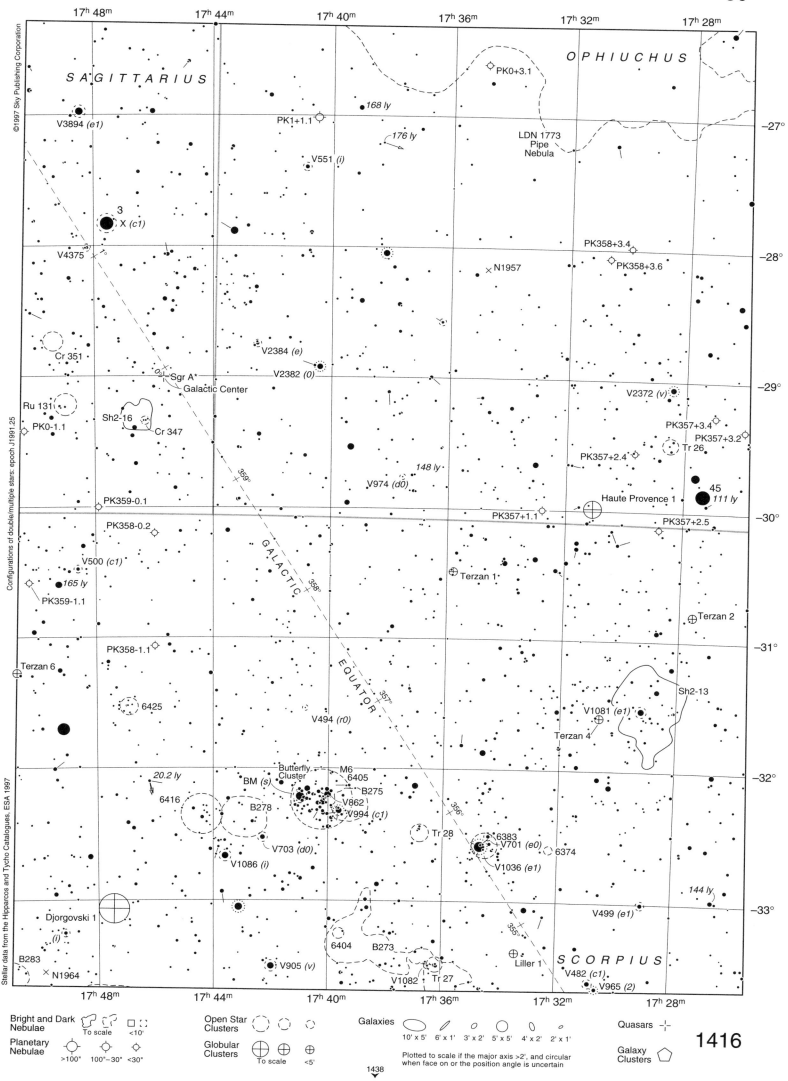

17ʰ 48ᵐ    17ʰ 44ᵐ    17ʰ 40ᵐ    17ʰ 36ᵐ    17ʰ 32ᵐ    17ʰ 28ᵐ

©1997 Sky Publishing Corporation

O P H I U C H U S

PK0+3.1

S A G I T T A R I U S

V3894 (e1)

168 ly

PK1+1.1

−27°

176 ly

LDN 1773
Pipe
Nebula

V551 (i)

3
X (c1)

PK358+3.4

V4375

N1957

PK358+3.6

−28°

Cr 351

V2384 (e)

V2382 (0)

V2372 (v)

Sgr A*
Galactic Center

PK357+3.4

−29°

Ru 131

PK357+3.2

Configurations of double/multiple stars: epoch J1991.25

PK0-1.1

Sh2-16

Tr 26

Cr 347

PK357+2.4

359°

148 ly

PK359-0.1

V974 (d0)

45
111 ly

Haute Provence 1

PK357+1.1

PK357+2.5

−30°

PK358-0.2

V500 (c1)

G A L A C T I C

Terzan 1

165 ly

358°

PK359-1.1

Terzan 2

PK358-1.1

−31°

Terzan 6

E Q U A T O R

Sh2-13

6425

357°

V1081 (e1)

V494 (r0)

Terzan 4

20.2 ly

Stellar data from the Hipparcos and Tycho Catalogues, ESA 1997

6416

Butterfly
Cluster

M6
6405

BM (s)

B275

−32°

B278

V862

V994 (c1)

356°

Tr 28

6383
+V701 (e0)

6374

V703 (d0)

V1036 (e1)

V1086 (i)

144 ly

Djorgovski 1

355°

V499 (e1)

−33°

(i)

6404

B273

B283

Liller 1

S C O R P I U S

N1964

V905 (v)

V482 (c1)

V1082    Tr 27

V965 (2)

17ʰ 48ᵐ    17ʰ 44ᵐ    17ʰ 40ᵐ    17ʰ 36ᵐ    17ʰ 32ᵐ    17ʰ 28ᵐ

Bright and Dark
Nebulae          To scale    <10'

Open Star
Clusters

Galaxies

Quasars

Planetary
Nebulae
>100"  100"−30"  <30"

Globular
Clusters
To scale    <5'

10' x 5'   6' x 1'   3' x 2'   5' x 5'   4' x 2'   2' x 1'

Plotted to scale if the major axis >2', and circular
when face on or the position angle is uncertain

Galaxy
Clusters

1416

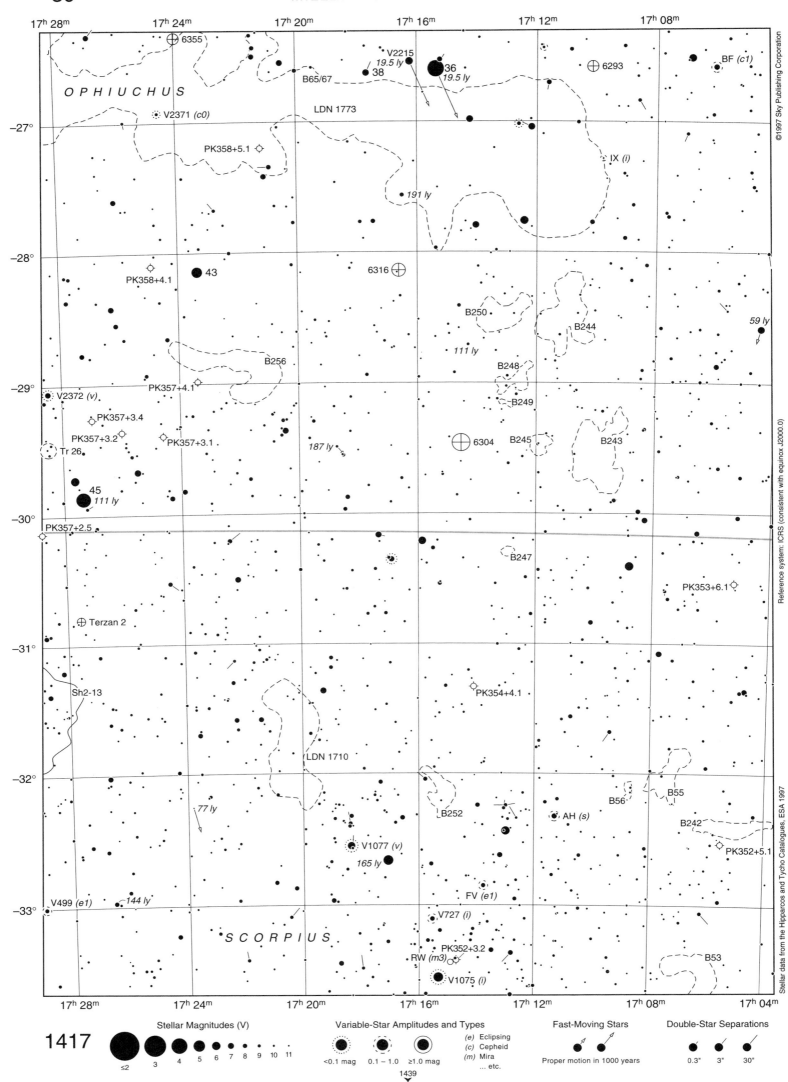

©1997 Sky Publishing Corporation

Reference system: ICRS (consistent with equinox J2000.0)

Stellar data from the Hipparcos and Tycho Catalogues, ESA 1997

OPHIUCHUS

SCORPIUS

6355

V2215
19.5 ly

38

36
19.5 ly

B65/67

LDN 1773

6293

BF (c1)

V2371 (c0)

PK358+5.1

191 ly

IX (i)

43

6316

B250

B244

59 ly

111 ly

B256

B248

B249

PK357+4.1

V2372 (v)

PK357+3.4

6304

B245

B243

PK357+3.2

PK357+3.1

187 ly

Tr 26

45
111 ly

PK357+2.5

B247

PK353+6.1

Terzan 2

Sh2-13

PK354+4.1

LDN 1710

B55

B56

77 ly

B252

AH (s)

B242

V1077 (v)

PK352+5.1

165 ly

FV (e1)

V499 (e1)

144 ly

V727 (i)

PK352+3.2

RW (m3)

V1075 (i)

Stellar Magnitudes (V)

≤2   3   4   5   6   7   8   9  10  11

Variable-Star Amplitudes and Types

<0.1 mag    0.1 − 1.0    ≥1.0 mag

(e) Eclipsing
(c) Cepheid
(m) Mira
... etc.

Fast-Moving Stars

Proper motion in 1000 years

Double-Star Separations

0.3"   3"   30"

# MILLENNIUM STAR ATLAS

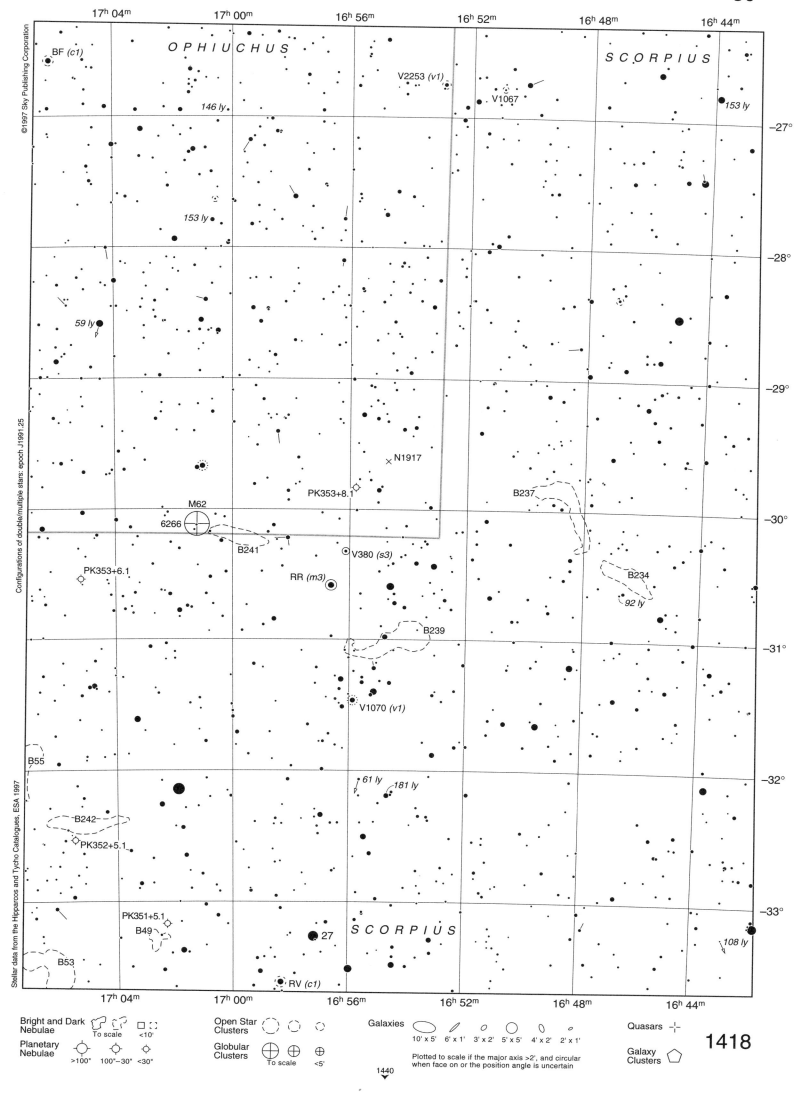

OPHIUCHUS

SCORPIUS

©1997 Sky Publishing Corporation

Configurations of double/multiple stars: epoch J1991.25

Stellar data from the Hipparcos and Tycho Catalogues, ESA 1997

17ʰ 04ᵐ    17ʰ 00ᵐ    16ʰ 56ᵐ    16ʰ 52ᵐ    16ʰ 48ᵐ    16ʰ 44ᵐ

BF (c1)

V2253 (v1)

V1067

153 ly

146 ly

−27°

153 ly

59 ly

−28°

−29°

N1917

PK353+8.1

B237

M62
6266

B241

B234

92 ly

−30°

V380 (s3)

PK353+6.1

RR (m3)

B239

−31°

V1070 (v1)

B55

61 ly

181 ly

−32°

B242

PK352+5.1

108 ly

PK351+5.1

B49

27

SCORPIUS

−33°

B53

RV (c1)

17ʰ 04ᵐ    17ʰ 00ᵐ    16ʰ 56ᵐ    16ʰ 52ᵐ    16ʰ 48ᵐ    16ʰ 44ᵐ

| Bright and Dark Nebulae | To scale | <10' |
| Planetary Nebulae | >100" | 100"–30" | <30" |

| Open Star Clusters | | |
| Globular Clusters | To scale | <5' |

Galaxies   10' x 5'   6' x 1'   3' x 2'   5' x 5'   4' x 2'   2' x 1'

Plotted to scale if the major axis >2', and circular when face on or the position angle is uncertain

Quasars

Galaxy Clusters

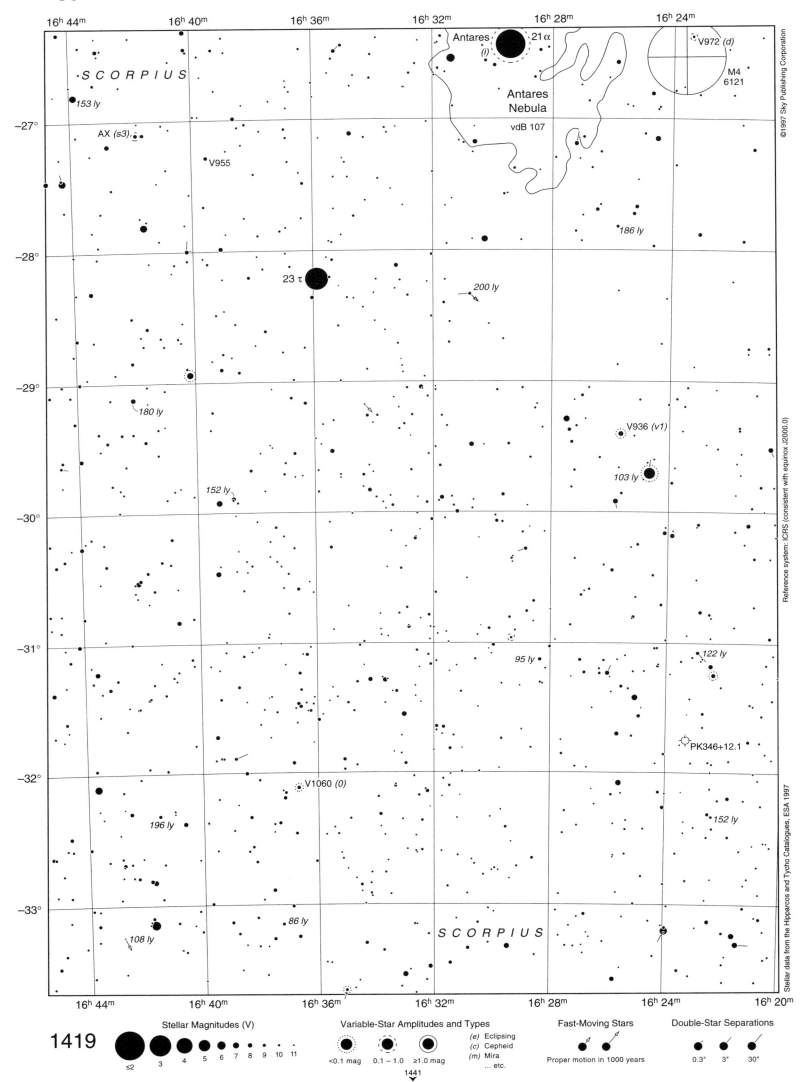

©1997 Sky Publishing Corporation

Reference system: ICRS (consistent with equinox J2000.0)

Stellar data from the Hipparcos and Tycho Catalogues, ESA 1997

S C O R P I U S

Antares 21 α
(i)

Antares
Nebula

vdB 107

V972 (d)

M4
6121

153 ly

AX (s3)

V955

186 ly

23 τ

200 ly

180 ly

V936 (v1)

103 ly

152 ly

95 ly

122 ly

PK346+12.1

V1060 (0)

196 ly

152 ly

108 ly

86 ly

S C O R P I U S

**1419**

Stellar Magnitudes (V)

≤2  3  4  5  6  7  8  9  10  11

Variable-Star Amplitudes and Types

<0.1 mag   0.1 – 1.0   ≥1.0 mag

1441

(e) Eclipsing
(c) Cepheid
(m) Mira
... etc.

Fast-Moving Stars

Proper motion in 1000 years

Double-Star Separations

0.3"   3"   30"

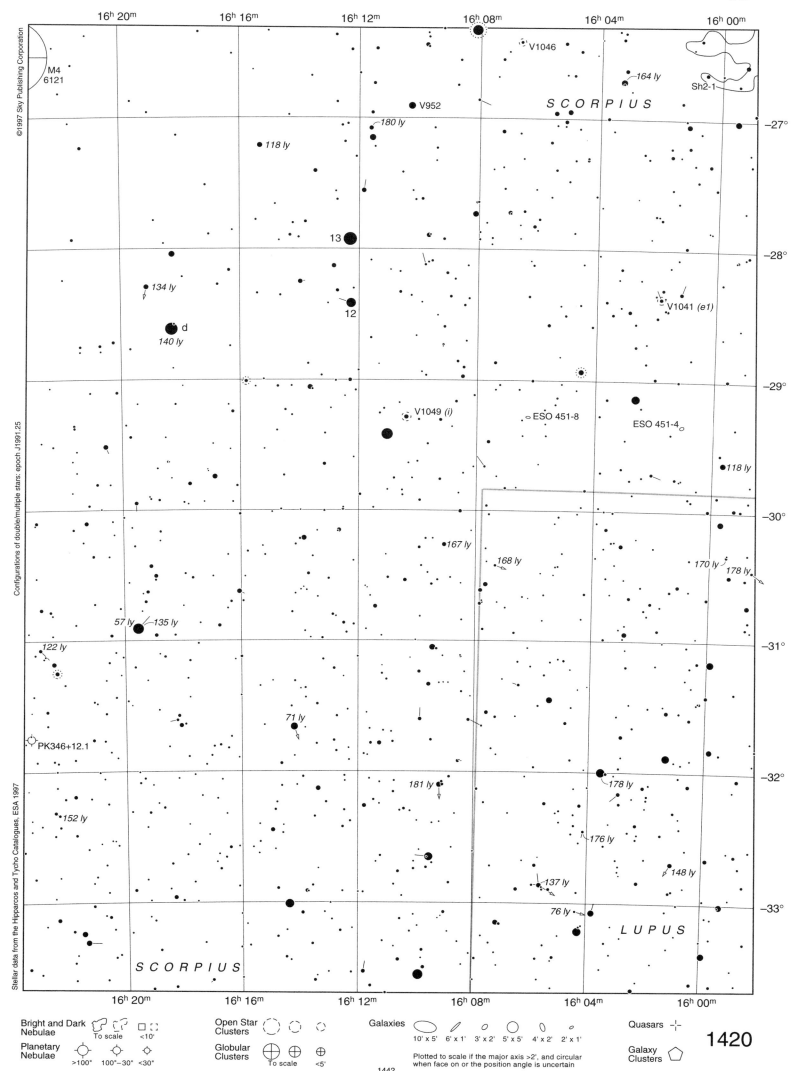

16h 20m    16h 16m    16h 12m    16h 08m    16h 04m    16h 00m

M4
6121

V1046

164 ly

Sh2-1

V952

S C O R P I U S

180 ly

118 ly

13

134 ly

12

V1041 (e1)

d
140 ly

V1049 (i)

ESO 451-8

ESO 451-4

118 ly

167 ly

168 ly

170 ly
178 ly

57 ly    135 ly

122 ly

71 ly

PK346+12.1

181 ly

178 ly

152 ly

176 ly

148 ly

137 ly

76 ly

L U P U S

S C O R P I U S

−27°

−28°

−29°

−30°

−31°

−32°

−33°

16h 20m    16h 16m    16h 12m    16h 08m    16h 04m    16h 00m

Bright and Dark
Nebulae          To scale    <10'

Planetary
Nebulae     >100"  100"-30"  <30"

Open Star
Clusters

Globular
Clusters     To scale    <5'

Galaxies

10' x 5'  6' x 1'  3' x 2'  5' x 5'  4' x 2'  2' x 1'

Plotted to scale if the major axis >2', and circular
when face on or the position angle is uncertain

Quasars

Galaxy
Clusters

1420

1442

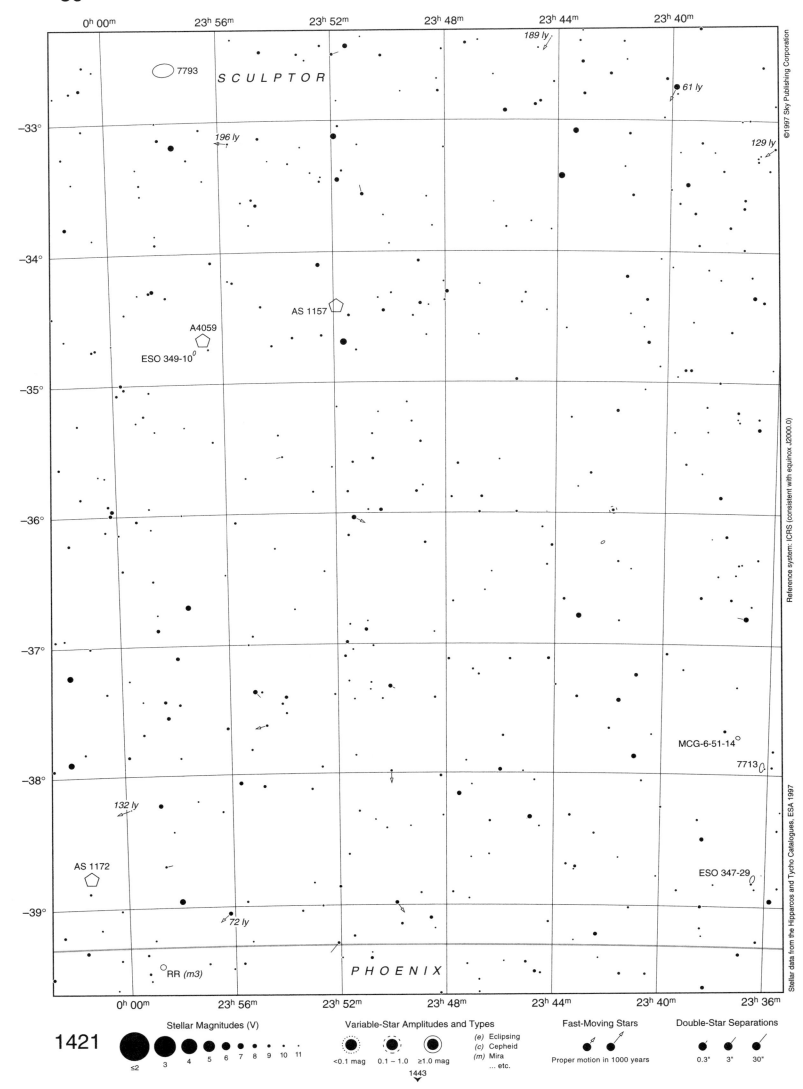

1399

S C U L P T O R

7793

189 ly

61 ly

196 ly

129 ly

−33°

−34°

AS 1157

A4059

ESO 349-10

−35°

−36°

−37°

MCG-6-51-14

7713

−38°

132 ly

AS 1172

ESO 347-29

−39°

72 ly

P H O E N I X

RR (m3)

1421

**Stellar Magnitudes (V)**

≤2   3   4   5   6   7   8   9   10   11

**Variable-Star Amplitudes and Types**

<0.1 mag    0.1 – 1.0    ≥1.0 mag

(e) Eclipsing
(c) Cepheid
(m) Mira
... etc.

1443

**Fast-Moving Stars**

Proper motion in 1000 years

**Double-Star Separations**

0.3"    3"    30"

©1997 Sky Publishing Corporation

Reference system: ICRS (consistent with equinox J2000.0)

Stellar data from the Hipparcos and Tycho Catalogues, ESA 1997

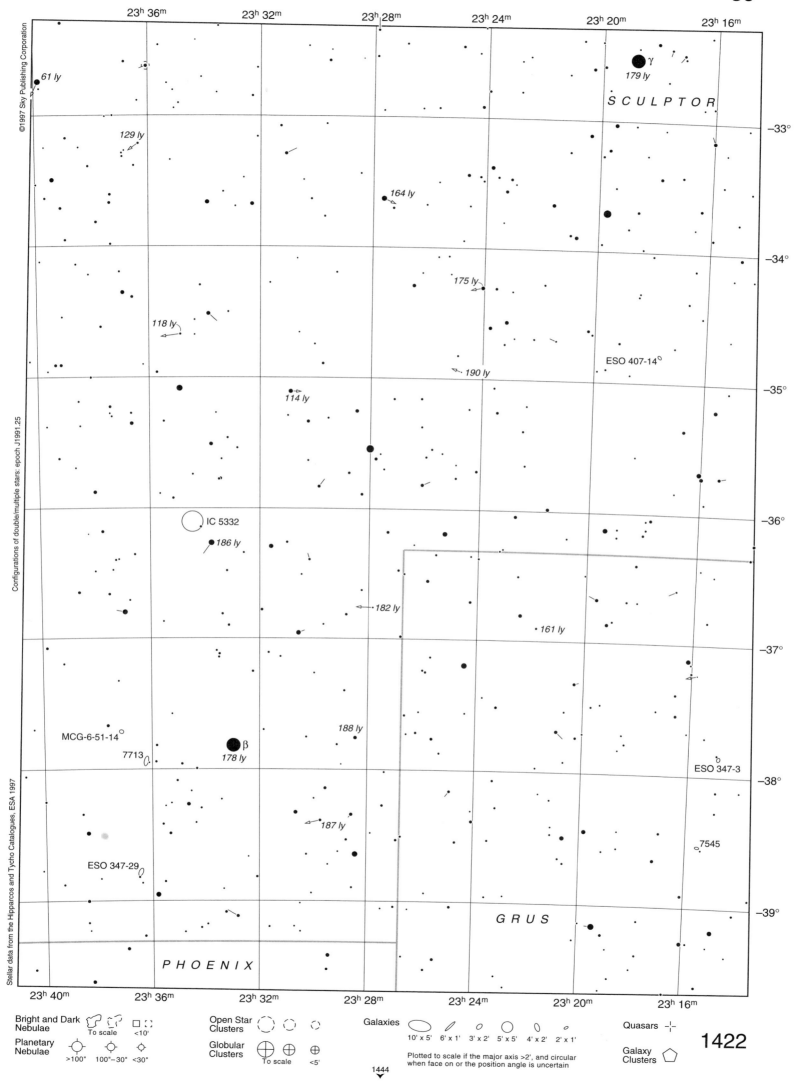

©1997 Sky Publishing Corporation

Configurations of double/multiple stars: epoch J1991.25

Stellar data from the Hipparcos and Tycho Catalogues, ESA 1997

S C U L P T O R

γ
179 ly

61 ly

129 ly

164 ly

175 ly

118 ly

ESO 407-14

190 ly

114 ly

IC 5332

186 ly

182 ly

161 ly

188 ly

MCG-6-51-14

ESO 347-3

7713

β
178 ly

187 ly

7545

ESO 347-29

G R U S

P H O E N I X

23h 36m   23h 32m   23h 28m   23h 24m   23h 20m   23h 16m

−33°

−34°

−35°

−36°

−37°

−38°

−39°

23h 40m   23h 36m   23h 32m   23h 28m   23h 24m   23h 20m   23h 16m

| Bright and Dark Nebulae | | | Open Star Clusters | | | Galaxies | | | | | | Quasars |
|---|---|---|---|---|---|---|---|---|---|---|---|---|
| To scale | <10' | | | | | 10' x 5' | 6' x 1' | 3' x 2' | 5' x 5' | 4' x 2' | 2' x 1' | |
| Planetary Nebulae | | | Globular Clusters | | | | | | | | | Galaxy Clusters |
| >100" | 100"−30" | <30" | To scale | <5' | | Plotted to scale if the major axis >2', and circular when face on or the position angle is uncertain | | | | | | |

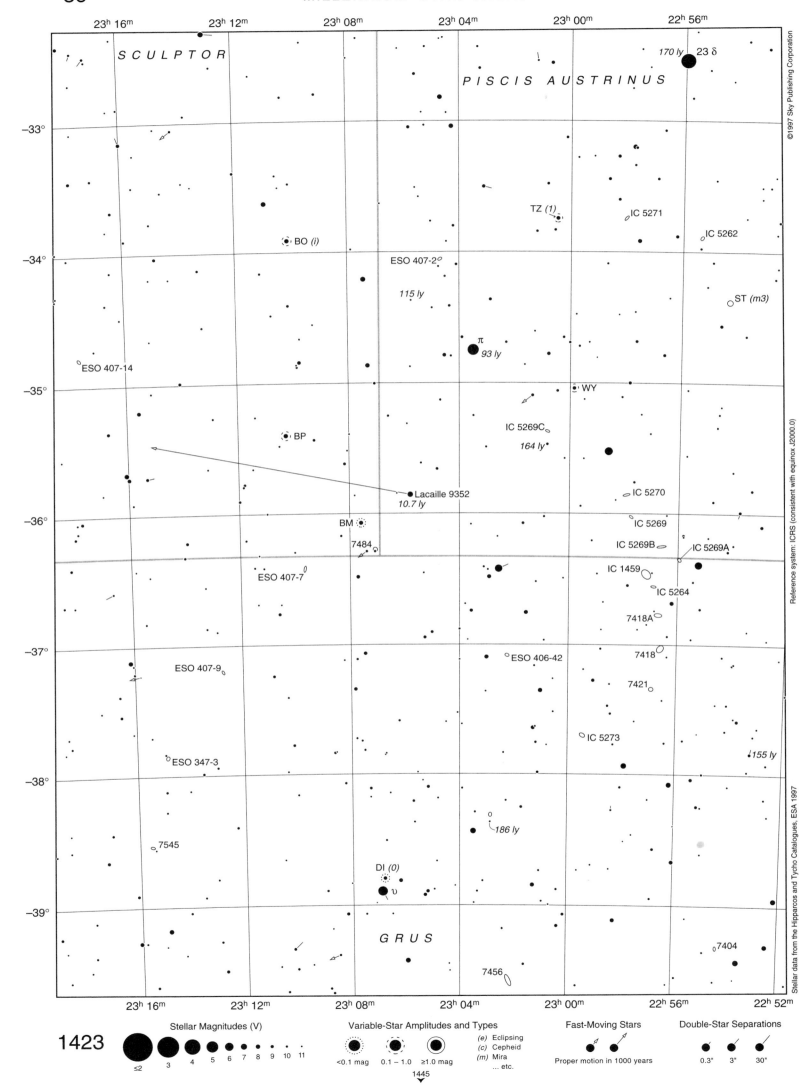

©1997 Sky Publishing Corporation

Reference system: ICRS (consistent with equinox J2000.0)

Stellar data from the Hipparcos and Tycho Catalogues, ESA 1997

SCULPTOR

PISCIS AUSTRINUS

170 ly   23 δ

TZ (1)

IC 5271

IC 5262

BO (i)

ESO 407-2

ST (m3)

115 ly

π
93 ly

ESO 407-14

WY

IC 5269C

BP

164 ly

Lacaille 9352
10.7 ly

IC 5270

BM

IC 5269

7484

IC 5269B       IC 5269A

ESO 407-7

IC 1459

IC 5264

7418A

ESO 407-9

7418

ESO 406-42

7421

IC 5273

ESO 347-3

155 ly

7545

186 ly

DI (0)

υ

GRUS

7404

7456

1423

**Stellar Magnitudes (V)**

≤2   3   4   5   6   7   8   9  10  11

**Variable-Star Amplitudes and Types**

<0.1 mag   0.1 – 1.0   ≥1.0 mag

(e) Eclipsing
(c) Cepheid
(m) Mira
... etc.

**Fast-Moving Stars**

Proper motion in 1000 years

**Double-Star Separations**

0.3"   3"   30"

1445

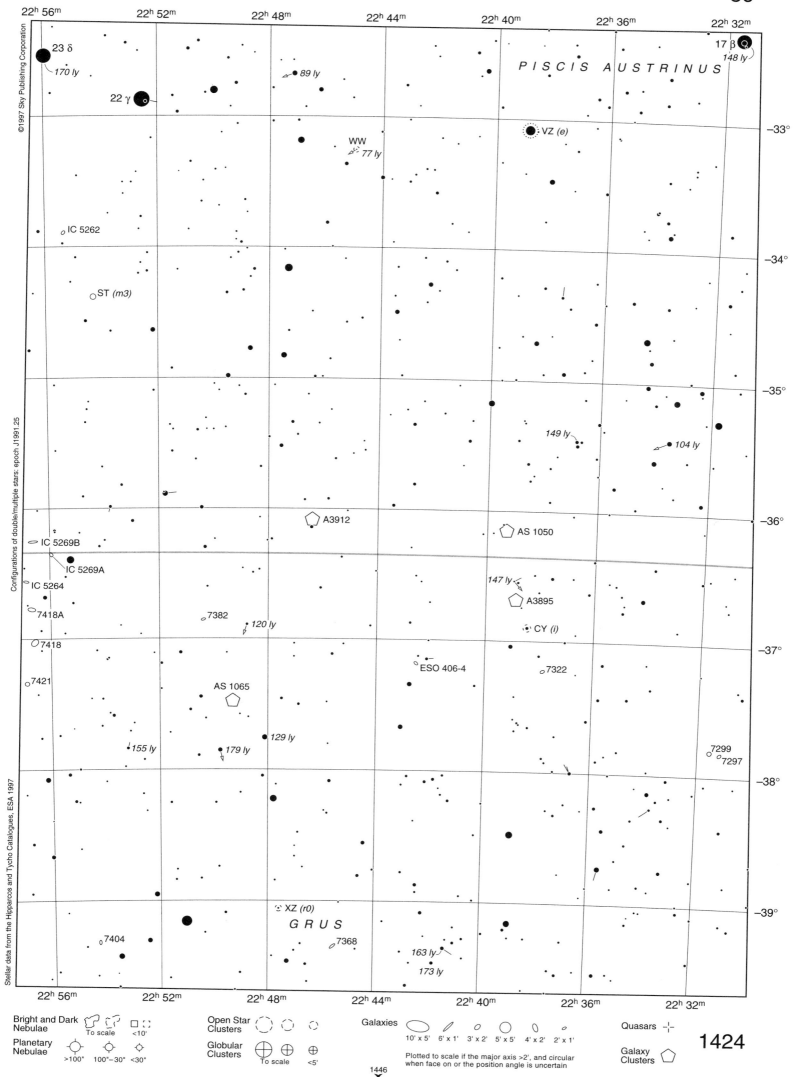

22h 56m    22h 52m    22h 48m    22h 44m    22h 40m    22h 36m    22h 32m

23 δ
170 ly
22 γ
89 ly
PISCIS AUSTRINUS
17 β
148 ly
−33°
VZ (e)
WW
77 ly
IC 5262
−34°
ST (m3)
−35°
149 ly
104 ly
A3912
AS 1050
−36°
IC 5269B
147 ly
IC 5269A
A3895
IC 5264
CY (i)
7418A
7382
120 ly
7418
ESO 406-4
7322
−37°
7421
AS 1065
7299
7297
129 ly
155 ly
179 ly
−38°
XZ (r0)
GRUS
−39°
7404
7368
163 ly
173 ly

22h 56m    22h 52m    22h 48m    22h 44m    22h 40m    22h 36m    22h 32m

| Bright and Dark Nebulae | | | Open Star Clusters | | | Galaxies | | | | | | Quasars |
|---|---|---|---|---|---|---|---|---|---|---|---|---|
| To scale | | <10' | | | | 10' x 5' | 6' x 1' | 3' x 2' | 5' x 5' | 4' x 2' | 2' x 1' | |
| Planetary Nebulae | | | Globular Clusters | | | | | | | | | Galaxy Clusters |
| >100" | 100"−30" | <30" | | To scale | <5' | | | | | | | |

Plotted to scale if the major axis >2', and circular when face on or the position angle is uncertain

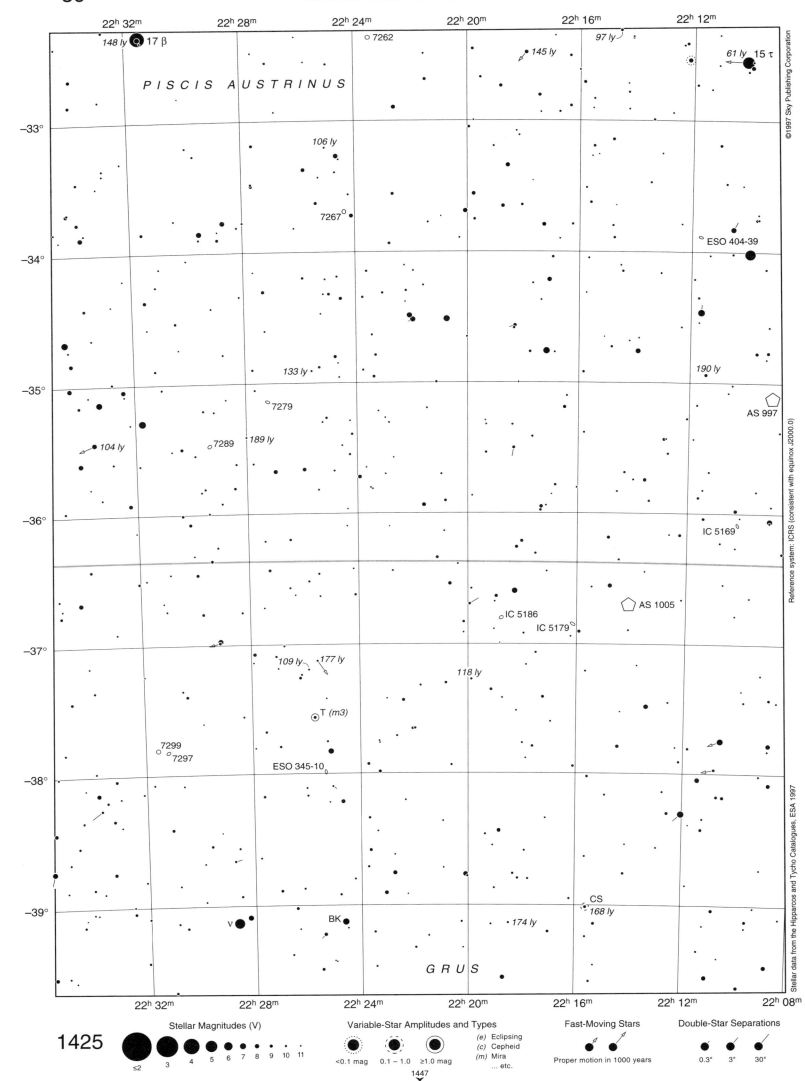

PISCIS AUSTRINUS

148 ly  17 β

7262

97 ly

145 ly

61 ly  15 τ

−33°

106 ly

7267

ESO 404-39

−34°

133 ly

190 ly

−35°

7279

AS 997

104 ly  7289  189 ly

−36°

IC 5169

IC 5186

AS 1005

IC 5179

−37°

109 ly  177 ly

118 ly

T (m3)

7299

ESO 345-10

7297

−38°

CS

168 ly

−39°

ν  BK

174 ly

G R U S

©1997 Sky Publishing Corporation

Reference system: ICRS (consistent with equinox J2000.0)

Stellar data from the Hipparcos and Tycho Catalogues, ESA 1997

Stellar Magnitudes (V)

≤2  3  4  5  6  7  8  9  10  11

Variable-Star Amplitudes and Types

<0.1 mag  0.1 – 1.0  ≥1.0 mag

(e) Eclipsing
(c) Cepheid
(m) Mira
... etc.

Fast-Moving Stars

Proper motion in 1000 years

Double-Star Separations

0.3"  3"  30"

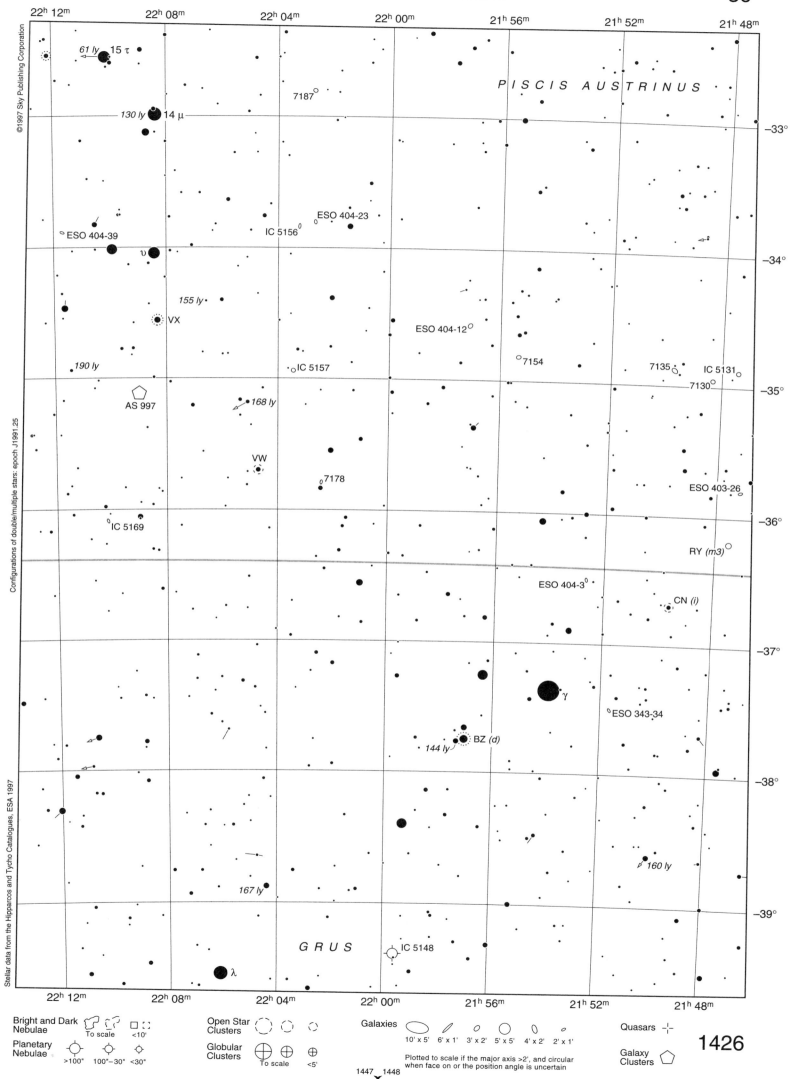

22h 12m   22h 08m   22h 04m   22h 00m   21h 56m   21h 52m   21h 48m

*PISCIS AUSTRINUS*

−33°
−34°
−35°
−36°
−37°
−38°
−39°

61 ly   15 τ
130 ly   14 μ
7187
ESO 404-23
IC 5156
ESO 404-39
υ
155 ly
VX
ESO 404-12
7154
7135   IC 5131
7130
190 ly
AS 997
168 ly
VW
7178
ESO 403-26
IC 5169
ESO 404-3
CN (i)
RY (m3)
γ
ESO 343-34
BZ (d)
144 ly
160 ly
167 ly
*GRUS*   IC 5148
λ

| Bright and Dark Nebulae | | | | Open Star Clusters | | | Galaxies | | | | | | Quasars |
| To scale | | <10' | | | | | 10' x 5' | 6' x 1' | 3' x 2' | 5' x 5' | 4' x 2' | 2' x 1' | |
| Planetary Nebulae | | | | Globular Clusters | | | | | | | | | Galaxy Clusters |
| >100" | 100"–30" | <30" | | To scale | | <5' | | | | | | | |

Plotted to scale if the major axis >2', and circular when face on or the position angle is uncertain

**1426**

1447  1448

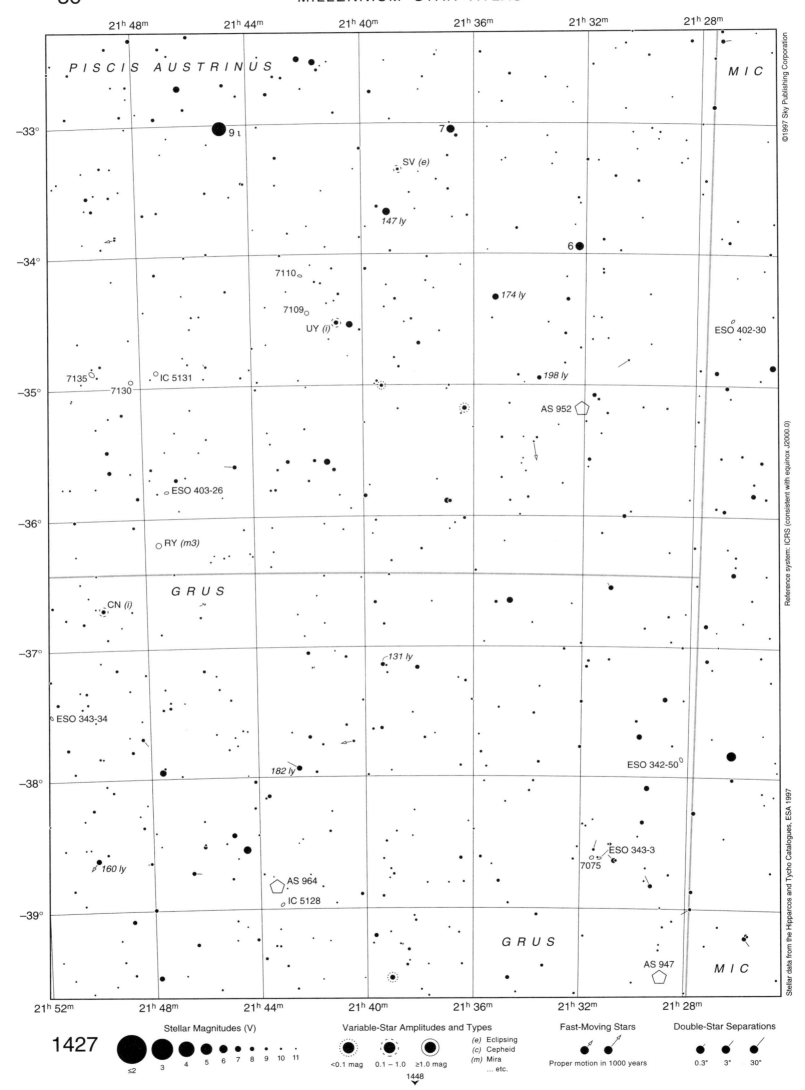

©1997 Sky Publishing Corporation

Reference system: ICRS (consistent with equinox J2000.0)

Stellar data from the Hipparcos and Tycho Catalogues, ESA 1997

1427

Stellar Magnitudes (V)

≤2   3   4   5   6   7   8   9   10   11

Variable-Star Amplitudes and Types

<0.1 mag    0.1 − 1.0    ≥1.0 mag

(e) Eclipsing
(c) Cepheid
(m) Mira
... etc.

Fast-Moving Stars

Proper motion in 1000 years

Double-Star Separations

0.3"    3"    30"

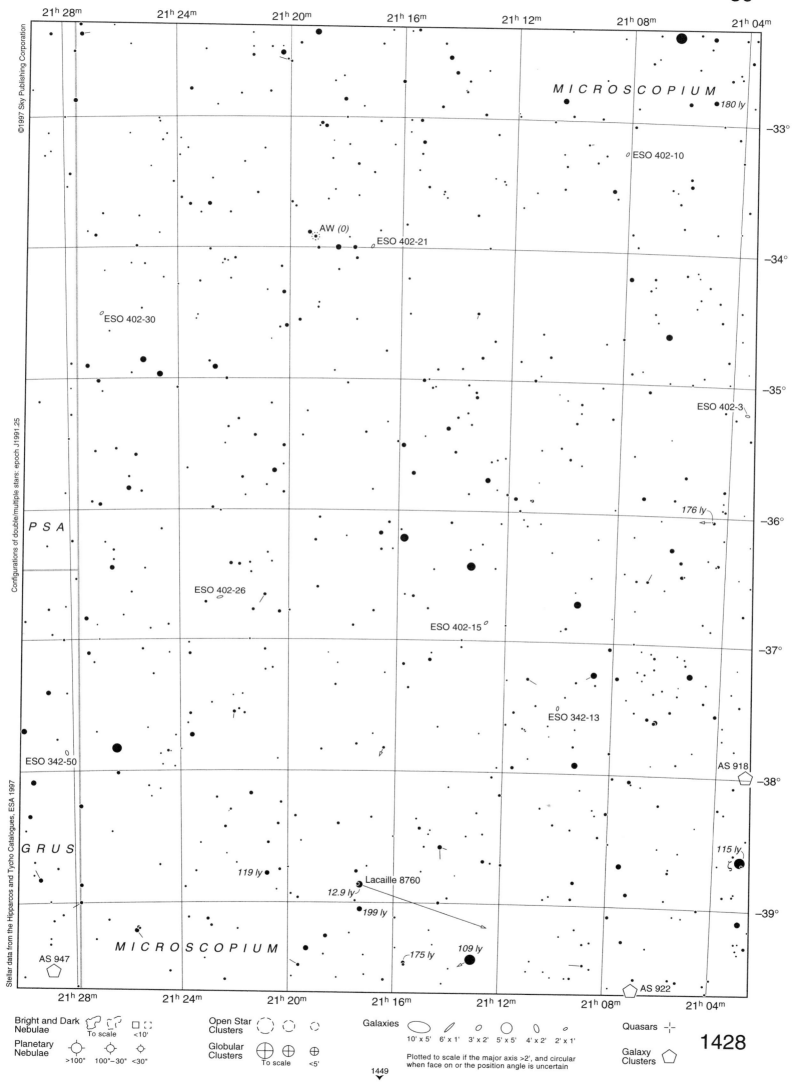

Configurations of double/multiple stars: epoch J1991.25

Stellar data from the Hipparcos and Tycho Catalogues, ESA 1997

21ʰ 28ᵐ  21ʰ 24ᵐ  21ʰ 20ᵐ  21ʰ 16ᵐ  21ʰ 12ᵐ  21ʰ 08ᵐ  21ʰ 04ᵐ

M I C R O S C O P I U M

180 ly

−33°

ESO 402-10

AW (0)
ESO 402-21

−34°

ESO 402-30

ESO 402-3

−35°

P S A

176 ly

−36°

ESO 402-26

ESO 402-15

−37°

ESO 342-13

ESO 342-50

AS 918

−38°

G R U S

115 ly

119 ly

Lacaille 8760
12.9 ly

199 ly

−39°

M I C R O S C O P I U M

175 ly    109 ly

AS 947

AS 922

21ʰ 28ᵐ  21ʰ 24ᵐ  21ʰ 20ᵐ  21ʰ 16ᵐ  21ʰ 12ᵐ  21ʰ 08ᵐ  21ʰ 04ᵐ

Bright and Dark
Nebulae              To scale     <10'

Planetary
Nebulae        >100"   100"–30"   <30"

Open Star
Clusters

Globular
Clusters       To scale    <5'

Galaxies

10' x 5'  6' x 1'  3' x 2'  5' x 5'  4' x 2'  2' x 1'

Plotted to scale if the major axis >2', and circular
when face on or the position angle is uncertain

Quasars  −|−

Galaxy
Clusters

1428

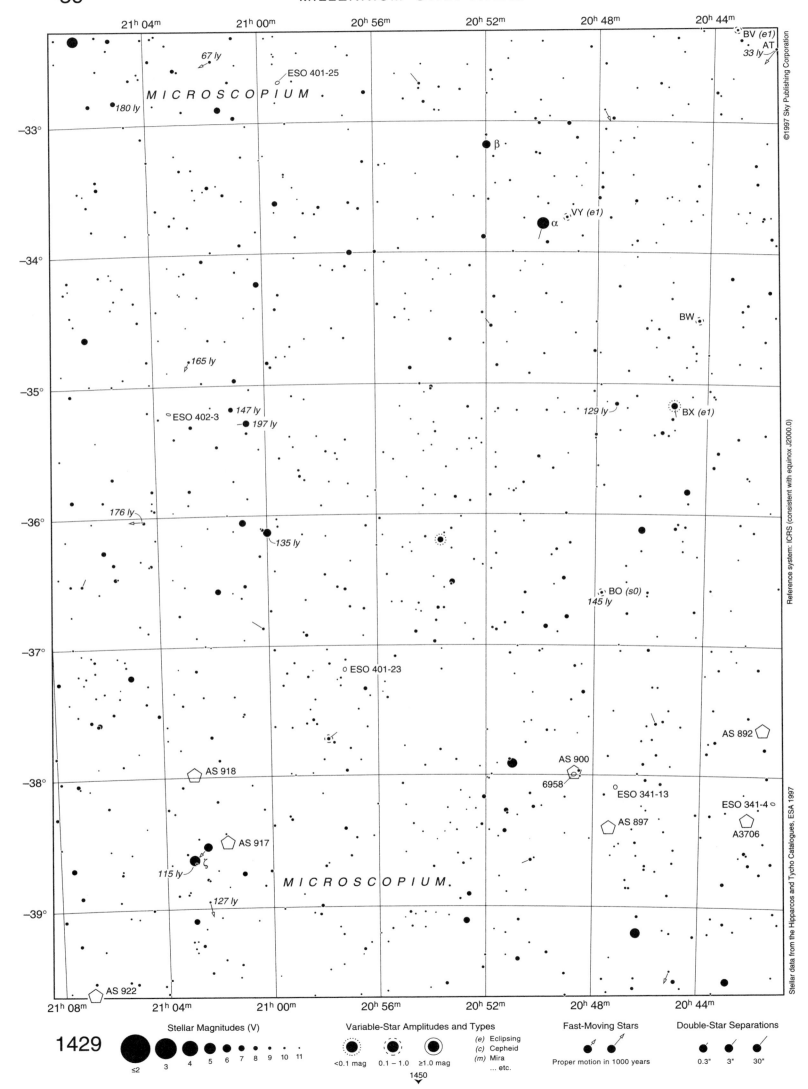

MICROSCOPIUM

MICROSCOPIUM.

67 ly

ESO 401-25

180 ly

β

VY (e1)

α

BW

165 ly

ESO 402-3    147 ly    BX (e1)

197 ly    129 ly

176 ly

135 ly    BO (s0)    145 ly

ESO 401-23

AS 892

AS 900    AS 897

AS 918    6958    ESO 341-13    ESO 341-4

AS 917    A3706

ζ

115 ly

127 ly

AS 922

1429    Stellar Magnitudes (V)    Variable-Star Amplitudes and Types    Fast-Moving Stars    Double-Star Separations

≤2    3    4    5  6  7  8  9  10  11

<0.1 mag    0.1 – 1.0    ≥1.0 mag    (e) Eclipsing
(c) Cepheid
(m) Mira
... etc.    Proper motion in 1000 years    0.3"    3"    30"

1450

# MILLENNIUM STAR ATLAS

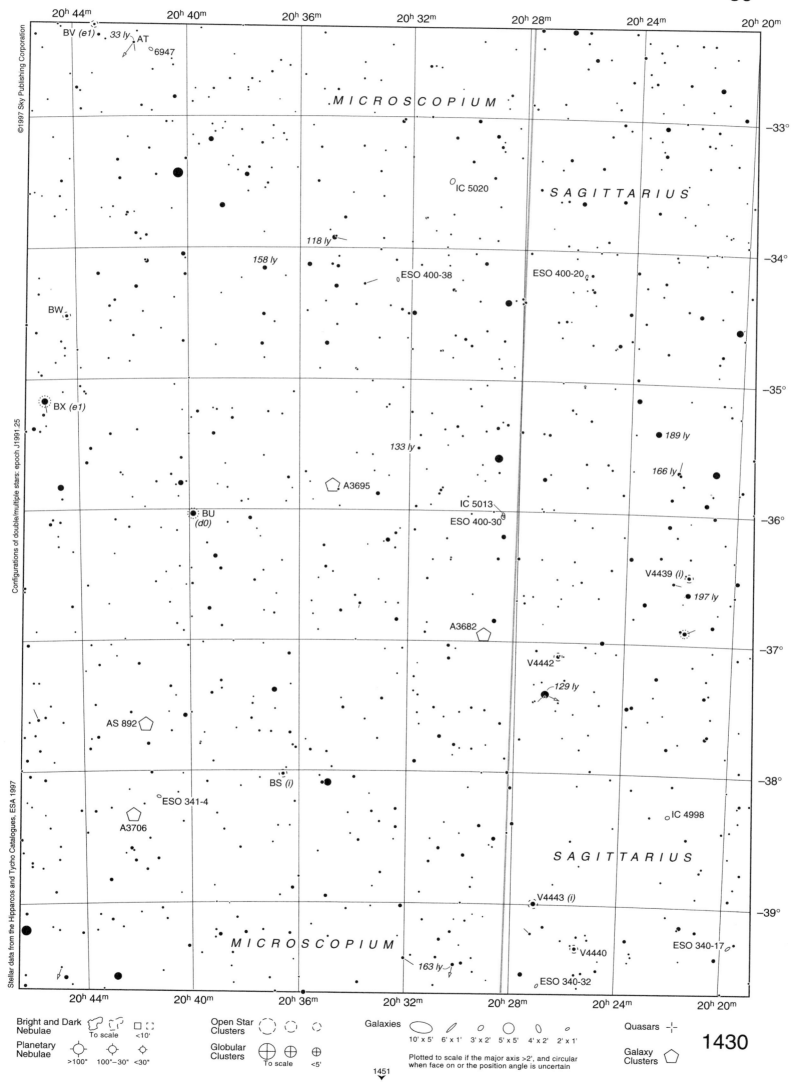

©1997 Sky Publishing Corporation

Configurations of double/multiple stars: epoch J1991.25

Stellar data from the Hipparcos and Tycho Catalogues, ESA 1997

20h 44m    20h 40m    20h 36m    20h 32m    20h 28m    20h 24m    20h 20m

BV (e1)   33 ly   AT   6947

MICROSCOPIUM

−33°

SAGITTARIUS

IC 5020

118 ly

158 ly    ESO 400-38    ESO 400-20

−34°

BW

BX (e1)

189 ly

166 ly

133 ly

A3695

IC 5013

BU (d0)    ESO 400-30

−36°

V4439 (i)

197 ly

A3682

V4442

129 ly

AS 892

−37°

BS (i)

−38°

ESO 341-4    IC 4998

A3706

SAGITTARIUS

V4443 (i)

−39°

MICROSCOPIUM

163 ly    V4440    ESO 340-17

ESO 340-32

20h 44m    20h 40m    20h 36m    20h 32m    20h 28m    20h 24m    20h 20m

Bright and Dark Nebulae    To scale   <10'

Planetary Nebulae   >100"   100"−30"   <30"

Open Star Clusters

Globular Clusters   To scale   <5'

Galaxies   10' x 5'   6' x 1'   3' x 2'   5' x 5'   4' x 2'   2' x 1'

Plotted to scale if the major axis >2', and circular when face on or the position angle is uncertain

Quasars

Galaxy Clusters

**1430**

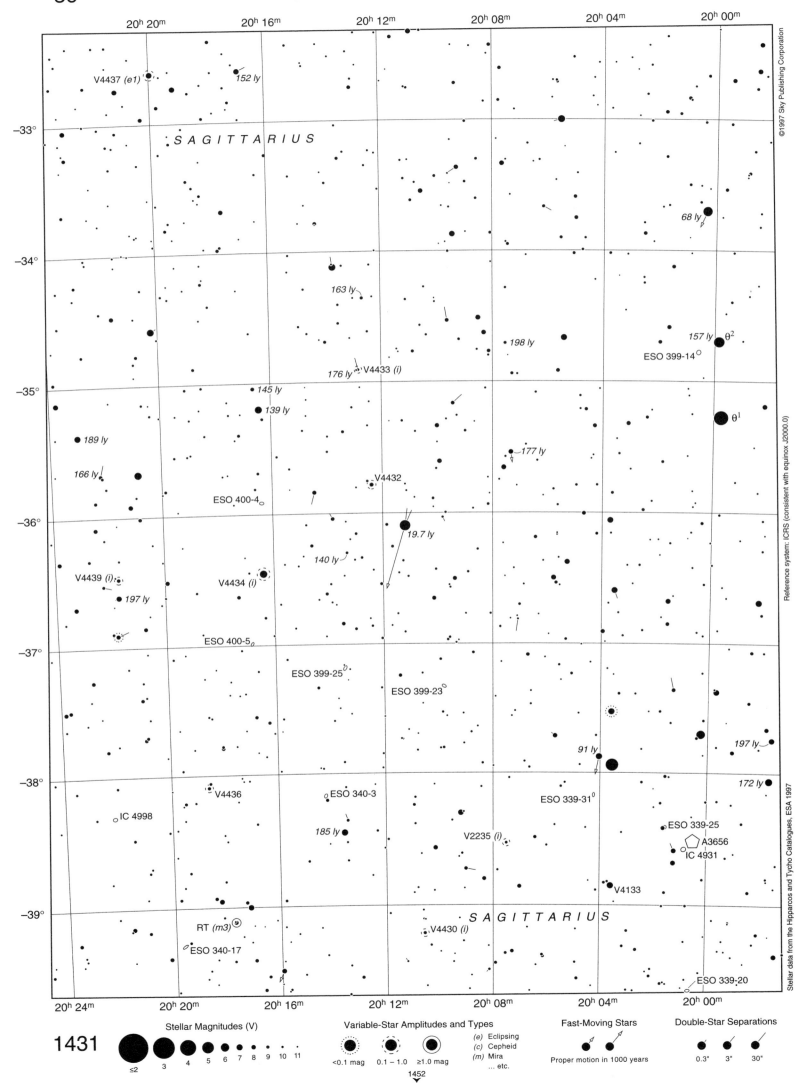

SAGITTARIUS

V4437 (e1)    152 ly

68 ly

163 ly

198 ly    157 ly  θ²
                   ESO 399-14

176 ly  V4433 (i)

145 ly
139 ly                              θ¹

189 ly

166 ly                     177 ly

                V4432

ESO 400-4

                19.7 ly

V4439 (i)      140 ly

V4434 (i)

197 ly

ESO 400-5

        ESO 399-25
                ESO 399-23

                                    197 ly
                        91 ly

                                    172 ly

V4436           ESO 340-3          ESO 339-31

IC 4998                                ESO 339-25
                                        A3656
        185 ly       V2235 (i)        IC 4931

                                V4133

SAGITTARIUS

RT (m3)         V4430 (i)
ESO 340-17

                                    ESO 339-20

Stellar Magnitudes (V)

≤2  3  4  5  6  7  8  9 10 11

Variable-Star Amplitudes and Types

<0.1 mag   0.1 – 1.0   ≥1.0 mag

(e) Eclipsing
(c) Cepheid
(m) Mira
... etc.

Fast-Moving Stars

Proper motion in 1000 years

Double-Star Separations

0.3"   3"   30"

# MILLENNIUM STAR ATLAS

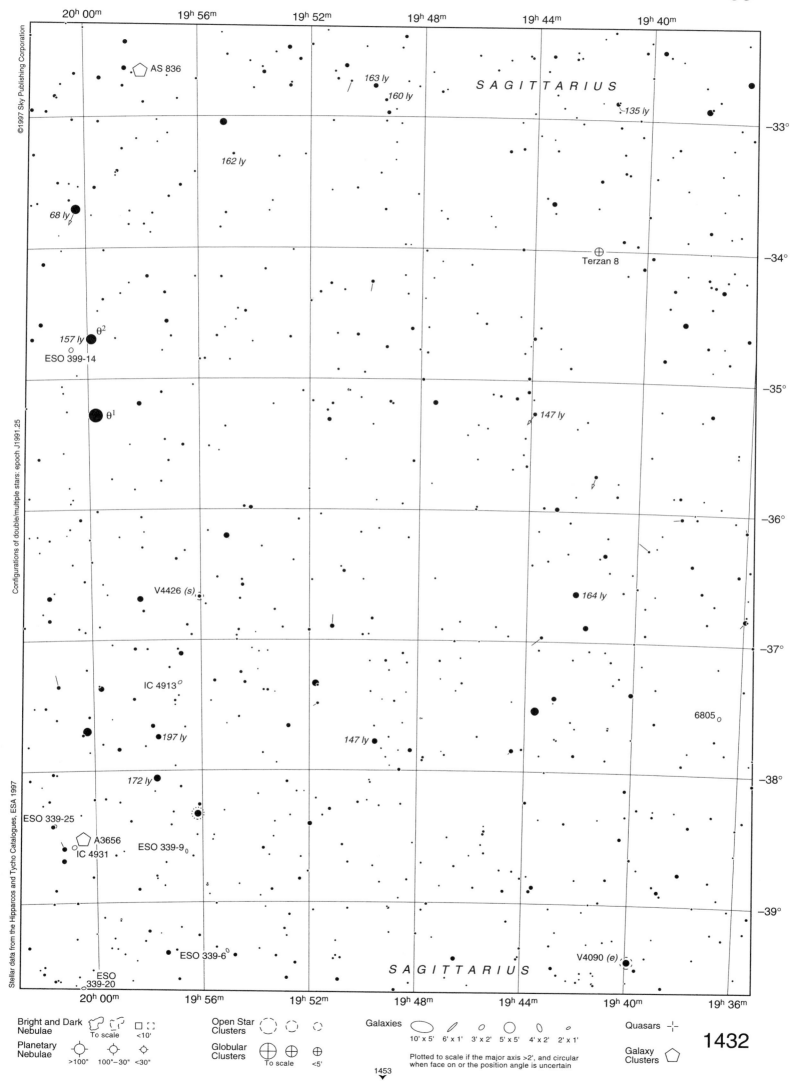

Configurations of double/multiple stars: epoch J1991.25

Stellar data from the Hipparcos and Tycho Catalogues, ESA 1997

AS 836

163 ly

160 ly

*SAGITTARIUS*

−135 ly

−33°

162 ly

68 ly

−34°

Terzan 8

157 ly θ²

ESO 399-14

−35°

θ¹

147 ly

−36°

V4426 (s)

164 ly

IC 4913

−37°

197 ly

147 ly

6805

172 ly

−38°

ESO 339-25

A3656

ESO 339-9

IC 4931

−39°

ESO 339-6

ESO 339-20

*SAGITTARIUS*

V4090 (e)

| Bright and Dark Nebulae | Open Star Clusters | Galaxies | Quasars |
| --- | --- | --- | --- |

To scale   <10'

Planetary Nebulae   >100"   100"−30"   <30"

Globular Clusters   To scale   <5'

Galaxies   10' x 5'   6' x 1'   3' x 2'   5' x 5'   4' x 2'   2' x 1'

Plotted to scale if the major axis >2', and circular when face on or the position angle is uncertain

Galaxy Clusters

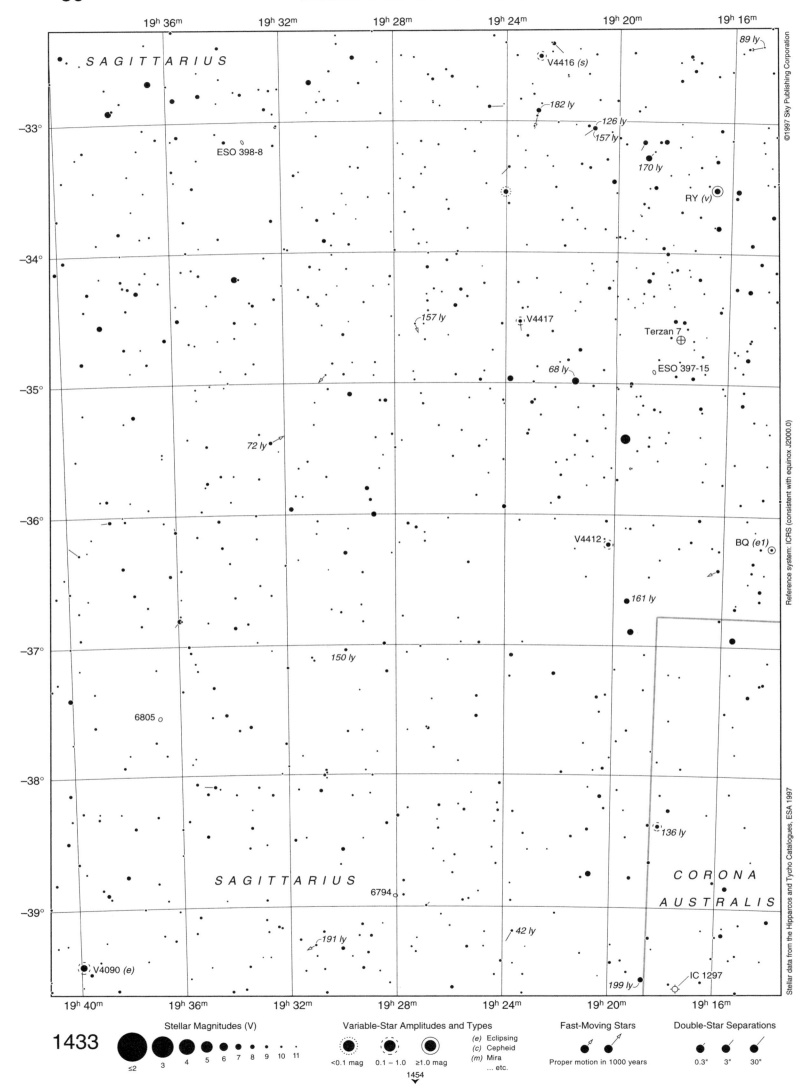

**1433**

| Stellar Magnitudes (V) | Variable-Star Amplitudes and Types | Fast-Moving Stars | Double-Star Separations |
|---|---|---|---|
| ≤2  3  4  5  6  7  8  9  10  11 | <0.1 mag   0.1 – 1.0   ≥1.0 mag | Proper motion in 1000 years | 0.3″   3″   30″ |

(e) Eclipsing
(c) Cepheid
(m) Mira
... etc.

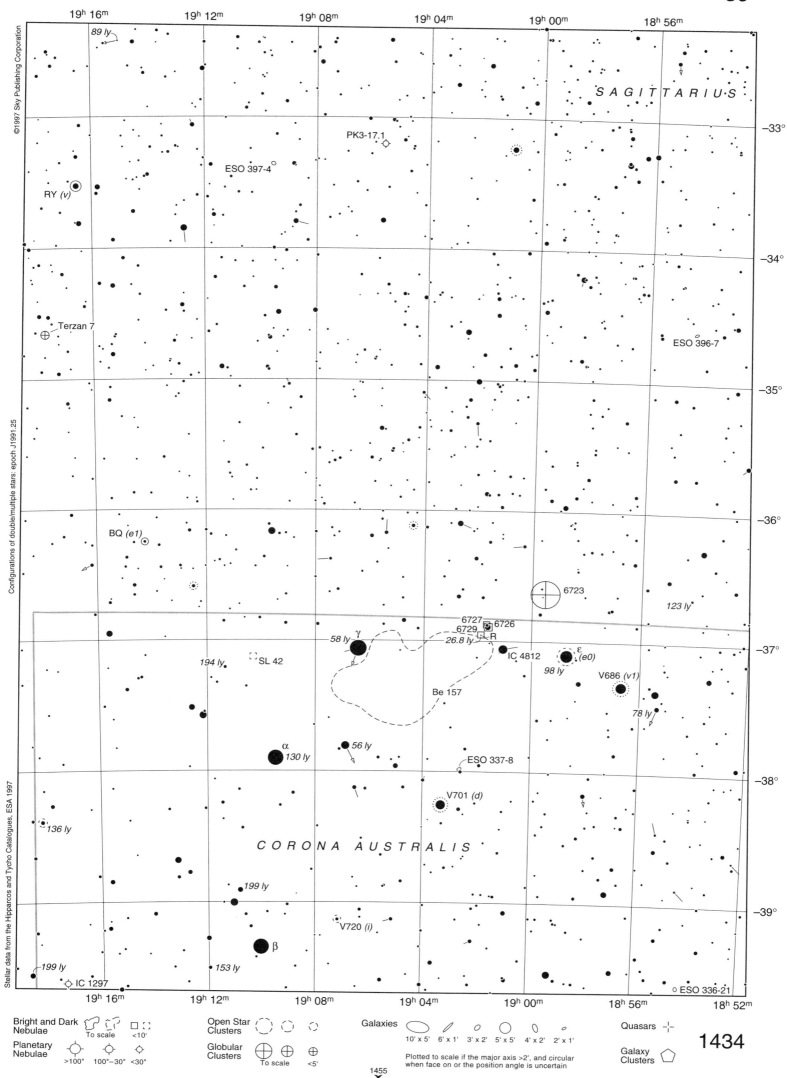

19h 16m   19h 12m   19h 08m   19h 04m   19h 00m   18h 56m

89 ly

S A G I T T A R I U S

−33°

PK3-17.1

ESO 397-4

RY (v)

−34°

Terzan 7

ESO 396-7

−35°

−36°

BQ (e1)

6723

123 ly

6727   6726
6729   R

58 ly   γ

26.8 ly

IC 4812   ε (e0)

−37°

194 ly   SL 42

98 ly

V686 (v1)

Be 157

78 ly

α   56 ly
130 ly

ESO 337-8

−38°

V701 (d)

136 ly

C O R O N A   A U S T R A L I S

199 ly

−39°

V720 (i)

β

199 ly   153 ly

IC 1297   ESO 336-21

19h 16m   19h 12m   19h 08m   19h 04m   19h 00m   18h 56m   18h 52m

Bright and Dark
Nebulae
To scale   <10'

Planetary
Nebulae
>100"   100"-30"   <30"

Open Star
Clusters

Globular
Clusters
To scale   <5'

Galaxies
10' x 5'   6' x 1'   3' x 2'   5' x 5'   4' x 2'   2' x 1'

Plotted to scale if the major axis >2', and circular
when face on or the position angle is uncertain

Quasars

Galaxy
Clusters

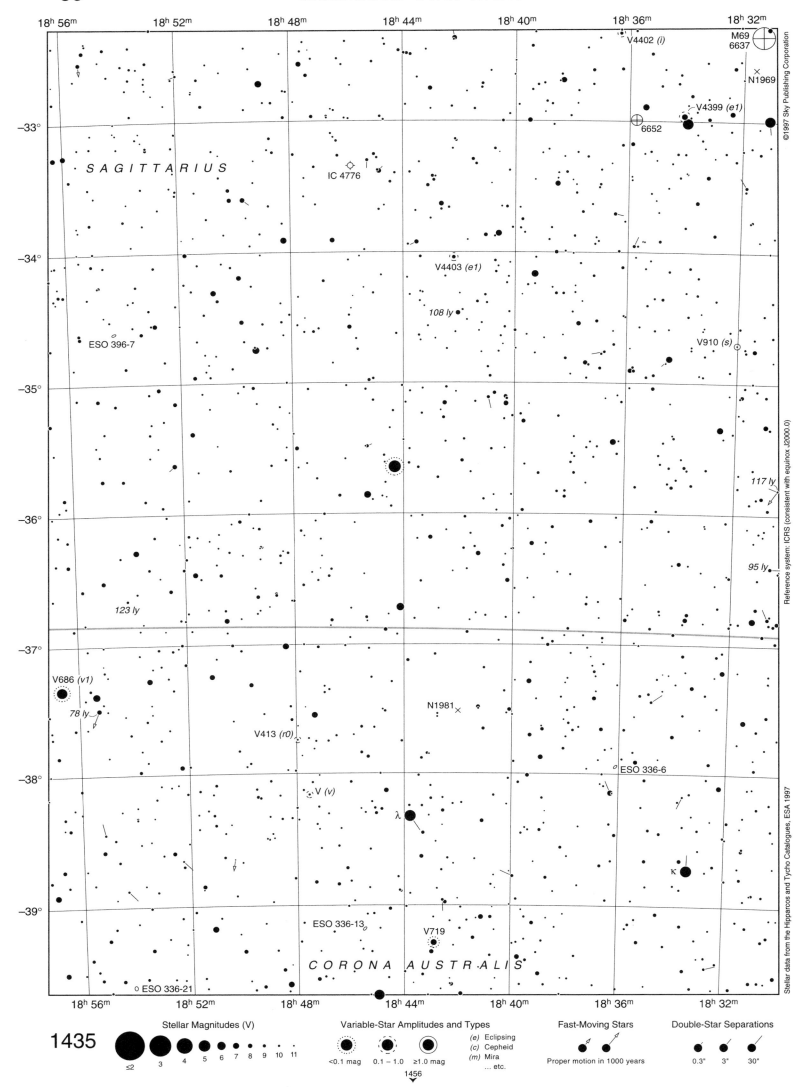

Reference system: ICRS (consistent with equinox J2000.0)

Stellar data from the Hipparcos and Tycho Catalogues, ESA 1997

**1435**

Stellar Magnitudes (V)

≤2   3   4   5   6   7   8   9   10   11

Variable-Star Amplitudes and Types

<0.1 mag   0.1 – 1.0   ≥1.0 mag

*(e)* Eclipsing
*(c)* Cepheid
*(m)* Mira
... etc.

Fast-Moving Stars

Proper motion in 1000 years

Double-Star Separations

0.3"   3"   30"

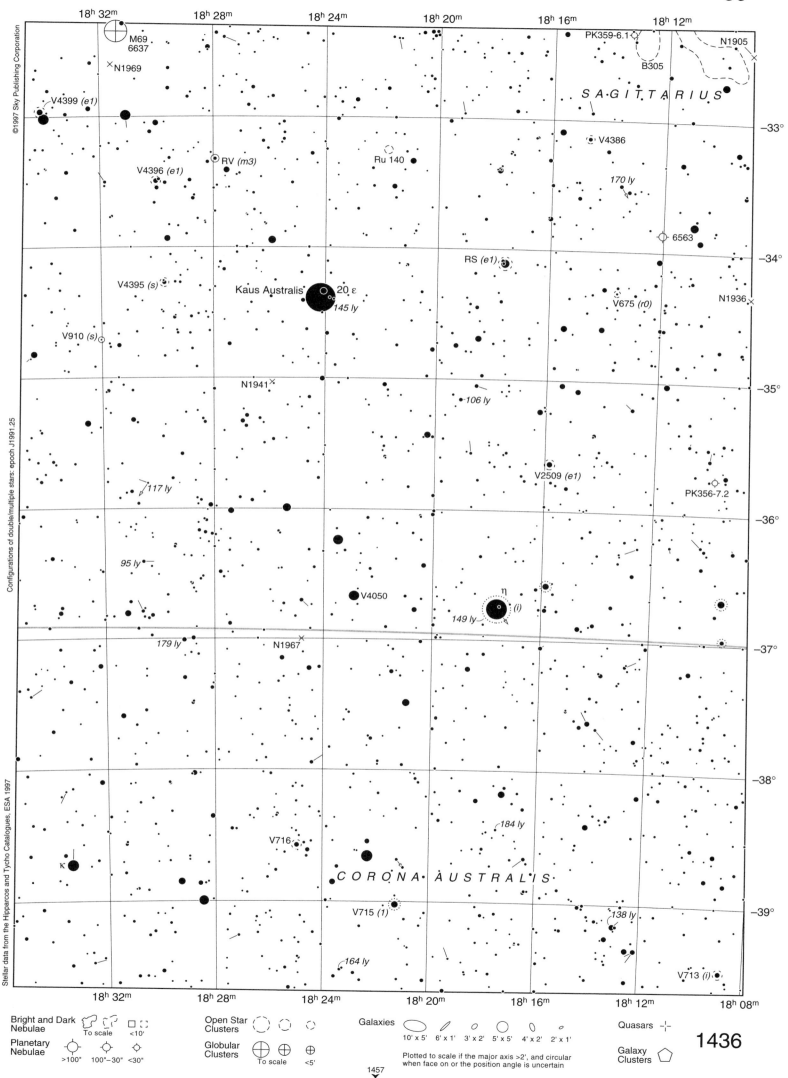

18h 32m     18h 28m     18h 24m     18h 20m     18h 16m     18h 12m

M69
6637

N1969

V4399 (e1)

PK359-6.1
N1905
B305

SAGITTARIUS

−33°

RV (m3)
V4396 (e1)

Ru 140

V4386

170 ly

6563

V4395 (s)

Kaus Australis    20 ε
145 ly

RS (e1)

V675 (r0)

N1936

−34°

V910 (s)

N1941

106 ly

−35°

V2509 (e1)

PK356-7.2

117 ly

−36°

95 ly

V4050

η
(i)
149 ly

179 ly     N1967

−37°

−38°

184 ly

V716

κ

CORONA AUSTRALIS

138 ly

−39°

V715 (1)

164 ly

V713 (i)

18h 32m     18h 28m     18h 24m     18h 20m     18h 16m     18h 12m     18h 08m

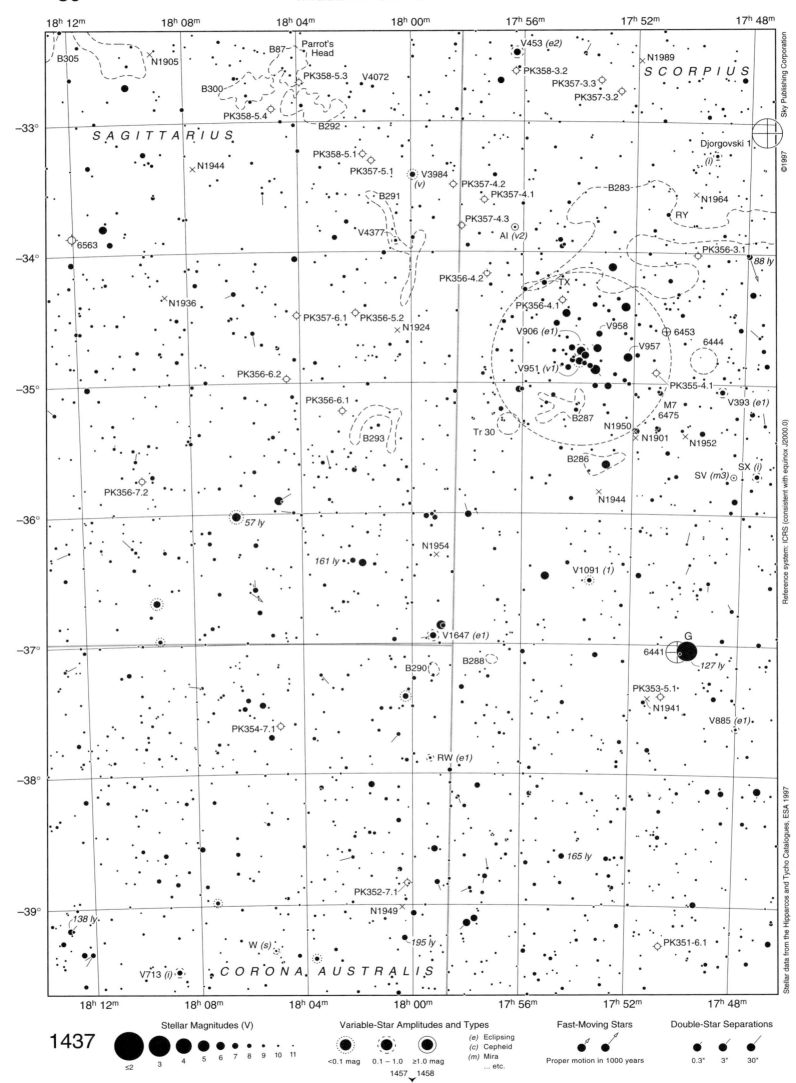

Sky Publishing Corporation
©1997
Reference system: ICRS (consistent with equinox J2000.0)
Stellar data from the Hipparcos and Tycho Catalogues, ESA 1997

1437

**Stellar Magnitudes (V)**
≤2   3   4   5   6   7   8   9   10   11

**Variable-Star Amplitudes and Types**
<0.1 mag   0.1 – 1.0   ≥1.0 mag
1457   1458

(e) Eclipsing
(c) Cepheid
(m) Mira
... etc.

**Fast-Moving Stars**
Proper motion in 1000 years

**Double-Star Separations**
0.3"   3"   30"

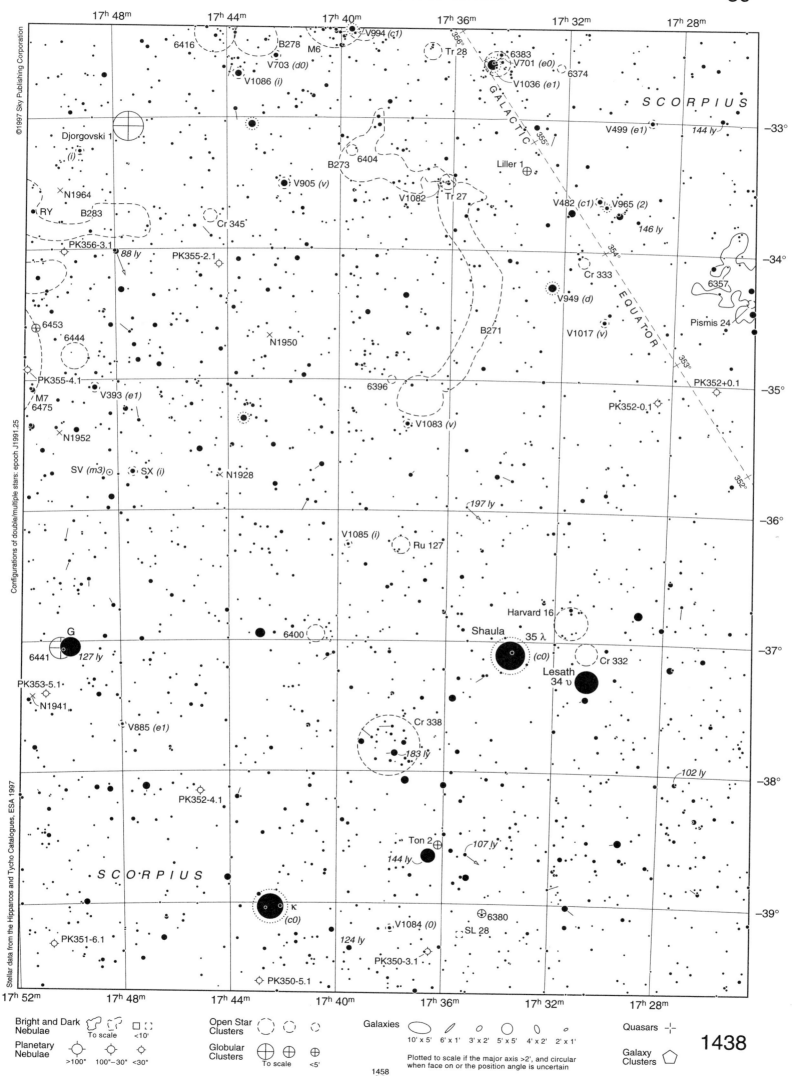

SCORPIUS

SCORPIUS

17h 48m      17h 44m      17h 40m      17h 36m      17h 32m      17h 28m

6416
B278    M6
V994 (c1)
Tr 28
V703 (d0)
V1086 (i)
6383
V701 (e0)
6374
V1036 (e1)
Djorgovski 1
(i)
V499 (e1)      144 ly
−33°
N1964
RY    B283
B273    6404
Liller 1
V905 (v)
V1082    Tr 27
V482 (c1)    V965 (2)
146 ly
PK356-3.1
88 ly    PK355-2.1
Cr 345
Cr 333
V949 (d)
−34°
6453
6444
N1950
B271
V1017 (v)
6357
Pismis 24
PK355-4.1
6396
PK352+0.1
353°
−35°
M7    V393 (e1)
6475
PK352-0.1
N1952
V1083 (v)
SV (m3)    SX (i)    N1928
197 ly
352°
−36°
V1085 (i)
Ru 127
Harvard 16
G    6400
Shaula    35 λ
6441    127 ly
(c0)
Cr 332
Lesath
34 υ
−37°
PK353-5.1
N1941
V885 (e1)
Cr 338
183 ly
102 ly
−38°
PK352-4.1
Ton 2
107 ly
144 ly
SCORPIUS
6380
κ
V1084 (0)
(c0)    SL 28
PK351-6.1
124 ly
PK350-3.1
PK350-5.1

17h 52m      17h 48m      17h 44m      17h 40m      17h 36m      17h 32m      17h 28m

1438

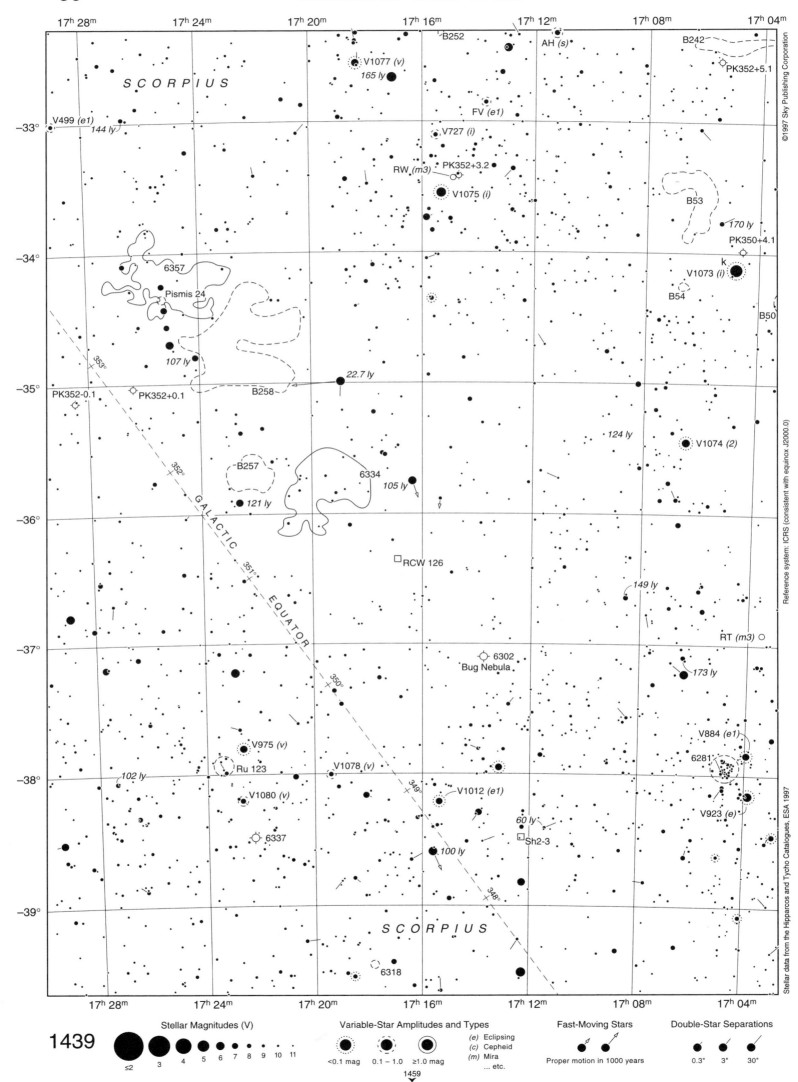

1439

Stellar Magnitudes (V)

≤2   3   4   5   6   7   8   9   10   11

Variable-Star Amplitudes and Types

<0.1 mag    0.1 − 1.0    ≥1.0 mag

(e) Eclipsing
(c) Cepheid
(m) Mira
... etc.

Fast-Moving Stars

Proper motion in 1000 years

Double-Star Separations

0.3"    3"    30"

1459

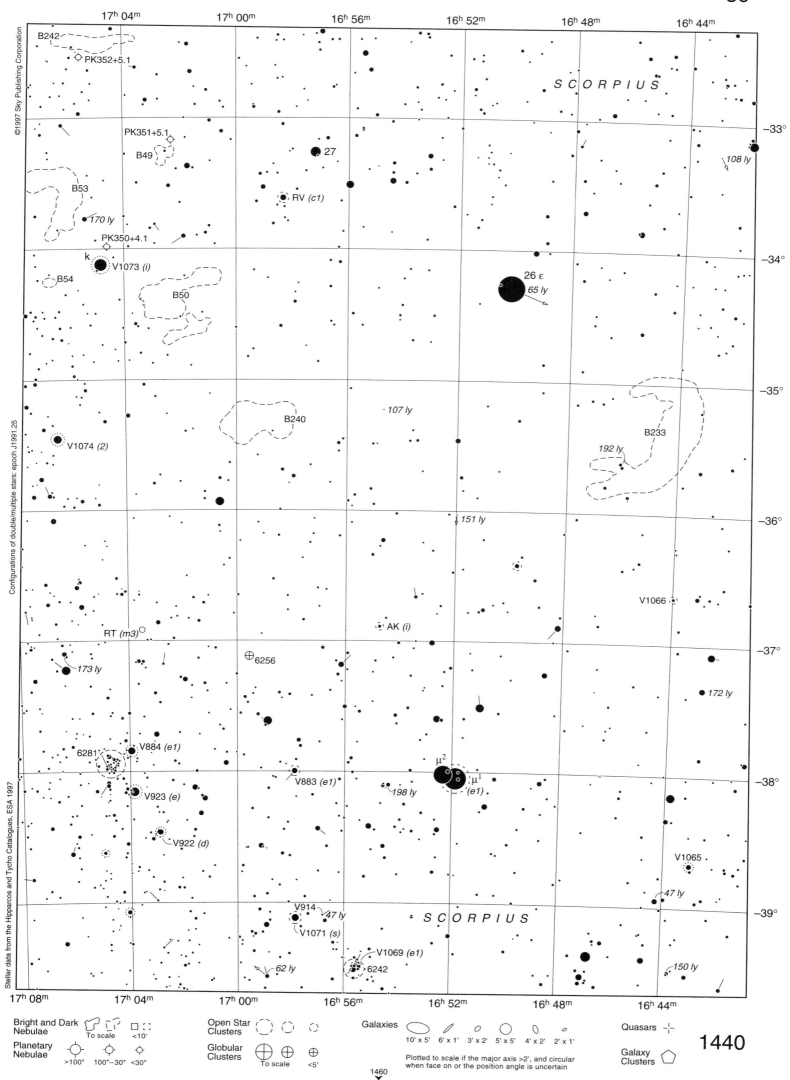

©1997 Sky Publishing Corporation

Configurations of double/multiple stars: epoch J1991.25

Stellar data from the Hipparcos and Tycho Catalogues, ESA 1997

SCORPIUS

−33°

−34°

−35°

−36°

−37°

−38°

−39°

17ʰ 04ᵐ   17ʰ 00ᵐ   16ʰ 56ᵐ   16ʰ 52ᵐ   16ʰ 48ᵐ   16ʰ 44ᵐ

17ʰ 08ᵐ   17ʰ 04ᵐ   17ʰ 00ᵐ   16ʰ 56ᵐ   16ʰ 52ᵐ   16ʰ 48ᵐ   16ʰ 44ᵐ

B242
PK352+5.1
PK351+5.1
B49
B53
170 ly
PK350+4.1
k   V1073 (i)
B54
B50
27
RV (c1)
26 ε
65 ly
107 ly
B240
B233
192 ly
151 ly
V1074 (2)
V1066
AK (i)
RT (m3)
173 ly
⊕ 6256
172 ly
V884 (e1)
6281
μ²
V883 (e1)
μ¹
(e1)
V923 (e)
198 ly
V922 (d)
V1065
V914   47 ly
V1071 (s)
47 ly
SCORPIUS
V1069 (e1)
62 ly   6242
150 ly

Bright and Dark Nebulae    ⊓ ⊔ To scale   □ <10'
Planetary Nebulae    ⬦ >100"   ⬦ 100"−30"   ⬦ <30"
Open Star Clusters   ⬡ ⬡ ⬡
Globular Clusters   ⊕ ⊕ To scale   ⊕ <5'
Galaxies   ⬭ ⬯ ◦ ◯ ⬮ ◦   10' x 5'   6' x 1'   3' x 2'   5' x 5'   4' x 2'   2' x 1'
Plotted to scale if the major axis >2', and circular when face on or the position angle is uncertain
Quasars   −⊢−
Galaxy Clusters   ⬠

1440

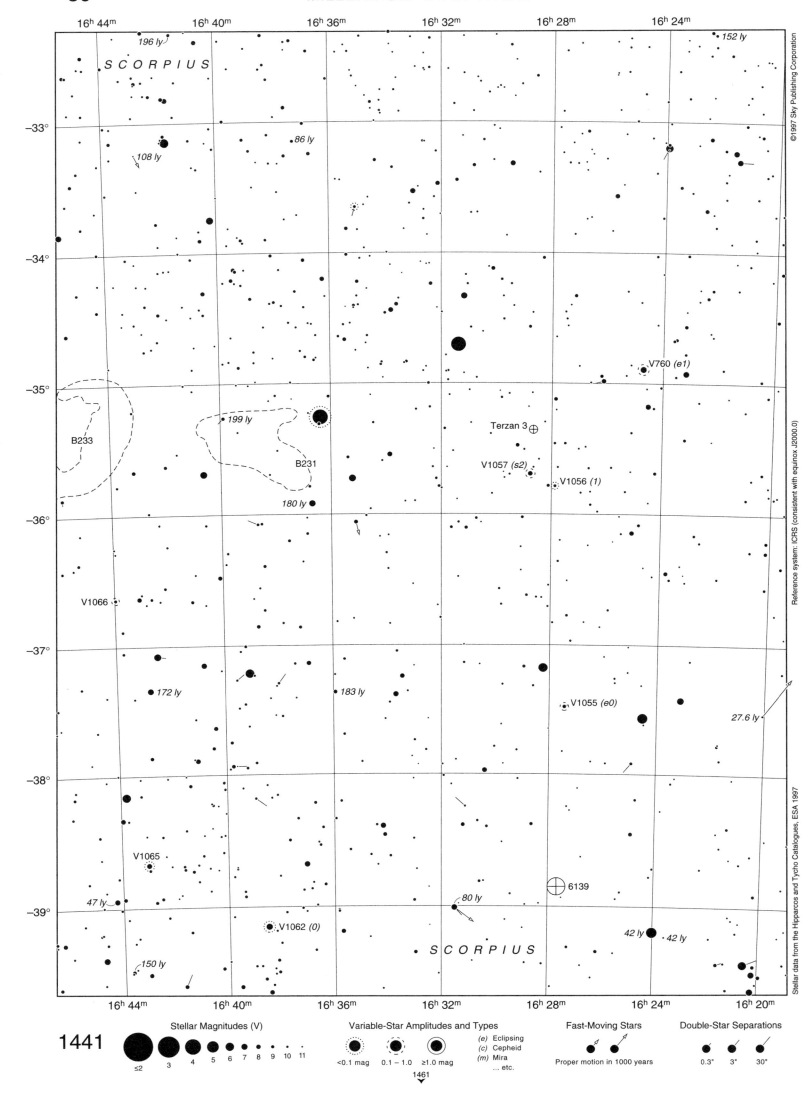

Reference system: ICRS (consistent with equinox J2000.0)

Stellar data from the Hipparcos and Tycho Catalogues, ESA 1997

SCORPIUS

196 ly
108 ly
86 ly
152 ly

B233
199 ly
B231
180 ly

V760 (e1)
Terzan 3
V1057 (s2)
V1056 (1)

V1066
V1055 (e0)
172 ly
183 ly
27.6 ly

V1065
47 ly
6139
80 ly
V1062 (0)
42 ly   42 ly
150 ly

SCORPIUS

**1441**

**Stellar Magnitudes (V)**
≤2   3   4   5   6   7   8   9  10  11

**Variable-Star Amplitudes and Types**
<0.1 mag   0.1 − 1.0   ≥1.0 mag
(e) Eclipsing
(c) Cepheid
(m) Mira
... etc.

**Fast-Moving Stars**
Proper motion in 1000 years

**Double-Star Separations**
0.3"   3"   30"

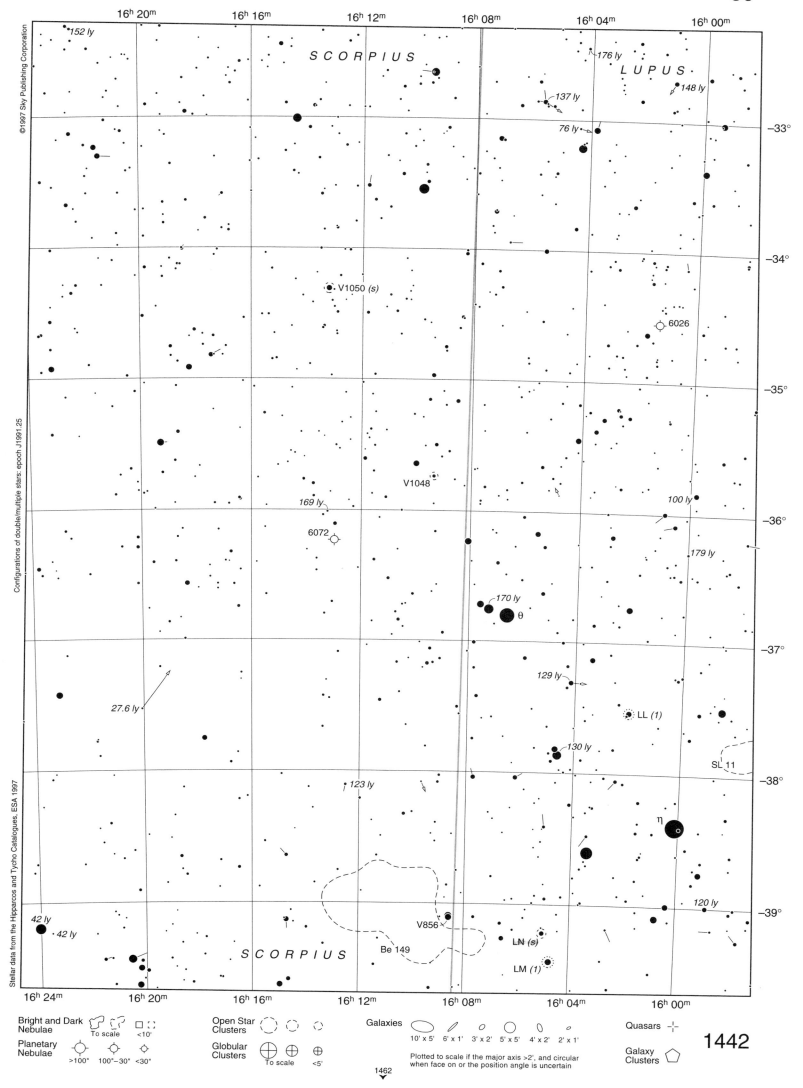

Configurations of double/multiple stars: epoch J1991.25

Stellar data from the Hipparcos and Tycho Catalogues, ESA 1997

SCORPIUS

LUPUS

152 ly

176 ly

148 ly

137 ly

76 ly

−33°

V1050 (s)

6026

−34°

−35°

V1048

169 ly

100 ly

6072

−36°

179 ly

170 ly

θ

−37°

129 ly

LL (1)

27.6 ly

130 ly

SL 11

−38°

123 ly

η

42 ly

120 ly

42 ly

−39°

V856

SCORPIUS

LN (s)

Be 149

LM (1)

16h 24m   16h 20m   16h 16m   16h 12m   16h 08m   16h 04m   16h 00m

| Bright and Dark Nebulae | Open Star Clusters | Galaxies | Quasars |
| Planetary Nebulae | Globular Clusters | | Galaxy Clusters |

Bright and Dark Nebulae    To scale    <10'

Planetary Nebulae    >100"   100"–30"   <30"

Open Star Clusters

Globular Clusters    To scale    <5'

Galaxies    10' x 5'   6' x 1'   3' x 2'   5' x 5'   4' x 2'   2' x 1'

Plotted to scale if the major axis >2', and circular when face on or the position angle is uncertain

Quasars

Galaxy Clusters

1442

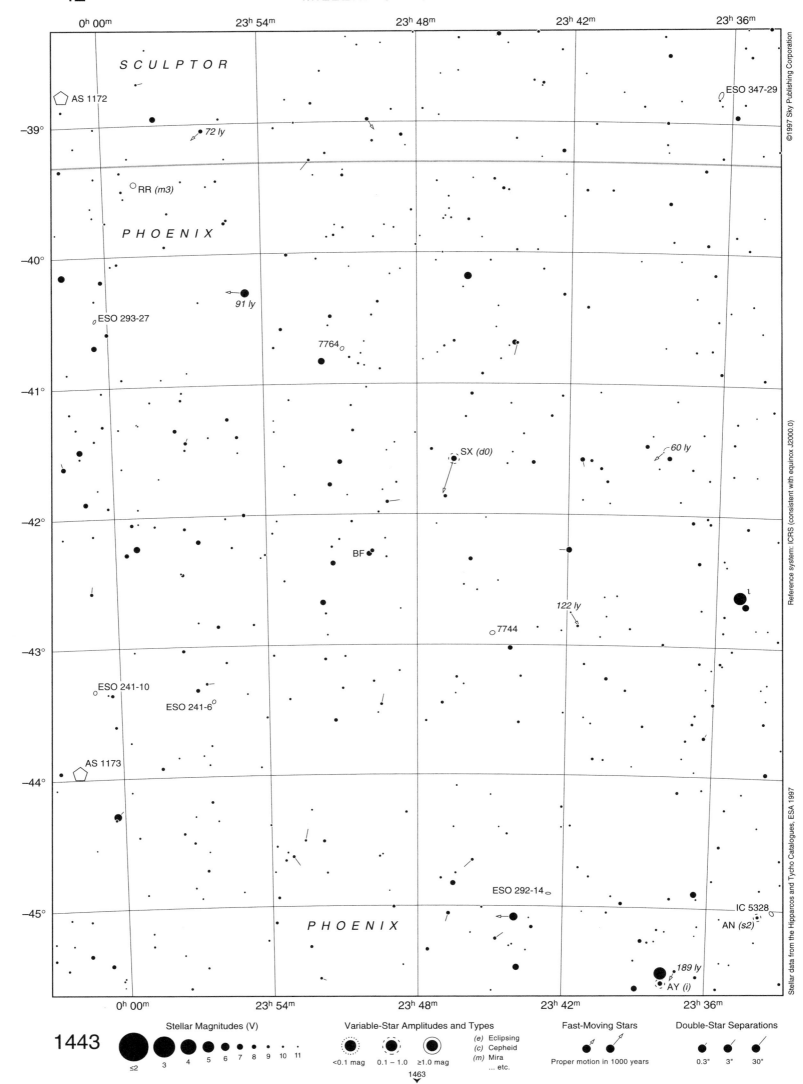

©1997 Sky Publishing Corporation

Reference system: ICRS (consistent with equinox J2000.0)

Stellar data from the Hipparcos and Tycho Catalogues, ESA 1997

Stellar Magnitudes (V)

≤2  3  4  5  6  7  8  9  10  11

Variable-Star Amplitudes and Types

<0.1 mag    0.1 – 1.0    ≥1.0 mag

(e) Eclipsing
(c) Cepheid
(m) Mira
... etc.

1463

Fast-Moving Stars

Proper motion in 1000 years

Double-Star Separations

0.3"    3"    30"

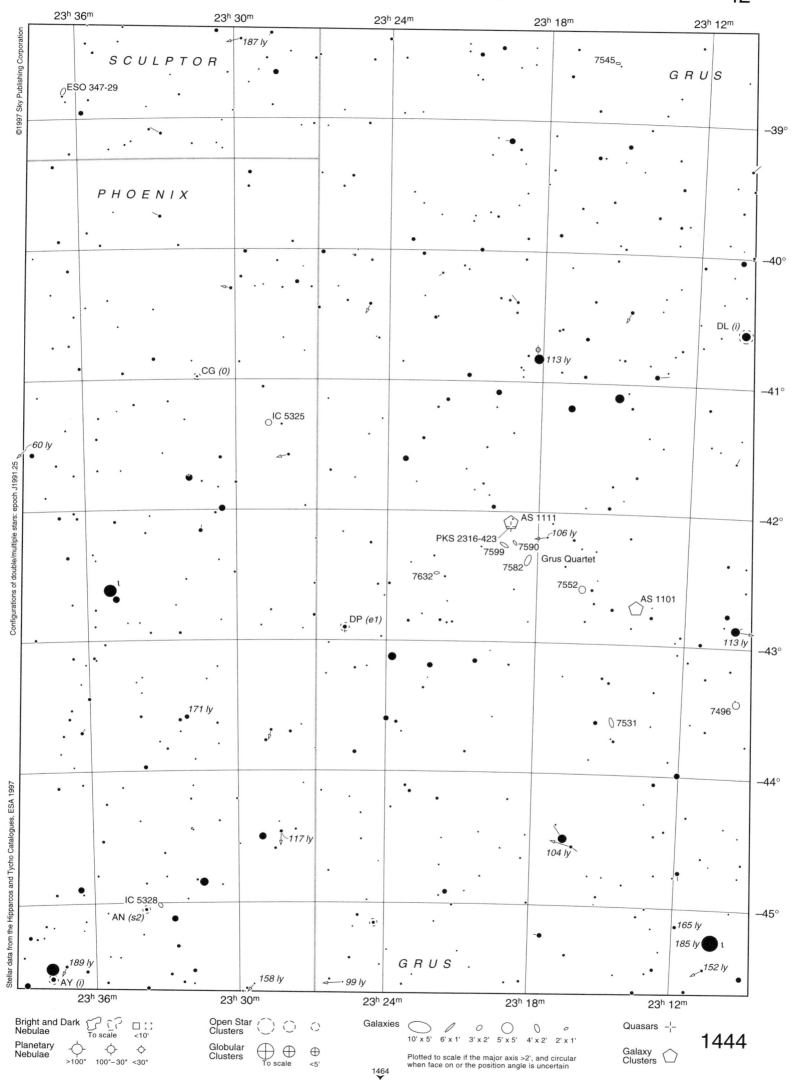

Stellar data from the Hipparcos and Tycho Catalogues, ESA 1997

Configurations of double/multiple stars: epoch J1991.25

23h 36m    23h 30m    23h 24m    23h 18m    23h 12m

S C U L P T O R

G R U S

ESO 347-29

7545

P H O E N I X

−39°

−40°

DL (i)

CG (0)

φ 113 ly

−41°

IC 5325

60 ly

AS 1111

PKS 2316-423    106 ly
7599   7590
7632   7582   Grus Quartet
7552
AS 1101

−42°

ι

DP (e1)

113 ly

−43°

171 ly

7496
7531

−44°

117 ly

104 ly

IC 5328

165 ly
185 ly ι

AN (s2)

189 ly
AY (i)

G R U S

158 ly    99 ly    152 ly

−45°

23h 36m    23h 30m    23h 24m    23h 18m    23h 12m

Bright and Dark Nebulae     Open Star Clusters     Galaxies     Quasars

To scale    <10'     To scale    <10'

Planetary Nebulae    Globular Clusters     10' x 5'  6' x 1'  3' x 2'  5' x 5'  2' x 1'  2' x 1'     Galaxy Clusters

>100"  100"–30"  <30"     To scale  <5'

Plotted to scale if the major axis >2', and circular when face on or the position angle is uncertain

1444

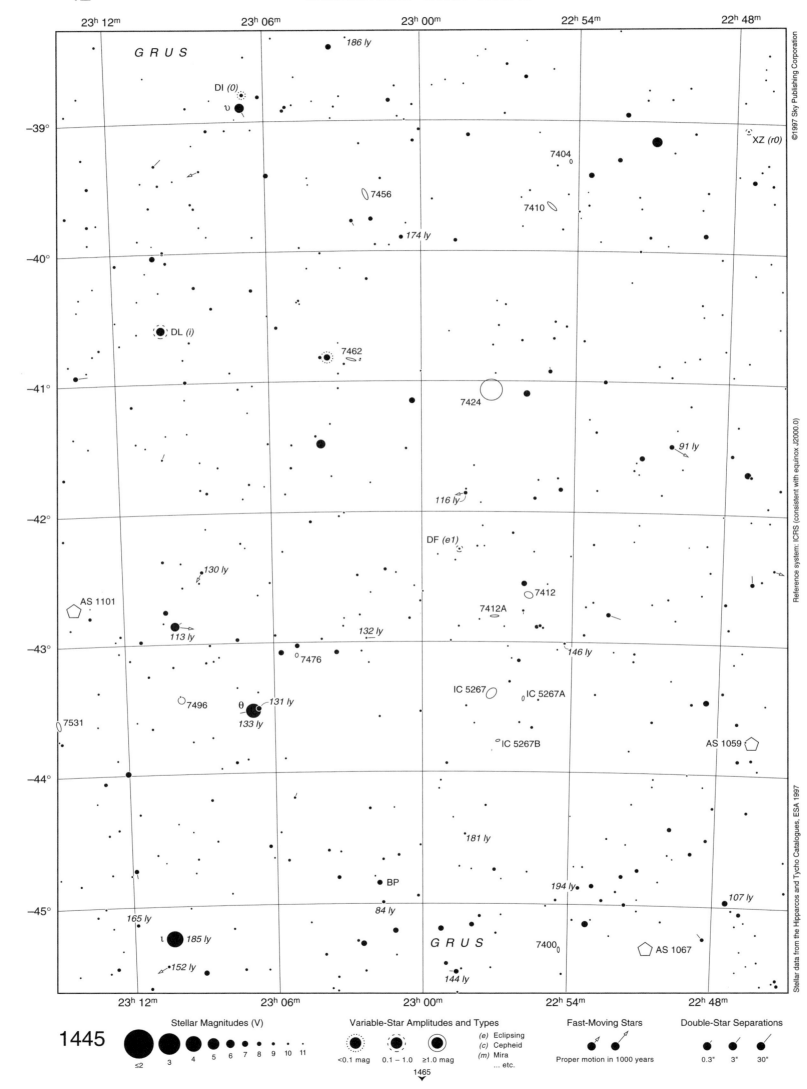

GRUS

DI (0)

υ

186 ly

XZ (r0)

7404

7410

7456

174 ly

−39°

DL (i)

7462

7424

91 ly

−40°

116 ly

−41°

DF (e1)

130 ly

AS 1101

7412

7412A

113 ly

132 ly

146 ly

−42°

7476

7496

θ     131 ly

7531     133 ly

IC 5267     IC 5267A

IC 5267B

AS 1059

−43°

181 ly

BP

194 ly

107 ly

84 ly

165 ly

GRUS

−44°

ι     185 ly

7400

AS 1067

152 ly

144 ly

−45°

©1997 Sky Publishing Corporation

Reference system: ICRS (consistent with equinox J2000.0)

Stellar data from the Hipparcos and Tycho Catalogues, ESA 1997

1445

Stellar Magnitudes (V)

≤2    3    4    5    6    7    8    9    10    11

Variable-Star Amplitudes and Types

<0.1 mag    0.1 – 1.0    ≥1.0 mag

(e) Eclipsing
(c) Cepheid
(m) Mira
... etc.

1465

Fast-Moving Stars

Proper motion in 1000 years

Double-Star Separations

0.3"    3"    30"

# MILLENNIUM STAR ATLAS

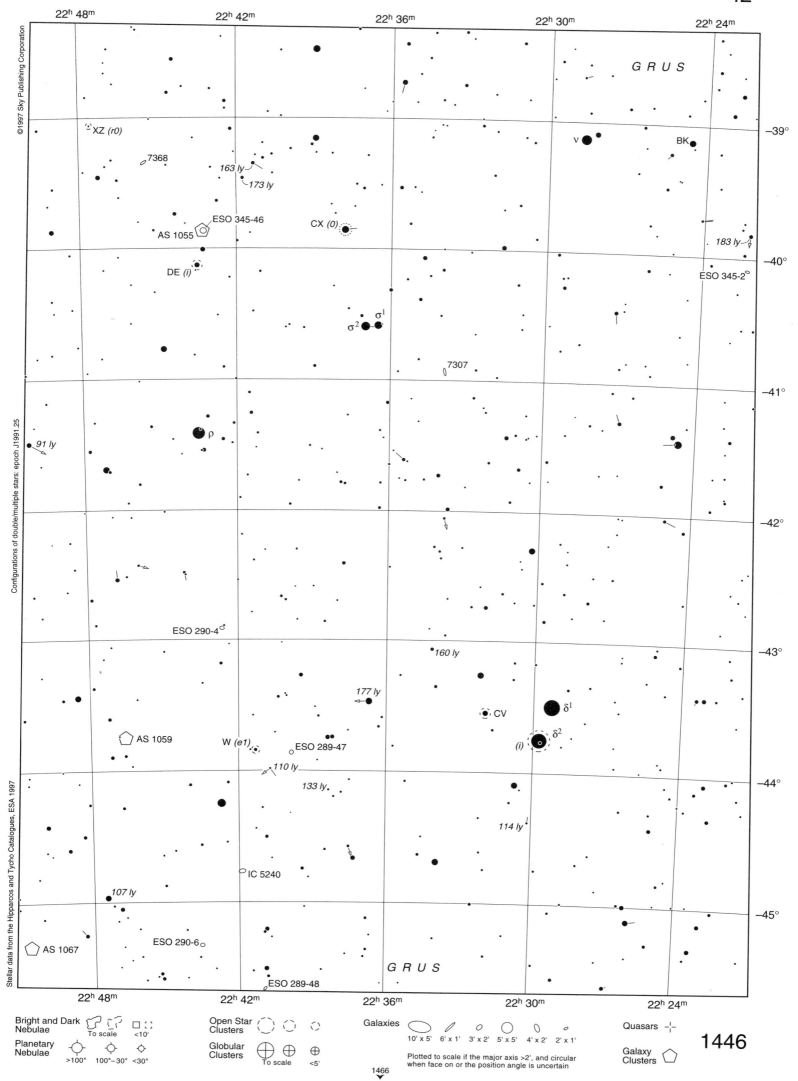

©1997 Sky Publishing Corporation

Configurations of double/multiple stars: epoch J1991.25

Stellar data from the Hipparcos and Tycho Catalogues, ESA 1997

22h 48m    22h 42m    22h 36m    22h 30m    22h 24m

GRUS

XZ (r0)

7368

163 ly
173 ly

ESO 345-46
AS 1055

CX (0)

ν

BK

183 ly

ESO 345-2

DE (i)

−39°

−40°

σ²  σ¹

7307

ρ

91 ly

−41°

−42°

ESO 290-4

160 ly

−43°

177 ly

AS 1059

CV

δ¹

W (e1)
ESO 289-47

(i)    δ²

110 ly

133 ly

−44°

114 ly

IC 5240

107 ly

AS 1067

ESO 290-6

GRUS

ESO 289-48

−45°

22h 48m    22h 42m    22h 36m    22h 30m    22h 24m

| Bright and Dark Nebulae | Open Star Clusters | Galaxies | Quasars |
|---|---|---|---|

To scale    <10'

Planetary Nebulae
>100"  100"−30"  <30"

Globular Clusters
To scale    <5'

10' x 5'  6' x 1'  3' x 2'  5' x 5'  4' x 2'  2' x 1'

Plotted to scale if the major axis >2', and circular when face on or the position angle is uncertain

Galaxy Clusters

1446

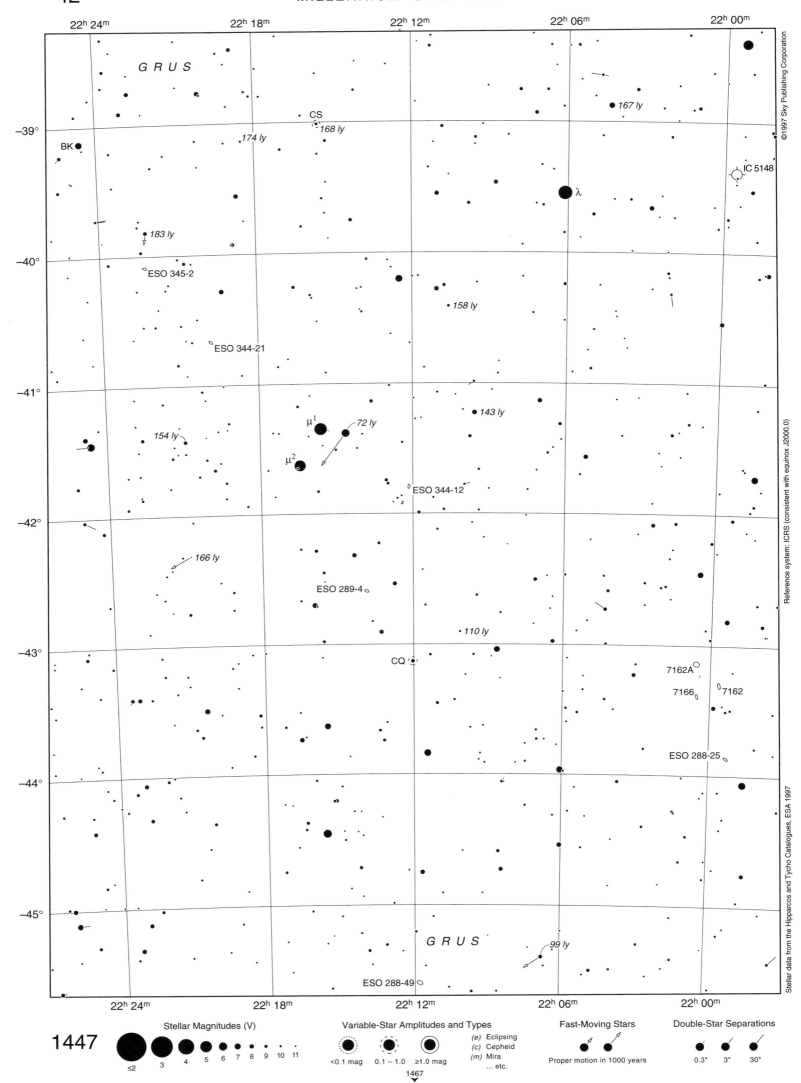

©1997 Sky Publishing Corporation

Reference system: ICRS (consistent with equinox J2000.0)

Stellar data from the Hipparcos and Tycho Catalogues, ESA 1997

22h 24m    22h 18m    22h 12m    22h 06m    22h 00m

GRUS

CS
168 ly
174 ly
BK ●
167 ly

IC 5148

λ

183 ly

ESO 345-2

158 ly

ESO 344-21

μ¹
72 ly
143 ly
154 ly
μ²
ESO 344-12

166 ly

ESO 289-4

110 ly

CQ
7162A
7166  7162

ESO 288-25

GRUS
99 ly

ESO 288-49

−39°
−40°
−41°
−42°
−43°
−44°
−45°

22h 24m    22h 18m    22h 12m    22h 06m    22h 00m

1447

Stellar Magnitudes (V)
≤2  3  4  5  6  7  8  9  10  11

Variable-Star Amplitudes and Types
<0.1 mag   0.1 – 1.0   ≥1.0 mag

(e) Eclipsing
(c) Cepheid
(m) Mira
... etc.

Fast-Moving Stars
Proper motion in 1000 years

Double-Star Separations
0.3"   3"   30"

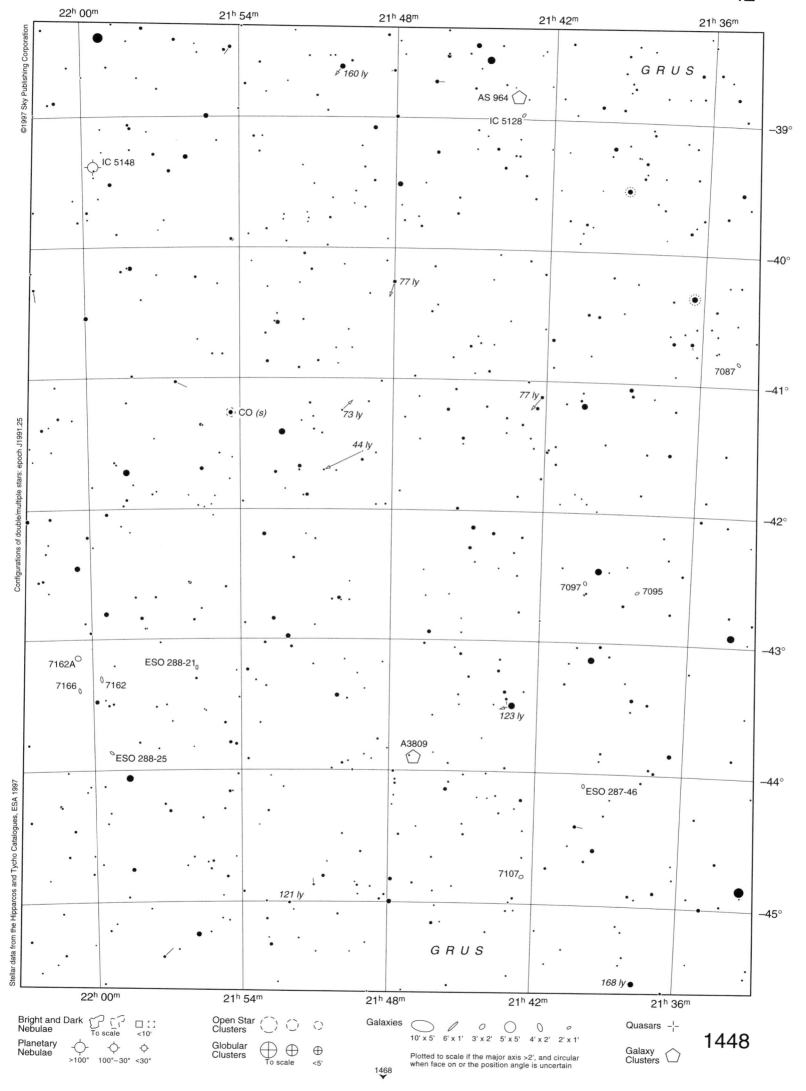

# MILLENNIUM STAR ATLAS

©1997 Sky Publishing Corporation

Configurations of double/multiple stars: epoch J1991.25

Stellar data from the Hipparcos and Tycho Catalogues, ESA 1997

22h 00m    21h 54m    21h 48m    21h 42m    21h 36m

G R U S

AS 964

IC 5128

IC 5148

−39°

160 ly

77 ly

−40°

7087

CO (s)

77 ly

73 ly

−41°

44 ly

−42°

7097    7095

−43°

7162A

ESO 288-21

7166    7162

123 ly

ESO 288-25

A3809

−44°

ESO 287-46

7107

121 ly    −45°

G R U S

168 ly

| Bright and Dark Nebulae | Open Star Clusters | Galaxies | Quasars |
|---|---|---|---|

To scale    <10'

Planetary Nebulae

>100"  100"−30"  <30"

Globular Clusters

To scale    <5'

10' x 5'  6' x 1'  3' x 2'  5' x 5'  4' x 2'  2' x 1'

Plotted to scale if the major axis >2', and circular when face on or the position angle is uncertain

Galaxy Clusters

1448

1468

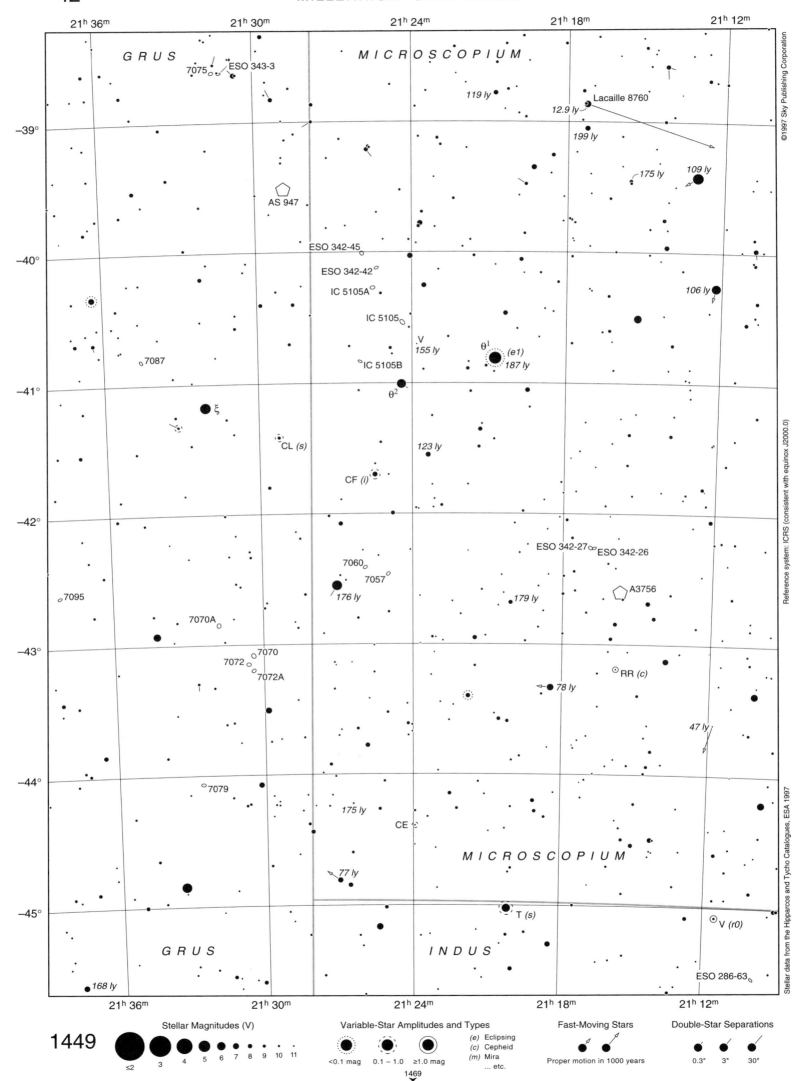

©1997 Sky Publishing Corporation

Reference system: ICRS (consistent with equinox J2000.0)

Stellar data from the Hipparcos and Tycho Catalogues, ESA 1997

GRUS

MICROSCOPIUM

7075  ESO 343-3

119 ly

Lacaille 8760
12.9 ly
199 ly

175 ly    109 ly

AS 947

ESO 342-45

ESO 342-42

IC 5105A

106 ly

IC 5105

V
155 ly     θ¹  (e1)
                187 ly
IC 5105B

θ²

7087

ξ

CL (s)

123 ly

CF (i)

ESO 342-27  ESO 342-26

7060
    7057           A3756
176 ly        179 ly

7095

7070A

RR (c)

7070
7072        78 ly
7072A

47 ly

7079

175 ly

CE

MICROSCOPIUM

77 ly

T (s)

GRUS          INDUS          V (r0)

168 ly                          ESO 286-63

1449

Stellar Magnitudes (V)

≤2  3  4  5  6  7  8  9  10  11

Variable-Star Amplitudes and Types

<0.1 mag   0.1 – 1.0   ≥1.0 mag

(e) Eclipsing
(c) Cepheid
(m) Mira
... etc.

Fast-Moving Stars

Proper motion in 1000 years

Double-Star Separations

0.3"   3"   30"

1469

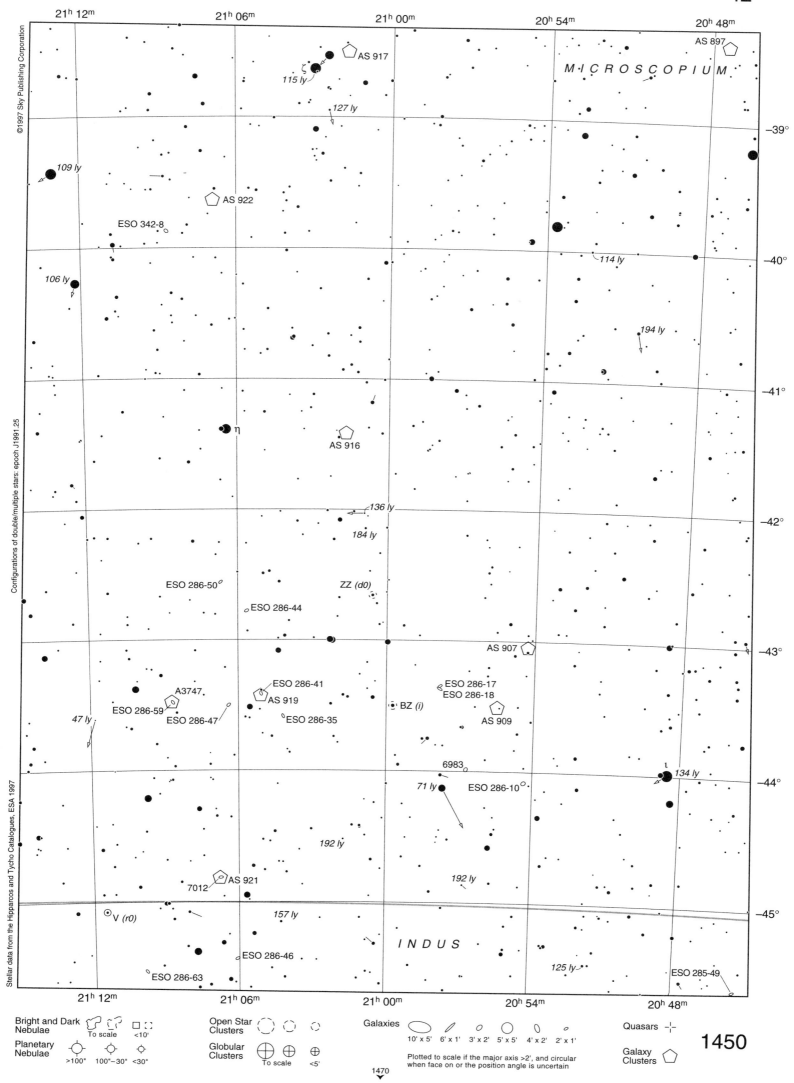

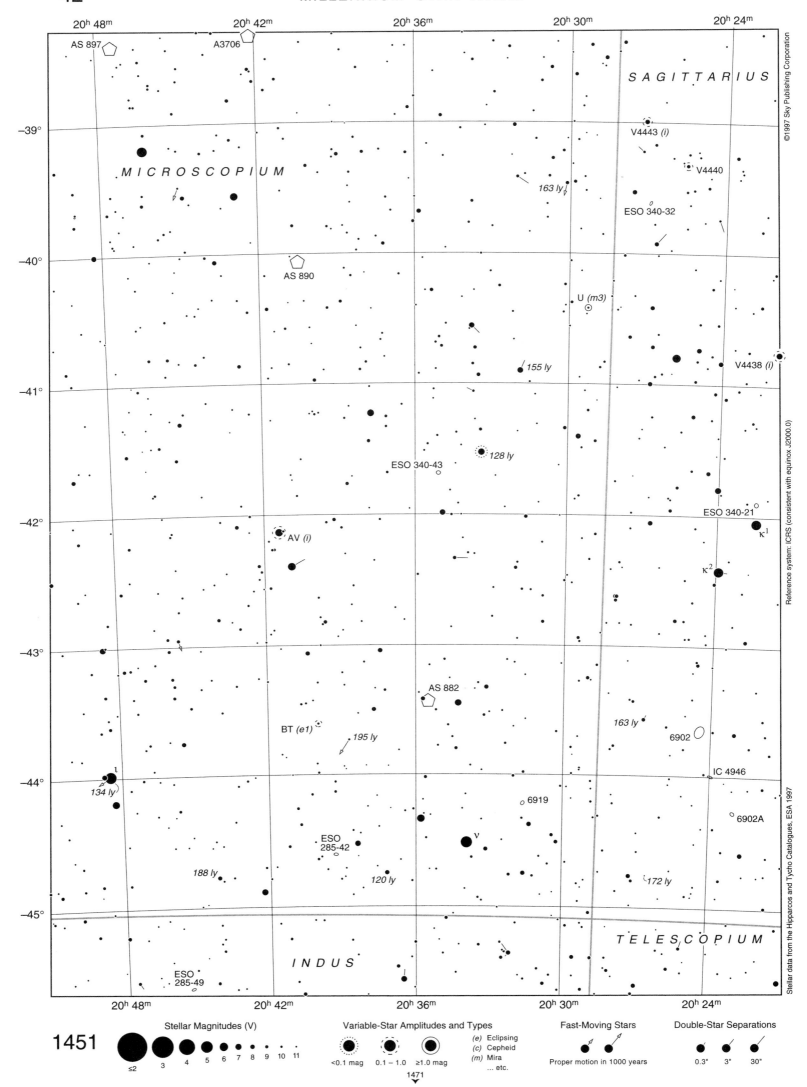

AS 897

A3706

SAGITTARIUS

V4443 (i)

MICROSCOPIUM

V4440

163 ly

ESO 340-32

AS 890

U (m3)

155 ly

V4438 (i)

128 ly

ESO 340-43

ESO 340-21

κ¹

AV (i)

κ²

AS 882

BT (e1)

163 ly

6902

195 ly

IC 4946

ι

134 ly

6919

6902A

ESO 285-42

ν

188 ly

120 ly

172 ly

TELESCOPIUM

INDUS

ESO 285-49

©1997 Sky Publishing Corporation

Reference system: ICRS (consistent with equinox J2000.0)

Stellar data from the Hipparcos and Tycho Catalogues, ESA 1997

**1451**

### Stellar Magnitudes (V)

≤2  3  4  5  6  7  8  9  10  11

### Variable-Star Amplitudes and Types

<0.1 mag   0.1 – 1.0   ≥1.0 mag

(e) Eclipsing
(c) Cepheid
(m) Mira
... etc.

1471

### Fast-Moving Stars

Proper motion in 1000 years

### Double-Star Separations

0.3"  3"  30"

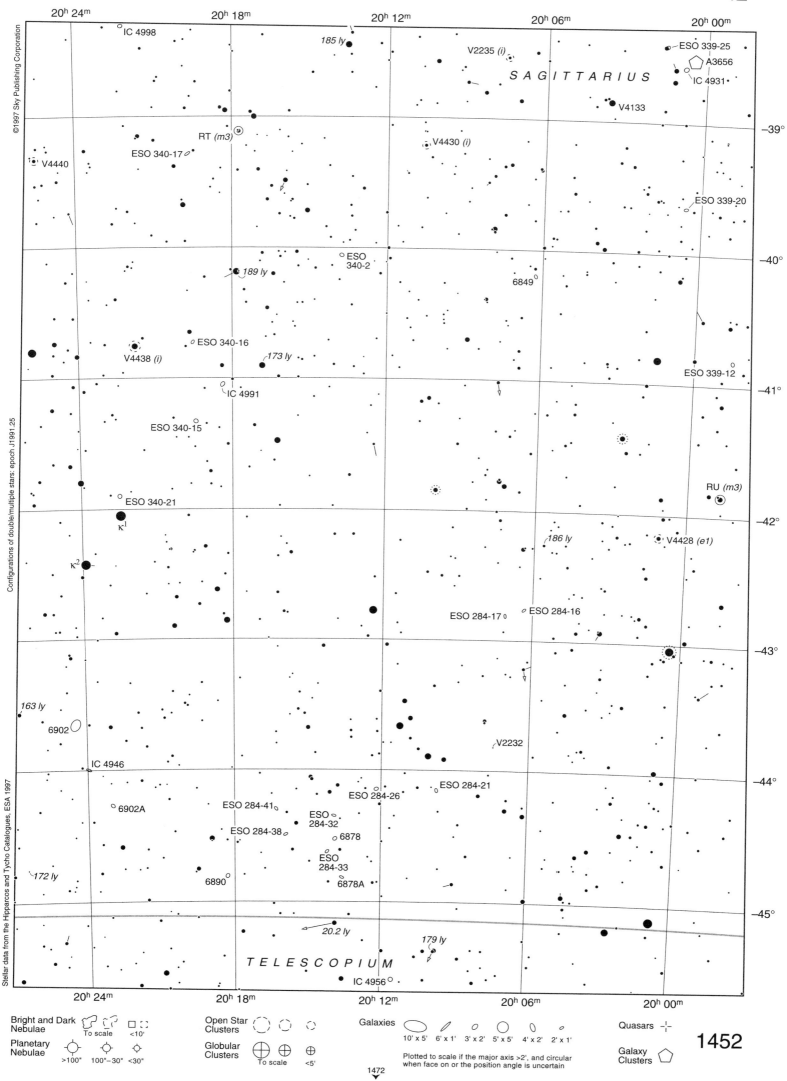

20h 24m   20h 18m   20h 12m   20h 06m   20h 00m

IC 4998

185 ly

V2235 (i)                ESO 339-25
                         A3656
        S A G I T T A R I U S      IC 4931

                    V4133

−39°

RT (m3)
ESO 340-17              V4430 (i)

V4440                                         ESO 339-20

                    ESO
                    340-2
                              6849                −40°
        189 ly

        ESO 340-16
V4438 (i)        173 ly                              ESO 339-12

        IC 4991                                   −41°

ESO 340-15                                         RU (m3)

ESO 340-21                                         −42°
κ¹                              186 ly        V4428 (e1)

κ²
                         ESO 284-17 ∘  ∘ ESO 284-16

                                              −43°

163 ly
6902

IC 4946                          V2232
                                              −44°
6902A                ESO 284-26  ∘ ESO 284-21
        ESO 284-41 ∘
        ESO 284-38 ∘  ESO
                     284-32
                     ∘ 6878
6890        ESO
            284-33
            6878A
                                              −45°

        20.2 ly
                179 ly
T E L E S C O P I U M
172 ly                IC 4956

20h 24m   20h 18m   20h 12m   20h 06m   20h 00m

Bright and Dark
Nebulae
                To scale        <10'

Planetary
Nebulae
        >100"  100"–30"  <30'

Open Star
Clusters

Globular
Clusters
        To scale   <5'

Galaxies

10' x 5'  6' x 1'  3' x 2'  5' x 5'  4' x 2'  2' x 1'

Plotted to scale if the major axis >2', and circular
when face on or the position angle is uncertain

Quasars  –⊢–

Galaxy
Clusters

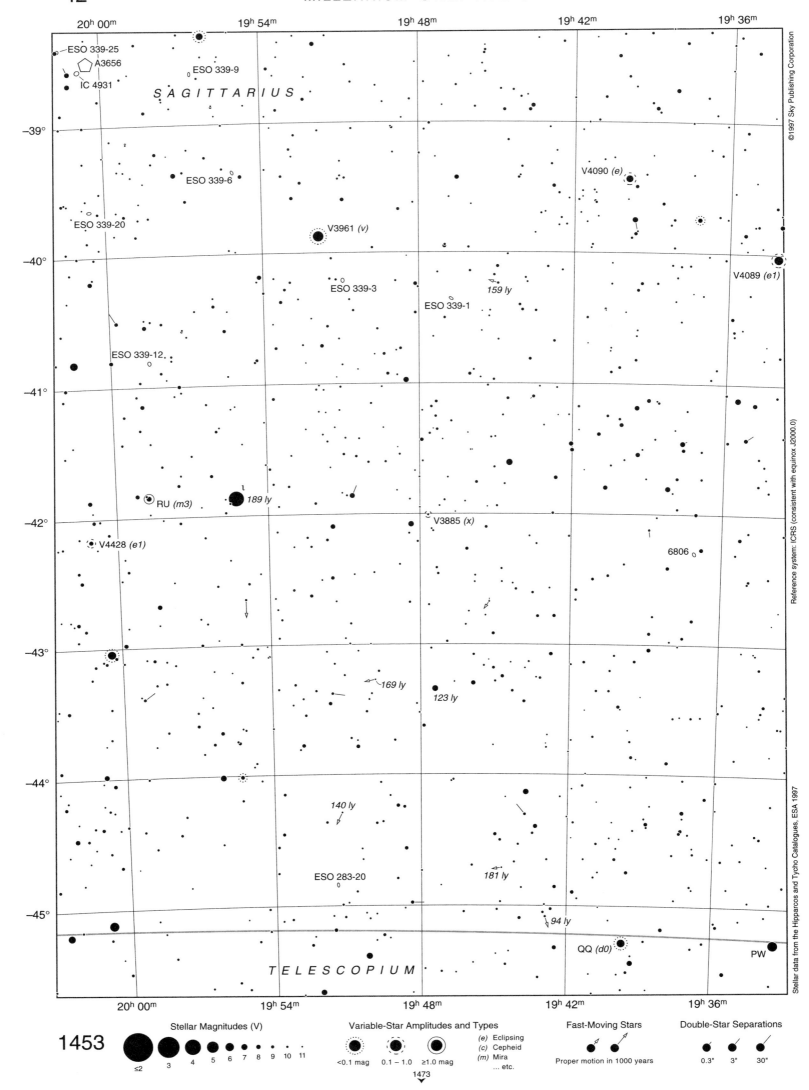

©1997 Sky Publishing Corporation

Reference system: ICRS (consistent with equinox J2000.0)

Stellar data from the Hipparcos and Tycho Catalogues, ESA 1997

20h 00m    19h 54m    19h 48m    19h 42m    19h 36m

ESO 339-25
A3656
IC 4931
ESO 339-9

*S A G I T T A R I U S*

ESO 339-6

ESO 339-20

V4090 (e)

−39°

V3961 (v)

ESO 339-3

159 ly

ESO 339-1

−40°

V4089 (e1)

ESO 339-12

−41°

RU (m3)        189 ly

V3885 (x)

−42°

V4428 (e1)

6806

169 ly

123 ly

−43°

140 ly

ESO 283-20

181 ly

94 ly

−44°

QQ (d0)        PW

*T E L E S C O P I U M*

−45°

20h 00m    19h 54m    19h 48m    19h 42m    19h 36m

1453

**Stellar Magnitudes (V)**

≤2   3   4   5   6   7   8   9   10   11

**Variable-Star Amplitudes and Types**

<0.1 mag    0.1 − 1.0    ≥1.0 mag

(e) Eclipsing
(c) Cepheid
(m) Mira
... etc.

1473

**Fast-Moving Stars**

Proper motion in 1000 years

**Double-Star Separations**

0.3"    3"    30"

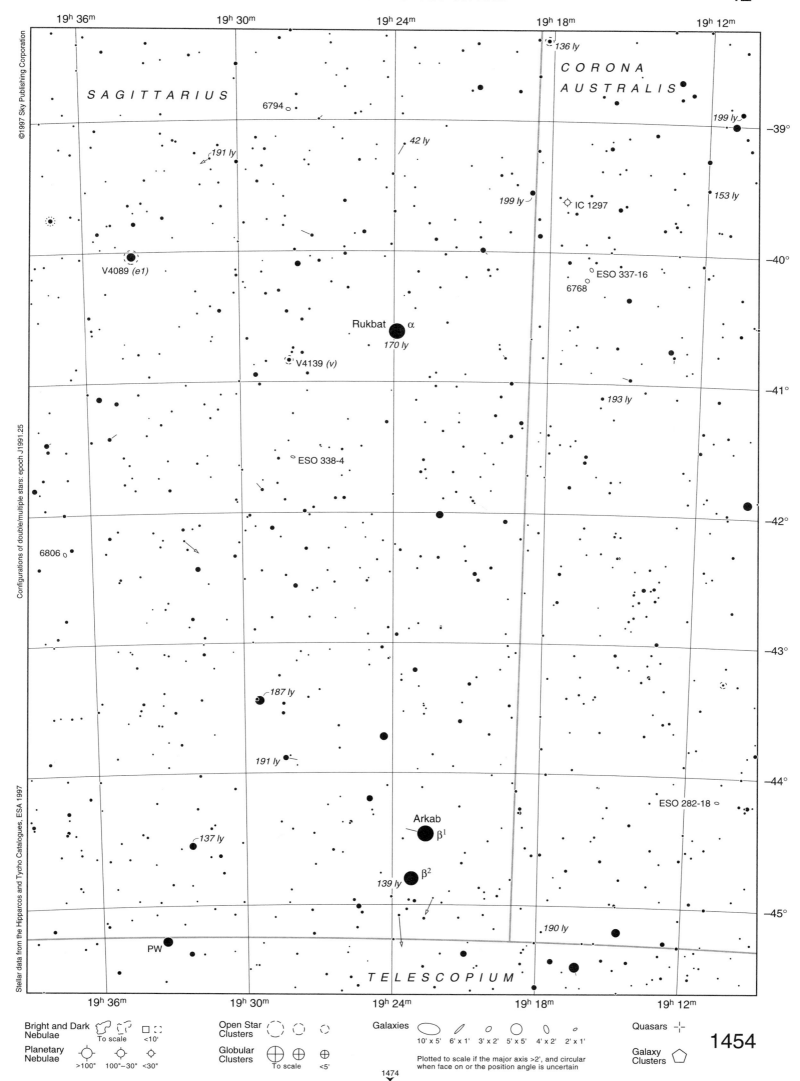

19h 36m    19h 30m    19h 24m    19h 18m    19h 12m

C O R O N A
A U S T R A L I S

S A G I T T A R I U S

6794

136 ly
199 ly
153 ly

191 ly

42 ly

199 ly        IC 1297

−39°

V4089 (e1)

ESO 337-16
6768

−40°

Rukbat    α
170 ly

V4139 (v)

193 ly

−41°

ESO 338-4

−42°

6806

−43°

187 ly

191 ly

ESO 282-18

−44°

Arkab
β¹

137 ly

β²
139 ly

190 ly

−45°

PW

T E L E S C O P I U M

19h 36m    19h 30m    19h 24m    19h 18m    19h 12m

| Bright and Dark Nebulae | Open Star Clusters | Galaxies | Quasars |
| Planetary Nebulae | Globular Clusters | | Galaxy Clusters |

Bright and Dark Nebulae    To scale    <10'
Open Star Clusters
Globular Clusters    To scale    <5'
Planetary Nebulae    >100"    100"–30"    <30"
Galaxies    10' x 5'    6' x 1'    3' x 2'    5' x 5'    4' x 2'    2' x 1'
Plotted to scale if the major axis >2', and circular when face on or the position angle is uncertain
Quasars
Galaxy Clusters

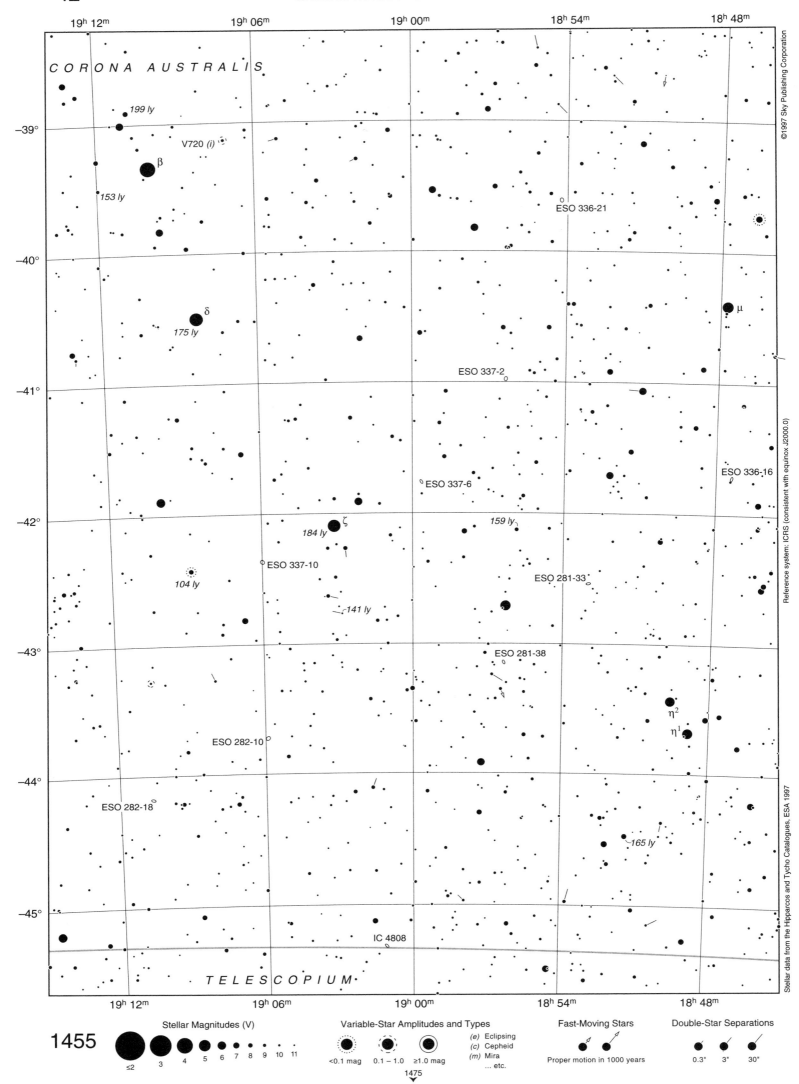

CORONA AUSTRALIS

TELESCOPIUM

©1997 Sky Publishing Corporation

Reference system: ICRS (consistent with equinox J2000.0)

Stellar data from the Hipparcos and Tycho Catalogues, ESA 1997

1455

**Stellar Magnitudes (V)**

≤2  3  4  5  6  7  8  9  10  11

**Variable-Star Amplitudes and Types**

<0.1 mag   0.1 – 1.0   ≥1.0 mag

(e) Eclipsing
(c) Cepheid
(m) Mira
... etc.

**Fast-Moving Stars**

Proper motion in 1000 years

**Double-Star Separations**

0.3"   3"   30"

1475

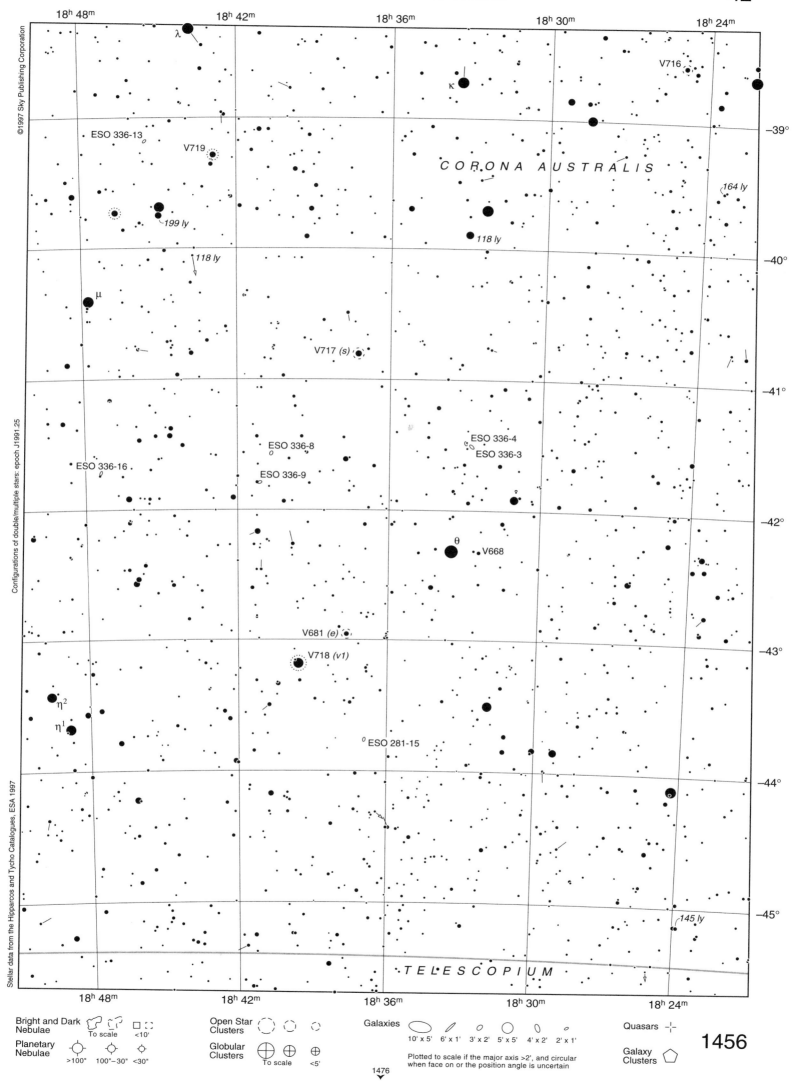

18ʰ 48ᵐ    18ʰ 42ᵐ    18ʰ 36ᵐ    18ʰ 30ᵐ    18ʰ 24ᵐ

−39°

λ

V716

κ

ESO 336-13

V719

CORONA AUSTRALIS

164 ly

199 ly

118 ly

118 ly

μ

−40°

V717 (s)

−41°

ESO 336-8

ESO 336-4

ESO 336-16

ESO 336-3

ESO 336-9

−42°

θ    V668

V681 (e)

−43°

V718 (v1)

η²

η¹

ESO 281-15

−44°

145 ly

−45°

TELESCOPIUM

18ʰ 48ᵐ    18ʰ 42ᵐ    18ʰ 36ᵐ    18ʰ 30ᵐ    18ʰ 24ᵐ

Bright and Dark Nebulae          Open Star Clusters          Galaxies          Quasars
To scale    <10'                                                10' x 5'  6' x 1'  3' x 2'  5' x 5'  4' x 2'  2' x 1'

Planetary Nebulae          Globular Clusters                                    Galaxy Clusters
>100"  100"–30"  <30"    To scale   <5'          Plotted to scale if the major axis >2', and circular
                                                  when face on or the position angle is uncertain

1456

1476

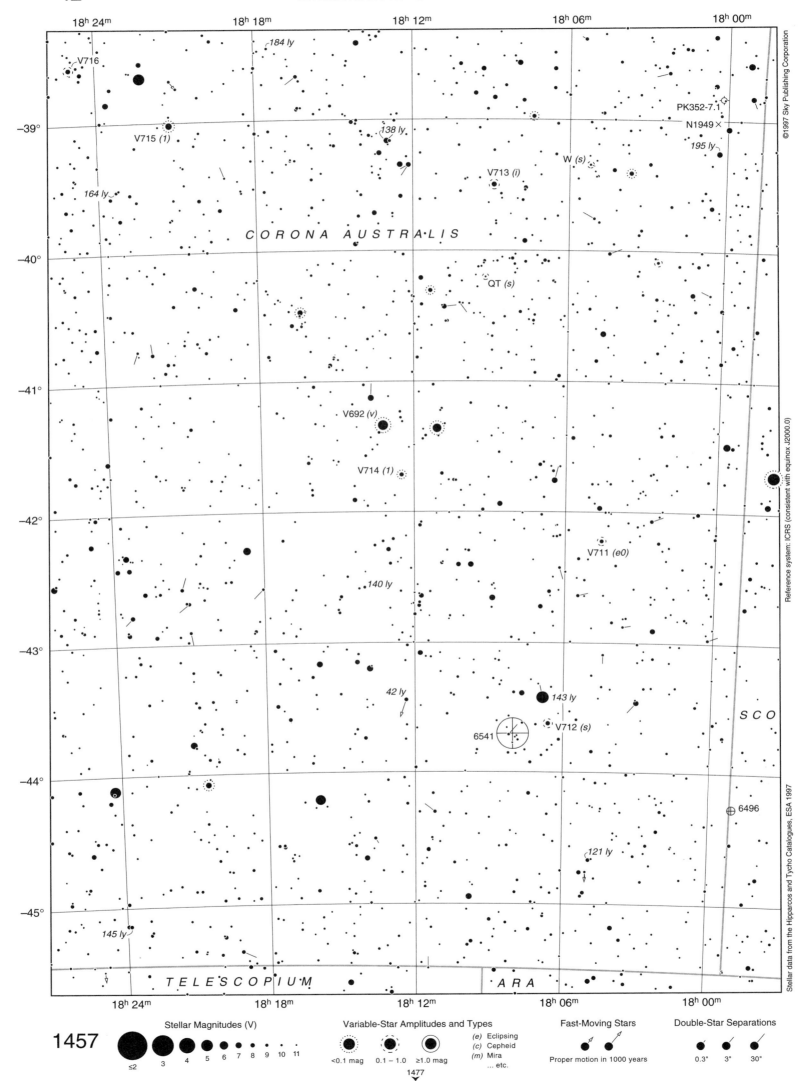

©1997 Sky Publishing Corporation

Reference system: ICRS (consistent with equinox J2000.0)

Stellar data from the Hipparcos and Tycho Catalogues, ESA 1997

1457

Stellar Magnitudes (V)

≤2  3  4  5  6  7  8  9  10  11

Variable-Star Amplitudes and Types

<0.1 mag   0.1 – 1.0   ≥1.0 mag

(e) Eclipsing
(c) Cepheid
(m) Mira
... etc.

Fast-Moving Stars

Proper motion in 1000 years

Double-Star Separations

0.3"  3"  30"

1477

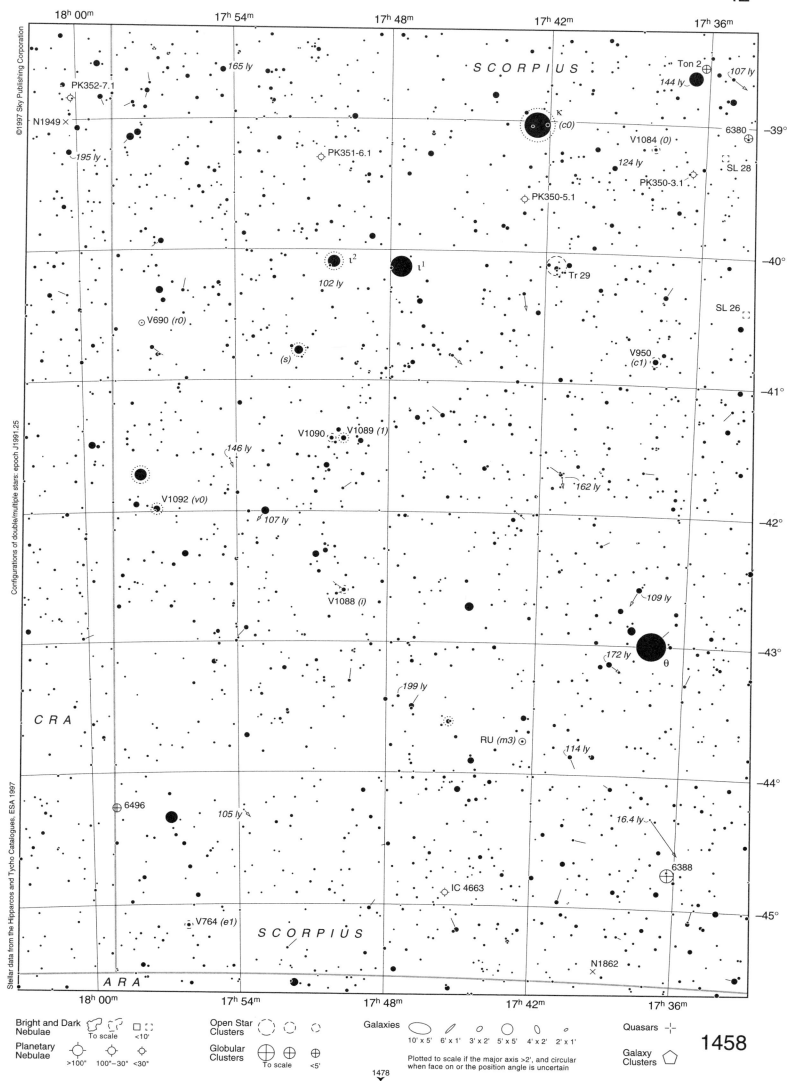

Configurations of double/multiple stars: epoch J1991.25

Stellar data from the Hipparcos and Tycho Catalogues, ESA 1997

SCORPIUS

Ton 2
144 ly
107 ly

PK352-7.1
N1949 ×
165 ly
6380
−39°
195 ly
PK351-6.1
κ (c0)
V1084 (0)
124 ly
SL 28
PK350-3.1
PK350-5.1

ι² 
102 ly
ι¹
Tr 29
−40°
SL 26
V690 (r0)
(s)
V950 (c1)

V1090  V1089 (1)
146 ly
−41°
162 ly

V1092 (v0)
107 ly
−42°

V1088 (i)
109 ly

172 ly
θ
−43°

199 ly

CRA
RU (m3)
114 ly
−44°

6496
105 ly
16.4 ly
6388
−45°

IC 4663

V764 (e1)
SCORPIUS
N1862 ×

ARA

Bright and Dark Nebulae
To scale   <10'
Planetary Nebulae
>100"   100"−30"   <30"

Open Star Clusters
Globular Clusters
To scale   <5'

Galaxies
10' x 5'   6' x 1'   3' x 2'   5' x 5'   4' x 2'   2' x 1'
Plotted to scale if the major axis >2', and circular when face on or the position angle is uncertain

Quasars

Galaxy Clusters

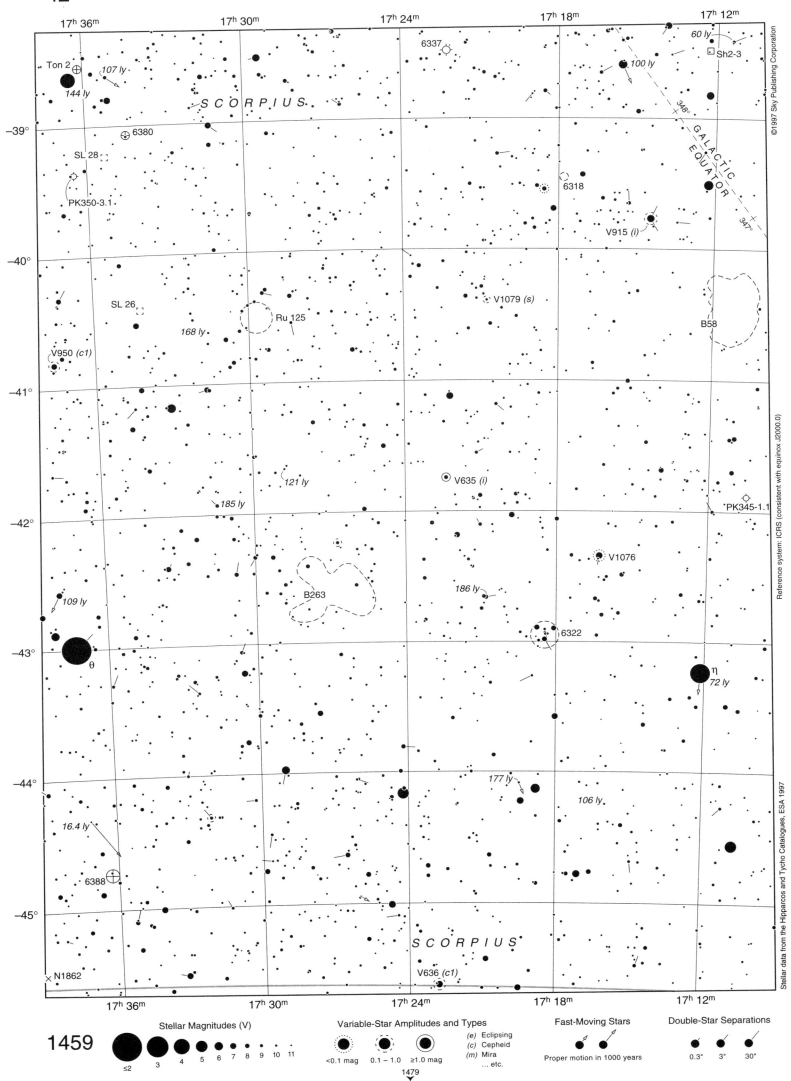

17ʰ 36ᵐ    17ʰ 30ᵐ    17ʰ 24ᵐ    17ʰ 18ᵐ    17ʰ 12ᵐ

Ton 2
107 ly
144 ly

60 ly
Sh2-3
100 ly
348°
347°

SCORPIUS

6337

⊕ 6380

SL 28

PK350-3.1

6318

V915 (i)

−39°

GALACTIC EQUATOR

−40°

SL 26

Ru 125
168 ly

V1079 (s)

B58

V950 (c1)

−41°

121 ly

V635 (i)

PK345-1.1

185 ly

−42°

B263

186 ly

V1076

6322

109 ly

θ

η
72 ly

−43°

177 ly
106 ly

−44°

16.4 ly

6388

−45°

SCORPIUS

× N1862

V636 (c1)

17ʰ 36ᵐ    17ʰ 30ᵐ    17ʰ 24ᵐ    17ʰ 18ᵐ    17ʰ 12ᵐ

1459

Stellar Magnitudes (V)

≤2   3   4   5   6   7   8   9   10   11

Variable-Star Amplitudes and Types

<0.1 mag    0.1 – 1.0    ≥1.0 mag

(e) Eclipsing
(c) Cepheid
(m) Mira
... etc.

1479

Fast-Moving Stars

Proper motion in 1000 years

Double-Star Separations

0.3"   3"   30"

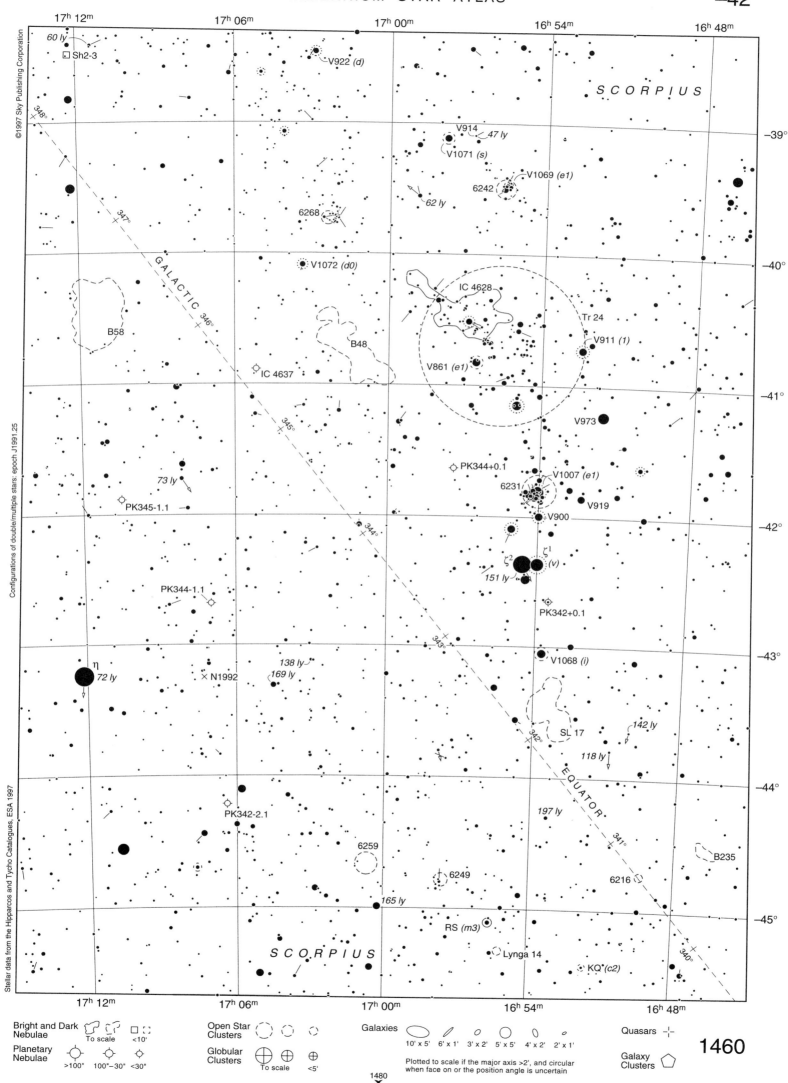

17ʰ 12ᵐ   17ʰ 06ᵐ   17ʰ 00ᵐ   16ʰ 54ᵐ   16ʰ 48ᵐ

−39°
−40°
−41°
−42°
−43°
−44°
−45°

60 ly
□ Sh2-3

V922 (d)

SCORPIUS

V914   47 ly
V1071 (s)
V1069 (e1)
6242

62 ly

6268

GALACTIC
348°
347°
346°
345°
344°
343°
342°
341°
340°

B58

B48

V1072 (d0)

IC 4628

Tr 24

V911 (1)

IC 4637

V861 (e1)

V973

PK344+0.1
V1007 (e1)
6231
V919
73 ly
PK345-1.1
V900

PK344-1.1

ζ²   ζ¹ (v)
151 ly

PK342+0.1

V1068 (i)

η   72 ly
× N1992   138 ly
169 ly

SL 17   142 ly

EQUATOR

197 ly   118 ly

PK342-2.1

B235

6259
6249
6216
165 ly

RS (m3)

SCORPIUS
Lynga 14
KQ (c2)

17ʰ 12ᵐ   17ʰ 06ᵐ   17ʰ 00ᵐ   16ʰ 54ᵐ   16ʰ 48ᵐ

Bright and Dark Nebulae   To scale   <10'
Planetary Nebulae   >100"   100"–30"   <30"

Open Star Clusters
Globular Clusters   To scale   <5'

Galaxies
10' x 5'   6' x 1'   3' x 2'   5' x 5'   4' x 2'   2' x 1'
Plotted to scale if the major axis >2', and circular when face on or the position angle is uncertain

Quasars   ‑|‑

Galaxy Clusters

1460

1480

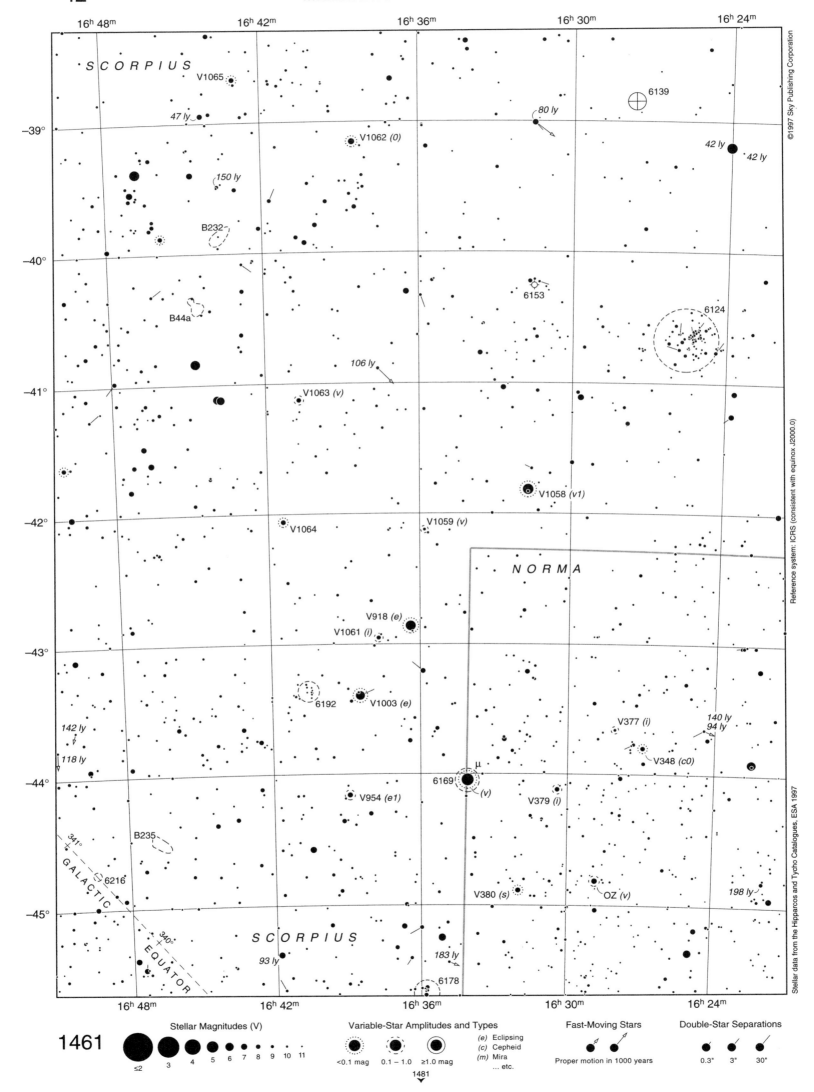

©1997 Sky Publishing Corporation

Reference system: ICRS (consistent with equinox J2000.0)

Stellar data from the Hipparcos and Tycho Catalogues, ESA 1997

SCORPIUS

V1065

47 ly

150 ly

V1062 (0)

6139

80 ly

42 ly    42 ly

B232

B44a

6153

6124

106 ly

V1063 (v)

V1058 (v1)

V1064

V1059 (v)

NORMA

V918 (e)

V1061 (i)

6192    V1003 (e)

V377 (i)

140 ly
94 ly

V348 (c0)

142 ly

118 ly

μ
6169
(v)

V954 (e1)

V379 (i)

B235

341°

GALACTIC

6216

V380 (s)

OZ (v)

198 ly

EQUATOR

340°

SCORPIUS

93 ly

183 ly

6178

Stellar Magnitudes (V)

≤2    3    4    5    6    7    8    9   10   11

Variable-Star Amplitudes and Types

<0.1 mag    0.1 – 1.0    ≥1.0 mag

(e) Eclipsing
(c) Cepheid
(m) Mira
... etc.

Fast-Moving Stars

Proper motion in 1000 years

Double-Star Separations

0.3"    3"    30"

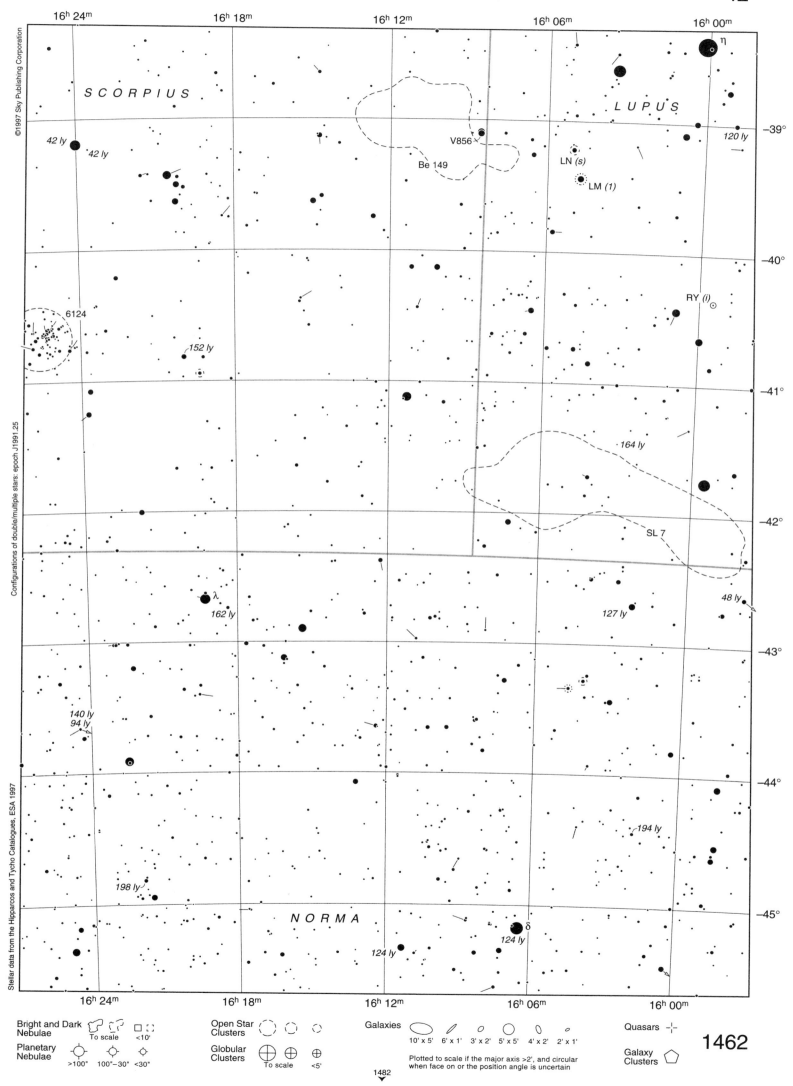

16h 24m    16h 18m    16h 12m    16h 06m    16h 00m

S C O R P I U S

L U P U S

−39°

42 ly    42 ly

V856
Be 149

LN (s)

LM (1)

120 ly

−40°

RY (i)

6124

152 ly

−41°

164 ly

λ
162 ly

SL 7

−42°

127 ly

48 ly

−43°

140 ly
94 ly

194 ly

−44°

198 ly

N O R M A

δ
124 ly

124 ly

−45°

16h 24m    16h 18m    16h 12m    16h 06m    16h 00m

Bright and Dark
Nebulae
To scale    <10'

Open Star
Clusters

Galaxies

10' x 5'   6' x 1'   3' x 2'   5' x 5'   4' x 2'   2' x 1'

Quasars

1462

Planetary
Nebulae
>100"   100"–30"   <30"

Globular
Clusters
To scale    <5'

Plotted to scale if the major axis >2', and circular
when face on or the position angle is uncertain

Galaxy
Clusters

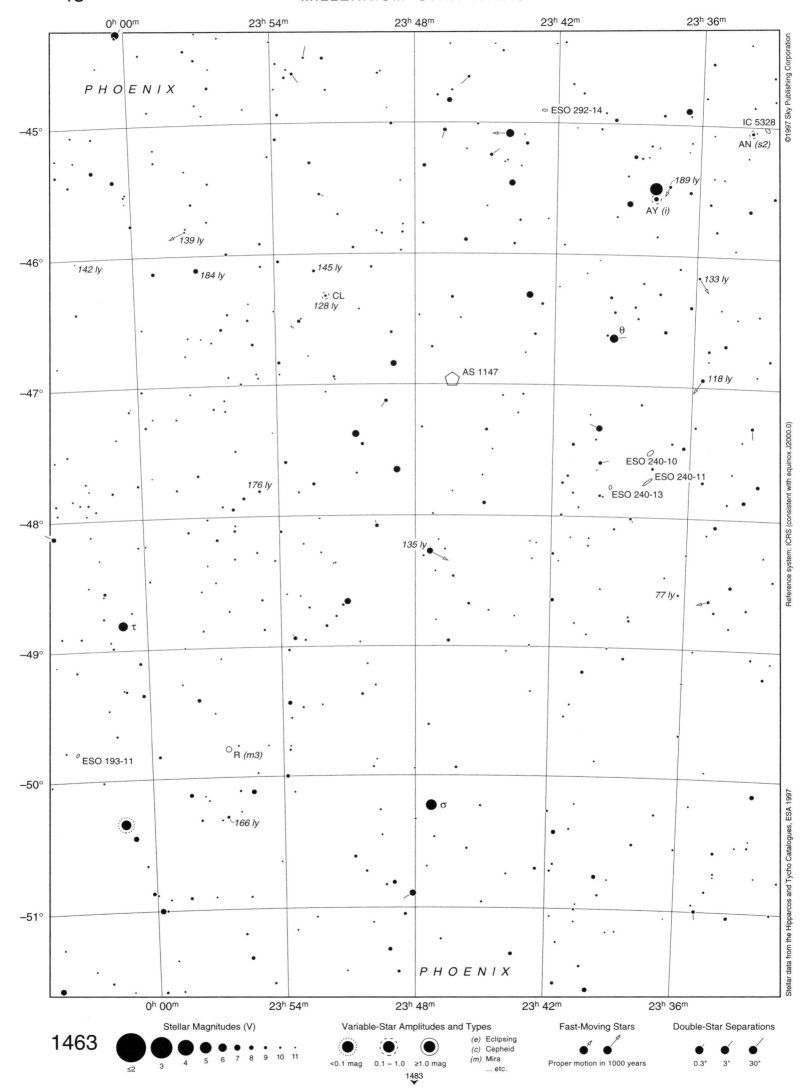

PHOENIX

−45°

ESO 292-14

IC 5328

AN (s2)

189 ly

AY (i)

139 ly

142 ly

−46°

184 ly

145 ly

133 ly

CL
128 ly

θ

AS 1147

118 ly

−47°

ESO 240-10

ESO 240-11

176 ly

ESO 240-13

−48°

135 ly

77 ly

τ

−49°

ESO 193-11

R (m3)

−50°

σ

166 ly

−51°

PHOENIX

©1997 Sky Publishing Corporation

Reference system: ICRS (consistent with equinox J2000.0)

Stellar data from the Hipparcos and Tycho Catalogues, ESA 1997

1463

Stellar Magnitudes (V)

≤2   3   4   5   6   7   8   9  10  11

Variable-Star Amplitudes and Types

<0.1 mag   0.1 – 1.0   ≥1.0 mag

(e) Eclipsing
(c) Cepheid
(m) Mira
... etc.

Fast-Moving Stars

Proper motion in 1000 years

Double-Star Separations

0.3"   3"   30"

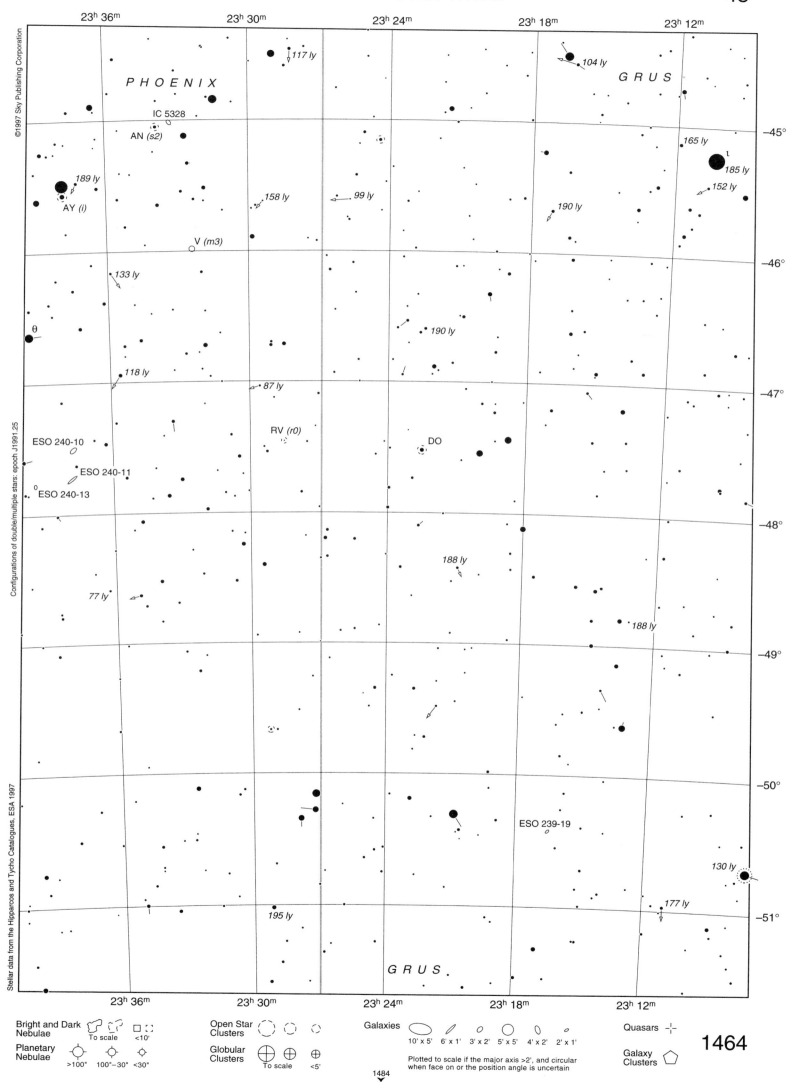

23h 36m    23h 30m    23h 24m    23h 18m    23h 12m

P H O E N I X

G R U S

117 ly

104 ly

IC 5328

AN (s2)

−45°

165 ly

ι
185 ly

189 ly

AY (i)

158 ly

99 ly

190 ly

152 ly

133 ly

190 ly

−46°

θ

V (m3)

118 ly

87 ly

−47°

RV (r0)

DO

ESO 240-10

ESO 240-11

ESO 240-13

188 ly

−48°

77 ly

188 ly

−49°

ESO 239-19

−50°

130 ly

195 ly

177 ly

−51°

G R U S

23h 36m    23h 30m    23h 24m    23h 18m    23h 12m

| Bright and Dark Nebulae | | | Open Star Clusters | | | Galaxies | | | | | | Quasars |
|---|---|---|---|---|---|---|---|---|---|---|---|---|
| To scale | <10' | | | | | 10' x 5' | 6' x 1' | 3' x 2' | 5' x 5' | 4' x 2' | 2' x 1' | |
| Planetary Nebulae | | | Globular Clusters | | | | | | | | | Galaxy Clusters |
| >100" | 100"–30" | <30" | To scale | <5' | | Plotted to scale if the major axis >2', and circular when face on or the position angle is uncertain | | | | | | |

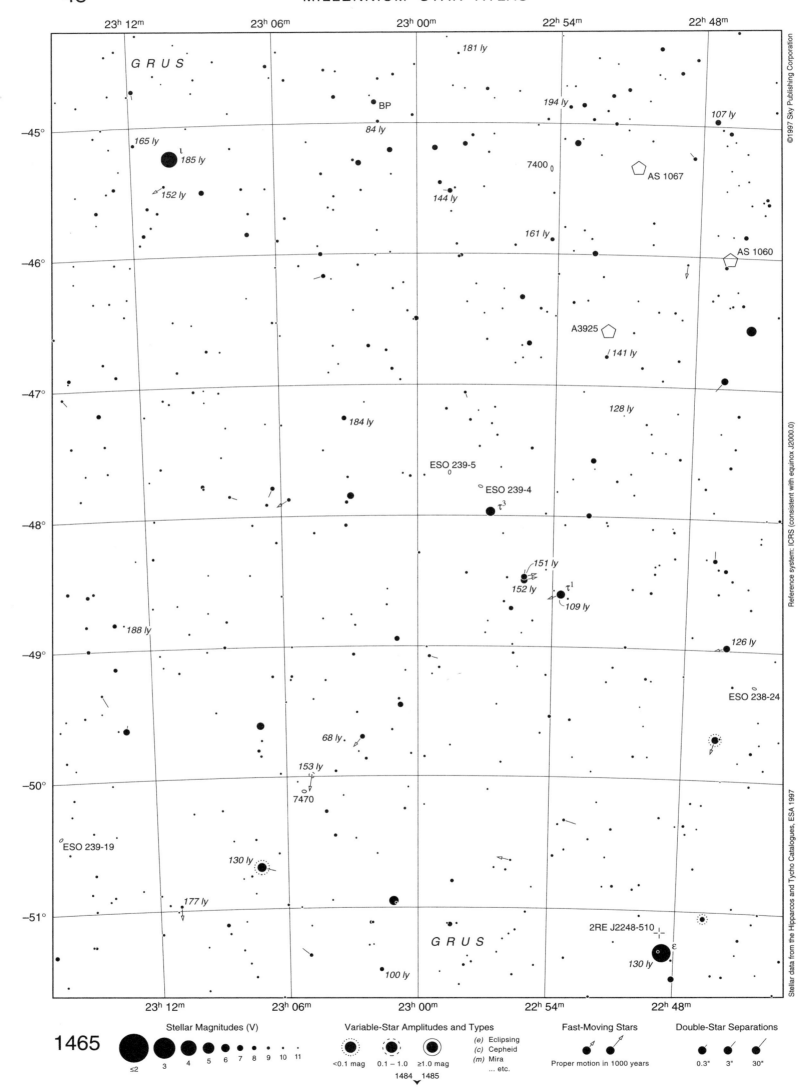

GRUS

181 ly

BP

194 ly

107 ly

84 ly

165 ly

ι

185 ly

7400

AS 1067

152 ly

144 ly

161 ly

AS 1060

A3925

141 ly

128 ly

184 ly

ESO 239-5

ESO 239-4

τ³

151 ly

152 ly

τ¹

109 ly

188 ly

126 ly

ESO 238-24

68 ly

153 ly

7470

ESO 239-19

130 ly

177 ly

2RE J2248-510

ε

130 ly

GRUS

100 ly

Stellar Magnitudes (V)

≤2   3   4   5   6   7   8   9   10   11

Variable-Star Amplitudes and Types

<0.1 mag   0.1 – 1.0   ≥1.0 mag

1484   1485

(e) Eclipsing
(c) Cepheid
(m) Mira
... etc.

Fast-Moving Stars

Proper motion in 1000 years

Double-Star Separations

0.3"   3"   30"

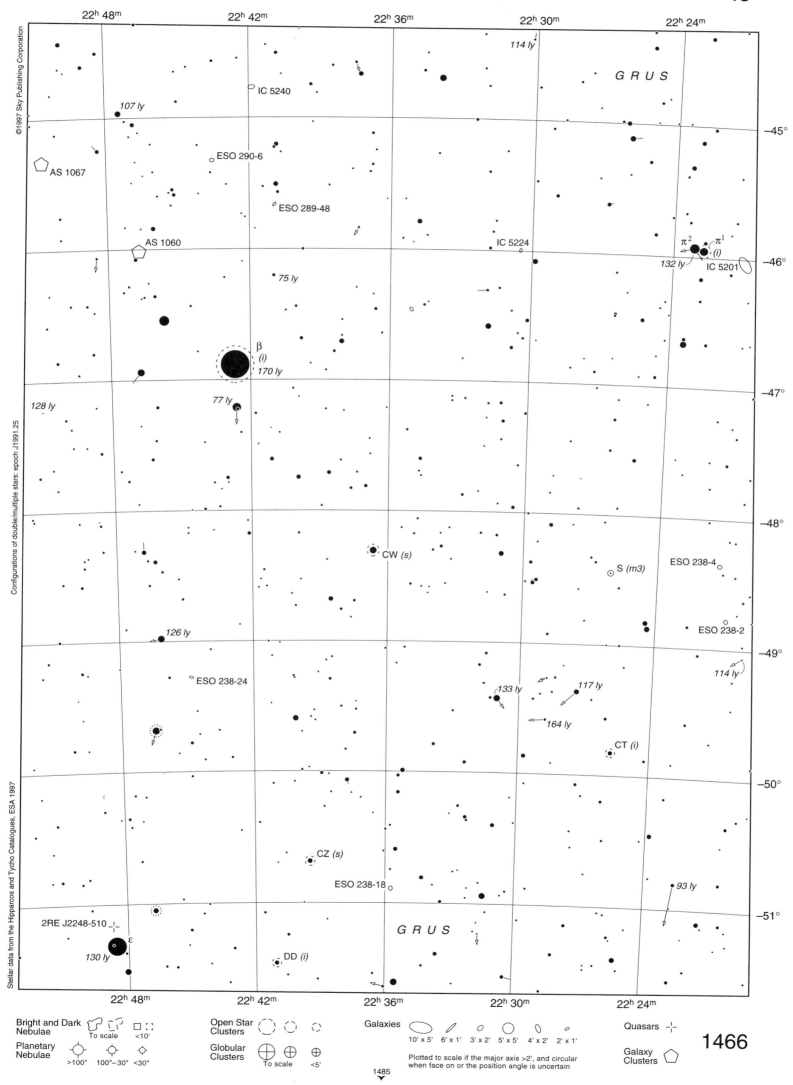

22h 48m    22h 42m    22h 36m    22h 30m    22h 24m

*G R U S*

114 ly

IC 5240

107 ly

AS 1067

ESO 290-6

ESO 289-48

−45°

AS 1060

IC 5224

π² π¹
(i)
132 ly
IC 5201

−46°

75 ly

β
(i)
170 ly

128 ly

77 ly

−47°

−48°

CW (s)

S (m3)

ESO 238-4

ESO 238-2

126 ly

ESO 238-24

−49°

133 ly

117 ly

164 ly

114 ly

CT (i)

−50°

CZ (s)

ESO 238-18

93 ly

2RE J2248-510

*G R U S*

−51°

ε
130 ly

DD (i)

22h 48m    22h 42m    22h 36m    22h 30m    22h 24m

| Bright and Dark Nebulae | | | Open Star Clusters | | | Galaxies | | | | | | Quasars |
|---|---|---|---|---|---|---|---|---|---|---|---|---|

To scale   <10'

Planetary Nebulae
>100"   100"–30"   <30'

Globular Clusters
To scale   <5'

Galaxies
10' x 5'   6' x 1'   3' x 2'   5' x 5'   4' x 2'   2' x 1'

Plotted to scale if the major axis >2', and circular when face on or the position angle is uncertain

Galaxy Clusters

1466

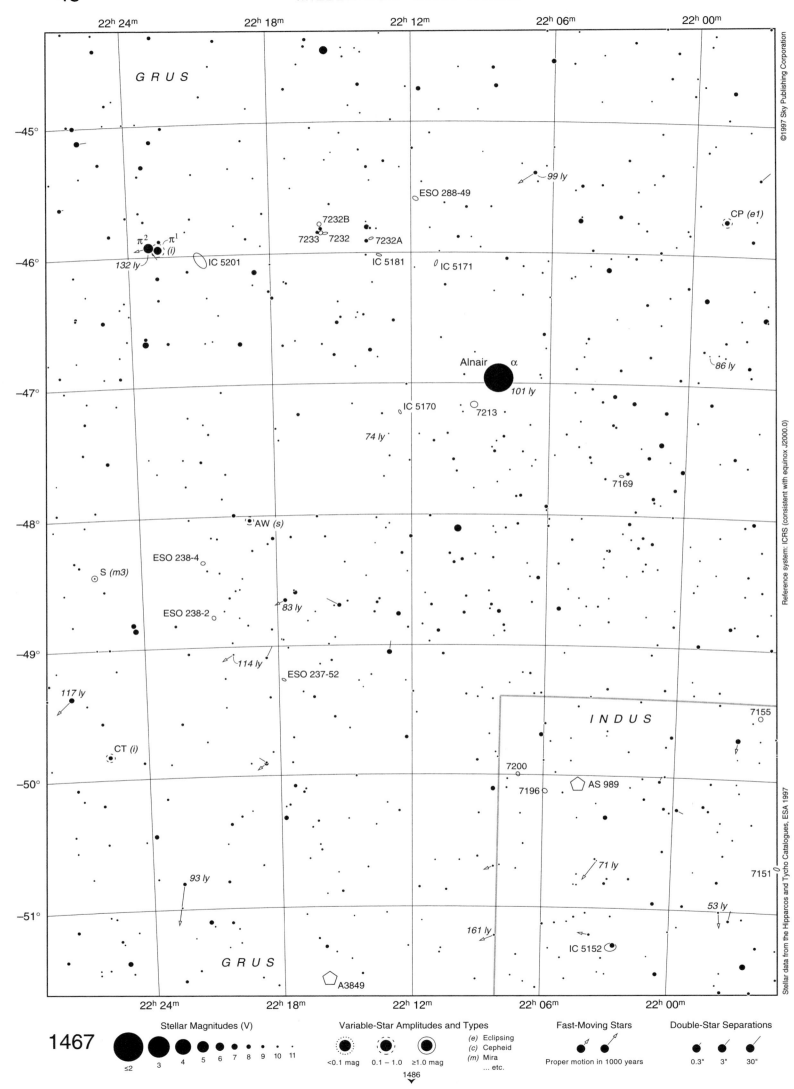

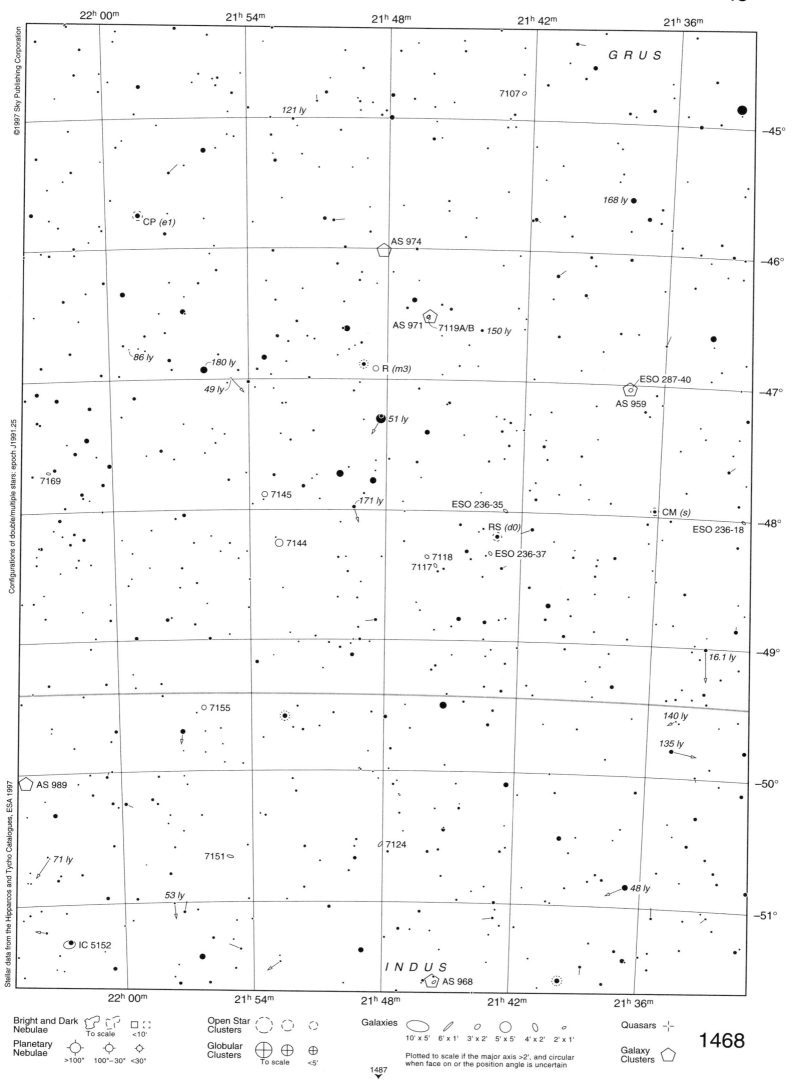

22h 00m          21h 54m          21h 48m          21h 42m          21h 36m

GRUS

7107

121 ly

−45°

168 ly

CP (e1)

AS 974

−46°

AS 971    7119A/B    150 ly

86 ly          180 ly

R (m3)

49 ly

ESO 287-40

AS 959

−47°

51 ly

7169

7145          171 ly

ESO 236-35

CM (s)

−48°

7144                    RS (d0)

ESO 236-18

7118    ESO 236-37

7117

−49°

16.1 ly

7155

140 ly

135 ly

AS 989

−50°

7124

71 ly

7151

53 ly          48 ly

−51°

IC 5152

INDUS

AS 968

22h 00m          21h 54m          21h 48m          21h 42m          21h 36m

| Bright and Dark Nebulae | | | Open Star Clusters | | | Galaxies | | | | | | | Quasars |
|---|---|---|---|---|---|---|---|---|---|---|---|---|---|
| To scale | <10' | | | | | 10' x 5' | 6' x 1' | 3' x 2' | 5' x 5' | 4' x 2' | 2' x 1' | | |
| Planetary Nebulae | | | Globular Clusters | | | | | | | | | | Galaxy Clusters |
| >100" | 100"–30" | <30" | To scale | <5' | | Plotted to scale if the major axis >2', and circular when face on or the position angle is uncertain | | | | | | | |

1468

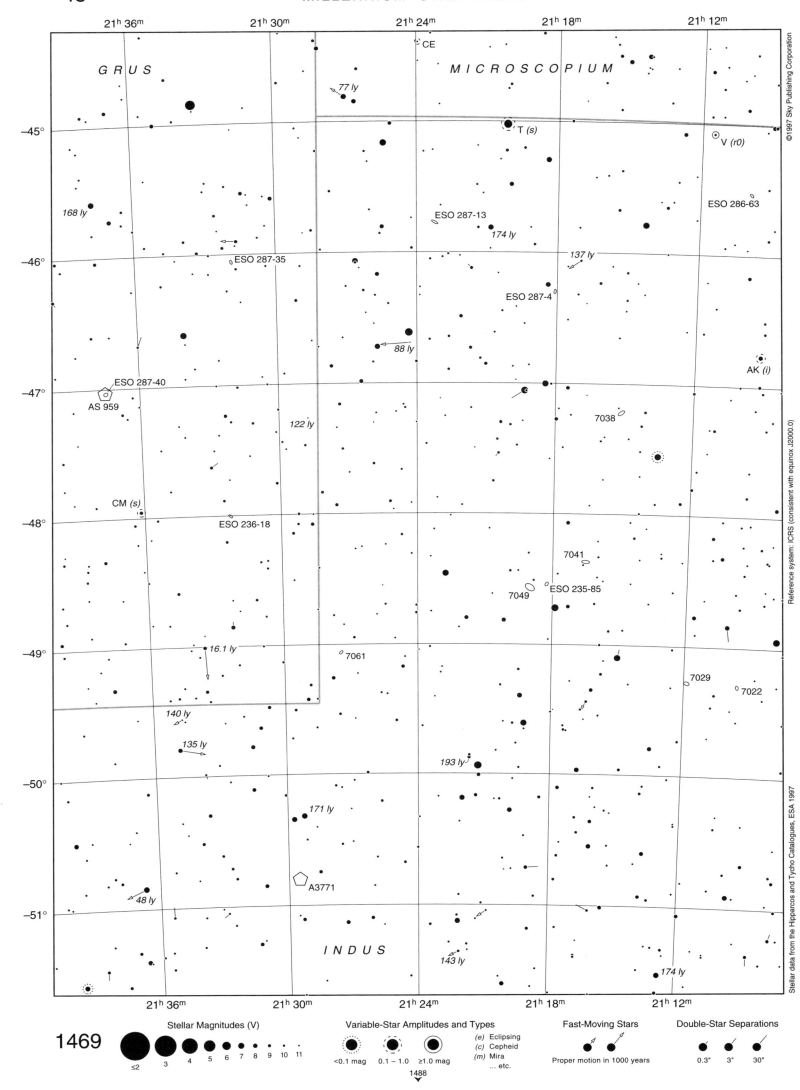

# MILLENNIUM STAR ATLAS

GRUS

MICROSCOPIUM

CE

77 ly

T (s)

V (r0)

168 ly

ESO 286-63

ESO 287-13

174 ly

ESO 287-35

137 ly

ESO 287-4

88 ly

AK (i)

ESO 287-40

7038

AS 959

122 ly

7041

CM (s)

ESO 236-18

7049   ESO 235-85

16.1 ly

7061

7029

7022

140 ly

135 ly

193 ly

171 ly

A3771

143 ly

48 ly

174 ly

INDUS

Reference system: ICRS (consistent with equinox J2000.0)

Stellar data from the Hipparcos and Tycho Catalogues, ESA 1997

## Stellar Magnitudes (V)

1469

≤2   3   4   5   6   7   8   9   10   11

## Variable-Star Amplitudes and Types

<0.1 mag   0.1 – 1.0   ≥1.0 mag

(e) Eclipsing
(c) Cepheid
(m) Mira
… etc.

1488

## Fast-Moving Stars

Proper motion in 1000 years

## Double-Star Separations

0.3"   3"   30"

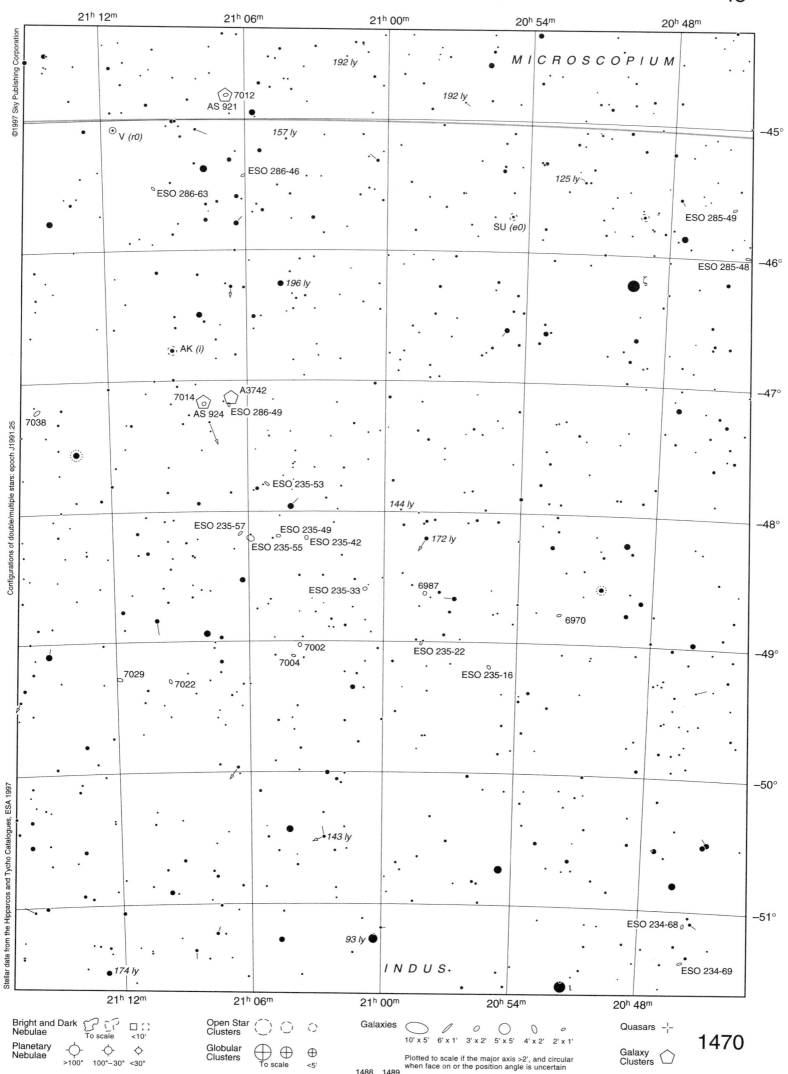

21h 12m   21h 06m   21h 00m   20h 54m   20h 48m

*M I C R O S C O P I U M*

*192 ly*

7012
AS 921

*192 ly*

V *(r0)*

*157 ly*

*125 ly*

ESO 286-46

ESO 286-63

ESO 285-49

SU *(e0)*

ESO 285-48          −46°

ζ

*196 ly*

AK *(i)*

7014        A3742        −47°
AS 924   ESO 286-49

7038

ESO 235-53

*144 ly*          −48°

ESO 235-57        ESO 235-49
ESO 235-55   ESO 235-42

*172 ly*

ESO 235-33        6987

6970

7002
7004        ESO 235-22          −49°

7029        ESO 235-16
7022

−50°

*143 ly*

−51°
ESO 234-68

*93 ly*

*I N D U S*        ESO 234-69

*174 ly*        ι

21h 12m   21h 06m   21h 00m   20h 54m   20h 48m

Bright and Dark
Nebulae                                 Open Star                                Galaxies                                                          Quasars
                    To scale     <10'     Clusters                                                                                                                1470
Planetary                               Globular                                10' x 5'  6' x 1'  3' x 2'  5' x 5'  4' x 2'  2' x 1'        Galaxy
Nebulae                                 Clusters                                                                                            Clusters
    >100"  100"−30"  <30"               To scale    <5'        Plotted to scale if the major axis >2', and circular
                                                               when face on or the position angle is uncertain

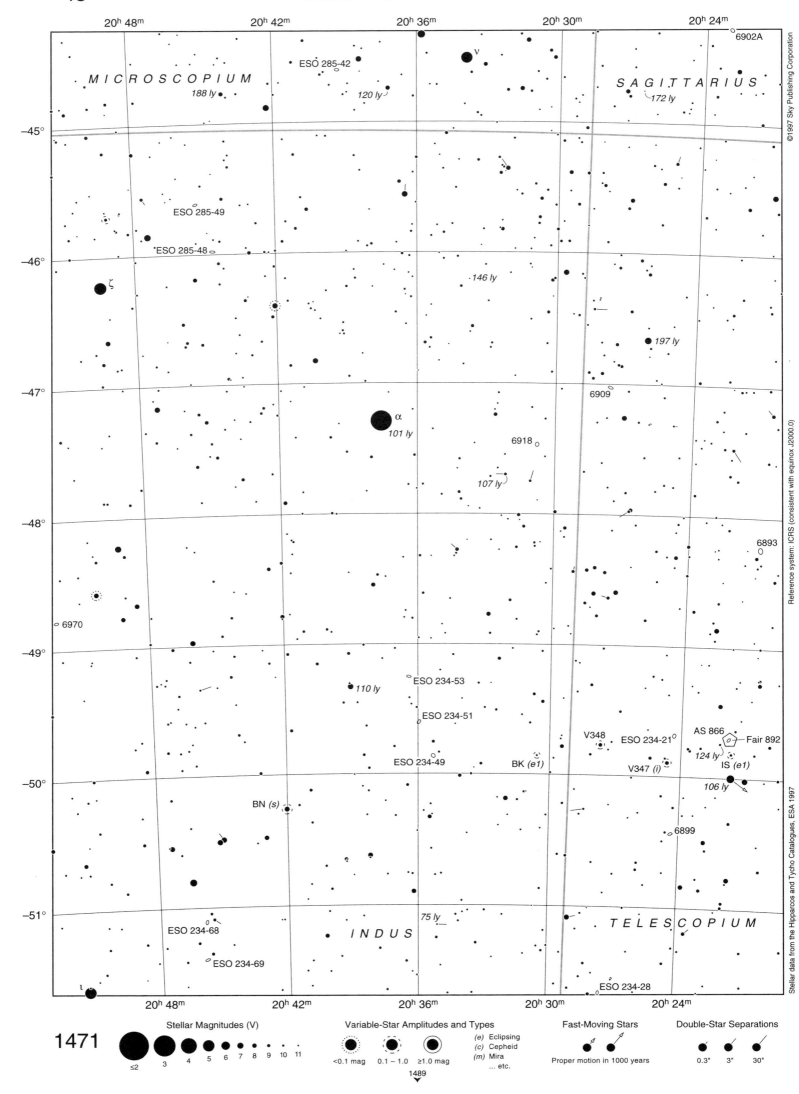

Reference system: ICRS (consistent with equinox J2000.0)

Stellar data from the Hipparcos and Tycho Catalogues, ESA 1997

MICROSCOPIUM

SAGITTARIUS

6902A

ν

ESO 285-42

188 ly

120 ly

172 ly

ESO 285-49

ESO 285-48

ζ

146 ly

197 ly

6909

α
101 ly

6918

107 ly

6893

6970

ESO 234-53

ESO 234-51

110 ly

V348     ESO 234-21

AS 866

Fair 892

ESO 234-49

BK (e1)

V347 (i)

124 ly

IS (e1)

106 ly

BN (s)

6899

ESO 234-68

INDUS

75 ly

TELESCOPIUM

ESO 234-69

ι

ESO 234-28

**1471**

Stellar Magnitudes (V)

≤2    3    4    5    6    7    8    9    10    11

Variable-Star Amplitudes and Types

<0.1 mag    0.1 – 1.0    ≥1.0 mag

(e) Eclipsing
(c) Cepheid
(m) Mira
... etc.

Fast-Moving Stars

Proper motion in 1000 years

Double-Star Separations

0.3"    3"    30"

1489

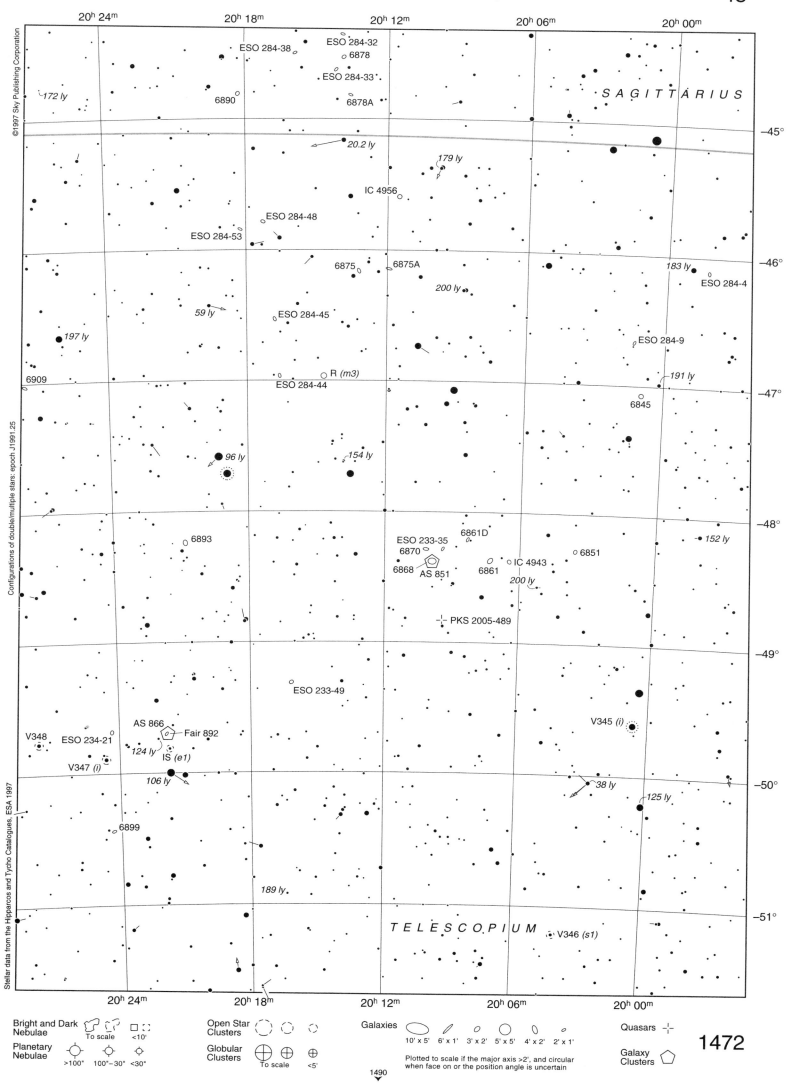

SAGITTARIUS

ESO 284-38
ESO 284-32
6878
ESO 284-33
6890
6878A
172 ly
20.2 ly
179 ly
IC 4956
ESO 284-48
ESO 284-53
183 ly
ESO 284-4
6875
6875A
200 ly
59 ly
ESO 284-45
197 ly
ESO 284-9
R (m3)
191 ly
6909
ESO 284-44
6845
96 ly
154 ly
152 ly
6893
ESO 233-35
6861D
6870
6851
6868
AS 851
IC 4943
6861
200 ly
PKS 2005-489
ESO 233-49
AS 866
V348
ESO 234-21
Fair 892
V345 (i)
124 ly
IS (e1)
V347 (i)
106 ly
38 ly
125 ly
6899
189 ly
TELESCOPIUM
V346 (s1)

20h 24m
20h 18m
20h 12m
20h 06m
20h 00m

−45°
−46°
−47°
−48°
−49°
−50°
−51°

20h 24m
20h 18m
20h 12m
20h 06m
20h 00m

Bright and Dark Nebulae
To scale    <10'
Planetary Nebulae
>100"   100"−30"   <30"

Open Star Clusters
Globular Clusters
To scale    <5'

Galaxies
10' x 5'   6' x 1'   3' x 2'   5' x 5'   4' x 2'   2' x 1'
Plotted to scale if the major axis >2', and circular when face on or the position angle is uncertain

Quasars

Galaxy Clusters

1472

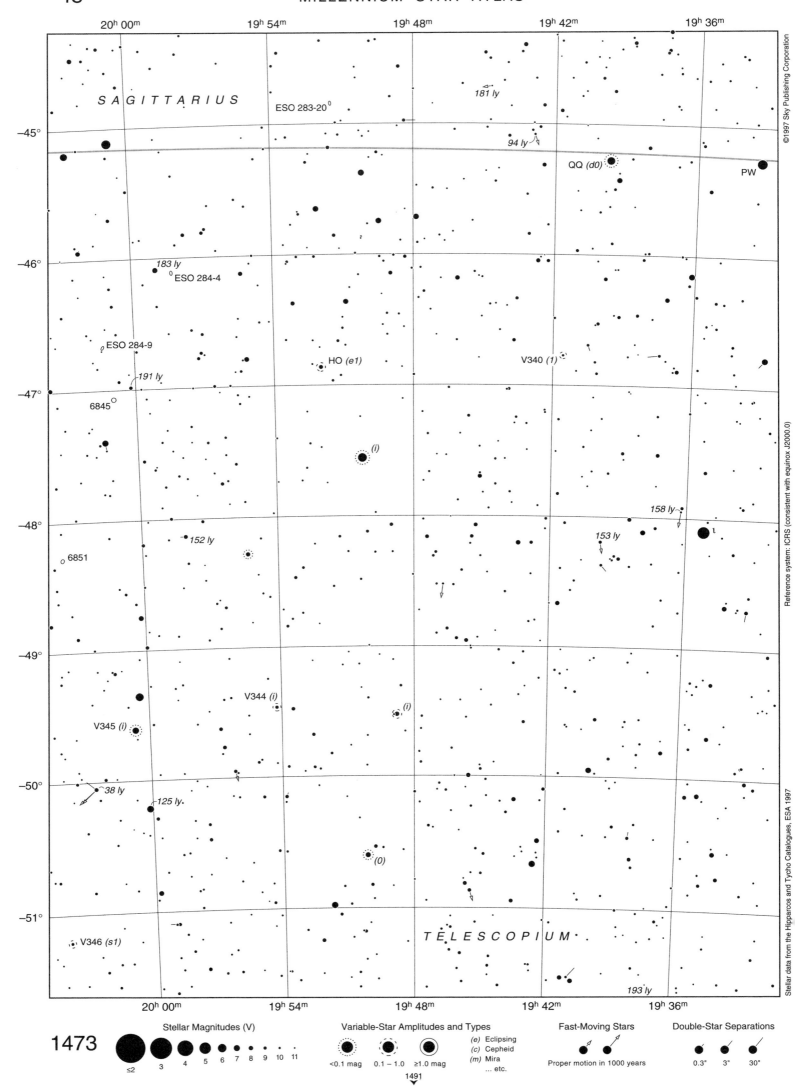

SAGITTARIUS

ESO 283-20

181 ly

94 ly

QQ (d0)

PW

183 ly
ESO 284-4

ESO 284-9

191 ly

6845

HO (e1)

V340 (1)

(i)

158 ly

152 ly

153 ly

ι

6851

V344 (i)

(i)

V345 (i)

38 ly

125 ly

(0)

TELESCOPIUM

V346 (s1)

193 ly

Stellar Magnitudes (V)

≤2    3    4    5    6   7  8  9 10 11

Variable-Star Amplitudes and Types

<0.1 mag    0.1 – 1.0    ≥1.0 mag

(e) Eclipsing
(c) Cepheid
(m) Mira
... etc.

Fast-Moving Stars

Proper motion in 1000 years

Double-Star Separations

0.3"    3"    30"

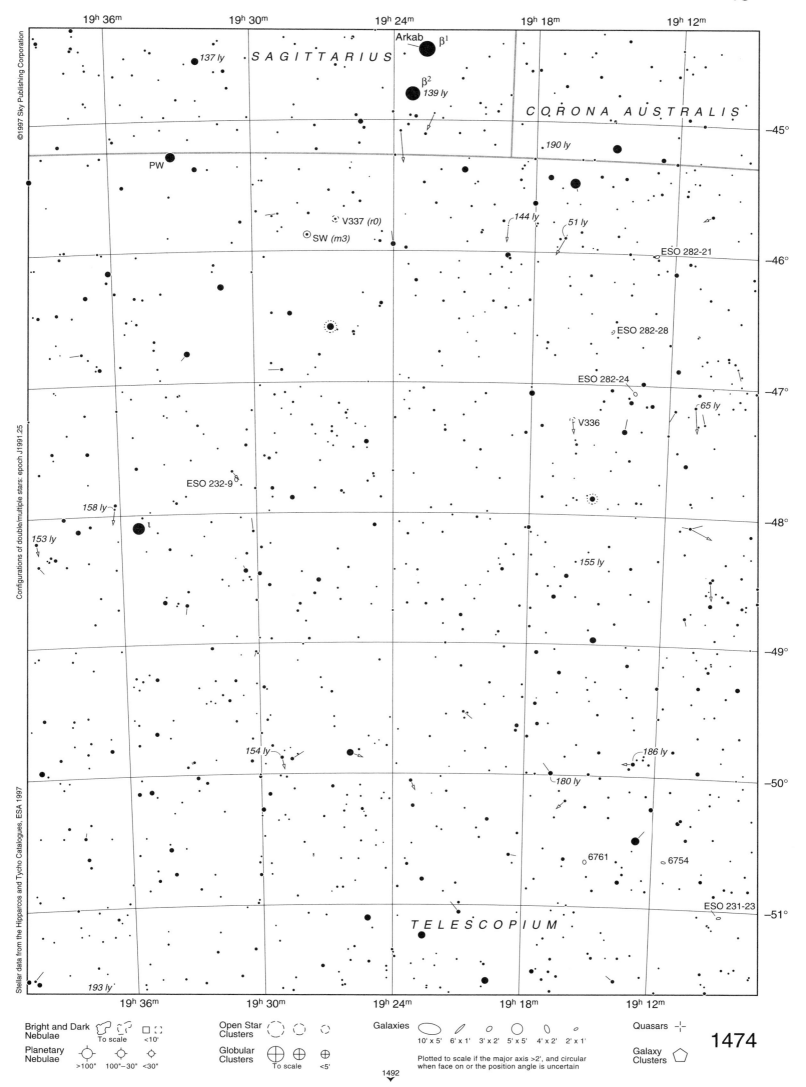

19h 36m    19h 30m    19h 24m    19h 18m    19h 12m

SAGITTARIUS
Arkab   β¹
137 ly
β²
139 ly
CORONA AUSTRALIS
−45°
PW
190 ly
V337 (r0)
SW (m3)
144 ly    51 ly
ESO 282-21    −46°
ESO 282-28
ESO 282-24
65 ly
V336
−47°
ESO 232-9
158 ly
153 ly    ι
155 ly    −48°
−49°
154 ly
186 ly
180 ly    −50°
6761    6754
ESO 231-23    −51°
TELESCOPIUM
193 ly

19h 36m    19h 30m    19h 24m    19h 18m    19h 12m

Bright and Dark Nebulae
To scale    <10'

Planetary Nebulae
>100"   100"−30"   <30"

Open Star Clusters

Globular Clusters
To scale    <5'

Galaxies
10' x 5'   6' x 1'   3' x 2'   5' x 5'   4' x 2'   2' x 1'

Plotted to scale if the major axis >2', and circular when face on or the position angle is uncertain

Quasars

Galaxy Clusters

1474

# MILLENNIUM STAR ATLAS

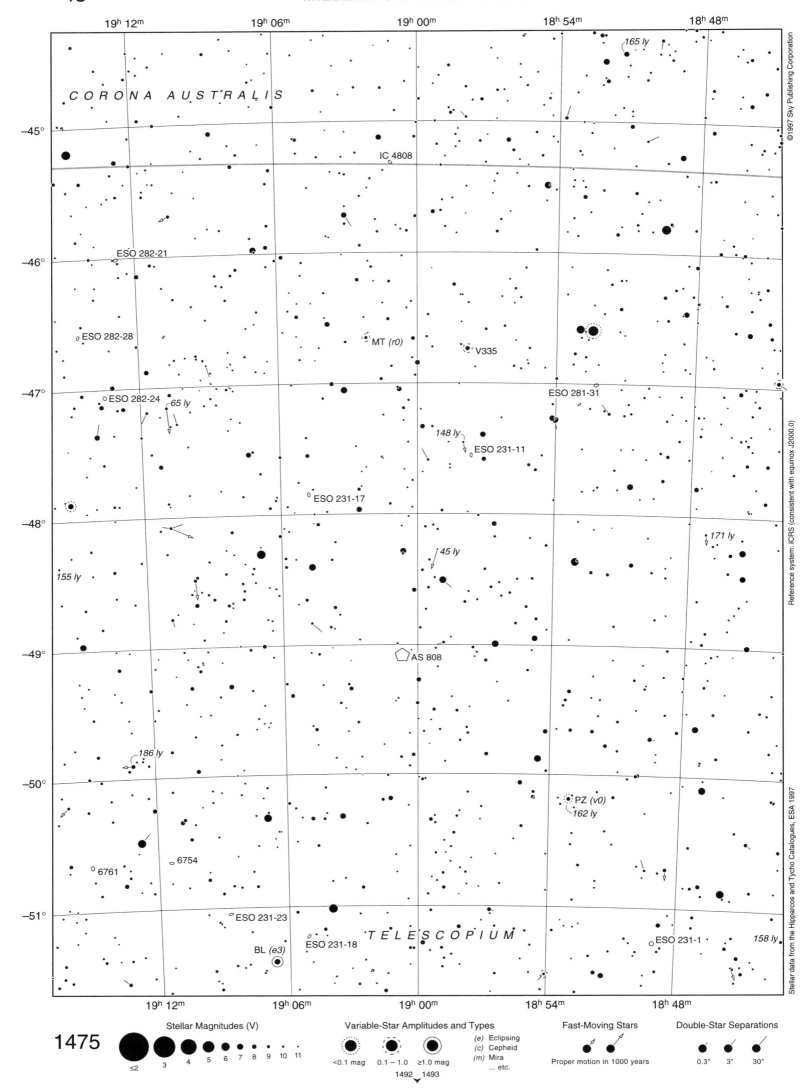

CORONA AUSTRALIS

IC 4808

ESO 282-21

ESO 282-28

ESO 282-24

65 ly

MT (r0)

V335

ESO 281-31

148 ly

ESO 231-11

ESO 231-17

165 ly

171 ly

45 ly

155 ly

AS 808

186 ly

PZ (v0)

162 ly

6754

6761

ESO 231-23

ESO 231-18

TELESCOPIUM

ESO 231-1

158 ly

BL (e3)

©1997 Sky Publishing Corporation

Reference system: ICRS (consistent with equinox J2000.0)

Stellar data from the Hipparcos and Tycho Catalogues, ESA 1997

1475

### Stellar Magnitudes (V)
≤2  3  4  5  6  7  8  9  10  11

### Variable-Star Amplitudes and Types
<0.1 mag   0.1 – 1.0   ≥1.0 mag
1492   1493

(e) Eclipsing
(c) Cepheid
(m) Mira
... etc.

### Fast-Moving Stars
Proper motion in 1000 years

### Double-Star Separations
0.3"   3"   30"

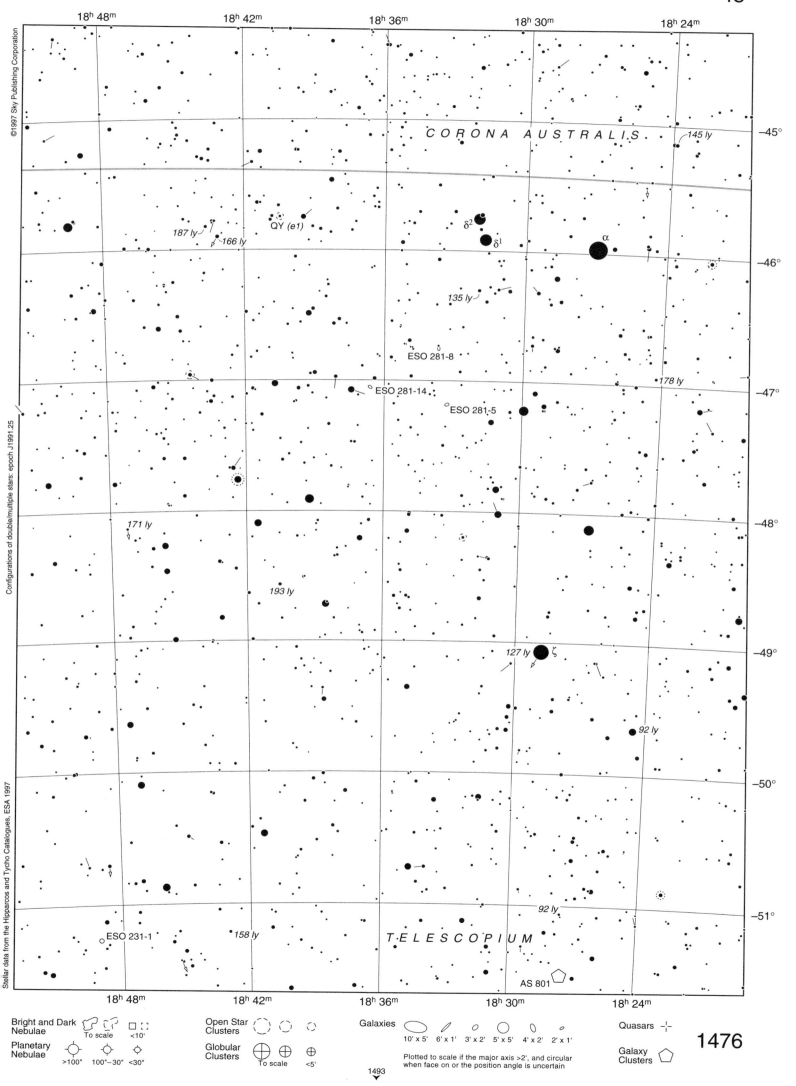

CORONA AUSTRALIS

145 ly

−45°

QY (e1)

187 ly

166 ly

δ²

δ¹

α

−46°

135 ly

ʋ
ESO 281-8

ESO 281-14

178 ly

−47°

ESO 281-5

171 ly

−48°

193 ly

127 ly   ζ

−49°

92 ly

92 ly

−50°

TELESCOPIUM

ESO 231-1

158 ly

−51°

AS 801

18ʰ 48ᵐ    18ʰ 42ᵐ    18ʰ 36ᵐ    18ʰ 30ᵐ    18ʰ 24ᵐ

**Bright and Dark Nebulae**
To scale   <10'

**Planetary Nebulae**
>100"   100"−30"   <30"

**Open Star Clusters**

**Globular Clusters**
To scale   <5'

**Galaxies**
10' x 5'   6' x 1'   3' x 2'   5' x 5'   4' x 2'   2' x 1'

Plotted to scale if the major axis >2', and circular when face on or the position angle is uncertain

**Quasars**

**Galaxy Clusters**

# MILLENNIUM STAR ATLAS

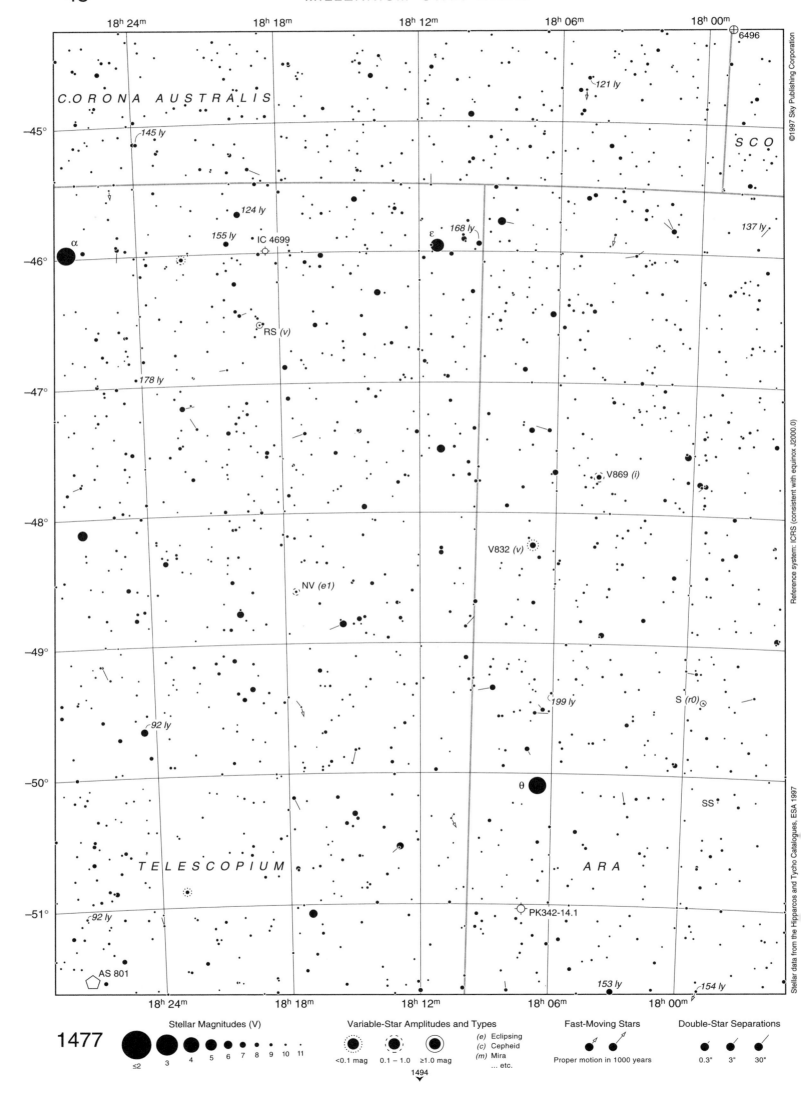

CORONA AUSTRALIS

SCO

145 ly

124 ly

155 ly

IC 4699

ε   168 ly

137 ly

α

−46°

RS (v)

178 ly

V869 (i)

V832 (v)

NV (e1)

S (r0)

92 ly

199 ly

θ

SS

TELESCOPIUM

ARA

92 ly

PK342-14.1

AS 801

153 ly

154 ly

121 ly

6496

**1477**

**Stellar Magnitudes (V)**

≤2   3   4   5   6   7   8   9   10   11

**Variable-Star Amplitudes and Types**

<0.1 mag   0.1 − 1.0   ≥1.0 mag

(e) Eclipsing
(c) Cepheid
(m) Mira
... etc.

**Fast-Moving Stars**

Proper motion in 1000 years

**Double-Star Separations**

0.3"   3"   30"

1494

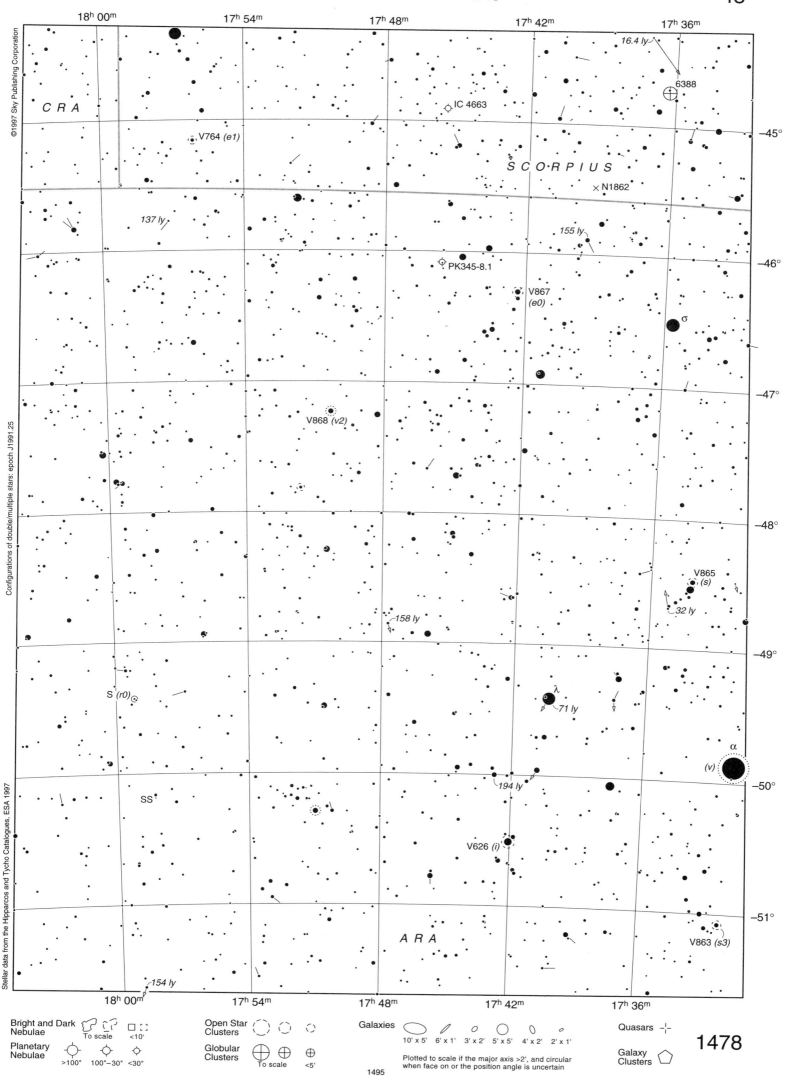

CRA

SCORPIUS

IC 4663

V764 (e1)

16.4 ly

6388

×N1862

137 ly

155 ly

PK345-8.1

V867
(e0)

σ

V868 (v2)

V865
(s)

32 ly

158 ly

S (r0)

λ

71 ly

α

(v)

SS

194 ly

V626 (i)

ARA

V863 (s3)

154 ly

−45°

−46°

−47°

−48°

−49°

−50°

−51°

18h 00m          17h 54m          17h 48m          17h 42m          17h 36m

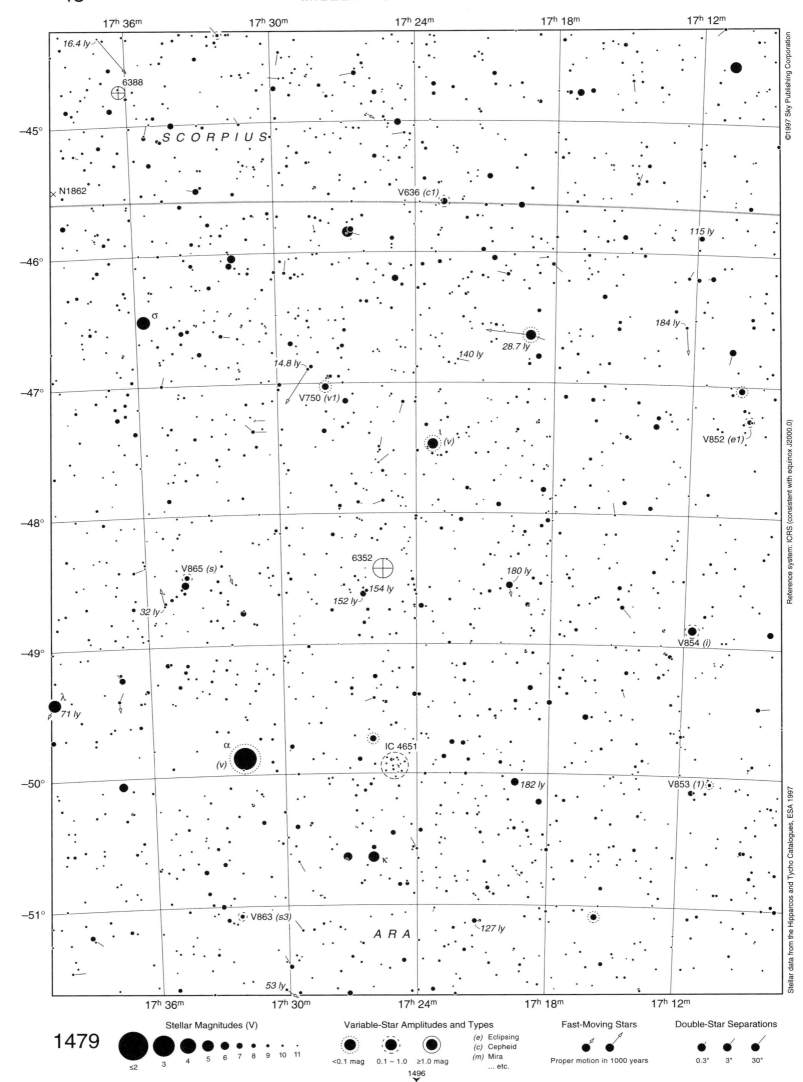

1479

Stellar Magnitudes (V)

≤2   3   4   5   6   7   8   9   10   11

Variable-Star Amplitudes and Types

<0.1 mag    0.1 – 1.0    ≥1.0 mag

(e) Eclipsing
(c) Cepheid
(m) Mira
... etc.

Fast-Moving Stars

Proper motion in 1000 years

Double-Star Separations

0.3"    3"    30"

1496
▽

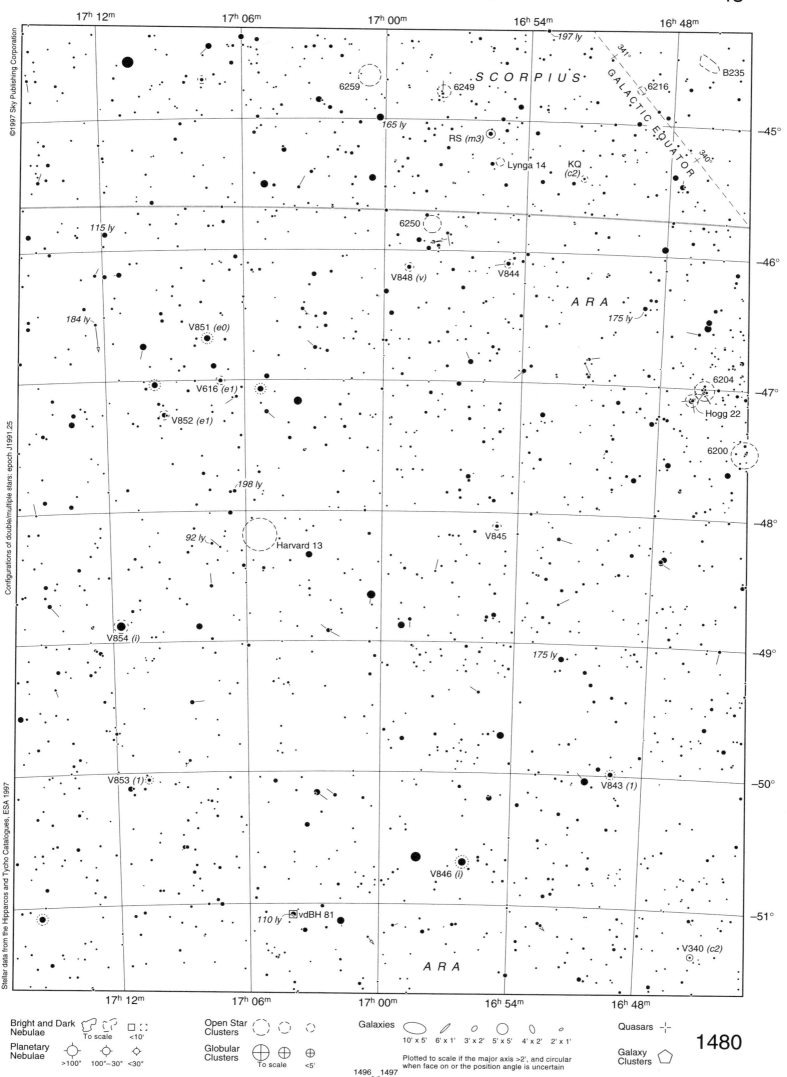

17h 12m    17h 06m    17h 00m    16h 54m    16h 48m

197 ly

B235

SCORPIUS

6259    6249    6216

GALACTIC EQUATOR
341°
340°

165 ly    −45°

RS (m3)

Lynga 14    KQ
(c2)

6250    −46°

V848 (v)    V844

ARA
175 ly

115 ly

184 ly

V851 (e0)

V616 (e1)    6204    −47°

Hogg 22

V852 (e1)

6200

198 ly

92 ly    V845    −48°
Harvard 13

175 ly    −49°

V854 (i)

V853 (1)    V843 (1)    −50°

V846 (i)

110 ly    vdBH 81    −51°

V340 (c2)
ARA

17h 12m    17h 06m    17h 00m    16h 54m    16h 48m

Bright and Dark
Nebulae                    Open Star          Galaxies                                    Quasars
        To scale    <10'    Clusters                                                                    Galaxy
Planetary                                                                 10' x 5'  6' x 1'  3' x 2'  5' x 5'  4' x 2'  2' x 1'      Clusters
Nebulae                    Globular
    >100"  100"–30"  <30"   Clusters                   Plotted to scale if the major axis >2', and circular
                    To scale  <5'        when face on or the position angle is uncertain

**1480**

1496   1497

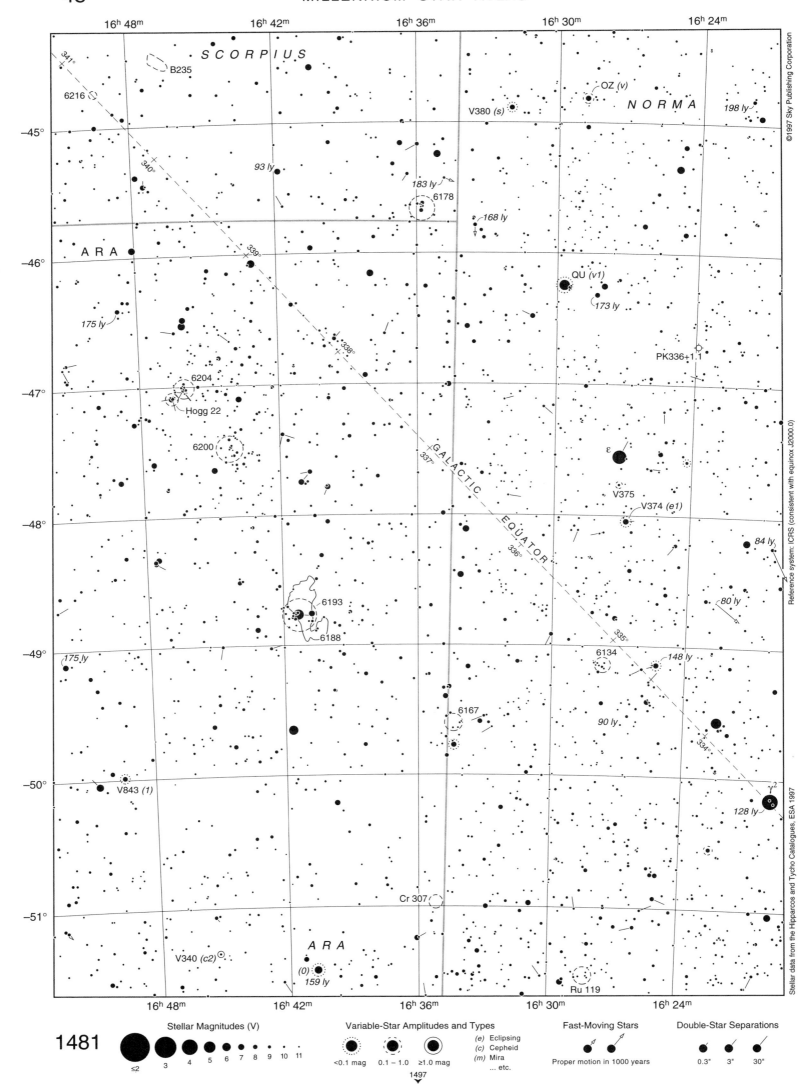

SCORPIUS

B235

6216

NORMA

OZ (v)

V380 (s)

198 ly

93 ly

183 ly

6178

168 ly

ARA

339°

QU (v1)

173 ly

175 ly

338°

PK336+1.1

6204

Hogg 22

ε

6200

337° GALACTIC

V375

V374 (e1)

84 ly

EQUATOR

80 ly

336°

6193

6188

6134

148 ly

175 ly

6167

90 ly

334°

V843 (1)

335°

γ²

128 ly

Cr 307

V340 (c2)

ARA

(0)

159 ly

Ru 119

1481

Stellar Magnitudes (V)

≤2    3    4    5   6   7  8  9 10 11

Variable-Star Amplitudes and Types

<0.1 mag   0.1 – 1.0   ≥1.0 mag

(e) Eclipsing
(c) Cepheid
(m) Mira
... etc.

Fast-Moving Stars

Proper motion in 1000 years

Double-Star Separations

0.3"    3"    30"

1497

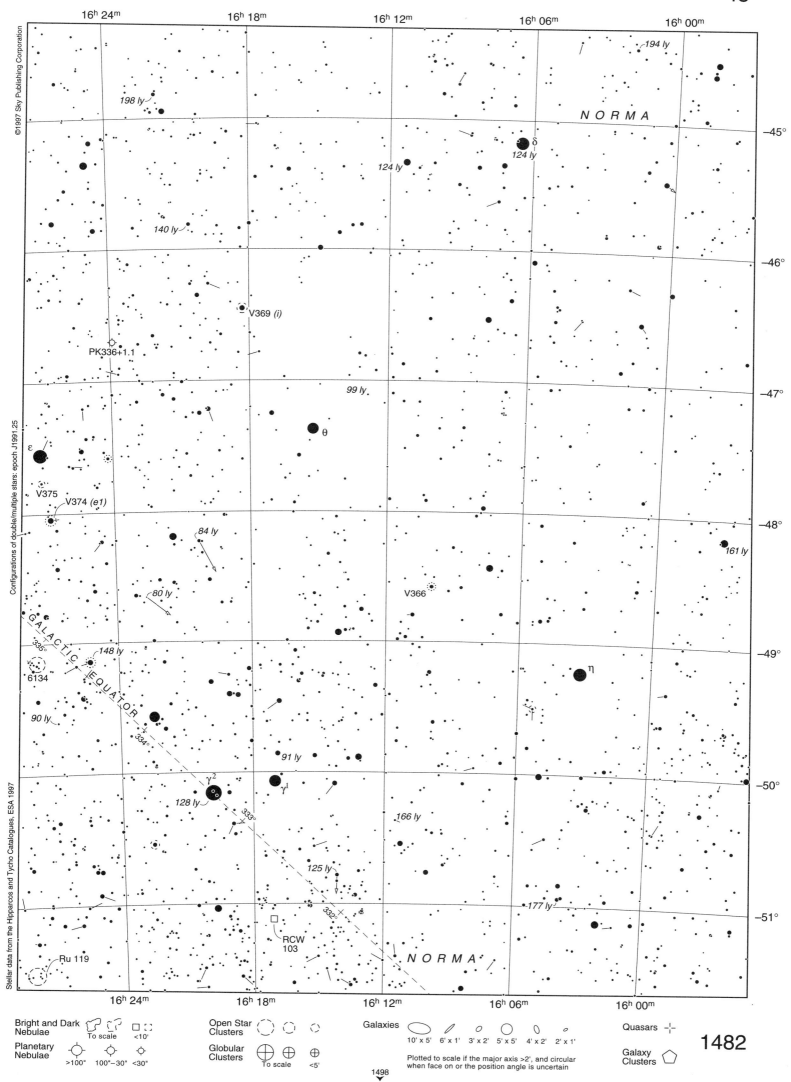

16h 24m   16h 18m   16h 12m   16h 06m   16h 00m

©1997 Sky Publishing Corporation

Configurations of double/multiple stars: epoch J1991.25

Stellar data from the Hipparcos and Tycho Catalogues, ESA 1997

N O R M A

194 ly

198 ly

δ
124 ly
124 ly

140 ly

−45°

−46°

V369 (i)

PK336+1.1

99 ly

θ

ε

V375
V374 (e1)

84 ly

161 ly

V366

−47°

−48°

80 ly

GALACTIC EQUATOR

335°

148 ly

6134

334°

90 ly

η

91 ly

−49°

γ²
128 ly

γ¹

333°

166 ly

−50°

125 ly

332°

177 ly

RCW
103

−51°

Ru 119

N O R M A

16h 24m   16h 18m   16h 12m   16h 06m   16h 00m

Bright and Dark Nebulae    To scale    <10'

Open Star Clusters    Galaxies

Quasars

Planetary Nebulae    >100"   100"–30"   <30'

Globular Clusters    To scale    <5'

10' x 5'   6' x 1'   3' x 2'   5' x 5'   4' x 2'   2' x 1'

Plotted to scale if the major axis >2', and circular when face on or the position angle is uncertain

Galaxy Clusters

1482

1498

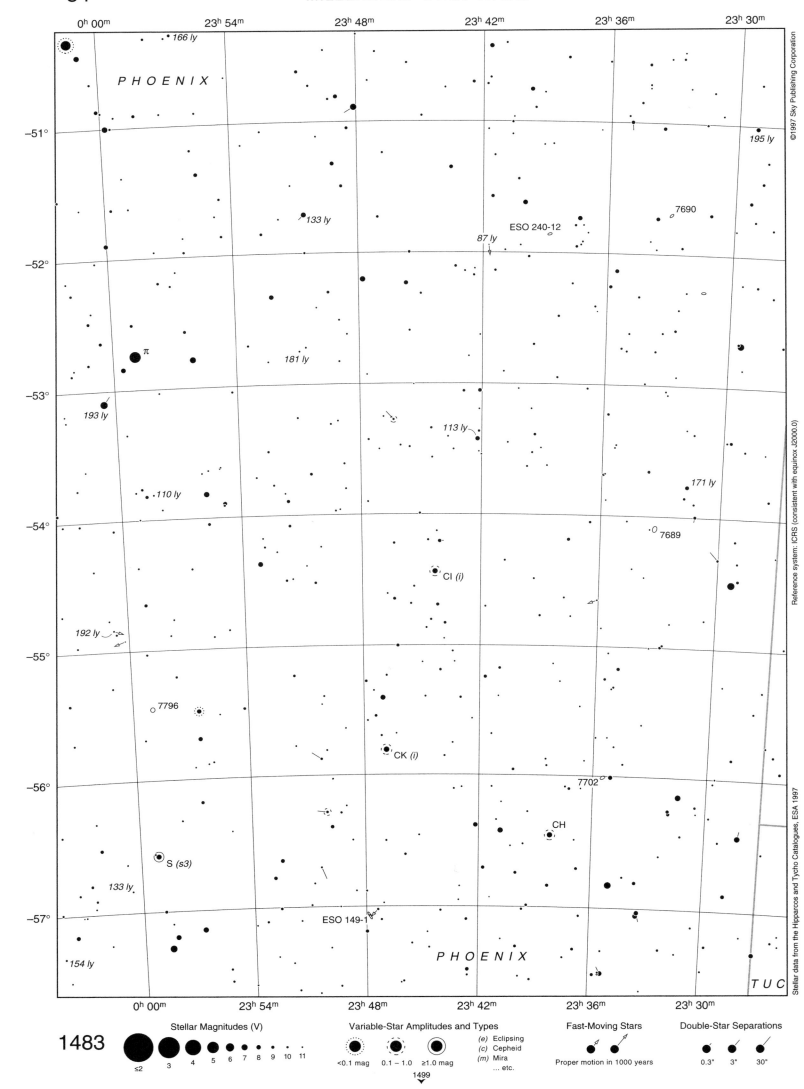

1483

Stellar Magnitudes (V)
≤2  3  4  5  6  7  8  9  10  11

Variable-Star Amplitudes and Types
<0.1 mag   0.1 – 1.0   ≥1.0 mag
(e) Eclipsing
(c) Cepheid
(m) Mira
... etc.

Fast-Moving Stars
Proper motion in 1000 years

Double-Star Separations
0.3"   3"   30"

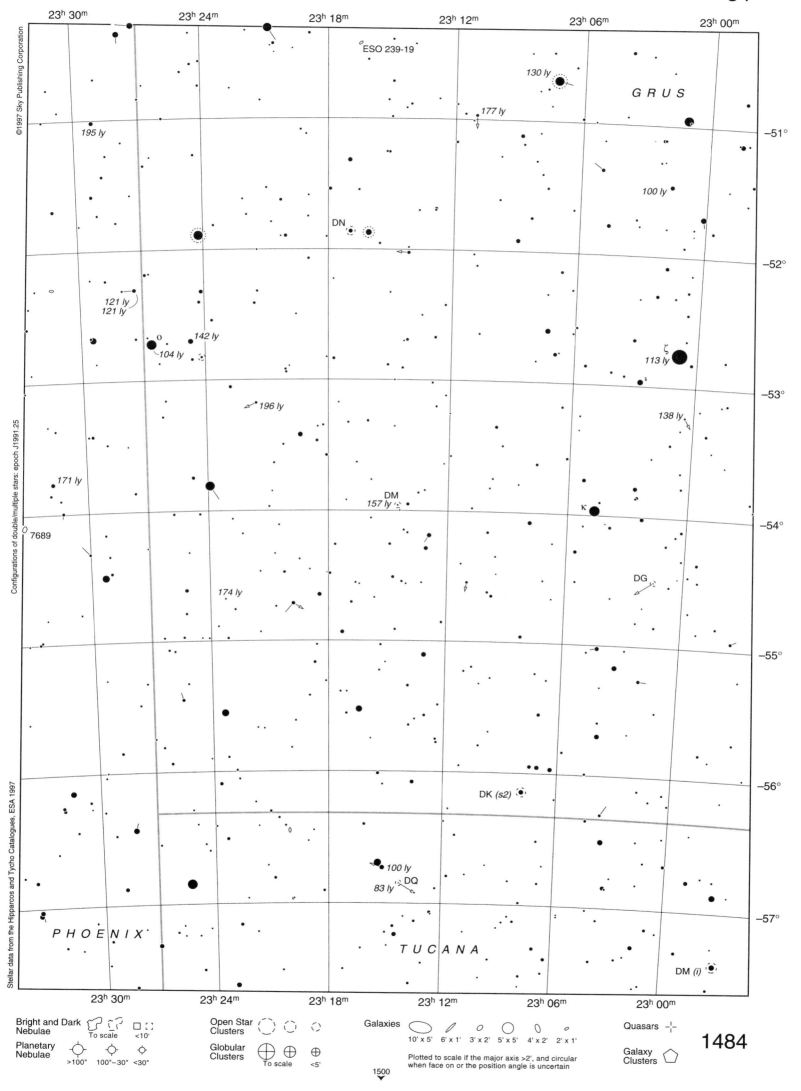

23h 30m    23h 24m    23h 18m    23h 12m    23h 06m    23h 00m

ESO 239-19

130 ly

177 ly

G R U S

195 ly

100 ly

−51°

DN

−52°

121 ly
121 ly

o    142 ly

104 ly

ζ
113 ly

196 ly

138 ly

171 ly

DM
157 ly

κ

−54°

7689

DG

174 ly

−55°

DK (s2)

−56°

100 ly

DQ
83 ly

−57°

P H O E N I X

T U C A N A

DM (i)

23h 30m    23h 24m    23h 18m    23h 12m    23h 06m    23h 00m

Bright and Dark
Nebulae        To scale    <10'

Open Star
Clusters

Galaxies

Quasars —|—

Planetary
Nebulae    >100"  100"−30"  <30"

Globular
Clusters    To scale    <5'

10' x 5'   6' x 1'   3' x 2'   5' x 5'   4' x 2'   2' x 1'

Plotted to scale if the major axis >2', and circular
when face on or the position angle is uncertain

Galaxy
Clusters

1484

1500

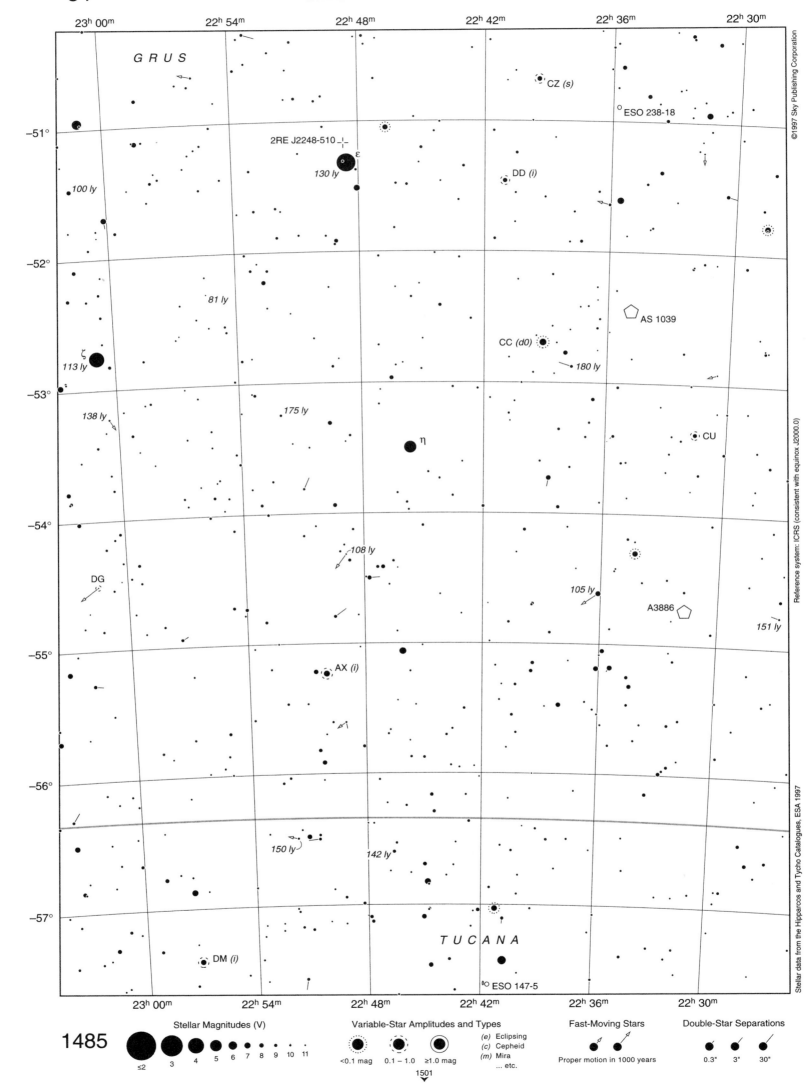

GRUS

CZ *(s)*

ESO 238-18

2RE J2248-510

ε

130 ly

DD *(i)*

100 ly

81 ly

AS 1039

CC *(d0)*

180 ly

ζ

113 ly

138 ly

175 ly

η

CU

DG

108 ly

105 ly

A3886

151 ly

AX *(i)*

150 ly

142 ly

TUCANA

DM *(i)*

ESO 147-5

©1997 Sky Publishing Corporation

Reference system: ICRS (consistent with equinox J2000.0)

Stellar data from the Hipparcos and Tycho Catalogues, ESA 1997

1485

Stellar Magnitudes (V)

≤2   3   4   5   6   7   8   9   10   11

Variable-Star Amplitudes and Types

<0.1 mag    0.1 – 1.0    ≥1.0 mag

*(e)* Eclipsing
*(c)* Cepheid
*(m)* Mira
... etc.

Fast-Moving Stars

Proper motion in 1000 years

Double-Star Separations

0.3"   3"   30"

# MILLENNIUM STAR ATLAS

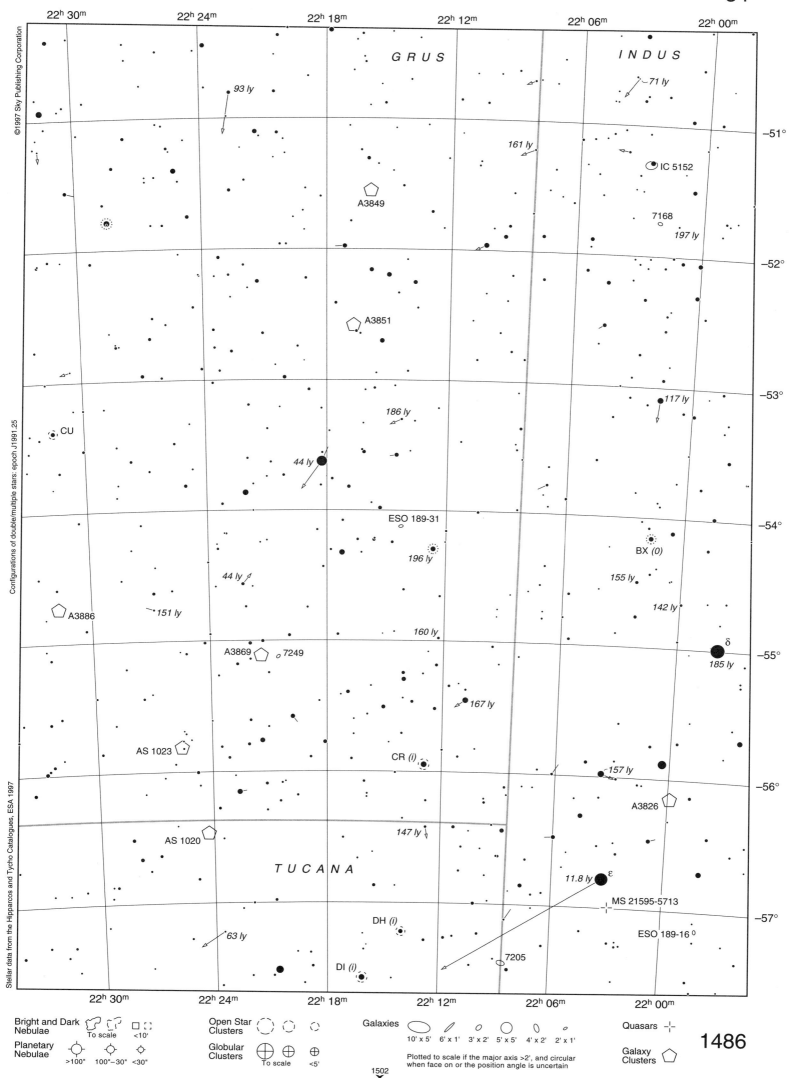

©1997 Sky Publishing Corporation

Configurations of double/multiple stars: epoch J1991.25

Stellar data from the Hipparcos and Tycho Catalogues, ESA 1997

22h 30m    22h 24m    22h 18m    22h 12m    22h 06m    22h 00m

*G R U S*          *I N D U S*

71 ly

−51°

161 ly

93 ly

IC 5152

A3849

7168

197 ly

−52°

A3851

186 ly

117 ly

−53°

CU

44 ly

ESO 189-31

−54°

196 ly

BX (0)

155 ly

44 ly

142 ly

A3886

151 ly

160 ly

δ

A3869   7249

185 ly

−55°

167 ly

AS 1023

CR (i)

157 ly

−56°

A3826

AS 1020

147 ly

*T U C A N A*

11.8 ly   ε

MS 21595-5713

DH (i)

−57°

63 ly

ESO 189-16

DI (i)

7205

22h 30m    22h 24m    22h 18m    22h 12m    22h 06m    22h 00m

**Bright and Dark Nebulae**   To scale   <10'

**Planetary Nebulae**   >100"   100"–30"   <30"

**Open Star Clusters**

**Globular Clusters**   To scale   <5'

**Galaxies**   10' x 5'   6' x 1'   3' x 2'   5' x 5'   4' x 2'   2' x 1'

Plotted to scale if the major axis >2', and circular when face on or the position angle is uncertain

**Quasars**

**Galaxy Clusters**

**1486**

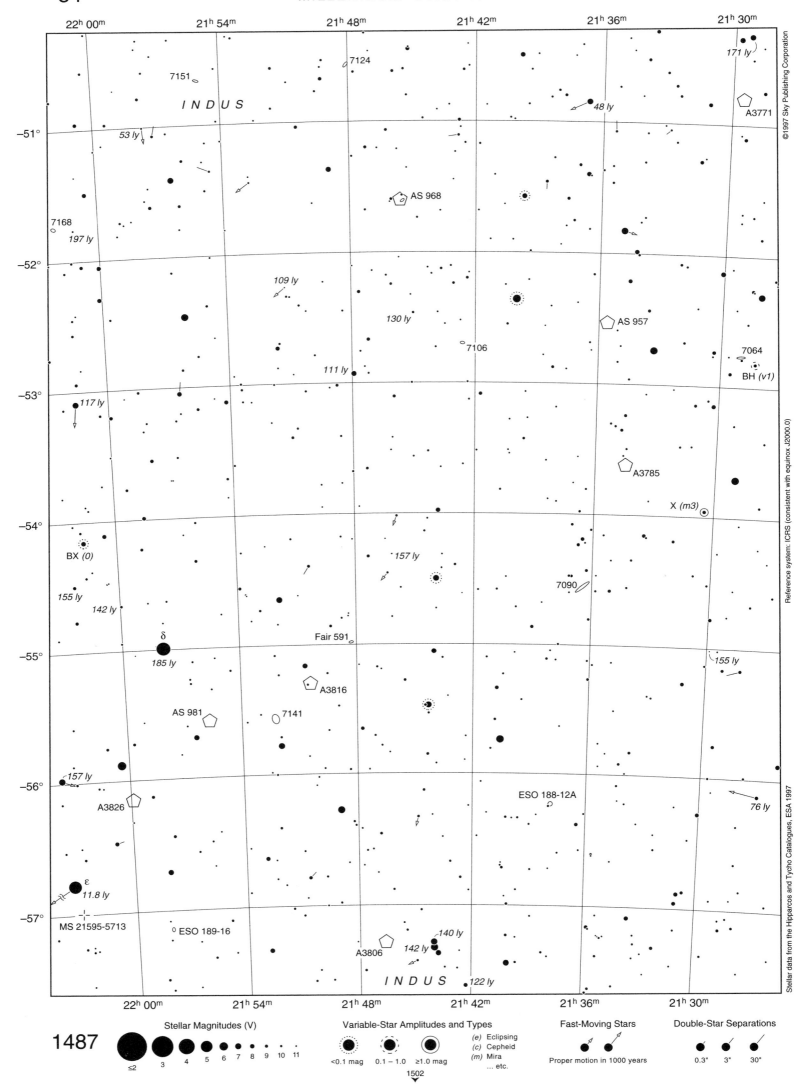

INDUS

7151

7124

48 ly
A3771
171 ly

53 ly

AS 968

7168
197 ly

109 ly

130 ly

7106
AS 957

7064
BH (v1)

111 ly

117 ly

A3785

X (m3)

BX (0)

157 ly

7090

155 ly
142 ly

δ
185 ly

Fair 591

155 ly

A3816

AS 981
7141

ESO 188-12A

157 ly

A3826

76 ly

ε
11.8 ly

MS 21595-5713
ESO 189-16

140 ly
A3806
142 ly

INDUS
122 ly

1487

Stellar Magnitudes (V)

≤2  3  4  5  6 7 8 9 10 11

Variable-Star Amplitudes and Types

<0.1 mag    0.1 – 1.0    ≥1.0 mag

(e) Eclipsing
(c) Cepheid
(m) Mira
... etc.

Fast-Moving Stars

Proper motion in 1000 years

Double-Star Separations

0.3"   3"   30"

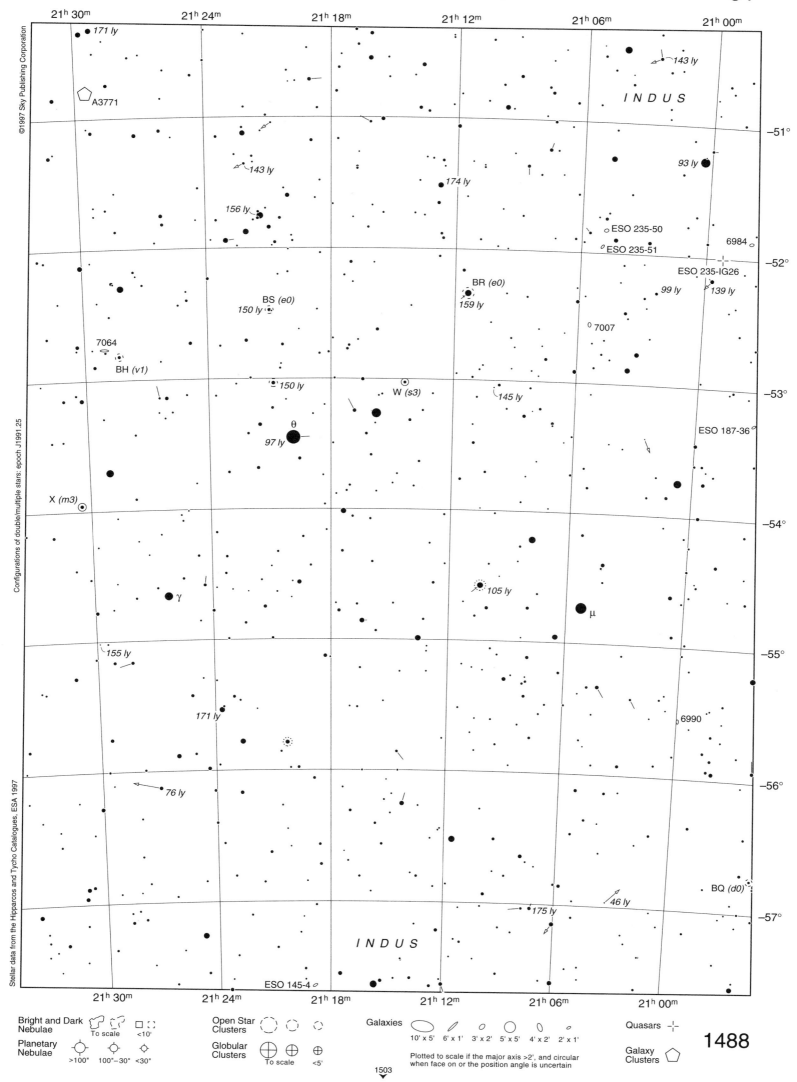

21h 30m    21h 24m    21h 18m    21h 12m    21h 06m    21h 00m

171 ly

A3771

*I N D U S*

143 ly

−51°

143 ly

93 ly

156 ly

174 ly

ESO 235-50

ESO 235-51

6984

−52°

ESO 235-IG26

BR (e0)
159 ly

99 ly

139 ly

BS (e0)
150 ly

7007

7064

BH (v1)

150 ly

W (s3)

145 ly

−53°

θ
97 ly

ESO 187-36

X (m3)

γ

105 ly

μ

−54°

155 ly

−55°

171 ly

6990

76 ly

BQ (d0)

46 ly

175 ly

−56°

*I N D U S*

−57°

ESO 145-4

21h 30m    21h 24m    21h 18m    21h 12m    21h 06m    21h 00m

Bright and Dark
Nebulae

To scale    <10'

Planetary
Nebulae

>100"  100"–30"  <30"

Open Star
Clusters

Globular
Clusters

To scale    <5'

Galaxies

10' x 5'  6' x 1'  3' x 2'  5' x 5'  4' x 2'  2' x 1'

Plotted to scale if the major axis >2', and circular
when face on or the position angle is uncertain

Quasars

Galaxy
Clusters

1488

1503

# MILLENNIUM STAR ATLAS

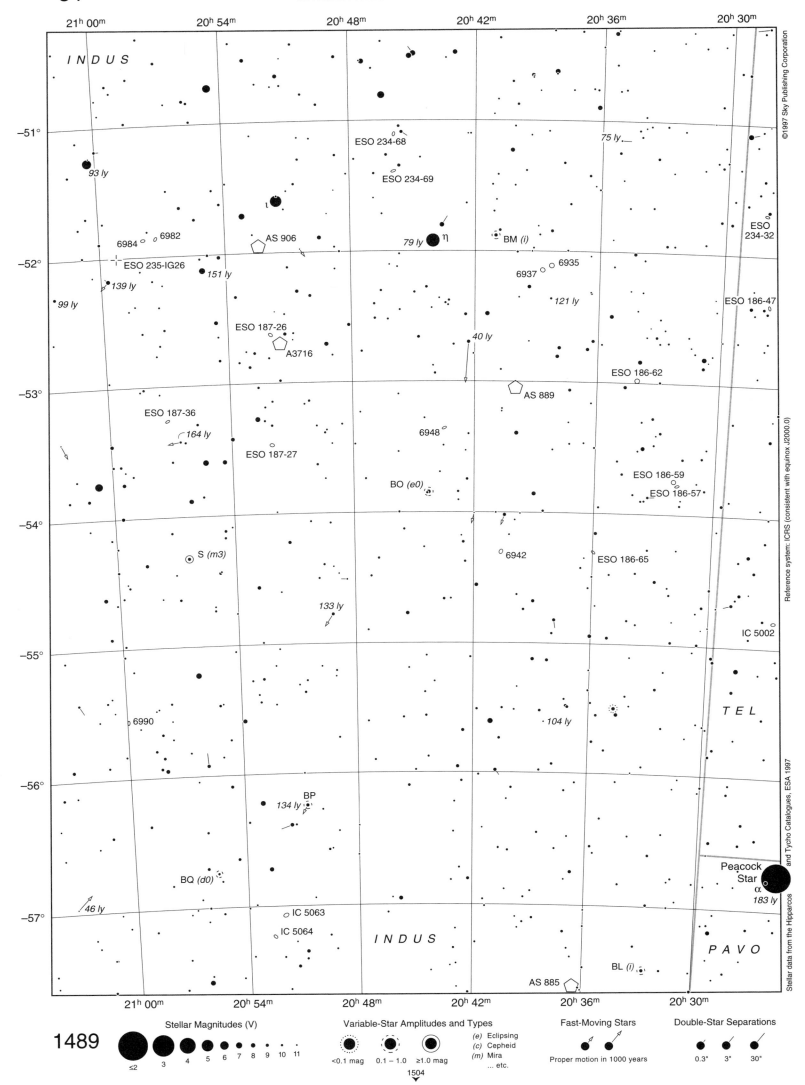

©1997 Sky Publishing Corporation

Reference system: ICRS (consistent with equinox J2000.0)

Stellar data from the Hipparcos and Tycho Catalogues, ESA 1997

*I N D U S*

ESO 234-68

ESO 234-69

*75 ly*

ESO 234-32

*93 ly*

ι

6984  6982

AS 906

*79 ly*  η

BM *(i)*

ESO 234-32

ESO 235-IG26

*151 ly*

6937  6935

ESO 186-47

*139 ly*

*99 ly*

*121 ly*

ESO 187-26

A3716

*40 ly*

ESO 186-62

AS 889

ESO 187-36

*164 ly*

6948

ESO 187-27

ESO 186-59

ESO 186-57

BO *(e0)*

S *(m3)*

6942

ESO 186-65

*133 ly*

IC 5002

*T E L*

6990

*104 ly*

BP

*134 ly*

BQ *(d0)*

Peacock
Star
α
*183 ly*

*46 ly*

IC 5063

IC 5064

*I N D U S*

*P A V O*

BL *(i)*

AS 885

## Stellar Magnitudes (V)

≤2  3  4  5  6  7  8  9  10  11

## Variable-Star Amplitudes and Types

<0.1 mag   0.1 – 1.0   ≥1.0 mag

*(e)* Eclipsing
*(c)* Cepheid
*(m)* Mira
... etc.

## Fast-Moving Stars

Proper motion in 1000 years

## Double-Star Separations

0.3"  3"  30"

# MILLENNIUM STAR ATLAS

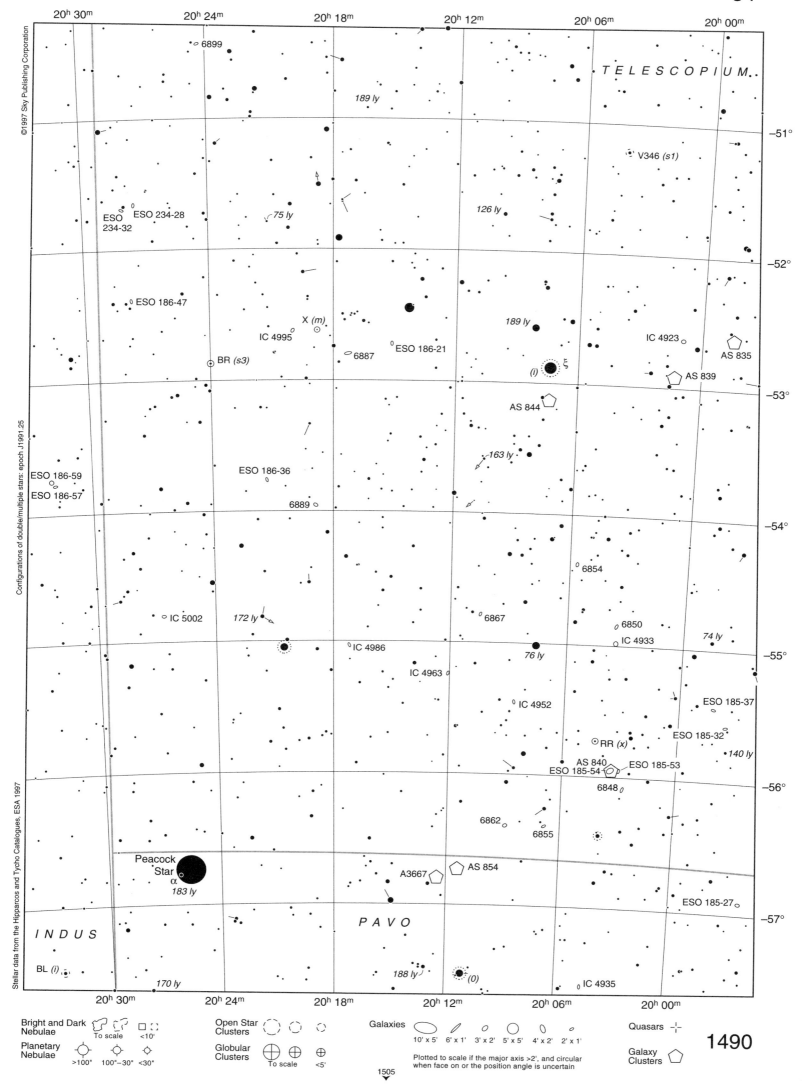

©1997 Sky Publishing Corporation

Configurations of double/multiple stars: epoch J1991.25

Stellar data from the Hipparcos and Tycho Catalogues, ESA 1997

T E L E S C O P I U M

I N D U S

P A V O

6899

189 ly

V346 (s1)

126 ly

ESO 234-28
ESO 234-32

75 ly

ESO 186-47

X (m)
IC 4995

189 ly

IC 4923

AS 835

ESO 186-21

ξ
(i)

AS 839

6887

BR (s3)

AS 844

163 ly

ESO 186-36

ESO 186-59
ESO 186-57

6889

6854

IC 5002

172 ly

6867

6850
IC 4933

74 ly

IC 4986

76 ly

IC 4963

ESO 185-37

IC 4952

ESO 185-32

RR (x)

140 ly

AS 840
ESO 185-54    ESO 185-53

6848

6862

6855

Peacock
Star
α
183 ly

A3667    AS 854

ESO 185-27

BL (i)

188 ly    (0)

IC 4935

170 ly

## Legend

| Bright and Dark Nebulae | | To scale | | <10' |
|---|---|---|---|---|

Planetary Nebulae   >100"  100"–30"  <30"

Open Star Clusters

Globular Clusters   To scale  <5'

Galaxies   10' x 5'   6' x 1'   3' x 2'   5' x 5'   4' x 2'   2' x 1'

Plotted to scale if the major axis >2', and circular when face on or the position angle is uncertain

Quasars

Galaxy Clusters

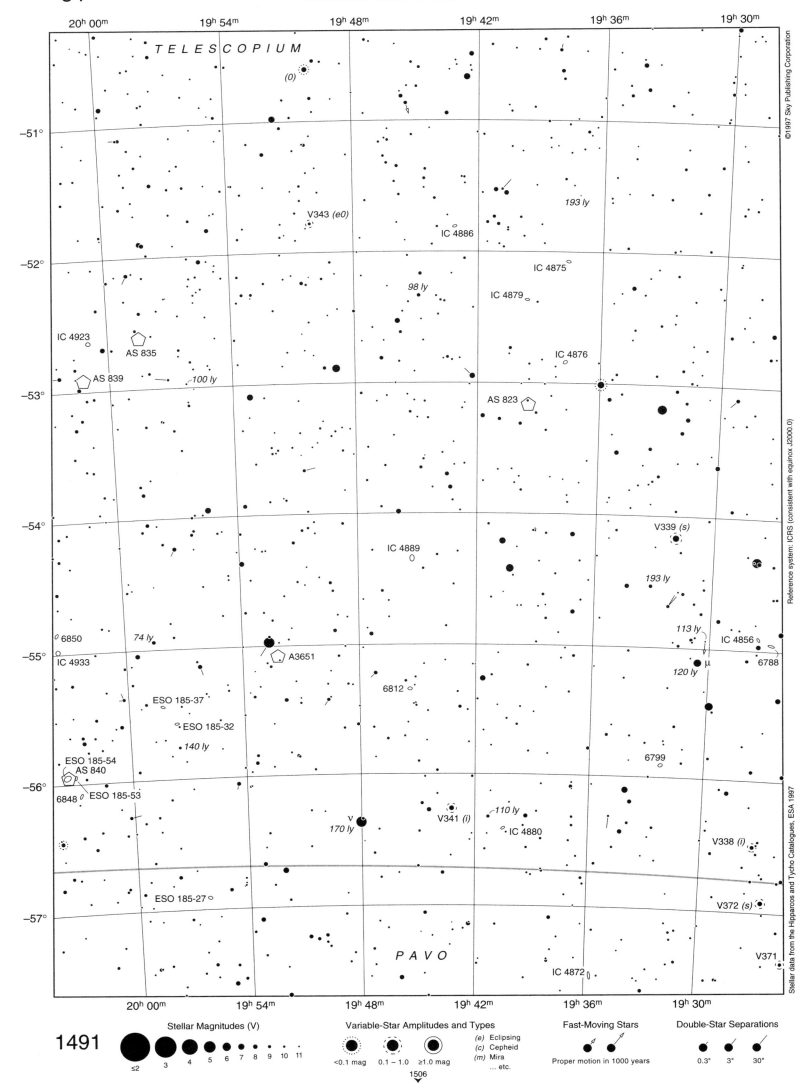

TELESCOPIUM

*(0)*

V343 *(e0)*

IC 4886

*193 ly*

IC 4875

*98 ly*

IC 4879

IC 4923

AS 835

IC 4876

AS 839

*100 ly*

AS 823

V339 *(s)*

IC 4889

*193 ly*

*113 ly*

IC 4856

*0* 6850

*74 ly*

6788

IC 4933

A3651

μ

*120 ly*

6812

ESO 185-37

ESO 185-32

6799

*140 ly*

ESO 185-54

AS 840

ν

V341 *(i)*

*110 ly*

V338 *(i)*

6848 *0* ESO 185-53

*170 ly*

IC 4880

ESO 185-27

V372 *(s)*

PAVO

V371

IC 4872

**1491**

Stellar Magnitudes (V)

≤2  3  4  5  6  7  8  9  10  11

Variable-Star Amplitudes and Types

<0.1 mag  0.1 – 1.0  ≥1.0 mag

*(e)* Eclipsing
*(c)* Cepheid
*(m)* Mira
... etc.

Fast-Moving Stars

Proper motion in 1000 years

Double-Star Separations

0.3"  3"  30"

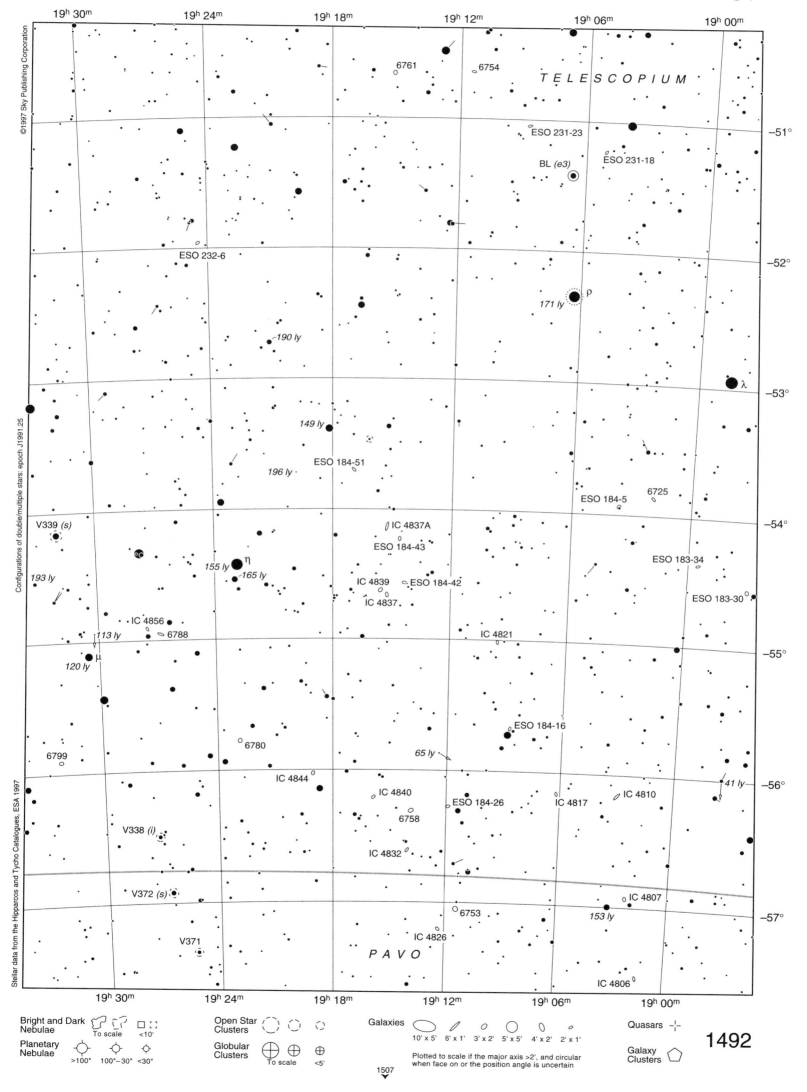

19h 30m  19h 24m  19h 18m  19h 12m  19h 06m  19h 00m

−51°
−52°
−53°
−54°
−55°
−56°
−57°

*T E L E S C O P I U M*

6761
6754

ESO 231-23

BL *(e3)*
ESO 231-18

ESO 232-6

ρ
*171 ly*

λ

*190 ly*

*149 ly*

ESO 184-51
*196 ly*

6725
ESO 184-5

IC 4837A
ESO 184-43

ESO 183-34

V339 *(s)*

η
*155 ly*
*165 ly*

IC 4839
ESO 184-42
IC 4837

ESO 183-30

*193 ly*

IC 4856
6788
*113 ly*

IC 4821

μ
*120 ly*

ESO 184-16

6799

6780

*65 ly*

*41 ly*

IC 4844

IC 4840

ESO 184-26
IC 4817
IC 4810

6758

V338 *(i)*

IC 4832

IC 4807
V372 *(s)*

6753
*153 ly*

V371

IC 4826

*P A V O*

IC 4806

19h 30m  19h 24m  19h 18m  19h 12m  19h 06m  19h 00m

| Bright and Dark Nebulae | To scale | <10' |
| Planetary Nebulae | >100" 100"−30" <30" | |

Open Star Clusters

Globular Clusters · To scale · <5'

Galaxies
10' x 5'  6' x 1'  3' x 2'  5' x 5'  4' x 2'  2' x 1'

Plotted to scale if the major axis >2', and circular when face on or the position angle is uncertain

Quasars

Galaxy Clusters

1492

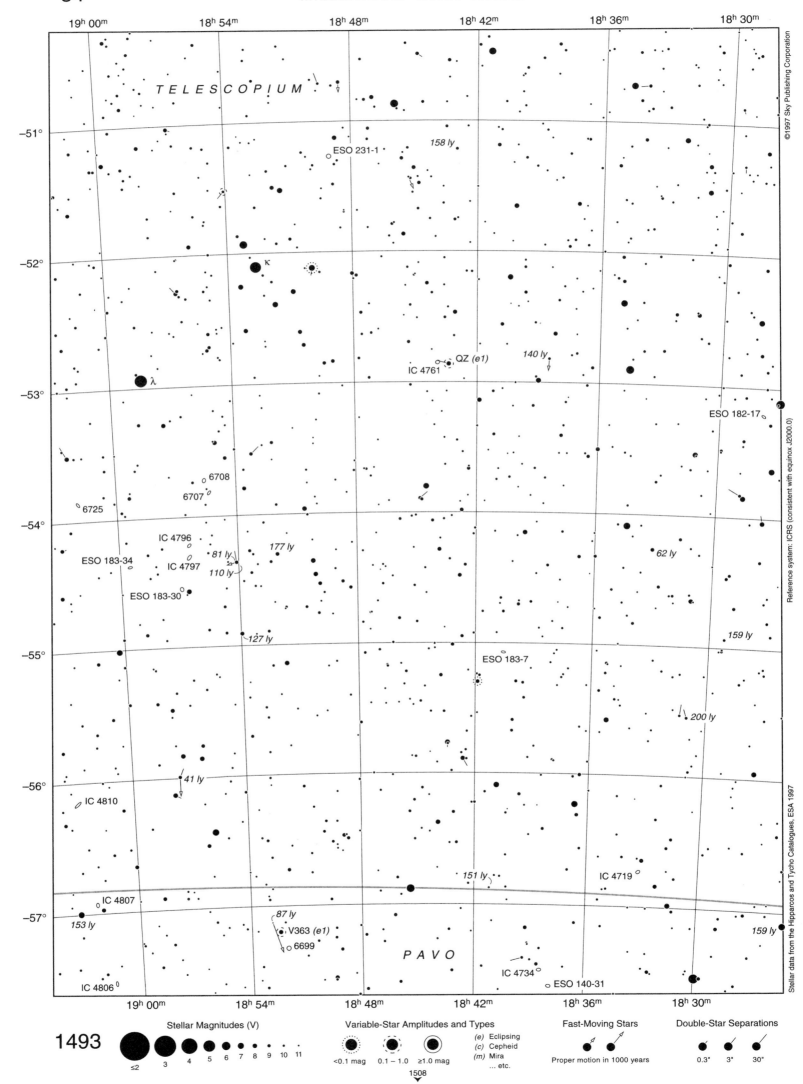

©1997 Sky Publishing Corporation

Reference system: ICRS (consistent with equinox J2000.0)

Stellar data from the Hipparcos and Tycho Catalogues, ESA 1997

TELESCOPIUM

ESO 231-1

158 ly

κ

λ

IC 4761    QZ (e1)

140 ly

ESO 182-17

6708
6707

6725

IC 4796

ESO 183-34    81 ly    177 ly

IC 4797    110 ly    62 ly

ESO 183-30

127 ly

ESO 183-7

159 ly

200 ly

41 ly

IC 4810

151 ly    IC 4719

IC 4807

153 ly    87 ly

V363 (e1)    159 ly

6699    PAVO

IC 4734

IC 4806    ESO 140-31

1493

Stellar Magnitudes (V)

≤2   3   4   5   6   7   8   9   10   11

Variable-Star Amplitudes and Types

<0.1 mag   0.1 – 1.0   ≥1.0 mag

(e) Eclipsing
(c) Cepheid
(m) Mira
... etc.

Fast-Moving Stars

Proper motion in 1000 years

Double-Star Separations

0.3"   3"   30"

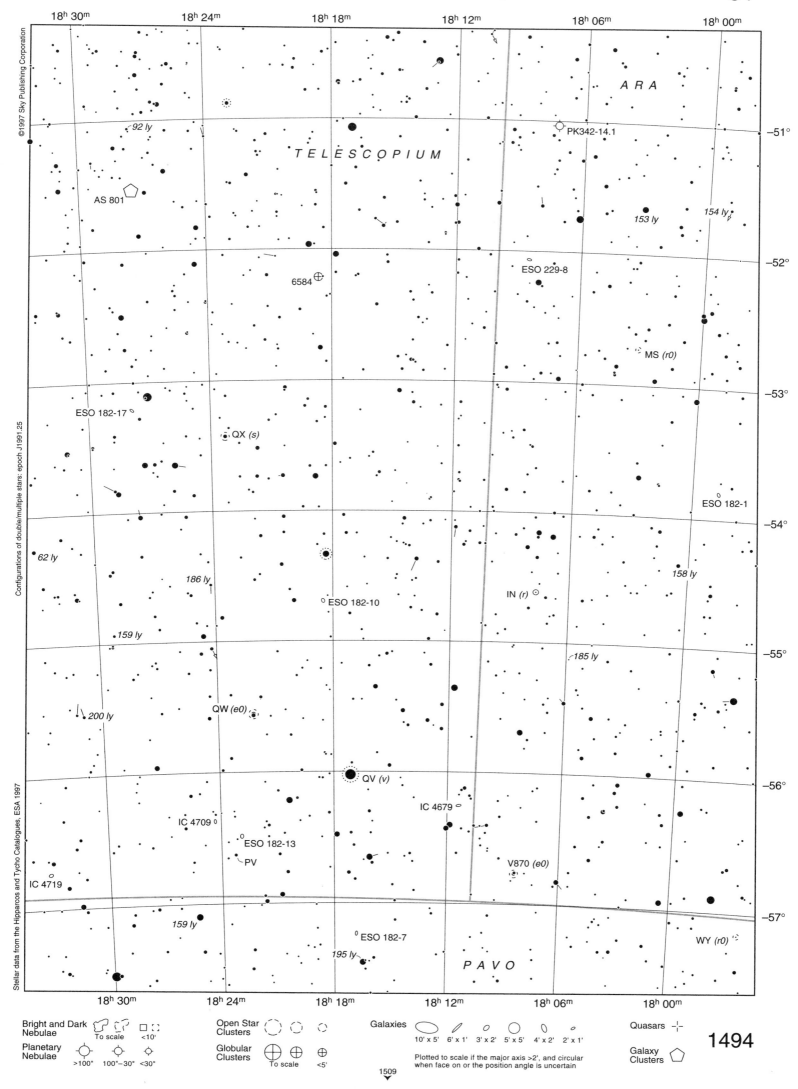

18ʰ 30ᵐ    18ʰ 24ᵐ    18ʰ 18ᵐ    18ʰ 12ᵐ    18ʰ 06ᵐ    18ʰ 00ᵐ

A R A

T E L E S C O P I U M

PK342-14.1

92 ly

AS 801

153 ly    154 ly

−51°

6584

ESO 229-8

−52°

MS (r0)

ESO 182-17

−53°

QX (s)

ESO 182-1

62 ly

−54°

186 ly

ESO 182-10

IN (r)

158 ly

159 ly

−55°

185 ly

200 ly

QW (e0)

QV (v)

−56°

IC 4679

IC 4709

ESO 182-13

V870 (e0)

PV

IC 4719

−57°

159 ly

ESO 182-7

WY (r0)

195 ly

P A V O

18ʰ 30ᵐ    18ʰ 24ᵐ    18ʰ 18ᵐ    18ʰ 12ᵐ    18ʰ 06ᵐ    18ʰ 00ᵐ

Bright and Dark Nebulae    To scale    <10'

Open Star Clusters

Galaxies

Quasars

Planetary Nebulae    >100"    100"–30"    <30"

Globular Clusters    To scale    <5'

10' x 5'   6' x 1'   3' x 2'   5' x 5'   4' x 2'   2' x 1'

Galaxy Clusters

Plotted to scale if the major axis >2', and circular when face on or the position angle is uncertain

1494

1509

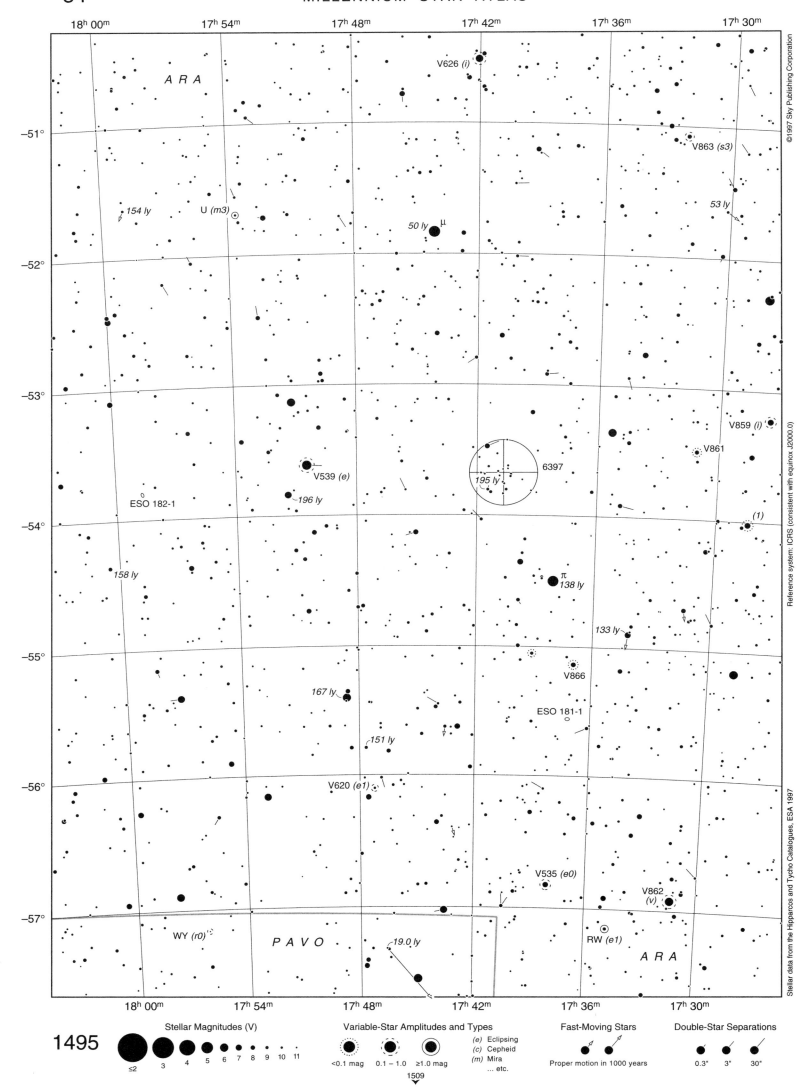

ARA

V626 (i)

V863 (s3)

154 ly

U (m3)

50 ly    μ

53 ly

V859 (i)

V861

6397

V539 (e)

195 ly

ESO 182-1

196 ly

(1)

158 ly

π
138 ly

133 ly

V866

167 ly

ESO 181-1

151 ly

V620 (e1)

V535 (e0)

V862
(v)

WY (r0)

PAVO

19.0 ly

RW (e1)

ARA

1495

Stellar Magnitudes (V)

≤2    3    4    5    6    7    8    9    10    11

Variable-Star Amplitudes and Types

<0.1 mag    0.1 – 1.0    ≥1.0 mag

(e) Eclipsing
(c) Cepheid
(m) Mira
... etc.

Fast-Moving Stars

Proper motion in 1000 years

Double-Star Separations

0.3"    3"    30"

# MILLENNIUM STAR ATLAS

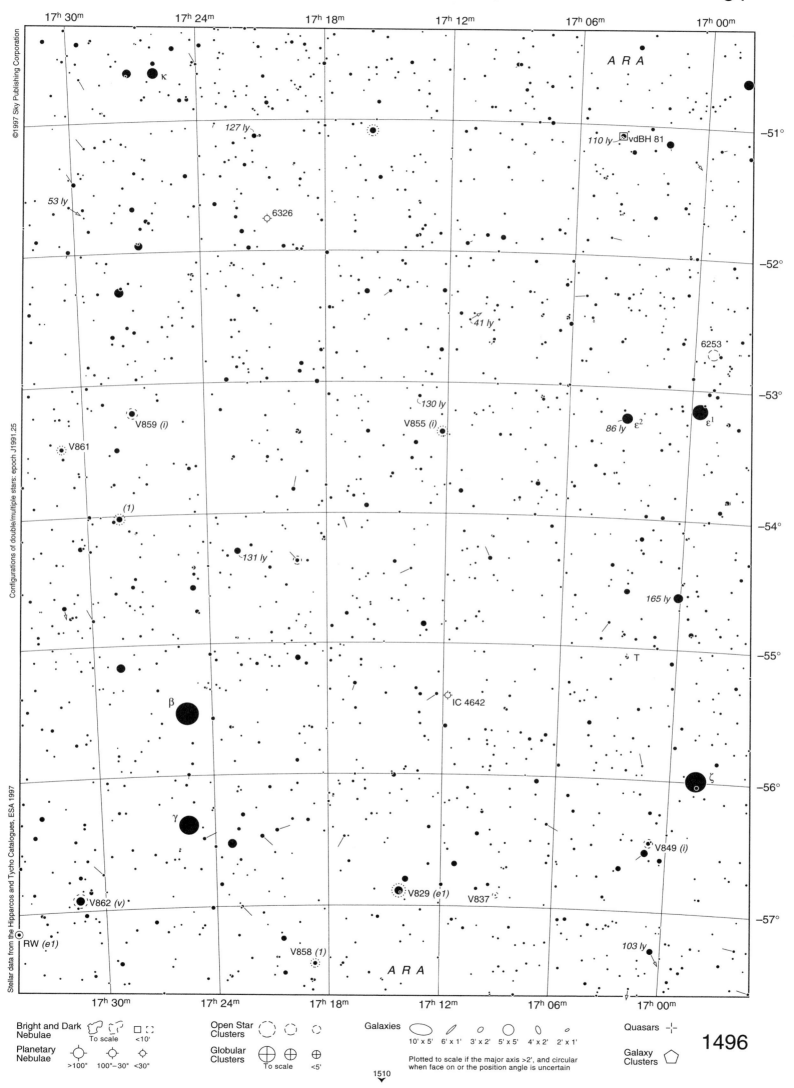

ARA

127 ly

110 ly vdBH 81

53 ly

6326

41 ly

6253

130 ly

V859 (i)

V855 (i)

ε²

ε¹

86 ly

V861

(1)

131 ly

165 ly

T

β

IC 4642

ζ

γ

V849 (i)

V862 (v)

V829 (e1)

V837

RW (e1)

V858 (1)

ARA

103 ly

| Bright and Dark Nebulae | Open Star Clusters | Galaxies | Quasars −┤┤− |
| To scale □ [□] <10' | ◯ ◯ ◯ | ◯ / ○ ◯ ○ ○ | |
| Planetary Nebulae | Globular Clusters | 10' x 5'  6' x 1'  3' x 2'  5' x 5'  4' x 2'  2' x 1' | Galaxy Clusters ⬠ |
| ◉ ◇ ◇ | ⊕ ⊕ ⊕ | | |
| >100"  100"−30"  <30" | To scale <5' | Plotted to scale if the major axis >2', and circular when face on or the position angle is uncertain | |

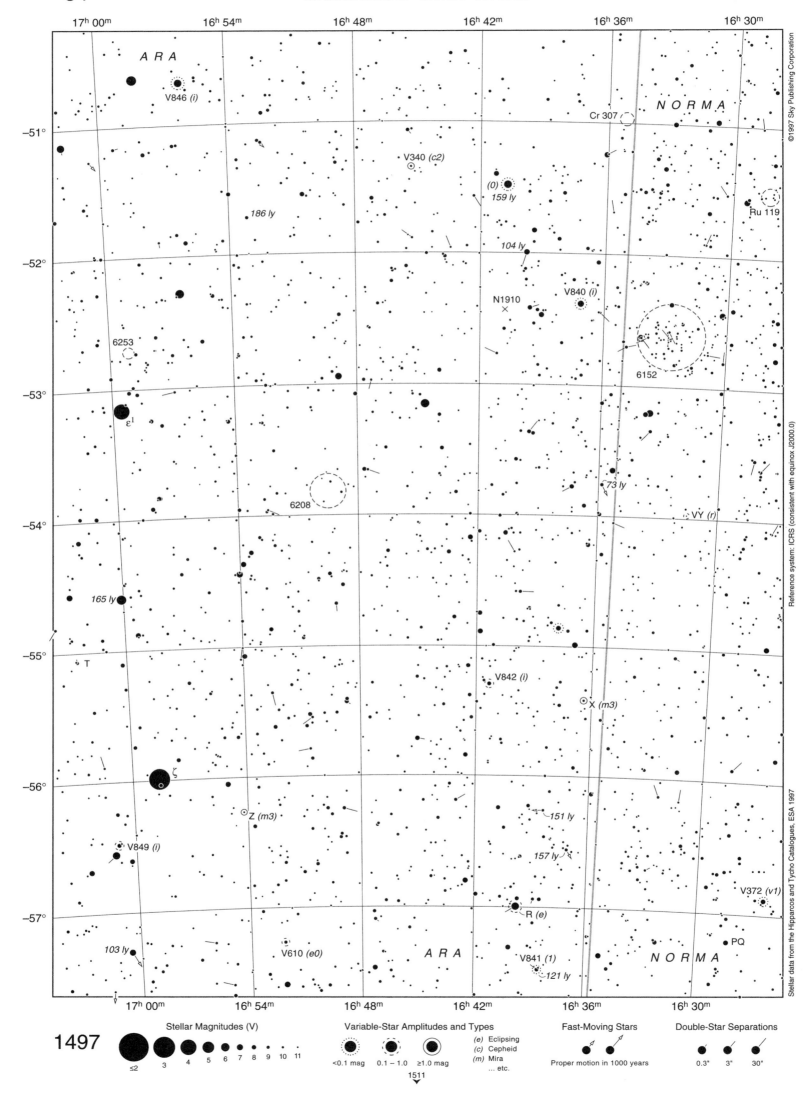

©1997 Sky Publishing Corporation

Reference system: ICRS (consistent with equinox J2000.0)

Stellar data from the Hipparcos and Tycho Catalogues, ESA 1997

**1497**

Stellar Magnitudes (V)

≤2  3  4  5  6  7  8  9  10  11

Variable-Star Amplitudes and Types

<0.1 mag    0.1 – 1.0    ≥1.0 mag

(e) Eclipsing
(c) Cepheid
(m) Mira
... etc.

Fast-Moving Stars

Proper motion in 1000 years

Double-Star Separations

0.3"    3"    30"

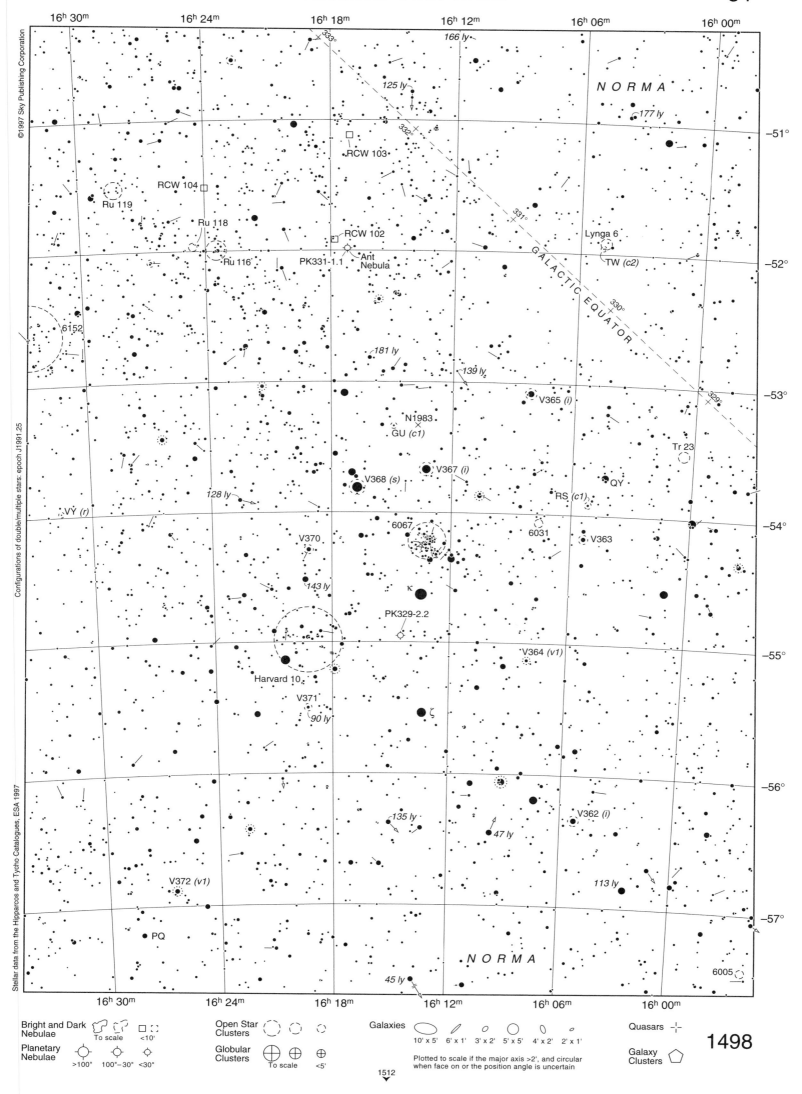

©1997 Sky Publishing Corporation

Configurations of double/multiple stars: epoch J1991.25

Stellar data from the Hipparcos and Tycho Catalogues, ESA 1997

NORMA

16h 30m  16h 24m  16h 18m  16h 12m  16h 06m  16h 00m

333°
166 ly
125 ly
177 ly
−51°

RCW 103
332°
RCW 104
Ru 119
331°
Ru 118
Lynga 6
−52°
RCW 102
Ru 116
TW (c2)
PK331-1.1
Ant
Nebula
GALACTIC EQUATOR
330°

6152
181 ly
139 ly
−53°
V365 (i)
329°
N1983
GU (c1)
Tr 23
V367 (i)
QY
V368 (s)
RS (c1)
VY (r)
128 ly
6067
6031
−54°
V370
V363
143 ly
κ
PK329-2.2
Harvard 10
V364 (v1)
−55°
V371
ζ
90 ly

135 ly
47 ly
V362 (i)
−56°

V372 (v1)
113 ly
−57°
PQ
NORMA
6005
45 ly

16h 30m  16h 24m  16h 18m  16h 12m  16h 06m  16h 00m

Bright and Dark Nebulae
To scale  <10'
Open Star Clusters
Galaxies
10' x 5'  6' x 1'  3' x 2'  5' x 5'  4' x 2'  2' x 1'
Quasars

Planetary Nebulae
>100"  100"–30"  <30"
Globular Clusters
To scale  <5'
Plotted to scale if the major axis >2', and circular when face on or the position angle is uncertain
Galaxy Clusters

1498

1512

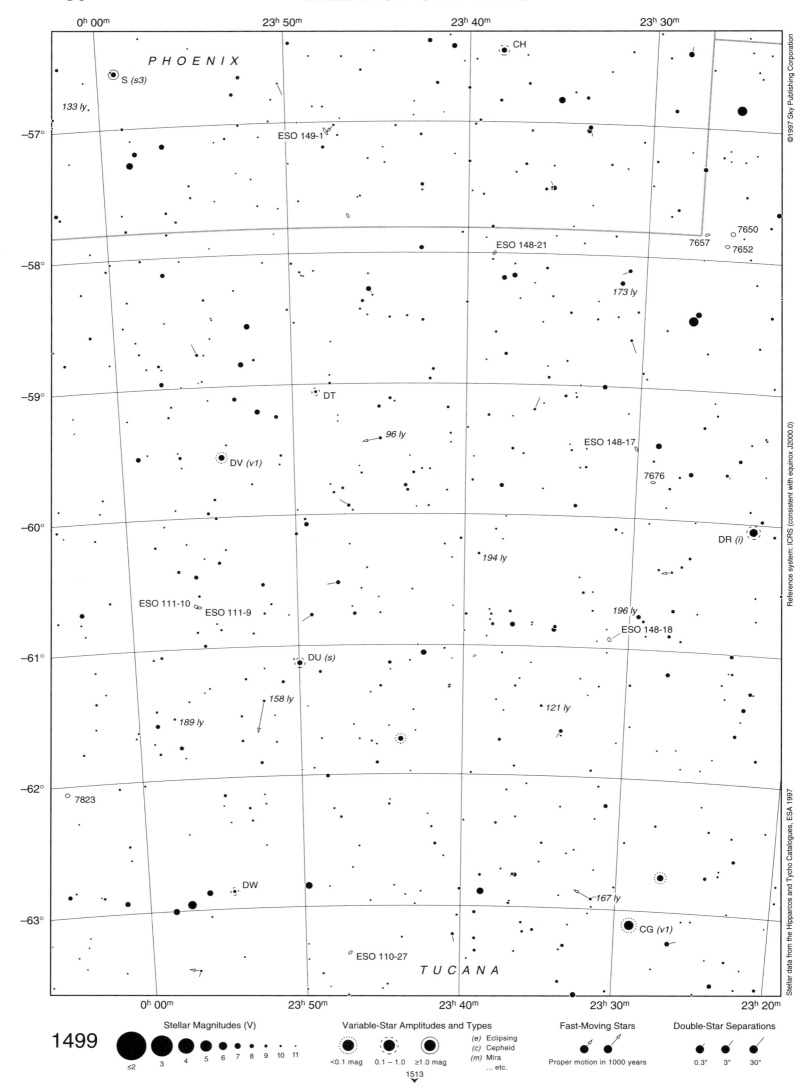

©1997 Sky Publishing Corporation

Reference system: ICRS (consistent with equinox J2000.0)

Stellar data from the Hipparcos and Tycho Catalogues, ESA 1997

PHOENIX

S (s3)

133 ly

CH

ESO 149-1

ESO 148-21

7650
7657        7652

173 ly

DT

96 ly

ESO 148-17

7676

DV (v1)

DR (i)

194 ly

196 ly

ESO 111-10    ESO 111-9

ESO 148-18

DU (s)

121 ly

158 ly

189 ly

7823

167 ly

DW

CG (v1)

ESO 110-27

T U C A N A

Stellar Magnitudes (V)

≤2   3   4   5   6   7   8  9 10 11

Variable-Star Amplitudes and Types

<0.1 mag   0.1 – 1.0   ≥1.0 mag

(e) Eclipsing
(c) Cepheid
(m) Mira
... etc.

Fast-Moving Stars

Proper motion in 1000 years

Double-Star Separations

0.3"    3"    30"

# MILLENNIUM STAR ATLAS

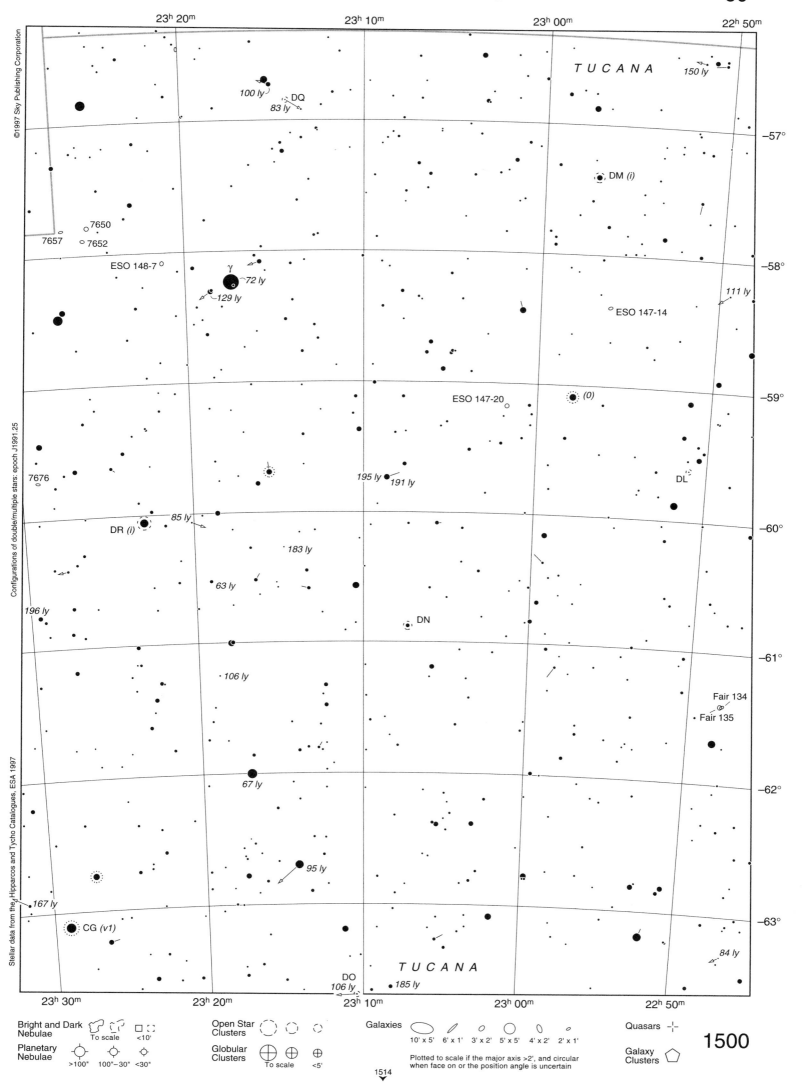

Configurations of double/multiple stars: epoch J1991.25

Stellar data from the Hipparcos and Tycho Catalogues, ESA 1997

*T U C A N A*

150 ly

23h 20m    23h 10m    23h 00m    22h 50m

DM *(i)*

−57°

100 ly    DQ
83 ly

7650
7652
7657

ESO 148-7    −58°
γ
72 ly    111 ly
129 ly    ESO 147-14

ESO 147-20    *(0)*    −59°

7676    DL
195 ly    191 ly

DR *(i)*    85 ly    −60°

183 ly
63 ly
196 ly
DN

−61°
106 ly

Fair 134
Fair 135

67 ly    −62°

95 ly

167 ly    −63°
CG *(v1)*

84 ly

*T U C A N A*

DO
106 ly    185 ly

23h 30m    23h 20m    23h 10m    23h 00m    22h 50m

| Bright and Dark Nebulae | Open Star Clusters | Galaxies | Quasars |
|---|---|---|---|

To scale    <10'

Planetary Nebulae
>100"    100"–30"    <30"

Globular Clusters
To scale    <5'

Galaxies
10' x 5'    6' x 1'    3' x 2'    5' x 5'    4' x 2'    2' x 1'

Plotted to scale if the major axis >2', and circular when face on or the position angle is uncertain

Galaxy Clusters

**1500**

MILLENNIUM STAR ATLAS

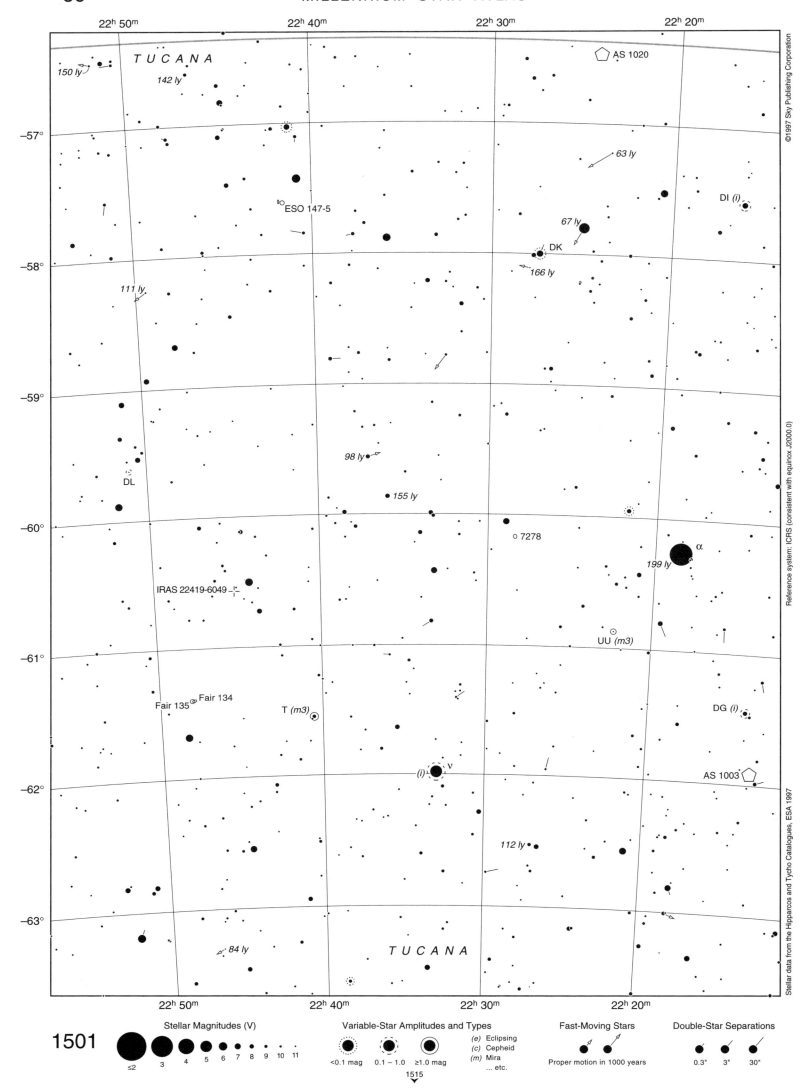

T U C A N A

22ʰ 50ᵐ   22ʰ 40ᵐ   22ʰ 30ᵐ   22ʰ 20ᵐ

AS 1020

150 ly
142 ly

−57°

63 ly

ESO 147-5

DI (i)

67 ly

DK

−58°

166 ly

111 ly

98 ly

−59°

DL

155 ly

o 7278

−60°

α

199 ly

IRAS 22419-6049

UU (m3)

−61°

Fair 135   Fair 134

DG (i)

T (m3)

(i)   v

AS 1003

−62°

112 ly

−63°

84 ly

T U C A N A

22ʰ 50ᵐ   22ʰ 40ᵐ   22ʰ 30ᵐ   22ʰ 20ᵐ

1501

Stellar Magnitudes (V)

≤2   3   4   5   6   7   8   9   10   11

Variable-Star Amplitudes and Types

<0.1 mag   0.1 – 1.0   ≥1.0 mag

(e) Eclipsing
(c) Cepheid
(m) Mira
... etc.

Fast-Moving Stars

Proper motion in 1000 years

Double-Star Separations

0.3"   3"   30"

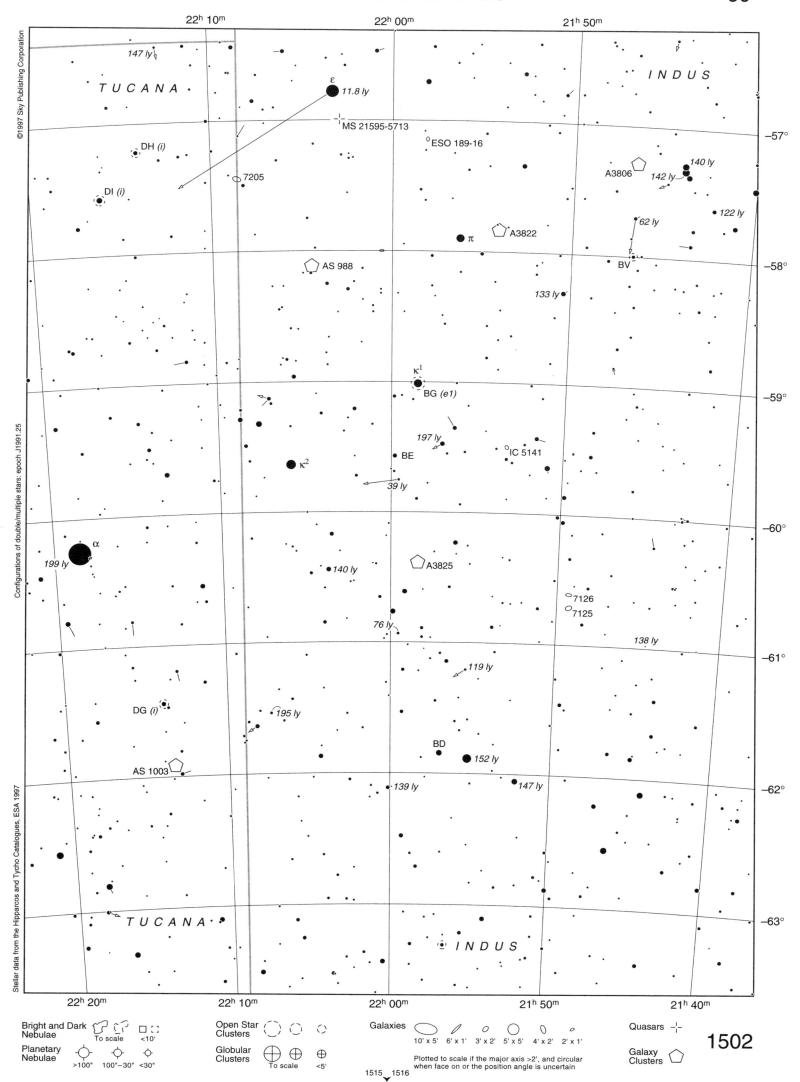

Configurations of double/multiple stars: epoch J1991.25

Stellar data from the Hipparcos and Tycho Catalogues, ESA 1997

*I N D U S*

*T U C A N A*

147 ly

ε  11.8 ly

MS 21595-5713

−57°

DH (i)

ESO 189-16

A3806

140 ly

142 ly

DI (i)

7205

122 ly

62 ly

π   A3822

BV

AS 988

−58°

133 ly

κ¹

BG (e1)

−59°

197 ly

κ²

BE

IC 5141

39 ly

−60°

α

140 ly   A3825

199 ly

7126

7125

76 ly

138 ly

−61°

119 ly

DG (i)

195 ly

BD

AS 1003

152 ly

147 ly

−62°

139 ly

*T U C A N A*

−63°

*I N D U S*

22h 10m   22h 00m   21h 50m

22h 20m   22h 10m   22h 00m   21h 50m   21h 40m

| Bright and Dark Nebulae | Open Star Clusters | Galaxies | Quasars |
| To scale   <10' | To scale   <5' | 10' x 5'   6' x 1'   3' x 2'   5' x 5'   4' x 2'   2' x 1' | |
| Planetary Nebulae | Globular Clusters | | Galaxy Clusters |
| >100"   100"−30"   <30" | To scale   <5' | Plotted to scale if the major axis >2', and circular when face on or the position angle is uncertain | |

1502

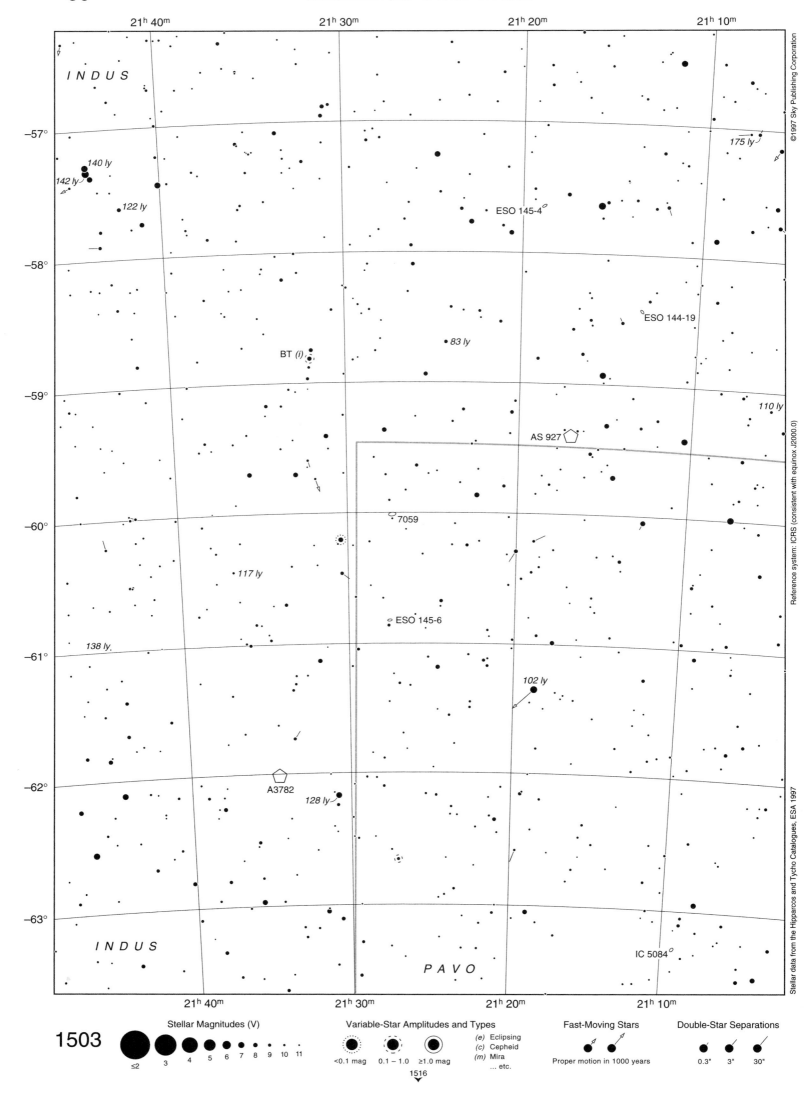

I N D U S

21ʰ 40ᵐ      21ʰ 30ᵐ      21ʰ 20ᵐ      21ʰ 10ᵐ

−57°

175 ly

140 ly
142 ly
122 ly

ESO 145-4

−58°

ESO 144-19

83 ly

BT (i)

−59°

110 ly

AS 927

7059

−60°

117 ly

ESO 145-6

138 ly

102 ly

−61°

A3782

−62°

128 ly

I N D U S

IC 5084

−63°

P A V O

21ʰ 40ᵐ      21ʰ 30ᵐ      21ʰ 20ᵐ      21ʰ 10ᵐ

1503

Stellar Magnitudes (V)

≤2   3   4   5   6   7   8   9  10  11

Variable-Star Amplitudes and Types

<0.1 mag   0.1 – 1.0   ≥1.0 mag

(e) Eclipsing
(c) Cepheid
(m) Mira
... etc.

Fast-Moving Stars

Proper motion in 1000 years

Double-Star Separations

0.3"   3"   30"

1516

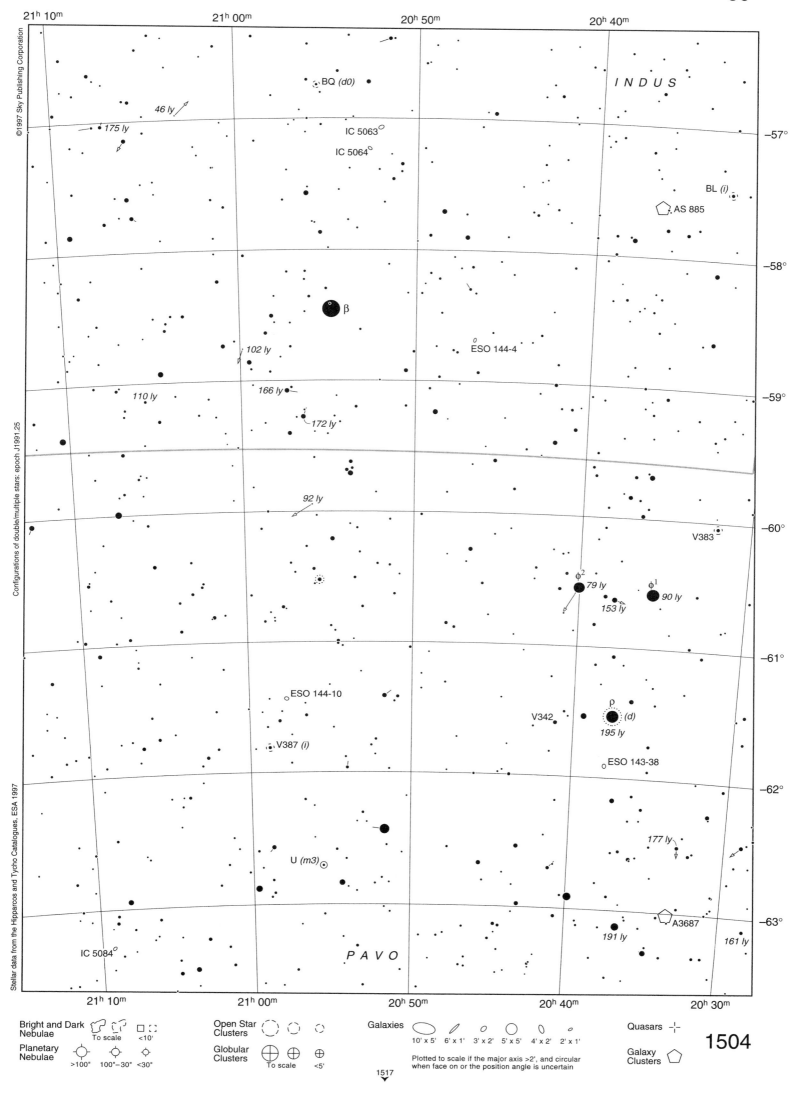

21h 10m · 21h 00m · 20h 50m · 20h 40m

I N D U S

BQ (d0)

46 ly

175 ly

IC 5063

IC 5064

BL (i)

AS 885

−57°

−58°

β

102 ly

ESO 144-4

110 ly

166 ly

172 ly

92 ly

−59°

−60°

V383

φ² 79 ly

153 ly

φ¹ 90 ly

−61°

ESO 144-10

ρ

V342

(d)

195 ly

V387 (i)

ESO 143-38

−62°

177 ly

U (m3)

A3687

191 ly

161 ly

−63°

IC 5084

P A V O

21h 10m · 21h 00m · 20h 50m · 20h 40m · 20h 30m

Bright and Dark Nebulae | To scale | <10'
Planetary Nebulae | >100" | 100"−30" | <30'

Open Star Clusters
Globular Clusters | To scale | <5'

Galaxies | 10' x 5' | 6' x 1' | 3' x 2' | 5' x 5' | 4' x 2' | 2' x 1'
Plotted to scale if the major axis >2', and circular when face on or the position angle is uncertain

Quasars
Galaxy Clusters

**1504**

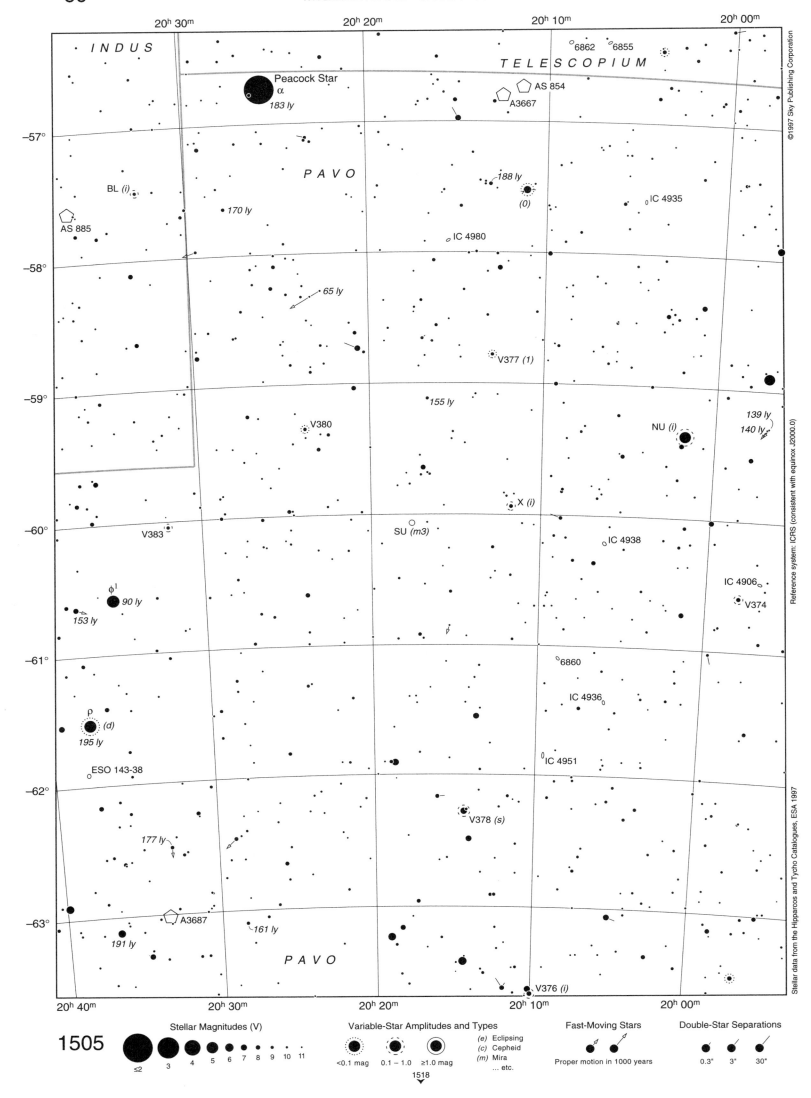

20ʰ 30ᵐ　　　　　　20ʰ 20ᵐ　　　　　　20ʰ 10ᵐ　　　　　　20ʰ 00ᵐ

I N D U S

T E L E S C O P I U M

°6862  °6855

Peacock Star
α
*183 ly*

AS 854
A3667

°IC 4935

P A V O

BL *(i)*

*188 ly*
*(0)*

*170 ly*

AS 885

°IC 4980

−57°

−58°

*65 ly*

V377 *(1)*

*155 ly*

−59°

V380

NU *(i)*

*139 ly*
*140 ly*

X *(i)*

V383

SU *(m3)*

−60°

IC 4938

IC 4906°
V374

φ¹  *90 ly*

*153 ly*

°6860

−61°

IC 4936°

ρ
*(d)*
*195 ly*

°IC 4951

°ESO 143-38

−62°

V378 *(s)*

*177 ly*

A3687

*161 ly*

*191 ly*

P A V O

−63°

V376 *(i)*

20ʰ 40ᵐ　　　　　　20ʰ 30ᵐ　　　　　　20ʰ 20ᵐ　　　　　　20ʰ 10ᵐ　　　　　　20ʰ 00ᵐ

Stellar Magnitudes (V)

≤2　3　4　5　6　7　8　9　10　11

Variable-Star Amplitudes and Types

<0.1 mag　0.1 − 1.0　≥1.0 mag

*(e)* Eclipsing
*(c)* Cepheid
*(m)* Mira
... etc.

Fast-Moving Stars

Proper motion in 1000 years

Double-Star Separations

0.3"　3"　30"

1505

# MILLENNIUM STAR ATLAS

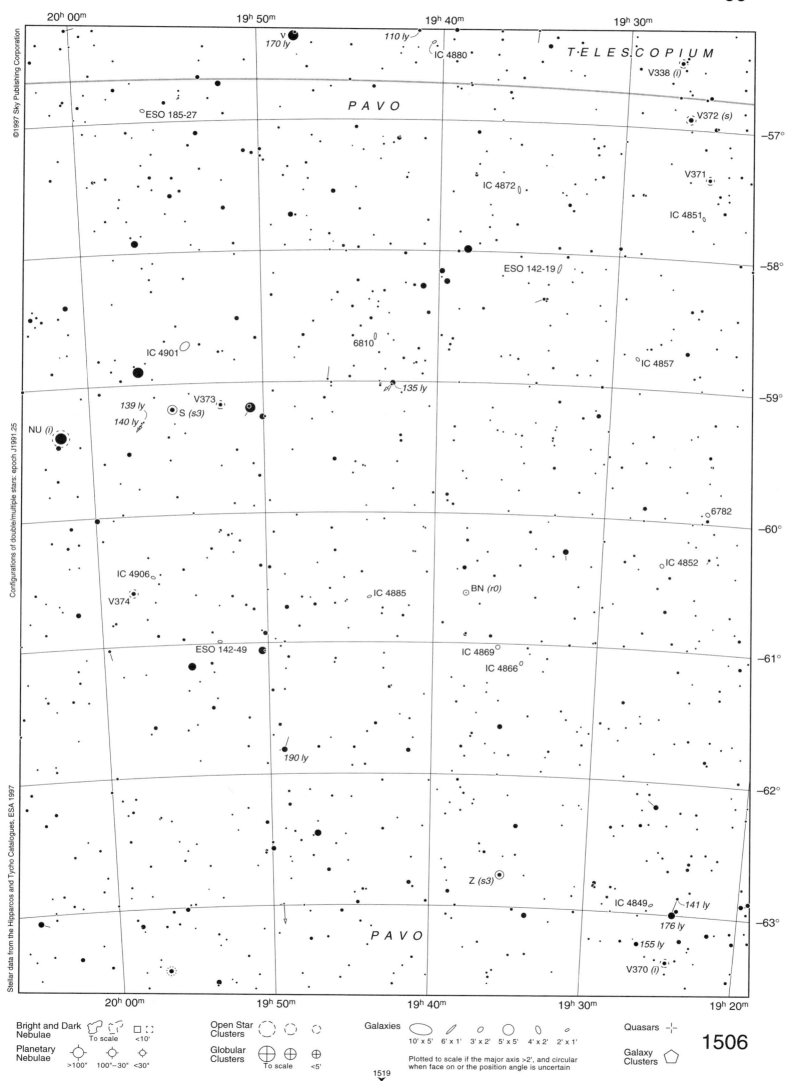

20ʰ 00ᵐ   19ʰ 50ᵐ   19ʰ 40ᵐ   19ʰ 30ᵐ

*TELESCOPIUM*

V
170 ly
110 ly
IC 4880
V338 (i)

*PAVO*

ESO 185-27
V372 (s)

−57°

IC 4872
V371

IC 4851

−58°

IC 4872

ESO 142-19

6810

ESO 185-27

IC 4901
IC 4857

−59°

139 ly
V373
140 ly
S (s3)
135 ly

NU (i)

6782

−60°

IC 4906
IC 4852

V374
IC 4885
BN (r0)

ESO 142-49
IC 4869
IC 4866

−61°

190 ly

−62°

Z (s3)

IC 4849
141 ly

176 ly

−63°

155 ly

*PAVO*

V370 (i)

20ʰ 00ᵐ   19ʰ 50ᵐ   19ʰ 40ᵐ   19ʰ 30ᵐ   19ʰ 20ᵐ

Bright and Dark Nebulae
To scale    <10'

Planetary Nebulae
>100"   100"−30"   <30"

Open Star Clusters

Globular Clusters
To scale    <5'

Galaxies
10' x 5'   6' x 1'   3' x 2'   5' x 5'   4' x 2'   2' x 1'

Plotted to scale if the major axis >2', and circular when face on or the position angle is uncertain

Quasars

Galaxy Clusters

**1506**

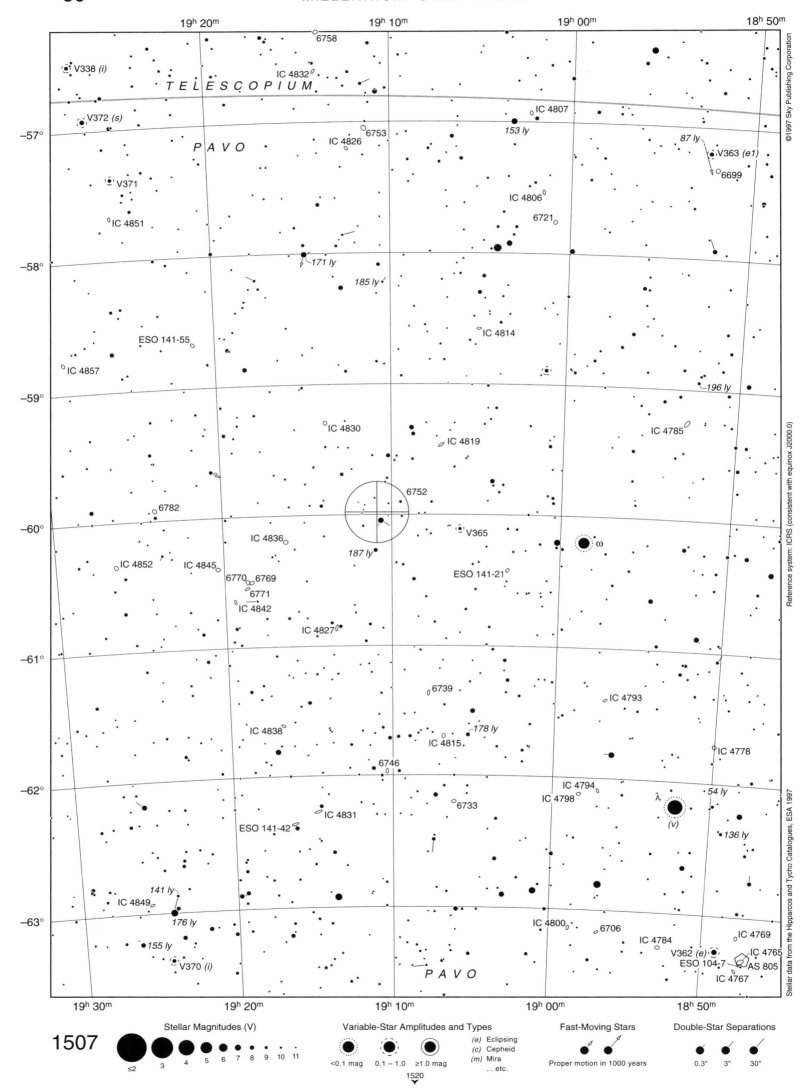

©1997 Sky Publishing Corporation

Reference system: ICRS (consistent with equinox J2000.0)

Stellar data from the Hipparcos and Tycho Catalogues, ESA 1997

1507

Stellar Magnitudes (V)
≤2  3  4  5  6  7  8  9  10  11

Variable-Star Amplitudes and Types
<0.1 mag   0.1 – 1.0   ≥1.0 mag
(e) Eclipsing
(c) Cepheid
(m) Mira
... etc.

Fast-Moving Stars
Proper motion in 1000 years

Double-Star Separations
0.3"  3"  30"

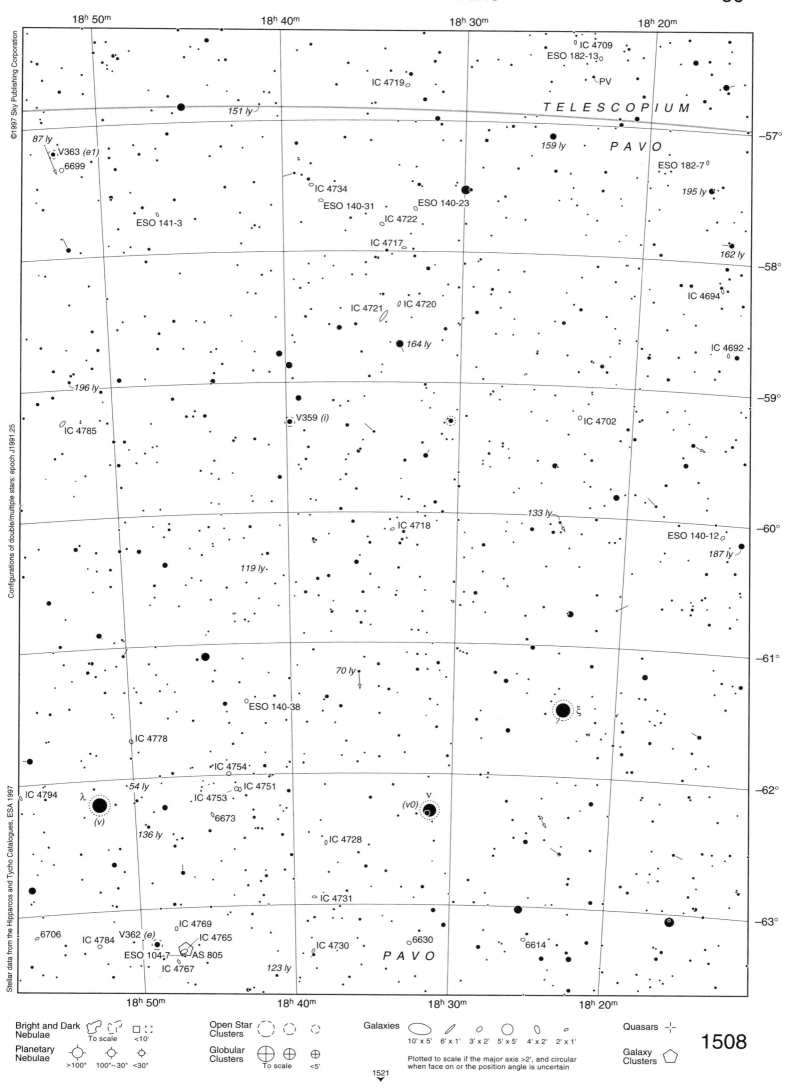

18ʰ 50ᵐ  18ʰ 40ᵐ  18ʰ 30ᵐ  18ʰ 20ᵐ

IC 4709
ESO 182-13
IC 4719
PV
TELESCOPIUM
151 ly
−57°
87 ly
V363 (e1)
6699
159 ly
PAVO
ESO 182-7
IC 4734
ESO 140-31
ESO 140-23
195 ly
ESO 141-3
IC 4722
IC 4717
162 ly
−58°
IC 4694
IC 4721
IC 4720
IC 4692
164 ly
196 ly
−59°
IC 4785
V359 (i)
IC 4702
133 ly
IC 4718
ESO 140-12
−60°
187 ly
119 ly
−61°
70 ly
ESO 140-38
ξ
IC 4778
IC 4754
−62°
IC 4794
λ
54 ly
IC 4751
ν
IC 4753
(v0)
(v)
6673
136 ly
IC 4728
IC 4731
−63°
6706
IC 4769
IC 4784
V362 (e)
IC 4765
6630
6614
ESO 104-7
AS 805
IC 4730
PAVO
IC 4767
123 ly

18ʰ 50ᵐ  18ʰ 40ᵐ  18ʰ 30ᵐ  18ʰ 20ᵐ

| Bright and Dark Nebulae | | | Open Star Clusters | | | Galaxies | | | | | | Quasars |
|---|---|---|---|---|---|---|---|---|---|---|---|---|
| To scale | <10' | | To scale | <10' | | 10' x 5' | 6' x 1' | 3' x 2' | 5' x 5' | 4' x 2' | 2' x 1' | |
| Planetary Nebulae | | | Globular Clusters | | | | | | | | | Galaxy Clusters |
| >100" | 100"–30" | <30" | To scale | <5' | | Plotted to scale if the major axis >2', and circular when face on or the position angle is uncertain | | | | | | |

**1508**

−60°

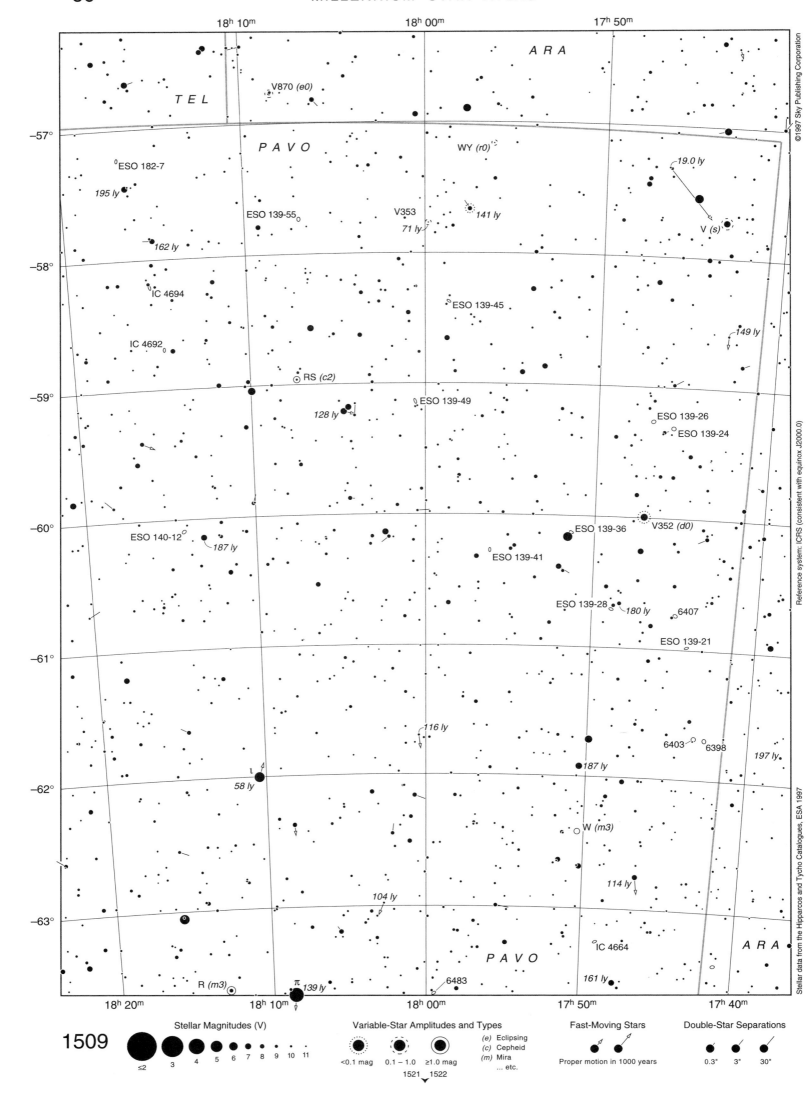

A R A

T E L

V870 (e0)

P A V O

WY (r0)

0 ESO 182-7

195 ly

V353

141 ly

19.0 ly

ESO 139-55

71 ly

V (s)

162 ly

IC 4694

ESO 139-45

149 ly

IC 4692 0

RS (c2)

128 ly

ESO 139-49

ESO 139-26

ESO 139-24

V352 (d0)

ESO 140-12

ESO 139-36

187 ly

0 ESO 139-41

ESO 139-28

180 ly

6407

ESO 139-21

116 ly

6403

6398

197 ly

ι

187 ly

58 ly

W (m3)

114 ly

104 ly

IC 4664

P A V O

A R A

R (m3)

π

6483

161 ly

139 ly

18h 20m        18h 10m        18h 00m        17h 50m        17h 40m

−57°

−58°

−59°

−60°

−61°

−62°

−63°

1509

Stellar Magnitudes (V)

≤2    3    4    5    6    7    8    9    10    11

Variable-Star Amplitudes and Types

<0.1 mag    0.1 – 1.0 mag    ≥1.0 mag

(e) Eclipsing
(c) Cepheid
(m) Mira
... etc.

Fast-Moving Stars

Proper motion in 1000 years

Double-Star Separations

0.3"    3"    30"

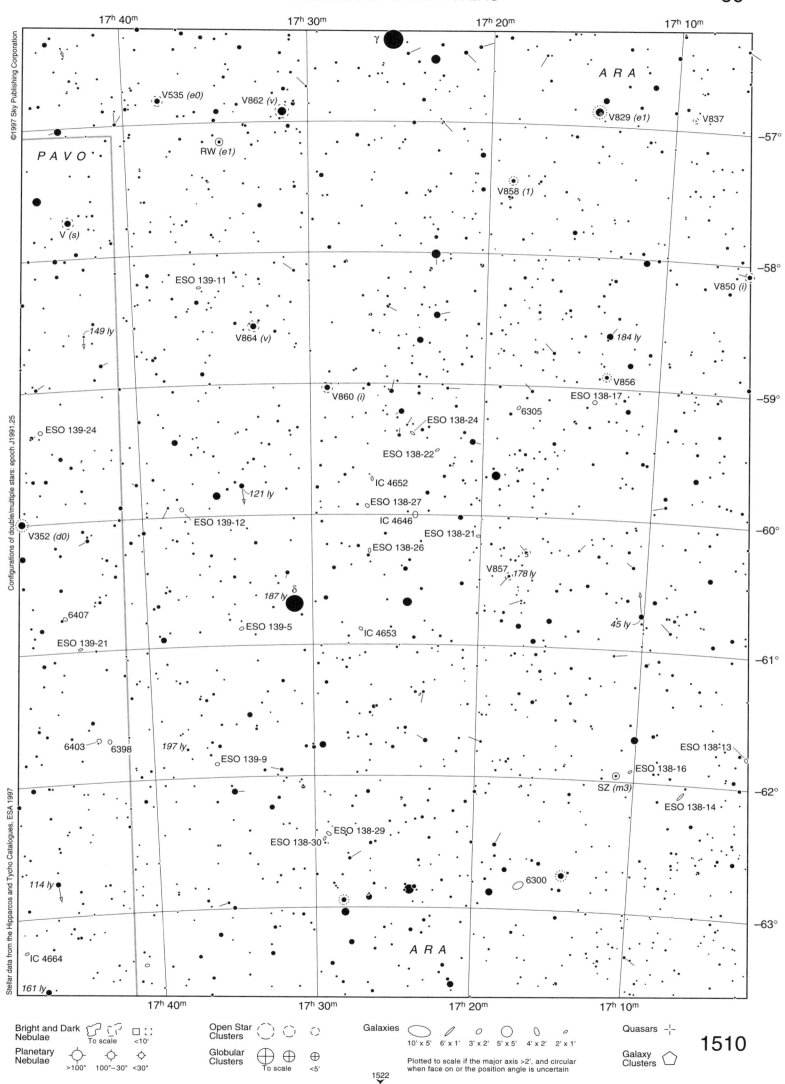

Configurations of double/multiple stars: epoch J1991.25

Stellar data from the Hipparcos and Tycho Catalogues, ESA 1997

17ʰ 40ᵐ     17ʰ 30ᵐ     17ʰ 20ᵐ     17ʰ 10ᵐ

γ

*A R A*

V535 *(e0)*     V862 *(v)*

V829 *(e1)*     V837

−57°

*P A V O*

RW *(e1)*

V858 *(1)*

V⁻ *(s)*

−58°

ESO 139-11

V864 *(v)*     149 ly

184 ly

V856

ESO 138-17

V860 *(i)*

ESO 138-24     6305

−59°

ESO 139-24

ESO 138-22

IC 4652

121 ly     ESO 138-27

ESO 139-12     IC 4646     ESO 138-21

V352 *(d0)*     ESO 138-26

V857     178 ly

6407     187 ly  δ

45 ly

ESO 139-5     IC 4653

ESO 139-21

−60°

6403     6398     197 ly

ESO 139-9     ESO 138-13

ESO 138-16

SZ *(m3)*

−61°

ESO 138-14

ESO 138-29

ESO 138-30

114 ly

6300

−62°

IC 4664

*A R A*

161 ly

−63°

17ʰ 40ᵐ     17ʰ 30ᵐ     17ʰ 20ᵐ     17ʰ 10ᵐ

−60°                    MILLENNIUM STAR ATLAS

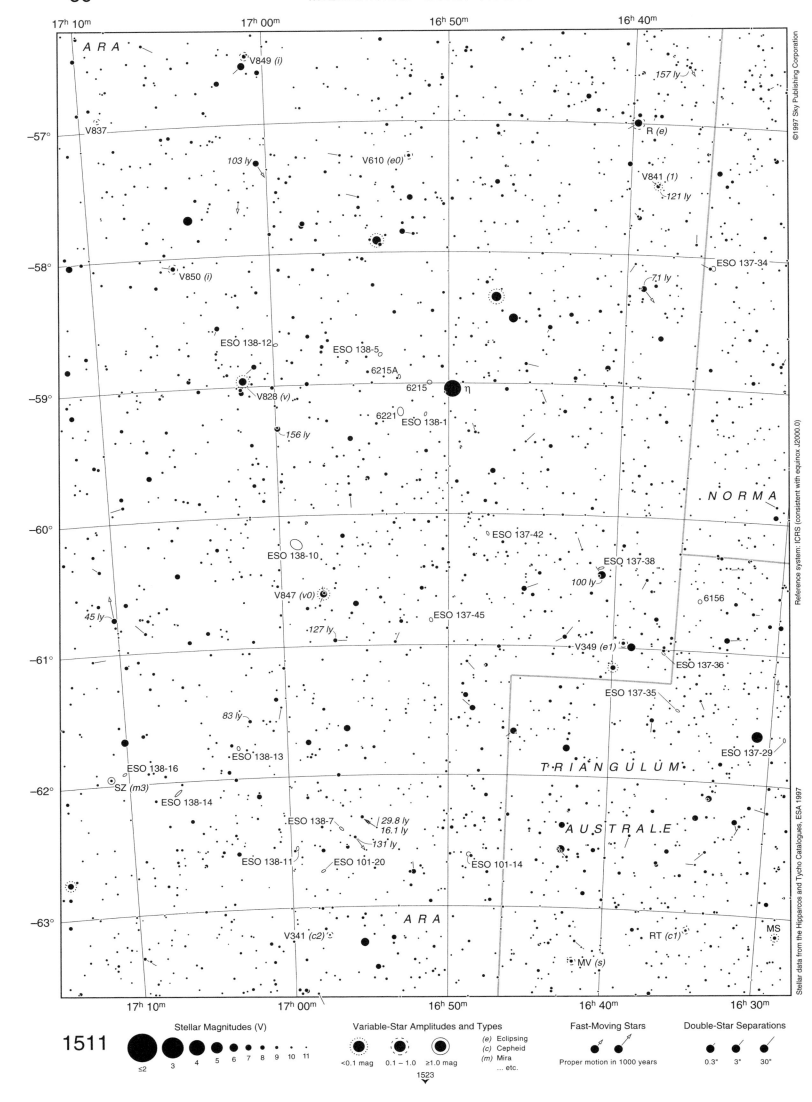

©1997 Sky Publishing Corporation

Reference system: ICRS (consistent with equinox J2000.0)

Stellar data from the Hipparcos and Tycho Catalogues, ESA 1997

1511

Stellar Magnitudes (V)
≤2  3  4  5  6  7  8  9  10  11

Variable-Star Amplitudes and Types
<0.1 mag   0.1 − 1.0   ≥1.0 mag

(e) Eclipsing
(c) Cepheid
(m) Mira
... etc.

Fast-Moving Stars
Proper motion in 1000 years

Double-Star Separations
0.3"   3"   30"

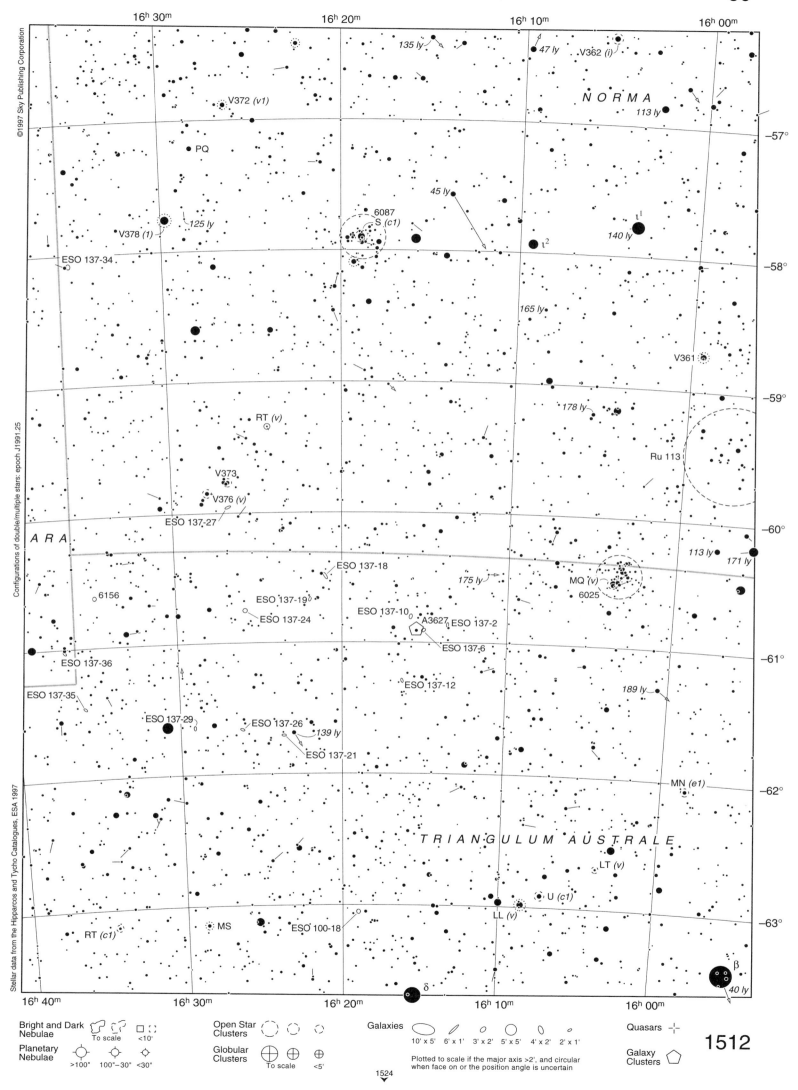

©1997 Sky Publishing Corporation

Configurations of double/multiple stars: epoch J1991.25

Stellar data from the Hipparcos and Tycho Catalogues, ESA 1997

16h 30m  16h 20m  16h 10m  16h 00m

135 ly
47 ly
V362 (i)
N O R M A
113 ly

−57°

V372 (v1)

PQ

45 ly
6087
S (c1)
ι¹
140 ly
V378 (1)
125 ly
ι²

ESO 137-34

−58°

165 ly

V361

RT (v)

178 ly

−59°

Ru 113

V373
V376 (v)
ESO 137-27

A R A

−60°

6156
ESO 137-18
175 ly
MQ (v)
6025
113 ly
171 ly

ESO 137-19
ESO 137-24
ESO 137-10
A3627  ESO 137-2
ESO 137-6

ESO 137-36

ESO 137-12
189 ly

ESO 137-35

−61°

ESO 137-29
ESO 137-26
139 ly
ESO 137-21

MN (e1)

−62°

T R I A N G U L U M   A U S T R A L E

LT (v)

U (c1)
LL (v)

−63°

RT (c1)
MS
ESO 100-18

δ
β
40 ly

16h 40m  16h 30m  16h 20m  16h 10m  16h 00m

Bright and Dark Nebulae — To scale — <10'
Open Star Clusters
Galaxies — 10' x 5'  6' x 1'  3' x 2'  5' x 5'  4' x 2'  2' x 1'
Quasars

Planetary Nebulae — >100"  100"–30"  <30'
Globular Clusters — To scale — <5'
Plotted to scale if the major axis >2', and circular when face on or the position angle is uncertain
Galaxy Clusters

## 1512

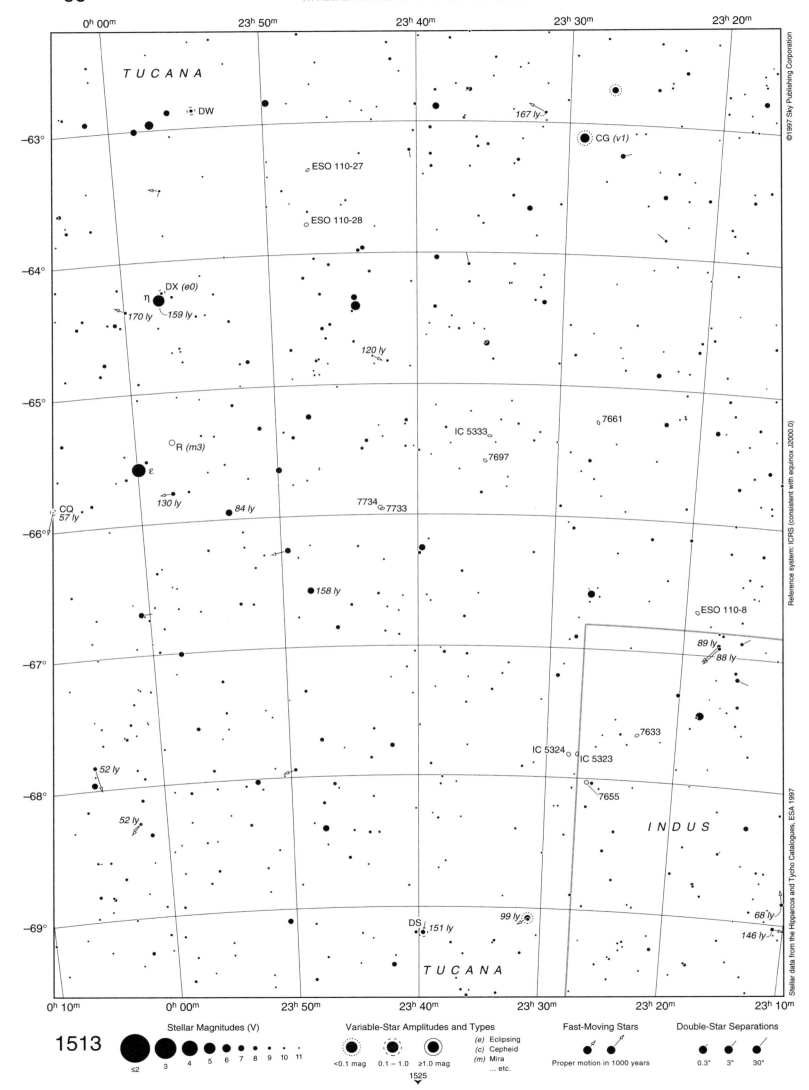

©1997 Sky Publishing Corporation

Reference system: ICRS (consistent with equinox J2000.0)

Stellar data from the Hipparcos and Tycho Catalogues, ESA 1997

T U C A N A

DW

ESO 110-27

ESO 110-28

167 ly

CG (v1)

DX (e0)

η

170 ly    159 ly

120 ly

R (m3)

ε

7661

IC 5333

7697

CQ
57 ly

130 ly

84 ly

7734  7733

158 ly

ESO 110-8

89 ly

88 ly

7633

IC 5324    IC 5323

7655

52 ly

I N D U S

52 ly

99 ly

68 ly

DS    151 ly

146 ly

T U C A N A

| Stellar Magnitudes (V) | Variable-Star Amplitudes and Types | Fast-Moving Stars | Double-Star Separations |
|---|---|---|---|

≤2   3   4   5   6   7   8   9   10   11

<0.1 mag    0.1 – 1.0    ≥1.0 mag

(e) Eclipsing
(c) Cepheid
(m) Mira
... etc.

Proper motion in 1000 years

0.3"    3"    30"

1525

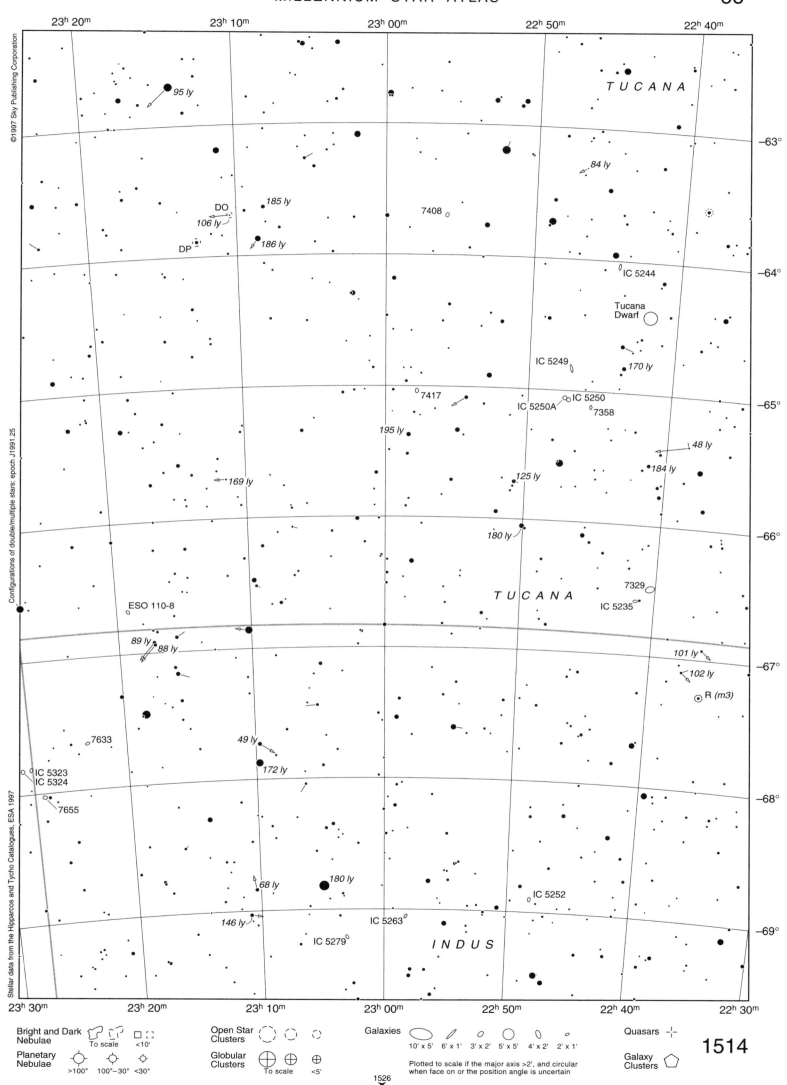

23h 20m   23h 10m   23h 00m   22h 50m   22h 40m

*T U C A N A*

95 ly

−63°

84 ly

DO
106 ly
185 ly

7408

DP
186 ly

IC 5244

−64°

Tucana
Dwarf

IC 5249
170 ly

7417
IC 5250
IC 5250A
7358

−65°

195 ly
48 ly
184 ly

169 ly
125 ly

180 ly

−66°

*T U C A N A*

7329
IC 5235

ESO 110-8

89 ly
88 ly
101 ly
102 ly

−67°

R (m3)

7633

49 ly

IC 5323
IC 5324

172 ly

7655

−68°

68 ly
180 ly

IC 5252

146 ly

IC 5263

IC 5279
*I N D U S*

−69°

23h 30m   23h 20m   23h 10m   23h 00m   22h 50m   22h 40m   22h 30m

Bright and Dark
Nebulae
To scale   <10'

Planetary
Nebulae
>100"   100"−30"   <30"

Open Star
Clusters

Globular
Clusters
To scale   <5'

Galaxies
10' x 5'   6' x 1'   3' x 2'   5' x 5'   4' x 2'   2' x 1'

Plotted to scale if the major axis >2', and circular
when face on or the position angle is uncertain

Quasars

Galaxy
Clusters

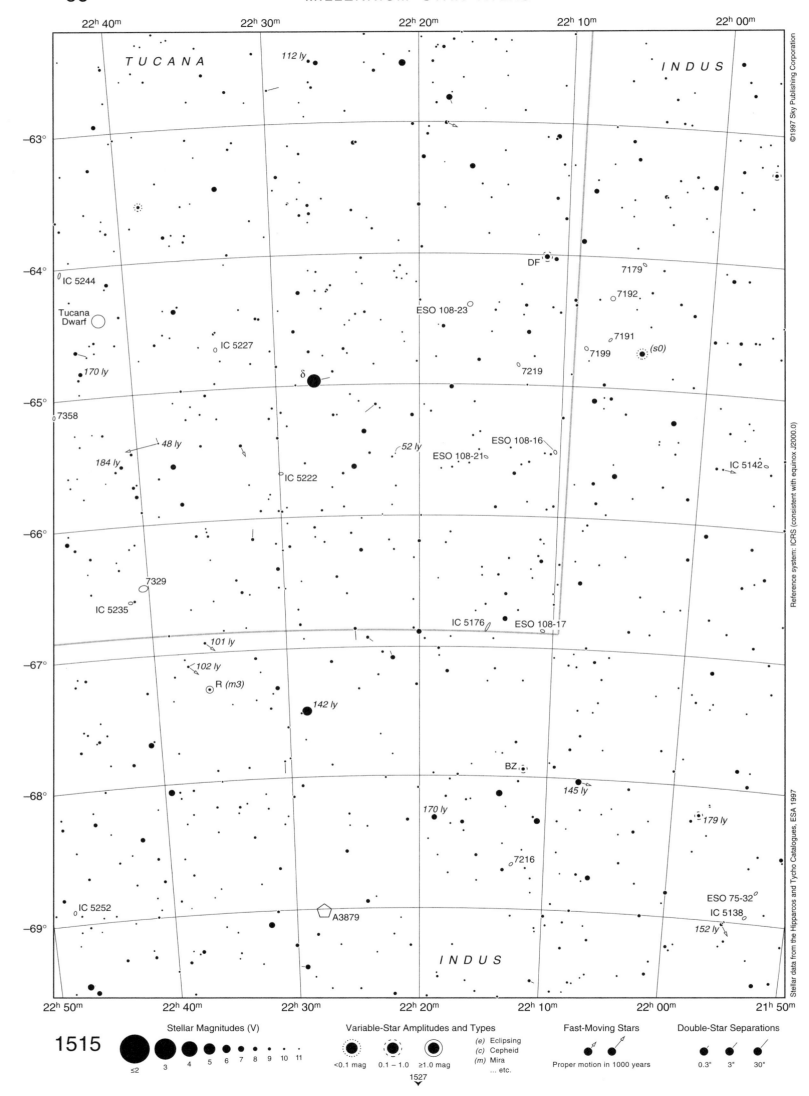

TUCANA

INDUS

112 ly

IC 5244

Tucana
Dwarf

170 ly

IC 5227

δ

7358

48 ly

184 ly

IC 5222

ESO 108-23

7179

7192

7191

7199        (s0)

7219

DF

ESO 108-16

ESO 108-21

52 ly

IC 5142

7329

IC 5235

IC 5176

ESO 108-17

101 ly

102 ly

R (m3)

142 ly

BZ

145 ly

170 ly

179 ly

7216

IC 5252

A3879

ESO 75-32

IC 5138

152 ly

INDUS

−63°
−64°
−65°
−66°
−67°
−68°
−69°

©1997 Sky Publishing Corporation

Reference system: ICRS (consistent with equinox J2000.0)

Stellar data from the Hipparcos and Tycho Catalogues, ESA 1997

1515

**Stellar Magnitudes (V)**

≤2   3   4   5   6   7   8   9   10   11

**Variable-Star Amplitudes and Types**

<0.1 mag   0.1 – 1.0   ≥1.0 mag

(e) Eclipsing
(c) Cepheid
(m) Mira
... etc.

1527

**Fast-Moving Stars**

Proper motion in 1000 years

**Double-Star Separations**

0.3"   3"   30"

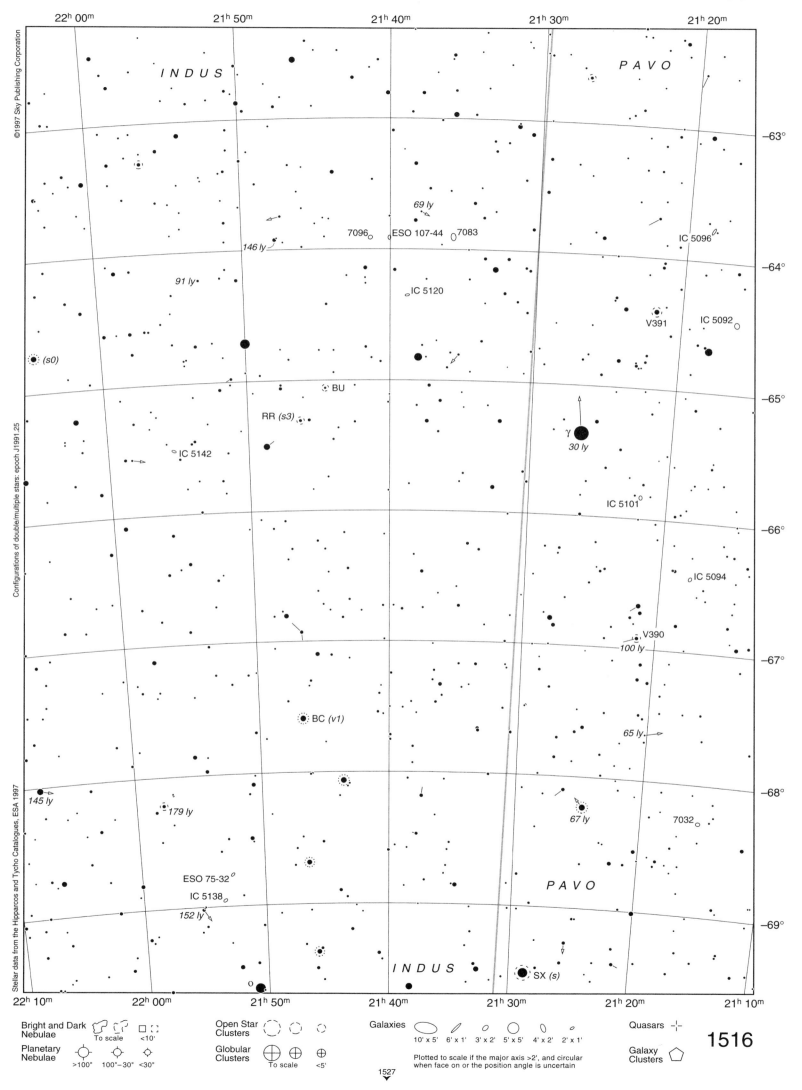

22h 00m   21h 50m   21h 40m   21h 30m   21h 20m

I N D U S

P A V O

© 1997 Sky Publishing Corporation

Configurations of double/multiple stars: epoch J1991.25

Stellar data from the Hipparcos and Tycho Catalogues, ESA 1997

−63°

69 ly

7096   ESO 107-44   7083

146 ly

IC 5096

−64°

91 ly

IC 5120

V391

IC 5092

(s0)

BU

−65°

RR (s3)

γ

30 ly

IC 5142

IC 5101

−66°

IC 5094

V390
100 ly

−67°

BC (v1)

65 ly

145 ly

−68°

179 ly

67 ly

7032

ESO 75-32

P A V O

IC 5138

152 ly

−69°

I N D U S

SX (s)

22h 10m   22h 00m   21h 50m   21h 40m   21h 30m   21h 20m   21h 10m

Bright and Dark Nebulae
To scale   <10'

Open Star Clusters

Galaxies
10' x 5'   6' x 1'   3' x 2'   5' x 5'   4' x 2'   2' x 1'

Quasars

1516

Planetary Nebulae
>100"   100"–30"   <30"

Globular Clusters
To scale   <5'

Plotted to scale if the major axis >2', and circular when face on or the position angle is uncertain

Galaxy Clusters

1527

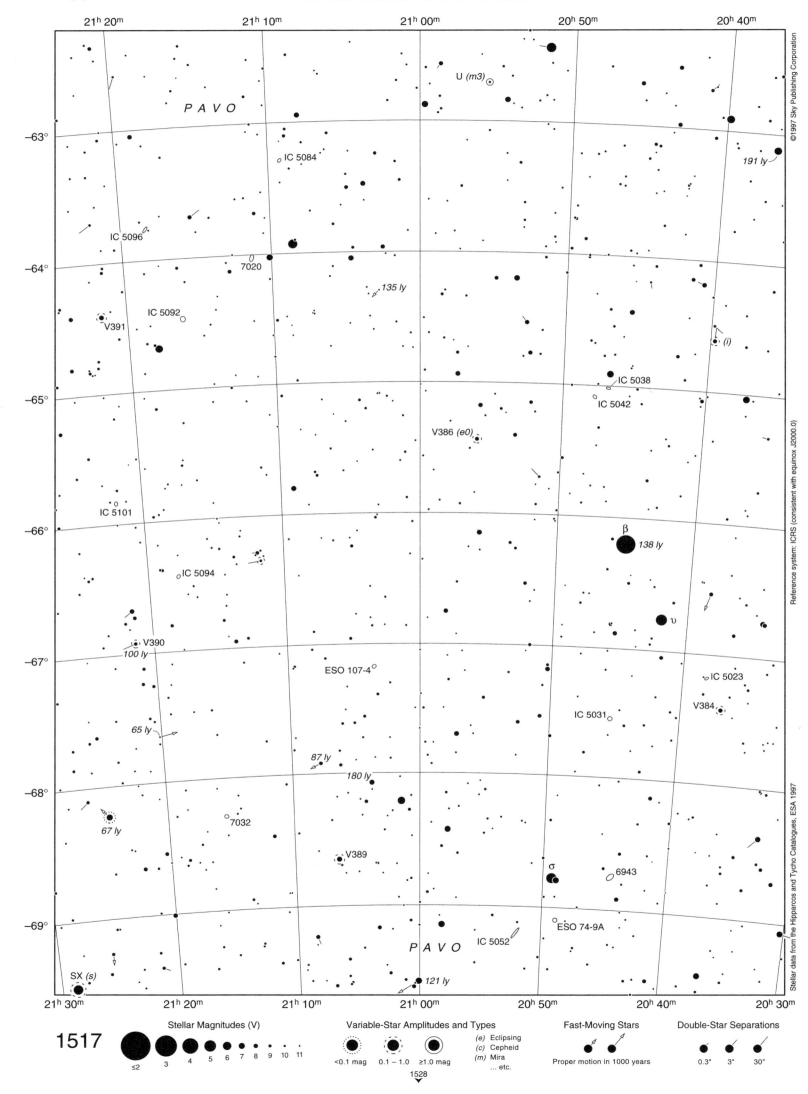

PAVO

IC 5084

IC 5096

7020

135 ly

V391　IC 5092

IC 5038
IC 5042

V386 (e0)

IC 5101

β　138 ly

IC 5094

υ

V390
100 ly

ESO 107-4

IC 5023

65 ly

IC 5031　V384

87 ly

180 ly

7032

67 ly

V389

σ　6943

ESO 74-9A

PAVO
IC 5052

SX (s)

121 ly

U (m3)

© 1997 Sky Publishing Corporation

Reference system: ICRS (consistent with equinox J2000.0)

Stellar data from the Hipparcos and Tycho Catalogues, ESA 1997

Stellar Magnitudes (V)

≤2　3　4　5　6　7　8　9　10　11

Variable-Star Amplitudes and Types

<0.1 mag　0.1 − 1.0　≥1.0 mag

(e) Eclipsing
(c) Cepheid
(m) Mira
... etc.

1528

Fast-Moving Stars

Proper motion in 1000 years

Double-Star Separations

0.3"　3"　30"

# MILLENNIUM STAR ATLAS

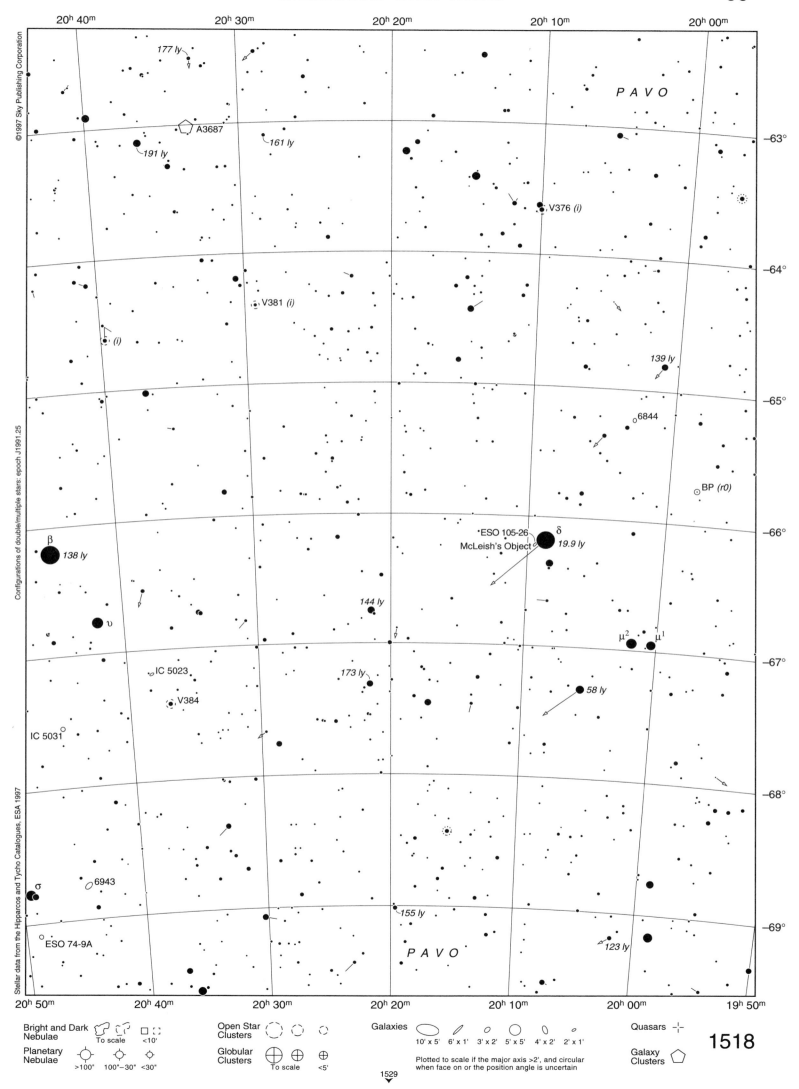

©1997 Sky Publishing Corporation

Configurations of double/multiple stars: epoch J1991.25

Stellar data from the Hipparcos and Tycho Catalogues, ESA 1997

20ʰ 40ᵐ  20ʰ 30ᵐ  20ʰ 20ᵐ  20ʰ 10ᵐ  20ʰ 00ᵐ

PAVO

177 ly

A3687

191 ly

161 ly

−63°

V376 (i)

−64°

V381 (i)

(i)

139 ly

−65°

6844

BP (r0)

β  138 ly

ESO 105-26  δ
McLeish's Object  19.9 ly

−66°

144 ly

υ

μ²  μ¹

−67°

IC 5023

173 ly

58 ly

V384

IC 5031

−68°

σ  6943

155 ly

−69°

ESO 74-9A

PAVO  123 ly

20ʰ 50ᵐ  20ʰ 40ᵐ  20ʰ 30ᵐ  20ʰ 20ᵐ  20ʰ 10ᵐ  20ʰ 00ᵐ  19ʰ 50ᵐ

| Bright and Dark Nebulae | | To scale | | <10' | | Open Star Clusters | To scale | | <5' | Galaxies | | | | | | Quasars |
|---|---|---|---|---|---|---|---|---|---|---|---|---|---|---|---|---|

Bright and Dark Nebulae  To scale  <10'

Planetary Nebulae  >100"  100"−30"  <30"

Open Star Clusters

Globular Clusters  To scale  <5'

Galaxies  10' x 5'  6' x 1'  3' x 2'  5' x 5'  4' x 2'  2' x 1'

Plotted to scale if the major axis >2', and circular when face on or the position angle is uncertain

Quasars

Galaxy Clusters

1518

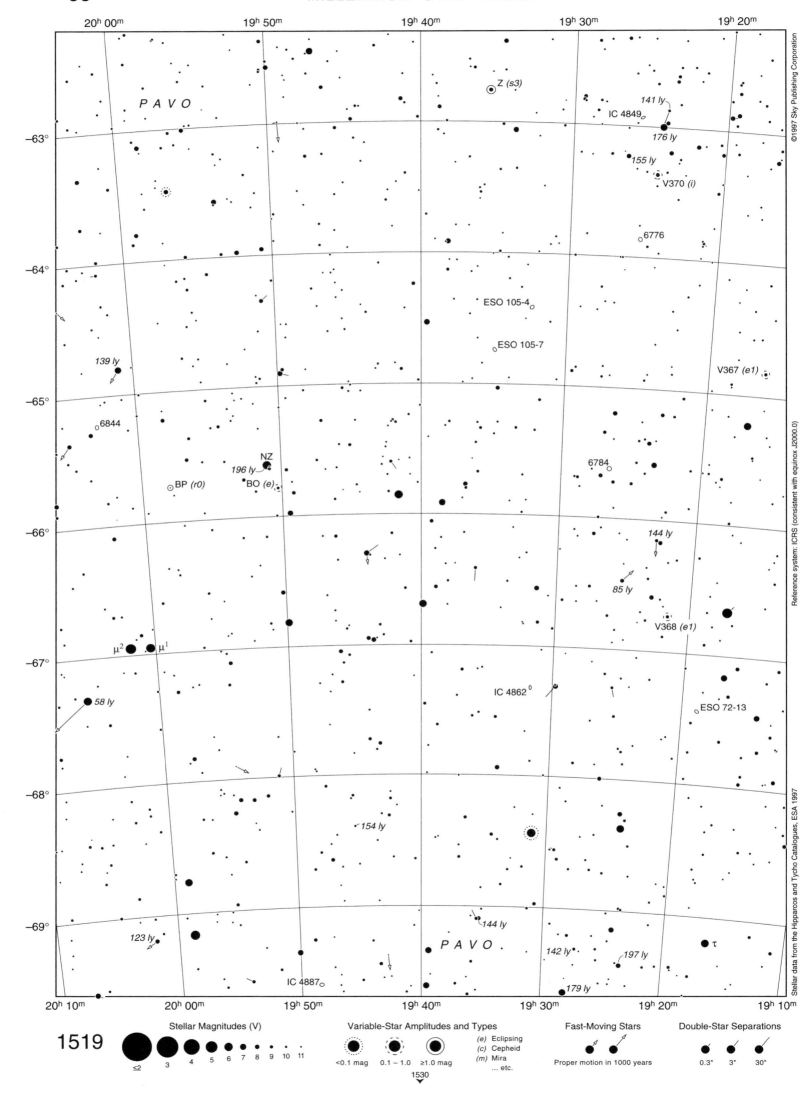

©1997 Sky Publishing Corporation

Reference system: ICRS (consistent with equinox J2000.0)

Stellar data from the Hipparcos and Tycho Catalogues, ESA 1997

PAVO

Z (s3)

141 ly
IC 4849
176 ly
155 ly
V370 (i)

6776

ESO 105-4

ESO 105-7

V367 (e1)

139 ly

6844

NZ
196 ly
BP (r0)
BO (e)

6784

144 ly

85 ly

V368 (e1)

μ² μ¹

IC 4862

ESO 72-13

58 ly

154 ly

144 ly

PAVO

142 ly
197 ly
τ

123 ly

179 ly

IC 4887

1519

Stellar Magnitudes (V)

≤2  3  4  5  6  7  8  9  10  11

Variable-Star Amplitudes and Types

<0.1 mag    0.1 – 1.0    ≥1.0 mag

(e) Eclipsing
(c) Cepheid
(m) Mira
... etc.

1530

Fast-Moving Stars

Proper motion in 1000 years

Double-Star Separations

0.3"  3"  30"

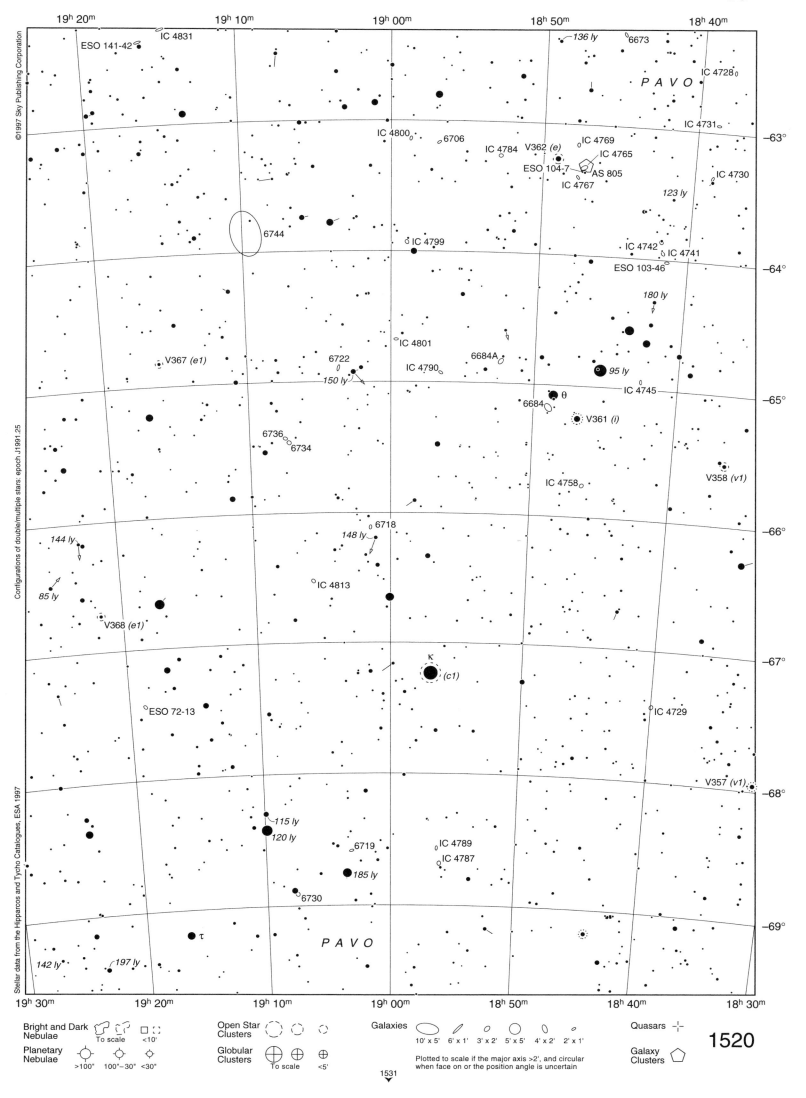

19h 20m     19h 10m     19h 00m     18h 50m     18h 40m

−63°
−64°
−65°
−66°
−67°
−68°
−69°

19h 30m     19h 20m     19h 10m     19h 00m     18h 50m     18h 40m     18h 30m

ESO 141-42   IC 4831

136 ly   6673

P A V O

IC 4728

IC 4731

IC 4800   6706   IC 4784   V362 (e)   IC 4769   IC 4765
ESO 104-7   AS 805   IC 4767
IC 4730
123 ly

6744   IC 4799   IC 4742   IC 4741
ESO 103-46

180 ly

V367 (e1)   6722   IC 4801   6684A   95 ly
150 ly   IC 4790   IC 4745
6684   θ
V361 (i)
6736   6734
V358 (v1)
IC 4758

6718
144 ly   148 ly
IC 4813
85 ly
V368 (e1)
κ
(c1)
ESO 72-13   IC 4729

V357 (v1)

115 ly
120 ly   6719   IC 4789
IC 4787
185 ly
6730

τ
P A V O
142 ly   197 ly

Bright and Dark Nebulae
To scale   <10'

Open Star Clusters

Galaxies   10' x 5'   6' x 1'   3' x 2'   5' x 5'   4' x 2'   2' x 1'

Quasars

Planetary Nebulae   >100"   100"−30"   <30"

Globular Clusters   To scale   <5'

Plotted to scale if the major axis >2', and circular when face on or the position angle is uncertain

Galaxy Clusters

1520

1531

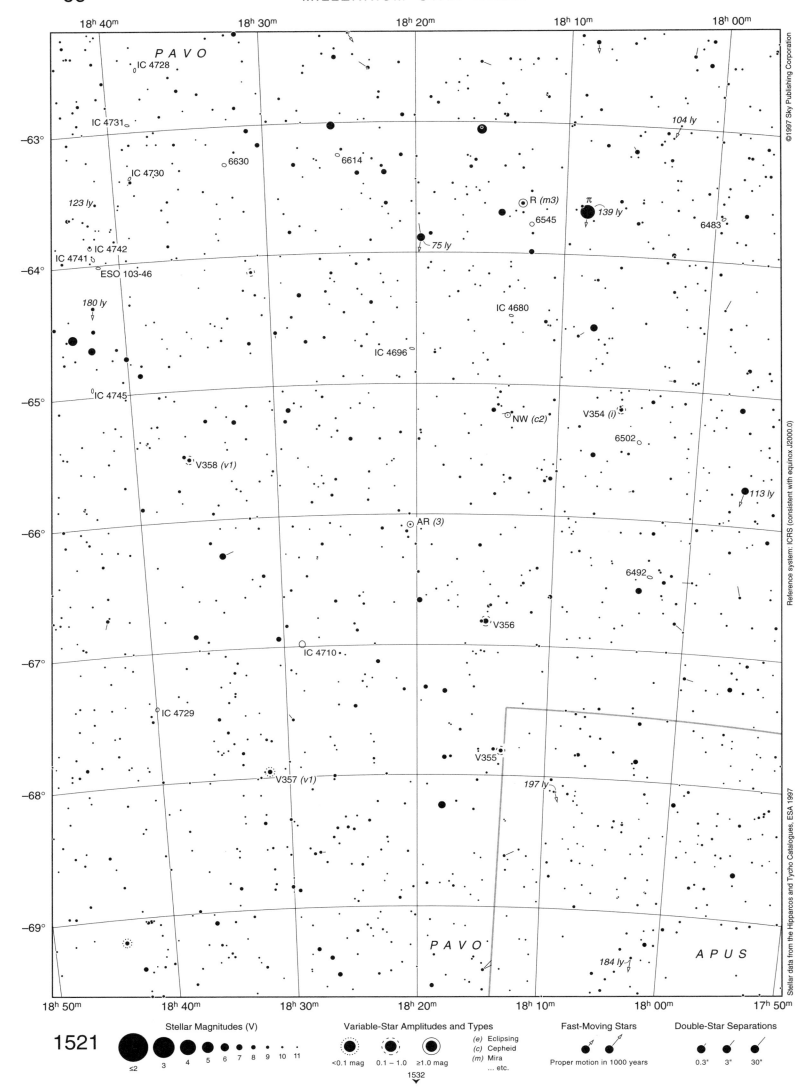

©1997 Sky Publishing Corporation

Reference system: ICRS (consistent with equinox J2000.0)

Stellar data from the Hipparcos and Tycho Catalogues, ESA 1997

PAVO

IC 4728
IC 4731
IC 4730
123 ly
IC 4742
IC 4741
ESO 103-46
180 ly
IC 4745
V358 (v1)
IC 4729

6630
6614

R (m3)
6545
π
139 ly
104 ly
6483
75 ly

IC 4680
IC 4696

NW (c2)
V354 (i)
6502
113 ly

AR (3)
6492
V356
IC 4710

V355
197 ly

V357 (v1)

PAVO
184 ly
APUS

18ʰ 40ᵐ   18ʰ 30ᵐ   18ʰ 20ᵐ   18ʰ 10ᵐ   18ʰ 00ᵐ

−63°
−64°
−65°
−66°
−67°
−68°
−69°

18ʰ 50ᵐ   18ʰ 40ᵐ   18ʰ 30ᵐ   18ʰ 20ᵐ   18ʰ 10ᵐ   18ʰ 00ᵐ   17ʰ 50ᵐ

1521

Stellar Magnitudes (V)

≤2   3   4   5   6   7   8   9   10   11

Variable-Star Amplitudes and Types

<0.1 mag   0.1 – 1.0   ≥1.0 mag

(e) Eclipsing
(c) Cepheid
(m) Mira
... etc.

Fast-Moving Stars

Proper motion in 1000 years

Double-Star Separations

0.3"   3"   30"

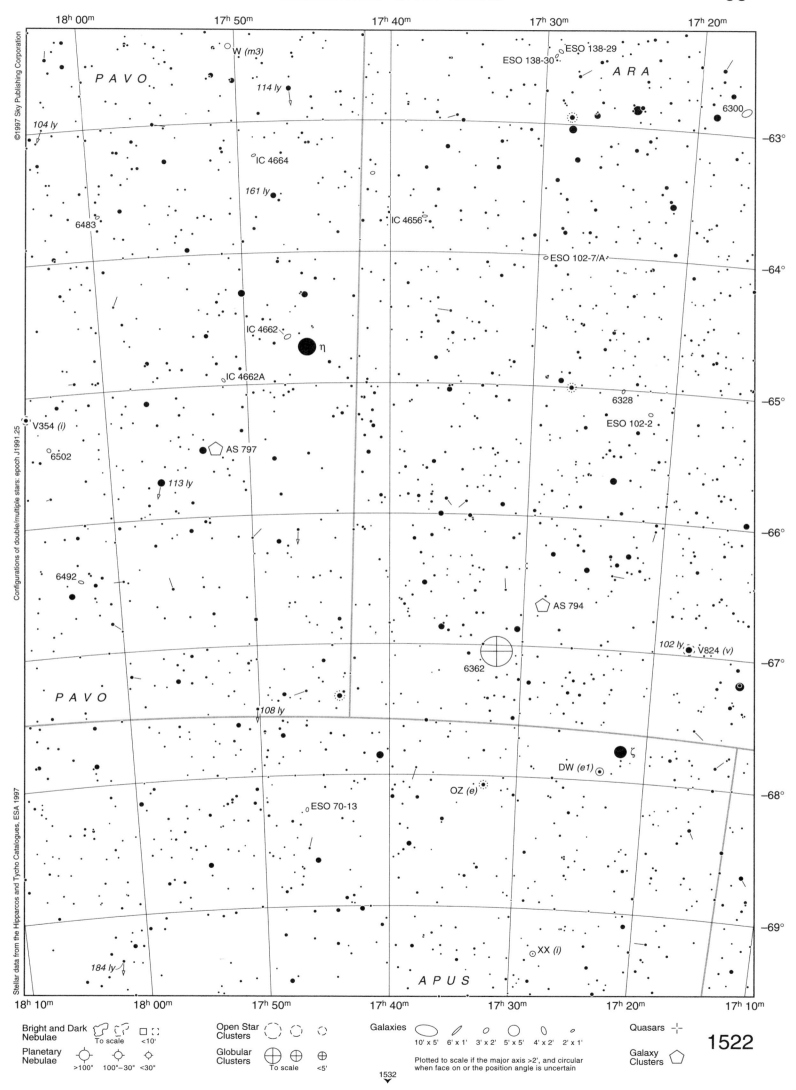

18h 00m
17h 50m
17h 40m
17h 30m
17h 20m

W (m3)
PAVO
114 ly
ARA
ESO 138-29
ESO 138-30
6300

−63°
104 ly
IC 4664
161 ly
6483
IC 4656
ESO 102-7/A
−64°
IC 4662
η
ESO 102-2
IC 4662A
6328
−65°
V354 (i)
6502
AS 797
ESO 102-2
113 ly
−66°
6492
AS 794
102 ly V824 (v)
6362
−67°
PAVO
108 ly
ζ
DW (e1)
OZ (e)
−68°
ESO 70-13
−69°
184 ly
XX (i)
APUS

18h 10m
18h 00m
17h 50m
17h 40m
17h 30m
17h 20m
17h 10m

Bright and Dark
Nebulae
To scale
<10'

Planetary
Nebulae
>100"  100"–30"  <30"

Open Star
Clusters

Globular
Clusters
To scale
<5'

Galaxies
10' x 5'   6' x 1'   3' x 2'   5' x 5'   4' x 2'   2' x 1'

Plotted to scale if the major axis >2', and circular
when face on or the position angle is uncertain

Quasars

Galaxy
Clusters

1522

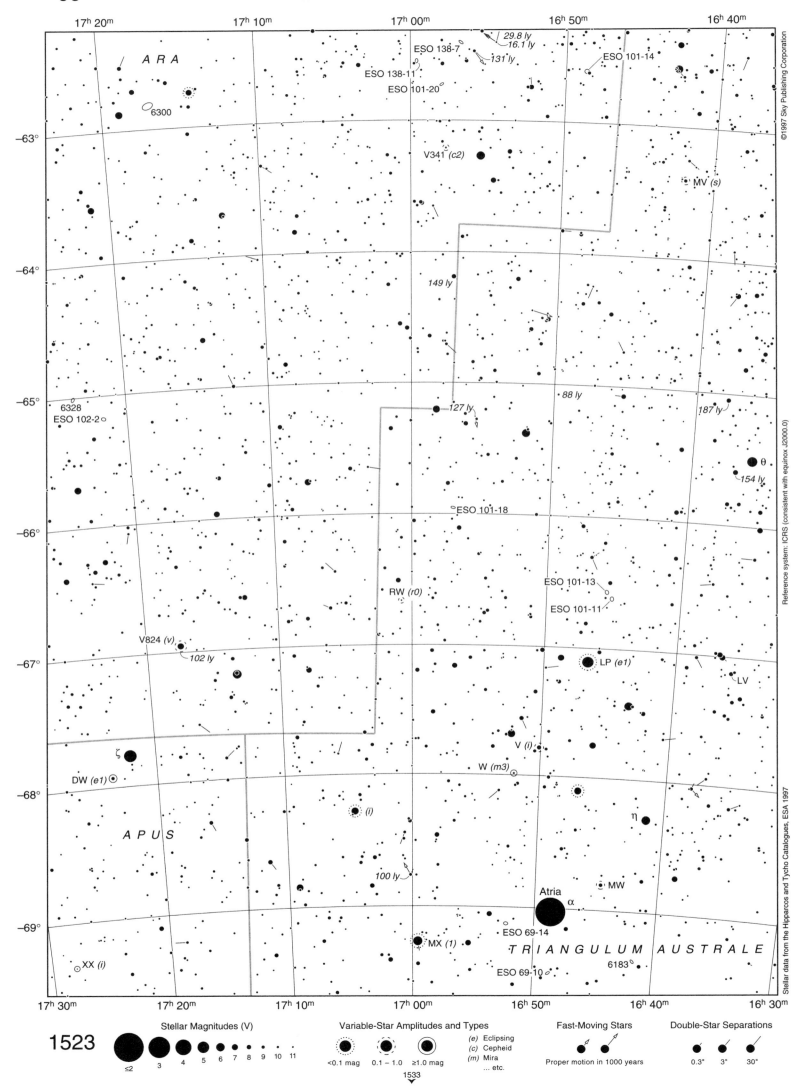

©1997 Sky Publishing Corporation

Reference system: ICRS (consistent with equinox J2000.0)

Stellar data from the Hipparcos and Tycho Catalogues, ESA 1997

**1523**

Stellar Magnitudes (V)

≤2  3  4  5  6  7  8  9  10  11

Variable-Star Amplitudes and Types

<0.1 mag   0.1 – 1.0   ≥1.0 mag

(e) Eclipsing
(c) Cepheid
(m) Mira
… etc.

Fast-Moving Stars

Proper motion in 1000 years

Double-Star Separations

0.3"   3"   30"

1533

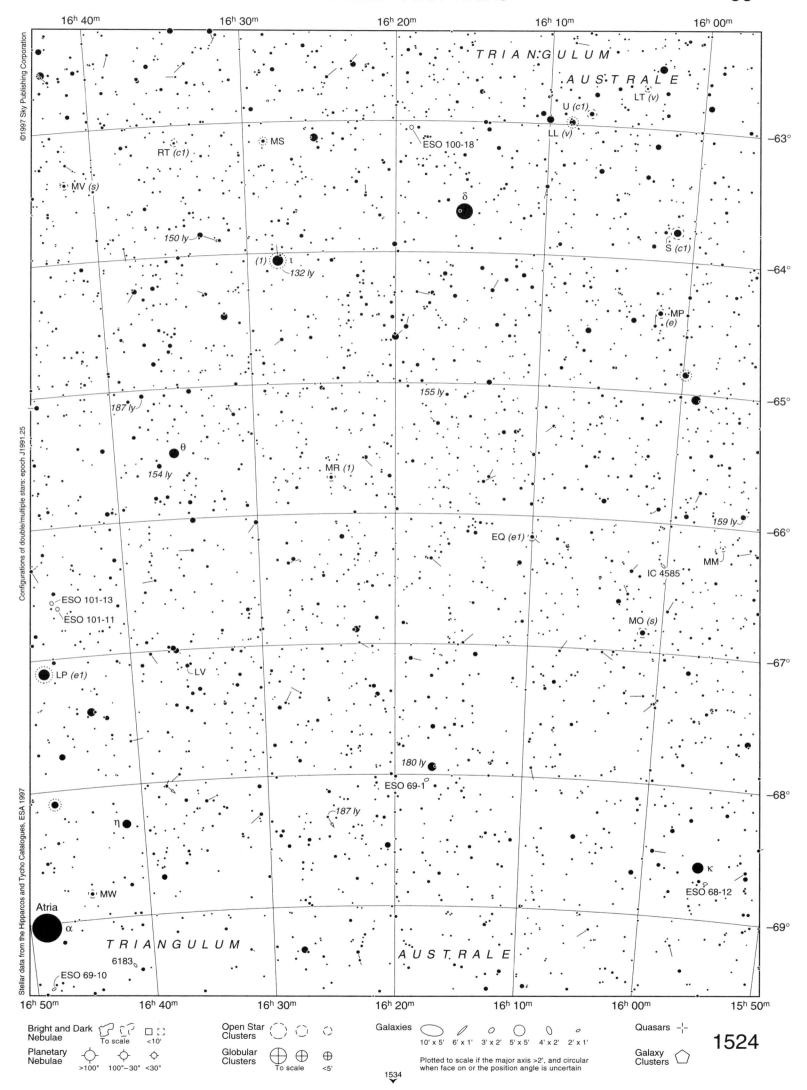

16ʰ 40ᵐ  16ʰ 30ᵐ  16ʰ 20ᵐ  16ʰ 10ᵐ  16ʰ 00ᵐ

−63°
−64°
−65°
−66°
−67°
−68°
−69°

16ʰ 50ᵐ  16ʰ 40ᵐ  16ʰ 30ᵐ  16ʰ 20ᵐ  16ʰ 10ᵐ  16ʰ 00ᵐ  15ʰ 50ᵐ

*TRIANGULUM*
*AUSTRALE*
LT (v)
U (c1)
LL (v)
ESO 100-18
MS
RT (c1)
δ
MV (s)
S (c1)
150 ly
(1) ι
132 ly
MP (e)
187 ly
155 ly
159 ly
θ
154 ly
MR (1)
EQ (e1)
MM
IC 4585
ESO 101-13
ESO 101-11
MO (s)
LP (e1)
LV
180 ly
ESO 69-1
187 ly
η
κ
MW
ESO 68-12
Atria
α
*TRIANGULUM*
*AUSTRALE*
6183
ESO 69-10

Bright and Dark Nebulae
To scale    <10'

Planetary Nebulae
>100"  100"−30"  <30"

Open Star Clusters

Globular Clusters
To scale    <5'

Galaxies
10' x 5'  6' x 1'  3' x 2'  5' x 5'  4' x 2'  2' x 1'

Plotted to scale if the major axis >2', and circular when face on or the position angle is uncertain

Quasars

Galaxy Clusters

1524

1513

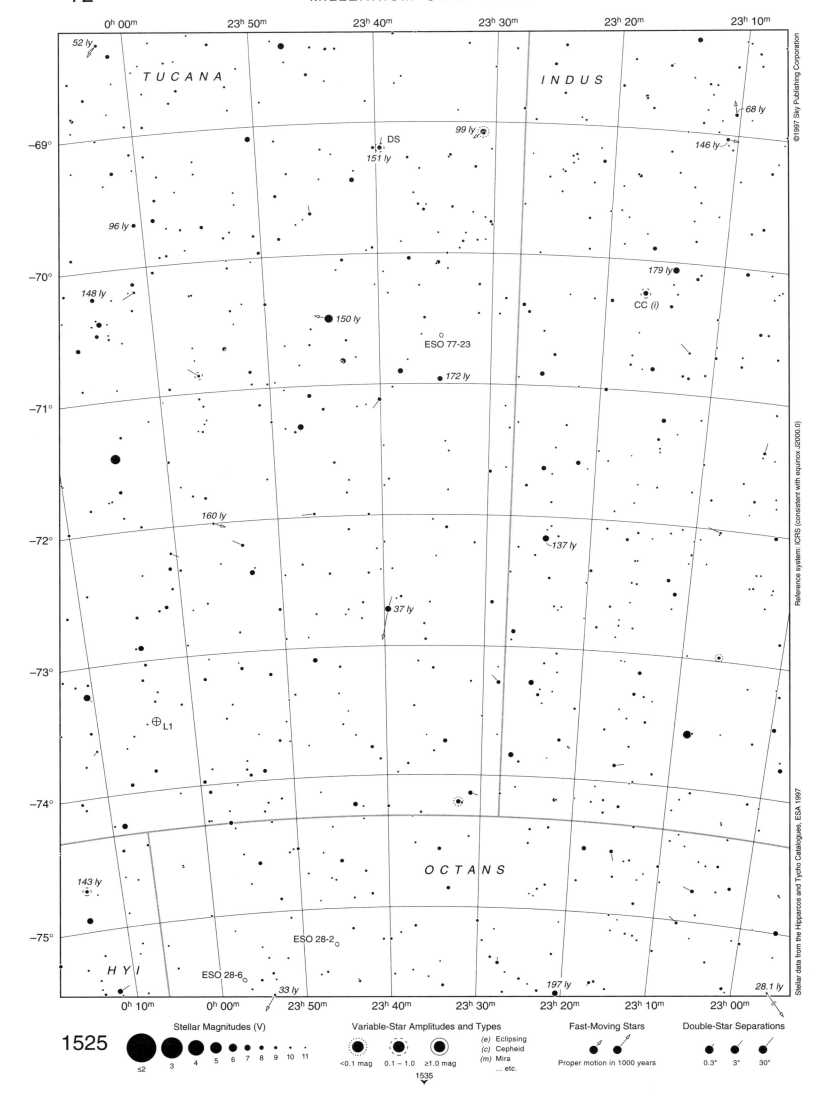

©1997 Sky Publishing Corporation

Reference system: ICRS (consistent with equinox J2000.0)

Stellar data from the Hipparcos and Tycho Catalogues, ESA 1997

52 ly

*T U C A N A*

*I N D U S*

68 ly

99 ly

146 ly

DS

151 ly

96 ly

179 ly

148 ly

CC (i)

150 ly

ESO 77-23

172 ly

160 ly

137 ly

37 ly

⊕ L1

143 ly

*O C T A N S*

ESO 28-2

ESO 28-6

33 ly

197 ly

28.1 ly

*H Y I*

-69°

-70°

-71°

-72°

-73°

-74°

-75°

0ʰ 00ᵐ   23ʰ 50ᵐ   23ʰ 40ᵐ   23ʰ 30ᵐ   23ʰ 20ᵐ   23ʰ 10ᵐ

0ʰ 10ᵐ   0ʰ 00ᵐ   23ʰ 50ᵐ   23ʰ 40ᵐ   23ʰ 30ᵐ   23ʰ 20ᵐ   23ʰ 00ᵐ

1525

Stellar Magnitudes (V)

≤2   3   4   5   6   7   8   9   10   11

Variable-Star Amplitudes and Types

<0.1 mag   0.1 – 1.0   ≥1.0 mag

(e) Eclipsing
(c) Cepheid
(m) Mira
... etc.

Fast-Moving Stars

Proper motion in 1000 years

Double-Star Separations

0.3"   3"   30"

1535

# MILLENNIUM STAR ATLAS

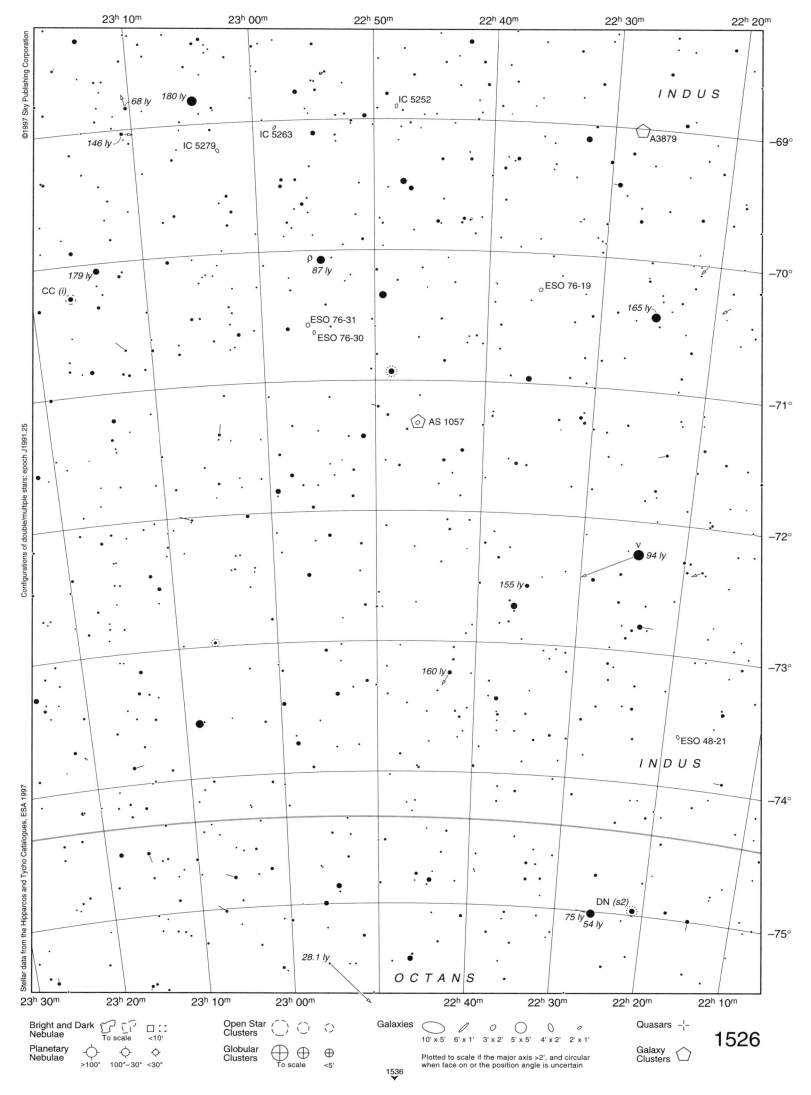

I N D U S

IC 5252

A3879

IC 5263

IC 5279

ρ
87 ly

ESO 76-19

CC (i)

179 ly

165 ly

ESO 76-31
ESO 76-30

AS 1057

ν
94 ly

155 ly

160 ly

ESO 48-21

I N D U S

DN (s2)

75 ly
54 ly

28.1 ly

O C T A N S

68 ly    180 ly

146 ly

**Bright and Dark Nebulae**  To scale  <10'

**Planetary Nebulae**  >100"  100"−30"  <30"

**Open Star Clusters**  To scale

**Globular Clusters**  To scale  <5'

**Galaxies**  10' x 5'  6' x 1'  3' x 2'  5' x 5'  4' x 2'  2' x 1'
Plotted to scale if the major axis >2', and circular when face on or the position angle is uncertain

**Quasars**

**Galaxy Clusters**

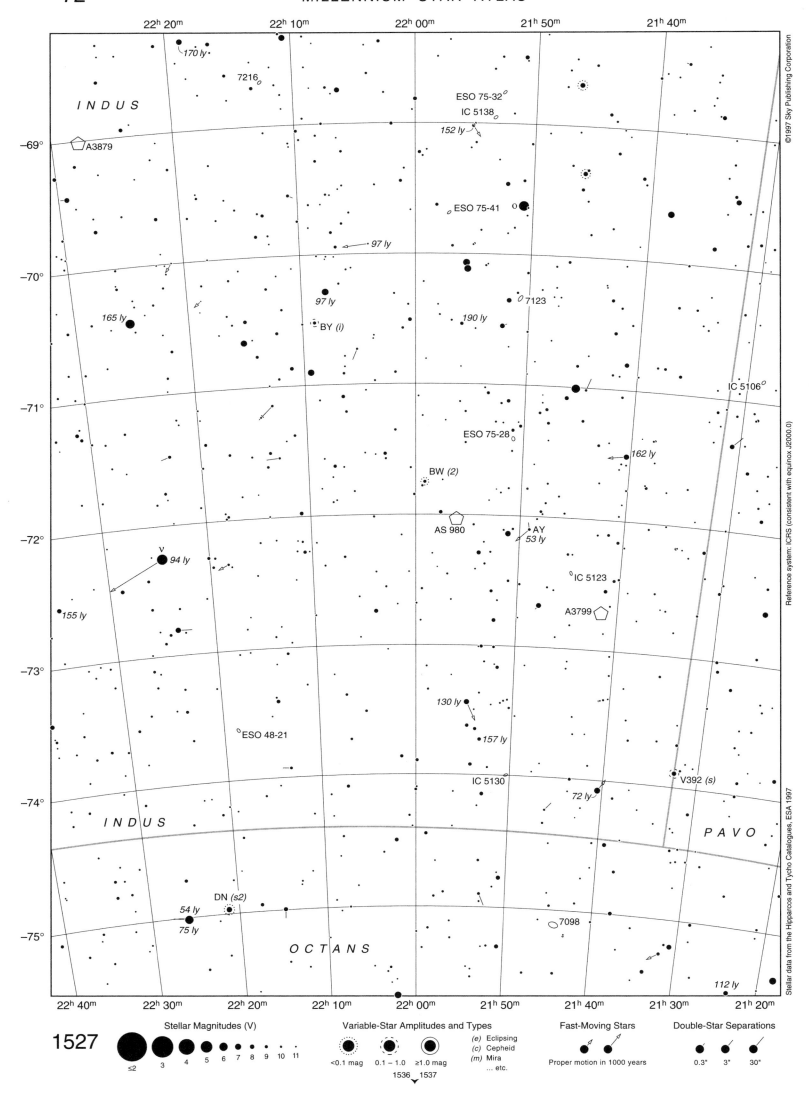

©1997 Sky Publishing Corporation

Reference system: ICRS (consistent with equinox J2000.0)

Stellar data from the Hipparcos and Tycho Catalogues, ESA 1997

INDUS

170 ly

7216

ESO 75-32
IC 5138
152 ly

A3879

ESO 75-41

97 ly

97 ly
BY (i)

7123

165 ly

190 ly

IC 5106

ESO 75-28

162 ly

BW (2)

AS 980

AY
53 ly

ν
94 ly

IC 5123

A3799

155 ly

ESO 48-21

130 ly

157 ly

IC 5130

V392 (s)

72 ly

INDUS

PAVO

DN (s2)

54 ly

75 ly

7098

OCTANS

112 ly

**1527**

Stellar Magnitudes (V)

≤2   3   4   5   6   7   8   9   10   11

Variable-Star Amplitudes and Types

<0.1 mag   0.1 – 1.0   ≥1.0 mag

1536   1537

(e) Eclipsing
(c) Cepheid
(m) Mira
... etc.

Fast-Moving Stars

Proper motion in 1000 years

Double-Star Separations

0.3"   3"   30"

# MILLENNIUM STAR ATLAS

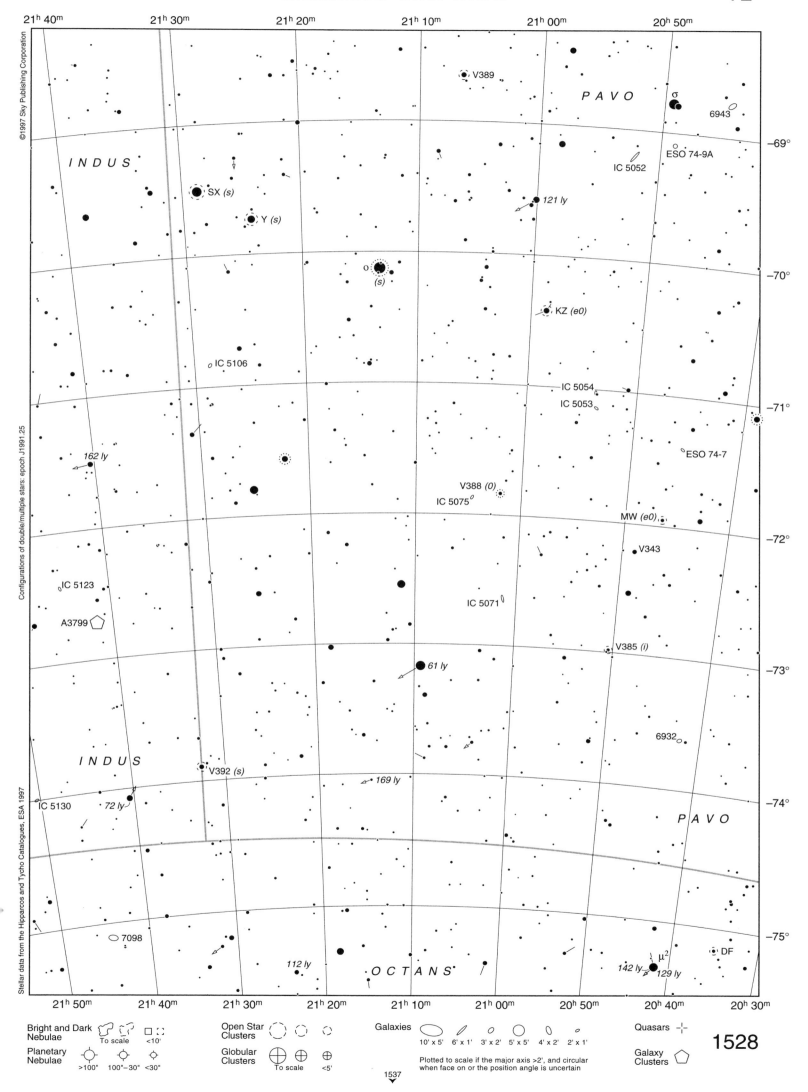

Configurations of double/multiple stars: epoch J1991.25

Stellar data from the Hipparcos and Tycho Catalogues, ESA 1997

P A V O

I N D U S

SX *(s)*

Y *(s)*

o *(s)*

V389

σ

6943

ESO 74-9A

IC 5052

*121 ly*

KZ *(e0)*

IC 5106

IC 5054

IC 5053

ESO 74-7

*162 ly*

V388 *(0)*

IC 5075

MW *(e0)*

V343

IC 5123

IC 5071

A3799

V385 *(i)*

*61 ly*

6932

I N D U S

V392 *(s)*

*169 ly*

IC 5130

*72 ly*

P A V O

7098

*112 ly*

O C T A N S

μ²

DF

*142 ly*  *129 ly*

| 21ʰ 40ᵐ | 21ʰ 30ᵐ | 21ʰ 20ᵐ | 21ʰ 10ᵐ | 21ʰ 00ᵐ | 20ʰ 50ᵐ |
|---|---|---|---|---|---|

−69°

−70°

−71°

−72°

−73°

−74°

−75°

| 21ʰ 50ᵐ | 21ʰ 40ᵐ | 21ʰ 30ᵐ | 21ʰ 20ᵐ | 21ʰ 10ᵐ | 21ʰ 00ᵐ | 20ʰ 50ᵐ | 20ʰ 40ᵐ | 20ʰ 30ᵐ |
|---|---|---|---|---|---|---|---|---|

Bright and Dark
Nebulae
To scale    <10'

Planetary
Nebulae
>100"  100"−30"  <30"

Open Star
Clusters

Globular
Clusters
To scale    <5'

Galaxies
10' x 5'   6' x 1'   3' x 2'   5' x 5'   4' x 2'   2' x 1'

Plotted to scale if the major axis >2', and circular
when face on or the position angle is uncertain

Quasars

Galaxy
Clusters

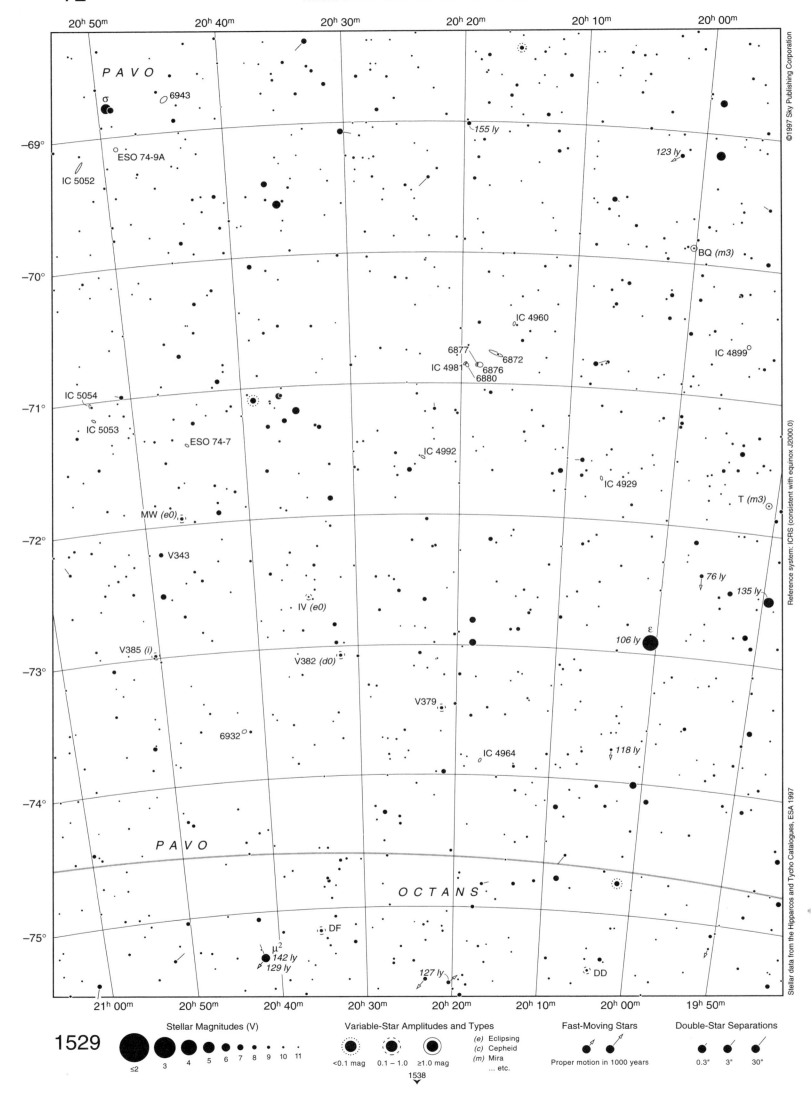

©1997 Sky Publishing Corporation

Reference system: ICRS (consistent with equinox J2000.0)

Stellar data from the Hipparcos and Tycho Catalogues, ESA 1997

1529

Stellar Magnitudes (V)

≤2   3   4   5   6   7   8   9  10  11

Variable-Star Amplitudes and Types

<0.1 mag    0.1 – 1.0    ≥1.0 mag

(e) Eclipsing
(c) Cepheid
(m) Mira
... etc.

Fast-Moving Stars

Proper motion in 1000 years

Double-Star Separations

0.3"    3"    30"

▼
1538

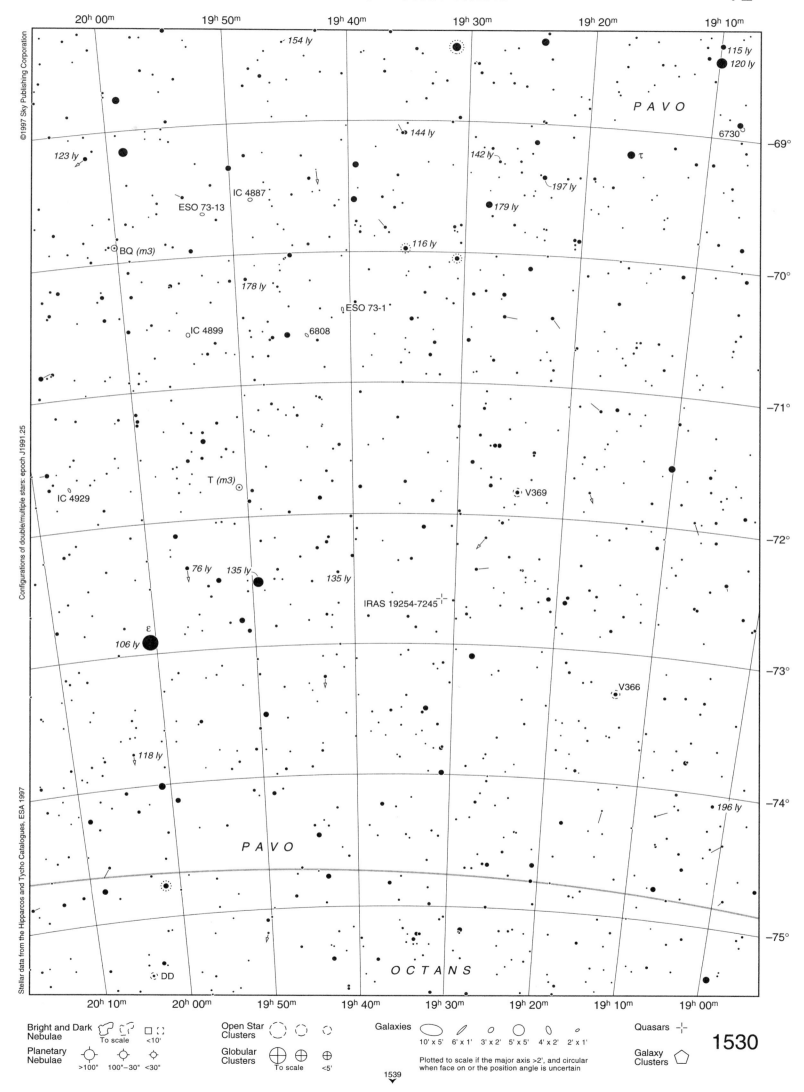

20h 00m    19h 50m    19h 40m    19h 30m    19h 20m    19h 10m

154 ly

115 ly
120 ly

P A V O

144 ly

−69°

142 ly

6730

123 ly

197 ly

τ

IC 4887
ESO 73-13          179 ly

BQ (m3)          116 ly

−70°

178 ly

ESO 73-1

IC 4899    6808

−71°

T (m3)

IC 4929              V369

−72°

76 ly   135 ly      135 ly

IRAS 19254-7245

ε

106 ly

V366

118 ly

196 ly

−73°

−74°

P A V O

DD

−75°

O C T A N S

20h 10m    20h 00m    19h 50m    19h 40m    19h 30m    19h 20m    19h 10m    19h 00m

Bright and Dark Nebulae
To scale      <10'

Planetary Nebulae
>100"   100"–30"   <30"

Open Star Clusters

Globular Clusters
To scale      <5'

Galaxies
10' x 5'   6' x 1'   3' x 2'   5' x 5'   4' x 2'   2' x 1'
Plotted to scale if the major axis >2', and circular when face on or the position angle is uncertain

Quasars

Galaxy Clusters

1530

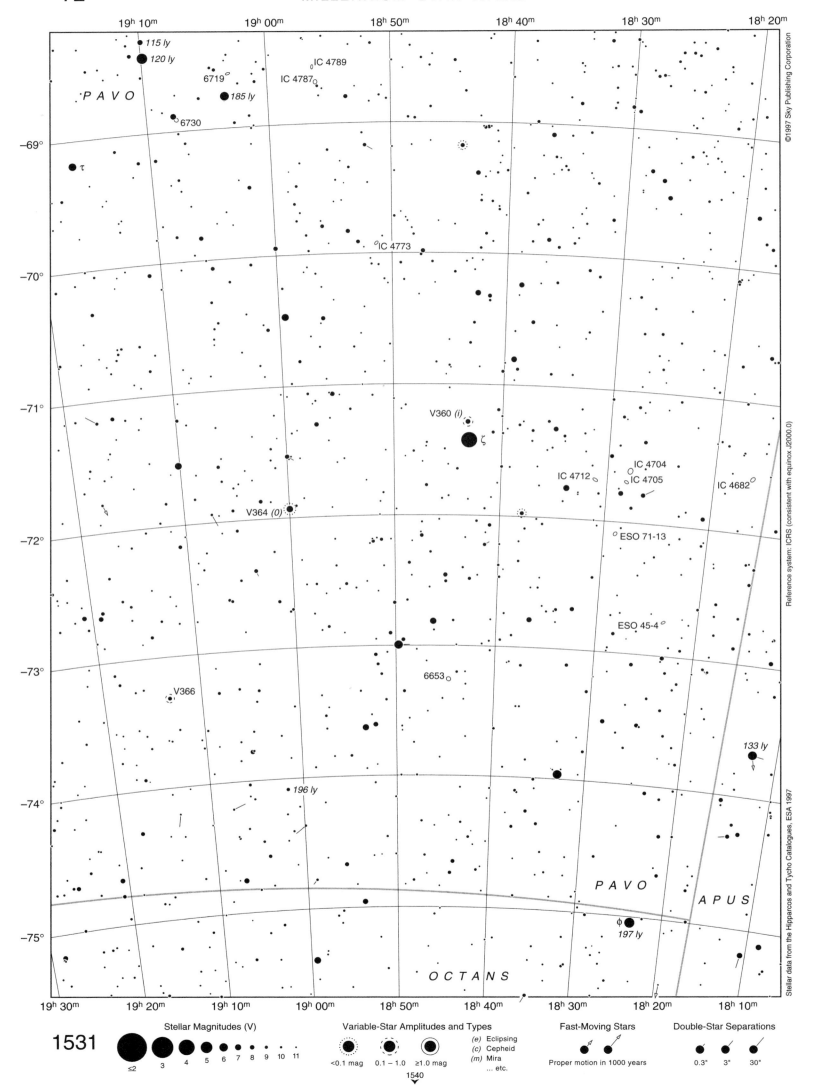

©1997 Sky Publishing Corporation

Reference system: ICRS (consistent with equinox J2000.0)

Stellar data from the Hipparcos and Tycho Catalogues, ESA 1997

P A V O

115 ly

120 ly

6719

IC 4789

IC 4787

185 ly

6730

τ

IC 4773

−69°

−70°

V360 (i)

ζ

IC 4704

IC 4712

IC 4705

IC 4682

−71°

V364 (0)

ESO 71-13

−72°

ESO 45-4

133 ly

V366

−73°

6653

196 ly

−74°

P A V O

A P U S

φ

197 ly

−75°

O C T A N S

19h 30m  19h 20m  19h 10m  19h 00m  18h 50m  18h 40m  18h 30m  18h 20m  18h 10m

19h 10m  19h 00m  18h 50m  18h 40m  18h 30m  18h 20m

1531

Stellar Magnitudes (V)

≤2  3  4  5  6  7  8  9  10  11

Variable-Star Amplitudes and Types

<0.1 mag  0.1 – 1.0  ≥1.0 mag

(e) Eclipsing
(c) Cepheid
(m) Mira
... etc.

1540

Fast-Moving Stars

Proper motion in 1000 years

Double-Star Separations

0.3"  3"  30"

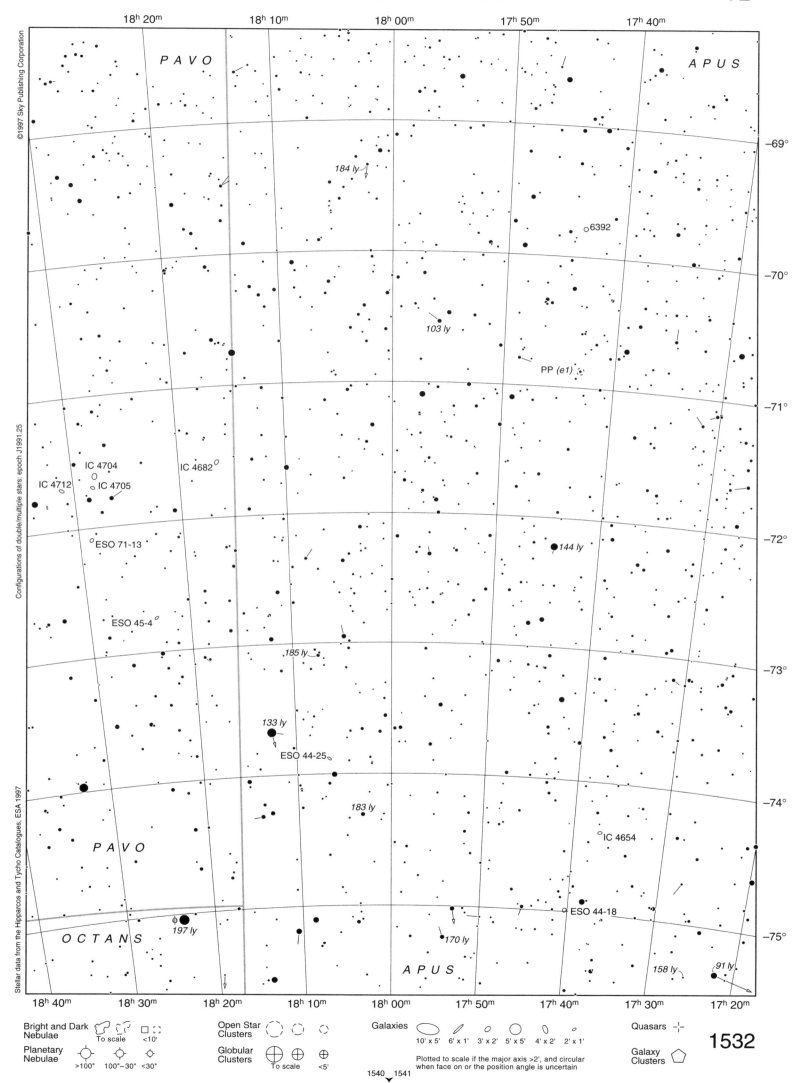

18ʰ 20ᵐ  18ʰ 10ᵐ  18ʰ 00ᵐ  17ʰ 50ᵐ  17ʰ 40ᵐ

−69°
−70°
−71°
−72°
−73°
−74°
−75°

P A V O

A P U S

6392

184 ly

103 ly

PP (e1)

IC 4704
IC 4682
IC 4712
IC 4705

ESO 71-13

144 ly

ESO 45-4

185 ly

133 ly

ESO 44-25

183 ly

IC 4654

P A V O

φ
197 ly

O C T A N S

ESO 44-18

170 ly

A P U S

158 ly

91 ly

18ʰ 40ᵐ  18ʰ 30ᵐ  18ʰ 20ᵐ  18ʰ 10ᵐ  18ʰ 00ᵐ  17ʰ 50ᵐ  17ʰ 40ᵐ  17ʰ 30ᵐ  17ʰ 20ᵐ

| Bright and Dark Nebulae | Open Star Clusters | Galaxies | Quasars |

To scale   <10'

Planetary Nebulae
>100"  100"−30"  <30"

Globular Clusters
To scale   <5'

10' x 5'  6' x 1'  3' x 2'  5' x 5'  4' x 2'  2' x 1'

Plotted to scale if the major axis >2', and circular
when face on or the position angle is uncertain

Galaxy Clusters

## 1532

# MILLENNIUM STAR ATLAS

-72°

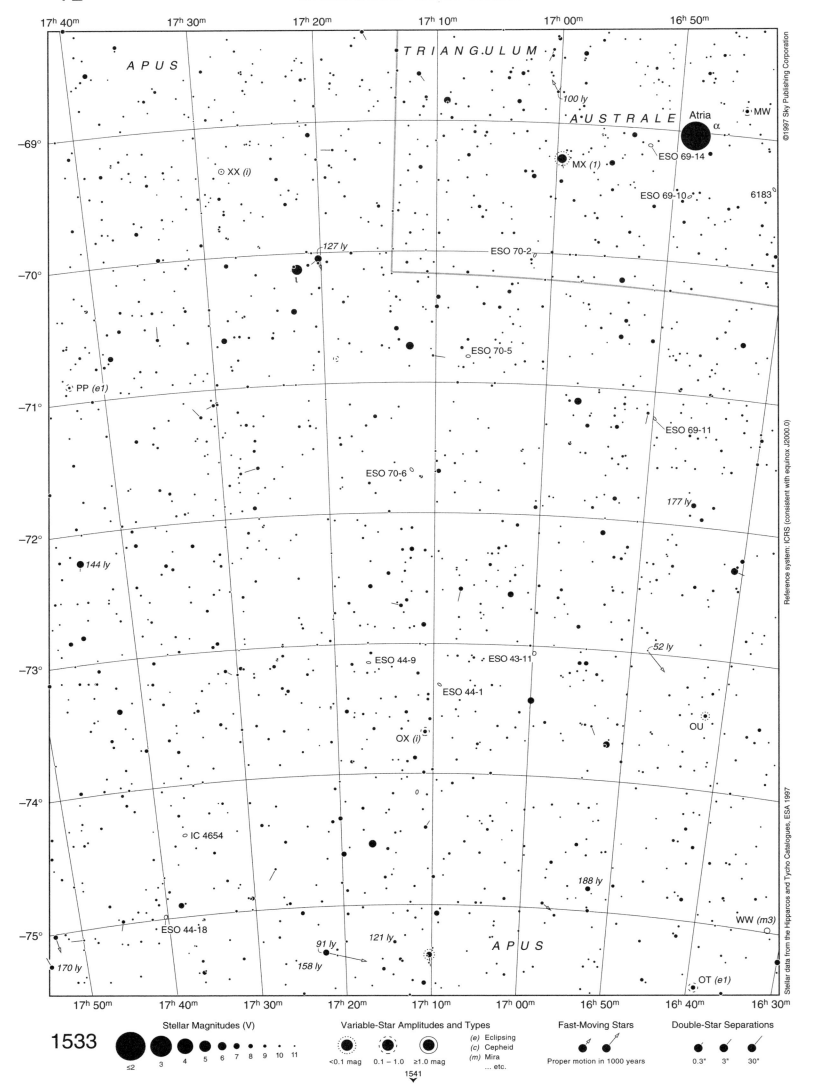

Reference system: ICRS (consistent with equinox J2000.0)

Stellar data from the Hipparcos and Tycho Catalogues, ESA 1997

APUS

TRIANGULUM

AUSTRALE

Atria α

MW

100 ly

MX (1)

ESO 69-14

ESO 69-10

6183

XX (i)

ESO 70-2

127 ly

ι

ESO 70-5

PP (e1)

ESO 69-11

ESO 70-6

177 ly

144 ly

52 ly

ESO 44-9

ESO 43-11

ESO 44-1

OX (i)

OU

IC 4654

188 ly

WW (m3)

ESO 44-18

121 ly

APUS

91 ly

OT (e1)

170 ly

158 ly

1533

## Stellar Magnitudes (V)

≤2   3   4   5   6   7   8   9   10   11

## Variable-Star Amplitudes and Types

<0.1 mag    0.1 – 1.0    ≥1.0 mag

(e) Eclipsing
(c) Cepheid
(m) Mira
... etc.

## Fast-Moving Stars

Proper motion in 1000 years

## Double-Star Separations

0.3"    3"    30"

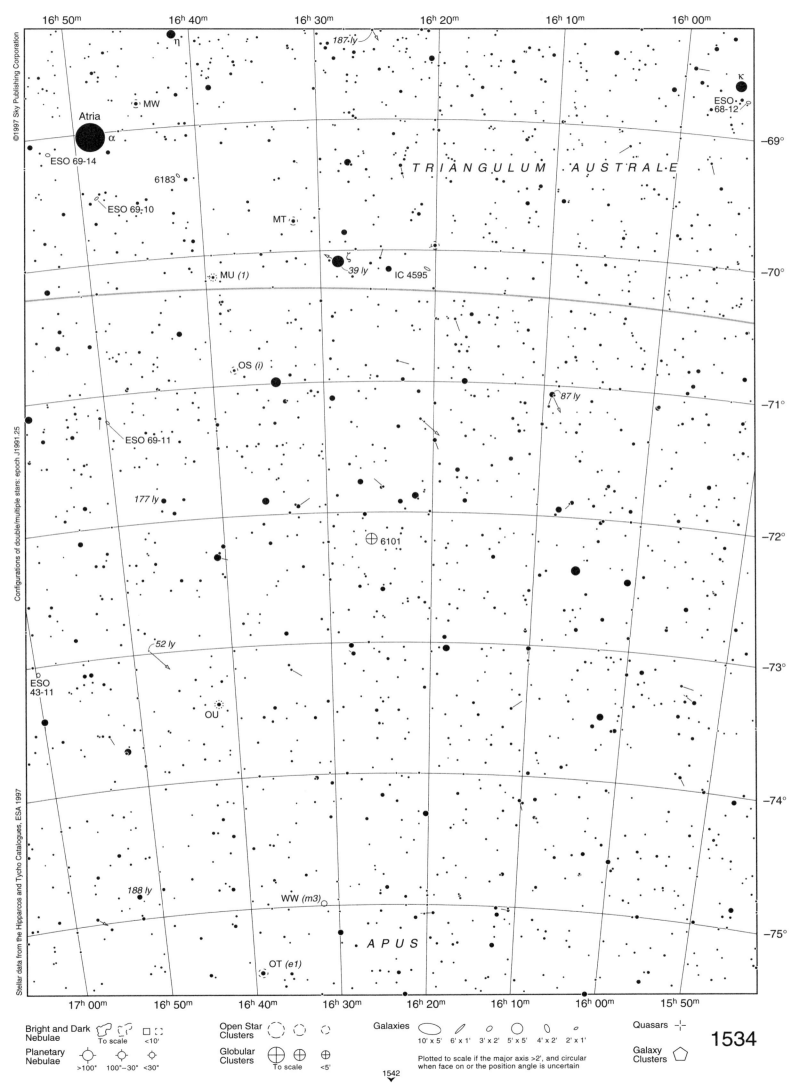

16ʰ 50ᵐ   16ʰ 40ᵐ   16ʰ 30ᵐ   16ʰ 20ᵐ   16ʰ 10ᵐ   16ʰ 00ᵐ

η

κ

ESO
68-12

MW

Atria

α

ESO 69-14

TRIANGULUM AUSTRALE

−69°

6183

ESO 69-10

MT

MU (1)

ζ

39 ly

IC 4595

−70°

OS (i)

87 ly

ESO 69-11

−71°

177 ly

6101

−72°

52 ly

−73°

ESO
43-11

OU

−74°

188 ly

WW (m3)

−75°

APUS

OT (e1)

17ʰ 00ᵐ   16ʰ 50ᵐ   16ʰ 40ᵐ   16ʰ 30ᵐ   16ʰ 20ᵐ   16ʰ 10ᵐ   16ʰ 00ᵐ   15ʰ 50ᵐ

187 ly

| | | | | | | |
|---|---|---|---|---|---|---|---|
| Bright and Dark Nebulae | To scale | <10' | | | | | Quasars |
| Planetary Nebulae | >100" 100"−30" <30" | | | | | | Galaxy Clusters |
| | | Open Star Clusters | | Galaxies | 10' x 5'  6' x 1'  3' x 2'  5' x 5'  4' x 2'  2' x 1' | | |
| | | Globular Clusters | To scale  <5' | | | | |

Plotted to scale if the major axis >2', and circular
when face on or the position angle is uncertain

1534

1542

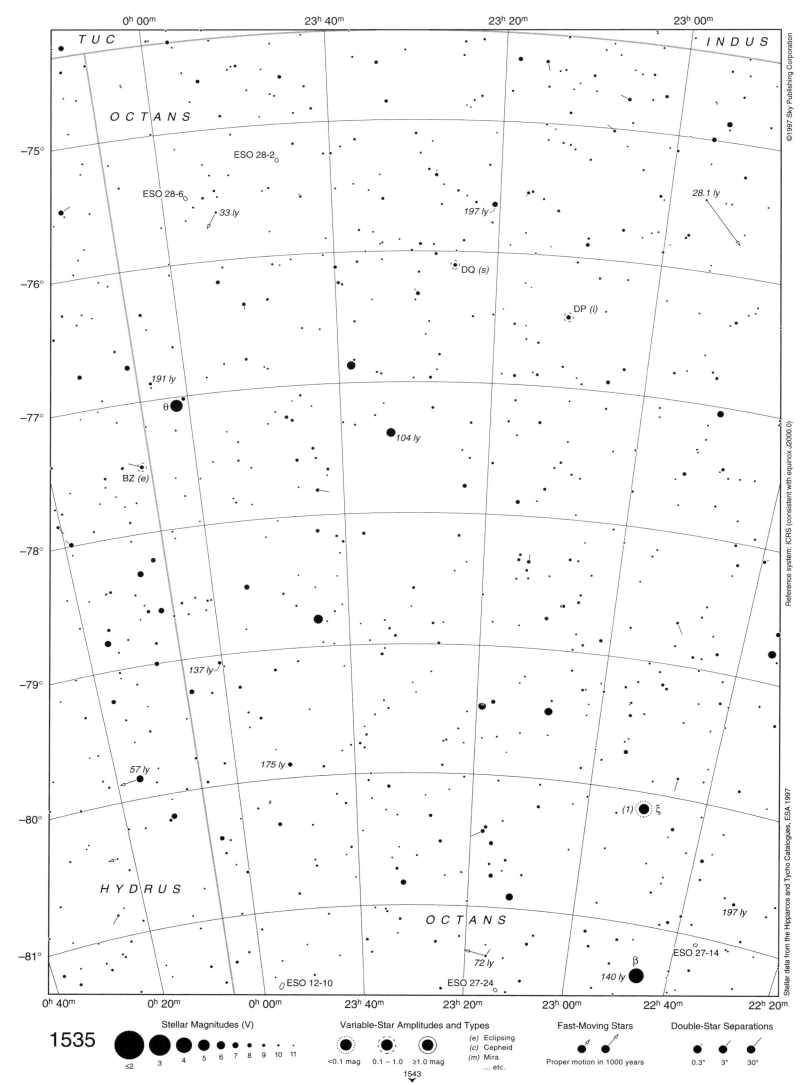

©1997 Sky Publishing Corporation

Reference system: ICRS (consistent with equinox J2000.0)

Stellar data from the Hipparcos and Tycho Catalogues, ESA 1997

TUC                    INDUS

OCTANS

ESO 28-2

ESO 28-6

33 ly

197 ly

DQ (s)

DP (i)

28.1 ly

191 ly

θ

104 ly

BZ (e)

137 ly

57 ly

175 ly

(1)  ξ

HYDRUS

OCTANS

197 ly

72 ly

ESO 27-14

β

140 ly

ESO 12-10

ESO 27-24

0ʰ 40ᵐ   0ʰ 20ᵐ   0ʰ 00ᵐ   23ʰ 40ᵐ   23ʰ 20ᵐ   23ʰ 00ᵐ   22ʰ 40ᵐ   22ʰ 20ᵐ

1535

Stellar Magnitudes (V)

≤2   3   4   5   6   7   8   9   10   11

Variable-Star Amplitudes and Types

<0.1 mag   0.1 − 1.0   ≥1.0 mag

(e) Eclipsing
(c) Cepheid
(m) Mira
... etc.

Fast-Moving Stars

Proper motion in 1000 years

Double-Star Separations

0.3"   3"   30"

1543

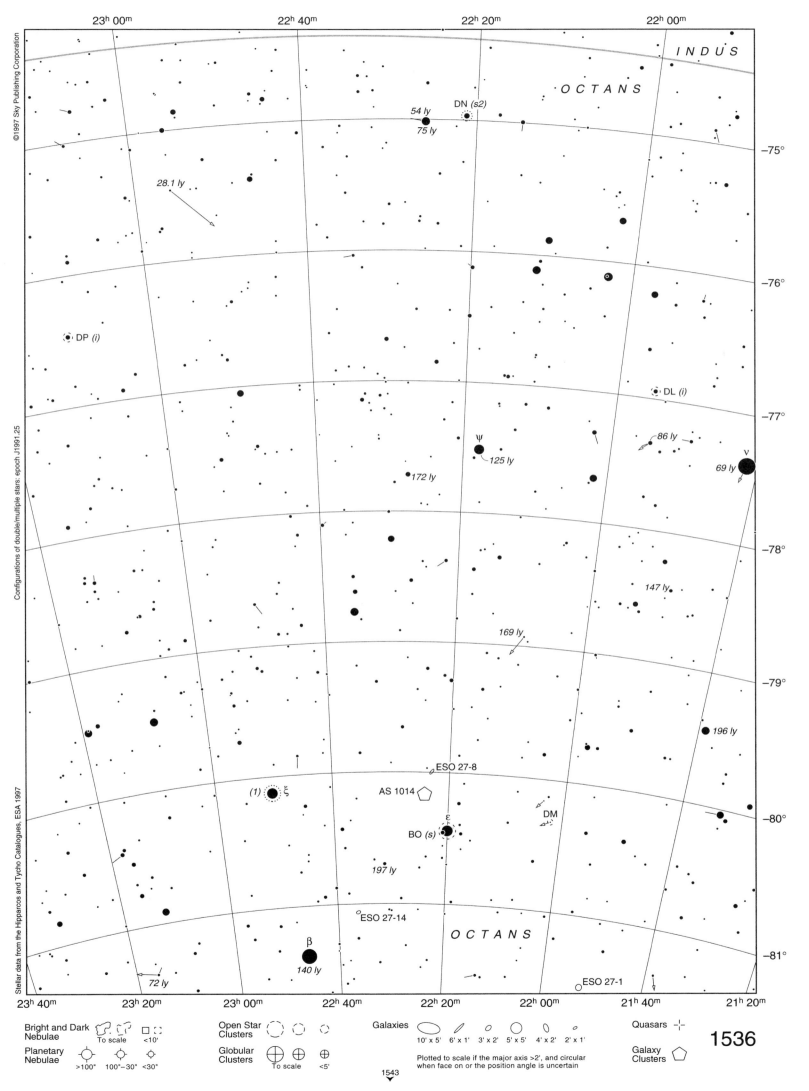

© 1997 Sky Publishing Corporation

Configurations of double/multiple stars: epoch J1991.25

Stellar data from the Hipparcos and Tycho Catalogues, ESA 1997

23ʰ 00ᵐ  22ʰ 40ᵐ  22ʰ 20ᵐ  22ʰ 00ᵐ

INDUS

OCTANS

DN (s2)

54 ly
75 ly

−75°

28.1 ly

−76°

DP (i)

DL (i)

−77°

86 ly

ψ
125 ly

ν
69 ly

172 ly

−78°

147 ly

169 ly

−79°

196 ly

ESO 27-8

(1) ξ

AS 1014

DM

−80°

ε
BO (s)

197 ly

ESO 27-14

OCTANS

β
140 ly

ESO 27-1

−81°

72 ly

23ʰ 40ᵐ  23ʰ 20ᵐ  23ʰ 00ᵐ  22ʰ 40ᵐ  22ʰ 20ᵐ  22ʰ 00ᵐ  21ʰ 40ᵐ  21ʰ 20ᵐ

Bright and Dark Nebulae    To scale    <10'

Open Star Clusters

Galaxies
10' x 5'   6' x 1'   3' x 2'   5' x 5'   4' x 2'   2' x 1'

Quasars

Planetary Nebulae    >100"   100"-30"   <30"

Globular Clusters    To scale    <5'

Plotted to scale if the major axis >2', and circular when face on or the position angle is uncertain

Galaxy Clusters

1536

1543

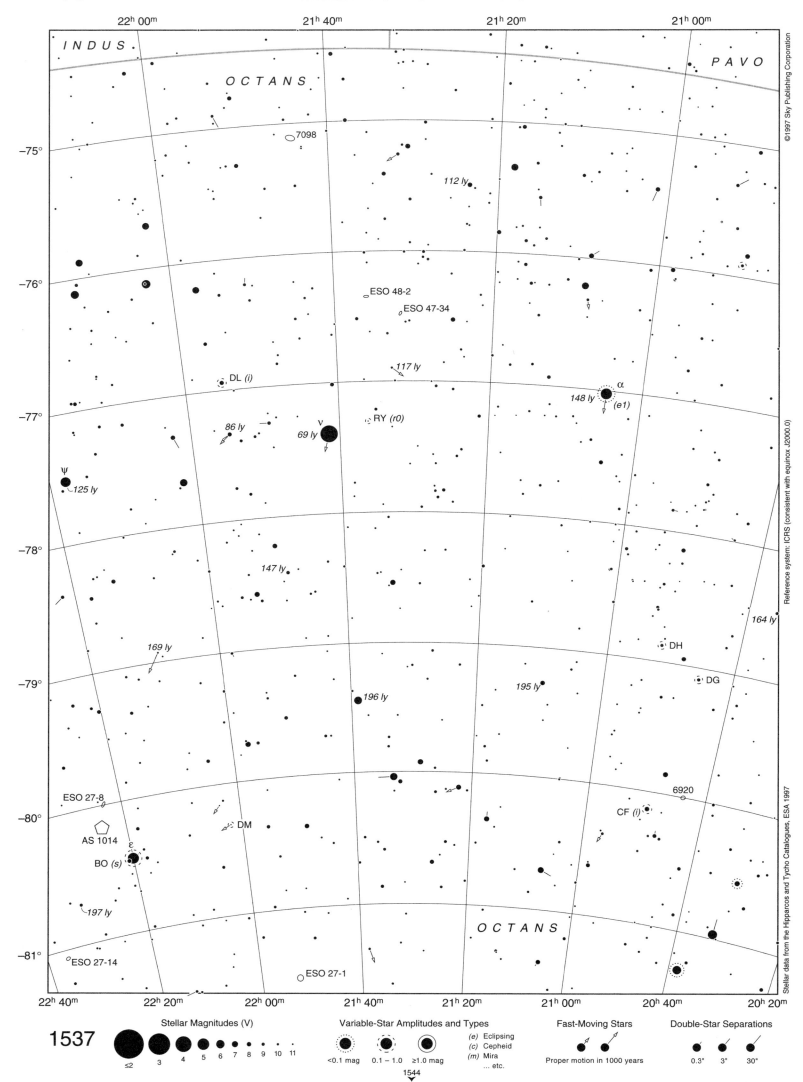

INDUS

OCTANS

PAVO

7098

112 ly

ESO 48-2

ESO 47-34

117 ly

DL (i)

α
148 ly
(e1)

86 ly

ν

RY (r0)

69 ly

ψ
125 ly

147 ly

164 ly

169 ly

DH

DG

195 ly

196 ly

6920

ESO 27-8

CF (i)

AS 1014

ε

DM

BO (s)

197 ly

OCTANS

ESO 27-14

ESO 27-1

1537

Stellar Magnitudes (V)

≤2    3    4    5   6  7  8  9  10  11

Variable-Star Amplitudes and Types

<0.1 mag    0.1 – 1.0    ≥1.0 mag

(e) Eclipsing
(c) Cepheid
(m) Mira
... etc.

1544

Fast-Moving Stars

Proper motion in 1000 years

Double-Star Separations

0.3"    3"    30"

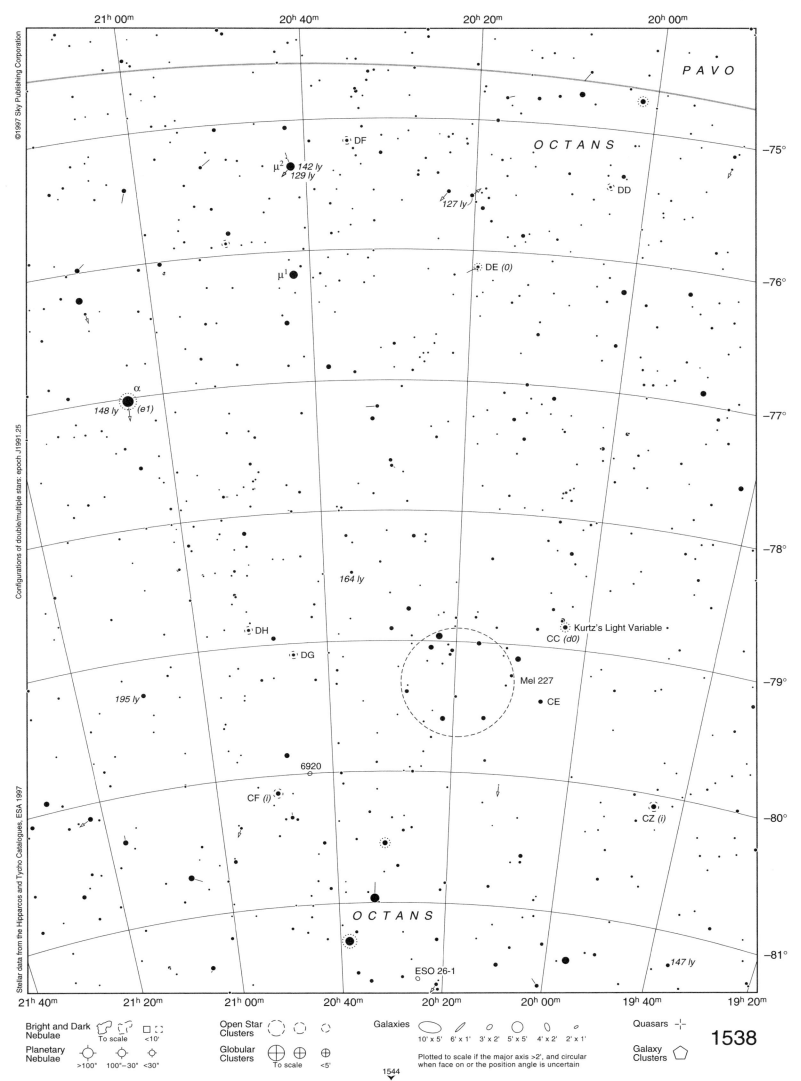

P A V O

O C T A N S

−75°

DF

μ² 142 ly
   129 ly

127 ly

DD

μ¹

DE (0)

−76°

α
148 ly    (e1)

−77°

164 ly

−78°

DH                    Kurtz's Light Variable
                      CC (d0)
DG
                      Mel 227
195 ly                       CE        −79°

6920

CF (i)
                                       CZ (i)
                                       −80°

O C T A N S

                                       −81°
ESO 26-1                      147 ly

21ʰ 40ᵐ   21ʰ 20ᵐ   21ʰ 00ᵐ   20ʰ 40ᵐ   20ʰ 20ᵐ   20ʰ 00ᵐ   19ʰ 40ᵐ   19ʰ 20ᵐ

Bright and Dark Nebulae    Open Star Clusters    Galaxies          Quasars
To scale   <10'                                  10' x 5'  6' x 1'  3' x 2'  5' x 5'  4' x 2'  2' x 1'
Planetary Nebulae          Globular Clusters                       Galaxy Clusters
>100"  100"–30"  <30"      To scale   <5'        Plotted to scale if the major axis >2', and circular
                                                 when face on or the position angle is uncertain

1538

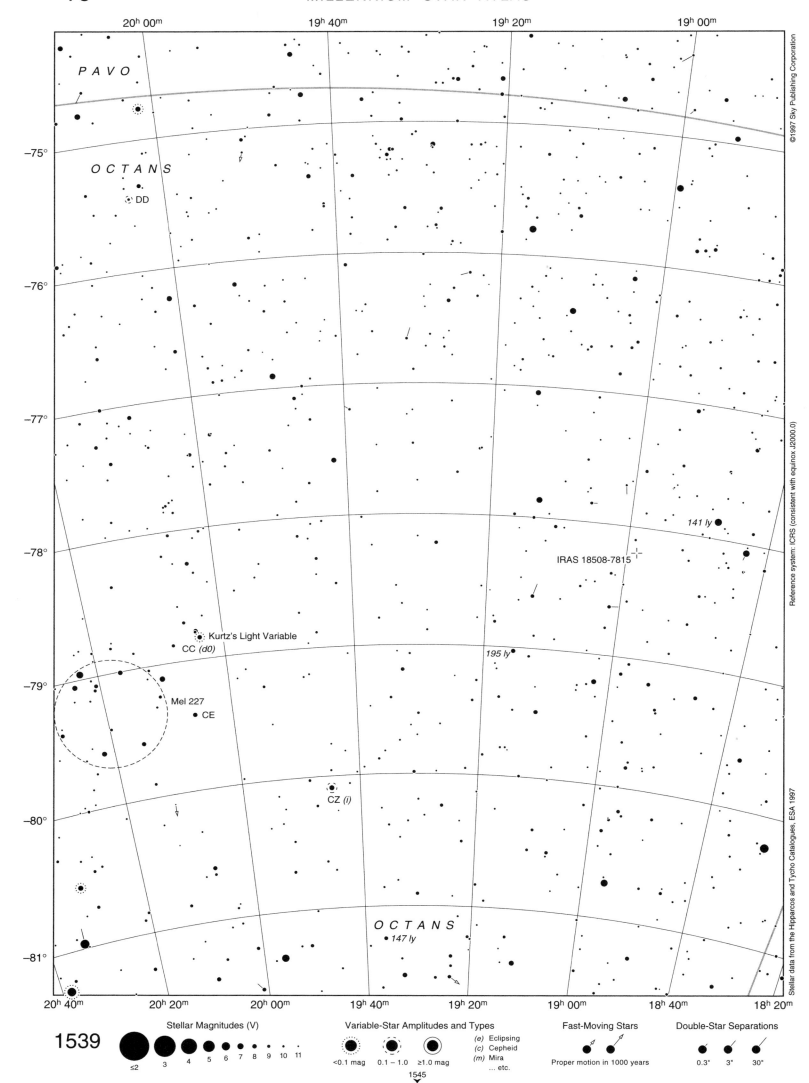

PAVO

OCTANS

DD

−75°

−76°

−77°

141 ly

−78°

IRAS 18508-7815

Kurtz's Light Variable
CC (d0)

195 ly

−79°
Mel 227
CE

CZ (i)

−80°

OCTANS

147 ly

−81°

20h 00m    19h 40m    19h 20m    19h 00m

20h 40m    20h 20m    20h 00m    19h 40m    19h 20m    19h 00m    18h 40m    18h 20m

1539

Stellar Magnitudes (V)

≤2   3   4   5   6   7   8   9   10   11

Variable-Star Amplitudes and Types

<0.1 mag   0.1 − 1.0   ≥1.0 mag

(e) Eclipsing
(c) Cepheid
(m) Mira
... etc.

Fast-Moving Stars

Proper motion in 1000 years

Double-Star Separations

0.3"   3"   30"

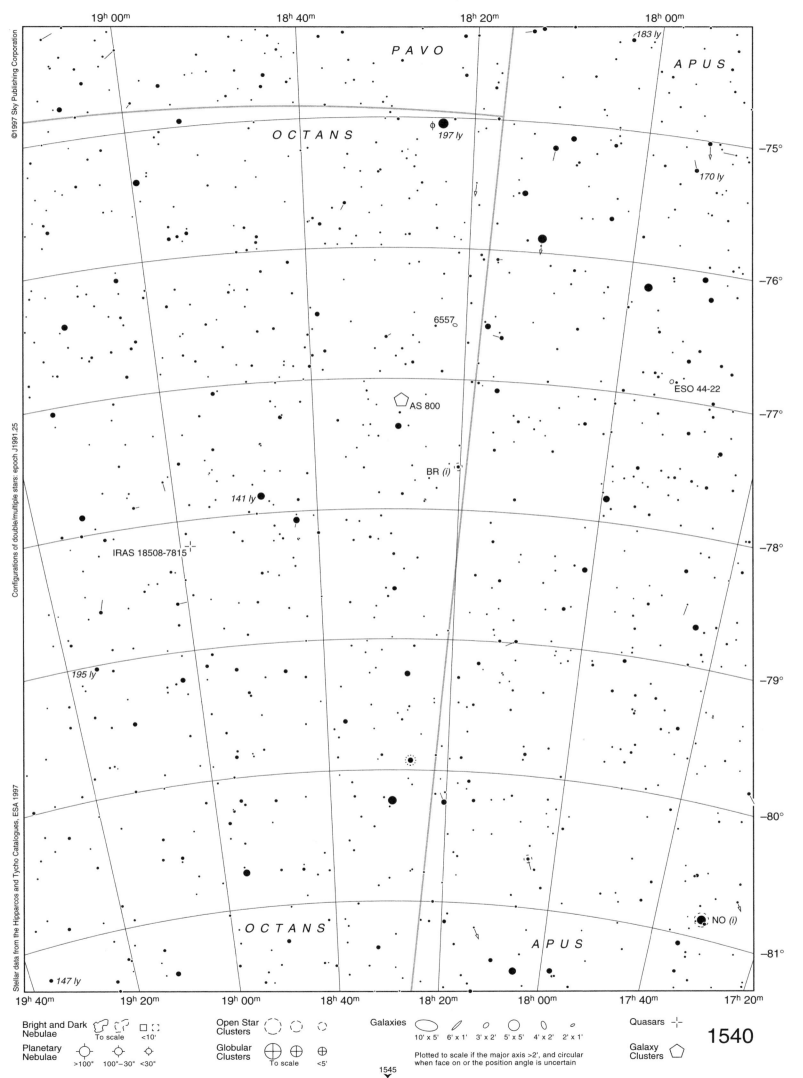

PAVO

APUS

OCTANS

φ 197 ly

183 ly

−75°

170 ly

−76°

6557

ESO 44-22

−77°

AS 800

BR (i)

141 ly

195 ly

IRAS 18508-7815

−78°

−79°

−80°

OCTANS

APUS

NO (i)

147 ly

−81°

| | | | |
|---|---|---|---|
| Bright and Dark Nebulae | To scale    <10' | Open Star Clusters | Galaxies    10' x 5'   6' x 1'   3' x 2'   5' x 5'   4' x 2'   2' x 1' |

Planetary Nebulae    >100"   100"–30"   <30"

Globular Clusters    To scale   <5'

Plotted to scale if the major axis >2', and circular when face on or the position angle is uncertain

Quasars

Galaxy Clusters

1540

1533

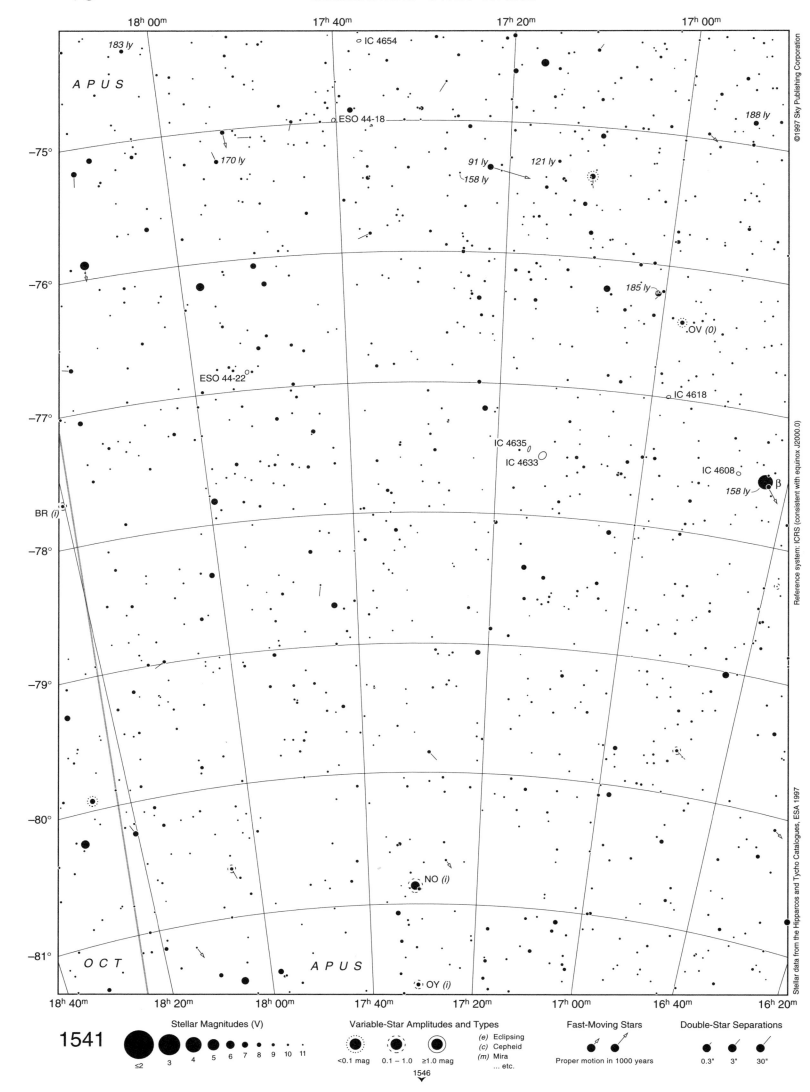

Reference system: ICRS (consistent with equinox J2000.0)

Stellar data from the Hipparcos and Tycho Catalogues, ESA 1997

1541

**Stellar Magnitudes (V)**

≤2  3  4  5  6  7  8  9  10  11

**Variable-Star Amplitudes and Types**

<0.1 mag   0.1 – 1.0   ≥1.0 mag

(e) Eclipsing
(c) Cepheid
(m) Mira
... etc.

1546

**Fast-Moving Stars**

Proper motion in 1000 years

**Double-Star Separations**

0.3"   3"   30"

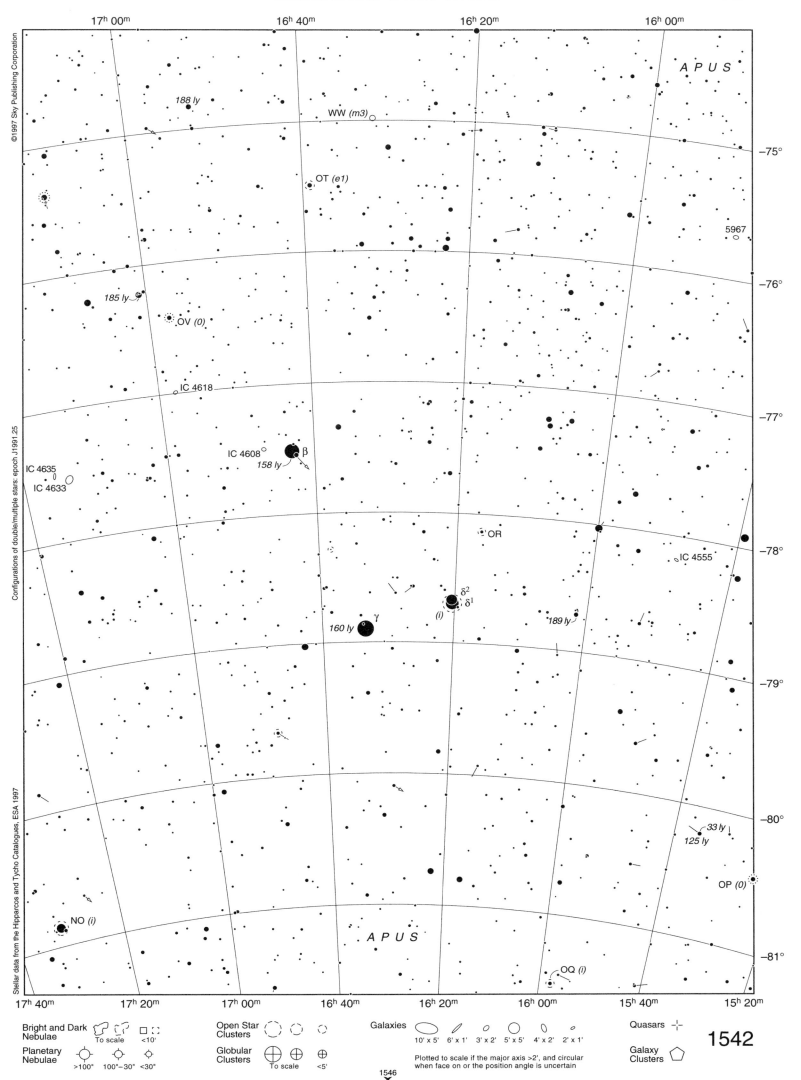

APUS

188 ly

WW (m3)

OT (e1)

5967

185 ly

OV (0)

IC 4618

IC 4608

IC 4635

IC 4633

β

158 ly

OR

IC 4555

δ²

δ¹

(i)

189 ly

γ

160 ly

33 ly

125 ly

OP (0)

NO (i)

APUS

OQ (i)

17ʰ 00ᵐ    16ʰ 40ᵐ    16ʰ 20ᵐ    16ʰ 00ᵐ

17ʰ 40ᵐ   17ʰ 20ᵐ   17ʰ 00ᵐ   16ʰ 40ᵐ   16ʰ 20ᵐ   16ʰ 00ᵐ   15ʰ 40ᵐ   15ʰ 20ᵐ

−75°

−76°

−77°

−78°

−79°

−80°

−81°

Bright and Dark Nebulae
To scale    <10'

Planetary Nebulae
>100"  100"–30"  <30"

Open Star Clusters

Globular Clusters
To scale    <5'

Galaxies
10' x 5'  6' x 1'  3' x 2'  5' x 5'  4' x 2'  2' x 1'

Plotted to scale if the major axis >2', and circular when face on or the position angle is uncertain

Quasars

Galaxy Clusters

1542

1546

−84°

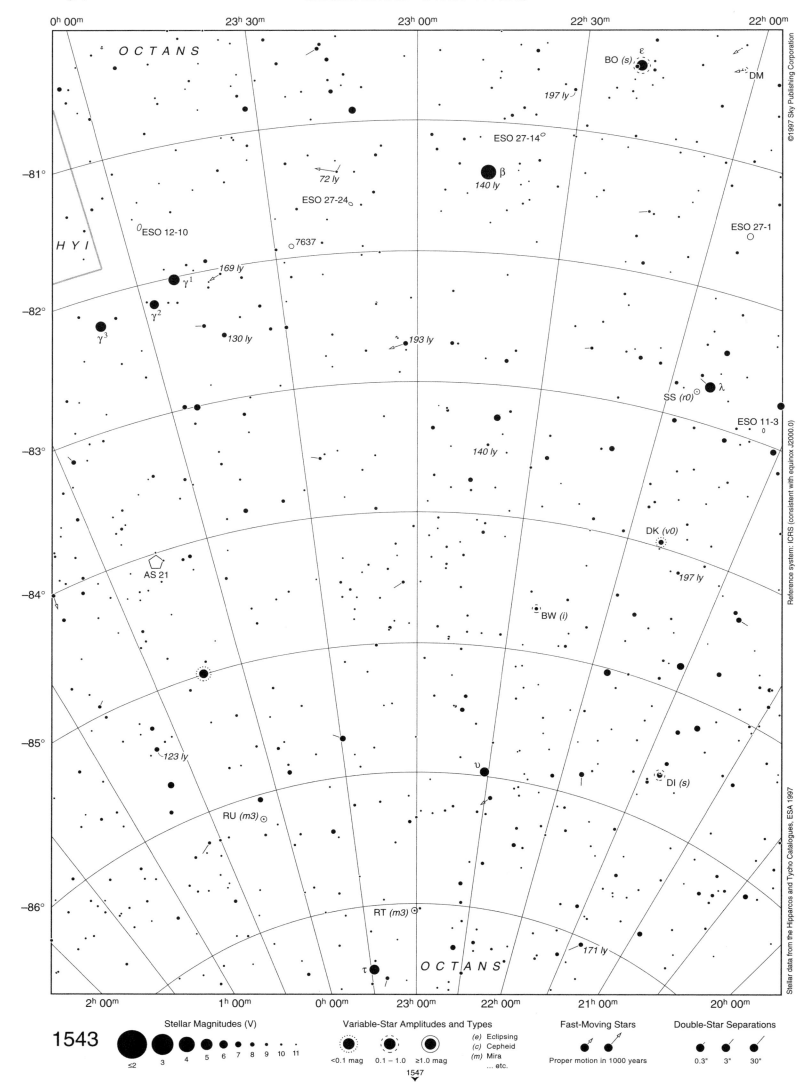

O C T A N S

H Y I

ESO 12-10

γ¹  169 ly

γ²

γ³  130 ly

7637

ESO 27-24

72 ly

ESO 27-14

β  140 ly

197 ly

BO (s)  ε

DM

ESO 27-1

193 ly

SS (r0)  λ

ESO 11-3

140 ly

DK (v0)

197 ly

AS 21

BW (i)

123 ly

υ

DI (s)

RU (m3)

RT (m3)

τ

O C T A N S

171 ly

0ʰ 00ᵐ  23ʰ 30ᵐ  23ʰ 00ᵐ  22ʰ 30ᵐ  22ʰ 00ᵐ

2ʰ 00ᵐ  1ʰ 00ᵐ  0ʰ 00ᵐ  23ʰ 00ᵐ  22ʰ 00ᵐ  21ʰ 00ᵐ  20ʰ 00ᵐ

−81°  −82°  −83°  −84°  −85°  −86°

©1997 Sky Publishing Corporation

Reference system: ICRS (consistent with equinox J2000.0)

Stellar data from the Hipparcos and Tycho Catalogues, ESA 1997

**1543**

Stellar Magnitudes (V)

≤2  3  4  5  6  7  8  9  10  11

Variable-Star Amplitudes and Types

<0.1 mag  0.1 – 1.0  ≥1.0 mag

(e) Eclipsing
(c) Cepheid
(m) Mira
... etc.

Fast-Moving Stars

Proper motion in 1000 years

Double-Star Separations

0.3"  3"  30"

# MILLENNIUM STAR ATLAS

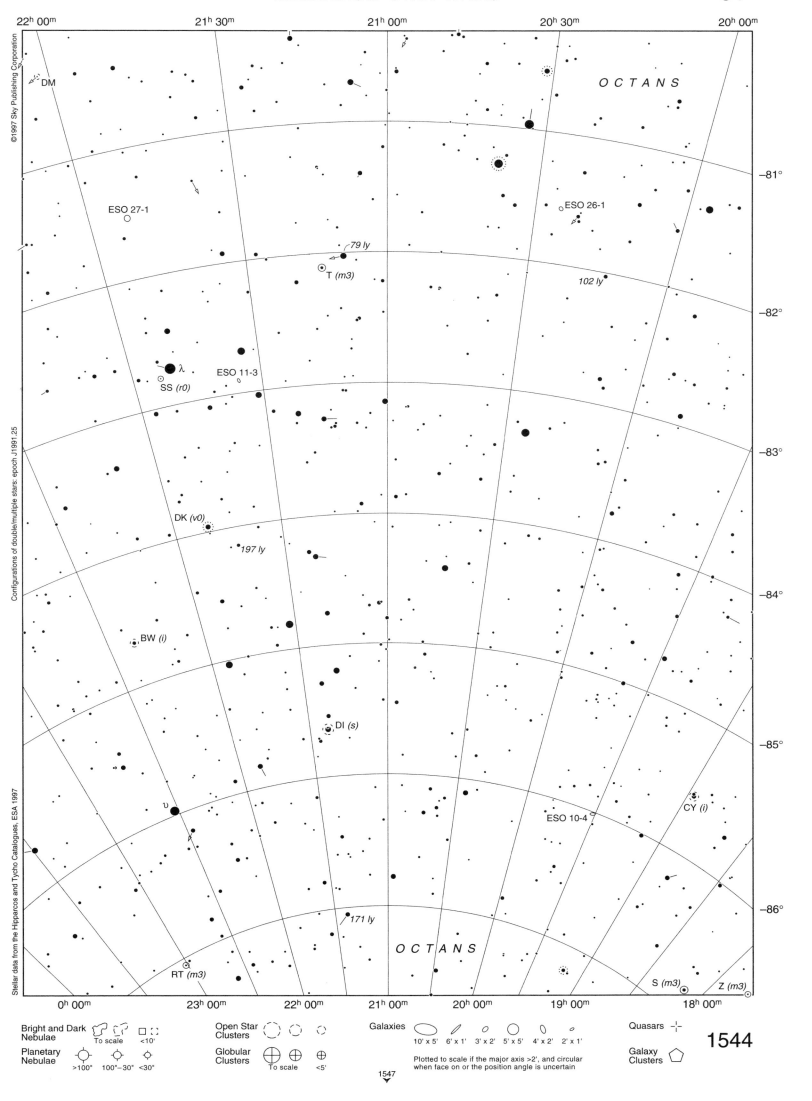

22h 00m  21h 30m  21h 00m  20h 30m  20h 00m

DM

OCTANS

−81°

ESO 27-1

ESO 26-1

79 ly

T (m3)

102 ly

−82°

λ

ESO 11-3

SS (r0)

−83°

DK (v0)

197 ly

−84°

BW (i)

DI (s)

−85°

υ

CY (i)

ESO 10-4

171 ly

−86°

OCTANS

RT (m3)

S (m3)   Z (m3)

0h 00m  23h 00m  22h 00m  21h 00m  20h 00m  19h 00m  18h 00m

**Bright and Dark Nebulae**  To scale  <10'

**Planetary Nebulae**  >100"  100"–30"  <30'

**Open Star Clusters**

**Globular Clusters**  To scale  <5'

**Galaxies**  10' x 5'  6' x 1'  3' x 2'  5' x 5'  4' x 2'  2' x 1'

Plotted to scale if the major axis >2', and circular when face on or the position angle is uncertain

**Quasars**

**Galaxy Clusters**

1544

−84° MILLENNIUM STAR ATLAS

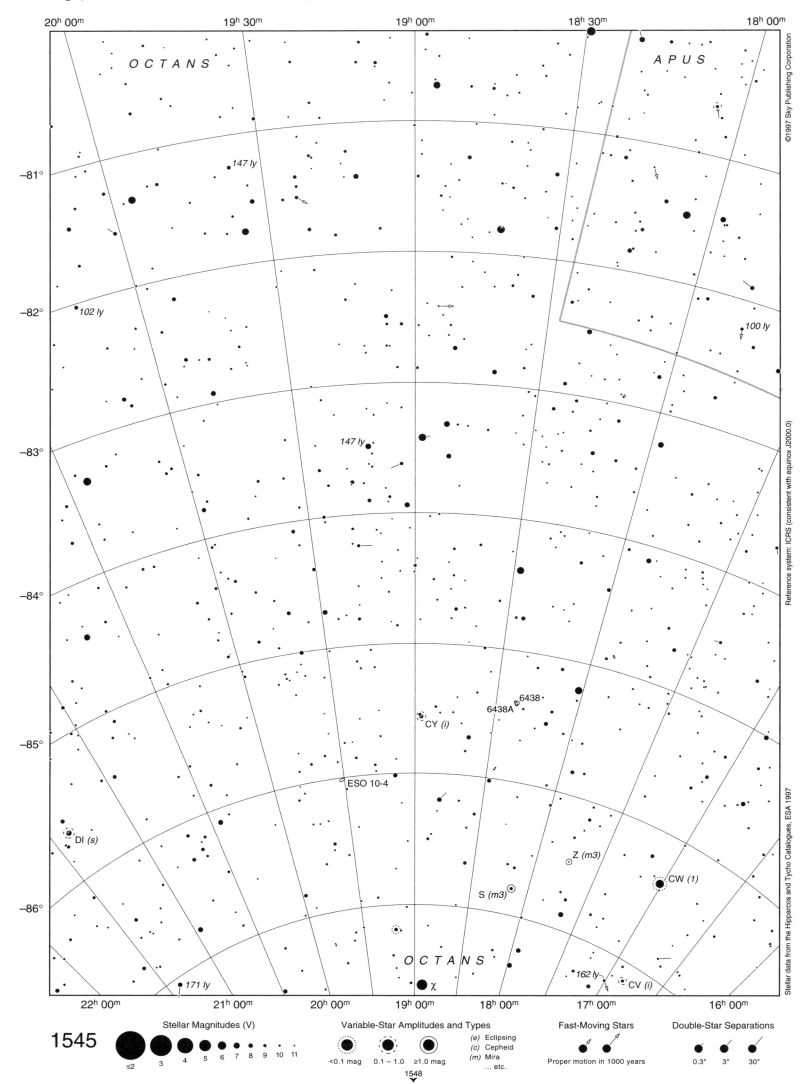

OCTANS

APUS

147 ly

102 ly

100 ly

147 ly

6438
6438A

CY (i)

ESO 10-4

DI (s)

Z (m3)

CW (1)

S (m3)

OCTANS

χ

162 ly

CV (i)

171 ly

©1997 Sky Publishing Corporation

Reference system: ICRS (consistent with equinox J2000.0)

Stellar data from the Hipparcos and Tycho Catalogues, ESA 1997

1545

Stellar Magnitudes (V)

≤2  3  4  5  6  7  8  9  10  11

Variable-Star Amplitudes and Types

<0.1 mag   0.1 − 1.0   ≥1.0 mag

(e) Eclipsing
(c) Cepheid
(m) Mira
... etc.

Fast-Moving Stars

Proper motion in 1000 years

Double-Star Separations

0.3"   3"   30"

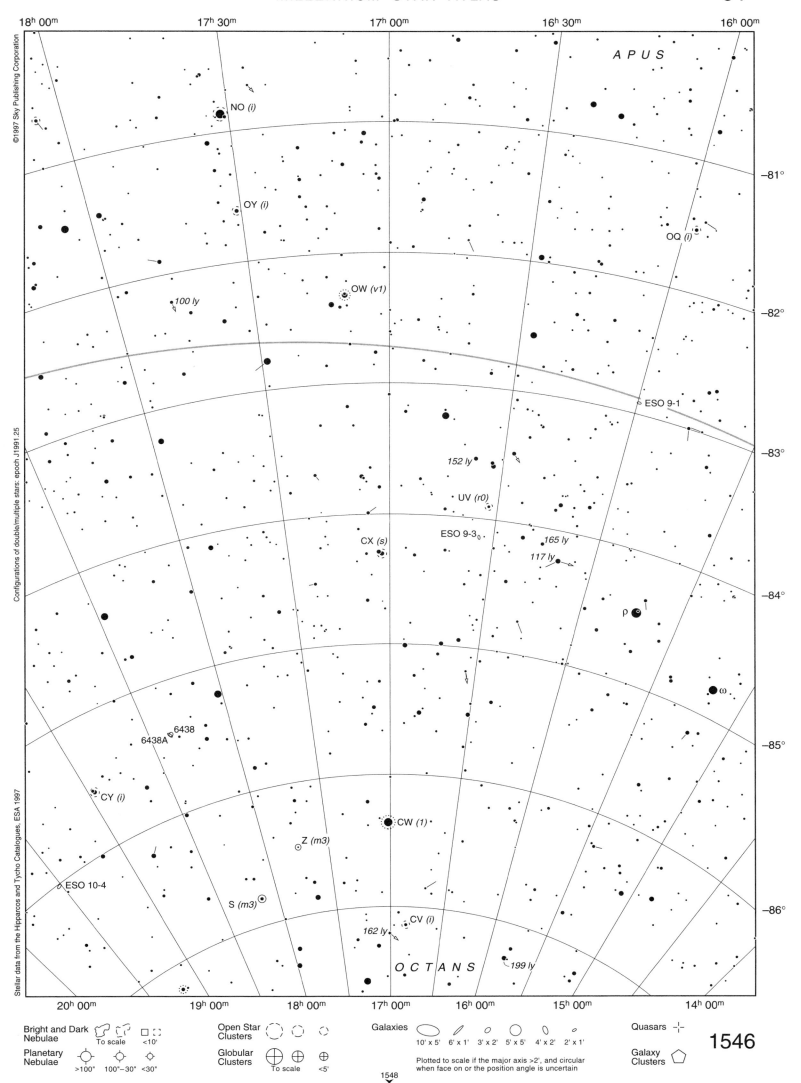

*A P U S*

NO *(i)*

OY *(i)*

OQ *(i)*

OW *(v1)*

*100 ly*

ESO 9-1

*152 ly*

UV *(r0)*

ESO 9-3₀

CX *(s)*

*165 ly*

*117 ly*

ρ

ω

6438
6438A

CY *(i)*

CW *(1)*

Z *(m3)*

ESO 10-4

S *(m3)*

CV *(i)*

*162 ly*

*O C T A N S*

*199 ly*

−81°

−82°

−83°

−84°

−85°

−86°

| | | | | | |
|---|---|---|---|---|---|
| 18ʰ 00ᵐ | 17ʰ 30ᵐ | 17ʰ 00ᵐ | 16ʰ 30ᵐ | 16ʰ 00ᵐ |

20ʰ 00ᵐ  19ʰ 00ᵐ  18ʰ 00ᵐ  17ʰ 00ᵐ  16ʰ 00ᵐ  15ʰ 00ᵐ  14ʰ 00ᵐ

Bright and Dark
Nebulae
To scale  <10'

Planetary
Nebulae
>100"  100"–30"  <30"

Open Star
Clusters

Globular
Clusters
To scale  <5'

Galaxies
10' x 5'  6' x 1'  3' x 2'  5' x 5'  4' x 2'  2' x 1'

Plotted to scale if the major axis >2', and circular
when face on or the position angle is uncertain

Quasars

Galaxy
Clusters

1546

1548

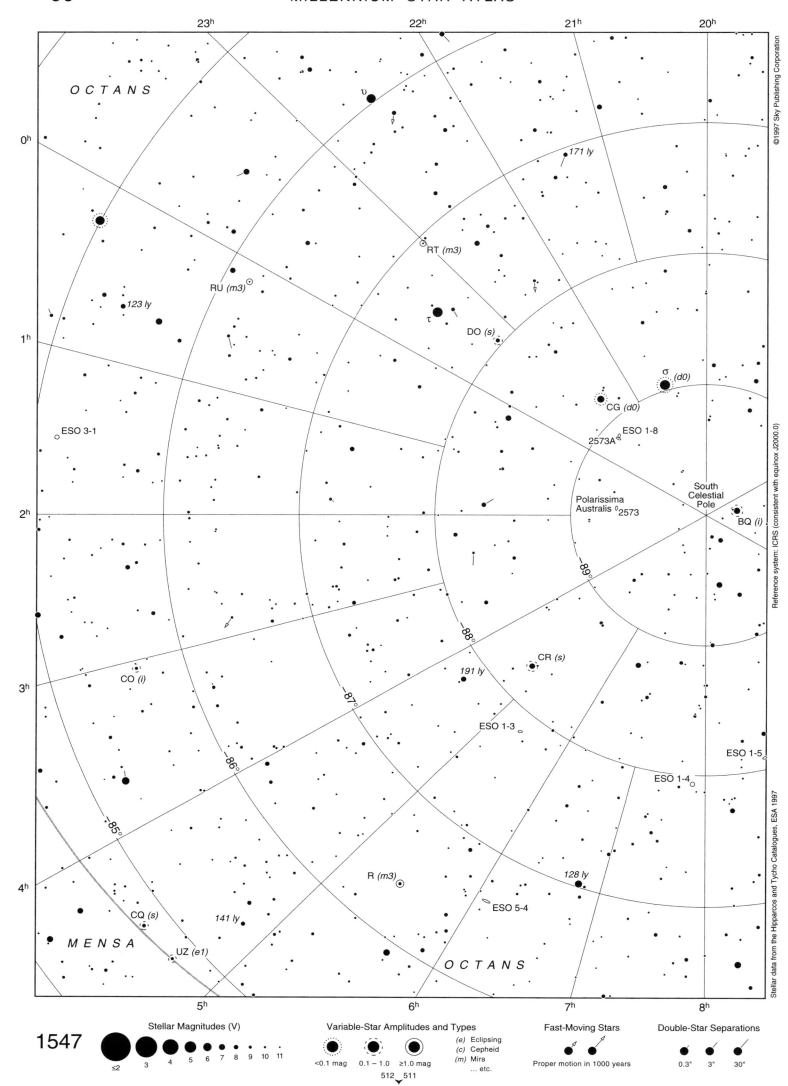

# MILLENNIUM STAR ATLAS

**−90°**

Reference system: ICRS (consistent with equinox J2000.0)

Stellar data from the Hipparcos and Tycho Catalogues, ESA 1997

OCTANS

υ

RT *(m3)*

RU *(m3)*

*123 ly*

*171 ly*

τ

DO *(s)*

σ *(d0)*

CG *(d0)*

ESO 1-8

2573A

ESO 3-1

South
Celestial
Pole

Polarissima
Australis ₀2573

BQ *(i)*

89°

88°

87°

86°

85°

CO *(i)*

CR *(s)*

ESO 1-3

*191 ly*

ESO 1-5

ESO 1-4

MENSA

CQ *(s)*

*141 ly*

UZ *(e1)*

R *(m3)*

ESO 5-4

*128 ly*

OCTANS

**1547**

## Stellar Magnitudes (V)

≤2    3    4    5    6    7    8    9    10    11

## Variable-Star Amplitudes and Types

<0.1 mag    0.1 – 1.0    ≥1.0 mag

512  511

*(e)* Eclipsing
*(c)* Cepheid
*(m)* Mira
… etc.

## Fast-Moving Stars

Proper motion in 1000 years

## Double-Star Separations

0.3"    3"    30"

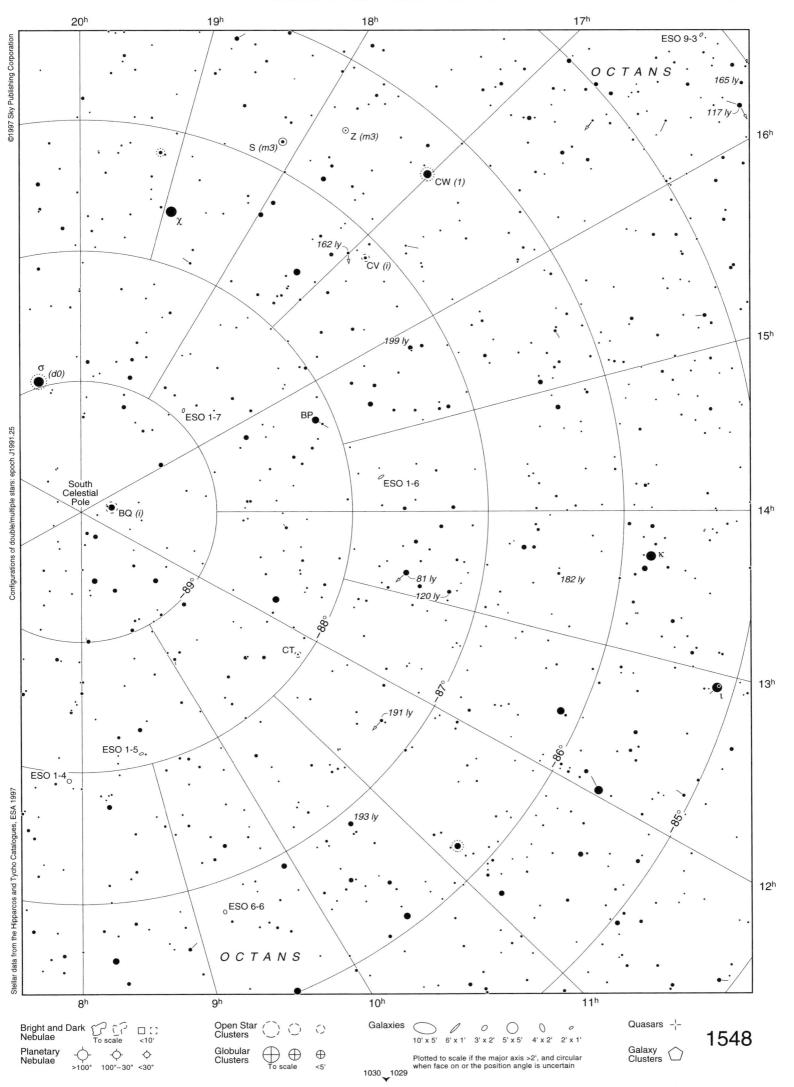

Bright and Dark Nebulae

To scale   <10'

Planetary Nebulae

>100"   100"–30"   <30"

Open Star Clusters

Globular Clusters

To scale   <5'

Galaxies

10' x 5'   6' x 1'   3' x 2'   5' x 5'   4' x 2'   2' x 1'

Plotted to scale if the major axis >2', and circular when face on or the position angle is uncertain

Quasars

Galaxy Clusters

1548

# INDEX TO SELECTED OBJECTS

THESE LISTINGS PROVIDE quick pointers to those charts that contain stars and nonstellar objects with popular names and many other benchmarks in the sky. Generally just a single chart number is given, indicating the chart on which the object is most nearly centered. Any star or object near a chart's edge can be found on at least one adjacent chart as well. Multiple chart numbers are given for a few large nebulae that extend across several charts.

Charts 1–516 are found in Volume I, which includes a more extensive index of bright stars by constellation and Bayer (Greek) letter. Charts 517–1032 are in Volume II, and charts 1033–1548 in Volume III.

## SPECIAL ASTRONOMICAL NAMES

## COMMON NAMES OF BRIGHT STARS

## THE MESSIER CATALOGUE

# CHART KEYS

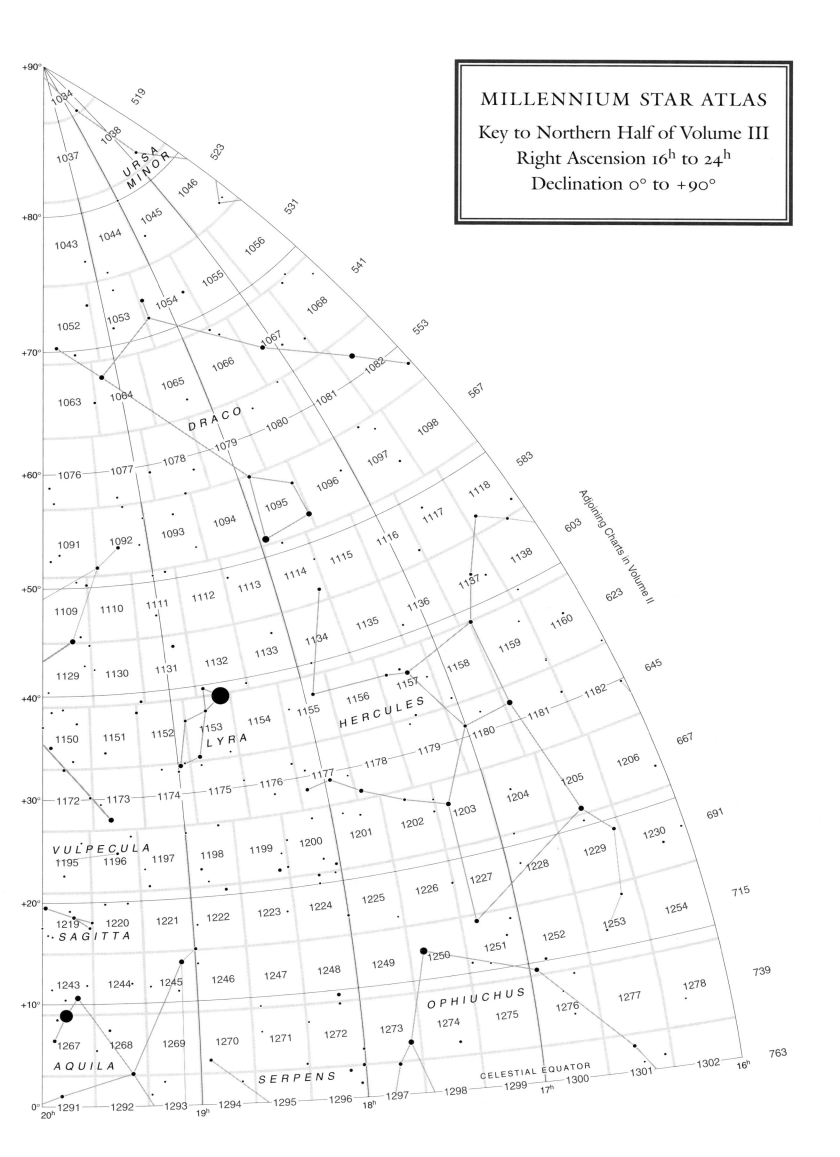

MILLENNIUM STAR ATLAS

Key to Southern Half of Volume III

Right Ascension 16ʰ to 24ʰ

Declination 0° to −90°

CARTOGRAPHY *The charts for this atlas were prepared electronically on a Sigma Tech Pentium System using Borland Turbo Basic. Final adjustments were made in Adobe Illustrator and the book was composed in QuarkXPress on a Power Macintosh computer system.*

PREPRESS *Electronic preparation was carried out by Dartmouth Publishing, Inc., Watertown, Massachusetts, and World Color Book Services, Taunton, Massachusetts.*

PRINTING *The atlas was printed at World Color Book Services on a Cottrell web press, using direct-to-plate technology.*

PAPER *The book paper is Finch Fine 70# text stock, manufactured by Finch, Pruyn, & Co., Glens Falls, New York, and supplied by Pratt Paper Company, Boston, Massachusetts. The endleaf stock is Multicolor Slate Blue from Permalin Products, New York, New York.*

BINDING *Binding and slipcase manufacture were handled by World Color Book Services. The material is Skivertex Ubonga.*

TYPEFACES *The typefaces used are Galliard text with Mantinia display, designed by Matthew Carter. Helvetica, designed by M. Miedinger, is used in the charts, diagrams, and graphs.*

BOOK DESIGN *Typography, binding, and slipcase design are by Christopher Kuntze.*